THIRD EDITION

AutoCAD 2000

with Lab Applications

S. R. KYLES

Addison
Wesley
Longman

Don Mills, Ontario   Reading, Massachusetts   Melo Park, California   New York
Wokingham, England   Amsterdam   Bonn   Sydney   Singapore   Tokyo   Madrid
San Juan   Paris   Seoul   Milan   Mexico City   Tapei

Canadian Cataloguing in Publication Data

Kyles, S.R. (Shannon R.)
   AutoCAD with lab applications : release 2000

3rd ed.
Previous ed. Published under title: AutoCAD with 2D and 3D lab applications.
Includes index.
ISBN 0-201-69815-3

1. AutoCAD (computer file). 2. Engineering design — Computer Programs. I. Title. II. Title: AutoCAD with 2D and 3D Lab applications.

T385.K95 2000   620".0042"02855369   C99-932737-2

© 2000 Addison Wesley Longman Ltd.
Pearson Education Canada

ALL RIGHTS RESERVED
No part of this book may be reproduced in any form without permission in writing from the publisher.

TRADEMARKS
AutoCAD®, AutoLISP®, AutoShade®, and AutoSURF® are registered trademarks of Autodesk Inc. dBase® is a registered trademark of dBase Inc. IBM®, IBM/PC/XT/AT, and IBM PS/2 are registered trademarks of International Business Machines. Lotus® and 1-2-3® are registered trademarks of Lotus Development Corporation. MS-DOS®, and Windows® are registered trademarks of the Microsoft Corporation. OS/2® is a registered trademark of International Business Machines Corporation. Windows® is a registered trademark of the Microsoft Corporation. Corel VENTURA™ Publisher and WordPerfect® are registered trademarks of The Corel Corporation.

ISBN 0-201-69815-3

Vice-President, Editorial Director: Michael Young
Acquisitions Editor: David Stover
Developmental Editor: Marta Tomins
Copy Editor: David Peebles
Production Editor: Sarah Dann
Production Coordinator: Wendy Moran
Art Director: Mary Opper
Cover Design: Anthony Cheung
Page Layout: Shannon Kyles

1 2 3 4 5   04 03 02 01 00

Printed and bound in Canada.

Table of Contents

Preface. vi
Acknowledgements viii
Introduction x

Chapter 1 Introductory Geometry and Setting Up
Setting UCS, LIMITS, SNAP, and GRID 1
Entry of Points Using Coordinates and Digitizing 6
Coordinate Entry Using Absolute, Relative, and Polar
 Values. 6
Coordinate Entry Using Digitizing 9
Geometry Commands. 10
View Commands 13
The REGEN and REDRAW Commands 16
The UNITS Command 17
Prelab 21
Exercises. 26
Challenger 34

Chapter 2 Help Files, CHAMFER, OSNAP, ERASE, TRIM, and BREAK
Help Files 37
SNAP and GRID 39
Point Entry and OSNAP 41
The ERASE Command 48
The CHAMFER Command 49
Prelab 50
Exercises 55
Challenger 60

Chapter 3 Entity Commands with Width
The TRACE Command 61
The PLINE Command 62
The PEDIT Command 65
The POLYGON Command. 67
The DONUT Command 69
Filling Irregular Shapes. 69
The TEXT Command 69
The MLINE Command (multilines) 71
Prelab 72
Exercises. 77
Challenger 82

Chapter 4 Object Selection and Editing
Selecting Objects Within the EDIT Command. 83
Editing Commands. 86
Editing with Grips 94
Setting LINETYPEs 97
Changing LTSCALE 99
Prelab A 100
Prelab B 102
Exercises. 105
Challenger 110

Chapter 5 STRETCH, TRIM, EXTEND, OFFSET, and ARRAY
Removing and Adding Objects 113
Editing Commands 115
Prelab. 129
Exercises 133
Challenger 141

Chapter 6 Entity Properties: Layers, Colors, and Linetypes
About LAYERs 143
Creating a New Layer 144
Changing LTSCALE 148
The Match Properties Command 148
CHPROP and CHANGE with Layers. 149
Changing the State of the Layers 151
The LAYER Command 151
Prelab. 153
Exercises 158
Challenger 164

Chapter 7 Dimensioning
About Dimensioning 165
Entering Dimensions 167
Dimension Styles 171
The Lines and Arrows Menu 172
The Fit Dialog Box 173
The Text Tab 175
Using Dimension Style Families 177
Editing Dimensions 180
When All Else Fails 180
Prelab. 181
Exercises 188
Challenger 194

Chapter 8 Text
Linear Text 195
Paragraph Text 199
Text Styles and Fonts 201
Editing TEXT and DTEXT 204
Making Isometric Lettering 206
Using LEADER to Create Notations 207
Prelab. 209
Exercises 215
Challenger 220

Chapter 9 HATCH and SKETCH
The HATCH Command 221
The BHATCH Command 222
Solid Hatches 228
Editing Hatches 228
The SKETCH Command 229
Point Filters 230
Prelab A 234
Prelab B 236
Exercises 240
Challenger 247

Chapter 10 Blocks and Wblocks
The BLOCK Command 252
The INSERT Command 253
The WBLOCK Command. 255
The MINSERT Command 258
Editing Blocks. 258
Compiling Drawings with BLOCK 260
Blocks, Wblocks, Color, and Layers 260
Prelab. 264
Exercises 269
Challenger 274

Chapter 11 Setting Up Drawings and PSPACE
Set Up and Scale for Simple 2D Drawings 275
Using Blocks to Compile Drawings. 277
Using Paper space to Compile Drawings 280
Paper space and Tilemode. 281
Scaling Views Within a Drawing 284
The VPLAYER Command. 285
Dimensioning in Paper space 286
The MVSETUP Command 286
Prelab A 288
Prelab B 297
Exercises 303
Challenger 308

Chapter 12 2D Review and Final Drawings
Review. 309
Problems. 310
Quiz 312
Final Drawings 327

Chapter 13 POINTS, DIVIDE, MEASURE, INQUIRY, and System Variables
Point Display or PDMODE Options 333
Using Divide and Measure 334
The SPLINE Command 337
Inquiry Commands 338
Creating Multiline Styles 344
Editing Multilines 346
Prelab. 348
Exercises 353
Challenger 357

Chapter 14 Creating Attributes
Introduction 359
Attributes for Title Blocks and Notations. . . . 359
Defining the Attributes. 360
Editing Attribute Definitions 362
Displaying Attributes 364
Creating Attributes for Data Extraction 365
Prelab A 366
Prelab B 369
Exercises 374
Challenger 378

Chapter 15 Editing and Extracting Attributes
Editing Attributes Attached to Blocks 379
The ATTEDIT Command 379
Data Extraction 383
Prelab 387
Exercises 391
Challenger 395

Chapter 16 Isometric and Orthographic Drawings
Isometric Views 397
Prelab A 400
Creating Orthographic Views 404
Prelab B 407
Exercises 410
Challenger 414

Chapter 17 File Formats and Management
What are Slides? 415
The MSLIDE Command 416
The VSLIDE Command. 417
Script Files 419
Exporting AutoCAD Files. 422
Importing Files to AutoCAD 423
Prelab A 424
Managing Larger Files 426
Groups 427
Prelab B 429
Exercises 432
Challenger 436

Chapter 18 Advanced Blocking, Xrefs, and Tracking
Advanced Blocking 437
Xrefs or External Reference Files 439
The XBIND Command 444
Tracking 445
Prelab. 446
Exercises 450
Challenger 457

Chapter 19 Final Tests and Projects
Section 1: On-Screen Problems 459
Section 2: Review 464
Final Drawings 474
Challenger 480

Chapter 20 Moving into 3D and Views
Generating 3D Models 481
VIEWPORTS or VPORTS 481
Orienting Views Within VPORTS 485
3D Icons 489
Entering X, Y, and Z Coordinates 489
Prelab. 492
Exercises 494
Challenger 497

Chapter 21 User Coordinate System
The UCS Command 500
Saving and Restoring UCS. 502
The UCS Icon 503
Prelab. 506
Exercises 511
Challenger 515

Chapter 22 3DFACE and X, Y, and Z Filters
Generating 3D Images 517
3DFACE 517
3DFACE Example 519
The EDGE Command 520
The HIDE Command 521
The SHADE Command 522
X, Y, and Z Filters 524
Auto Tracking 525
Prelab 526
Exercises 530
Challenger 534

Chapter 23 Extruding 2D Shapes into 3D Shapes
The ELEVation Command 537
The THICKNESS Command 538
Changing Existing ELEVATION 539
Creating Thickened Objects 541
VPOINT, VPORTS and VIEW 541
Prelab 544
Exercises 548
Challenger 553

Chapter 24 Dynamic View, Scripts and Slides
AutoCAD's Model Space 555
Using DVIEW Options 557
Slides and Scripts 566
Prelab 569
Exercises 573
Challenger 577

Chapter 25 Surfacing
Surfaces in a CAD Environment 579
Surface Display 579
3D Polyline Meshes 580
Surface of Revolution or REVSURF 584
Tabulated Surfaces or TABSURF 587
Edge Surfaces or EDGESURF 588
3DPOLY or 3D PLINEs 589
Prelab 590
Exercises 595
Challenger 604

Chapter 26 Paper Space, Model Space and Drawings
Model Space and Paper Space 605
Paper Space 605
Tilemode 607
MVIEW 608
Entering the Title Block 612
Scaling Views Within a Drawing 612
Editing Floating Viewports 614
Locking the Zoom Factor Within a Viewport 614
Prelab 615
Exercises 627
Challenger 631

Chapter 27 3D Shapes, PFACE and Mesh
More 3D Entities in AutoCAD 633
3D Commands 633
Using 3D Objects 637
The PFACE Command 639
3DMESH 640
Using PEDIT to Edit 3DMESH 641
Prelab 645
Exercises 649
Challenger 653

Chapter 28 Three-Dimensional Solids
What Are Solids? 655
Creating Solid Objects 656
Modifying Solid Objects 660
Filleting and Chamfering Solids 662
Prelab 666
Exercises 671
Challenger 679

Chapter 29 Revolving, Extruding and Sectioning in 3D Solids
The REVOLVE Command 681
The EXTRUDE Command 683
The SECTION Command 684
The SLICE Command 685
Prelab 687
Exercises 691
Challenger 695

Chapter 30 Editing Solids, Regions, and 3D Objects
The 3DARRAY Command 697
The MIRROR3D Command 699
The ROTATE3D Command 701
MOVE and COPY in 3D 702
Prelab 705
Exercises 708
Challenger 713

Chapter 31 Regions and Mass Properties Calculations
Regions 715
The REGION Command 716
The AREA Command 718
Mass Properties 719
The MASSPROP Command 719
Prelab 723
Exercises 726
Challenger 730

Chapter 32 Managing and Exporting Models
Components of Large Models 731
Wildcards 736
Making Listing Easier 737
Model Documentation 737
Management Considerations 738
Transferring Large Drawings 738
Exporting Files 739
DXF Graphics Transfer Example 740

Importing DXF Files. 740
Files You May Want to Transfer with the Drawing File . 742
Model Management 742
Prelab. 743
Exercises 745
Challenger 749

Chapter 33 Dimensioning 3D Parts
3D Dimensioning 751
Prelab. 754
Exercises 756
Challenger 760

Chapter 34 Final Projects
Final Tests 761
3D Review 763
Final Projects. 777
Exercises 778

Appendix A
Glossary of Terms. 785

Appendix B
File Extensions 793

Appendix C
Abbreviations and Aliases. 795

Appendix D
Plotting and Printing. 796

Appendix E
AutoCAD's Standard Hatch Patterns 804

Appendix F
AutoCAD's Standard Fonts 805

Index. 807
Icons 817, 819

Preface

AutoCAD® remains the world's leading design software, and the software most often chosen in colleges and universities. Architects, engineers and technologists need to be able to use CAD (computer-aided design) as effectively as they use pencils and pens.

Earlier versions of this text have been class tested in both college and university settings by literally thousands of students. Notations and exercise enhancements reflect both student and instructor feedback. In addition, the text has been used extensively by distance education students who learn on their own, virtually "by the book." The set up of this book makes it perfect for use as a classroom text, or by an individual in a self-teaching environment.

The main text of each chapter in *AutoCAD® with Lab Applications* deals with a different aspect of the software, providing illustrations, examples, and information on how to access the commands. The text is complete and considers all options in each command structure, so can be used not only as a textbook but also as a reference. This version of the book is written for AutoCAD® Release 2000, but the labs and examples are applicable to releases 13 and 14 as well. Software platforms can differ among various labs within a college or university and students may also have different software at home. *AutoCAD® with Lab Applications* will help students work in any AutoCAD® environment.

Prelabs Each chapter has a Prelab designed to give students opportunity to practice what has just been explained. The Prelabs are detailed examples that explain the functions step-by-step. Students should be able to complete the Prelabs without assistance. In a situation in which there is no lecture time, the student may be requested to read the chapter and complete the prelab *before* the lab so that any difficult questions can be addressed once the fundamentals of each chapter have been grasped. Where there is ample time for labs and lectures, the Prelabs can be used to gain a better understanding of the subject and/or additional help.

Exercises Each chapter closes with several exercises. The Practice Exercise has been developed for those students who have limited time—one hour or less—or merely need a warm-up. Following the Practice Exercise are exercises that relate to four major disciplines: architectural, civil, electrical and mechanical engineering. Each has been tested in a learning environment to provide a challenging but not impossible exercise for a two-hour lab. In many cases some flexibility is built in; the student can produce all or part of the final example. All commands needed to complete the end of chapter exercises will have been introduced.

The Challenger exercise at the end of each chapter is provided for those students who are eager to become masters of AutoCAD and have the time and equipment to practice; or for those students who have prior knowledge of the software but need to attend classes for necessary credits. It is designed to prevent boredom for those who need a challenge.

Organization

Not all of the commands necessary to complete the exercises have been included in the Challenger examples. Students attempting the Challenger will either know what the commands are, or will have a strong sense of what they are and where to find them.

The book is organized into three sections. The first twelve chapters are at the introductory level. By the end of Chapter 12 students should be able to produce a 2D drawing of any given shape.as well as a plot of the drawing.

The next seven chapters are provided for further study in AutoCAD as an intermediate stage. These chapters will help students understand the software better, enabling them to use some of the nongraphic data. For those who have completed the first twelve chapters, the next seven chapters, plus six or seven of the Challenger exercises, could be considered an intermediate course.

Chapters 20-34 progress into drawing and design in the 3D realm. Based upon the groundwork established in 2D, the same AutoCAD concepts plus additional ones are explored and applied in the more advanced 3D realm.

Other Releases

This book covers AutoCAD Release 2000. Most of the information is also relevant to the earlier Releases, 12, 13 and 14. The command structures have been expanded in Release 2000, but the options have remained largely the same. Many system interfaces have been added to Release 2000. These are explained in the introduction and can be modified to suit the home or school environment.

The student who has Release 13 or 14 at home will find that most of the commands have remained the same, but the menus are often different. Drawings completed in earlier versions of AutoCAD can be brought up in Release 2000 and then saved for Release 14 by changing the file type in the Save command. For those who have only limited RAM and clock speed, Release 12 can be used in the DOS version by using the command line equivalents listed with each command. This textbook can be used in virtually any environment.

Testing

Each section has a list of questions to test the student's understanding of the text. For on-terminal testing, each chapter has at least 5 exercises and as many as 25 exercises that can be given as a dexterity and time limited example.

Over 300 complete drawings help users fine-tune their skills and practice what they have learned in order to become AutoCAD experts. *AutoCAD with Lab Applications* is a book that will teach you how to use AutoCAD 2000 as effectively as possible and remain a useful reference in years to come.

Acknowledgments

The exercises in this book went through many years of student testing at Mohawk College. Since the first edition appeared in January 1993, there have been many positive suggestions and many bits of constructive criticism. I would like to thank all my students for working with me on the development of new projects, and for proofing tutorials and exercises. I would like to thank Denise Serafin for her excellent job proofreading; Peter Mann of Mohawk College for his encouragement and generous offers of help with architectural examples; Philip Morias of ADS for his help with new plotting parameters; and Dan Gamble for his tireless efforts to match graphics with engineering.

Illustrations of projects showing industry standards have been generously provided by Sylvia Smith of UMA Engineering Limited in Edmonton, Alberta; Jim Ellis at Micro-Rel in Arizona; Dave Umbach at Tarsons, Benckerhoff, Gore, and Storrie Incorporated; and Andy Slupecki of Dundas, Ontario.

I would also like to thank the following people who supplied very useful and constructive comments on the material: Barbara Bang of North Dakota State College of Science; Jag Mohan of Sheridan College; Curtis Rhodes of the University of Southern California; Tom Hyde of Kirkwood College, USA; Roger Winn of University College of Cape Breton; John Bonacci of the University of Toronto; Dennis Short of Purdue University; and Don Bird of Ricks College. Ron Doleman, formerly of AddisonWesley Longman Canada, was a wonderful influence and source of good cheer.

In addition, I would like to thank Sarah Dann; the production editor, Marta Tomins, the developmental editor; David Stover, the acquisitions editor; and David Peebles, the copy editor, for their help in producing this book.

S. R. Kyles

August 1999

Introduction

AutoCAD is a very popular, flexible software system that allows the user to create both 2-dimensional and 3-dimensional models and drawings.

For those who are familiar with computers, learning AutoCAD will be easy, simply because they are aware of the typical response structure and the format of their system. This release focuses on many more *Windows* functions, including the Multiple Document Environment which allows various drawing sessions to be opened concurrently, providing the computer hardware is sufficient.

If you are computer-literate, glance through the next few pages to see if there is anything in AutoCAD that looks different from the programs with which you are familiar. If you are not used to working with computers, read the next few pages carefully before starting on Chapter 1.

Using This Book

System Prompts and User Responses

In this book, the system command information will be shown in this style:

```
Command:
Specify first point:
Specify second point or [Undo]:
```

The user responses (what you should type in) will be shown in bold:

```
Command: LINE
Specify first point: 0,0
Specify second point or [Undo]: 5,3
```

The Enter or Return Key

At the end of each command or entry on the command line, use the Enter key (symbolized by ⏎) to signal the end of:

- A command entry:

  Command:**LINE**⏎

- A coordinate entry:

  Specify first point:**2,4**⏎

- A value:

  New fillet radius.0000:**3**⏎

- Text:

  Text:**All Holes 2.00R Unless Noted**⏎

Please note that the ⏎ will not be shown at the end of every entry; it will only be used when the user should press ⏎ rather than entering any other response.

Floppy Disks

In order to access AutoCAD in a learning environment, you may need a floppy disk in the A: drive. And in order to store your files, you will definitely need floppy disks—usually two—one for the file itself and one for a backup file.

Zip drives, Jazz drives, and CD writers are also available for storing larger files. These will not probably be necessary until the 3D segment of the book.

Floppy disks are very inexpensive and "cheap" memory devises. Always be sure to keep at least two copies of every file that you do. Three copies is a better idea. You can reuse old floppies by either erasing all information or reformatting. Format your floppy in the following way:

Danger

Formatting a disk will erase all data on the disk. Make sure that the disk contains no necessary information before formatting.

DOS Command

FORMAT A: This will format a 1.2 meg disk on a 1.2 meg drive or a 1.44 meg disk in a 1.44 meg drive. It is rare to need to format a floppy disk these days, but it does happen.

If you are using a **B:** drive just substitute **B:** for **A:**.

Starting AutoCAD

Your Windows environment should have been set up so that a double click on this application icon will bring up AutoCAD 2000.

You will automatically be placed in the Drawing Editor.

Unfortunately, there is no way of guaranteeing how the last user has left the screen, so you may not have the necessary toolbars. If your screen is not the same as shown below, you can either open toolbars in the View pull-down menu (page xiv) or move them to where you want them (page xv).

Danger

If your floppy has already been formatted and has information on it, do not reformat, unless you want to erase all the information on the disk.

The Windows Drawing Editor

The initial Windows screen contains the menu bar, the status bar, the drawing window or graphics area, and several toolbars. Toolbars contain icons that represent commands.

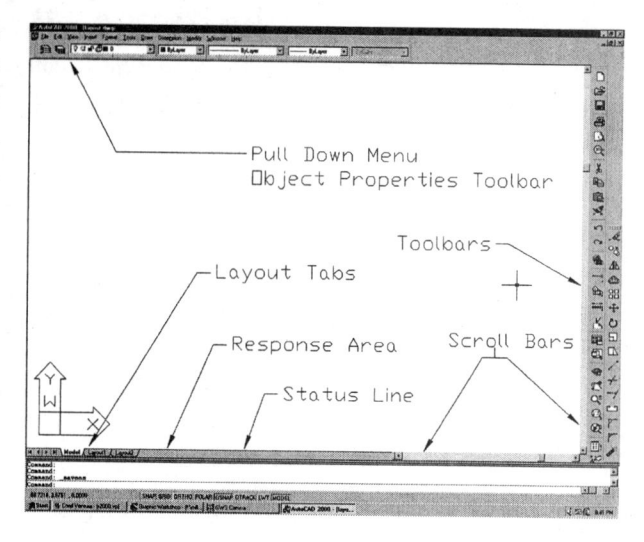

The menu bar contains the pull-down menus. The status bar displays the cursor coordinates and the status modes such as Grid and Snap. Mode names are always visible in the status bar as selectable buttons. Click the buttons to toggle the modes. The command line in Windows is "floating," that is, it may be dragged to any location on the screen.

> **Notes**
>
> To turn off your scroll bars or change the colors on your screen, use the Tools pull-down menu, the Options dialog box, and Display.

Keyboard and Mouse Functions

Pointing Devices for Both Windows and DOS

There are many different kinds of pointing devices or "mice" on the market. Some have two or three buttons, others have as many as twenty. Two buttons are adequate for most operations.

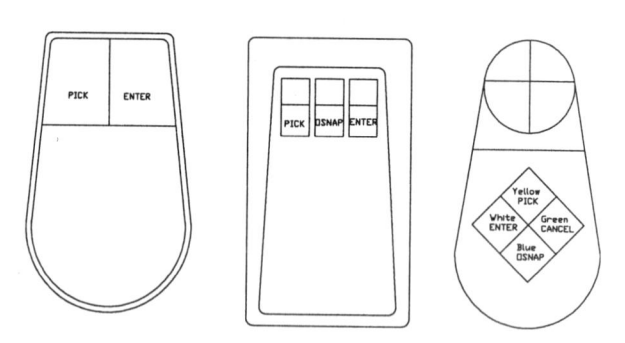

The Pick Button

On all mice there will be a point or command indicator or *pick button*; on a three-button mouse, it is usually on the left side of the device.

The pick button is used to indicate the command you want to access either from the on-screen menu or from the digitizer tablet. It is also used to indicate point positions.

The Enter Button

Another button on the mouse will have the function of the ⏎ key (Enter or Return) on the keyboard. This signals the end of a command. There is also a right-click facility in Release 2000 that accesses functions associated with each command. This can be turned off under the Tools pull down menu, Options, and User Preferences.

xii   INTRODUCTION

Other Buttons

Other buttons can mean **Escape, OSNAP**, or other commands.

The mouse (or "puck") is intended to work in conjunction with the keyboard for the entry of commands.

Before entering commands, be sure you have a "Command:" prompt. *To return to the command prompt use Escape. The Escape key is on the top left of your keyboard.*

Function Buttons for Both Windows and DOS

To become familiar with the function keys, move the mouse around the screen noting the movement of the crosshairs. Find the F buttons or function keys on the top or side of your keyboard.

DOS		Windows
Now press **F6**.	You will notice that the numbers on the status line are moving as you move the mouse. These are the *X* and *Y* values.	5.0000,0.0000
Now press **F9**.	You will notice that the numbers are snapping to even values. In DOS, the word Snap is in the status line; in Windows, the SNAP will be highlighted.	SNAP
Now press **F7**.	You will see a grid on the screen.	GRID

F8 is used with linear commands to create lines at right angles. Once you are in the LINE command, try using **F8** or Ortho within the command to get lines vertical and horizontal.

Type in **LINE** at the command prompt. With the pick button, pick a spot on the screen. Then use ORTHO.

```
Command:LINE
Specify first point: (pick the screen)
```

ORTHO

Now press **F8**. Your lines will only be created on a vertical or horizontal.

Press the ⏎ key to exit from the line command.

```
Specify second point or [Undo]:⏎
```

Many commands invoke a system response that shows an alphanumeric screen with related data. To exit from the alphanumeric screen onto the graphics screen, you can use **F1** in DOS or pick the command close box at the top of the alphanumeric overlay.

Type in the word **HELP** at the command prompt:

```
Command:HELP
```

To exit from Help, pick OK or the command close box:

INTRODUCTION xiii

Many systems provide *toggle switches* by means of function keys. These allow the user to turn a specific function on and off simply by pressing the key. In Windows these functions can be accessed through icons as well. The function switches are:

Flip Screen	COORDS	GRID	ORTHO	SNAP
F1	F6	F7	F8	F9

When entering commands, you can use the function keys at any time either before or within a command.

Entering Commands and Coordinates

You can enter information either through the keyboard or through your mouse or pointing device. There are also toolbars and icons that help to access the information. You can enter a command by typing it in at the command prompt or you can use the pointing device to pick up commands from:

- The pull-down menus in the menu bar
- The icons from the toolbars
- The Tablet menu on the digitizing board (where available)
- The screen menu where loaded

Windows Toolbars

Toolbars are groups of icons or tools compiled according to application. Toolbars can be on screen or not, and can be either on the top or side of your screen or floating. The tools on the toolbars now have a default flat look. A border will appear on the icons or tools when you "roll over" the tool with your cursor. "Coolbar" is the name given to the animated behaviour of the toolbar, i.e., the fact that it displays a border.

Accessing Windows Toolbars

Toolbars can be accessed through the View pull-down menu.

Pick View, then Toolbars, then the toolbar that you need.

To remove a toolbar from your screen, use the icon on the top right of the toolbar.

Notes
Tools are sometimes called icons. An application icon opens a software package, a tool is an icon that invokes a command.

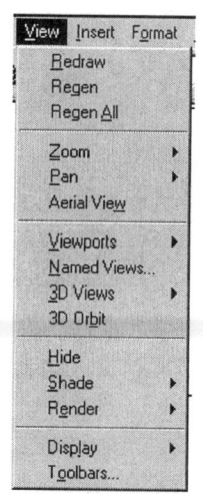

Notes
The toolbar dialog box is under a different menu on every new release of AutoCAD. There is no apparent reason for this.

xiv   INTRODUCTION

Using Windows Toolbars

Toolbars contain tools that represent commands. When you move the pointing device over a tool, Tooltips below the cursor display the name of the tool. Pick that tool to invoke the command.

Placing Toolbars

The Standard toolbar is visible by default. It carries frequently used tools such as Zoom, Redraw, and Undo. You can display multiple toolbars on-screen at once, change their contents, resize them, and dock or float them. A ***docked toolbar*** attaches to any edge of the graphics window. A ***floating toolbar*** can lie anywhere on the application screen, and it can be resized and does not overlap with the drawing window.

To Dock a Toolbar

1. Position the cursor on the caption, and press the pick button on the pointing device.

2. Drag the toolbar to a dock location at the top, bottom, or either side of the drawing window.

3. When the outline of the toolbar appears in the docking area, release the pick button.

To place the toolbar in a docking region without docking it, hold down the **Ctrl** key as you drag.

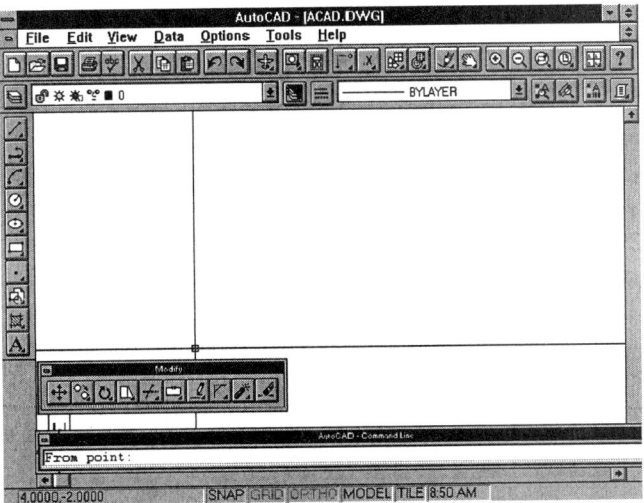

Releasing a Toolbar

To get the toolbar off the screen, choose the control menu box on the top right corner.

The Windows Command Window

Like the toolbars, the Windows command line or response area can be moved and docked. By default the command window is a floating window with a caption and frame.

You can move the floating command window anywhere on the screen and change its width and height with the pointing device. This window is also dockable within the AutoCAD application window. Dock the command window by dragging it until it is over the top or bottom dock regions of the application window. Undock the window by selecting any part of its border and dragging it away from the dock region until it has a thick outline. Drop it to make it a floating window.

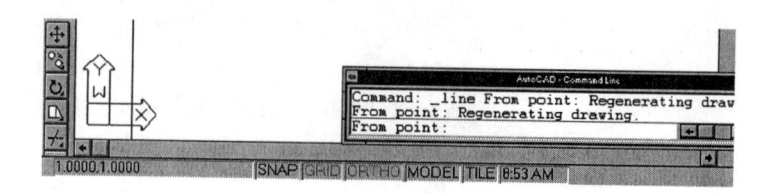

You can resize the commmand window vertically and horizontally, both with the pointing device and with the splitter bar located at the top edge of the window when docked on the bottom and on the bottom edge when docked at the top. Resizing and docking the command window can help you to create more space for your drawings on-screen.

Scroll Bars

In most Windows applications there are *scroll bars* that advance the file you are viewing. Each scroll bar has arrows that indicate a move up or down. To access an area not displayed, either pick on the up or down arrow until the information is displayed or pick the box within the scroll bar and move it quickly up and down the screen.

Scroll bars can be either vertical or horizontal. In Windows, the scroll bars on the top and bottom move the file across the screen in the same way that a PAN does.

Menus

In Windows, AutoCAD divides the command set by default between menus and toolbars. You can work exclusively with menus by loading a menu file that contains the full command set or by typing in the commands.

When AutoCAD was running in DOS, the commands were all available either in the screen menu or in the pull-down menus. In Release 2000 the screen menu is once again available under the Tools menu, Options and Display. You can use either the toolbars or the screen menu, or both if you have an extremely large screen.

Screen Menus

The screen menu is a set of submenus to the right of the drawing window. It contains the full AutoCAD command set.

To load the screen menu in Windows:

1. Pick the Tools pull down menu.
2. Select Options.
3. Pick the Display tab from the Options dialog box, then Display Screen menu.

Pull-down Menus

Pull-down menus are used to access many of the same commands that are found on the buttons, screen menu, and by typing. Place your cursor on the menu bar, pick the menu that you want, then pick the command or submenu that you want.

Reading the Pull-down Menus

Under each separate menu you can access commands, subcommands, and dialog boxes. For example, in the View menu, if you choose Redraw, you are simply invoking that command. With the ZOOM command, you are led to a submenu of ZOOM options. The triangle indicates that there is another "flyout" menu.

The third type of pull-down menu choice has three dots following the entry, meaning a dialog box is invoked either immediately or after an object is selected. In View, the dialog box menu choices include Named Views, which brings up the Named Views dialog box, where you can modify the number of named views on your file.

Opening or Accessing Drawings

Once you have accessed the Drawing Editor, you can start drawing and later save your work under a specified name in a specified directory. If you have a drawing started in AutoCAD Release 13, 14, or some earlier version, you can use OPEN to work on it.

Opening Existing Drawings

The command line equivalent is **OPEN**.

In Windows, under File Name double-click the file name in the list of files. Use the scroll bars to access other files. To access other directories, pick the down arrow beside the words " Look in:". You can also type in the drawing name by picking the long white box, then typing in the name of the file. If you prefer to type in both the directory and the name. type that into the File Name box.

Starting a New File

If you would like to start a new file, access the same File menu and choose New.

Before the new file is created, you can choose a default drawing file environment and/or enter the name of the file that you wish to create.

```
Command:_new
Enter template file name or [. (For none)] <acad,dwt>:
```

The .DWT extension stands for drawing template.

The default file environment can be either the ACAD.DWT standard file or a prototype file that contains all the settings for a specific application. Once you are familiar with AutoCAD, you can save drawing templates that contain plotter information, layer information, groups, blocks, linetypes, and other standard information so that you don't need to set up your file from scratch each time.

Recovering Files

If you have a problem with retrieving a file in the Open command, you may need to Recover the file. Usually these problems are caused by either bad diskettes or removing the floppy disk from the drive before AutoCAD has completely exited from the file. If you need to Restore a file, simply choose Recover from theDrawing Utilities menu. In Release 2000, the OPEN command should automatically repair any damaged files, but if this doesn't work, try RECOVER.

You do *not* need to Recover the file every time you load it.

> **Notes**
> If you are taking drawings from a Windows environment to a DOS environment, often the menu is loaded with the drawing. Thus, when loading a Windows drawing in DOS, you may need to load the menu file as well. Type **MENU** at the command prompt.

Saving Files

Computers have a tendency to lose information at the worst possible times. It is suggested that when you are using AutoCAD you save your files at least every hour.

The first time you save a drawing, you will be prompted for the name of the file before it saves. If you have already entered the name of the current file under the New option in the File, then AutoCAD simply saves the file under the given name and directory and you will not be prompted for a name.

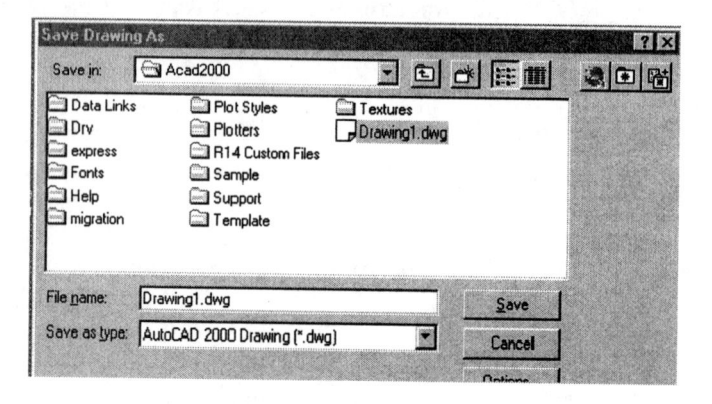

To save a named file, use SAVE.
1. Type in the word SAVE at the command prompt.
2. From the File menu, choose SAVE. In the Save Drawing As dialog box, enter the new drawing name. Then choose OK.

> **Notes**
> File names should be less than eight characters long and without dots (.), backslashes (\), or spaces.

Choose Save every subsequent time you would like to save the drawing, and the drawing will automatically be saved under this specified file name.

If you specified a directory and file when you signed on, use SAVE to save the file under this name.

To save the file under a new name or on a different directory, choose Save As from the File pull-down menu.

To change the directory, double-click on the directory listing that you want. The line reading "Look In:" must reflect the directory chosen.

To enter the name of a file, pick the File area and type the name in.

To Exit the file and Save it at the same time, type in End at the command line.

You can save a file as a different release of AutoCAD by specifying the File type. Specify the release you need under the Save As Type box in the Save As dialog box.

> **Notes**
> To save a file so it can be read in Release 12, type in SAVEASR12, and enter the file name. You may lose some hatch or text objects.

Changing the Drawing Name or Directory

If you want to change the drawing name or directory, use Save As. If you have been addressing C: while creating your drawing, you can save the file onto a floppy disk before exiting the file by using Save As; then pick A: or B: for the directory or drive.

Browsing Through Files

The Browse/Search dialog box displays small images of drawings in the directory you specify. Use the options on the dialog box to sort images by file type and change the size of the images. Click an image to select it.

Exiting AutoCAD

Once you have saved the file, you can exit AutoCAD either by picking the button on the right or by picking EXIT from the File menu.

The command line equivalent is **QUIT**.

Do not remove your floppy disk from the drive before you have completely exited from AutoCAD.

Entering Commands

When you enter commands at the command prompt, AutoCAD displays a set of options or a dialog box. Many commands have a series of options, for example the FILLET command:

```
Command:FILLET
Current settings: Mode = Trim, Radius = 0.500
Select first object or [Polyline/Radius/Trim]:
```

The default is to choose the first object that you would like to have filleted. If you would like to choose one of the options, simply type in the first letter of the option at the command line and the option will be invoked. For example, if you would like to change the Radius of the fillet, simply type in **R** and you will be prompted for the size of the radius.

```
Select first object or [Polyline/Radius/Trim]:R
Specify fillet radius <0.50>:6
```

Then enter the size of radius that you require.

Values Versus Coordinates

In many commands you will be prompted for coordinates or a position on the screen. These are *X,Y* (and, in 3D, *Z*) coordinates.

```
Command:LINE
Specify first point:2,3                    Coordinates
Specify second point:4,3
```

If you are asked to specify a radius or diameter, or a distance such as the length of a line or the width of a linetype, this is a value that is expressed with only one number.

```
Radius <1.000>:3                           Values
Offset distance <0.5000>:12
```

Object Selection Prior to Command Entry

Once you are in the Graphics Editor, commands are entered either through the menus or icons with the pick button or by the keyboard. If you should pick the graphics screen without first invoking a command, you will create an object selection box that can be used for editing commands. (See Chapters 4 and 5.)

Window

If you pick anywhere on the screen and then pick to the right, either above or below the first pick, you will be creating a window. Every object that is fully within that window will be selected. (See Chapter 4.)

Crossing

If you pick anywhere on the screen and then pick a second point to the left of the first point, you will be creating a crossing window. This selection window selects all objects fully or partially within its borders. (See Chapter 4.)

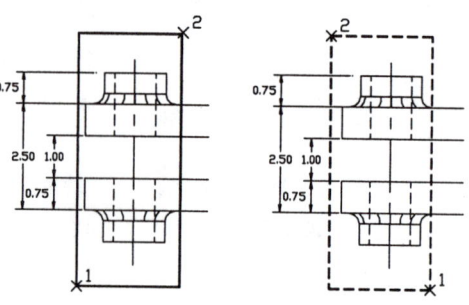

In the left side of the illustration above (pick 1 and pick 2) create a window that would identify all of the objects completely contained in it; the dimensions and the horizontal lines extending to the right would not be included. On the right, the crossing, picking right to left, identifies the whole set of objects on the screen. If this set of picks is followed by a Modify command such as MOVE, ERASE, COPY, then all of the objects would be selected.

Objects

If you select an object on screen without invoking a command first, small squares called *grips* will appear on the object or objects you select. These are for editing the object. (See Chapter 4 .)

If you have selected objects either through a window, through a crossing window, or as an individual object selection, and you do not want to edit the objects at the time, simply continue to enter the next command and the selection will be ignored.

Help Files

When first entering AutoCAD, many people have a tendency to press the space bar before starting work on the file. This will invoke the Help files. If you are not familiar with computers, this can be rather disconcerting.

To exit the Help files and continue with the drawing press **Escape** a few times until the dialog box disappears.

Accessing Commands

Typing in the Commands

You can type in commands instead of picking them from menus, but they must be spelled correctly! Any commands on-screen that are followed by a colon can be typed in.

You cannot access the menus by typing in the menu titles (note that menu selections are not followed by colons). In DOS, if you type in **EDIT** by mistake, it will convert your screen to alphanumeric format because you have entered Edit, the DOS editor. Pick the command close box or File Exit to return to the graphics screen.

Speeding Up Your Entries

The space bar on the keyboard and the enter button on the pointing device, when used with a "Command:" prompt, will bring back the last command entered. Effective use of this technique can greatly enhance your speed when entering LINEs etc.

Right-Click Shortcut Menus

The right-click button in AutoCAD has always meant "Enter" or the end of the command. This option makes normal geometry very quick and easy to enter. For those who are used to a Windows environment as opposed to an AutoCAD environment, the right-click facility means options connected to the commands that are currently running. If you want to use the right-click facilities, you can set this variable under the Tools pull down menu. Choose Options, the User Preferences tab, then make sure there is a check beside *Shortcut menus in drawing area*.

With the right-click shortcut options off, the right-click means that the previous command will be repeated. With the right-click shortcuts menus on, and no command in use, the right-click offers the default menu.

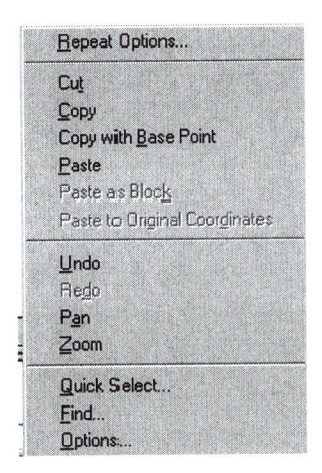

This menu offers part of the Edit pull down menu, part of the View menu, and some Tools. Other right-click menus are available for the Edit commands, and many of the draw and view commands. The right-click menus can also be customised. The customisation is set under the Options> User Preferences.

Options Dialog Box

In previous releases and in many other Windows programs this dialog box is called Preferences. The Options set up your screen display, the drawing environment, and the system. If you find the color of the screen difficult to work with, change it under Tools> Options> Display Color.

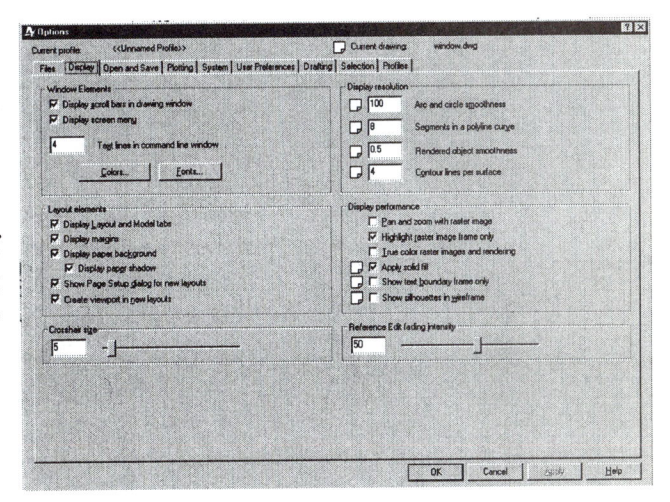

INTRODUCTION xxi

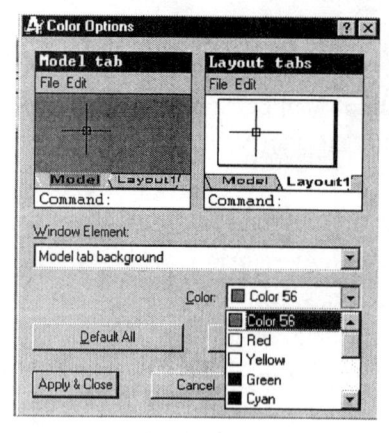

Once in color, choose the color that you would like, then Apply and Close. This will be the background color until it is next changed.

If you are using the Copy and Paste facilities under the Edit menu, you may find that a white background is the best for you. If you are using AutoCAD strictly for drawing purposes, then a black background, or at least a dark color is what you will need.

Command Aliases

Many commands can be accessed by simply typing the first letter of the command.

L = LINE   E = ERASE
A = ARC   Z = ZOOM
C = CIRCLE   P = PAN

Saving and Exiting

SAVE   QUIT or EXIT
Makes a copy   Exits without saving

When you use AutoCAD, the system is generating a temporary file on the drive that you are accessing. *Do not remove your floppy disk until you have saved and exited the Drawing Editor.* In Release 2000 the theory is that the file will not be corrupted if you remove the diskette before you exit AutoCAD. Personally, I prefer to play safe. When you are working on a computer, all bets are off on what might happen next.

When working in an environment where the computer is accessible to others, there is always the possibility that someone, for whatever reason, will QUIT or EXIT your file if you leave it unattended. It is also possible that a severe storm or power surge could cut off the electricity temporarily, thereby erasing your file. So it is good practice to perform a SAVE every half-hour or hour, to reduce the amount of work you may accidentally lose. Lightning also has a very annoying habit of "cooking" your computer, whether it is turned on or not. When you buy your computer, it is a good idea to purchase a surge-suppressing power bar for plugging it in.

I don't believe that I have ever met anyone who has driven the same car for 20 years. Cars break down and need to be replaced. Computers are made of the same materials and by the same processes as the cars, and yet everyone is shocked and traumatized when *a computer* breaks down. It is only a matter of time before your computer's hard drive gets a virus, breaks down, is stolen, or explodes. If you do not have a complete backup of everything that you had, then you are likely to be upset for a long time.

The only way to improve your AutoCAD skills is by practicing. There is a wide variety of exercises in this book. The more you do, the better you will get.

1 Introductory Geometry and Setting Up

Upon completion of this chapter, you should be able to:

1. Set the UCS origin
2. Change the screen LIMITS, SNAP, and GRID
3. Use coordinate entry methods
4. Create simple geometry using LINE, ARC, CIRCLE, and FILLET
5. Use the Display commands ZOOM and PAN
6. Set up the UNITS

This book describes AutoCAD Release 2000. If you are not familiar with the platform — WINDOWS 95, 98 or NT — you are using, read the preface for your platform before continuing with the specific AutoCAD commands in this chapter.

The text is designed for AutoCAD Release 2000, however, much of the information is relevant to Release 12, 13 and 14. Most of the commands are the same as in the earlier releases if typed in.

Setting UCS, LIMITS, SNAP, and GRID

Once you have entered the Drawing Editor, AutoCAD establishes a default working environment. This includes LIMITS set at 12 x 9 units, (the default setting is decimal units), GRID set at one dot per unit, and SNAP set at one-unit increments. This drawing environment is stored in a drawing called ACAD.DWG, which is loaded as a default prototype for new files.

You will probably want to change these defaults for every design you do. To make a drawing on paper, the paper size can be set when you are ready to plot.

Notes

If you pick at the command prompt, a rectangle will be started. Pick again to return to the Command prompt.

AutoCAD uses Cartesian coordinates for point entry. The points are set around a determined origin at *X*0, *Y*0, *Z*0. All points to the right of the 0,0 are positive *X*; all points to the left are negative X. All points above 0,0 are positive *Y*; all points below are negative *Y*.

Moving the cursor around the screen with the Coordinates ON (**F6** or COORDS), you will notice that the 0,0 position is at the bottom left corner of your screen.

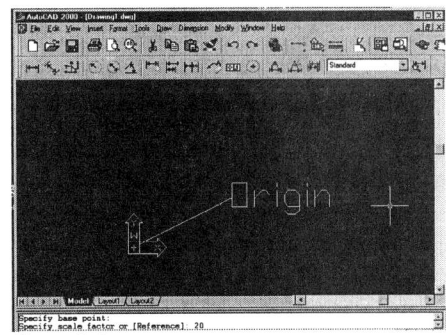

Figure 1-1

Choosing the Origin with UCS

The origin should be the most easily accessible point on the design. If a large percentage of the dimensions on a model stem from one point, it should be made the origin. The reason for

Introductory Geometry and Setting Up   **1**

this is that the coordinate readout on the top of the screen is there to help you find your position. The placement of the origin is important to establish a base for your readouts. It is advisable to have the drawing or part start at 0,0 so that the dimensions of the drawing match the coordinate readout on the screen. To move 0,0 from the bottom of the screen use the UCS command with the Origin option as follows:

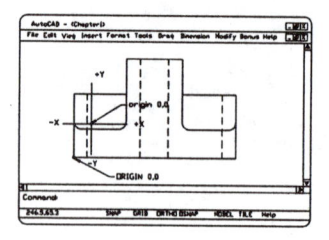

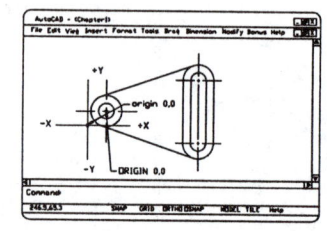

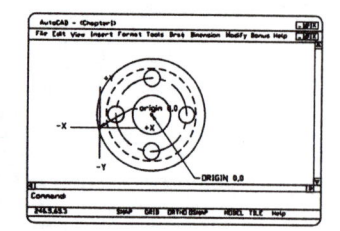

Figure 1-2

UCS stands for *user coordinate system*. This system allows placement of the origin anywhere on the screen for easy identification of 0,0. To place the origin at the positions shown in the above illustration, use UCS with the option New and pick the position on the screen as shown. Because many options on the pull-down menus are not relevant at this stage, simply type in UCS at the command prompt.

```
Command: UCS
Enter an option [New/Move/orthoGraphic/Prev/Restore/Save/
   Del/Apply/?/World] <World>: N
Specify origin of new UCS or
   [Zaxis/3point/OBject/Face/View/X/Y/Z]<0,0,0>: (pick a point
   on the screen)
```

> **Danger**
>
> If you press the space bar before entering any other command just as you open the file, the system will offer you the HELP files. To get the HELP files off screen, press "Esc" Escape to return to the Command prompt.

For a rectangular part, a point further up on the bottom left is a good idea. For a symmetrical part, the center of the screen is a good idea.

If the model or drawing is larger than 12 inches, you must set the screen to the size needed.

All drawings and models in AutoCAD should be created at a full-size scale of 1:1. Plotting to a scale factor other than 1:1 is done when you want to scale a drawing to fit a piece of paper.

The LIMITS Command

The LIMITS command is used to set up the screen to accept the lengths of lines and arcs you need. LIMITS sets the size of your screen and the area covered by the screen grid.

Here are some examples of LIMITS which you may set:

● = the position of the origin

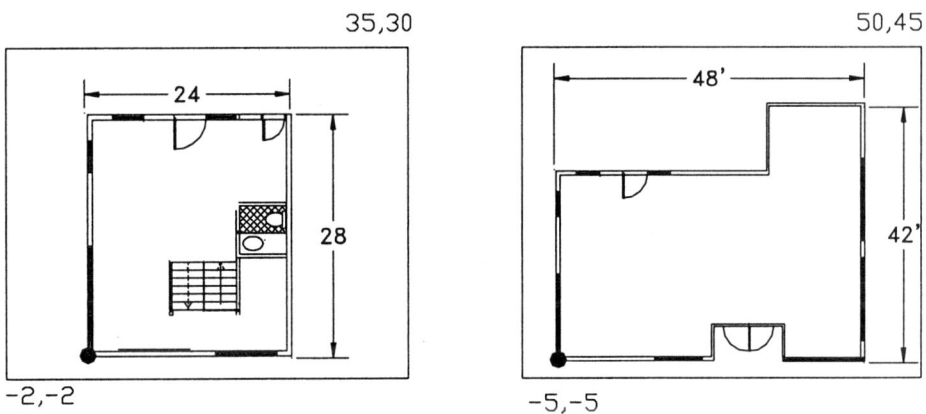

35,30

50,45

-2,-2

-5,-5

In architectural applications, dimensions are either
interior or exterior. The origin is often at the bottom left.

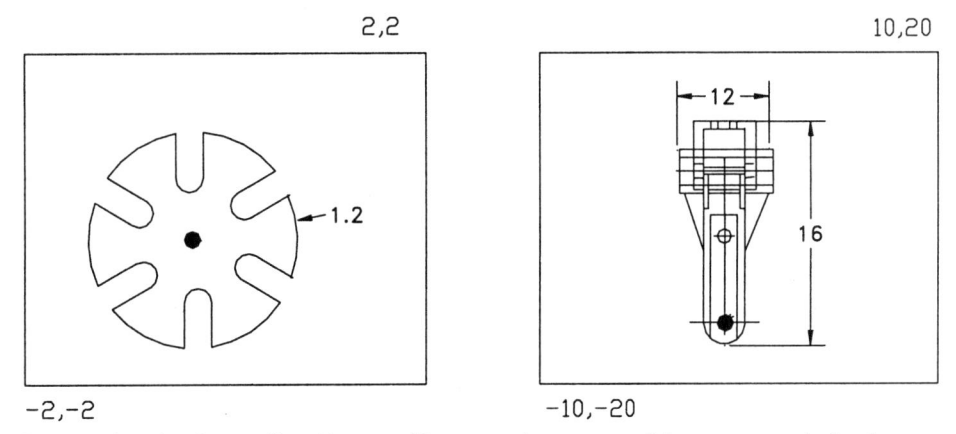

2,2

10,20

-2,-2

-10,-20

In mechanical applications, the parts are often symmetrical
so the origin is found on the part for easy measuring.

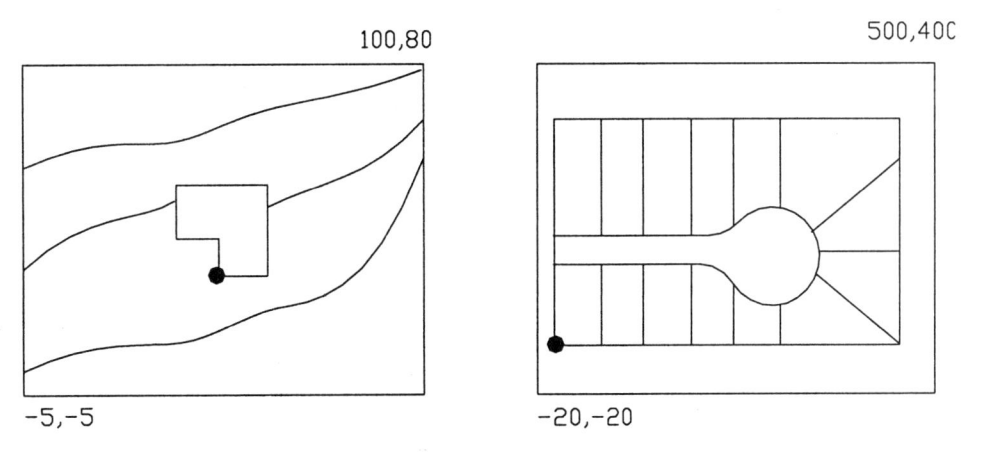

100,80

500,400

-5,-5

-20,-20

In civil applications, large sizes are often needed
The origin or 0,0 is usually on the bottom left.

Figure 1-3

Introductory Geometry and Setting Up   **3**

LIMITS sets a flexible general size for your drawing. You can set limits only on the X Y plane, not in Z. To find LIMITS:

> **Toolbar** No button for this command.
>
> **Pull Down Menu** From the Format menu, pick Drawing Limits.

The command line equivalent is **LIMITS**.

Setting LIMITS does not limit your model; it merely lets you determine how big the finished product might be. Should the design change, you can change the LIMITS at any time.

If you set square limits, e.g. 10 × 10, you will use only part of the screen, because the screen's *X* value is larger than the *Y*.

If you choose the ON option you cannot work outside the area defined by the LIMITS command. You can choose OFF to have the grid extend to the edges of your screen.

Once the LIMITS are set, you may want to set up a GRID and SNAP.

ZOOM All allows you to view the size you have chosen. To make sure the limits and zoom are correct, press **F6** (Function button 6 on the top of your keyboard) and move the cursor around. The coordinates should change. The Coords function is a three way toggle, off, absolute coordinates, and incremental coordinates.

$$8.2578, 0.1673, 0.0000$$

> **Notes**
> If your GRID is not covering your screen, simply invoke the LIMITS command and pick the bottom left and top right of your screen.

Setting start-up SNAP and GRID

SNAP will set an increment that the cursor will move by.

GRID will set a visual aid to help you place objects. The GRID is often set to twice the SNAP value. The grid will extend over the area given by the LIMITS command. If the grid setting is too small for the screen limits, an error message will be issued: "Grid too dense to be displayed." Change the GRID spacing to a larger value.

To find GRID and SNAP:

> **Toolbar** Double click SNAP and GRID on the status bar at the bottom of the screen to turn them off or on.
>
> **Pull Down menu** From the Tools menu, choose Drawing Aids.

The command line equivalent is **SNAP** or **GRID**.

4 CHAPTER ONE

Setting a Drawing Boundary

Setting LIMITS sets up an invisible boundary that helps fit the drawing to paper at the scale chosen.

Example A1: A house that is 40′ × 36′.

```
Command:LIMITS
Reset Model space limits
Specify lower left corner or [ON/OFF]<0'-0",0'-0">:-5',-5'
Specify upper right corner <12.0000,9.0000>:45',40'
Command:ZOOM
[All/Center/Dynamic/Extents/Left/Previous/Scale/Window]<real
   time>:ALL
Command:SNAP
Specify snap spacing (X) or
   [ON/OFF/Aspect/Rotate/Style/Type]<1.0000>:1
Command:GRID
Specify grid spacing or [ON/OFF/Snap/Aspect]<0>:5
```

These settings will provide plenty of viewing space on either side of the drawing and allow you to enter the units by decimal point. The smallest integer picked will be one unit. This can be changed at any time.

Example M1: A template that is 220 mm × 160 mm.

```
Command:LIMITS
Reset Model space limits
Specify lower left corner or [ON/OFF]<0.0000,0.0000>:-5,-40
Specify upper right corner<12.0000,9.0000>:240,180
Command:ZOOM
[All/Center/Dynamic/Extents/Left/Previous/Scale/Window]<real
   time>:ALL
Command:SNAP
Specify snap spacing (X) or
   [ON/OFF/Aspect/Rotate/Style/Type]<1.0000>:5
Command:GRID
Specify grid spacing or [ON/OFF/Snap/Aspect]<0>:10
```

These settings will provide plenty of viewing space on either side of the model and allow a minimum five-unit integer entry.

Example C1: An intersection that is 15 m × 12 m.

```
Command:LIMITS
Reset Model space limits
Specify lower left corner or [ON/OFF]<0.0000,0.0000>:-5,-5
Specify upper right corner<12.0000,9.0000>:20,15
Command:ZOOM
[All/Center/Dynamic/Extents/Left/Previous/Scale/Window]<real
   time>:ALL
Command:SNAP
```

```
           Specify snap spacing (X) or
             [ON/OFF/Aspect/Rotate/Style/Type]<1.0000>:1
           Command:GRID
           Specify grid spacing or [ON/OFF/Snap/Aspect]<0>:2
```

Entry of Points Using Coordinates and Digitizing

All parts of geometry are entered by means of points. **Lines** have two points each. **Circles** have a center point and a point determining the radius. **Arcs** have a center point, a radius point, a start point, and an end point.

There are three ways of entering points:

- Entering them by coordinates: absolute values, relative values, or polar values
- Picking them on the screen, with or without SNAP, also called *digitizing*
- Entering them relative to existing geometry

In this chapter we will look only at the first two methods of point entry. The LINE command will be used to illustrate coordinate entries.

The LINE Command

Find LINE as follows:

> **Toolbar** From the Draw toolbar, choose the Line button.
>
> **Pull Down menu** From the Draw menu, choose LINE.

Notes: Entering **U** at the command prompt will undo the last command.

The command line equivalent is **LINE** or the command alias **L**.

```
           Command:LINE
                 or
           Command:L
```

To create a LINE, you will need to know where it starts, and where it ends. Pick two or more points on the screen or enter the coordinates. Terminate the command by pressing ↵ (the Return or Enter key).

Coordinate Entry Using Absolute, Relative, and Polar Values

The coordinates of an item, the X, Y, and Z values, can be entered either relative to the origin — the absolute value of the line — or relative to the last point entered — the incremental value.

Absolute Value Entries

In this method, the origin of the model or drawing does not change: the objects are placed relative to the origin. To enter the absolute value of an item, type in the X value, then the Y value, separated by a comma. Press ↵ to signal the end of the coordinate entry.

```
           Command:LINE
           Specify first point:0,0
           Specify next point:4,0 (from the absolute position of 0,0 to
             the absolute position of 4,0)
```

6   CHAPTER ONE

Relative Value Entries

To enter an incremental or relative value, type the **@** symbol (**Shift-2**) before the number. @ means "from the last point."

```
Command:LINE
Specify first point:2,3
Specify next point or [Undo]:@4,0 (from the absolute position
   of 2,3 to a position 4 units in positive X from this point)
```

Try this example:

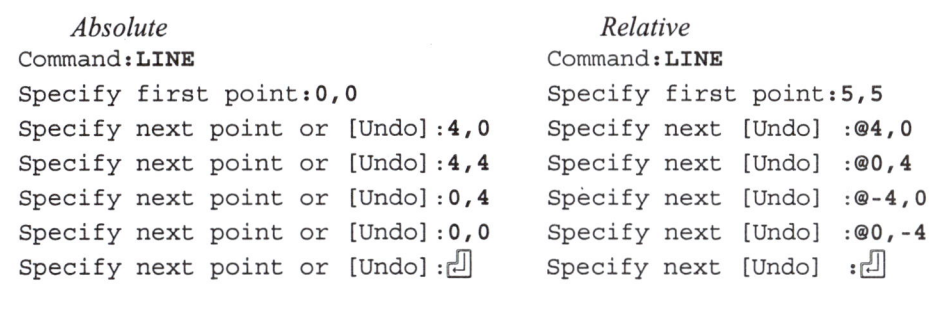

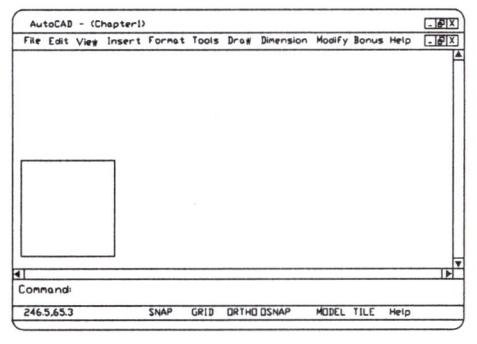

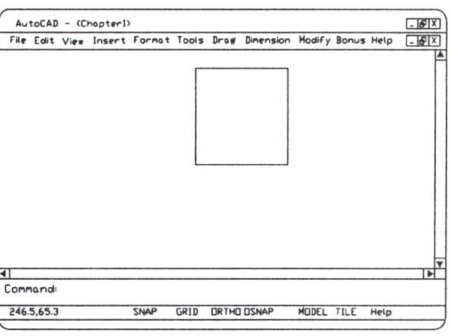

Absolute	*Relative*
`Command:LINE`	`Command:LINE`
`Specify first point:0,0`	`Specify first point:5,5`
`Specify next point or [Undo]:4,0`	`Specify next [Undo] :@4,0`
`Specify next point or [Undo]:4,4`	`Specify next [Undo] :@0,4`
`Specify next point or [Undo]:0,4`	`Specify next [Undo] :@-4,0`
`Specify next point or [Undo]:0,0`	`Specify next [Undo] :@0,-4`
`Specify next point or [Undo]:↵`	`Specify next [Undo] :↵`

Absolute   Relative

Figure 1-4

The first example will give you a four-unit square starting at 0,0. The second will give you a four-unit square starting at 5,5.

To draw a line from point 5,6 to point 8.3,6 use either of the following.

Absolute	*Relative*
`Command:LINE`	`Command:LINE`
`Specify first point:5,6`	`Specify first point:5,6`
`Specify next point or [Undo]:8.3,6`	`Specify next [Undo] :@3.3,0`

In choosing between the absolute and the incremental method, the deciding factor is what you know. If you know that the final point is going to be 8.3,6, use the absolute value. If you know that the line is going to be 3.3 units in positive *X* from the last point, then enter the incremental coordinates.

Introductory Geometry and Setting Up   **7**

Try these examples:

Absolute	*Relative*
Command:**LINE**	Command:**LINE**
First point:**0,0**	First point:**7,5**
Next point:**2,0**	Next point:**@2,0**
Next point:**2,3**	Next point:**@0,3**
Next point:**4,3**	Next point:**@2,0**
Next point:**4,2**	Next point:**@0,-1**
Next point:**6,2**	Next point:**@2,0**
Next point:**6,4**	Next point:**@0,2**
Next point:**0,4**	Next point:**@-6,0**
Next point:**0,0**	Next point:**@0,-4**
Next point:⏎	Next point:⏎

The objects should look like this, one starting at 0,0 and the other starting at 7,5:

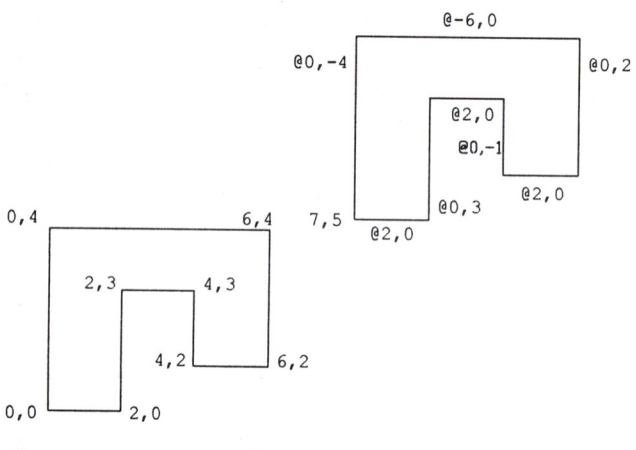

Figure 1-5

Polar Value Entries

Polar coordinates allow you to enter an item, relative to the last item, at a specified length and angle. Angles are normally calculated counterclockwise from the positive X direction as shown in figure 1-6.

Command:**LINE**
Specify first point:**3,4**
Specify next point or [Undo] :**@4<45**

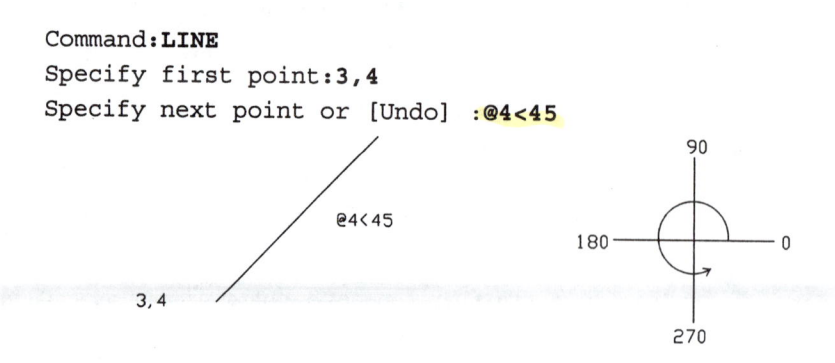

Figure 1-6

Where: @ = relative to the last point
4 = the length of the line
< = angle
45 = the angle that the line will be drawn at; all angles are calculated counterclockwise

Try this example:

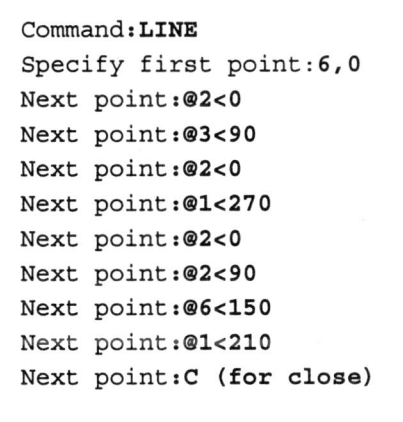

```
Command:LINE
Specify first point:6,0
Next point:@2<0
Next point:@3<90
Next point:@2<0
Next point:@1<270
Next point:@2<0
Next point:@2<90
Next point:@6<150
Next point:@1<210
Next point:C (for close)
```

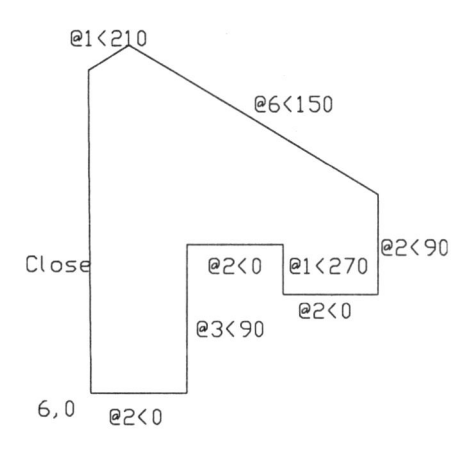

Figure 1-7

As noted above, angles are calculated counter-clockwise from the furthest point in positive *X*.

Coordinate Entry Using Digitizing

The "pick" button on the mouse will enter a point every time you press it while in a geometry command. You can make your digitizing or picking of points much easier and much more accurate by using the SNAP function.

With SNAP you can draw lines, arcs or circles at preset integers. If you set the snap to .25, all entries will be rounded to the nearest .25 interval as follows:

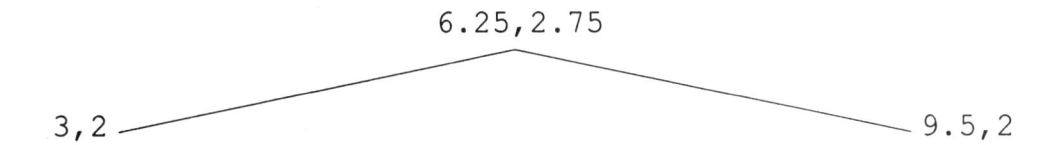

Figure 1-8

Try repeating the previous exercises using the mouse and setting the SNAP value to 1. If the coordinate readout does not move, press **F6**. Remember that it is a three-way toggle; Off, Absolute, and Incremental. Incremental works only within a draw command.

If you set SNAP to 1, all the points you digitize or pick from the screen will be accurate to one-unit integers. You cannot be accurate without using SNAP.

Do not make the mistake of thinking that the grid will help to place items on the screen. The grid is for visual reference only.

ORTHO Mode

With the ORTHO option (F8 or the ORTHO button), lines can only be drawn vertically or horizontally. Set SNAP at .25 and enter the following:

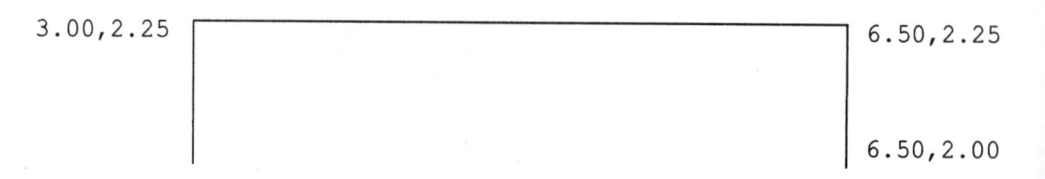

```
3.00,2.25 ┌─────────────────────┐ 6.50,2.25
          │                     │
                                │ 6.50,2.00
```

Figure 1-9

You will notice that the cursor only goes vertically and horizontally. By pressing **F8**, you will be able to draw diagonal lines again.

The GRID (**F7** or the GRID button) will give you a visual display of distance.

You can use any of the above methods in combination at any time.

Geometry Commands

The LINE Command

The LINE command is as simple as the above examples indicate. Indicate, with either a pick on the screen or a coordinate position, where each point should be. Any combination of points is accepted. Use ⏎ at the end of any coordinate entries.

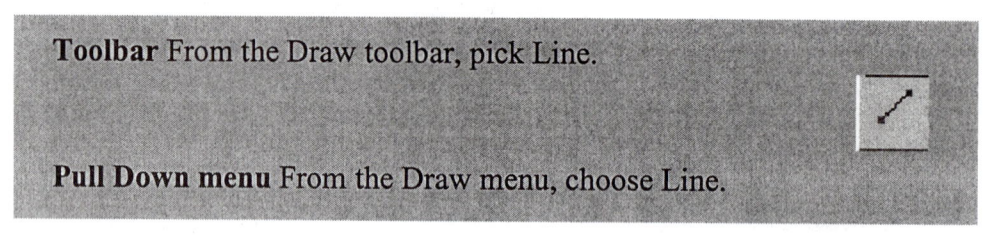

> **Toolbar** From the Draw toolbar, pick Line.
>
> **Pull Down menu** From the Draw menu, choose Line.

The command line equivalent is **LINE** or **L**.

```
Command:LINE
Specify first point: (pick a point)
Specify next point or (Undo):@3<250
Specify next point or (Undo): (pick another point)
Specify next point or (Undo):⏎ (Then Enter)
```

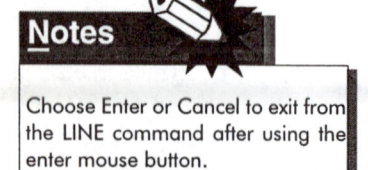

Notes: Remove right click menu with Tools, Options, User Preferences, Right Click Customization.

When drawing lines, you are creating objects that are described by two points: a beginning and an end. Any number of points can be entered in the LINE command with each point joined to the last by a separate line. If you have entered five or six points in a single command, any of the lines can be erased.

Notes: Choose Enter or Cancel to exit from the LINE command after using the enter mouse button.

LINE Options

C will close the string of lines with a line from the last point to the first point.

U will undo the last entered point.

.X, .Y, .Z are dealt with in Chapter 9.

The CIRCLE Command

Drawing a CIRCLE you are also describing an object that has two points; a center and a radius. The ARC has four points: a center, a radius, a start, and an end. The CIRCLE command will prompt you for the information needed to complete the circle. The command is:

> **Toolbar** From the Draw toolbar, choose the Circle command.
>
> **Pull Down menu** From the Draw menu, choose Circle - Center,Radius.

The command line equivalent is **CIRCLE** or **C**.

```
Command: CIRCLE
Specify center point for circle or [3P/2P/Ttr (tan tan
   radius)]: (pick a point)
Specify Radius of Circle or Diameter: (pick another point or
   type in a radius value)
```

Where:
- **3P** = a circle fit through three points
- **2P** = a circle fit through two points
- **Ttr** = a circle that is tangent on its diameter to two selected objects indicated with a specified radius
- **Center point** = the default circle which is described by a center point and a radius, in that order
- **Diameter or Radius** = the default circle specified by a radius; or type **D** to specify a diameter
- **DRAG** = the drag mode; the circle will expand and contract following the movement of the cursor

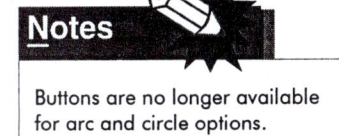

Notes

Buttons are no longer available for arc and circle options.

Options appear when you type in **C** or **CIRCLE**. When picking CIRCLE from either the screen menu or the pull-down menu, you will be prompted for one of the options listed above. All of the options for creating circles are shown on page 24.

The ARC Command

Arcs are also created by using options to control how the ARC is entered. The default is to define the first, then the second, then the third or final point of an arc. The command is:

> **Toolbar** From the Draw toolbar, choose the Arc button
>
> **Pull Down menu** From the Draw menu, choose Arc - 3 point.

The command line equivalent is **ARC** or **A**.

```
Command: ARC
ARC Specify start point of arc or [CEnter]: (pick a point)
Specify second point of arc or [CEnter/ENd]: (pick another
   point)
Specify end point of arc: (pick another point)
```

Introductory Geometry and Setting Up

Where: **CEnter** = an option to pick a center point

Start point: = the default first point to create an arc stretched through three points

ENd = an option to pick the end point

There are many variations on the ARC command, illustrated on page 25.

You can access all arc options through the Draw Pull Down menu under arc. Should you want to enter the options at the command line, simply type in the option that you want as follows:

> **Notes**
> The key to using ARC is to determine what is not known and choose the options that work.

```
Command:ARC
ARC Specify start point of arc or [CEnter]: (pick 1)
Specify second point of arc
or [CEnter/ENd]:EN
Specify end point of arc: (pick 2)
Specify center point of arc or
[Angle/Direction/Radius]:R
Specify radius of arc: (pick 3)
```

Figure 1-10

The FILLET Command

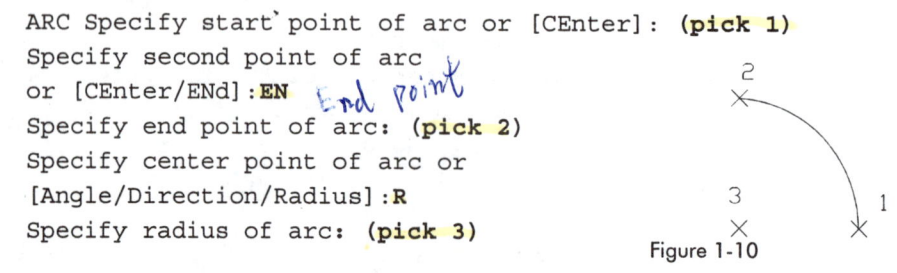

The FILLET command provides an easy way to place an arc between two existing objects, usually lines. FILLET can also be used with Radius 0 to clean up corners and connect lines to an apex.

> **Windows** From the Modify toolbar, choose the Fillet button. 
>
> **Pull Down menu** From the Modify menu, choose Fillet.

The command line equivalent is **FILLET**.

```
Command:FILLET
Current settings: Mode = Trim,
Radius = <5.0000>
Select first object or [Polyline
/Radius/Trim]: (pick 1)
Select second object: (pick 2)
```

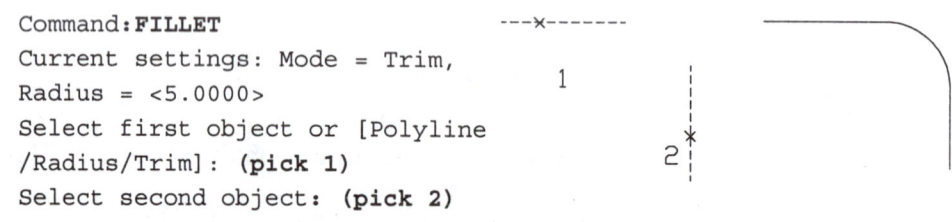

Figure 1-11

To change the radius choose **R**.

> **Notes**
> To restart the previous command at the command prompt, press ↵.

```
Command:FILLET
Current settings: Mode = Trim,
Radius = <5.0000>
Select first object or [Polyline
/Radius/Trim]:R
Specify fillet radius:12
```

12   CHAPTER ONE

View Commands

The View menu and toolbar offer commands which will change the display of the model or drawing relative to the screen. Commands from the View menu will not change the coordinates or position of the model or the database. They only change the way you look at it. The following commands appear in the View menu:

ZOOM	=	magnifies a section of the screen
PAN	=	moves the model across the screen without changing the magnification factor (zoom)
REDRAW	=	updates the view and clears off blips (pick marks — see pg 16) and erase marks
REGEN	=	recomputes the file

The ZOOM Command

ZOOM is accessed by typing it on the command line, using the slider bars on the top and bottom of the screen, or using the pull-down menus or the standard toolbar. For the Zoom options on the toolbar, hold the Zoom Out button down and the options will be shown. The following is the list of options for the ZOOM command.

```
Command:ZOOM
Specify corner of window, enter a scale factor (nX or nXP), or
[All/Center/Dynamic/Extents/Previous/Scale/Window]<real time>:
```

Where:			
	A	=	**All.** Expands or shrinks the model or drawing to fit onto the screen relative to your limits
	C	=	**Center.** Centers the model on the screen; you must enter a magnification factor or "height"
	D	=	**Dynamic.** Creates a dynamic display of the item for zooming
	E	=	**Extents.** Expands or shrinks the model or drawing to fit all of the objects on screen
	P	=	**Previous.** Returns you to the Previous zoom factor
	Realtime	=	**Real time.** Zooms interactively to a logical extent. Activate with either the button or a right click
	W	=	**Window.** Describes by two diagonal points a rectangle around the area you want to view
	Scale nX	=	specifies a percentage of the existing size
	Scale nXP	=	specifies a size relative to paper space

ZOOM In, Out and Realtime are not invoked by the first letter of the word as are the above options. Use the buttons, the right click, or the pull down menu for these choices.

Scale works like this: .8x will display an image at 80% of its current size; .5x will display an image at half the current size; and 2x will display an image twice the size of the current size.

Zooming In and Out

Zooming in doubles the size of the image, zooming out reduces the image by half.

Zoom Limits shows the screen limits.

Toolbar From the standard toolbar, choose ZOOM In ZOOM Out. Or ZOOM Realtime

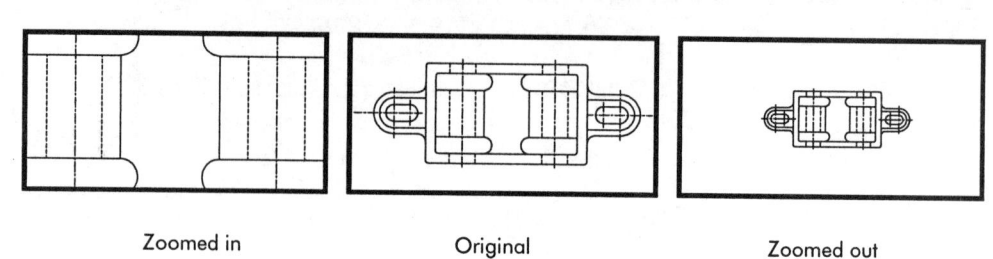

Zoomed in   Original   Zoomed out

Figure 1-12

ZOOM Window

To zoom into an area by specifying its boundaries, use Window.

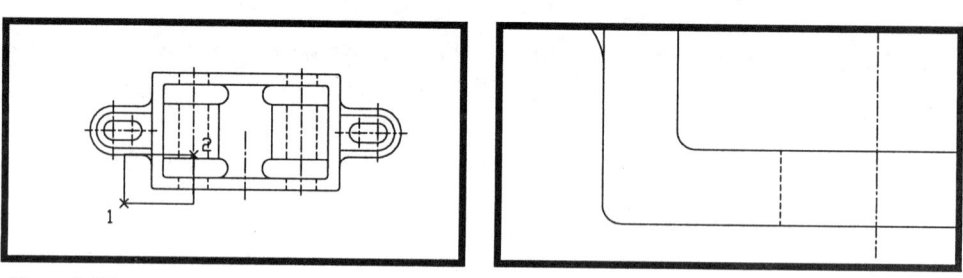

Figure 1-13

```
Command: ZOOM
Specify corner of window, enter a scale factor (nX or nXP), or
[All/Center/Dynamic/Extents/Previous/Scale/Window]<real time>: W
Specify first corner: (pick 1)
Specify opposite corner: (pick 2)
```

ZOOM All

To display the entire drawing, use ZOOM All.

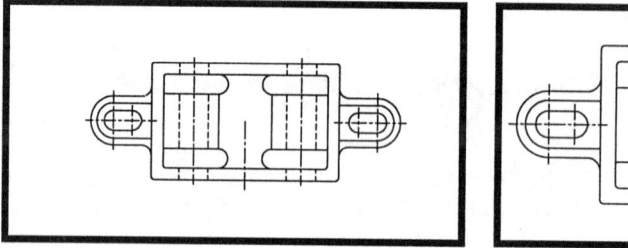

Figure 1-14

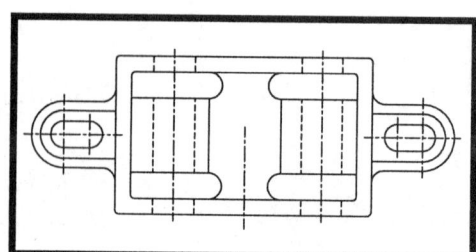

```
Command: ZOOM All
Specify corner of window, enter a scale factor (nX or nXP), or
[All/Center/Dynamic/Extents/Previous/Scale/Window]<real time>: A
```

Zoom Relative to the Current Size

To scale a view relative to the current size, use the x. To double the size of the current view use **2x; to reduce the view to 75% use .75x**.

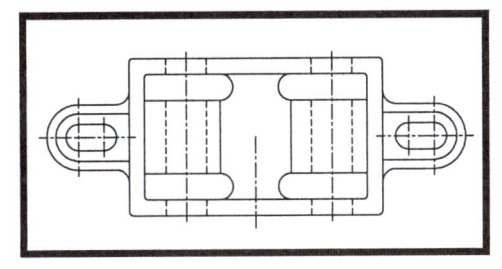

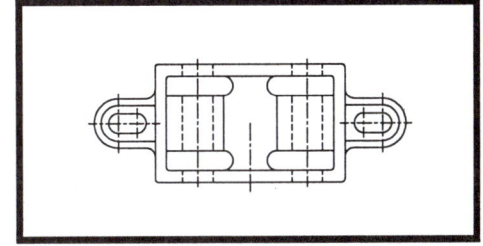

Figure 1-15

```
Command: ZOOM
Specify corner of window, enter a scale factor (nX or nXP), or
[All/Center/Dynamic/Extents/Previous/Scale/Window]<real
   time>:.75X (this is the same as Zoom Out)
```

Zoom Relative to the Drawing Limits

To scale the view to twice the drawing limits use **2**. To display the image at half the full size use **.5**.

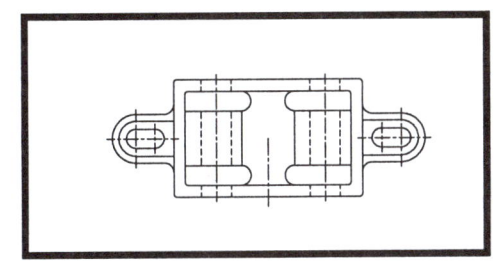

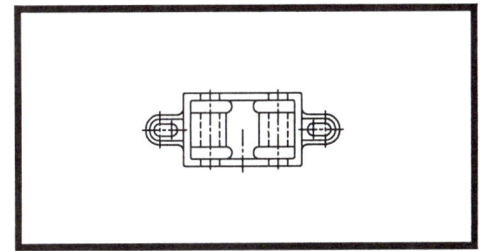

Figure 1-16

```
Command: ZOOM
Specify corner of window, enter a scale factor (nX or nXP), or
[All/Center/Dynamic/Extents/Previous/Scale/Window]<real
   time>:.5
```

The PAN Command

To move the view across the screen without changing the display size, use PAN.

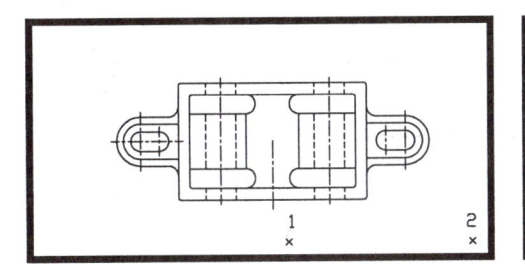

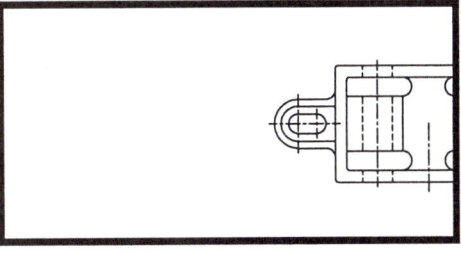

Figure 1-17

```
Command: PAN
Press ESC or ENTER to exit, or right-click to display
   shortcuts.
```

Introductory Geometry and Setting Up   **15**

> **Toolbar** From the Standard Toolbar choose the PAN button, or use the scroll bars on the side and bottom of the screen.

The command line equivalent is **PAN** or **P**.

PAN and ZOOM

The PAN command moves the model across the screen, while ZOOM magnifies the model within the screen. The database, i.e., the 0,0,0 point and associated coordinate points, remain the same.

If you want to see an area not currently in view but with the same magnification factor, use PAN to translate the data across the screen without changing the magnification. PAN and ZOOM may take a bit of time to do depending on the size of your memory and how much data you have on screen.

Transparent View Commands

ZOOM and PAN can be entered at the command line, or they can be accessed through the buttons or screen menu. If accessing the commands from the Pull Down menu, ZOOM and PAN can be used within a command sequence. If you are in the middle of a line sequence and need to access a certain area for accuracy, choose the ZOOM Window button without exiting from LINE.

Windows Scroll Bars

Windows slider bars can be used instead of the PAN command. To move the drawing up, pick the "down" arrow on the vertical slider bar. To move the drawing to the left, pick the right arrow on the slider bar. If you have a smaller screen, you may want to have the slider bars not displayed. To remove them from the screen, choose the Tools menu, then Options, then Display. Remove the checkmark from the box beside "Display Scroll Bars."

> **Notes**
> Preferences is called Options in this release, and is found under the Tools menu. To change scroll bar display, use Options.

The REGEN and REDRAW Commands

While your data is always available, to save space in RAM, it is not always completely generated. Thus, the use of ZOOM or PAN sometimes results in a screen regeneration.

The REDRAW command cleans the screen and redraws any information that may be absent due to previous erasing or changes in the position of objects. It refreshes the screen from the available generated data.

While you are creating a model, the screen may fill up with a series of small items called *blips*, which look like tiny crosses. These indicate position markers, where you have digitized or picked a spot on the screen. (Blips can be turned off by typing **BLIPMODE** at the command prompt, followed by **OFF**.)

To clean the screen, you can use the REDRAW command by typing in **R** or using REDRAW on the View menu. If your grid is properly set, pressing **F7** twice (GRID on, GRID off) provides another method.

In the illustration at the right, the blips have been removed:

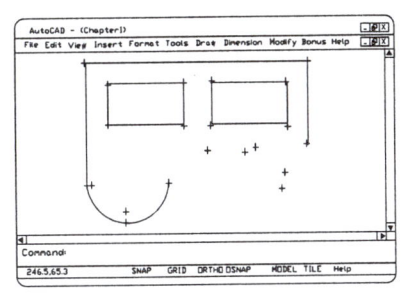

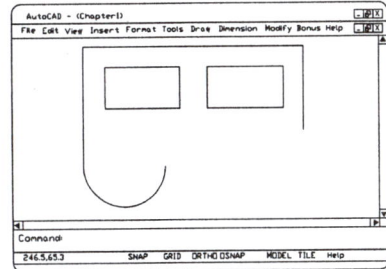

Figure 1-18

The REGEN command actually regenerates all the data, and takes much longer. REGEN is used to update arc and circle displays to make the objects look more rounded. If you pick up an arc or circle in a ZOOM Window command, it is not rounded but octagonal, or at least "squared" rather than rounded at the corners. To have a better image of the circle, try REGEN. This will update the display of an arc or circle relative to the current magnification factor and display a superior image.

The UNITS Command

In AutoCAD it is suggested that you draw everything at full scale or 1:1 scale, and plot the drawing at the required scale factor later. The type of units chosen determines how AutoCAD interprets coordinate and angle entries.

AutoCAD offers various types of units of measure for entering into drawings. Before setting up the parameters of the drawing, first set up the units so that the readout displays the required units. Decimal mode may be used for metric units and for inch or foot units. When plotting to paper, if you want the number to represent an inch on the final plot, choose inches in the PLOT command. If you want the decimal to represent millimeters, choose mm in the PLOT command.

The scientific, decimal, and fractional modes simply equate one drawing unit to one displayed unit. The engineering and architectural modes assume that one drawing unit equals one inch. The decimal mode makes no assumptions.

Use these settings in UNITS to set up your drawing and they will be reflected properly in the final plot.

The UNITS command can be accessed either through the command line or through the DDUNITS dialog box from the Pull Down menu.

> **Toolbar** There is no button for this command.
>
> **Pull Down menu** From the Format menu, choose UNITS.

The command line equivalent is **UNITS** or **DDUNITS**.

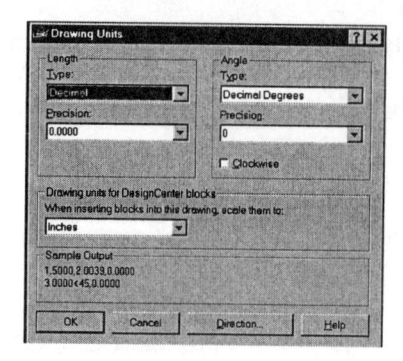

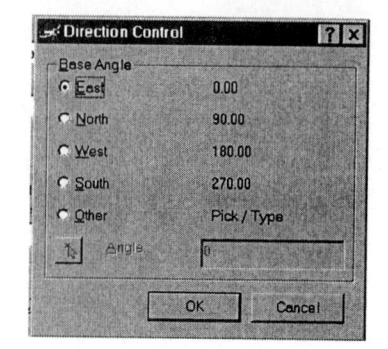

Figure 1-19

From the dialog box, choose the units readout that you require by picking the down arrow under type. Choose the precision by picking the arrow beside 0.0000; then choose the desired accuracy. For surveying, the direction is important, so a direction dialog box is provided. Choose the appropriate readout for your discipline. Once completed, pick OK.

Here are some of the options that you can choose:

```
Report formats:
    1. Scientific      1.55E+01
    2. Decimal         15.50
    3. Engineering     1-3.58"
    4. Architectural   1'-3 1/2"
    5. Fractional      15 1/2
```

Decimal (Option 2)

This option changes the amount of decimals shown on the status line and in your dimensions. Once the type of unit you want to use is selected, you can then choose the precision.

1.00

1.000000

Bear in mind that your SNAP values (page 39) may be to a different decimal point than your readout. This readout in no way influences the accuracy of your drawing.

Architectural (Option 4)

When Architectural (i.e. imperial) units are chosen, inches are your preferred unit: when you enter a number, - 1 or 2 - this means 1 inch or 2 inches, not 1 foot or 2 feet.

When using architectural measurements, each numerical entry is accepted as an inch. The ' and " symbols must be used to differentiate between feet (') and inches ("). The status line readout puts a hyphen between the foot and the inches, when typing in the point, place the hyphen between the inches and the fraction of an inch. Following is an example of an architectural unit input using the LINE command.

```
Command:LINE
Specify first point:2,3 (X 2 inches, Y 3 inches)
Specify next point or (Undo):@4',0 (4 feet in X and none in Y)
Specify next point or (Undo):@0,2'3 (none in X and 2 feet 3
   inches in Y)
Specify next point or (Undo):@3'4-1/2",0 (3 feet 4 1/2 inches
   in X and none in Y)
```

All angles will be measured in decimal degrees in a counterclockwise direction. If you want to change this option, check the box for clockwise in the units dialog box, and change the appropriate system of angle measurement.

Usually the default is decimal degrees.

Do not worry about the paper size until you are ready to plot.

Notes

The hyphen (-) in the architectural point entry is not the same as in the architectural readout on the status line.

Scientific (Option 1)

In scientific notation, the E is the exponent factor of 10 and is shown with a plus sign. The quantity of 4.1325E+6 is read as 4132500. This notation is used when numbers are very large, such as in astronomy or physics. Its use reduces the need for a large number of trailing zeros.

Engineering (Option 3)

Often in civil engineering there is a need to express feet and inches without fractions. With this option, you can do exactly that.

   3' 4 3/4" = 3' 4.75"

In fact, with engineering units, the inch symbol is not required. Therefore, you are able to place objects in inches with good precision.

```
Command:LINE
Specify first point:4'3.5,0 (4 feet 3 1/2 inches in X and 0 in
   Y)
Specify next point or (Undo):@4.4,0 (4 4/10 inches in X and
   none in Y)
```

Fractional (Option 5)

With fractional units the information is entered as a fraction with a slash (/). For mixed numbers a hyphen (-) must be added with the slash (/).

```
Command:LINE
Specify first point:1-1/2,2-3/4
Specify next point or (Undo):@3/4,0
```

Choose the required precision from the next prompt.

Surveying

The surveyor's "compass rose" is much the same as a ship's compass — divided into four parts with the top being north, the left being west, etc. Angles are expressed in 90 degree quadrants.

The quadrant between north and east, for example, starts at 0 degrees due east and progresses 90 degrees to due north. To express 25 decimal degrees using AutoCAD's default origin for angles, enter **N25d0'0''E**. You may omit null minutes and/or seconds and enter **N25dE**.

When entering this measurement, do not use spaces.

```
Command:L
Specify first point:0,0
Specify next point or (Undo):@38<S44d14'9"W
```

Measuring Angles

AutoCAD's default setting for angles is zero degrees at due east. You may change this zero-degree reference point to due north, due west, or due south. These are the only four positions offered by the UNITS command. To orient the zero reference at an angle other than those specified, you can change the user coordinate system (UCS) as explained later.

CLOCKWISE OR COUNTERCLOCKWISE: These two angle rotations can be applied to all angles. The rotation always starts at the zero reference point.

UNTRANSLATED ANGLES: If the UNITS command is set to a nondecimal angular mode (e.g. radians), an angle can be preceded by a < to enter a measurement counterclockwise from three o'clock.

If an angle measurement direction or origin has been changed, enter < before an angle measurement to have the angle measured counter clockwise from three o'clock.

USING UNITS EFFECTIVELY: Remember that the UNITS command does not operate like the SNAP command. The status line will indicate the position relative to the units that were specified, but points will not be entered exactly at the position specified without setting the SNAP.

The units can be changed when beginning a model or drawing, or when entering all or part of a model. For example, in a floor layout at 1:1 decimal units, you can switch to architectural units and then scale the entire model by 12. See Chapter 11 for plotting scales.

Prelab 1 Using LINE, ARC, CIRCLE and FILLET

Open AutoCAD. If AutoCAD is already running, pick File from the Pull Down menu, then New to start a new file.

Step 1 Set the LIMITS to 100,60, GRID to 10, SNAP to 5. Use the Tools Pull Down menu to do this under Drafting Settings. Then pick ZOOM All from the View pull-down menu or the button. Or the command line, type **LIMITS**, then **SNAP**, then **GRID**. Type in the **BOLD**.

```
Command:LIMITS
Reset model space limits
Specify lower left corner or [ON/OFF]
<0.0000,0.0000>:↵
Specify upper right corner
<12.0000,9.0000>:100,60
Command:SNAP
Specify snap spacing (X) or
[ON/OFF/Aspect/Rotate/Style/
   Type]<1.0000>:5
Command:GRID
Specify grid spacing or [ON/OFF/Snap/Aspect]<1.0000>:10
Command: (from the View Pull Down menu, pick ZOOM All)
```

Notes
If you pick on the screen without a command, a box will start to be drawn Pick again, and you will return to the Command prompt.

Toolbar From the Draw toolbar, choose the Circle button.

Pull Down menu From the Draw menu, choose Circle-Center,Radius.

Step 2 Start by drawing circles. With the first one, use the Pull Down menu.

With the second, use the command alias. With the third, use the pull-down menu. The command line equivalent is **CIRCLE** or **C**.

```
Command:CIRCLE
Specify center point for circle or
[3P/2P/Ttr (tan tan radius)]:25,30
Specify Radius of Circle or Diameter:10
Command:C
Specify center point for circle or [3P/2P/Ttr (tan tan
   radius)]: 70,40
Specify Radius of Circle or Diameter: (pick a point 5
   units straight over from the point shown)
Command:↵ (the enter key retrieves the previous
   command)
Specify center point for circle or [3P/2P/Ttr (tan tan
   radius)]:70,20
Specify Radius of Circle or Diameter:5
```

Introductory Geometry and Setting Up

Step 3 Now use ARC with the option Start,End,Radius to create an arc. Use the Pull Down menu. Make sure that SNAP is on. The word SNAP should be highlighted on the status line. If not, press **F9** or the Snap button.

Toolbar From the Draw toolbar, choose the Arc button.

The command line equivalent is **ARC**.

```
Command:ARC From the Draw Pull Down
menu, pick Arc, then
Start, End, Radius
ARC Specify start point of arc or
[CEnter]: (pick 1)
Specify end point of arc: (pick 2)
Specify Radius: (pick 3)
```

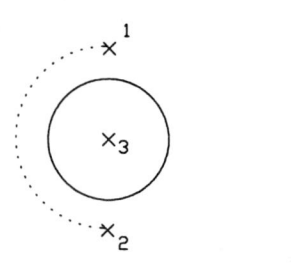

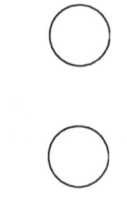

Step 4 With the SNAP still on, add the other two arcs. Type in **A** at the command prompt to access the command.

```
Command:A
ARC Specify start point of arc or [CEnter]: (pick 4)
Specify second point of arc or
[CEnter/ENd]:EN
Specify end point of arc: (pick 5)
Specify center point of arc or
[Angle/Direction/Radius]: (pick 6)
Command:
ARC Specify start point of arc or
[CEnter]: (pick 7)
Specify second point of arc or
[CEnter/ENd]:EN
Specify end point of arc: (pick 8)
Specify center point of arc or
[Angle/Direction/Radius]:  (pick 9)
```

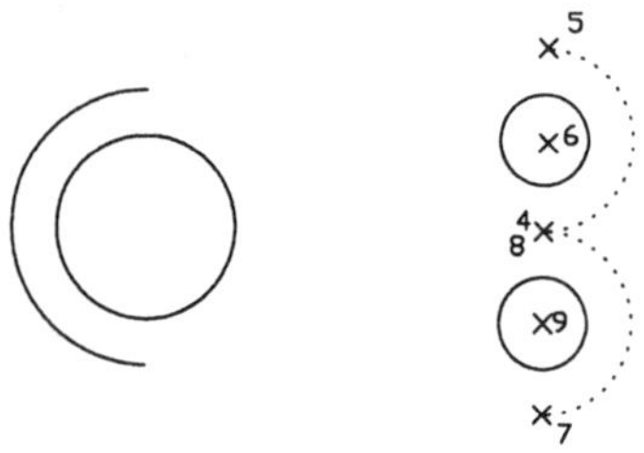

Step 5 Now draw in the lines from the ends of the arcs.

```
Command:LINE
Specify first point: (pick 10)
Specify next point or (Undo):(pick 11)
Specify next point or (Undo):
Command:L
Specify first point: (pick 12)
Specify next point or (Undo): (pick 13)
Specify next point or (Undo):
```

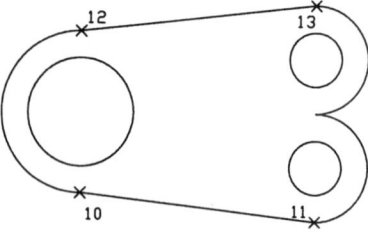

Step 6   Use the FILLET command to complete the drawing.

> **Toolbar** From the Modify toolbar, choose the Fillet button.
>
> **Pull Down menu** From the Modify menu, choose Fillet.

```
Command: FILLET
Current settings: Mode = Trim,
Radius = <5.0000>
Select first object or [Polyline
/Radius/Trim]: r
Specify fillet radius <1.000>:15
Command:FILLET
Current settings: Mode = Trim,
Radius = <5.0000>
Select first object or [Polyline
/Radius/Trim]: (pick 14)
Select second object: (pick 15)
```

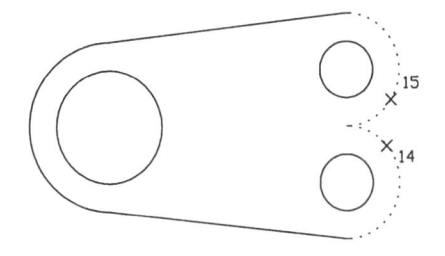

Turn your SNAP off if the arcs are too difficult to pick.

Your drawing should look like this.

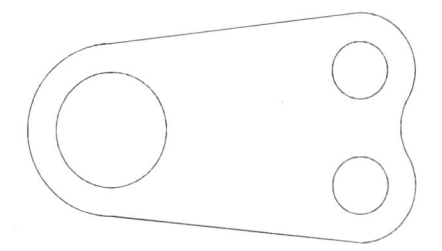

To save the file, access the File Pull Down menu. Choose SAVE. See the Introduction for details.

Circle Draw Menu

Center Radius
If you know the center and the radius

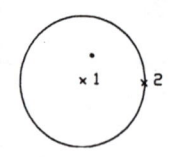

Command: **CIRCLE**
Specify center point for circle or [3P/2P/Ttr (tan tan radius)]: **(pick 1)**
Specify Radius of Circle or Diameter: **(pick 2)**

Center Diameter
If you know the center and the diameter

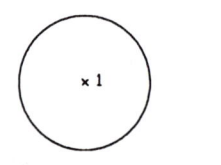

Command: **CIRCLE**
Specify center point for circle or [3P/2P/Ttr (tan tan radius)]: **(pick 1)**
Specify Radius of Circle or Diameter: **D**
Specify Radius of Circle or Diameter: **(pick 2)**

2-Point

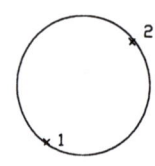

Command: **CIRCLE**
Specify center point for circle or [3P/2P/Ttr (tan tan radius)]: **2P**
Specify first end point on circle's diameter: **(pick 1)**

3-Point

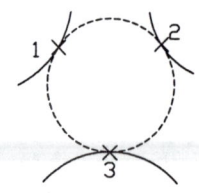

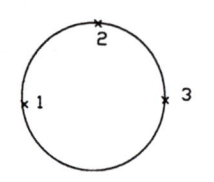

Command: **CIRCLE**
Specify center point for circle or [3P/2P/Ttr (tan tan radius)]: **3P**
Specify first end point on circle's diameter: **(pick 1)**
Specify second end point on circle's diameter: **(pick 2)**
Specify third end point on circle's diameter: **(pick 2)**

TTR

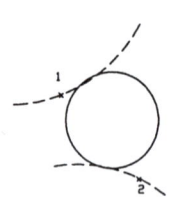

Command: **CIRCLE**
Specify center point for circle or [3P/2P/Ttr (tan tan radius)]: **ttr**
Specify point on object for first tangent of circle: **(pick 1)**
Specify point on object for second tangent of circle: **(pick 2)**

TTT

Command: **CIRCLE**
Specify center point for circle or [3P/2P/Ttr (tan tan radius)]: **3P**
Specify first end point on circle's diameter: **(pick 1)**

Fillet

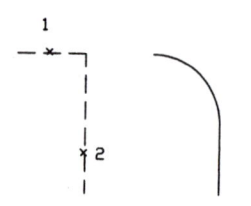

Command: **FILLET**
Current settings: Mode = Trim, Radius = <5.0000>
Select first object or [Polyline/Radius/Trim]: **r**
Specify fillet radius <1.000>: **15**
Command: **FILLET**
Current settings: Mode = Trim, Radius = <5.0000>
Select first object or [Polyline/Radius/Trim]: **(pick 1)**
Select second object: **(pick 2)**

24 CHAPTER ONE

Arc Draw Menu

3-point

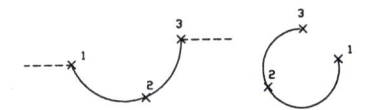

ARC Specify start point of arc or
   [CEnter]: **(pick 1)**
Specify second point of arc or
   [CEnter/ENd]: **(pick 2)**
Specify end point of arc: **(pick 3)**

Start, Center, Angle

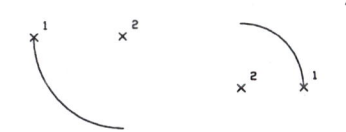

ARC Specify start point of arc
   or[CEnter]: **(pick 1)**
Specify center point of arc:**(pick 2)**
Specify angle: **90**

Start, End, Angle

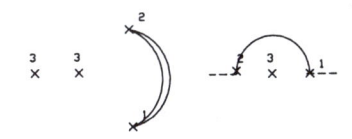

ARC Specify start point of arc or
   [CEnter]: **(pick 1)**
Specify end point of arc:**(pick 2)**
Specify Angle: **(pick 3)**

Start, End, Direction

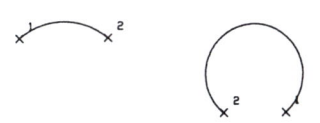

ARC Specify start point of arc
   or [CEnter]: **(pick 1)**
Specify end point of arc:**(pick 2)**
Specify Direction: **(pick 3)**

Center, Start, Angle

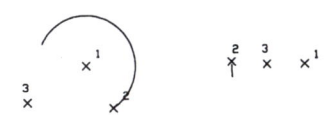

ARC Specify center point of arc
   : **(pick 1)**
Specify start point of arc:**(pick 2)**
Specify angle: **(pick 3)**

Start, Center, End

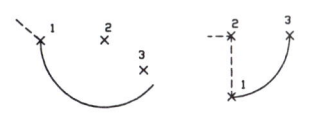

ARC Specify start point of arc
   or[CEnter]: **(pick 1)**
Specify center point of arc:**(pick 2)**
Specify end of arc: **(pick 3)**

Start, Center, Length of Chord

ARC Specify start point of arc
   or[CEnter]: **(pick 1)**
Specify center point of arc:**(pick 2)**
Specify length of chord: **(pick 3)**

Start, End, Radius

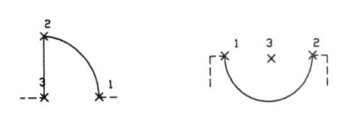

ARC Specify start point of arc
   or[CEnter]: **(pick 1)**
Specify end point of arc:**(pick 2)**
Specify Radius: **(pick 3)**

Center, Start, End

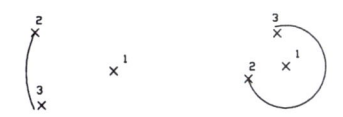

ARC Specify center point of arc
   : **(pick 1)**
Specify start point of arc:**(pick 2)**
Specify end of arc: **(pick 3)**

Center, Start, Length

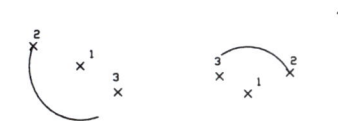

ARC Specify center point of arc
   : **(pick 1)**
Specify start point of arc:**(pick 2)**
Specify length of chord: **(pick 3)**

Introductory Geometry and Setting Up

Practice Exercise 1

For these exercises you may not need to change your limits, but you may need to change your SNAP and GRID. Save each as a different drawing.

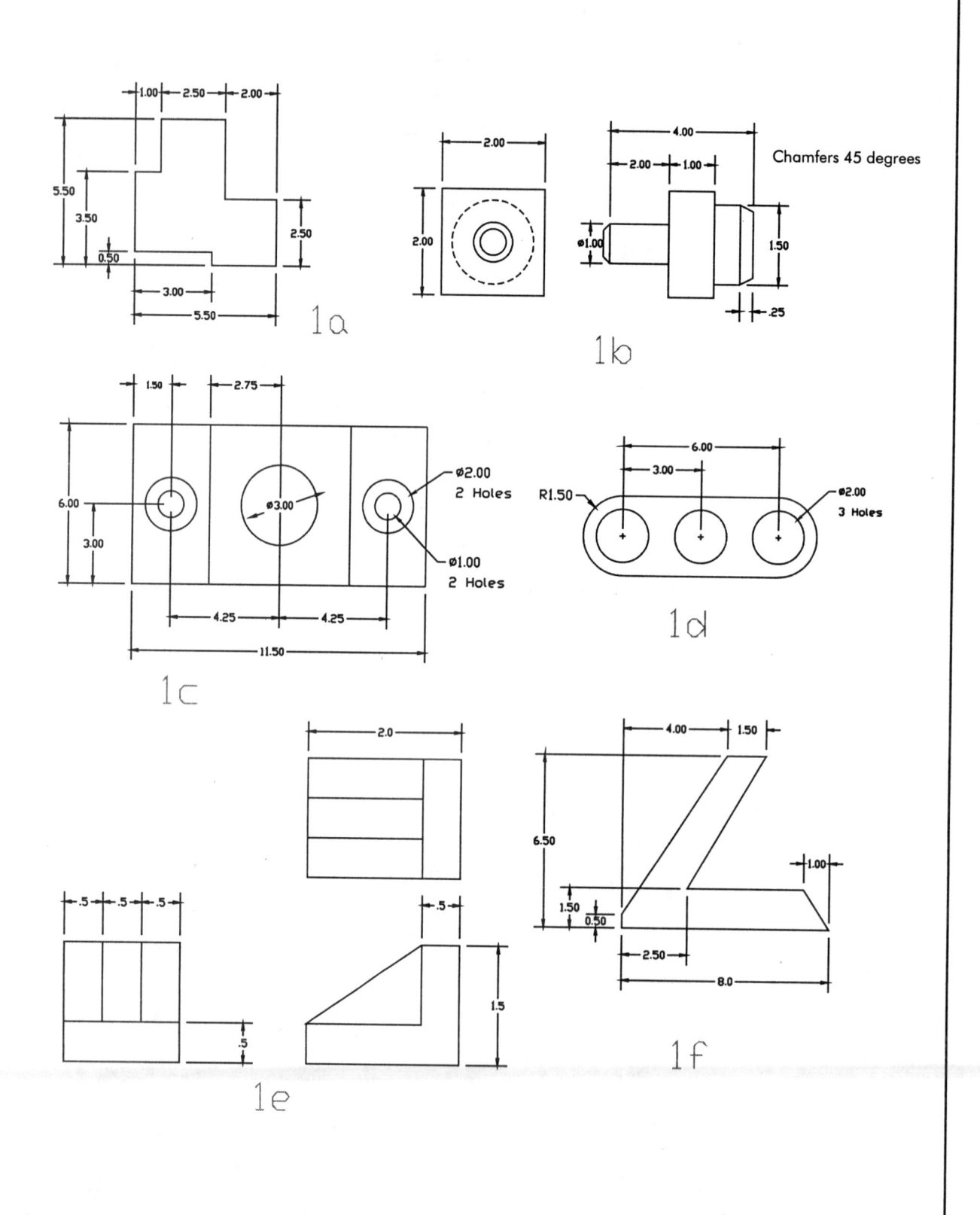

Exercise A1

Set up your screen using UNITS, LIMITS, GRID, and SNAP, then use LINE to add in the floor plan outline as shown. If you get finished early, the remainder of the interior walls are on Exercise A5.

```
Command:UNITS, Architectural, 1
Command:LIMITS
Reset model space limits
Specify lower left corner or [ON/OFF]
<0.0000,0.0000>:-3',-3'
Specify upper right corner
<12.0000,9.0000>:45',38'
Command:SNAP
Specify snap spacing (X) or
[ON/OFF/Aspect/Rotate/Style/
   Type]<1.0000>:1
Command:GRID
Specify grid spacing or [ON/OFF/Snap/Aspect]<1.0000>:6
Command: (from the View Pull Down menu, pick ZOOM All)
```

When you are finished, SAVE the file as **SECONDFL**.

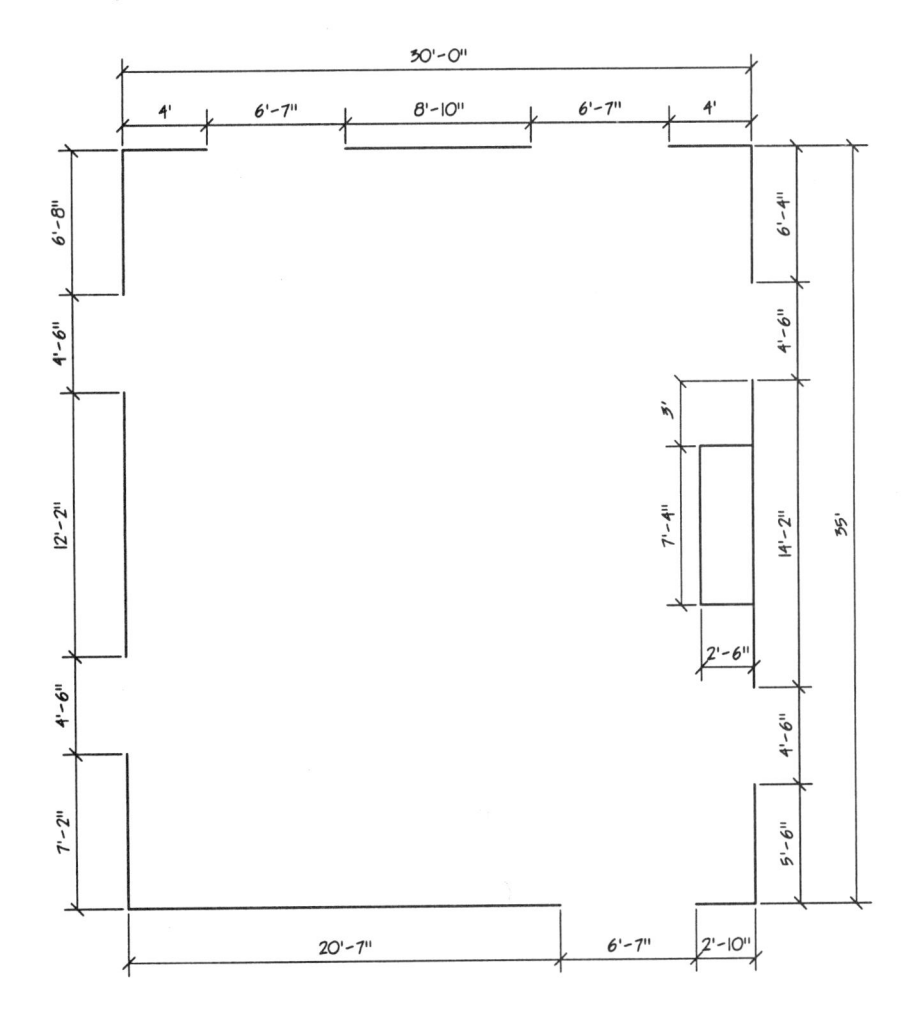

Introductory Geometry and Setting Up 27

Exercise C1

```
Command:LIMITS
Reset model space limits
Specify lower left corner or [ON/OFF]
<0.0000,0.0000>:-5,-5
Specify upper right corner
<12.0000,9.0000>:35,25
Command:SNAP
Specify snap spacing (X) or
[ON/OFF/Aspect/Rotate/Style/
   Type]<1.0000>:1
Command:GRID
Specify grid spacing or [ON/OFF/Snap/Aspect]<1.0000>:5
Command: (from the View Pull Down menu, pick ZOOM All)
```

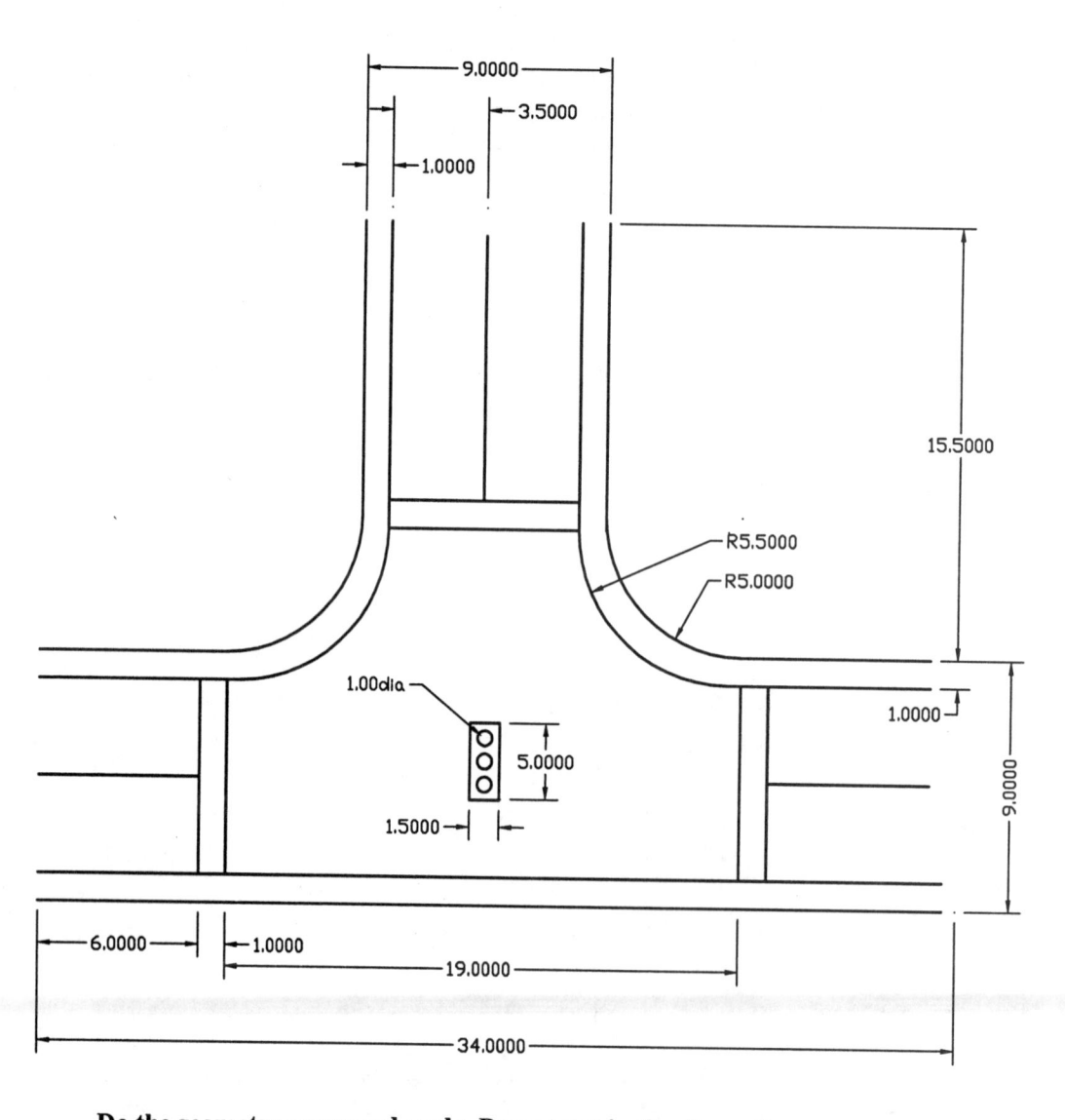

Do the geometry commands only. Do not put in the dimensions.

28 CHAPTER ONE

Hints for C1

Use the following commands to complete the exercise.

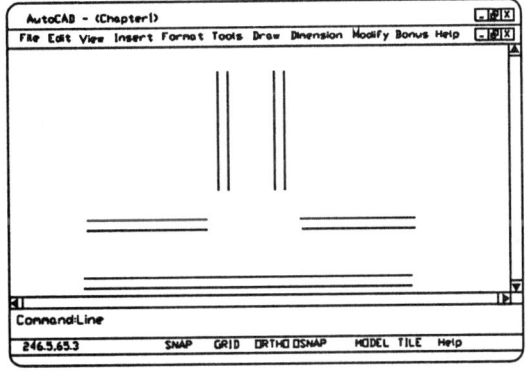

Lines
With your snap on draw the lines

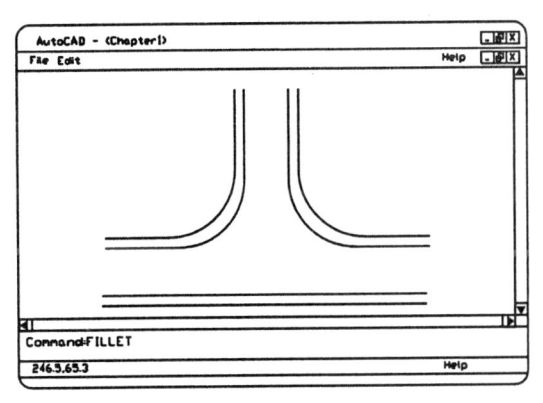

Fillets
Fillets are under the EDIT menu
Change the Radius

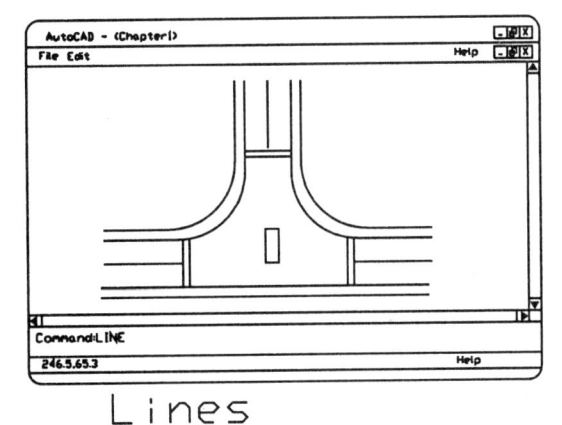

Lines
Change your snap for more accuracy

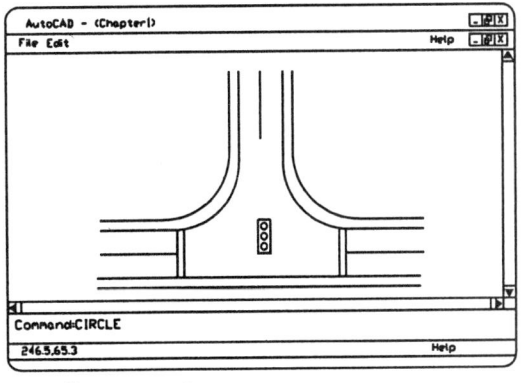

Circles
Use CENtre RADius for circles
Use drag to change the radius

Make sure you have a "**Command:**" prompt before starting a new command. If you do not, use ESC to return to the "**Command:**" prompt..

ARC, LINE, and CIRCLE are under the Draw menu. FILLET is under the Modify menu.

When you are finished use **SAVE**. This will save the drawing on your floppy disk.

Type in the name of the file in the box beside File Name.

Introductory Geometry and Setting Up

Exercise E1

```
Command:LIMITS
Reset model space limits
Specify lower left corner or [ON/OFF]
<0.0000,0.0000>:-1,-1
Specify upper right corner
<12.0000,9.0000>:⏎
Command:SNAP
Specify snap spacing (X) or
[ON/OFF/Aspect/Rotate/Style/
   Type]<1.0000>:.5
Command:GRID
Specify grid spacing or [ON/OFF/Snap/Aspect]<1.0000>:1
Command: (from the View Pull Down menu, pick ZOOM All)
```

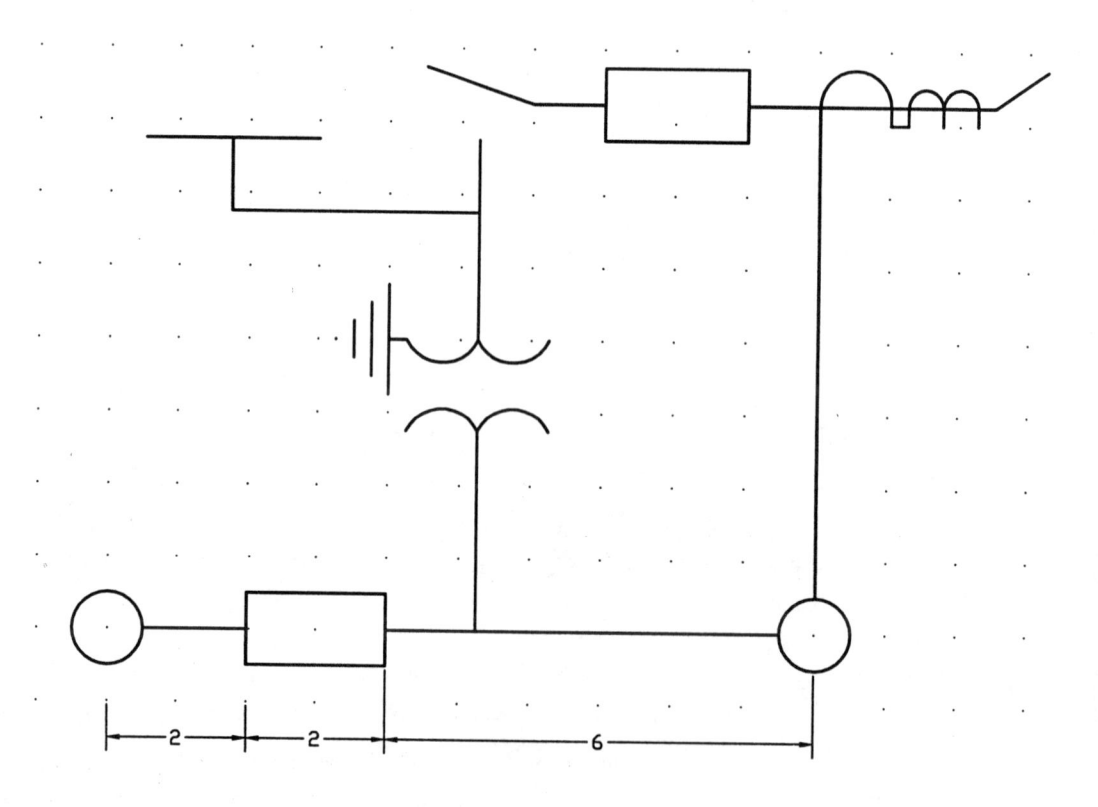

Do the geometry commands only. Do not put in the dimensions.

Hints for E1

Use the following commands to complete the exercise.

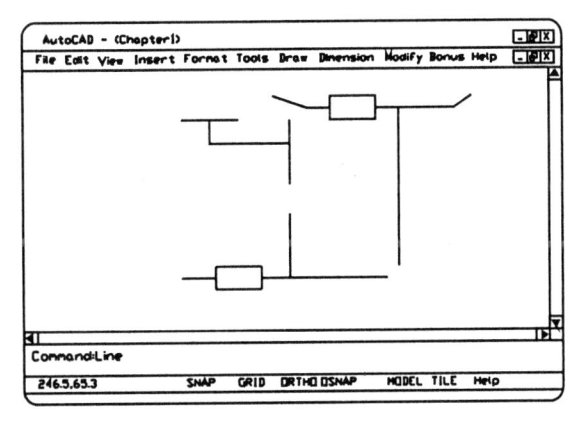

Lines
With your snap on draw the lines

Circles
Add the CIRCLES where needed

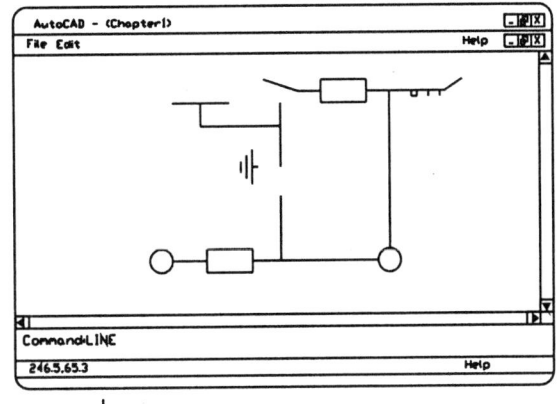

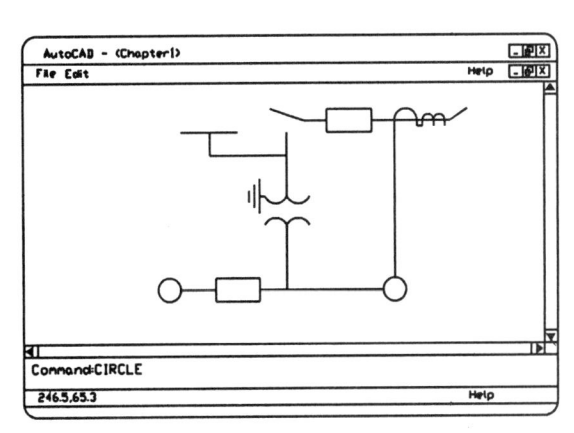

Lines
Change your snap for more accuracy

Arcs
Use Arc 3point
Use drag to change the radius

Make sure you have a "**Command:**" prompt before starting a new command. If you do not, use ESC to return to the "**Command:**" prompt..

ARC, LINE, and CIRCLE are under the Draw menu. FILLET is under the Modify menu.

When you are finished use **SAVE**. This will save the drawing on your floppy disk.

Type in the name of the file in the box beside File Name.

Introductory Geometry and Setting Up   **31**

Exercise M1

```
Command:LIMITS
Reset model space limits
Specify lower left corner or [ON/OFF]
<0.0000,0.0000>:-10,-40
Specify upper right corner
<12.0000,9.0000>:220,110
Command:SNAP
Specify snap spacing (X) or
[ON/OFF/Aspect/Rotate/Style/
   Type]<1.0000>:5
Command:GRID
Specify grid spacing or [ON/OFF/Snap/Aspect]<1.0000>:10
Command: (from the View Pull Down menu, pick ZOOM All)
```

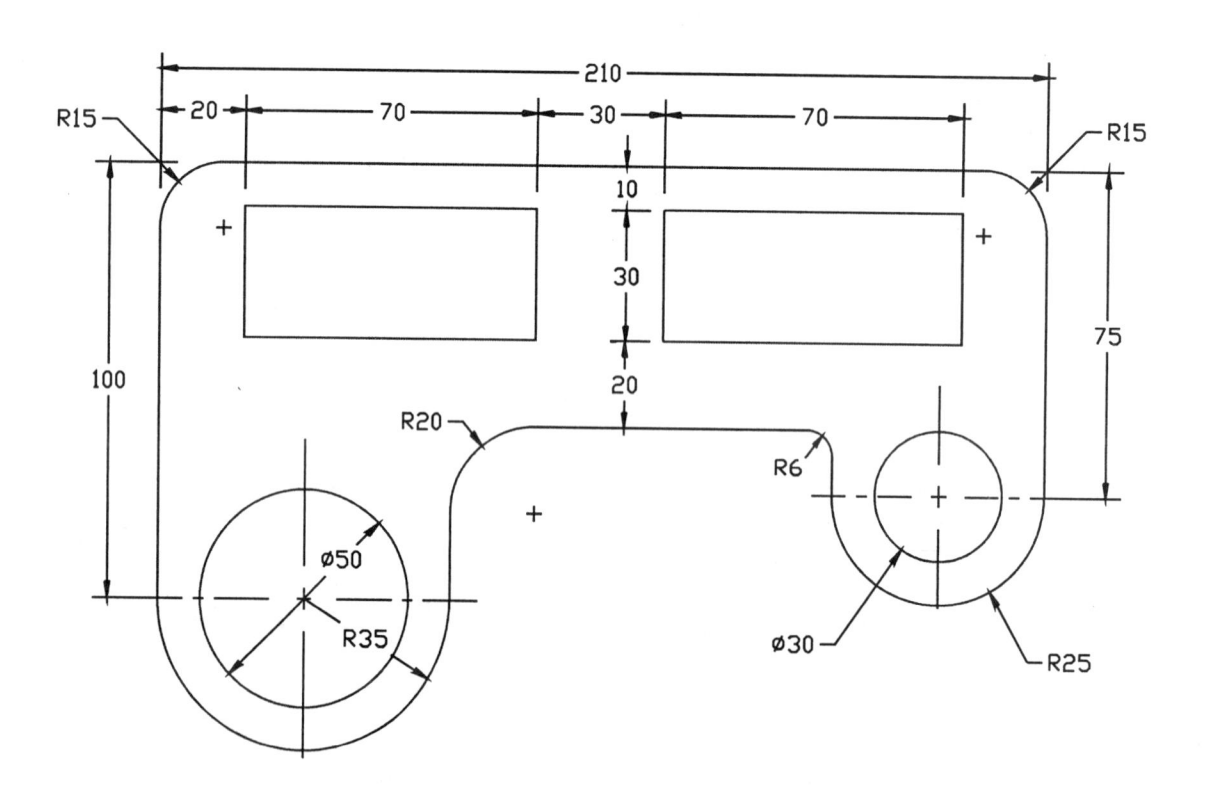

Do the geometry only. No dimensions are needed yet.

Hints for M1

Use the following commands to complete the exercise.

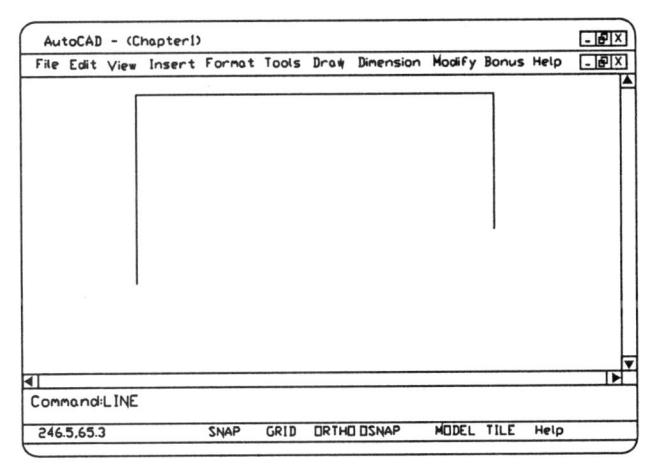

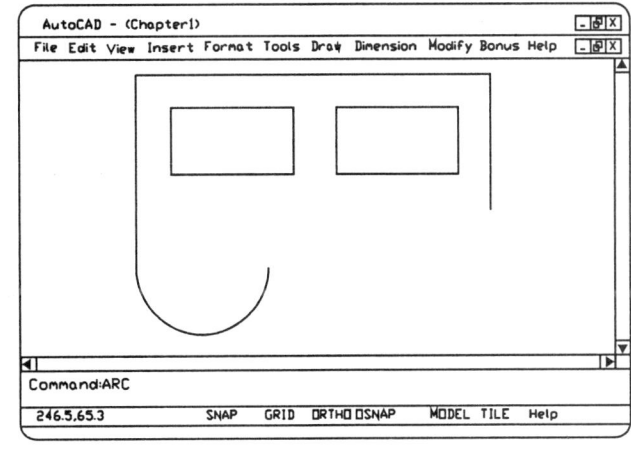

Lines
With SNAP on, draw the lines
make sure your co-ords are on F6.

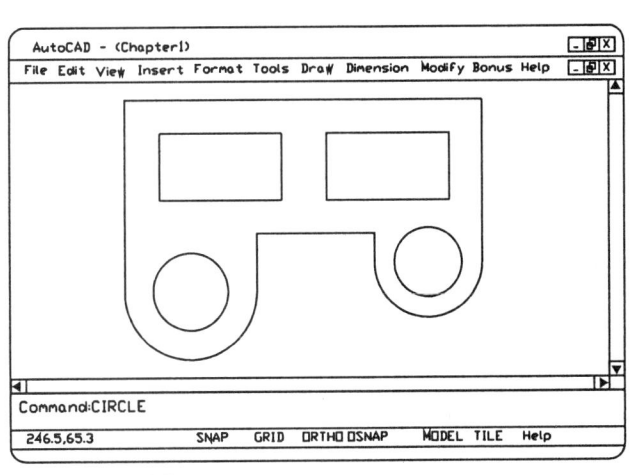

ARCs
With SNAP on, draw the arcs
start, end, radius

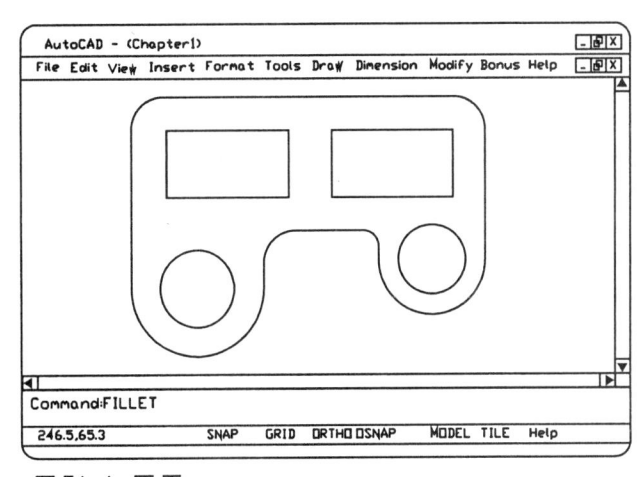

CIRCLEs
Use the SNAP to line up
the centers of the circles

FILLETs
Change the radius
then add the fillets

Make sure you have a "**Command:**" prompt before starting a new command. If you do not, use ESC to return to the "**Command:**" prompt..

ARC, LINE, and CIRCLE are under the Draw menu. FILLET is under the Modify menu.

When you are finished use **SAVE**. This will save the drawing on your floppy disk.

Type in the name of the file in the box beside File Name.

Challenger 1A

If you have taken AutoCAD before, try these.

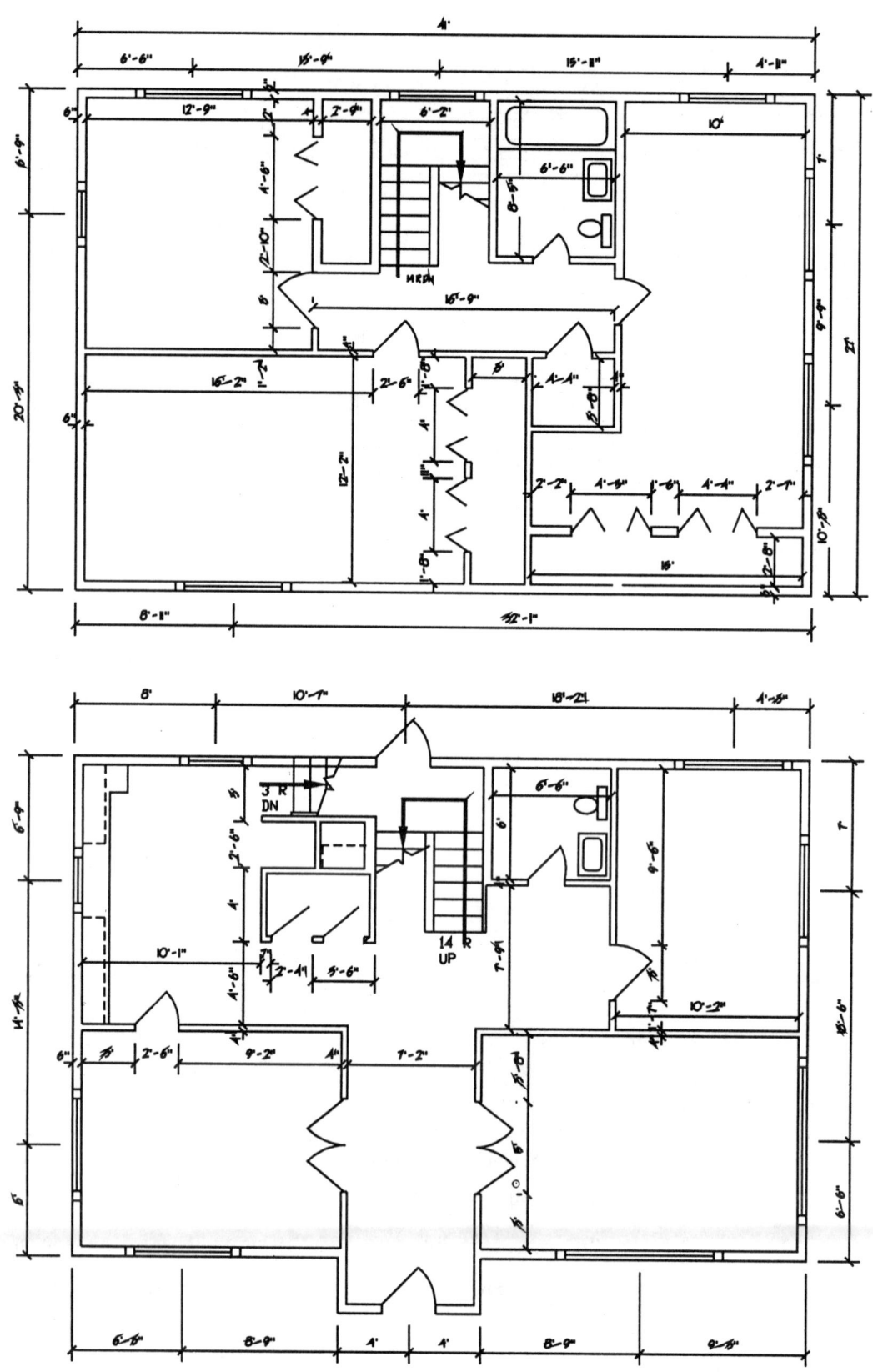

Challenger 1B

These exercises will help you with your skills.

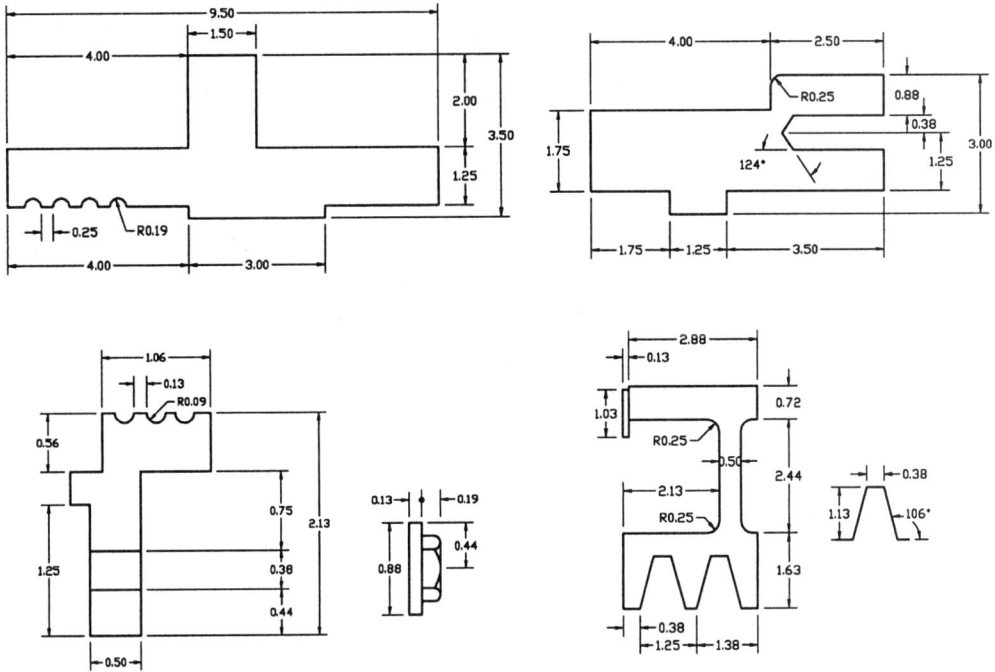

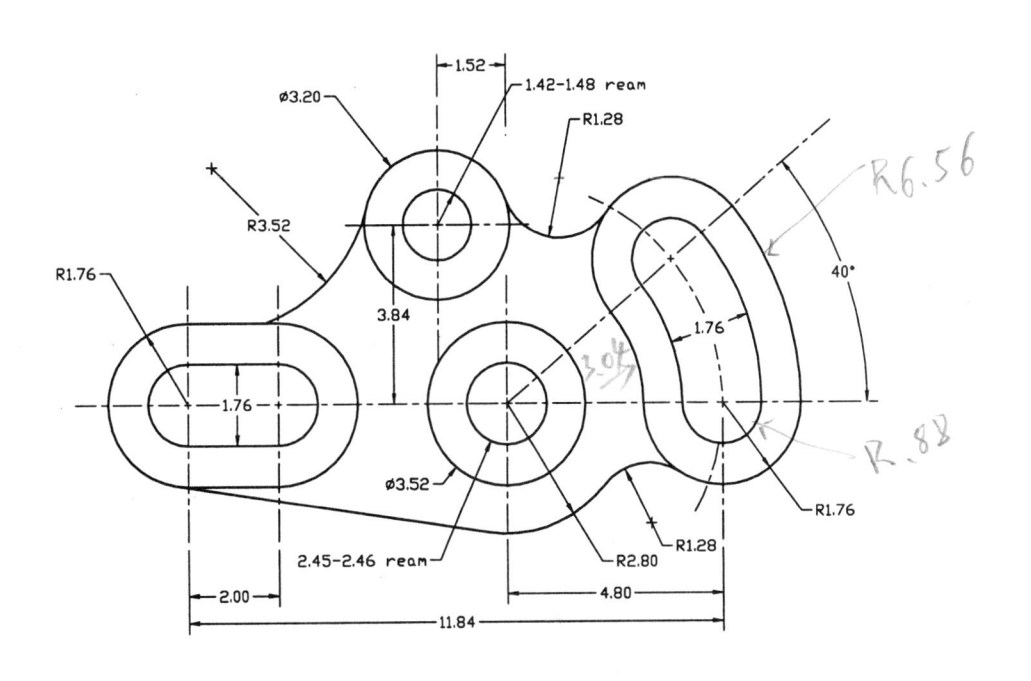

Challenger 1C

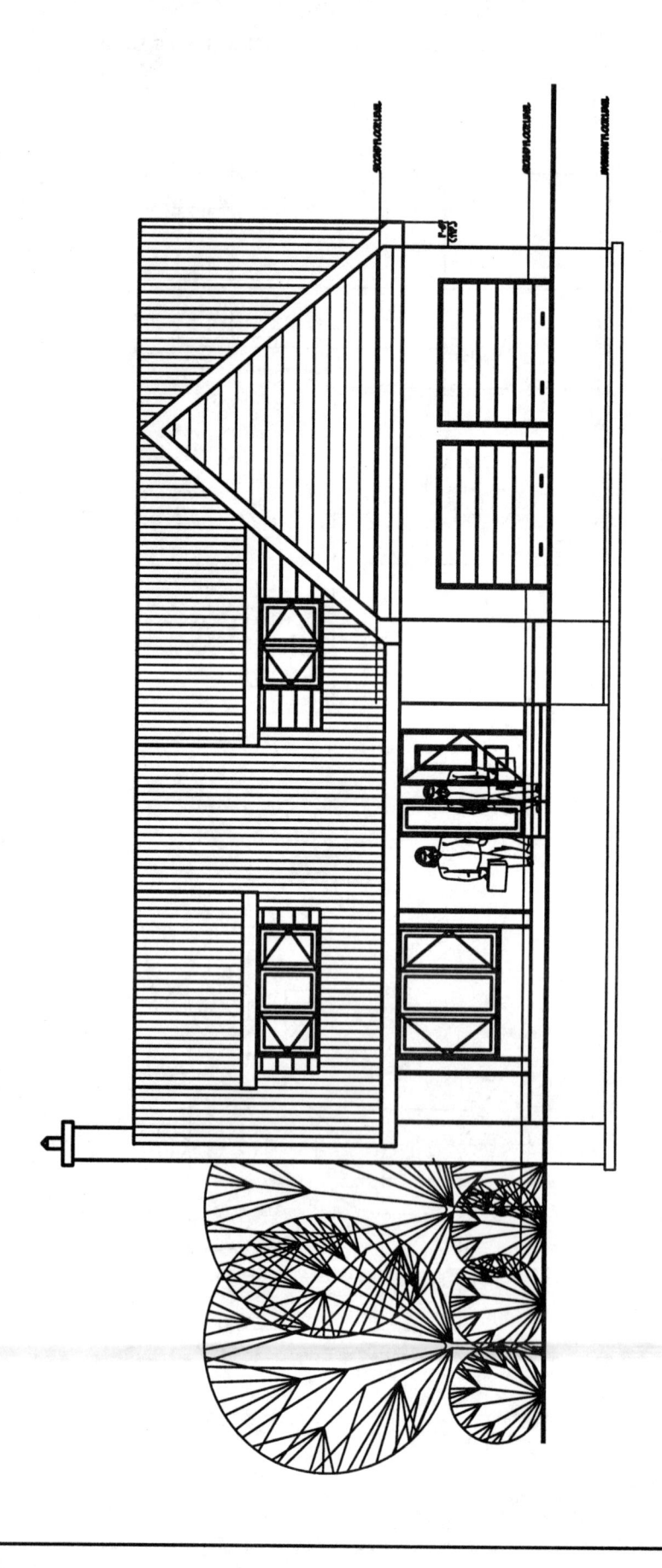

CHAPTER ONE

2

Help Files, CHAMFER, OSNAP, ERASE, TRIM, and BREAK

Upon completion of this chapter, you should be able to:

1. Retrieve on-line documentation or Help files
2. Use the commands GRID and SNAP effectively
3. Use OSNAP both within a command and as a setting
4. Use TRIM and BREAK to erase portions of objects
5. Use ERASE to remove whole objects
6. Use the CHAMFER command

OBJECTIVES

Help Files

Once you have learned how to sign on to the system and have located all the menus, you can learn the system from on-screen documentation from this point on. The Help files have two main functions.

Function #1

The first function serves as an index of commands. When looking for a command that will change the magnification of the data on the screen, you may be able to spot it by using the following.

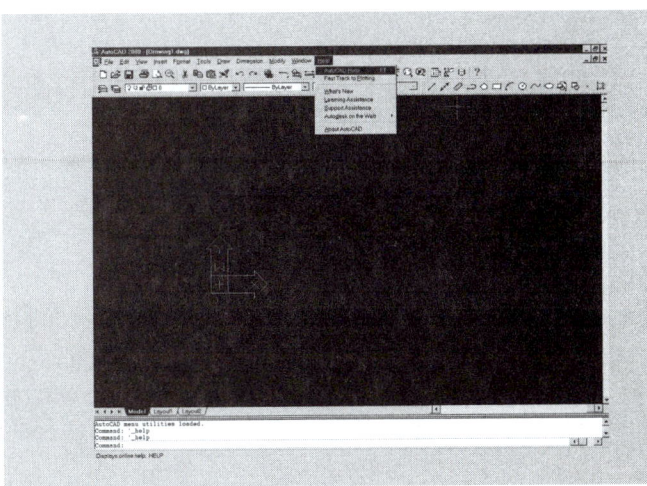

Pull Down menu Choose Help from the Pull Down menu, then AutoCAD Help, or use ? as follows:

    Command:?

Choose **Index** from the tabs listed along the top of the folders, then type in the word that you would like help with, or scroll through the

If you have just opened a new file in AutoCAD, you can get to the help files simply by pressing the space bar before entering a command.

Use the X on the top right of the dialogue box to take the box off your screen.

The Help Index will give you a listing of the various commands which are available on the system. Use the scroll bar to look at the commands (the scroll bar is described in the Introduction, page xvii). By reading the various command names, you may be able to identify a word that is similar in meaning to the one you are after.

If you have completed what you are expected to complete for the day, use Help to become familiar with more of the commands.

If the command is shown with an apostrophe before it, as in 'ZOOM, it may be used within a current command. For example, if you are in the LINE command and would like to ZOOM Window on an area, choose ZOOM from the pull-down menu, perform the operation, and continue with the LINE command. Commands marked in this way are called *transparent commands*.

' = transparent command

Function #2

The second function of the Help files permits you to quickly retrieve information about a specific command. AutoCAD responds to any command by a series of prompts. The Help files will explain those prompts.

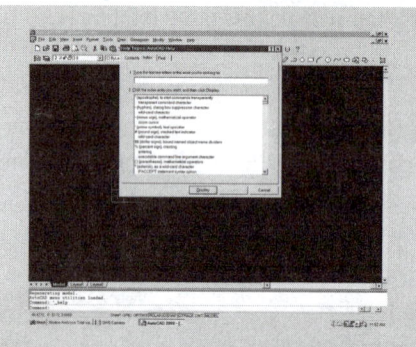

Toolbar Choose Help, Help Topics. For example, to find out about the ARC command, find the ARC submenu on the slide bar. Pick ARC, then Go To, then pick Show Topics.

Often there are several options indicated. If you want to see information about the command, choose the option that specifies the word "command".

Choose Display to see the topics indicated
Choose Cancel to exit from Help   or   **Pick the X in the top right corner to exit.**

On any version of AutoCAD, the Help files will explain the syntax or command line sequence and the prompts and options of each command. With a little practice, you will be able to understand the Help files and use them for commands that you have not already used.

Angle Brackets

Within the command strings are the options associated with the commands. You will notice that one of the options is contained in angle brackets. In any prompt the information offered in angle brackets, <>, is the default. This is what the command will do if you do not specify something else.

In the case of the ARC command, it will accept a **Start point** unless you tell it that you want something else.

```
Command:ARC
Specify start point of arc or [CEnter]:
```

Exiting from the Help Menu

In the first two or three weeks of classes, students often press the space bar before they enter any command. If you do this immediately after you have signed on, the system will offer you the Help files. If this should happen, press ESCape or pick the X on the top right of the dialog box to exit from Help.

Help files are also useful once you have learned AutoCAD and you switch to a system using a different release of the program.

SNAP and GRID

In AutoCAD, always draw the objects at a scale of 1:1. The LIMITS command is one way to set up the screen.

LIMITS	defines the general size that you want the model to be.
ZOOM All	allows you to view the size chosen. To make sure it has changed, press **F6** and move the cursor around.
SNAP	will set an increment that the cursor will move to.
GRID	will set a visual aid to help place objects.

If you prefer, you can turn LIMITS off and work with no set space. SNAP can be used without setting LIMITS. The SNAP command sets a spacing for point entries and restricts cursor movements to the preset integer. The GRID command places dots on the screen, providing a visual framework.

Click SNAP and GRID on the bottom of your screen to invoke them. Double click them in all previous versions of AutoCAD.

The SNAP (**F9**) and GRID (**F7**) functions act as toggles, but can be modified through the command system. Type in your choice of GRID or SNAP, then type the desired spacing length. The **Aspect Ratio** (X vs. Y) will be equal ($X = Y$) unless you change it.

The SNAP Command

SNAP allows you to indicate points or positions on the screen at preset regular integers. It also allows a rotated or isometric drawing to be entered. In the following example of a simple lug section, we will set a snap as a guide to draw in both the horizontal and the angled section of the part.

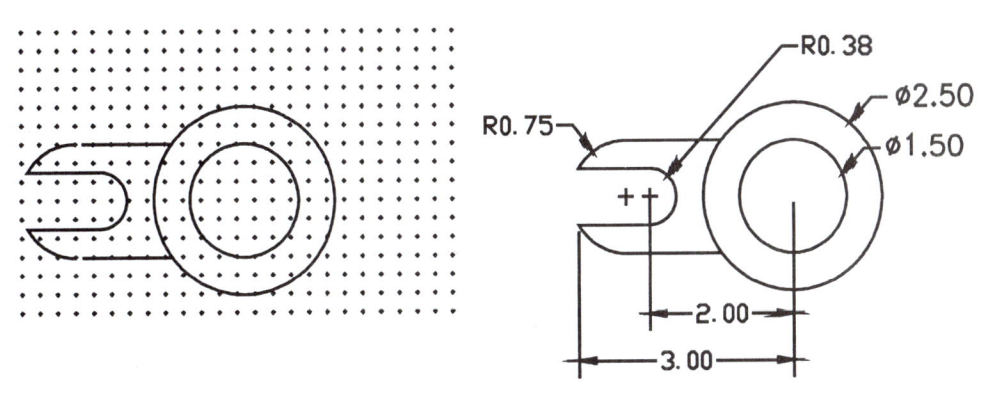

Figure 2-1

First set SNAP and GRID to .25 units. Then draw in Figure 2-1.

Next rotate SNAP by 45 degrees and set the base point in the center of the large circle. The GRID will follow the SNAP angle. The crosshairs will remain perpendicular, but are seen at an angle.

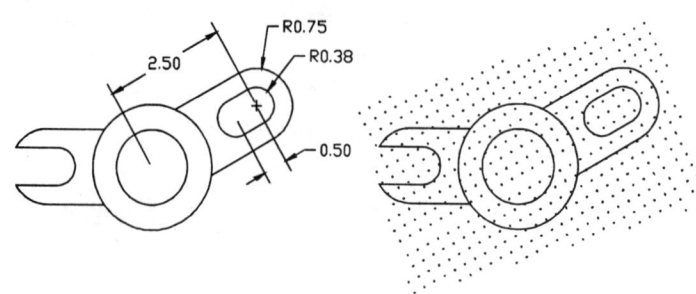

Figure 2-2

```
Command:SNAP
Specify snap spacing or
  [ON/OFF/Aspect/Rotate/Style/Type]<0.500>:R
Specify base point<0'-0.00",0'-0.00">:CEN of (pick the circle)
Specify rotation angle<0.00>:45
```

Where: **On**   = SNAP activated or turned on
       Off   = SNAP turned off
       Aspect = the option of changing the X value with relation to the Y value
       Rotate = the option of rotating SNAP for drawing on a given angle
       Style   = the option of changing the style from Standard to Isometric, thus allowing isometric drawing
       Type   = the option of having either polar or rectangular grids

The GRID Command

The **GRID** command sets a visual aid for drawing. The grid size will follow the snap size unless changed using GRID. To change the relative X, Y value, use Aspect.

```
Command:GRID
Specify grid spacing(X) or [ON/OFF/Snap/Aspect]<0.000>:A
Specify the horizontal spacing (X) <0.5000>:1
Specify the vertical spacing (Y) <0.500>:2
```

Where: **On**   = GRID activated or turned on
       Off   = GRID turned off
       Value = the spacing
       Aspect = the option of changing the relative X and Y values

Notes

GRID and SNAP can be changed at any time during the creation of a drawing.

Using the Drawing Aids Dialog Box

The dialog box can be used to rotate SNAP and GRID as well. The box is transparent, and therefore can be used to change the SNAP in the middle of another command. To change the snap angle and base point in the dialog box:

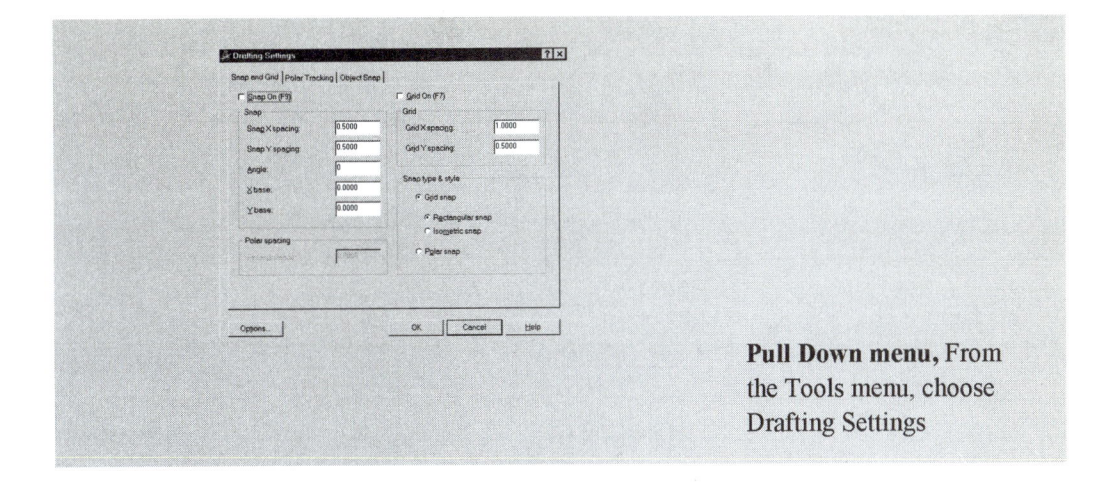

Pull Down menu, From the Tools menu, choose Drafting Settings

The command line equivalent is **DDRMODES**.

1. In the Snap Angle box, enter 45, for 45 degrees.
2. Change the *X* and *Y* coordinate values in the X Base and Y Base boxes to change the base point for the rotation.
3. Choose OK to make the changes happen.

To return to standard snap and grid values, choose 0 degrees and 0,0 for the angle and base points. You can pick the Snap, Grid, and Ortho modes on or off by picking the box On. Options on the bottom left will allow you to change OSNAPs, and many other settings. These options are only available if you have entered via the Pull Down menu.

Point Entry and OSNAP

Point Entry

In most CAD systems, there are three basic ways to enter points:

PICKING   If you pick or digitize a point on the Pull Down, the object will be placed at exactly the point indicated. The SNAP command can be used to access a point at a preset integer to increase your accuracy. The GRID and ORTHO commands can also help the entry process.

COORDINATE ENTRY   You can enter absolute, relative, or polar coordinates in any order.

ENTITY SELECTION, OBJECT SNAP, OR OSNAP   This allows you to use existing objects on Pull Down to create your file. Accessing points on existing objects is called using OSNAPs.

OSNAP: Object SNAP

Object Snaps allow you to specify precise points on objects in order to create or edit objects. Osnaps can be used with any command that requires a "point."

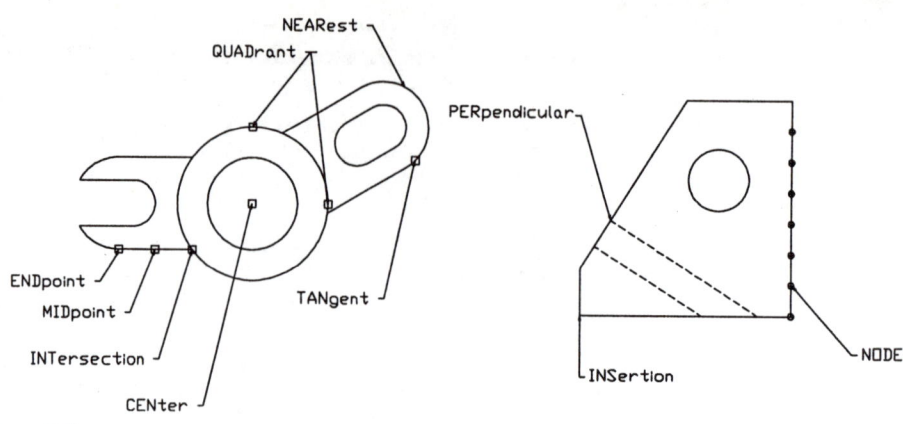

Figure 2-3

AutoCAD has 15 Object Snap modes that allow you to specify precise points on objects such as circles or lines. Following is a short description of the available Object Snaps (see Figure 2-3). The capitalized letters are those needed when typing in the option.

APPint	(apparent intersection) snaps to a real or imaginary intersection of two objects.
CENter	snaps to the center of an arc or circle.
ENDpoint	snaps to the closest end of any object.
EXTention	snaps to a point along the extension of a line or arc.
FROM	establishes a temporary reference point from the parameters of an existing objects.
INSertion	snaps to the insertion point of a block.
INTersection	snaps to the intersection of two items.
MIDpoint	snaps to the midpoint of a selected item.
NEARest	snaps to a point on an object nearest to the digitized point.
NODE	snaps to a point created by POINT, DIVIDE, or MEASURE.
NONE	turns the Object Snap mode off.
PARallel	draws a line parallel to an existing line
PERpendicular	snaps to a 90 degree angle to an existing line.
QUADrant	snaps to the 0, 90, 180, or 270 degree point on an arc, circle, or ellipse.
Quick	snaps to the first snap point found; it must be used in conjunction with other OSNAPs.
TANgent	snaps to the tangent of an arc or circle.

Accessing OSNAPs

OSNAPs can be accessed in one of 4 ways:

1. There may be a designated button on your mouse. Often if you hold the "SHIFT" button on your keyboard down and use the right click button on your mouse, an OSNAP menu will appear where your cursor is.

Hold the SHIFT key down

on your keyboard, and

right click on the mouse.

2. Type in the first few letters of the OSNAP mode.
3. Choose Object Snap from the Drafting Settings..., Settings under the Tools menu.
4. Object Snap buttons

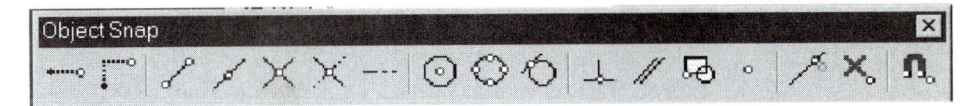

Using OSNAPs

This lifting socket will illustrate how to use Object Snaps within the command line. First, two circles are drawn and then lines are added TANgent to the circles and from the QUADrant of the circles.

```
Command: (pick Draw menu) CIRCLE CEN RAD
Specify center point for circle or
  [3P/2P/Ttr (tan tan radius)]: 0,0
Specify Radius of Circle or Diameter:1.5
Command:C
Specify center point for circle or
  [3P/2P/Ttr (tan tan radius)]:9,4
Specify Radius of Circle or Diameter:3
Command:PAN (pan the objects onto the
  screen)
```

Figure 2-4

TANgent creates a tangent to the identified object from the last object. This creates an object tangent to a circle or arc.

```
Command:LINE
Specify first point:TANgent to (pick 1)
Specify next point or (Undo):
TANgent to (pick 2)
```

AutoCAD will calculate the tangent for you; just pick which side of the object the tangent should be on.

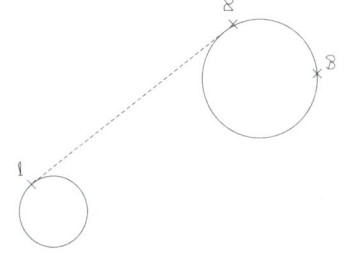

Figure 2-5

QUADrant takes the top, the bottom, or the far right or left of a specified circle or arc.

```
Command:LINE
Specify first point:QUADrant of (pick 3)
Specify next point or (Undo):@0,-10
```

Help Files, CHAMFER, OSNAP, ERASE, TRIM, and BREAK   **43**

CENter takes the center of an arc or circle. Only items with a defined radius can have a center point.

ENDpoint takes the closest end point. All lines are made up of two end points. Circles have one end point, and arcs have two.

When finding the CENter of the arcs and circles, pick the object itself, rather than the spot where the center might be; the system will calculate that for you.

```
Command:CIRCLE
Specify center point for circle or [3P/2P/Ttr (tan tan
   radius)]:CENter of (pick 4)
Specify Radius of Circle or Diameter:.55
Command:CIRCLE
Specify center point:CENter of (pick 5)
Specify Radius of Circle or Diameter:1.5

Command:ARC
ARC Specify start point of arc or
  [Center]:-1.5,-5
Specify end point of arc:ENDpoint of (pick 6)
Specify Radius:15
```

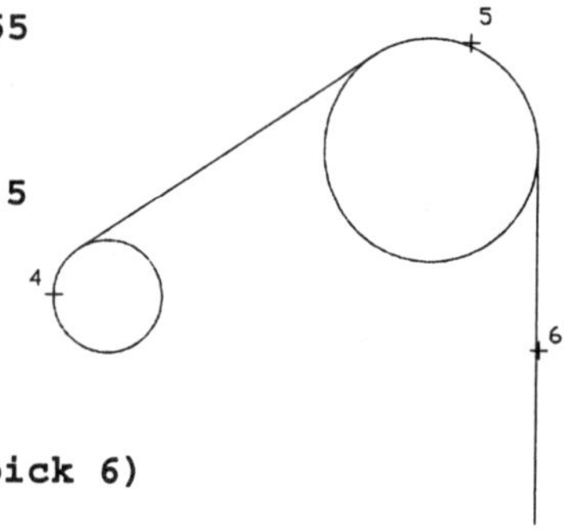

Figure 2-6

PERpendicular forms a normal to an identified object.

```
Command:LINE
Specify first point:ENDpoint of (pick 7)
Specify next point or (Undo):
 QUADrant of (pick 8)
Specify next point or (Undo):↵
Command:LINE
Specify first point:QUADrant of (pick 9)
Specify next point or (Undo):@0,-2.5
Specify next point or (Undo):
 PERpendicular to (pick 10)
Specify next point or (Undo):↵
```

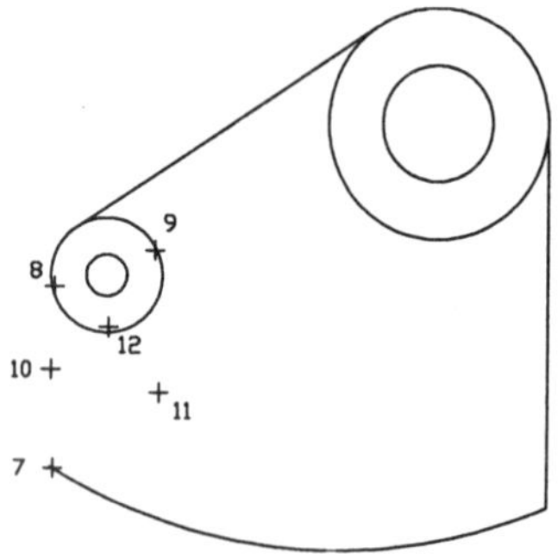

Figure 2-7

ERASE the short line between points 9 and 11. Add an arc going from point 11 tangent to the lower quadrant of the circle.

```
Command:ARC
ARC Specify start point of arc or[CEnter]
 :ENDpoint of (pick 11)
Specify end point of arc:TANgent to (pick 12
Specify Radius:10
```

Then use TRIM to trim off the unnecessary pieces.

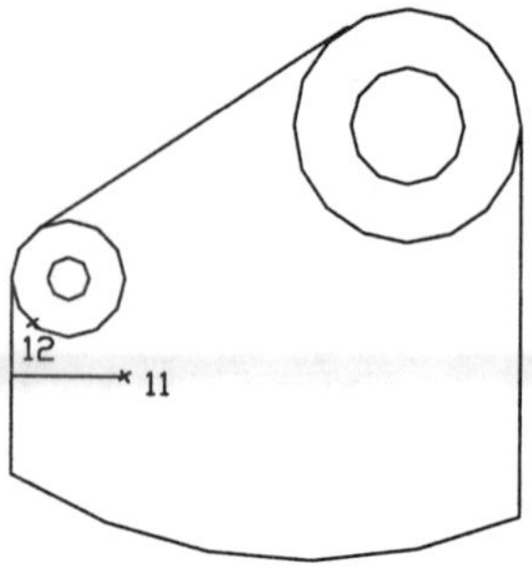

Figure 2-8

44 CHAPTER TWO

TRIM is used to remove portions of existing objects between specified cutting edges. Notice that TRIM goes to the closest intersection. TRIM will be discussed at length in Chapter 5.

```
Command:TRIM
Current settings: Projection=UCS Edge=None
Select cutting edges...
Select objects: (pick 13)
Select objects: (pick 14)
Select objects: (pick 15)
Select objects: (pick 16)
Select objects:⏎ (no more cutting edges
   are needed)
<Select object to trim>Project/Edge/Undo:
   (pick the dotted lines)
```

Figure 2-8

With the exception of APPint, QUICK, NONE, and FROM, the OSNAP modes not illustrated above are fit into the command strings exactly as those shown — before the object selection digitize.

APParent Intersection

APPint (apparent intersection) snaps to a real or visual 3D intersection formed by objects you select or by an extension of those objects. (A *visual intersection* occurs when objects appear to meet in the current view but do not actually intersect in 3D space.)

```
Command:LINE
Specify first point:APPint of (pick 1 and
   pick 2)
Specify next point or (Undo):END of (pick 3)
```

Figure 2-9

FROM

From establishes a temporary reference point as a basis for specifying subsequent points. It is usually used in combination with other object snaps and relative coordinates.

To establish a point that is 2 units in the *X* direction and 3 units in the *Y* direction from the middle of an existing line, use the following.

```
Command:LINE
Specify first point:FROM
Base point:MID of (pick 1)
   <offset>:@2,3
```

Figure 2-10

NONE

None is used to turn off the current running object snap. The aperture will disappear from the cursor and no object snap will take place. This is used when typing in osnaps to override an existing osnap.

EXTension

Like the APPINT object snap, this projects a line or arc and offers a point along it. Using LINE, activate the EXTension osnap and move your cursor over an existing line or arc; a cross should appear to show that this is the line or arc that you have chosen. Then move your cursor along what might be the extension of that line and a dotted line will appear showing that you are on the correct path. Pick a point to start your LINE.

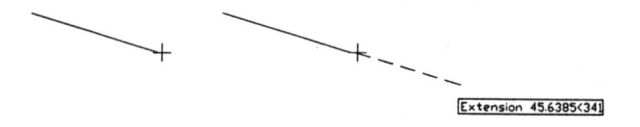

Figure 2-11

PARallel

PARallel Snap helps draw a line parallel to an existing line. Using the LINE command, pick the first point of a new line. Move your cursor over the line to be paralleled and pause until a small cross indicates that AutoCAD has accepted that line as a guide. Move the cursor to a point approximately parallel to the guide line, and the cross will be replaced with a parrallel sign showing that the new line will be parallel.

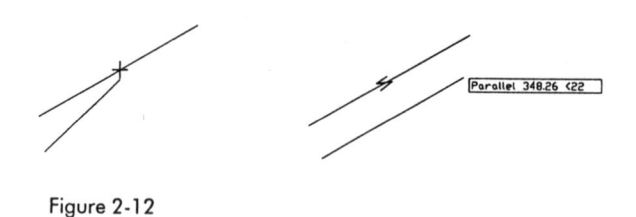

Figure 2-12

Using OSNAPs with the BREAK Command

Like TRIM, BREAK is used to remove portions of existing objects.

Once BREAK is invoked, you are prompted to choose the object to BREAK. You can break the object from the point chosen on the object and a second point, taking the selection digitize as a first point. Or you can choose the object and then specify **F** to choose a different break point.

OSNAPs are used to define points, often intersections, between any two objects: arcs, lines, circles, etc. The objects must be identified in the area of the intersection, preferably where the objects actually intersect.

The BREAK Command

BREAK is found under the Modify menu in both the Toolbar and the Pull Down menu.

```
Command:BREAK
Select object: (pick 1)
Enter second point (or F for first
  point):F
Enter first point:CENter of (pick 2)
Enter second point:INTersection of (pick 3)
```

Figure 2-13

Danger

With Object Snaps on, you will snap to whatever settings are current. Squares and triangles will shown up on your objects as you move your cursor when Object Snaps are on. Toggle them off on the status line.

The first pick indicates the object itself and should be placed where the system cannot mistake it for any other object.

The second pick indicates the first point at which the item will be broken.

When breaking circles, break points are measured counterclockwise from the pick point.

Change your automatic object snap settings with this menu.

Turn them on and off by clicking the word OSNAP on the status bar.

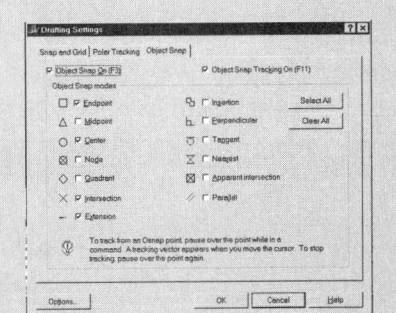

Toolbar From the Tools menu, choose Drafting Settings then the Object Snap settings.

Auto SNAP Mode

If you use the Object Snap automatic settings with the above menu, AutoCAD understands that every time you approach an object with your cursor, you want the Object Snaps (Mid, End, CEN) to be shown and snapped to. Use NONE to override the automatic settings.

```
Command:OSNAP
```

This brings up the above menu.

Aperture Size

To change the size of the aperture, use Tools menu, Options, then Drafting or:

```
Command:APERTURE
Object snap target height (1-50 pixels)<10>:6
```

Help Files, CHAMFER, OSNAP, ERASE, TRIM, and BREAK   47

Object Selection Cycling

The selection pick box can touch more than one object at a time. At any "Select objects:" prompt, hold Ctrl down before picking, then each pick will select the object chosen and add it to the list.

The ERASE Command

The ERASE command will take objects out of the file. There are several options to help you choose items. You can pick the objects individually, or pick either a *window* or a *crossing* to indicate your selection set.

```
Command: ERASE
Select objects: (use either individual items, Window, or
    Crossing)
```

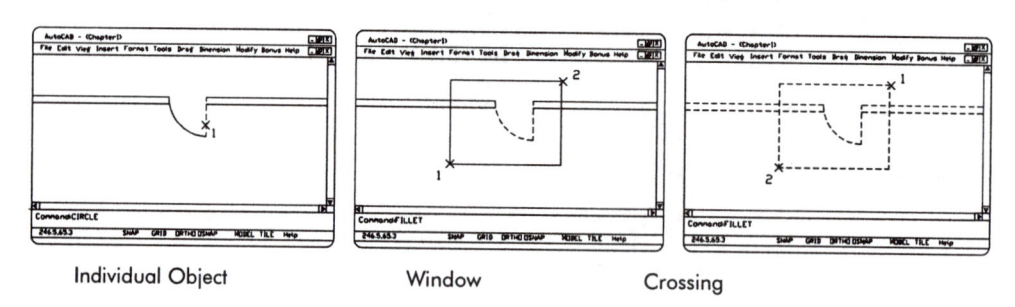

Figure 2-14

In the first illustration, the user has indicated only the door; therefore, this is the only object to be erased.

In the second illustration, a window is indicated by picking from left to right. All objects *totally contained* in the window will be erased.

In the third illustration, a crossing is indicated by picking from right to left. All objects *either entirely or partly crossing* the rectangle will be erased. Press ⏎ to have the objects disappear.

Other options are discussed in Chapter 4.

Undoing an ERASE

If you have just erased an object or group of objects and then realize that you should not have, you can use the OOPS command to bring back the erased items.

```
Command: ERASE
Select objects: (pick 1, pick 2)
Select objects: ⏎
Command: OOPS (all erased objects will reappear)
```

The CHAMFER Command

The CHAMFER command is very similar to the FILLET command. Both commands modify the connection between two objects. With FILLET you can create a curved fillet ending relative to a defined radius. With CHAMFER you can create a chamfered edge relative to a defined distance.

To find CHAMFER:

> **Toolbar** From the Modify menu, choose the CHAMFER button.
> **Pull Down** From the Modify menu, choose Chamfer.

The command line equivalent is **CHAMFER**.

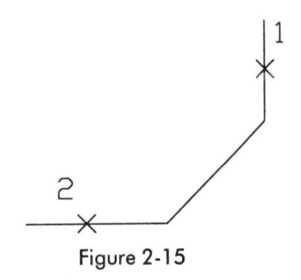

Figure 2-15

```
Command: CHAMFER
(Trim mode) Current chamfer Dist1 = 1.00, Dist2 = 1.00
Select first line [Polyline/Distance/Angle/Trim/Method] >:D
Specify first chamfer distance<1.00>:2
Specify second chamfer distance<2.00>:⏎
Command:⏎ (restarts command)
(Trim mode) Current chamfer Dist1 = 1.00, Dist2 = 1.00
Select first line [Polyline/Distance/Angle/Trim/Method]: (pick 1)
Select second line: (pick 2)
```

Where: **Polyline** = can create chamfered edges on all sides of a closed polyline
Distance = allows you to set a distance
Angle = allows you to set different angles for the two sides
Trim = allows you to have the objects either trimmed when chamfered or not trimmed when chamfered
Method = allows you to choose either two distances or an angle and a distance

Prelab 2 Using OSNAP and TRIM

Step 1 Start a new file and set the screen size to 35,25 with either LIMITS or ZOOM Scale. No GRID or SNAP is needed for this example. (You make the entries shown in **BOLD**)

```
Command:LIMITS
Reset model space limits
Specify lower left corner or [ON/OFF]
 <0.0000,0.0000>:-10,-40
Specify upper right corner
 <12.0000,9.0000>:220,110
Command: (pick View, Zoom All)
```

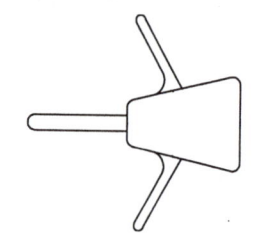

Step 2 Start by drawing circles. With the first one, use the Pull Down menu. With the second, use the command alias. With the third, use the pull-down menu.

```
Command:(Pull Down menu)CIRCLE CENTER RADIUS
Specify center point for circle or[3P/2P/Ttr(tan tan rad)]: 0,0
Specify Radius of Circle or Diameter:1
Command:C
Specify center point for circle or:13,2
Specify Radius of Circle or Diameter:1
Command:⏎
Specify center point for circle or:13,-2
Specify Radius of Circle or Diameter:1
Command:Z
Specify corner of window, enter a scale factor (nX or nXP), or
 [All/Center/Dynamic/Extents/Previous/Scale/Window]<real time>:
  (pick 1)
Other corner: (pick 2)
```

Notes

If you can't see your draw toolbar, use the View screen menu, then Toolbars, then Draw.

Step 3 Now use the LINE command with the Object Snaps to access the appropriate points on the identified objects. Access the OSNAPs by the mouse buttons, from the Tools menu, or by typing them in. Use the Pull Down menu or the button to first find the LINE command.

```
Command:(From the Draw menu)LINE
Specify first point:TANgent to (pick 3)
Specify next point or (Undo):TANgent to (pick 4)
Specify next point or (Undo):⏎
Command:L
Specify first point:QUADrant of (pick 5)
Specify next point or (Undo):
PERpendicular to (pick 6)
Specify next point or (Undo):⏎
Command:(space bar)
Specify first point:QUADrant of (pick 7)
Specify next point or (Undo):PERpendcular to (pick 8)
Specify next point or (Undo):⏎
```

Step 4 Use TRIM to remove the portions of the existing objects not wanted on the final drawings. TRIM can be found under the Modify menu.

```
Command:TRIM
Current settings: Projection=UCS Edge=None
Select cutting edges...
Select objects: (pick 9)
Select objects: (pick 10)
Select objects:↵
<Select object to trim>Project/Edge/Undo: (pick 11)
Select object to trim:↵
```

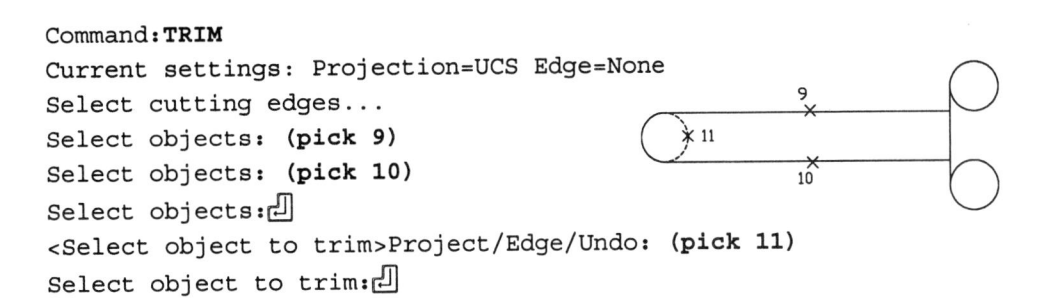

Step 5 Use the PAN command to translate the view to the left, and add some more circles.

```
Command:PAN
Press ESC or Enter to exit,
 or right-click to display shortcut menu:
 (pick 12)
Second point: (pick 13)


Command:(pick Draw)CIRCLE CEN RAD
Specify center point for circle or
 [3P/2P/Ttr(tan tan rad)]:26,-5
Specify Radius:1
Command:C
Specify center point for circle or
 [3P/2P/Ttr(tan tan rad)]:26,5
Specify Radius:1
```

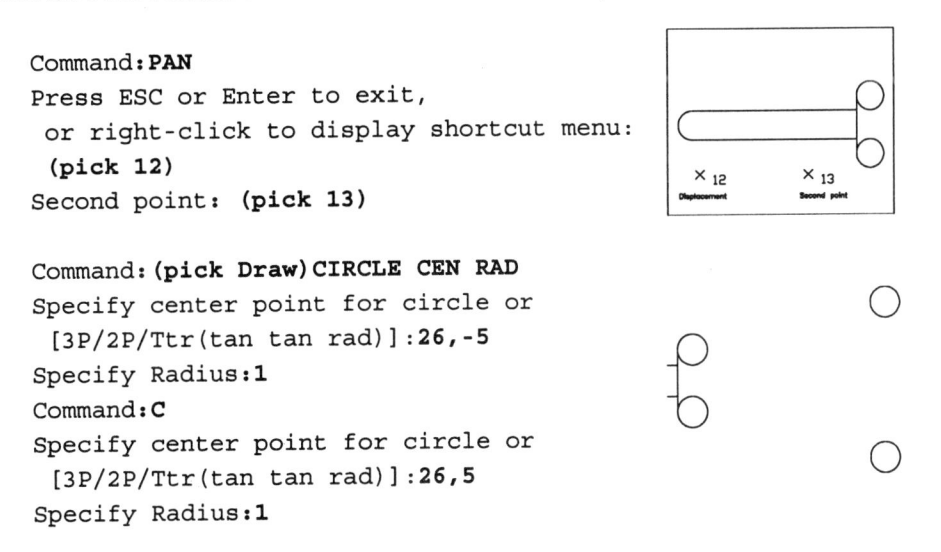

Use PAN to get the objects fully on screen as they are in this example.

Step 6 Now using the two new circles, create lines between the circles. First use the OSNAP command under the Assist menu to set the OSNAP to TANgent. Notice that the aperture is already on the crosshairs.

```
Command:OSNAP Osnap mode:TANgent
Command:(From the Draw menu)LINE
Specify first point: (pick 14)
Specify next point or (Undo): (pick 15)
Specify next point or (Undo):↵
Command:L
Specify first point: (pick 16)
Specify next point or (Undo): (pick 17)
Specify next point or (Undo):↵
Command:(space bar)
Specify first point: (pick 18)
Specify next point or (Undo): (pick 19)
Specify next point or (Undo):↵
```

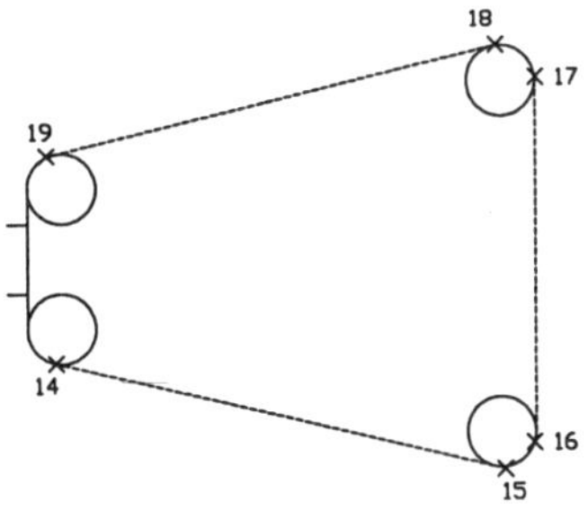

Toggle your OSNAP OFF on the status line.

Step 7 Use the TRIM command to remove portions of the circles.

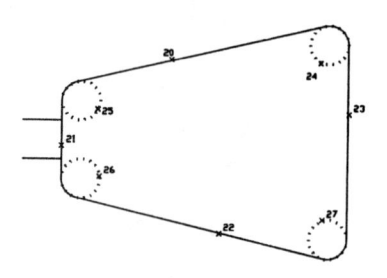

```
Command:TRIM
Current settings: Projection=UCS Edge=None
Select cutting edges...
Select objects: (pick 20, 21, 22, 23)
Select objects:⏎
<Select object to trim>Project/Edge/Undo:(pick 24, 25, 26, 27)
Select object to trim:⏎
```

Step 8 Use the Zoom command to reduce the drawing to 50% of the current size and create lines from the midpoints of the identified lines at the angles shown.

```
Command:Z
Specify corner of window, enter a scale factor (nX or nXP), or
  [All/Center/Dynamic/Extents/Previous/Scale/Window]<real
    time>:.5X
Command:L
Specify first point:MID of (pick 28)
Specify next point or (Undo):@10<120
Specify next point or (Undo):⏎
Command:(space bar)
Specify first point:MID of (pick 29)
Specify next point or (Undo):@10<240
Specify next point or (Undo):⏎
```

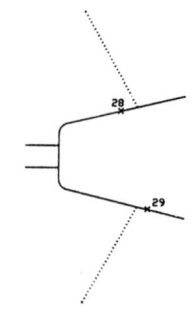

Step 9 Create circles on the ends of the identified lines using END to help specify the end point.

```
Command:CIRCLE
Specify center point for circle or
  [3P/2P/Ttr (tan tan radius)]:2P
Specify first end point on circle's
  diameter:END of (pick 30)
Second point on diameter:@-2,0
Command:C
Specify center point for circle or
  [3P/2P/Ttr (tan tan radius)]:2P
Specify first end point on circle's
  diameter:END of (pick 31)
Second point on diameter:@-2,0
```

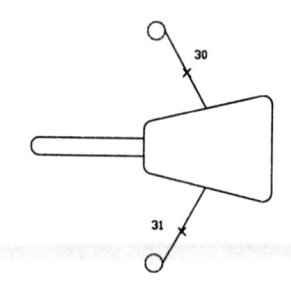

Step 10   This next command is extremely useful and difficult to do by hand. You will be making two lines tangent from the two circles at a specified angle and length.

```
Command:L
Specify first point:TAN of (pick 32)
Specify next point or (Undo):@10<300
Specify next point or (Undo):↵
Command:(space bar)
Specify first point:TAN of (pick 33)
Specify next point or (Undo):@10<60
Specify next point or (Undo):↵
```

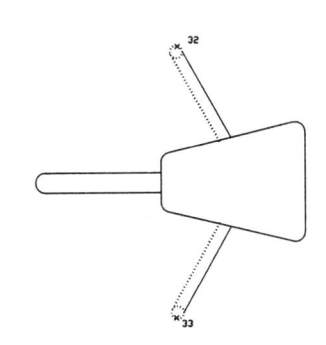

The lines are parallel to the first lines drawn.

Step 11   Object snaps are also sometimes part of the command as in CIRCLE TTR. Use this option to place the two circles as shown.

```
Command:CIRCLE
Specify center point for circle or
  [3P/2P/Ttr (tan tan radius)]:ttr
Specify point on object for first
  tangent of circle:(pick 34)
Specify point on object for second
  tangent of circle:(pick 35)
Radius:2
Command:C
3P/2P/TTR/<Center point>:TTR
First tangent: (pick 36)
Second tangent: (pick 37)
Radius:2
```

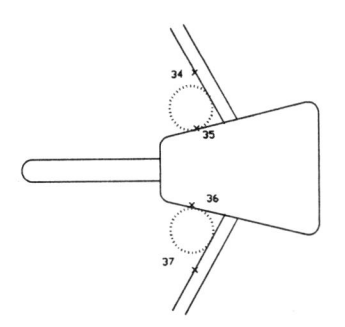

Step 12   Finally we will use the TRIM command to trim off all of the unwanted geometry. Many cutting edges can be used at once. TRIM using the cutting edges shown in Figure (a) to remove the portions of objects in Figure (b).

```
Command:TRIM
Select cutting edges:
Select objects:(pick objects in (a)
  with crossing)
Select objects:↵
Select object to trim:(pick objects
  in (b))
Select object to trim:↵
```

When completed, your object should look like this. It is a plan view of a crowd control unit.

Command and Function Summary

BREAK is used to erase a portion of an existing object.

CHAMFER is used to trim two intersecting lines at a specified distance from their intersection and connect the intersecting lines by a new line segment.

ERASE erases selected objects.

HELP files are used to access information about a selected command.

Object SNAPs are used to access particular points on existing objects during other commands.

PAN is used to shift the view of your drawing without changing the magnification.

REDRAW refreshes the screen display and removes blips.

REGEN regenerates the entire file.

Practice Exercise 2

These exercises will help you with object snaps and TRIM.

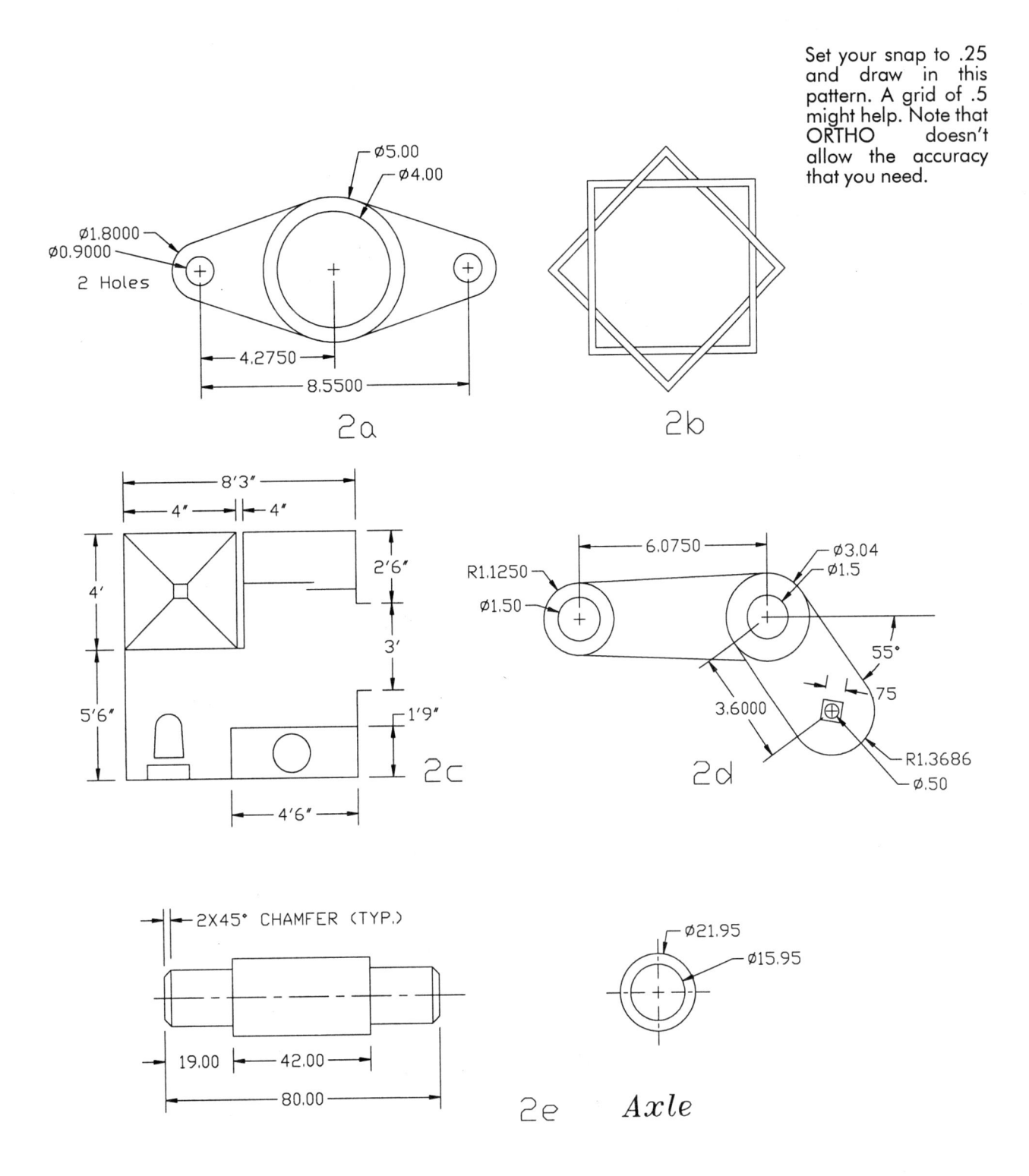

Set your snap to .25 and draw in this pattern. A grid of .5 might help. Note that ORTHO doesn't allow the accuracy that you need.

2a

2b

2c

2d

2e *Axle*

Help Files, CHAMFER, OSNAP, ERASE, TRIM, and BREAK

Exercise A2

You will need PAN and ZOOM to place these interior walls.

```
Command: UNITS, 4, 1 (press ↵, accepting the default on the
    other settings until you return to the command prompt)
Command: LIMITS -3',-3' 45',38'
Command: SNAP 6
Command: GRID 24
```

Use **F6** to get your coordinates to move.
When you are finished, SAVE the file as FIRSTFL.

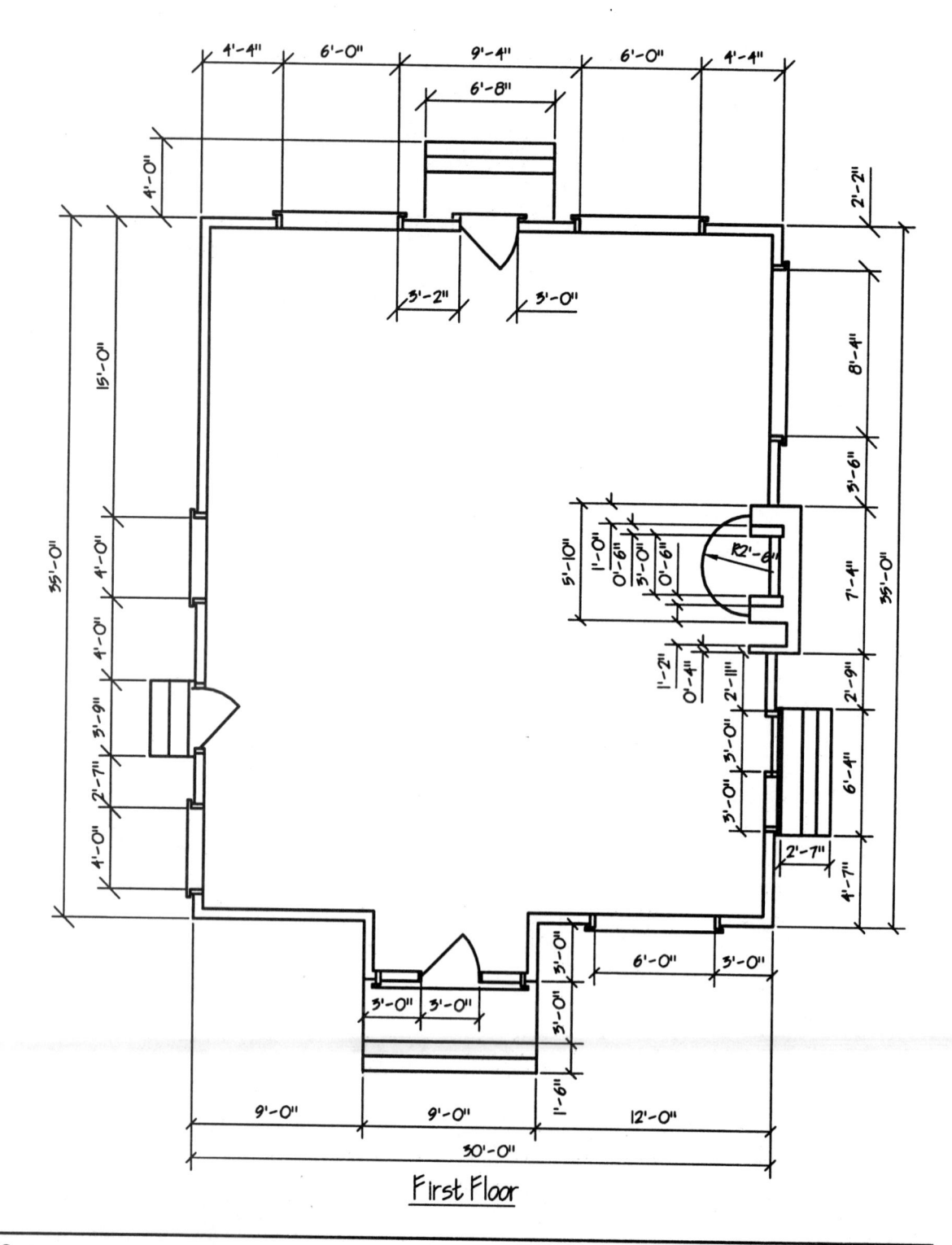

First Floor

CHAPTER TWO

Exercise C2

Set up your file as follows:
 LIMITS -5,-5
          60,40
 SNAP 1
 GRID 5
 ZOOM All

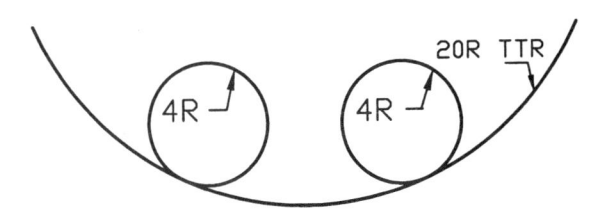

Make the sidewalk 2.5 wide, and place the deep end lines by the diving board about 7 feet away from the edge.

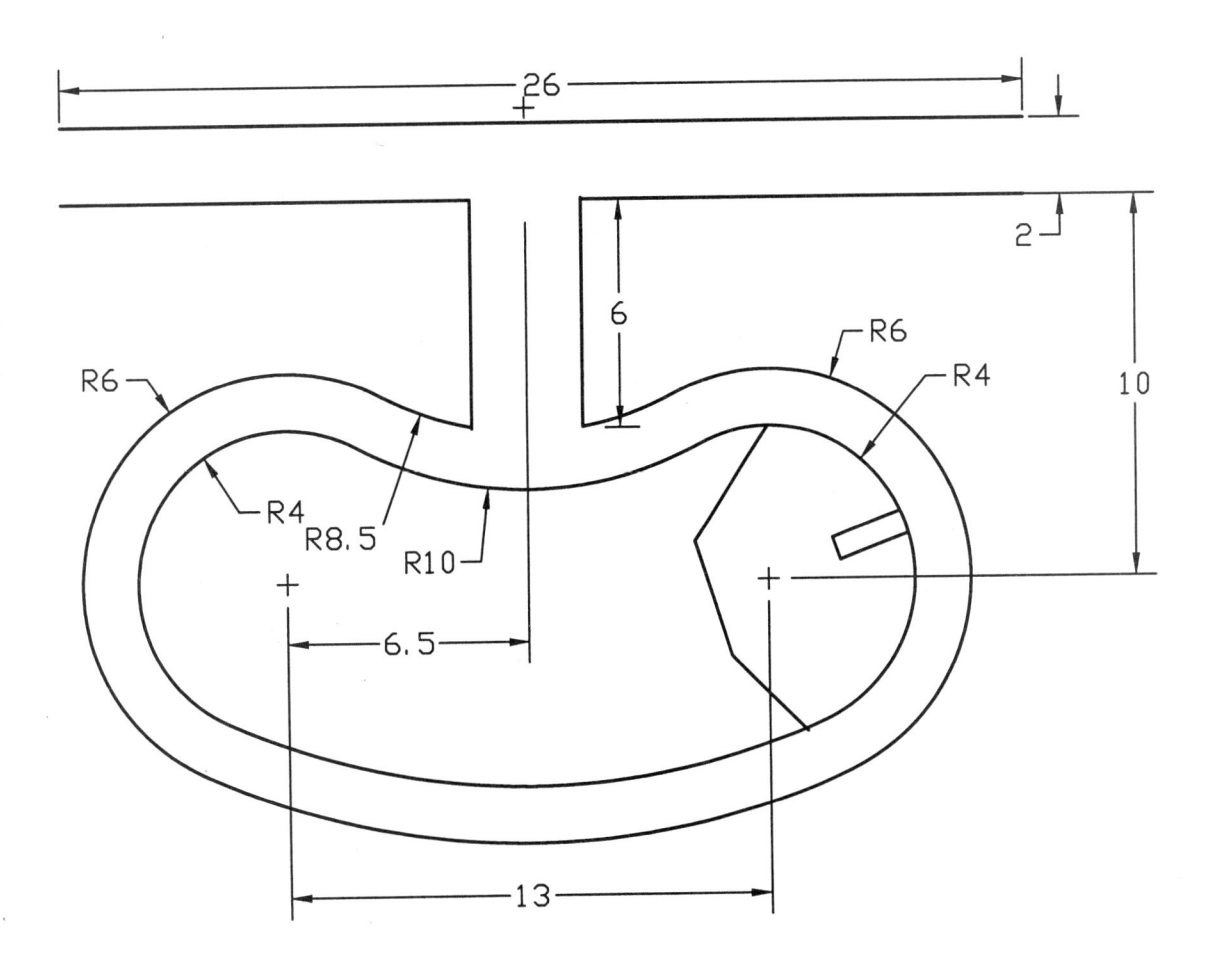

Use OSNAP to enter objects correctly in this swimming pool design.

Place two circles at 4R, then two circles at 6R. You will need CIRCLE TTR (tangent tangent radius) to connect them.

Use NEAR to place the diving board.

Help Files, CHAMFER, OSNAP, ERASE, TRIM, and BREAK

Exercise E2

Set up a file as follows:

                    LIMITS -5,-5
                          45,30
SNAP **1**
GRID **5**
ZOOM **All**

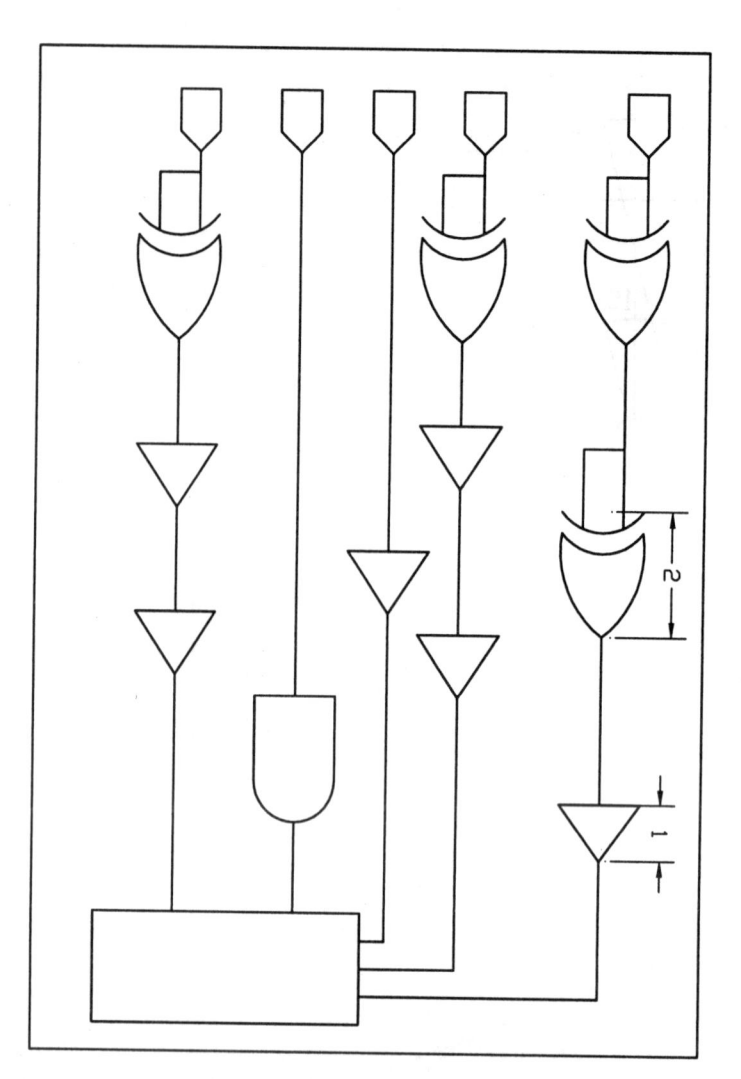

Use LINE for the outline of the schematic. Then change the SNAP to .5 and enter the lines for the top line. Use the space bar to speed up entry. Put the arcs in, overlapping the lines, and use BREAK to create a good corner.

Use ZOOM to get a good look at your work. PAN the drawing over to complete an adjacent section.

Practice on Exercise M2 if you finish early.

Exercise M2

Set up a separate file for each of the following. No changes in limits, snap, or grid are required for the first one; set the limits to top right 150,100 for the second. Use ZOOM Window, ZOOM All, and PAN to access the geometry. Place the objects using the OSNAPs. Use TRIM to remove unwanted lines.

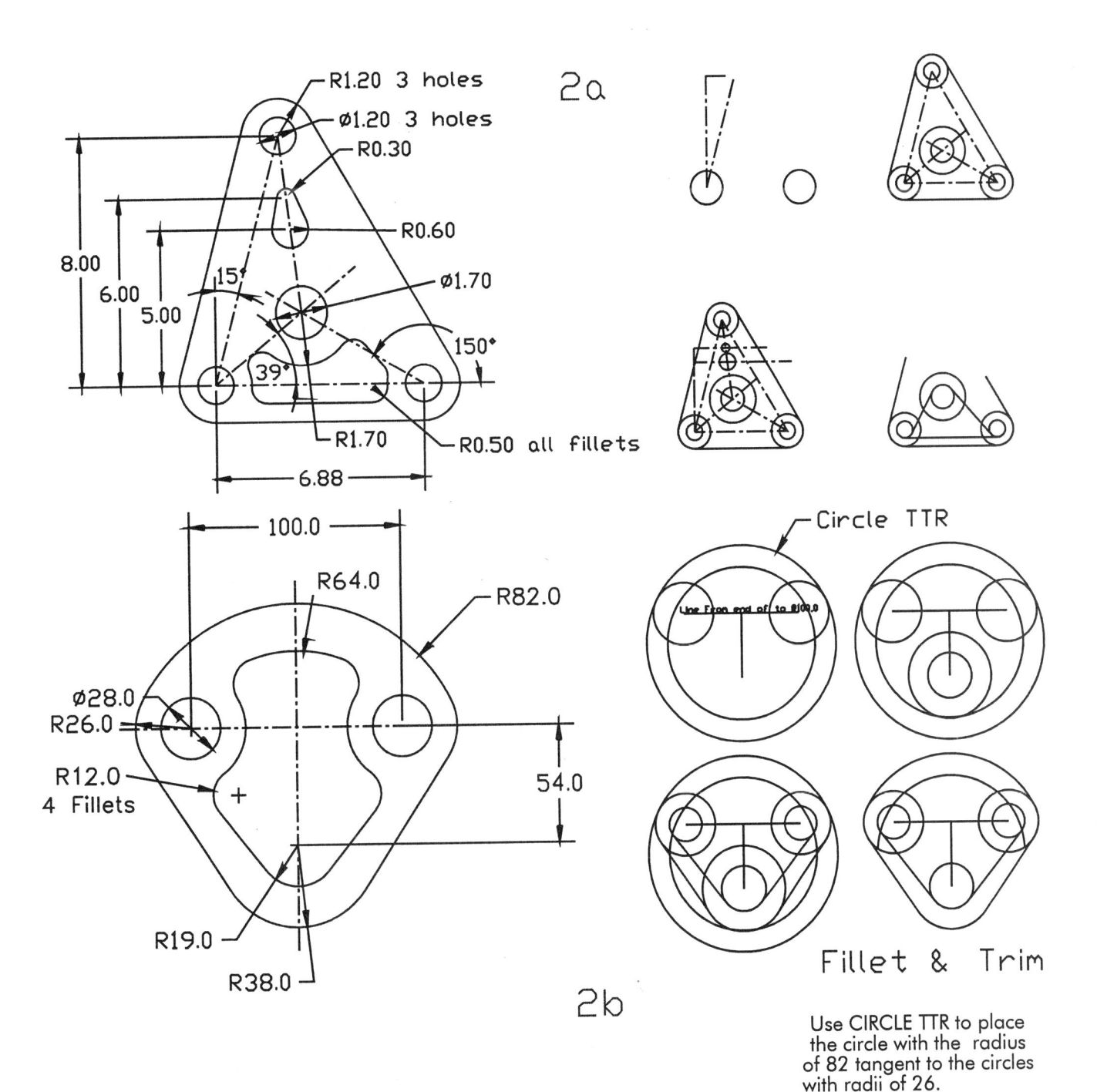

MECHANICAL

2a

- R1.20 3 holes
- Ø1.20 3 holes
- R0.30
- R0.60
- 15°
- Ø1.70
- 150°
- 39°
- R1.70
- R0.50 all fillets
- 8.00
- 6.00
- 5.00
- 6.88

2b

- 100.0
- R64.0
- R82.0
- Ø28.0
- R26.0
- R12.0 4 Fillets
- 54.0
- R19.0
- R38.0

Circle TTR

Line from end of to Ø100.0

Fillet & Trim

Use CIRCLE TTR to place the circle with the radius of 82 tangent to the circles with radii of 26.

Help Files, CHAMFER, OSNAP, ERASE, TRIM, and BREAK

Challenger 2

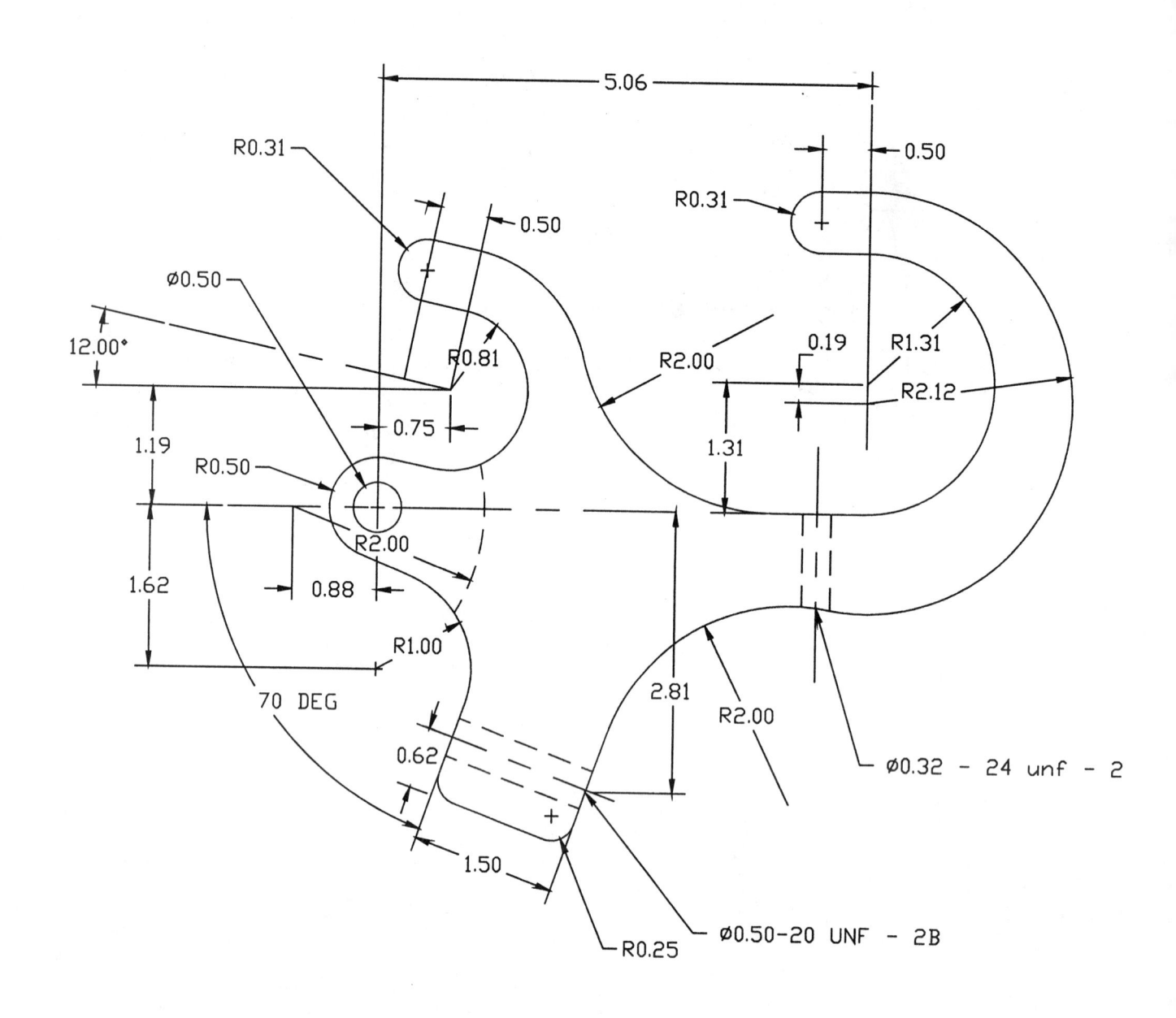

This is an excellent OSNAP exercise.

Use LINE, ARC, CIRCLE, FILLET, OFFSET (Chapter 4), and BREAK to create this model. Your origin should be the center of the small circle.

3 Entity Commands with Width

Upon completion of this chapter, you should be able to:

1. Create a TRACE
2. Create a polyline PLINE with acceptable corners and widths
3. Edit a pline using PEDIT to change the width and curve factors
4. Create a POLYGON
5. Create a SOLID
6. Create a DONUT with a specific width
7. Enter simple TEXT
8. Add Multilines with the MLINE command

The TRACE Command

The TRACE command makes a thickened line with bevelled or mitred corners. Traces are drawn in the same way as lines, from point to point; the difference is that a width must be specified.

Toolbar This command is not available through the toolbar.

Pull Down This command is no longer available through the Pull Down menus.

At the command line enter **TRACE**.

```
Command:TRACE
Specify trace width<0.0500>:.1
Specify start point:5,.5
Specify next point:11,.5
```

The line segment created will show up one pick behind because AutoCAD is calculating the mitre to the next edge. If you want to keep this mitre, draw in an extra segment to have the mitre calculated, then erase it as in the following examples.

```
Command:TRACE
Specify trace width<0.1000>:.2
From point: (pick 1)
Specify start point: (pick 2)
Specify next point: (pick 3)
Specify next point: (pick 4)
Specify next point: (pick 5)
Specify next point: (pick 6)
Specify next point:↵
```

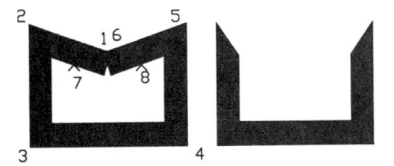

Figure 3-1

Each segment of the trace is a separate entity once it is placed, and thus the segments adjacent to the mitred edges can be erased to provide a final mitred edge.

```
Command: ERASE
Select objects: (pick 7, 8)
Select objects:↵
```

To create a closed square with TRACE, start halfway down the side of the square and continue around so that all sides have square corners.

The disadvantage of TRACE is that it cannot be edited. To create thick lines that can be edited, use PLINE.

The PLINE Command

A *pline* or polyline is a single-drawing entity that includes line and curve sections that may vary in thickness, and may be edited using PEDIT for the Spline and Fit curve options to create contour lines or airfoils. The individual segments are connected at vertices; the direction, tangency, and line width are stored at each vertex.

The PLINE command can create rectangles as single entities as well as curved segments of varying thickness.

> **Toolbar** From the Draw toolbar, pick the Polyline button.
>
> **Pull Down** From the Draw menu, pick Polyline.

The command line equivalent is **PLINE**.

```
Command: PLINE
Specify start point: (pick a point)
Current line width is 0.0000
Specify next point or
 [Arc/Close/Halfwidth/Length/Undo/Width]:
```

Where: **Arc** = a change from line entry to arc entry
        Close = a closed pline, in which the first point will be joined to the last entered point in the pline to make a closed object; more than two points are needed to have a closed pline
        Halfwidth = a specified halfwidth on either side of the pline vector
        Length = the length of the pline
        Undo = an undo of the last point entered
        Width = a specified width of the line or arc segments on either side of the pline vector

The first PLINE command prompt asks for a point at which the pline will start.

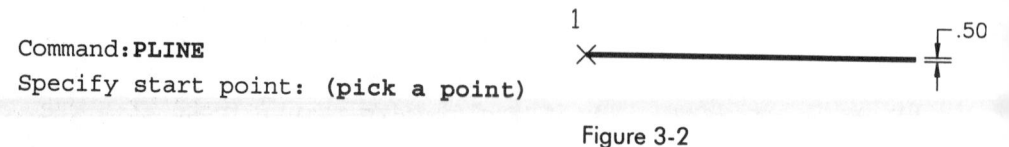

```
Command: PLINE
Specify start point: (pick a point)
```

Figure 3-2

You *must* enter the first point, after which you can choose one of the options (Width, Arc, etc.).

The next command default is to enter the second point, "<Endpoint of line>." If you pick a second point, this assumes a straight segment or a line. If you continue picking points, the object created will look like a series of lines, but it will be a single object that can be edited using PEDIT or other editing commands.

To change the width of a pline, enter the first point and then specify width by entering **W** or picking Width from the side menu. The system will prompt you for both the beginning and the end width. If these are the same, press ⏎ to accept the default.

```
Command:PLINE
Specify start point:0,0
Current line width is 0.0000 units
Specify next point or [Arc/Close/Halfwidth/Length/Undo/Width]:W
Specify starting width<0.0000>:.25
Specify ending width<0.2500>:⏎
Specify next point or [Arc/Close/Halfwidth/Length/Undo/Width]:
   11,0
```

You can continue drawing with this line at the current thickness or change it at any time.

```
Specify next point or
   [Arc/Close/Halfwidth/Length/Undo/
   Width]:11,8.5
Specify next point or [Arc/Close/
   Halfwidth/Length/Undo/Width]:0,8.5
Specify next point or [Arc/Close/
   Halfwidth/Length/Undo/Width]:C
```

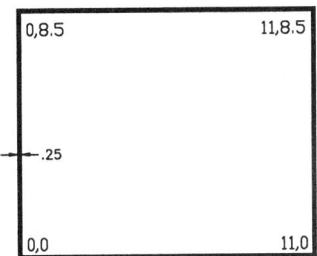

Figure 3-3

To achieve a perfect corner on a box or rectangle, use the Close option. This will attach the first point to the last entered point and create a clean, bevelled corner.

```
Command:PLINE
Specify start point:2,2
Current line width is 4.00 units
Specify next point or [Arc/Close/Halfwidth/Length/Undo/Width]:W
Specify starting width<4.00>:.25
Specify ending width<0.25>:⏎ (don't pick)
```

Do not pick! If you pick, you will create an object similar to that of Figure 3-4. There, the second pick was assumed to be the width of the end point of your pline, measured from the first entered point.

Pick 2 is generally inside the triangle.

Figure 3-4

Entity Commands with Width   **63**

PLINE with Varying Width

You can create objects such as arrows using one PLINE with a series of different segments with varying widths. You can change the width at every vertex.

```
Command:PLINE
Specify start point: (pick 1)
Current line width is 4.00 units
Specify next point or [Arc/Close/Halfwidth/Length/Undo/Width]:W
Specify starting width<4.00>:0
Specify ending width<4.00>:.35
Specify next point or [Arc/Close/Halfwidth/
Length/Undo/Width]: (pick 2)
Specify next point or [Arc/Close/Halfwidth/Length/Undo/Width]:W
Specify starting width<0.35>:.10
Specify ending width<0.10>:.10
Specify next point or [Arc/Close/Halfwidth/Length/Undo/Width]:
 (pick 3)
```

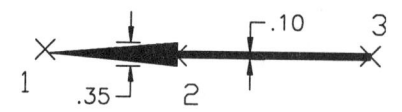

Figure 3-5

Using PLINE Effectively

There are a few tricks with PLINE that will make the entered plines perfect. First, let us look at creating good corners.

Remember that the points entered for a pline are considered to be vertices. This means the pline is to be calculated as a series of points entered with a specific sequence in mind.

Figure 3-6

While creating a PLINE, you are creating only one object that is fit through a series of points at a defined width. As the pline changes direction, the end of each pline is calculated relative to the points or vertices used to create it. If a thickened pline is created with just two points, its ends are calculated perpendicular to the pline vector. If three points are used to create a pline, the end of the pline that attaches to a segment going in another direction is calculated to create a sharp corner. As shown in Figure 3-6, the ends of the plines are perpendicular to the direction of the pline itself. When entering plines, do not pick a point twice in the same spot; this will create a corner that has two perpendicular ends as shown in Figure 3-7. To get the corners to close properly, only one pick per corner is needed.

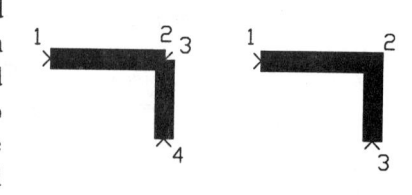

Figure 3-7

The Fill Option

If a drawing is becoming too dark, or is taking a long time to regenerate after ZOOM commands, you may want to use the FILL command. This allows the lines to show the edges of your pline, but the pline will not be filled in.

Figure 3-8 demonstrates how the FILL option can change the appearance of a pline. On the left, the FILL is off; on the right, the FILL is on.

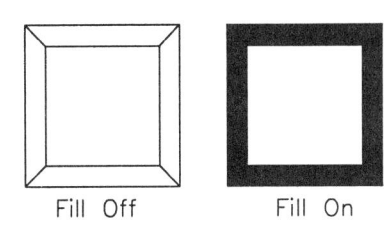

Fill Off   Fill On

Figure 3-8

You need to use the REGEN command to see the effect of turning Fill on and off. Turn FILL off for quicker draft plots.

Fillet and Chamfer with Polylines

Both the FILLET and the CHAMFER command have polyline options that apply to all the vertices or corners.

Polyarcs

The PLINE command can be used to create arcs within polyline segments or on their own. The Arc options are:

```
Command: PLINE
Specify start point: (pick a point)
Current line width is 0.1000
Specify next point or [Arc/Close/
  Halfwidth/Length/Undo/Width]: A
Angle/CEnter/CLose/Direction/Halfwidth/
  Line/Radius/Second point/Undo/Width]:
```

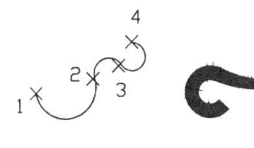

Figure 3-9

Notes

If your Polyarc is not working, create an arc using the ARC command and then make it a polyarc with PEDIT.

The command default is to create a two-point arc. Once the first arc segment is in, the system assumes that you want to continue with a series of arcs until the **L** option is entered, which will return you to a line segment.

The PEDIT Command

One of the great advantages of PLINE is that, once the pline is entered, it can be modified using PEDIT (Polyline Edit).

In the introductory stages, this command sequence is used most often to change the width of a pline. In Figure 3-10, the border is edited from .25 units to .10 units.

The PEDIT command changes the width of all the segments of the identified pline.

> **Toolbar** From the Modify II toolbar, choose the Polyline Edit button
>
> **Pull Down** From the Modify menu, choose Polyline.

The command line equivalent is **PEDIT**.

Entity Commands with Width   **65**

```
Command:PEDIT
Select polyline: (pick the polyline)
Enter an option [Close/Join/Width/Edit
 Vertex/Fitcurve/Spline/Decurve/ Ltype
 gen/Undo:W
Specify new width for all segments:.10
Enter an option [Close/Join/Width/Edit
 Vertex/Fitcurve/Spline/DecurveLtype
 gen/Undo] :⏎
```

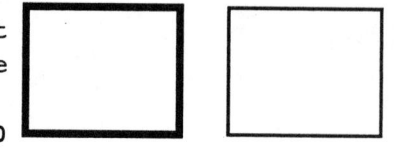

Figure 3-10

More segments can be added to the pline by using the Join option. This will add lines or arcs to a pline which can then be edited for width. Below, the arc and the two lines identified by picks 2, 3, and 4 are added to the pline selected with the first pick before the command option Join. Only segments with a common end point can be joined.

```
Command:PEDIT
Select polyline: (pick 1)
Enter an option [Close/Join/Width/Edit
 Vertex/Fit curve/Spline/Decurve/Ltype
 gen/Undo] :J
Select objects: (pick 2)
Select objects: (pick 3)
Select objects: (pick 4)
Select object:⏎
Enter an option [Close/Join/Width/Edit
 Vertex/Fit curve/Spline/DecurveLtype gen/Undo] :⏎
```

Figure 3-11

You can change polylines back to regular lines by using the command EXPLODE. This will also remove the width given.

If you apply PEDIT to an object that is not a polyline, you will be given the option of turning it into one. Then use Join.

PEDIT with Spline and Fit Curve

To create contour lines and other items used in surveying, among other fields, a pline can be modified to become a spline or fit a curve through a series of points. Splines and spline editing will be dealt with in more detail in Chapter 13. For purposes of this chapter, use PEDIT to fit a curve through a series of vertices.

The Spline curve option of PEDIT will edit the pline according to the series of points used to create it. Make sure you use the Close option when entering the pline to get a continuous spline.

The Fit curve option of PEDIT will create continuous curves through a series of points.

Figure 3-12

Figure 3-12 shows two "airfoil" shapes. The plines are closed and were drawn without a width.

In the upper example, the Spline option was used to create a smooth curve using the points as a guide.

66 CHAPTER THREE

In the lower example, the Fit curve option was used, and the resulting curve is much more choppy.

The Spline option, on the other hand, uses the points as a guide but has a degree of continuity through each of the adjacent points.

If you need to be quite specific about spline generation, you can change the curve of the spline with the SPLINETYPE system variable.

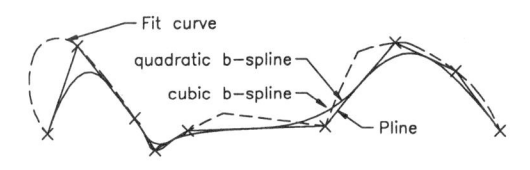

Figure 3-13

```
Command:SPLINETYPE
New value for the SPLINETYPE <6>:5
```

The default is a cubic B-spline <6>. A quadratic B-spline can be achieved by changing the variable to 5.

The POLYGON Command

The POLYGON command is like a PLINE in that you are creating an object that has many vertices.

Toolbar From the Draw toolbar, choose the Polygon flyout, then Polygon.

Pull Down From the Draw menu, choose Polygon.

The command line equivalent is **POLYGON**.

```
Command:POLYGON
Enter number of sides<4>:5
Specify center of polygon or [Edge]:
  (pick a center point)
Enter an option [Inscribed in circle/
  Circumscribed about circle] <I>:I
Specify radius of circle:1.5
```

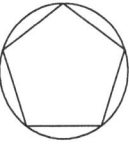

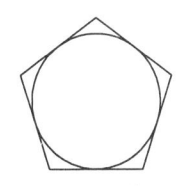

Inscribed   Circumscribed

Figure 3-14

Hexagons

In mechanical drawing, hexagons (six-sided regular polygons) are quite common.

If you need to draw a hexagon that is measured by *the distance across the flats* choose the option Circumscribed about circle. The diameter across the circle will equal the distance across the flats.

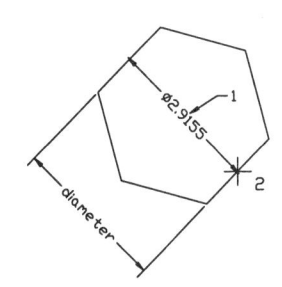

Figure 3-15

Entity Commands with Width   **67**

```
Command: POLYGON
Enter number of sides<4>:6
Specify center of polygon or [Edge]: (pick center)
Enter an option [Inscribed in circle/
 Circumscribed about circle] <I>:C
Radius of circle:(pick 2)
```

You can also use the polygon command to draw regular polygons by specifying *the length of an edge*.

```
Command: POLYGON
Enter number of sides<4>:6
Specify center of polygon or [Edge]:E
Specify first endpoint of edge: (pick 1)
Specify second endpoint of edge:@4<0
```

Figure 3-16

The SOLID Command

The SOLID command creates a polygon filled with the currently selected color. The Fill On option will fill in the solid with each screen regeneration, while the Fill Off option will display only an outline for quicker redraws.

The command line equivalent is **SOLID**.

Notes
Do not confuse SOLID with the SOLIDS option given under the Draw menus.

Toolbar From the Surfaces toolbar, choose SOLID button.

Pull Down From the Draw Pull Down menu, choose Surfaces then 2D SOLID.

The command line equivalent is **SOLID**.

```
Command: SOLID
Specify first point: (pick 1)
Specify second point: (pick 2)
Specify third point: (pick 3)
Specify fourth point or [Exit]:
   (pick 4)
Third point:↵
```

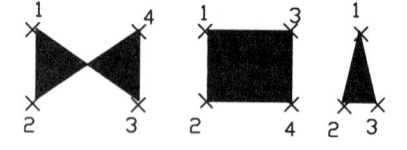

Figure 3-17

If you continue to digitize after the fourth entry, the system will continue to add to the original entity until you terminate with ↵. To create a triangle, use ↵ after the third point prompt.

The order in which points are entered is very important. Figure 3-18 provides some examples.

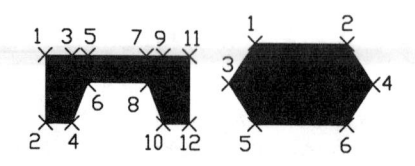

Figure 3-18

68 CHAPTER THREE

The DONUT Command

The DONUT command is used to create a thick or solid circle. The inside diameter is used to determine the hole of the doughnut. Use an inside diameter of zero to create a solid circle; use a larger diameter to create a ring. Once DONUT is active, a doughnut will be drawn every time you digitize until you press ⏎.

The DONUT command can be accessed through the Draw pull down menus or by typing it in.

```
Command:DONUT
Specify inside diameter of donut<.5>:0
Specify outside diameter<1.0>:2
Specify center of donut or <exit>:
  (pick 1)
Specify center of donut or <exit>:
  (pick 2)
Specify center of donut or <exit>:⏎
```

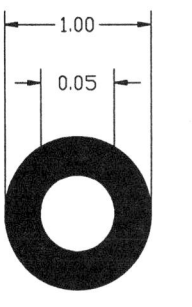

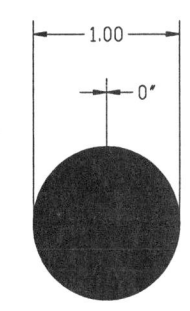

Figure 3-19

Filling Irregular Shapes

The BHATCH command can be useful when you are trying to fill an irregular shape. With Release 2000, there is a solid fill pattern that will fill any shape with any color. Pick BHATCH, then Pattern, then Solid. For more information on HATCH and BHATCH see Chapter 9.

The TEXT Command

Chapter 8 deals with many aspects of text, including text style, editing, fonts, and a wide variety of text alignments. Here we introduce simple, one-line text entry. Paragraph text entry is found in Chapter 8. Use TEXT from the command line or DTEXT from the pull down menus. The commands are the same except that DTEXT will allow you to see the text as it is written on the screen. DTEXT allows for multiple lines of text, so there are two things to remember. First, you will be prompted for the next line of text until you use the enter key on the keyboard to exit the command. Second, if you use ESCape to exit from DTEXT you will lose all of your text.

Both the commands **TEXT** and **DTEXT** will place strings of characters on your drawing. When entering text, AutoCAD will prompt you to choose a height for each character, a rotation angle for your string, and a point at which to place the text string on the model or drawing.

To access TEXT:

> **Toolbar** From the Draw toolbar, neither TEXT nor DTEXT are available.
>
> **Pull Down** From the Draw menu, pick Text, then Single-Line Text.

The command line equivalent is **TEXT**.

```
Command:TEXT
Current text style: "Standard" Text height 0.200
Specify start point [Justify/Style]:J
Align/Fit/Center/Middle/Right/TL/TC/TR/ML/MC/MR/BL/BC/BR:
```

Entity Commands with Width 69

Where: **Justify** = placement of the text
Style = switches the style of the letters; the styles must be loaded in AutoCAD to be accessible
Align = an alignment by the end points of the baseline; the aspect ratio (X versus Y) will correspond to the preset distance
Center = the center point of the baseline; this option will center the text on the point indicated
Fit = an adjustment of width only of the characters that are to be fit or "stretched" between the indicated points
Middle = a placement of the text around the point , i.e the top and bottom of the text are centered as well as the sides
Right = an alignment with the right side of the text

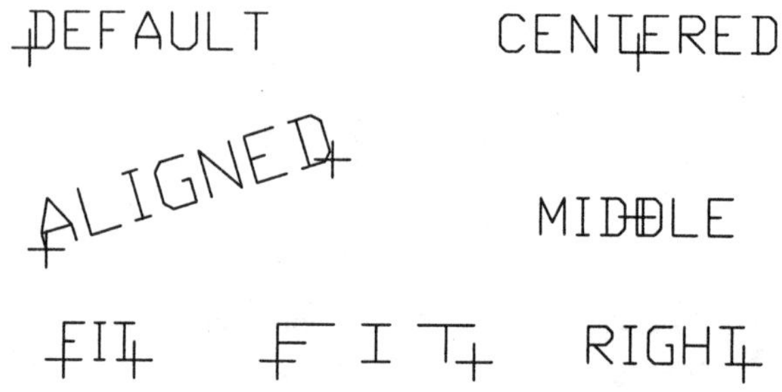

Figure 3-20

The initials TL, TC, etc. stand for other alignments. See Chapter 8.

The examples in Figure 3-20 demonstrate the standard justifications.

The default is left justification at the baseline of the text string.

Once you have chosen a point at which to place your text, the command will prompt you for the height of the letters, the rotation angle, and the text or string of characters itself.

```
Command:TEXT
Current text style: "Standard" Text height 0.200
Specify start point [Justify/Style]: (pick 1)
Specify height <.2000>:.15
Specify rotation angle of text <0>:↵ (to accept the default)
Enter text:Scale:
Enter text:↵
Command:↵
Current text style: "Standard" Text height 0.150
Specify start point [Justify/Style]: (pick 2)
Specify height<.2000>:.25
Specify rotation angle of text <0>:↵
Enter text:1/4"=1'0"
Enter text:↵
```

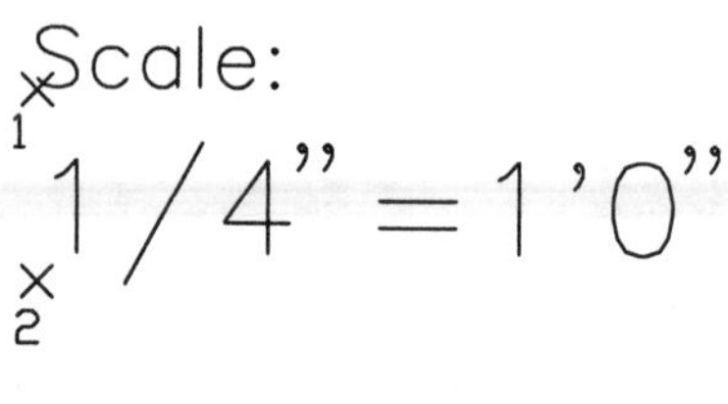

Figure 3-21

Multilines

The MLINE or multiline command is used to create multiple, parallel lines.

> **Toolbar** From the Draw toolbar, choose the Multiline button.
>
> **Pull Down** From the Draw menu, choose <u>M</u>ultiline.

The command line equivalent is **MLINE**.

MLINE is particularly useful for drawing walls and other architectural features. From a specified point, AutoCAD draws a multiline segment using the current multiline style, and continues to prompt for other points. Like LINE, using Undo undoes the last vertex point on the multiline. If you create a multiline with two or more segments, the Close option will be included in the command string.

```
Command:MLINE
Current settings; Justification  = Top, Scale = 1.00,
  Style = Standard
Specify start point or [Justification
 /Scale/STyle]: (pick 1)
Specify next point: (pick 2)
Specify next point or
 [Close/Undo]:(pick 3)
Specify next point or
 [Close/Undo]: (pick 4)
Specify next point or
 [Close/Undo] :C
```

Justification

This option determines how the multiline is drawn between the points you specify.

Enter Justification type [Top/Zero/Bottom] <Top>:

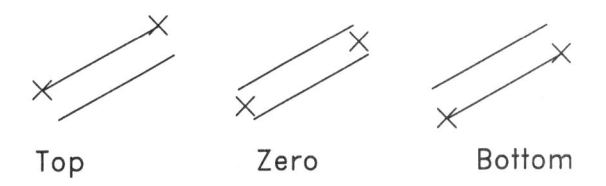

Top   Zero   Bottom

Scale

This option determines the distance between the two lines of the multiline.

The scale is based on the width established in the multiline style.

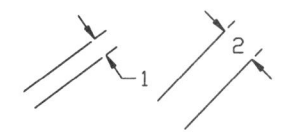

Style

Specifies a style. For more information see Chapter 13.

Prelab 3 Using PLINE and SOLID

By using PLINE and SOLID effectively, we can create a presentation view of a small cabin with a staircase and a fireplace.

Step 1 First change the units to Architectural. At the command prompt type **UNITS**.

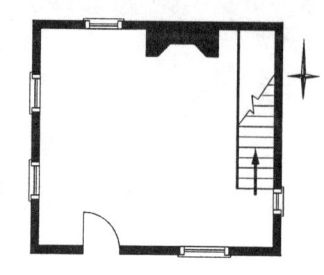

```
Command:UNITS
Report formats:Architectural
Denominator of smallest fraction to display:1/4
```

Step 2 Make your LIMITS -2', -2' by 22', 18'.

Put the SNAP at 12" or 1' to enter the outline of the cabin as shown.

```
Command:LIMITS
Reset model space limits
Specify lower left corner or [ON/OFF]
   <0.0000,0.0000>: -2',-2'
Specify upper right corner
   <12.0000,9.0000>:22',18'
```

Step 3 Add the PLINEs in, as shown on the illustration.

Things really get complicated when you start to dimension this.

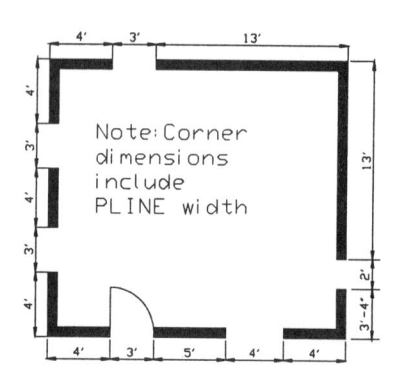

Note: Corner dimensions include PLINE width

Notes
Since PLINEs are created along a center line with width added to *both* sides, be sure to deduct half the wall thickness to obtain the correct wall length.

Toolbar From the Draw toolbar choose Polyline.

Pull Down From the Draw menu, choose Polyline.

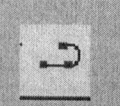

```
Command:PLINE
Specify start point:4',0
Current line width is 0.00 units
Specify next point or [Arc/Close/Halfwidth/Length/Undo/Width]:W
Specify starting width<0.00>:8
Specify ending width<8.00>:↵
Specify next point or
   [Arc/Close/Halfwidth/Length/Undo/Width]:0,0
Specify next point or
   [Arc/Close/Halfwidth/Length/Undo/Width]:0,4'
Specify next point or
   [Arc/Close/Halfwidth/Length/Undo/Width]:↵
```

72 CHAPTER THREE

Step 4   Now use ZOOM Window to get a closer look at the northeast corner of the building. Add the lines as shown, with PLINE width at 2″.

> **Toolbar** From the standard toolbar, pick Zoom Window. 
>
> **Pull Down** From the View menu, choose Zoom Window.

Once sufficiently zoomed, enter the staircase with PLINE.

Notes

PLINEs are entered from their MIDDLE point, so calculations will need to be adjusted.

```
Command:PLINE
Specify start point:16'8",5'
Current line width is 8.00 units
Specify next point or [Arc/Close/
 Halfwidth/Length/Undo/Width]:W
Specify starting width<8.00>:2
Specify ending width<2.00>:↵
Specify next point or [Arc/Close/
 Halfwidth/Length/Undo/Width]:
  16'8",17'6"
```

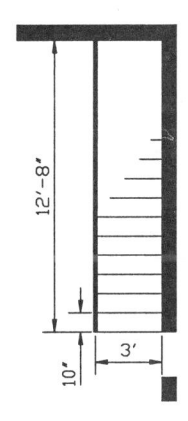

Step 5   Now use PLINE to place an arrow pointing up the stairs.

```
Command:PLINE
Specify start point:18'2",4'6"
Current line width is 2.00 units
Specify next point or [Arc/Close/Halfwidth
 /Length/Undo/Width] :18'2",7'
Specify next point or [Arc/Close/Halfwidth
 /Length/Undo/Width]:W
Specify starting width<4.00>:7
Specify ending width<7.00>:0
Specify next point or [Arc/Close/Halfwidth
 /Length/Undo/Width] :18'2",8'
Specify next point or [Arc/Close/Halfwidth
 /Length/Undo/Width] :↵
```

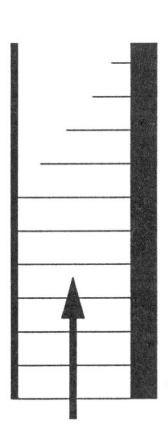

Step 6   Now use PLINE to create a break line on the staircase.

```
Command:PLINE
Specify start point: (pick 1)
Current line width is 0.00 units
Specify next point or [Arc/Close/
Halfwidth/Length/Undo/Width]:
(pick 2, 3, 4, 5, 6, 7 in sequence)
```

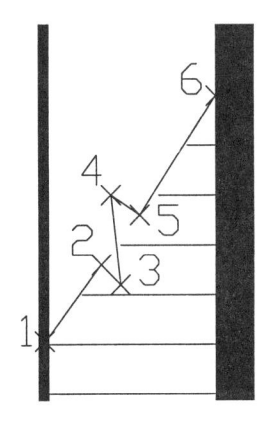

Entity Commands with Width   **73**

Step 7   Now use PAN to move the drawing to the right, at the same scale factor, and then use SOLID to create a fireplace.

> **Toolbar** From the standard toolbar, choose PAN. Then from the Surfaces toolbar, choose Solid.
>
> **Pull Down** From the View menu, choose Pan. Then from the Draw menu, choose Surfaces, then 2D Solid.

```
Command: SOLID
Specify first point: (pick 1)
Specify second point: (pick 2)
Specify third point: (pick 3)
Specify fourth point or [Exit]:(pick 4)
Specify third point: (pick 5)
Specify fourth point or [Exit]:(pick 6)
Specify third point: (pick 7)
Specify fourth point or [Exit]:(pick 8)
Specify third point: (pick 9)
Specify fourth point or [Exit]:(pick 10)
Specify third point: (pick 11)
Specify fourth point or [Exit]:(pick 12)
Specify third point:
```

Step 8   Use PAN again to move the drawing over to the left so that you can create a "north arrow" outside of the building. Draw in a vertical line at 3 feet, and a horizontal line at 1.5 feet across the lower section as shown.

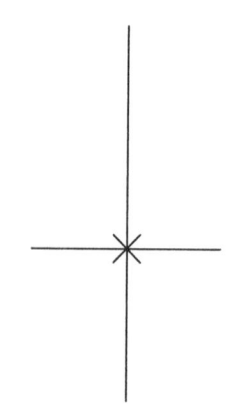

Step 9   Then, with your SNAP still set to 2, draw in two diagonal lines through the intersection. Now use SOLID to fill in the sides of the north arrow.

```
Command: SOLID
Specify first point: (pick 1)
Specify second point: (pick 2)
Specify third point: (pick 3)
Specify fourth point or [Exit]:
Specify third point:
```

Step 10 Finally, add lines for windows, and your simple floor plan is complete.

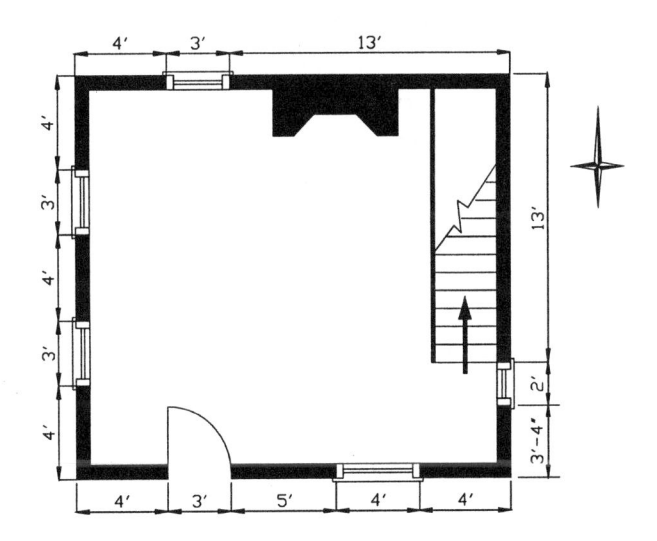

Step 11 Now PAN your view over and, using the same overall dimensions, add a second floor plan with MLINE. The MLINE will act like a polyline; the lines are one unit. Change the Scale of the exterior walls to 8″ and the interior walls to 4″.

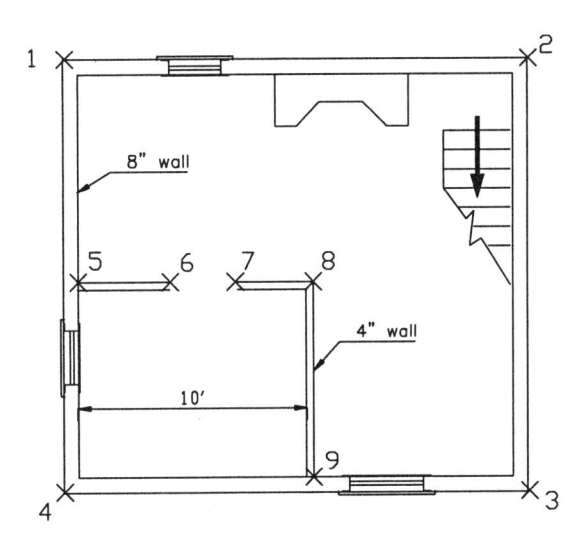

Entity Commands with Width **75**

Command and Function Summary

DONUT creates filled circles or rings.

PEDIT is used to edit the PLINEs.

PLINE creates lines with multiple segments in varying widths.

POLYGON is used to create polygons with equal sides, having anywhere from 3 to 1024 sides.

SOLID creates filled polygons.

TEXT is used to place text or lettering on drawings.

TRACE is used to make thick lines with mitred corners.

Here is a small paper cabinet just for practice.

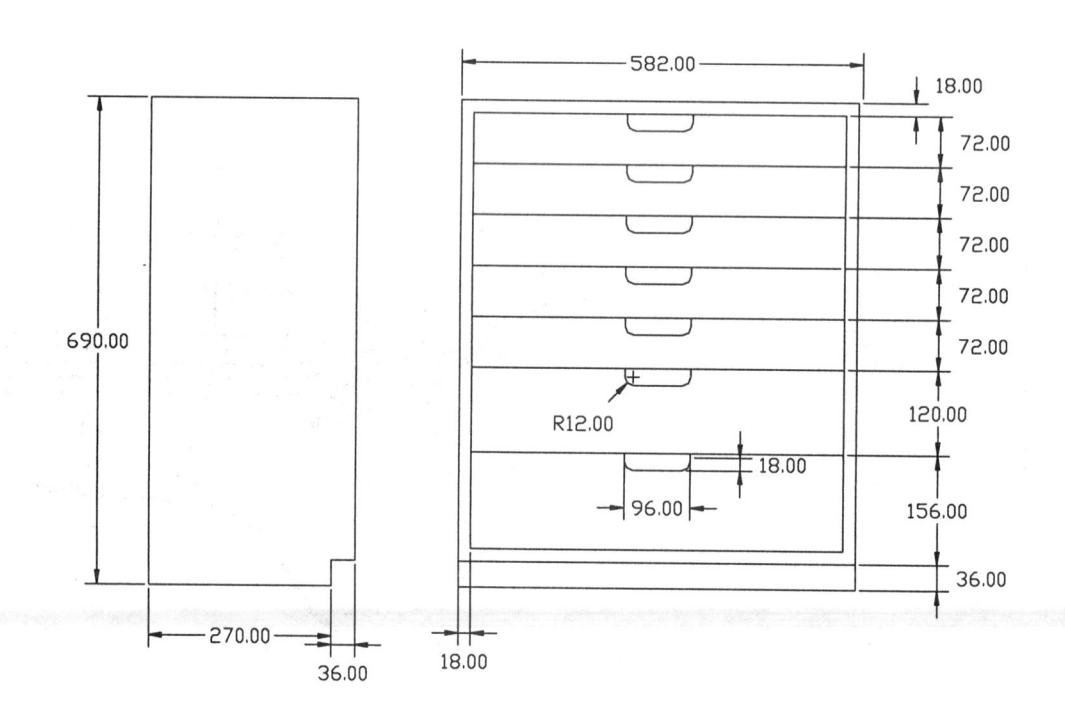

Practice Exercise 3

Use PLINE, SOLID, and DONUT to create this map. Then use DONUT and BREAK with the OSNAP QUADrant to create the elevation marker.

POLYGON can be used to create the bolt.

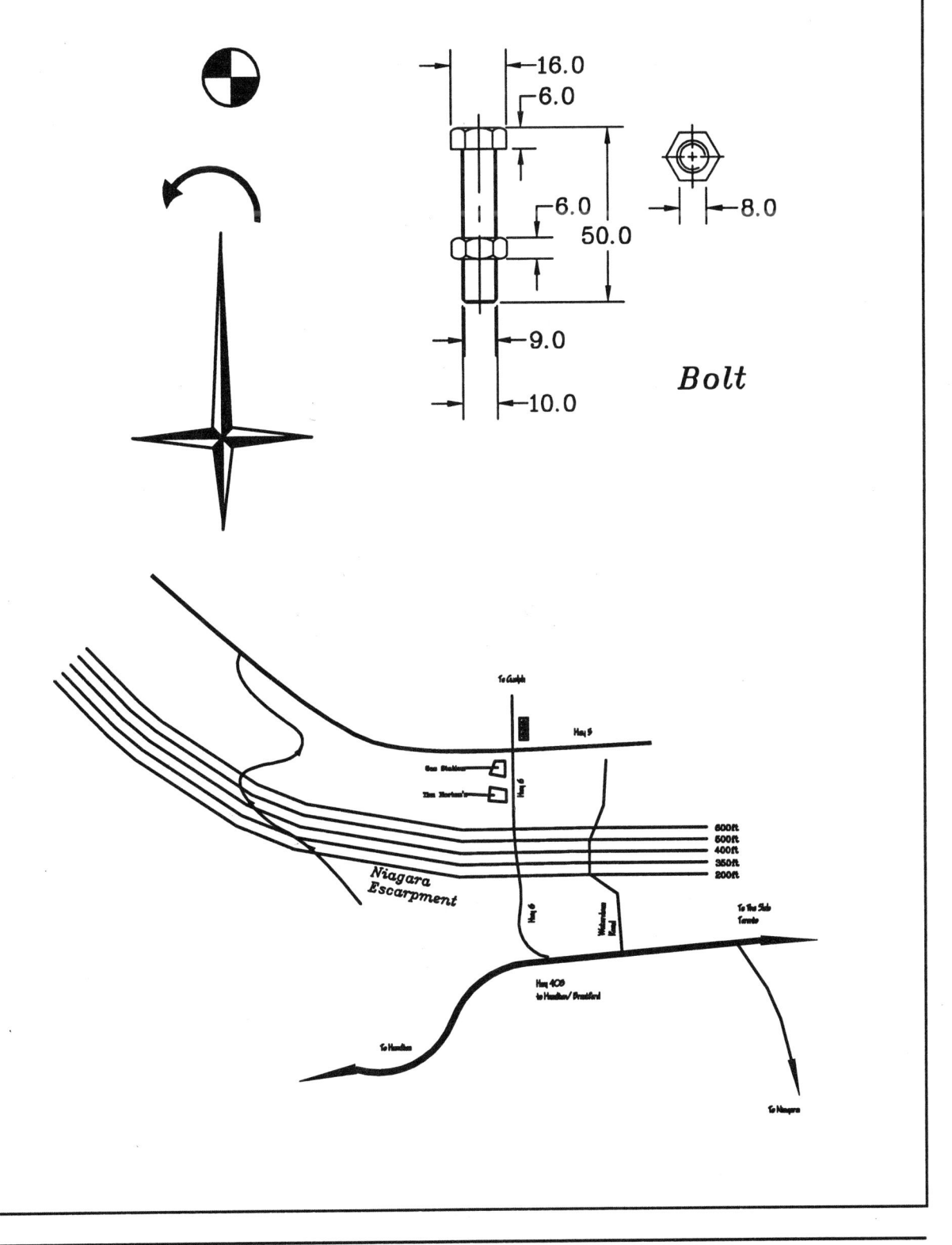

Bolt

Exercise A3

Using the dimensions from the floor plan in Chapter 2, use PLINE to create this presentation floor plan. Make the outside walls 8″ thick and the inside walls 5″ thick. Add a fireplace using SOLID, and columns to support the terrace roof with DONUT. Save the file as FLOORP. Open a new file to create the title block below. Save it under the name of ATITLE.

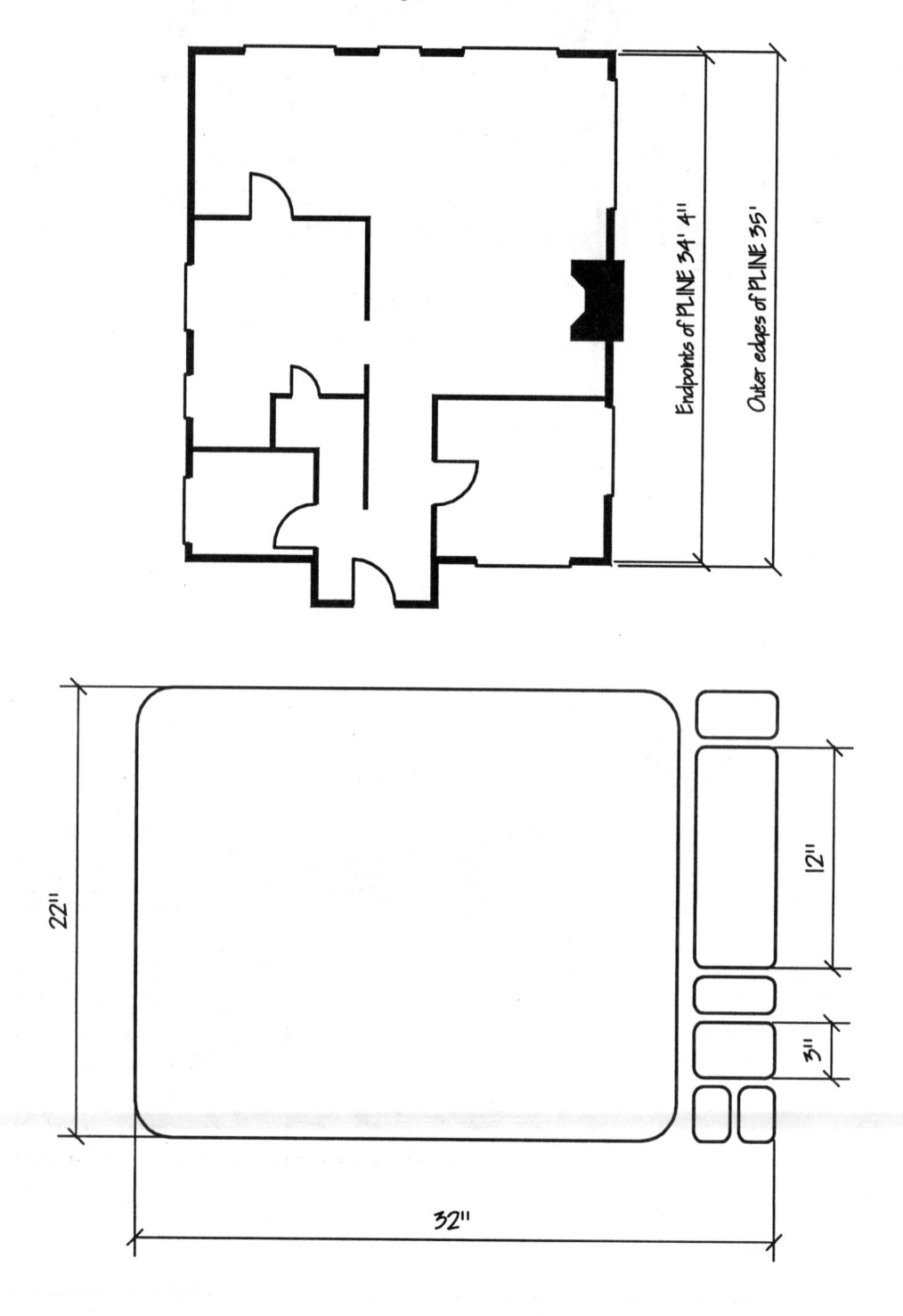

Never use more than eight characters in a file name. Do not use spaces, slashes /, or dots. The manuals tell you that you can use as many characters as you want, but you will have trouble later if you use more than eight.

Exercise C3

Use surveyor's units to create the lot plan shown below. Save this as file LOT. Then create the titleblock and call it CTITLE. Finally make a file called NORTH for the north arrow. For help on accessing surveyor's units, see Chapter 1.

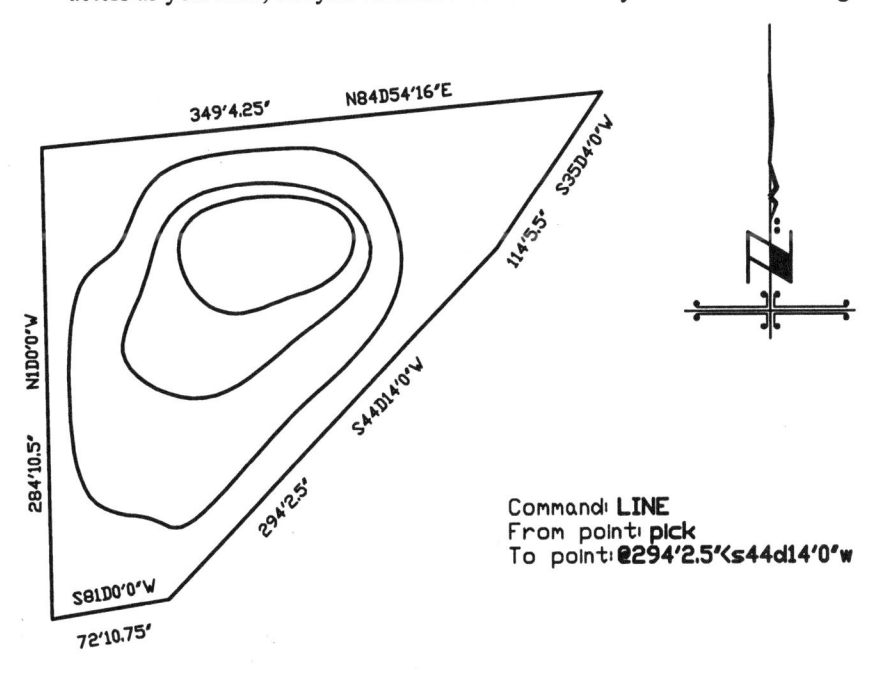

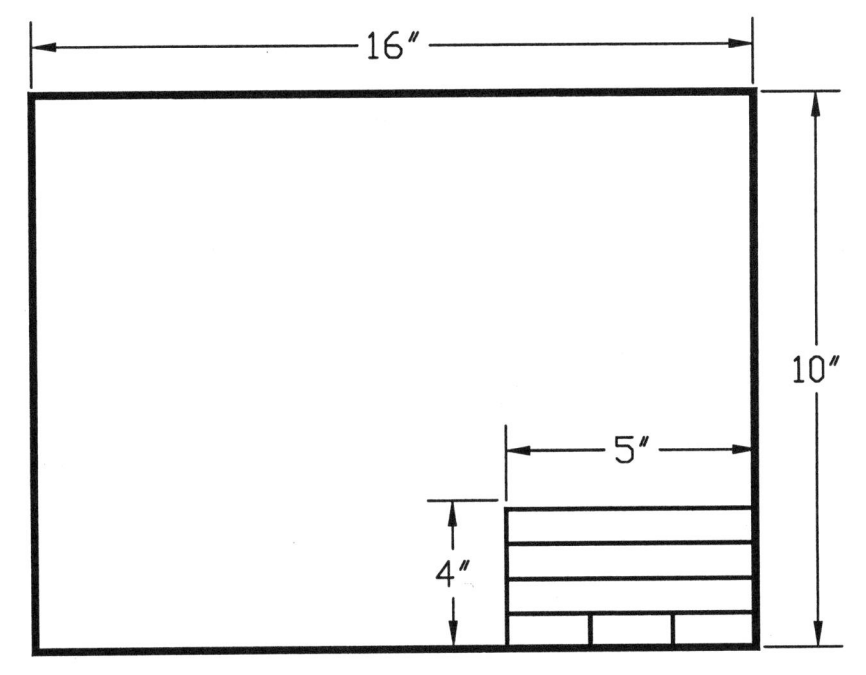

Never use more than eight characters in a file name. Do not use spaces, slashes /, or dots. The manuals tell you that you can use as many characters as you want, but you will have trouble later if you use more than eight.

```
Command: LINE
From point: pick
To point: @294'2.5"<s44d14'0"w
```

Entity Commands with Width   79

Exercise E3

Create the schematic below and save it as E3. Then use PLINE to draw the title block and save it as ETITLE.

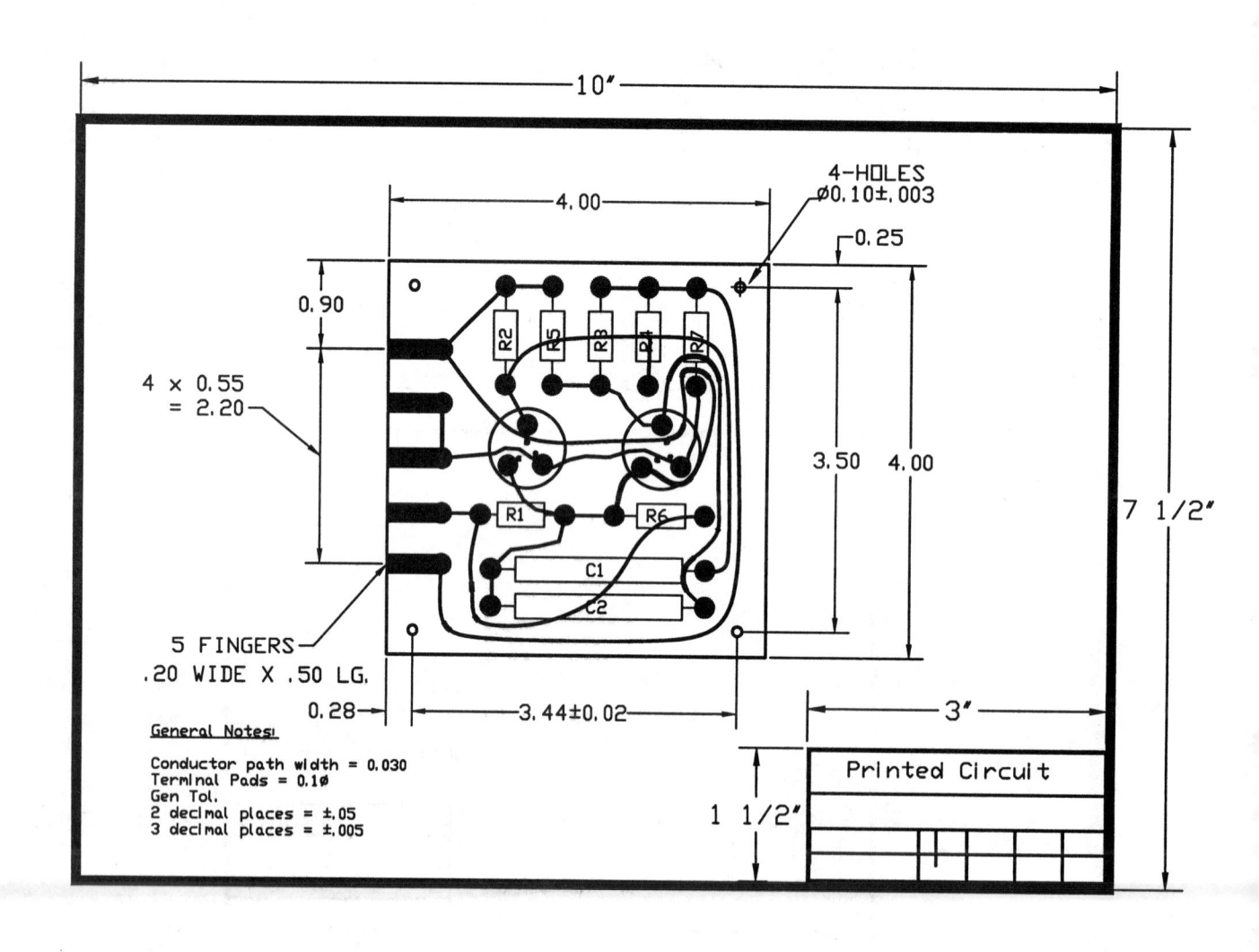

Never use more than eight characters in a file name. Do not use spaces, slashes /, or dots. The manuals tell you that you can use as many characters as you want, but you will have trouble later if you use more than eight.

Exercise M3

Draw the lifting screw assembly shown below using PLINE and SOLID. Save the file as M3. Then open a new file and draw the title block and border shown below. Save this as MTITLE.

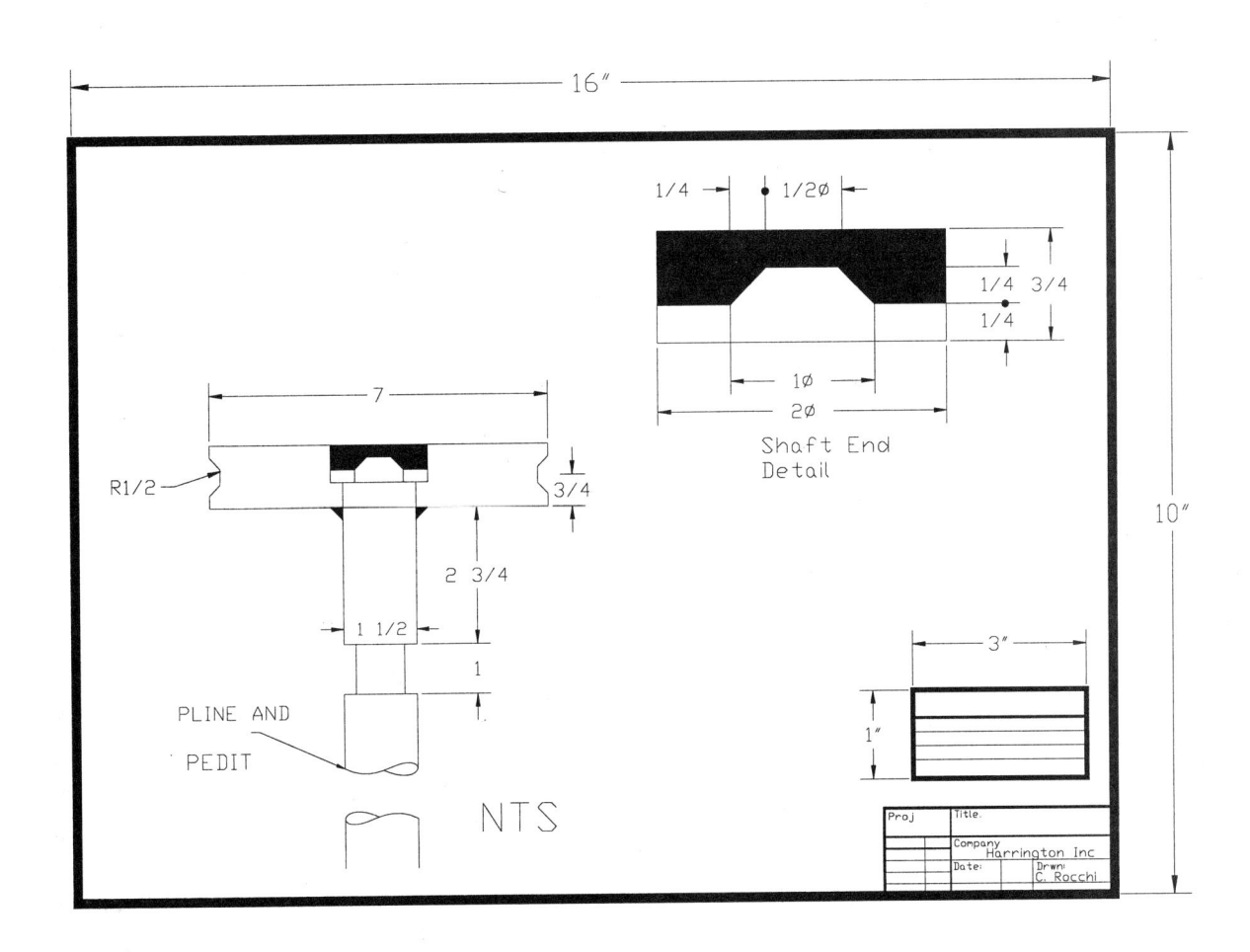

Never use more than eight characters in a file name. Do not use spaces, slashes /, or dots. The manuals tell you that you can use as many characters as you want, but you will have trouble later if you use more than eight.

Challenger 3

Draw the ball bearing shown below using PLINE, DONUT, and SOLID. Save the file as CH3.

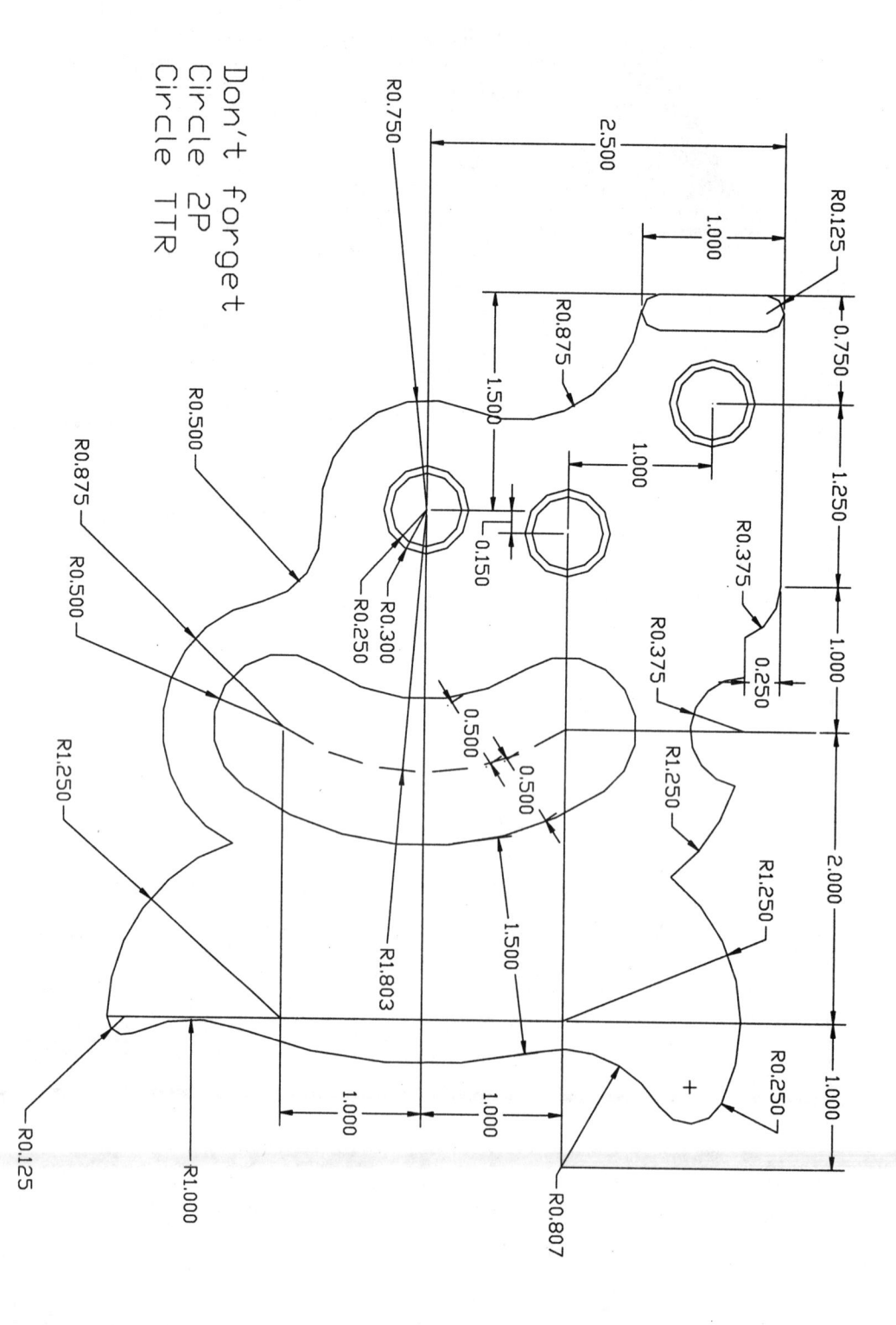

4 Object Selection and Editing

Upon completion of this chapter, you should be able to:

1. Use the various options for selecting objects
2. Edit objects with the MOVE command
3. Edit objects with the COPY command
4. Edit objects with the MIRROR command
5. ROTATE objects
6. SCALE objects
7. Use grips to edit objects
8. Change the LINETYPE

Once objects are drawn on the screen, editing commands under the Modify menu or toolbar are used to cut down on drawing time. When editing, OSNAP is particularly important to get the exact position of objects when they are moved, copied, or rotated.

Selecting Objects Within the Edit Command

In virtually every editing command, you will be prompted to "select objects." This makes sense, because the editing command will change the position or the parameters of objects, and thus the system needs to know which objects you want to change. As you select items, they become highlighted (dotted lines).

Objects can be selected in a variety of ways. If you are selecting the object after you have invoked the command you can select the objects by:

- Digitizing the desired item with the cursor "pick box"
- Indicating a group of items with the Crossing option
- Indicating a group of items with the Window option
- Indicating a series of items with Fence
- Indicating a group of items with CPolygon
- Indicating a group of items with WPolygon
- Indicating the last entered item using the Last option
- Indicating the previous selection set with Previous
- Indicating all objects by typing in **ALL**

Once you have identified your selection set or chosen the objects that are to be edited, AutoCAD will keep prompting you to select objects to be added or removed from the selection set. To continue with the Edit command after selecting objects, press ↵ to signal the end of object selection.

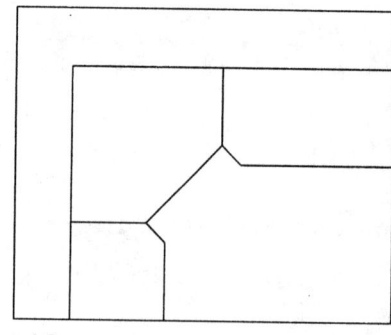

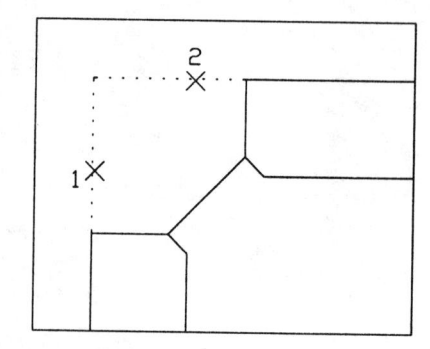

Figure 4-1

The object selection default is to select the items one by one.

```
Select objects: (pick 1, 2)
```

Only the two objects selected will be affected by the editing command.

Selection Windows

You can also select the objects by drawing a rectangular window area in response to the "Select objects:" prompts.

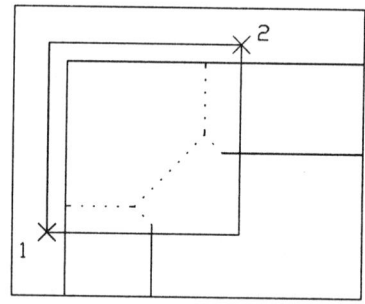

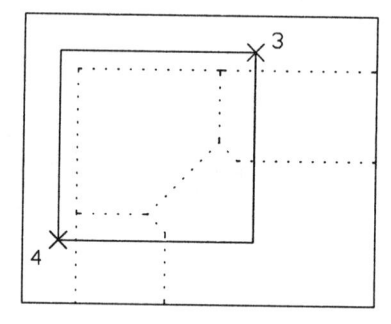

Figure 4-2

```
Select objects: (pick 1)
Specify opposite corner: (pick 2)
Select objects: (pick 3)
Other corner: (pick 4)
```

In Figure 4-2 the first selection is a Window; the second is a Crossing box. Dragging the window from left to right (Window selection box) identifies only the objects completely enclosed in the rectangle. Dragging the window from right to left (Crossing selection box) identifies objects within the window as well as any objects that cross into the selection area.

Sometimes while trying to indicate a Window or Crossing, your selection picks up an object rather than starting the window or crossing. To specify that you want a Window you can also specify Window from the menu or by typing in **W**. You can specify Crossing from the menu or by typing in **C**. In both cases you will be prompted for the other corner once your selection pick doesn't select an object.

Selection Polygons

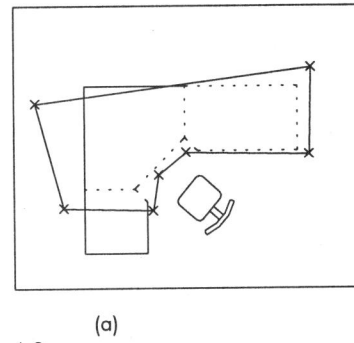

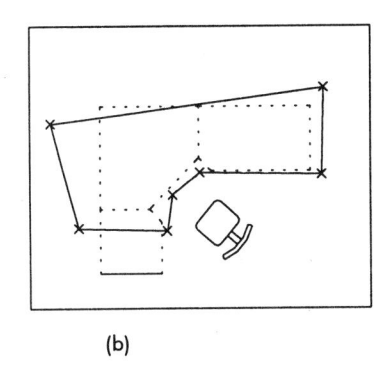

Figure 4-3

To select objects in an irregularly shaped area, use Window Polygon or Crossing Polygon. With the WPolygon option (Figure 4-3(a)) the objects contained within the polygon are chosen. With the CPolygon option (Figure 4-3(b)), all objects touching the three- or four-sided polygon will be picked up. Up to 16 points can be used on the polygon.

```
Select objects:WP (Window Polygon) (pick points as in
   Figure 4-3(a))
Select objects:CP (Crossing Polygon) (pick points as in
   Figure 4-3(b))
```

Selection Lines or Fence

With the Fence option, the objects touching the fence line will be picked up. Fence is useful for nonadjacent objects.

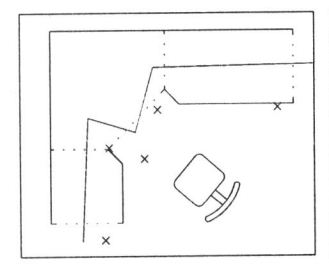

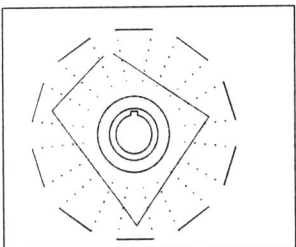

Figure 4-4

```
Select objects:F (Fence) (pick points)
```

Last and Previous

To identify the same selection set just used, type in **P** for Previous. To identify for editing the last object entered, type in **L** for Last.

```
Select objects:L (Last)
Select objects:P (Previous)
```

Editing Commands

Object Selection Cycling

In cases where a selection pick box touches more than one object, AutoCAD normally selects the most recent object. To avoid picking many times in an area with many overlapping objects, enter **Ctrl** before picking, then repeatedly pick at the location where multiple objects lie. Press the Enter key to exit object cycling.

You can use any of the above methods for object selection in any of the editing commands. The following examples show how to choose first the command, and then the selection set. Choosing the selection set first is covered on page 94.

The COPY Command

The COPY command takes an item or group of items and places a copy at another location or at multiple locations.

Danger

Do NOT use they Copy function under the Edit menu. This is a Windows function that takes a series of objects from one software package to another. It is NOT an AutoCAD function. When using the HELP files, make sure you have the right COPY function.

Toolbar From the Modify toolbar, choose Copy.

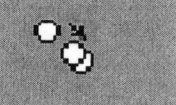

Pull Down From the Modify menu, choose Copy.

The command line equivalent is **COPY**.

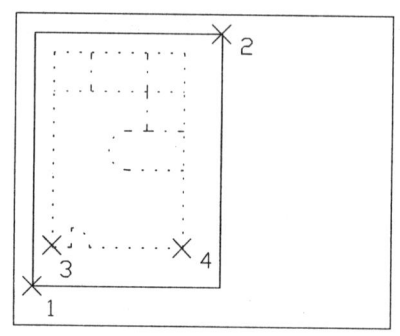

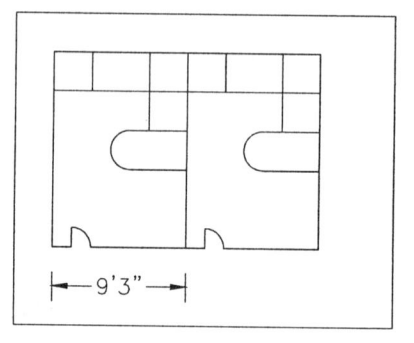

Figure 4-5

```
Command:COPY
Select objects: (pick 1, 2)
Select objects:↵
Specify base point or displacement,or[Multiple]:END of (pick 3)
Specify second point of displacement or <use first point as
   displacement>:END of (pick 4)
```

In the example of Figure 4-5, an incremental value could be used provided you know the exact location of the displacement in relation to the base point. For example:

```
Second point of displacement:@9'3",0
```

COPY Multiple

The COPY command can be used to place multiple copies of objects at random spacing. Once the objects have been selected, the command prompts for either the base point or the Multiple option.

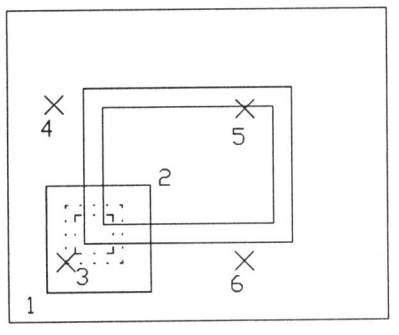

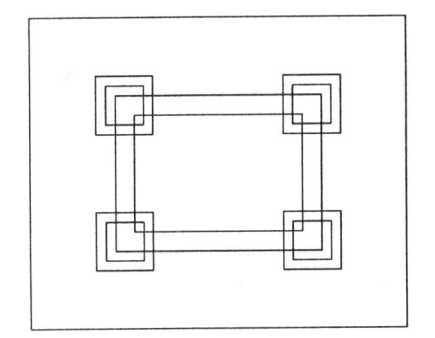

Figure 4-6

```
Command: COPY
Select objects: (pick 1)
Other corner: (pick 2)
Select objects: ↵
Specify base point or displacement, or [Multiple]:M
Specify base point:END (pick 3) (from)
Specify second point of displacement or <use first point as
   displacement>:(pick 4, 5, 6) (to)
```

> **Notes**
> Autodesk has unaccountably tripled the amount of words in the prompts. In COPY, the first point is "from" the next is "to".

All displacements are relative to the first base point, so choose that point carefully. In Figure 4-6 the end point of the bottom left corner is chosen as the base point. This point is referenced each time the object is to be placed.

The MOVE Command

The MOVE command moves an object or series of objects from one point to another, relative to a defined point on the object or a base point.

> **Toolbar** From the Modify toolbar, choose Move.
> **Pull Down** From the Modify menu, choose Move.

The command line equivalent is **MOVE** or **M**.

> **Notes**
> In Figure 4-7, pick 3 is where the objects are coming from, and pick 4 is where they are going to. These points need not be ON the objects moved.

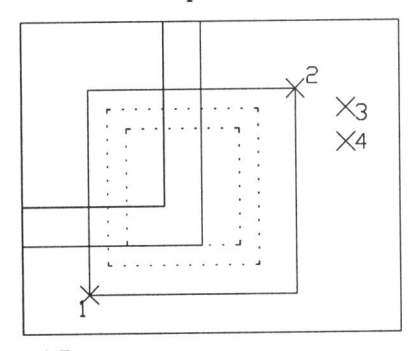

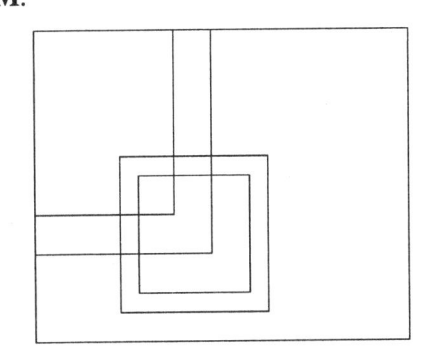

Figure 4-7

```
Command: MOVE
Select objects: (pick 1)
Specify opposite corner: (pick 2)
Select objects: ↵
Specify base point or displacement: (pick 3) (from where)
Specify second point of displacement or <use first point as
   displacement>: (pick 4) (to where)
```

MOVE Using Incremental Values

In Figure 4-8, the base point could have been picked up anywhere on the screen. The second point, @-2,0, describes a point two units in negative *X* from the current position, wherever that may be. The point given is a relative or incremental point.

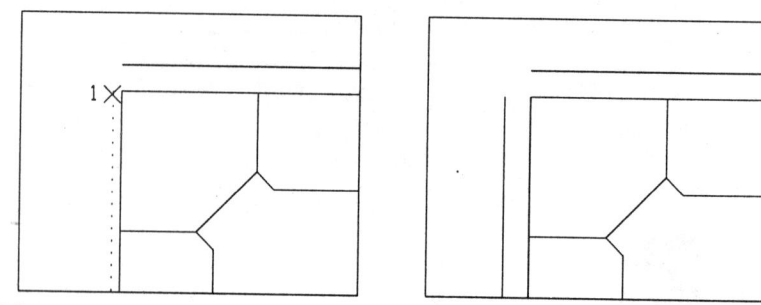

Figure 4-8

```
Command: MOVE
Select objects: (pick 1)
Select objects:
Specify base point or displacement: 0,0
Specify second point of displacement or <use first point as
   displacement>: @-2,0
```

Moving Objects to 0,0

To move a selected group of objects from their current position to 0,0, first identify the selection set. Identify which point will be finally 0,0. Use 0,0 as the displacement. Since the exact end point of that object must be at 0,0, use END (end point). The displacement is given as an absolute value.

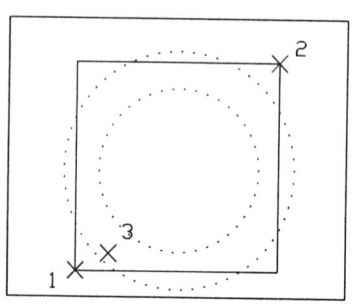

Figure 4-9

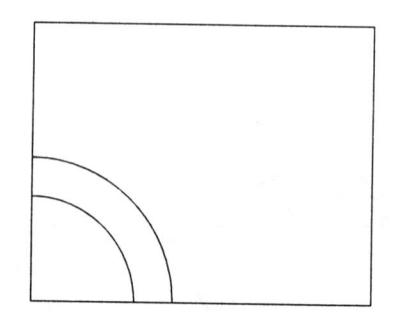

```
Command: MOVE
Select objects: (pick 1)
Specify opposite corner: (pick 2)
Select objects:
Specify base point or displacement: (pick 3) (from wherever)
Specify second point of displacement or <use first point as
   displacement>: 0,0   (to 0,0)
```

88 CHAPTER FOUR

You may wonder: What is the difference between the PAN command and the MOVE command?

PAN moves the screen viewing area. It is a display command. After the PAN command is finished, the parameters or the coordinates of each object will be the same: even though they appear to have moved, they have only moved relative to the screen. MOVE, on the other hand, actually moves the items from one point to another so that the coordinates of the objects change.

The MIRROR Command

The MIRROR command creates a mirror image of an item or group of items through a specified mirroring plane selected by a real or imaginary line.

After you have executed this command, you are prompted to either delete the old objects or keep them. Thus, to "flip" a series of objects, delete the old objects and you will only retain the mirror image.

> **Toolbar** From the Modify toolbar, choose Mirror.
>
> **Pull Down** From the Modify menu, choose Mirror.

The command line equivalent is **MIRROR**.

In Figure 4-10, the object is mirrored through a *mirroring-plane object* or *mirroring plane* — picks 3 and 4 — placed at the halfway point of the final object. The mirroring plane was deleted after the operation.

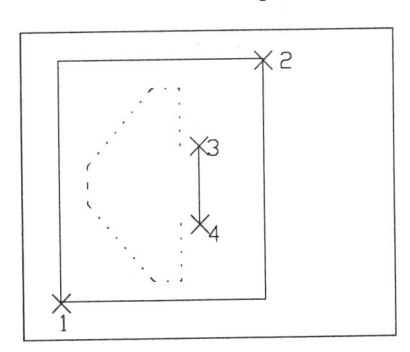

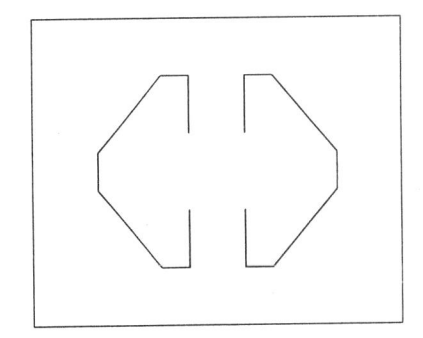

Figure 4-10

```
Command:MIRROR
Select objects: (pick 1)
Specify opposite corner: (pick 2)
Select objects:
Specify first point of mirroring plane:END of (pick 3)
Specify second point of mirroring plane:END of (pick 4)
Delete source objects? [Yes/No] <N>:
```

If existing objects can be used to describe the mirroring plane, use them.

In Figure 4-11, the mirroring plane is calculated from the center of the circle, in the center at the bottom. With ORTHO on, the mirroring plane would be easier to identify.

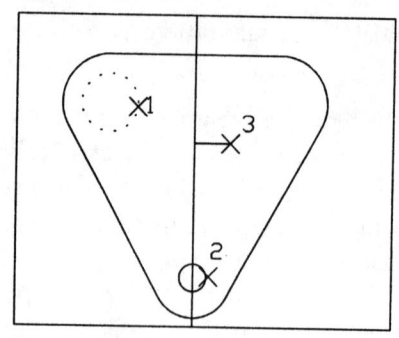

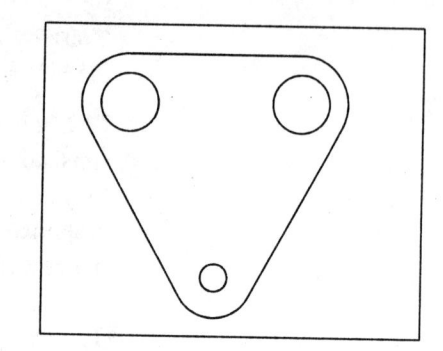

Figure 4-11

```
Command:MIRROR
Select objects: (pick 1)
Select objects:⏎
Specify first point of mirroring plane:CEN of (pick 2)
Specify second point of mirroring plane: (pick 3) (use Ortho)
Delete source objects? [Yes/No]<N>:⏎
```

Mirroring Using Absolute Values

If no object is accessible as a mirroring-plane base point, one can calculate the distance using the coordinates, and pick them on the screen. The mirroring plane can be indicated by picking points or by entering values, as demonstrated in Figure 4-12.

When MIRROR prompts for a point, any kind of point may be entered.

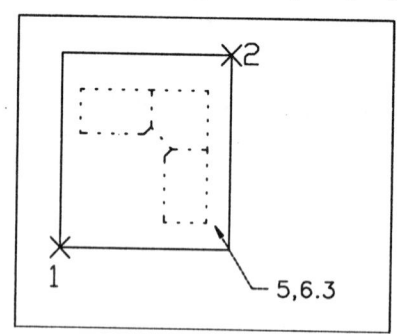

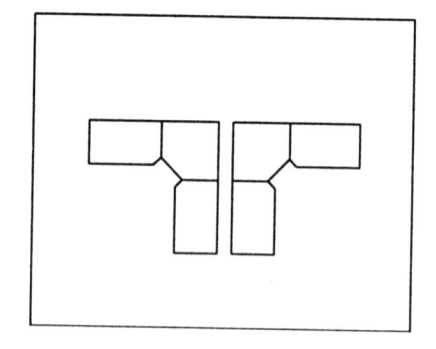

Figure 4-12

```
Command:MIRROR
Select objects: (pick 1, 2)
Select objects:⏎
Specify first point of mirroring plane:5,6.3
Specify second point of mirroring plane:@0,3
Delete source objects? [Yes/No]<N>:⏎
```

In Figure 4-12, the point 5,6.3 was chosen because it is 1.5 units in the X direction past the desk, allowing for a 3-unit space between the desks.

Mirrored Text

The MIRRTEXT variable allows you to set text while either creating mirror-image (backwards) text, or simply copying it.

```
Command:MIRRTEXT
Enter new value for MIRRTEXT <1>:
0 Retains text direction    1 Mirrors the text
```

The ROTATE Command

The ROTATE command rotates an object or series of objects around a specified base point. Using the command sequence of Figure 4-13, the objects are rotated 45 degrees around a point in the middle of the object itself. To view the rotation of the object, move the cursor in a circle around the base point.

Toolbar From the Modify toolbar, choose Rotate.

Pull Down From the Modify menu, choose Rotate.

The command line equivalent is **ROTATE**.

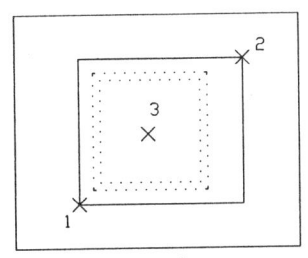

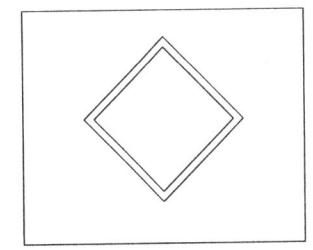

Figure 4-13

```
Command:ROTATE
Current positive angle in UCS: ANGDIR=clockwise ANGBASE=0
Select objects: (pick 1)
Specify opposite corner: (pick 2)
Select objects:⏎
Specify base point: (pick 3) (use SNAP for accuracy)
Specify rotation angle or [Reference]:45
```

In Figure 4-14, the objects were first copied from the position on the front wall, then rotated relative to the base point at the ENDpoint of the window so the selection fits perfectly into the space provided.

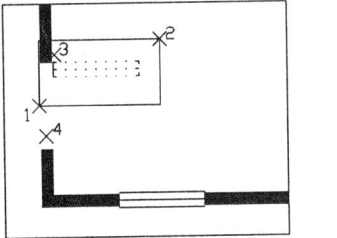

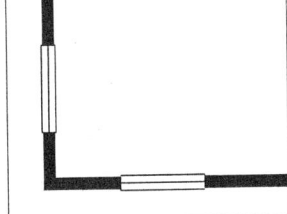

Figure 4-14

Object Selection and Editing

```
Command:ROTATE
Current positive angle in UCS: ANGDIR=clockwise ANGBASE=0
Select objects: (pick 1)
Specify opposite corner: (pick 2)
Select objects:↵
Specify base point:END of (pick 3)
Specify rotation angle or [Reference]: (pick 4) (use ORTHO F8
   for accuracy)
```

COPY and ROTATE to Create a New Object

In Figure 4-15, the objects are copied in the same place, then rotated around a point identified as the middle of the object.

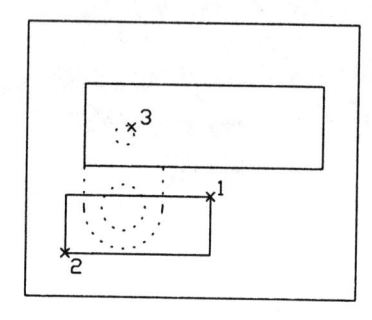

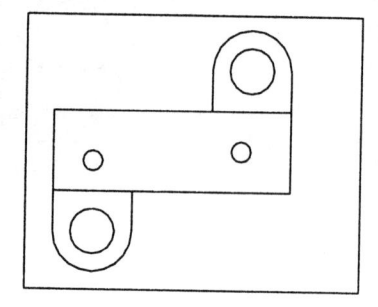

Figure 4-15

```
Command:COPY
Select objects: (pick 1)
Specify opposite corner: (pick 2)
Select objects: (pick 3)
Select objects:↵
Specify base point or displacement,or [Multiple]:0,0
Specify second point of displacement or <use first point as
   displacement:0,0
```

This command makes a duplicate copy of the arc, two circles, and two lines at the same spot. Use Previous to identify the first selection set *but not the copy*.

```
Command:ROTATE
Current positive angle in UCS: ANGDIR=clockwise ANGBASE=0
Select objects:P (this will take the previous selection set)
Select objects:↵
Specify base point: (pick 4)
Specify rotation angle or [Reference]:180
```

Rotating Using a Reference

Use the reference option to rotate something when you are not sure what the angle is, but you know the desired final angle.

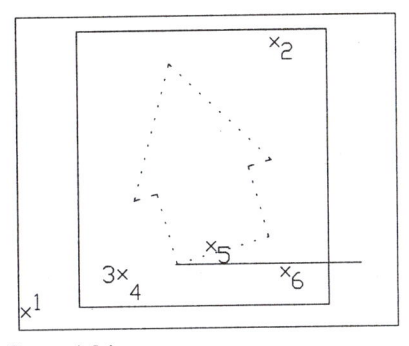

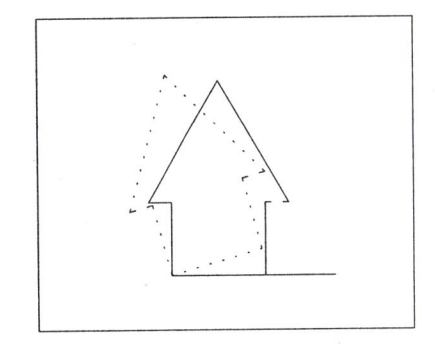

Figure 4-16

```
Command: ROTATE
Current positive angle in UCS: ANGDIR=clockwise ANGBASE=0
Select objects: (pick 1)
Specify opposite corner: (pick 2)
Select objects:↵
Specify base point:(END of pick 3)
Specify rotation angle or [Reference]:R
Specify the reference angle <0>:(END of pick 4)
Specify second point:(END of pick 5)
Specify the new angle:(END of pick 6)
```

See Prelab 4B for ROTATE/COPY using grips.

The SCALE Command

The SCALE command is very similar to those described above. You select objects, pick a base point, then enter a scale factor. Not surprisingly, a scale factor more than 1:1 will make the image bigger. A scale factor less than 1:1 will make it smaller.

> **Toolbar** From the Modify toolbar, choose the Scale.
>
> **Pull Down** From the Modify menu, choose Scale.

The command line equivalent is **SCALE**.

```
Command: SCALE
Select objects: (use an object selection method)
Specify base point: (pick a point, usually on the object)
Specify scale factor or [Reference]:3
```

Problems with Editing

How do you easily remove objects that have been moved, copied, or mirrored to the wrong place?

The Undo command negates the previous command. Almost any type of command can be undone. Typing **U** ↵ will undo any number of commands back to the beginning of the current editing session. All the commands are stored in the order in which they were performed.

```
Command:U ↵ SCALE
Command:U ↵ ROTATE
```

Repeat until you have removed all the objects that are incorrect.

UNDO is similar to U, but UNDO offers more power and is more dangerous. UNDO will prompt for the number of commands to be undone and undo them in a single operation. For example, to undo the last five entries, type **UNDO 5**.

To override an UNDO, use REDO. This command must directly follow the UNDO command.

```
Command:U ↵ SCALE
Command:REDO (this will restore the information just undone)
```

What happens when you move or copy a group of objects and they disappear?

Use **U** ↵ to undo the command, or **ZOOM A** to view the spot to which it was moved or copied.

During the COPY or MOVE command, you may have pressed ↵ when the system was prompting for the base point. Remember to read the prompts, then give the needed information.

It is a good idea to save the model or drawing with SAVE before doing extensive editing. If you undo more than expected, you can quit and reload the original file.

Getting Good Results the First Time

Always use SNAP, OSNAP, or actual coordinates to pick base points. If a reference object is needed to complete an editing command (for example, a line in the MIRROR command), insert it, reference it with OSNAP, then erase it.

Editing with Grips

The commands demonstrated above were chosen before the objects were selected. With the aid of grips, you can use the SELECT command to select objects, then use the editing commands or the grip modes to edit them.

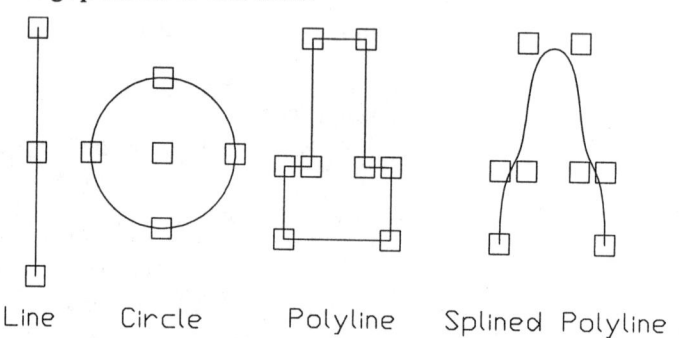

Line   Circle   Polyline   Splined Polyline

Figure 4-17

Figure 4-17 shows where the grips would be placed on a variety of objects. Grips allow you to combine objects and command selection and thereby edit more quickly.

Grip Modes

Object and command selection can be combined by using the grip modes — Stretch, Move, Rotate, Scale, and Mirror. Once you have identified the selection set, you identify a base point or *hot grip*.

When the hot grip is chosen, it turns a solid color. The grip modes will then be loaded and you can then edit using one of the five modes.

Use the space bar or Enter key to toggle through the modes, or type in the first two letters of the mode. For example, to reach Scale mode from another mode, keep pressing ⏎ until Scale appears, or enter **SC**.

If the grip mode does not work on your system, type **GRIPS** and then enter **1**.

> **Notes**
> Clear Grips by pressing ESCape twice, or by accessing a new command either through buttons or menus.

Grips Example

First draw in a series of lines as shown.

At the command prompt pick up the two objects on the right. The grips will appear in blue on the set of objects.

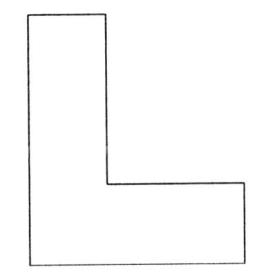

Figure 4-18

```
Command: (pick 1, 2)
```

The cursor snaps to any grip over which it is moved. Select the top right grip to act as the base point for the edit.

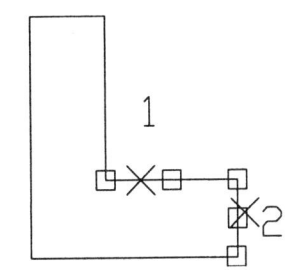

Figure 4-19

```
Command: (pick 3) (pick the right
  corner of the object)
```

The base grip will be identified with a solid color, probably red.

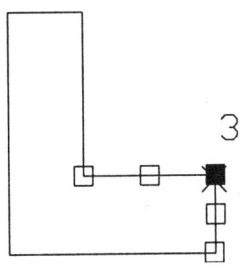

Figure 4-20

Now that you have the base point highlighted, the grip modes appear and you can choose one. First use Stretch. Pick the point for the displacement of the specified objects.

```
Command:**STRETCH**
Specify stretch point or [Base
  point/Copy/Undo/eXit]:
  (pick 4)
```

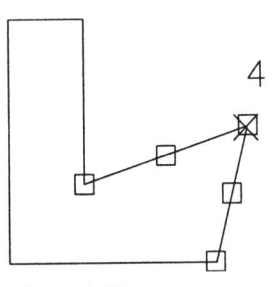

Figure 4-21

Now pick up the upper left objects to be moved plus the base point.

```
Command: (pick 5, 6) (the objects
  to be moved)
Command: (pick 7) (the base point
  or hot point)
```

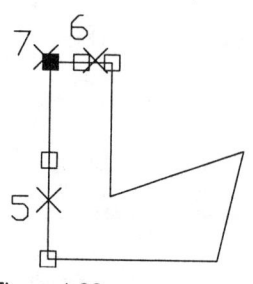

Figure 4-22

Once you have chosen the base point, the grip mode is invoked, starting with Stretch. Use ⏎ to advance to the next mode, which is Move. Then pick the displacement point for the objects to move to.

```
Command:**STRETCH**⏎
Command:**MOVE**
Specify move point or [Base
  point/Copy/Undo/ eXit]: (pick 8)
```

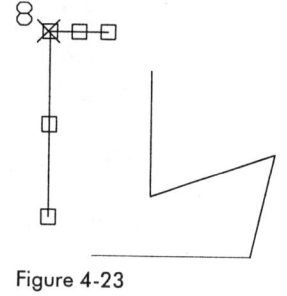

Figure 4-23

Again use **Esc** to remove the grips from the objects.

Now we will rotate one object.

Pick the lowest horizontal line once to pick the object and then at the corner to identify the base point.

```
Command: (pick 9) (the object to
  be rotated)
Command: (pick 10) (the base
  point)
```

Figure 4-24

You will be in the grip mode. Use ⏎ to toggle to rotate.

```
Command:**STRETCH**⏎
Command:**MOVE**⏎
Command:**ROTATE**
Specify rotation angle or [Base
  point/Copy/Undo/eXit]:-10
```

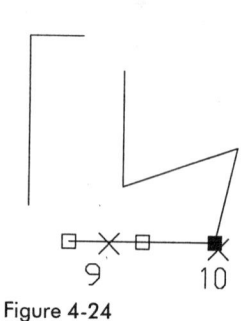

Figure 4-25

96 CHAPTER FOUR

For Scale, use the same sequence. Pick the objects, pick the base point, then enter the scale factor. You can type in **SC** to get Scale rather than toggling through.

```
Command: (pick 11, 12, 13)
Command:**STRETCH**SC
Command:**SCALE**
Specify scale factor or [Base
   point/Copy/Undo/eXit]:.5
```

Figure 4-26

Finally, the mirror mode allows you to mirror the objects, but doesn't allow you to keep the original selection set. Only the mirrored image is left.

```
Command: (pick 14, 15)
Command: (pick 16)
Command:**STRETCH**MI
Command:**MIRROR**
Specify second point or [Base
   point/Copy/Undo/Exit]: (pick 17)
```

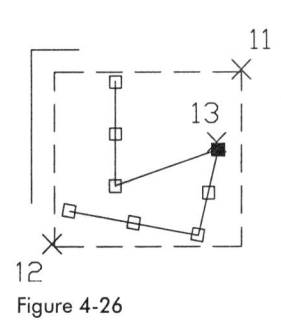

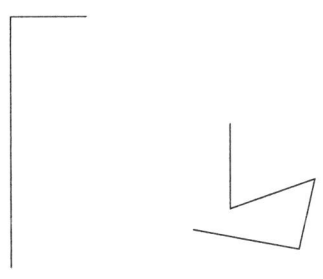

Figure 4-27

Editing with grips should make your editing much faster.

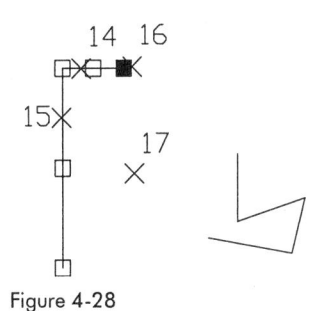

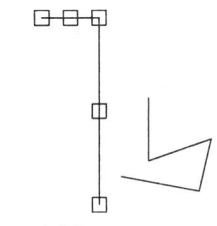

Figure 4-28

Figure 4-29

Setting LINETYPEs

AutoCAD offers the standard different types of lines — center, hidden, and dashed — in addition to many variations to make drawings more legible and more attractive. The *linetypes* are not loaded with the default AutoCAD drawing, so for you to use them they must be loaded into the file.

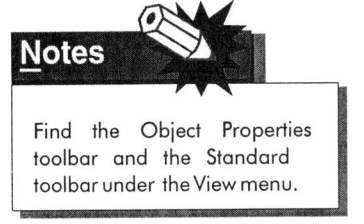

Notes

Find the Object Properties toolbar and the Standard toolbar under the View menu.

Toolbar From the Object Properties toolbar, choose Linetype.

Pull Down From the Format menu, choose Li_n_etype...

The command line equivalent is **LINETYPE**.

Object Selection and Editing **97**

Both the command line and the Pull Down menu will offer you the dialog box.

Command: **LINETYPE**

The dialog box is the easiest way to access the linetypes.

From the linetypes listed, pick the one you require. If the linetype you require is not listed, choose Load.

Choose the linetypes that you would like to load, then pick OK.

You will then return to the main menu. If you want to use the new linetype to draw with, pick the Current button from the top of the menu. This will set the current linetype for subsequently drawn objects.

For each linetype there are three listings. For example:

- Hidden = 3 dashes per inch
- Hidden2 = 6 dashes per inch
- HiddenX2 = 1 1/2 dashes per inch

You may use these to modify the appearance of your lines. As well, you can go to the bottom of the dialog box and change the Current Object linetype setting, if the lines that you are entering are not to your specific size.

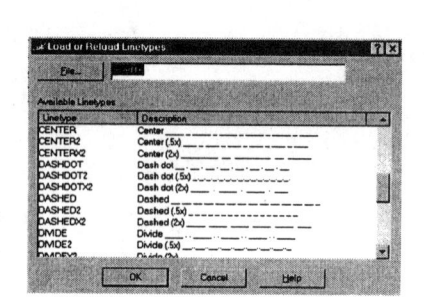

There are two sets of line scales in *AutoCAD 2000*. The Global setting is used for all the linetypes on the screen. The Current object setting is just for the one object. If these settings aren't visible on your Linetype menu, choose Details from the bottom of the screen.

The command line LINETYPE will take you directly to the dialog box.

Loading all linetypes

As with all Windows lists, load many or all linetypes by selecting one linetype, then holding Shift down to select another. All linetypes between the first and second linetypes chosen will be loaded.

To load two or three linetypes that are not adjacent, use the Control key (Ctrl) instead of the Shift key.

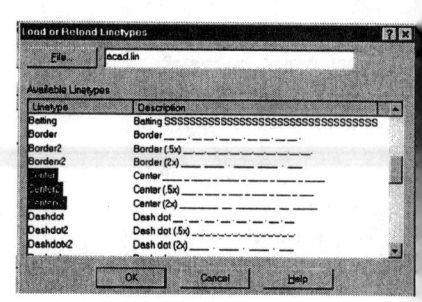

All objects that you draw will now be in linetype Hidden. If you cannot see them, change the LTSCALE as seen below.

Again, it is MUCH easier to use the linetype icon than to use the command strings in this case.

Prototype Drawings

To avoid loading linetypes for every drawing, open ACAD.DWG, the prototype for new drawings. Load all the linetypes. Save the changes, then exit. Linetypes require little memory, so it is easier if they are always loaded.

Changing LTSCALE

Depending on the size of your object, linetypes that are not continuous may show up as such. This is because the scale of the drawing is too large or too small.

All scales are set to be viewed on a 12" x 9" screen. This means that a hidden line, for example, will show up with three long dashes for every actual inch of line. If your screen is showing a line which is 200 units in length, this means there are 600 actual segments to that line. Obviously, you can't see 600 segments of a line on a screen that is 14 inches wide, so the line will appear to be continuous.

To see it properly you need to change the scale of the screen display. The Global linetype scale is changed under the Linetype icon. Change the Global setting for all lines. You can also type in LTSCALE at the command prompt.

Danger

Be sure to set your linetype back to BYLAYER when you are finished using Hidden.

```
Command: LTSCALE
Enter new linetype scale factor <1.000>:13
```

To determine the LTSCALE of the screen, start with the scale of the drawing. If a floor plan is to be drawn at 1/4"=1'0", then the scale is 1/48: try 48 for the LTSCALE. If you have not determined the scale of a drawing yet and simply want a screen display, find the furthest point in X and divide by 12. If you have set up the screen but have not as yet entered any points or geometry, take the furthest limit in positive X and divide by 12. If the limits are 200,160, then the LTSCALE will be 200/12, or approximately 15. If your limits are 3,3 then your LTSCALE will be 3/12, or .25.

Prelab 4A Using ROTATE, COPY and MIRROR

First we'll make a roller arm. Open a new file, keep the settings the same, and draw in two circles — one with a radius of .5, the other with a radius of .75 as shown. Use SNAP to access the same center.

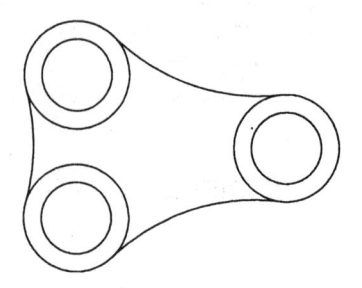

Step 1

```
Command:C
Specify center point for circle or
[3P/2P/Ttr(tan tan rad)]: (pick 1)
Specify Radius of circle or
    Diameter:.5
Command:C
Specify center point for circle or
[3P/2P/Ttr(tan tan rad)]: (pick 1)
Specify Radius of circle or Diameter:.75
```

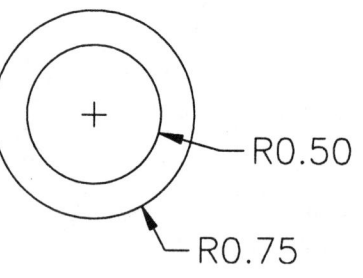

Step 2 Now MOVE these from wherever they are on the screen to 0,0.

```
Command:MOVE
Select objects: (pick 1, 2)
Specify base point:CEN (pick 3)
Specify second point of displacement
or <use first point as displacement>:0,0
```

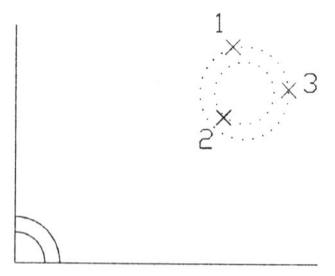

Step 3 Now PAN the objects across the screen so you can see them, and use COPY to place another set of circles.

```
Command:PAN   (pick 1)   (pick 2)
```

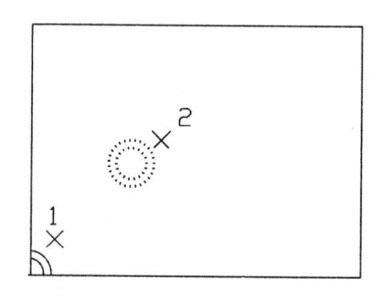

```
Command:COPY
Select objects: (pick 1, 2)
Specify base point or displacement,
   or [Multiple]:CEN of (pick 2)
Specify second point of displacement
or <use first point as displacement:
   @3,1
```

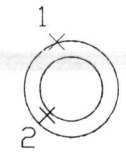

100   CHAPTER FOUR

Step 4   Now use MIRROR to get the third arc in.

```
Command:MIRROR
Select objects: (pick 1)
Specify opposite corner:(pick 2)
Select objects:↵
Specify first point of mirror line:
CEN of(pick 3)
Specify second point: (pick 4)
Delete source objects?[Yes/No]<N>:↵
```

Set ORTHO on if it makes it any easier.

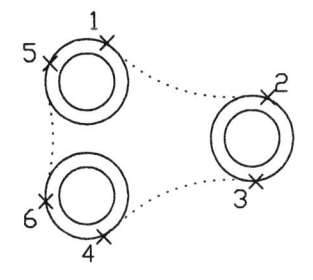

Step 5   Use FILLET to create the arcs between the parts.

```
Command:FILLET
Current settings: Mode = Trim,Radius = <5.0000>
Select first object or [Polyline/Radius/Trim]:r
Specify fillet radius <1.000>:3
Command:FILLET
Current settings: Mode = Trim,Radius = <5.0000>
Select first object or [Polyline/Radius/Trim]: (pick 1)
Select second object: (pick 2)
```

(pick 3 to 6) as shown

Your drawing should look like this.

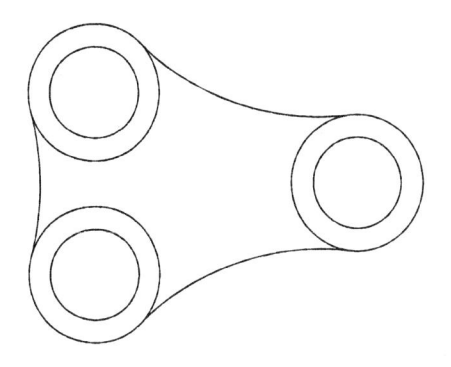

Object Selection and Editing   **101**

Prelab 4B Using ROTATE, COPY and MIRROR

In this example we will make a bay window using ROTATE, COPY, and MIRROR. First change your units to architectural — use UNITS.

Step 1 Use LINE to draw in the window itself.

```
Command:LINE
Specify start point:0,0
Specify next point or (Undo):8,0
Specify next point or (Undo):
(continue drawing the window)

Command:ZOOM    All

Command:ZOOM    .8X
```

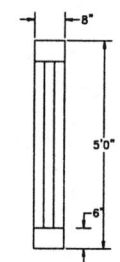

Step 2 Use PLINE to create the wall section.

```
Command:PLINE
Specify start point:MID of( pick 1)
Current line-width is 0.0000
Specify next point or
 [Arc/Close/Halfwidth/Length/Undo/
 Width]:W
Specify starting width<0.1000>:8
Specify ending width<8.000>:↵
Specify next point or
 [Arc/Close/Halfwidth/Length/Undo/
 Width]:@0,-12
Specify next point or [Arc/Close/Halfwidth/Length/Undo/
 Width]:@12<315
Specify next point or [Arc/Close/Halfwidth/Length/Undo/
 Width]:↵
```

Step 3 Use COPY to get a copy of the window to the end of the PLINE.

```
Command:COPY
Select objects:W (pick 1, 2)
Specify base point or displacement, or
   [Multiple]: MID of (pick 3)
Specify second point of displacement
or <use first point as displacement>:
 END of (pick 4)
```

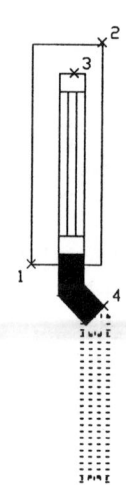

It is important to use the OSNAPs MID and END to get

the correct point of reference on the window.

Step 4   Now use ROTATE to rotate the window at 45 degrees.

```
Command:ROTATE
Select objects:W (pick 1, 2)
Specify base point:MID of (pick 3)
Specify rotation angle or
   [Reference]:45
```

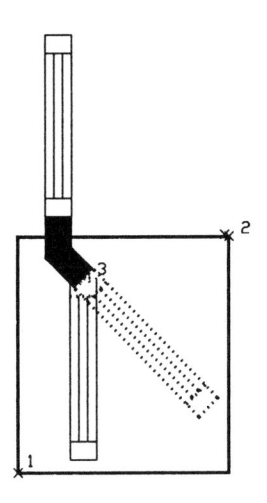

Step 5   Finally use MIRROR to create the other half of the image. Again, make sure that your OSNAPs are used.

```
Command:MIRROR
Select objects:W (pick 1, 2)
Specify first point of mirroring
plane:MID of (pick 3)
Specify second point of mirroring
plane: (pick 4)
Delete source objects {Yes/No]<N>:
```

Put ORTHO on if it makes it easier.

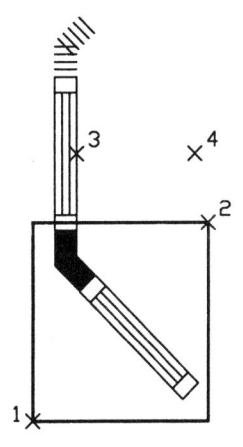

Your window should look like this:

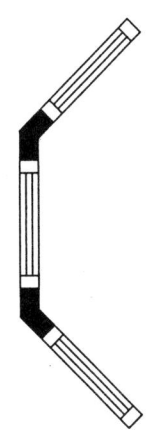

Object Selection and Editing   **103**

Command and Function Summary

COPY is used to make one copy or a series of copies of selected objects at random spacing.

Crossing is an object selection method which picks up all objects that cross over into the selected rectangle.

Grips speed up the editing process, allowing you to use the pointing device to combine object and command selection.

Fence is an object selection method that identifies any object that is touched by the Fence line.

LINETYPE is used to create, load, or set to a variety of different linetypes.

LTSCALE is used to change the scale of the linetypes relative to the drawing.

MIRROR is used to make a mirror image of selected objects through a specified mirroring line.

MOVE is used to move selected objects from one position to another along an identified vector.

Crossing Polygon is an object selection method that identifies any object contained within the defined polygon.

Window Polygon is an object selection method that identifies any object that crosses into the defined polygon.

ROTATE is used to rotate objects around an identified base point.

UNDO or **U** is used to undo the commands in reverse order of entry.

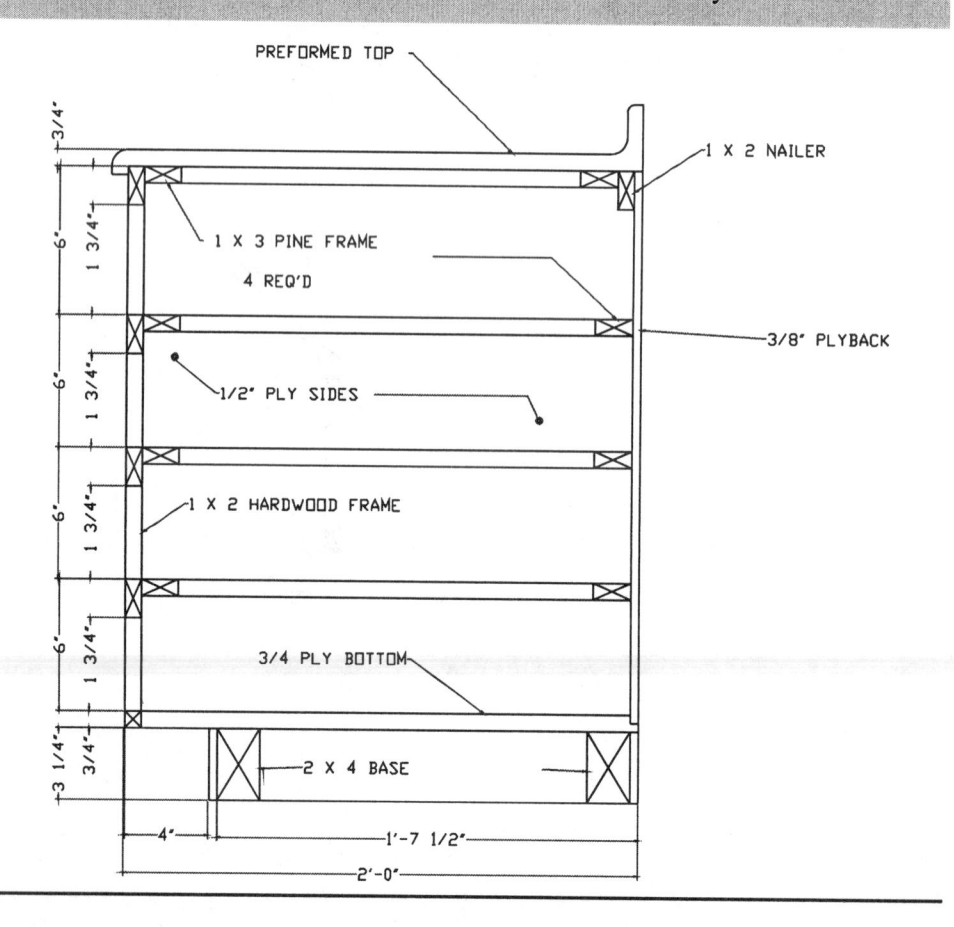

Practice Exercise 4

Use COPY, ROTATE, MIRROR, and MOVE to complete these drawings. No dimensions are needed.

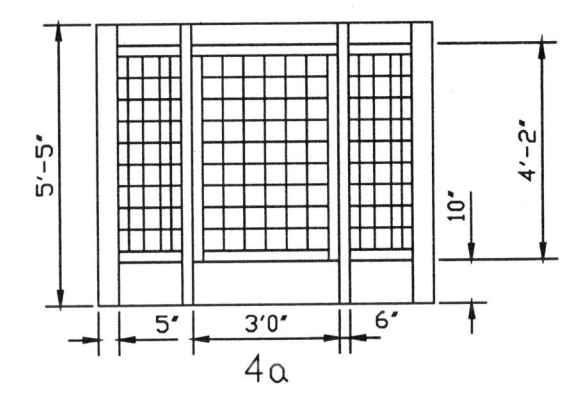

4a

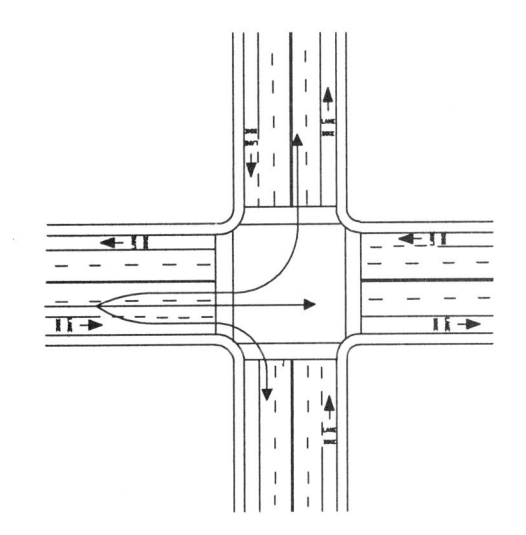

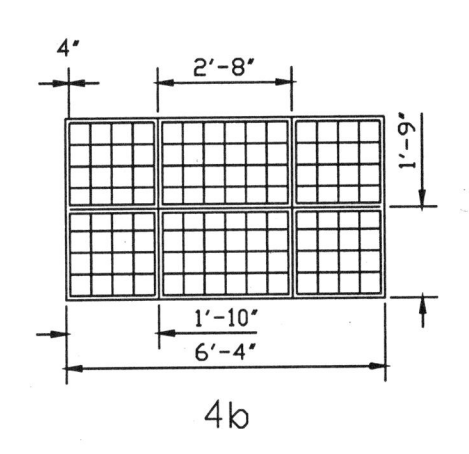

4b

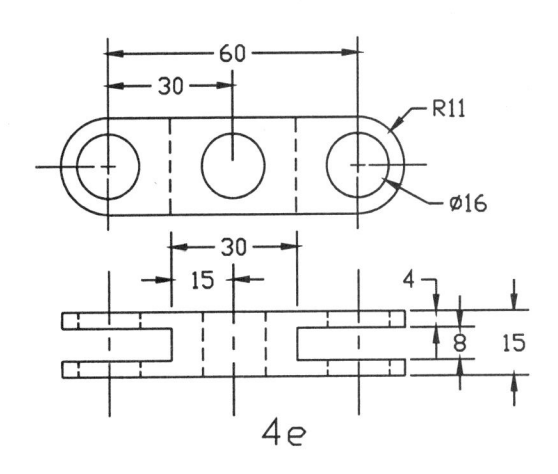

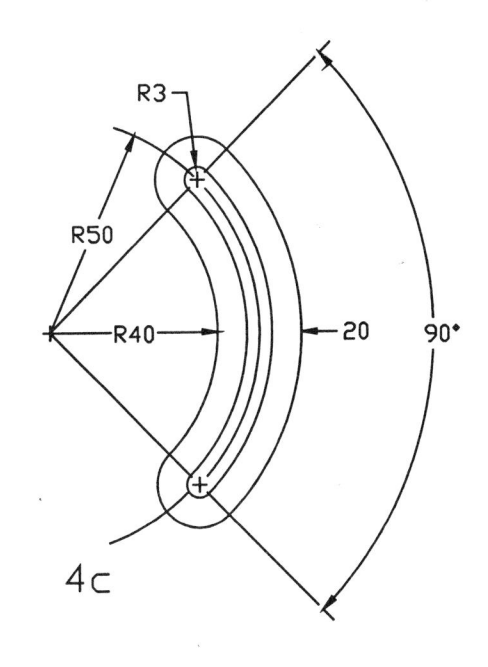

4c

4d

4e

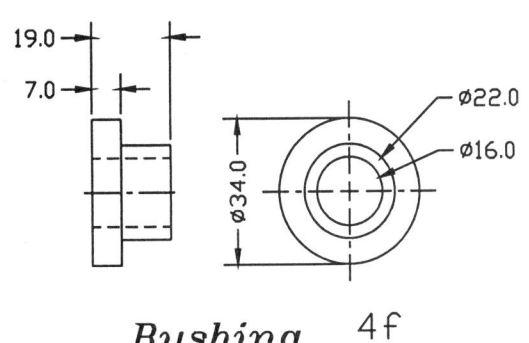

Bushing 4f

Exercise A4

Open FIRSTFL, the file you created earlier. Use LINE to draw in one window. Then use COPY, ROTATE, and MIRROR to place the windows within the walls. SNAP can be useful for drawing the windows. Be sure to use the OSNAPs when placing them.

Leave a 2″ gap between the exterior wall and the ledge of the window. This will be filled in with a veneer hatch in Chapter 8.

When the first floor is completed, start the second. All dimensions are in Chapter 7 Architectural example.

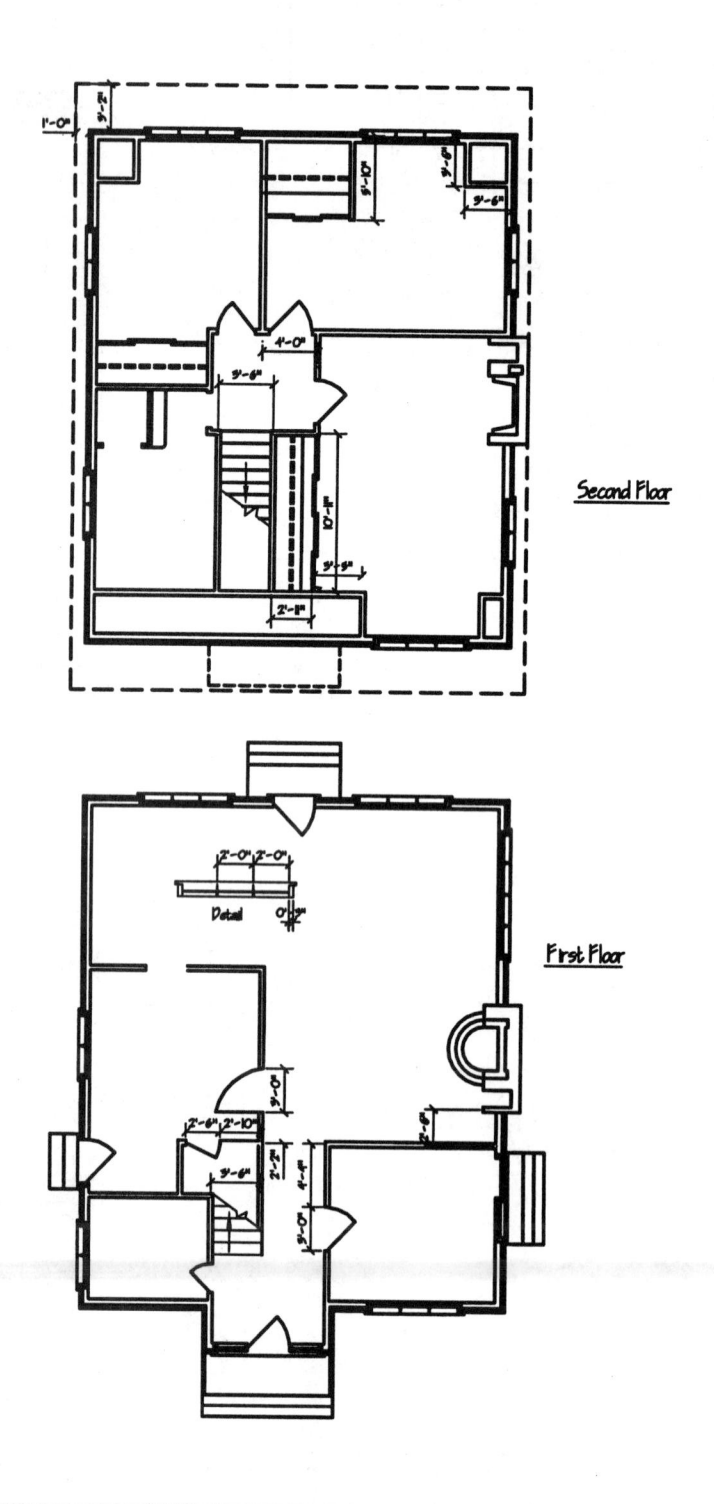

Second Floor

First Floor

Exercise C4

For this exercise, use MIRROR and COPY for the road, COPY and ROTATE for the trees, and MIRROR for the fire hydrant. The scale in this case is metric.

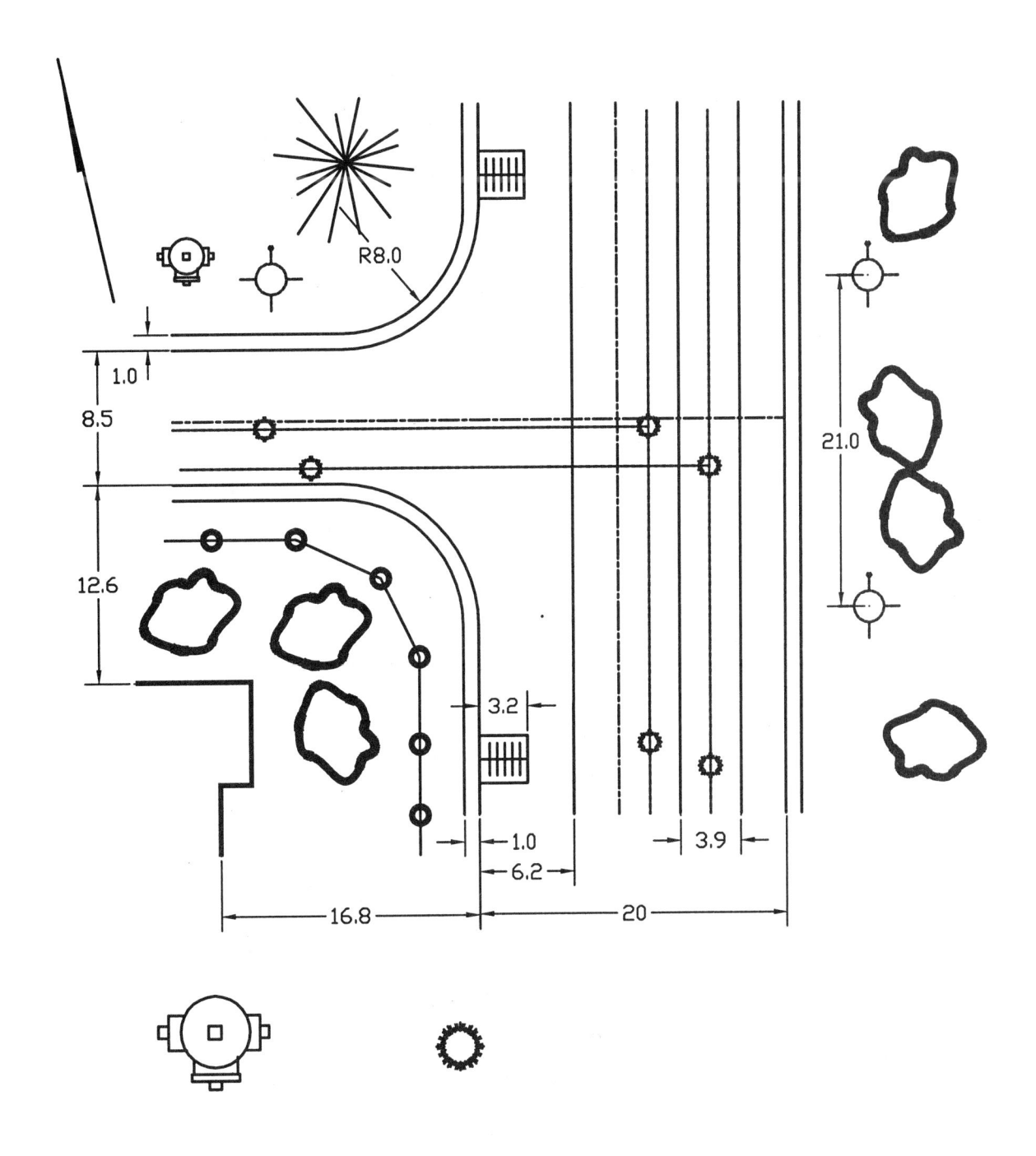

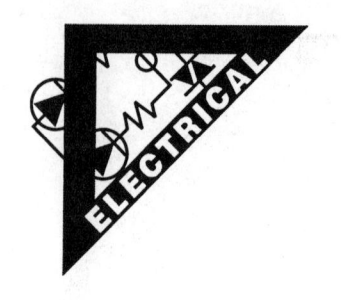

Exercise E4

Use COPY, COPY ROTATE with Grips, MIRROR, and MOVE to complete this schematic. Use OSNAP to access the end points of objects and the midpoints of objects. Create the symbols first, then put them in.

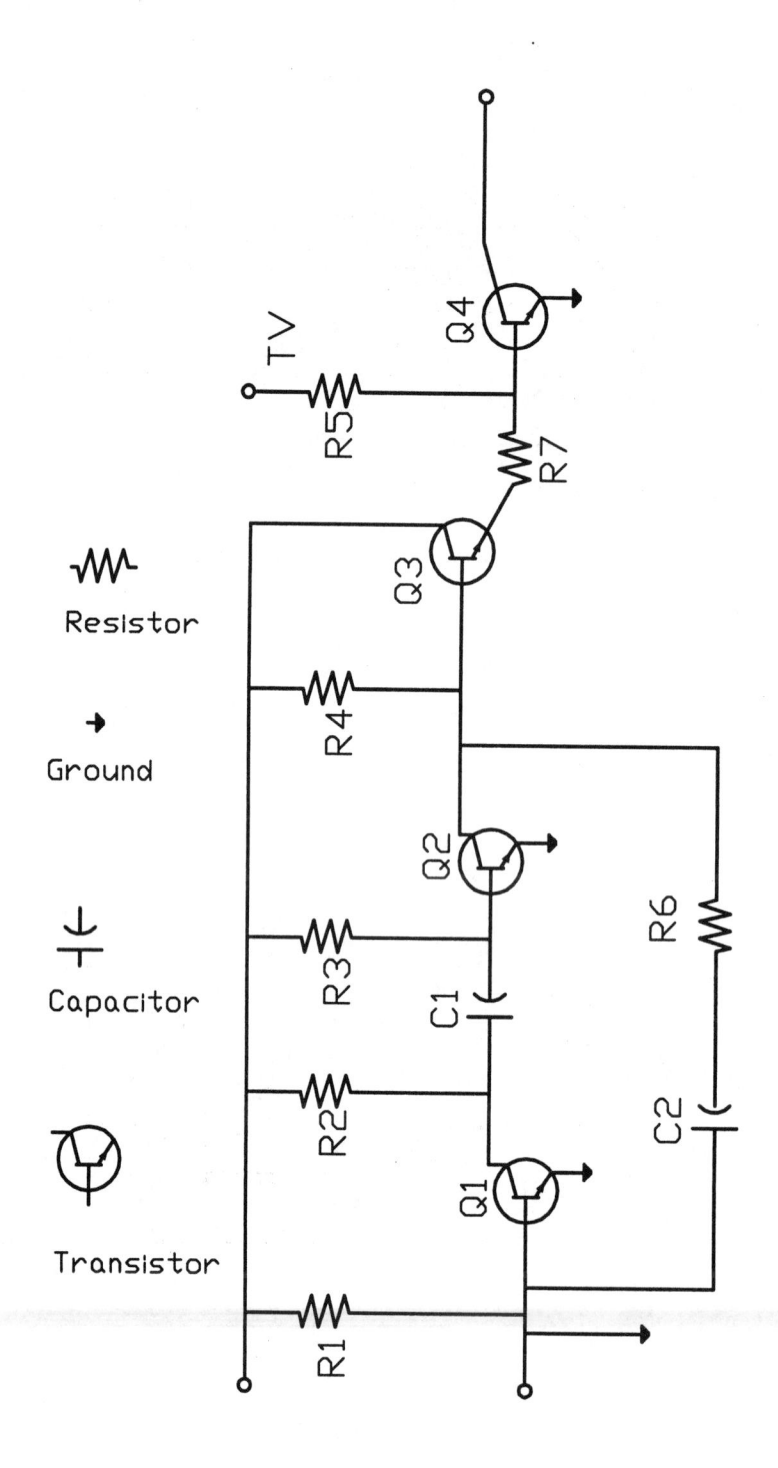

Exercise M4

Use COPY, MIRROR, MOVE, and TRIM to complete these drawings.

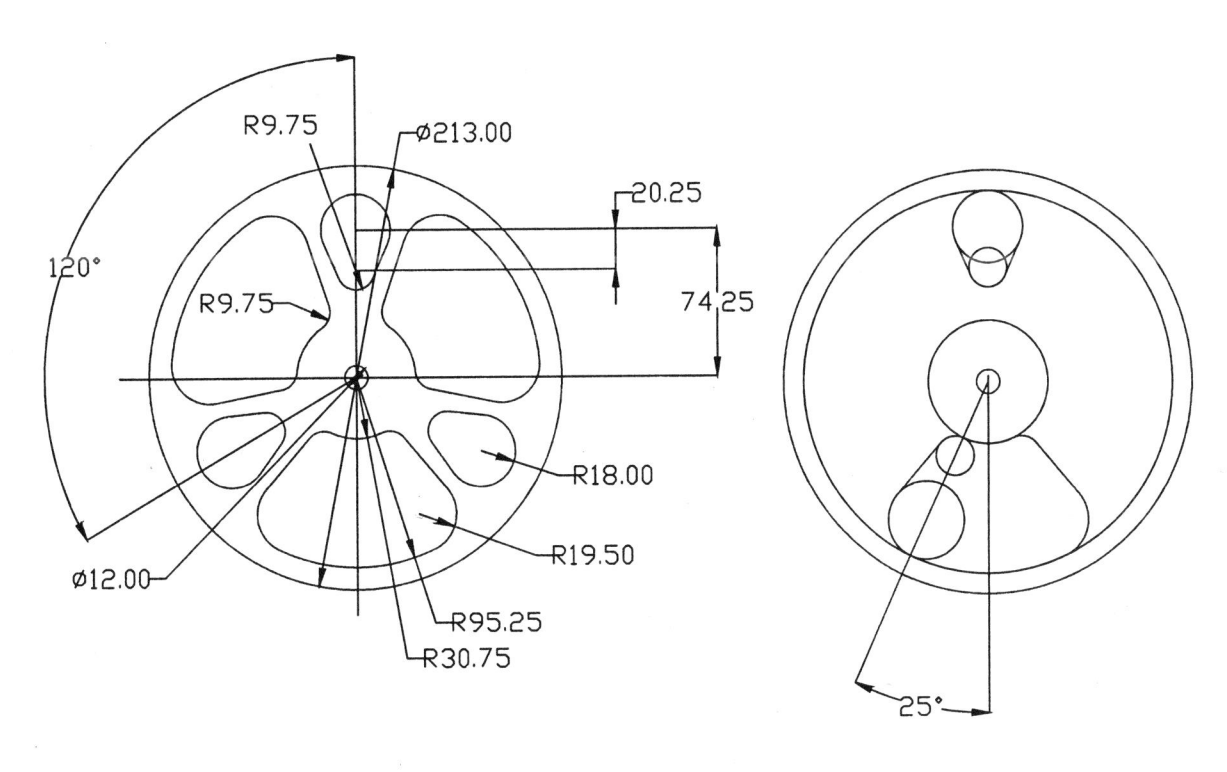

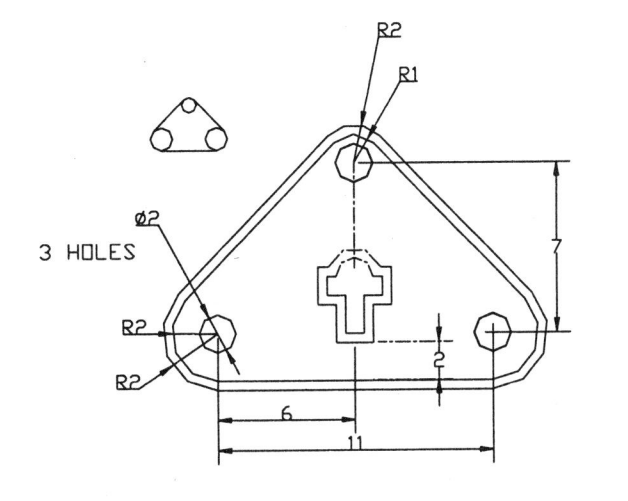

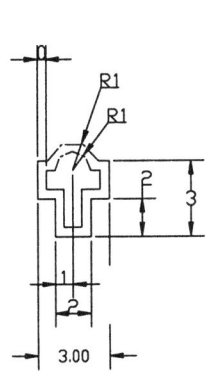

Challenger 4A

View from the side to gain maximum use of the screen.

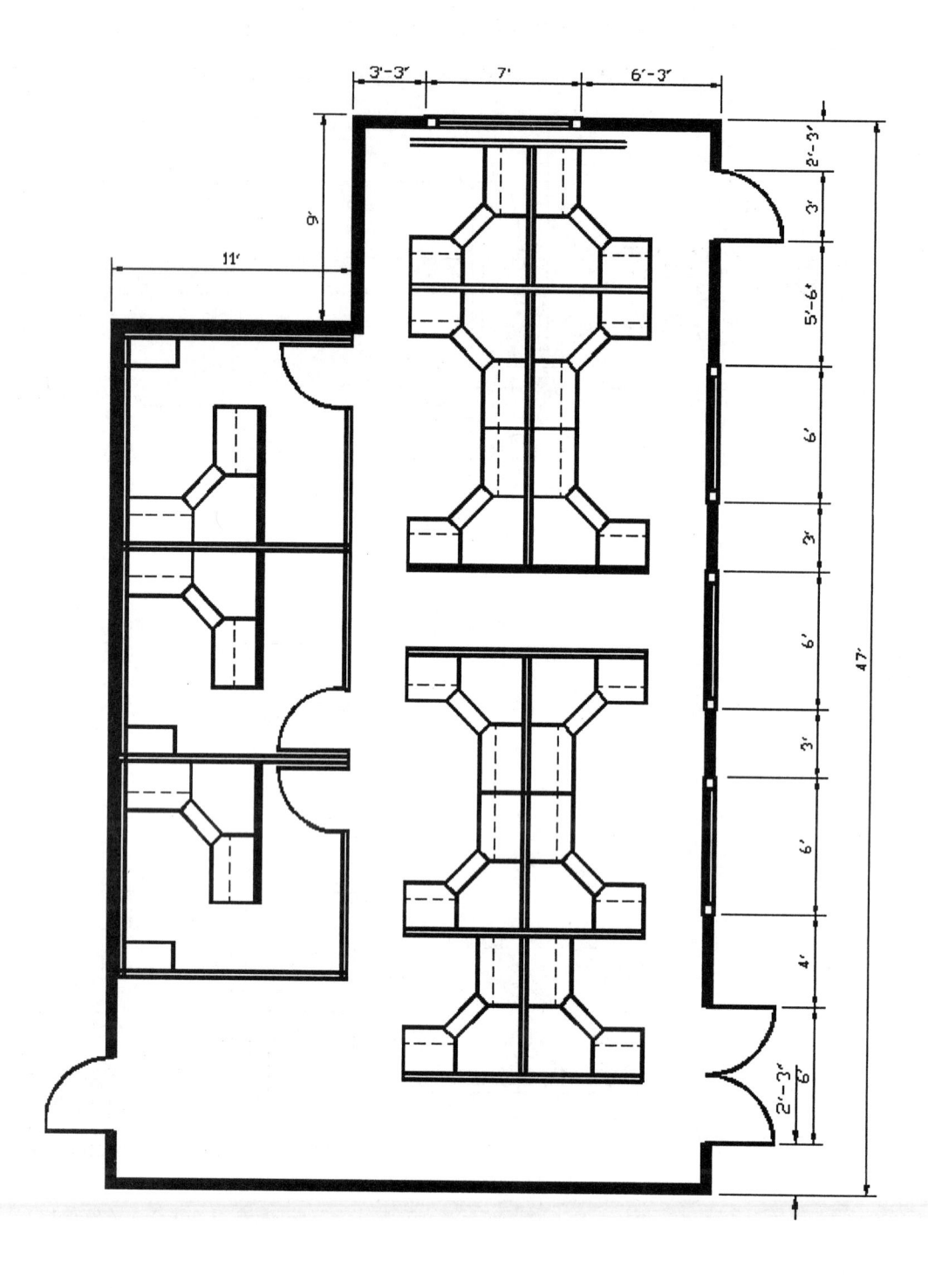

110 CHAPTER FOUR

Hints on Challenger 4A

In this example, change to architectural units with a Snap value of 3. Remember, any number entered without a foot (') or inch ('') symbol will be accepted as inches. It should be easy to draw with SNAP and GRID on.

The drawing is of modular furniture. Create the offices by using lines. The panels separating the offices are 3 inches thick. Be sure to leave enough space for them.

Use ROTATE, COPY, and MOVE to create the offices exactly as you see them.

PLINE can be used to make the exterior walls easier to see.

Do not dimension.

Make the filing cabinet 18" by 24".

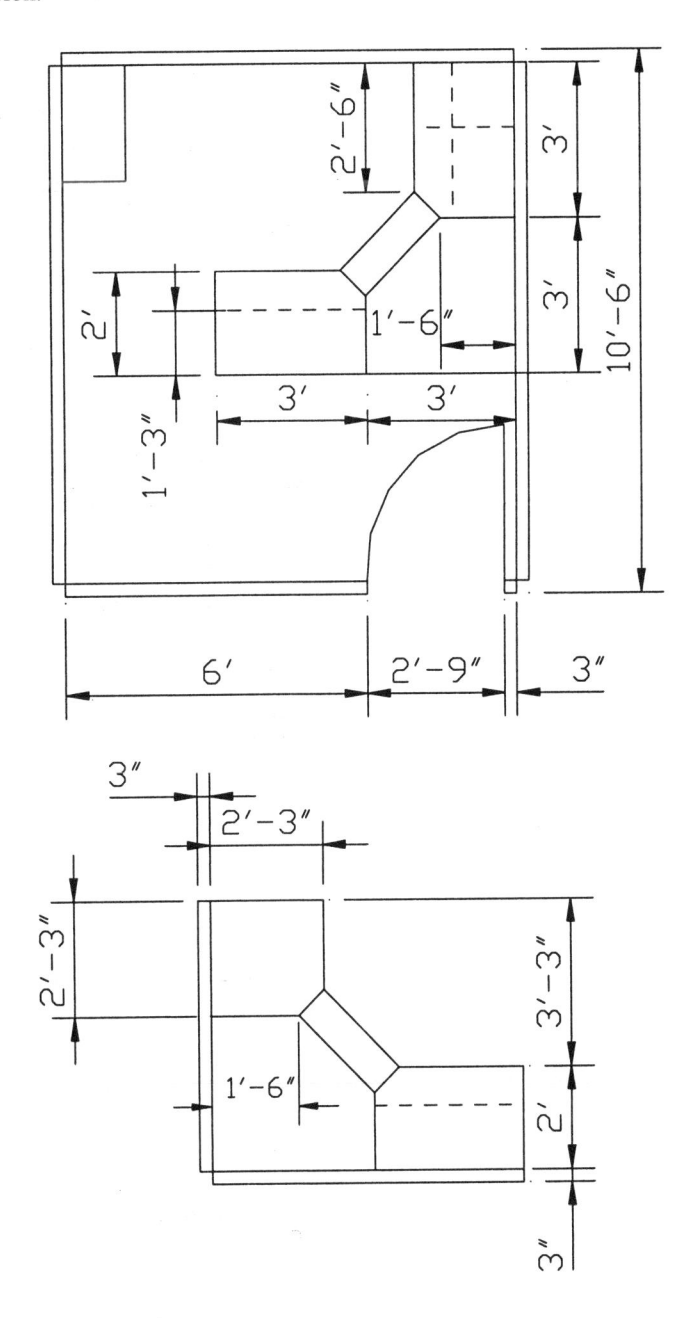

When finished with this drawing, save it so you can edit it later with STRETCH, as well as dimension it as shown in Chapter 7.

Object Selection and Editing

Challenger 4B

These commercial windows should give you some experience with editing commands.

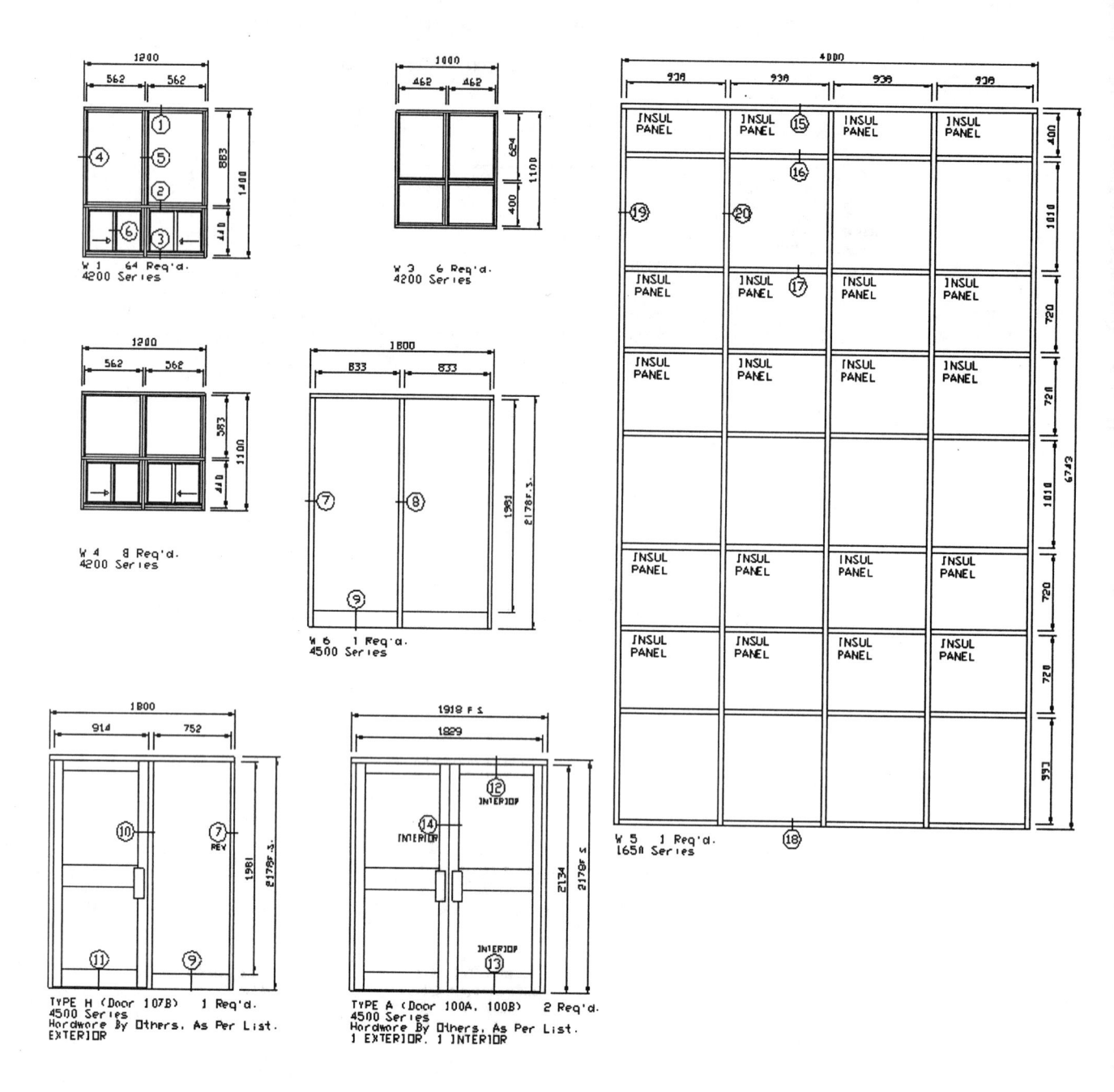

5

STRETCH, TRIM, EXTEND, OFFSET, and ARRAY

Upon completion of this chapter, you should be able to:

1. Use the Remove and Add Selection Set options
2. Edit objects using STRETCH, TRIM, EXTEND, OFFSET, and ARRAY
3. Use the ALIGN command

OBJECTIVES

Removing and Adding Objects

Chapter 4 looked at identifying objects for a selection set using Window and Crossing, Window Polygon, Crossing Polygon , Previous and Last. Now we will discuss removing objects from the selection set and addingobjects that have been removed.

> **Select Objects** In previous releases of AutoCAD, the object selection methods were avaialable on the Pull Down menu and from a toolbar. Since most people use Window (from left to right) and Crossing (from right to left), and have used windows in so many other programs, these options have been removed from the display screen, but are still available with editing commands.

Remove Option

The Remove option allows for objects to be removed from the selection set. Use Remove when a group of objects has been identified with Window or Crossing and a few need to be deleted from this selection set. Once this option is chosen, the "Select objects:" prompt changes to a "Remove objects:" prompt. Note that you can use Window and Crossing within the Remove option.

To copy just the lines and solids in the electrical symbol in Figure 5-1 you could pick each object separately (four picks) or identify the whole set with Window, then remove the circle (three picks).

The command line equivalent is **REMOVE** or **R** . Object selection methods can only be typed in.

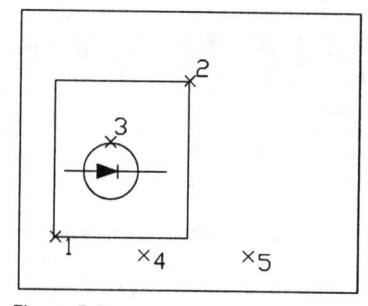

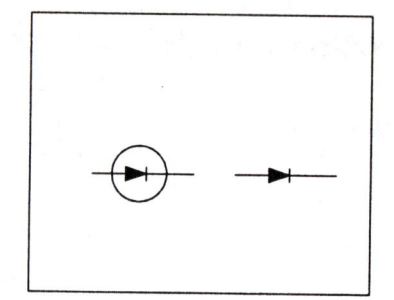

Figure 5-1

```
Command:COPY
Select objects: (pick 1)
Select opposite corner: (pick 2)
Select objects:R
Remove objects: (pick 3)
Remove objects:⏎
Specify base point or displacement, or [Multiple]:(pick 4)
Specify second point of displacement
 or <use first point as displacement>: (pick 5)
```

Add Option

If objects have been removed and should be added back into the selection set, use Add. Use Add to change the prompt from "Remove Objects:" to "Select objects:", then continue to add objects to the selection set. The command line equivalent is ADD or A.

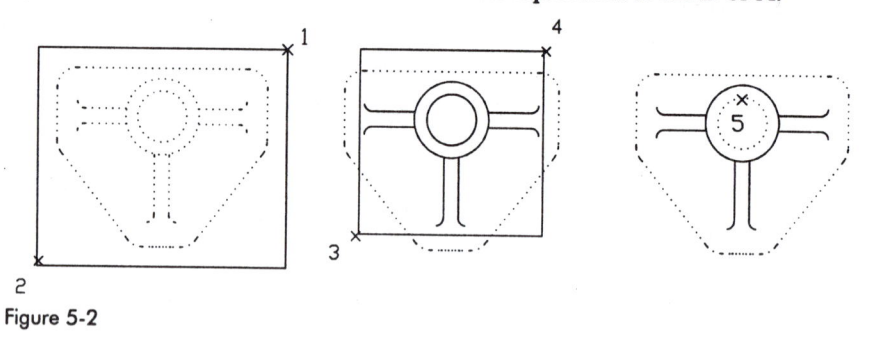

Figure 5-2

```
Command:COPY
Select objects: (pick 1)
Specify opposite corner: (pick 2)
Select objects:R
Remove objects: (pick 3)
Other corner: (pick 4)
Remove objects:A
Select objects: (pick 5)
Select objects:⏎
Specify base point or displacement, or [Multiple]:(pick 6)
Specify second point of displacement
 or <use first point as displacement>:   (continue with command)
```

You may alternate between Remove and Add until you are satisfied with the objects in the selection set.

Editing Commands

These editing commands are similar to those discussed in Chapter 4, but have a more intricate structure. Keep reading the prompts for maximum efficiency.

Like the commands offered in Chapter 4, these can be found under the Modify Pull-Down menu and under the Modify toolbar, and by typing them in with aliases.

Toolbar From the View Pull Down menu, choose Toolbars, then Modify. From this toolbar, choose Stretch, Trim, etc. Remember that you can turn the toolbars off and on.

Pull Down From the Modify menu, choose the command you want.

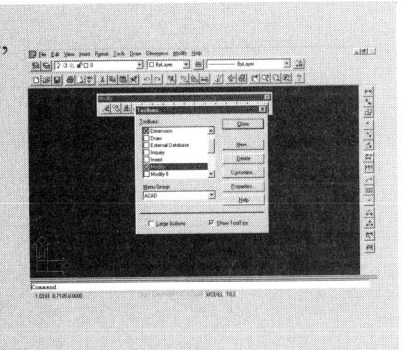

The STRETCH Command

The STRETCH command is used to make lines, plines, and other linear objects either shorter or longer. It repositions the selected side of an existing object or group of objects relative to a new point or position.

First select which *portion* of an object you would like to redefine with a Crossing Window or CPOLY (Crossing POLYgon), then place it in the new position. The object will be redrawn relative to the new end point while the unselected point will remain at its original position, acting as an anchor for the selected adjoining lines.

> **Notes**
> You must use a Crossing Window with STRETCH.

Toolbar From the Modify toolbar, pick Stretch.

Pull Down From the Modify menu, pick Stretch.

The command line equivalent is **STRETCH**.

Figure 5-3

```
Command:STRETCH
Select objects to stretch by crossing-window or polygon ...
Select objects: (pick 1)
Other corner: (pick 2) (the right side of the objects was
  picked up)
Select objects:⏎
Specify base point or displacement: (pick 3)
Specify second point of displacement: (pick 4)
```

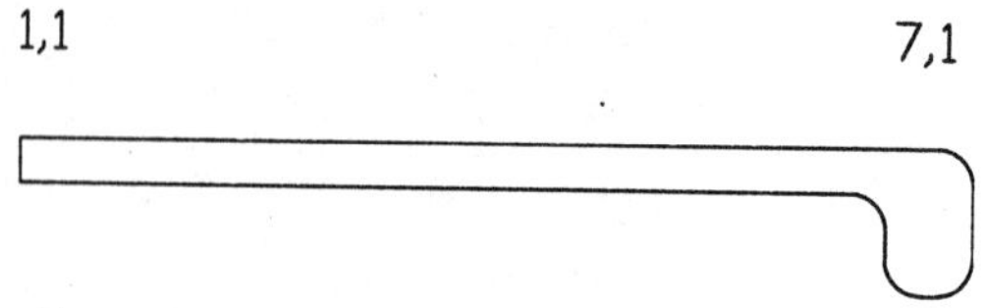

1,1   7,1

Figure 5-4

Note that if the STRETCH command is taken from the pull-down menu or the toolbar, the Crossing option is automatic. All objects in the Crossing are highlighted when they are chosen.

Only the right side of the object is affected by the command above, because only the right-side point was picked up with the Crossing option.

The LINE can also be made shorter or diagonal through changing the position of the second point.

```
Base point:7,1              Base point:7,1
New point:@-4,0             New point:@-4,3
```

1,1   3,1   3,3
                              1,1

Figure 5-5

The first point has not changed; the item has been stretched by identifying one point and moving it in relation to the original point.

Stretching Circles and Arcs

Circles are moved as full circles — stretching a circle does not create an ellipse. One end of an arc can be picked up and stretched into a different radius.

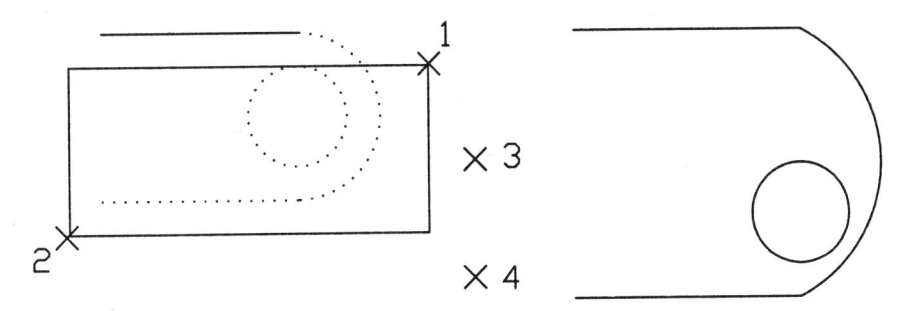

Figure 5-6

```
Command: STRETCH
Select objects to stretch by crossing-window or polygon ...
Select objects: (pick 1)
Other corner: (pick 2)
Select objects:↵
Specify base point or displacement: (pick 3)
Specify second point of displacement: (pick 4)
```

Stretching Using Remove

Objects removed from the selection set will not be stretched.

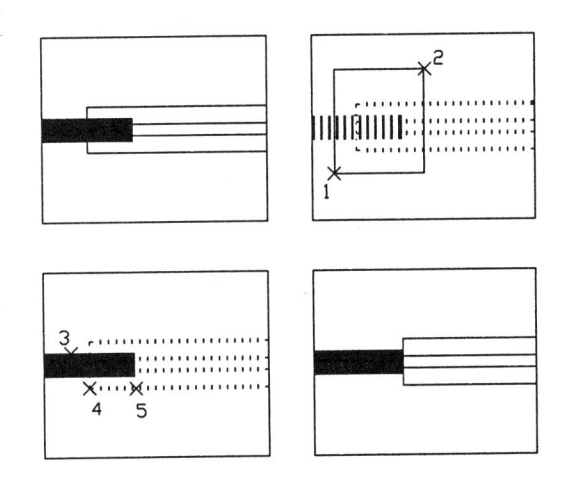

Figure 5-7

```
Command: STRETCH
Select objects to stretch by crossing-window or polygon ...
Select objects: (pick 1)
Other corner: (pick 2)
Select objects:↵
Select objects: R (Remove)
Remove objects: (pick 3) (indicates that pline is not to be
    stretched)
Remove objects:↵ (indicates no more items on the list)
Specify base point or displacement: (pick 4)
Specify second point of displacement: (pick 5)
```

The objects identified will be "loaded on the cursor" and will move along with the cursor while identifying the new point.

In this example, notice that the door opening retains its width when the walls on either side are selected and stretched.

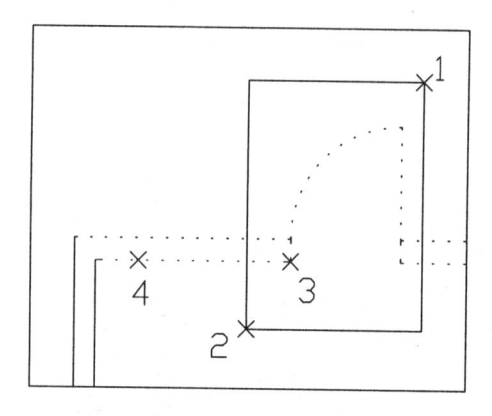

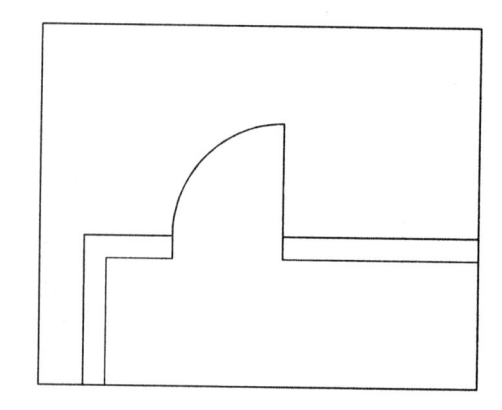

Figure 5-8

> **Danger**
>
> If you pick all the objects with your Crossing selection, you will MOVE the objects instead of STRETCHing them. Choose only the side of the object that you would like to stretch.

```
Command: STRETCH
Select objects to stretch by crossing-window or polygon ...
Select objects: (pick 1)
Other corner: (pick 2)
Select objects:↵
Specify base point or displacement: (pick 3)
Specify second point of displacement: (pick 4)
```

Use ORTHO to make sure that the walls remain straight.

It is advisable to use STRETCH or EXTEND (see page 120) when making an object fit into a larger space than was originally intended. It is *not* a good idea to add extra lines.

The TRIM Command

The TRIM command is used to cut off an object or a series of objects at their intersection with a boundary or cutting edge. While you have already used TRIM on individual objects, you can also use it on multiple objects.

The cutting edge or boundary must already exist on the drawing before you can use TRIM.

In this example, the horizontal lines will be trimmed to the diagonal line which has been defined as the cutting edge. Notice that the cutting line is to be chosen first. It becomes highlighted when chosen.

> **Toolbar** From the Modify toolbar, pick Trim.
>
> **Pull Down** From the Modify menu, pick Trim.

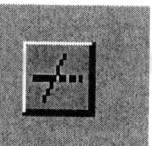

The command line equivalent is **TRIM**.

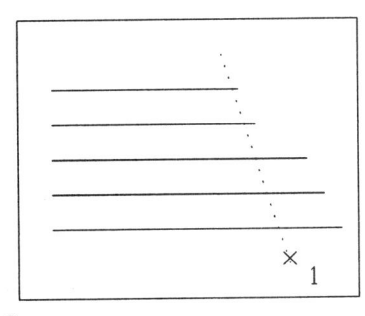

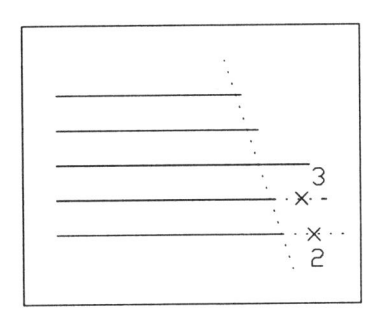

Figure 5-9

```
Command:TRIM
Current settings Projection=UCS, Edge=None
Select cutting edges...
Select objects: (pick 1)
Select objects:⏎ (no more cutting edges are needed)
Select object to trim or [Project/Edge/Undo]: (pick 2)
Select object to trim or [Project/Edge/Undo]: (pick 3)
Select object to trim or [Project/Edge/Undo]: (select the
   remaining objects)
```

The first pick(s) indicates the cutting edge. Use ⏎ to continue when the cutting edges have been selected. The following picks are those items which will be trimmed to this edge. Any number of objects can be trimmed. Using Fence at the "Select objects to trim:" prompt can greatly speed the process.

The objects are trimmed from the end chosen to the closest cutting edge. Choose the segments to be trimmed away.

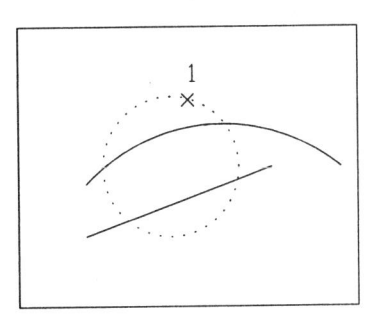

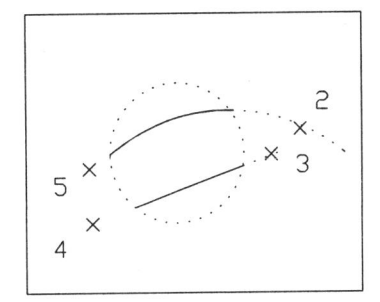

Figure 5-10

```
Command:TRIM
Current settings Projection=UCS, Edge=None
Select cutting edges...
Select objects: (pick 1)
Select objects:⏎ (no more cutting edges are needed)
Select object to trim or [Project/Edge/Undo]: (pick 2)
Select object to trim or [Project/Edge/Undo]: (pick 3 to 5)
```

STRETCH, TRIM, EXTEND, OFFSET, and ARRAY

You can also use Window to select the cutting edges.

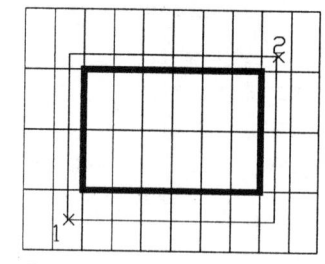

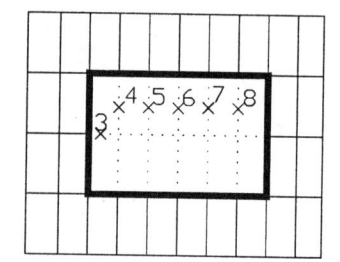

Figure 5-11

```
Command:TRIM
Current settings Projection=UCS, Edge=None
Select cutting edges...
Select objects: (pick 1, pick 2)
Select objects:↵ (no more cutting edges are needed)
Select object to trim or [Project/Edge/Undo]: (pick 2 to 8)
```

You can also choose multiple objects as the cutting edges. In the following example, all of the objects are considered cutting edges.

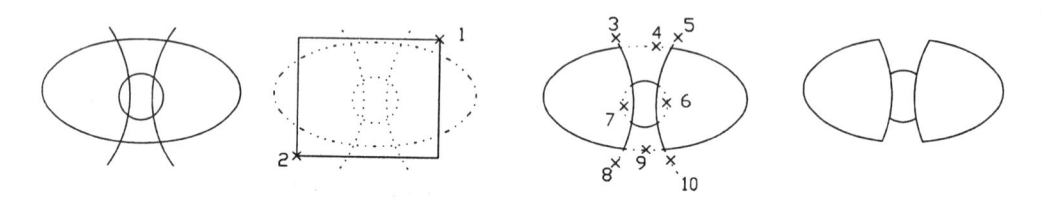

Figure 5-12

```
Command:TRIM
Current settings Projection=UCS, Edge=None
Select cutting edges...
Select objects: (pick 1)
Other corner: (pick 2)
Select objects:↵
Select object to trim or [Project/Edge/Undo]: (pick 3 to 10)
```

The EXTEND Command

The EXTEND command also uses a boundary (or boundaries), but uses it as the item to extend objects to. In this example, the boundary is clearly the diagonal line. Once picked, it will be highlighted.

Toolbar From the Modify toolbar, pick Extend.

Pull Down From the Modify menu, pick Extend.

The command line equivalent is **EXTEND**.

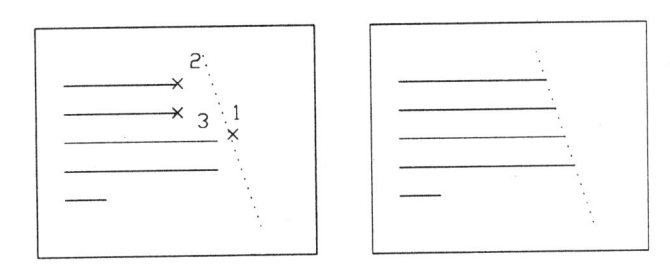

Figure 5-13

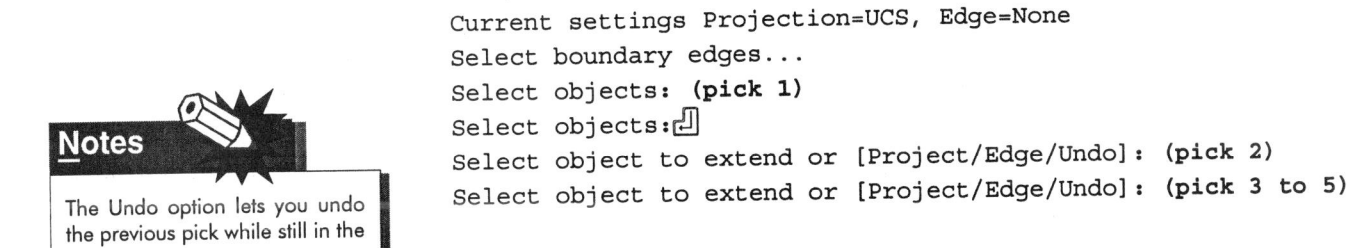

```
Command: EXTEND
Current settings Projection=UCS, Edge=None
Select boundary edges...
Select objects: (pick 1)
Select objects: ↵
Select object to extend or [Project/Edge/Undo]: (pick 2)
Select object to extend or [Project/Edge/Undo]: (pick 3 to 5)
```

Notes

The Undo option lets you undo the previous pick while still in the command.

In this example, the LINEs are extended to the closest boundary selected. More than one boundary can be chosen for objects to extend to, and the closest end point will always be extended to the boundary chosen. The Fence option is also useful here.

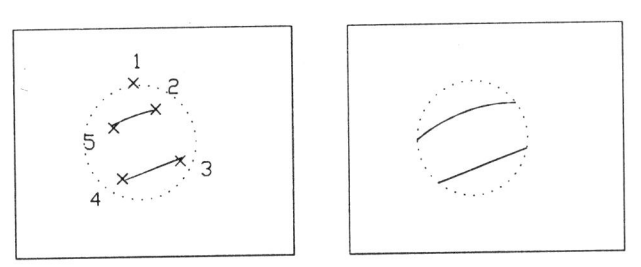

Figure 5-14

```
Command: EXTEND
Current settings Projection=UCS, Edge=None
Select boundary edges...
Select objects: (pick 1)
Select objects: ↵
Select object to extend or [Project/Edge/Undo]: (pick 2 to 5)
```

TRIM and EXTEND with Implied Intersections

Implied intersections are the points where two objects would intersect if they were either extended or trimmed. You can trim objects using their implied intersections as cutting edges for the trim, and extend objects using their implied intersection as the boundary.

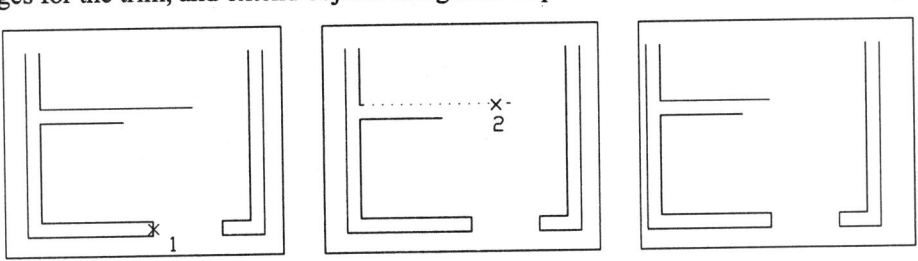

Figure 5-15

STRETCH, TRIM, EXTEND, OFFSET, and ARRAY **121**

```
Command: TRIM
Current settings Projection=UCS, Edge=None
Select cutting edges...
Select objects: (pick 1)
Select objects:⏎ (no more cutting edges are needed)
Select object to trim or [Project/Edge/Undo]:E
Enter an implied edge extension mode [Extend/No extend]:E
Select object to trim or [Project/Edge/Undo]: (pick 2)
Select object to trim or [Project/Edge/Undo]:⏎
```

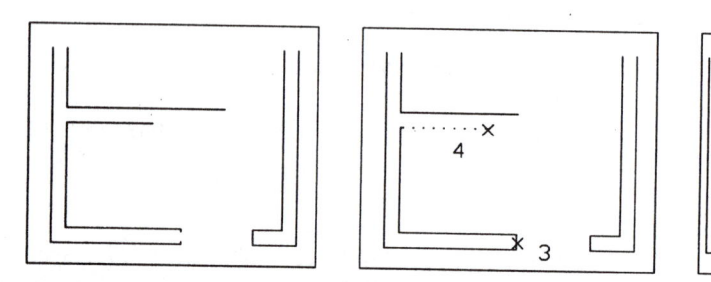

Figure 5-16

```
Command: EXTEND
Current settings Projection=UCS, Edge=None
Select boundary edges...
Select objects: (pick 3)
Select objects:⏎
Select object to extend [Project/Edge/Undo]:E
Enter an implied edge extension mode [Extend/No extend]:E
Select object to extend or [Project/Edge/Undo]: (pick 4)
Select object to extend or [Project/Edge/Undo]:⏎
```

What Can Go Wrong with TRIM and EXTEND

If AutoCAD responds with:

No edges selected = you have chosen an object that cannot be referenced as a boundary or cutting edge. TRACE, TEXT, and hatching are not valid boundaries and will be rejected.

Cannot extend this entity = the object chosen cannot be extended. For example, if you choose a complete circle, this cannot extended.

Entity does not intersect an edge = the object does not line up with the edge selected. Try using FILLET Radius 0. Arcs continue their radius and may curve away from the boundary.

The OFFSET Command

OFFSET is arguably the most often used editing command on the system. It is similar to the parallel object snap function, but with OFFSET you can specify a distance.

OFFSET copies an object parallel to an existing object at a given distance. Any number of objects can be offset at the specified distance within one command string. Note that the OFFSET command works only in the *X-Y* plane.

> **Toolbar** From the Modify toolbar, pick Offset.
>
> **Pull Down** From the Modify menu, choose Offset.

The command line equivalent is **OFFSET**.

Offset first requires the offset distance — the distance that all of the objects will be offset by. It doesn't matter how far away the pick point is from the offset object; only the side is important.

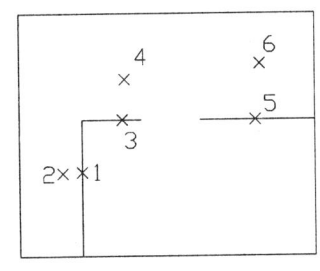

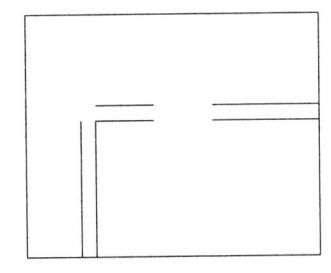

Figure 5-17

```
Command:OFFSET
Specify offset distance or [Through]<Through>:8
Select object to offset or <exit>: (pick 1)
Specify point on side to offset: (pick 2)
Select object to offset or <exit>: (pick 3)
Specify point on side to offset: (pick 4)
Select object to offset or <exit> : (continue to pick points
   and sides)
```

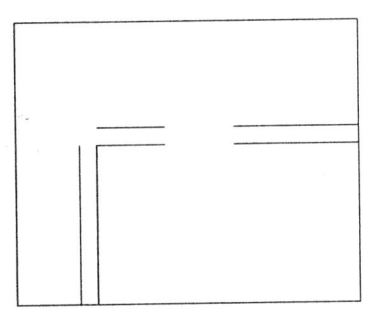

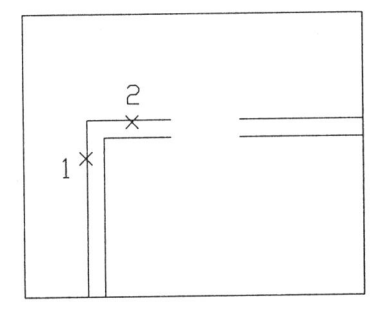

The prompts for the objects to offset and the side to offset will continue in a paired sequence until you press ↵. Next, clean up the corners with FILLET Radius 0.

Figure 5-18

```
Command:FILLET
Current settings: Mode = Trim,Radius = <5.0000>
Select first object or [Polyline/Radius/Trim]: r
Specify fillet radius <1.000>:0 (then FILLET, pick 1, pick 2)
```

OFFSET with the Through Option

The Through option in OFFSET is used to specify a point through which you would like the offset calculated, as opposed to having a specified distance.

Offsetting a circle or an arc will result in the second object having the same center, but the radius will be larger or smaller by the offset distance. The center point does not change; only the size of the circle or arc changes.

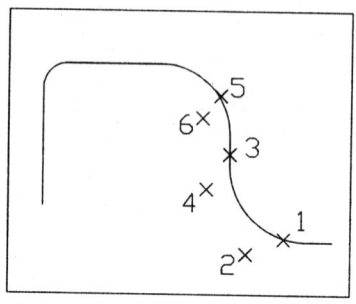

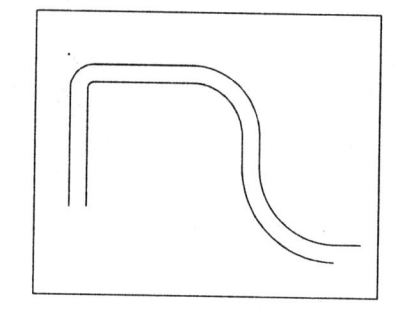

Figure 5-19

```
Command: OFFSET
Specify offset distance or [Through]<Through>: t
Select object to offset or <exit>: (pick 1)
Specify through point: (pick 2)
Select object to offset or <exit>: (pick 3)
Specify through point: (pick 4)
```

Offsetting PLINEs

Similarly, with plines that are fit into curves or splines, the resulting object is fit through the same series of points at an offset distance. The inside offset spline will be defined by the same number of vertices, but the distance between the vertices will be different.

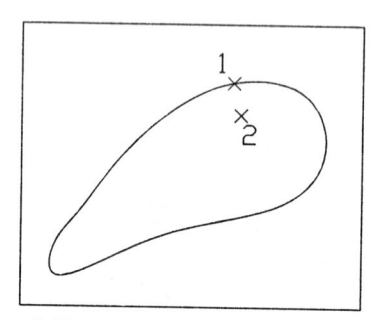

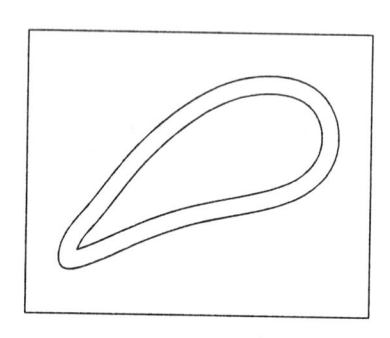

Figure 5-20

```
Command: OFFSET
Specify offset distance or [Through]<Through>: 1
Select object to offset or <exit>: (pick 1)
Specify point on side to offset: (pick 2)
Select object to offset or <exit>:
```

The ARRAY Command (Polar)

The ARRAY command makes circular (polar) or rectangular patterns of selected objects by copying them along or around an identified point. You are prompted first for the objects that are to be arrayed, then for the type of array — polar or rectangular. Finally you are asked to specify how many objects are to be in the array and how they are to be spaced.

In this polar array example, the object (a chair) is arrayed around the center of the larger circle (a table) at equal distances through 360 degrees, rotating the copies in line with the center point.

> **Toolbar** From the Modify Toolbar, pick Array.
>
> **Pull Down** From the Modify menu, choose Array, then Polar.

The command line equivalent is **ARRAY**.

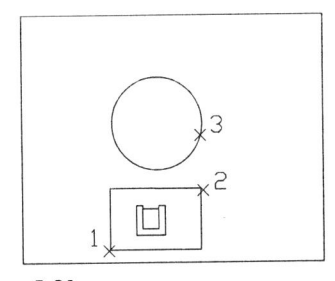

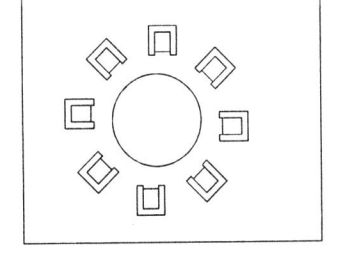

Figure 5-21

```
Command:ARRAY
Select objects: (pick 1)
Other corner: (pick 2)
Select objects: ↵ (indicates that no more are needed)
Enter the type of array [Rectangular/Polar]<R>:P
Specify center point of array:CENter of (pick 3)
Enter the number of items in the array:8
Specify the angle to fill (+=CCW,-=CW)<360>:↵ (accepts default
   of 360)
Rotate arrayed objects [Yes/No]<Y>:↵ (accepts default)
```

Polar Arrays with Incremental Angles

With a polar array, you can specify the incremental angle between each object rather than the total distance if you prefer.

You must know both the angle that you need between items and the number of items.

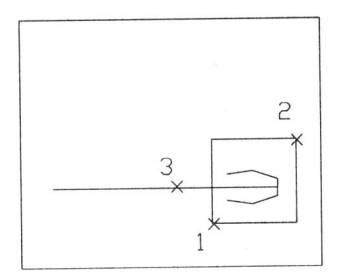

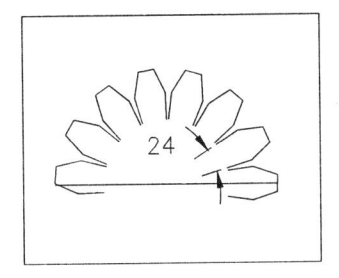

Figure 5-22

Respond with a **0** when prompted for the angle to fill, and you will be asked for the incremental angle.

```
Command:ARRAY
Select objects: (pick 1)
Other corner: (pick 2)
Select objects:⏎ (indicates no more objects are needed)
Enter the type of array [Rectangular/Polar]<R>:P
Specify center point of array:MIDpoint of (pick 3)
Enter the number of items:8
Specify the angle to fill (+=CCW,-=CW)<360>:0 (indicates
  incremental angle)
Specify the angle between items (+=CCW,-=CW):24
Rotate arrayed objects? [Yes/No]<Y>:⏎ (accepts default)
```

If you don't know the number of items but you know what the final angle and the angle between items is, use:

```
Specify center point of array:MIDpoint of (pick)
Enter the number of items:⏎
Specify the angle to fill (+=CCW,-=CW)<360>:180
Specify the angle between items (+=CCW,-=CW):24
Rotate arrayed objects? [Yes/No]<Y>:⏎
```

The ARRAY Command (Rectangular)

The Rectangular option of the ARRAY command prompts for the number of rows (copies in the *Y* direction) and the number of columns (copies in the *X* direction). Then you are prompted for the distance between the copies in rows and columns. This is the center-to-center distance, useful for both building trades and mechanical engineering.

> **Toolbar** From the Modify toolbar, pick Rectangular Array.
>
> **Pull Down** From the Modify menu, pick Array, then Rectangular.

The command line equivalent is **ARRAY**.

In the following diagram, the objects are ARRAYed along *X* or in columns. Note the distance between the columns includes the halfwidth of the item itself.

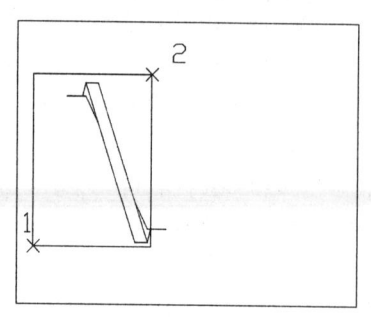

Figure 5-23

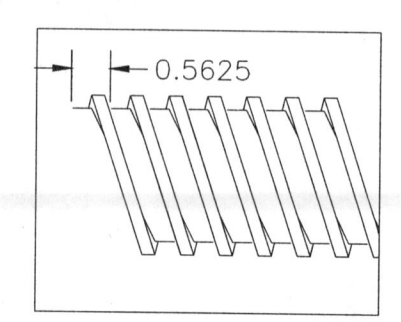

ARRAY: Single Row or Column

```
Command:ARRAY
Select objects: (pick 1)
Other corner: (pick 2)
Select objects:⏎Enter the n
Enter the type of array [Rectangular/Polar]<R>:⏎
Enter the number of rows(--)<1>:⏎ (accepts the default of 1)
Enter the number of columns(|||)<1>:7
Enter the distance between the columns:.5625
```

When doing layouts that contain many objects in both the X and the Y direction, specify both rows and columns. In specifying the number of rows and columns, the total number is indicated.

ARRAY: Multiple Rows and Columns

If you have a chair that is 24 inches wide and you want an aisle of 18 inches between it and the next chair, the spacing would be the width of the chair plus the width of the aisle (24 +

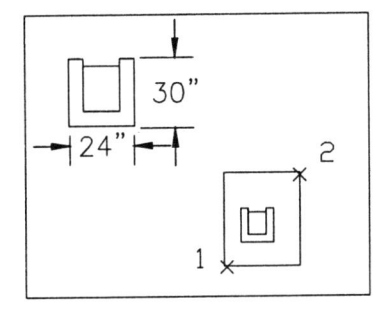

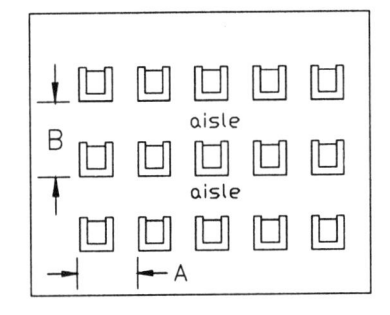

Figure 5-24

18 = 3'6'').

```
Command:ARRAY
Select objects: (pick 1)
Other corner: (pick 2)
Select objects:⏎
Enter the type of array [Rectangular/Polar]<R>:⏎
Enter the number of rows(--)<1>:3
Enter the number of columns(|||)<1>:5
Enter the distance between the rows:60 (distance B)
Enter the distance between the columns:42 (distance A)
```

A negative distance will place the array in a negative direction: to the left if columns, and down from the original if rows.

ARRAY with Unit Cell

Unit cell satisfies the distance between rows and columns with a resultant distance of X and Y. The object arrays the directions the unit cell window has selected.

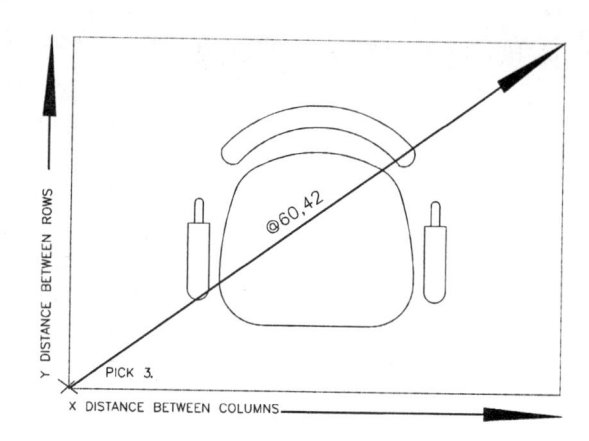

```
Command: ARRAY
Select objects: (pick 1)
Other corner: (pick 2)
Select objects: ↵
Enter the type of array [Rectangular/Polar]<R>: ↵
Enter the number of rows(--)<1>: 3
Enter the number of columns(||||)<1>: 5
Enter the distance between the rows<--->: (pick 3)
Specify opposite corner: @60,42
```

Figure 5-25

Align

Align moves and rotates objects to align with other objects, either in 2D or 3D. Align uses up to three pairs of source and destination points. The first set of points defines a move for the objects. The second set of points can define either a 2D or 3D transformation and rotation of the objects. The third set of points defines an unambiguous 3D transformation of the objects.

Toolbar None

Pull Down From the Modify menu, pick 3D operations, then ALIGN.

The command line equivalent is **ALIGN**.

```
Command: ALIGN
Select objects: (pick the upper set
   of objects)
Select objects: ↵
Specify 1st source point: (pick 1)
Specify 1st destination point: (pick
   2)
Specify 2nd source point: (pick 3)
Specify 2nd destination point: (pick
   4)
3rd source point: ↵
3rd destination point: ↵
```

This is largely a 3D command, but can come in useful in 2D as well.

Prelab 5 Editing Commands

This example will illustrate how to use ARRAY, TRIM, EXTEND, and OFFSET to create a backyard pool.

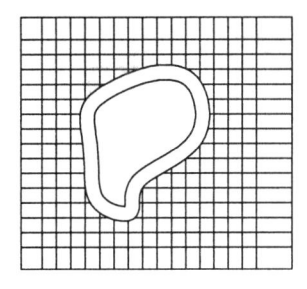

Step 1 Set LIMITS to -1,-1 and 40,30 or place your UCS origin on screen.

Set GRID to 2 and SNAP to 1. ZOOM All.

Step 2 Create a line from 0,0 to 0,28, and ARRAY it to make 16.

```
Command:L
Specify start point:0,0
Specify next point or [Undo]:0,28
Specify next point or [Undo]:⏎
Command:ARRAY
Select objects:L
Select objects:⏎
Enter the type of array [Rectangular/Polar]<R>:R
Enter the number of rows (---)<1>:⏎
Enter the number of columns (|||)<1>:16
Enter the distance between columns (|||):2
```

Step 3 Create a line from 0,0 to 30,0 and ARRAY it by 15 to make a rectangular grid (the patio stones).

```
Command:L
Specify start point:0,0
Specify next point or [Undo]:30,0
Specify next point or [Undo]:⏎
Command:ARRAY
Select objects:L
Select objects:⏎
Enter the type of array [Rectangular/Polar]<R>:⏎
Enter the number of rows (---)<1>:15
Enter the number of columns (|||)<1>:⏎
Enter the distance between rows (|||):2
```

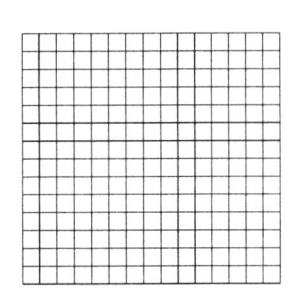

STRETCH, TRIM, EXTEND, OFFSET, and ARRAY

Make a PLINE and use PEDIT to create a pool shape.

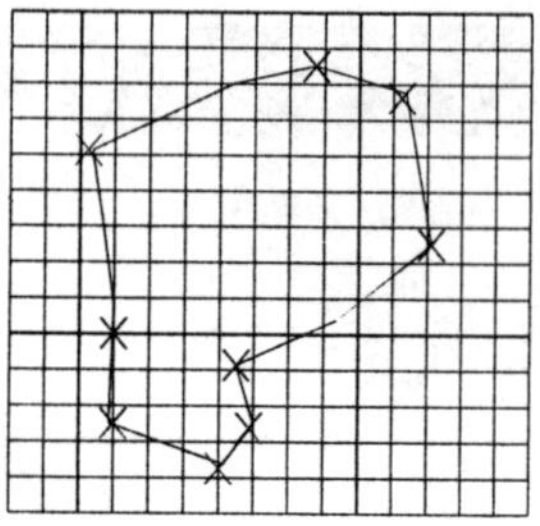

```
Command: PLINE
Specify start point: (pick 1)
Current line width is 0.1000
Specify next point or [Arc/Close/
Halfwidth/Length/Undo/Width]: (pick
 points 1 to whatever)
Specify next point or [Arc/Close/
Halfwidth/Length/Undo/Width]:C
Command: PEDIT
Select polyline:L
Enter an option [Close/Join/Width/Edit vertex/Fit curve/Ltype
  gen/Spline curve/Decurve/Undo]:S
Enter an option [Close/Join/Width/Edit vertex/Fit curve/Ltype
  gen/Spline curve/Decurve/Undo]:⏎
```

Step 4 Now OFFSET the pool shape to create a pool border.

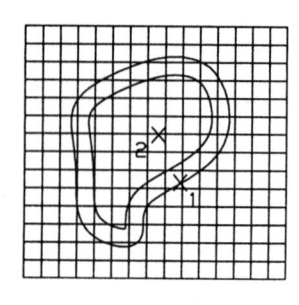

```
Command: OFFSET
Specify offset distance or
  [Through]:2
Select object to offset or <exit>:
  (pick 1)
 Specify point on side to offset:
  (pick 2)
Select object to offset or <exit>:⏎
```

Step 5 Now use trim to remove the lines from the patio stones within the pool.

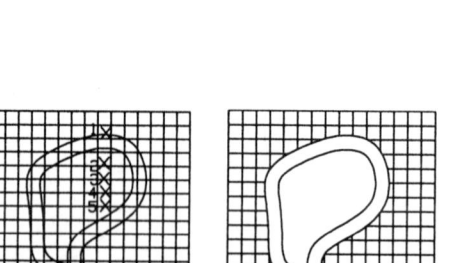

```
Command: TRIM
Current settings
  Projection=UCS, Edge=None
Select cutting edges...:
  (pick 1)
Select objects:⏎
<Select object to trim> Undo:FENCE (pick
  points 2 to whatever)
```

Step 6 Use OFFSET to create a set of larger patio stones on the outside of the original stones as a border.

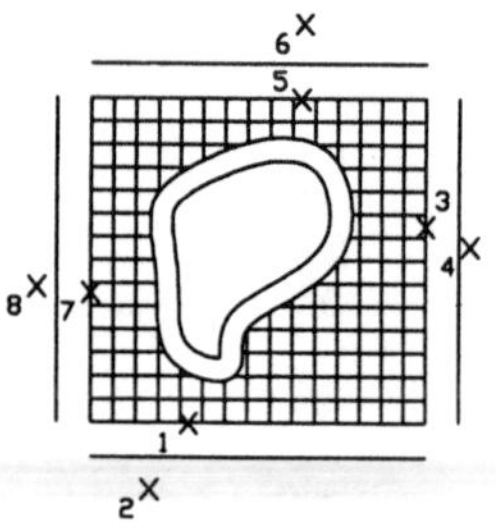

```
Command: OFFSET
Specify offset distance or [Through]:3
Select object to offset or <exit>:
 (pick 1)
Specify point on side to offset: (pick 2)
Select object to offset or <exit>: (complete picks indicated)
```

130 CHAPTER FIVE

Use FILLET to make the corners square.

```
Command: FILLET
Current settings: Mode = Trim, Radius = <5.0000>
Select first object or [Polyline/Radius/Trim]: (pick line)
Specify second object: (pick another line)
```

Now use EXTEND to extend the lines from the existing stones to the new boundary.

```
Command: EXTEND
Current settings Projection=UCS,
Edge=None
Select boundary edges...
Select objects: (pick 1 to 4)
Select objects: ↵
Select object to extend or [Project/
  Edge/Undo]: (pick 5 and so on)
```
Hint: Fence can be used.

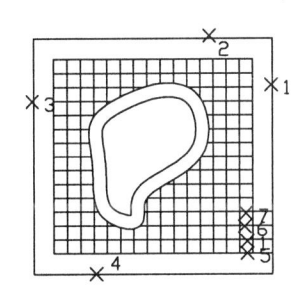

Step 7   Now STRETCH the stones on the right just one unit further.

```
Command: STRETCH
Select objects to stretch by
crossing-window or polygon...
Select objects:C
First corner: (pick 1)
Other corner: (pick 2)
Select objects:↵
Specify base point or displacement: (pick 3)
Specify second point of displacement:@1,0
```

Now you have a completed exterior pool area with 2×2 stones, 2×3 stones and 2×4 stones.

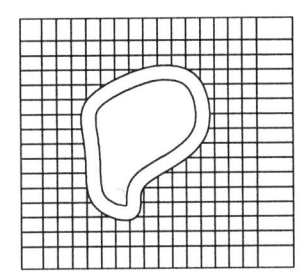

Command and Function Summary

Add is an object selection option that allows you to keep adding to your selection set after the Remove option has been used.

ARRAY makes copies of an entity in either a polar or a rectangular pattern.

EXTEND is used to extend an object or a series of objects to reach a selected boundary.

OFFSET makes a copy of an entity parallel to and at a specified distance from that entity.

STRETCH changes the length or width of an object or group of objects by stretching the parameters of one side of the object.

TRIM is used to trim an object or a series of objects to reach a selected cutting line.

Note: You are now at the point where you can draw the geometry for almost any part. The only way to speed your understanding is through practice, not only in your own discipline but in all. Do as many of the exercises in this chapter as possible. Remember to save your files!

This is the base of a clock which will be be under the COMMANDS for the next few chapters. Do it if you have time.

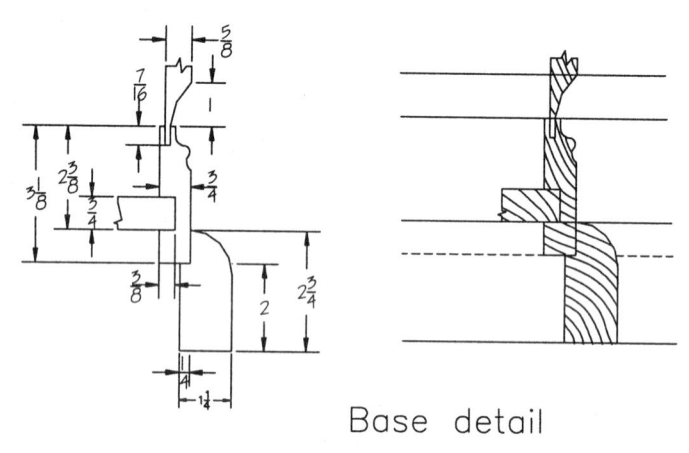

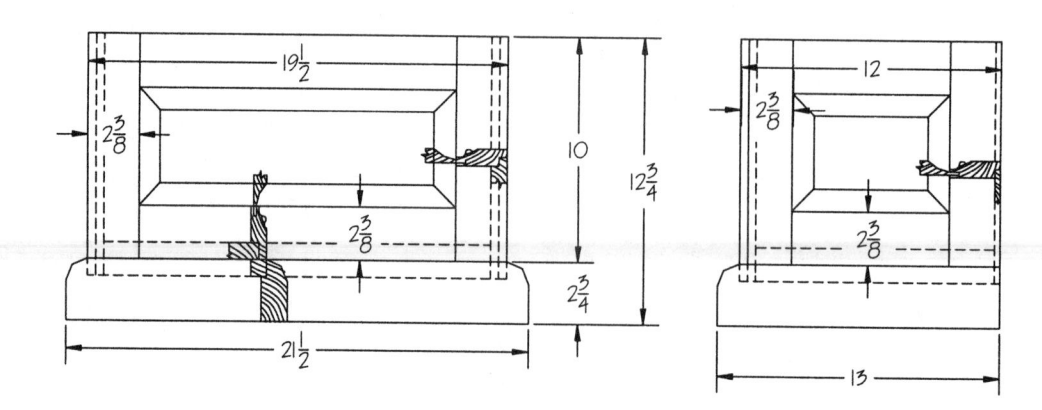

Base detail

Practice Exercise 5A

Use the editing commands to complete these mechanical examples.

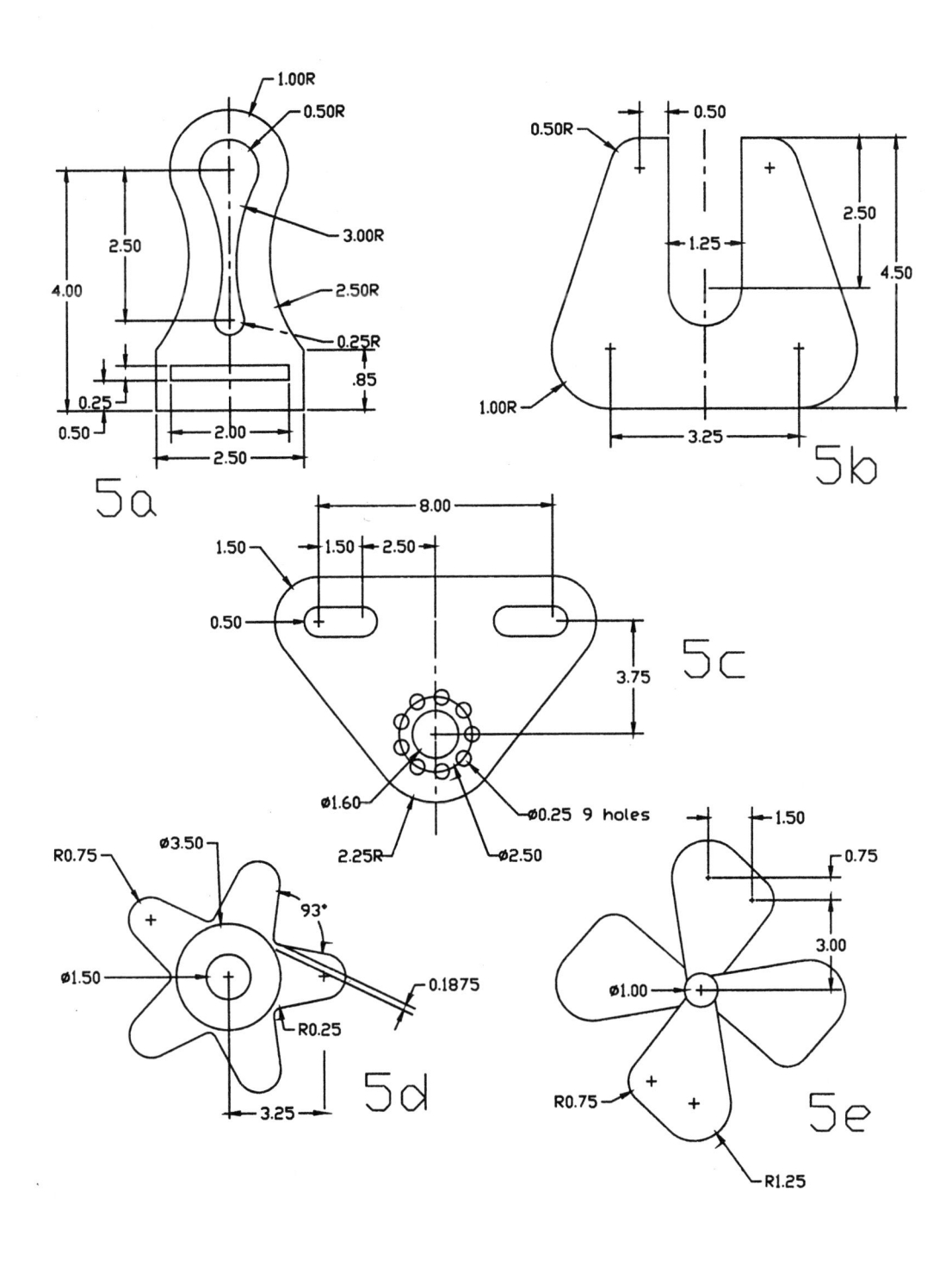

5a

5b

5c

5d

5e

STRETCH, TRIM, EXTEND, OFFSET, and ARRAY

Practice Exercise 5B

In the digital display use SOLID to make the numerals, then DONUT, CIRCLE, LINE, and FILLET to complete the drawing.

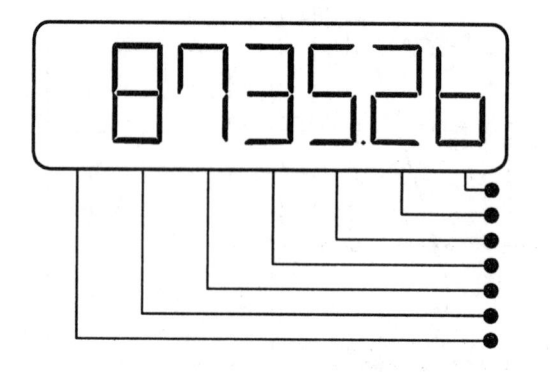

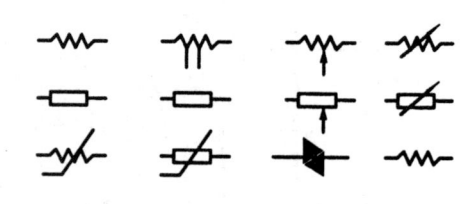

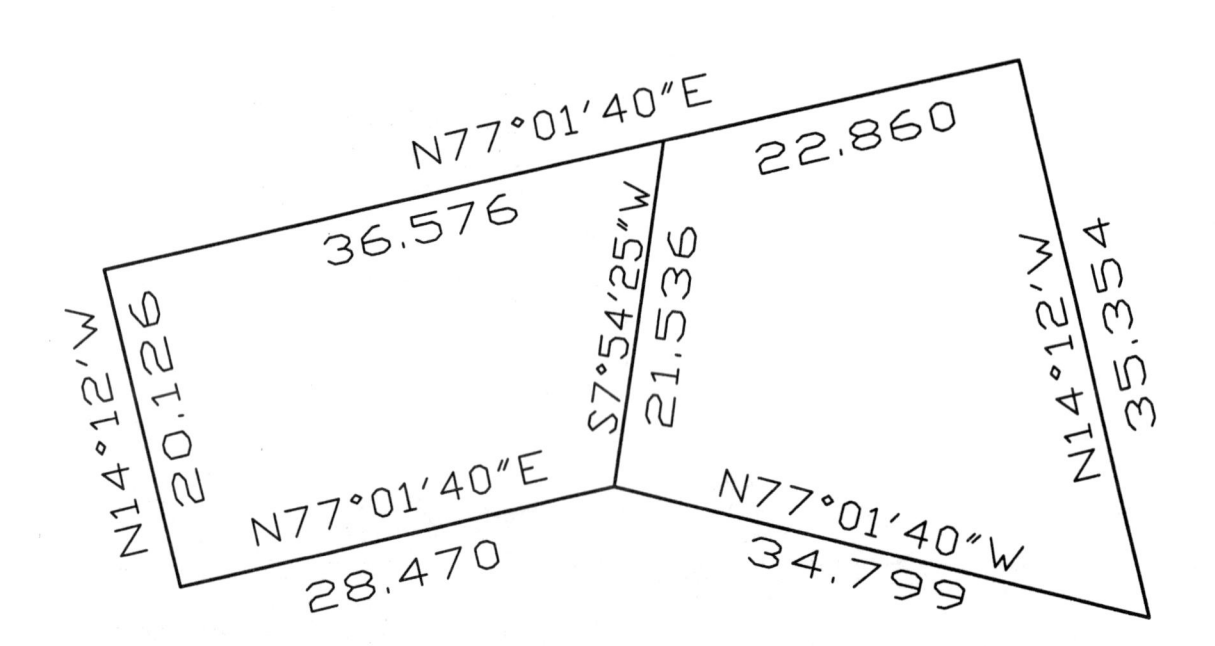

Practice Exercise 5C

OFFSET and ARRAY will be useful for these examples.

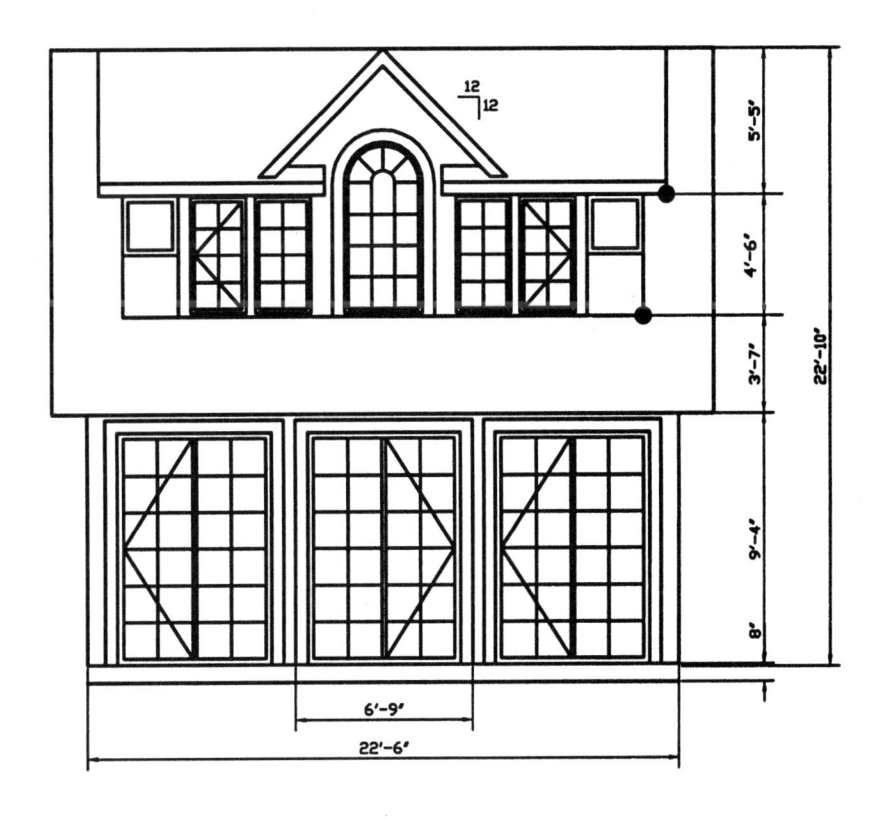

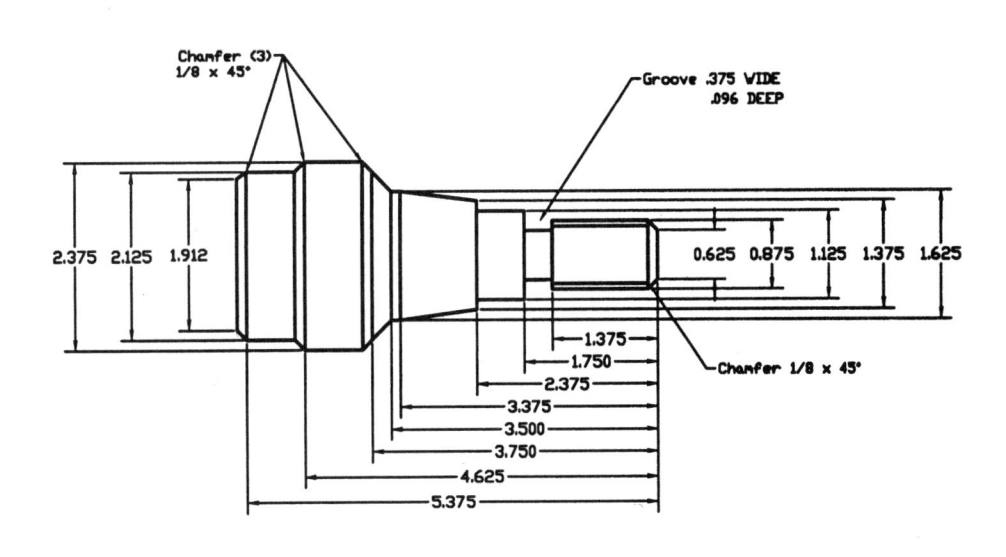

Exercise A5

Using the files from the previous chapters, for the interior walls of the second floor use OFFSET and FILLET. If you are not happy with some of the design features, use STRETCH to move things around. Use ARRAY to place the upper stairs.
If time permits, draw in the bathrooms on this floor and on the first floor.

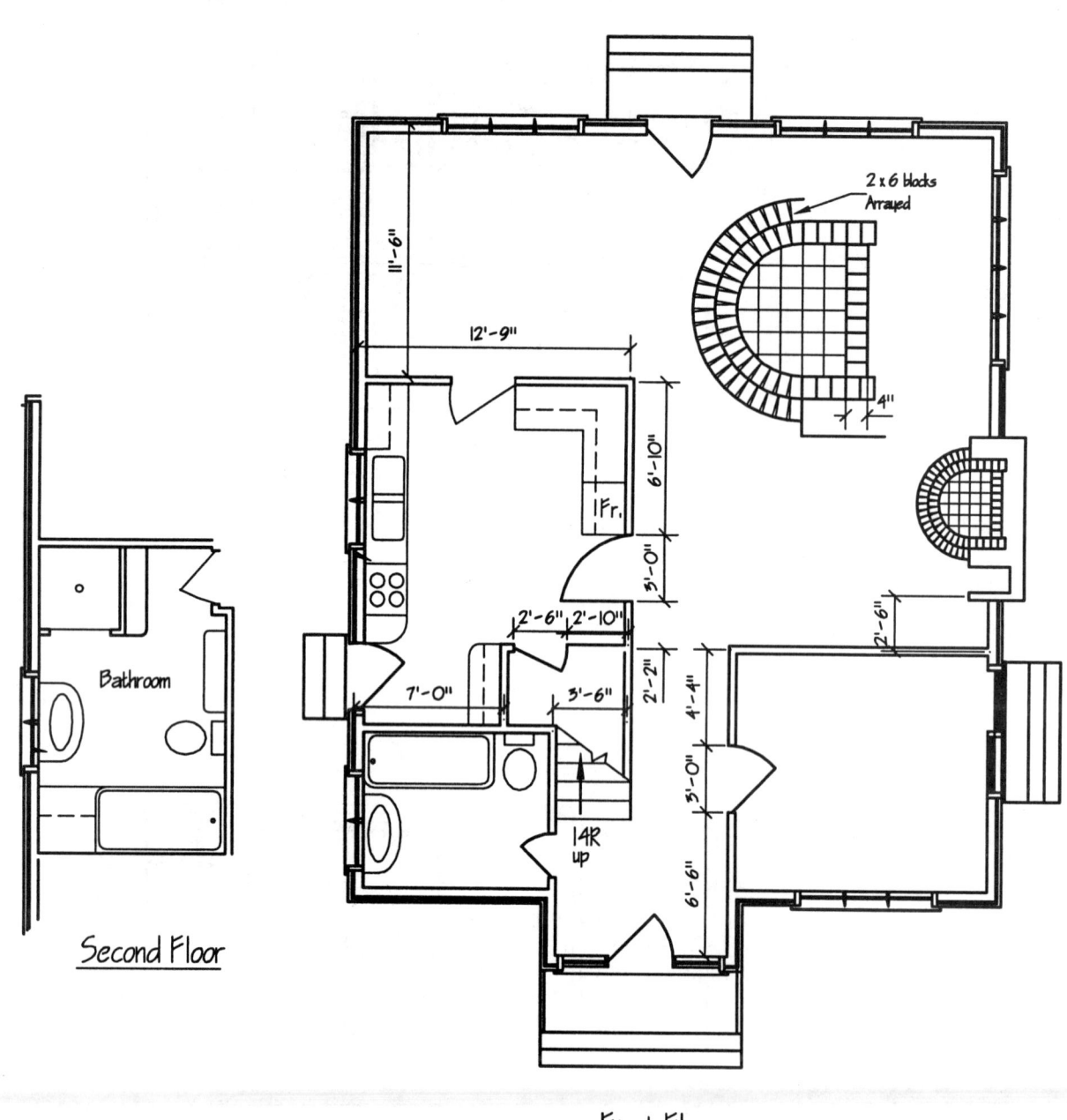

Second Floor

First Floor

136 CHAPTER FIVE

Exercise C5

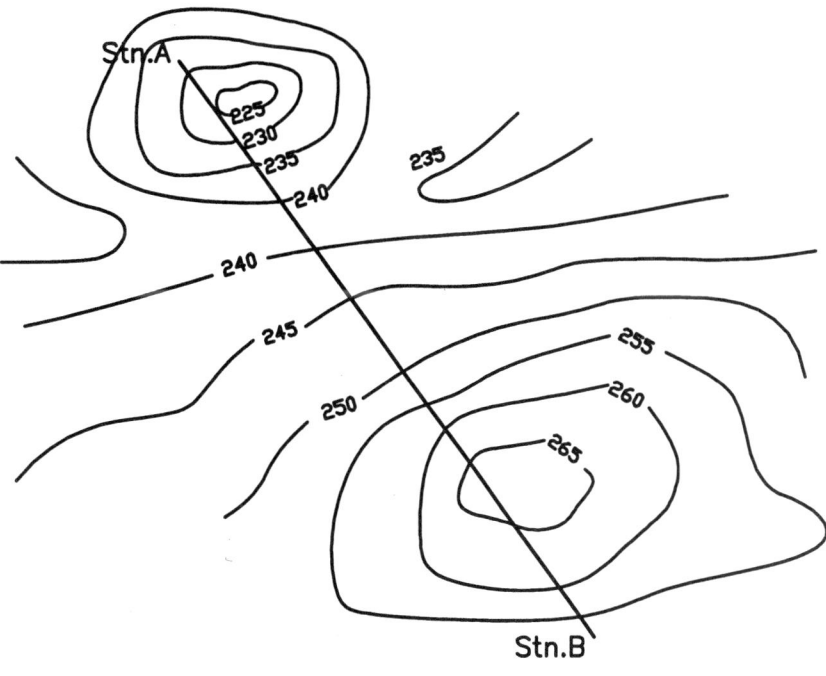

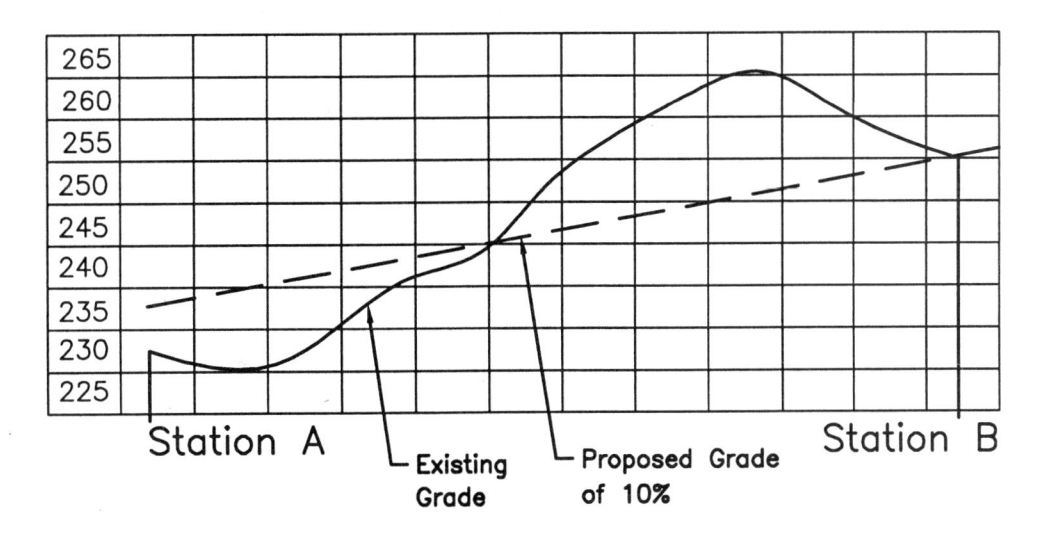

The polylines are contours showing the existing ground elevations for a proposed roadway. Use PEDIT to create smooth polylines. The original ground elevations are shown with contours at 5.00 m intervals.

The same drawing shows a profile route of the highway running from station A to station B at +10.00. On the profile, plot the highway elevations as well as the original road elevations.

STRETCH, TRIM, EXTEND, OFFSET, and ARRAY

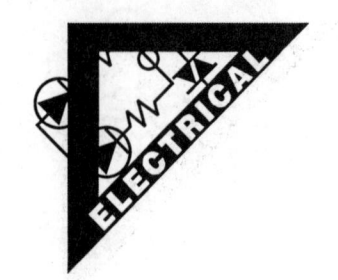

Exercise E5

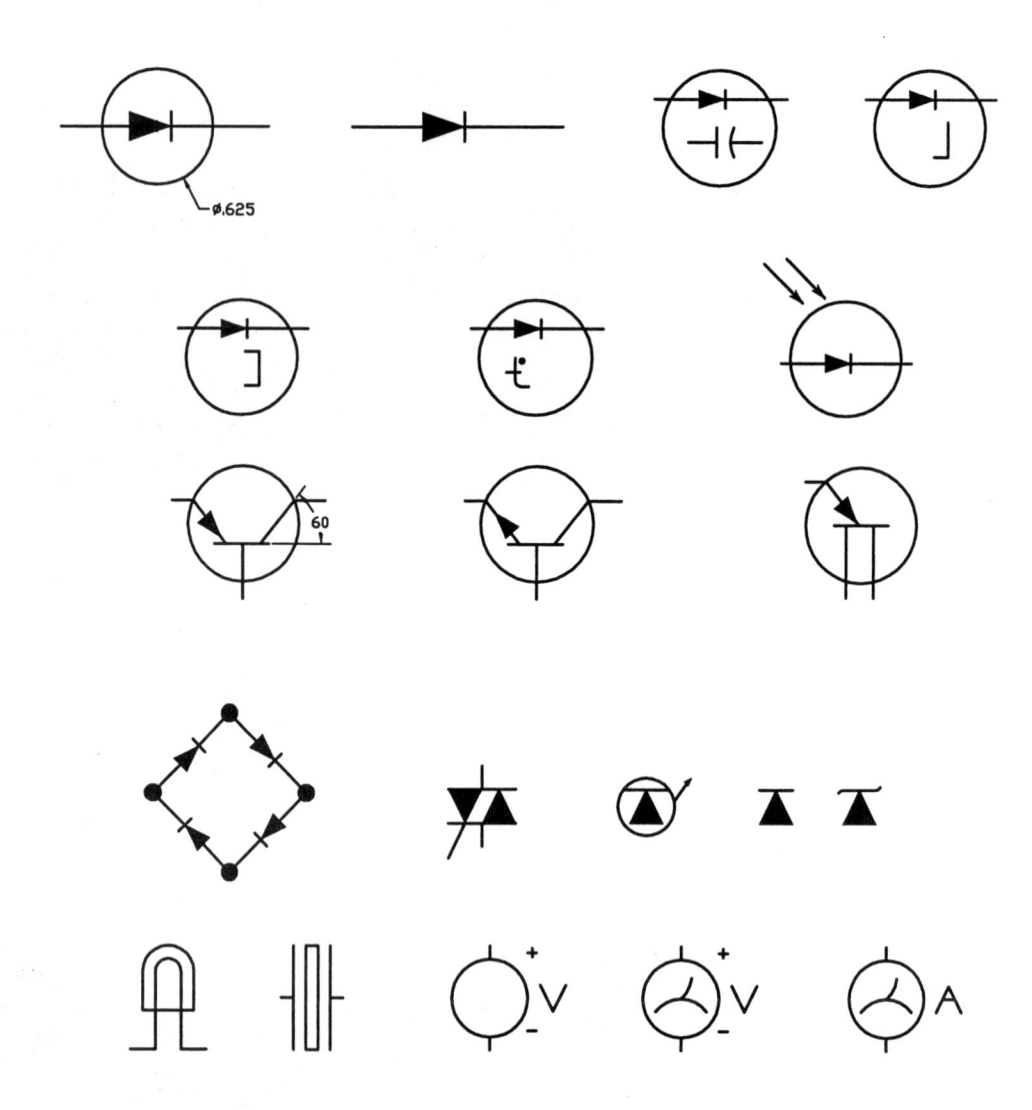

Create these symbols with the editing commands; use COPY, ROTATE, and MOVE to draw the parts more efficiently. Use the SCALE command to change the relative size of the PLINE when you enter it as an arrow.

When you are finished, use the symbols to create a logical schematic.

Exercise M5

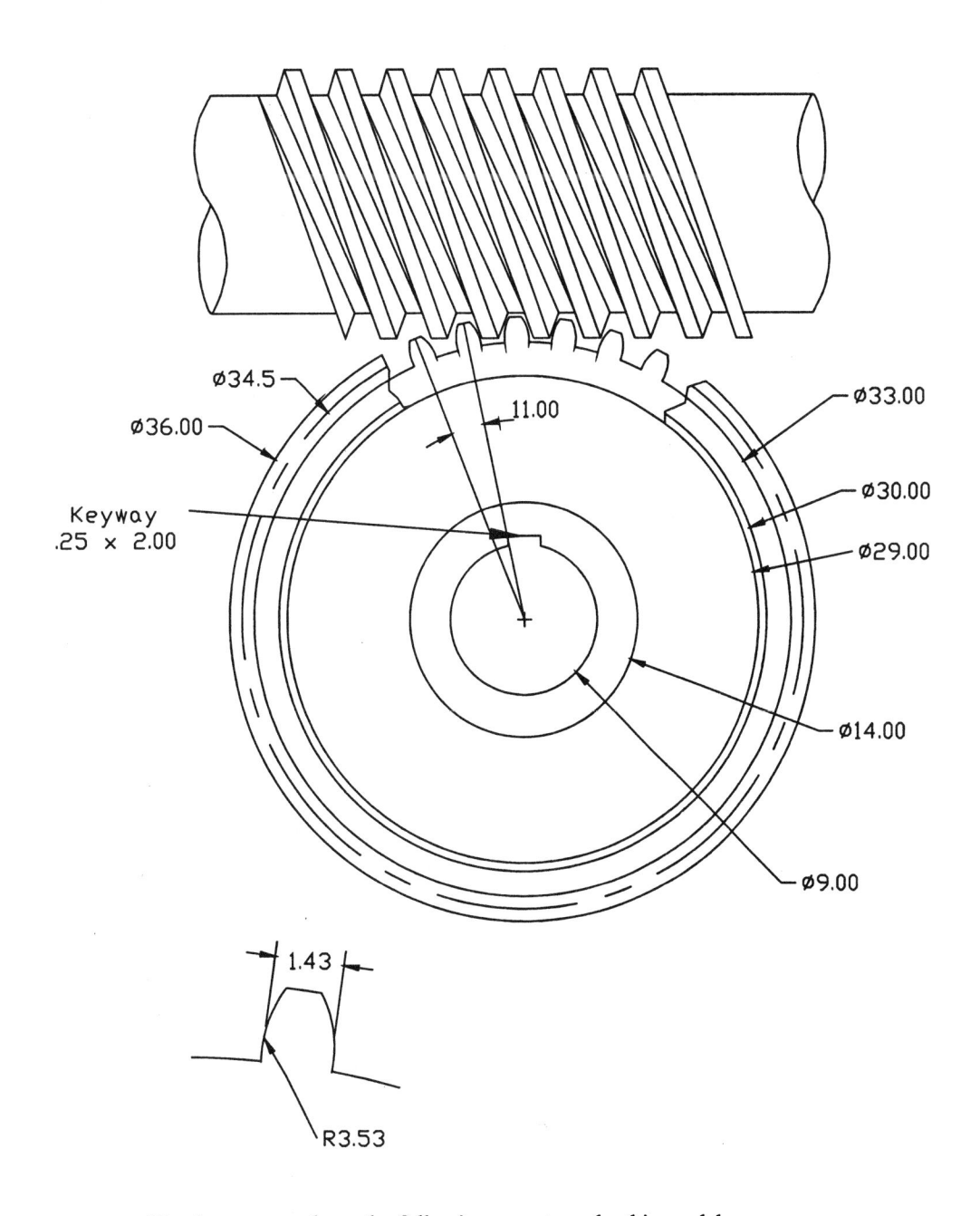

Ø34.5
Ø36.00
11.00
Ø33.00
Ø30.00
Ø29.00
Keyway
.25 x 2.00
Ø14.00
Ø9.00

1.43
R3.53

Use the commands on the following page to make this model.

Once you are finished, SAVE or END so you can add dimensions in a future exercise.

STRETCH, TRIM, EXTEND, OFFSET, and ARRAY

Hints on M5

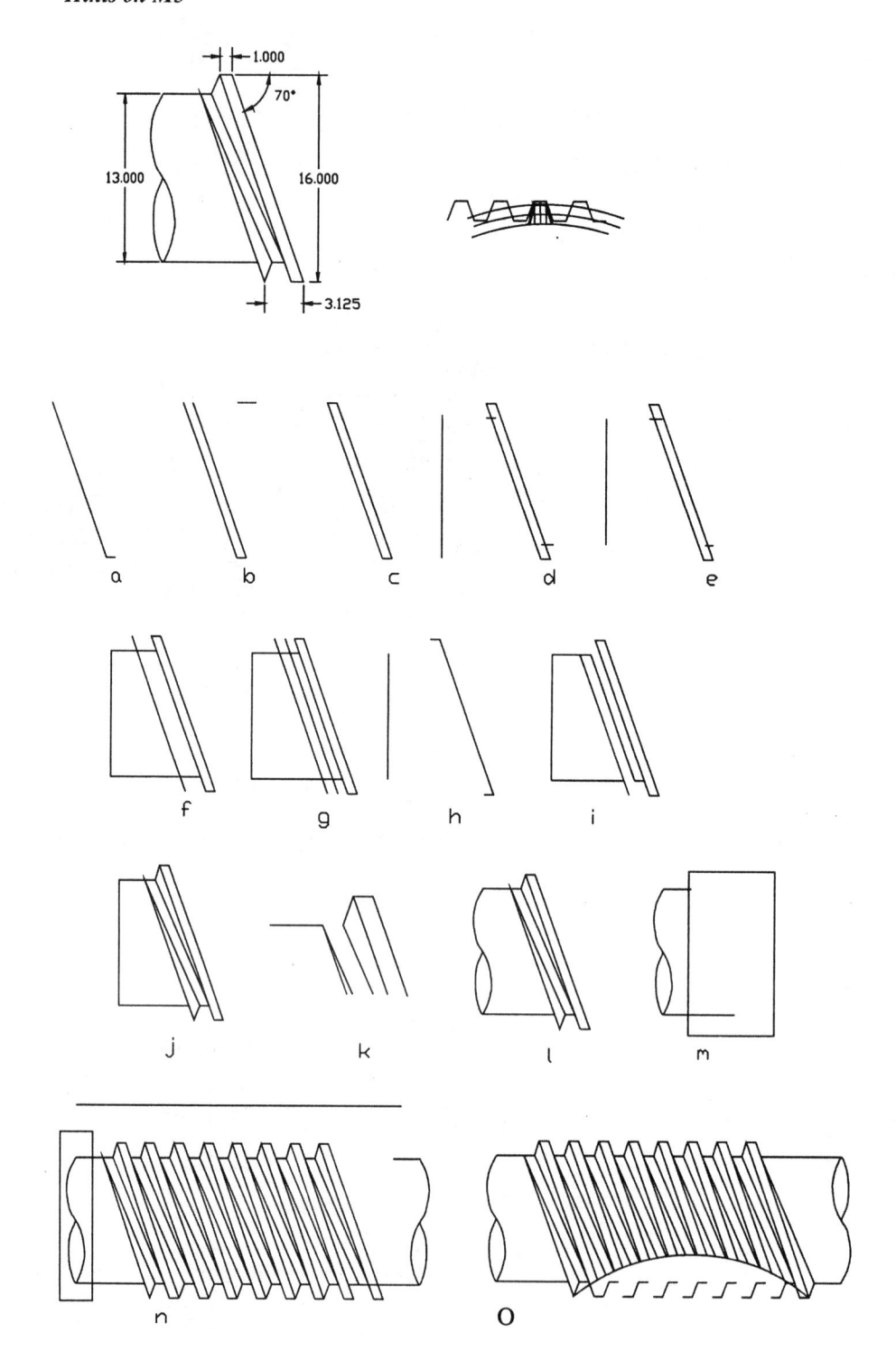

a. Draw the first line. b. OFFSET at the specified distance. c. Add the bottom line. d. OFFSET again to the top at 16 units, and draw in the line for the end. e. Use OFFSET to create the top and bottom, then TRIM. f. to i. OFFSET and TRIM. j. Draw the lines as shown. k. Draw in the small line section. l. and m. Use ARRAY to create a line of teeth. Then finish the part.

Challenger 5

This is an interesting part that you can do in 3D later.

The section and details are on the next page.

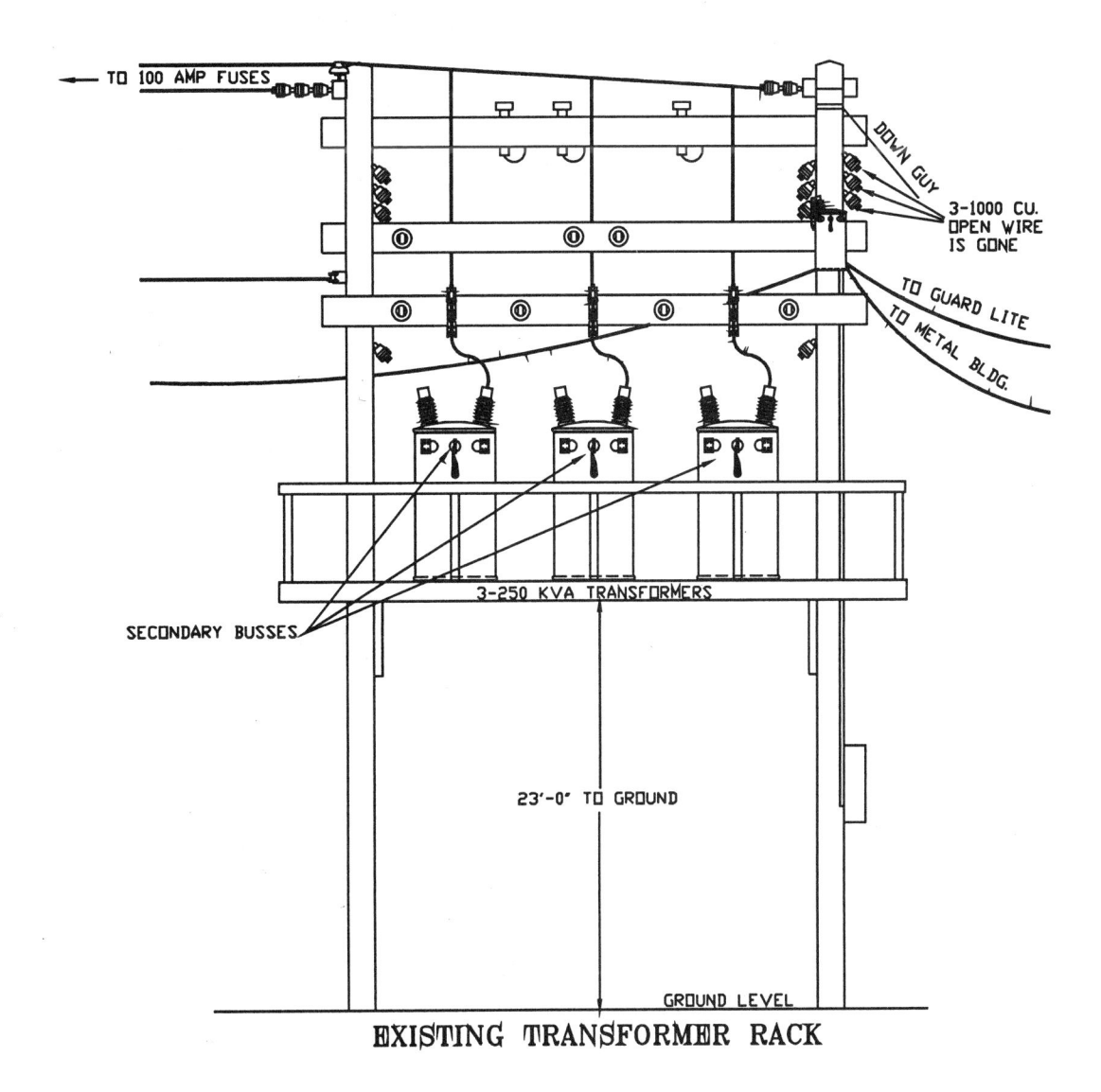

(drawing labels)

- TO 100 AMP FUSES
- DOWN GUY
- 3-1000 CU. OPEN WIRE IS GONE
- TO GUARD LITE
- TO METAL BLDG.
- SECONDARY BUSSES
- 3-250 KVA TRANSFORMERS
- 23'-0" TO GROUND
- GROUND LEVEL

EXISTING TRANSFORMER RACK

The individual parts are actually quite simple to draw. Once drawn, they can be copied and rotated to fit the illustration. See the next page for overall measurements.

STRETCH, TRIM, EXTEND, OFFSET, and ARRAY

Hints on Challenger 5

Use the overall dimensions above to create the individual items, then place them using MOVE, COPY, MIRROR, and ROTATE.

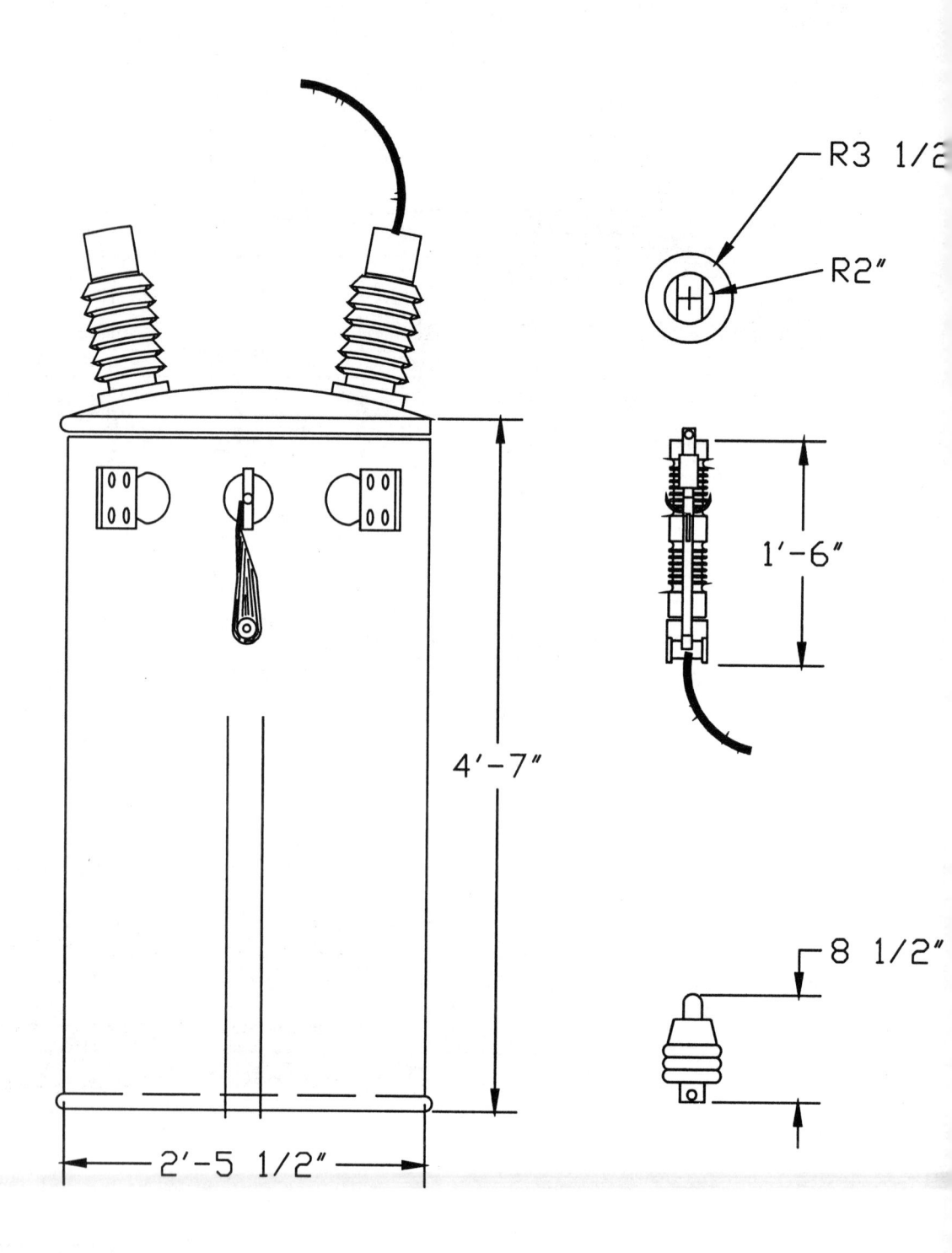

R3 1/2
R2"
1'-6"
4'-7"
8 1/2"
2'-5 1/2"

142 CHAPTER FIVE

6 Entity Properties: Layers, Colors, and Linetypes

Upon completion of this chapter, you should be able to:

1. Set up LAYERs and create geometry on them
2. Set colors to layers and use the COLOR command
3. Set LINETYPEs to layers and use the LINETYPE command
4. Change the properties of objects
5. List the properties of objects
6. Freeze/thaw and ON/OFF the LAYER
7. Lock and unlock layers

About LAYERs

The LAYER command allows you to control the drawing by means of visible entities. In a sense, it is like a set of transparencies or acetate overlays that contain different colors and linestyles which may be either visible or invisible. Layering is a powerful organizational tool and should be used on all drawings.

In AutoCAD, different colors and linetypes can be associated with different layers. To help complete the database, these layers can be either displayed or undisplayed, active or inactive, accessible or inaccessible. The number of layers you can use is unlimited.

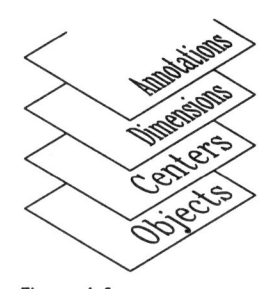

Figure 6-1

Using LAYERs

Both the Pull Down menu and the toolbar take you to the dialog box or you can type in DDLMODES or LAYER. On the left is the dialog box without details, on the right the details of the current layer are shown.

> **Toolbar** Pick the Layer button from the Object Properties toolbar.
>
> **Pull Down** Under the Format menu, choose Layer...

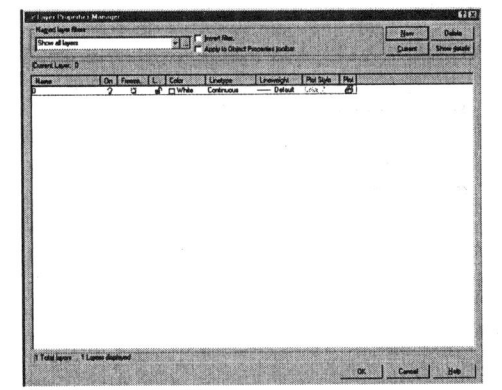

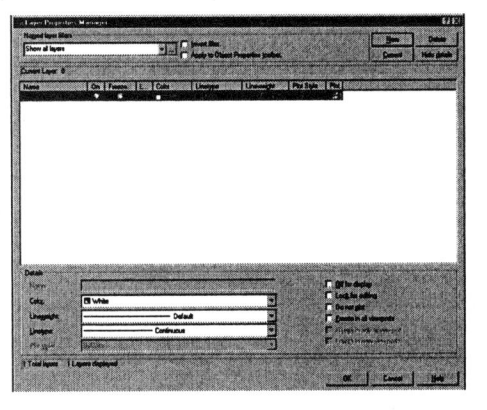

Entity Properties: Layers, Colors, and Linetypes **143**

The Layer Properties dialog box will help you to view the layers, change the colors, turn layers off, freeze and thaw them, and lock or unlock them.

Current	Sets the highlighted layer to current — the one you are working on.
Name	The name of the layer; no spaces or dots allowed.
Show all layers	Which layers are visible, some can be filtered out.
O... Or On	Sets the selected layers off or on, which makes the layer invisible or visible.
F... Freeze	Freezes selected layers, making them invisible and not regenerated, or thaws (unfreezes) them. This Freeze is for model space layers.
Active VP Freeze	This paper space oriented option shows freezing and thawing in selected layers in the current viewport.
New VP Freeze	This shows freeze or thaw in selected layers in a new viewport.
L... Or Lock	Locks selected layers, making them visible but not accessible, or unlocks them.
C... Or Color	The color set to that layer. All of the choices along the top so far have been toggle switches, on or off; this allows you to choose a color.
Linetype	The linetype of the layer.
New	Allows you to enter a new layer starting with the layer name.
Delete	Allows you to delete a layer if there are no objects in it.
OK	Exits from the layer dialog box while saving changes.
Show Details	Offers more information on the status of the highlighted layer.
Cancel	Cancels the layer changes or additions you have made.
Help	Provides help files on the layer functions.

Creating a New Layer

Pick the button for New on the top right side of the layer dialog box, and you will see a new layer appear in the list. Type in the name for the layer to override Layer1, the default name. A layer name can have up to 31 characters, but eight characters is all you need. There are only spaces for ten layers in the display box provided, but you may enter as many layers as you like and the screen will scroll down.

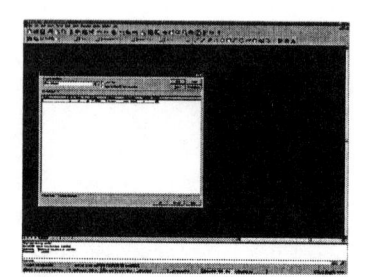

Figure 6-2

```
Command: (pick DDLMODES or layer button)
(Pick New)
(Type in layer name)
```

Once the name is entered the layer will be added to the layer list. The next time you enter the dialog box it will be listed alphabetically.

When typing layer names, keep the following rules in mind:

1. Use no spaces in the names. For example, to indicate the layer for a side bracket use **SIDE-BR**.
2. Use no slashes (/ or \) or periods (.), as the system will not accept them.
3. You may enter as many as 31 characters for a layer name, but you will only be able to read eight letters on the Status line. Try to keep the entry to that many characters.

Activating Layers for Changes

In order to change the name, state, color, linetype, or lock value of the layer, it must be identified or selected. Move the cursor to the layer name and pick it. The layer's line should be highlighted.

When selecting more than one layer for changes, use the regular Windows method for identifying multiple objects: use the Shift key to highlight all layers including the top one and the bottom one that you choose, and the Ctrl key to highlight multiple layers individually. If more than one layer is selected, or no layers are, nothing is highlighted. You must be careful of having more than one layer highlighted, as the Set color and Set linetype options will affect all highlighted objects.

Changing a Layer Name

If you should type in the name incorrectly, double click the name from the list. The area now activated will turn blue. Now move your cursor away from the line, and the name itself should be highlighted. Type in a new name or revise the current name. The new name will replace the old.

```
Command: (pick Layers)
(double click the layer from the list)
(type in a new name)
```

Figure 6-3

If you have created a layer that will never be used, delete it with Delete.

Making a LAYER Current

In order to draw on a layer you must make it *current*. Activate the layer that you would like to have current, and pick the word Current.

```
Command: (pick Layers)
(pick the layer from the list)
(pick Current)
```

The top line of the layer dialog box will show the current layer name. While working on a drawing or model, you can easily check to see what layer is current by reading the Object Properties toolbar. All of your work from this point on will be in the current layer.

It is a good idea to always have your object properties toolbar visible.

Changing Layer Color

First select the layer or layers that you would like to be in a particular color, then pick one of the boxes under the letter C.... This will invoke the Select Color dialog box. From the dialog box pick a color that you would like, or enter a color name or number in the Color text box at the bottom of the box.

```
Command: (pick Layers)
(pick the layer from the list)
(pick the box under C ... Or Color)
(pick a color)
(pick OK)
```

When you pick the color that you want, the color will be shown in the Color text box on the bottom of the screen. Anyone who has trouble seeing colors on the screen can also type in the number of the color in the text box. Instead of yellow, type 2.

All computers use the same number code for the first seven colors.

1 = red

2 = yellow

3 = green

4 = cyan

5 = blue

6 = magenta

7 = black or white

8 = Grey

Once you have chosen the desired color, select it by picking OK. You will then return to the Layer Properties menu.

Setting Color Independent of Layer

You can set a color using the COLOR command. This will override your Layer Color setting. To do this, type in the word **COLOR** at the command prompt, or pick the color button on the Object Properties toolbar, just to the right of the layer display.

> **Danger**
> If your objects are being entered in a color different than your layer setting, you have set a color in the COLOR command. Set the COLOR setting back to Bylayer.

Command: **COLOR**

All subsequent objects will be drawn in this color. Keep the COLOR command set to Bylayer and you should have no problem.

Loading LINETYPEs

In addition to colors, you can also have linetypes associated with each layer. All linetypes are not loaded with the default AutoCAD drawing, and thus may not be available under the listing of linetypes in the dialog box. To use different linetypes, they must be loaded into the file.

The command line equivalent is **LINETYPE**.

Toolbar From the Object Properties toolbar, pick the Linetype icon.

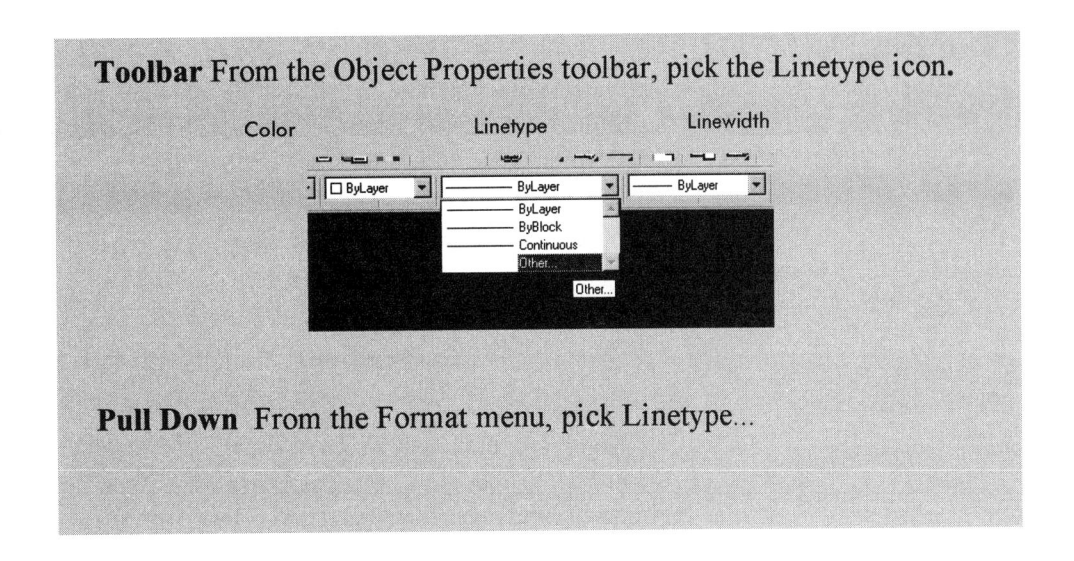

Pull Down From the Format menu, pick Linetype...

```
Command: LINETYPE
```

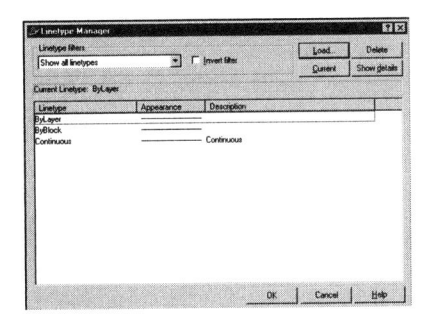

Figure 6-4

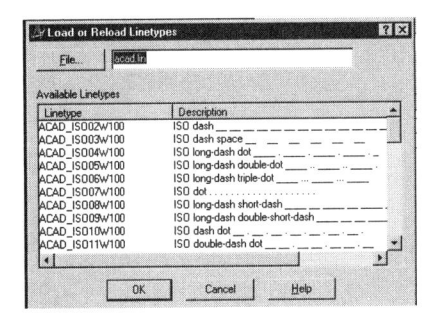

Figure 6-5

In order to add the hidden linetype on the layer dialog box, load the linetypes through the dialog box with Load.

Pick Load, choose the linetypes that you require either with the help of Shift or Control, then choose OK. Shift will add all linetypes from the first linetype chosen to the last linetype chosen, Control (Ctrl) will allow individual picks.

If you want all of the linetypes always loaded, open the ACAD.DWG file, load the linetypes, then SAVE the file as ACAD.DWG. This will update the AutoCAD prototype file and make the linetypes always available.

Once the linetype is loaded, you can go back to the layer control dialog box, by picking the Layer button from along the top of the screen, and choose the linetype in the same way you chose your color.

All future geometry added to this layer will use this linetype. If the linetype is the hidden type, all entities in that layer will be in hidden lines, unless they are overridden by the LINE-TYPE command. **Until you are sure of what you are doing, both the Color setting and the Linetype setting should be Bylayer.**

Changing LTSCALE

Depending on the size of the object, the hidden lines may not show up as hidden. If this is the case, either the objects that you thought were on that layer are not, or the scale of the drawing is too large or too small for the linetype to show. You will need to change the linetype scale relative to the current drawing.

The command line equivalent is **LTSCALE**.

```
Command:LTSCALE
Enter new linetype scale factor<1.00>:12
```

To determine the LTSCALE of the screen, take the furthest point in X and divide by 12. If you have defined the screen but have not as yet entered any points or geometry, take the furthest limit in positive X and divide by 12. If the limits are 200,160, the LTSCALE will be 200/12 or approximately 14. If the limits are 3, LTSCALE will be 3/12 or .25.

LTSCALE is often linked to the Hatch scale and text scale.

Using LTSCALE will cause your file to regenerate.

The Match Properties Command

The Match Properties command will take the linetype, color and linetype scale of a selected object and apply those properties to any other objects that you choose.

> **Toolbar** From the Standard Toolbar, pick the Match Properties button.

The command line equivalent is MATCHPROP or PAINTER

```
Command:-MATCHPROP
Select source object: (pick 1)
Current active settings = Color Layer Ltype Ltscale Lineweight
   Thickness Plotstyle Text Dim Hatch
Select destination object(s) or [Settings]: (pick 2)
```

In figure 6-6, the first or source object is in a hidden line and the second object is in a continuous line. After the command, the second object will also be in a hidden line.

All of the properties listed — Color, Layer etc — will update in the second object as well. This command can radically change your database, so be careful when you use it, particularly in layer control.

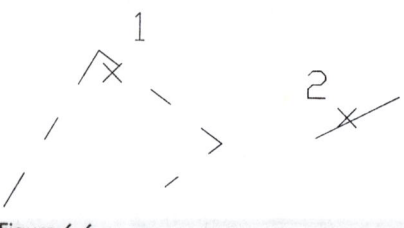

Figure 6-6

What Can Go Wrong with LAYER, COLOR, and LINETYPE

When working with LINETYPE and COLOR, keep in mind that both can be changed independent of LAYER. This means that if COLOR, for example, is set to Red, all the geometry will show up as red even if the current layer is blue. Similarly, if the LINETYPE is set to Hidden, all of the lines will be hidden lines, even if the current layer asks for center lines. When picking layer names for changing color, linetype, freezing, etc., make sure that *only* the layers you want to change are highlighted in blue. You must pick the layer again to deselect it. LINETYPE and COLOR should be set to Bylayer.

CHPROP and CHANGE with LAYERs

To change the properties of entities individually — the color, linetype, or layer — use CHPROP (CHange PROPerties), or the DDCHPROP dialog box.

Danger
If you set a color or LINETYPE under the COLOR or LINETYPE commands, they will override your layer setting.

Toolbar There is no longer a button for this command.

The command line equivalent is **CHPROP**.

The dialog box will help you to change the properties of the selected object. Under General are all of the properties listed in the CHPROP command. Under Geometry are all of the points, angles, radii, etc. associated with the object.

Note:
While the dialog boxes can show a list of all the properties of the objects, using the command string to change properties is usually far quicker.

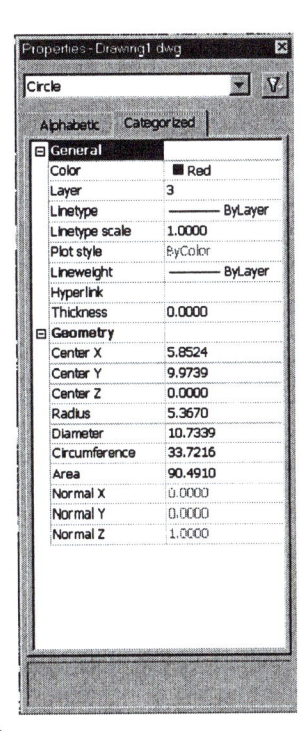

Figure 6-7

Entity Properties: Layers, Colors, and Linetypes **149**

With the dialog box you are prompted to pick the objects you would like modified; then you can choose Layer, Color, Linetype, Thickness, etc. and type in the new value. If you use the command line, here is the sequence.

```
Command:CHPROP
Select objects:(pick an object)
Select objects:↵
Enter property to change
   [Color/LAyer/LType/LtScale/Thickness]:C
Enter new color <bylayer>:Red
Enter property to change
   [Color/LAyer/LType/LtScale/Thickness]:LT
Enter new linetype <hidden>:Center
Enter property to change
   [Color/LAyer/LType/LtScale/Thickness]:↵
```

If your objects are not showing up in the color or linetype that you expected, change them all back to BYLAYER.

```
Command:CHPROP
Select objects:ALL
Select objects:↵
Enter property to change
   [Color/LAyer/LType/LtScale/Thickness]:C
Enter new color <varies>:BYLAYER
Enter property to change
   [Color/LAyer/LType/LtScale/Thickness]:LT
Enter new linetype <varies>:BYLAYER
Enter property to change
   [Color/LAyer/LType/LtScale/Thickness]:↵
```

If everything changes to the correct color and linetype, check to see that COLOR and LINETYPE on the object properties toolbar are set to Bylayer as well.

If objects still do not show the color or linetype expected, they are probably in the wrong layer. Again, use CHPROP.

```
Command:CHPROP
Select objects: (pick 1, 2) (pick the objects to change)
Select objects:↵
Change what property(Color/LAyer/LType/LtScale/Thickness)?:LA
New layer <varies>:HIDDENLINES (for example)
Change what property(Color/LAyer/LType/LtScale/Thickness)?:↵
```

The CHANGE command can also be used to change the properties of objects.

If things are still not as you want them, try REGEN. If this does not work, there is something wrong with the entity itself. Use the properties dialog box (above) to show you the properties and position of the object or objects not reacting to the above commands. Often you will find the objects are not on the layer that you thought they were.

Changing the State of the Layers

Once the layers are loaded, and objects have been placed in them, you can have them displayed or not displayed, displayed but not editable, and completely turned off. In Windows, you can access the state of the layers either through the dialog box or through the icons.

On/Off

Turning off a layer will make that specific layer invisible. To turn it off, pick the lightbulb under On. If the lightbulb is yellow, it is on. If it is dark, then the layer will be off.

Freeze/Thaw

Freezing a layer will tell AutoCAD to ignore any entities on the specified layers when regenerating the drawing, as well as making the layer invisible. When the drawing gets quite large, this option is used to save time in regenerating by removing items that will not be viewed. It is usually better to use Freeze than Off.

Frozen layers must be Thawed before they can be viewed or plotted.

To Freeze and Thaw, use the Layer dialog box. The state of the layer will be reflected by an F if it is frozen, and a dot (.) if it is not.

Lock/Unlock

This facility will help you to place objects relative to other objects without taking the chance of editing those objects. Locking prevents editing on visible objects.

To lock the layers choose Lock from the dialog box. This may be shown as an L on the State column.

Plotting and paper space status of layers will be dealt with in Chapter 11 when viewports are introduced.

The LAYER Command

In a perfect world, you would probably always use the dialog box. For many reasons, however, sometimes dialog boxes may not work. This could be a hardware problem, which is usually associated with the graphics card, or it could be because certain functions are disabled. You may also find it faster to key in the single letters to change the layer. In any case, if you cannot use the dialog box, use the LAYER command (type -**LAYER**).

```
Command:-LAYER
[?/Make/Set/New/On/OFF/Color/Ltype/LWeight/Plot/Freeze/Thaw/
  LOck/Unlock]:N
Enter name list for new layer(s):ELECTRIC
[?/Make/Set/New/On/OFF/Color/Ltype/LWeight/Plot/Freeze/Thaw/
  LOck/Unlock]:C
Enter color name or number (1-255):1
Enter name list of layer(s) for color 1(red)<0>:ELECTRIC
[?/Make/Set/New/On/OFF/Color/Ltype/LWeight/Plot/Freeze/Thaw/
  LOck/Unlock]:⏎
```

None of the LAYER options take effect until you have exited the command. Use ⏎ to exit the command. If you want to look at the list of layers, use the ? option. AutoCAD then prompts for the layers you want listed. The wildcard * can be used to list all of the layers, or to search for specific layers if you have more than one screen's worth of layers.

Layer Filtering

Sometimes you may want only certain layers to be listed in the Layer Control dialog box. The Filter option allows you to limit which layers are listed. You can filter on the basis of:

- Layer names, colors, and linetypes
- Whether the layers are on or off
- Whether they are frozen or thawed
- Whether they are locked or unlocked
- Whether they have plot or don't plot status
- Whether they contain objects or not
- Whether they are part of externally referenced (xref) drawings

To Filter a Layer

Open the Layer Control dialog box.

In the Layer Properties Manager under the Named Layer Filters area, choose the [...] button.

In the Named Layer Filters dialog box, select or enter layer property settings.

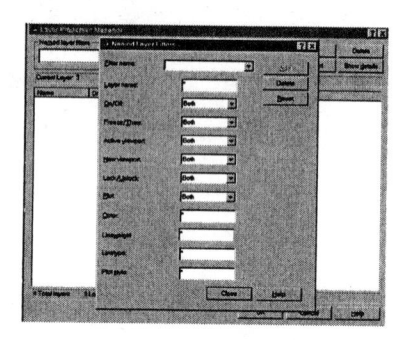

Figure 6-9

Layer Management

The default layer is 0. If you enter any dimensions, you will also create a layer called Defpoints. Neither of these layers is renamable. The Defpoints layer does not plot.

While creating a model in AutoCAD, keep in mind that other people may want to work with your file at some point. Layers should therefore be named in a logical, straightforward manner. Also, keep your LINETYPE and COLOR command set to Bylayer.

Many industries have developed layering standards so that there is no question about where objects will be located. If you are starting work with a company, make sure that you know what the layering standards for the company are, and find out whether there are any standards outside of the company that you should be aware of.

If you do not use the layer names suggested in the exercises, at least make sure your names are logical.

Freezing layers when you are not using them will save a great deal of time with larger models. Until they are regenerated, layers that have been frozen will not display when they are thawed.

Prelab 6 Layers, Colors, and Linetypes

In this example we will make an adjustable bearing with hidden lines and center lines.

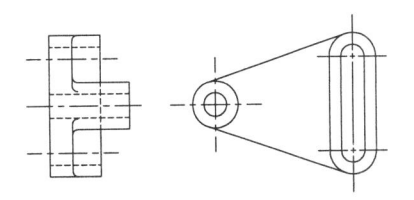

Step 1   First set up your layers

> **Toolbar** Choose the Layer button: 
>
> **Pull Down** Choose Format, then Layer.

In the Layer Name text box enter the following:

LINES
HIDDEN
CENTER
DASHED

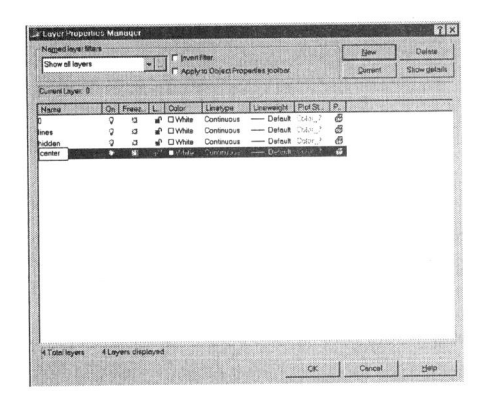

Step 2   Once the names are loaded, change the color of each layer by picking the layer name and then picking the Set color button. An overlay menu will offer you a selection of colors. Choose a color for that layer.

- **LINES**   White
- **HIDDEN**   Yellow
- **CENTER**   Red

Step 3   Now load and set the linetypes. Press OK on the layer menu, then:

> **Toolbar** Pick the Linetype button from the Object Properties toolbar: 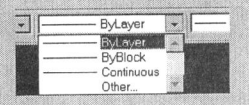
>
> **Pull Down** From the Format menu, pick Linetype.

Step 4   Now that the linetypes have been loaded, return to the Layer pull-down menu and load the linetypes onto the appropriate layer.

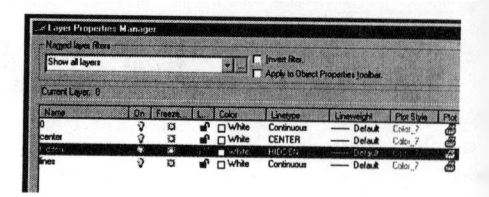

Toolbar Choose the Layer button:

Pull Down Choose Format, then Layer.

Activate the HIDDEN layer, press LINETYPE, then choose the hidden linetype from the list. Press OK. Deactivate the hidden layer by picking it again, then activate the Center layer and set the center linetype to that layer. Use OK to exit from the Set Linetype dialog box, then OK again to exit from the Layer Control dialog box.

Step 5   Now that the layers are ready, use the same menu to make the LINEs layer current.

Your screen should look like this:

Step 6   Now with the LINEs layer current, draw in the front view of the adjustable bearing as shown. Do not draw in the dimensions.

The limits and grid are not important in this drawing, but a snap of .25 would help to place the objects quickly. If you want the origin or 0,0 to be the center of the left circle, use UCS to place the origin about 2 inches up and 2 inches over from the bottom of the screen.

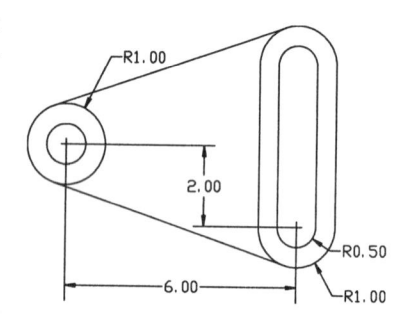

Use LINE and CIRCLE with OSNAPs to create the objects.

Step 7   Now return to the pull-down menu and make the CENTER layer current.

Draw in the lines as shown. They should be a different color as well as a different linetype.

Try changing the LTSCALE to see if there is any noticeable difference in the center lines.

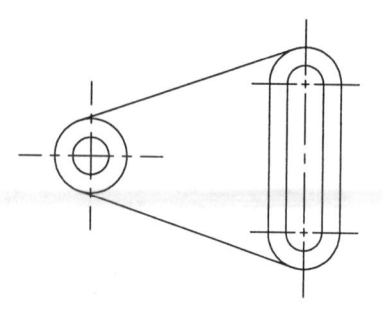

```
Command:LTSCALE
New scale factor<1.00>:1.5
```

Step 8 Return to the pull-down menu and make the LINEs layer current to draw in the side view as shown. You will need to use PAN to move the front view over. You can use LIMITS and pick the bottom left and upper right corners.

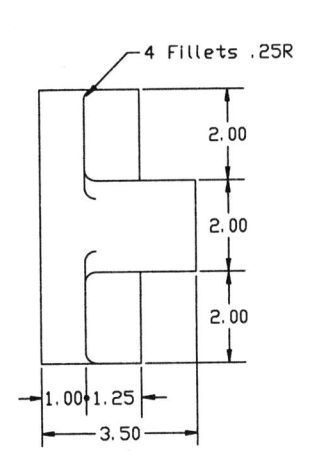

Step 9 Now return to your pull-down menu and make the HIDDEN layer current to place the hidden lines as shown. They should be a different color as well as a different linetype.

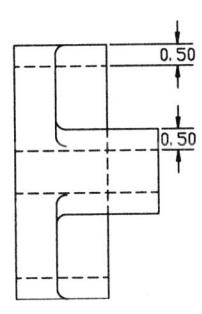

Step 10 Now make the CENTER layer current and add the center lines as shown. Again, a SNAP would be of use in this view. If the SNAP is too big, make it smaller.

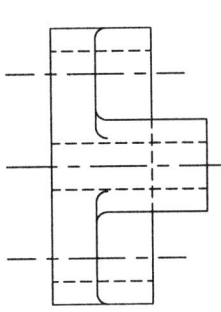

Step 11 Return to the layer pull-down menu and change the colors of the layers to see if you can make it look nicer. If the colors remain the same as you change the layer color, it is because the current color of an object is overriding the layer color. Set color back to Bylayer, then use CHPROP to change all of the objects to be colored Bylayer.

Step 12 We are now going to play with the Lock/Unlock facility to see how it works. It may be time to save the file — just in case.

```
Command: SAVE
(enter a name in the dialog box)
```

On the 'DDLMODE, select the layers for the hidden lines and the center lines, then pick Lock. In Windows, pick the Lock icon and then pick the center and hidden layers.

Entity Properties: Layers, Colors, and Linetypes

Once the layers are locked, you will be able to see them, but you will no longer be able to edit them. Make sure the LINEs layer is current before you start.

Name	On	Freeze..	L...	Color	Linetype
0	♀	✲	🔓	☐ White	Continuous
center	♀	✲	🔒	■ Red	CENTER
hidden	♀	✲	🔒	☐ Yellow	HIDDEN
lines	♀	✲	🔓	☐ White	Continuous

Current Layer: lines

Step 13 Now back in the drawing or model, from the Modify menu pick Properties and change the color of the LINEs layer to blue.

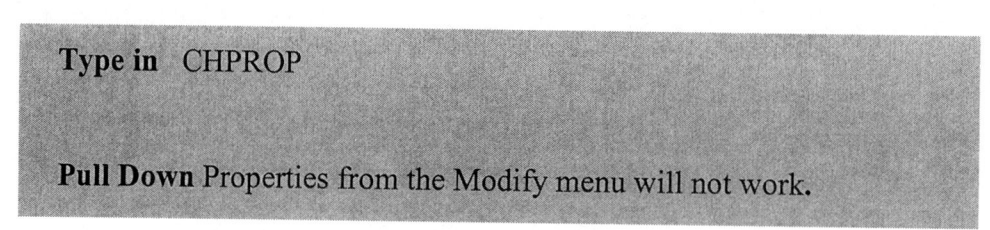

> **Type in** CHPROP
>
> **Pull Down** Properties from the Modify menu will not work.

Pick all of the objects on screen with either a window or a crossing. Type in the following.

```
Command:CHPROP
Select objects:ALL
56 objects on locked layers
Select objects: ⏎
Enter property to change
   [Color/LAyer/LType/ltScale/Thickness]:C
Enter new color <varies>:blue
Enter property to change
   [Color/LAyer/LType/LtScale/Thickness]:⏎
```

Notice that only the objects on the LINEs layer were changed, because the other layers were locked.

Step 14 Try turning Off and On, and Freezing and Thawing, the layers. The data for the layers is still on file, but the information is not displayed.

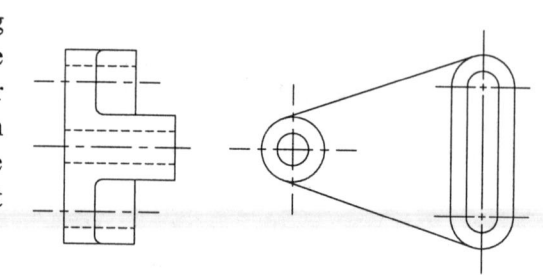

156 CHAPTER SIX

Command and Function Summary

CHANGE allows the user to change various aspects of the chosen objects.

CHPROP allows the user to change the properties of objects.

COLOR allows the user to set a new current color. This overrides the layer color.

LINETYPE allows the user to set a current linetype.

LA or LAYER allows the user to set the current layer.

MATCH PROPERTIES allows the user to apply the properties of an object to other objects.

Practice Exercise 6

While drawing in these mechanical parts, have different layers for the center lines and for the hidden lines.

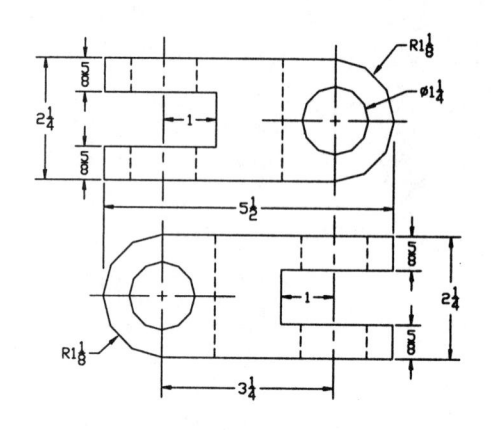

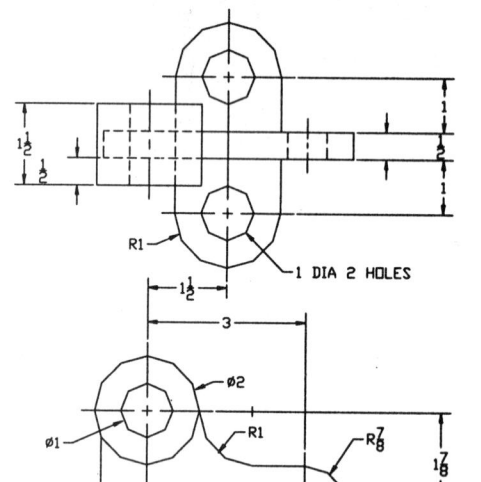

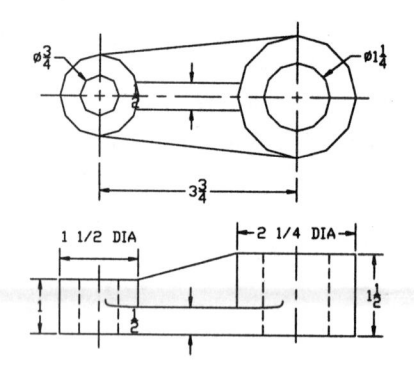

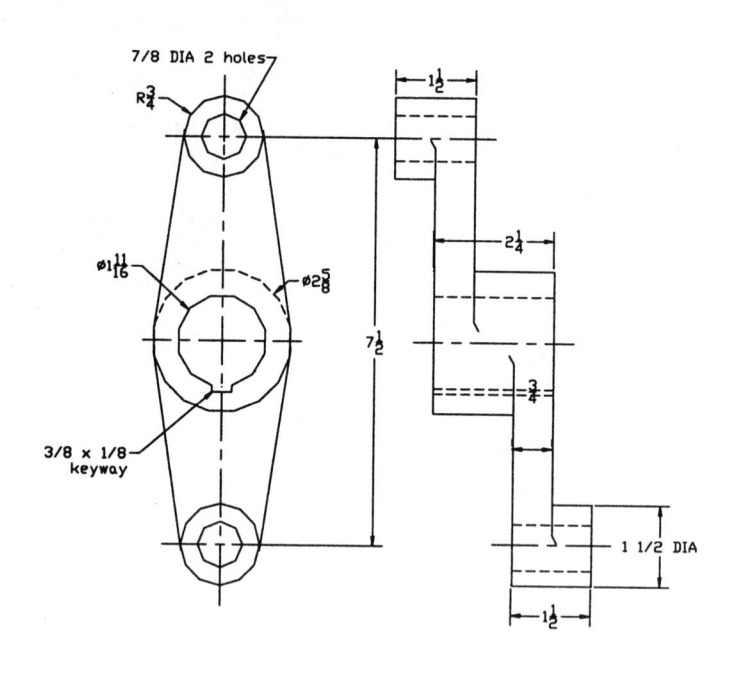

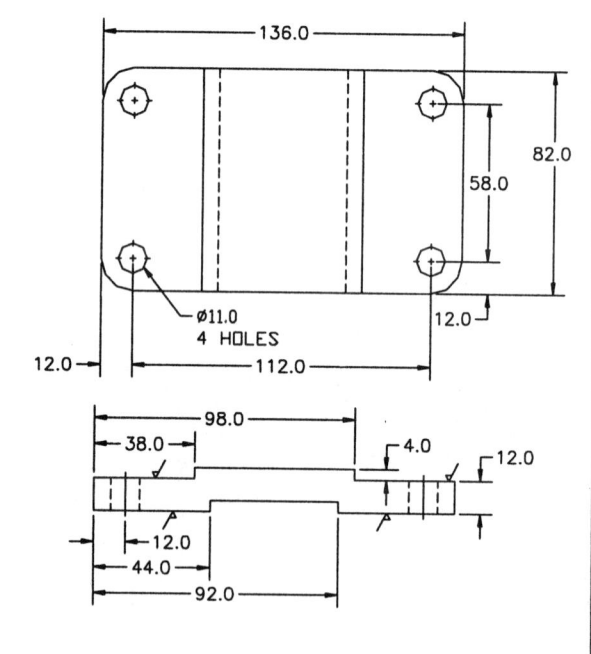

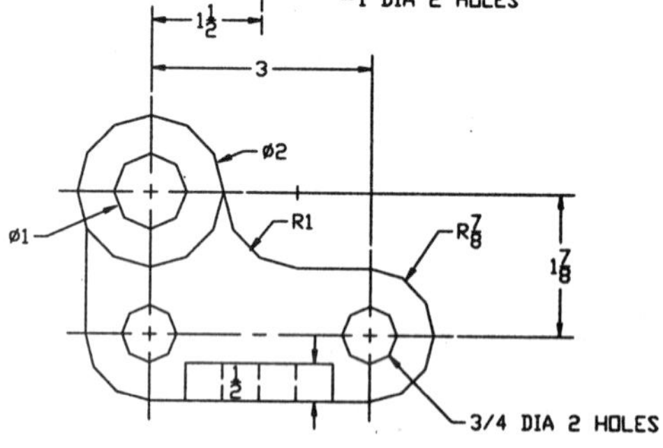

Exercise A6

Open FIRSTFL. Create new layers for Doors, Windows, Foundation, and Elevation. Use CHPROP to place the existing windows in the Windows layer. Use LINETYPE to load the linetype Hidden. In the LAYER pull-down menu, make the FOUNDATION layer current and draw in a foundation at 16″ around the first floor plan as shown in previous exercises. Change the LTSCALE to 48 to make the hidden lines visible.

Freeze the Foundation layer and make the Elevation layer current. Using the floor plans, draw in at least one elevation.

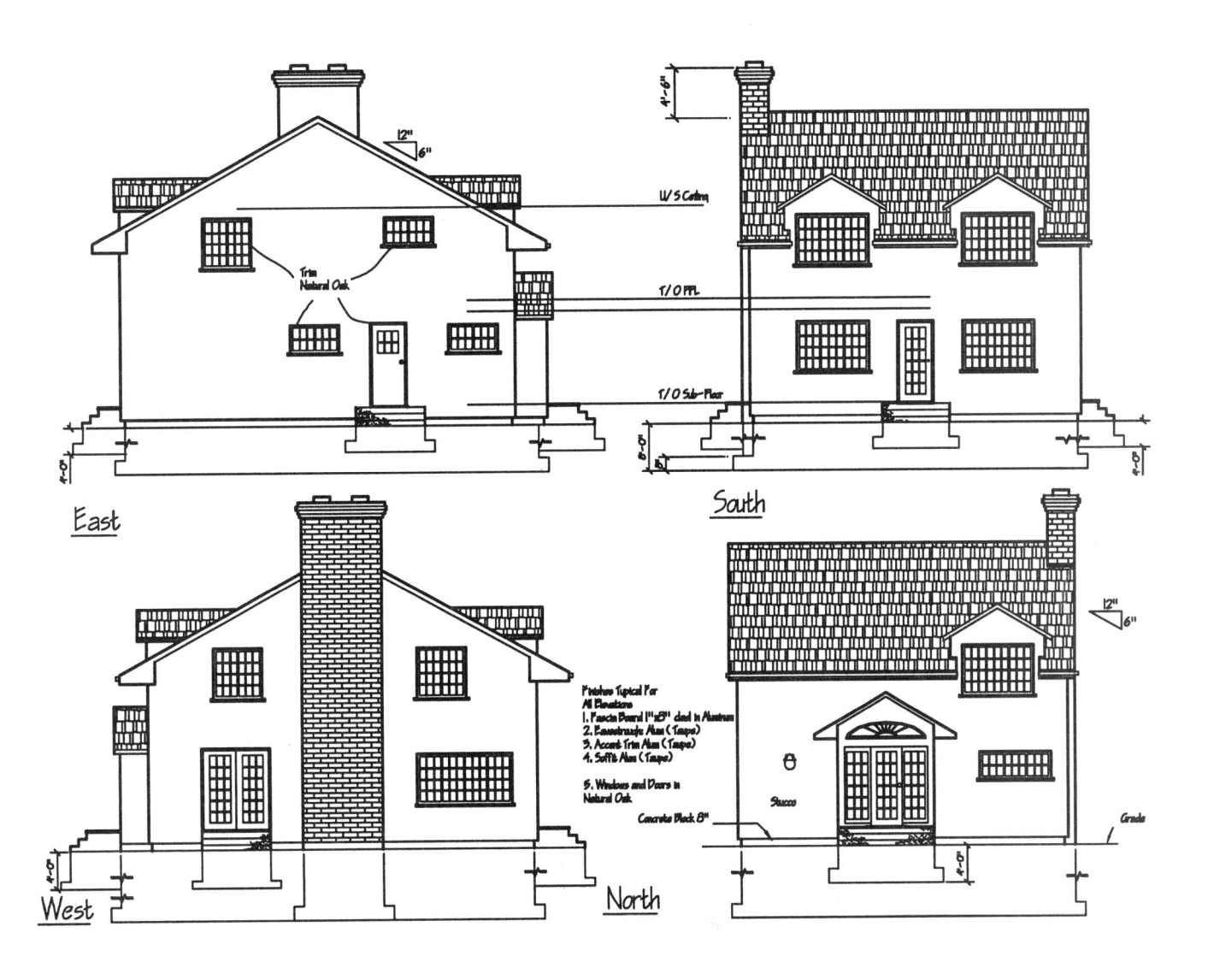

Exercise C6

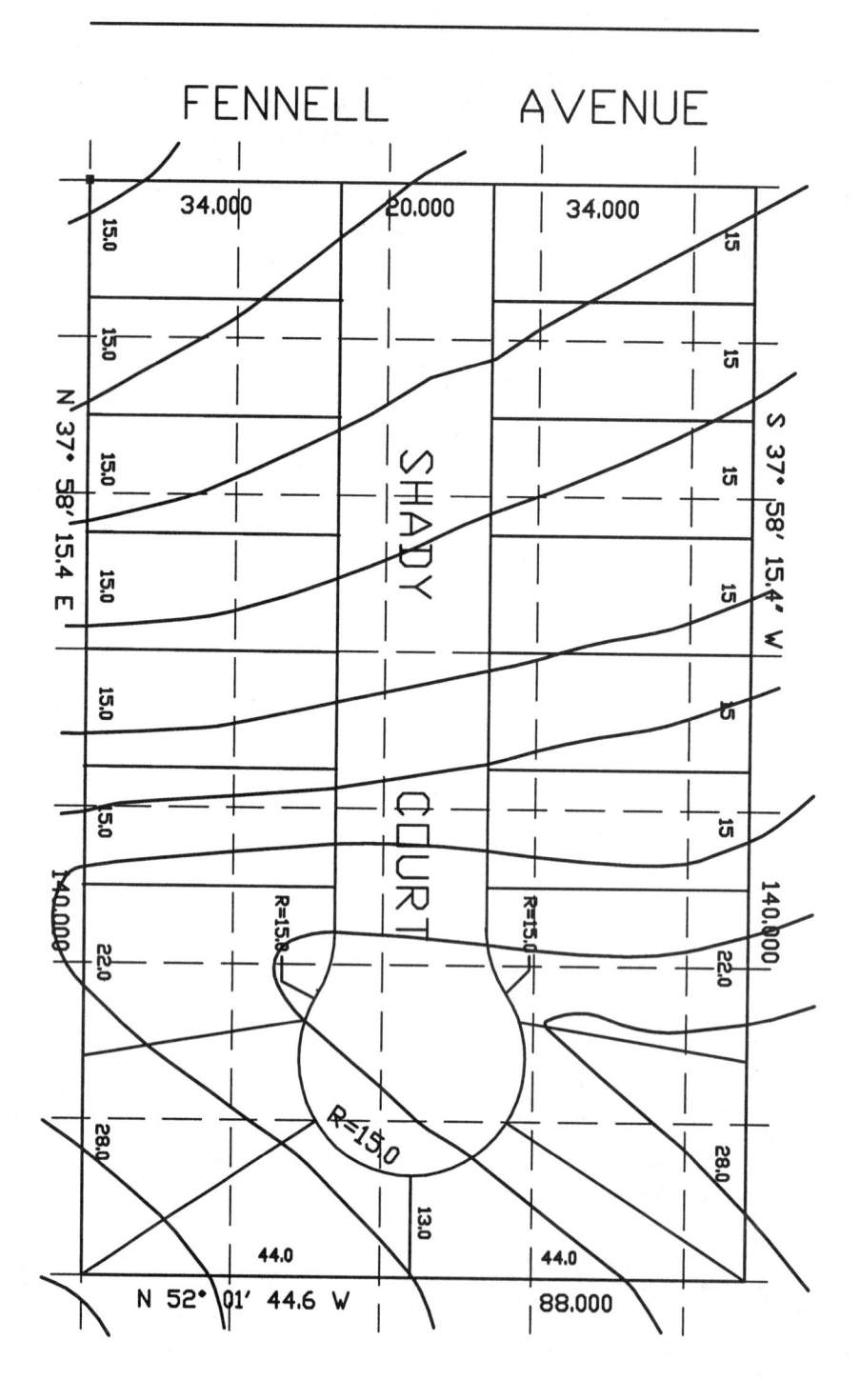

Hints on C6

First create the geometry for this court. Change the units to surveying units.

Use OFFSET as much as possible. Do not forget the OSNAP commands.

Now you can add the grid to the overall design. Add the hidden linetype under the LINETYPE command, then create a new layer for the grid. Use OFFSET to create the grid.

To generate the contours, use PLINE with PEDIT and the Spline function. You can also experiment with the OFFSET command on a spline in this case. Once the spline is in, it can be trimmed to the proper size.

Going Further

Put each lot on a separate layer for use in a GIS package later.

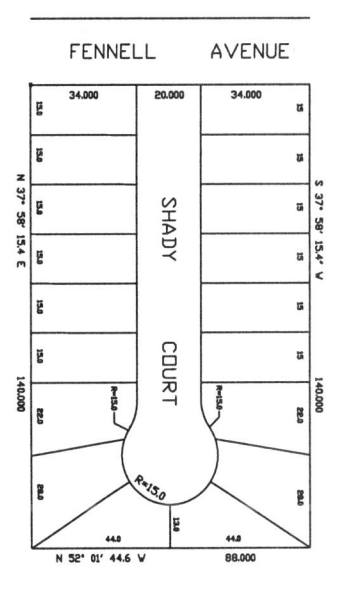

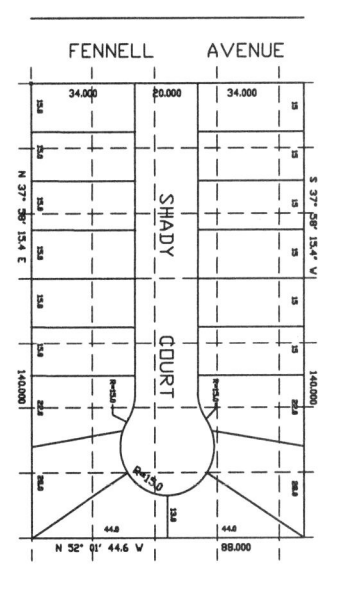

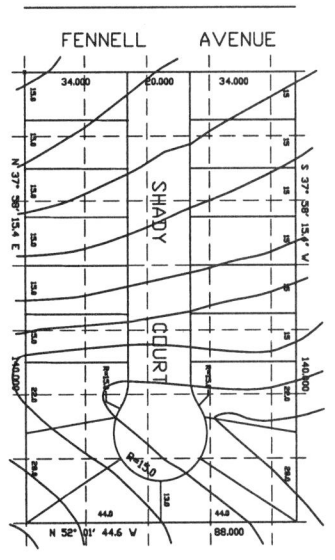

Entity Properties: Layers, Colors, and Linetypes   **161**

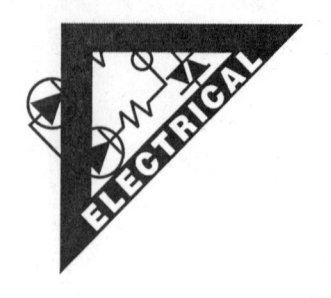

Exercise E6

This circuit diagram is created with LINE, CIRCLE, and PLINE. The text is placed by simply using DTEXT.

Create a new layer for the conductors. Put each conductor path on a different layer. Finally, enter the text.

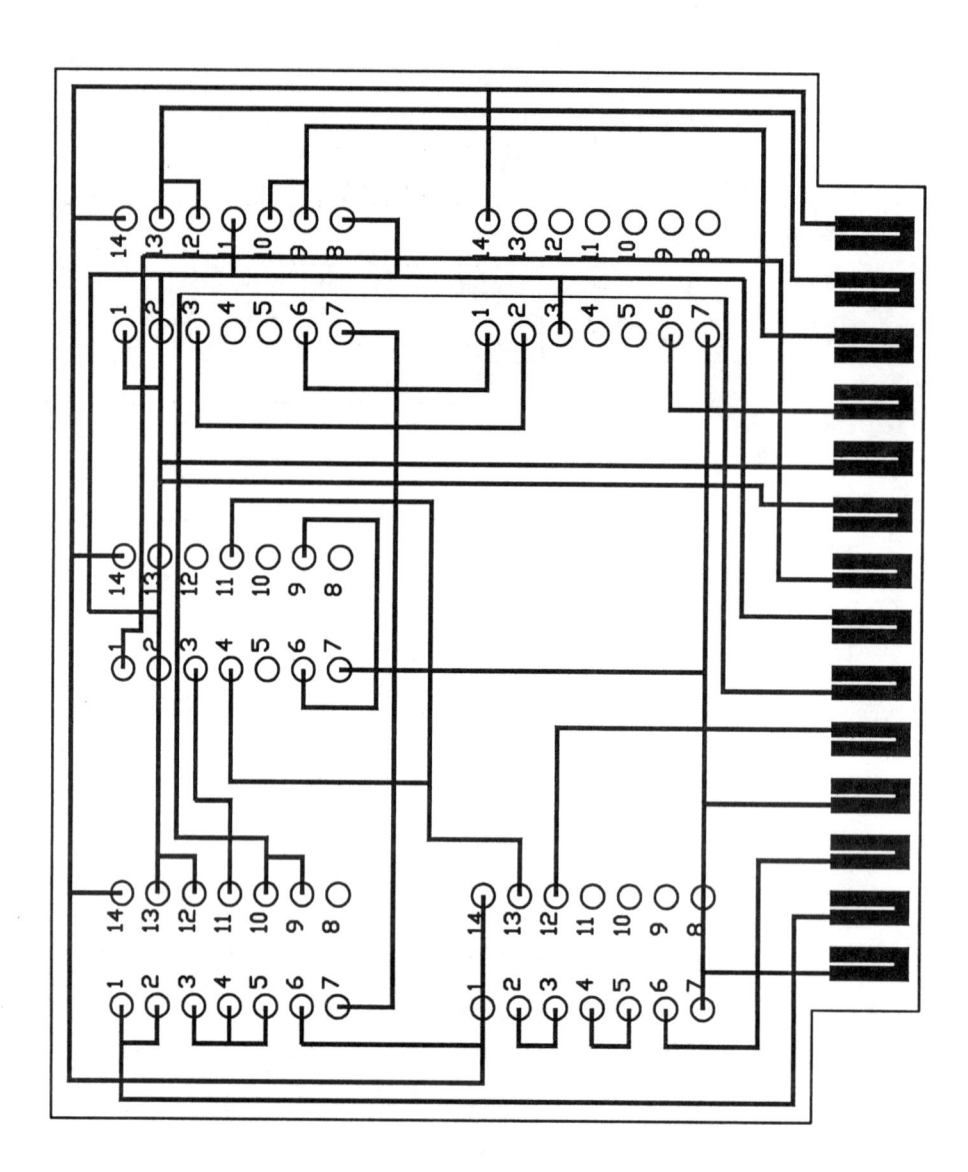

Hints on E6

To get the numbers in exactly as you want them, create one number, then use COPY with Multiple and SNAP to place the character in even rows. Use the CHANGE or DDEDIT commands to change the actual number once it has been placed.

Exercise M6

LIMITS 12,9
GRID .5
SNAP Various

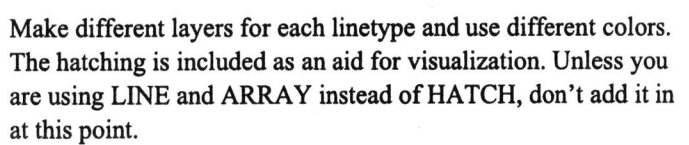

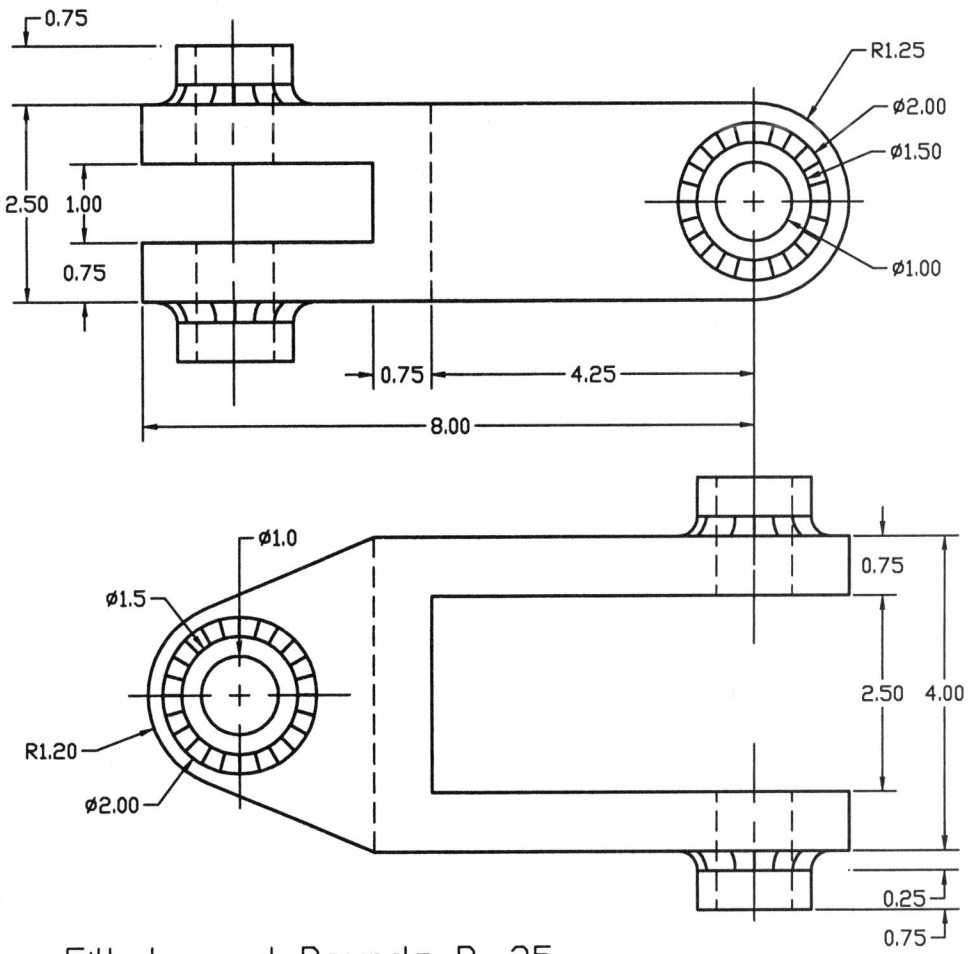

Make different layers for each linetype and use different colors. The hatching is included as an aid for visualization. Unless you are using LINE and ARRAY instead of HATCH, don't add it in at this point.

Fillets and Rounds R .25

Suggested Layer Schedule

Name	Color	Linetype
0	White	Continuous
One	Red	Continuous
Center	Blue	Center
Hidden	12	Hidden

Challenger 6

Use the editing commands to create the brickwork and block work on this gothic window. To create the hatch, freeze the layer that contains the brickwork and have just the boundary showing.

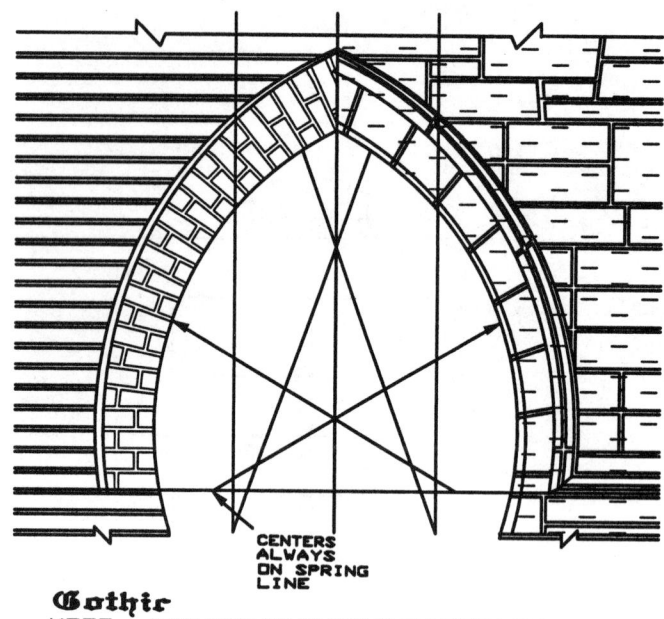

Gothic

CENTERS ALWAYS ON SPRING LINE

NOTE : STONE JOINTS MAY BE HANDLED IN A VARIETY OF WAYS
THIS IS ONE ILLUSTRATION

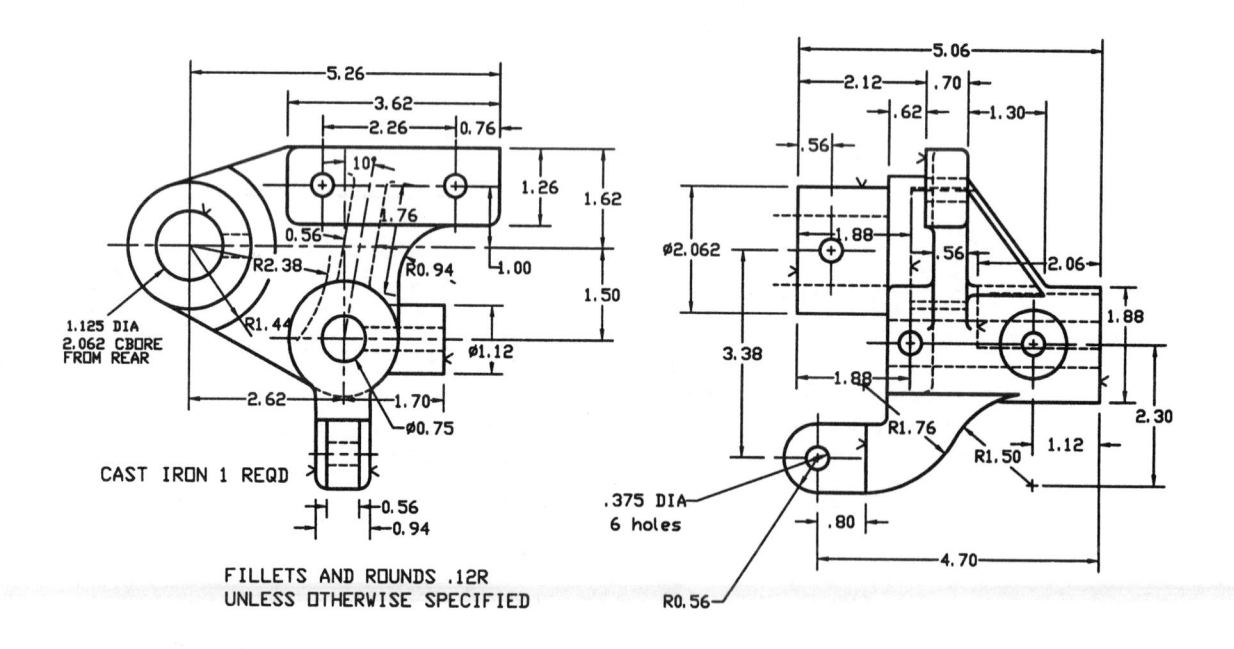

CAST IRON 1 REQD

FILLETS AND ROUNDS .12R
UNLESS OTHERWISE SPECIFIED

.375 DIA
6 holes

7 Dimensioning

Upon completion of this chapter, you should be able to:

1. Set up a dimensioning style, using the DDIM dialog box
2. Add vertical, horizontal, and aligned dimensions
3. Add diameter and radius dimensions
4. Add baseline and continuous dimensions
5. Use DIMSTYLE, UPDate, and OVERRIDE to alter the dimensions

About Dimensioning

While the objects are being created, the size of the object is being programmed with the part's geometry. Lines, circles, arcs, etc. should be created perfectly every time. If you get into the habit of creating data in a lazy or slapdash manner, it will catch up with you later when dimensioning the drawing.

Dimensioning shows the measurements, the locations, and the angles of objects. The dimensioning commands are designed to extract the sizes that are already programmed with the part, and display them in accepted formats. Every discipline has a different set of drawing protocols. The dimensioning variables and dimension styles are used to set the dimensions to the required parameters.

AutoCAD offers a wide variety of ways to produce linear, baseline, radial, diameter, and angular dimensions. This illustration shows some of the basic dimension types.

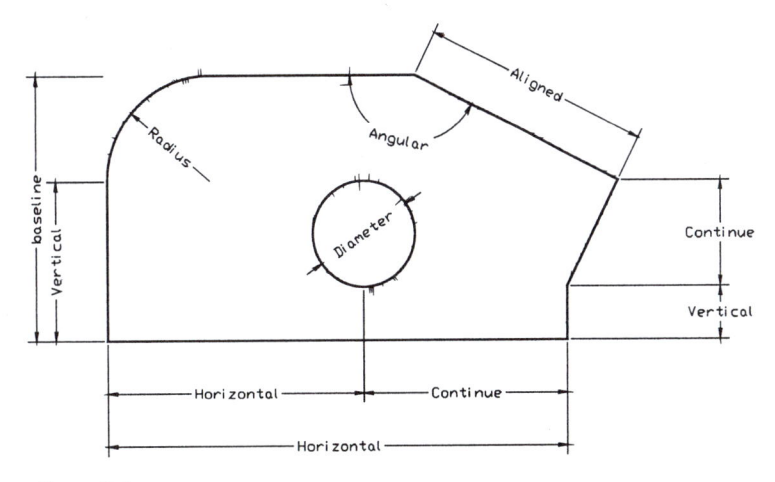

Figure 7-1

Dimensioning Components

Every dimension has several components. The ***dimension text*** states how big the object is. The ***dimension line*** holds the dimension text. The ***extension line*** extends from the object to the dimension line. The extension line is ***offset*** by .06 or 1/16 of an inch from the part itself and should extend .12 or 1/8 inch past the dimension line.

This illustration shows the components of a dimension.

The point at which you start your dimension is the reference point or ***definition point***. AutoCAD automatically puts a gap between this point and the start of the extension line. AutoCAD also creates a layer for this point called *defpoints* that does not plot.

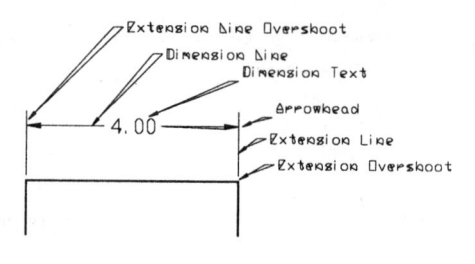

Figure 7-2

Dimension Mode

Prior to Release 14, you had to enter the dimension mode in order to create dimensions. This is no longer necessary. While you can use the command DIM to access the DIM mode commands, including UPDate, the dimensioning commands and variables are now available directly from the command line. As well, dimensions in Release 2000 are run more from the pull-down menus and set up more in dialog boxes than in earlier releases.

The dimension variables found in previous releases are still available through the DIM mode, but the Dimension style function has been developed to make dimensioning easier. To add dimensions and accept the default or standard dimension style, simply access the dimensions through the Dimensioning pull-down menu, or dimensioning in the dimension toolbar.

Figure 7-3

Accessing Linear Dimensions

To access the screen menus and the dimensioning toolbar.

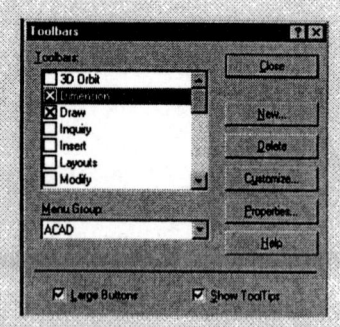

Toolbar From the View Pull Down menu, pick Toolbars, then Dimension to get the toolbar shown above.

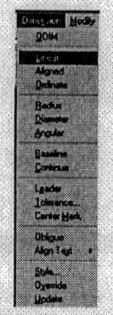

Pull Down If you only need a few dimensions, the Pull Down menu is fine.

Entering Dimensions

Horizontal and Vertical Dimensions

Like the Window and Crossing options, horizontal and vertical dimensions can be placed simply by using the LINEAR command, and they will show up at the desired spot depending on the extension line origins that you set or the point where you select an object. To override the horizontal or vertical default, choose **V** or **H**.

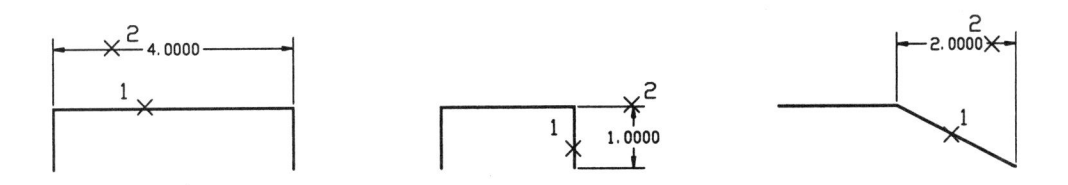

Figure 7-4

Once you have accessed the LINEAR command, you will be prompted for the first extension line origin. Press ↵ to select the first line rather than the two extension lines.

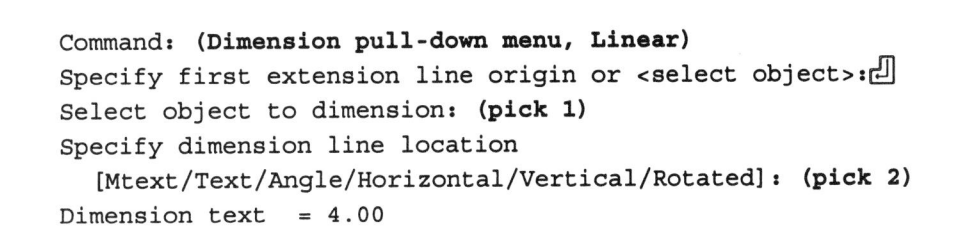

```
Command: (Dimension pull-down menu, Linear)
Specify first extension line origin or <select object>:↵
Select object to dimension: (pick 1)
Specify dimension line location
   [Mtext/Text/Angle/Horizontal/Vertical/Rotated]: (pick 2)
Dimension text  = 4.00
```

In all three examples, the extension offshoot is shown because of the position of the adjoining lines. In the next two examples, the first extension line is picked, then the second, and finally the placement of the dimension line is picked. In these, you would lose the extension line gap distance if you simply chose the object itself. Use SNAP and OSNAP for accuracy.

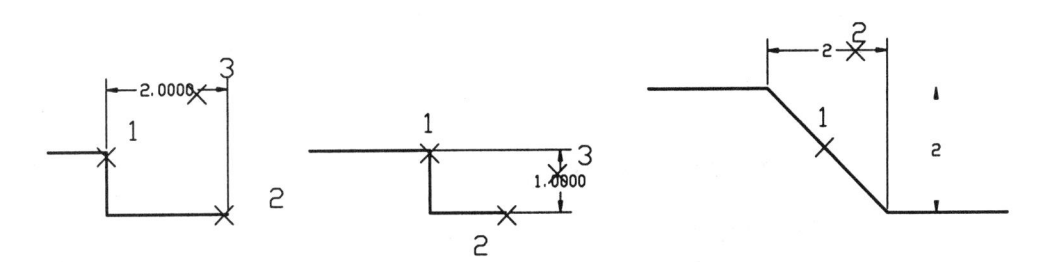

Figure 7-5

Before specifying the dimension line location, you are prompted to change the dimension text (Text), the text angle (Angle), the dimension direction (Horizontal or Vertical), or the dimension line angle (Rotated).

In the third illustration above, either the horizontal length or the vertical could be taken. Move your cursor to the position the dimension should be in, then pick the spot.

Dimensioning   **167**

```
Command: (Dimension pull-down menu, Linear)
Specify first extension line origin or <select object>:
Select object to dimension: (pick 1)
Dimension line location or[ Text/Angle/Horizontal/Vertical/
   Rotated]: (pick 2)
```

- To rotate the extension lines, type **R** for rotate.
- To override the horizontal or vertical default, type **H** or **V**.
- To override the text, type **T**.
- To rotate the text within the dimension line, type **A** for angle.

Aligned Dimensions

If the line is on an angle and you would like to rotate the dimension, use Aligned.

> **Toolbar** From the Dimension toolbar, choose Aligned.
>
> **Pull Down** From the Dimensioning menu, choose Aligned.

```
Command: (Dimension pull-down menu,
   Aligned)
Specify first extension line origin or
   <select object>: (pick 1)
Specify second extension line origin:(pick 2)
Specify dimension line location
 or [Mtext/Text/Angle]: (pick 3)
Dimension text = 2.8284
```

Figure 7-6

Like the vertical and horizontal, you can also simply choose the line itself to be dimensioned. To dimension circles, choose the circle and the end points of the diameter will be chosen for the end of the extension lines.

```
Command: _DIMALIGNED
Specify first extension line origin or RETURN to select:
Select object to dimension: (pick 1)
Specify dimension line location or [Mtext/Text/Angle]: (pick 2)
Dimension text = 2.8284
```

To change the unit readout, change the dimension style (see page 175).

168 CHAPTER SEVEN

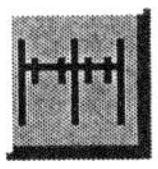

Continued Dimensions

Once you have either a horizontal, a vertical, or an aligned dimension, you can create baseline or continued dimensions.

```
Command: _DIMLINEAR
Specify first
   extension line
   origin or <select
   object>: (pick 1)
Specify second
   extension line
   origin: (pick 2)
Specify dimension
   line location [M/T
   /A/H/V/R]: (pick 3)
Command: _DIMCONTINUE
   (pull-down menu)
Specify a second extension line origin or [Undo/Select]
   <Select>: (pick 4)
Dimension text = 4.5000
Specify a second extension line origin or [Undo/Select]
   <Select>: (pick 5)
```

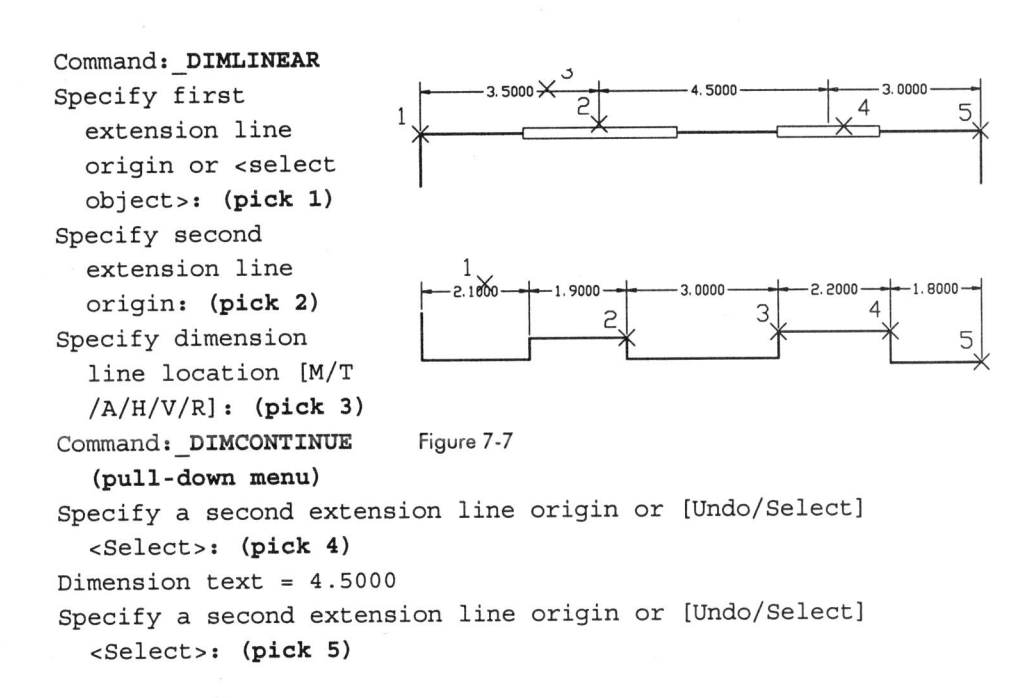

Figure 7-7

Notes

The distance between the dimension lines for both the continued dimensions and the baseline dimensions are set with the DDIM dialog box or the DIMension VARiables.

Continued dimensions are multiple dimensions placed end to end. The first example continues from the dimension just put in. Choose a dimension that was entered earlier as the dimension object to have the successive dimensions line up with.

```
Command: _DIMCONTINUE
Specify a second extension line origin or [Undo/Select]
   <Select> :⏎
Select object to dimension: (pick 1)
```

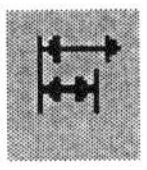

Baseline Dimensions

Similarly, for baseline dimensions, create the first dimension and continue from there.

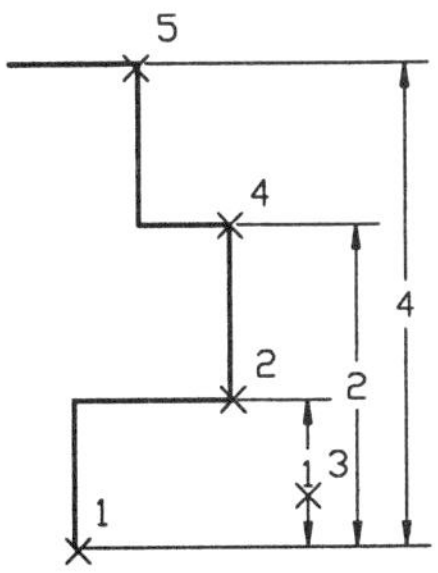

```
Command: _DIMLINEAR (pick from the toolbar)
Specify first extension line origin or
<select object>: (pick 1)
Specify second extension line origin: (pick 2)
Specify dimension line location
   [Mtext/Text/Angle/Horizontal/Vertical/
   Rotated]: (pick 3)
Dimension text = 1
Command: _DIMBASELINE
Specify a second extension line origin or
   [Undo/Select]<select>: (pick 4)
Specify a second extension line origin or
   [Undo/Select]<select>: (pick 5)
```

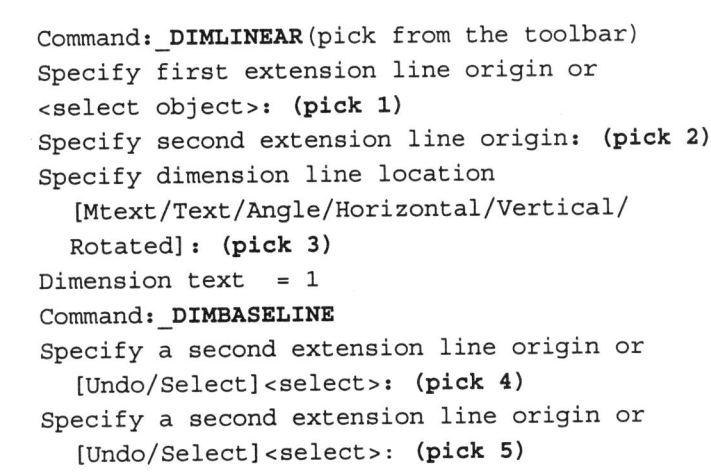

Figure 7-8

Dimensioning **169**

In both continued and baseline dimensions, if AutoCAD can't fit text and arrows between extension lines it will place the text on the side picked second. Use DIMTIX to override this, or set it up in the Dimension Style dialog box (page 175).

Radial Dimensions

A *radial dimension* measures the diameter and radius of an arc or circle. The dimension will be placed according to the current dimension style or setup. Radial dimensions and diameter dimensions are very tricky.

```
Command: (Dimension menu, Radius)
Select arc or circle: (pick 1 — the arc)
Specify dimension line location or [Mtext/
 Text/Angle]: (pick 2 — the spot for the
 radius)
```

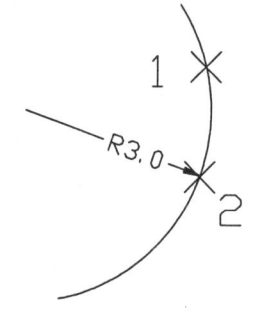

Figure 7-9

Dimradius can be used on both circles and arcs. Overriding text styles or Dimension Variables are often needed to place the text within the object where it belongs.

Use DIMTIX and DIMTOFL to place the text where needed, or to change the format and annotation options of the Modify Dimension Styles dialog box.

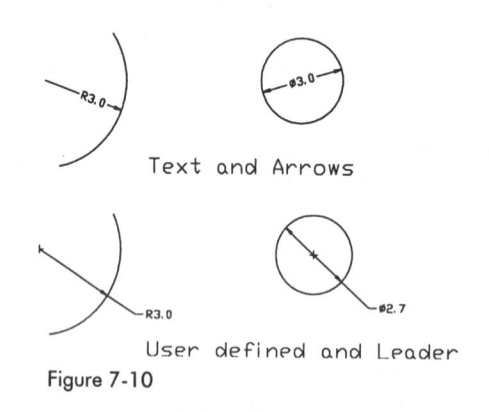

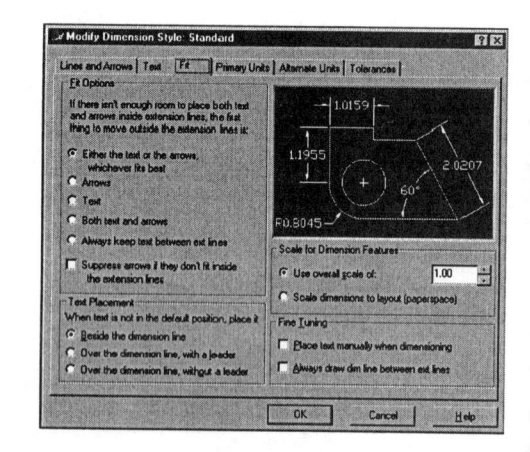

Figure 7-10

Figure 7-11

Diameter dimensions are affected by the same dimension variables as the radius dimensions. Use the Fine Tuning area if you are having difficulty.

```
Command: _DIMDIAMETER
Select arc or circle: (pick 1)
Specify dimension line location
 [Mtext/(Text/Angle]: (pick 2)
```

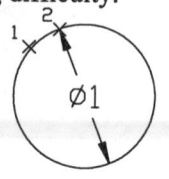

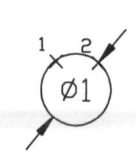

As in the linear commands, the text and the text angle can both be changed.

Figure 7-12

Angular Dimensions

The angular dimension command measures the angle between two nonparallel lines or three points. It can also measure the angle around a portion of a circle or the angle subtended by an arc.

The angle defined is determined by the placement of the dimension line.

```
Command: _DIMANGULAR
Select arc, circle, line, or
   <specify vertex>: (pick 1)
Select second line: (pick 2)
Specify dimension arc line
   location or [Mtext/Text/
   Angle]: (pick 3)
```

Notes
You can MIRROR a dimension to place it outside of the circle if you really get fed up.

The dimension line for the angular measurement is an arc that spans the measured angle and passes through the measured point.

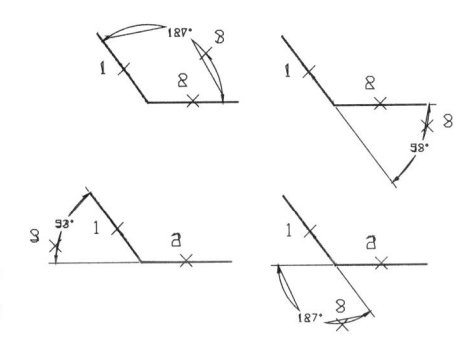

Figure 7-13

Dimension Styles

Controlling Dimension Style

A *dimension style* is a named group of settings that determines the appearance of the dimension. Every dimension has an associated dimension style. If no style is applied before dimensioning, the Standard or default style is used. The style controls the unit readout, the text style, the color, the linetype scale, and many other factors.

In earlier releases of AutoCAD, the UNITS command controlled the dimension units; in Release 2000 this command does not affect the units of the dimensions. They are determined by the dimension style.

Dimension styles are used to manage all variables. Once you have created a new style, it becomes the *parent* of a *style family*.

Toolbar From the Dimensioning toolbar, choose Dimension Style.

Pull Down From either the Dimension menu or the Format menu, choose Style.

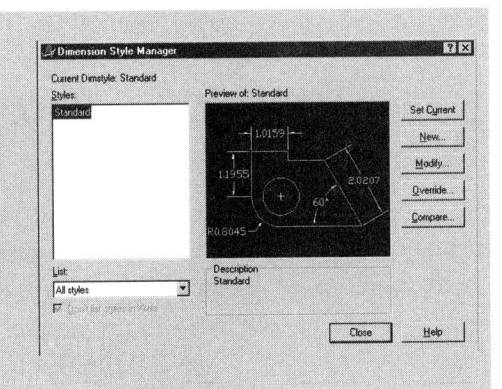

To create a parent dimension style:

The command line equivalent is **DDIM**.

```
Command: DDIM
```

Dimensioning **171**

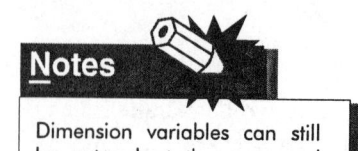

> **Notes**
>
> Dimension variables can still be entered at the command prompt.

Dimension styles are controlled through the DDIM dialog boxes. These take the place of many of the dimension variables.

To create a new style, enter a style name in the Name box and pick Save. Changes that you make with the Modify Dimension Style menu will be filed with the saved name.

The Lines and Arrows Menu

The Lines and arrows menu allows you to set the size and shape of the lines and arrows on your dimension lines.

In the Modify Dimension Style dialog box, pick the Lines and Arrows tab at the top of the screen.

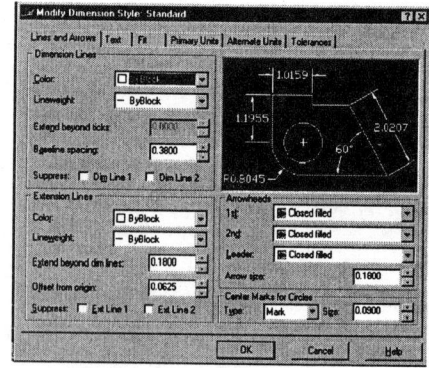

Figure 7-14

Scale or Dimscale

The overall size of the dimensions is determined in the Fit tab of the Modify Dimension Style dialog box. If you change the Overall scale, you will change the arrowhead size, the extension line gap, the extension line overshoot, and the gap between the dimension and the dimension line. It is a much better idea to change the overall scale than to change each size individually.

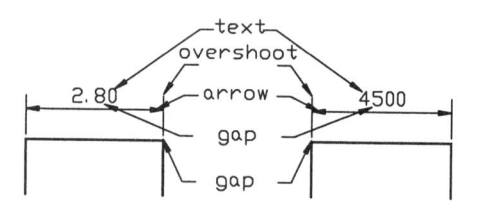

Figure 7-15

If you change the dimscale, all of these factors will change. If you change just the text size or just the arrowhead size, all of the other parameters will remain the same.

Paper space dimensions are dealt with in Chapter 11.

Arrowheads

First chose the arrowhead style that you need. The size of the Arrowhead is listed below. The styles can be changed by simply picking the current style, then choosing a new style from the available menu.

To enter a user-defined arrowhead style you must first define the objects, then block them using the BLOCK command. See Chapter 10.

```
Arrowheads
     None (DIMASZ 0)
←—2—→ Closed
◆—2—◆ Dot
←—2—← Closed Filled
∕—2—∕ Tick (DIMTSZ)
←—2—← Open
○—2—○ Origin Indication
←—2—→ Right Angle
⋈—2—⋈ User Arrow (DIMBLK)
```
Figure 7-16

172   CHAPTER SEVEN

Center Marks

In order to change the center mark style, choose the appropriate style from the list.

To add a center to an arc or circle, pick Center Mark from the dimension list, then pick the circle. These are not real "center lines," and are placed on the current layer.

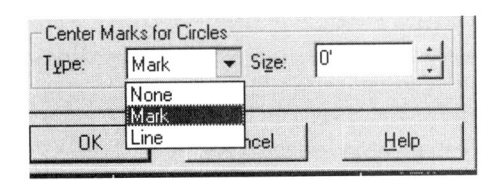

Figure 7-17

Figure 7-18

Suppressing Extension and Dimension Lines

In the geometry area, you can also cause either the extension line or the dimension line and arrowheads to be omitted. This is referred to as *suppressing* the extension or dimension lines. You can suppress both extension and dimension line in one command. Remember to return it to the previous setting.

To return to the main dimension style menu, choose OK. To cancel the changes that you have made, choose Cancel. To read the help files on this menu, choose Help.

You can change the color of the dimension lines and the text within this menu as well.

Figure 7-19

Figure 7-20

The Fit Dialog Box

The Fit dialog box will allow you to define the position of the dimension text, arrowheads, and leader lines relative to the dimension and extension lines. To open the Fit dialog box:

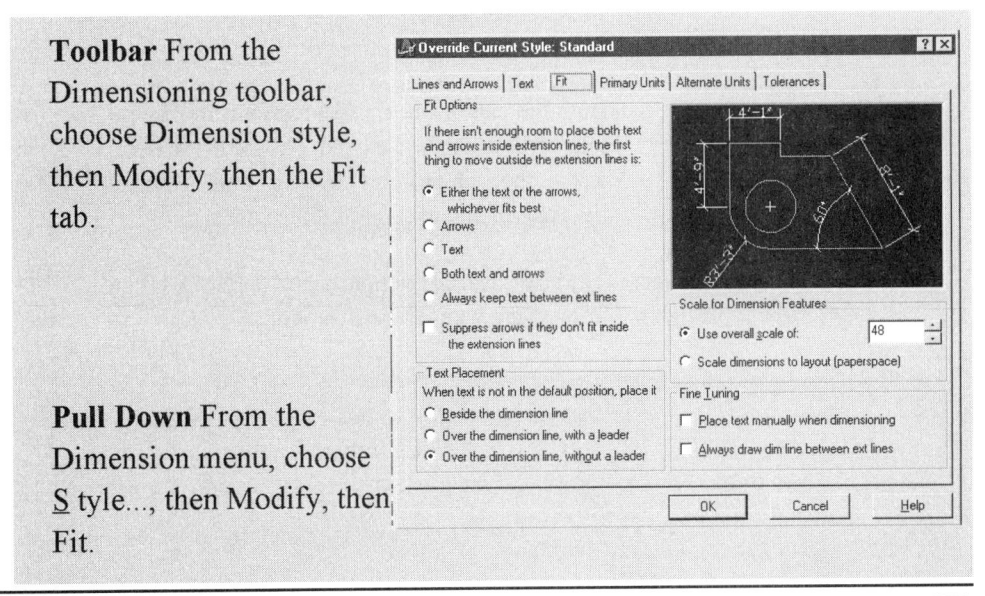

Toolbar From the Dimensioning toolbar, choose Dimension style, then Modify, then the Fit tab.

Pull Down From the Dimension menu, choose Style..., then Modify, then Fit.

Dimensioning **173**

Best Fit

Many factors influence how arrowheads and dimension text fit within the extension lines. If possible, both text and arrowheads are accommodated between the extension lines no matter what fit option you choose, and AutoCAD will try to provide the "best fit." If you want to override the Best Fit, there are certain options.

If the best fit forces the text and arrowheads outside of the extension lines, you can have the line at least forced within the extension lines.

This was done in previous releases with the DIMTOFL DIM Var.

AutoCAD will follow the format set in the Fit dialog box where possible, but once again this is determined by the sizes of the objects involved. If you set the text-fit options so that text only is meant to fit within the extensions, AutoCAD will include both text and arrows within the extension lines if there is room for both.

Usually the Arrows option is only used where there are more than three characters in the text string.

You can spend a lot of time trying to get dimensions to fit properly. If worse comes to worse, use a Leader line.

Text Orientation

Orientation of text is an important feature for dimensions. If you are doing civil or architectural drawings, the standard is to read vertical dimensions from the right with the text above the line as well.

Both the text inside and the text outside the extension lines can be changed. The results will follow the dimension lines in both vertical dimensions and in aligned dimensions.

The text is placed over the line with DIMTAD on or by using vertical justification.

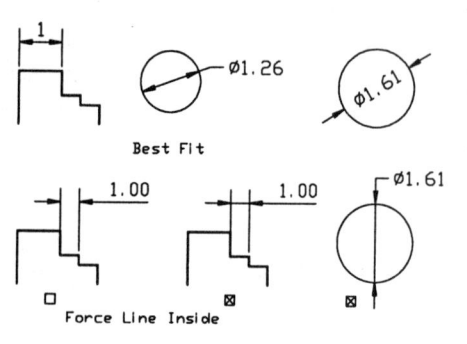

Figure 7-21

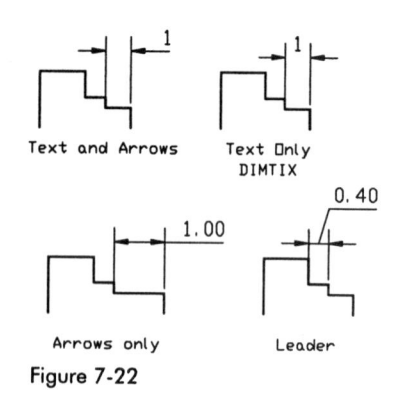

Figure 7-22

Figure 7-23

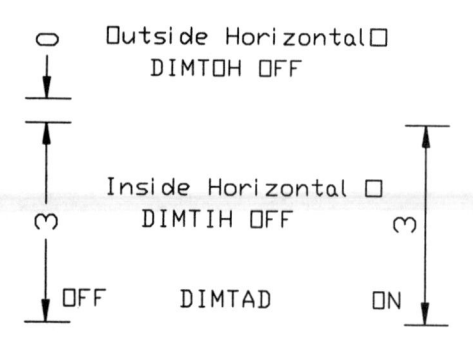

Figure 7-24

174 CHAPTER SEVEN

The Text Tab

The Text dialog box will allow you to control the dimension text with respect to the unit readout, alternate units, tolerances, text style, gap, color, and rounding-off value.

To open the Annotation dialog box:

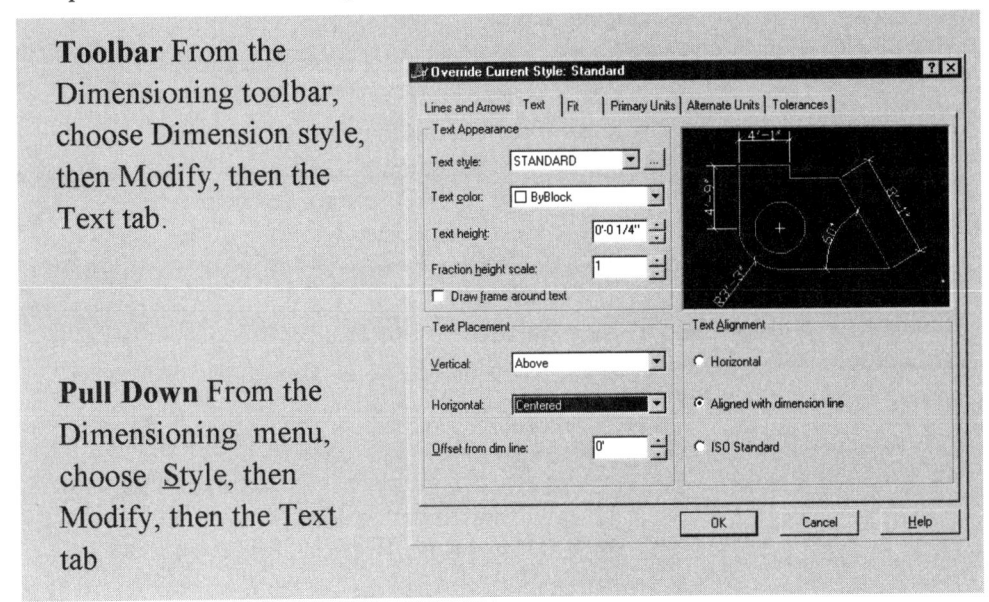

Toolbar From the Dimensioning toolbar, choose Dimension style, then Modify, then the Text tab.

Pull Down From the Dimensioning menu, choose Style, then Modify, then the Text tab

Vertical Justification

ANSI specifications generally have the text horizontal. There are a number of variables that can be used together to achieve the dimension required.

Both of the illustrations with circles show text not horizontal. The text can also be all outside the dimension lines.

The text can be fit above the dimension line or within the dimension line.

You will need to play around with the variables to see what combination suits your purpose.

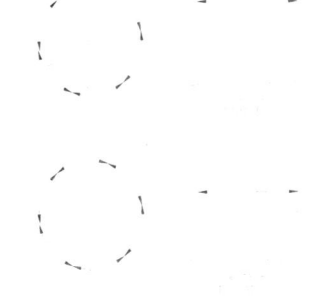

Figure 7-25

Horizontal Justification

You can also change the horizontal justification of the text. Generally speaking, the text should be in the center of the dimension line. Use the options shown to change this.

If there is only one dimension that needs to be changed, you can use STRETCH to move it out of the way.

In dimension text you must also consider prefixes and suffixes, alternate units, and lateral tolerances.

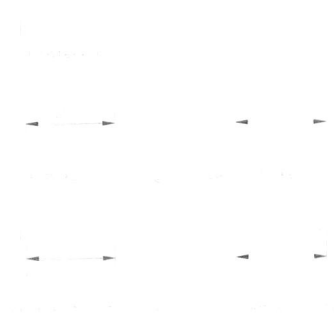

Figure 7-26   Figure 7-27

Dimensioning **175**

Alternate Units

Alternate units can be either imperial or metric, or they can represent another specific unit difference. The alternate unit will be shown in parentheses beside the primary unit readout. In the Annotation dialog box you can also control the degrees of accuracy of the alternate unit and the factor of the alternate unit.

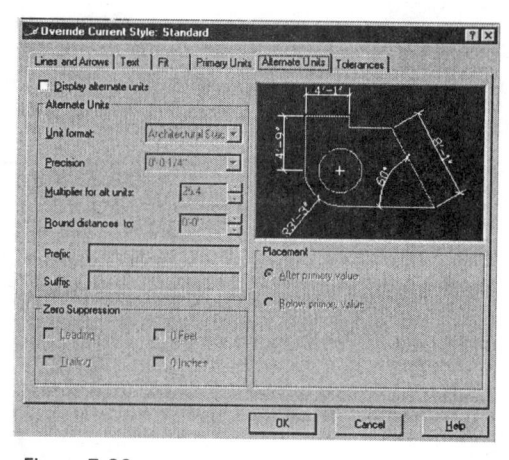

Figure 7-28

Primary Units

This will determine the main dimension values. With these units can be stored suffixes and prefixes such as diameter symbols, four holes, etc. As well, zero suppression is controlled and tolerances are set with this menu. Finally, you set the precision of the readout and the global measurement scale or a length scaling factor for dimensions created in paper space.

Select a unit type from the list for all dimension types except angular. For angular dimensions, select an angle type from the Angles list.

Under Precision, you choose the precision value for the primary units. Under Tolerance, select the precision value for the tolerance values.

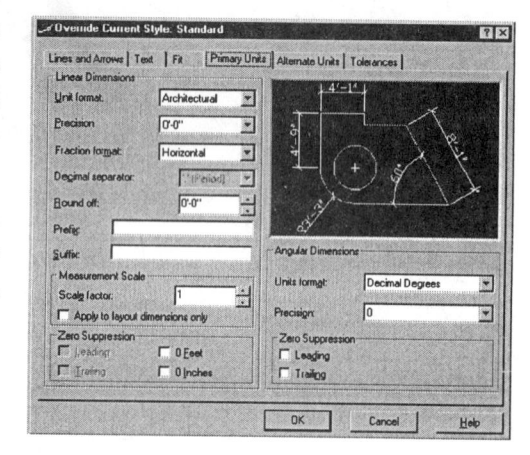

Figure 7-29

Suppressing Zeros in Primary Units

You can suppress both leading and trailing zeros. With suppression of the leading zeros, 0.0400 becomes .0400. With suppression of the trailing zeros, 0.0400 becomes 0.04. If you suppress both, 0.0400 becomes .04. This option replaces DIMZIN.

Suppressing zeros is most important in dimensions using feet and inches. Here are some examples of how the options work.

Option	Effect	Examples		
0 feet and 0 inches	Suppresses zero feet and zero inches	1/2''	6''	1'-0 3/4''
No options	Includes zero feet and zero inches	0'-0 1/2''	0'-6''	1'-0 3/4''
0 inches	Suppresses zero inches (includes zero feet)	0'-0 1/2''	0'-6''	1'-0 3/4''
0 feet	Suppresses zero feet (includes zero inches)	1/2''	6''	1'-0 3/4''

176 CHAPTER SEVEN

Tolerances

In the manufacturing sector, tolerances are often used to control the degree of accuracy required for certain applications. The tolerances show the largest and smallest permissible deviation on the manufacturing.

To add tolerances, choose the tolerance area of the annotation menu and choose the method required. Upper and lower tolerances can be specified.

The types of tolerances can also be specified. In the illustration here, the first dimension is created with symmetrical or bilateral tolerancing and the second is created with the Limits option. Again, there are many variables that can be set in the tolerancing area to create the desired dimension style.

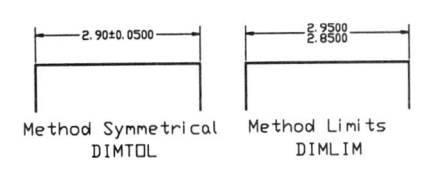

Figure 7-30

Dimension Text Style

In the Dimension text style area under the Text tab, you can modify both the font and the size of the text. Keep in mind that if you change the text size this will change *only* the size of the text; it will not change the size of the arrowheads or any of the other variables changed in the Scale option.

Before you select a style, it must be loaded using the STYLE command. See Chapter 8.

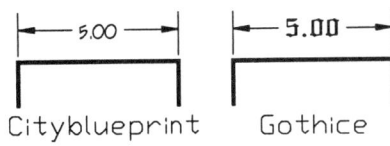

Figure 7-31

In choosing a text style for dimensions, keep in mind that certain fonts, such as Standard and Cityblueprint, are more readable than others, such as Gothic. The more intricate the font, the more difficult it will be to read and the more space it will take up on disk.

Rounding Off Dimensions

You can control the precision of dimensions by using the Round off area of the annotation menu. All dimension types can be rounded off, except for angular dimensions. The number of digits that follow the decimal point can be set under the Primary Units area or under Alternate units and Tolerancing units. The rounding-off value will be within this decimal value.

This option was performed in previous releases with the DIMRND DIM Var.

Using Dimension Style Families

Once you have made all of the changes necessary for a dimensioning style, you must save it as a particular style. Change the name in the Dimension Styles dialog box. This will be your parent style. Each style contains a font, just as layers contain a color and a linetype. Changes to the style alter all text within that style.

If there are certain options that you would like to change for some dimensions, you can make the changes and save them under the parent style. An example would be tolerancing on all of the radius or diameter dimensions but not on any of the linear dimensions. In this case, create a *family member style* that will allow tolerancing only on these dimension types.

Saving Dimension Styles

Open the Dimension Styles dialog box.

> **Toolbar** From the Dimensioning Toolbar, choose Dimension Style.
>
> **Pull Down** From the Dimension menu, choose Style.

Once you have opened the Dimension Style dialog box, pick the New button and create a new dimension style. Add the name for your new dimension style, use Copy of Standard to start, then pick Continue to set the parameters for your style for your dimensions. Use OK to save.

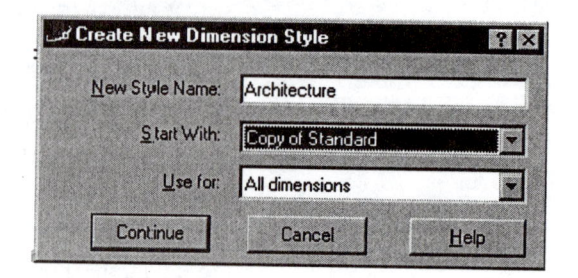

Overriding Styles

DIMOVERRIDE overrides dimensioning system variable settings associated with a dimension object, but doesn't affect the current dimension style.

Some of the dimensioning variables, such as extension line suppression and forcing text within extension lines, apply to only certain dimensions on the drawing. In a case like this, a dimension override would be appropriate.

An override is equivalent to changing a certain dimension variable without changing the overall style of the dimensions. To override existing dimensions, you can use the DIMOVERRIDE command to change only dimensions that you select.

```
Command: DIMOVERRIDE
Enter dimension variable name to override or [Clear
    overrides]: (enter C or a variable )
```

If you enter a dimensioning system variable name, AutoCAD redisplays the "Current value, New value:" prompt. If you press ⏎, AutoCAD prompts:

```
Select objects:
```
AutoCAD applies the overrides to the selected dimension objects.

UPDATING Existing Dimensions

There are three basic categories of ways to update your dimensions.

Dim:UPDate will update the selected dimensions relative to the changes that you have made either in the dimension variables or on the Dimension Styles dialog box.

Command:**DIMSTYLE** will do the same.

DIMOVERRIDE will let you update the selected dimensions or clear all of the dimension variables that are not the Standard dimensions on the selected dimensions.

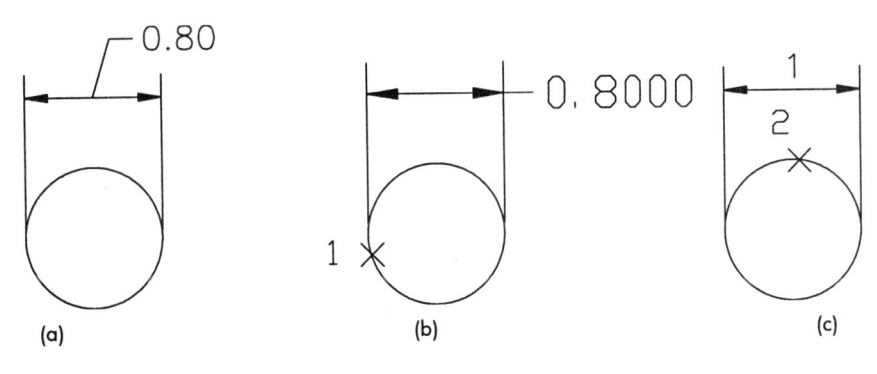

Figure 7-32

The aligned dimension on the left reflects some changes in the Dimension Styles dialog box. In Figure 7-32(b), DIMOVERRIDE was used; in Figure 7-32(c), DIMSTYLE Apply was used.

```
Command:DIMOVERRIDE
Enter dimension variable to override or [Clear overrides]:C
Select objects: (pick 1)
```

This has cleared all of the dimension variables that are currently set.

UPDate can be used to override a dimension variable in a few selected dimensions, without affecting the other dimensions. For example, DIMTIH (Text Inside the arrowheads Horizontal).

```
Command:DIMTIH
Enter new value for DIMTIH <OFF>:on
Command:DIM
Dim:UPD
Select objects:(pick 1)
Select objects:↵
```

This should get you started on the way to good dimensions.

Dimensioning   179

Editing Dimensions

Text

If you pick Properties from the Modify pull-down menu and select a dimension, you are given the Modify Dimension dialog box. Pick the box that offers what you would like to change. If you would like to change just the text, type **DIM**⏎, then **NEWTEXT**. Then enter the characters that you would like to have in the text string. Choose OK, and you will be prompted to pick the dimension that you would like to change.

The DIMTEDIT Command

Moves and rotates dimension text.

> **Toolbar** From the Dimensioning toolbar, choose Dimension Text Edit.
>
> **Pull Down** From the Dimension menu, choose Align Text.

The command line equivalent is **DIMTEDIT**.

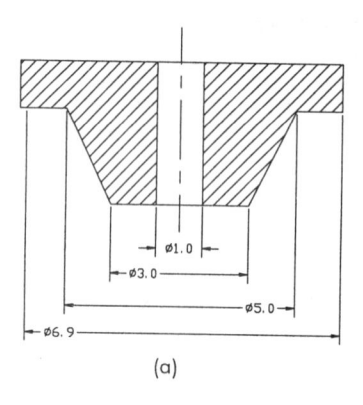

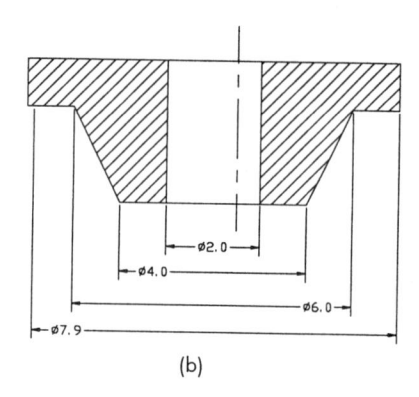

Figure 7-33

DIMTEDIT edits the position of the text with Left/Right/Home or Angle.

Under the Annotation dialog box is the heading Prefix. You can add the prefix **%%c** for the diameter sign to add diameter signs to all of the dimensions shown.

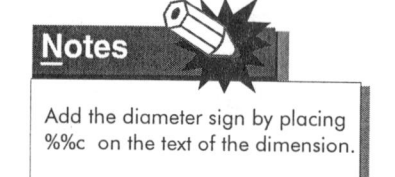

Stretch

You can also stretch the object and have the dimensions automatically updated as in Figure 7-33(b). The STRETCH command can be used in the same way that DIMEDIT is used to move the text across the dimension line.

EXTEND and TRIM can also be used to have the dimensions show up *exactly* correctly.

Dimensioning can be quite annoying at first. If you have changed a series of dimension variables, and/or a series of options in the DDIM dialog box, you may find it just too cumbersome to try to figure out what is happening.

In this case, save the file, and open a new one. Use the INSERT command to insert the file into a fresh drawing environment. Use EXPLODE to revert the block into individual parts, and start again with your dimensioning variables.

See Chapter 10 for more details.

> **Notes**
> Add the diameter sign by placing %%c on the text of the dimension.

When All Else Fails

Prelab 7 Dimensioning

Step 1 Quickly draw the part as shown. The dimensions are shown for your convenience in this illustration, but do not try to add them yet. It will help with your placement later if the center of the lower left arc is drawn on a SNAP point. SNAP could be set to .25.

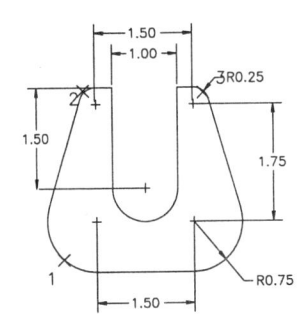

> **Notes**
> Systems may have different default factors. If you are *not* getting what is shown, just continue.

Step 2 Once the part is drawn in, let's take a look at what a dimension would look like using the standard dimensioning format.

Before starting dimensioning, create a layer called Dims, make it red, and make it current.

Now set your Object Snap to ENDpoint and CENter. The Object Snap dialog box is hidden in the Drafting Settings box under Tools.

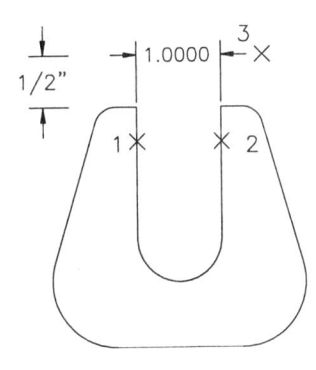

> **Notes**
> For Dimensioning icons, pick the View Pull Down menu, then Toolbars, then Dimension.

> **Toolbar** From the Dimensioning toolbar, choose Linear.
>
> **Pull Down** From the Dimension menu, choose Linear.

```
Command:DIMLINEAR
Specify first extension line origin or <select object>:END of
   (pick 1)
Specify second extension line origin:END of (pick 2)
Specify dimension line location or
   [Mtext/Text/Angle/Horizontal/Vertical/Rotated]: (pick 3)
Dimension text = 1.0000
```

The dimension line should be 1/2 inch away from the object line. With SNAP set at .25, this should be easy to place.

Step 3 Four decimal points of accuracy are not needed, and the scale of the dimensions is larger than needed. The next step is to make a dimension style that will incorporate the changes. First, access the area of the Dimension Style dialog box, create a style called Mechanical, and Continue to change the precision.

> **Toolbar** From the Dimensioning toolbar, choose Dimension Style, then New, then Continue.
>
> **Pull Down** From the Dimension menu, choose Style, then New, then Continue.

Having set up your Mechanical style, now set the Precision to two decimal places under the Primary Units tab.

Now pick the Fit tab, and change the Overall scale to .75 as shown on the right below.

Pick OK to return to the Dimension Style Dialog box.

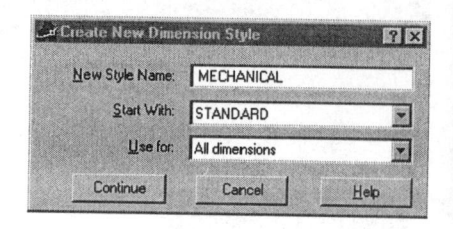

Make sure that your new dimension style is current by choosing the Set Current button, then Close the dialog box.

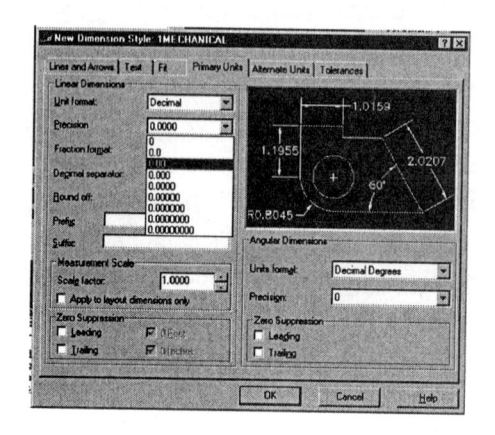

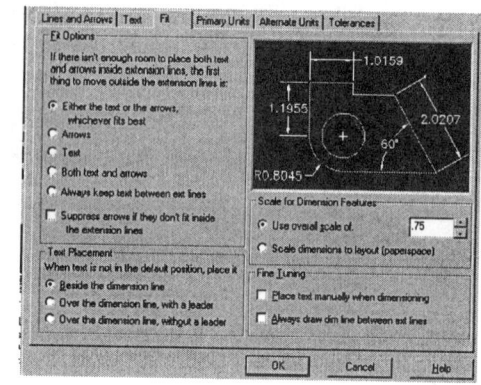

Step 4 The dimension will be updated to the new style.

If the dimension is not a different color, you may not have your Dims layer current.

Make sure all of your dimensions go onto the Dims layer.

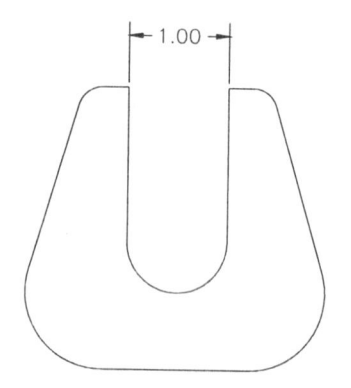

Step 5 Now that the style has been set, add the linear dimensions. First create the horizontal dimension between the centers of the two arcs on the top, then create the vertical dimension on the right.

Toolbar From the Dimensioning toolbar, choose Linear.

Pull Down From the Dimension menu, choose Linear.

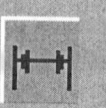

```
Command:DIMLINEAR
Specify first extension line origin
   or <select object>:CEN of (pick 1)
Specify second extension line
   origin:CEN of (pick 2)
Specify dimension line location or
   [Mtext/Text/Angle/Horizontal/
   Vertical/Rotated]:(pick 3)
Command:⏎
Specify first extension line origin
   or <select object>:CEN of (pick 4)
Specify second extension line
   origin:CEN of (pick 5)
Specify dimension line location or
   [Mtext/Text/Angle/Horizontal/Vertical/
   Rotated]: (pick 6)
```

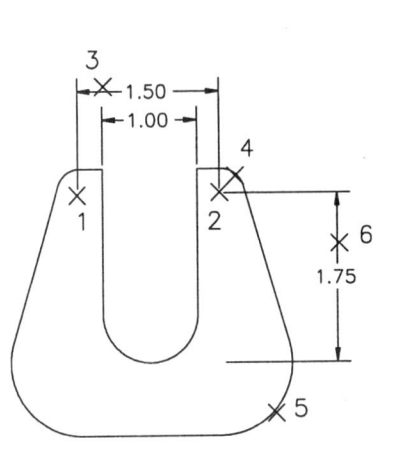

Add the other vertical and horizontal dimensions in the same manner.

```
Command:DIMLINEAR
Specify first extension line origin
   or <select object>:END of(pick 1)
Specify second extension line
   origin:CEN of (pick 2)
Specify dimension line location or
   {Mtext/Text/Angle/Horizontal/
   Vertical/Rotated]:(pick 3)
Command:⏎
Specify first extension line origin
   or <select object>:CEN of (pick 4)
Specify second extension line
   origin:CEN of (pick 5)
Specify dimension line location or
   [Mtext/Text/Angle/Horizontal/Vertical/
   Rotated]: (pick 6)
```

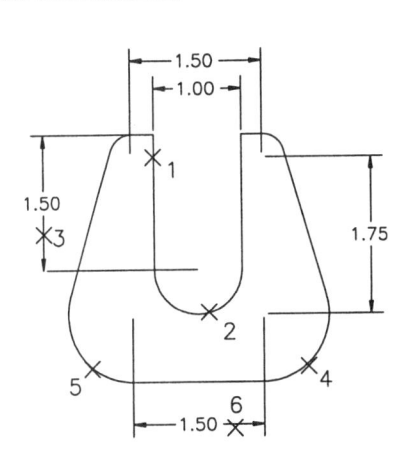

> **Toolbar** From the Dimension toolbar, choose Radius.
>
> **Pull Down** From the Dimension menu choose Radius.

Step 6   Now add the radial dimensions. When you pick radial for the dimensions, you can move the leader line either inside or outside the radius. Place the radii outside the object as shown.

Dimensioning   **183**

Notes

Again, some systems may have defaults set to avoid this problem. If your radius was entered correctly the first time, continue to Step 9.

```
Command: _DIMRADIUS
Select arc or circle: (pick 1)
Specify dimension line location or
   [Mtext/Text/Angle]: (pick 2)
Command: _DIMRADIUS
Select arc or circle: (pick 3)
Specify dimension line location or
   [Mtext/(Text/Angle]: (pick 4)
```

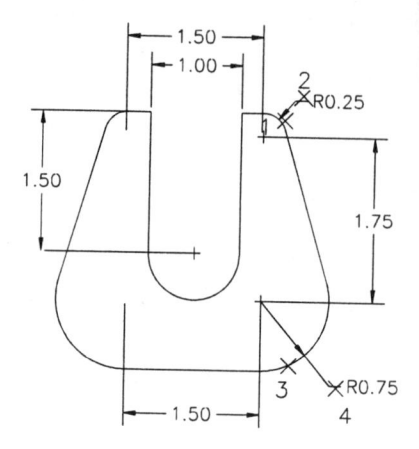

Step 7 Your dimensions are fine, now add center marks. From either the Pull Down menu or the toolbar, choose Center Mark.

> **Toolbar** From the Dimensioning toolbar, choose Center Mark
>
> **Pull Down** From the Dimension menu, pick Center Mark.

```
Command: _DIMCENTER
Select arc or circle: (pick the radii)
```

Step 8 The dimensions added are associative dimensions. This means that, if you have entered all the dimensions and then find that they are the wrong scale or the wrong units, that the arrowheads should be ticks, or some other problem, you can edit the dimensions singly or in groups with the aid of the UPDATE command.

The dimensions are entered relative to the points that you have identified. These are called defpoints, and there is a special layer created for them under your layer menu. This layer does not plot, so be careful not to make it current.

This means that you can also STRETCH the part and the dimensions will automatically update.

184 CHAPTER SEVEN

Now we will stretch the object using the STRETCH command, and see how the dimensions react.

> **Toolbar** From the Modify toolbar, choose STRETCH.
>
> **Pull Down** From the Modify menu, choose STRETCH.

```
Command: STRETCH
Select objects to stretch by window
...
Select objects:C
First corner: (pick 1)
Other corner: (pick 2)
Select objects:↵
Base point: (pick 3)
New point:@1<90 (or pick 4)
```

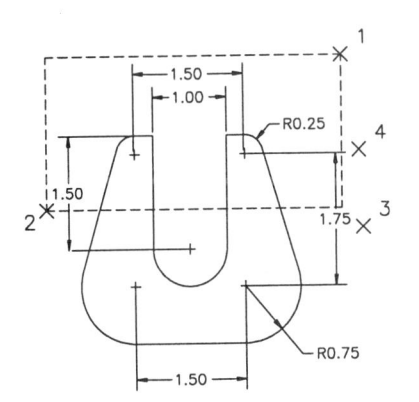

The resulting object should look like this.

Your objects should stretch and the vertical dimension should change.

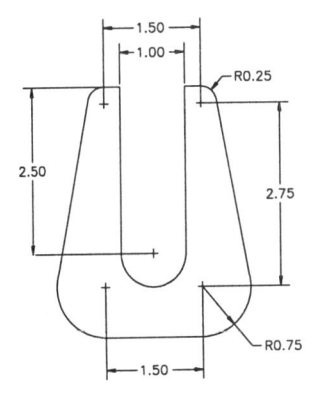

Step 11 Finally, what if the dimensions should really be in fractional rather than decimal? You can change the dimension style and apply it to the current drawing.

First, save the drawing so that you have two copies, one that will have fractions and one with decimals.
From the File menu, choose SAVE_AS. Name the file PRELAB7.

The next step is to make a new dimension style that incorporates the necessary changes. First, access the Dimension Style dialog box to change the dimension style.

From the main dialog box, pick new. Then on the top line enter the new name for your dimension style. Mechanical will be the standard that you are changing.

Once this is entered, pick Continue to change the units to fractions.

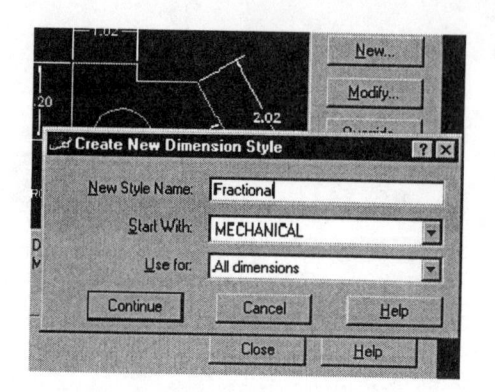

Now under Primary Units tab, change the Unit Format to fractional.

To exit the dialog box, pick OK until you are at the Dimension Styles dialog box.

Set the current style to Fractional and close the dialog box.

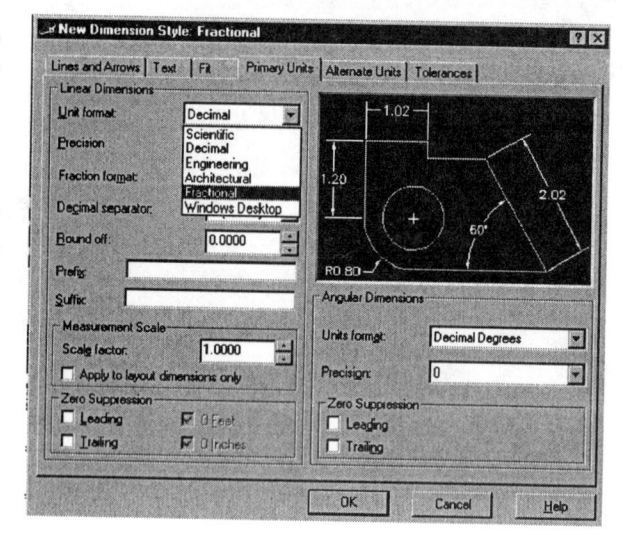

To update all of your dimensions to fractional, use the UPDate command. At the command prompt, change the mode to dimensioning mode, then use UPD.

```
Command:DIM
Dim:UPD
Select objects: (pick all the objects with crossing or window)
Select objects:
```

The dimension should update to the current style.

The final drawing should look like this.

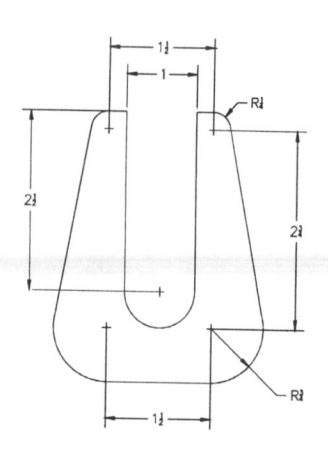

Command and Function Summary

Dimension Style dialog box allows the user to create a dimension style that will be used on all subsequent dimensions.

Geometry dialog box allows the user to control the appearance of the dimension line, extension lines, arrowheads and center marks for lines, and the scale of the dimension.

Scale or **Dimscale** controls the overall size of the dimensions.

Arrowheads controls the size and style of the arrowheads.

Center Marks controls the size and style of the center marks.

Extension and **Dimension Lines** controls the display of the relevant lines.

Format dialog box allows you to define the position of the dimension text, arrowheads, and leader lines relative to the dimension and extension lines.

Best Fit controls the placement of the text relative to the arrowheads and extension lines.

Text Orientation controls both the text inside and the text outside the extension lines.

Vertical Justification fits the dimension text above the dimension line or within the dimension line.

Horizontal Justification controls the horizontal justification of the text.

Annotation dialog box allows the user to control the unit readout, alternate units, tolerances, text style, gap, color, and rounding-off value.

Alternate Units controls alternate units.

Primary Units determines the main dimension values.

Suppressing Zeros controls the number of zeros in both the primary units and the alternate units readouts.

Tolerances allows and controls reading of tolerances.

Dimension Text Style controls the style of the text.

Rounding off allows you to round the dimensions off to the desired unit readout.

DIMANGULAR allows you to add aligned dimensions.

DIMBASELINE allows you to add baseline dimensions.

DIMCONTINUE allows you to add continued dimensions.

DIMDIAMETER allows you to add diameter dimensions.

DIMLINEAR allows you to enter dimensions either vertically or horizontally.

DIMRADIUS allows you to add radial dimensions.

DIMSTYLE allows you to edit or update the current style.

UPD in the DIM mode allows you to update the dimensions to the current style.

Practice Exercise 7

The upper section is a roof assembly for fire-rating. The lower are simple mechanical parts that should help with your dimensioning skills.

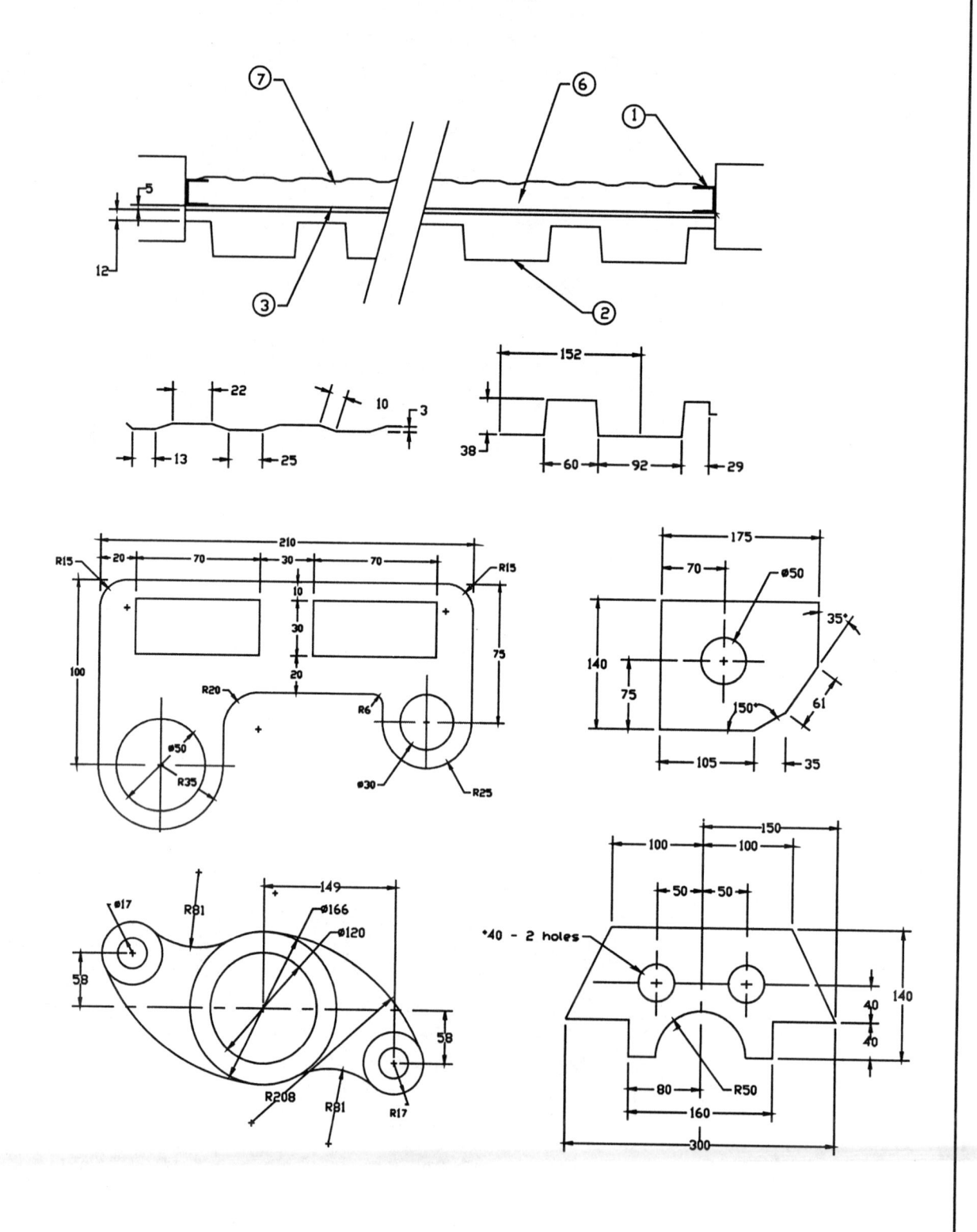

Exercise A7

Open the file SECONDFL. Create a layer called DIM2 and make it current; be sure to change the color so that it is easier to distinguish the extension lines from the object lines. Create the dimensions as shown, dimensioning to the MIDpoint of the windows and doors on the second floor. The first line of dimensions should be to the center of the wall partitions.

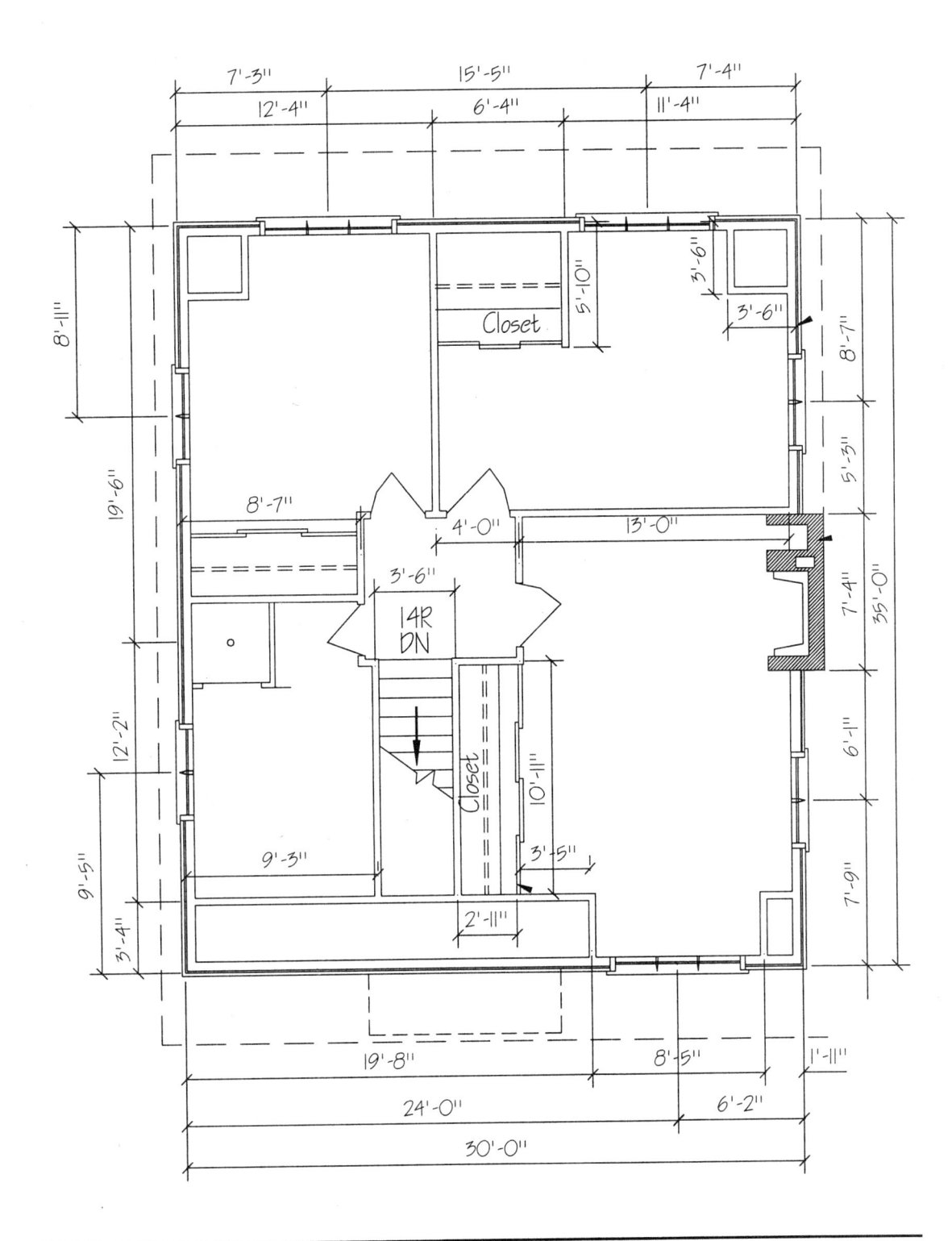

Dimensioning 189

Exercise A7 (cont.)

Now open FIRSTFL. Create a layer called DIM1 and make it both current and a different color. Place dimensions on the first floor.

Be sure to save both files when the dimensioning is complete.

Always use object snaps to place the dimensions accurately on the feature being dimensioned. Set the OSNAP mode to ENDpoint if most of your horizontal and vertical dimensions are from the ends of objects.

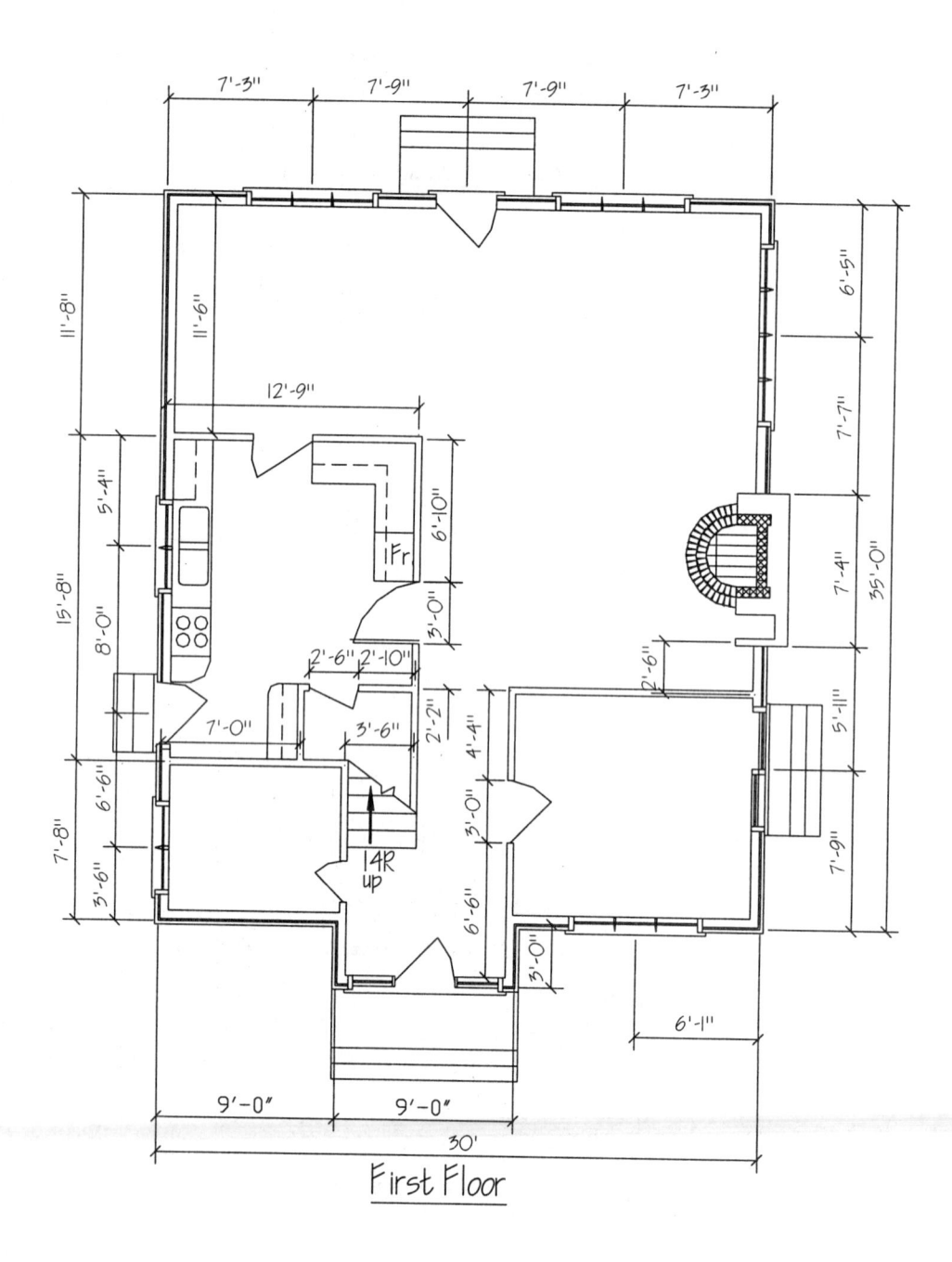

First Floor

Exercise C7

Create this footing drawing using different layers for the footings.

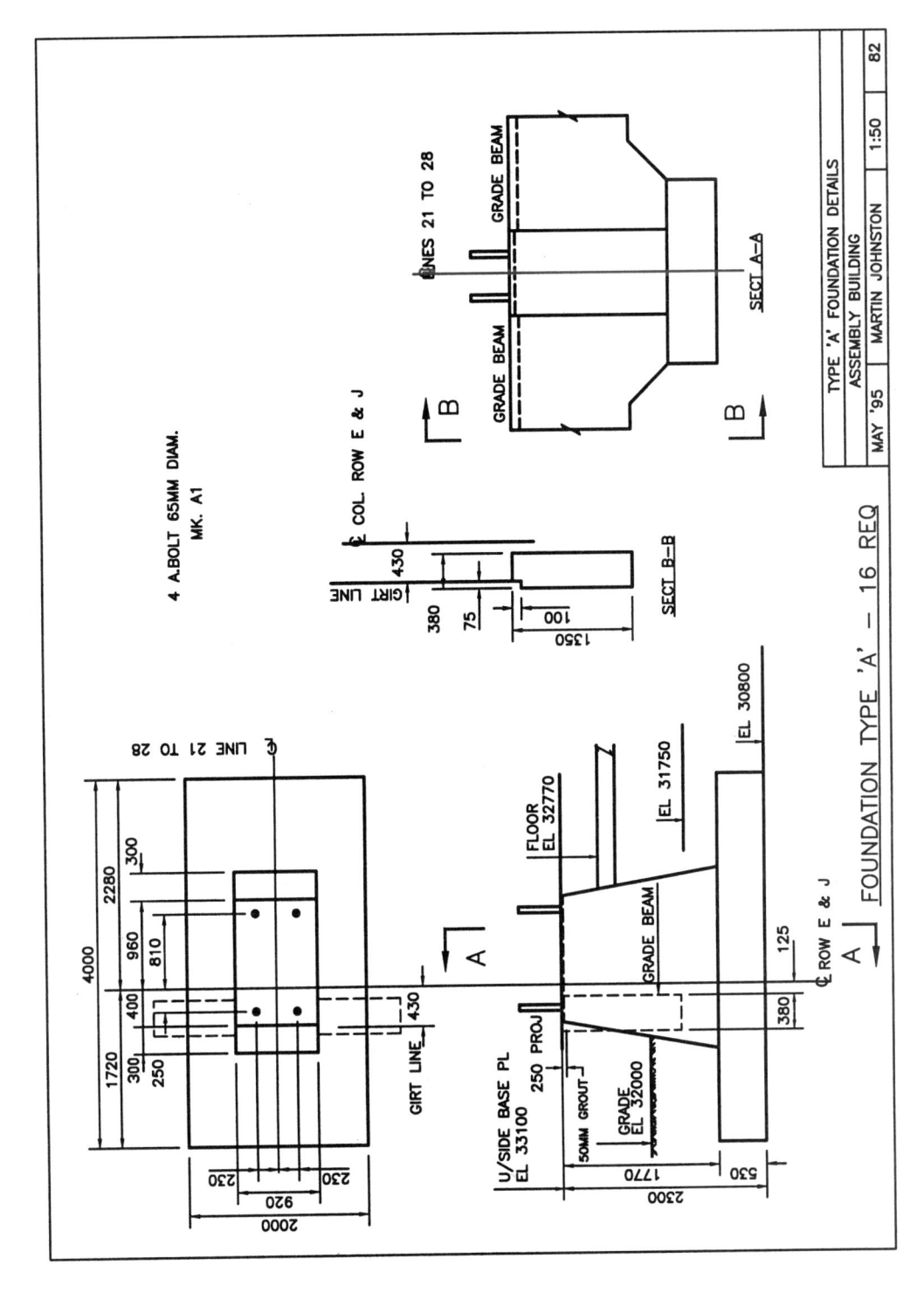

Exercise E7

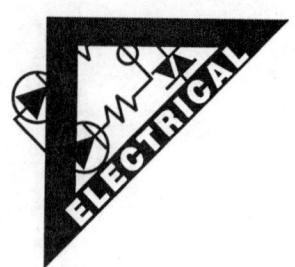

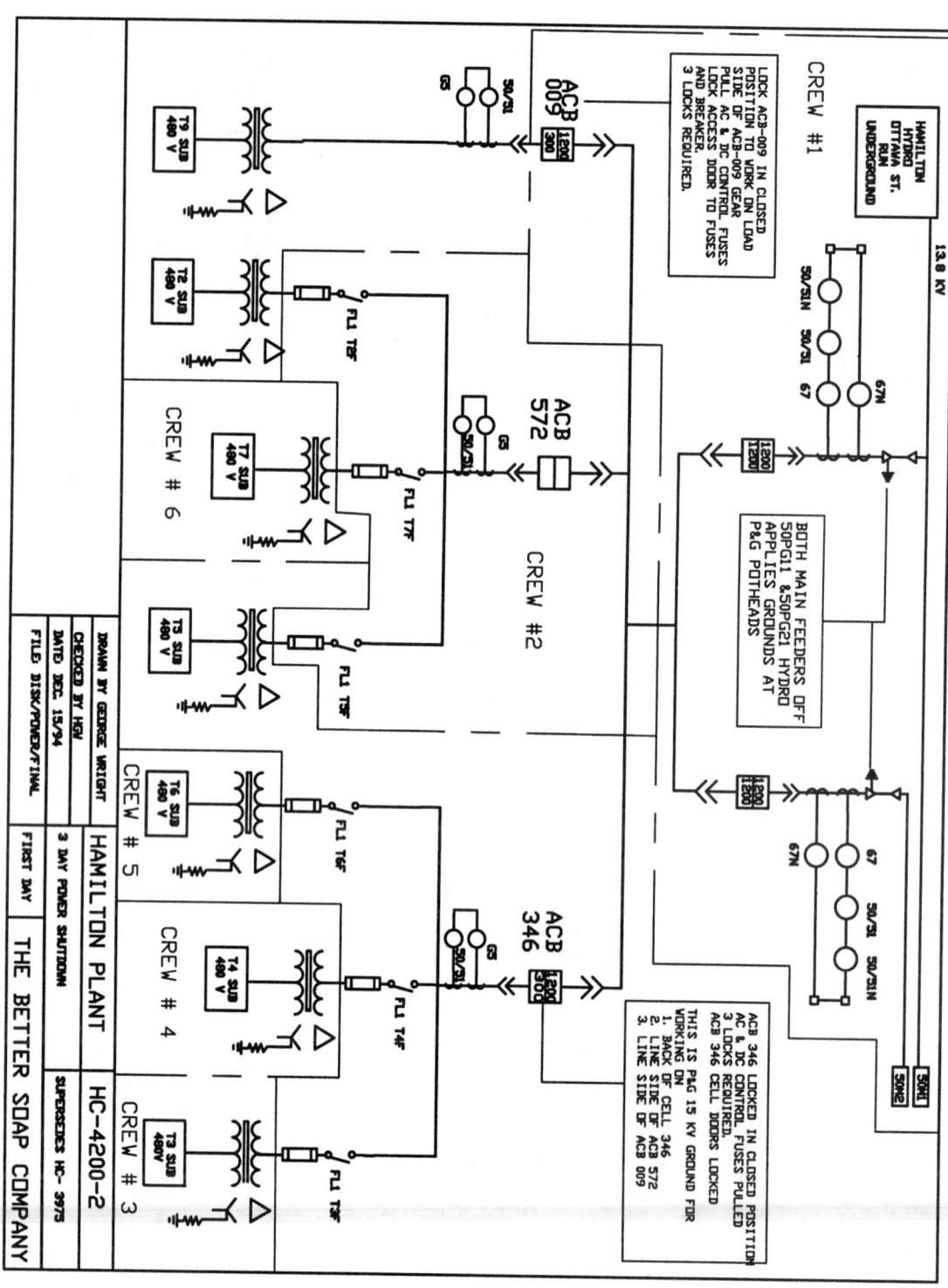

Exercise M7

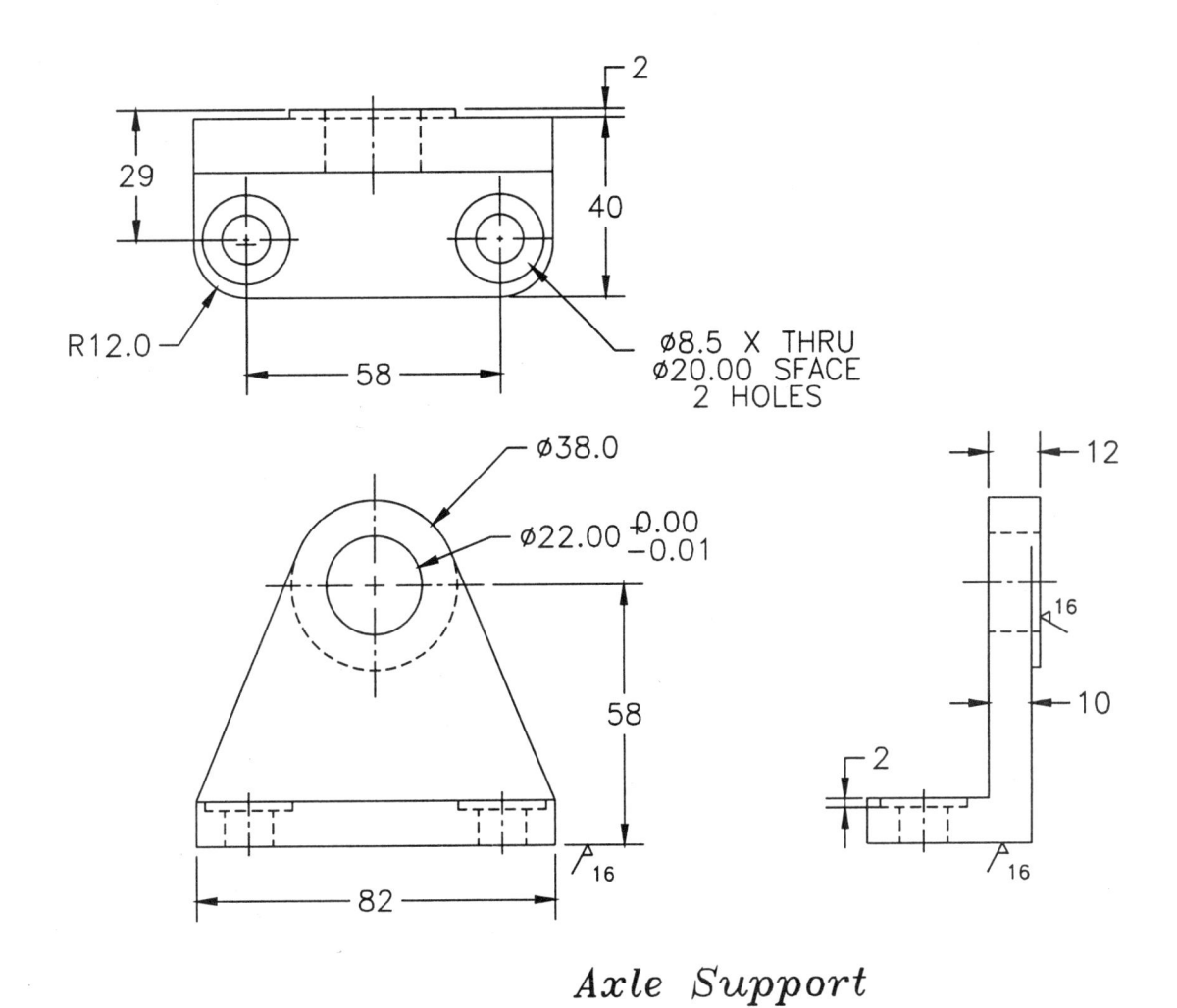

Axle Support

Set up the file with several different layers: Object, Hidden, Center, and Dimensions. Draw the objects, making sure that all lines line up with the corresponding views. Add center lines, hidden lines, and object lines on the appropriate views. Then add dimensions, making sure that the dimension lines also line up with the corresponding views.

Challenger 7

Be sure to use different layers.

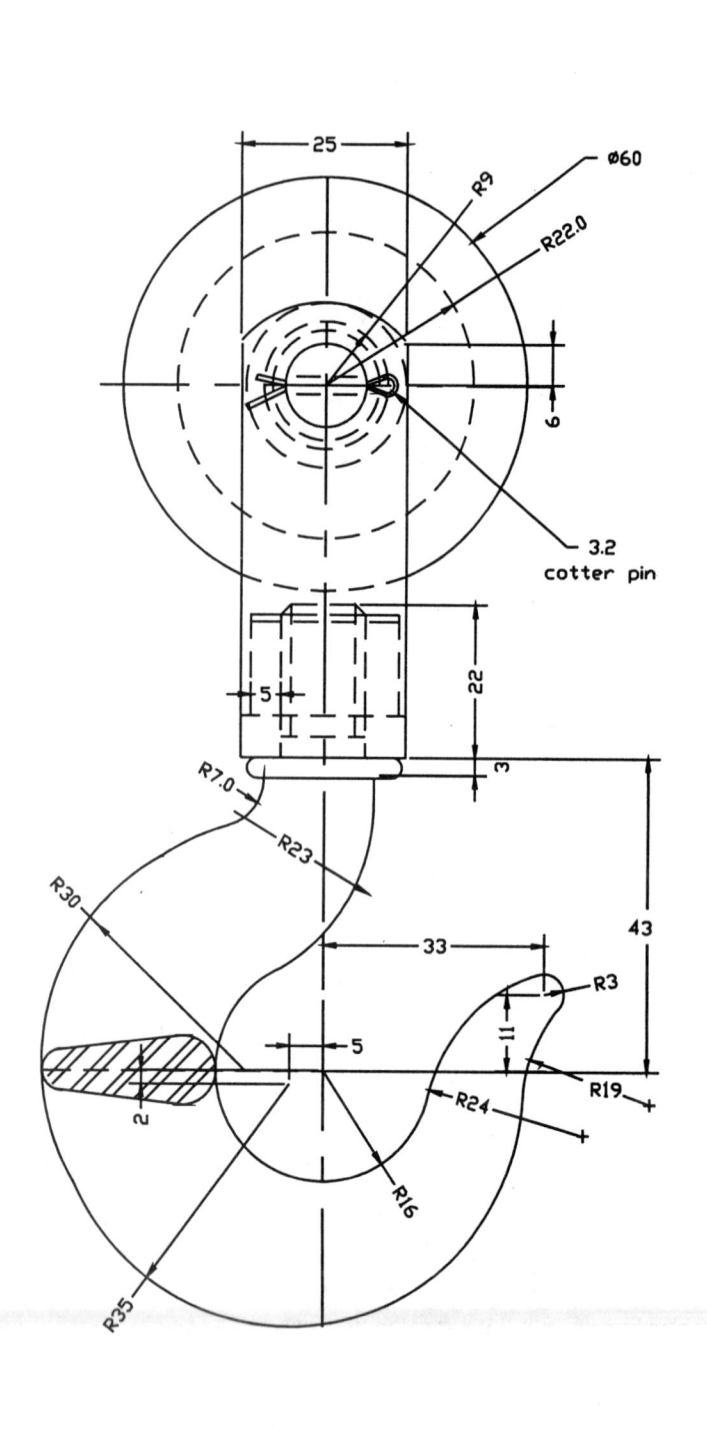

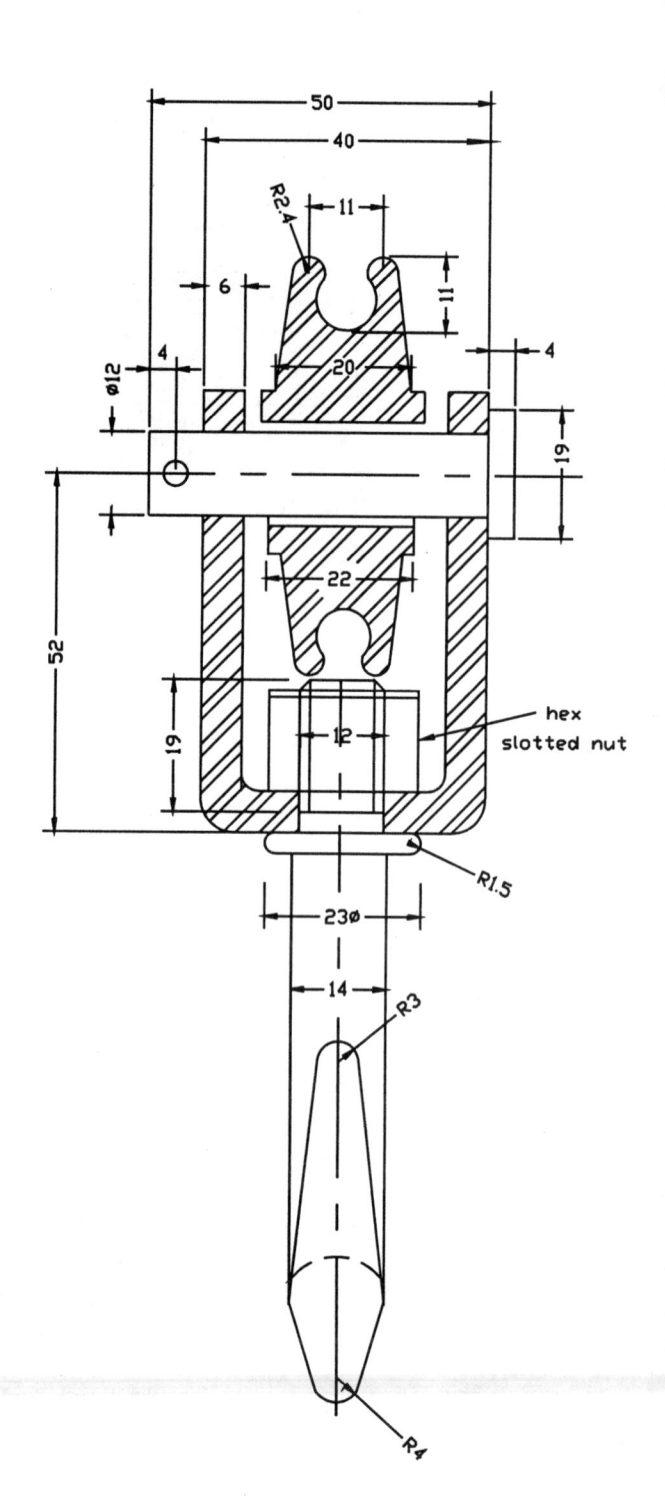

8 Text

Upon completion of this chapter, you should be able to:

1. Place linear text in any size at any rotation angle
2. Place paragraph text
3. Create and change collections of formats to make a text style
4. Change existing text
5. Set up an isometric text

AutoCAD provides two basic ways to create text. *Linear text* places simple entries of one or two lines. For longer entries *paragraph text* is used. Text is entered in the current text style, which incorporates the current format and font settings. With Release 2000, however, there are several methods of saving and controlling alternate text styles.

Linear Text

As stated in Chapter 3, the commands TEXT and DTEXT will place strings of characters on your drawing. When entering text, AutoCAD will prompt you to choose a height for each character, a rotation angle for the string, and a point at which to place the text string on the model or drawing. Many people prefer DTEXT or Single Line Text from the Pull Down menu, as with it you can see the style and placement of the text as it is entered. For DTEXT, see page 197.

The TEXT Command

> **Toolbar** There is no button for TEXT or DTEXT in this release.
>
> **Pull Down** There is no command on the Pull Down menu for TEXT, only DTEXT.

The command line equivalent is **TEXT**.

The TEXT command is as follows:

```
Command:TEXT
Specify start point of text or [Justify/Style]:J
Enter an option
   Align/Center/Fit/Middle/Right/TL/TC/TR/ML/MC/MR/BL/BC/BR:
```

Where: **Justify** = the placement of the text
Style = controls the style of the letters; the styles must be loaded in AutoCAD to be accessible
Align = an alignment by the end points of the baseline; the aspect ratio (X vs. Y) will correspond to the preset distance
Center = the center point of the baseline; this option will fit the text through the center point indicated
Fit = an adjustment of width only of the characters that are to be fit or "stretched" between the indicated points
Middle = a placement of the text around the point, i.e., the top and bottom of the text are centered as well as the sides
Right = an alignment with the right side of the text

The examples in Figure 8-1 demonstrate the standard justifications. The default is left justification at the baseline of the text string.

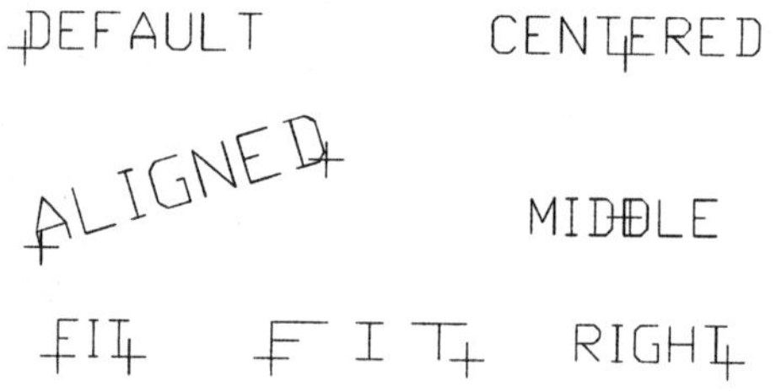

Height can be chosen by picking a point to indicate the height, or by typing in a number.

The double-initialled justification options are as follows:

TL = top left
TC = top center
TR = top right
ML = middle left
MC = middle center
MR = middle right
BL = bottom left
BC = bottom center
BR = bottom right

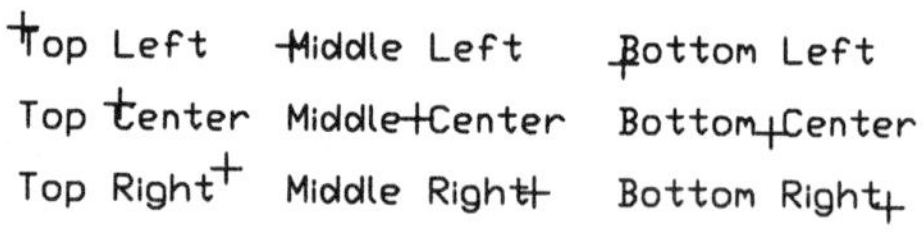

Figure 8-1

Figure 8-2

Once you have chosen a point at which to place your text, the command will prompt you for the height of the letters, the rotation angle, and the text or string of characters itself.

A text *string* is one line of text.

```
Command: TEXT
Specify Start point or [Justify/
Style]: C
Specify center point: (pick 1)
Specify height<.2000>:.5
Specify rotation angle <0>:⏎ (to accept the default)
Enter text: Front Elevation
```

Figure 8-3

In this example, the justify option Center was chosen, so the other options for placement were bypassed. If Justify had been chosen, the following line would have been offered:

196 CHAPTER EIGHT

```
Align/Center/Fit/Middle/Right/TL/TC/TR/ML/MC/MR/BL/BC/BR:
```

If TEXT was the last command entered, pressing ⏎ at the "Specify start point [Justify/Style]:" prompt skips the prompts for height and rotation angle and immediately displays the "Enter text:" prompt. The text is placed directly beneath the previous line of text.

The DTEXT Command

When using the TEXT command, you will see the text string only at the bottom of the screen in the "Command:" prompt area. The DTEXT or Dynamic TEXT command allows the text to be displayed on the screen as you enter it. Many people find this a more useful format. DTEXT always displays text as left-justified on the screen (default) regardless of the format chosen. The justification will be corrected when the command is finished.

As in the ZOOM Dynamic command, there are those who will argue that the D stands for Difficult instead of Dynamic, because, once entered, it is more difficult to get out of. The advantage is that it allows you to enter text more quickly. The DTEXT command automatically offers you a second string for text. Press ⏎ to exit from the command. To find DTEXT:

The command line equivalent is **DTEXT**.

> **Toolbar** There is no button for DTEXT in this release.
>
> **Pull Down** From the Draw menu, choose Text and then Single-line Text.

```
Command: DTEXT
Specify start point or [Justify/Style]: (pick 1)
Specify height <.5000>: .25
Specify rotation angle <0>: ⏎ (to accept the default)
Enter text: Scale
Enter text: (pick 2)
Enter text: Date
Enter text: (pick 3)
(etc.)
```

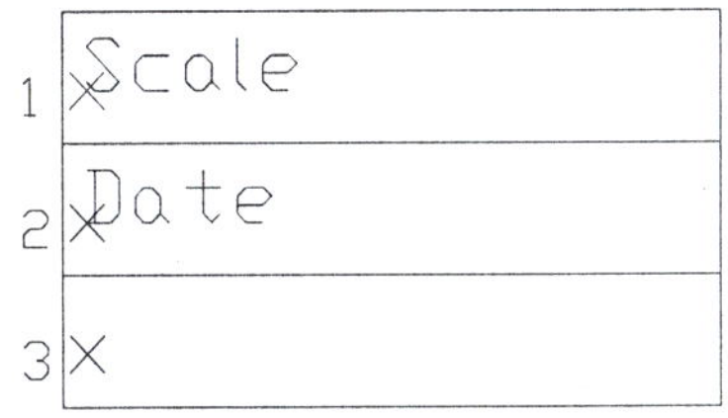

To exit from DTEXT, use:

```
Enter text: ⏎
```

Figure 8-4

> **Danger**
>
> If you use ESCape to quit the DTEXT command, you will loose all the text you entered. Always use ⏎ to exit from the DTEXT or TEXT commands.

You can also reposition your cursor and start a string of text in another area of the screen at any point within the command, by simply choosing another point. This lets you position text of a similar height in various places of your drawing with one DTEXT command. The pull-down menus are disabled throughout this command.

Text **197**

Special Character Fonts

You can underscore, overscore, or include a special character by including control information in the text string.

%%u = underscore
%%o = overscore   *overscore* (overscored)
%%d = degree symbol
%%p = plus-minus tolerance symbol
%%c = diameter symbol
%%nnn = ASCII characters — example: %%123 %%125 = { }

When using special character fonts with the DTEXT command, the special characters will be displayed as you type, i.e., **%%uFront Elevation%%u**. The entry will be updated to the desired text once the command is finished.

```
Command: DTEXT
Specify start point or [Justify/Style]: R
Right side: (pick 1)
Specify height<.2500>: ↵
Specify rotation angle<0>: ↵
Enter text: %%u%%c25 4 holes
Enter text: ↵
```

⌀25 4 holes

Figure 8-5

Multiline Text

A new text string will line up with the previously entered text string, if there are no changes in the base point or justification options in both the TEXT and the DTEXT command. If Center is chosen, all of the text will be centered (see Figure 8-6 (b)); if no option is chosen, all strings will be left-justified (see Figure 8-6 (a)). Your last string of text will be highlighted to show where the next line will be lined up.

All fillets are Radius .5
Both sides

Autodesk, Inc
Sausolito CA
USA

(a)   (b)

Figure 8-6

If you do not want your text to line up with the last string entered, simply identify a new start point.

The DTEXT command allows multiline text in one command. In TEXT use ↵ to reenter the command after the first text string, then ↵ to accept the default position, size, and rotation.

Once your text has been entered, it is accepted as one item and can be edited using any of the edit commands, such as COPY, MOVE, ERASE, ROTATE, AND ARRAY. To edit the text itself, use DDEDIT, DDMODIFY, or CHANGE.

Paragraph Text

Paragraph text or MTEXT is for long, complex entries that have many lines of text. Any number of text lines or paragraphs can be entered to fit within a specified width. The paragraphs form a single object that can be moved, rotated, copied, erased, mirrored, stretched, or scaled. This is the default text command under the Draw toolbar in Release 2000.

You can apply overscoring, underlining, fonts, color, and text height to any individual character, word, or phrase of the paragraph.

Creating paragraph text is a lot more flexible, but slightly more difficult than entering single line text. Text is entered in the Edit Mtext dialog box. This editor can be changed using the MTEXTED system variable. Use Preferences to set up a different editor. If you are using a system with limited RAM and limited speed, the ability to have your text spell checked does not make up for the time necessary to access the MTEXT dialog box every time you want to add a string of text. For large paragraphs, however, this is a real advantage.

Paragraph Text for Windows

The Edit MText dialog box is a very efficient way to set properties that affect the entire paragraph or selected text. As in a word processor, you should set the width before you create the text. The paragraph will be displayed in a dialog box within the specified width. The text will wrap or spill in the direction defined by the current attachment setting. The text boundary can be realigned. To create paragraph text:

From the Text flyout on the Draw Pull Down menu, choose Multiline text, or the button shown on the toolbar. This will invoke the MTEXT command.

Toolbar From the Draw toolbar, choose this button:

Pull Down From the Draw menu, choose Multiline Text.

The command line equivalent is **MTEXT**.

You will be prompted to specify the insertion base point for the text as follows:

```
Command:MTEXT
Current text style: STANDARD Text height: 0.2000
Specify first corner or [Height/Justify/Line
   Spacing/Rotation/Style/Width]: (pick a point where the text
   will start)
```

Next you specify the width of the text by using one of the following methods:

- To define a diagonally opposite corner of a rectangular text boundary, specify a point.
- To define only the width of the text boundary, enter **W** and specify a width value. Entering **0** causes the text to extend horizontally until you press ↵.
- Properties and Find/Replace tabs offer more settings.

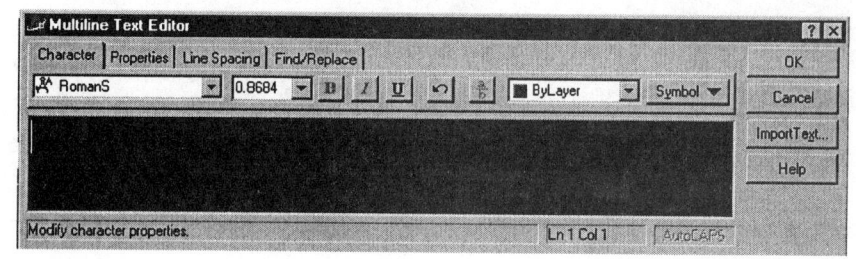

Figure 8-7

The width of the text that you have chosen will be reflected on the dialog box. Type in the text you would like placed at the specified location on your file, then choose OK to write it to the file.

The text can be typed in as in a word processor; it will wrap according to the width chosen.

To edit the color of one word or phrase, or to have it underlined or overscored, select the text by "wiping" the mouse over it, then choose Overscore, Underline, or Color.

Some fonts cannot be displayed in the Edit MText dialog box. If text isn't shown, select a substitute font to represent the original font, then choose OK. When you are finished editing, the original font selected appears in the graphics area.

The text will wrap according to the size of lettering that you have chosen. When you have finished typing in the information you need, pick OK to have it placed in the area on your screen that you earlier specified.

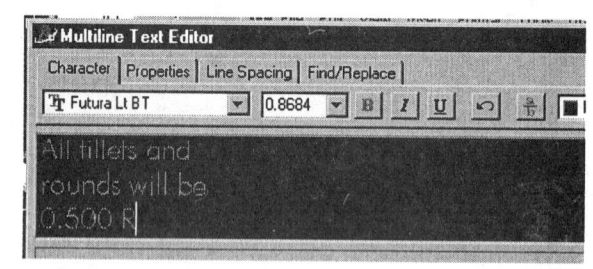

Figure 8-8

MTEXT Options

Other options of the MTEXT command are as follows:

Justify   controls the boundary alignment of your text. The option you select determines both text justification and text spill in relation to the text boundary. According to the option chosen, the text will justify to the right, the left, or the center.

TL/TC/TR/ML/MC/MR/BL/BC/BR:

200   CHAPTER EIGHT

Rotation	specifies the rotation angle for the text boundary.	
Style	specifies the text style for the paragraph text.	
Height	specifies the height of the uppercase text.	
Direction	specifies the direction of the paragraph text object. This will create vertical text, not rotated text.	
Width	specifies the width of the text boundary.	

Text Styles and Fonts

Text styles are what the user names the style of the lettering chosen. *Fonts* are the style or design of the letters and numbers used to create the text string. The fonts can be supplied by AutoCAD or a third-party developer. A text style is stored with not only the lettering style but also a group of characteristic settings.

Setting	*Default*	*Description*
Style name	Romans	Name of up to 31 characters
Font file	ROMANS.TXT	File associated with font
Height	0	Character height
Width	1	Expansion or compression of characters (aspect ratio)
Obliquing factor	0	Slant of individual characters
Backward	No	Orientation of text (for mirrored images)
Upside down	No	Orientation of text
Vertical	No	Vertical, not rotated

The *obliquing factor* is the angle of the text characters themselves, i.e., the slant.

Here are some examples of what your text will look like.

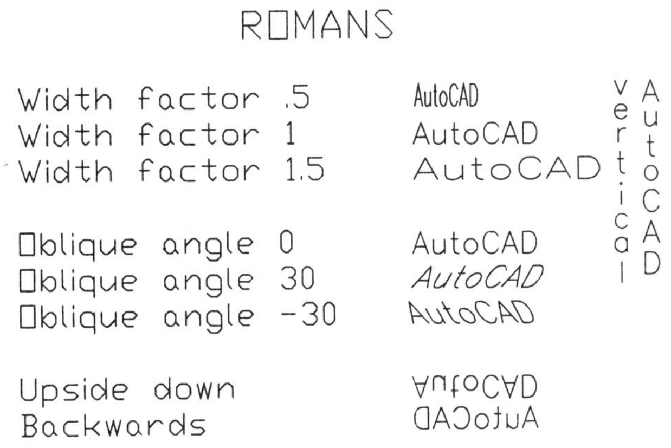

Figure 8-9

Note that the options Height and Width are in fact the *aspect ratio*, or relative *X-Y* value, of the text. If you change the Height of the text with the STYLE command, you forfeit the flexibility of changing it in the TEXT command. It is recommended that, while you are learning AutoCAD, you *never change the height of the text in the STYLE command*, because there are many instances — such as with dimensions and annotations — where this will cause you great inconvenience.

The Vertical option places text vertically. To rotate a text string, *do not* change Vertical in the STYLE command; rather, change the rotation angle in the TEXT command.

Using Text Styles

Each text style takes a font file from the AutoCAD list. The style is saved with the font style. If you change the font or vertical property of an existing style, all text using that style is regenerated using the new font or orientation. For MText objects, other properties change as well. When you change other properties of the text style such as height or obliquing angle, the text already created in that style using TEXT and DTEXT does not update, but all text created subsequently will reflect those changes.

The default style is STANDARD using the TXT.SHX font. To use any other type of lettering you must load or create that style.

To create a text style:

> **Pull Down** From the Format menu, choose Text Style.

The command line equivalent is **STYLE**.

Both the Pull Down menu and typing will give you this dialog box.

First identify the name you would like to assign the text font, then pick the font you want to use.

Height can be specified in this style box, or within the command itself. It is MUCH better to assign the height in the TEXT or DTEXT command than here.

Notes

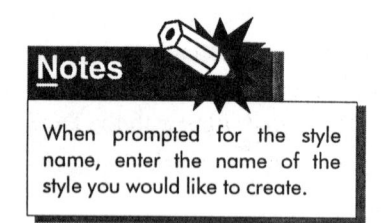

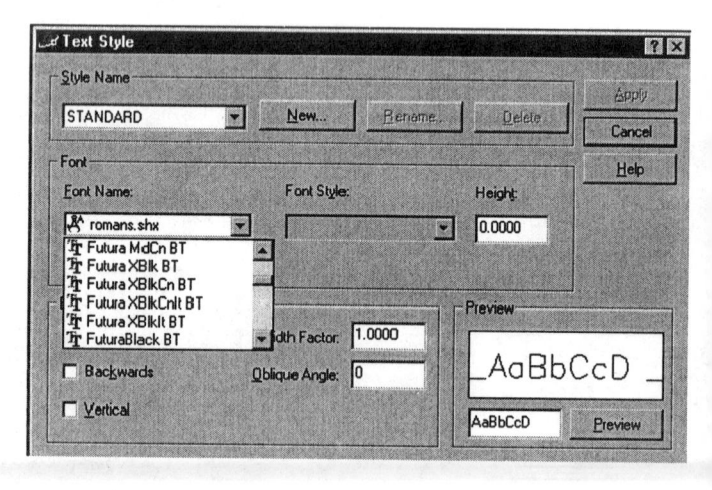

When prompted for the style name, enter the name of the style you would like to create.

Figure 8-10

202 CHAPTER EIGHT

Change other settings as needed.

This will now be the current text font and will remain so until you change it.

Once the text style is created, you can use it as often as you like, then change the style or create a new one. To make the text style current simply pick it from your Style listing.

Select the name of the style you want to use, then choose OK to exit the dialog box. In Figure 8-11 you can see that the name for the text font is entirely your own choosing; you can use the name of the font itself, or if it helps, use the intended location, for example, Title block text.

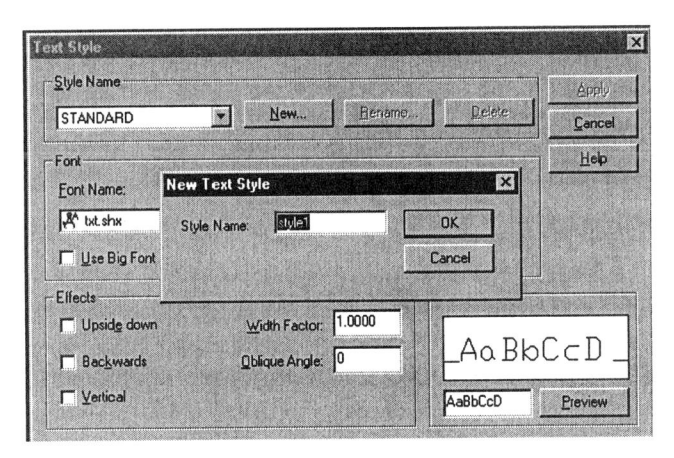

Figure 8-11

Other Text Fonts

A font is the particular style or design of the text characters. AutoCAD comes with a list of available fonts as seen in Figure 8-10. In addition to AutoCAD's standard list, you can also load TrueType or Adobe Type 1 PostScript fonts from third-party vendors.

First install the PostScript or TrueType fonts according to the vendor's instructions. Then copy the fonts to the AutoCAD font submenu.

TEXTFILL and FFLIMIT variables are used to manage and control these font files.

The Unicode character encoding standard is also available in Release 2000. Unicode formats can contain up to 65,535 characters. The Big fonts option on the Select Font File menu is invoked for this purpose and largely contains Asian characters.

Notes

If you use a third-party font, be aware that other AutoCAD users may not have it installed. This makes transferring of files complex. The font files have an extension of .shp, .shx, .pfb, or .pfm. Add these files to your disk when transferring.

Using Text Fonts

Now that you have been working with AutoCAD for some weeks, you should be becoming aware that the amount of disk space the file for a drawing occupies is directly related to the number of lines on the drawing. Take a look at your floppy disk files with the DOS command DIR A:, and you will see that the exercise file for Chapter 7 is much larger than the file for Chapter 1.

AutoCAD's text fonts are made up of a series of small line segments. Each style uses a different number of line segments. The more complicated the style, the more line segments there will be, and the more disk space the text uses. While the Gothic letters are attractive, they take up a lot of space and are not appropriate for many jobs. In addition, regeneration time is much longer, particularly in paper space. Therefore, to avoid overloading the disk, before choosing a font try to determine which is best suited to your job. Begin with a simple font; then, when you are finished, change the style's font to a more complex font.

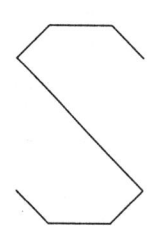

Monotext
7 line segments

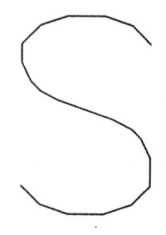

Roman Simplex
19 line segments

English Gothic
70 line segments

Figure 8-12

In Figure 8-12, you can see that the Gothic letter has ten times the amount of lines as the Monotext; it may be appropriate for a title, but not for a notation or a dimension.

Since text takes up memory space, to save time during regenerations it is a good idea to have a separate layer for text and freeze it.

The QTEXT Command

If you have 128 meg of RAM you will not need QTEXT. If you are finding that your redraw times increase with the amount of text you add, try QTEXT.

If you want to save time, but do not want to freeze the layer for text because you need to position objects in reference to the text, try QTEXT. This command can be accessed both in the Drawing Aids dialog box and at the command line with **QTEXT**. Use REGEN to update your screen both with QTEXT on and QTEXT off.

QTEXT places a rectangle of the approximate size of the text in the space provided for the text. Text characters are made up of vectors, and thus occupy a lot of memory; when text is replaced with a simple rectangle, only four lines need to be regenerated per text string. This will save a lot of time during editing commands, zooms, and regenerations.

Remember to turn QTEXT off before plotting, or only the rectangles will plot.

Editing TEXT and DTEXT

A text string is considered an object and can therefore be moved, copied, changed into different layers, and created in different colors. You can also alter the text string itself as well as the height, the rotation angle, and the style of the characters.

Text objects also provide grips for moving, scaling, and rotating. A paragraph text has grips at the four corners of the text boundary and, in some cases, at the attachment point. Line text provides a grip at the lower left corner and another at the alignment point. (Review Chapter 4 for more information on grips.)

Osnap INSERT is the insertion point to grab your text by the point you selected to create the text.

Editing Line Text

You can change both the text characteristics and the text string with the CHANGE command. This is useful for changing many lines of text, particularly when making charts. DDEDIT and DDMODIFY make editing single strings of text much easier.

```
Command: CHANGE
Select objects: (pick 1)
Select objects:↵
Specify change point or [Properties]:↵
Specify new TEXT insertion point <no change>:↵
Enter new text style <STANDARD>:ROMANT (part 1, Figure 8-13)
Specify new height <5.0000>:10 (part 2)
Specify new rotation angle <0>:30 (part 3)
Enter new text <AutoCLAD>:AutoCAD (part 4)
```

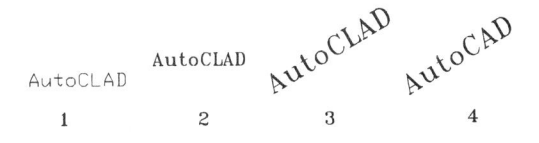

Figure 8-13

This command gives you the options to change all of the variables in the TEXT command as shown in Figure 8-13.

If you pick more than one string, the command will repeat the prompts for each string.

The DDEDIT Command

In long strings of text, DDEDIT makes the editing process much easier. You can change only the text, not the formatting or properties of the text.

To edit the text string content:

> **Toolbar** From the Modify toolbar, choose choose Edit Text.
>
> **Pull Down** From the Modify menu, choose Text.

The command line equivalent is DDEDIT.

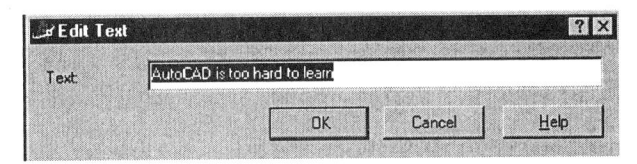

Figure 8-14

Select the line text object that you would like to edit. Pick the text where you want it to be changed, or type over or reenter the text, then choose OK to have it updated. Pressing Backspace will delete the highlighted text.

Select another line of text, or press ↵ to exit the command.

If you have chosen multiline text, you will be returned to the Multiline Text editor.

Figure 8-15

Modifying all the Properties

If you want to change more than the text line content, use DDMODIFY. This works on only one string of text at a time, but offers you a variety of things to change.

To edit the text string:

> **Toolbar** There is no button for properties in this release.
>
> **Pull down** From the Modify menu, choose Properties.

The command line equivalent is DDMODIFY.

This works similarly to the CHANGE command in that you can change all of the properties associated with the line of text.

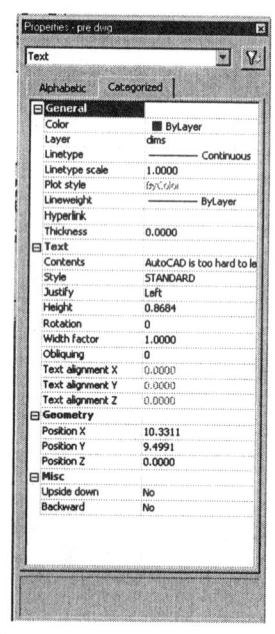

Figure 8-16

Making Isometric Lettering

As mentioned earlier, SNAP sets a spacing for point entries, and GRID places a dot grid on the screen. SNAP allows you to indicate points or positions on the screen at preset regular integers. SNAP also allows a rotated or isometric drawing to be entered. Once entered, you need to change the obluquing angle of the text to make it look isometric.

206 CHAPTER EIGHT

```
Command: SNAP
Specify snap spacing or [ON/OFF/Aspect/Rotate/Style/Type]:R↵
Specify base point <0'-0.00",0'-0.00">:↵
Specify rotation angle <0.00>:45↵  (will rotate at 45 degrees)
```

The GRID and SNAP can be changed at any time during a drawing. This is particularly important in creating text, because text is often close to, but not on, an existing item or line.

To create isometric lettering, change the SNAP to Isometric. Then change the obliquing angle in the STYLE command to be either 30 or -30. This will adjust the slant. Then enter your letters using Fit.

Isometric Lettering — An Exercise

Use your own initials to fill in the spaces on the cube.

Step 1 Change the SNAP style to Isometric, and draw in a cube.

Step 2 Pick a font from the Pull-Down menu - Format, then Text Style. (Roman, Standard, or Monotext are the best for this purpose). Next change the obliquing angle to 30. This is calculated by measuring the angle from the horizontal. Use Fit to place the text.

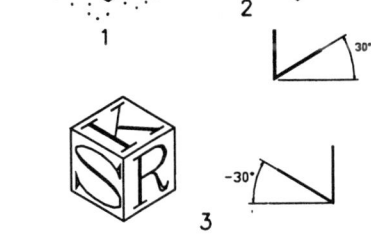

Figure 8-16

Step 3 Pick the same font, and change the obliquing angle to -30. Use Fit to place the text. Use your own judgment to create the last letter.

Using LEADER to Create Notations

The LEADER command in the Dimension menu gives you the facility of creating text with a leader line or series of leader lines and an arrowhead. The leader arrowhead emanates from the point picked. The command is as follows:

```
Command: LEADER
Specify leader start point: (pick 1)
Specify next point: (pick 2)
Specify next point or [Annotation/Format/Undo]<Annotation>:
  (pick 3)
Specify next point or [Annotation/Format/Undo]<Annotation>:↵
Enter first line of
  annotation text:24.00%%c
  %%p0.02
MText:↵
```

You can enter as many points on the leader line as are necessary.

All special text characters can be used in this dimension as well.

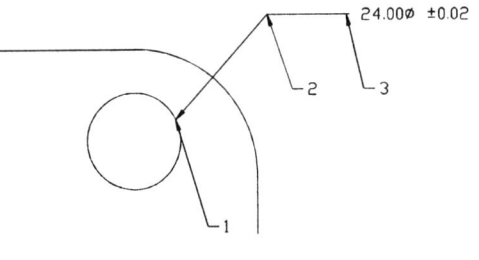

Figure 8-17

Text **207**

The arrowhead size is set in the dimension style or with DIMSCALE or DIMASZ.

To enter multiple lines of text, either keep typing at the "MText:" prompt, or enter at the "Annotation (or RETURN for options):" prompt. If you choose the latter, you will enter the text editor and can continue entering text using it.

The options of Leader include:

Tolerance offers a control frame containing geometric tolerances using the Geometric Tolerances dialog box.
Copy copies text, a text paragraph, a block, or a feature control frame to the leader line.
Block inserts a block at the end of the leader line.
Format controls the way the leader is drawn and whether it has an arrowhead. Options include Spline, Straight, and Arrow.

To enter a leader line without related text, enter a single blank space when you are prompted for the dimension text. This can be done with all dimension entries.

As in the LINE command, you can use **U** to undo the previous point entry without exiting the command.

Prelab 8 Using Text and Text Styles

In this lab we will create a title block.

Step 1 Use PLINE and LINE to create this title block. If you set the SNAP to .25 to start, it will make drawing easier. Change the SNAP as needed.

The lower left area will be for Scale, Date, etc., the central area will be for the company title, which is "3D Design Studio," and the top area will be for revisions.

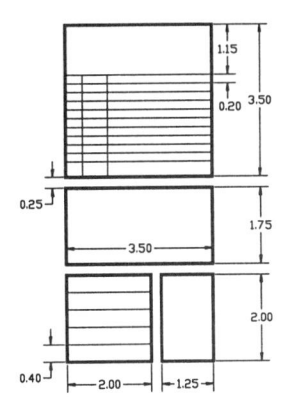

Step 2 Set up a text style.

Pull Down From the Format menu, choose Text Style.

The command line equivalent is **STYLE**.

Command:**STYLE**

This will invoke the dialog box.

Slide the bar up until you find Futura. Choose this font, or another if this is not available; then choose Apply and then Close to return to the command prompt.

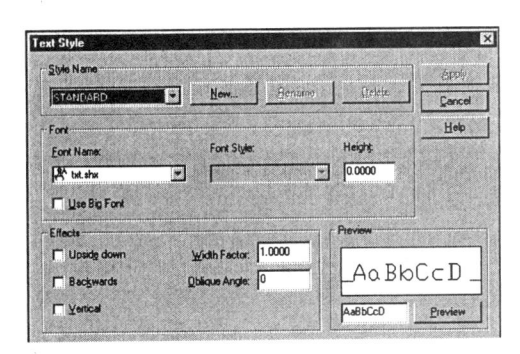

Step 3 Set up DTEXT.

Pull Down From the Draw menu, pick Text, then Single Line Text.

The command line equivalent is **DTEXT**.

```
Command:DTEXT
Specify start point or [Justify/Style]:
  (pick 1)
Specify height <.5000>:.1
Specify rotation angle <0>:↵
Enter text:Scale (pick 2)
Enter text:Drawn By (pick 3)
Enter text:Checked By (pick 4)
Enter text:Date (pick 5)
Enter text:Date of Print
Enter text:↵
```

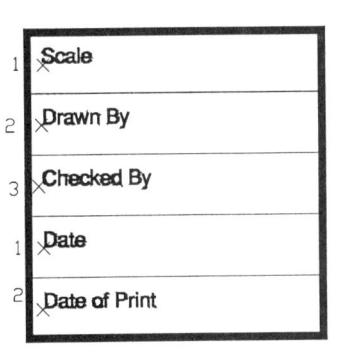

Text 209

Step 4 The lettering is a bit large, so use the CHANGE command to make the letters a bit smaller. You can change them with DDMODIFY, but for this operation CHANGE is quicker.

```
ommand:CHANGE
Select objects: (pick 1, 2, 3, 4, 5)
Select objects:⏎
Specify change point or [Properties]:⏎
Specify new TEXT insertion point
  <no change>:⏎
Enter new text style <STANDARD>:⏎
Specify new height <5.0000>:.08
Specify new rotation angle <0>:⏎
Enter new text <Scale>:(keep pressing ⏎
  until you have changed all the sizes
  and exited from CHANGE)
```

Scale	×1
Drawn By	×2
Checked By	×3
Date	×4
Date of Print	×5

Step 5 Now use the MOVE command to move the text up a bit.

```
Command:MOVE
Select objects:P
Select objects:⏎
Specify base point or
  displacement: (pick 1)
Specify second point as
  displacement: (pick 2)
```

Scale	
Drawn By	
Checked By	
Date	×1 ×2
Date of Print	

Step 6 For the other text in this box, create a new text style and add the text as shown. The text font illustrated is Cityblueprint.

> **Pull Down** From the Draw menu, choose Text, then Single-Line Text.

The command line equivalent is **STYLE**.

Then add the text as either DTEXT or single-line text.

Scale	As noted
Drawn By	S. Kyles
Checked By	D. Blackman
Date	04/01/98
Date of Print	04/28/98

Step 7   Now make a cube with isometric lettering. Change SNAP and GRID to draw in the cube.

From the Format menu, pick Drawing Aids. Change the rotation angle of the SNAP to 30.

```
Command: SNAP
Specify snap spacing or [ON/OFF/Aspect/Rotate/Style/Type]:R
Specify base point <0'-0.00",0'-0.00">:
Specify rotation angle <0.00>:30  (will rotate at 30 degrees)
```

The grid size will follow the snap size unless changed by the GRID command.

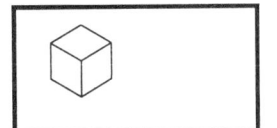

Use the line command to draw in the cube.

Step 8   Now use the STYLE command to load the ROMANT font and change the obliquing angle in order to load letters onto an isometric plane.

From the Format menu choose Text Style.

```
Command: STYLE
```

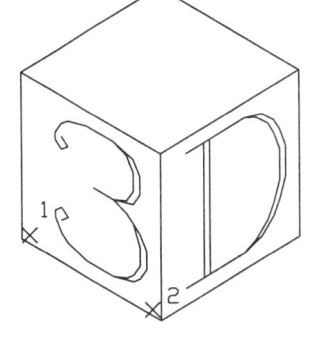

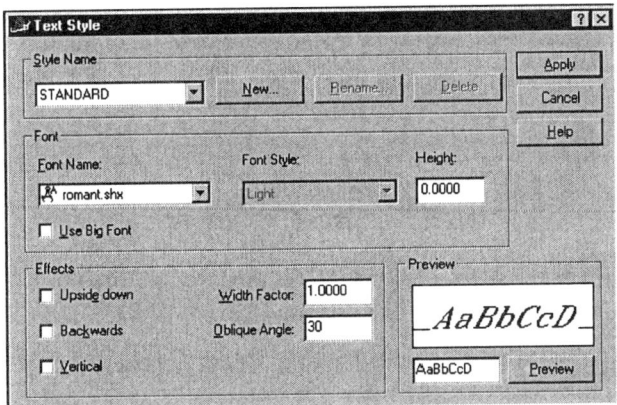

Now change the obliquing angle to -30 and add the second line.

```
Command: STYLE
```

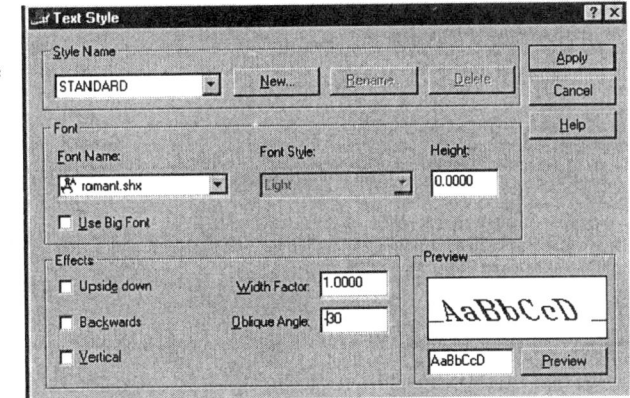

Text   **211**

Step 9   Change the obliquing angle of the ROMANT font to 0 and add the title and address using the Center option. Set SNAP back to normal before you start.

```
Command: SNAP
Specify snap spacing or [ON/OFF/Aspect/Rotate/Style/Type]: S ↵
Isometric/Standard: S
Increment<1.00>: ↵

Command: STYLE
```

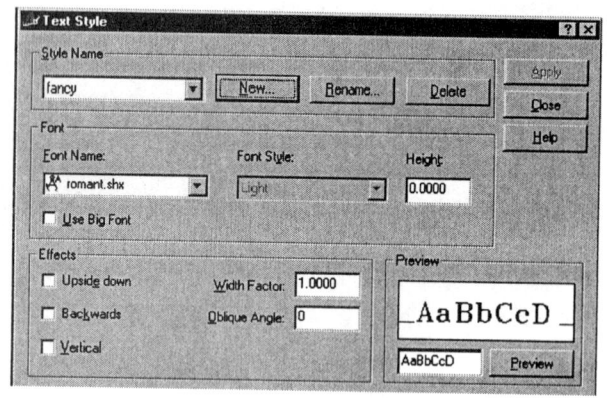

```
Command: DTEXT
Specify start point or [Justify/Style]: C
Specify Center point of text: (pick 1)
Specify height <.5000>: .1
Specify rotation angle <0>: ↵
Enter text: Design Studio
Enter text: Slip Gate Road
Enter text: Frog Hollow
Enter text: New Hampshire
Enter text: ↵
```

Step 10   Use PAN to move the screen down so that you can change the STYLE to Italic and add the notes regarding the revisions. Use the dialog boxes to change the style.

Do not change any options.

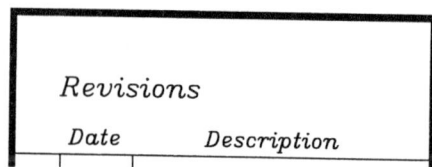

```
Command: DTEXT
Specify start point or [Justify/Style]: (pick the first point)
Specify height <1.5000>: ↵
Specify rotation angle< 0>: ↵
Enter text: Revisions (pick again)
Text: Date (pick again)
Text: Description
Text: ↵
```

Step 11 Now create another box above the Revisions box, and add a paragraph of text regarding the date of tender for the drawing. Use PLINE to quickly draw in a rectangle. Then change the style to Romans. Finally add a paragraph of text using MTEXT.

Change style or font first.

> **Toolbar** From the Draw menu, choose Text.
>
> **Pull Down** From the Draw menu, choose Text, then Multiline.

The command line equivalent is **MTEXT**.

    Command:MTEXT

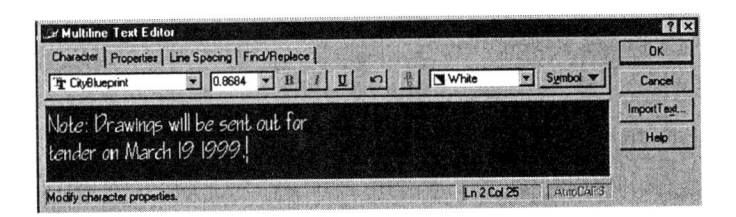

Step 12 Use ZOOM All to view your title block.

Change some of your text using DDEDIT and file it for future use under the name PRE-LAB8.

You will need this title block for the Prelab in Chapter 11, so don't lose it!

Command and Function Summary

DDEDIT edits multiple lines of text and attribute definitions.

DDMODIFY edits text and properties of multiline text.

DTEXT creates text and displays it on screen while it is being created.

MTEXT creates paragraph text.

QTEXT allows the text to be displayed as a box to save regeneration time.

STYLE controls the style of the characters..

TEXT creates text in single line format.

Practice Exercise 8

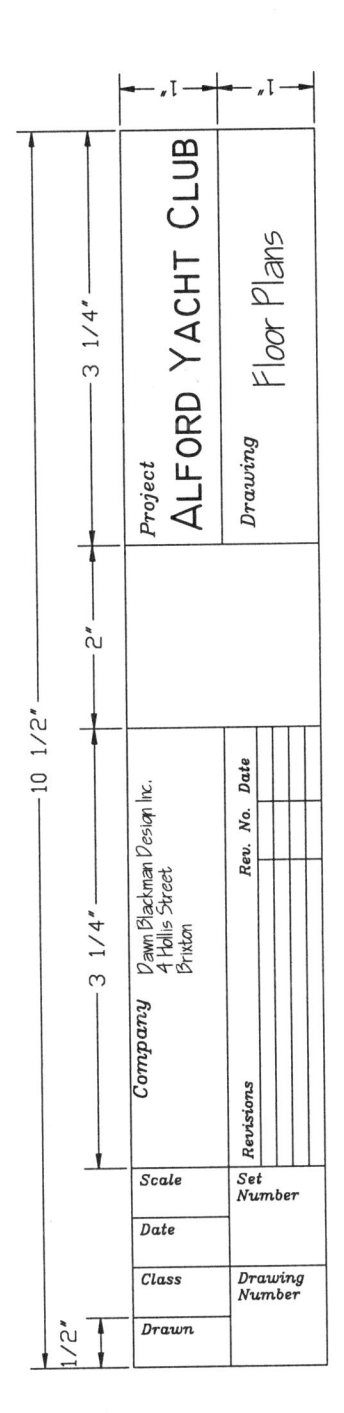

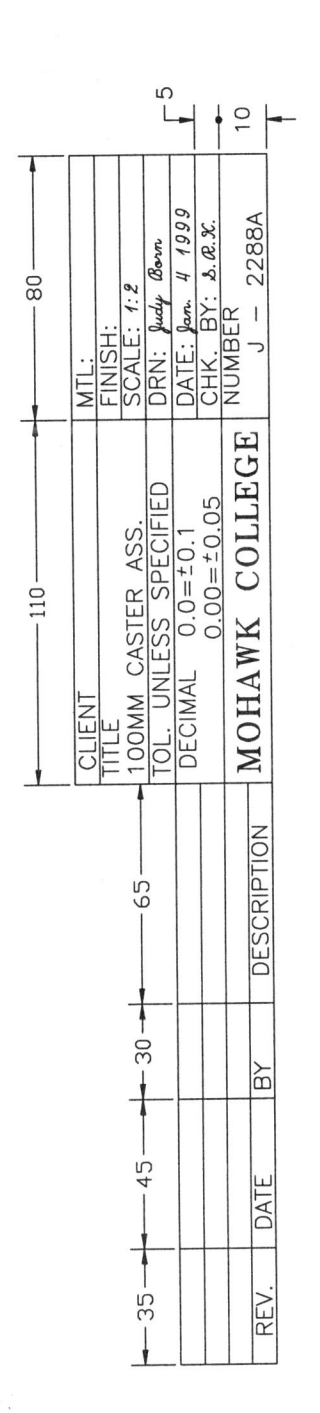

Use a PLINE to make the outer edges. Remember to use Close for the corners. Use at least three different lettering styles. Do not forget to change SNAP to line up the lettering.

If you prefer another style of title block, that is fine, as long as it is acceptable by your department.

Exercise A8

Retrieve the model called A1SHEET. Using the TEXT and DTEXT commands plus the Set style option, enter the text in the title block as shown. Retrieve the files FIRSTFL and SECONDFL and add the view titles at a size of 1'6''. Then add the necessary notations for things like closets, stair risers, and room titles.

Since this is relatively easy, use the remainder of the lab time to create the interior finish. Offset at .5 and FILLET Rad 0 is the easiest way.

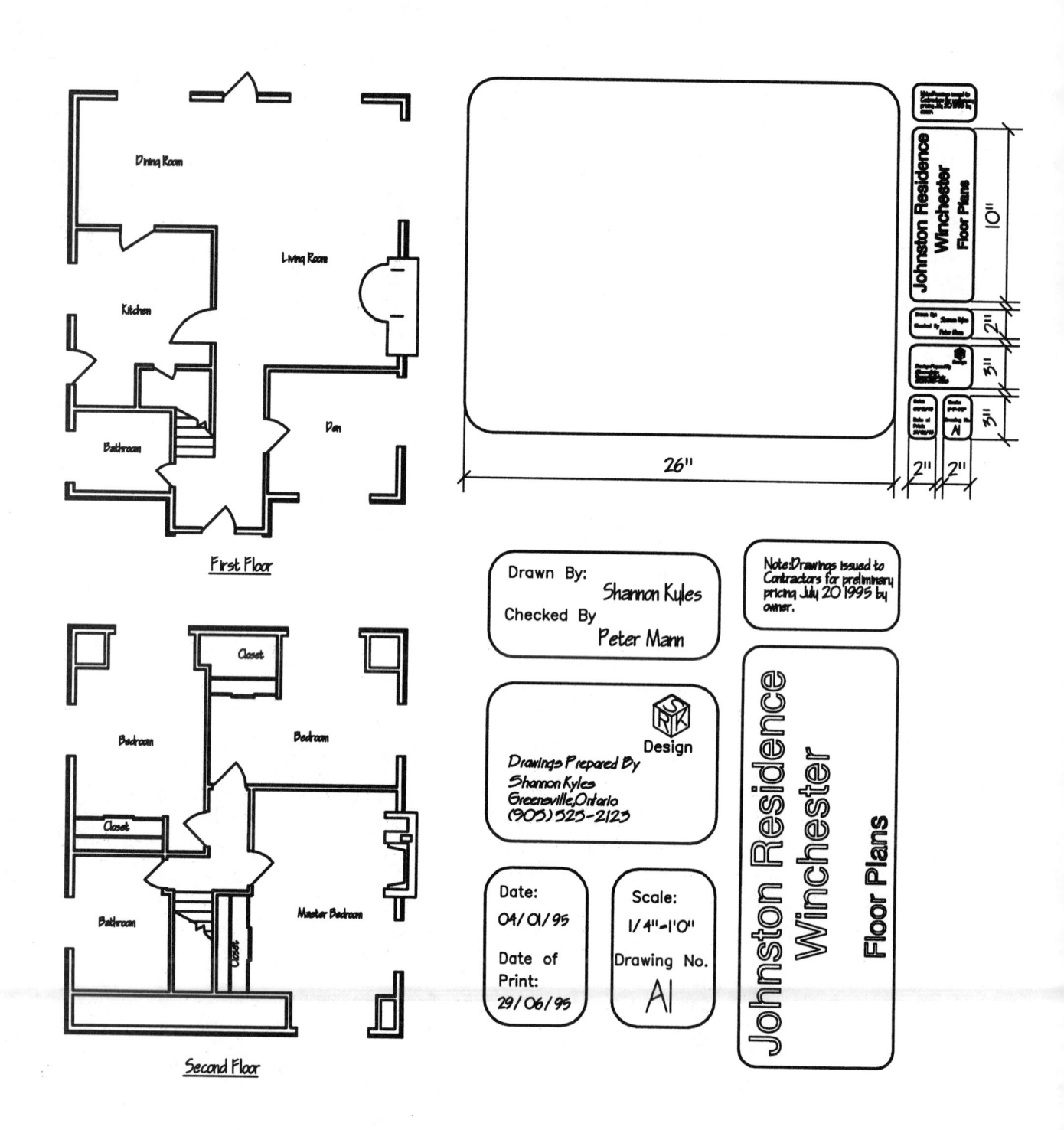

Exercise C8

Draw the title block in first, then draw in the foundations.
Sizes for footings are in Exercises noted.

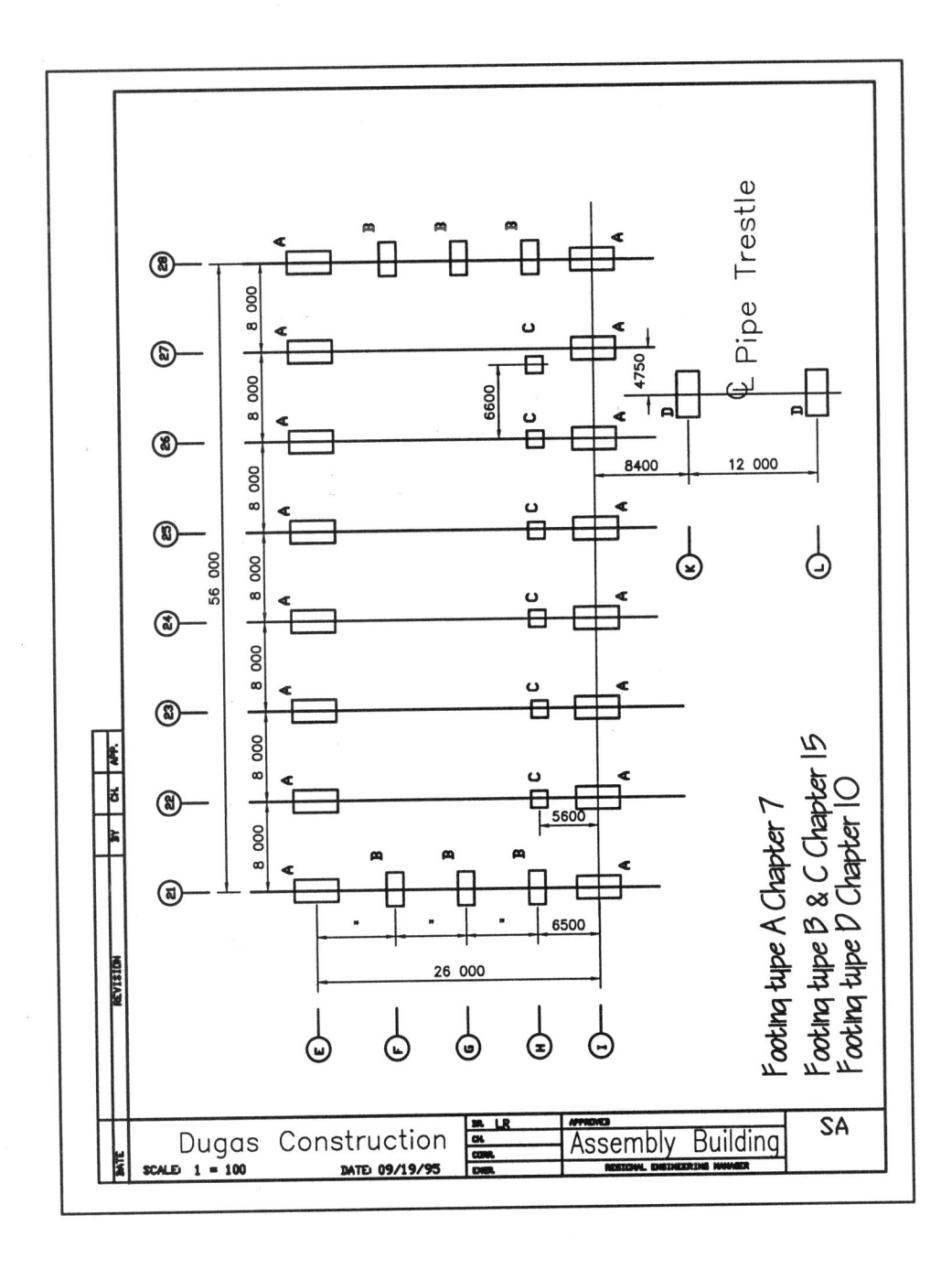

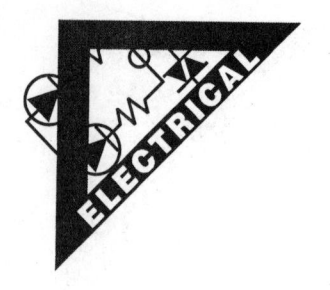

Exercise E8

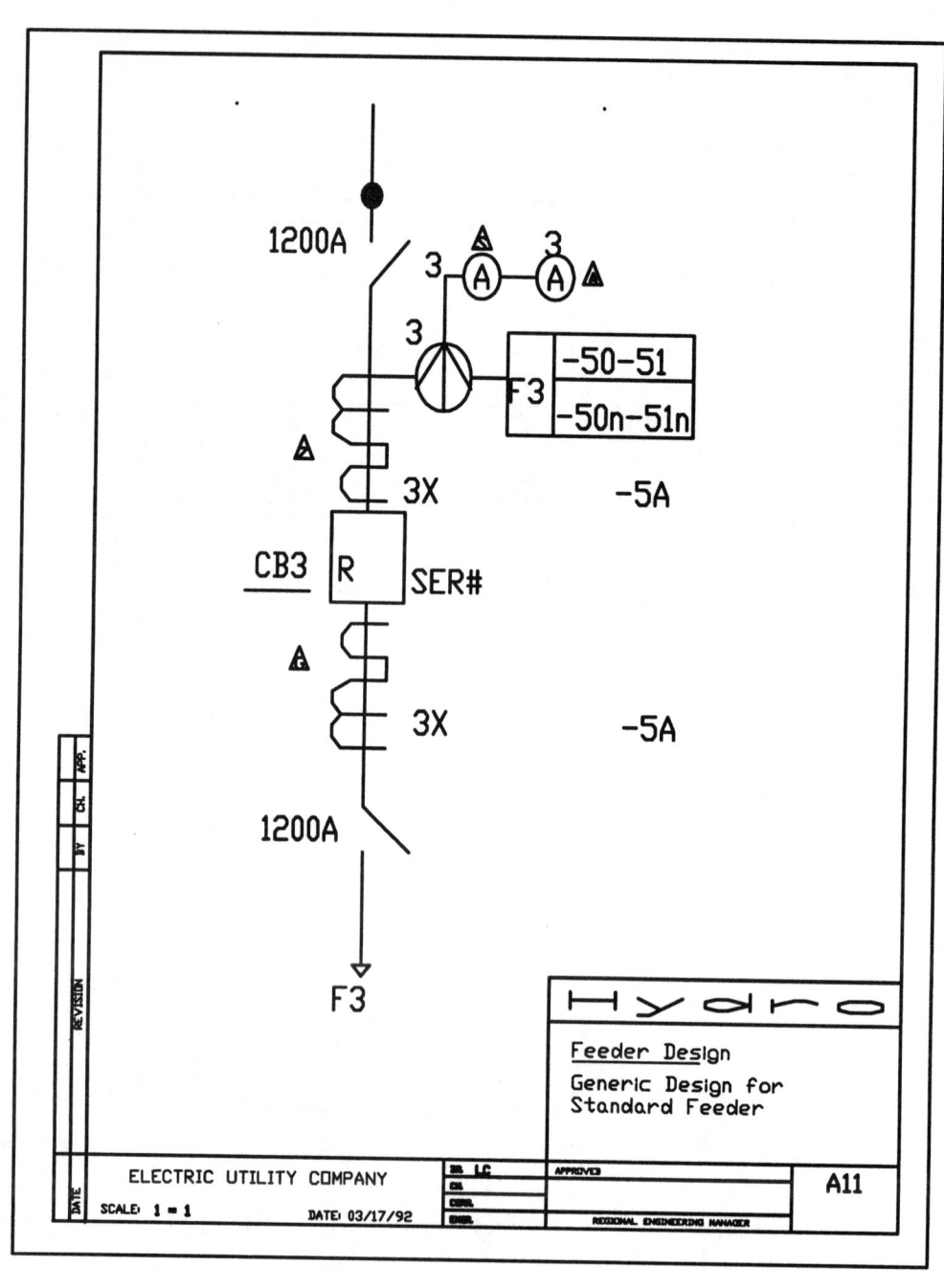

Draw the title block in first, then add the text. Once this is completed, you can start on the drawing and add the notations.

Exercise M8

Draw the title block in first, and add the text. Once this is completed, you can start on the drawing and add the notations.

Change the SNAP to get the isometric in easily.

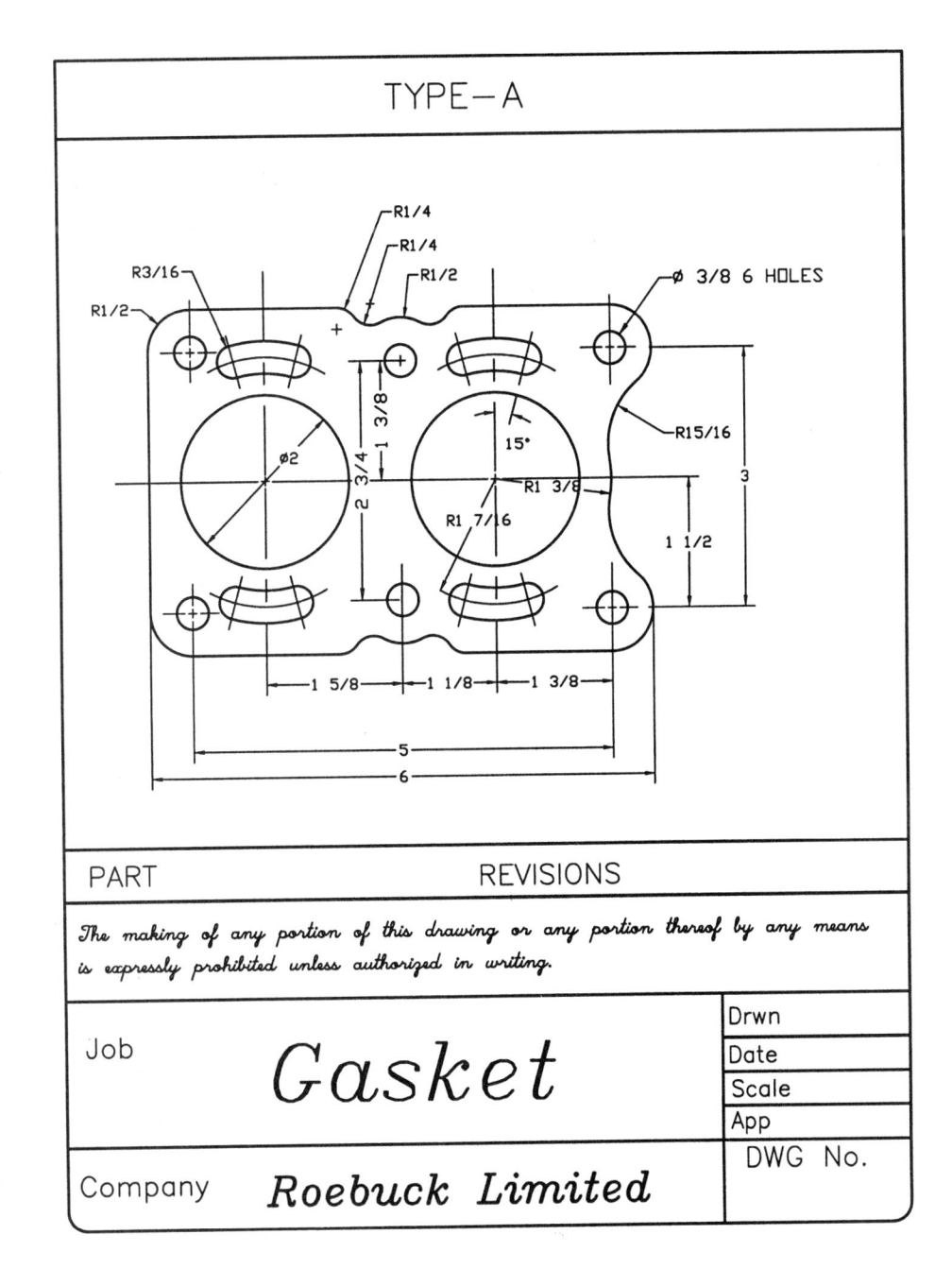

Challenger 8

These architectural details will be useful later.

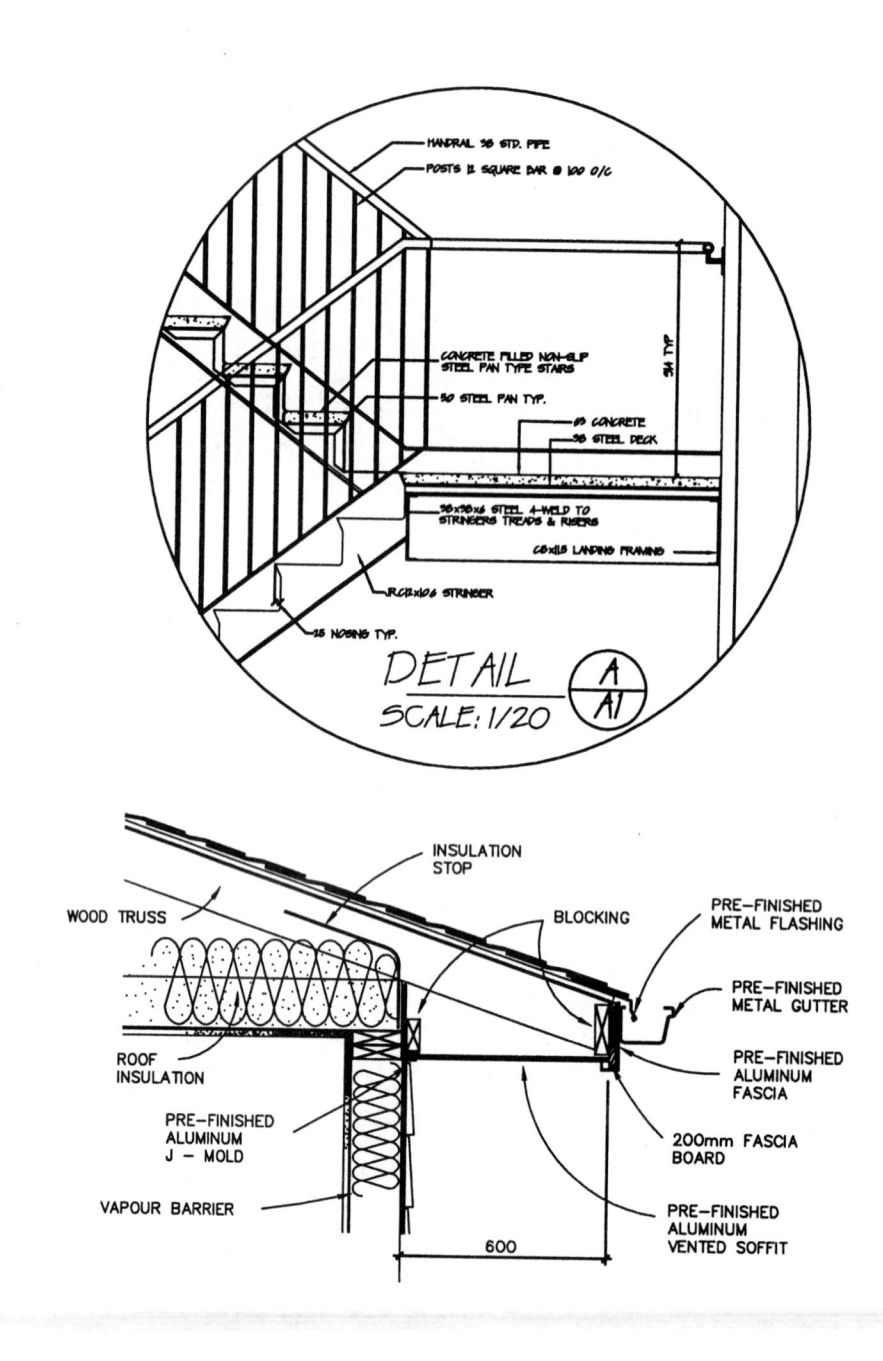

(Many thanks to UMA for this drawing.)

9 HATCH and SKETCH

Upon completion of this chapter, you should be able to:

1. Use the HATCH command
2. Use BHATCH with the dialog box
3. Edit existing hatches
4. Use the SKETCH command
5. Use point filters

The HATCH Command

The HATCH command fills an area with a specified pattern. It creates a nonassociative hatch pattern which will not update when the boundaries are updated. (The BHATCH command, described in the next section, creates a hatch pattern that will be updated along with the associated boundary.) Unless otherwise specified, HATCH combines the lines that make up the hatch into a block.

The HATCH command is accessed through the command prompt only; no button or pull down command is available.

To start, you must create a boundary for the hatch. The geometry must be perfect: the corners must all meet, and there must be no gaps or overlapping items. Closed polylines, circles, and ellipses can be selected as single objects for hatch generation. The hatch command is found only by typing it in.

The default hatch pattern is a 45 degree angle.

Enter **HATCH** at the command line.

```
Command:HATCH
Enter pattern name or [?/Solid/User
   defined] <ANSI31>:
Specify a scale for the pattern<1>:
Specify an angle for the pattern <0>:
Select objects to define hatch boundary
   or <direct hatch>,
Select objects: (pick 1)
Select objects:
```

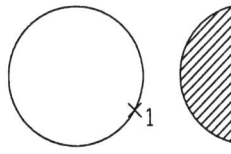

Figure 9-1

In order to create a HATCH, you need four basic parameters: the pattern, the size, the rotation angle, and the items which are to be hatched.

Objects can be selected by individual selection, Window, Crossing, or any of the other object selection methods.

Direct Hatch

This option allows you to define the boundary of the hatch within the HATCH command. You can either retain the boundary or not. AutoCAD prompts for points until the boundary is complete. Both line and arc segments can be added to the boundary. Pressing ⏎ ends the command and creates the hatch.

If you opt not to retain the boundary, only the hatch pattern is drawn. This is useful for areas where only a hatch, not a boundary, is required as in the concrete hatch and the steel hatch patterns shown in Figure 9-2.

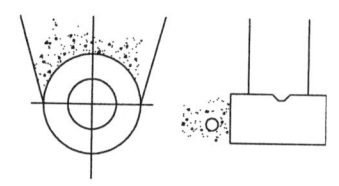

Figure 9-2

```
Command: HATCH
Enter pattern name or [?/Solid/User
defined] <ANSI31>:⏎
Specify a scale for the pattern <1>:⏎
Specify an angle for the pattern <0>:⏎
Select objects to define hatch
boundary or <direct hatch>,
Select objects:⏎
Retain polyline boundary? <n>:⏎
Specify start point: (pick a point)
Specify next point or [Arc/Close/Length/Undo]:
   (pick the remaining points)
Specify start point for new
boundary or <apply hatch>:⏎
```

Figure 9-3

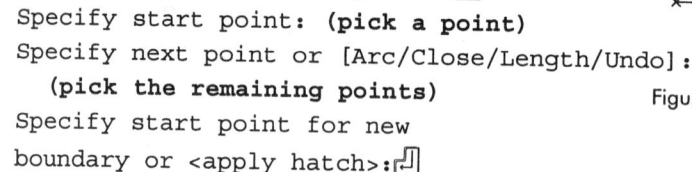

You can either choose one of the existing hatch patterns, or create a series of straight, parallel lines to form your own hatch pattern by selecting the User option. List the HATCH patterns in the HATCH command with the **?**.

```
Command: HATCH
Enter pattern name or [?/Solid/User
defined] <ANSI31>:?
```

Scale, Patterns, Rotation angle, and Style for HATCH are the same as for BHATCH.

The BHATCH Command

BHATCH (Boundary Hatch) fills an enclosed area with an associative hatch pattern that will update when the boundaries are modified. In addition, BHATCH allows you to preview the hatch pattern and adjust the definition or options of the hatch such as scale and angle. BHATCH is accessed through a dialog box.

Toolbar From the Draw toolbar, choose this button:

Pull Down From the Draw menu, choose Hatch...

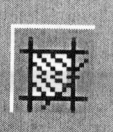

The BHatch Dialog Box

The command line equivalent is **BHATCH**.

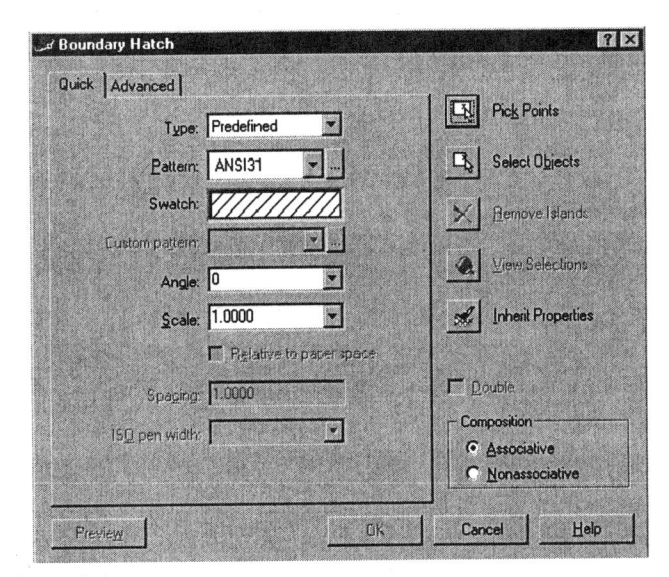

Figure 9-4

The BHatch dialog box controls every aspect of the hatch pattern, and under the Advanced option you can create a new boundary.

Type	tells you if it is a user defined or an AutoCAD defined hatch.
Pattern	controls the ACAD standard hatch patterns. Hatch patterns are listed by name in the dialog box. Pick the down arrow to view the available patterns. This area lists only the names of the patterns.
Swatch	illustrates the pattern.
Custom Pattern	iIllustrates a custom pattern.
Angle	controls the angle of the hatch patterns.
Scale	shows the scale of the pattern to be used. The default scale factor is 1. This means that the hatch is calculated to be displayed at the default screen size or an 11″ × 8 1/2″ sheet.
Relative to Paper Space	sets the properties specific to the paper space parameters.
Spacing	is for user-defined hatch patterns; it refers to the distance between the first line and the second. This option is only available if User-defined is selected in the Pattern Type box.
ISO Pen Width	controls the pen width if an ISO pattern is chosen from the Pattern list.

Each hatch pattern has a specific number of lines per inch. For example, the ANSI31 pattern generates three lines per inch at a scale of 1:1. If you have changed the limits and the model is larger than 11 units in X, you *must* change the scale factor.

When working in inch units, the scale factor of the hatch should be the maximum X value of the screen divided by 12, the same as the scale factor for LTSCALE. For example, limits at 0,0 and 24,18 would be a scale factor of 2.

Danger

If you do not adjust your scale factor, AutoCAD will attempt to create the hatch at the default scale. There is a good chance you will run out of room on your floppy disk and be forced to exit from the file. Save your file before hatching, and preview the hatch just in case.

HATCH and SKETCH   **223**

Other scale sizes are shown in Figure 9-5. Remember, if you are using architectural units or feet and inches, each unit is an inch, not a foot.

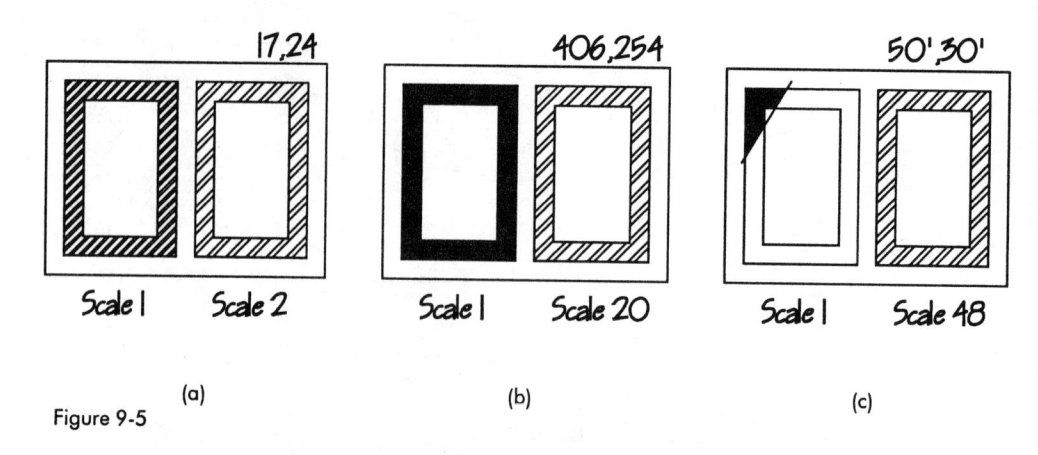

Figure 9-5

If you do not change the scale factor, there will be far too many lines to view, and the lines from the patterns will quickly fill up space on your disk. If you have not changed the scale factor, and the pattern is much too small, then it is possible you will have a system crash or be forced to exit your file. AutoCAD will make an attempt to save everything on your file up to the point where the hatch started, but there is no guarantee. You can be sure that, if this is going to happen, it will happen 20 minutes before the drawing is due.

Always use the Preview Hatch option just in case or create a small test pattern on the screen, about 1″ × 1″ relative to the real size or actual vectored inches of the screen, i.e., not relative to the limits but to the screen. You can tell by the test pattern if the scale is appropriate. If, on the other hand, the test area is totally filled in or remains blank, the scale needs to be changed.

Usually, people add hatches because they are going to be plotting onto paper. The hatch scale should be determined by the size of the final drawing, not the size of the object being hatched. If you have to change the scale of a hatch, keep in mind the final size of the plot as well as the size of the drawing relative to the screen.

In Chapter 11, there is a discussion on scale with regard to the size of the hatch and linetype scales and the size of the drawing. Before producing the final drawings, check that chapter to see that the hatch is accurate.

Angle If you are picking a hatch from the pull-down menu, the rotation angle will be exactly as shown. For example, Figure 9-6(a) uses ANSI33, which is displayed at an angle of 45 degrees. To pick this pattern as it appears on the screen, do not change the rotation angle; leave it at zero, because that is the angle of the pattern itself.

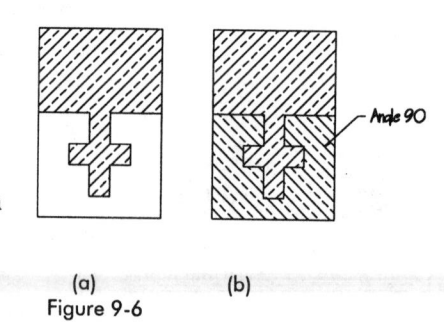

Figure 9-6

Figure 9-6(b) has ANSI33 at the default rotation and at a rotation angle of 90 degrees.

When using user-defined hatch patterns, the rotation angle is calculated at a horizontal, rotating counterclockwise.

When using user-defined hatch patterns, the rotation angle is calculated at a horizontal, rotating counterclockwise.

Identifying the Boundary

For many students, this is where the difficulties begin, because objects must form a perfect boundary.

The problem many students encounter is that lines, circles, and other objects are sometimes not entered accurately. SNAP and OSNAP are not always used effectively and consequently the lines are crooked, do not have tidy intersections with adjacent items, or are otherwise defective. This means that these objects do not provide an adequate boundary for hatching.

Poor entry of objects will lead to other problems as well. If you have what appears to be four objects on the screen, there should be only four objects (or one polyline) on the screen. If you list the objects using Window and have more than four objects, you may have trouble.

Figure 9-7

```
Command:LIST
Select objects:(pick 1) Other Corner: (pick 2) 7 found
```

If your hatch doesn't work because the point picked is outside the boundary or the boundary can't be identified, clean up your geometry and be more careful next time.

There are two basic ways of identifying the boundaries: by picking points and by selecting objects.

Pick Points   identifies a boundary from existing objects that form an enclosed area. AutoCAD defines the boundary by analyzing all the closed objects in the area. Once you have chosen the Pick Points option, the dialog box disappears and AutoCAD prompts for point specification.

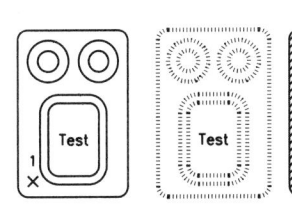

Figure 9-8

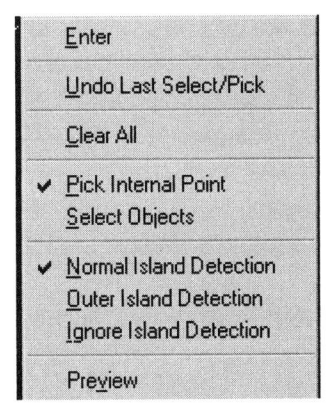

```
Command:BHATCH
(choose Pick Points)
Select internal point: (pick 1)
Select internal point:↵
(choose Preview, then OK)
```

HATCH and SKETCH   **225**

Select Objects allows the user to identify the boundary by object selection rather than as an internal point. Sometimes both Select objects and Pick Points can be used successfully to identify one hatch boundary.

```
Command: BHATCH
(choose Select Objects)
Select internal point: (pick 1)
Other corner: (pick 2)
Select internal point:↵
(choose Preview, then Apply)
```

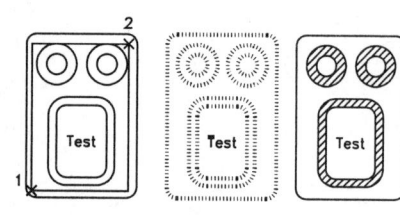

Figure 9-9

In both cases, the geometry must form a continuous boundary.

The opposite happens if your boundary is on normal.

Preview displays the hatching before it is applied. This can save a lot of time and a lot of grief if you have not set the scale properly.

Inherent Properties allows the user to apply the properties of an existing BHATCH to a new boundary. The hatch style, rotation angle, and scale will all be applied to the new area. Once the Inherent Properties box is chosen, the dialog box disappears and the user is prompted to indicate the hatch pattern.

When the hatch has been identified, the dialog box returns so that Pick Points or Select Objects can be chosen.

Remove Islands removes from the boundary set objects defined as islands by the Pick Points option.

```
Command: BHATCH
(choose Pick Points)
Select internal point: (pick 1)
Select internal point:↵
(choose Select Objects)
Select internal point: (pick 2,3)
Select internal point:↵
(Preview — get the upper hatch)
(choose Remove Islands)
Select internal point: (pick 4)
(Preview — get the lower hatch)
```

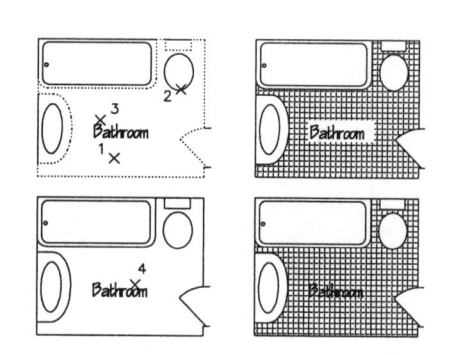

Figure 9-10

226 CHAPTER NINE

Advanced Options Dialog Box

This dialog box controls the definition of the boundary set.

Object Type AutoCAD's hatches are created either in regions or in polylines.

Boundary Set In large drawings this option allows the user to define certain objects or areas as the boundary set rather than taking all of the objects on screen. This saves time in producing boundaries.

Island detection style Once your data is correct, Window the objects you want to hatch, and the hatch pattern you have chosen will fill the boundary starting from the outer boundary. If there are closed boundaries within the outer boundary, the default is to have the hatch show up on alternating boundaries.

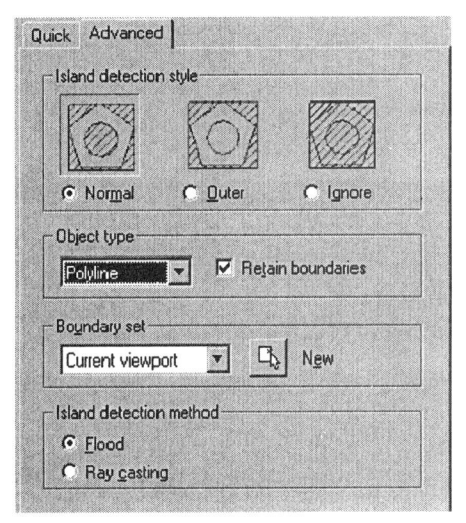

Figure 9-11

Hatching concave curves and multiple circles can cause hatching discrepancies.

Ray Casting controls the way AutoCAD defines a hatch boundary. It helps to define boundaries when difficulties occur. If you encounter the prompt "Outside boundaries:" try the Ray Casting options.

Flood Controls how AutoCAD identifies your islands.

Figure 9-12

If Ray Casting is giving you bad results, try Flood.

HATCH and SKETCH 227

Solid Hatches

Release 14 and 2000 allow for solids in undulating boundaries. Pick the Solid option either from the Hatch options or from the BHATCH dialog box under pattern.
The solid will take on the current color.

```
Command: HATCH
Enter pattern name or [?/Solid/
 User defined] <ANSI31>: s
Select objects to define boundary
  or <direct hatch>
Select objects: (pick 1)
Select objects:
```

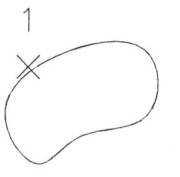

Figure 9-13

Editing Hatches

There are two ways of editing associative hatching. The first is to edit the boundaries; the second is to edit the actual hatch itself.

Editing Boundaries

With associative hatching, the hatch will update when the boundaries are changed.

```
Command: STRETCH
Select objects: (pick 1)
Other corner: (pick 2)
Select objects:
Specify base point or displacement:
  (pick 3)
Specify  second point of
   displacement: (pick 4)
```

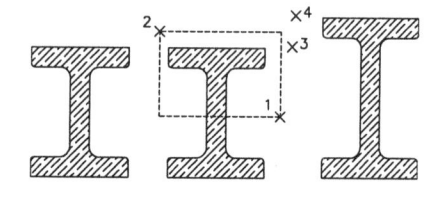

Figure 9-14

The hatch has updated along with the boundaries.

Editing the Hatch Properties

The Hatchedit dialog box and command allow for the modification of the hatch itself.

Toolbar From the Modify toolbar, choose the Hatch button:

Pull Down From either the Properties or the Modify menu, choose Object, then Hatch.

The command line equivalent is **HATCHEDIT**.

AutoCAD first prompts you to select the hatch object to be edited. Once this is done, the Hatchedit dialog box is invoked and you can choose the properties to be edited.

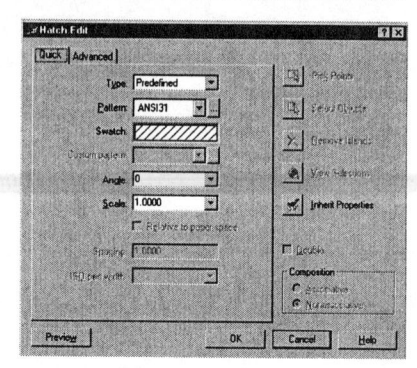

Figure 9-15

228 CHAPTER NINE

Figure 9-16(a) shows the base hatch. In (b), the pattern has been changed from ANSI35 to ANSI38. In (c), the scale of the hatch in (a) has been changed.

Most of the options are the same as those in the BHATCH command and dialog box.

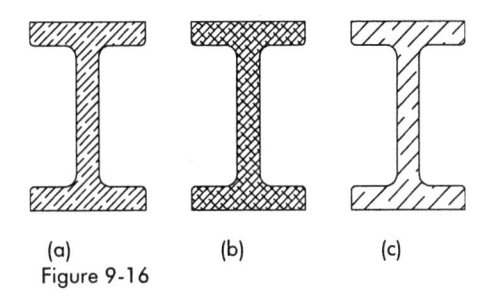

(a) (b) (c)
Figure 9-16

The SKETCH Command

The SKETCH command is included in this chapter because, like HATCH, it is often used to make final notations on drawings before they are plotted. In addition, just as the HATCH command has a tendency to take up a lot of room on a disk, the SKETCH command can also take up more room than expected on a disk because it can contain so many vectors.

SKETCH provides freehand sketching capabilities on a drawing. The motion of the mouse or digitizer determines the position of the sketch segments; the accuracy of the sketch segments is determined within the command.

The SKETCH command will prompt the user for the increment, or the distance between segments; for smoother curves, use smaller increments. The command is as follows:

Toolbar There is no button for this command.

Pull Down There is no command for sketch in the pull down menu.

The command line equivalent is **SKETCH**.

```
Command:SKETCH
Record increment <0.01>:.1
Sketch, Pen eXit Quit Record
   Erase Connect:P
Sketch:
```

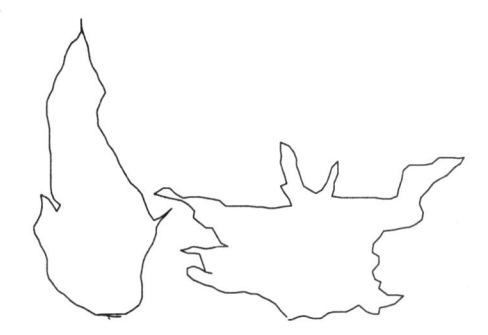

Where: **Pen** = the pen being lowered. The system prompts to put your "pen down"; whatever move you make with your cursor will be recorded. **P** a second time will lift the pen up.

eXit = the end of the command. **X** will exit from the Sketch command, retaining all segments created up to that point.

Quit = a cancellation of the segments to date. **Q** will leave SKETCH without saving the segments you have drawn.

Record = a save of all the lines drawn so far. **R** will make a permanent record of your lines without exiting from the command.

Erase = an erasing of some of the line segments drawn. **E** will allow you to erase lines from a certain point; it acts as a "backspace" over segments created.

Connect = a continuation of a previous sketch. **C** lets you pick up sketch again at the last entered end point after it has been ended.

Segments are not recorded on the disk until you use the Record option. Because each segment is added as a separate object and can take up a lot of room on a disk, the computer will offer a series of warning beeps to let you know that you are moving too quickly or that the disk is full. Raise your pen, press pick, and record your lines to date before continuing.

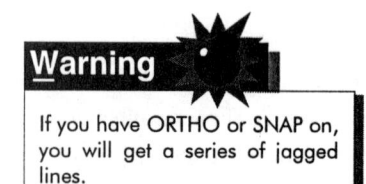

> **Warning**
> If you have ORTHO or SNAP on, you will get a series of jagged lines.

The SKPOLY Variable

AutoCAD captures sketching as a series of independent lines. Setting the SKPOLY system variable to a nonzero value produces a polyline for each contiguous sequence of sketched lines, rather than multiple line objects. This will save space on your disk.

Point Filters

X, Y, and Z *point filters* are used to make the entry of geometry easier.

With OSNAPs, the user can extract both the X and the Y value of points that are part of existing geometry; when you access the CENter of a circle, you are extracting the X and Y coordinates of that point. With point filters, you can extract just the X or just the Y value. Just as with the OSNAP entries, a space must be entered after your filter option if you are typing it in.

```
Command:LINE
Specify first point:.X (space) of MIDdle of (space)
```

In Figure 9-18, assume that you have the circle and the line. Now you want to place a doughnut at the X value of the center of the circle and the Y value of the top point on the line.

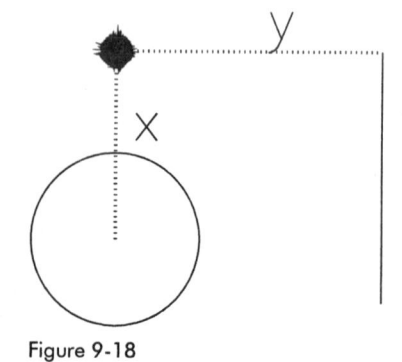

```
Command:DONUT
Inside diameter <0.5000>:0
Outside diameter <1.0000>:1
Center of doughnut:.X (space) of CENter of (pick the circle)
   (this gets the X value)
(Need YZ):.Y (space) of END of (pick the line) (this gets the Y
   value)
(Need Z):0 (positions the circle in the middle of the Z0 plane)
```

Figure 9-18

In Figure 9-19, assume that you have the vertical and diagonal LINEs and are trying to construct the PLINE starting at the same *X* value as the middle of the diagonal line, and the same *Y* value as the top of the vertical line.

```
Command:PLINE
From point:.X of MIDdle of (pick the
   diagonal)
(Need YZ):.y of END of (pick the
   vertical)
(Need Z):0
(complete the PLINE with options
   desired)
```

Figure 9-19

For MIDdle of and END of, the OSNAPs were used.

Rather than using filters, you could have created a horizontal line from the top of the vertical line and a vertical line from the middle of the diagonal line, and then started the PLINE from the INTersection of the two construction lines. But filters are much easier when you get used to them, and you don't need to either create or erase construction lines.

Using X, Y, and Z Filters

Filters "copy" coordinates of existing geometry.

With the construction lines, the draftsman lines up one view with another using a straight edge.

In English, you might say "Let's draw a horizontal line here, taking this other line and lining the straight edge up with it."

With the CAD drawing, the user picks points on the other views to have the computer calculate the perfect spot on the new view.

An English translation might be "Let's enter a line here, taking the *X* value of the end of this object and adding a *Y* of 1."

Or, even better, "Let's enter a line here, taking the *X* value of this line and the *Y* value of that."

Now you have determined the first point of the line and you simply need to put in the second point.

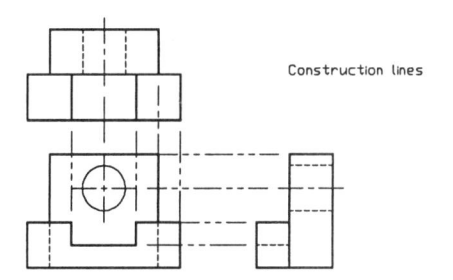

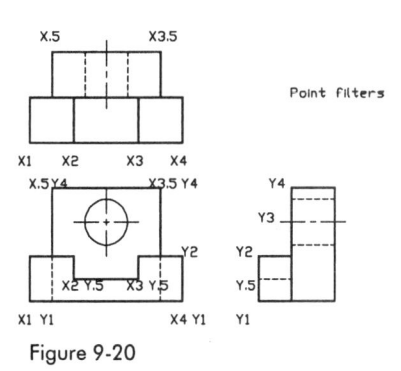

Figure 9-20

On a part where the views are all on regular increments, the SNAP might be just as easy to use. But on a part where there are areas not on SNAP points, this offers two great advantages:

1. The drawing will be made much quicker, because you don't have to go to LIST or ID to pick up the point needed.
2. The accuracy will be far greater, because you can trust the system to enter the correct number instead of you figuring it out, writing it down so you won't forget, and then typing it in. In the three steps needed to determine and enter a coordinate, there may be a high rate of errors.

Point filters work much the same way as OSNAP, in that you are asking for a point or parameter on something that already exists. The difference is that you are asking for only the X or the Y or the Z value instead of all of the coordinates attached to a particular object.

When used with OSNAP, filters filter out only the coordinate that you need.

Filters Without OSNAPs

If you are using a point in space to reference your filter, the value requested — .X or .Y — is taken from the point that you actually pick. If your SNAP is on, you will pick the coordinate with a preset integer; if not, you will pick exactly the point that you hit on the Z0 plane of the UCS.

If you are referencing an object with the use of one of the OSNAPS — CENter, ENDpoint, MIDdle, etc. — you must request first the filter desired, .X or .Y.

Entering Filters

A space must be entered after your filter option if you are typing it in. When you hit the space bar or ⏎ after this entry, your screen will show **.X of** or **.Y of**. Then you can pick the OSNAP that suits your purpose.

```
Command:LINE
Specify first point:.X of ENDpoint of (pick 1) (this gets the X
   value)
```

Instead of ENDpoint or MIDdle of an object, you are asking for only the X value or the Y value of the specific portion of the object you have chosen.

To call up the filter, pick .X or .Y from the LINE menu, or type in .X or .Y. (Don't forget the **period.**) AutoCAD will then pick up only the X or Y value of the point indicated. Once you have picked up the value you require, you are prompted to fill in the other coordinates needed to complete the point.

The following is an easy exercise illustrating two-dimensional point filters.

X, Y Filters — An Exercise

We will just create a cross section of a simple bushing.

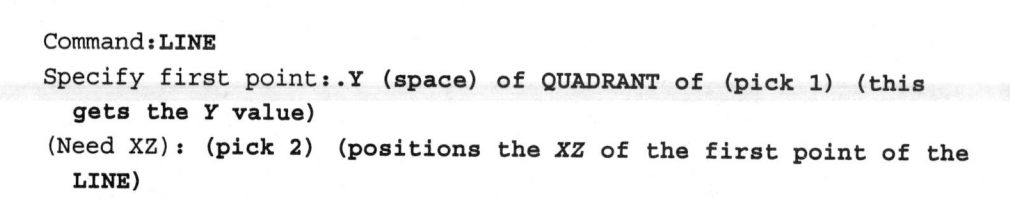

Step 1 First create three concentric circles on the left side of the screen. Keep the SNAP off so that you will not be tempted to use SNAPs rather than filters.

Step 2 Now extract the Y value of the top circle to create the first line of the section.

```
Command:LINE
Specify first point:.Y (space) of QUADRANT of (pick 1) (this
   gets the Y value)
(Need XZ): (pick 2) (positions the XZ of the first point of the
   LINE)
```

```
        To point:.Y of QUADrant of (pick 3)
        (Need XZ): (press F8 = ORTHO on)
          (pick 4) (positions the first LINE)
        To point:⏎
```

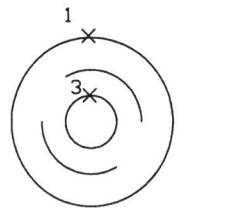

Make sure that ORTHO is on when placing the lower point on the line.

Step 3 Pick a spot to the right on your screen, then extract the *Y* value of the central hidden line circle. If you knew the length of the bushing, you could enter that, but for this exercise simply pick a point in space.

```
        Command:LINE
        Specify first point:⏎ (this will pick the last point entered)
        To point: (pick 5)
        To point:.Y of QUADrant of (pick 6)
          (this gets the Y value)
        (Need XZ): (pick 7)
        To point:⏎
```

Step 4 Now add the horizontal line at any distance between the two verticals.

```
        Command:LINE
        Specify first point:⏎ (this will pick the last point entered)
        To point: (pick 8)
        To point:.Y of ENDpoint of (pick 9)
          (this gets the Y value)
        (Need XZ): (pick 10)
        To point:ENDpoint of (pick 9 again)
        To point:⏎
```

Step 5 Now that this section is in, you could of course simply mirror it through the center point. But you already know how to do that, so try to create the bottom half using both *X* and *Y* filters.

```
        Command:LINE
        Specify first point:.X of ENDpoint of (pick 11)
        (Need YZ):.Y of QUADrant of (pick 12)
        (Need Z):0
        To point:.Y of QUADrant of (pick 13)
        (Need XZ): (pick 14) (ORTHO should
          still be on)
        To point:⏎
```

Step 6 Using both *X* and *Y* filters finish the rest of the cross section.

Each point is going to need an *X* and a *Y* value.

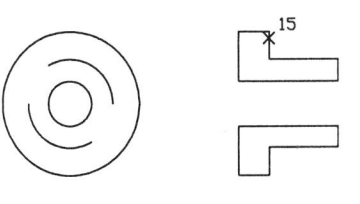

HATCH and SKETCH   **233**

Prelab 9A Point Filters

Looking at the drawing on the right, you can see that the side view would be easy to create once the front view is done, simply by lining up the horizontal lines with existing lines on the front view. Instead of using construction lines, try point filters.

For a really accurate model, *X,Y* filters are the easiest method.

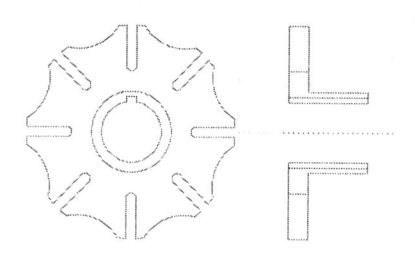

Step 1 Generate the geometry on the right using LINEs, ARCs, EXTEND, CIRCLE, and ARRAY. Make the center of the circle at 0,0.

The easiest way to approach it would be to draw the two inner CIRCLEs plus the keyway, then draw one of the exterior scallops completely and ARRAY it.

Once completed, you can start entering the cross section using the existing geometry as a guide.

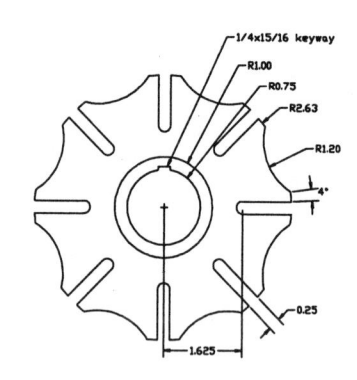

Step 2 Now add the vertical line from the top of the section to the center.

```
Command:F8 (= ORTHO on)
Command:LINE
Specify first point:
.Y of ENDpoint (pick 1)
(Need XZ):4,0
To point:.Y of QUADrant of (pick 2)
(Need XZ): (pick 3)
To point:@2,0 (gives the length of
  the line at 2 in X)
To point:⏎
```

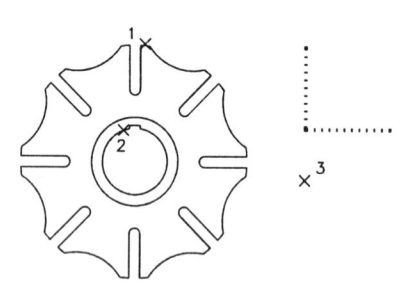

Step 3 Continue adding the horizontal lines across the bottom.

```
Command:LINE
Specify first point:ENDpoint of
  (pick 4)
To point:.Y of ENDpoint of (pick 5)
(Need XZ): (pick 6)
To point:@-1.5,0
To point:⏎
```

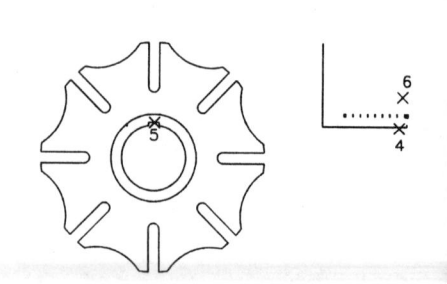

ORTHO should still be on.

234 CHAPTER NINE

Step 4 Continue adding lines.

```
Command:LINE
Specify first point:ENDpoint of
  (pick 7)
To point:.Y of ENDpoint of (pick 8)
(Need XZ): (pick 9)
To point:@-.5,0
To point:↵
```

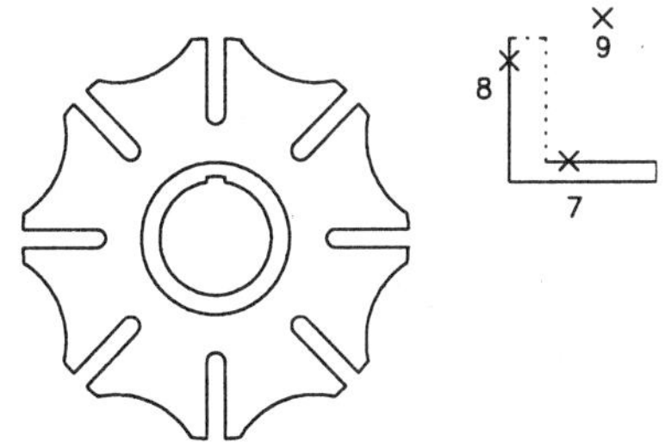

Step 5 Add the final two lines.

```
Command:LINE
Specify firstpoint:.Y of ENDpoint of (pick 10)
(Need XZ):NEAR (pick 11)
To point:PERpendicular to (pick 12)
Command:LINE
To point:.Y of QUADrant of (pick 13)
(Need XZ):NEAR (pick 14)
To point:PERpendicular to (pick 15)
To point:↵
```

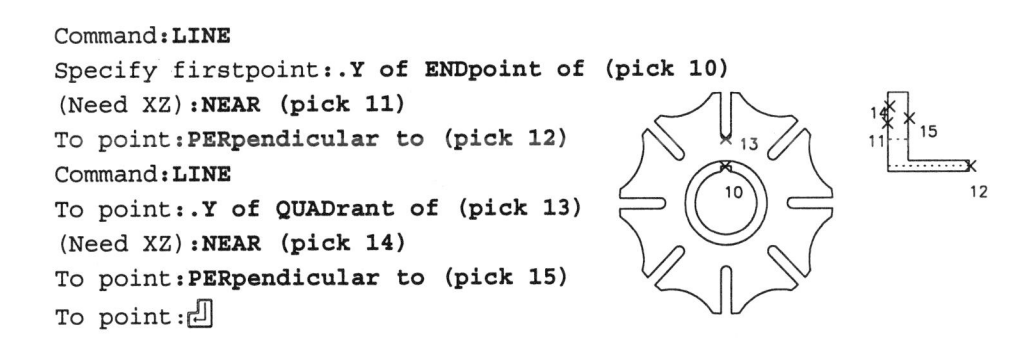

Remember that the default for a filter is to pick the point in space that you have picked. The filter won't pick up a portion of an existing object without the help of an OSNAP.

Step 6 Now that all of the lines are in, mirror the part through the center of the circle.

Erase the keyway line on the lower section. Use BHATCH to hatch the sectioned area and then add any lines needed to make it look like the illustration above Step 1.

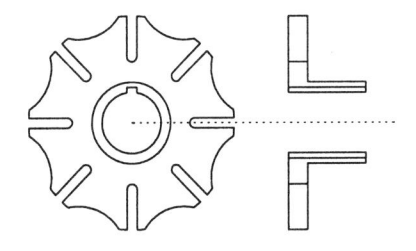

Once you understand this concept, object snap tracking is much easier. See page 445 for AutoCAD's Automatic tracking.

HATCH and SKETCH   **235**

Prelab 9B Hatch Using BHATCH

Step 1 In order to make this half-section assembly drawing, quickly draw up the part as shown. Notice that the increments are all in .25 units, so a SNAP of .25 may be of use.

Use ARC SER or CIRCLEs and TRIM.

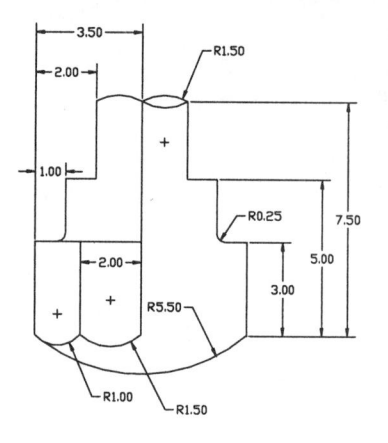

Step 2 Once this is completed, draw in the second half as shown.

You'll have to draw the full 180 degree arc and trim the dotted lines.

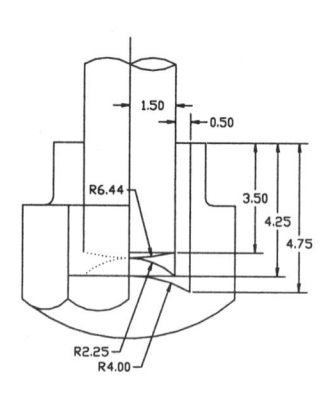

Step 3 Now access the BHATCH dialog box.

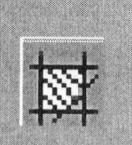

> **Toolbar** From the Draw toolbar, choose this button:
>
> **Pull Down** From the Draw menu, choose Hatch...

The command line equivalent is **BHATCH**.

This is the Boundary Hatch menu. From it, choose ANSI31.

        Command: (pick ANSI31)

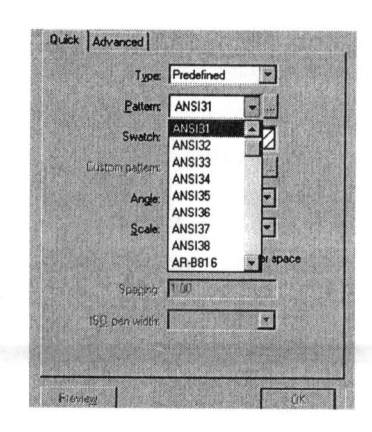

Now choose the ANSI32 pattern from the list.

        Command: (pick ANSI32)

236 CHAPTER NINE

Step 4 Once you have chosen this pattern, you can choose the Pick Points option and choose the appropriate area.

```
Command: (pick Pick Points)
```

The dialog boxes have disappeared, and the part is visible. On your command line you will see the prompt:

```
Select internal point: (pick 1, 2)
```

Indicate by picking inside the areas that you would like hatched. The area boundary will be highlighted, showing where the hatch will go.

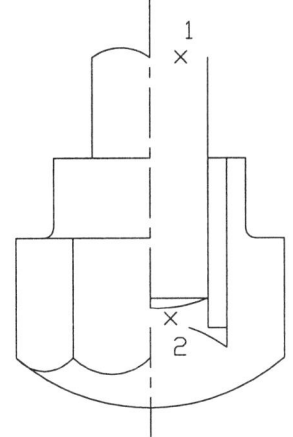

Make sure the same areas as shown are highlighted; if not, recheck your geometry.

Step 5 When you have pressed ⏎ to indicate the end of the selection set, you will be given a menu. Choose Preview to make sure that it is OK. If satisfied, press ⏎ and return to the menu, then press Apply and the hatch will appear in the areas indicated.

```
Command: (pick Preview Hatch)
Command: ⏎
Command: (pick Apply)
```

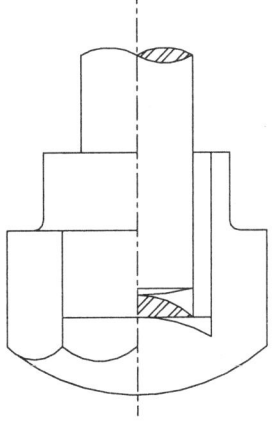

Step 6 On the next hatch, follow the same menus with the following responses.

```
Command: (pick Draw, Hatch ...)
(pick ANSI32)
(choose ANSI35)
(pick Points, pick 3)
(pick Apply)
```

You will get the hatch pattern in the area shown.

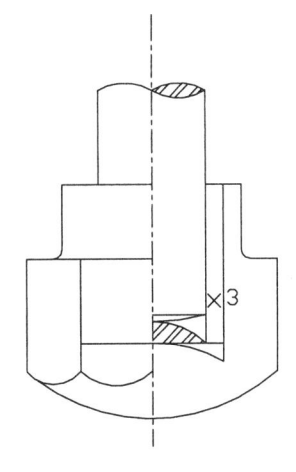

HATCH and SKETCH   **237**

Step 7 For the final hatch, use the user-defined hatch patterns. Notice that the highlighted menu choices will differ according to the options you choose.

```
Command:(pick Draw, Hatch ...)
(user-defined hatch pattern)
Angle 135
Spacing .25
(OK)
(pick Points)
```

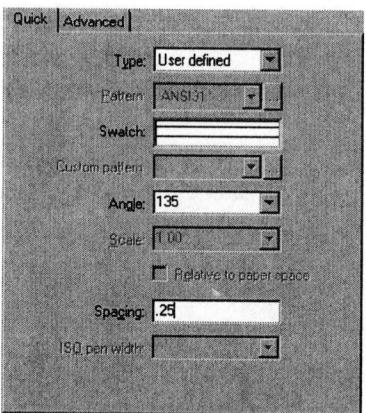

The ANSI31 hatch is the same, but try this one just for the practice.

Your final part should look like this.

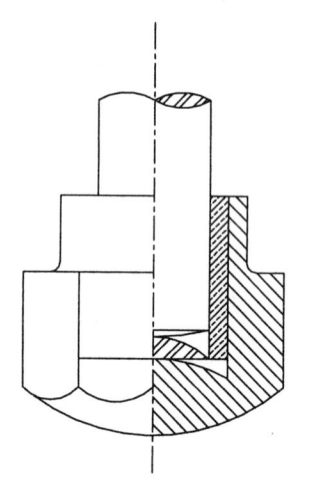

238 CHAPTER NINE

Command and Function Summary

BHATCH fills an enclosed area with an associative hatch pattern.

Point Filters filter an X, Y or Z value, from an existing point on an object for defining a point on a new object.

HATCH fills an area with a hatch pattern.

SKETCH creates a series of freehand line segments.

Practice Exercise 9

Use the HATCH command to complete these examples. Change the angle of the user pattern to 55 degrees if there is an angle on the object line that is 45 degrees.

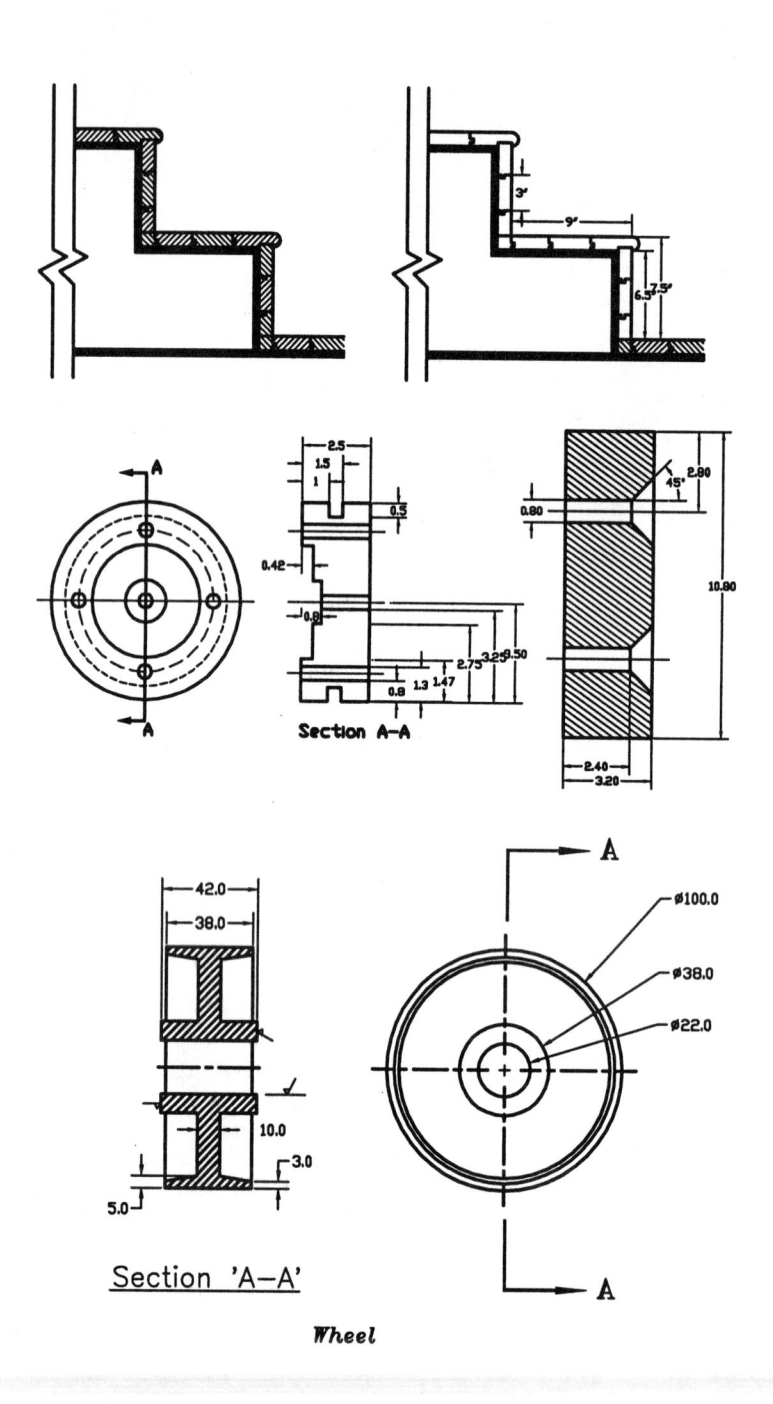

Section A-A

Section 'A-A'

Wheel

Exercise A9

Open FIRSTFL and create layers called Veneer, Fireplace, and Firebrick. Make veneer current and draw in the outline for the veneer. Use HATCH with ANSI31 at a scale of 48 to fill it in. On the fireplace, draw in the outlines with the appropriate layer and fill in the areas as shown. Do the same for the second floor.

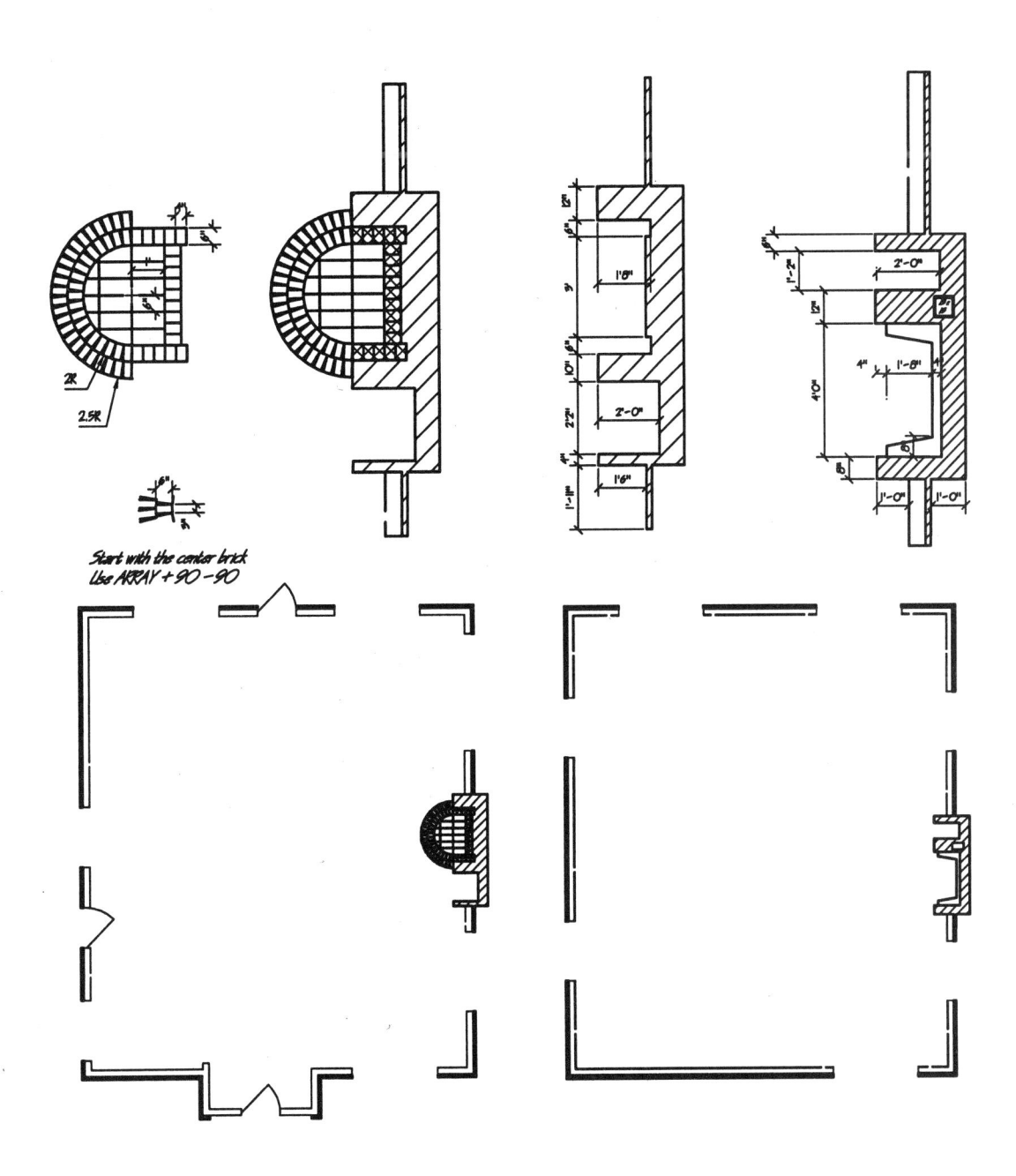

Exercise C9

Cavity Wall at Corner Parapet

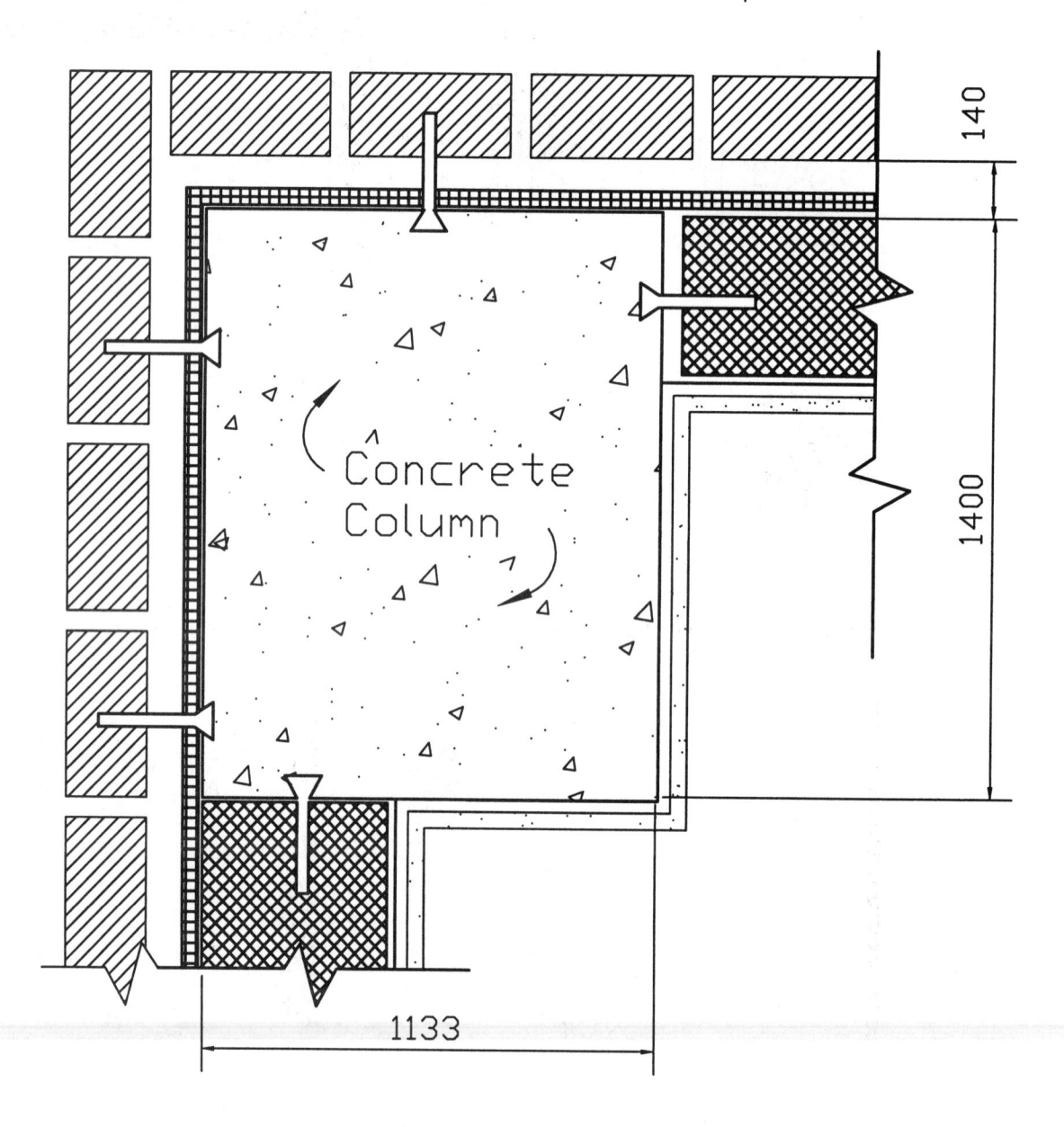

140

1400

1133

Hints on Exercise C9

Turn off the layer of sections you are not using when creating hatches. Remember you will need to change the hatch scale factor because the area is large.

Keep the text within the boundary when hatching, and it will be accepted as a separate boundary. If you are finished early, add a layer for the mortar, the pins, and the notations.

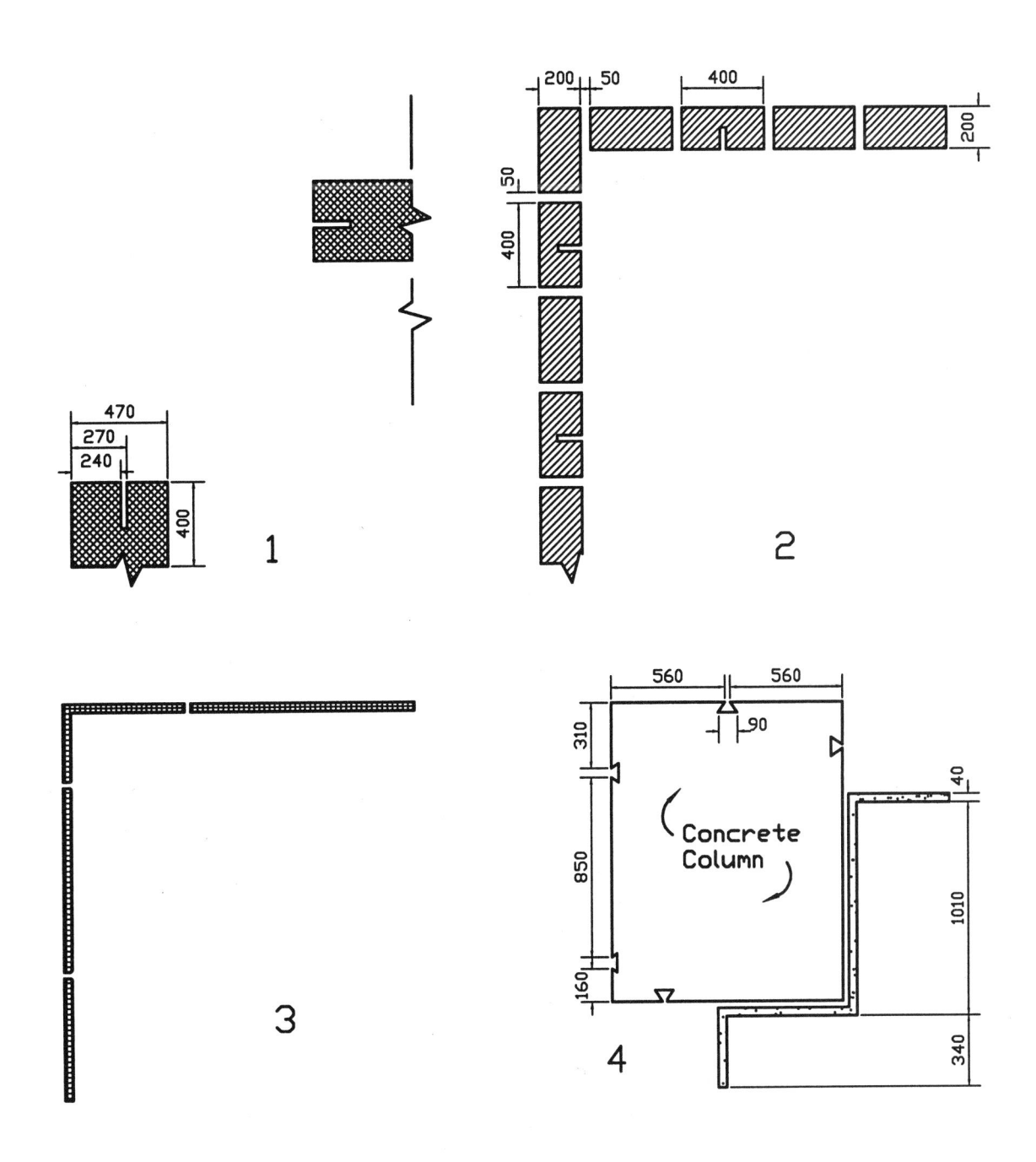

HATCH and SKETCH

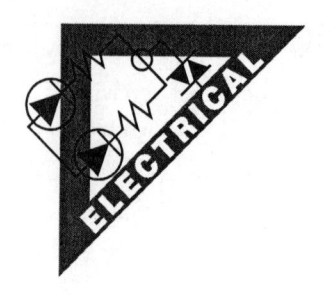

Exercise E9

This layout should fit on an 8.5″×11″ sheet.

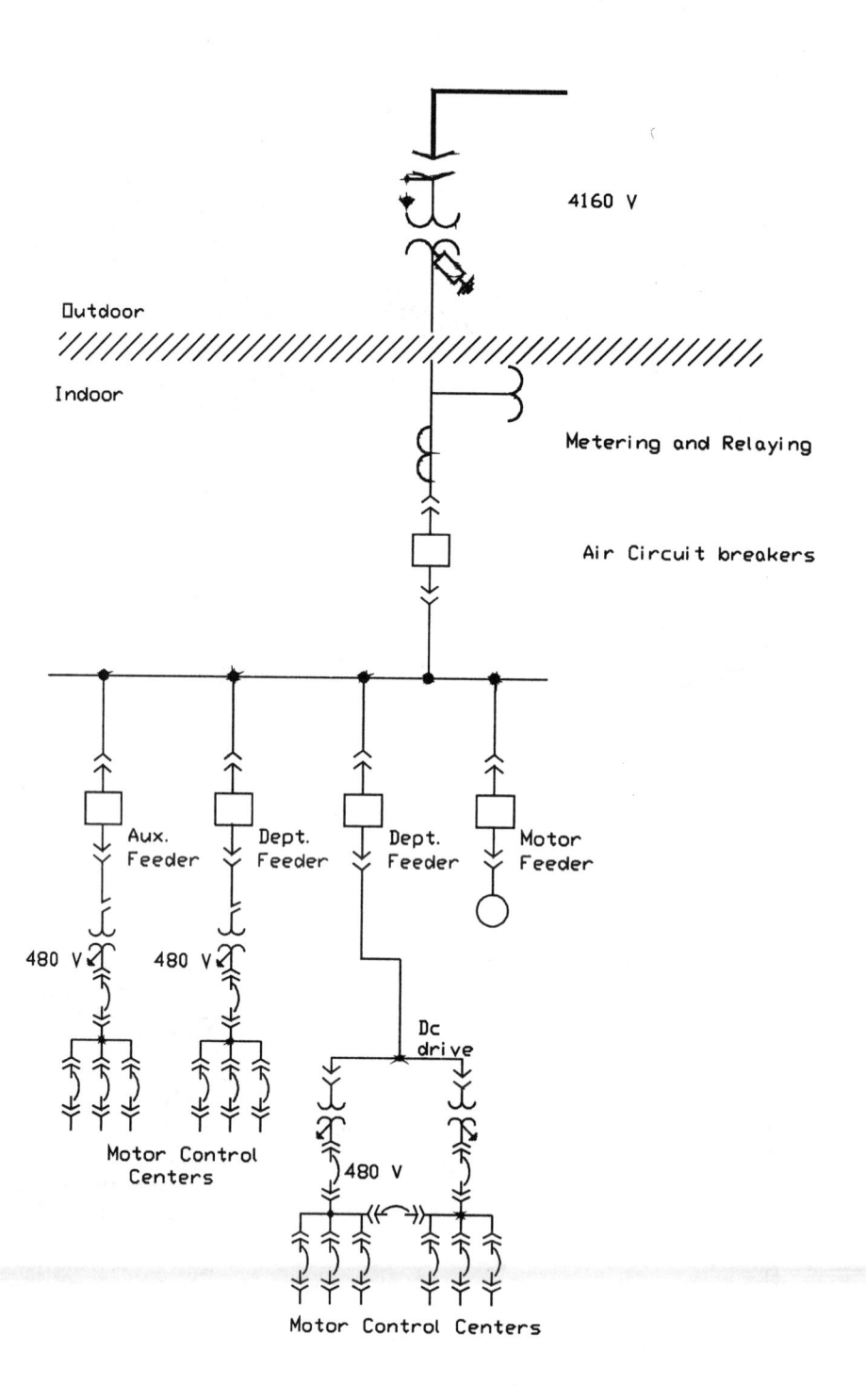

4160 V

Outdoor

Indoor

Metering and Relaying

Air Circuit breakers

Aux. Feeder

Dept. Feeder

Dept. Feeder

Motor Feeder

480 V

480 V

Dc drive

Motor Control Centers

480 V

Motor Control Centers

Exercise M9

Complete the drawing as in "Hints on Exercise M9" (page 246; use the dimensions listed there). Separate layers can be useful.

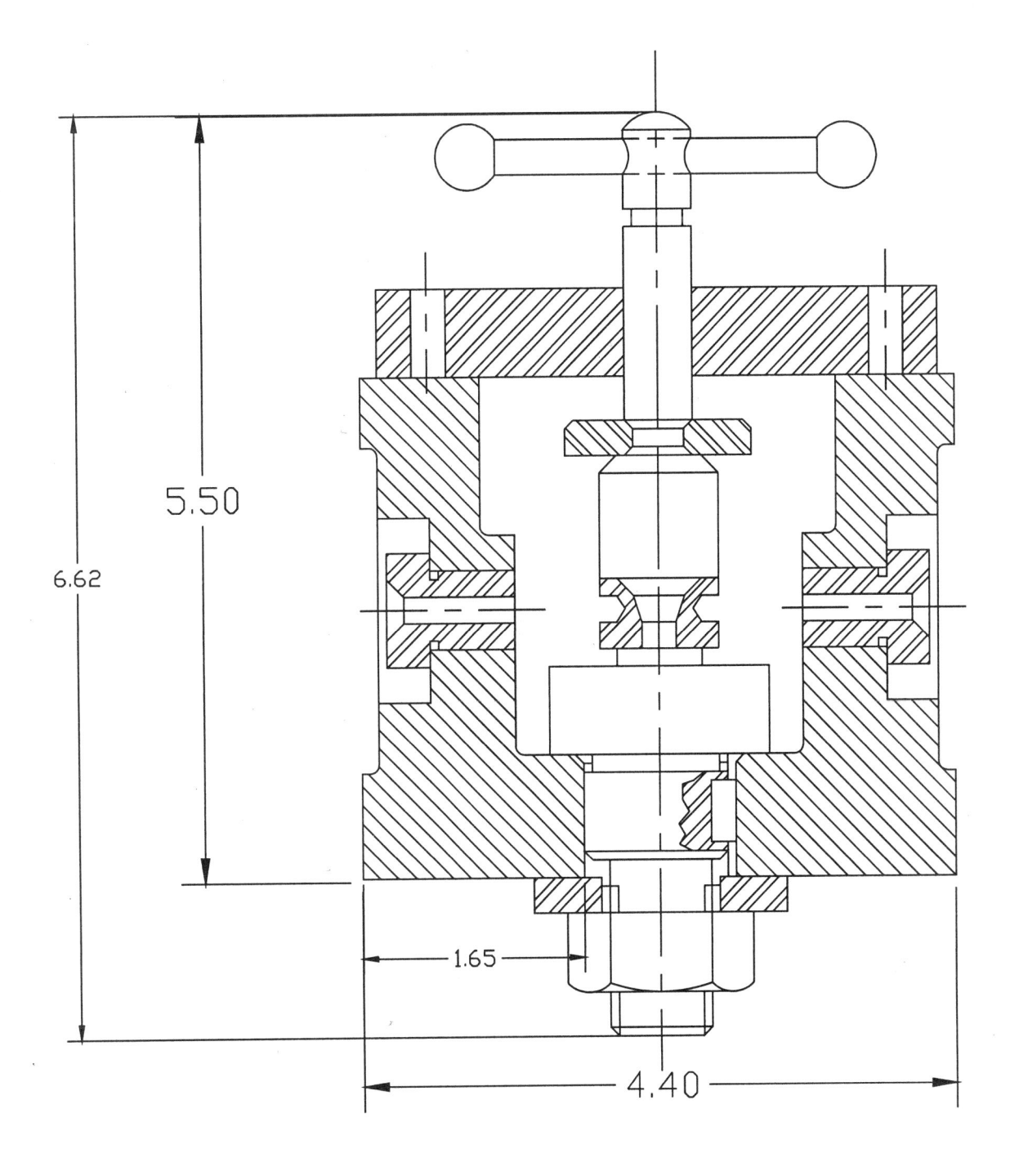

Hints on Exercise M9

Use the Pick Points option in the HATCH command to fill in the various boundaries. You will need to rotate one hatch by 90 degrees. Please note that the dimensions indicated are for you to create the part only.

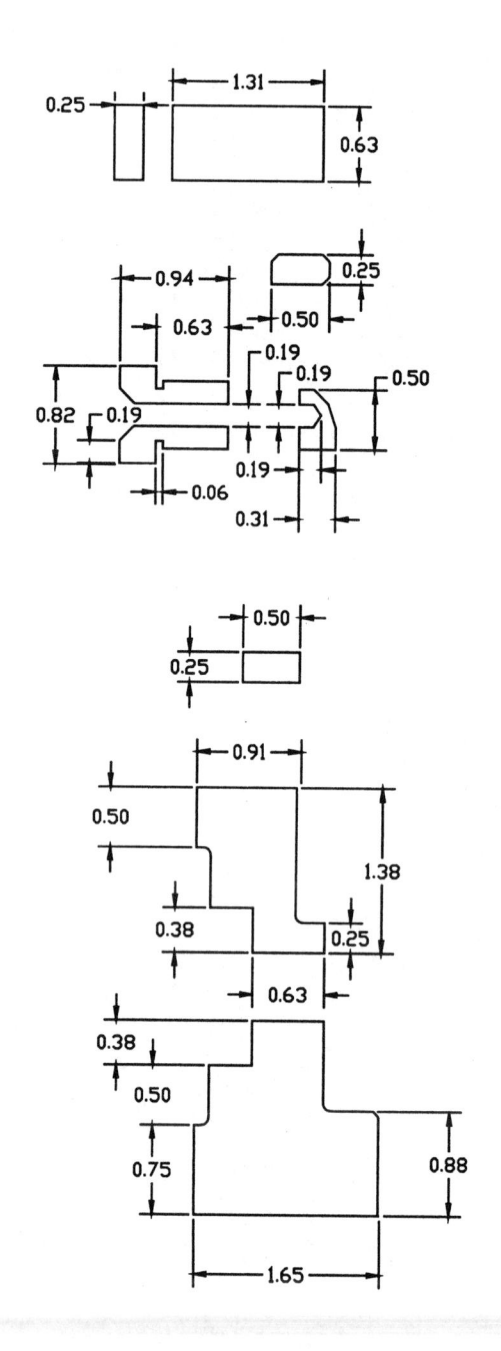

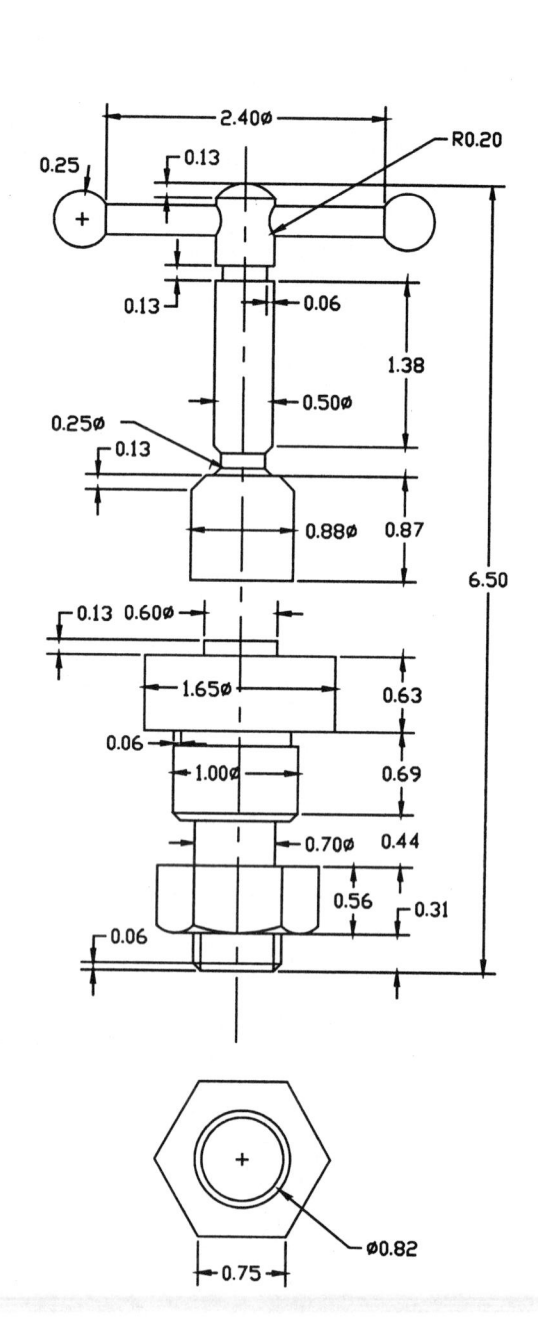

Challenger 9A

LIMITS: 20',15'
SNAP: 6"
GRID: 1'
ZOOM: All

Dimensions are on the following page.

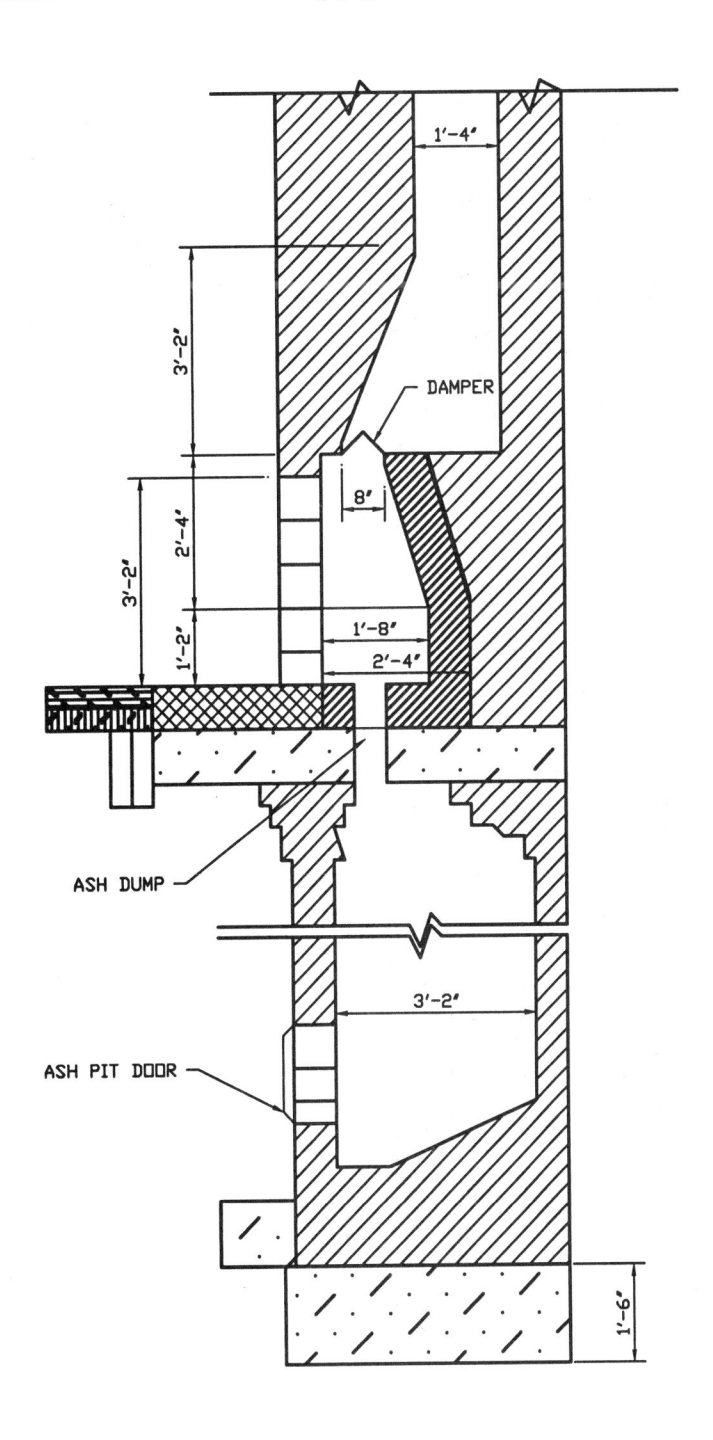

Hints on Challenger 9A

These sections do not need to be on separate layers after Release 11. It may be a good idea, however, to create different layers for insul-brick for estimating purposes later.

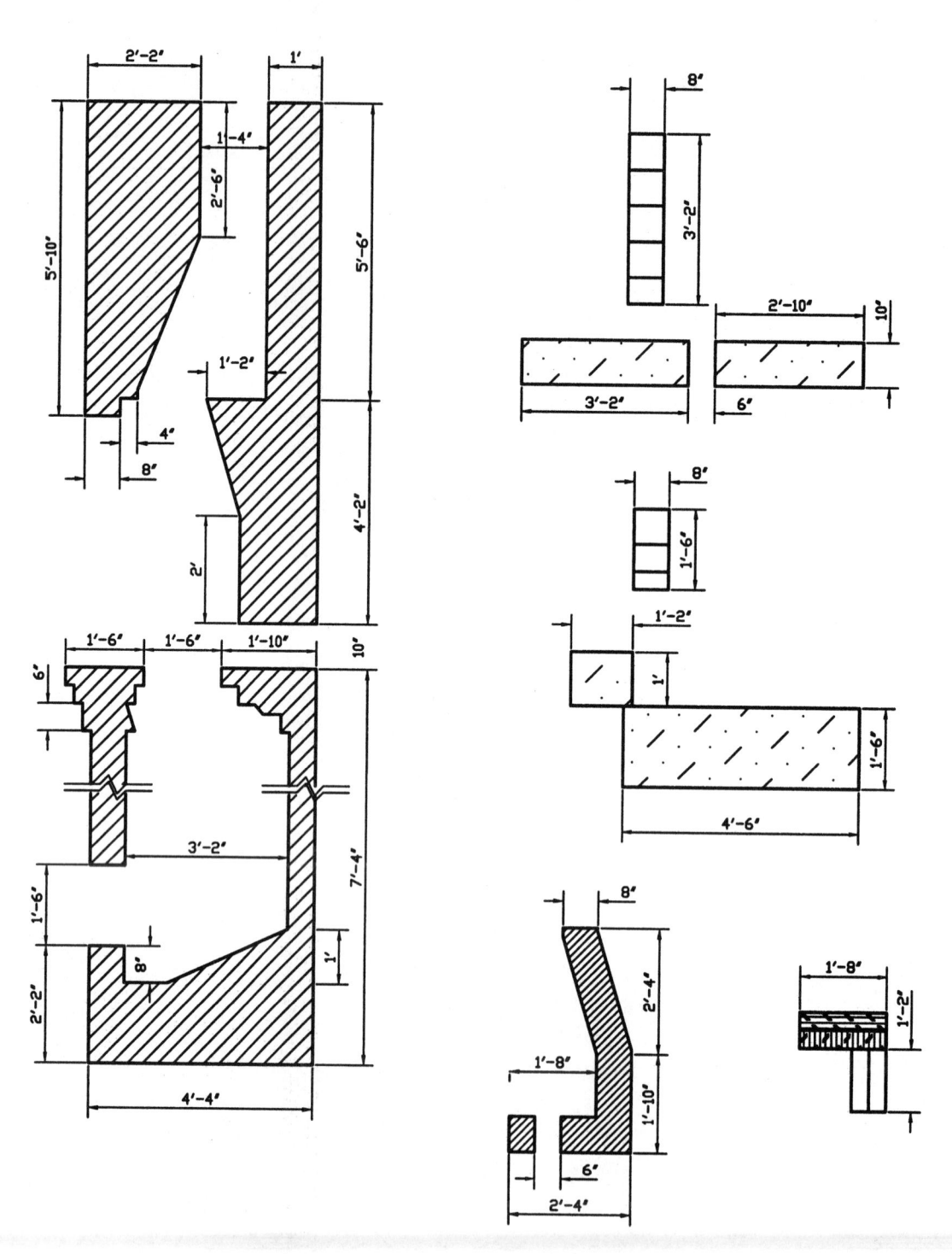

Use the Pick Points option of the HATCH command to access the different areas to hatch. You will need to change the rotation on at least one pattern. If you are using architectural units, make sure that you change your hatch scale factor to at least 12 (1″ = 1′0″).

Challenger 9B

This second example will give you experience with multiple hatches.

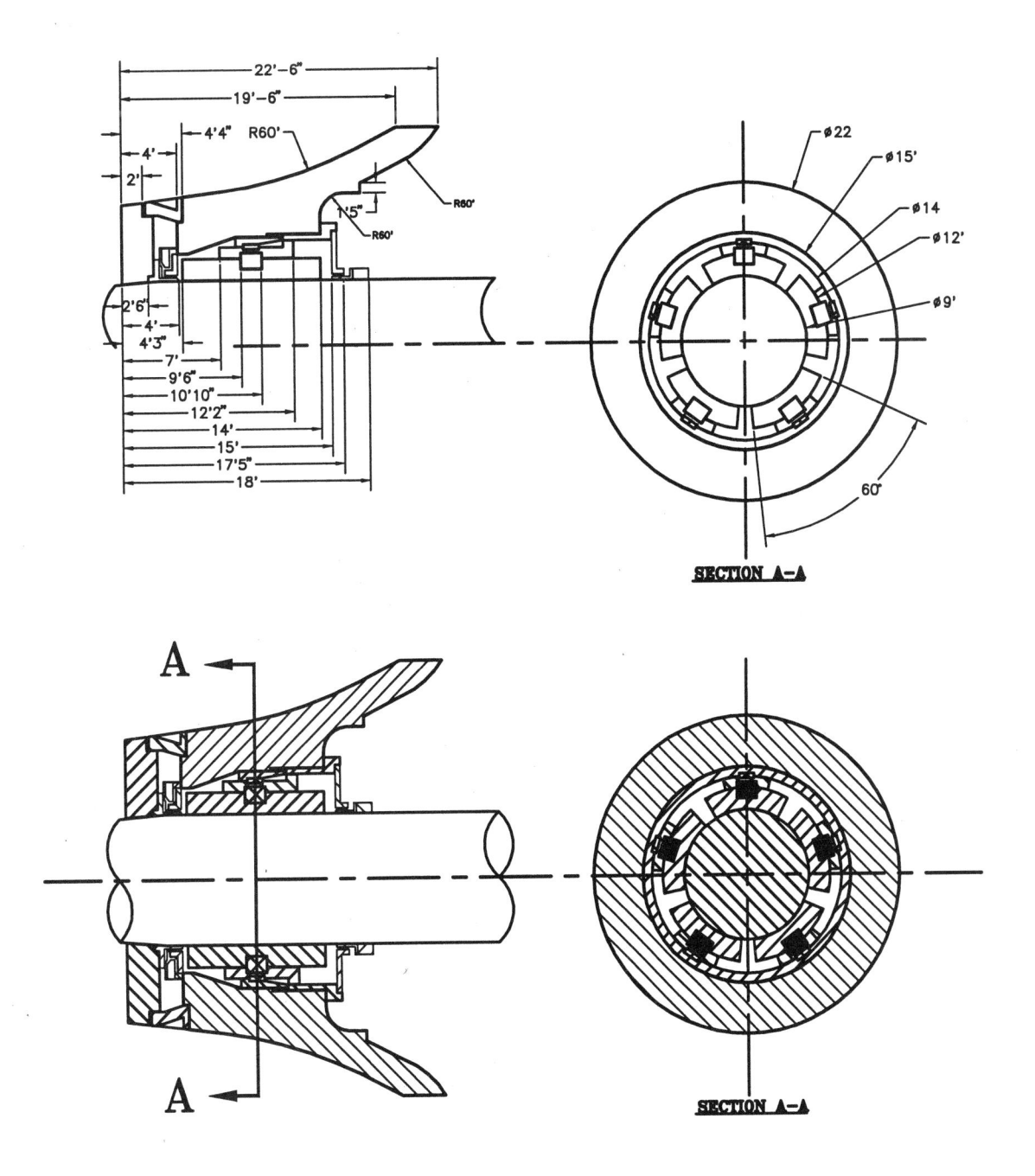

Challenger 9C

This drawing can be compiled with the illustrations on page 250, 358, and the top detail on 220 to make a complete commercial stair design.

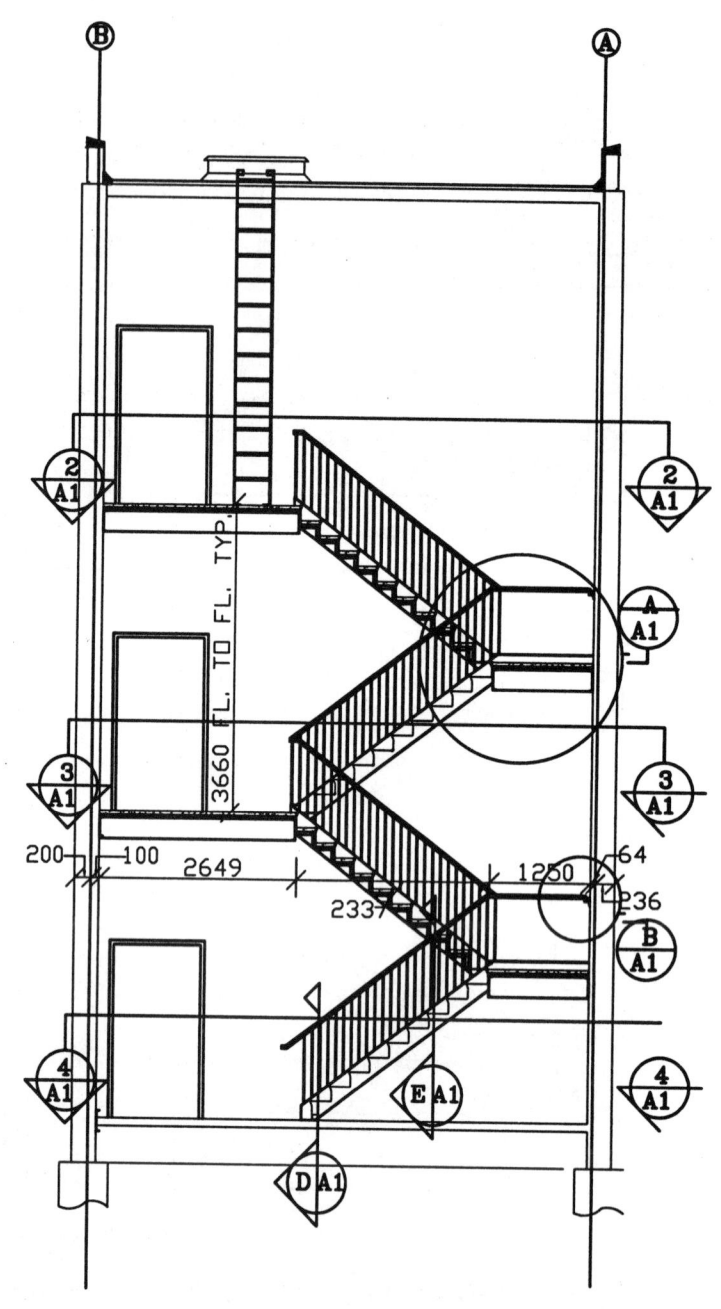

STAIR LAYOUT—SECTION

250　CHAPTER NINE

10 Blocks and Wblocks

Upon completion of this chapter, you should be able to:

1. Create a block
2. Create a wblock
3. INSERT both blocks and wblocks
4. EXPLODE blocks and wblocks
5. Update existing blocks
6. Use COLOR, LAYERS, and other data with blocks

Introduction

For the past ten chapters, you have been working on AutoCAD models and drawings as individual sets of data. The geometry was entered relative to a specific origin, and consisted of a variety of geometric and text information.

You have also seen that LAYERs are important as a management tool for keeping portions of the file separate for viewing purposes.

Another important management tool is *blocking*. With BLOCKs, the CAD operator can create a library of parts that can be used repeatedly. The operator can also have a library of drawing conventions such as title blocks, section markers, typical details, and other views that might be found on many drawings.

By using BLOCKs on large projects, you can cut down design time by creating portions of the drawing separately and then assembling them on a final drawing.

In a manufacturing environment, models or drawings of bolts, plugs, fasteners, and other standard parts are kept in a central database, and you would insert the object you needed rather than drawing it onto a new drawing. In architecture, a firm would have a library of staircase details, plumbing fixtures, windows and doors, and other often-used objects. In City Hall, there would be road signs, traffic lights, major service components, and other common symbols. In electrical applications, all the symbols for electrical components would be on file, so that the drawings would in fact be compiled more than drawn.

There are two types of blocks used in AutoCAD. An *internal block* created with the BLOCK command is part of the base drawing and cannot be accessed except within the drawing. An *external block* or *wblock* is a drawing file.

Any drawing file can be inserted onto another drawing file at any time.

Dimensions and Hatches are also considered blocks by AutoCAD, but these are not made with the BLOCK commands.

The five commands that are connected with blocks are:

BLOCK   creates an internal block.

WBLOCK   creates a .DWG file or external block.

INSERT   inserts either a block or a wblock (external drawing file).

MINSERT   inserts blocks in rectangular arrays like the ARRAY command.

EXPLODE   reverts the blocked data back to individual objects.

The BLOCK Command

The BLOCK command is used to create a grouping or set of objects that are identified by a given name. Once blocked, an object can be inserted into your drawing many times. Blocks created with the BLOCK command are internal, i.e. available only within the current file. To make them accessible in other files you must use WBLOCK.

Internal blocks are used on drawings where an object or group of objects needs to be accessed a number of times. Instead of ZOOM All and COPY, the BLOCK command allows you to store a set of objects under a given name for insertion at any time.

> **Toolbar** From the Draw toolbar, choose this button. 
>
> **Pull Down** From the Draw menu, choose Block, then Make.

An example could be chairs for an office layout. Let us take a variation of the layout from Challenger 4. Assume that the layout is complete except for the chairs.

The command line equivalent is **BLOCK** or **-BLOCK** for no dialog box.

```
Command:-BLOCK
Enter block name or [?]:STENO
Specify insertion base point:
 MID of (pick 1)
Select objects: (pick 2)
Other corner: (pick 3)
Select objects:↵
```

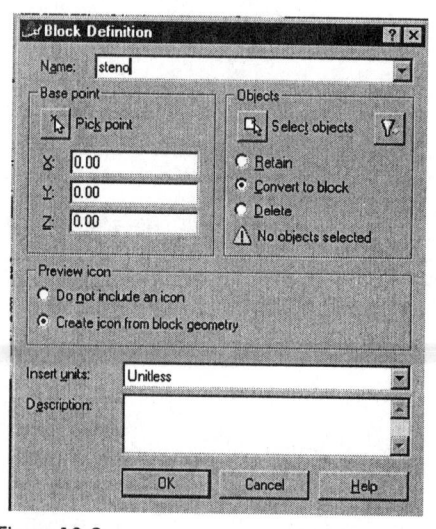

Notes
If you don't like dialog boxes, most can be turned off by adding a -, for example, -block, -insert.

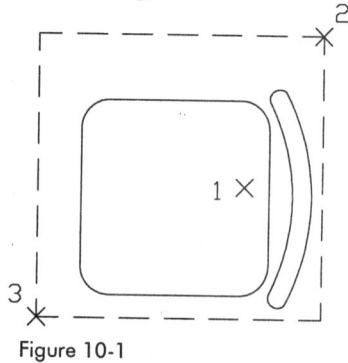

Notes
If you use -BLOCK, your block will disappear. With the dialog box, it will only change colour.

Figure 10-1

Figure 10-2

The "insertion base point" on this object is particularly important, because it is the point of reference for inserting, much like the base point in the COPY or MOVE command. If this point is placed logically on the object, the insertion of the block should be perfect every time.

Once the first command is completed, you can create another object and block it under a different name.

252   CHAPTER TEN

```
Command:-BLOCK
Enter block name or [?]:ARMSTENO
Specify insertion base point:MID of
   (pick 4)
Select objects: (pick 5)
Other corner: (pick 6)
Select objects:↵
```

The blocks are now complete and you are ready to insert them into a drawing.

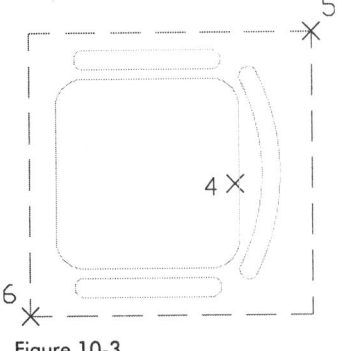

Figure 10-3

The INSERT Command

The INSERT command is used to place previously defined blocks into the current drawing.

Toolbar From the Draw toolbar, choose this button:

Pull Down From the Insert menu, choose Block...

The command line equivalent is **INSERT** or **-INSERT** for no dialog box.

```
Command:-INSERT
Enter block name or [?]:Steno
Specify insertion point or
   [Scale/X/Y/Z/Rotate/PScale/PX/PY/PZ
   /PRotate]: (pick 1)
Enter X scale factor, specify opposite
   corner, or [Corner/XYZ] <1>:↵
Enter Y scale factor <use X scale
   factor>:↵
Specify rotation angle <0>: (move your
   cursor around until the chair is
   properly positioned, then pick)
```

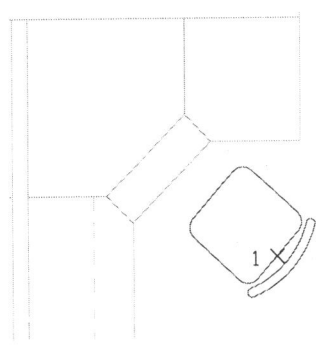

Figure 10-4

If "Invalid Block Name" is displayed, check to see that there is not another block with this name.

The X scale factor defaults to 1. Any number smaller than 1 will make the block smaller than its original size; any larger number will make it larger than the original.

The Y scale factor defaults to X. If you make the X value 2, the Y value will also be 2, unless you change it. Changing the Y value relative to the X value will distort the image of the original block.

The rotation angle is a counterclockwise rotation around the insertion base point.

Inserting blocks is much like using COPY, except that you identify objects by a given name and not a pick.

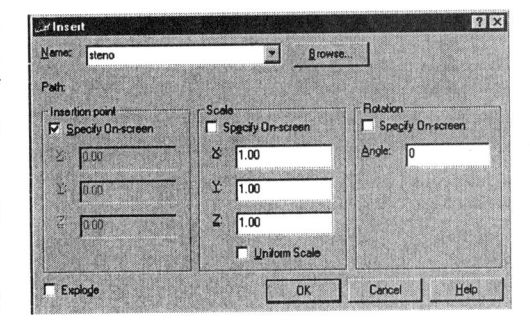

Figure 10-5

Blocks and Wblocks

```
Command: INSERT
Enter block name or [?]:Steno
Specify insertion point or
 [Scale/X/Y/Z/Rotate/PScale/PX/
 PY/PZ/PRotate]: (pick 2)
Enter X scale factor, specify
 opposite corner, or [Corner/XYZ]:⏎
Y scale factor <use X scale factor>:⏎
Specify rotation angle <0>:
 (move and pick)
```

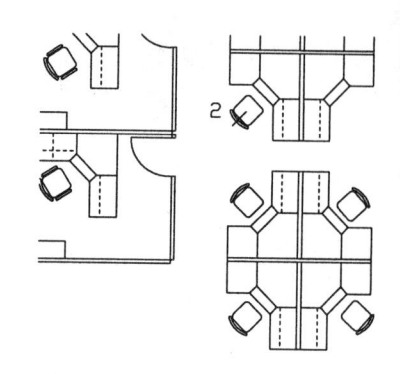

Figure 10-6

Now that the layout is complete, we could add a title block. This would be a drawing file already on disk.

Inserting External Blocks

Once the BLOCK or drawing has been INSERTed into the file, it is referred to as the *block instance*. The original still exists in memory, but a copy of it has been put in the current drawing. This is similar to a rubber stamp and the stamp impression. On the office layout there are now two identified blocks and many block instances.

Let us take the title block from Chapter 8. First we must find out the name of the file.

Listing Block Files

Use the following to get a listing of files.

> **Toolbar** From the INSERT dialog box, pick the arrow beside Name. A list of the blocks in your file should appear immediately.
>
> Use Browse from the dialog box to get a listing of the dates of your drawings. This icon will list the date.

Inserting the Block

Now insert the title block onto the file using your drawing from chapter 8.

Use DDINSERT to place the title block onto the file.

```
Command:-INSERT
Enter block name (or ?)<STENO>:
 a:title
Specify insertion point or
 [Scale/X/Y/Z/Rotate/PScale/PX/
 PY/PZ/PRotate]: (pick 1)
Enter X scale factor, specify
 opposite corner, or [Corner/XYZ]:⏎
Y scale factor <use X scale factor:⏎
Specify rotation angle <0>::⏎
```

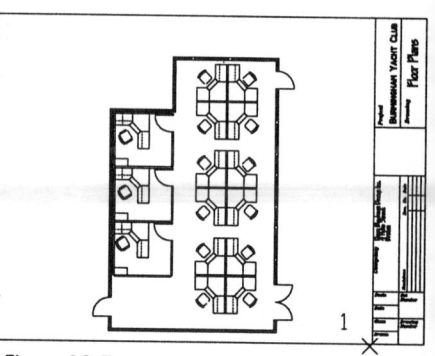

Figure 10-7

Notes

You can insert a drawing file onto your current drawing at any time.

254 CHAPTER TEN

The WBLOCK Command

BLOCKs exist within the drawing and cannot be accessed except within the base drawing. This is why they are referred to as internal blocks.

WBLOCKs are separate files. They are stored separately as drawing files on your disk and have the extension .DWG. They do *not* need to be blocked.

Any file on disk can be inserted as a wblock into any drawing.

WBLOCK is used when you want to take only a portion of an existing file and use it on another file. Because the wblocks exist outside of the current file, they are referred to as external blocks.

An example of WBLOCK use is the extraction of a "north arrow" from a drawing for use on another drawing.

To start, you must open the file that contains the information that you would like to export as a block. Then access the WBLOCK command.

> **Toolbar** There is no button for WBLOCK.
>
> **Pull Down** From the File menu, choose EXPORT, then save with .dwg

The command line equivalent is **WBLOCK**.

```
Command: -WBLOCK
Enter name of existing block or
 [=(Block=output file)/*(whole
drawing)] <define new drawing>:
A:NORTH
Block name (or ?):↵
Specify insertion base point: (pick 1)
Select objects: (pick 2)
Specify opposite corner: (pick 3)
Select objects:↵
```

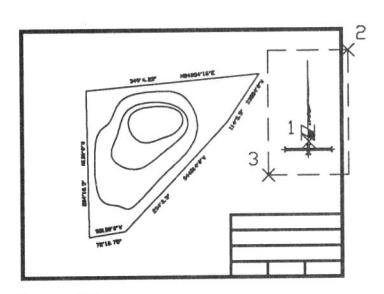

Figure 10-8

Once you have chosen the WBLOCK command, the Create Drawing File dialog box will be invoked. Enter the name of the file in the File Name box.

When you press ↵, the dialog box will disappear and the command will continue.

When you are identifying the file name, be sure to type in the drive or directory as well.

To check to see that the file is in the directory, list the files by shelling to DOS and using the DIR command or My Computer in WINDOWS.

```
Command: SHELL
OS Command: ↵
Command: DIR
File specification: *.DWG
```

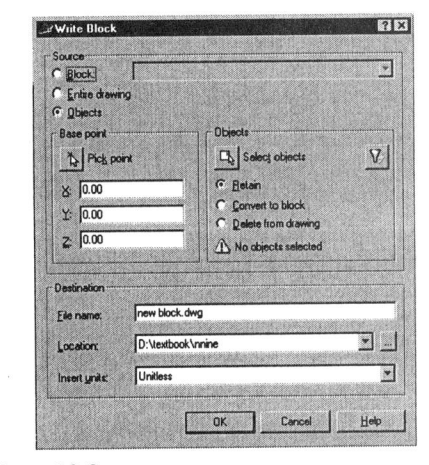

Figure 10-9

To place this file on another drawing, open the drawing and use INSERT.

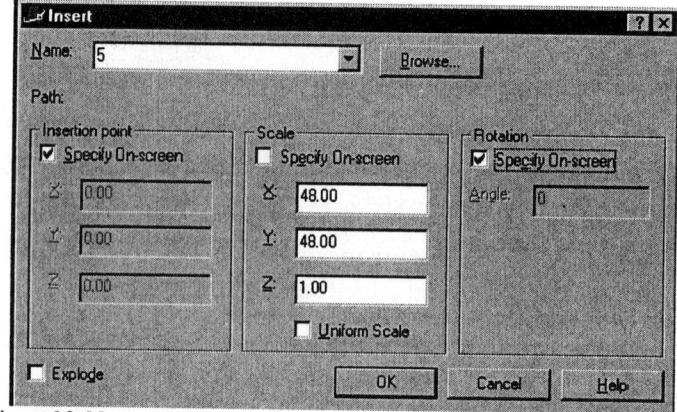

Figure 10-11

or

```
Command: -INSERT
Enter block name or [?]:A:NORTH
Specify insertion point or
 [Scale/X/Y/Z/Rotate/PScale/PX/
 PY/PZ/PRotate]: (pick 1)
Enter X scale factor, specify
 opposite corner, or [Corner/XYZ]:48
Y scale factor <use X scale factor>:⏎
Specify rotation angle <0>:36
```

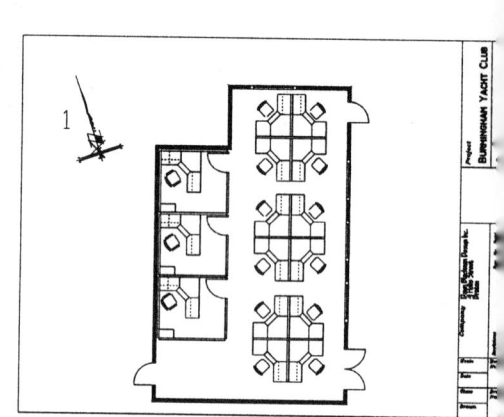

Figure 10-12

Inserting Existing Drawings as Blocks

The origin or 0,0 of the drawing is the default base point for drawings inserted into the current drawing. To change the default, open the original drawing and use BASE to specify a different insertion base point. AutoCAD uses the new base point the next time the drawing is inserted.

Using a BLOCK to Create a WBLOCK

If you have already created a block internally called N-ARROW and would like to have this block written to an external file saved as NORTH on your A: drive, use the following.

```
Command:WBLOCK
File name:A:NORTH
Block name or [?]:N-ARROW
```

This will take the internal block N-ARROW and create an external file called A:NORTH.

The insertion base point from your original block will be identified as the insertion base point of the file or wblock as well.

The listing gives you the name of the drawing, the extension showing that it is a .DWG file or drawing file, the size of the file, and the date and time when it was created.

If you want to use a portion of a file in another file, repeat this process, but press ⏎ at the "Block name or [?]:" prompt. Now you are prompted for the base point and selected objects.

WBLOCK with =

After entering the name of the wblock, entering an equal sign specifies that the existing block and the output file shall have the same name. If no block of that name exists in the drawing, AutoCAD redisplays the "Block name or [?]:" prompt.

*WBLOCK with ***

Entering an asterisk (*) writes the entire drawing to the new output file, except for unreferenced symbols. AutoCAD writes model space objects to model space and paper space objects to paper space.

Scaling Wblocks

Title blocks, north arrows, and other drawing symbols should be created at a scale of 1:1. For example, a title block could be perhaps 12 × 4 inches; a north arrow could be 3 inches; a section marker could be 1 inch.

When these are inserted onto a file, the scale of the block should be expanded to fit the size of the drawing. In the floor plan above, the drawing might be plotted at a scale of 1/4″=1′0″ or 1/48 of the actual size of the floor plan. The north arrow would then be inserted at a scale of 48.

```
Command:-INSERT
Enter block name or [?]:A:NORTH
Specify insertion point or[Scale/X/Y/Z/Rotate/PScale/PX/
 PY/PZ/PRotate]: (pick 1)
Enter X scale factor, specify opposite corner, or
   [Corner/XYZ]:48
Y scale factor <use X scale factor>:⏎
Specify rotation angle <0>: (move and pick)
```

In mechanical, if the final drawing is to be 1:20 and you are drawing in millimeters, insert the drawing symbols at 20 so that they will be the correct size on the drawing when plotted at 1/20 of that size or 1:20.

Charts of appropriate sizes are given in Chapter 11. For the exercises today, simply adjust the size to fit.

The MINSERT Command

MINSERT is used to insert multiple block instances of a block in a rectangular array. The command melds the INSERT command with the ARRAY command. If used properly, this can be a very useful command.

> **Toolbar** There is no button for MINSERT.
>
> **Pull Down** There is no menu choice for MINSERT.

The command line equivalent is **MINSERT**.

```
Command:MINSERT
Enter block name or [?]<STENO>:↵
Specify insertion point or
 [Scale/X/Y/Z/Rotate/PScale/PX/
 PY/PZ/PRotate]: (pick 1)
Enter X scale factor, specify
 opposite corner, or [Corner/XYZ]:↵
Y scale factor <use X scale factor>:↵
Specify rotation angle <0>:90
Enter number of rows (----)<1>:3
Enter number of columns (|||):6
Enter distance between rows
 Or specify unit cell (---):4'
Specify distance between columns:5'
```

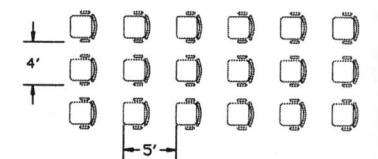

Figure 10-13

Minserted blocks cannot be individually edited or exploded. If you erase one, you erase them all.

Editing Blocks

Once a block has been placed in a file, it is edited as a single entity. An entity select pick will pick the whole block. If you pick up one object on the block, the whole block will be selected. Try moving a block instance to the left.

```
Command:MOVE
Select objects: (pick 1)
Select objects:↵
Specify base point or displacement:
  (pick 2)
Displacement: (pick 3)
```

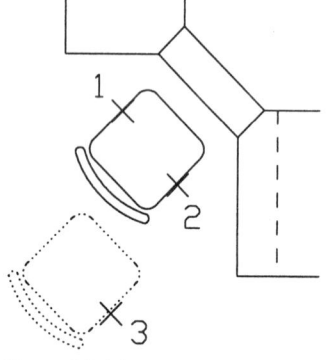

Figure 10-14

Notice that your block moves as a unit. If you erase a block, only one pick point is needed to identify the block. Move the block back to its original position by using **U** ↵.

If you want to edit or change the block once it has been inserted, you will need to return the block to its original objects. The EXPLODE command is used for this purpose.

258 CHAPTER TEN

The EXPLODE Command

The EXPLODE command reduces an object to its original entities. A block can be exploded into its original parts, a polyline or polygon can be exploded into line or arc segments, and a dimension can be exploded into lines, arrowheads, and text.

Title blocks are generally saved with only the general information such as Scale, Date, etc., and not the information regarding the specific drawing. If you would like to change any of the information already on the drawing, use EXPLODE and then CHANGE or DDEDIT.

> **Toolbar** From the Modify toolbar, choose this button:
>
> **Pull Down** From the Modify menu, choose E\underline{x}plode.

The command line equivalent is **EXPLODE**.

```
Command: EXPLODE
Select objects: (pick the
   block instance)
```

Now use CHANGE or DDEDIT to change the text as shown.

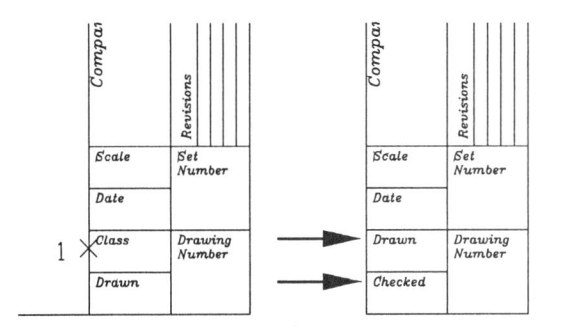

Figure 10-15

If you are inserting a block or wblock and know you want to change portions of it later, type * before the block name or pick the box Explode on the dialog box. This inserts the block as separate entities that can be edited. The * helps avoid the EXPLODE command. You are not given the option of changing the scale factor if you pre-explode the block.

```
Command: INSERT
Block name or [?] <BUSHING>:*TITLE
Insertion point: (pick a point)
Rotation angle<0>:
```

Now, if you try to edit anything on the inserted BLOCK, it will be identified as a single unit even though it is a block instance.

Updating Blocks

There can be only one definition of a block under each specific name within a file. Should you change or update the original block, the new block instances will be the new block and the old block instances will update. This can be very useful.

For example, if you have shown the drawing of the office layout to your client, and he or she has decided to specify a different chair, explode one chair. Make the changes and block it again under the same name, using the same insertion point to update the other chairs.

Blocks and Wblocks **259**

```
Command:EXPLODE
Select objects: (pick the block
    instance 1)
```

The block of the chair will now revert back to the original lines and arcs used to create it.

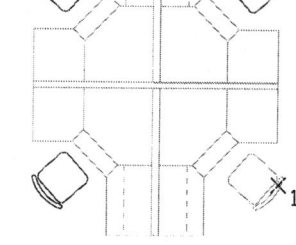

Figure 10-16

Now make the changes to the chair that you would like to see.

Because the chairs in the layout have all been rotated, make sure that you rotate the new block back to the original rotation angle before reblocking.

Once complete, use BLOCK to resave the chair under the original name.

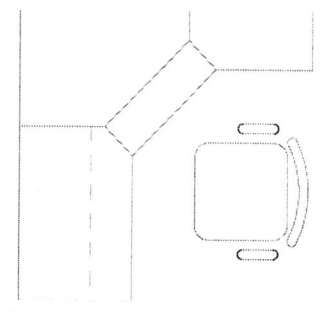

Figure 10-17

```
Command:-BLOCK
Enter block name or [?]:STENO
Block STENO already exists. Redefine it?<N>:Y
Insertion base point:MID of (pick 1)
Select objects: (pick the objects)
```

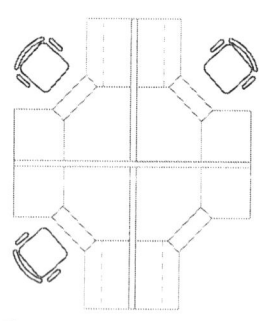

Figure 10-16

Compiling Drawings with BLOCK

Drawings are often compiled as opposed to being drawn. Generally you would have title blocks and symbols and details already on file. In an architectural firm you would find libraries of parts such as plumbing details, light fixtures, windows, doors, etc. already on file and you simply need to insert them rather than draw them in again.

It is a good idea always to compile drawings on the current file of the most important drawing. That way, if there are changes to the base plan, they can be made on the current drawing and then replotted rather than having to recompile the drawing many times. Chapter 11 deals more in detail with compiling of drawings.

Blocks, Wblocks, Color, and Layers

You may have noticed that the default layer is 0, and that this layer cannot be renamed or deleted. Layer 0, the universal layer, cannot be changed because it is used extensively with regard to BYBLOCK and BYLAYER settings for color and linetype. The layers blocks sit on and the color of the block can be set either bylayer or byblock.

Once you have created a number of blocks or wblocks, file management becomes more difficult, because you must remember the size of the blocks as well as the directory they are in and the layer they are on.

If items are created on a layer other than 0 in a wblock, these new layers will be added to the list of layers in the current file when the wblock file is inserted.

All objects on layer 0 will be automatically placed on the current layer of the drawing on screen, and will assume the current layer color and linetype when the block is inserted. These are not necessarily added bylayer. If color or linetype are not set bylayer, the current setting overrides the layer setting. To check to see what the current settings are, use the STATUS command or pick Object Creation (DDEMODES) from the Data menu.

If you want a particular wblock to always have a specific layer, linetype, and color, assign it explicitly; do not leave it on layer 0.

To illustrate this point, make sure that your current layer DIMS has a different color than white, then insert a drawing from one of the first tutorials. The drawing called TEMPLATE is a good choice, because it is quite small.

```
Command: INSERT
Enter block name or [?]: Template
Specify insertion point or [Scale/X/Y/Z/Rotate/PScale/PX/
 PY/PZ/PRotate]: (pick a point)
Enter X scale factor, specify opposite corner, or
    [Corner/XYZ]:⏎
Y scale factor <use X scale factor>:⏎
Specify rotation angle <0>:⏎
Command: (pick Zoom All from the Display pull-down menu)
```

Notice that your template file is in the current layer color. If you use LIST to find out the parameters of the model, you will see that the layer for the block is listed as the current layer.

> **Danger**
>
> If you start your drawing from a floppy disk, remember not to remove your floppy disks while you are in the AutoCAD drawing editor. If you do, you may be creating bad clusters on your disk which will eventually cause a crash.

Byblock

If color and linetype are defined by the Byblock option in the original file, the colors and linetypes can be changed once the file is inserted. If you want the color and linetype of the wblock to always assume those of the layer on which it is inserted, use bylayer rather than byblock as the setting for the color and linetype.

Once a block has been inserted, the objects will retain the original layers. Neither CHANGE nor CHPROP can be used to alter the layer of a portion of a block. You must first explode the block in order to change the layers on the block entities.

Naming Blocks, Wblocks, and Layers

From the previous discussion you can see that if five wblocks are inserted into a file, and each one has five separate and unique layer names, you will have a file with 25 different layer names. This can be a problem and a terrific waste of time. When creating drawings, try to use standard layer names to avoid problems. You may think layer names such as 1 and 2 or A and B are easier to enter and that you will remember what is in each layer as you are working.

You won't!

Furthermore, when you insert several drawings, you can bet on having problems with data management.

Using the date on the readout to locate files is useful, but every time you retrieve a file and then END or SAVE it, the date will change.

When working on large projects that have several different files and several different layers, it is a good idea to keep a project designation sheet containing the names of all of the files needed, the date they were last updated, the names of all layers, and what is contained within those layers. This will save you a lot of time later trying to figure out the database you are dealing with.

Accessing Files for Inserting

If you are using floppy disks, you should copy all of the files either onto the hard drive or onto your working floppy disk before inserting them onto a base drawing.

If you have two or three files on different disks, make sure you are writing to the C: drive, then copy the files to a clean new disk and insert them.

Removing Unwanted Blocks

Each time a block or drawing file (wblock) is inserted into a file, a copy of it is placed in the drawing memory or default area. If you want to clean your file, you must PURGE the blocks. The PURGE command will erase all unused blocks, layers, text styles, linetypes, etc. from a file. Any blocks, layers, etc. that have been brought into the file but never used can be purged. It erases the information from the file defaults and settings.

If you don't PURGE the memory of the original drawing file or wblock before you insert a new one, the old block file will be inserted, even if you have created a new file.

When a drawing file or wblock is inserted, then erased, the copy of the wblock remains in memory in case it is needed again. The original file *must* be purged in order to accept a new file.

The PURGE Command

PURGE removes unused named references, such as unused blocks or layers from the database.

If you are inserting an updated drawing file and you keep getting the original file, use PURGE.

```
Command: PURGE
Enter type of unused objects to purge
 [Blocks/Dimstyles/LAyers/LTypes/PLotstyles/SHapes/textSTyles/
  Mlinestyles/All]:A
Enter names to purge <*>:
```

Danger
Never name an internal block and an external block the same name.

If you press function button 2 on the keyboard (F2) you will be able to see the listing as it scrolls.

Once the old block is purged, you can enter the new or updated one.

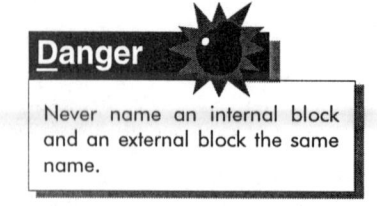

```
Command:-INSERT
Enter block name or [?]<STENO>: A:TITLE
 Etc.
```

This gives you the new title block.

Another way to insert an updated block is to use FILENAME=. This will indicate that the file has been updated, and the base file will search for the updated file. A message will be displayed stating that the block has been redefined.

```
Command:-INSERT
Enter block name or [?]:TITLE=
```

This command sequence will insert the new copy of the file called TITLE instead of the old one. Using PURGE, however, is a better use of memory.

Tips

Objects must be visible to be included in the block, but they can be on many layers. If you are trying to block information from only one layer, turn the others off for easy selecting.

When in doubt, use 0,0 as the insertion point. If all of the files are created at a 1:1 scale, the data will always fit.

If you have inserted the wrong block, undo it, and the block reference on the file will be deleted as well. This is the same as undoing a HATCH rather than erasing it.

Paper Space Objects

When you insert an entire object into the current drawing, any paper space objects will not be included in the current drawing's block definition. To use the paper space objects in another drawing, open the original drawing file and use BLOCK to define the paper space objects as a block. The block will then be included in the original drawing database when you insert the drawing into another drawing.

Creating a Symbol Library

There are various methods of creating a symbol library. This will help you to define a library of parts that can be accessed to compile your drawings.

1. Create a directory on your disk, e.g. SYM, and make individual files.
2. As above, except draw all the symbols on one sheet and WBLOCK them individually to the disk.
3. Draw all the symbols on one sheet, calling the drawing ELEC-SYM or MEC-SYM, and block them individually. Save the drawing. To access the symbols, simply insert the file ELEC-SYM into your current drawing at 0,0 and then use DDINSERT to access the block you want.

Also note that you can insert an old file if you want some blocks from it. Use ESC when asked for the insertion point. This loads the drawing but only into the database, saving much time on regenerations. Once you have extracted the blocks you want, you can purge the old file or WBLOCK.

Prelab 10 BLOCK, WBLOCK, INSERT, and MINSERT

In this lab we will draw a standard lot, block it, insert it both as an individual lot and as a survey, and insert the title block from Chapter 8.

Step 1 Draw in a rectangle that is 40 × 30. Use ZOOM to get it on screen, and then ZOOM by .5X. Add the house as shown.

```
Command:L
Specify first point:0,0
Specify next point:30,0
Specify next point:30,40
Specify next point:0,40
Specify next point:C
Command:Z
All/Center/Dynamic/Extents/Left/
   Previous/Vmax/Window/X/XP:A
Command:Z
All/Center/Dynamic/Extents/Left/
   Previous/Vmax/Window/X/XP:.5X
```

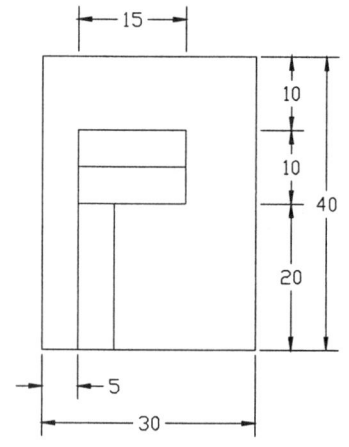

Step 2 Use BLOCK to create a block of this data.

> **Toolbar** From the Draw toolbar, choose this button: 
>
> **Pull Down** From the Draw menu, choose Block, then Make.

The command line equivalent is **BLOCK**.

```
Command:BLOCK
Enter block name or [?]:LOT
Specify insertion base point:0,0
Select objects: (pick 1)
Specify opposite corner: (pick 2)
Select objects:↵
```

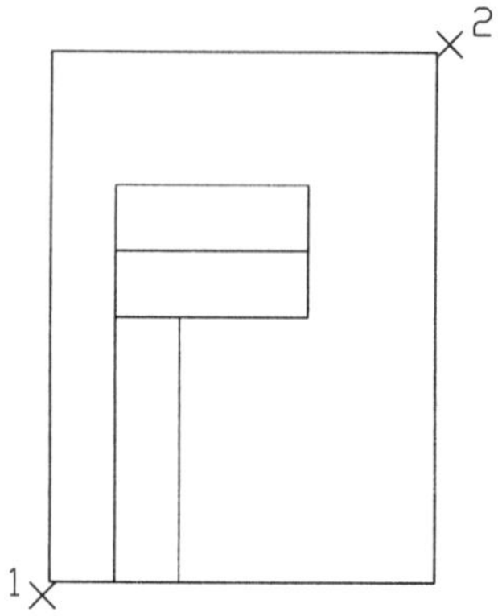

The object will disappear from the screen.

Step 3 Now use INSERT to place the block back on the screen.

> **Toolbar** From the Draw toolbar, choose this button: 
>
> **Pull Down** From the Insert menu pick Block...

At the command prompt, type **INSERT**.

```
Command: INSERT
Enter block name or [?]:LOT
Specify insertion point or
   [Scale/X/Y/Z/Rotate/PScale/PX/
  PY/PZ/PRotate]: (pick the lower
  left of your screen)
Enter X scale factor, specify
  opposite corner, or
  [Corner/XYZ]:↵
Y scale factor <use X scale
  factor>:↵
Specify rotation angle <0>:↵
```

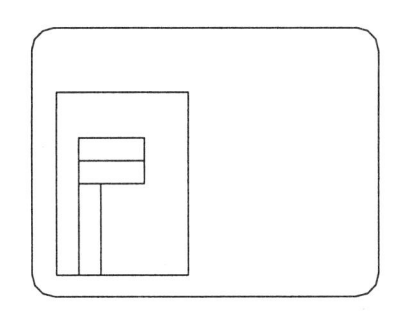

Step 4 Create a new layer called SURVEY with color set to Magenta. Make it current.

```
CREATE LAYER SURVEY
```

Step 5 Use the MINSERT command to place a survey on the page.

> Type in MINSERT at the Command: prompt.

```
Command: MINSERT
Enter block name or [?]:LOT
Specify insertion point or
   [Scale/X/Y/Z/Rotate/PScale/PX/
  PY/PZ/PRotate]: (pick 1)
Enter X scale factor, specify
  opposite corner, or
  [Corner/XYZ]:.25
Y scale factor <use X scale
  factor>:↵
Specify rotation angle <0>:↵
Specify number of rows (----)<1>:↵
Specify number of columns (|||):6
Enter distance between the columns (|||):7.5
```

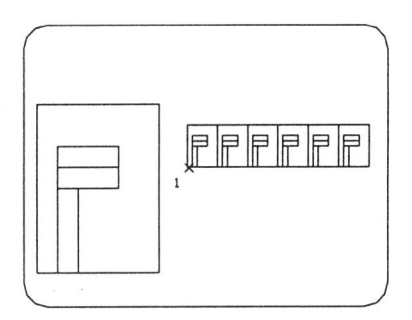

Blocks and Wblocks **265**

Step 6   Use MINSERT again to place the lots on the other side of the street.

```
Command:-MINSERT
Enter block name or [?]:LOT
Specify insertion point or
   [Scale/X/Y/Z/Rotate/PScale/PX/
PY/PZ/PRotate]: (pick 2)
Enter X scale factor, specify
   opposite corner, or [Corner/XYZ]
   <0.25>:↵
Y scale factor <use X scale factor>:↵
Specify rotation angle <0>:180
Specify number of rows (----)<1>:↵
Specify number of columns (|||):6
Distance between the columns (|||):7.5
```

If the two surveys are not perfectly aligned, use MOVE to move one of them. Window is not needed; an object selection pick is all that is needed to pick up the parts.

Step 7   Now insert the title block from Prelab 8. Use INSERT to find the file.

```
Command:-INSERT
Enter block name or [?]:A:EXAMP8
Specify insertion point or
   [Scale/X/Y/Z/Rotate/PScale/PX/
PY/PZ/PRotate]: (pick 1)
Enter X scale factor, specify
   opposite corner, or
   [Corner/XYZ]:3
Y scale factor <use X scale
   factor>:↵
Specify rotation angle <0>:↵
```

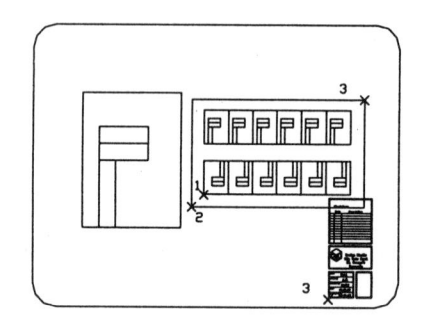

Notice that the date and names may be wrong on the inserted title block. If you try to use CHANGE to change the text, the entire entity will be chosen. You must first EXPLODE the block instance before you can change the text.

```
Command:EXPLODE
Select Block/Polyline/Dimension: (pick the block or L for last)
```

Now use to DDEDIT to update the data.

Notice that the title block originally inserted took on the current layer, which was SURVEY, but once exploded it went back to layer 0.

266   CHAPTER TEN

Step 8   Now that you have this drawing complete, what happens if you would like to use a block that is in this drawing on another file? Use WBLOCK to make a named internal block an external file on your disk.

> **Toolbar** There is no button for WBLOCK.
>
> **Pull Down** Use File, Export, then save with a .dwg extension.

```
Command:-WBLOCK
File name:A:LOT
Block name or [?]:LOT
```

This will take the block LOT and create a file of it. Check to see that this has been written to a file by using Utilities or DIR A:.

```
Command: (pick Files, List)
```

OR:

```
Command:DIR
Name of directory:A:
```

Your listing should include a file called LOT.DWG.

Step 9   Now what happens if you would like to use a portion of this drawing on another file? Use WBLOCK to take a portion of this file and have it accessible on other files.

```
Command:WBLOCK
Enter name of existing block or [=(Block=output file)/*(whole
drawing)] <define new drawing>:A:SURVEY
Block name (or ?):↵
Specify insertion base point: (pick 1)
Select objects: (pick 2)
Specify opposite corner: (pick 3)
Select objects:↵
  Command: (pick Files, List)
```

Now save your file. Start a new file called SURVEY2. Use DDINSERT to insert the file SURVEY.

In DDLMODES note the addition of the layer SURVEY.

Remember: *A file is not a block until it is inserted into another file.* You do not need to block a drawing to insert it into another file.

Blocks and Wblocks   **267**

Command and Function Summary

BLOCK creates an identified group of objects for insertion within the current file.

EXPLODE breaks a compound object such as a block, a dimension, a hatch, or a pline into its component objects.

INSERT allows you to insert predefined blocks and drawing files (wblocks).

MINSERT inserts multiple instances of a block in a rectangular array.

PURGE allows you to remove any layers, blocks, linetypes, text files, or shape files that you have entered into your file and not used.

WBLOCK creates an external block or .DWG file from specified objects on the screen.

Practice Exercise 10

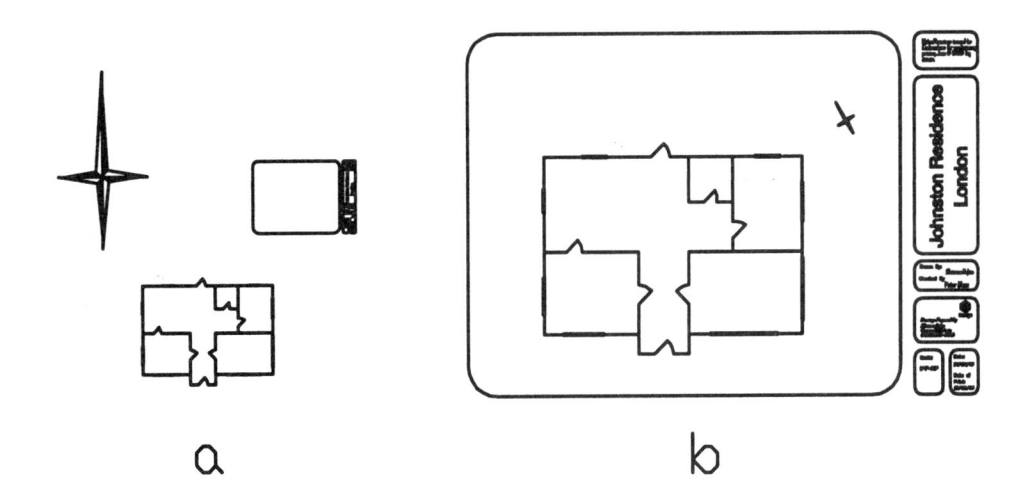

1. Draw the first house. BLOCK it. INSERT it at different scale factors and aspect ratios. Using the same block, create some row housing with MINSERT.
2. a. Draw a north arrow (or retrieve it from Chapter 3) and file it as a separate file. Draw a very simple house plan at 1:1. Draw a simple title block (Chapter 8) b. Open the floor plan. Insert the title block at a scale of 48. Insert the north arrow to fit.

Exercise A10

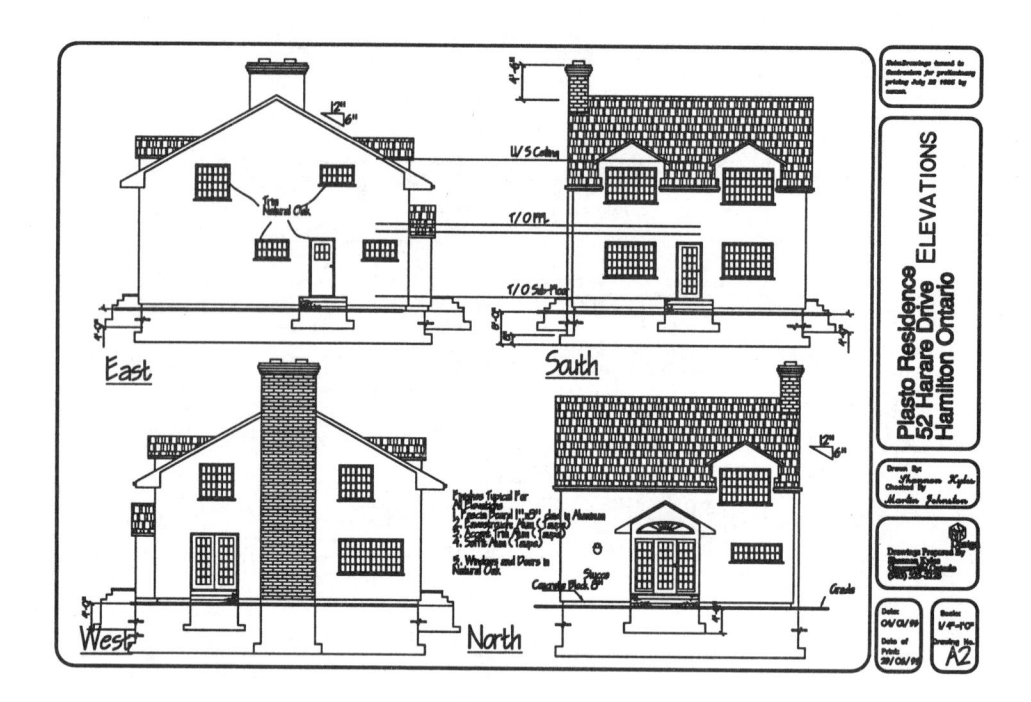

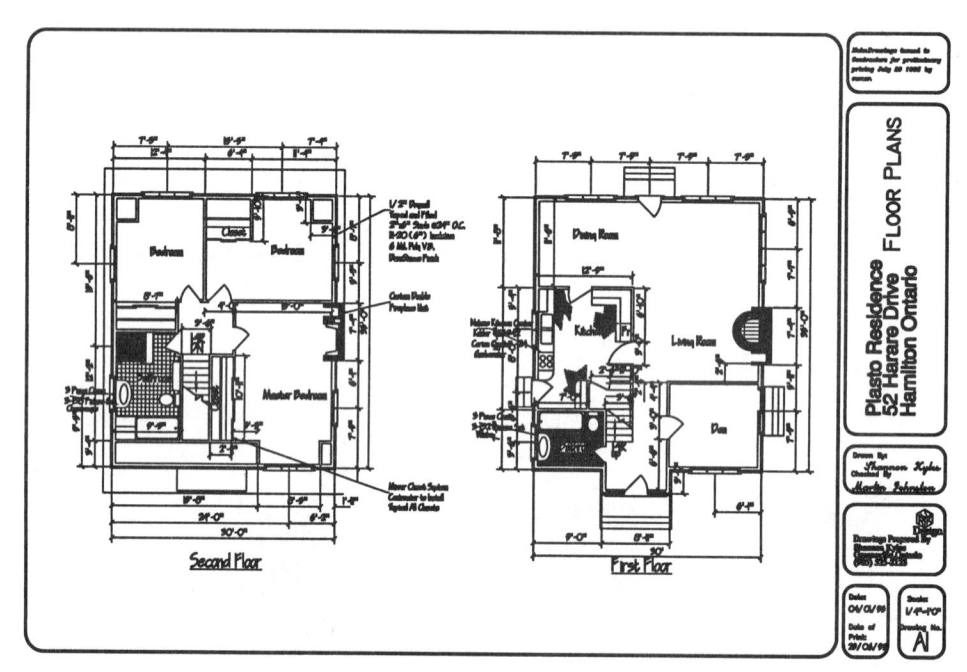

1. Retrieve your floor plan for the first floor.
2. Insert your floor plan for the second floor.
3. Insert the title block from Chapter 8 at a scale of 48.
4. Use SCALE to adjust the size of your title block to suit the paper size.
5. If there is room, insert the elevations — one or many — from Chapter 6. If not, insert the title block again using *NAME so that you can change the drawing number and the description.
6. Your drawing is now ready to plot.
7. Add any notations or titles at this point.

Exercise C10

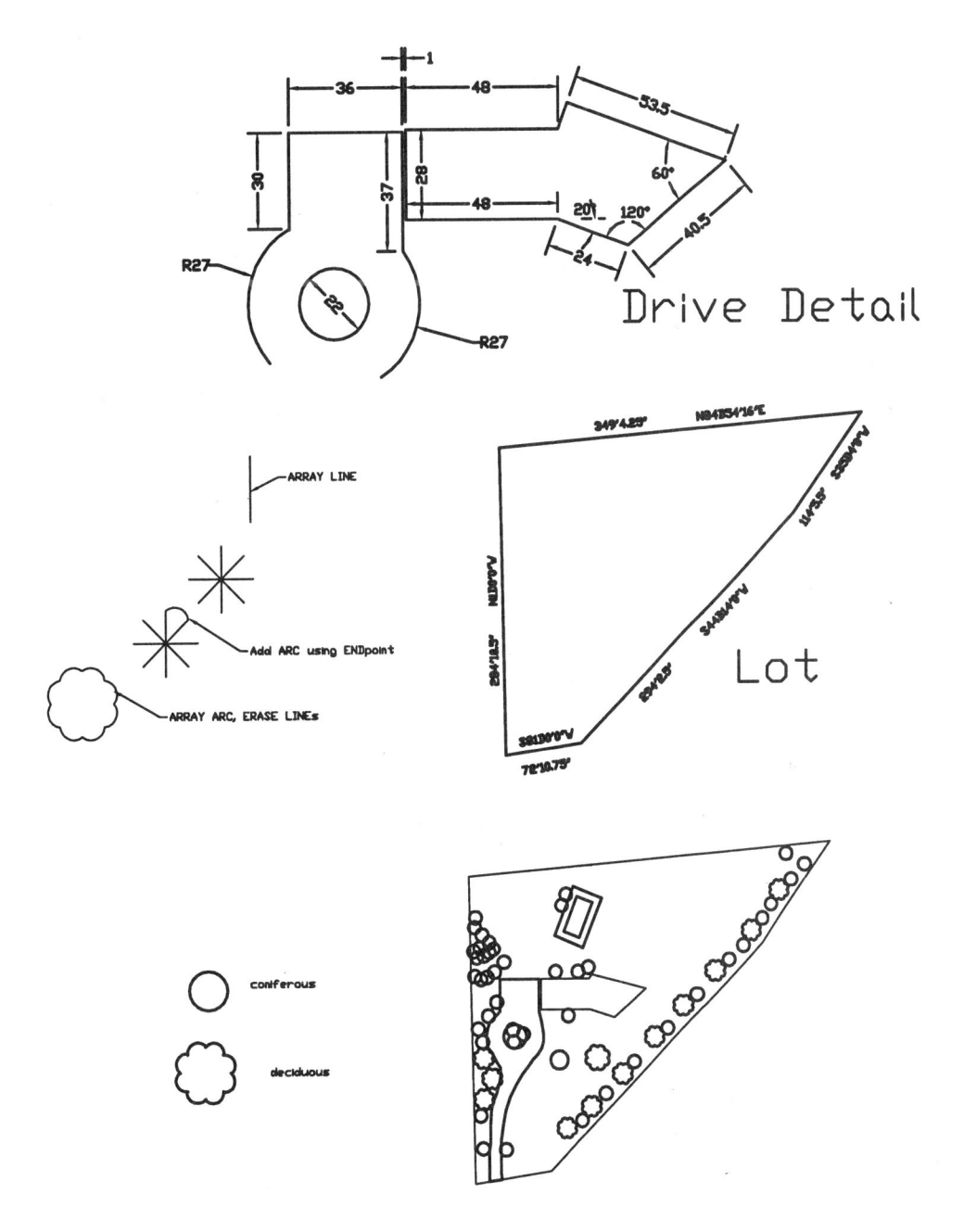

Drive Detail

Lot

- ARRAY LINE
- Add ARC using ENDpoint
- ARRAY ARC, ERASE LINEs

coniferous

deciduous

1. Draw the lot at the size suggested.
2. Place the house and driving circle on the property. Add a driveway.
3. Make a tree using ARRAY. Block it and name it DECID for deciduous. Make another for CONIFerous. INSERT the trees on the lot.

Blocks and Wblocks

Exercise E10

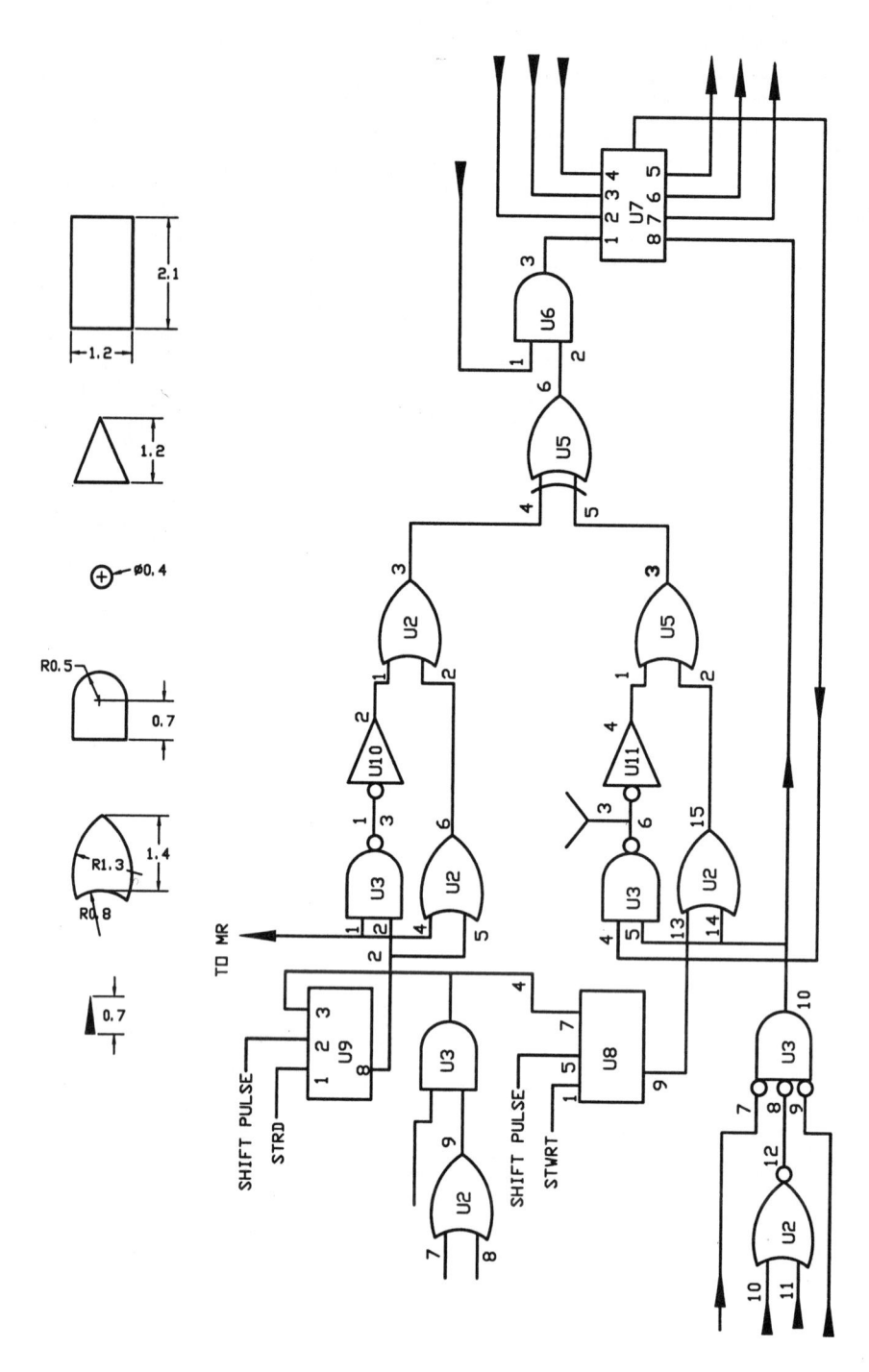

Create the blocks needed to make this computer logic diagram. Then insert the blocks and add the lines to create the layout.

If you have time, add a title block.

Exercise M10

Create the jig body, the jigleg, and the body on one file as shown.

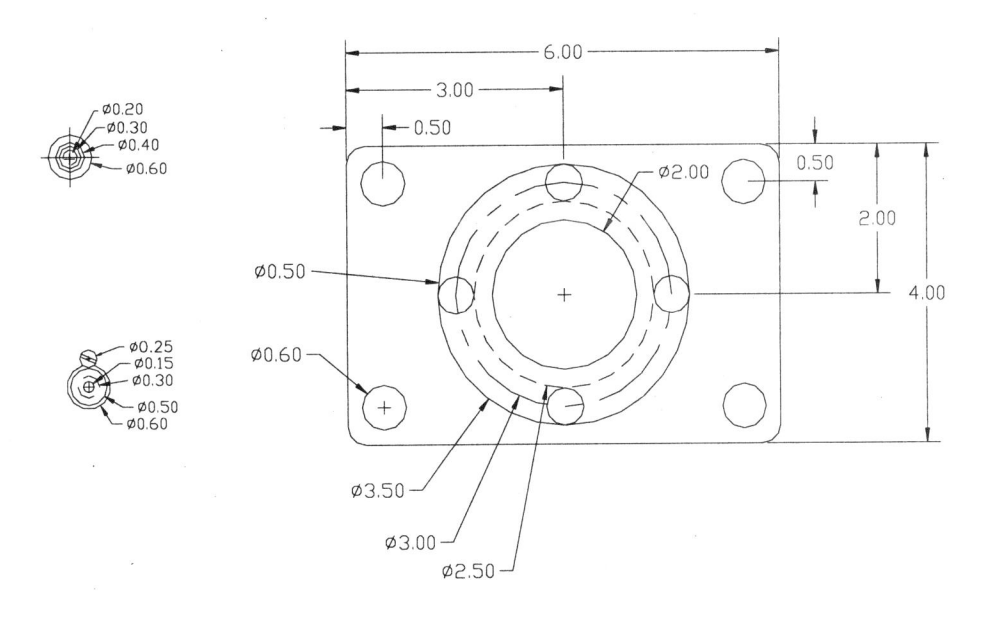

Block the jigleg as JIGLEG. Use the center of the circle as the insertion base point.

Block the bushing as BUSHING using the center of the large circle as the insertion base point.

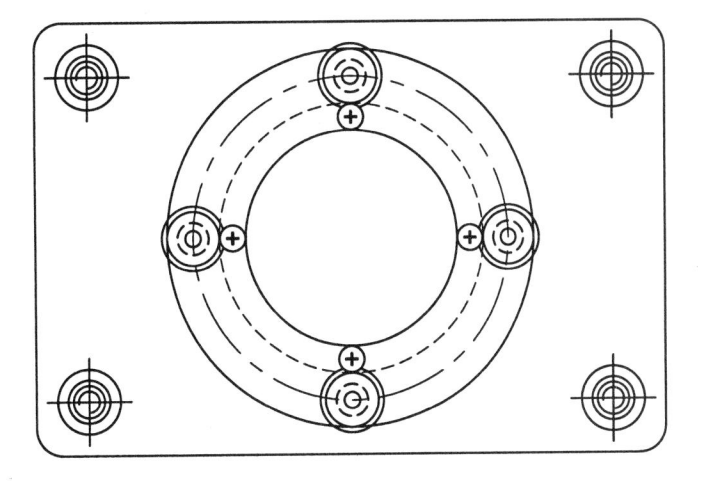

Once blocked, insert the jiglegs and bushings as shown in the above illustration.

Blocks and Wblocks 273

Challenger 10

Use the dimensions from the exercises listed to create files that can be merged into this final part. (Note: Pr-6 = Practice Exercise, Chapter 6; M-7= Mechanical Exercise, Chapter 7.)

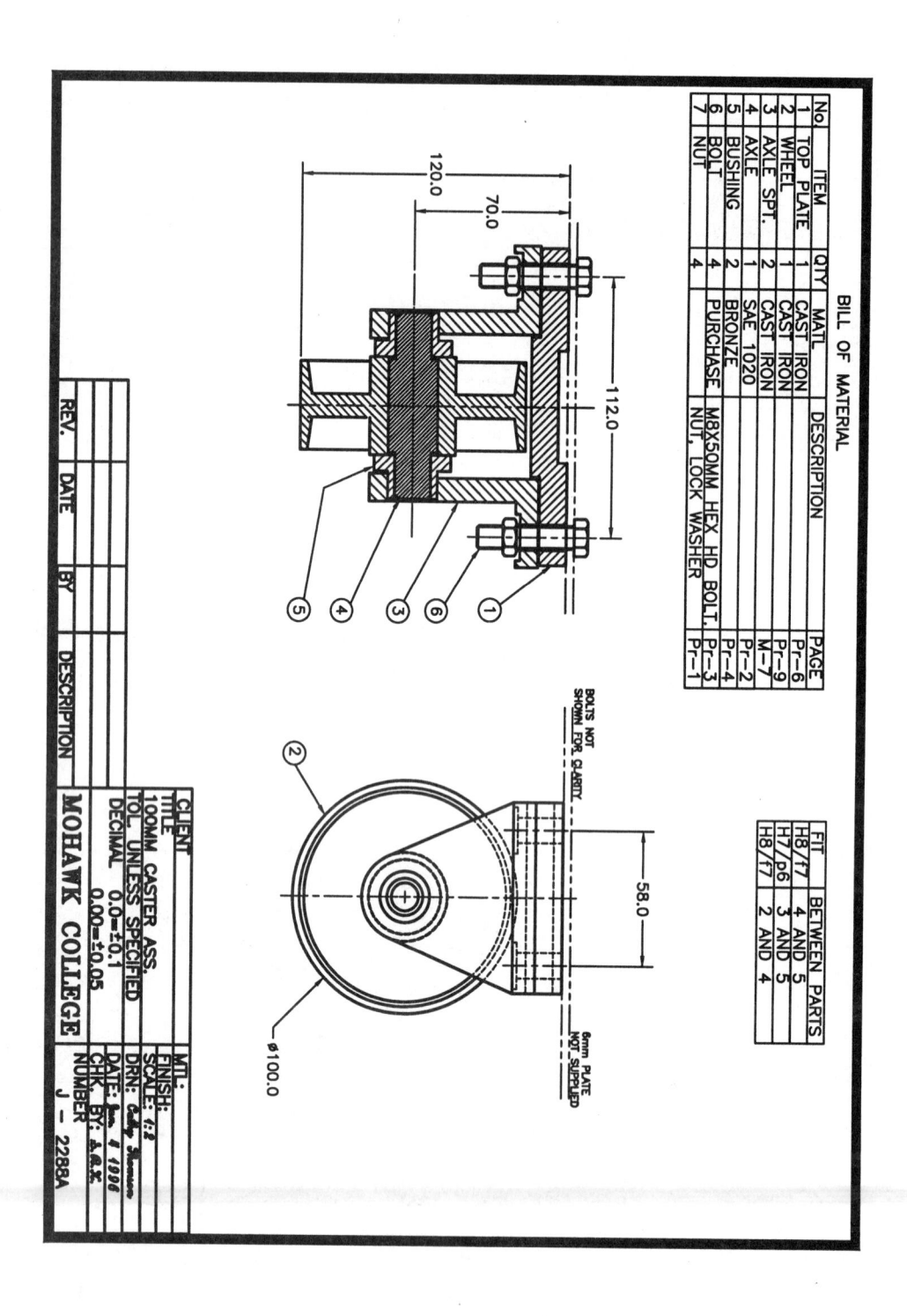

11 Setting Up Drawings and PSPACE

Upon completion of this chapter, you should be able to:

1. Create a plot of a single view
2. Set TEXT, HATCH, and LINETYPE sizes for any drawing
3. Use blocks to compile multi-view drawings
4. Use paper space and tilemode to access a paper environment
5. Use MVIEW to set up a drawing with four views on a standard title sheet
6. Use VPLAYER to have layers visible in selected viewports only
7. Use MVSETUP to lay out a drawing

Set Up and Scale for Simple 2D Drawings

For the past ten sessions, we have been working on AutoCAD models as individual sets of data. The geometry is being entered relative to the origin (0,0). The data, once entered to perfection, can then be used for a variety of purposes, including:

1. Computer-aided manufacturing (CAM)
2. Analysis
3. Downloading to a computer graphics program for marketing purposes
4. Downloading to a stereolithography system
5. Estimating and costing
6. Downloading as a drawing for communication to others

If the model is initially scaled to fit a paper, many of the above applications are complicated. With the model scaled at 1:1, all we need do is extract from the model the views we want to see on a drawing and then scale them appropriately.

There are two ways of creating a scaled plot; with and without paper space. To plot *without* paper space, draw the model at 1:1, then insert the title block at an appropriate scale factor and plot the file at a specific scale.

For example, say you have a layout for a house that is 40′ × 30′ and drawn in real units at a scale of 1:1. You want to have this plotted at 1/4″=1′0″. As you can see by Chart 1 (page 276), 1/4″=1′0″ is the same as 1/48.

Title Blocks

Your title block should be drawn at 1:1 as well. It must also be large enough to contain the floor plan. In this example it is set up for a 24 × 36 sheet. In order to have this visible at the correct scale on the layout, you can insert the title block at a scale of 48. Then, when plotting the model, use a plot scale of 1/48.

This is by far the best method of plotting and scaling, as it allows you to maintain the model at a scale factor of 1:1. For all of the information that requires scaling such as Overall Scale in the dimension style, HATCH, LINETYPE, TEXT Size, etc., 48 can be used.

Title Block, Dimension, Hatch, and Linetype Scale

The ANSI standard for the text in dimensions is 3/16″ or 5 mm. This is also the default for the dimension text in AutoCAD. This will need to be changed, however, if you are plotting the part or view at a scale different than 1:1. You want the part to be scaled, but you still want your dimension text to show up at 3/16″ on the paper.

To do this, you must determine the text size needed for each particular scale. Remember, by changing the DIMSCALE or resetting the Scale in the Dimension Style dialog box and then using the UPD command in the DIM mode, you can automatically change the size of the dimensions if they are not the correct size for the plot of your drawing.

Chart 1: Determining Scale for Drawings

Scale Factor		Decimal Value	Fraction
Architectural or Imperial			
3″=1′0″	3:12	.25	1/4
1″=1′0″	1:12	.0833333	1/12
1/2″=1′0″	.5:12	.0416666	1/24
1/4″=1′0″	.25:12	.0208333	1/48
3/16″=1′0″	.1875:12	.0156246	1/64
1/8″=1′0″	.125:12	.0104166	1/96
1/16″=1′0″	.0625:12	.0052083	1/192
Mechanical			
3/4″=1″	.75:1	.75	
1/2″=1″	.50:1	.5	
1/4″=1″	.25:1	.25	
Metric			
1:10		.1	
1:50		.02	
1:100		.01	
1:1000		.001	

The first step is to *determine* the scale factor for the plot, and change the overall dimension scale factor or the DIMSCALE and other notations to fit. You can also change your DIMTXT, but this is not advisable, because the arrowheads, overshoot, and other variables will not change with the text size.

On a simple drawing with only one scale factor, Chart 1 can be used to determine the plotting scale factor and the block insertion factor for title blocks and other blocks. To use this chart, first determine the final scale for the drawing, then work back from there.

For example, if you are creating a plot or drawing that will be 3/16″=1′0″, draw the floor plan at a scale of 1:1. Add the dimensions at a DIMSCALE of 64. Add the hatch at a scale of 64 (unless it is an architectural hatch), then insert the title block at a scale of 64. Finally, plot the drawing at a scale of 1/64.

Chart 1 will help you to scale the model correctly. The dimensions, text, hatch, and linetype must be scaled to fit the drawing.

Scaling the Text and Annotations

You will have noticed that, when creating text and dimensions, you often had to change the scale factors in order to see them correctly on the screen. This is even more of a difficulty when they are merged with a group of other files or views in a drawing at various scale factors.

If, for example, you want to make sure the text on the above floor plan is at 1/8'' on the final drawing, you would need to find the relationship between 1/8'' on the paper and the size of the text on the floor plan. If 1/4'' on the paper will be equivalent to 12 inches on the model, then 1/8'' or half of that value will be 6'' on the model. If you create your notations and dimensions at 6'' when creating the part, the final drawing at 1/4''=1'0'' will show text that is 1/8'' in height.

Text, dimensions, and related notations should be scaled to attain the appropriate size on the paper. Chart 2 (see next page) shows you at what sizes to scale your text to obtain the proper size on the final drawing. Find the size that you want your text to be, the scale you intend to use, and make the text the suggested size.

To use Chart 2, determine the final size of text that you require and set Dimension scale or DIMSCALE and text size accordingly. Again, do not forget you can change existing dimensions with UPD or create a new style and have it Applied (page 178).

For dimensions on a drawing that will be 1/4''=1'0'', change the DIMSCALE to:

```
DIM:DIMSCALE                    (or Use overall scale of 48 in the
Current value <.1800>:48         Dimension Modify dialog box
                                 under the Fit tab)
```

Or set overall scale in your Fit tab on the Modify Dimension dialog box.

If you take your final plot scale and multiply it by the default sizes and scale factors, you will arrive at workable scales and heights.

LTSCALE and HATCH Scale

While working with views to be placed on a drawing, you must also consider HATCH and LINETYPE. In creating these drawing aids for display on a screen, we determined that the scale for these functions should be the furthest value of X on your screen divided by 12. This provided a working area that was visible on the screen and easy enough to work with, without risking the possibility of filling the disk.

To place views onto a sheet of paper with the linetype and hatch at the proper paper format, use the same setting that you would for dimension scale or final plot scale.

Using Blocks to Compile Drawings

For plotting different drawings at different scale factors, you can insert drawings as blocks on a title block or another accepted drawing sheet. But though this will work, it is not recommended, because any changes will have to be made in the original file.

In the following drawing there are two separate files inserted onto a drawing sheet that is 36'' × 24''.

Chart 2: Dimension and Text Size

Plotted Text Size (Architectural or Imperial)	Scale	Text on the Model	DIMSCALE
1/8"	1/16"=1'0"	24"	192
	1/8"=1'0"	12"	96
	3/16"=1'0"	8"	64
	1/4"=1'0"	6"	48
	1/2"=1'0"	3"	24
	1"=1'0"	1.5"	12
1/4"	1/16"=1'0"	48"	192
	1/8"=1'0"	24"	96
	3/16"=1'0"	16"	64
	1/4"=1'0"	12"	48
	1/2"=1'0"	6"	24
	1"=1'0"	3"	12
3/16"	1/16"=1'0"	36"	192
	1/8"=1'0"	18"	96
	3/16"=1'0"	12"	64
	1/4"=1'0"	8"	48
	1/2"=1'0"	4.5"	24
	1"=1'0"	2.25"	12
Mechanical			
.25"	1:2	.5	2
	1:10	25.0	10
	2:1	.125	0.5
.125"	1:2	.25	2
	1:10	12.50	10
	2:1	.0625	0.5
.1875"	1:2	.375	2
	1:10	18.75	10
	2:1	.09375	0.5
Metric			
3 mm	1:10	30	10
	1:100	300	100
	1:500	1500	500

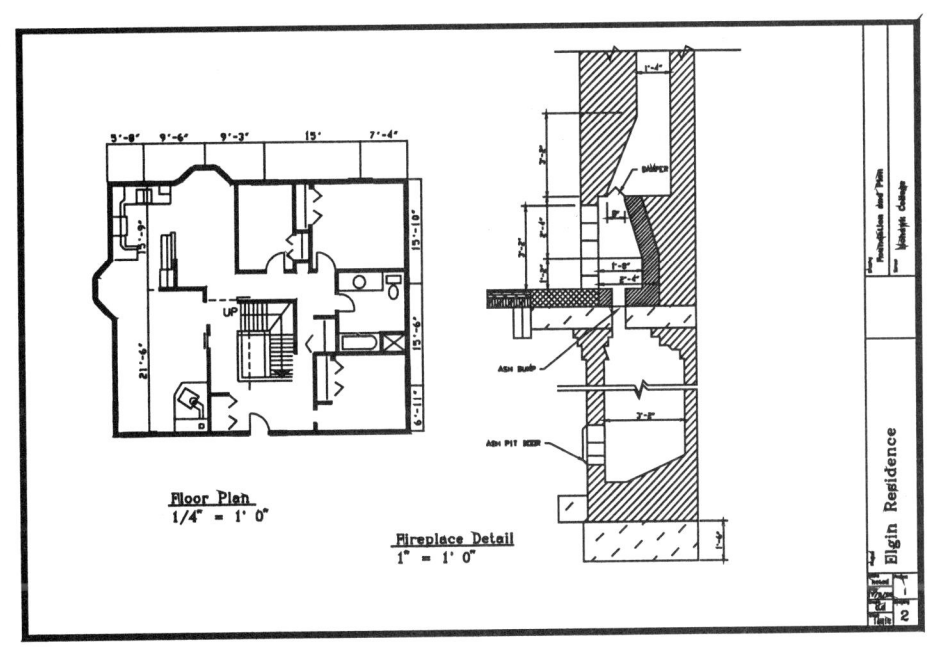

Figure 11-1

The drawing shown in Figure 11-1 consists of three separate stored files:

1. A title block at 36″ × 24″
2. A fireplace detail at 16′ vertically
3. A floor plan 35′ × 30′ (EXA6)

Since the floor plan is the most important view and the one most likely to have changes made, it is the base file. The other two files are inserted in. The floor plan was inserted at a scale of 48 and the fireplace, being a detail, was inserted at a scale factor of 4 times its original size, which will be 1″=1′-0″.

```
Command:-INSERT
Enter block name or [?]:Title
Specify insertion point or [Scale/X/Y/Z/Rotate/PScale/PX/
PY/PZ/PRotate]:0,0
Enter X scale factor, specify opposite corner, or
   [Corner/XYZ]:48
Y scale factor <use X scale factor>:↵
Specify rotation angle <0>:↵
```

This method of creating drawings is useful for many reasons. Often, you have details that can be used on various drawings. If the details were merged with each file plotted, this would take up a lot of room on your disk. Time and space are saved when details are kept as separate files and simply merged when a drawing is ready to be plotted. The drawing can be compiled with many views, plotted, and then erased.

If a drawing is to be plotted at many different scale factors, create dimension styles at those different sizes and have the correct dimension scale factor displayed on the drawing that is plotted.

You can insert drawings onto the title block and plot at a scale of 1:1, or you can insert the title block and details onto the main view and plot at a determined scale.

Setting Up Drawings and PSPACE   **279**

Reconfiguring for Extra Space

If you are working on extremely large files — in 3D this is particularly important — you can have temporary files and swap files located in a reserved directory of the hard drive to speed up REGENs, shading, etc. Use CFIGDHAR.EXE to place swap files on reserved directory if you have not already done so.

A batch file can be used to delete contents of these directories when AutoCAD is started.

Using Paper Space to Compile Drawings

The most efficient way to compile a drawing that has details to be shown at different scale factors is through paper space.

Essentially, *paper space* is a 2D document layout facility. Once the views are completed with all the dimensioning required, paper space takes these views and places them on a "paper" much like a cut-and-paste routine so that they can be compiled as a drawing. With paper space, you will be creating viewports so that you will have the views of the object set up on a 2D format. Paper space acts like a sheet of paper through which the object is seen; you can then annotate as if you were drawing on paper.

Paper space makes use of the multiple viewport facility shown in the 3D section of this book. Multiple viewports are used to place the various views of the objects onto different portions of paper layout both in 3D and in 2D.

With paper space, it is as if you have taken photographs of the model and now you are compiling them on a board or paper for use in communicating the information to someone else. The paper space limits are set to the size of the plotted sheet.

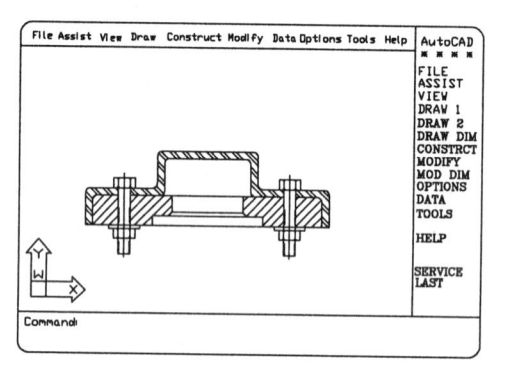

Model space   Paper space

Figure 11-2

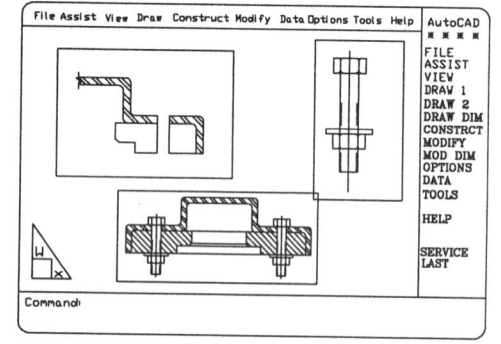

In Figure 11-2, the screen on the left is in *model space* and the screen on the right is in paper space. Both are filled with the same drawing. One has one view, the other has three.

In paper space the crosshairs cover the screen. In the view on the left you have a regular UCS icon; on the right there is the UCS paper space icon. In the screen on the left is one view of the drawing; on the right you have one screen cut into three sections.

The borders for the views will not be plotted on the final drawing if they are made on a different layer.

The main view of the part seen in the drawing on the right will be produced at a scale of 1:1. The details of the views will be produced at a scale of 2:1.

While you can create the same type of drawing with blocks, paper space not only is much easier to use than blocks, but also saves a lot of space both on your disk and on the drawing, because there are many fewer overlapping lines. When using blocks to compile a drawing, there are four sets of lines in a four-view drawing. With paper space, the data within the file is only one model, and thus the storage is much smaller.

To get into paper space, use **TILEMODE**.

Paper space and Tilemode

Getting from model space to paper space was quite simple, but with Release 2000 it has become cumbersome and annoying. There is no way to avoid the dialog boxes that are useful if you know a lot about plotting, but are just a nuisance if you don't.

> **Toolbar** On the status bar, click Model; it changes to PAPER.
>
> **Pull Down** From the Insert menu, choose Layout, then New.

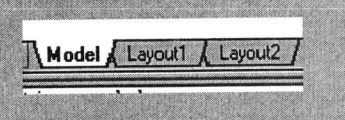

The command line equivalent is **TILEMODE**.

Danger

Do not leave plotting of your drawing to the day before it is due. Any system will have difficulty printing the first time. You need to know the final plotter destination and have the necessary driver before you can even start to plot.

```
Command: TILEMODE
Enter new value
for TILEMODE <1>: 0
Regenerating drawing.
```

The Page Setup dialog box appears. First pick your plotting device from the Plot tab, then pick your paper size from the Layout tab. If you are trying to set up a drawing, and all you have loaded are laser printers, you will need to get another plotter driver loaded before you can access any paper bigger than 11 x 17. Go to CONFIG, then load a plotter. See page 803.

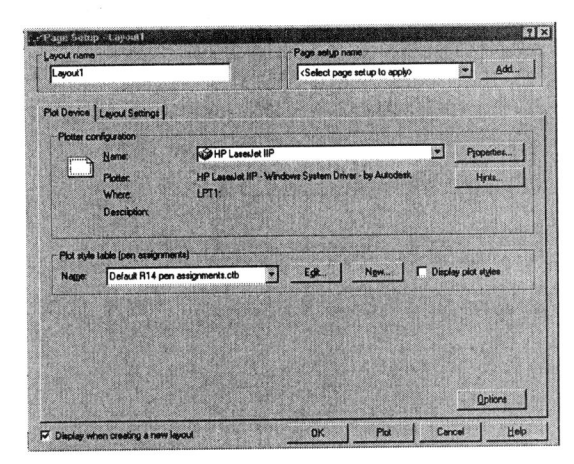

Figure 11-3

Floating Viewports or MVIEW

The MVIEW or Floating Viewports command is used to identify views that will be used in paper space. The screen before MVIEW is the same as a blank piece of paper. The MVIEW command or Floating Viewports option allows you to add views of the model to this paper format. The Page Set up dialog box in Figure 11-3 forces you to pick a paper size, then fits whatever is currently on screen into that paper. If you want something else, erase the views by using ERASE then picking the frame or border, and use MVIEW.

> **Toolbar** There is no button for MVIEW.
>
> **Pull Down** From the View menu, choose Viewports.

The command line equivalent is **MVIEW**.

The pull down menu offers the same choices as the command line;:1 Viewport, 2 Viewports, Restore, etc.

Once paper space has been accessed and the views have been made, you can toggle between model space and paper space quite readily. When you turn TILEMODE back on (returning to model space), AutoCAD restores the drawing as it was before paper space was entered.

When using the Floating Viewports or the MVIEW command, you can create various configurations of viewports, select viewports for hidden-line removal, and have different layers active in different viewports.

From the Viewports menu, choose the number of viewports you want. If you only want one, pick the lower left and upper right corner for the viewport. The default setting for the command line is one viewport. Always set a new layer for the border of the view.

```
Command:MVIEW
Specify corner of viewport or
  [ON/OFF/Fit/Hideplot/Lock/
  Object/Polygonal/Restore/2/3
  /4]: (pick 1)
Specify opposite corner: (pick 2)
```

Figure 11-4

You can use this single viewport to create a single view of the model for plotting and drawing purposes. The single view on screen contains the view of the model that was current in model space. If you want more than one view, choose another option. Other options more relevant to 3D work are covered in detail in the 3D version of this book.

The 2/3/4 Option

If you would like to open a few viewports at once, pick 2, 3, or 4 viewports from the menu.

```
Command:MVIEW
Specify corner of viewport or
  [ON/OFF/Fit/Hideplot/Lock/
  Object/Polygonal/Restore/2/
  3/4]:3
Fit/<First Point>:(pick 1)
Specify opposite corner:(pick 2)
```

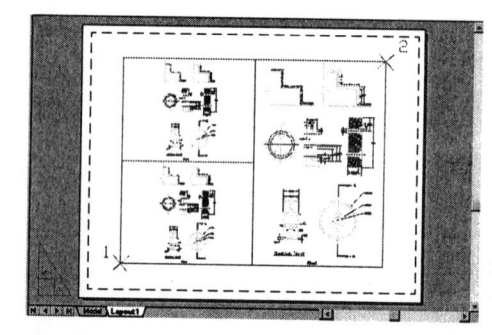

Figure 11-5

This will create a layout of three quadrants as shown. The view in each quadrant will be the view in the active viewport in model space. (If you only had one viewport, it will be that view.)

Using Model Space and Paper Space

TILEMODE On allows you to have one or more views of the model with the borders of the views side by side. You must be in model space.

TILEMODE Off allows you to move the views and place them on a page. (Going into TILEMODE Off will place you in paper space. Use MSPACE to toggle back.)

When TILEMODE is off, you can toggle from model space to paper space very easily using **MSPACE** or **MS** and **PSPACE** or **PS**.

```
Command:MSPACE (toggles back to model space)
Command:PSPACE (toggles back to paper space)
```

Paper space (PSPACE) only lets you access the paper view of the model. Model space (MSPACE) lets you access the model.

Tilemode on
Model space

Tilemode off
Paper space

Tilemode off
Model space

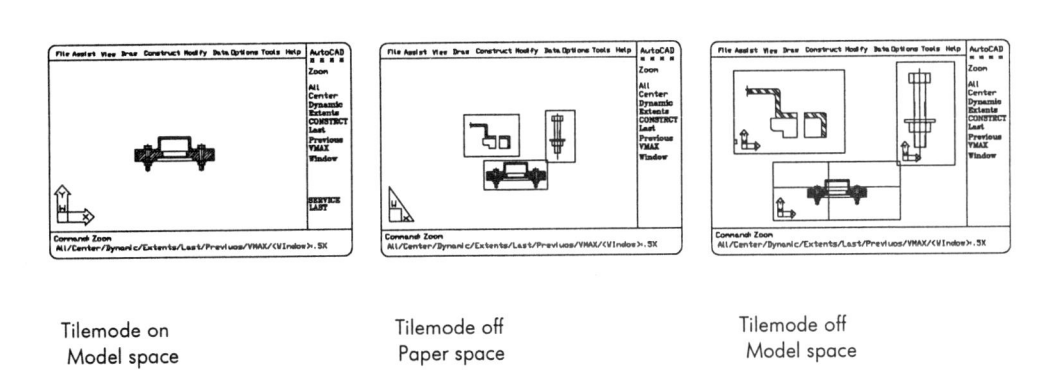

Figure 11-6

With TILEMODE off you can access the model through model space, or you can create the drawing in paper space. With TILEMODE on you can only access the model through model space.

When you use the ZOOM command in paper space, it affects the entire page or paper. A ZOOM .5X will result in the paper with the views intact at half the size that it was before.

When you use the ZOOM command in model space, the model or drawing within the view will be affected. Be careful not to ZOOM the views in model space after you have scaled them with ZOOM XP.

In model space you can PAN the objects within the viewports; in paper space the PAN command will affect the view of your paper environment.

Tilemode on
Model space

Tilemode off
Paper space

Tilemode off
Model space

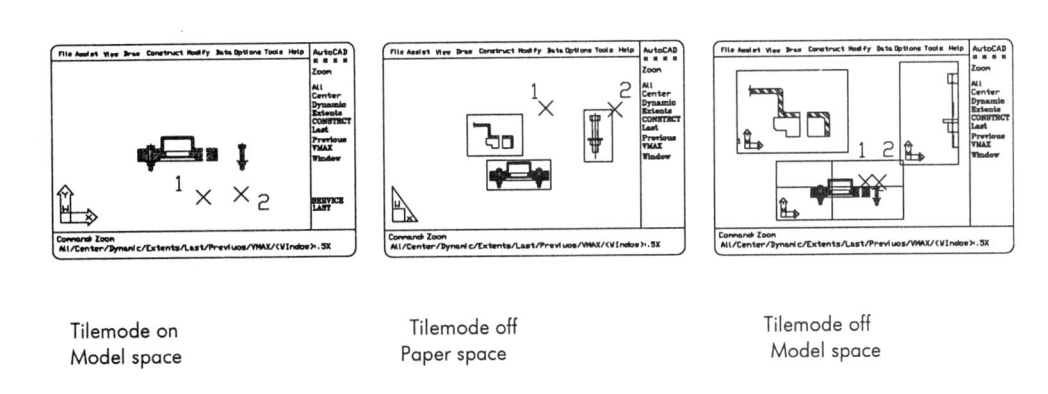

Figure 11-7

In model space the MOVE command will move the objects within the views. In paper space the MOVE command will move the views relative to the other views.

Setting Up Drawings and PSPACE   283

Manipulating the Views

You can use either construction lines (see hidden line) or point filters to move the information across the screen to line it up. The data contained within the views is accessible for reference either for filters or for OSNAPs, but is not accessible for editing purposes.

Any of the Modify commands will work on the viewports in paper space the same way that they work on the objects in model space. You can use MOVE, COPY, STRETCH, etc. to place the viewports where you want with the necessary information.

Scaling Views Within a Drawing

In model space, the command ZOOM All causes you to lose any relation to the actual scale of the part being designed; the image expands to fit the space provided. Use the ZOOM "times paper space" XP option to set the size for the drawing realtive to the paper.

While still in Tilemode Off, change your paper space environment back to model space, and set the zoom in the current viewport. To set the other viewports, simply pick those viewports, then use zoom again.

```
Command:MSPACE
Command:ZOOM
Specify corner of  window, enter a scale factor (nX or nXP) or
   [All/Center/Dynamic/Extents/Previous/Scale/Window]<real time>
   :.5XP
```

In paper space you want the views to be scaled to a relative size. Use the Zoom option XP to scale the object relative to the paper scale units. While the ZOOM option X scales the object relative to its current size within the viewport, the scale factor of XP gives you a zoom factor "times the paper scale" or relative to the paper and also relative to the actual part. Zoom XP scales can be seen in the following chart.

For a Scale Of	Use	Size Relative to Actual
1:1	ZOOM 1XP	1
1/2"=1"	ZOOM .5XP	1/2
1:50	ZOOM .02XP	1/50
1/4"=1'0"	ZOOM 1/48XP	1/(4 × 12)

A ZOOM of 2XP will result in a view twice the size of the original. You can use the scales on page 276 to determine the size of ZOOM needed.

LAYERs within Viewports

The easiest way to control your layers is within the active viewport.

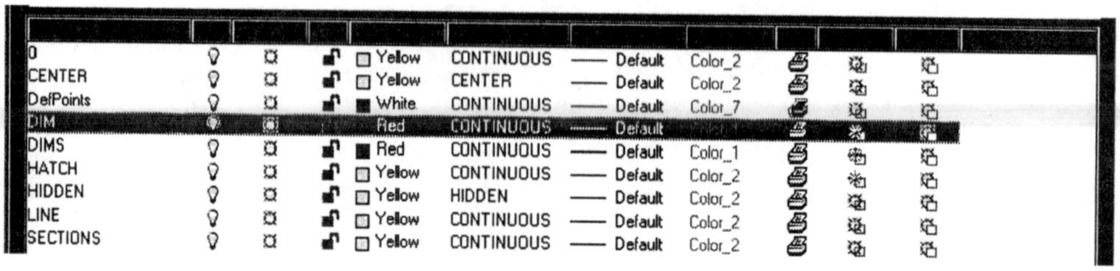

Figure 11-8

With model Space on, access the Layer dialog box, and pick the Active column to freeze or thaw layers within that viewport.

Each viewport can have what ever layers are necessary displayed.

Paper space dependant layers can only be accessed in paper space.

The New column freezes or thaws selected layers for all new objects you create.

The VPLAYER Command

Because you are using one model to create the drawing, and because each view of the drawing will contain dimensions and other information relative to that view and no others, you will need to be able to display certain layers in only one view of the drawing and not the others. VPLAYER allows you to do this.

The VPLAYER command also allows you to perform LAYER freezing in selected viewports rather than as a global command.

As with the Floating Viewports or MVIEW command, this command only shows up in paper space, when the TILEMODE is off (or set to 0). You can use VPLAYER in either model space or paper space TILEMODE 0, but the system will automatically switch to paper space if you try to use it in model space.

> **Toolbar and Pull Down** There is no button or menu choice for VPLAYER.

The command line equivalent is **VPLAYER**.

```
Command: VPLAYER
Enter an option [?/Freeze/Thaw/Reset/Newfrz/Vpvisdflt]:
```

Where:
- **?** = a request for a listing of the LAYERs that are frozen in any selected viewport
- **Freeze** = freeze a LAYER or LAYERs in selected viewports
- **Thaw** = the reverse of Freeze; turns on selected LAYERs in selected viewports
- **Newfrz** = creates a LAYER that is new in the VPLAYER command; this LAYER is created frozen in all viewports, and is primarily used for creating a LAYER to be viewed only in one viewport ever; you first create the LAYER, then you Thaw it in the desired viewport
- **Reset** = the default display for layers created in the LAYER command is Thawed; in the VPLAYER command, the display defaults to Frozen; with the Reset option, the layers are returned to their original default setting
- **Vpvisdflt** = set a default visibility for any layer in any viewport; this could be useful for Resetting the layers; determines the default visibility of all layers in existing viewports

```
Command:VPLAYER
Enter an option [Freeze/Thaw/Reset/Newfrz/Vpvisdflt]:N
New viewport frozen layer names:TITLE (name of the LAYER)
```

Reset the default display for layers created in the LAYER command is Thawed; in the VPLAYER command, the display defaults to Frozen; with the Reset option, the layers are returned to their original default setting

```
Command:VPLAYER
Enter an option [Freeze/Thaw/Reset/Newfrz/Vpvisdflt:R (Reset)
Layer(s) to Reset:0,DIM1,DIM2 (no space between names)
```

For most of the above options, none of the changes will take place until you complete the command.

The prompts allow you to choose the LAYER to be modified, and the objects to be selected for freezing. You can enter multiple LAYERs by putting commas between the layer names.

Dimensioning in Paper Space

To use different scales in different viewports on the same drawing, set the DIMSCALE value to 0. This is paper space scale, and will cause all dimensions to be shown in the default size regardless of the scale of the view. Once you have set the DIMSCALE to 0, you must update each viewport in MSPACE. Use the VPLAYER command to freeze dimension layers that appear in the wrong viewport.

The same is also true of LTSCALEs. To neutralize the effect of different scale factors in paper space, set the PSLTSCALE variable to ON and regenerate the file.

The MVSETUP Command

MVSETUP is a quick way to set up the specifications of a drawing.

In Model Space

In model space, MVSETUP can be used to set the units, type, drawing scale factor, and paper size. Using the settings you provide, AutoCAD draws a rectangular border at the drawing limits. If you are just starting a drawing this is not terribly useful, as it somewhat cuts down on your ZOOM capabilities. This is an old drawing attitude. It is better CAD practice to draw the object and add the title block and notations later. This will make better use of the screen.

In Paper Space

In paper space or with TILEMODE off (0), you insert one of several predefined title blocks into the drawing and create a set of floating viewports within this title block. You can specify a global scale as the ratio between the scale of the title block in paper space and the model geometry in model space.

The Floating Viewports menu is available only when TILEMODE is off or set to 0. The first prompt AutoCAD displays depends on the tilemode setting. In paper space find MVSETUP from the View menu.

> **Toolbar and Pull Down** There is no button or menu choice for MVSETUP.

The command line equivalent is **MVSETUP**.

```
Command:MVSETUP
Creating the default file mvsetup.dfs
Enter an option [Align/Create/Scale viewports/Options/Title
   block/Undo]:
```

Where: **Align**	=	(This option is explained below.)
Create	=	create viewports within the paper space environments
Scale viewports	=	adjust the scale factor of the objects displayed in the viewports; this functions like the ZOOM XP factor
Options	=	set the layer, limits, units, and Xrefs within each view
Title block	=	prepare paper space, orient the drawing by setting the origin, and create a drawing border and title block.

Align will provide the following prompt:

```
Enter an option [Angled/Horizontal/Vertical alignment/Rotate
   view/Undo]:
```

Where: **Align**	=	pan the view in a viewport so that it aligns with a basepoint in another viewport
Horizontal	=	pan the view in one viewport until it aligns horizontally with a basepoint in another view
Vertical alignment	=	pan the view in one viewport until it aligns vertically with a basepoint in another view
Rotate view	=	rotate the view in a viewport around a basepoint
Undo	=	undo the last option in the command

This method of preparing a drawing incorporates the VPLAYER, ZOOM XP, and MVIEW commands.

See Prelab 11B for a walk-through of the MVSETUP command.

Prelab 11A Architectural Example

In this example we will take a floor plan of a house that has a circular fireplace and a kitchen, and we will create one drawing sheet with a plan view and the two details described. Take you layout from chapter 10, or use another floor plan. This drawing will have three scales as follows:

Plan view of house	1/4"= 1'0"
Detail of fireplace	1' = 1'0"
Detail of kitchen	1/2" = 1'0"

Step 1   Retrieving the File

Retrieve the file on which you want to create a drawing.

It may be a good idea to make a simple sketch of the final drawing noting the view scales and the DIMSCALEs. The final drawing will be plotted on a 36" × 25" sheet.

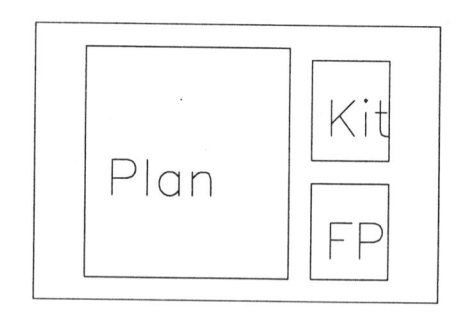

Step 2   Accessing Paper space

Assuming that the data is complete on the file, turn TILEMODE off and create a paper on which to place the views that you have decided on.

Paper space is a 2D document layout facility. You are now taking the file, laying out three rectangles on paper for the three desired views, and adding to the part geometry all of those things that relate to paper.

In order to create the viewports you must enter paper space.

> **Toolbar** On the status bar, double click MODEL. The toggle changes to PAPER.
>
> **Pull Down** Choose Paper space from the View menu.

The command line equivalent is **TILEMODE**.

Danger

The following is what will happen MOST of the time. Release 2000 has many variables in the plotting commands that can affect what you are dealing with. You can spend a few hours going through the AutoCAD Help files for plotting, but it is better to get help from someone who has plotted.

```
Command: TILEMODE
Enter new value
   for TILEMODE
   <1>:0
Regenerating
   drawing.
```

If this dialog box does not appear, go to the pull down menuInsert, then Layout. Establish a paper size to fit.

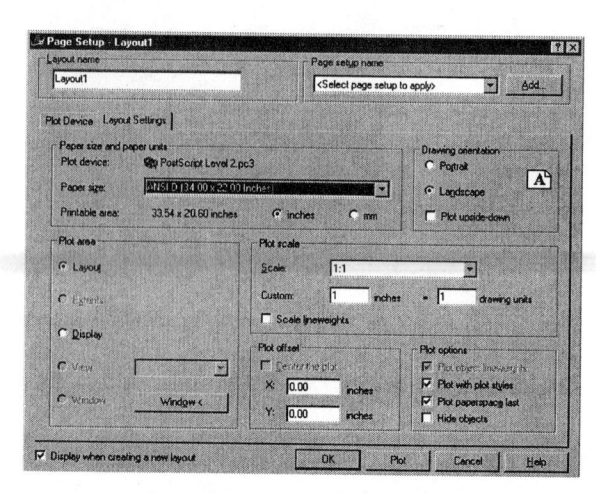

288   CHAPTER ELEVEN

Establish a paper size on your plotter at 34" by 22". If there is no size equivalent to 34 x 22, pick a new plotter. If there is no new plotter to pick, exit the dialog box and use CONFIG (page 803) to configure a new plotter.

Step 3 Setting Up Your File for Paper Space

First create the following layers, making BORDER current.

```
Command: Layers
Add layers with colors as shown.
Layer Name      Color       Color Number
DIM1            red         1
DIM2            yellow      2
DIM3            green       3
BORDER          magenta     6
PSPACE          blue        5
```

The model may be on many different layers. Those listed above are added for the PSPACE information.

Views of the model will be added to the paper in paper space. These views will have borders or frames. As the borders for the views will be frozen before plotting, make your BORDER layer current before adding the views so that the view borders will be in that layer.

> **Danger**
>
> If your plot works the first time, consider yourself a genius. Allow at least a few hours to get your first plot, and get someone to help you who has already been successful on THAT plotter. If anyone else uses it, you can assume that things will be messed up.

SNAP and GRID can be used to help place the views properly. If you are dealing with a roller plotter, you can use LIMITS to set the paper size in some cases.

```
Command: (make BORDER layer current in the Layer Prperties
  Manager)
Command: SNAP
Specify snap spacing or [ON/OFF/Aspect/Rotate/Style]<1">:.5
Command: GRID
Specify grid spacing or [ON/OFF/Value/Aspect} <2">:1
Command: ZOOM All
```

This will set the actual size of your paper. *If there is a view of your mdel on screen, erase it by picking the border.*

Step 4 Creating the Views

Now you can add your views relative to this paper using either the Floating Viewports or the command MVIEW. When setting up you will need to account for the mechanism of the plotter, again, depending on the plotter

> **Pull Down** From the View menu choose Floating Viewports.

The command line equivalent is MVIEW.

Setting Up Drawings and PSPACE **289**

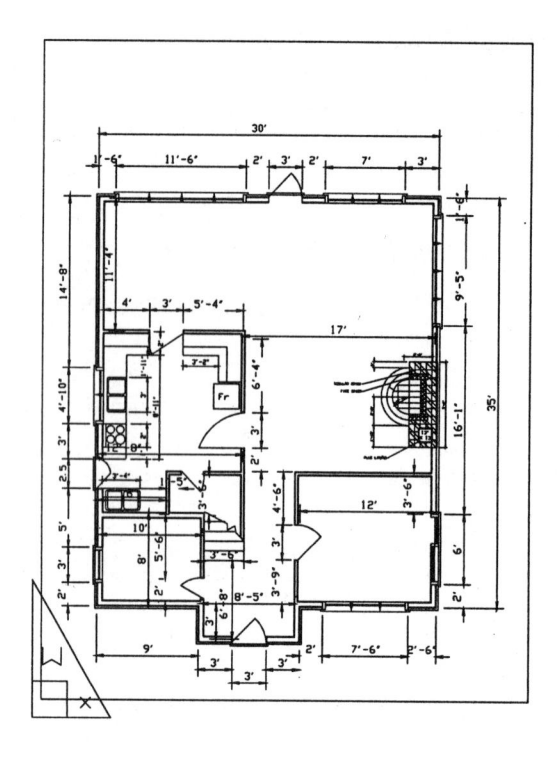

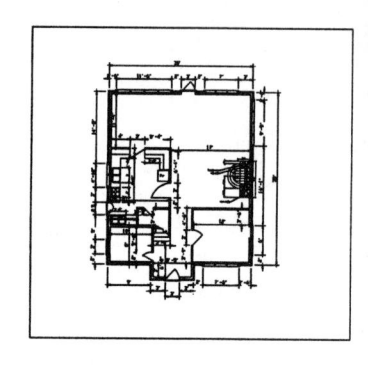

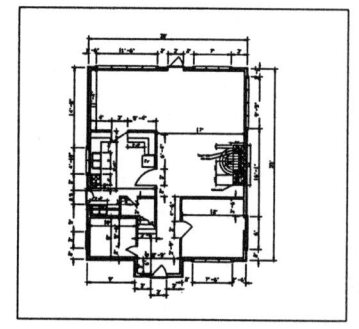

```
Command:MVIEW
Specify corner of viewport or [ON/OFF/Fit/
   Hideplot/Lock/Object/Polygonal/Restore/2/3/4]: 3.5,2
Specify opposite corner: 18,22
```

Add the two other views. Each view becomes an individual viewport entity.

```
Command:MVIEW
Specify corner of viewport or [ON/OFF/Fit/Hideplot
   /Lock/Object/Polygonal/Restore/2/3/4]: 20,2
Specify opposite corner: 31,11
Command:MVIEW
Specify corner of viewport or [ON/OFF/Fit/Hideplot
   /Lock/Object/Polygonal/Restore/2/3/4]: 20,12
Specify opposite corner: 31,22
```

Notice that your model space display is repeated in each viewport. The borders for the views are in layer BORDER, color magenta. If they are not, use CHPROP to put them in that layer.

Step 5 Setting the Zoom with ZOOM XP in the Plan View

We will decide on the scale of each view. Use ZOOM XP to scale each view relative to the viewport, and add dimensions and notations in each model space viewport.

Start with the plan view. Since this view is to be plotted at a scale of 1/4″=1′0″, the Overall scale and HATCH scale should be 48.

Toggle back to MSPACE so that you can access the information within the viewports.

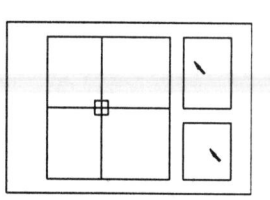

```
Command:MSPACE or MS
```

Notice that your crosshairs are in one view only. Pick the large view on the left to activate it for scaling and dimensioning.

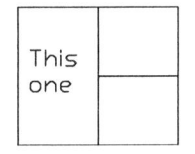

Use ZOOM XP (times paper space) to create a view of the plan at the size in which it will appear on the drawing.

```
Command: (pick the plan view)
Command:ZOOM
 Specify corner of  window, enter a scale factor (nX or nXP) or
    [All/Center/Dyn/Ext/Previous/Scale/Window] <real time> :W
(use Window and PAN to place the house within the viewport)
Command:Z
 Specify corner of  window, enter a scale factor (nX or nXP) or
    [All/Center/Dyn/Ext/Previous/Scale/Window] <real time>:1/48XP
Command:PAN (pan the view onto the screen if necessary)
```

The plan view should be correct. The dimensions should be on in layer DIM1. If not, use CHPROP or add the dimensions and notations now.

Step 6 Accessing the Fireplace Detail

In model space you can only access the information within the viewports; you can't PAN or ZOOM the viewport configuration. Therefore, toggle back to paper space in order to get a detail of the fireplace viewport. This will make dimensioning easier.

```
Command:PSPACE
Command:ZOOM (Window the view)
   (pick 1) (pick 2)
```

You are zooming in paper space only the lower right view.

Now in MSPACE within the viewport, use ZOOM W to get a general area of the fireplace, then ZOOM XP to get the correct scale of 1″=1′-0″.

```
Command:MSPACE
Command: (pick in the fireplace
 viewport)
Command:ZOOM (Window the fireplace)
First Corner: (pick 1)
Other Corner: (pick 2)
Command:ZOOM
 Specify corner of  window, enter
 a scale factor (nX or nXP, or
 [All..]<real time>:1/12XP
Command:PAN (use PAN to place
 the view correctly)
```

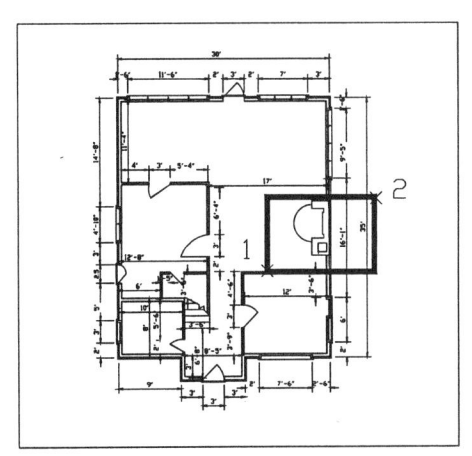

Setting Up Drawings and PSPACE   291

Step 7 *Dimensioning the Views*

This view is going to be 1″=1′0″, so change your DIMSCALE to 12, make layer DIM2 current, and create dimensions on the fireplace. Use the layer dialog box and the Active... viewport to Freeze DIM1 to get the first set of dimensions off the screen.

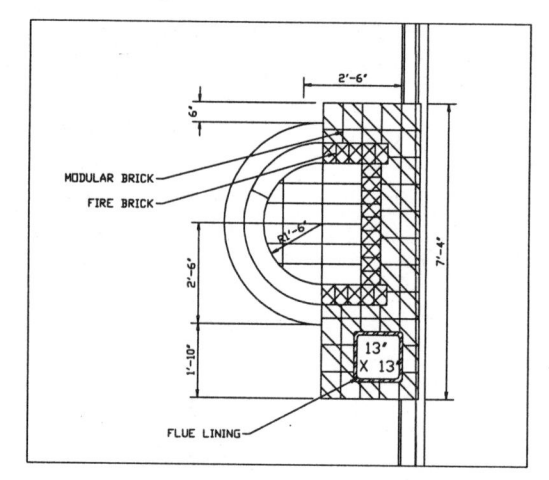

```
Command: (make DIM2 current, Freeze DIM1 in the Active
    viewport)
Command:MSPACE (you should be in MSPACE
    already, but if not, use MSPACE now)
Command:DIM
Dim:DIMSCALE
Scale factor <48>:12
Dim: (continue to add dimensions)
```

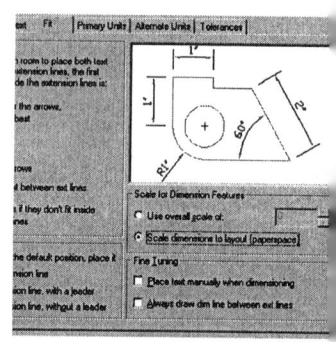

You can also use Scale to Paper space in the Fit tab.

Make the HATCHes on the same layer. The HATCH scale should be 12.

Once the view is complete, make the kitchen active and add dimensions there.

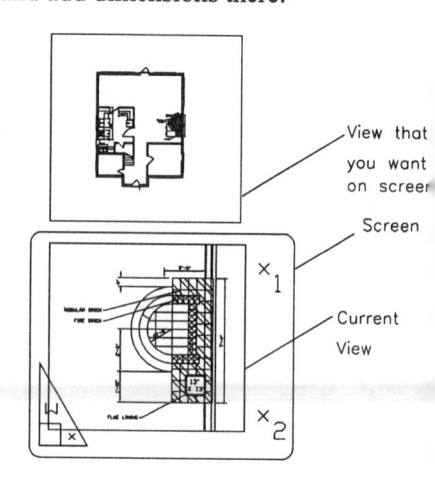

```
Command:PSPACE
Command:PAN
Displacement: (pick the top of the screen)
Second Point: (pick much lower on the screen)
```

Now use ZOOM XP to scale the view to 1/2"=1'0".

```
Command:MSPACE
Command:ZOOM
Specify corner of  window, enter a scale factor (nX or nXP) or
   [All/Center/Dyn/Ext/Previous/Scale/Window]<real time>:W
Specify first Corner: (pick 1)
Specify opposite Corner: (pick 2)
Command:ZOOM
 Specify corner of  window, enter a scale factor (nX or nXP) or
   [All/Center/Dyn/Ext/Previous/Scale/Window]<real time>:1/24XP
Command:PAN (use PAN to place the view correctly)
```

Make Layer DIM3 current and add the dimensions for the kitchen with a DIMSCALE of 24. Add any hatches or hidden lines at a scale of 24 as well.

You have dimensioned your views in the correct dimscale; now try DIMSCALE 0 and UPDate the views to see if there is any change. Set PSLTSCALE to 1.

Step 8 *Adjusting the Size of Your View (Optional)*

If the viewport is not large enough, return to paper space to STRETCH the size of the viewports to fit the views. Always adjust the size of the viewport rather than the scale of the view if possible. You may need to use ZOOM .7X in paper space to get the viewport configuration to fit more accessibly on the screen.

```
Command:PSPACE
Command:ZOOM
Specify corner of  window, enter
   a scale factor (nX or nXP) or
   [All/Center/Dyn/Ext/Previous/S
   cale/Window]<real time>.7X
Command:STRETCH
Select objects:C
Specify first corner: (pick 1)
Specify opposite corner: (pick
   2)
Select objects:↵
Specify base point: (pick 3)
New point: (pick 4)
```

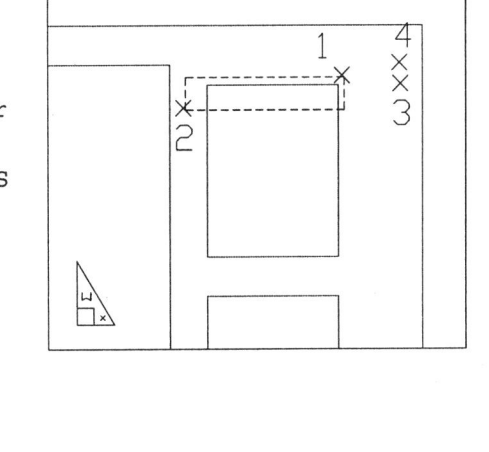

By picking up the outside edge of the viewport, you can stretch it as large or as small as you like. You can also use MOVE to place the view where you want it. Pick the border of the view at the "Select objects:" prompt.

Step 9 *Using VPLAYER to Freeze Layers in Certain Viewports*

The VPLAYER command performs LAYER freezing in selected viewports rather than as a global command. After ZOOM All, notice that the plan view has the dimensions for the kitchen and fireplace. The dimensions are on different layers at different scale factors.

Use VPLAYER to freeze DIM3 in the plan view and the fireplace view. First go to 'DDLMODES to thaw DIM1.

```
Command:Layers (thaw DIM1)
Command:VPLAYER
Enter an option [Freeze/Thaw/
Reset/Newfrz/Vpvisdflt:F
Layer(s) to Freeze:DIM3
All/Selected/<current>:S
Select objects: (pick the plan and
   the fireplace)
Enter an option [Freeze/Thaw
Reset/Newfrz/Vpvisdflt:⏎
```

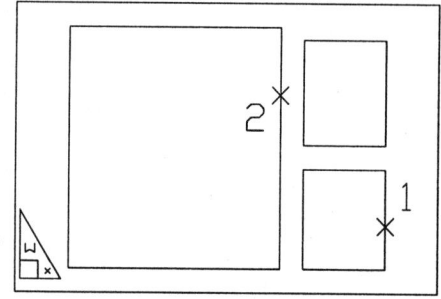

Once you become familiar with the command you can do all freezing and thawing in one command. Now freeze DIM2 in the kitchen and the plan, and DIM1 in the fireplace and kitchen.

```
Command:VPLAYER
Enter an option [Freeze/Thaw/Reset/Newfrz/Vpvisdflt:F
Layer(s) to Freeze:DIM2
All/Selected/<current>:S
Select objects: (pick the plan and kitchen)
Enter an option [Freeze/Thaw/Reset/Newfrz/Vpvisdflt:F
Layer(s) to Freeze:DIM1
All/Selected/<current>:S
Select objects: (pick the kitchen and fireplace)
Enter an option [Freeze/Thaw/Reset/Newfrz/Vpvisdflt:⏎
```

Having used the VPLAYER command, toggle back to MSPACE and use the layer dialog box to make the remainder of the layers frozen in the appropriate viewports.

Step 10 **Adding the Title Block and Drawing Notations**

Add a title block. You may have one from Tutorial 8; if not, draw in a title block in paper space. Make layer PSPACE current before you start. Use DIR A: to find the title block if you have one.

```
Command: (make PSPACE
layer current)
Command:INSERT
Enter block name or
   [?]:TB33X22 (or another
   title block)
Insertion point:3.5,.5
X scale factor<1>/Corner/XYZ:⏎
Y scale factor (default=X):⏎
Rotation angle<0>:⏎
Command: (move the title block if you need to)
```

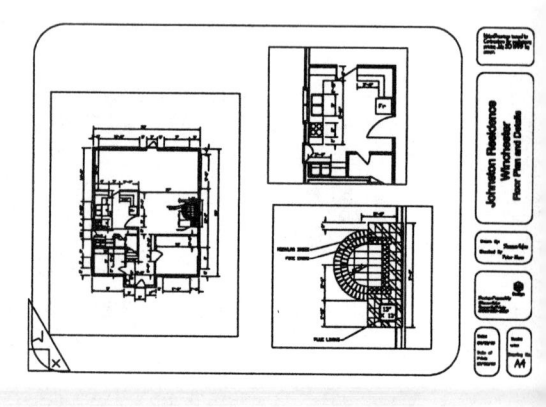

Make sure that your title block allows for the plotter's rollers; leave at least .5″ on three sides and 3″ on the left side.

If you want to reposition any of the views at this point, do so.

```
Command:MOVE
Select objects: (pick the border of the view)
Select objects:↵
Specify base point or displacement: (pick the border)
Specify second point of displacement: (pick a point where you
   would like the view)
```

Step 11 *Repositioning the Views with Point Filters (Optional)*

Filters can be used to help line up the views.

```
Command:MOVE
Select objects: (pick 1)
Select objects:↵
Specify base point or
   displacement:END of (pick 2)
Specify second point of
   displacement:.X of END of (pick 3)
Needs YZ:F8 (pick 4)
```

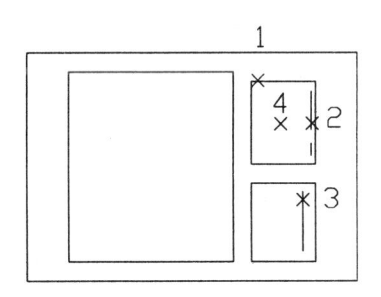

Points on objects within the view can be accessed as object snaps, but cannot be accessed for editing.

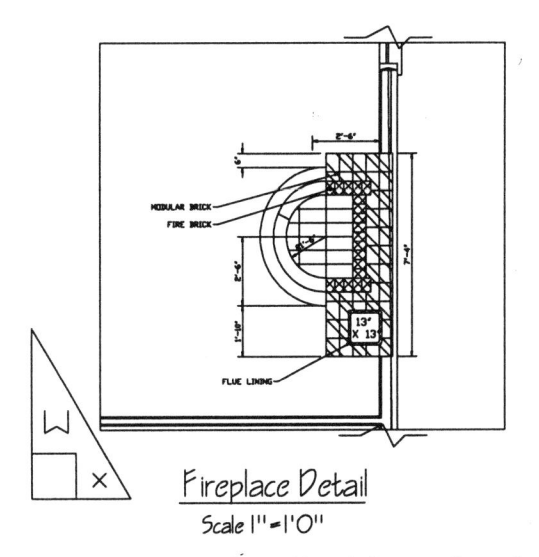

Remember that the borders will be turned off, so you will need break lines at the ends of the lines that will be cut as well as view titles and scales.

If you have entered a title block with incorrect information, change it now. If it is a block, you may need to explode it.

Setting Up Drawings and PSPACE **295**

Step 12 *Turning Off Paper space Frames or Borders*

The frames or borders for the tiles used to position the views are no longer necessary in the final drawing. Freeze layer **Borders** so that the view borders will be removed.

Your drawing is now ready to plot at a scale of 1:1.

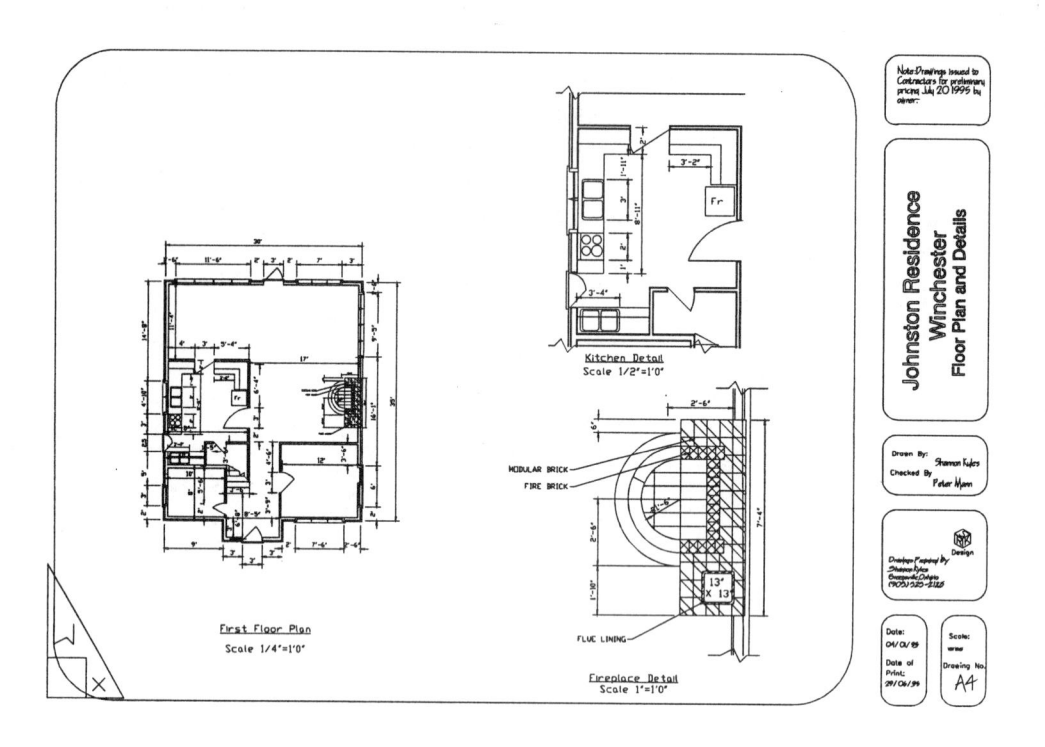

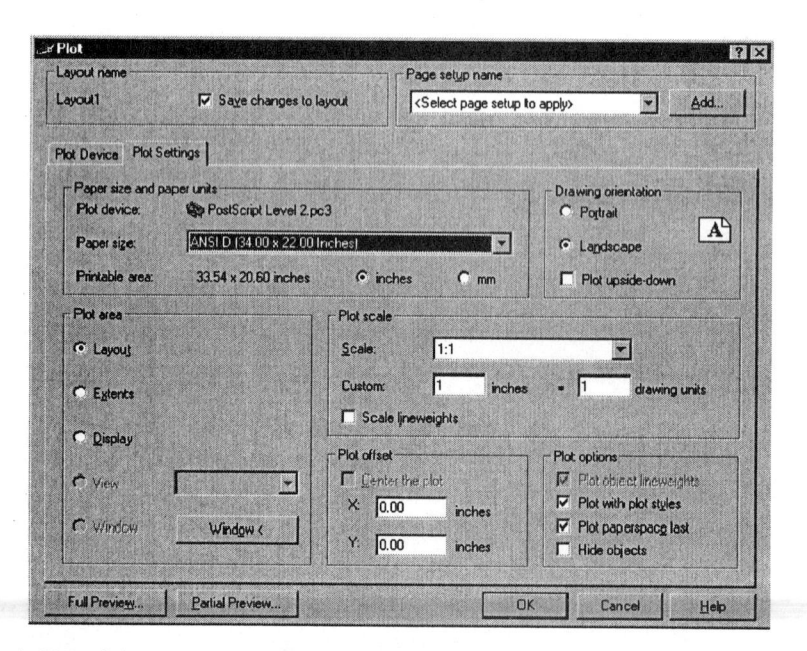

Read *ALL* of the options and change the ones you need. Usually, plotting to Plot Area of Window works best. *ALWAYS* preview the print before it goes out.

See page 796 for more information on plotting.

296 CHAPTER ELEVEN

Prelab 11B Mecahnical/Civil Drawing using MVSETUP

In this example we will take a structural steel drawing that has an end detail, a PAD detail, and a section detail. We will create one drawing in model space, then create several views in paper space.

Beam elevation   1/4''=1'0''

End elevation   1 1/4''=1'0''

Pad detail   6''=1'0''

Detail A   1 1/4''=1'0''

Step 1   Retrieving the File

Retrieve the file for the beam or quickly draw it up.

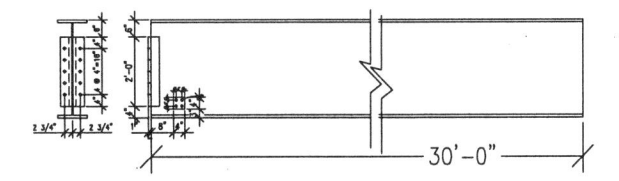

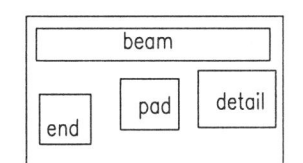

It may be a good idea to make a simple sketch of the final drawing noting the view scales and the DIMSCALEs. The final drawing will be plotted on an 8 1/2'' × 11'' sheet.

Step 2   Accessing Paper space

Assuming that the data is complete on the file, turn TILEMODE off and create a paper on which to place the views that you have decided on.

Paper space is a 2D document layout facility. You are now taking the file, laying out three rectangles on paper for the three desired views, and adding to the part geometry all of those things that relate to paper.

In order to create the viewports you must enter paper space.

> **Toolbar** On the stautus bar, double click MODEL. The toggle changes to PAPER.
>
> **Pull Down** From the View menu, choose Viewports.

```
Command: TILEMODE
New value for TILEMODE <1>:0
Entering paper space. Use MVIEW to insert model space
   viewports.
Regenerating drawing.
```

Don't panic! Your screen should be blank and you should have the paper space icon in the lower corner.

Step 3 *Setting Up Your File for Paper space*

First create the following layers, making PSPACE current.

```
Command:Layers
Add layers with colors as shown.
Layer Name      Color          Color Number
DIM2            yellow              2
DIM3            green               3
DIM4            cyan                4
PSPACE          blue                5
BORDER          magenta             6
```

The model may be on many different layers. Those listed above are added for the PSPACE information.

Views of the model will be added to the paper in paper space. These views will have borders or frames. The borders for the views will be frozen before plotting, so make your BORDER layer current before adding the views so that the view borders will be in that layer.

LIMITS can be set using MVSETUP, but GRID and SNAP are useful too, so use the normal commands to set up the drawing.

```
Command: (make PSPACE layer current)
Command:Set up your Page Setup for a 8.5 x 11 (your default
   will be whatever size your original drawing is made in; in
   this case 8.5 X 11)
Command:SNAP
Snap spacing or ON/OFF/Aspect/Rotate/Style <1">:.25
Command:GRID
ON/OFF/Value/Aspect/<2">:.5
Command:ZOOM
Specify corner of  window, enter a scale factor (nX or nXP) or
   [All/Center/Dyn/Ext/Previous/Scale/Window]<real time>:A
```

If you want to set the units and limits in MVSETUP, use the following.

Toolbar There is no button for MVSETUP.

```
Command:MVSETUP
Align/Create/Scale viewports/Options/Title block/Undo:
```

To change the options, use **O**, then:

To specify the current layer, use **L** for layer. Then enter the name **PSPACE**. If this layer is not already made, this command will make it, but you must go to the layer menu to make it current.

To reset the drawing limits, use **LI** for limits, then enter **Y**.

The size will adjust to slightly larger than the chosen title block.

To specify how drawing limits should be expressed, enter **U** for UNITS. Then enter **F** for feet, **I** for inches, **ME** for meters, or **MI** for millimeters.

Press ⏎ to return to the original prompt.

This will set the actual size of your paper. *There will still be nothing on your screen.*

Step 4 Adding the Title Block

Now you can add your title block and views relative to this paper using Floating Viewports and MVSETUP.

In the same command, enter **T** for Title block. Press ⏎ to display a list of standard paper sizes. Enter the number of the size you want to use, which would be:

```
Command:MVSETUP
Align/Create/Scale viewports/Options/Title block/Undo:T
Add/Delete/Redisplay/<Number of entry to load>:7
```

This will enter a preloaded title block.

Step 5 Adding the Viewports

From the same command, load the viewports.

```
Command:MVSETUP
Align/Create/Scale viewports/Options/Title block/Undo:C
Delete objects/Undo/<Create viewports>:⏎

Available Mview viewport layout options

0: None
1: Single
2: Std. Engineering
3: Array of Viewports

Redisplay/<Number of entry to load>:1
```

Add the three other views. Each view becomes an individual viewport entity.

Notice that your model space display is repeated in each viewport.

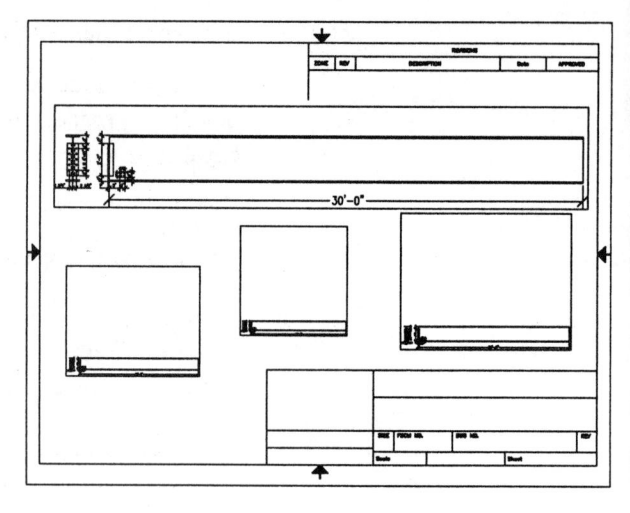

Step 6   **Scaling the Viewports**

You can scale the viewports using the MVSETUP command in PSPACE, but first you should go into MSPACE and ZOOM Window to get the approximate size that you want of each view.

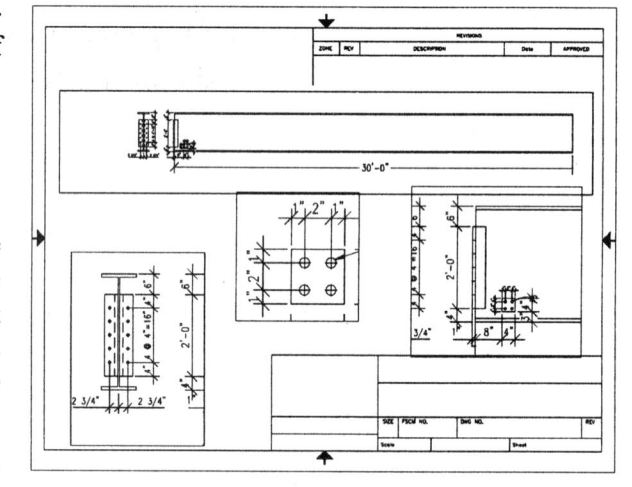

Command:**MSPACE**

Notice that the crosshairs are only in one view. Zoom into the approximate area that you want on that view, and then pick another view and ZOOM Window on it.

Now toggle back to PSPACE and use MVSETUP to scale the views to the exact scale that you want. Start with the beam view.

```
Command:MVSETUP
Align/Create/Scale viewports/Options/Title block/Undo:S
Select objects: (pick the full beam view)
Enter the ratio of paper space units to model space units ...
Number of paper space units <1.0>:1/48
Number of model space units <1.0>:1
Align/Create/Scale viewports/Options/Title block/Undo:S
```

1/16 will be the fraction for 1'1/4'', and 1/6 will be the fraction for 6''.

You may need to PAN the information over on the screen. You must be in MSPACE to PAN a view within a viewport.

```
Command:MSPACE
Command:PAN
```

Step 7 **Dimensioning Within the Views**

The dimensions for the beam should have been done in model space. Now that the views are all assembled, use DIMSCALE 0 with UPDATE to make all of the dimensions the same size within each viewport.

Using the Dimension style mode under the Data menu, access the Geometry menu, then activate the Scale to Paper space button.

Step 8 **Adjusting Layer Visibility**

Use the DDLMODE Layer dialog box to turn off the layers not needed in each viewport.

```
Command:MS (MSPACE must be on to access each individual view)
Command: (pick the beam detail)
```

Select the DIM2, DIM3, and DIM4 layers, then freeze within the viewport using the Active... Column under the Layer Properties Manager.

Do the same for the other views.

Make sure that all of the views contain the necessary information.

Step 9 **Turning the BORDER Layer Off**

The views should contain only the information needed. Use MOVE and STRETCH to make sure that the viewport boundaries are in the correct spot. You cannot change the size of the viewports once the BORDER layer is frozen.

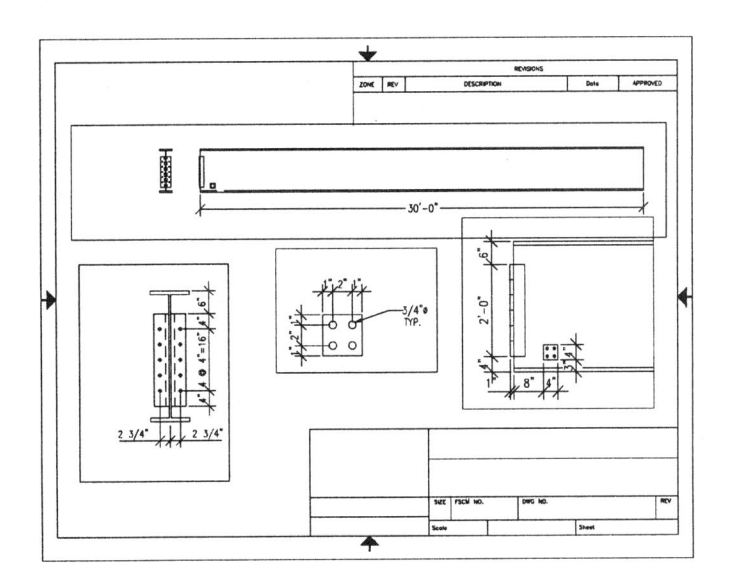

When everything is in correctly, freeze the BORDER layer.

Setting Up Drawings and PSPACE   **301**

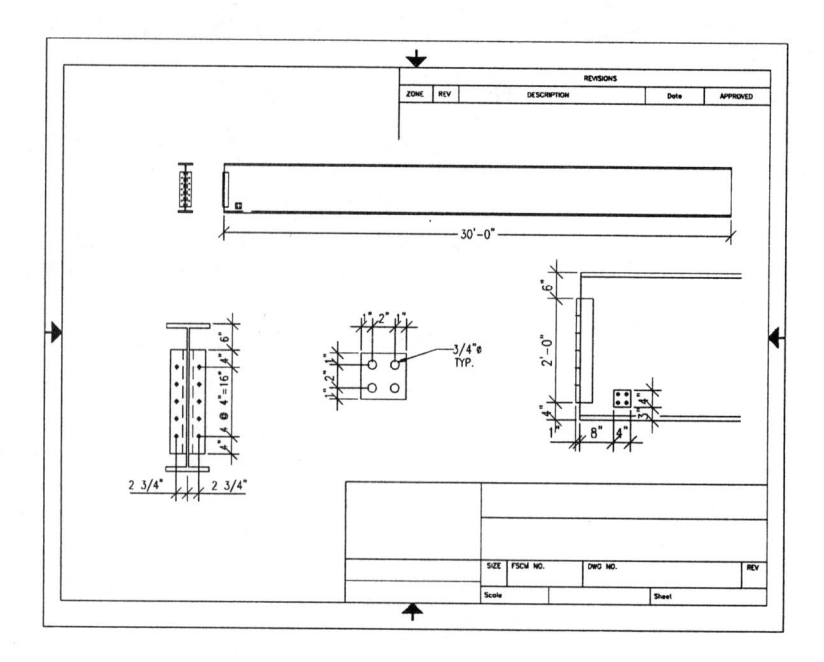

Step 10   Adding Notations

With the PSPACE layer current, add all of the information that you would need on a drawing such as view titles and scales. Fill in the title block.

Your drawing should now be ready to print.

For plotting parameters, see Appendix D, "Plotting and Printing" at the back of the book.

Practice Exercise 11

Create this drawing in model space, then use paper space and MVSETUP to create the final drawing.

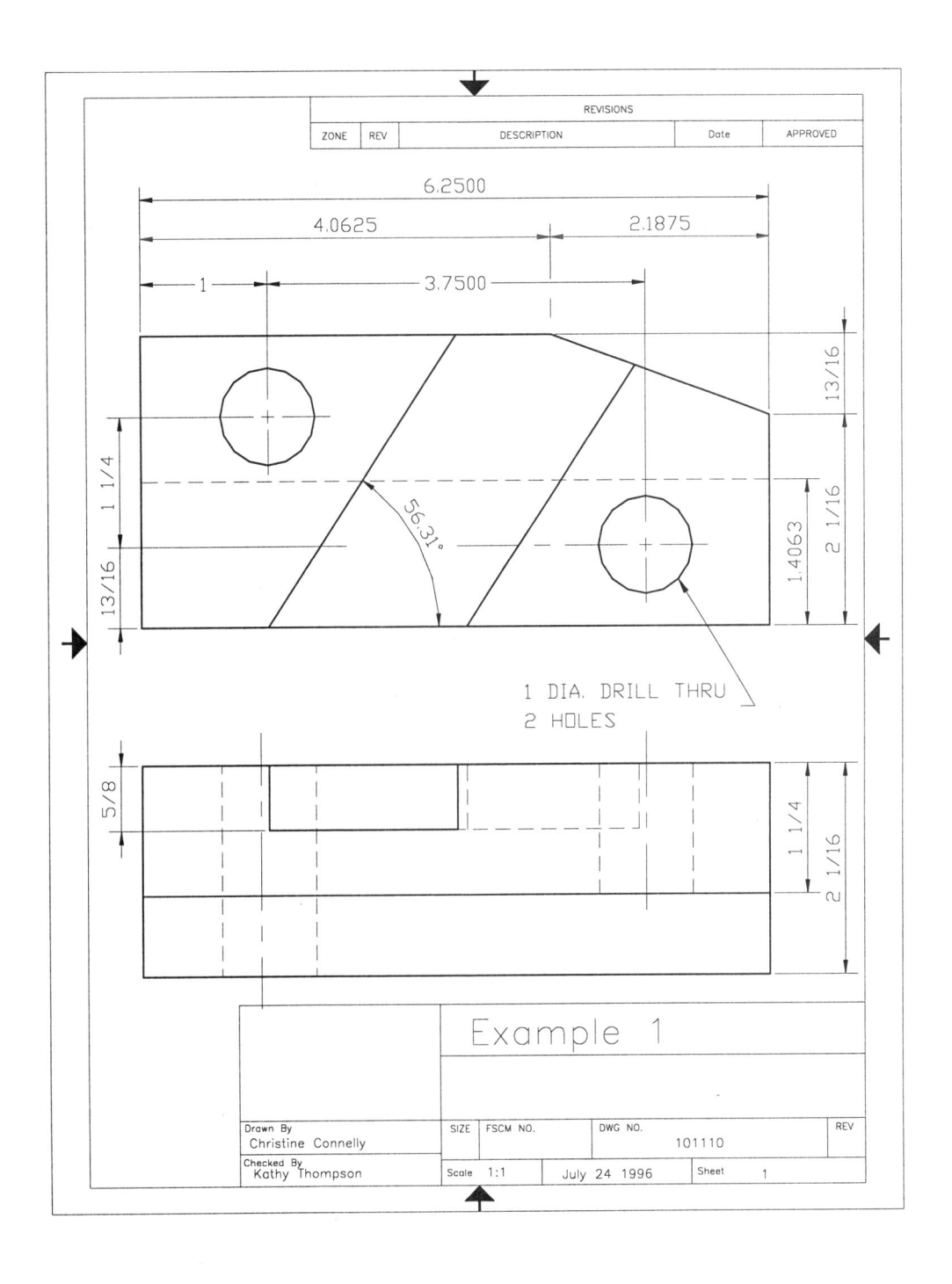

Exercise A11

Quickly draw up the staircase. Then use PSPACE to create two viewports, one for the full view and one for the detail. Add the title block in PSPACE and plot.

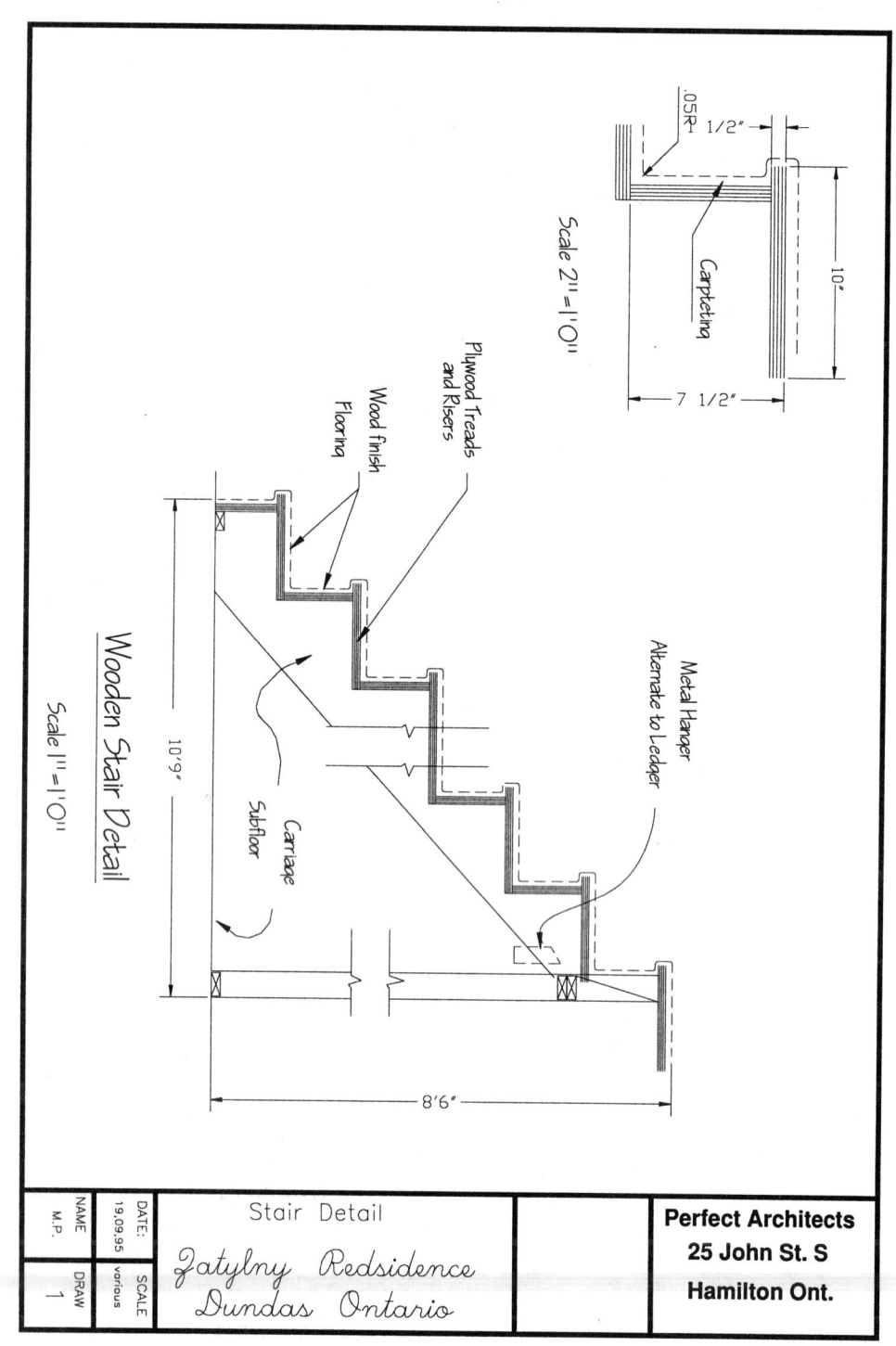

Exercise C11

Draw in the footing. Then turn tilemode off and add two viewports, one for the front and top, the other for a detail view. Use model space to create the dimensions in the appropriate dimscale, then add the views in paper space.

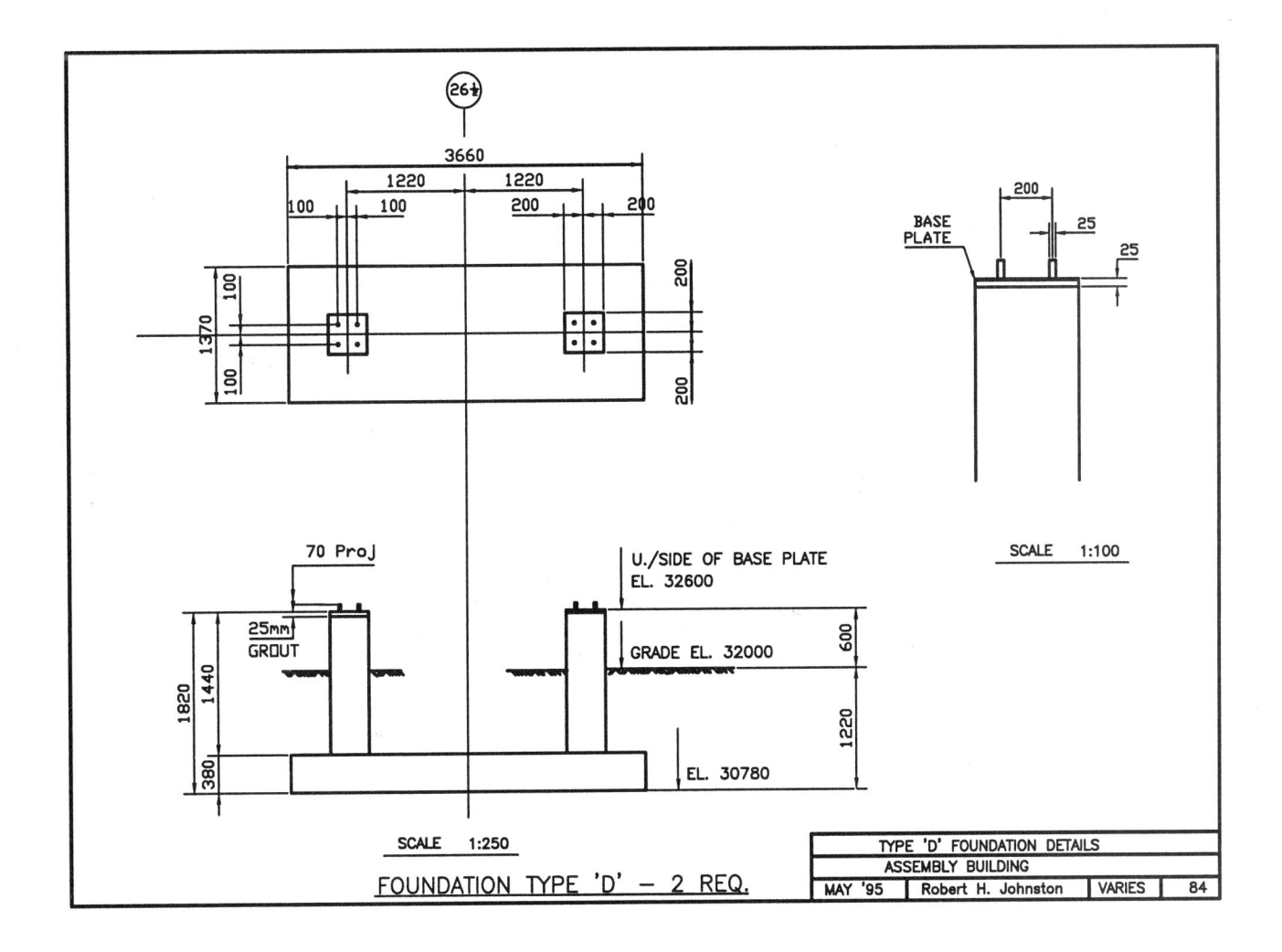

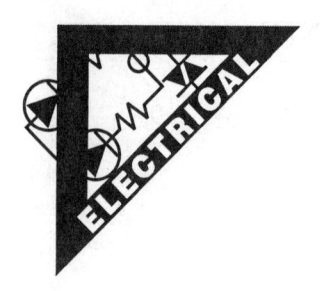

Exercise E11

Draw in the circuit, then use MVSETUP to place it on a metric title block.

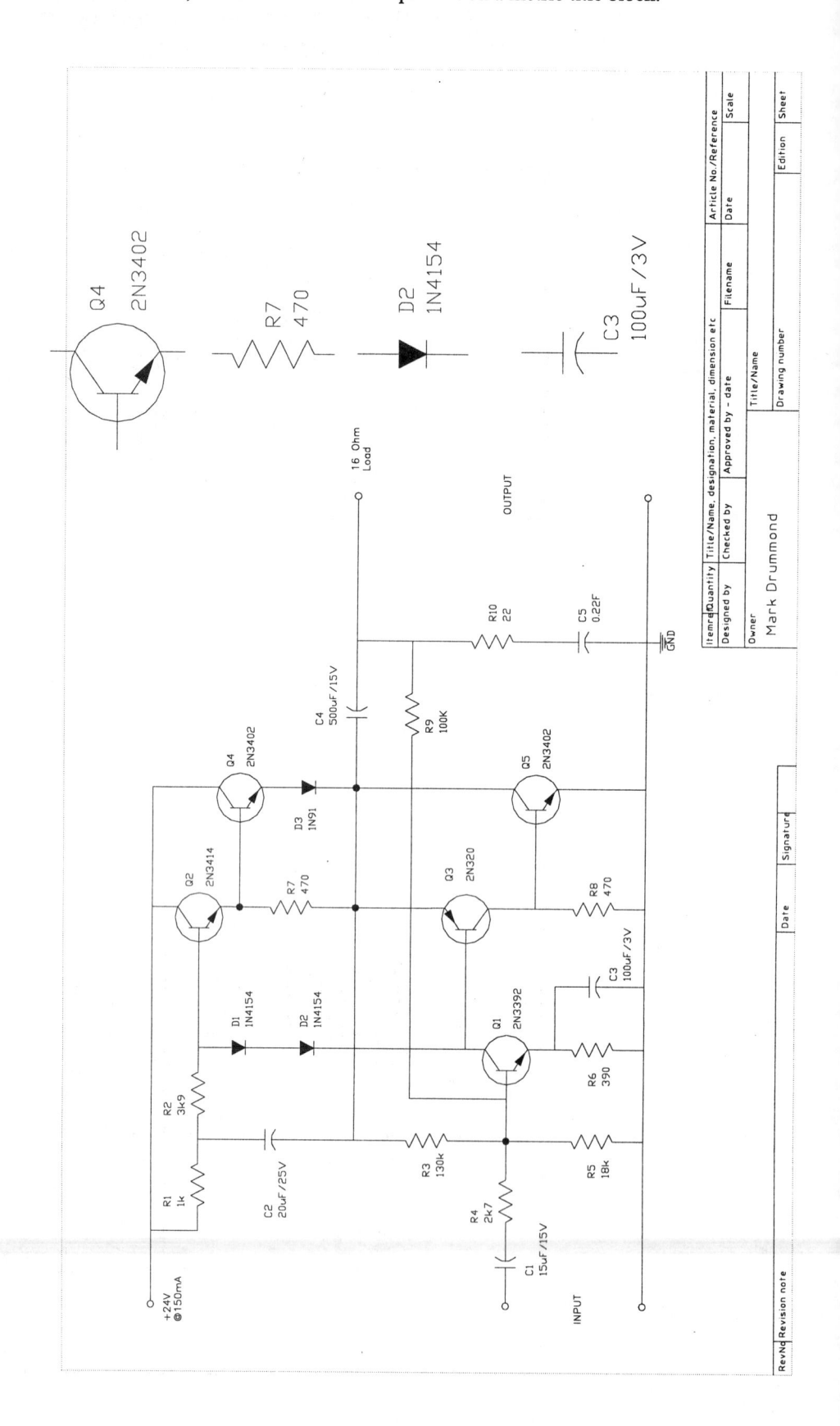

Exercise M11

Draw the body of the part and the pin at a scale of 1:1. Then create two viewports in paper space and dimension the parts in model space. Add a title block and print.

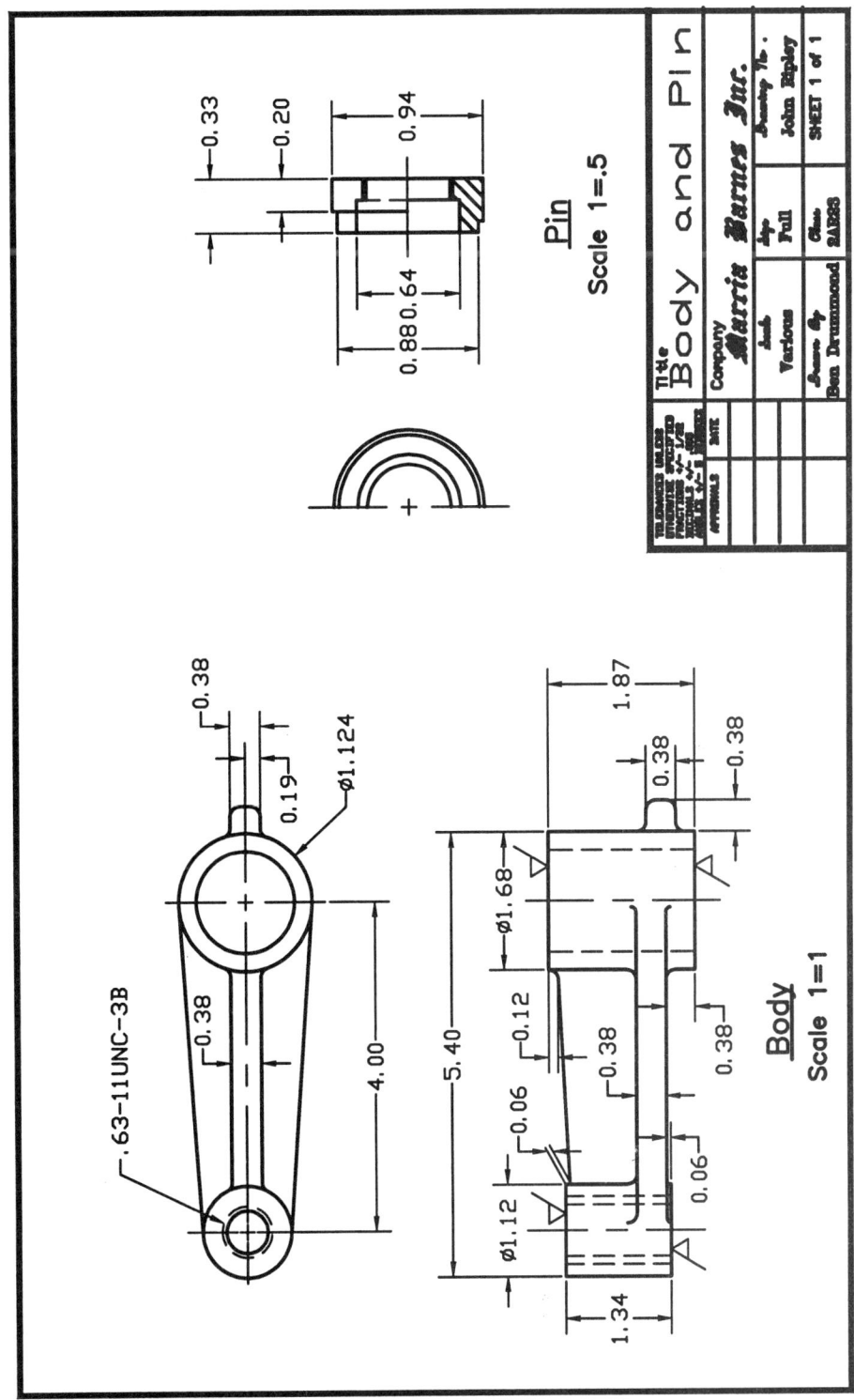

Challenger 11

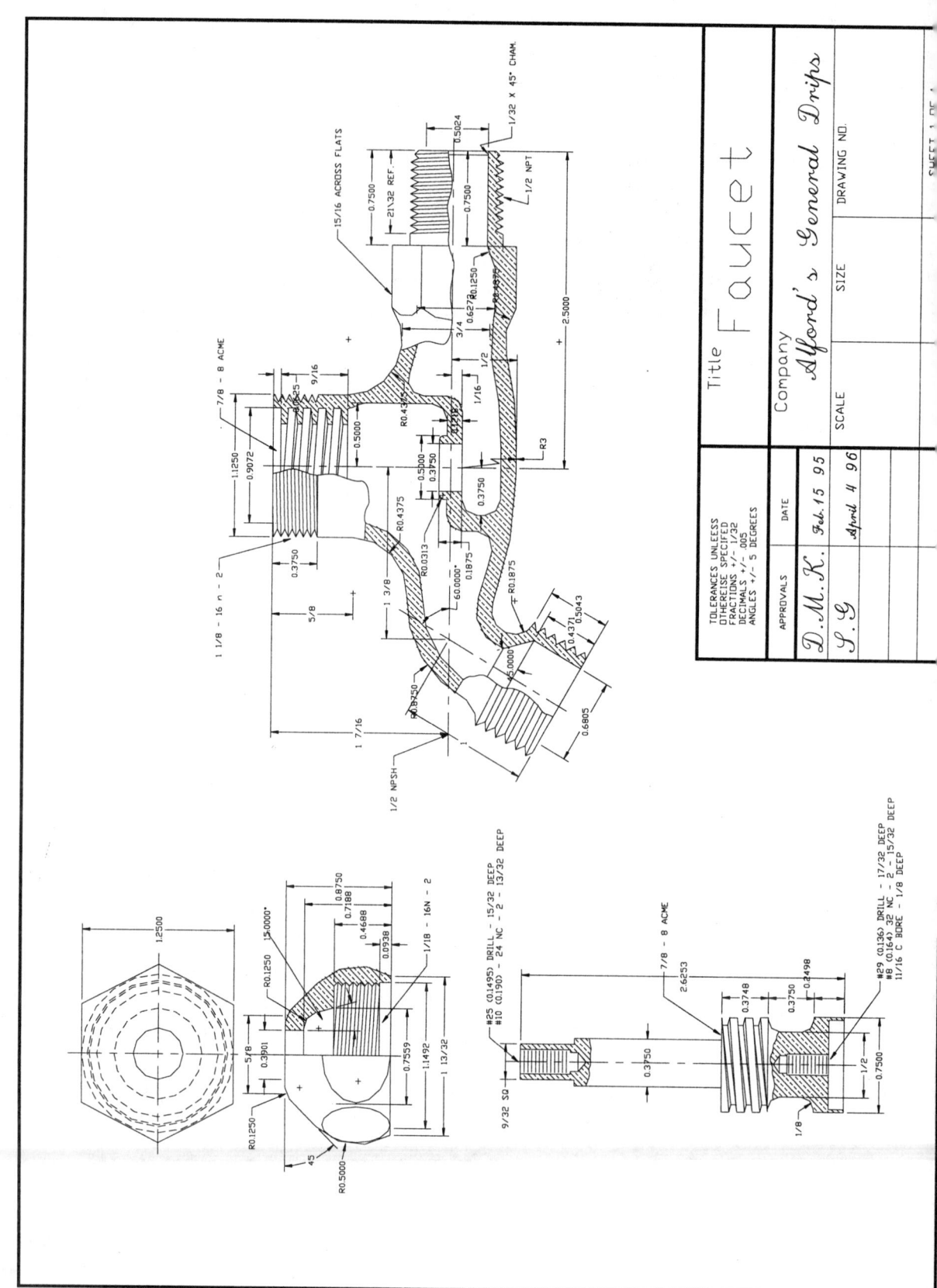

12 2D Review and Final Drawings

1. Review of creation of 2D drawings
2. Final practice in creating large drawings

OBJECTIVES

Review Each of the preceding eleven chapters has introduced a different aspect of AutoCAD software. You should now be capable of creating 2D drawings and plotting or printing them.

The real problems with any CAD system begin when you start compiling large drawings and multiview drawings. The drawings at the end of this chapter are included to help you practice creating large drawings.

Most people learn about file management the hard way. Most CAD users can tell you the tragic story of the first time they lost a very important drawing. In order to avoid joining the list of people who have lost their final drawings just before completion, stick by the following rules.

1. Always keep two backups of your files, not one, on separate disks.
2. Save the file every hour; this way, you will never lose more than one hour's work. You can also set the variable SAVETIME, for example to 15 minutes or 30 minutes, and AutoCAD will save the file automatically.
3. Save your drawings to the hard drive, then copy them to the two floppies. This will prevent file size errors.
4. Keep your disks away from magnets—cell phones and digitizers can contain magnets.
5. Never trust a computer.

If your files on the hard drive are too large to copy onto a floppy, it is usually because you have unwanted HATCH data or unwanted database records. To make the files smaller:

1. PURGE the file, then QSAVE it.
2. OPEN the file again.
3. QSAVE the file again.

Now list your files. You may find that the .DWG files are very much smaller than the .BAK files.

AutoCAD became the most popular CAD package in the world because it offered the most flexibility. The *only* way to become really proficient with the software is to practice. If you have time, it would benefit you a great deal to create *all* of the drawings in this chapter.

Problem 1

Draw the desk and panel unit shown, starting with the 0,0 at point A. Set Units to Architectural with a one-inch readout.

Refer to the drawing of the desk to answer the following questions.

1. What would be a reasonable "First point of mirror line" to create the desk unit in dashed lines? Be sure that you avoid creating duplicate panels or duplicate lines. Once you have identified the point, perform the MIRROR command.

    a. 0,1.5"

    b. -1.5,0"

    c. 0,3"

    d. -3,0"

2. What would be a reasonable "First point of mirror line" to create the desk units in hidden lines? Perform the MIRROR command.

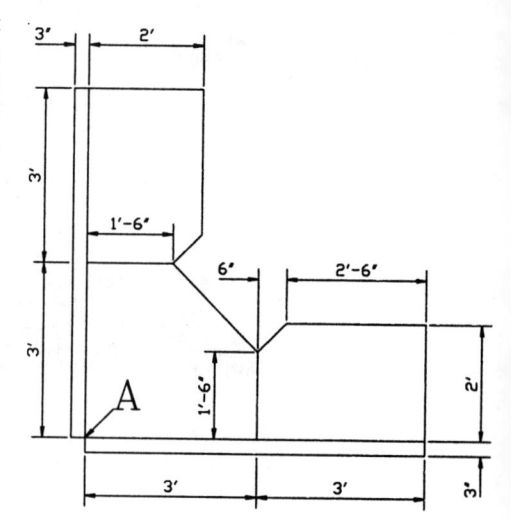

    a. 0,-1.5"

    b. -1.5,0"

    c. 0,-3"

    d. -3,0

3. What would be the absolute coordinate value of the midpoint of line B?

    a. 3'3",1'9"

    b. 2'3",2'3"

    c. 2'6",2'6"

    d. 2'3",2'6"

4. What would be the absolute coordinate value of the midpoint of line C?

    a. 3'3",1'0"

    b. 2'3",2'3"

    c. 3'3",1'9"

    d. 2'3",2'6"

5. What would be the absolute value of point D?

    a. -3'9",-2'3"

    b. -4'3",-2'0"

    c. -3'6",-2'3"

    d. -3'9",-2'0"

6. If drawn so that each desk unit is 3' in length and each connecting panel is 6' in length, how many lines are there?

    a. 52

    b. 48

    c. 44

    d. 40

Problem 2

Draw the object shown, locating the center of the 3.250 radius circle E at 5.000,5.000.

Use the UNITS command to set the units to decimal, with the number of digits to the right of the decimal point at 3.

Refer to the drawing on your screen to answer the following questions.

1. The total length of line segment D is:
    a. 18.127
    b. 17.239
    c. 17.238
    d. 16.986
    e. 16.374

2. The absolute coordinate value of the center of the 12.00 radius arc is:
    a. 24.245,23.456
    b. 23.464,22.259
    c. 22.231,22.497
    d. 21.321,22.497
    e. 20.437,23.267

3. The length of the 2.750 radius arc segment F is:
    a. 5.790
    b. 5.970
    c. 7.590
    d. 7.950
    e. 9.750

4. The distance from the center of the 3.250 radius arc E to the center of the 0.750 radius arc A is:
    a. 24.557
    b. 24.957
    c. 25.975
    d. 25.759
    e. 26.349

5. The circumference of the 4.00 diameter circle C is:
    a. 11.476
    b. 11.957
    c. 12.566
    d. 12.750
    e. 13.254

6. Using the center of the 12 unit radius arc A as a base point, scale the object in size by a scale factor of .333. The absolute value of the center of the 1.570 radius circle B is:
    a. 13.676,20.467
    b. 15.897,21.349
    c. 16.947,22.393
    d. 17.714,22.608
    e. 18.354,22.538

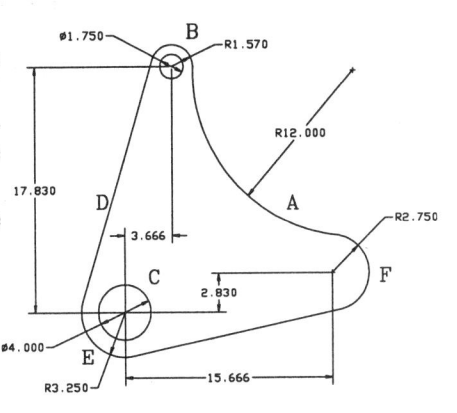

Quiz

Following are 104 questions that should provide a good review of the work performed so far.

Choose the response that is *most* correct.

1. Who makes the AutoCAD software?

    a. AutoCAD

    b. AutoDESK

    c. AutoSHADE

2. What does ORTHO do?

    a. SNAPs to a preset integer

    b. Allows only straight lines

    c. Allows only vertical and horizontal lines

3. What function do you use to see your position with relation to the origin?

    a. Status bar, double-click ORTHO

    b. Options menu, double-click ORTHO

    c. F6 or COORDS

4. What function sets your point picks to a preset integer?

    a. GRID

    b. SNAP

    c. ORTHO

5. How would you draw a line 3 units in length at 45 degrees?

    a. @3<45

    b. @3>45

    c. @45<3

6. What would be the final point in this line?

    From point: 3,4

    To point: @4,0

    To point: @0,3

    To point: @-2,0

    a. 9,7

    b. 7,9

    c. 5,7

7. What does the Object SNAP QUADrant do on a circle?

    a. SNAP to the top, bottom, and far left or right sides

    b. SNAP to a tangent

    c. SNAP to the center point

    d. SNAP to the end point

8. What does the C stand for in the CIRCLE command?

    a. Center

    b. Close

    c. Clip

9. What does the XP stand for in the ZOOM command?

    a. Times Paper space

    b. Across the Paper

    c. Return to Previous

10. What function does R perform in the Erase command?

    a. Replace

    b. Remove

    c. Restore

11. How do you cancel a command in progress?

    a. QUIT

    b. ESC

    c. ^C

    d. F1

12. Can you use the Object SNAP TANgent to create a line between two lines?

    a. Yes

    b. No

    c. Sometimes

13. How do you edit a polyline?

    a. CHANGE

    b. PEDIT

    c. EDIT

    d. CHPROP

14. How do you get a fully solid circle?

    a. SOLID

    b. FILLET Rad 0

    c. DONUT

15. Can you change the grid size once the drawing has started?

    a. Yes

    b. No

    c. Sometimes

16. Can you use the cursor to pick the points from the screen for the bottom left and top right of your limits?

    a. Yes

    b. No

17. Can you turn the limits off?

    a. Yes

    b. No

    c. Sometimes

18. Does a ZOOM All affect the size of your limits?

    a. Yes

    b. No

    c. Sometimes

19. What does U do?

    a. Erases the last line

    b. Edits the last erase

    c. Undoes the last command

20. How can you set AutoCAD to reference the ENDpoint of existing objects for more than one command?

    a. Running Object SNAP on the status bar under OSNAP

    b. OSNAP on the command line

    c. Object Snap under the Drafting Settings menu

    d. All of the above

    e. a. and b. above

21. What does the L stand for in selecting objects?

    a. LINE

    b. Last

    c. Lost

    d. Link

22. What command places multiple copies of objects in patterns that are either polar or rectangular?

    a. ROTATE

    b. ARRAY

    c. TWIST

23. What does the F stand for in BREAK?

    a. First point

    b. Freeze

    c. Find

    d. Flip Screen

24. How do you make many copies of an item at random placing?

    a. COPY Multiple

    b. ARRAY

    c. ROTATE

    d. MIRROR

25. EXTEND helps you to elongate items to reach what?

    a. A boundary

    b. A cutting line

    c. A corner

26. What do you need to create an OFFSET?

    a. An object, a distance, and a side to offset

    b. An object, a cutting line, and an edge

    c. An object, a center point, and an edge

27. What command allows you to break off and delete any overhangings beyond a cutting edge that you specify?

   a. TRIM

   b. BREAK

   c. EXTEND

28. Can you use a Crossing window to identify the cutting lines in the TRIM command?

   a. No

   b. Yes

   c. Only in paper space

29. Under what circumstances does the cursor turn into a box?

   a. When the zoom factor is too low

   b. When you are being prompted to Select Objects:

   c. When a prompt is missing

30. Can you use incremental values (@3,4) to describe the displacement in the MOVE command?

   a. Yes

   b. No

31. What two commands may automatically perform a REGEN on your file?

   a. ZOOM and PAN

   b. DISPLAY and EDIT

   c. MOVE and BREAK

32. What do the square brackets [ ] in a command string indicate?

   a. Options available in the command

   b. A preset integer

   c. The suggested size

   d. The current size

33. What does CP mean in the "select objects" prompt?

   a. Crossing Polygon

   b. Create Polygon

   c. Center of Polygon

34. Can you set two concurrent Running Object Snaps?

    a. No

    b. Yes

35. What does the command PURGE do?

    a. Exits AutoCAD and saves the file

    b. Cleans the file of all unused blocks, layers, and linetypes

    c. Erases WBLOCKS

36. What extension is used to identify a file made up solely of linetypes?

    A. .bak

    B. .ltp

    C. .lin

    D. .lon

37. Can you change the width of a pline once it has been entered?

    a. Yes

    b. No

    c. Sometimes

38. Must your mirroring line in the MIRROR command always be part of the object?

    a. Yes

    b. No

    c. Sometimes

39. What happens if you enter **UNDO 5**?

    a. The last five erases will be undone

    b. The last five commands will be undone

    c. The last five lines will be undone

40. Can you save your files into other versions of AutoCAD?

    a. Yes

    b. No

    c. Only in Paperspace

41. In the filename A:\first .dwg, what does A: stand for?

    a. The drive

    b. The directory

    c. The extension

42. In AutoCAD, which command do you use to get a listing of your files on the A: drive?

    a. List File Utility

    b. FILES

    c. DIR A:

    d. File Manager

43. Why would you copy a backup file into a drawing file?

    a. To get a newer version of the file

    b. To retreive and use an older version of the file

    c. To have a backup of the file.

44. How would you erase a drawing file from your disk?

    a. Shell to DOS then ERASE A:*.DWG

    b. In My Computer, open the diectory, highlight the file, then Delete.

    c. Both of the above

    d. None of the above

45. Why is it important not to remove your floppy disk from the drive while you are writing to it in AutoCAD?

    a. You may lose the address of the temporary file

    b. You may insert the wrong diskette later

    c. The RAM will not be able to retrieve the file

46. Why do people keep a copy of their files on their hard drive as well as on their floppies?

    a. In case of a virus.

    B. In case of a disk crash

    c. In case the computer is stolen

    D. All of the above

47. Can you rename layer 0 if it has no data in it?

    a. Yes

    b. No

    c. Sometimes

48. When using the STRETCH command, what is the system automatically set to if you pick the command from the screen menu?

    a. Crossing

    b. Window

    c. Last

    d. None of the above

49. If you stretch a circle, does it turn into an ellipse?

    a. Yes

    b. No

    c. Only with ORTHO on

50. If you change the rotation of GRID and SNAP, does the ORTHO rotate as well?

    a. Yes

    b. No

51. How would you determine the layer of an object?

    a. MATCHPROP

    b. LIST

    c. CHPROP

52. Why must you press ↵ once you have selected all of the objects that you need?

    a. To signal the end of the object selection

    b. To exit OSNAP

    c. To reset the cursor

53. If you have selected a Window full of objects for editing, but one item was picked up that you do not want to edit, how would you release it from the list?

    a. Release

    b. Remove

    c. Undo

54. If you have an item in one layer, but you want it to be on another layer, how can you alter it?

    a. CHPROP

    b. MATCHPROP

    c. DDLMODEs

    d. Both a and b

55. Which of the following conditions would prevent you from deleting a layer?

    a. There are objects in the layer

    b. The layer is frozen

    c. The layer is locked

56. How do you change the color of an object once it has been entered?

    a. Change the color in the layer command

    b. Use CHPROP to change the color

    c. Turn the layer off, then reenter

    d. All of the above

    e. Just a. and b. of the above

57. When you copy an object with the COPY command what properties does the new object have?

    a. The properties set by the current layer

    b. The Color and Linetype set in the Color and Linetype settings

    c. The properties of the source object

    d. Any properties you assign in the COPY command

58. Of what use is OK within the layer format?

    a. To exit the Layers dialog box

    b. To thaw layers

    c. To change colors

59. What wildcard can you use to load all the linetypes?

    a. ^F1

    b. *

    c. ?

60. If you have a set linetype, will this override your current layer linetype?

    a. Yes

    b. No

    c. Sometimes

61. What is the default setting for radius in FILLET?

    a. 0

    b. .5

    c. 1.0

    D. Whatever your system preferences was set to.

62. What CIRCLE option do you use to get the arc in the illustration on the right?

   a. 2 Point

   b. 3 Point

   c. Center Radius

   d. Center Diameter

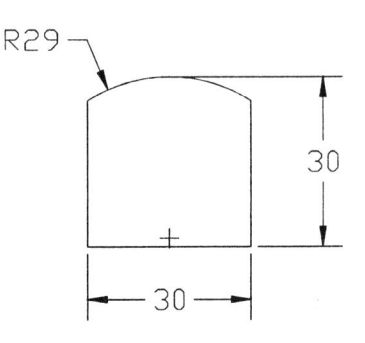

63. How do you change the size of the dashes in the hidden-line display?

   a. LINETYPE

   b. LTSCALE

   c. DIM VARs

64. What is the advantage of global Linetype scale?

   a. There is no advantage

   b. The Global Linetype Scale allows you to set the linetypes for different scales of drawings

   c. The Global Linetype gives a smaller file size

   d. Both c. and b.

65. If you create several styles under the same basic dimension style, what have you created?

   a. A file data replacement

   b. A dimension style family

   c. A dimension style triad

66. If you want to change any of these settings, what do you need to access?

   a. The Geometry dialog box

   b. The Dimension Style dialog box

   c. The Dimension Style icon menu

67. How do you use different text fonts in the dimension text area?

   a. Set to the new font before creating the dimensions

   b. Set a new font in the dimension style menu

   c. Use APPLY to set a style from the style menu

68. What command do you use to make an image appear at 70% of its current screen size for purposes of dimensioning?

    a. SCALE .7

    b. ZOOM .7X

    c. ZOOM 70

    d. ZOOM .7XP

69. Can you use more than one basic dimension style in a drawing?

    a. Yes

    b. No

    c. Sometimes

70. What command do you use if you have changed the unit readout and want to have your existing dimensions revised according to the current setting?

    a. APPLY

    b. OVERRIDE

    c. UPD

    d. All of the above

71. Why does text already entered become highlighted when the command TEXT or DTEXT is reentered?

    a. In case you want to replace it

    b. To indicate where to place the next paragraph

    c. To indicate where the text will default to line up

72. What is the purpose of QTEXT?

    a. QTEXT allows you to enter the text more quickly

    b. QTEXT allows for quicker REGENs

    c. QTEXT allows you to read the text as it is being entered

73. Can you pick the height with your cursor when entering text, or do you need to use a numeric entry?

    a. A numeric entry is needed

    b. Both cursor and numeric entries are allowed

    c. Only a numeric entry is allowed

74. When will the TEXT command not offer you a height option?

    a. When you have changed the aspect ratio in the Style

    b. When you have used your cursor to pick the first height

    c. When you are using QTEXT

75. What command do you use to change the type of letters that you would like to use?

    a. Text Style

    b. MTEXT

    c. DTEXT

    d. Object Creation

76. What does an obliquing angle do?

    a. Sets the angle of a string of text

    b. Sets the angle of a character

    c. Makes lines oblique

77. What command would you use to alter the spelling within your text string?

    a. CHPROP

    b. DDEDIT

    c. CHANGE

    d. Two of the above

78. Name two ways of repositioning text once entered.

    a. MOVE and CHANGE

    b. MOVE and COPY

    c. COPY and CHPROP

79. Which of these lettering styles takes up the most room on the disk?

    a. Gothic English

    b. Roman Simplex

    c. Monotext

    d. Standard

80. How do you change the position of a paragraph of text?

    a. Properties

    b. CHANGE

    c. MOVE

81. How do you create an associative hatch?

    a. BHATCH

    b. ASOHATCH

    c. AHATCH

82. Which standard are the hatch patterns derived from?

    a. ASCII

    b. ANSI

    c. CSA

83. Can you get a hatch pattern to ignore text?

    a. Yes

    b. No

84. How can you access the standard AutoCAD hatch patterns?

    a. Use HATCHSTYLE

    b. Use HATCH ?

    c. Use the Boundary Hatch dialog box

85. If you are using a User-defined hatch pattern, what will it be made up of?

    a. Lines

    b. Lines and points

    c. Lines and circles

86. What are the ISO standards?

    a. Isometric Ortho hatch patterns

    b. International Standards Organization

    c. Internal Set Organizer

87. Where does your drawing go to if you have been silly enough to crash your disk by not putting your HATCH in properly?

    a. The AutoCAD directory

    b. The root directory

    c. The directory that the drawing was in

88. Once hatches are in, how can you get them off the screen so your REDRAWs will not take so long?

    a. BLOCK them

    b. Turn the HATCH LAYER off

    c. Freeze the HATCH LAYER

89. If you stretch the boundary of the hatch, can you set the hatch to go with it?

    a. No

    b. Yes

90. Can you move a hatch?

    a. No

    b. Yes

91. What is an internal block?

    a. A block that is part of an existing file

    b. A block that exists on a floppy disk as a .DWG

    c. A block that is contained within another block

92. What symbol can you use to have the wblock placed on a file as separate entities?

    a. ^

    b. *

    c. #

93. How do you insert an external drawing file?

    a. WBLOCK

    b. BLOCK

    c. INSERT

94. How do you modify an entity on the block once it has been inserted?

    a. CHANGE the entity

    b. EDIT the entity

    c. EXPLODE the block

95. With what command do you erase blocks from your file that are not part of the file, but only part of the memory?

    a. DBLIST

    b. ERASE in DOS

    c. PURGE

    d. WBLOCK *

    e. c. and d.

96. Under what condition can you not SCALE a wblock instance?

    a. If the aspect ratio is changed

    b. If the entities have been changed

    c. If the object was inserted with MINSERT

    d. Both a. and c.

97. What happens to the LTSCALE of your external file block instance when it is inserted onto another drawing?

    a. It takes the LTSCALE of the original drawing

    b. It takes the LTSCALE of the current drawing

98. How can you get object lines on a plot thicker than dimension lines without using pline?

    a. Change the pens so that one is thicker

    b. Change the DIMLIN and UPD

    c. Change the LTSCALE

99. How do you change a drawing currently in architectural units into mechanical?

    a. Change the UNITS

    b. Change the DIMALT

    c. Change the drawing size

100. If you WBLOCK a model in paper space, must you be in paper space in the current model in order to insert it?

    a. Yes

    b. No

101. If you have the viewport frames or borders in the wrong layer in paper space, can you change them?

    a. Yes

    b. No

Final Drawings

Front Elevation

Final Drawings (cont.)

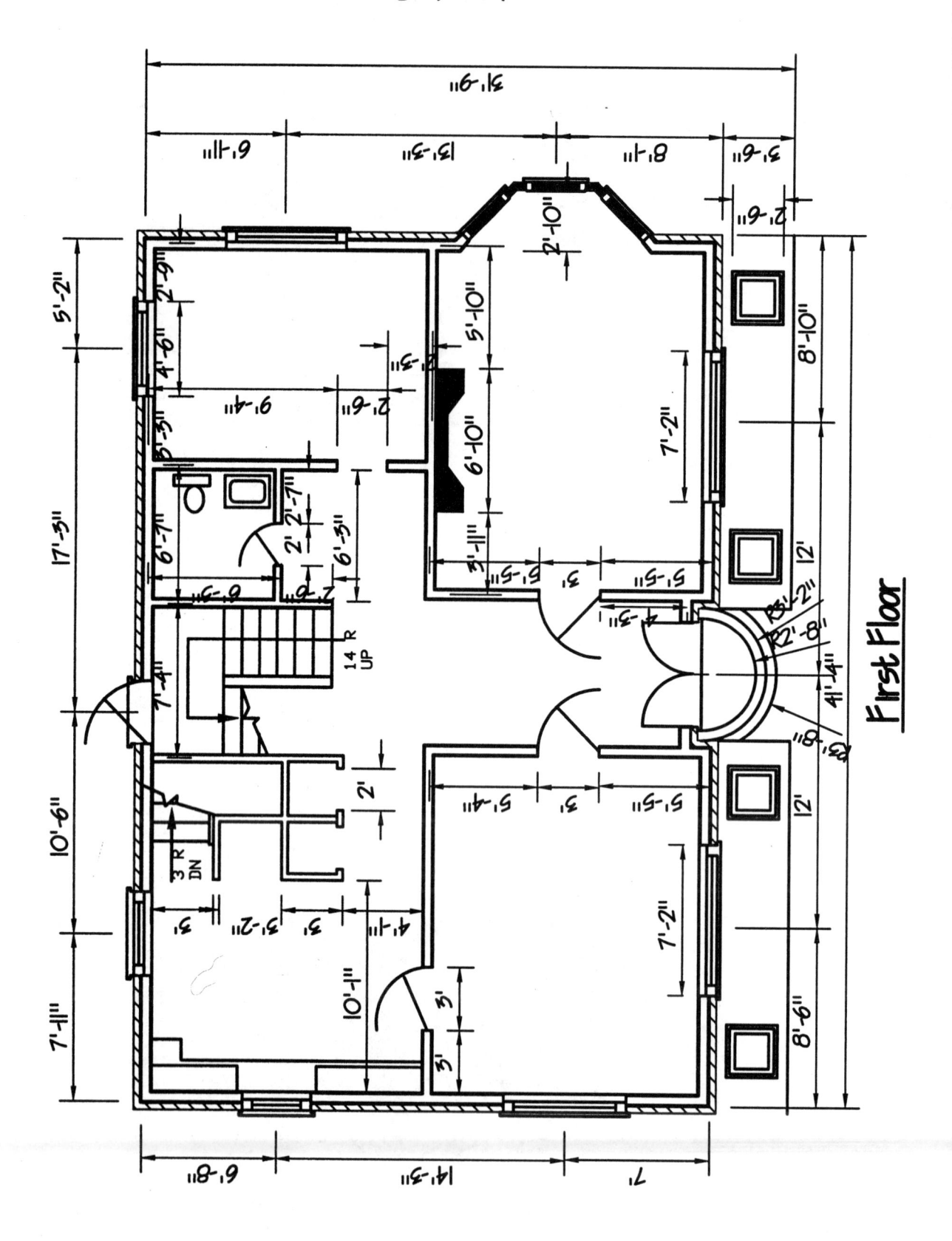

Second Floor

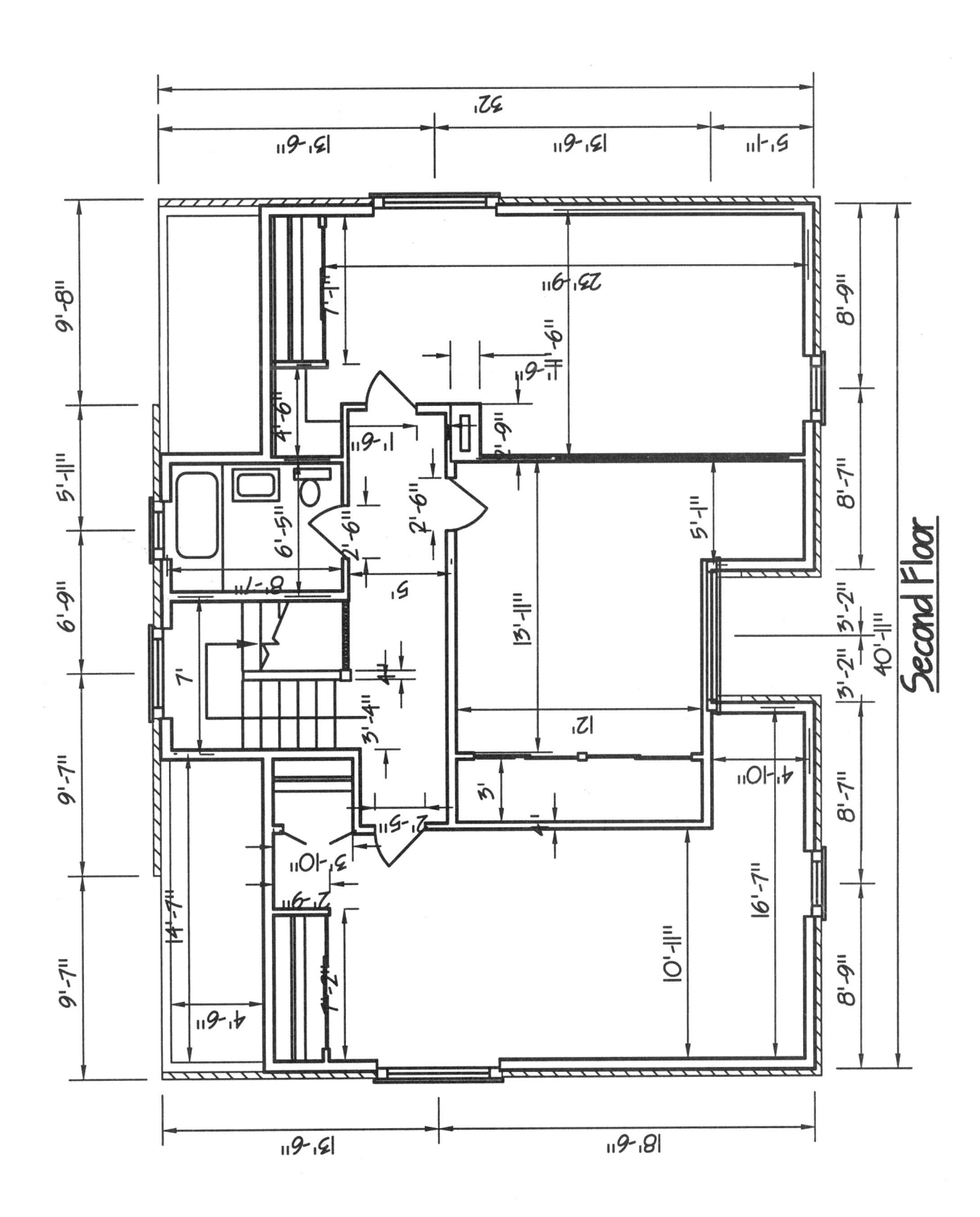

2D Review and Final Drawings

Final Drawings (cont.)

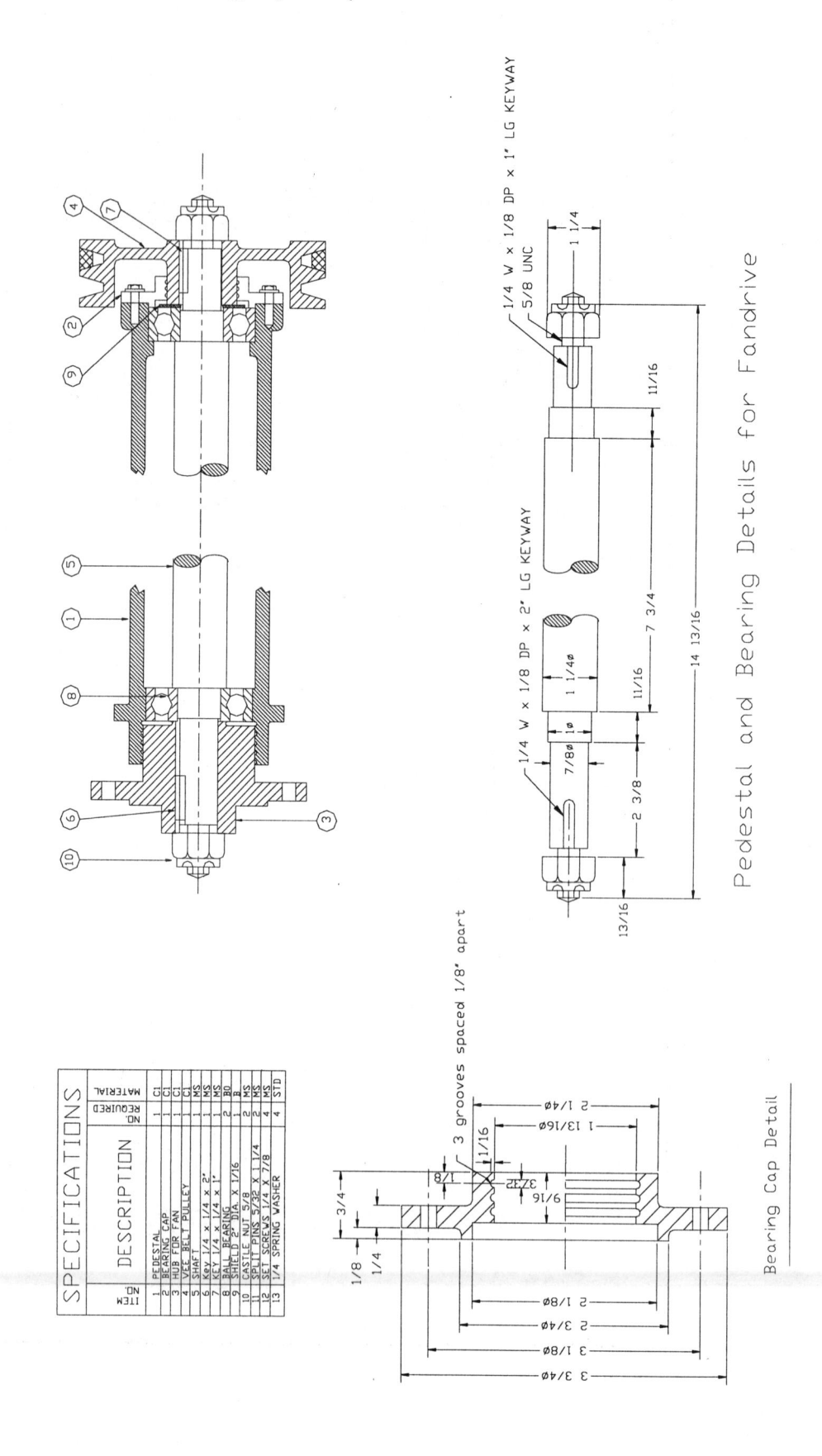

Pedestal and Bearing Details for Fandrive

Bearing Cap Detail

SPECIFICATIONS			
ITEM NO.	DESCRIPTION	NO. REQUIRED	MATERIAL
1	PEDESTAL	1	CI
2	BEARING CAP	1	CI
3	HUB FOR FAN	1	CI
4	VEE BELT PULLEY	1	CI
5	SHAFT 1/4 x 1/4 x 2"	1	MS
6	KEY 1/4 x 1/4 x 1"	1	MS
7	BALL BEARING	2	B0
8	SHIELD 2" DIA. x 1/16	1	B
9	CASTLE NUT 5/8	1	MS
10	SPLIT PINS 5/32 x 1 1/4	2	MS
11	SET SCREWS 1/4 x 7/8	4	MS
12	1/4 SPRING WASHER	4	STD

330 CHAPTER TWELVE

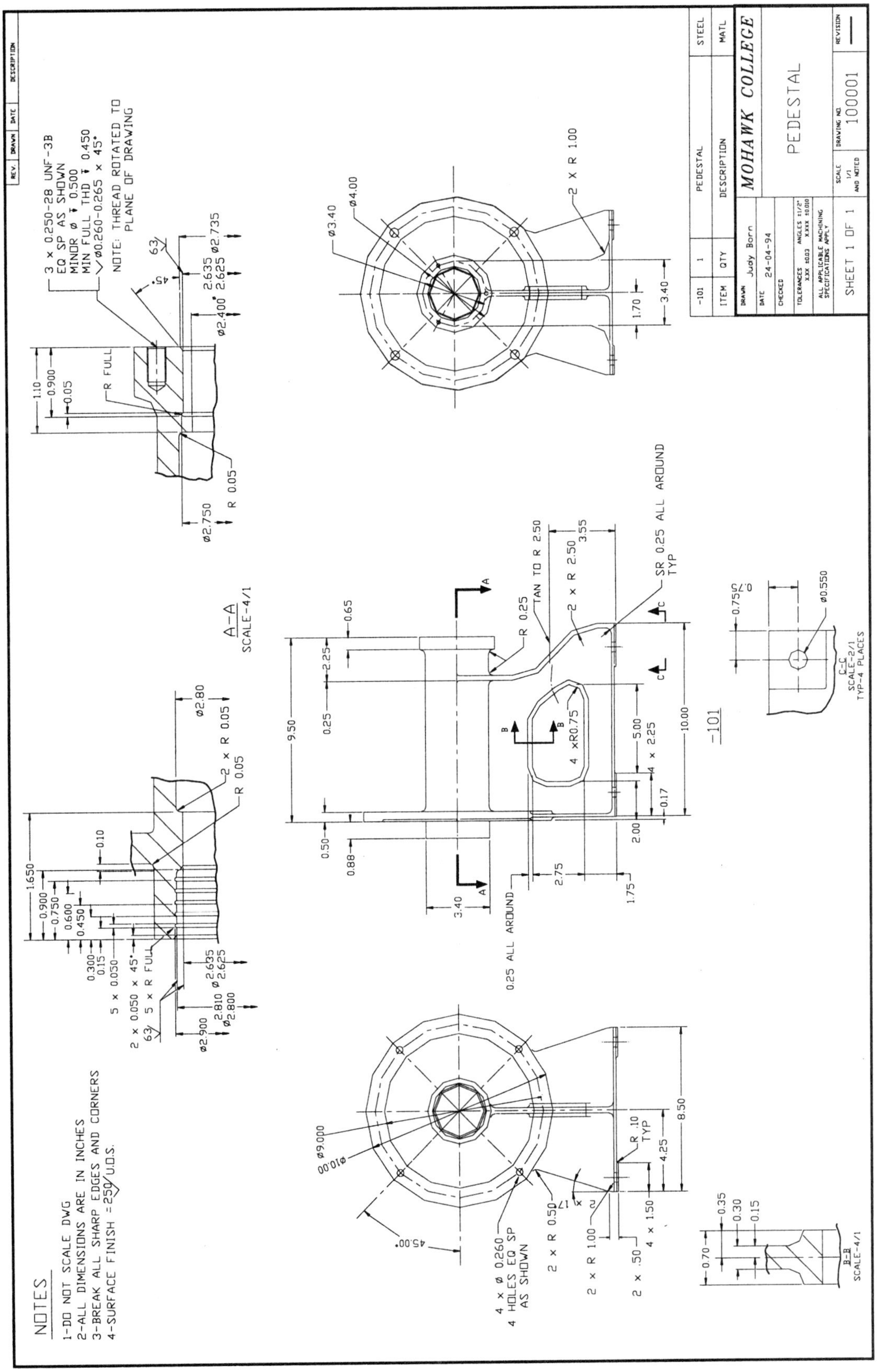
NOTES
1-DO NOT SCALE DWG
2-ALL DIMENSIONS ARE IN INCHES
3-BREAK ALL SHARP EDGES AND CORNERS
4-SURFACE FINISH = 250 U.O.S.
3 × 0.250-28 UNF-3B
EQ SP AS SHOWN
MINOR ⌀ ↧ 0.500
MIN FULL THD ↧ 0.450
⌀0.260-0.265 × 45°
NOTE: THREAD ROTATED TO PLANE OF DRAWING
A-A
SCALE-4/1
B-B
SCALE-4/1
C-C
SCALE-2/1
TYP-4 PLACES
-101
4 × ⌀ 0.260
4 HOLES EQ SP
AS SHOWN
2 × R 0.50
2 × R 1.00
2 × .50
4 × 1.50
R .10
TYP
2 X R 1.00
TAN TO R 2.50
2 × R 2.50
SR 0.25 ALL AROUND
TYP
0.25 ALL AROUND
R 0.25
4 ×R0.75
4 × 2.25
2 × R 0.05
R 0.05
R FULL
5 × 0.050
2 × 0.050 × 45°
5 × R FULL
⌀9.000
⌀10.00
⌀3.40
⌀4.00
⌀0.550
-101 | 1 | PEDESTAL | STEEL
ITEM | QTY | DESCRIPTION | MATL
DRAWN Judy Born
DATE 24-04-94
CHECKED
TOLERANCES XXX ±0.03 XXXX ±0.010 ANGLES ±1/2°
ALL APPLICABLE MACHINING SPECIFICATIONS APPLY
MOHAWK COLLEGE
PEDESTAL
SHEET 1 OF 1
SCALE 1/1 AND NOTED
DRAWING NO. 100001
REVISION
REV. DRAWN DATE DESCRIPTION

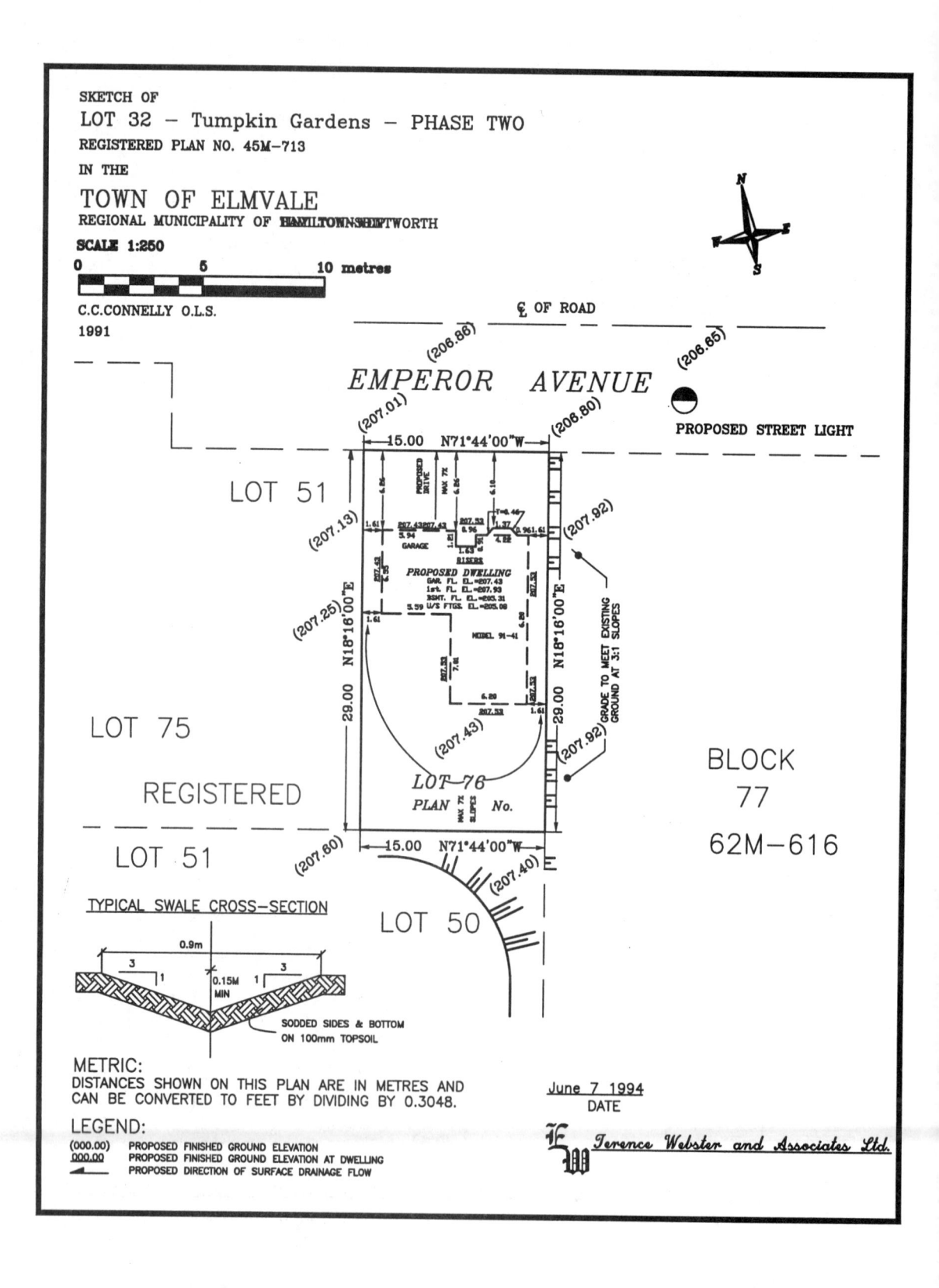

SKETCH OF
LOT 32 — Tumpkin Gardens — PHASE TWO
REGISTERED PLAN NO. 45M-713
IN THE
TOWN OF ELMVALE
REGIONAL MUNICIPALITY OF HAMILTON-WENTWORTH

SCALE 1:250

0   5   10 metres

C.C.CONNELLY O.L.S.
1991

¢ OF ROAD

EMPEROR AVENUE

● PROPOSED STREET LIGHT

LOT 51

(206.86) (206.65) (207.01) (206.80)

15.00 N71°44'00"W

PROPOSED DRIVE
MAX 7%

207.43 207.43
5.94
GARAGE
3 RISERS

PROPOSED DWELLING
GAR. FL. EL.=207.43
1st FL. EL.=207.93
BSMT. FL. EL.=205.31
U/S FTGS. EL.=205.08

MODEL 91-41

29.00 N18°16'00"E   29.00 N18°16'00"E

GRADE TO MEET EXISTING GROUND AT 3:1 SLOPES

(207.13) (207.25) (207.92) (207.92)

LOT 75

REGISTERED

LOT 51

LOT 76
PLAN No.
MAX 7% SLOPES

15.00 N71°44'00"W

(207.60) (207.40)

LOT 50

BLOCK 77
62M-616

TYPICAL SWALE CROSS-SECTION

0.9m
3 : 1   1 : 3
0.15M MIN
SODDED SIDES & BOTTOM
ON 100mm TOPSOIL

METRIC:
DISTANCES SHOWN ON THIS PLAN ARE IN METRES AND CAN BE CONVERTED TO FEET BY DIVIDING BY 0.3048.

LEGEND:
(000.00) PROPOSED FINISHED GROUND ELEVATION
000.00   PROPOSED FINISHED GROUND ELEVATION AT DWELLING
→   PROPOSED DIRECTION OF SURFACE DRAINAGE FLOW

June 7 1994
DATE

Terence Webster and Associates Ltd.

13 POINTS, DIVIDE, MEASURE, INQUIRY, and System Variables

Upon completion of this chapter, you should be able to:

1. Change the PDMODE and PDSIZE
2. Use DIVIDE and MEASURE to place points and/or multiple objects where desired within a model
3. Check the parameters and properties of objects within the model
4. Check the overall size of the model
5. Calculate the area of a model with AREA or Boundary
6. Use the time management facility
7. Use the system variables
8. Use the SPLINE command
9. Use MLSTYLE and MLEDIT commands

Point Display or PDMODE Options

Points are used in spline generation, in many 3D applications, and as node or reference points which you can snap to or offset from. When you divide or measure an object, points are used to show the divisions. You can set the style of the point and its size either relative to the screen or in absolute units.

> **Toolbar** There is no button for this function
> **Pull Down** From the Format menu, pick point style.

The command line equivalent for the dialog box is **DDPTYPE**.

To set the point size or style without using the dialog box, use PDMODE for the style and PDSIZE for the size.

Point Size

In PDSIZE, a positive number will represent the actual size in drawing units of the point. A negative number is taken as a relative percentage of the screen and a difference in the zoom factor will have no effect on the size of the point display.

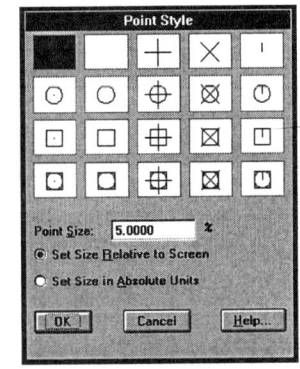

Figure 13-1

First choose whether you want the point to be relative to the screen or in absolute values. AutoCAD then stores the point size in the PDSIZE system variable. All points will be added relative to the new size, and all existing points will be updated according to this size upon the next regeneration.

Points, either created by MEASURE and DIVIDE or entered using the POINT command, can be accessed with the OSNAP option NODE. This is particularly important when entering blocks at specific points, or, in 3D, when finding centers for fillets, etc.

POINTS, DIVIDE, MEASURE, INQUIRY, and System Variables **333**

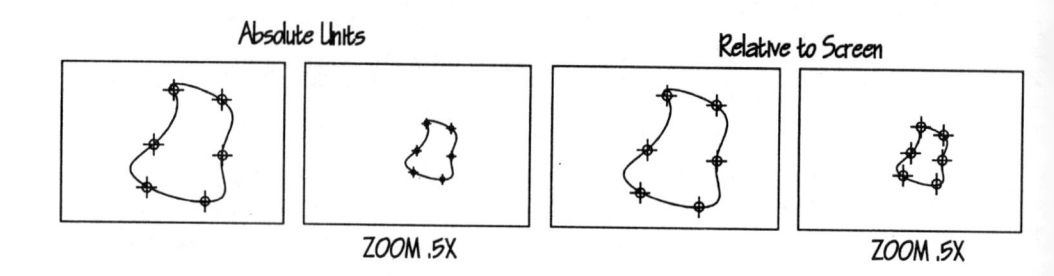

Figure 13-2

The points will then be added in at the points that are determined by either the DIVIDE or the MEASURE command.

Using DIVIDE and MEASURE

If you have an object or space that needs to be cut into equal pieces or portions, you can use DIVIDE or MEASURE.

DIVIDE will visually divide any linear element — an arc, a circle, a line, or a pline — into a specified number of equal parts.

MEASURE will visually measure a linear element into segments of a specified length.

The DIVIDE Command

DIVIDE places equally spaced point objects or blocks along the length or perimeter of an object.

> **Toolbar** There is no button available.
>
> **Pull Down** From the Draw menu, choose Point, then Divide.

The command line equivalent is **DIVIDE**.

DIVIDE with Points

Using the Point Style dialog box, set the current point to the one illustrated.

```
Command:DIVIDE
Select object to divide: (pick the object)
Enter the number of segments or [Block]:6
```

The selected object is not altered in any way, but there are points in the current style at regular intervals. The points become objects on the current model. They can be accessed with the OSNAP NODE.

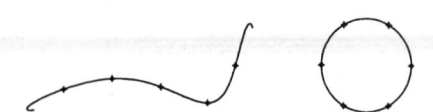

Figure 13-3

334 CHAPTER THIRTEEN

DIVIDE Using a BLOCK

DIVIDE can also be used with blocks. In the following example, a mullion block is used to divide a window into equally spaced sections. Both a curved window and a block called MULLION will be needed.

In Figure 13-4 we have a curved window and a block called MULLION, which is the shape of a mullion. The insertion point on the block is the middle of the bottom line.

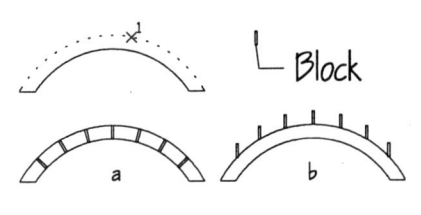

Figure 13-4

The command will place this block at regular intervals along the window. The base point of the block is very important. In *a* the mullion is placed on the lower arc and rotated, in *b* the mullion is placed on the upper arc without rotation.

```
Command:DIVIDE
Select object to divide: (pick 1)
Enter the number of segments or [Block]:B
Enter name of block to insert:MULLION
Align block with object?[Yes/No]: (Y for (a), N for (b))
Enter the number of segments:8
```

The MEASURE Command

The MEASURE command is very similar to the DIVIDE command in that it divides a specified object into a series of equal portions. The difference is that the equal portions are given a specific length, and thus there may be a portion of the object "left over" when the command is finished. Again, the MEASURE command works on lines, arcs, circles, and pline;, and again, the markers can be either points or blocks.

> **Toolbar** There is no button available.
> **Pull Down** From the Draw menu, choose Point, then Measure.

The command line equivalent is **MEASURE**.

MEASURE with Points

In the following example, use point display 4 or the vertical line in the dialog box, and change the length to be 18 m with PDSIZE 18. Then use MEASURE to divide a road illustrated by a pline, (a), into equally spaced lots, (b). The pline representing the road will be needed.

Type in the system variables **PDMODE** and **PDSIZE**.

```
Command:PDMODE
Select new point mode <1>:4
Command:PDSIZE
Enter new point size< 1.000>:18
Command:MEASURE
Select object to measure: (pick (a))
   Specify length of segment or [Block]: 15
```

We now have a road that is divided into equal portions of 15 m lengths with a depth of 18 m each. Notice that the road is created with pline and thus has line and arc segments.

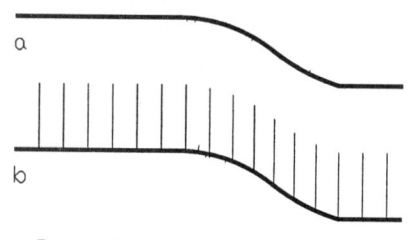

Figure 13-5

MEASURE Using BLOCKs

In the next example, we will place a block of a toilet along an existing wall. Both a LINE representing a 19′ wall and a BLOCK that represents a toilet will be needed.

Create a toilet that has an interior space of 3 × 5 feet.

Now BLOCK the toilet, making sure that the insertion base point leaves enough space for a 2 inch wall on the back and on the sides.

```
Command:BLOCK
Block name:TOILET
Insertion base point: corner
Select objects:WINDOW
```

Now use MEASURE to place the toilet along a 19 foot wall.

```
Command:MEASURE
Select object to measure: (pick 1)
  (take the left side of the 19' wall)
Specify length of segment or [Block]:B
Enter name of block to insert:TOILET
Align block with object? [Yes/No]:⏎
Specify length of segment:3'4"
```

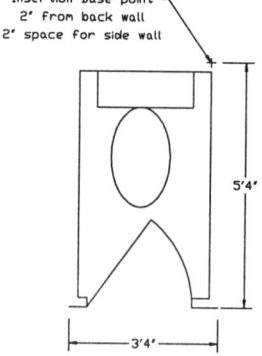

Figure 13-6

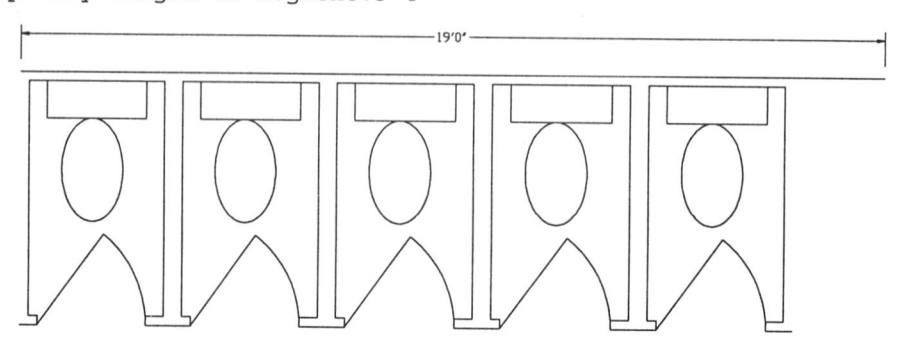

Figure 13-7

When creating the block to be used in a MEASURE command, be sure that you have no overlapping items.

If you use points in either the DIVIDE or the MEASURE command, you will have to change the PDMODE to be able to see the displayed points. Once placed, these points become objects in the file and will be affected by editing commands such as ERASE, MOVE, COPY, etc. If you do not change the PDMODE, these points may be difficult to see.

The SPLINE Command

In Chapter 3 we looked at polylines and how to edit them into splines. There is also now a command to create splines or smooth curved lines without accessing the PLINE command.

AutoCAD used the Nonuniform Rational B-Spline (NURBS) formula to describe the splines entered. A NURBS curve produces a smooth curve between control points; this spline can be either quadratic or cubic.

If you are creating a large drawing with multiple splines for mapping or airfoil design, a drawing containing splines uses less disk space and memory than a drawing with polylines. To access the SPLINE command:

> **Toolbar** From the Draw toolbar, choose Spline.
>
> **Pull Down** From the Draw menu, pick Spline.

The command line equivalent is **SPLINE**.

```
Command: SPLINE
Specify first point or [Object]: (pick 1)
Specify next point: (pick 2)
Specify next point or
[Close/Fit tolerance] <start point>:
    (pick 3 through 9)
Specify start tangent: (pick 10)
Specify end tangent: (pick 11)
```

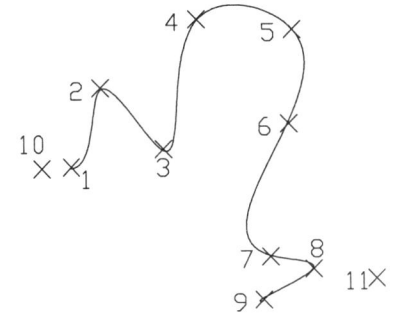

Figure 13-8

Entering Points

Enter points in to add additional spline curve segments until you press ⏎. Like the Line and PLINE commands, a **U** for Undo will remove the last entered point.

As the points are entered you can see the spline being created.

Start and End Tangency

The "Enter start tangent:" prompt specifies the tangency of the spline at the first point; the "Enter end tangent:" prompt does the same for the end point. You can specify tangency at both ends of the spline, and you can use either point, TANgent, or PERpendicular object snaps to make the spline tangent or perpendicular to existing objects.

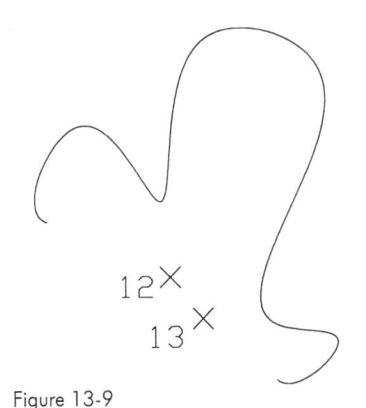

Figure 13-9

POINTS, DIVIDE, MEASURE, INQUIRY, and System Variables

```
                Specify start tangent: (pick 12)
                Specify end tangent: (pick 13)
```

Points 112, 13 and 14 are points of continuity for the spline curve.

Close

Like the POLYLINE command, the Close option defines the last point as coincident with the first and makes it tangent there.

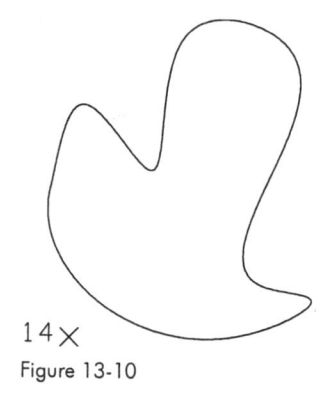

Figure 13-10

Fit Tolerance

This changes the tolerance for fitting the spline through the points. The number is higher or lower depending on how you want the spline to fit through the points.

Object

This option converts either 2D or 3D polylines into splines.

The SPLINEDIT Command

The SPLINEDIT command edits the spline object.

> **Toolbar** From the Modify menu, choose Splinedit. 
>
> **Pull Down** From the Modify menu, choose Object, then Spline.

The command line equivalent is **SPLINEDIT**.

The options for this edit command are similar to those of PEDIT.

Inquiry Commands

The Inquiry commands are used to see and list the parameters of a model.

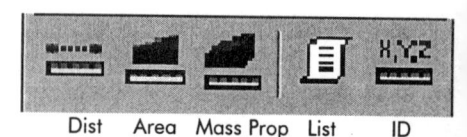

Dist   Area   Mass Prop   List   ID

AREA   computes the area of a closed polygon

DIST   computes the distance between two points

LIST   lists the position and properties of a specific object or group of objects

ID   identifies a point

STATUS displays a listing of all the statistics of a file along with other information

The AREA Command

AutoCAD offers built-in area computational abilities which also display the perimeter of the object calculated. This can be extremely useful for calculations of plines and irregular shapes.

AREA Using an Entity

On the right we have a pline that has been fit with a spline curve, and the area and perimeter are to be calculated. In this case an entity is chosen for the area option.

```
Command:AREA
Specify first corner point or [Object/Add/Subtract]:O
Select objects: (pick 1)
Area = 16.1434 Perimeter = 19.6824
```

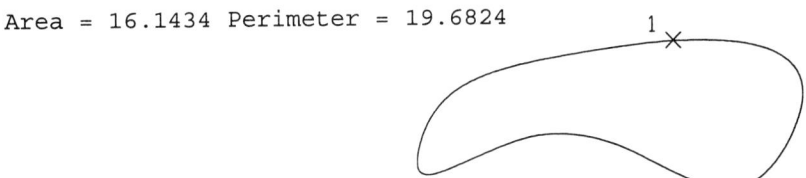

Figure 13-11

AREA Using Lines

When calculating a series of straight lines, the Point option is used, as in the following command sequence. OSNAPs are needed for accuracy.

```
Command:AREA
Specify first corner point or [Object/Add/Subtract]:
 END of (pick 1)
Specify next point or press ENTER for total:END of (pick 2)
Specify next point or press ENTER for total:END of (pick 3)
Specify next point or press ENTER for total:END of (pick 4)
Specify next point or press ENTER for total:END of (pick 5)
Specify next point or press ENTER for total:↵
Area = 67.5000 Perimeter = 31.1131
```

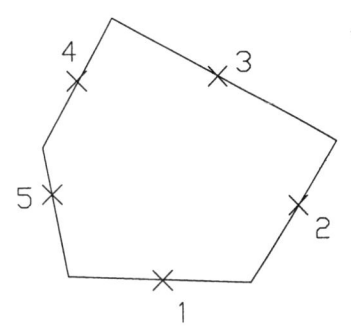

Figure 13-12

Subtract and Add with AREA

To calculate the net floor area of a bathroom, a drawing of a bathroom will be needed. Draw in a bathroom 8'6'' × 5'6'' as shown.

Set the osnap to ENDpoint and calculate the total floor area.

```
Command:OSNAP
Object snap modes:ENDpoint
```

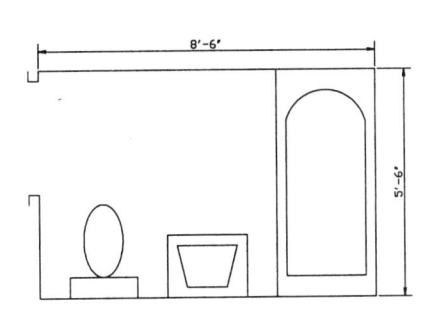

Figure 13-13

POINTS, DIVIDE, MEASURE, INQUIRY, and System Variables **339**

```
Command:AREA
Specify first corner point or
[Object/Add/Subtract]:A
First point: (pick 1)
Next point: (pick 2)
Next point: (pick 3)
Next point: (pick 4)
Next point:⏎
Area = 6732.00 square inches
(46.7500 square feet)
Perimeter = 28' 0"
Total area 6732.00 square inches
(46.75 square feet)
```

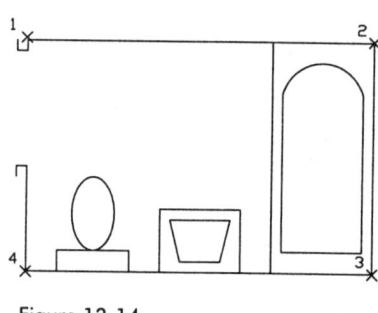

Figure 13-14

Without leaving the command, subtract the fixtures.

```
Specify first corner point or [Object/Add/Subtract]:S
(SUBTRACT mode)<First point/Object/Add: (pick 5)
(SUBTRACT mode) Next point: (pick 6)
(SUBTRACT mode) Next point: (pick 7)
(SUBTRACT mode) Next point: (pick 8)
(SUBTRACT mode) Next point:⏎
Area = 1980 square inches
(13.7500 square feet)
Perimeter = 16' 0"
Total area 4752 square inches
(33.0000 square feet)
```

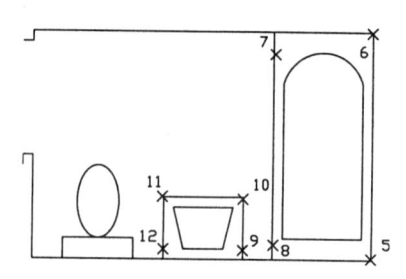

Figure 13-15

> **Notes**
> The wording in these commands is voluminous, just look for SUBTRACT mode or Add.

```
(SUBTRACT mode)<First point>/Object/Add: (pick 9)
(SUBTRACT mode) Next point: (pick 10)
(SUBTRACT mode) Next point: (pick 11)
(SUBTRACT mode) Next point: (pick 12)
(SUBTRACT mode) Next point:⏎
Area = 432 square inches (3.00 square feet) Perimeter = 7' 0"
Total area 4320 square inches (30.0000 square feet)

(SUBTRACT mode)<First point>/Entity/Add: (pick 13)
(SUBTRACT mode) Next point: (pick 14)
(SUBTRACT mode) Next point: (pick 15)
(SUBTRACT mode) Next point: (pick 16)
(SUBTRACT mode) Next point:⏎
Area = 126 square inches (0.8750
   square feet) Perimeter = 4' 6"
Total area 3852 square inches (26.75
   square feet)
```

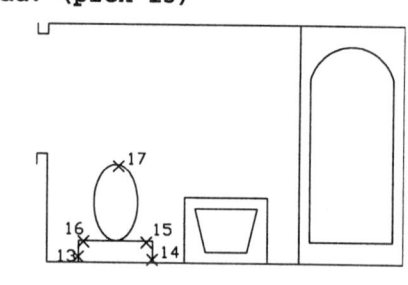

Figure 13-16

```
(SUBTRACT mode)<First point>/Object/Add:O
Select objects: (pick 17)
Area = 260 square inches (1.81 square feet) Length = 4' 2"
Total area 3592 square inches (24.94 square feet)
```

340 CHAPTER THIRTEEN

As you can see from the example above, points and Objects can be used together. With the SUBTRACT mode, subsequent area calculations are subtracted from the accumulated area. Use Add to enter the first area, then Subtract for the subsequent areas.

With the Add option, subsequent areas will be added to the accumulated area.

In 3D calculations, all of the points used for calculation must be on the same plane. The UCS can be changed to allow for this. The extrusion direction of entities must also be parallel with the current UCS.

AREA and PERIMETER are also system variables and can be viewed but not changed by displaying them. Use the SETVAR command to access the system variable. If you calculated an area, but neglected to jot it down, type **AREA** as the variable name and the last calculated area will be displayed. To find the length or circumference of a circle, arc, or pline, use the LIST command. Be sure to change the units to the desired values before entering the AREA command; otherwise the readings may be inaccurate.

The BOUNDARY Command

The BOUNDARY command creates a region or a polyline of a closed boundary. Specifying a boundary set can produce the boundary more quickly, because AutoCAD examines fewer objects when a boundary set is identified. For an example of how BOUNDARY works, see Prelab 13.

> **Toolbar** There is no button available.
>
> **Pull Down** From the Draw menu, choose Boundary...

The command line equivalent is **BOUNDARY**.

The DISTance Command

The DISTance command will give you the actual distance between two points. Remember that, when dealing with points in AutoCAD or any other CAD package, you can specify the points in three ways:

1. If they are associated with objects, by finding them with OSNAPs such as ENDpoint, MIDpoint, etc.
2. By picking on them on the screen, with or without the use of SNAP
3. By specifying their coordinates

When calculating DISTance, you can identify the points by any combination of the above. First enter the DIST command, then respond with the two points that identify the distance you want to know. It is better that you specify the exact points with either an OSNAP or a coordinate entry. As with the other commands, you will be offered the information relative to the current units specified.

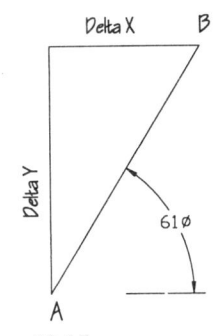

Figure 13-17

You will note that the readout contains not only the distance, but also the angle from the X-Y plane, and the length and width of the object.

POINTS, DIVIDE, MEASURE, INQUIRY, and System Variables

```
Command:DIST
Specify first point: (pick point A)
Specify second point: (pick point B)
Distance= 10.2956, Angle in X-Y Plane = 61, Angle from X-Y
   Plane = 0 Delta X = 5.0000 Delta Y = 9.0000 Delta Z = 0.0000
```

The LIST Command

We looked at LIST briefly in the first section of this book to establish the layer, color, and linetype properties of objects that had already been entered. In addition to this, LIST is an extremely useful command for the following purposes:

1. Cleaning up objects before hatching and editing
2. Finding out the angle of an existing LINE
3. Finding out the radius of a specified circle
4. Determining text fonts and sizes
5. Finding out if existing items were put in incorrectly or without the use of SNAP
6. Checking for incorrect dimensions

> **Notes**
> The properties command has similar information in a dialog format.

In 3D, LIST can be used to find out the current Z depth and extrusion length of an object as well as the properties listed above. LIST can also be used to show the number of objects within a specified window to check to see that the objects follow good CAD practice. In the following example, we will see how LIST can also be used to tell us if the dimension for an object is real or "fudged."

In Figure 13-18, there are two associative dimensions listed. To the eye, they look the same. They are identified by being highlighted in the DOT linetype.

Figure 13-18

Note the difference in the readouts after the LIST command has been used.

```
Command:LIST
Select objects: (pick the dimension)

                 DIMENSION Layer: dim
                 SPACE: Model Space
                 Handle = 1D14
type: horizontal
1st extension defining point:  X= 2.0000 Y= 4.5000 Z= 0.0000
2nd extension defining point:  X= 4.0000 Y= 3.5000 Z= 0.0000
dimension line defining point: X= 4.0000 Y= 2.5000 Z= 0.0000
default text position X= 3.875 Y= 2.5000 Z= 0.0000
default text
dimension style *UNNAMED

                 DIMENSION Layer: dim
                 SPACE: Model Space
                 Handle = 1D14
```

```
type: vertical
1st extension defining point:  X= 6.0000  Y= 8.5000  Z= 0.0000
2nd extension defining point:  X= 6.0000  Y= 3.0000  Z= 0.0000
dimension line defining point: X= 6.5000  Y= 2.5000  Z= 0.0000
default text position X= 6.500 Y= 5.7500  Z= 0.0000
dimension text modifier: 5.0000
dimension style *UNNAMED
```

You can see that the first dimension has been entered properly, and the text for the dimension is the default text. In the second dimension, however, the dimension text has been modified to read 5.0000. If you subtract the second extension defining point from the first in the Y value, you will notice that the actual distance should read 5.5000, but the dimension text has been altered before it was entered.

In addition to checking your own work to be sure that it is all entered correctly and that there are no overlapping items, with the LIST command you can check to see that the dimensions associated with the drawing you have on file are correct and not altered in any way. If the dimensions have been altered, check to see that *all* of the necessary dimensions have been altered.

Another great advantage of LIST is that it enables you to determine if there are overlapping lines when making hatches and dimensions. Use LIST, then Crossing, to see the number of objects overlapping.

The ID Command

The ID function is similar to the LIST function, in that it gives an exact position. The difference is that it gives an exact position of a point rather than an object. This command is used in 3D modelling more frequently than in 2D modelling, to determine the Z depth of items. In 2D this can be useful for finding out the exact position you are looking at on a ZOOMed screen, or for simply "getting your bearings." Keep in mind that, if you are picking a point in space, a snap can give a more usable readout.

The location of the point will be relative to the origin or 0,0,0 of the model. If a point in space is chosen, the Z depth will be the current elevation; if an object is chosen with an OSNAP, the actual Z depth of the object will be used.

ID can be used as a reference point for the next point entered using @:

```
Command: LINE
From point:@2,0 (starts the line 2 units in X from the ID
  point)
```

There are basically two ways of using ID. The first is to find the parameters of a point on the screen.

```
Command: ID
Specify point: (pick a point)
X = 34.6375    Y = 24.8758    Z = 0.0000
```

This will give the coordinates of a point in space in the defined units. The second is to locate a point by typing in the coordinates.

```
Command: ID
Specify point: 23,4,0
```

If BLIPMODE is on, you will get a blip on the screen at the exact location of the point entered. The blip will disappear with the next REDRAW.

The STATUS Command

Another useful command for determining what is happening is STATUS. As you become proficient with AutoCAD, you will find the STATUS command more and more useful, because it displays a listing of all the statistics of a file.

The STATUS command will also offer information on memory and the partition on the hard drive where your temporary file or .AC$ file is being stored. If you run out of space in this partition (in a classroom this is often the A: drive), the program will terminate after first saving your file.

STATUS is most often used by beginners to determine if the color setting is overriding the layer color setting.

Enter **STATUS** at the command prompt and read the status of your file.

Creating Multiline Styles

As seen in Chapter 3, multilines are multiple parallel lines. Multilines consist of between 1 and 16 parallel lines called elements. You can create and save multiline styles, or use the default style shown in Chapter 3. The color and linetype of each element of the multiline can be set, and the ends of multilines can be set with caps.

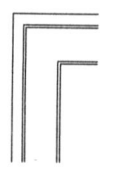

The MLSTYLE Command

Like dimension styles and text styles, multiline styles can be named and saved to control the elements and properties of each element.

> **Toolbar** There is no button available.
>
> **Pull Down** From the Format menu, pick Multiline style.

The command line equivalent is **MLSTYLE**.

The LINETYPE command loads the linetypes from the ACAD.LIN file. MSTYLE also loads the multilines from an external file called ACAD.MLN.

The dialog box displays the multiline style names, makes them current, loads them from a file, and saves, adds, and renames them.

Current	sets the current multiline style.
Add	adds the new style in the Name text box to the current list.
Name	creates a new multiline style. First define the elements, then enter a new name on this line and pick Save.
Description	adds a description of up to 255 characters to the name.
Load	loads a style from the library.

Here is an example of how to load a multiline style. We will use a typical northern exterior wall as an example.

Example

Step 1   Open the MLSTYLE dialog box.

Step 2   Pick the Element Properties button, and Add, using the Offset option to load the 5 line elements.

When using the offset option, the offset starts from 0.0 and continues both up and down from there. Offset the first line at 2.5 from 0 by highlighting it, then changing the number in the offset box, and highlighting again. Then add the offset of .5 by typing .5 in the offset box, then picking the Add button. To add a line, use Add. To change an offset, highlight, change and re-highlight.

Step 3   Once the lines are entered, use the color button to change the colors of the lines to correspond to the line widths of your plotter. These changes are the same as the color changes in layers. Assume that a red line is the thinnest, a yellow line is medium, and a green line is the thickest object line width. Pick OK when finished.

Step 4   In the MLSTYLE dialog box, pick the box beside the word, Name. Type in Extwall for your multiline style. Use Add to add the name to the current list.

Step 5   Use the new MLINE style to create an exterior wall.

Your MLINE will default to being justified at the outside of the veneer. Many residential designers prefer to have their home designs justified at the outside of the studwall. This will allow for greater accuracy when dimensioning the part for the framers. To do this, add a line in the dot linetype at a distance of positive 6.5. Then use Zero as the Justify option of the MLINE command. The dot line will not print, and the line will be justified at the center of the MLINE, or the edge of the wooden frame. To add straight line caps onto the wall, re-enter the MLSTYLE dialog box, and use the multiline properties button to add caps to the outer edges of the multiline. Use Save to save the MLINE style.

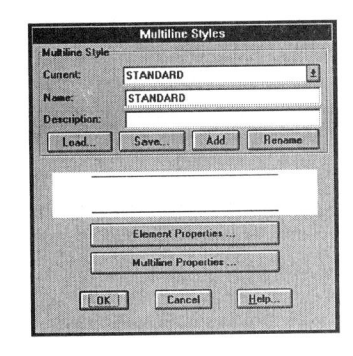

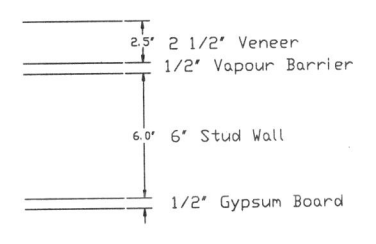

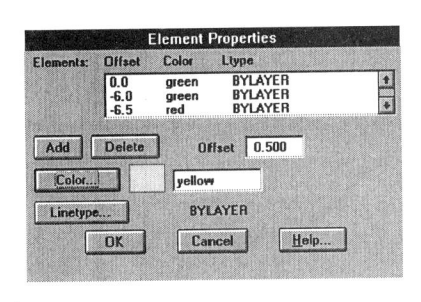

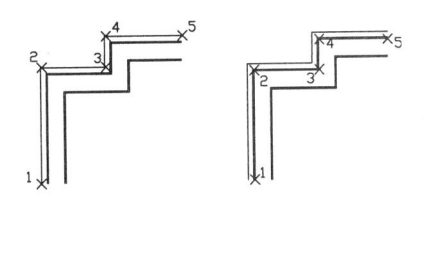

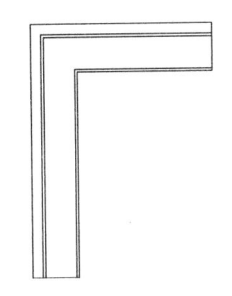

POINTS, DIVIDE, MEASURE, INQUIRY, and System Variables

Editing Multilines

Once a multiline is entered, it is considered to be single unit. Like polylines, multilines c be edited by adding and deleting vertices. In addition, you can control the display of cor joints and the intersection of the multilines. You can also edit multiline styles to change properties of individual line segments, or the end caps and background fill of fut multilines.

The MLEDIT Command

The Multiline Edit Tools dialog box controls intersections between multilines.

Toolbar From the Modufy menu, choose this button.

Pull Down From the Modify menu, choose Object, then Multiline.

The command line equivalent is **MLEDIT**.

Once the multilines are created, the dialog box is used to change the intersection or to add or delete a vertex or break.

The first column works on multilines that cross. The second on multilines that form a tee, the third on corner joints and vertices, and the fourth on multilines to be cut or welded.

The first two columns work on pairs of multilines, the second two work on single multilines.

In the first two columns, you can edit more than one intersection. You will be prompted as follows:

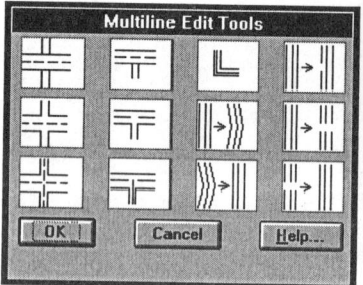

```
Select first mline: (pick one mline)
Select second mline: (pick an intersecting mline)
Select first mline: (pick another mline or U to erase the
   first)
```

Once you have selected the first MLINE, you will be prompted for the second MLINE. you enter U, AutoCAD undoes the closed cross intersection and displays the "Select firs MLINE" prompt.

Closed Cross creates a closed cross intersection between two multilines
Merged Cross Rejoins multiline segments that have been cut.

Open Cross creates an open cross intersection between two multilines, breaking all elements of the first multiline and only the outside element of the second multiline

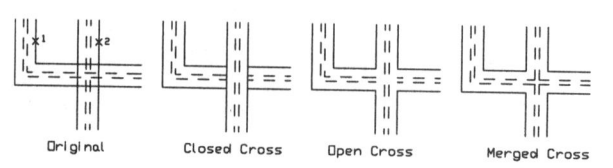

Original   Closed Cross   Open Cross   Merged Cross

346 CHAPTER THIRTEEN

Closed Tee	creates a closed intersection between two multilines, trimming or extending the first multiline to its intersection with the second multiline	
Open Tee	creates an open tee intersection between two multilines, trimming or extending the first multiline to its intersection with the second multiline	
Merged Tee	creates a merged tee intersection between two multilines, trimming or extending the first multiline to its intersection with the second multiline	

Corner Joint	creates a corner joint between multilines, trimming or extending the first multiline to its intersection with the second multiline	
Add Vertex	adds a vertex to a multiline	
Delete Vertex	deletes a vertex of a multiline	

Cut Single	cuts a single element of a multiline	
Cut All	cuts a multiline in two	
Weld All	rejoins multiline segments that have been cut	

POINTS, DIVIDE, MEASURE, INQUIRY, and System Variables

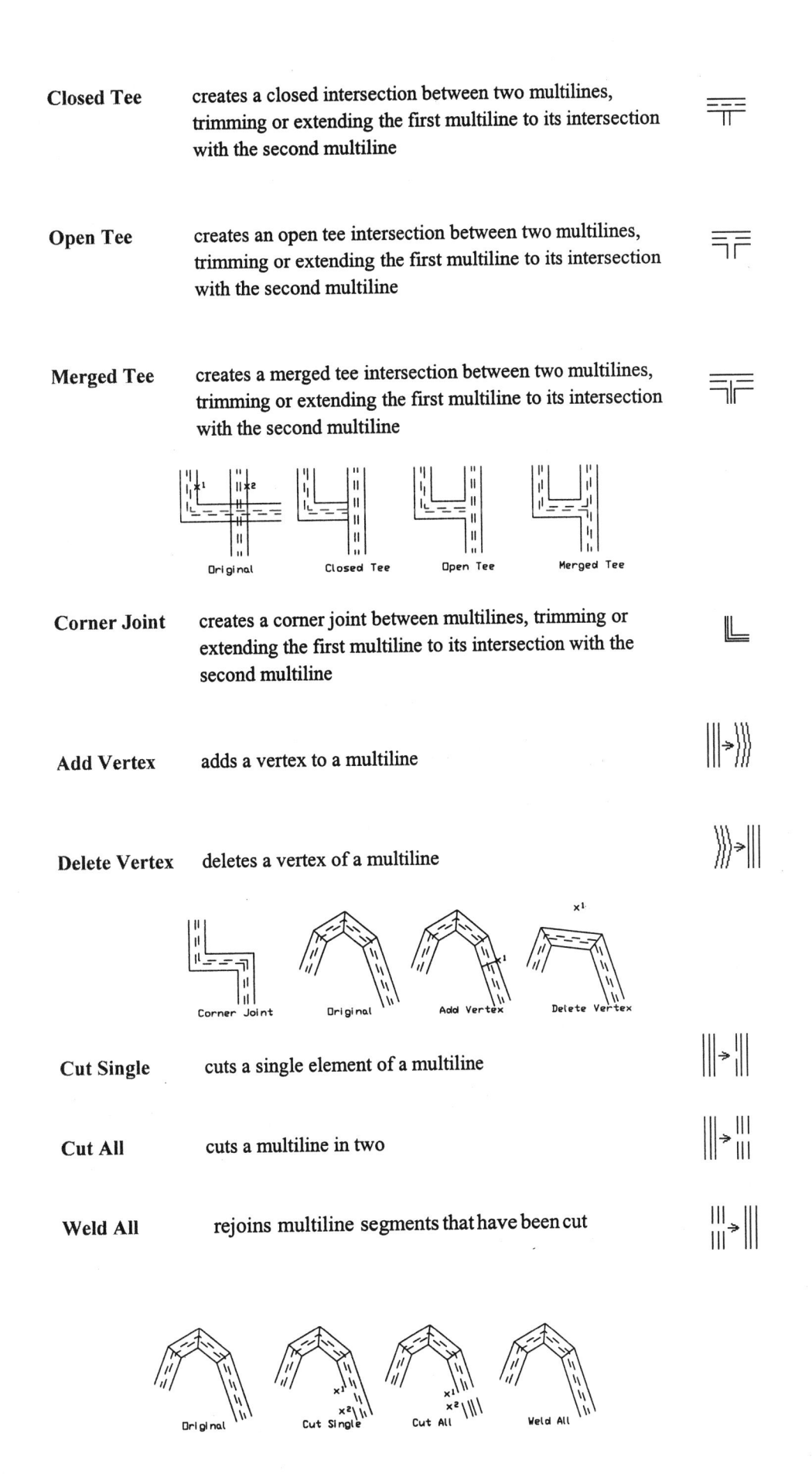

Prelab 13 Point Style, SPLINE, and Inquiry

This top view of a corner gusset is drawn using both a complex spline and a series of lines. In order to get the spline so that it can be edited later if necessary, we will put in the points as POINTS and generate the spline through the nodes. In order to see the points you will need to change both the PDMODE and the PDSIZE.

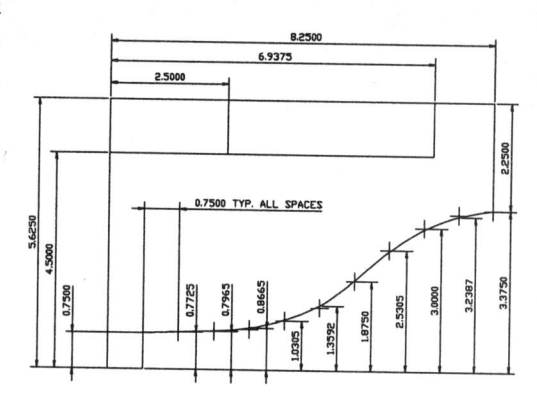

Step 1 Set up three layers, for POINTS, OBJECT, and DIMENSIONS. Make POINTS current. Then add points.

> **Toolbar** There is no button avaiable.
>
> **Pull Down** From the Format menu, choose Point Style.

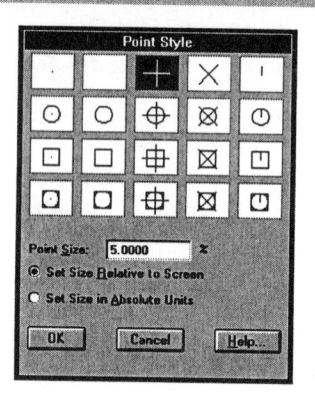

Make the top center or third point active, and change Size Relative to Screen to 5%.

Step 2 Add the points. The lower left corner will be 0,0.

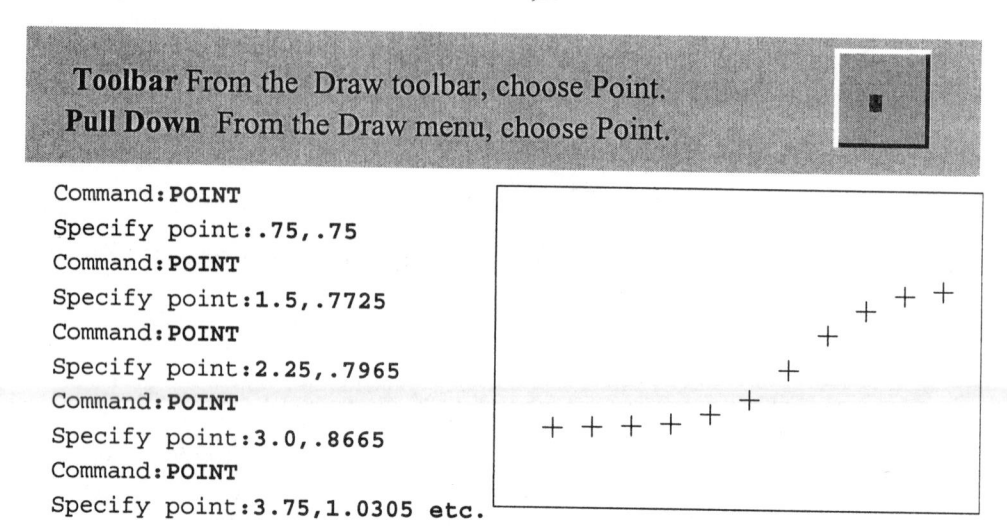

> **Toolbar** From the Draw toolbar, choose Point.
> **Pull Down** From the Draw menu, choose Point.

```
Command: POINT
Specify point: .75,.75
Command: POINT
Specify point: 1.5,.7725
Command: POINT
Specify point: 2.25,.7965
Command: POINT
Specify point: 3.0,.8665
Command: POINT
Specify point: 3.75,1.0305 etc.
```

348 CHAPTER THIRTEEN

Step 3   Change your OSNAP to NODE and use SPLINE to create a spline through all of the points.

> **Toolbar** There is no button for this.
>
> **Pull Down** From the Format menu choose Drafting Settings.

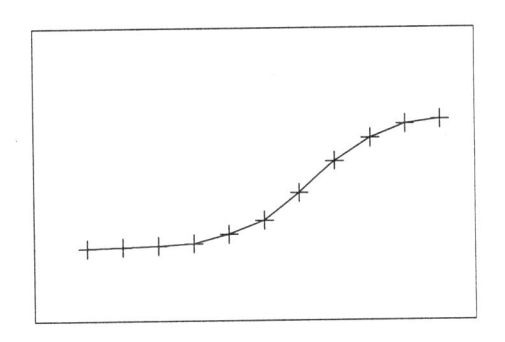

```
Command: OSNAP
Object snap modes: NODE
```

Now use SPLINE to create a spline through the identified points.

> **Toolbar** From the Draw toolbar, choose Spline.
>
> **Pull Down** From the Draw menu, choose Spline.

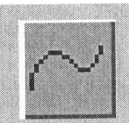

```
Command: SPLINE
Specify first point or [Object]: (pick the first point)
Specify next point: (pick the next point)
Specify next point or [Close, Fit Tolerance]: (pick the points
    in sequence)
Specify next point or [Close, Fit Tolerance]: (pick the last
    point)
Specify next point or [Close, Fit Tolerance]: ↵
Specify start tangent: (pick the first point)
Specify end tangent: (pick the last point)
```

Step 4   Using the drawing given at the beginning, add the outside lines.

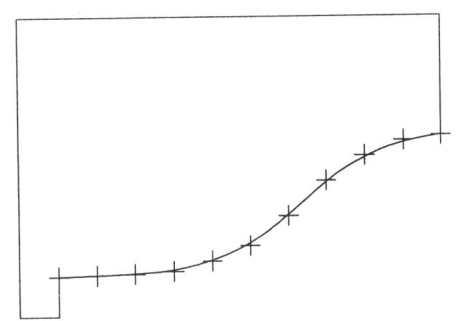

Step 5   Now use the Boundary option to help determine the area of the top of the part.

Pull Down From the Draw menu choose Boundary...

From the Boundary Creation dialog box, choose Make New Boundary Set.

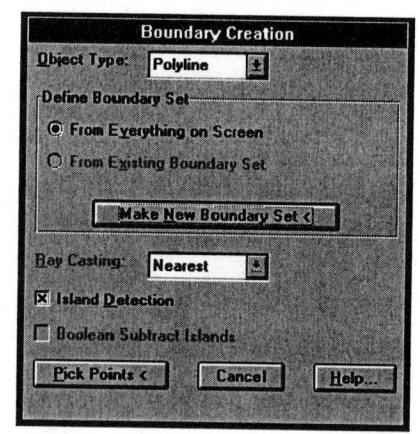

Now pick the lines and the spline.

Press ⏎ when you are finished and you will return to the Boundary Creation dialog box.

From the dialog box, pick "Pick points." You will be prompted to pick the internal point; choose the inside of the part.

A region will be created and you will have the area for the part.

If your system doesn't allow this, enter the AREA command, use the Object option, and **L** for LAST object.

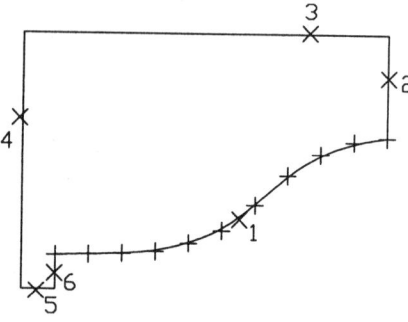

Step 6   Now list the properties of the spline and one of the point nodes.

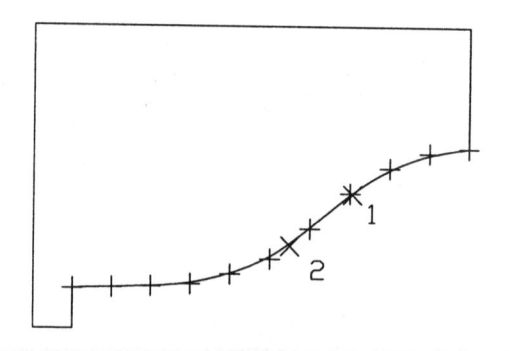

Toolbar From the Inquiry toolbar, choose List.

You will get a listing of the properties.

350   CHAPTER THIRTEEN

Step 7 Now add some points along the top edge of the part that correspond to the *X* measurement of all of the points. This is to double-check that all of your points are entered correctly. Use DDPTYPE to change the point style to the vertical line as shown.

> **Pull Down** From the Draw menu, choose Point, then Measure.

```
Command: MEASURE
Select object to measure:
   (pick 1)
Specify length of segment or
   [Block]:.75
```

Use Undo to remove the points once they have been used to double-check the lower points.

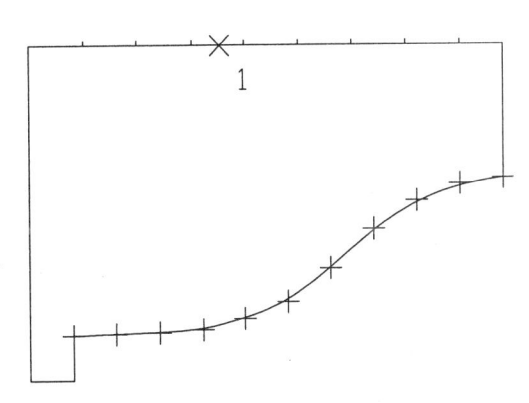

Step 8 Now add the remaining lines and dimensions to this view.

Step 9 Pan the screen over and, using the same method, draw in the front view of the gusset. The points will be much easier to enter if you make 0,0 the upper left corner. Move the first view up and out of the way.

When you are done, add a title block and notations to complete the drawing.

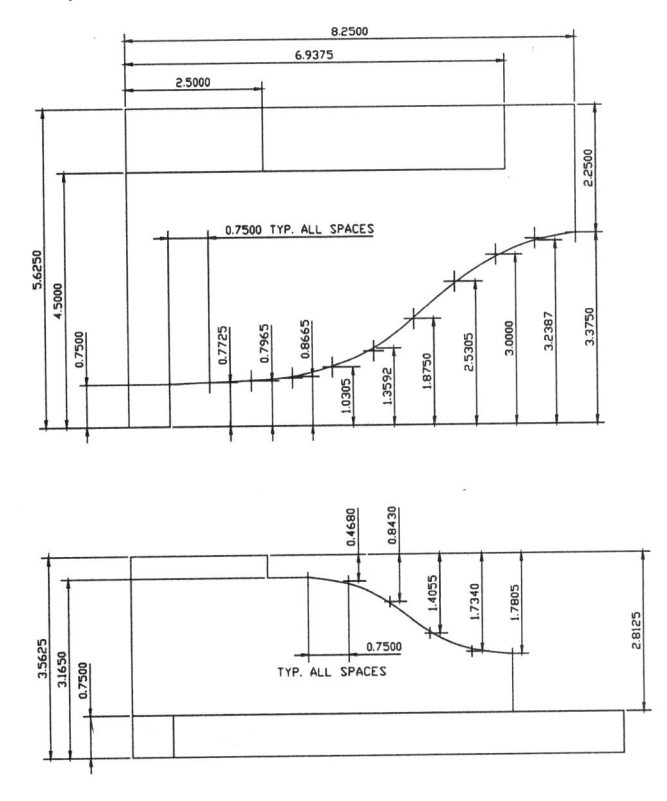

POINTS, DIVIDE, MEASURE, INQUIRY, and System Variables **351**

Command and Function Summary

AREA calculates the area and perimeter of objects or defined areas.

BOUNDARY creates a region or polyline of a closed boundary.

DIST measures the distance and angle between two points.

DDPTYPE specifies the display mode and size of point objects.

ID displays the coordinates of a location.

LIST displays database information for selected objects.

MLEDIT edits multiline intersections and vertices.

MLSTYLE sets multiline styles.

For practice, there will be part of a grandfather clock on this page every chapter until chapter 19.

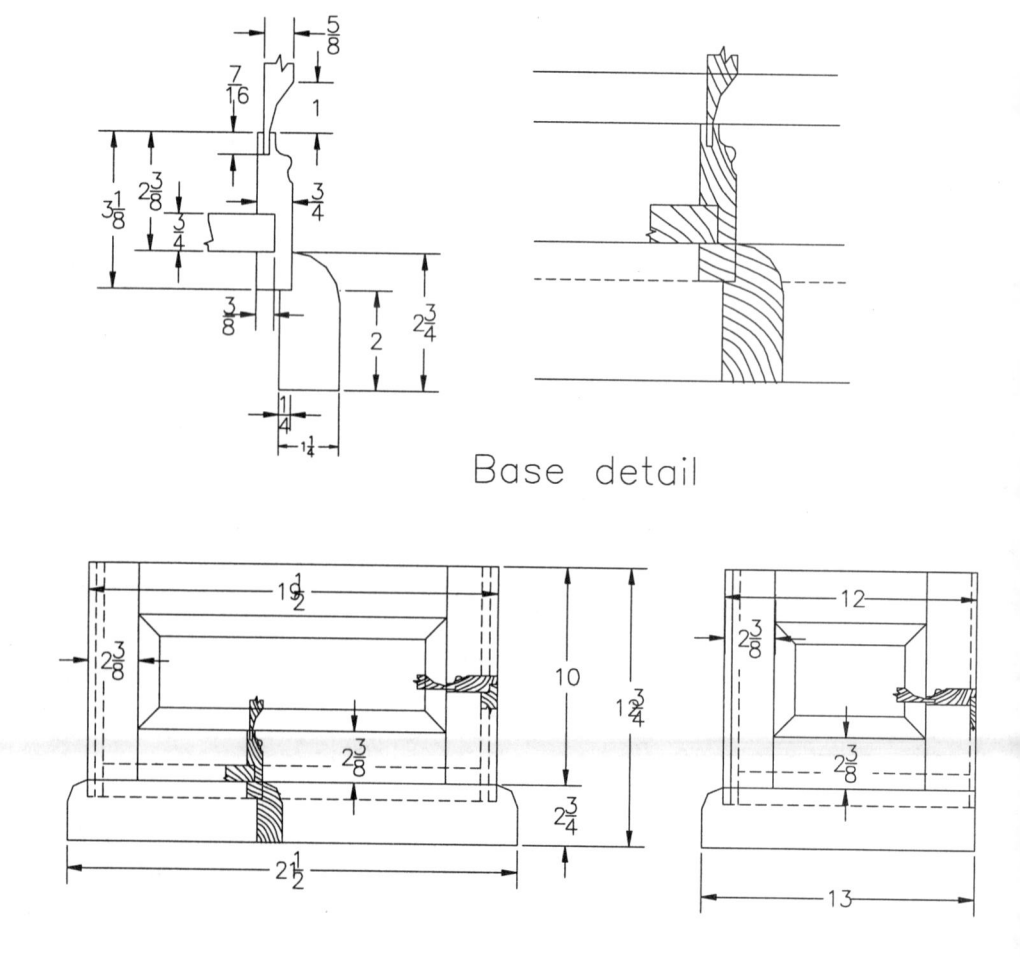

Base detail

Exercise A13

Step 1 Use DDPTYPE to load the point shown, then create nine points at a regular distance to form a decorative wall.

Step 2 Use SPLINE with the NODE OSNAP to join the points together into a spline element.

Step 3 Offset the spline at 8" and use LINE to close the ends so that the left end is perpendicular and the right end is horizontal.

Step 4 Use AREA with the Boundary option to figure out the area of the decorative wall.

Step 5 Create a rectangle 1" × 8". Block it making sure that the insertion base point is the middle of the bottom line.

Step 6 Use MEASURE to place the blocks at 8" intervals to illustrate decorative brick.

Step 7 Draw in the remainder of the room using MLSTYLE and MLEDIT where needed.

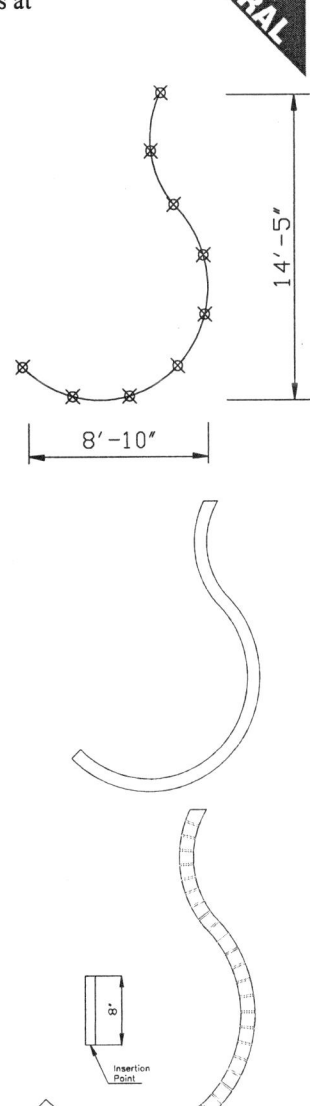

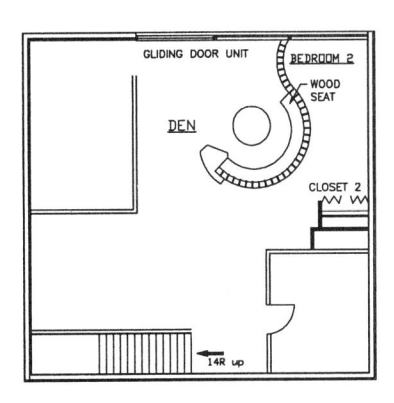

POINTS, DIVIDE, MEASURE, INQUIRY, and System Variables

Exercise C13

Step 1 Use SPLINE to create a riverbank fit through the following points.

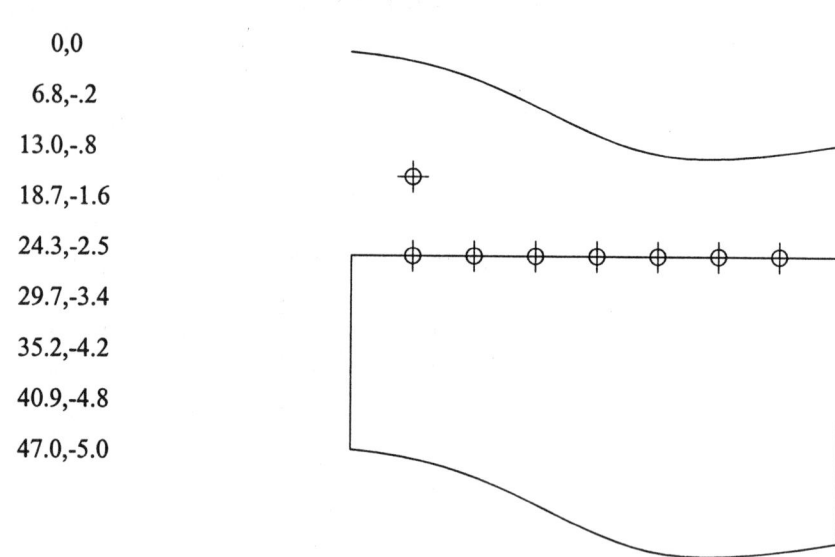

0,0
6.8,-.2
13.0,-.8
18.7,-1.6
24.3,-2.5
29.7,-3.4
35.2,-4.2
40.9,-4.8
47.0,-5.0

Step 2 Create a light as shown in the illustration and BLOCK it under the name LIGHT.

Step 3 Using DIVIDE, divide the riverbank into four equal sections. Use the OSNAP NODE to create lot lines between these sections and the road 21 m to the north of the river.

Step 4 Use MEASURE to place the lights along the roadway at spaces of 7 m each.

Step 5 Use the AREA command to calculate the total area of each lot. Make sure that you have the correct area, not an area with a straight line from the intersection of the lot line and the plines.

Step 6 Use LIST to find the length of road along the northern edge of these four lots. Use DIST to find the total length in a straight line from the southwest end of the first lot to the southeast end of the last lot.

If the southwest corner of the lots is at 0,0, what is the exact point at the centre of the four lots?

What is the total area taken up by the lots?

How much space have you left in your partition or RAM?

Exercise E13

Step 1   Use DIVIDE and MEASURE to create this partial drawing of electrical connectors in an oscilloscope. Use DIVIDE and MEASURE to place connections in both a circular and a linear fashion. In the linear example, the block was not rotated; in the circular, it was.

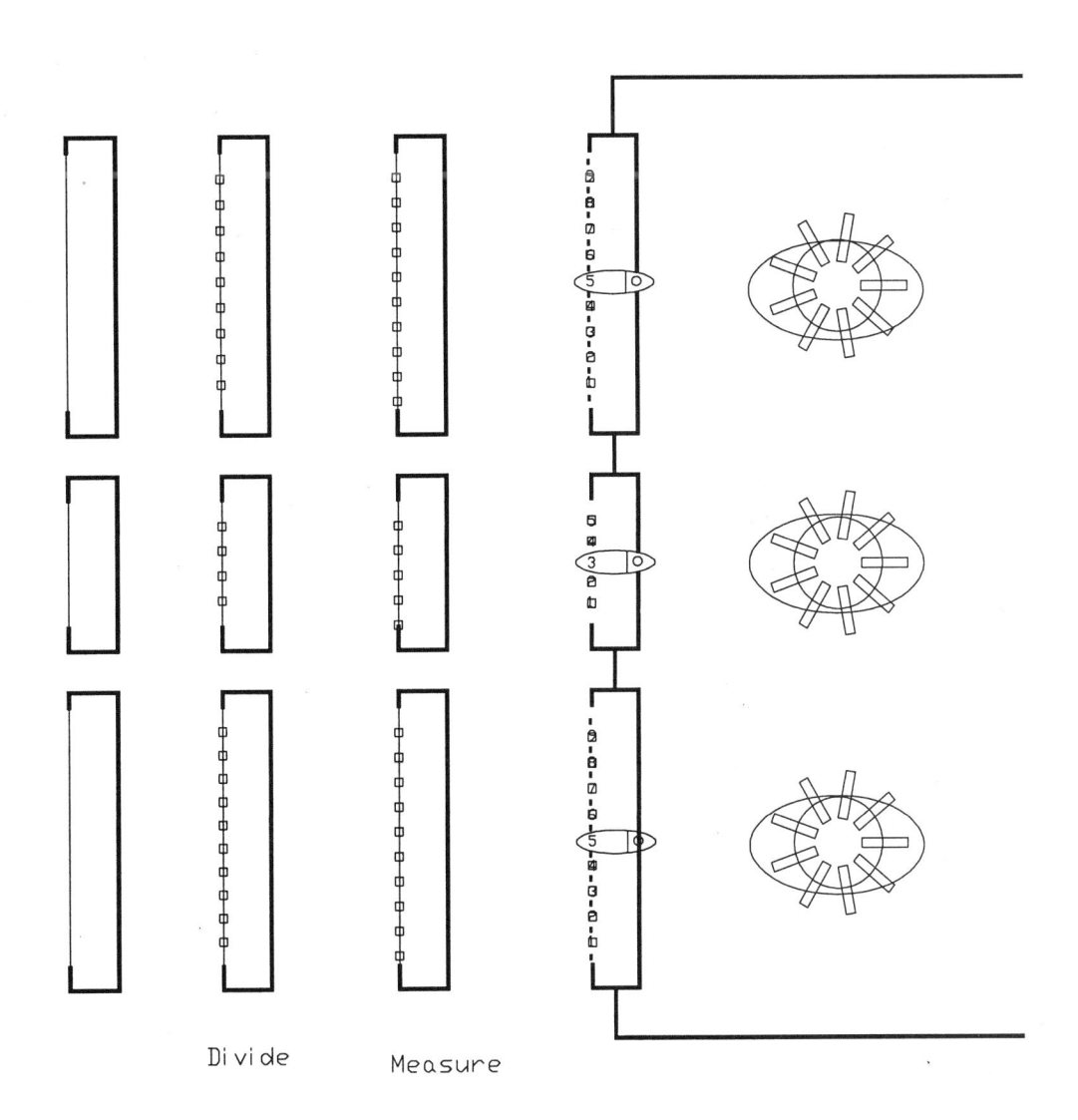

Divide   Measure

Step 2   Use LIST to find the length of the connections.
Use DIST to find the height of the schematic.

Exercise M13

Step 1 Draw the outlines for the sprocket shown. If the SNAP is set at .25 it will be quite simple.

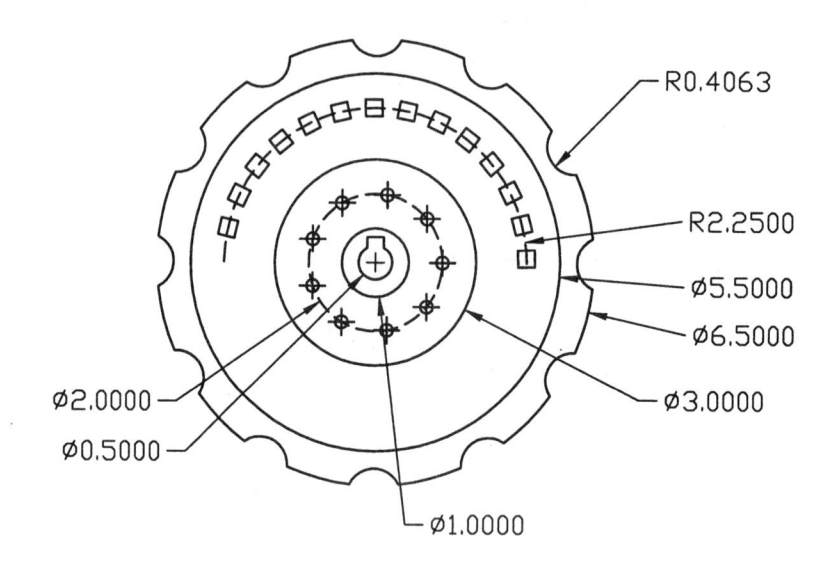

Step 2 Change the point display to 34 and use DIVIDE to place nine points to indicate the tap holes on the 1 unit radius center line.

Step 3 Create a block of a square .25 units by .25 units. Use MEASURE to place this block at a distance of .5 units along the 2.25 radius arc.

Step 4 Use the AREA command to calculate the total area of the sprocket, making sure to subtract the keyway.

Step 5 Use LIST to find the length of arc along the perimeter of the sprocket.

Use DIST to find the minimum distance between one square and another on the sprocket.

Use PEDIT and Join to find the outer perimeter of the entire object.

If the center of the sprocket is at 0,0, what is the exact location of the left side of the keyway opening?

What is the total area taken up by the squares?

How much space have you left in your partition or RAM?

Challenger 13A

Step 1   Use the SPLINE command to place the outline of this part. The points will need to be placed perfectly to get an even, undulating curve. Don't forget to use Close. If you find this too frustrating, draw the part using arcs, then change it to a spline (not a pline, but a spline).

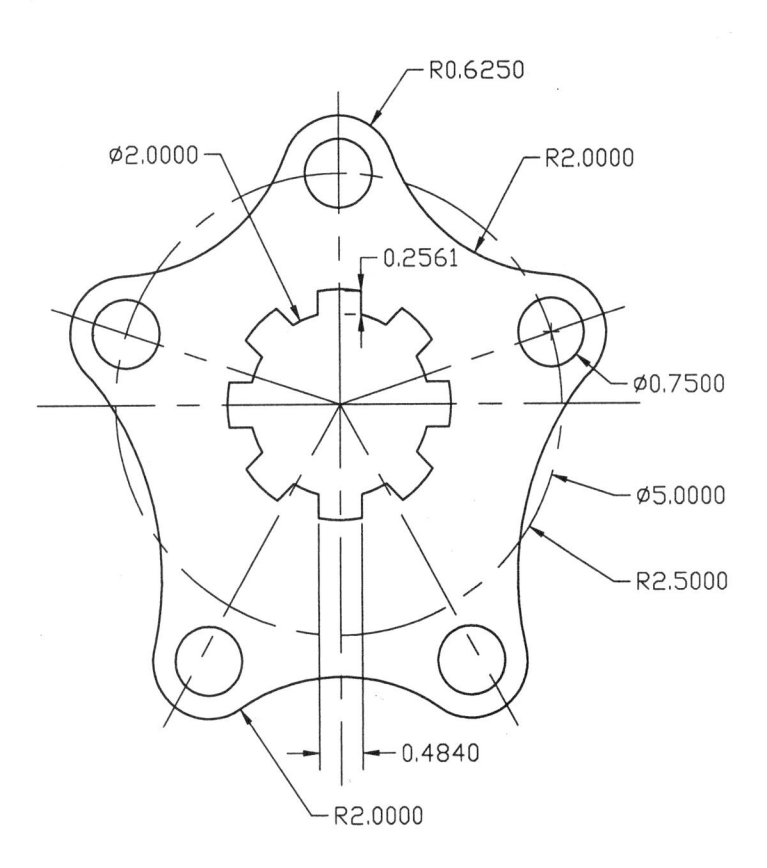

Step 2   Use Boundary and Area to discover the area of the surface of the part.

Challenger 13B

This illustration can be added to pages 220, 250, and 457 to create a complete commercial stair layout.

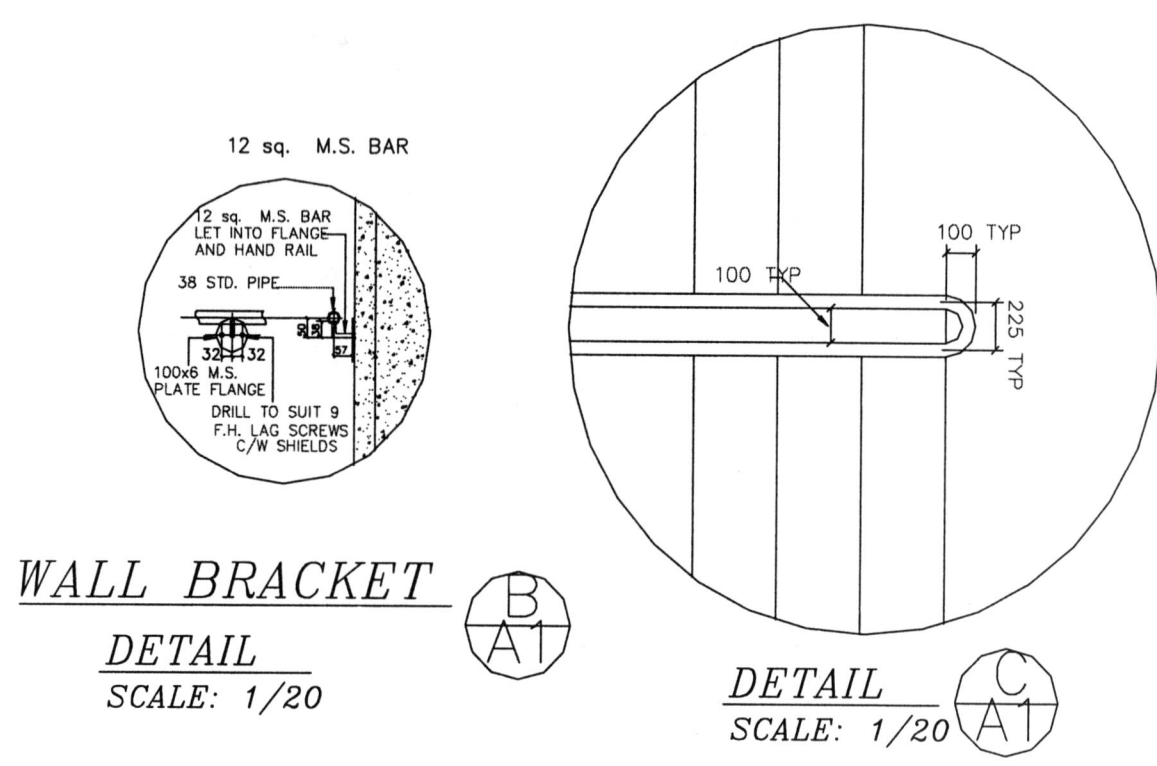

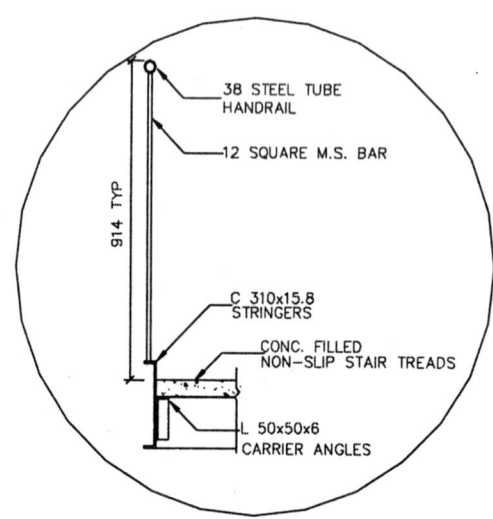

WALL BRACKET
DETAIL B/A1
SCALE: 1/20

DETAIL C/A1
SCALE: 1/20

DETAIL D/A1
SCALE: 1/20

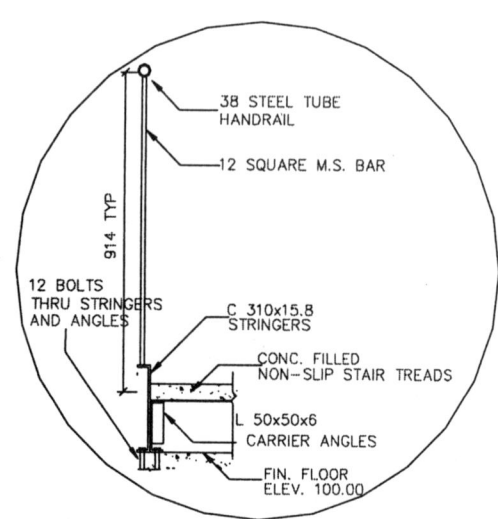

DETAIL E/A1
SCALE: 1/20

14 Creating Attributes

Upon completion of this chapter, you should be able to:

1. Define a series of attributes
2. Block the attributes
3. Insert the attributes onto a drawing
4. Use the ATTribute DIAlog boxes

OBJECTIVES

Introduction

In addition to creating geometry and drawings, AutoCAD allows for the generation of nongraphic information which can be accessed in the form of bills of materials, schedules, parts lists, and other data that is cross-referenced on the drawing. This data is not necessarily displayed on the drawing, but is filed with the drawing. This nongraphic intelligence is called an *attribute*. Attributes provide a label or tag that lets you attach text or other data to a block. Attributes can also be used to generate templates for fill-in-the-blanks situations such as on drawing notations and title blocks.

You can define *constant* attributes which have the same value for every occurrence in the block, and *invisible* attributes that are not displayed nor plotted.

When you define an attribute, you are creating a program to prompt the user for data. You decide what the user must enter by creating the prompts for the entry of data.

Attributes for Title Blocks and Notations

In a standard title block there are areas identified for such information as date, part number, drawing number, etc. These would be printed on the title block. The user would then fill in the information that pertains to the part being drawn.

If this were a computer-generated title block, without attributes, the user would need to zoom into each area, adjust the TEXT size and style, then enter the current data using TEXT.

With attributes the user is prompted for the current information when the block is inserted. All of the sizes for the inserted text are determined at the time the attribute is defined and blocked. So are the placement of the text and the lettering font. All the user needs to do is add the missing information for the customer, name of part, date, name of designer, etc.

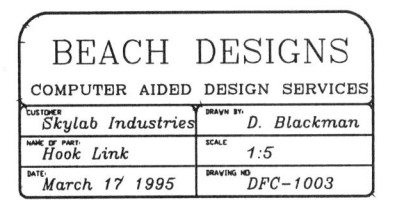

BEACH DESIGNS
COMPUTER AIDED DESIGN SERVICES
CUSTOMER: Skylab Industries   DRAWN BY: D. Blackman
NAME OF PART: Hook Link   SCALE: 1:5
DATE: March 17 1995   DRAWING NO: DFC-1003

Figure 14-1

In the title block in Figure 14-1, all the information relative to the current drawing has been added using attributes. If this title block had attributes, you could expect the following prompts in the INSERT command:

Creating Attributes   **359**

```
Command:-INSERT
Enter block name or [?]:TITLE
Specify insertion point or
  [Scale/X/Y/Z/Rotate/PScale/PX/PY/PZ/PRotate]:0,0
Enter X scale factor,specify opposite corner,or [Corner/XYZ]:⏎
Enter Y scale factor <use X scale factor>:⏎
Specify rotation angle <0>:⏎ (the same as block inserts)
Customer name<Skylab Industries>:⏎
Name of Part<>:Hook Link
Enter the current date (DD/MM/YY):17/03/96
Drawn by <E.C.Jones>:⏎
Scale <1:5>:⏎
Drawing no. DFC-####<>:DFC-1003
```

> **Notes**
> Use -insert and -attdef to avoid the dialog boxes. Typing is faster.

Notice that the INSERT command starts out the same as in Chapter 10, but there are prompts at the end that are specific to this title block. The prompts and the related information are what you create with the ATTDEF command or attribute dialog box (thankfully without the word Specify in it).

Defining the Attributes

Prior to creating the attributed block, think through the information you are likely to need. How much is needed and where? A bit of forethought can save hours of editing. In a title block the text font for the block titles (Name, Date, Drawn By) should be different from the text font for the current information. Before creating the attribute definitions, load the new text font.

To define the attribute use ATTDEF or the Attribute dialog box.

The ATTDEF Command

The ATTDEF command allows you to define an attribute. We will create the attribute definition for the date. Access the ATTDEF command through the command line.

```
Command:-ATTDEF
Current attribute modes -- Invisible-N, Constant-N, Verify-N,
  Preset-N
Enter an option to change [Invisible/Constant/Verify/Preset]
  <done>:⏎
```

Change the modes if you want the attribute to be constant, invisible, preset, or verified. In this case no change is necessary.

```
Enter attribute tag name:DATE
```

The *attribute tag* is a one-word summary of the subject of the attribute. In this case, you want to enter the current date onto an existing title block. The word DATE is used to summarize what you want from the attribute.

```
Enter attribute prompt:Enter the current date (DD/MM/YY)
```

The attribute prompt is what is actually going to appear on screen. This prompt asks you for the required information, in this case the date, and it should offer any further information that may be required in order to enter that information. With regard to the date, you probably want a standard format such as Day/Month/Year so that an entry such as 03/04/94 will be April 3 and not March 4.

```
Enter default attribute value:↵
```

The default attribute value is what the user will usually want to use. There is no default required for the date because, in most cases, it changes daily.

```
Specify start point of text or [Justify/Style]:J
```

Now that the you have identified what your attribute is going to say, you need to place it on the title block. Like the TEXT command, ATTDEF prompts for the position of the attribute.

```
Align/Center/Fit/Middle/Right/TL/TC/TR/ML/MC/MR/BL/BC/BR:M
Middle point: (pick a point in the center of the area reserved
   for the date)
Specify height <0.1800>:.25 (this sets the size of lettering.
   Make sure this is both logical and readable!)
Specify rotation angle <0>:↵
```

Text in the Standard font was used to define the text for the title block. The tag for the date attribute is in the Italic Complex Font. This is where the current date will appear.

Prelab 14A describes in detail the construction of a fully attributed title block.

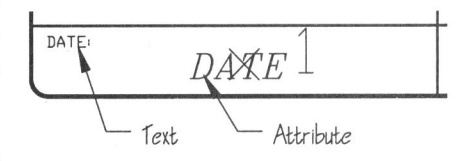

Figure 14-2

> **Notes**
> The Value box means default value.

Using the ATTribute DIAlog Box

There is no Toolbar button or Pull Down available, although there is one listed in the Help files.

The command line equivalent is **ATTDEF**.

In the dialog box in Figure 14-3, you can set the modes, tag information, prompt, location, and text style as described above. When Pick Point is chosen, the dialog box will disappear until the point is chosen, then reappear once the selection is made.

Any number of attributes can be added to or associated with each block, as long as the tag is different.

Use the TAB key or the mouse to change fields.

Figure 14-3

Enter the information as required. Choose pick point to pick the insertion point on the screen. Use Tab to advance, or the mouse.

Editing Attribute Definitions

If you have made an error in defining the attribute you can change the attribute definition with the CHANGE command or with the Edit Attribute Definition dialog box.

```
Command: CHANGE
Select objects: (pick the definition you wish to change)
Select objects:
```

You will be prompted for changes in the tag, prompt, and default values, etc. You can also use modify text to change attribute definitions.

Toolbar From the Modify toolbar, choose Edit Text.

Pull Down From the Modify menu, choose Object, then text.

The command line equivalent is **DDEDIT**.

> **Notes**
> CHANGE and DDEDIT alter the Attribute Definitions, not the attributed block.

```
Command: DDEDIT
<Select a TEXT or ATTDEF object>/Undo: (pick the ATTDEF)
```

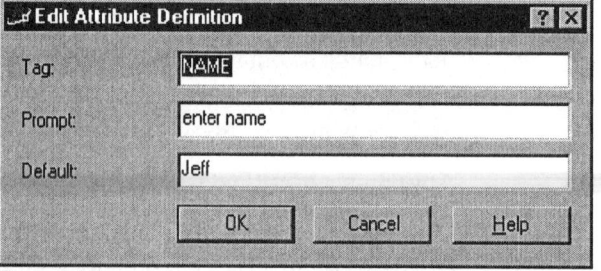

Figure 14-4

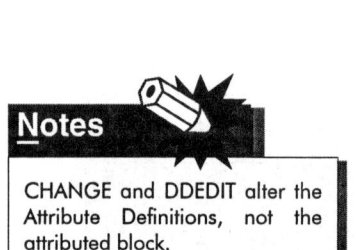

362 CHAPTER FOURTEEN

This will offer you three input boxes to change the Tag, Prompt, or Default value. Note how the Value is here called the Default. Press OK to complete the command.

BLOCKing the Attributes

Once the attributes are all defined, you must BLOCK the information in the order that you want your prompts to appear in by picking each attribute. If you use Window, you may be prompted in the reverse order, depending on where the Window starts.

Attributes can be used with both the BLOCK and the WBLOCK command.

Saving the file also saves the attribute information without using the BLOCK or WBLOCK commands.

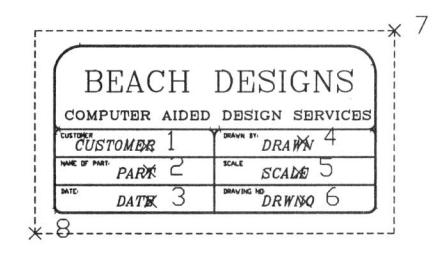

Figure 14-5

Inserting the Attributed Blocks

Having created the attributed block, you can now use INSERT to place it on your drawing. Once inserted, the block will contain the values for each attribute in that particular instance or application.

Using the ATTribute DIAlog Box

The Attribute dialog box will give you an automatic on-screen list of all the attribute data you have entered as soon as the INSERT command has been activated. You can then make any changes to the data on-screen. To activate the command, type ATTDIA at the command prompt, and make the variable active.

```
Command: ATTDIA
Enter new value for
ATTDIA <0>:1
```

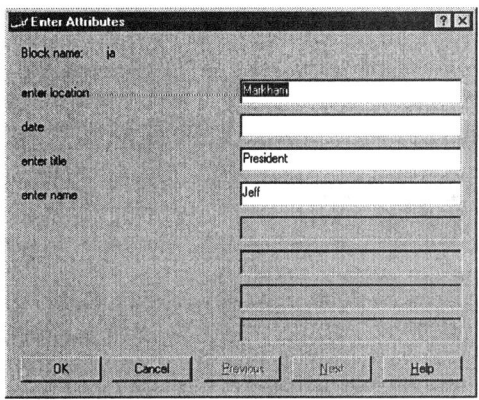

Figure 14-6

With ATTDIA at 0, the box does not display; with ATTDIA set to 1, it does.

The information in the box represents the default values. Just indicate which values you want to change by using the cursor arrow to highlight them. Then type in the new values and press OK to have the attributes display on the screen where placed.

This dialog box can be an advantage if there are a number of attributes that need to be coordinated.

Creating Attributes   **363**

Changing Attribute Definitions

While inserting the block, you may notice some errors in the block definitions. To change the attribute definitions at this point, use EXPLODE and then CHANGE. When you EXPLODE the attributed block, it will revert back to the tag format.

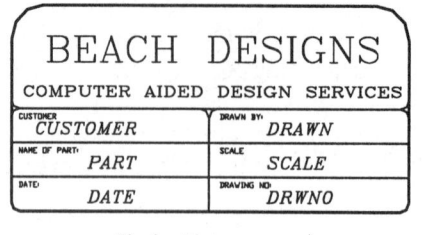

Block with tags   Attributed block

Figure 14-7

In Figure 14-7, we have the block with attribute tags on the left, and the inserted block with the instance values on the right.

If you use EXPLODE, you will return the attributed block to the attribute definitions, and only the tags will be shown. You can now use the CHANGE command or the Edit Attribute Definition dialog box to update the attribute definitions. Once changed, the attribute can be reblocked and reinserted.

```
Command: EXPLODE
Select block reference, polyline, dimension, or mesh: (pick 1)
Command: CHANGE
Select objects: (pick the block)
Select objects: ⏎ (etc.)
```

Displaying Attributes

When attributes are added to objects, they can be made universally invisible by setting the Invisible mode in the ATTDEF command, or you can make them invisible later using the ATTDISP command.

The ATTDISP Command

ATTDISP controls the display of attributes.

> **Pull Down** From the View menu, Display, then Attribute Display.

The command line equivalent is **ATTDISP**.

```
Command: ATTDISP
Enter attribute visibility setting [Normal/ON/OFF] <Normal>: OFF
```

Where: ON   = all attributes visible

           OFF   = all attributes invisible

           Normal = normal visibility set individually

Attribute Modes

If you want to INSERT the attributed blocks without having to turn the display off, you can have the attribute mode set to invisible. You can set these as follows to make attributed block insertion easier:

INVISIBLE	hides data associated with a BLOCK that does not need to be seen; for example, on a desk layout you may want to have the name of the current occupant for reference, but to provide specs for a decorator this is not necessary.
CONSTANT	makes an attribute uneditable; for example, the president's desk is always the president's desk even though the president may change.
VERIFY	allows you to take a final look at what you have entered prior to having it added to the drawing.
PRESET	is used when creating attributes that will always have the same value. This lets you insert a block that has an attribute or a set of attributes automatically attached to it. No user response is needed, because the attribute never changes. An example of this would be a part that would always maintain the same order number. The number would be inserted with the attribute, but the user is not prompted for any change.

Creating Attributes for Data Extraction

Attributes can be used both for title blocks and drawing notations and for occasions where the information can be downloaded to a price list or bill of materials. The attributes are all defined in the same way, and the extractions take place once the attributed blocks are all inserted.

Attributes are always associated with blocks. If you want an attributed block, first create the geometry for the final block, if there is any, then add the attributes. You will need to have lines and text as well as attributes in a title block, but you will not need geometry in an attributed block that is meant to extract room colors.

Prelab 14B gives an example of attributes used for extraction. Extracting attribute data is covered in Chapter 15.

Prelab 14A   Attributes for a Title Block

Step 1   Use LINE and PLINE to create the design for a standard title block. Use TEXT to enter the headings for each area. Use the parameters of this title block, or retrieve your title block from Chapter 8 to start.

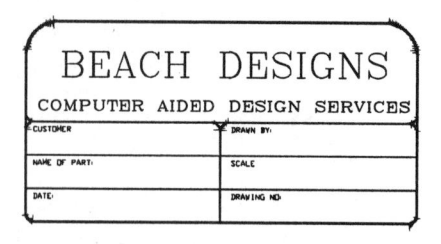

BEACH DESIGNS
COMPUTER AIDED DESIGN SERVICES

CUSTOMER DRAWN BY:
NAME OF PART: SCALE
DATE: DRAWING NO.

Step 2   Add the attribute definition for the part number.

You will probably want to set a new Style for the information to be added to the title block by attributes. Sometimes a new colour is required as well. Set these up using the STYLE command and either COLOR or LAYERS.

```
Command:ATTDEF
Current attribute modes:Invisible-N Constant-N Verify-V
  Preset-P
Enter an option to change [Invisible/Constant/Verify/Preset]
  <done>:↵
Enter attribute tag name:Part
Enter attribute prompt:Enter name of part
Enter default attribute value:HOOK
Justify/Style/<start point>:J
Align/Center/Fit/Middle/Right
 /TL/TC/TR/ML/MC/MR/BL/BC/BR:R
Right point: (pick 1)
Specify height <5.0000>:.25
Specify rotation angle <0>:↵
```

NAME OF PART: PART SCAL
DATE

Step 3   Now enter the attribute for the designer using the Attribute Definition dialog box.

> There is no toolbar button or Pull Down available.

The designer who created the block can use the default here, but if someone else wants to use this title block as well, they would simply enter their initials without using the default.

Step 4 Define the other attributes so that each area has an attribute tag.

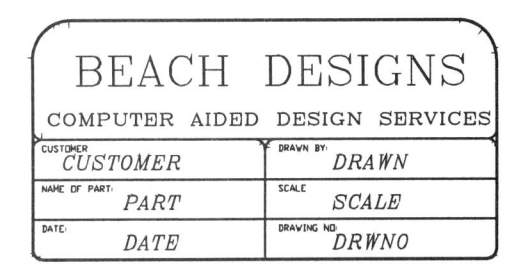

```
BEACH DESIGNS
COMPUTER AIDED DESIGN SERVICES
CUSTOMER: CUSTOMER      DRAWN BY: DRAWN
NAME OF PART: PART      SCALE: SCALE
DATE: DATE              DRAWING NO: DRWNO
```

The block is now finished. We can block it and insert it.

Step 5
```
Command:-BLOCK
Specify block name or [?]:TITLE
Specify insertion base point: (pick the corner)
Select objects: (pick attributes 1-6, then use Crossing to
   select the rest)
```

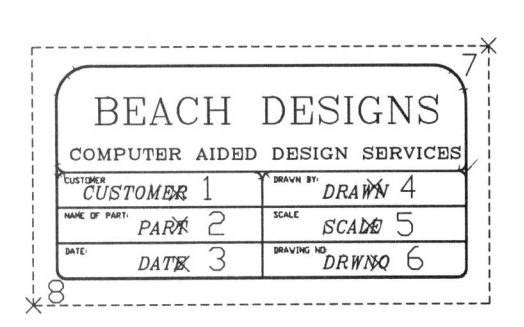

Creating Attributes **367**

Step 6   Insert the attributed block and check to see that you have specified the proper size of lettering and that prompts are clear. You can use ATTDIA if you like.

```
Command:INSERT
Enter block name or [?]:TITLE
Specify insertion point or
   [Scale/X/Y/Z/Rotate/PScale/PX/PY/PZ/PRotate]:0,0
Enter X scale factor,specify opposite corner,or [Corner/XYZ]:⏎
Enter Y scale factor <use X scale factor>:⏎
Specify rotation angle <0>:⏎ (the same as block inserts)
Customer name <Skylab Industries>:⏎
Name of Part <>:Hook Link
Enter the current date (DD/MM/YY):17/03/96
Drawn by <E.C.Jones>:⏎
Scale <1:5>:⏎
Drawing no. DFC-####<>:DFC-1003
```

Step 7   A good way of checking your attributed block is to have a fellow student insert the block and fill in the details of the attributes without your help. If he/she has any problem understanding the prompts, go back and edit it. While you may understand your prompts now, the fact that someone else doesn't understand them may indicate that you won't either after a few days.

Other areas you may want to adjust are the attribute text sizes. Use EXPLODE and then CHANGE or DDEDIT to adjust them.

```
Command:EXPLODE
Select block reference, polyline, dimension, or mesh: (pick 1)
Command:CHANGE
Select objects: (pick 1)
Select objects:⏎
```

Once changed, reblock the title block and reinsert it. To have the title block accessible for all files save the file as ATTITLE or use WBLOCK and take TITLE as the block.

Chapter 15 will illustrate how to edit the inserted attributed block.

Prelab 14B Defining, Blocking, and Inserting Attributes

In this tutorial, you will create a jig with a bushing and jigleg. In a manufacturing environment, it is usual to have items such as bushings purchased rather than made on-site to save both time and money. If you were to create a drawing of this part using these items, you could also have the ordering information stored as attributes with the block before it is inserted into the drawing.

Step 1   Draw up these very simple parts on different areas of your screen.

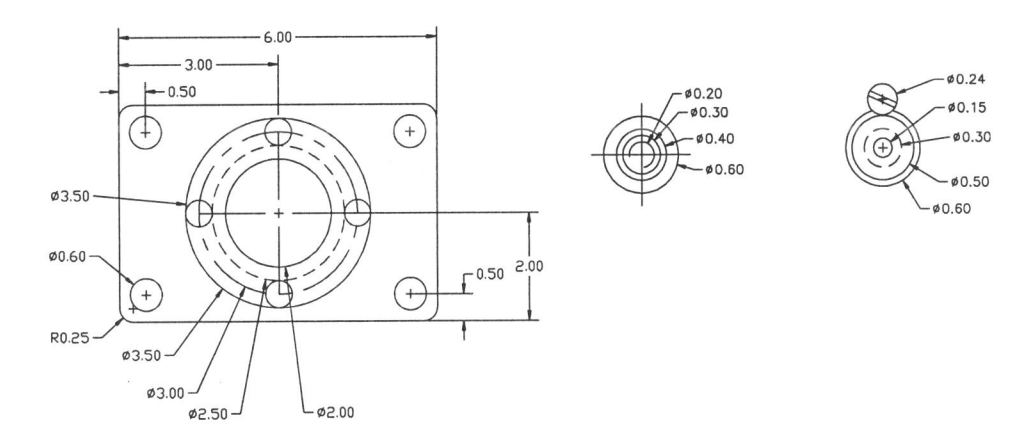

Step 2   If you wanted to create a bill of materials for these items, the information could include:

- Part Number
- Description
- Material
- Size
- Price

Then you would add the quantity and order the parts. The information listed above can be added as attributes to the block before it is blocked and then extracted later.

The words in this illustration are attribute tags, not text. No text is needed on this exercise.

Creating Attributes   **369**

Add the attributes for the part using these default factors:

Tag	Prompt	Default Value
Partno	Enter Part Number	JIG125
Descript	Enter Part Description	Jigleg
Material	Enter Material	Steel
Size	Enter Part Size	.60 × 1.25
Price	Enter Current Price	5.26

Enter this information with the ATTDEF command or with the Attribute Definition dialog box.

> At the command prompt type in ATTDEF or DDATTDEF.

```
Command:ATTDEF
Current attribute modes:Invisible-N Constant-N Verify-V
  Preset-P
Enter an option to change [Invisible/Constant/Verify/Preset]
  <done>:⏎
Enter attribute tag name:PARTNO
Enter attribute prompt:Enter Part Number
Enter default attribute value:JIG125
Justify/Style/<start point>:(pick a spot beside the part)
Specify height <5.0000>:10
Specify rotation angle <0>:⏎
```

When entering the next line for the attribute, the attribute definition will line up with the last entered line if you press ⏎ at the text justification line or simply choose OK on the dialog box.

```
Command:ATTDEF
Current attribute modes:Invisible-N Constant-N Verify-V
  Preset-P
Enter an option to change [Invisible/Constant/Verify/Preset]
  <done>:⏎
Enter attribute tag name:DESCRIPT
Enter attribute prompt:Enter Part Description
Enter default attribute value:JIgleg
Justify/Style/<start point>:⏎
Command:ATTDEF
 :⏎ :⏎
Enter attribute tag:MATERIAL
Enter attribute prompt:Enter Material
Enter default attribute value:Steel
Justify/Style/<start point>:⏎
```

Continue with the final two definitions until all five are complete.

Step 3 When all of the information has been added, create a block of the part with a new name to help you identify it as an attributed block.

```
Command:BLOCK
Block name (or ?):ATTJIGLG
Insertion base point: CENter of (pick 1)
Select objects: (pick 2, 3)
```

Remember that the block will disappear.

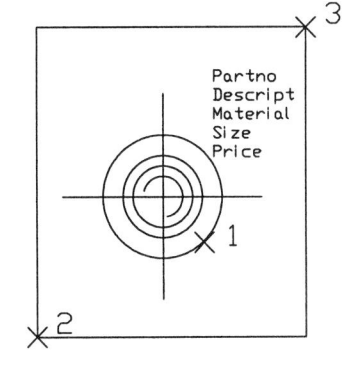

Step 4 Do the same with the bushing. Use the values listed below.

Tag	Prompt	Default Value
Partno	Enter Part Number	BU125
Descript	Enter Part Description	Stand. Bushing
Material	Enter Material	Steel
Size	Enter Part Size	.125 × .55
Price	Enter Current Price	3.29

Block the new file under the name ATTBUSH.

Step 5 Use ZOOM All to get the original file back onto the screen. Now insert four jiglegs and four bushings onto the file.

```
Command:INSERT
Block name (or ?):ATTJIGLG
Insertion point:CEN of (pick 1)
X scale factor <1>/Corner/XYZ:↵
Y scale factor (default = X):↵
Rotation angle <0>:↵
Enter Part Numbe r<JIG125>:↵
Enter Part Description< Jigleg>:↵
Enter Material <Steel>:↵
Enter Part Size <.60 x 1.25>:↵
Enter Current Price <5.26>:↵
```

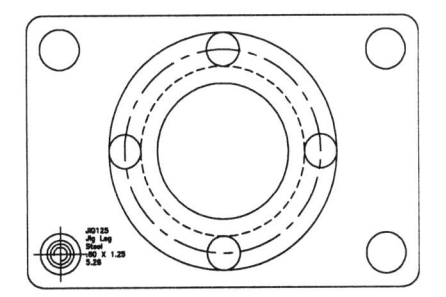

To get all four of these jiglegs placed, you could insert the object three more times or you could copy the existing block.

Step 6   Use the ATTribute DIAlog box to enter the final four parts.

```
Command:ATTDIA
New value for ATTDIA <0>:1
Command:INSERT
```

Rotate the bushings by 90 when inserting.

When all four bushing blocks have been entered, your file will look like this:

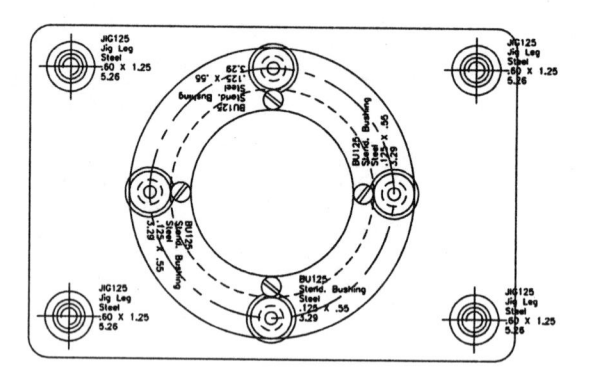

Notice that when you insert the bushings, the attributes will be rotated along with the geometry. This is of no importance, because the attributes will not be part of an overall drawing. In an electrical drawing, however, the attributes must be visible and legible; in this case, create attributed blocks for both directions. When attributes are added to parts, they are not usually printed or plotted.

Step 7   If you were just making a drawing, it would never look like this. Use ATTDISP to turn all of the attributes off.

```
Command:ATTDISP
Normal/On/Off <current value>:OFF
```

Command and Function Summary

ATTDEF creates an attribute definition that can be blocked and added to a drawing.

ATTDIA uses a dialog box to enter an attribute.

ATTDISP controls the display of attributes.

DDATTE edits inserted attribute blocks.

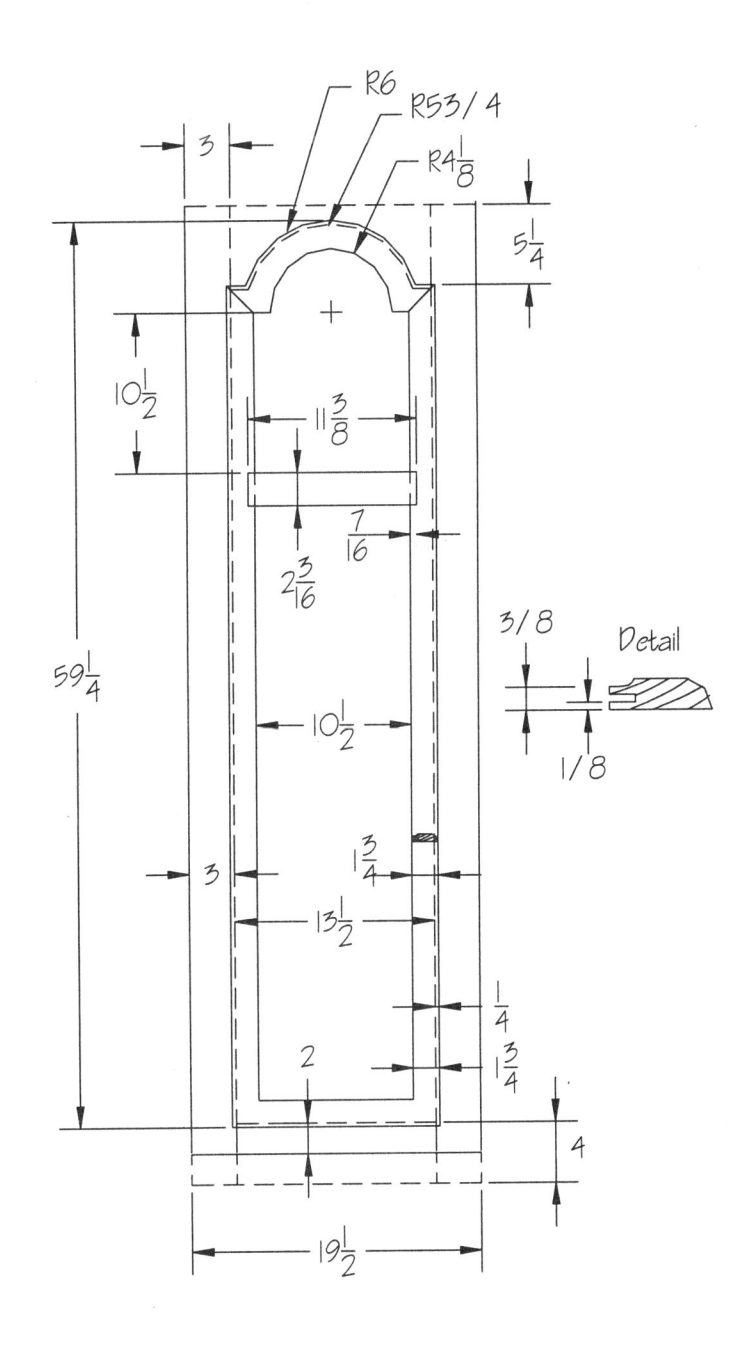

Exercise A14

Title Block Retrieve your title block from Chapter 8 or create a new one. Use ATTDEF to define the attributes.

Project		Drawing	Scale	Project
Project		Drawing info	Scale	Pro
			Date	
		School	Drawn	Drawing
		School	Drawn	DR#
			Class	

Block the attributes and title block. Insert it to see how it works.

Project		Drawing	Scale 1"=1'0"	Project
Elgin Residence		Foundation and Plan	Date 17/3/92	1
		School	Drawn G.G	Drawing
		Mohawk College	Class 1AT12	2

Room Finishes Create one block containing the indicated attributes. No geometry is needed with this block. Draw a simple floor plan, and work out the color scheme by inserting the block in all of the rooms.

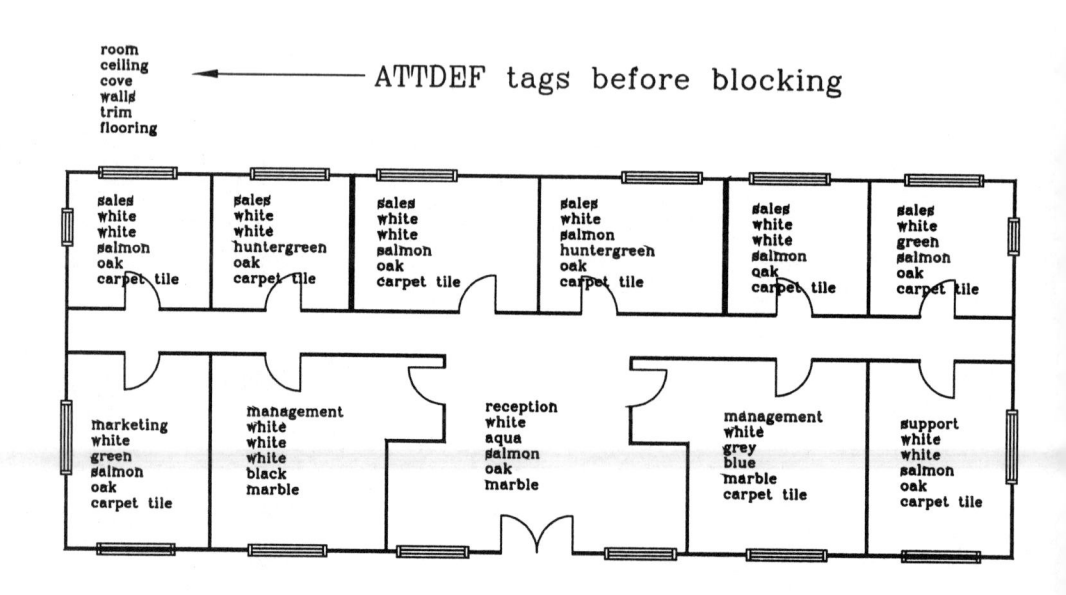

```
room
ceiling
cove         ←——— ATTDEF tags before blocking
walls
trim
flooring
```

Floor plan rooms:

- sales / white / white / salmon / oak / carpet tile
- sales / white / white / huntergreen / oak / carpet tile
- sales / white / white / salmon / oak / carpet tile
- sales / white / white / huntergreen / oak / carpet tile
- sales / white / white / salmon / oak / carpet tile
- sales / white / white / green / salmon / oak / carpet tile
- marketing / white / green / salmon / oak / carpet tile
- management / white / white / white / black / marble
- reception / white / aqua / salmon / oak / marble
- management / white / grey / blue / marble / carpet tile
- support / white / white / salmon / oak / carpet tile

374 CHAPTER FOURTEEN

Exercise C14

Title Retrieve your title block from Chapter 8 or create a new one.
Block Use ATTDEF to define the attributes.

Part	REVISIONS		
\multicolumn{4}{l}{The making of any copy of this drawing or any portion thereof by any means is expressly prohibited unless authorised in writing.}
Job		DWN	DRWN
		Date	DATE
	Job	Scale	Scale
		App.	App.
Company		DWG No.	
	Company		DRW#

Block the attributes and title block. Insert it to see how it works.

Part	REVISIONS		
\multicolumn{4}{l}{The making of any copy of this drawing or any portion thereof by any means is expressly prohibited unless authorised in writing.}
Job		DWN	C.S.Lewis
		Date	2/15/92
	Rebecca St & Ferguson	Scale	1:500
		App.	444
Company		DWG No.	
	Tiny Township		AA4

A Survey Draw a simple survey. Create attributes for the desired services and particulars as illustrated below. Block the attributes, then insert the block into each lot indicating the different lot numbers and services for each lot.

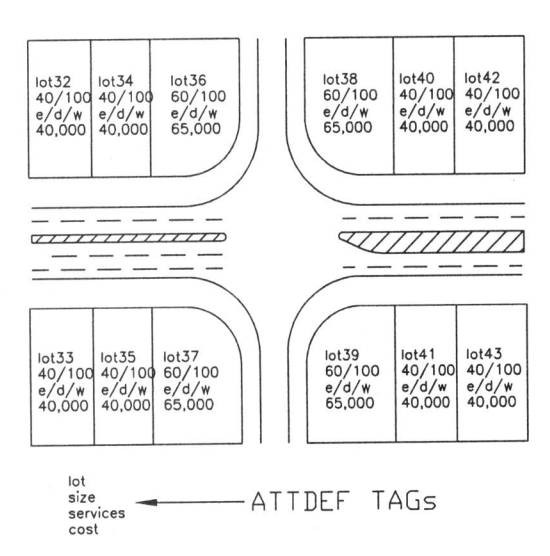

	lot32	lot34	lot36		lot38	lot40	lot42
	40/100	40/100	60/100		60/100	40/100	40/100
	e/d/w	e/d/w	e/d/w		e/d/w	e/d/w	e/d/w
	40,000	40,000	65,000		65,000	40,000	40,000

	lot33	lot35	lot37		lot39	lot41	lot43
	40/100	40/100	60/100		60/100	40/100	40/100
	e/d/w	e/d/w	e/d/w		e/d/w	e/d/w	e/d/w
	40,000	40,000	65,000		65,000	40,000	40,000

lot
size   ← ATTDEF TAGs
services
cost

Creating Attributes

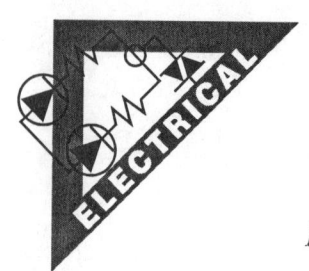

Exercise E14

Title Block — Retrieve your title block from Chapter 8 or create a new one. Use ATTDEF to define the attributes.

Block the attributes and title block. Insert it to see how it works.

Wiring Devices — Create four wiring devices with attributes containing color, price, and finish. Insert the blocks with attributes where necessary.

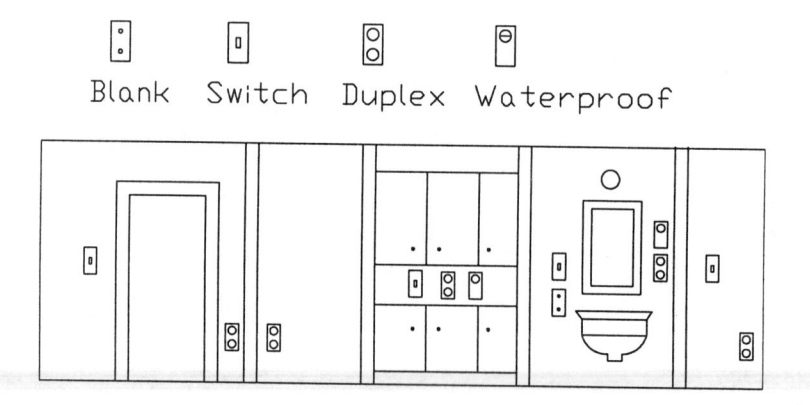

Blank   Switch   Duplex   Waterproof

Exercise M14

Title Block Retrieve your title block from Chapter 8 or create a new one. Use ATTDEF to define the attributes.

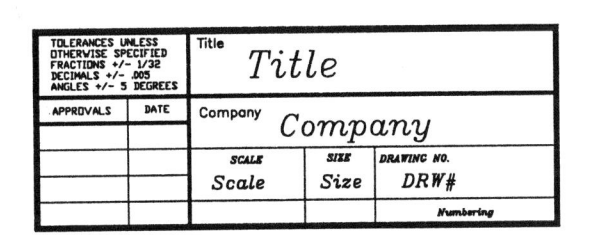

	Title		
TOLERANCES UNLESS OTHERWISE SPECIFIED FRACTIONS +/- 1/32 DECIMALS +/- .005 ANGLES +/- 5 DEGREES	*Title*		
APPROVALS DATE	Company *Company*		
	SCALE *Scale*	SIZE *Size*	DRAWING NO. *DRW#*
			Numbering

Block the attributes and title block. Insert it to see how it works.

	Title		
TOLERANCES UNLESS OTHERWISE SPECIFIED FRACTIONS +/- 1/32 DECIMALS +/- .005 ANGLES +/- 5 DEGREES	*Crane Hook*		
APPROVALS DATE	Company *Miller Inc*		
	SCALE *1=1*	SIZE *A4*	DRAWING NO. *ch-48*
			Sheet 1 of 1

Oiler Tray This is an assembly drawing for an oiler tray. Create one wire support rod. Add the part, part number, etc. as attributes. Then insert it six times on the drawing where needed.

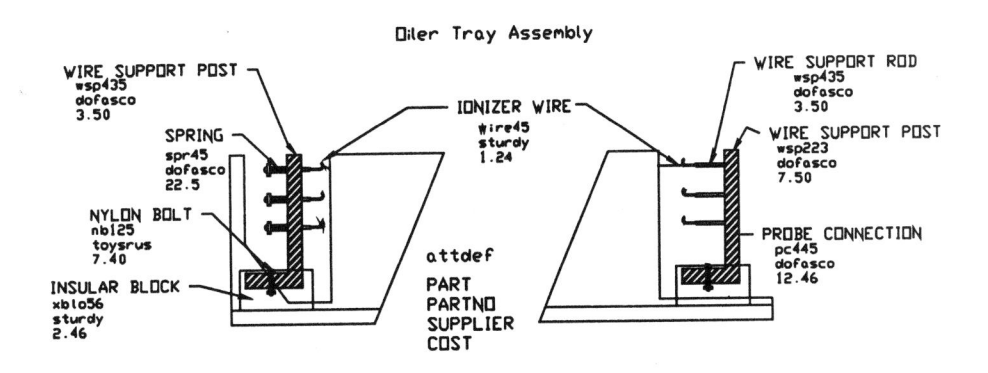

Oiler Tray Assembly

- WIRE SUPPORT POST — wsp435, dofasco, 3.50
- SPRING — spr45, dofasco, 22.5
- NYLON BOLT — nb125, toysrus, 7.40
- INSULAR BLOCK — xbl056, sturdy, 2.46
- IONIZER WIRE — wire45, sturdy, 1.24
- WIRE SUPPORT ROD — wsp435, dofasco, 3.50
- WIRE SUPPORT POST — wsp223, dofasco, 7.50
- PROBE CONNECTION — pc445, dofasco, 12.46

attdef
PART
PARTNO
SUPPLIER
COST

Do the same for each separate part. Create the geometry, add the attributes, and block them. Then insert them to complete the drawing.

Challenger 14

1. Draw the outline of a typical small office.
2. Draw two chairs, one slightly more complicated than the other, and two desks, one slightly larger than the other. Use the dimensions in Challenger 4.
3. Use ATTDEF to define the product number, description of the part, color, trim color, and price for the chairs, the desks, and the wall panels or dividers. Block each desk and each chair with their associated attributes separately.
4. Insert the windows and furnishings to make a full office layout.
5. Use ATTEXT to extract the product listing.

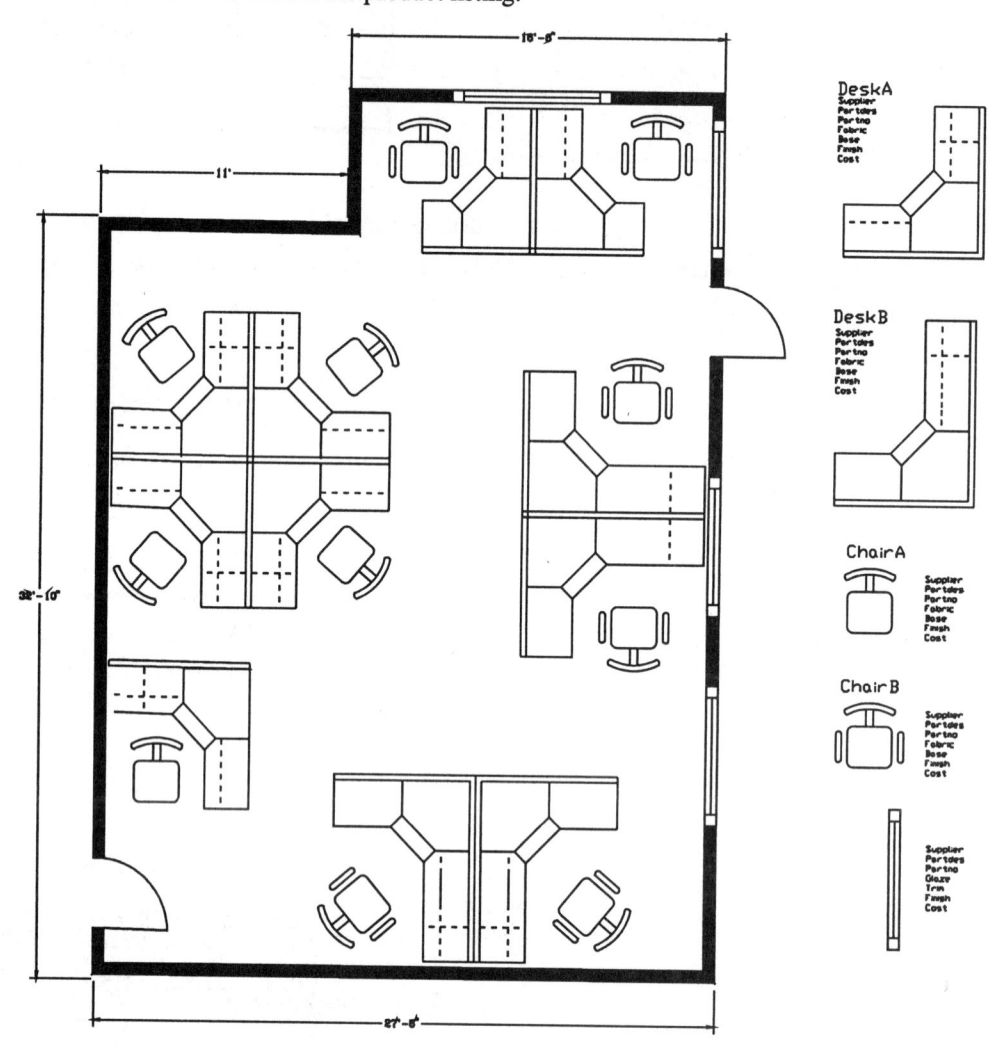

6. Take this attribute extract file into a spreadsheet or processing package that can produce a sum total for the price. Add applicable taxes, shipping of 10%, and $1200 installation charges to the total.

If you are using Lotus, you will need to PARSE the information before you can perform equations on it.

Then using the same office, change the color scheme of both the chairs and the offices. Change the trim to wood. This will reflect a different price for the entire office. Create another extract file and another quotation of the desks.

For a mechanical part of similar difficulty, see Challenger 15.

15 Editing and Extracting Attributes

Upon completion of this chapter, you should be able to:

1. Edit attributes
2. Extract attribute data to an ASCII format

Editing Attributes Attached to Blocks

As we saw in Chapter 14, you can use DDEDIT or Edit Text to edit an attribute definition before it is associated with a block.

Once the attributed block is in the drawing, you may want to edit the attributes that are already attached to a block and inserted in a drawing. To do this, use ATTEDIT.

CHANGE alters the characteristics of existing attribute *definitions* before they are blocked. Using the ATTEDIT command, you can change both the string value and the other characteristics of a blocked, inserted attribute.

The ATTEDIT Command

Toolbar From the Modify II toolbar, choose Edit Attribute.

Pull Down From the Modify menu, Attribute, then single.

The command line equivalent is **-ATTEDIT**.

You will be prompted to choose the block to edit.

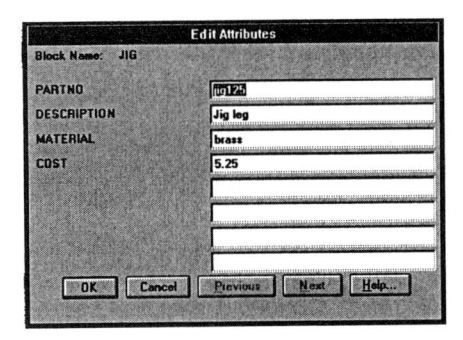

Figure 15-1

Use this dialog box the same way that you would use the Text Edit box. Change what you need to change, then pick OK.

Editing and Extracting Attributes **379**

Editing Individual Attributes

For example, to change the string value and color of just one attributed block, enter -ATTEDIT at the command line, then choose to edit one by one.

```
Edit attributes one at a time? [Yes/No]<Y>:↵
```

You will be notified as to how many of the selected attributes have been chosen and an X will appear on the attribute you are editing. You will be prompted for filtering of tags, block names, and value specifications; just press ↵ to accept all the attributes chosen.

Then you will be prompted for the following possible changes:

```
Enter block name specification <*>:↵
Enter attribute tag specification <*>:↵
Enter attribute value specification <*>:↵
Select Attributes:(Pick an Attribute)
Enter an option
   [Value/Position/Height/Angle/Style/Layer/Color/Next]<N>:
```

This will highlight the string values one by one and offer the user the possibility of changing each one as in the following options.

Where: **VAL** = attribute value (the text string or what it says)
       POS = position of the text
       Hgt = text height
       ANG = angle of the text
       Style = text style
       Lay = layer
       Color = color
       Next = next

The response to each option is similar to that of CHANGE. Be sure you are answering the question posed and you will be fine.

The most common change required is the value. This will change what the attribute actually reads. Accept the default <N> for the next attribute, and scroll through until you have the top attribute, which will be your part number, then make changes.

```
[Value/Position/Height/Angle/Style/Layer/Color/Next]<N>:V
Change or Replace:R
New string:JIG135
[Value/Position/Height/Angle/Style/Layer/Color/Next]<N>:C
New color:BLUE
[Value/Position/Height/Angle/Style/Layer/Color/Next]<N>:N
```

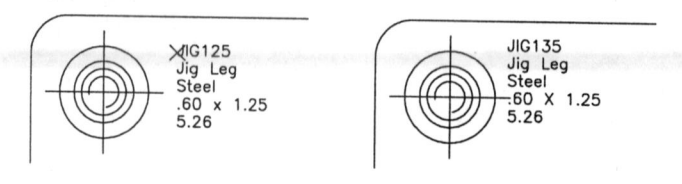

Figure 15-2

You can continue changing the attribute values, or use **Ctrl-C** to exit the command. The **N** option allows you to scroll on to the next attribute.

Editing Attributes Globally

When you are editing attributes with ATTEDIT one by one, you can change any of the values (orientation, text height, location, or string value); but when you perform a global edit, only the string value changes. A *global edit* is an edit that changes all of the attributes at once. A *string value* is the text actually created by the attributed block instance; a string of text is simply a line of characters. To access global editing:

> **Toolbar** From the Modify II toolbar, choose Edit Attribute.
>
> **Pull Down** From the Modify menu, Attribute, then Global.

The command line equivalent is **ATTEDIT**.

```
Command: -ATTEDIT
Edit attributes one at a time?<Y>:N
```

A positive response (**Y**) will identify and edit each attribute one by one. A negative response (**N**) will edit all of the attributes at once. It is easier, though not necessary, to have the attributes displayed when you are editing them. AutoCAD asks if only the visible ones are to be edited, then prompts for the parts of the attributes to be edited.

```
Enter block name specification <*>:
Enter attribute tag specification <*>:PARTNO
Enter attribute value specification <*>:
```

The * is a "wildcard" and indicates that all of the items will be changed. You can accept this default and change string values in all the blocks, under any tags and values. If you want to change just attribute values in one type of block or one tag, specify the desired tag or value to avoid cycling through all the rest. You can use the block name, the tag name, and the string value to limit the number of attributes that will be edited. In the example above, only the PARTNO will be changed.

Finally, you are asked to select which attributes to change. Window or Crossing can be used to identify the attributes, but these must be preceded by **W** for Window or **C** for Crossing at the "Select attributes:" prompt.

```
Select attributes:W
First corner: (pick 1)
Other corner: (pick 2)
5 attributes selected.
```

You will now be asked for the string to change.

Notes
When changing the string value, be sure to specify upper- or lowercase letters when needed.

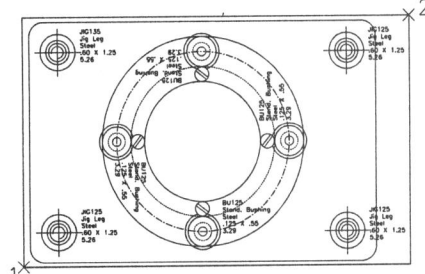

Figure 15-3

```
Enter string to change:JIG125 ("jig125" will not work)
Enter new string:JIG135
```

The ATTEDIT command changes the properties or value of the attribute once it has been inserted. The CHANGE command changes the tag, prompt, or default value of the attribute definition before it is blocked.

ATTEDIT for Global Edit — An Example

Attributes can also be copied and changed, which can save a lot of time.

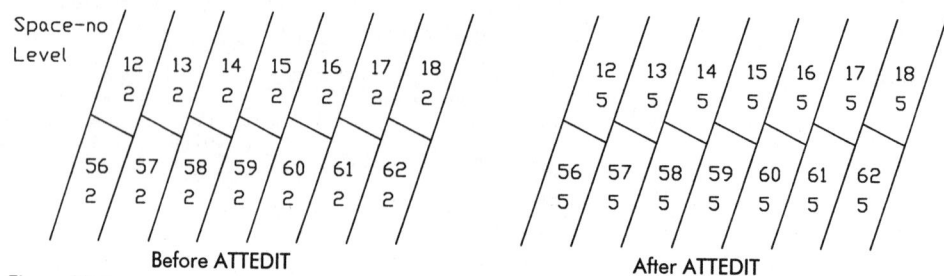

Figure 15-4

Step 1

Draw a series of parallel lines as in the illustration on the left. Create an attribute to define a space number and a level. Make the tag for the level LEVEL, and block the attributes under the name PARK. Insert the attributes as in the illustration on the left, making a series of different space numbers and keeping the level constant by accepting the default.

Step 2

Copy the parking lot over to the right. All of the attributed block instances will be copied as well.

Step 3

The second parking lot will be on level 5. The space number information will remain the same but the level will change.

Use ATTEDIT to quickly change all of the level specifications.

```
Command:ATTEDIT
Edit attributes one at a time? [Yes/No]<Y>:N
Global edit of attribute values.
Edit only attributes visible on screen?<Y>:↵
Enter block name specification <*>:PARK
Enter attribute tag specification <*>:LEVEL
Enter attribute value specification <*>:2
Select attributes:W
First corner: (pick 1)
Other corner: (pick 2)
14 attributes selected.
Enter string to change:2
Enter new string:5
```

Be careful to choose a string justification that will allow editing of the text, because the text string will be repositioned when the number of characters changes.

Data Extraction

Now that the data is entered correctly, you can have it printed out onto a spreadsheet or materials list by using the command ATTEXT. This operation does not change the drawing in any way, but takes the attribute data to applications such as EXCEL, Lotus 1-2-3, or your favorite word processor.

You must create a template file to tell AutoCAD how to structure the file that contains the extracted information. Once this is completed, use ATTEXT to extract the information.

Extract File Formats

There are three main formats for data extraction.

- **CDF** Comma-delimited format
- **SDF** Space-delimited format
- **DXF** Drawing interchange file

CDF (comma-delimited format) takes each attributed block and extracts the attributes into a record where each attribute is separated by a comma. The extract file would look like this:

```
JIG135,Jigleg,Steel,.60 x 1.25,5.26
```

SDF (space-delimited format) will, again, provide one line for each occurrence of each block. In this format, there are no commas, the template file must specify the length of field for each extract, and any data that exceeds this limit is truncated. The extract file should look like this:

```
JIG135    Jigleg    Steel    .60 x 1.25    5.26
```

Note the difference in the format of this file as opposed to that of the CDF file. Note also that the area where the description appears must be large enough to contain all the letters.

Both the CDF and the SDF file must be made with a template file.

DXF (drawing interchange file) is the format used by many third-party programmers for drawing enhancements, analysis programs, and related applications. The DXF format is also used for exchange of engineering data, geological data, and nesting routines, as well as the extraction of purely spatial information. The extract file will contain all of the information in the block, such as insertion point, rotation angle, and X,Y,Z values. This creates a file with a .DXX extension. On some systems, you can also specify a filename of .CON to send the attribute extract directly to the screen, or .PRN to send it to a printer. Make sure your printer is connected before you use .PRN.

Template Files

A *template file* identifies the structure of the extracted information. It specifies which attributes are to be extracted, what information is to be included, and what the extract file will look like.

The template file must have the extension .TXT. Each line of the template file specifies one field to be written in the extract file. The extract file will contain the information in the order given in the template file.

For the jigleg example using an SDF format, your extract file might look like this:

```
JIG        Jigleg          Steel    .60 x 1.25    5.26
JIG135     Jigleg          Steel    .60 x 1.25    5.26
BU135      Stand. Bushing  Steel    .125 x .55    3.29
BU135      Stand. Bushing  Steel    .125 x .55    3.29
```

The template file might look like this:

```
PARTNO C008000
DESCRIPT C015000
MATERIAL C008000
SIZE C008000
PRICE C008000
```

The template file is set up with the tag plus the code:

```
PARTNO C008000
```

Where: **PARTNO** = TAG
       C = character
       008 = 8 characters maximum in the jig name (C**008**000)
       000 = number of decimal places (none are needed for a character field)

If your entry consists exclusively of numbers, as in the case of the price, you can use an N, which will signify a numeric field. If there is anything other than numbers, you must use a C. If the entry contains both numbers and letters, use C. If you want the block name and the *X,Y* factors, use BL:.

	Field Name	C or N, Field Width of C or N, Decimal Places if N
Block name	BL:JIG1	C008000
Insertion point	BL:X	N007001
	BL:Y	N007001
	PARTNO	C008000
	DESCRIPT	C015000
Attribute tags	MATERIAL	C008000
	SIZE	C008000
	PRICE	C008000

Creating the Template File

Create the file using one of the following methods:

> **Toolbar** Access Notepad or similar text editor if you can.
>
> **Pull Down** None available; at the command line, enter SHELL.

```
Command: SHELL
OS Command: EDIT TEMPLATE.TXT
```

Type in the template file as outlined above using either the tags or the blocks. Then use ATTEXT to extract the file.

> **Toolbar** There is no button or pull down available.

The command line equivalent is **ATTEXT** or **DDATTEXT**.

Creating the Extract file

Once the template file has been created, you can extract the data using the command ATTEXT. This will ask for the name of the template file and the name of the extract file.

```
Command: ATTEXT
CDF, SDF, or DXF Attribute extract ? (or entities)<C>: SDF
Template file <default>: TEMPLATE (this is the template file you
   created)
Extract file name <JIG>: ⏎ (this is the extract file)
8 records in extract file.
```

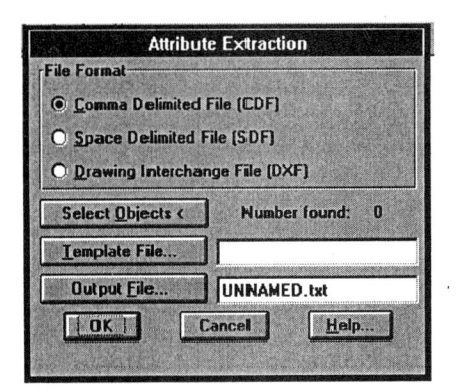

Figure 15-5

Editing and Extracting Attributes **385**

What Can Go Wrong with an ATTEXT

Field Overflow

On the readout after the ATTEXT command you may get a message saying:

```
Field overflow on line 3
```

This means that there are not enough spaces for characters in the template file. To remedy this situation, you must return to the template file and allow more characters in the field. For example, you may have allowed for only ten characters for the DESCRIPT tag:

```
DESCRIPT C010000
```

In this case the string value "Stand. Bushing" will be truncated, because it contains more than ten characters, and there will be a field overflow.

Extra Lines in File

When you are entering your template file, make sure that there are no extra lines in the file. Use a hard return on the last line of the text, but do not use a hard return after the final entry.

```
PARTNO   C008000[HRt]
DESCRIPT C015000[HRt]
MATERIAL C008000[HRt]
SIZE     C008000[HRt]
PRICE    C080000[HRt]
Use the down arrow to make sure there are no extra lines here.
```

> **Danger**
>
> The new file created by the ATTEXT command has the extension .TXT. Be sure that you do not have the same name for the template and the extract file; otherwise you will lose one of the files. There is no prompt to tell you that you are overwriting the first file.

Flow Chart for Creating ATTribute EXTracts

Start by creating the drawing and the attributes, and then create the template file. Alternatively you can start by creating the template file, as long as both the template and the attributed block instances are created when you use ATTEXT.

If you *start* by creating your template file, you can decide what information you need and then create the attributes to provide this information.

Create template a:template.txt → Create attributes → Use ATTEXT to extract data

OR:

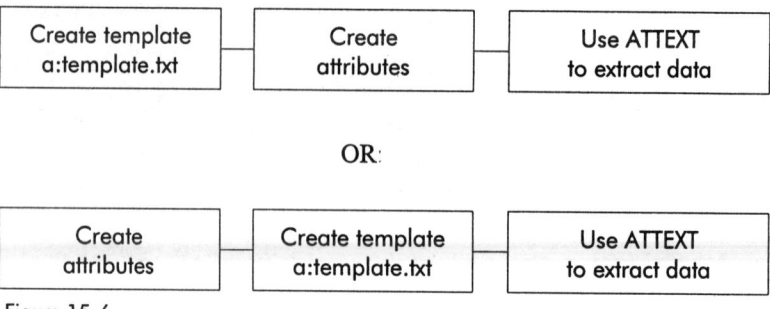

Create attributes → Create template a:template.txt → Use ATTEXT to extract data

Figure 15-6

Prelab 15 Editing and Extracting Attributes

Step 1 Retrieve your file from Prelab 16B. If your attributes are turned off, turn them back on with ATTDISP.

Step 2 Use the following command to change all of the part numbers for the bushing. The command line equivalent is **ATTEDIT**.

> **Toolbar** From the Modify II toolbar, choose Attedit.
>
> **Pull Down** From the Modify menu, choose Object, then Attribute.

```
Command:ATTEDIT
Edit attributes one at a time?<Y>:N
Global edit of attribute values.
Edit only attributes visible on
    screen?<Y>:↵
Block name specification
  <*>:ATTBUSH
Enter attribute tag specification <*>:↵
Enter attribute value specification <*>:↵
Select attributes:W
First corner: (pick 1)
Other corner: (pick 2)
20 attributes selected.
Enter string to change:BU125 ("BU" must be uppercase)
Enter new string:BU135
```

Use **INSERT ?** to find the name of the block if you think it may be different from ATTBUSH.

Notice that the prompts in ATTEDIT change with regard to the options chosen. In this example, it is a global edit, so *all* attributes will be changed at once. Since the attributes will not be highlighted, you are asked if the invisible attributes will be changed as well.

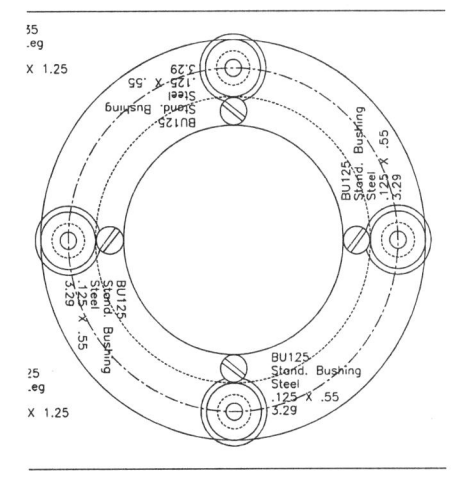

Editing and Extracting Attributes **387**

Step 3 Make a note of the tags of your attributes. If you have forgotten what they are, use LIST. Note the name of the tag exactly (no spelling errors are allowed).

Step 4 Now create a template file.
```
Command:SHELL
DOS Command:EDIT TEMPLATE.TXT

Command:EDIT
File to edit:TEMPLATE.TXT
  PARTNO   C008000
  DESCRIPT C020000
  MATERIAL C010000
  SIZE     C010000
  PRICE    C008000
^Z (Ctrl-Z)
Command:
```

The template file will be saved on your disk as TEMPLATE.TXT. TEMPLATE is the name of the file and can be changed; .TXT is the extension and must not be changed.

You have now written a template file for an extract. It uses the template file TEMPLATE.TXT and the attribute data to merge the files.

Step 5 Back at the Graphics screen, enter the ATTEXT command to extract the data into a separate file.

> **Toolbar** There is no button or pull down available

The command line equivalent is **ATTEXT**.

```
Command:ATTEXT
CDF, SDF, or DXF Attribute extract ? (or entities)<C>:SDF
Template file <default>:TEMPLATE
Extract file name <jig>:PRELAB13
8 records in extract file.
```

AutoCAD will tell you how many extracts you have. The extract filename will default to the drawing name unless changed. Make sure it is PRELAB13.

Step 6 Now take a look at your file in the editor. The file should be PRELAB13.TXT.

```
Command:SHELL
OS command:EDIT
File to edit:PRELAB13.TXT
```

```
JIG125    Jig Leg          Steel    .60 x 1.25    5.26
JIG125    Jig Leg          Steel    .60 x 1.25    5.26
JIG125    Jig Leg          Steel    .60 x 1.25    5.26
JIG125    Jig Leg          Steel    .60 x 1.25    5.26
BU135     Stand. Bushing   Steel    .125 x .55    3.29
BU135     Stand. Bushing   Steel    .125 x .55    3.29
BU135     Stand. Bushing   Steel    .125 x .55    3.29
BU135     Stand. Bushing   Steel    .125 x .55    3.29
```

Step 7   There are often a few problems with the file the first time through. Either your fields were not large enough, or you have forgotten one field. In this case, the description area could be a little larger.

```
Command: EDIT
```

> **DOS** Use EDIT (or SHELL) to adjust your template file. Then try ATTEXT again.

```
File to edit: TEMPLATE.TXT

PARTNO   C008000
DESCRIPT C020000  (change to C025000)
MATERIAL C010000
SIZE     C010000
PRICE    C008000
```

Step 8   Now use ATTEXT to extract the file again, and look at it to make sure that the description area has been made larger.

Bringing Up the ASCII File in Other Software Packages

You have created a document that is written in ASCII format. If you want to bring this up in WordPerfect, Microsoft Word, or any other program, you can simply enter it as you would any text file. If you want to bring this file into Lotus, use Import and then Parse the file to create a columnar format.

Save the current file as JIG and exit the file.

Step 9   Sometimes you want a Bill of Materials or Window Schedule from the available attributes entered back onto your drawing. Use MTEXT and the Import Text button.

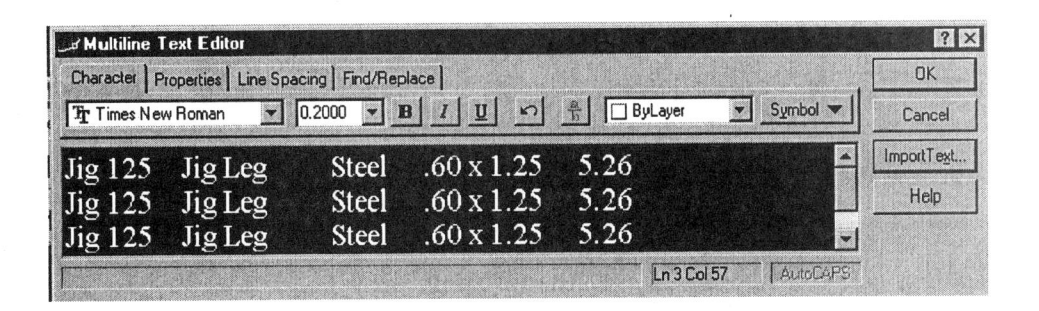

Editing and Extracting Attributes   **389**

Command and Function Summary

ATTEDIT edits the value of inserted attributes.

ATTEXT extracts information from attributes in your drawing file to a CDF, SDF, or DXF format.

DDATE opens a dialog box that allows you to edit inserted attribute blocks.

EDIT allows DOS users to create and edit a text file using the DOS editor.

Notepad allows Windows users to create text files.

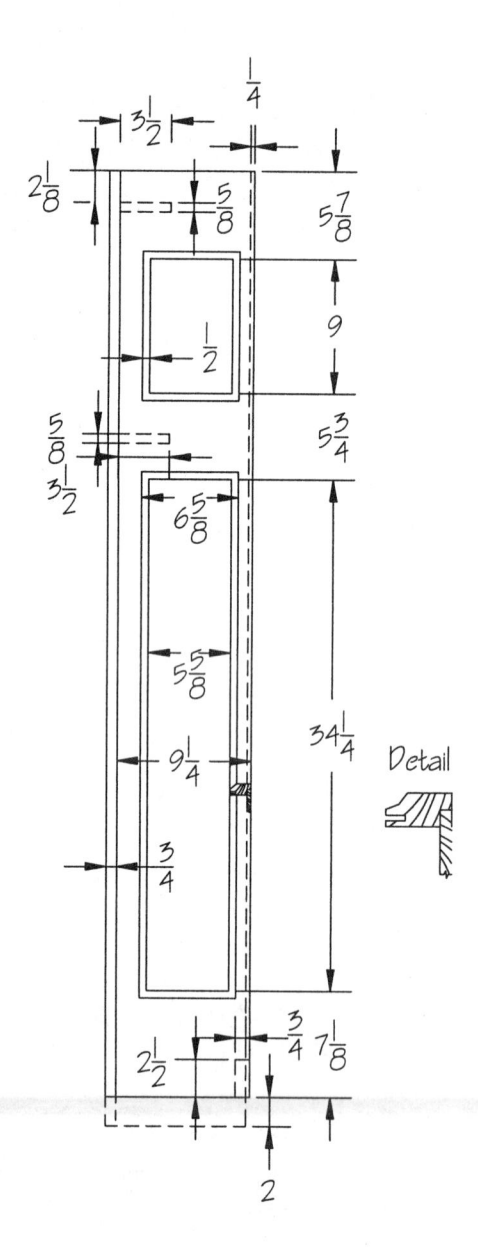

Right Side of Clock.

Exercise A15

Part 1 **Room Finishes**

In your floor plan layout, change all the carpet tile to linoleum. Change the black trim to navy.

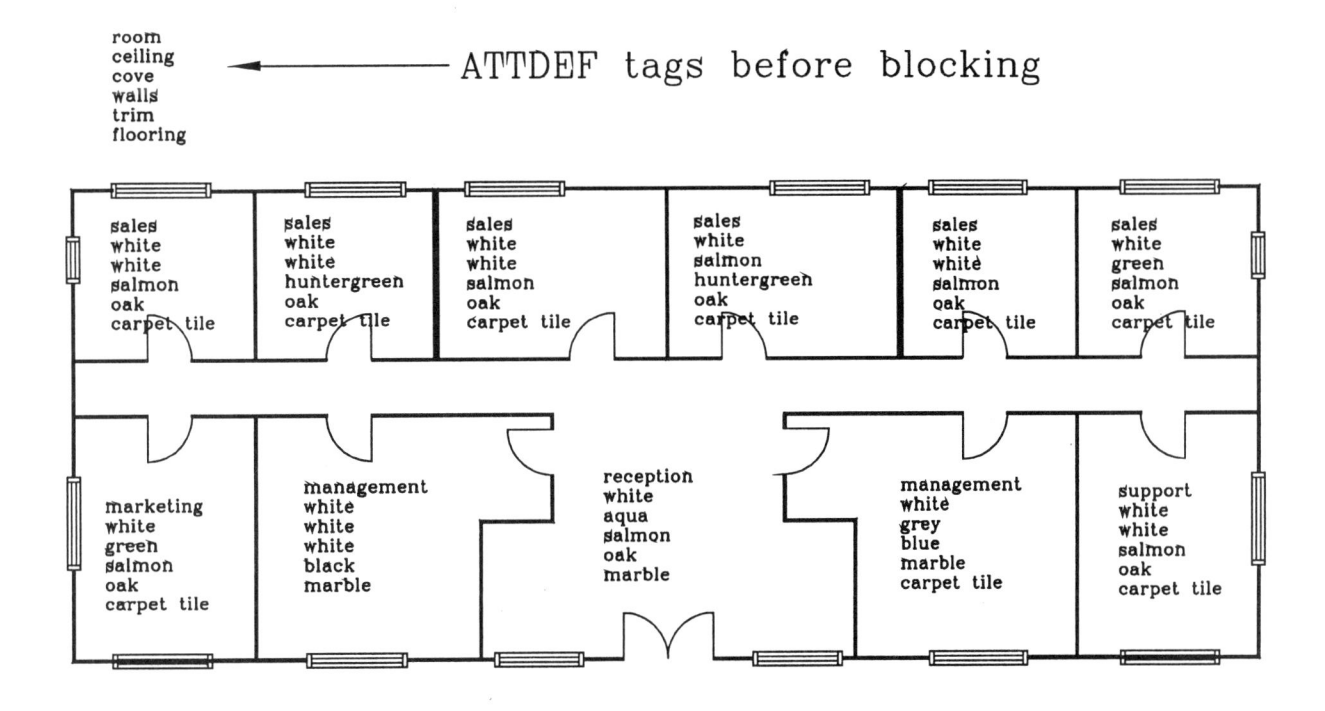

ATTDEF tags before blocking (pointing to):
- room
- ceiling
- cove
- walls
- trim
- flooring

Room finishes:

sales — white, white, salmon, oak, carpet tile

sales — white, white, huntergreen, oak, carpet tile

sales — white, white, salmon, oak, carpet tile

sales — white, salmon, huntergreen, oak, carpet tile

sales — white, white, salmon, oak, carpet tile

sales — white, green, salmon, oak, carpet tile

marketing — white, green, salmon, oak, carpet tile

management — white, white, white, black, marble

reception — white, aqua, salmon, oak, marble

management — white, grey, blue, marble, carpet tile

support — white, white, salmon, oak, carpet tile

Part 2 Then extract the attribute data onto an ASCII file, retrieve it into a word processing package such as WordPerfect, and print your color schedule.

Editing and Extracting Attributes

Exercise C15

Part 1 **A Survey**

On your survey, change the price of the 40,000 lots to 42,000. Then change the 65,000 to 67,000.

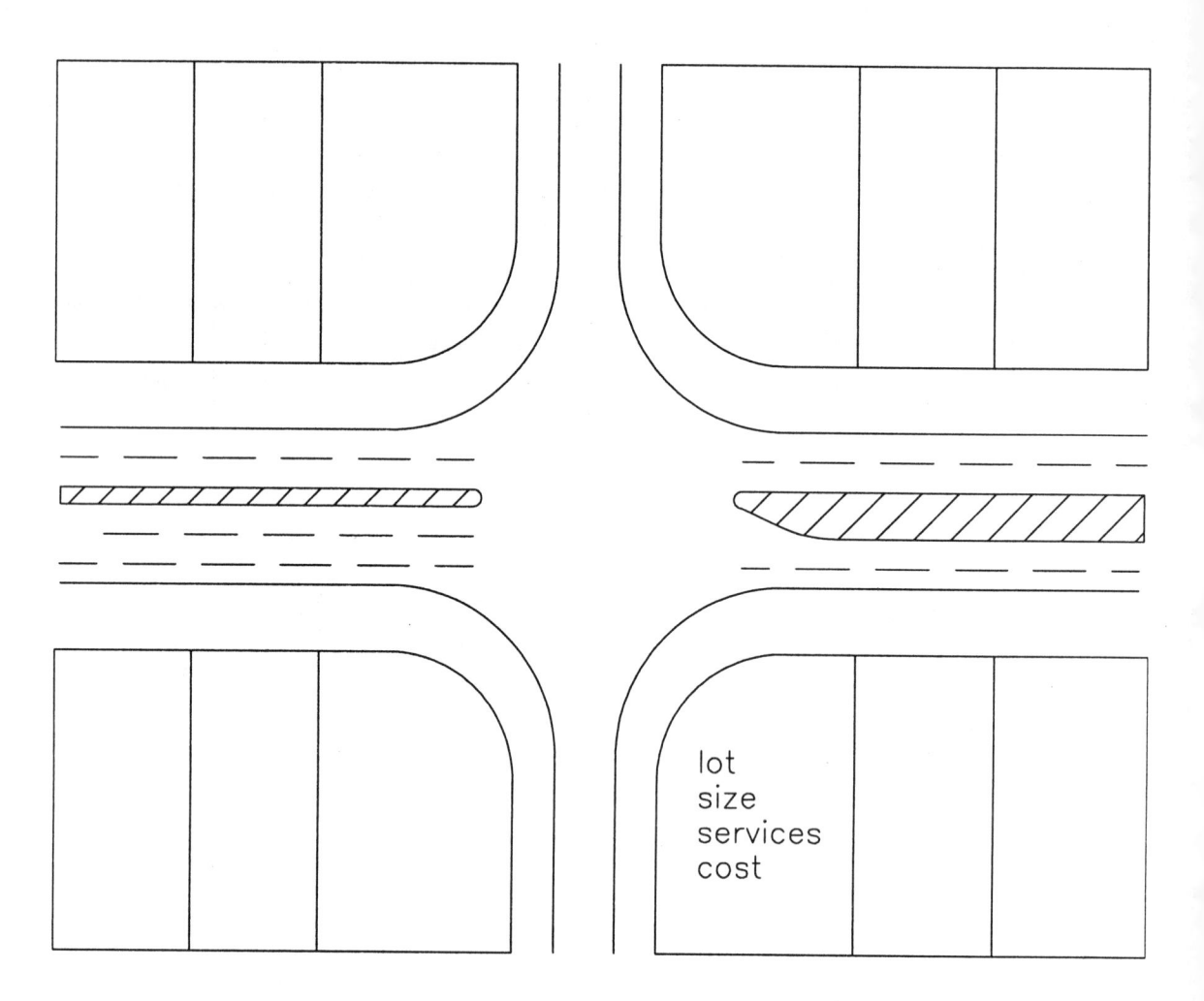

lot
size
services
cost

Part 2 Now extract the data into an ASCII file. Bring the file up in WordPerfect or a similar package, and create a listing of the lots and their values. Print the listings.

Exercise E15

Part 1 **Wiring Devices**

On your wall layout, change the color of all of the white fixtures to bone. Now change the prices by adding .15.

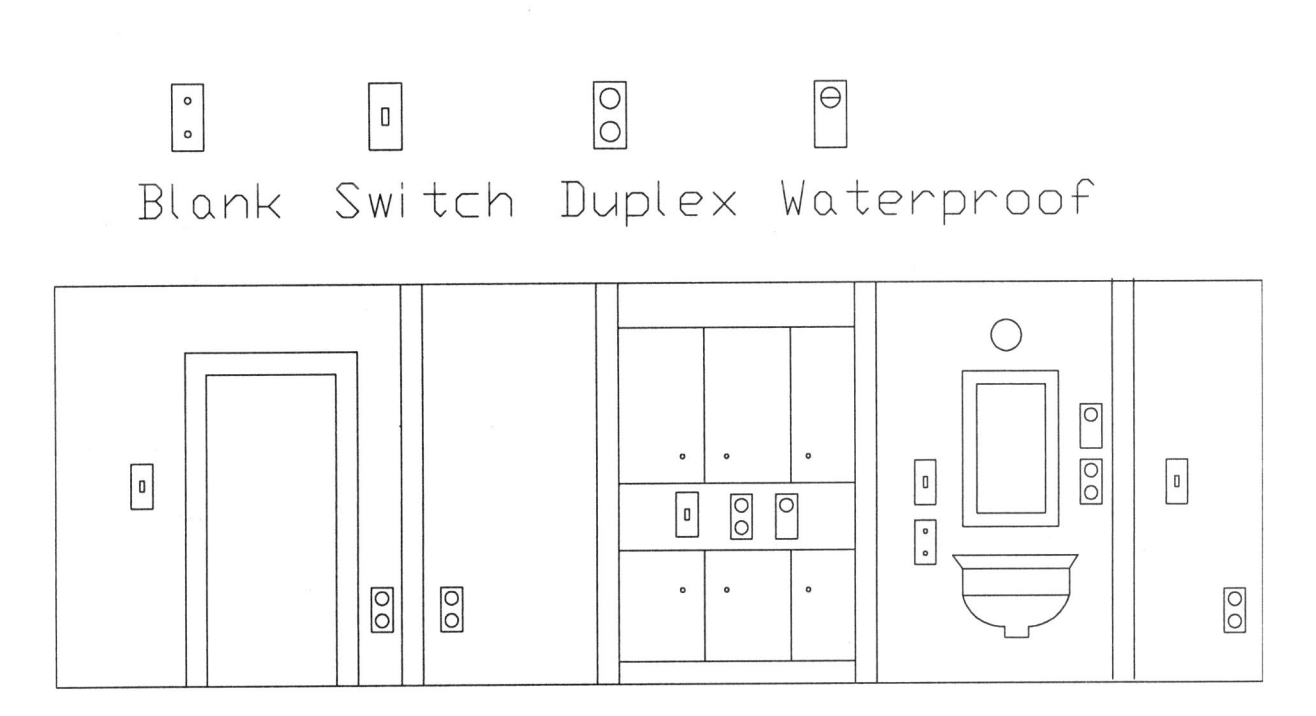

Part 2 Now extract this data into an ASCII format. Bring up the extract file into WordPerfect or a similar application. Create a full bill of materials.

Exercise M15

Part 1 **Oiler Tray**

Change the price of the wire support rod to 4.50. Change that of the nylon bolt to 8.25.

Oiler Tray Assembly

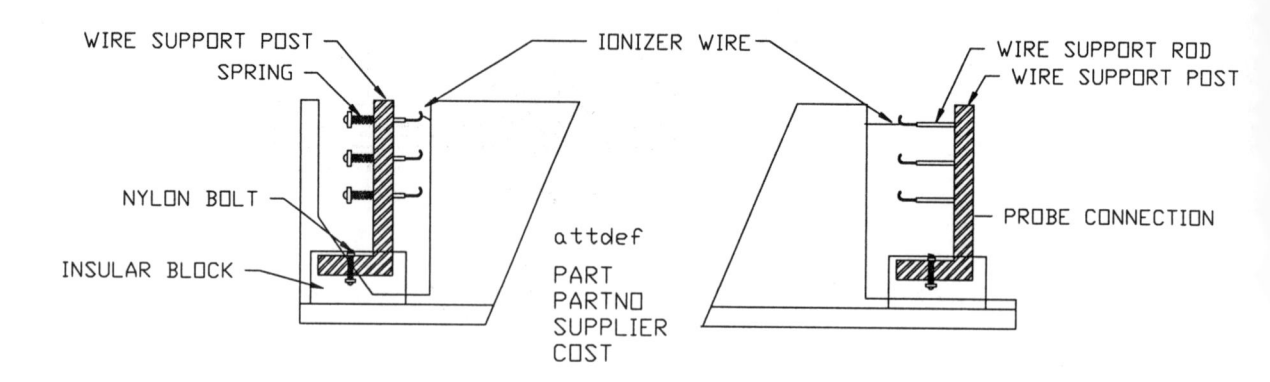

- WIRE SUPPORT POST
- SPRING
- IONIZER WIRE
- WIRE SUPPORT ROD
- WIRE SUPPORT POST
- NYLON BOLT
- PROBE CONNECTION
- INSULAR BLOCK

attdef
PART
PARTNO
SUPPLIER
COST

Part 2 Now extract the attribute data from all of the parts on this assembly into an ASCII file.

In Lotus or a similar package, create a spreadsheet for the costs of the parts. Print out a bill of materials.

Challenger 15A

1. Draw this airbrush nozzle. For each individual part, create attributes for part number, description, material, and cost. Block the attributes with the parts. Insert them back into the assembly.

2. Create a template file for the part numbers, material, description, and cost. Extract the file and create a bill of materials.

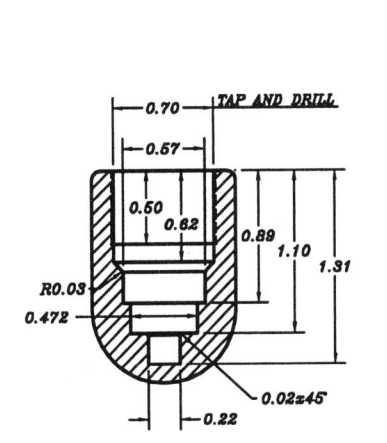

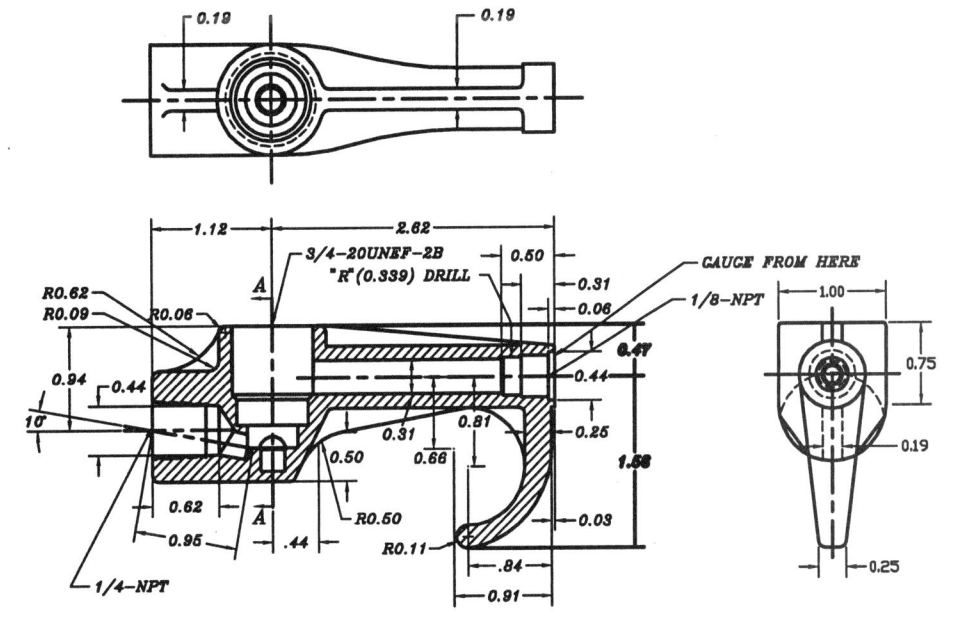

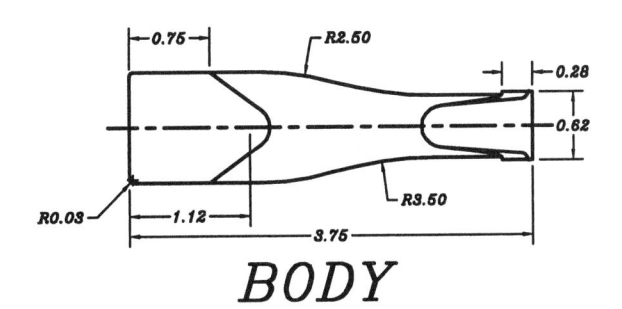

SECTION AA

BODY

Challenger 15B

Draw the part as shown. Block each object as a separate attributed file, and insert back into the drawing. Create a parts list from the various parts.

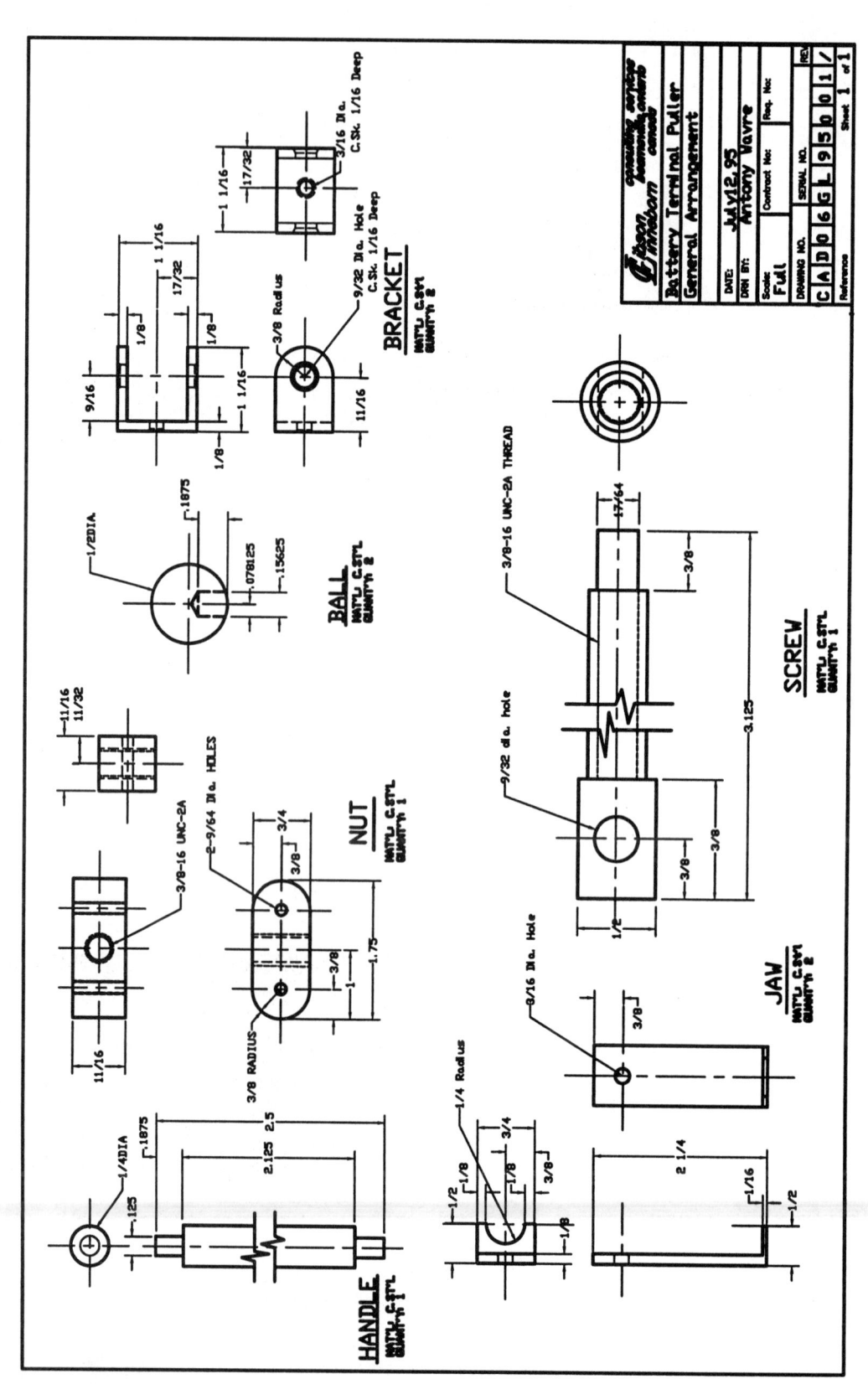

16 Isometric and Orthographic Drawings

Upon completion of this chapter, you should be able to:

1. Change SNAP to isometric to create isometric views
2. Use ISOPLANE to align arcs and circles to a certain plane
3. Change the obliquing angle of the text to create isometric text
4. Create orthographic views in 2D

Isometric Views

In AutoCAD, it is possible to create rotatable 3D models by means of more advanced commands. However, if you are only concerned with a 2D representation of a 3D model, similar to what you can get by drawing with pencil on paper, you will find it satisfactory to change SNAP and use the ISOPLANE commands. The results are not 3D, but look 3D. This method has the advantage of possibly enabling you to create an image much more quickly than you could with full 3D modelling techniques.

Changing the SNAP to Isometric

Remember from Chapter 1 that SNAP sets a spacing for point entries, and GRID places a dot grid on the screen.

SNAP allows for both rotated and isometric drawings to be entered. To access SNAP use either the command line or the Drawing Aids dialog box.

> **Toolbar** Not accessible through the toolbar
>
> **Pull Down** From the Tools menu, choose then Drawing Aids.

The command line equivalent is **SNAP**.

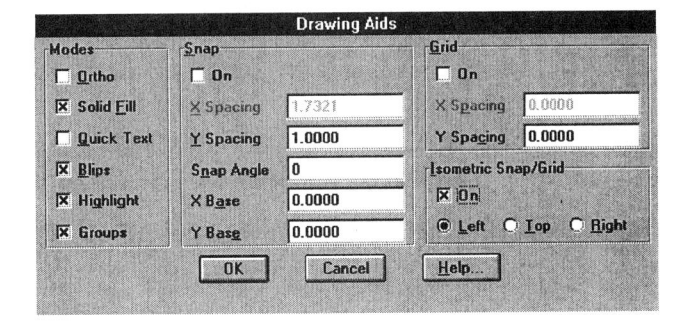

```
Command: SNAP
Snap spacing or ON/OFF/Aspect/Rotate/Style <1.0000>: S
Standard/Isometric <Standard>: I
Vertical spacing <0.4>:
```

Once you set SNAP you will notice that the grid is set at a 30 degree angle as well. The GRID size will follow the SNAP size unless changed. In addition, the crosshairs will be viewed at a 30 degree angle and ORTHO will also be isometric.

The easiest way to test the isometric snap is by drawing a simple cube on the screen with the aid of SNAP and GRID. The easiest way is to simply pick the points from the screen with the SNAP set to 1.

Follow the lines of the grid.

```
Command:LINE
Specify first point: (pick a point)
Specify next point or [Undo]:
(pick following the grid)
```

Now that you've seen how easy this is, how do you think coordinate entry reacts?

```
Command:LINE
Specify first point: (pick a point)
Specify next point or [Undo]:@2,0
Specify next point or [Undo]:@0,2
Specify next point or [Undo]:
```

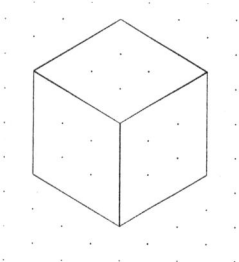

Figure 16-1

Notice that your line entries when using points from the screen SNAP to an isometric plane, but line entries using coordinates are not isometric.

Using ISOPLANE

Once you have entered the cube you will notice that the crosshairs line up with only one plane. Use ISOPLANE to get the crosshairs to line up with all three planes. Change the ISOPLANE through the Drawing Aids dialog box or by typing it in.

You can toggle to the next plane by using **Ctrl-E**. ISOPLANE is not available unless you have set SNAP to Isometric.

```
Command:ISOPLANE
Current isoplane: Left
Enter isometric plane setting
  [Left/Top/Right]<Top>:R
```

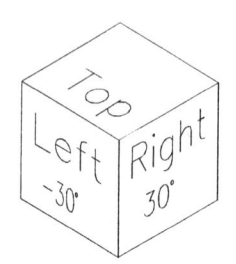

Figure 16-2

ISOPLANE will act as a toggle switch that toggles through the three planes and then off. ORTHO is useful when using ISOPLANE to make rectangular shapes.

Drawing Circles in Isometric

Lines can be entered quickly without ISOPLANE and with the use of the SNAP, but circles and arcs are entered relative to the actual *X,Y* plane, much like the line coordinate entry. In Figure 16-3(a), CIRCLE was used to create a circle, which on the isometric plane looks like an ellipse.

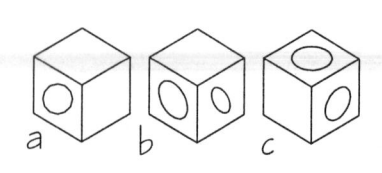

Figure 16-3

You will need to use ISOPLANE and ELLIPSE with the Isocircle option to create circles in the three standard isometric planes.

On the left cube, (a), a circle is drawn using the CIRCLE command.

The central circles shown on cube (b) are drawn relative to the left plane using the ELLIPSE command. The planes on cube (c) are toggled before the circles are added.

```
Command:ELLIPSE
Specify axis endpoint of ellipse or [Arc/Center/Isocircle]:I
Specify center of isocircle: (pick 1)
Specify radius of isocircle or [Diameter]: (pick 2)
```

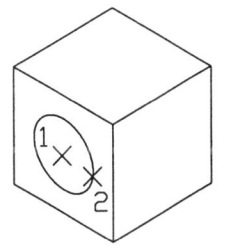

Figure 16-4

The current isoplane governs the plane in which the circle will be drawn; change the ISOPLANE to change the orientation of the circle.

Drawing LINEs at Angles

Because this is a 2D drawing, lines are drawn relative to the *X-Y* plane.

```
Command:LINE
Specify first point: (pick 1)
Specify next point or [Undo]:@1<0
Specify next point or [Undo]:↵
Command:LINE
Specify first point: (pick 2)
Specify next point or [Undo]:@1<30
Specify next point or [Undo]:↵
```

(a) (b)
Figure 16-5

Thus, lines drawn at angles will not be rotated relative to the ISOPLANE. In this illustration, the lines are drawn as rotated normal to the *X-Y* plane.

In order to add a line at an angle relative to the isoplane, add 30 degrees to the angle that you need.

```
Command:LINE
Specify first point: (pick a point)
Specify next point or [Undo]:@1<75
```

This will give you a line of 45 degrees relative to the current plane.

Prelab 16A An Isometric Example

This example will illustrate how to change SNAP and ISOPLANE, and how to use ELLIPSE with ISOCIRCLE to generate this simple part.

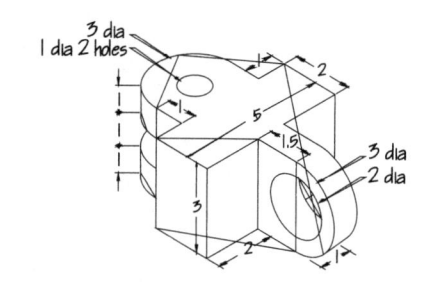

Step 1 Start by setting SNAP to isometric with a value of .5, and GRID to a value of 1. Then put in the lines as shown. Setting the coordinate readout to relative coordinates (F6) will help to attain the correct dimensions.

> **Pull Down** From the Tools menu, choose Drawing Aids.

The command line equivalent is **SNAP**.

```
Command:SNAP
Specify snap spacing or [ON/OFF/Rotate/Style/Type]<0.5000>:S
Enter snap grid style [Standard/Isometric]<I>:I
Specify vertical spacing <1.0>:.5
Command:GRID
Specify grid spacing (X) or [ON/OFF]:1
Command:LINE
Specify first point:
```

Add the lines as shown.

Step 2 Make sure that ISOPLANE is set to Left and add a circle using ELLIPSE.

```
Command:ISOPLANE
Current isoplane: Left
Enter isometric plane setting
[Left/Top/Right]<Top>:L
Command:ELLIPSE
Specify axis endpoint of ellipse or
[Arc/Center/Isocircle]:I
Specify center of isocircle: (pick 1)
Specify radius of isocircle or [Diameter]: (pick 2)
```

Now TRIM the left side of the circle to the two lines.

```
Command: TRIM
Select cutting edge(s) ...
Select objects: (pick 3)
Select objects: (pick 4)
Select objects: ⏎
Select object to trim or
   [Project/Edge/Undo]: (pick 5)
<Select object to trim>/Undo: ⏎
```

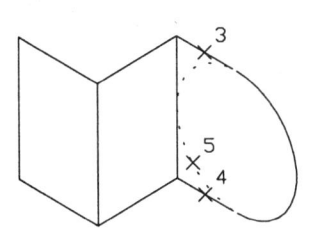

Step 3   Add the circle in the center of the arc, and then copy the arc, the circle, and the line onto the back plane. The dimensions are shown in the figure at the start of this Prelab.

```
Command: COPY
Select objects: (pick the arc, circle,
   and line)
Select objects: ⏎
Specify base point or displacement or
[Multiple]: (pick 6)
Specify second point of
displacement: (pick 7)
```

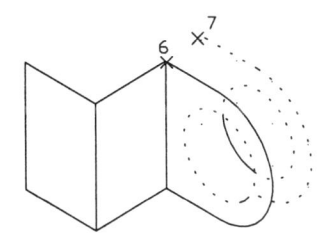

Step 4   The circle on the back plane needs to be trimmed behind the front plane. Remember that these objects are still only in 2D, so the TRIM command will work as it normally does.

```
Command: TRIM
Select cutting edge(s) ...
Select objects: (pick 8)
Select objects: ⏎
Select object to trim or Undo: (pick 9)
Select object to trim or Undo: ⏎
```

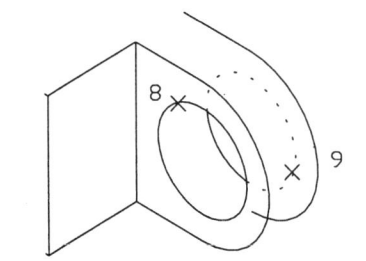

Step 5   With SNAP still on, create a line tangent to the first circle at a length of 1 unit at an angle of 30 degrees.

```
Command: LINE
Specify first point: TAN to (pick 10)
Specify next point or [Undo]: @1<30
Specify next point or [Undo]: ⏎
```

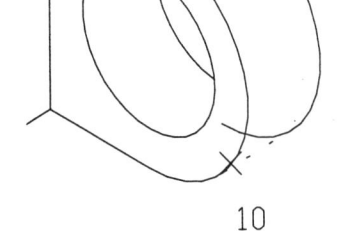

Step 6   Now trim the back arc to the line that you just entered.

```
Command: TRIM
Select cutting edge(s) ...
Select objects: (pick 11)
Select objects: ⏎
Select object to trim or Undo: (pick 12)
Select object to trim or Undo: ⏎
```

Isometric and Orthographic Drawings   **401**

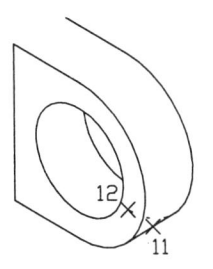

Step 7   Now using the crosshairs and SNAP, add the lines that make up the top and sides of the part.

The line visible through the hole in the part can be put in between two points, then trimmed.

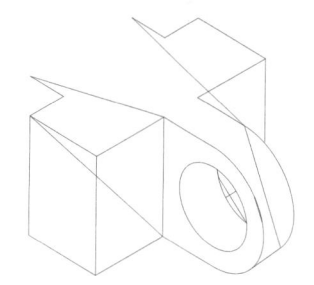

Step 8   Now change ISOPLANE to the top and add the circle along the top as shown.

```
Command:ISOPLANE
Current isoplane:Left
Enter isometric plane setting [Left
 /Top/Right]<Top>:⏎
```

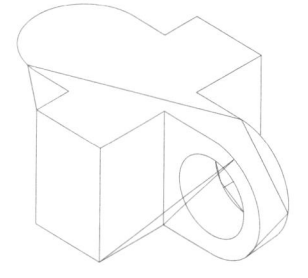

```
Command:ELLIPSE
Specify axis endpoint of ellipse or
 [Arc/Center/Isocircle]:I
Specify center of isocircle: (pick the center
 point)
Specify radius of isocircle or [Diameter]: (pick the end of
 the line)
```

Trim the circle as shown.

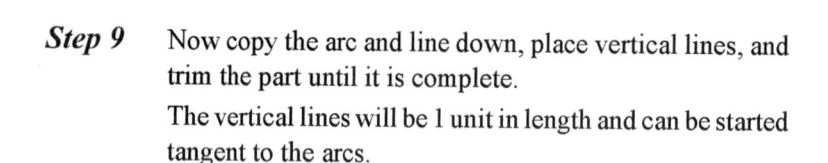

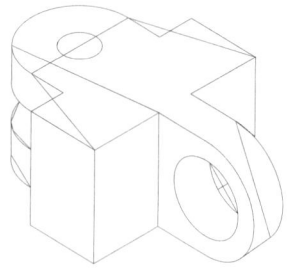

Step 9   Now copy the arc and line down, place vertical lines, and trim the part until it is complete.

The vertical lines will be 1 unit in length and can be started tangent to the arcs.

Finally, add the circle on the top for the hole.

Step 10   SNAP and ISOPLANE are set to isometric, but text will still be placed as circles would be placed, relative to the *X-Y* plane unless the obliquing angle is changed. We used isometric text in Chapter 8.

> **Pull Down** From the Format command, choose Text Style.

The command line equivalent is **STYLE**.

```
Command:STYLE
Text Style name <Monotxt>:NEG
Font File:CITYBLUEPRINT
Height <0.200>:⏎
Width <1.00>:⏎
Obliquing factor:-30
Backward <N>:⏎
Upside Down <N>:⏎
Vertical <N>:⏎
```

Now add your text using the Fit option.

```
Command:TEXT
Current text style:"NEG"
Height:0.2000
Specify start point of text or
   [Justify/Style]:F
Specify first endpoint of text
   baseline: (pick on the left)
Specify second endpoint of text
   baseline: (pick on the right)
Height <0.2000>:.7
Text:Top
```

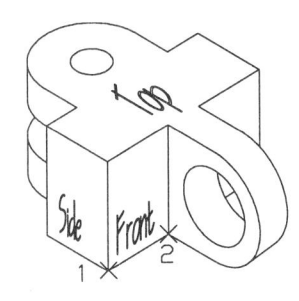

Create another text style called POS for positive, and change the obliquing angle to positive 90. Review Chapter 8 for more details.

When creating isometric text, use one of the fonts that is not already slanted such as Monotext, Standard, or any of the Roman fonts. The obliquing angle is calculated relative to the slant of the side.

Dimensioning isometric drawings can be quite tricky. Create an oblique text font, save it, and make it part of your dimension style. Use TEDIT if necessary.

Creating Orthographic Views

If you are drawing an object that needs to be seen in a number of views, you could — if you used advanced AutoCAD techniques — draw it in 3D, then generate multiple 2D views to fully define it in drawing format. Should you wish to create orthographic views starting in 2D, however, AutoCAD has many tools that can help you.

Traditionally, orthographic drawings include a set of views from mutually orthogonal lines of sight. The three most commonly drawn views are Top, Front, and Right Side as seen at right.

The top view is drawn above the front view because the two views share the dimension of width. The side view is placed beside the front view because the two views share the dimension of height.

In AutoCAD, point filters and layers can make this process simpler.

Using Layers with Construction Lines

You can use construction lines to line up the views. Point filters are quicker, and in many ways preferable, because they make better use of the computer; but until you become comfortable with point filters, use construction lines or ray line options.

Place construction lines on a separate layer so that you can freeze them later. Construction lines transfer the depth by projecting this value from the top view to the side view through a 45 degree angle.

Orthographic Projection — An Example

Here we will illustrate the procedure for determining the side view of this object with just the front and top views.

Set the drawing limits to 24 × 18. It is easiest to draw if the SNAP is set to 1 unit and GRID is on. ZOOM All will expand the file to the drawing limits.

The dimensions can be taken from the isometric view above.

To create the depth for the part, you can use a 45 degree *mitre line* (dotted line) and construction lines (hidden lines) to create construction lines to make sure they line up.

404 CHAPTER SIXTEEN

Adding Construction Lines from the Top View

The construction lines extend from the end of the lines on the top view, straight across to the diagonal line. This, in most cases, will not lie on a snap point, so use ORTHO to make the line straight; then make another line from the intersection of the diagonal line and the construction line straight down to line up with the bottom of the front view.

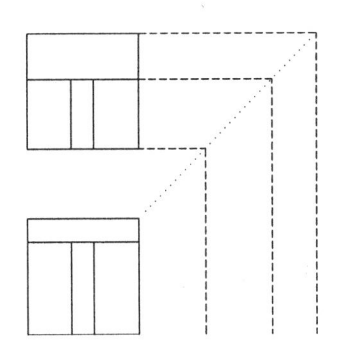

Adding Construction Lines from the Front View

On the front view, extend the construction lines straight across from the vertical points through to the far side of the existing construction lines.

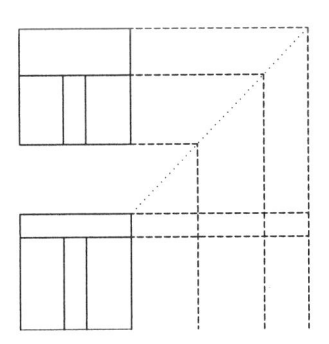

Finally, change your layer back to construction lines and draw in the outline of the part where the construction lines overlap.

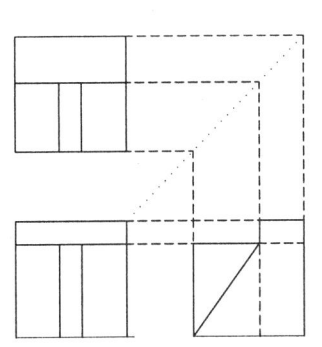

Turn the construction lines off and you will have the right side view.

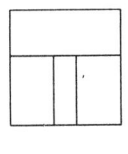

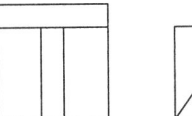

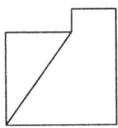

Isometric and Orthographic Drawings

Notes

Using OFFSET/FILLET and TRIM can be simpler.

You can now change SNAP to Isometric and draw in the isometric view. It is easiest to draw it in at a scale of 1:1. This will be far too large on the final drawing, so once it has been entered, scale the isometric to .66 of the original value.

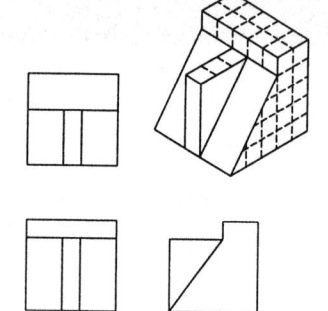

You now have a completed drawing.

Using another version of this rather simple formula, we will now create a top view from a front and side view.

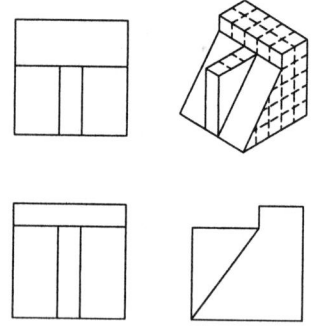

Prelab 16B Orthographic Projection

With the use of GRID and SNAP, orthographic projection of regular shapes is very simple. You may encounter trouble, however, when projecting arcs and ellipses as in the following example.

As you can see from the illustration, the arc in the right view is transformed into an ellipse in the Top view. You know the height of the arc from the front view, and the depth of the piece can be standardized with the use of construction lines. But how do you calculate the ellipse?

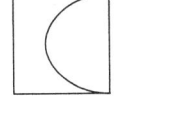

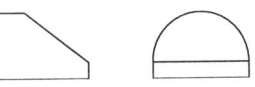

Step 1   First, draw in the part with simply the lines and the circles.

Step 2   Create a new layer for construction lines, and ensure that you change color and/or linetype. Make the new layer current. This is going to get a bit messy, so you might as well make the visualizing of the part as easy as possible.

Project the top horizontal and the right vertical lines on the front view to form a rectangle and draw in a line from the top projected to the furthest point on the right view.

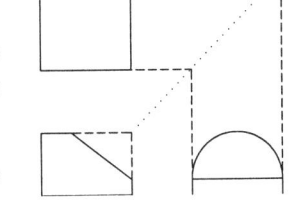

Draw in the rectangle of the outside of the top view using the construction lines, the SNAP, and the crosshairs.

Step 3   Now project a line from the right ENDpoint of the top horizontal line of the front view up through the top view (pick 1 and 2). Then project a line from the MIDpoint of the arc in the side view up through the 45 degree angle line (pick 3 and 4). Draw a horizontal line from the INTersection of the last line drawn and the 45 degree angle line to the first vertical projection line (pick 5 and 6).

```
Command:(F8 to put ORTHO on)
Command:LINE
Specify first point:END of (pick 1)
Specify next point or [Undo]: (pick 2)
Specify next point or [Undo]:↵
Command:LINE
Specify first point:QUAD of (pick 3)
Specify next point or [Undo]: (pick 4)
Specify next point or [Undo]:↵
Command:LINE
Specify first point:INT of (pick 5)
Specify next point or [Undo]:PER (Pick 6)
Specify next point or [Undo]:↵
```

This will create your first point, the left central axis of the ellipse.

Step 4   Now create another point on the ellipse using the same method. Draw a line from a random point (use NEAR) along the side on the sloping surface directly horizontal to the side view. Where this intersects, draw a line vertically to the 45 degree angle mark. Where this intersects, draw a line horizontally back to the Top view. Then draw a line from the first point vertically. The intersection with the previous line will be a correct point on the ellipse.

Isometric and Orthographic Drawings

Make sure your ORTHO is still on.

```
Command:LINE
Specify first point:NEAR (pick 1)
Specify next point or [Undo]: (pick 2)
Specify next point or [Undo]:↵
Command:LINE
Specify first point:INT of (pick 3)
Specify next point or [Undo]: (pick 4)
Specify next point or [Undo]:↵
Command:LINE
Specify first point:INT of (pick 5)
Specify next point or [Undo]: (pick 6)
Specify next point or [Undo]:↵
Command:LINE
Specify first point:INT of (pick 7)
Specify next point or [Undo]: (pick 8)
Specify next point or [Undo]:↵
```

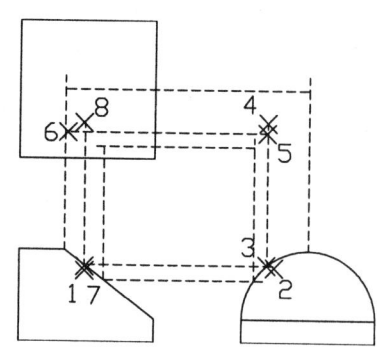

This will give you the second point of your ellipse. Identify another point in the same way.

Step 5 Now use the POINT command to create points at the intersection of the lines on the top view. Change your layer to the geometry layer before you start and turn ORTHO off. Setting SNAP to intersection will help.

```
Command:OSNAP
Object snap modes:INTersection
Command:POINT (pick the
   intersections)
```

Now MIRROR the points through the midpoint of the vertical line on the right.

Step 6 Finally, use the SPLINE command to create the spline. Use OFFSET with the distance of 2 to create a line, the endpoints of which will be used for the start and end tangent points.

With SPLINE, set Running Object Snap to both NODE and ENDpoint for easy access to endpoints.

Your part should be finished.

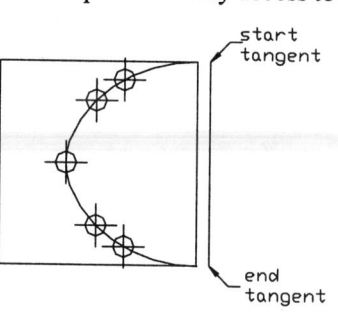

Command and Function Summary

ELLIPSE allows you to draw ellipses according to defined axes, or with the Isocircle option allows you to draw circles on receding planes.

ISOPLANE allows you to access any of the three planes in the SNAP's Isometric mode and set the axes to that plane.

SNAP with Style Isometric allows you to draw in isometrics. GRID, crosshairs, and **ORTHO** will change to isometric mode as well.

STYLE with a change in the obliquing angle allows text entry on a receding plane.

For the head of the clock, use these dimensions as a guide, or make up a style of your own.

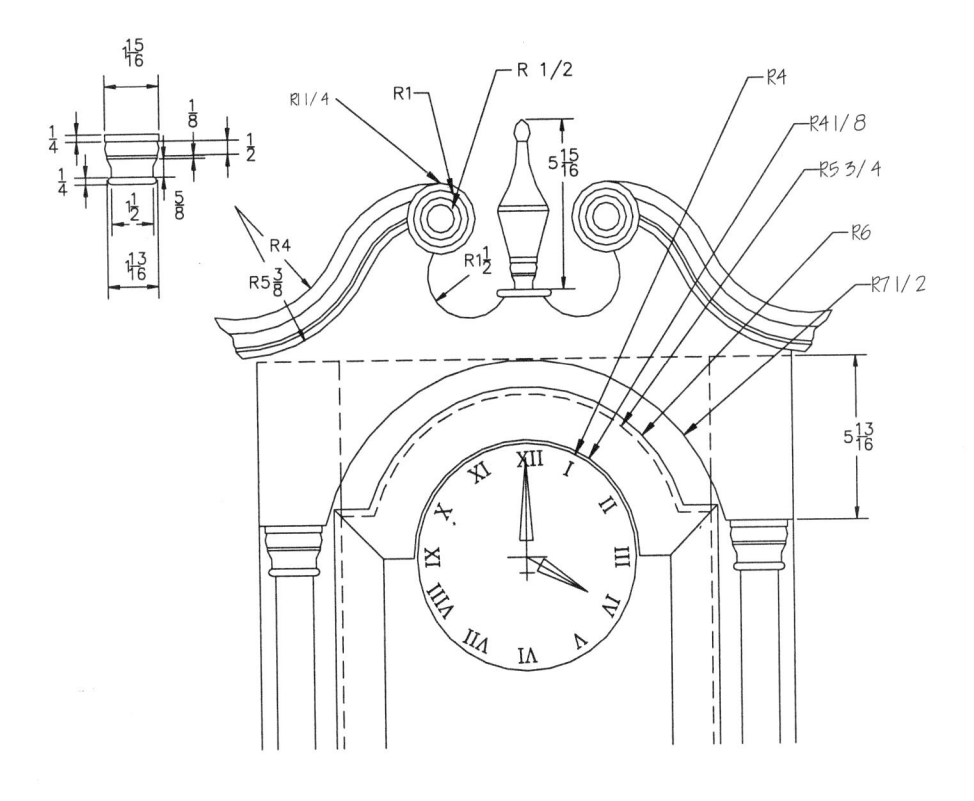

Isometric and Orthographic Drawings

Practice Exercise 16

For the four parts shown, create four views: the front, the top, the side, and the isometric. Be sure to create different layers for construction lines, and project the lines properly. When you are done, dimension.

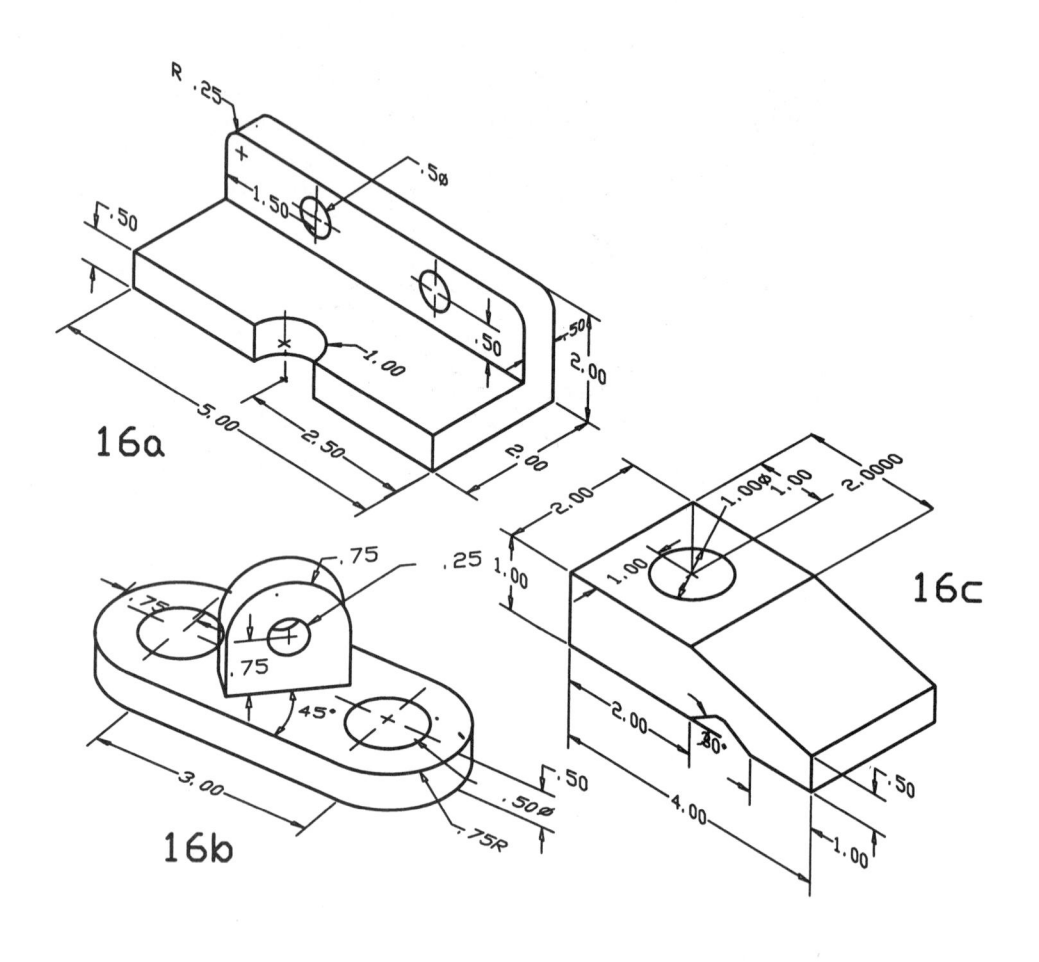

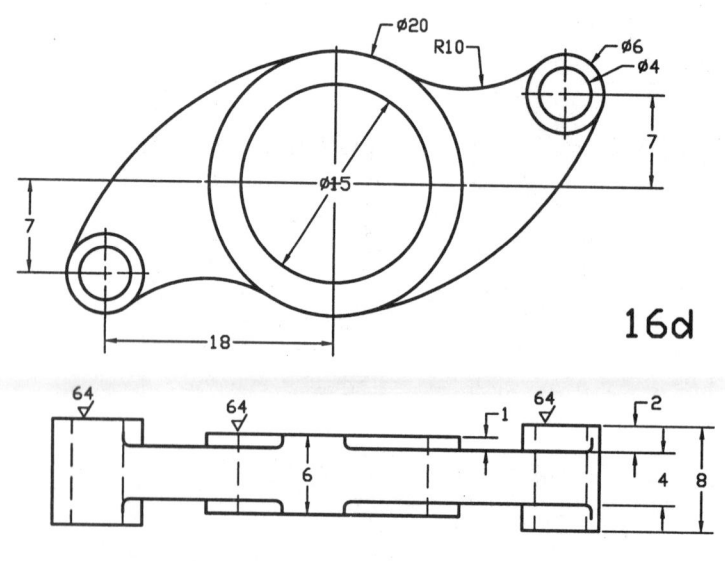

16a

16b

16c

Create side and isometric view

16d

Exercise A16

Use SNAP Isometric and the ELLIPSE command with Isocircle to create this standard stair detail. Make sure that the distance between the ballisters matches current code requirements.

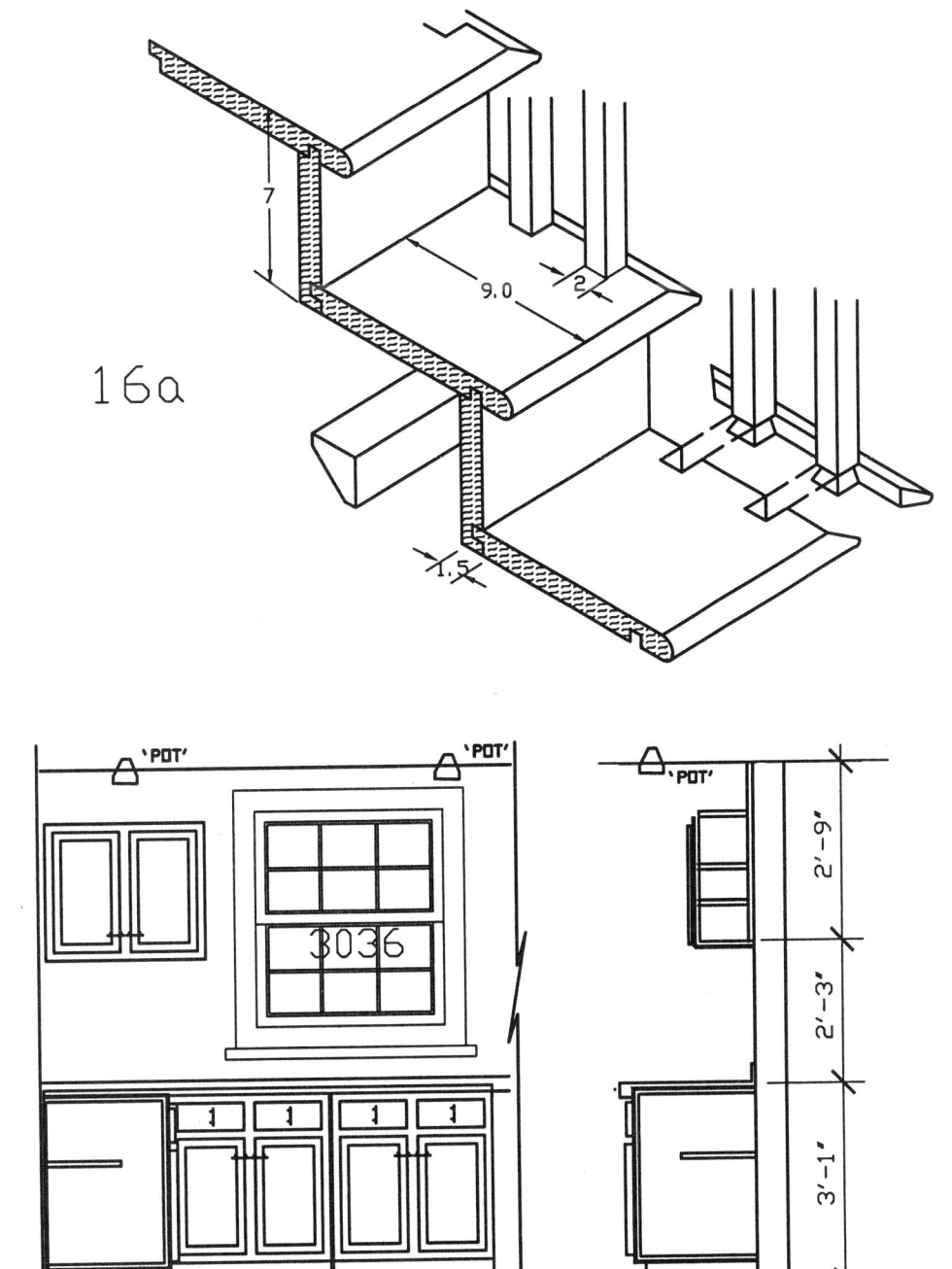

16a

16b   KITCHEN CABINETS
SCALE: 3/8"=1'-0"

Exercise C16

Using this typical wall detail, create an isometric view of the footings of a house 24' by 28'.

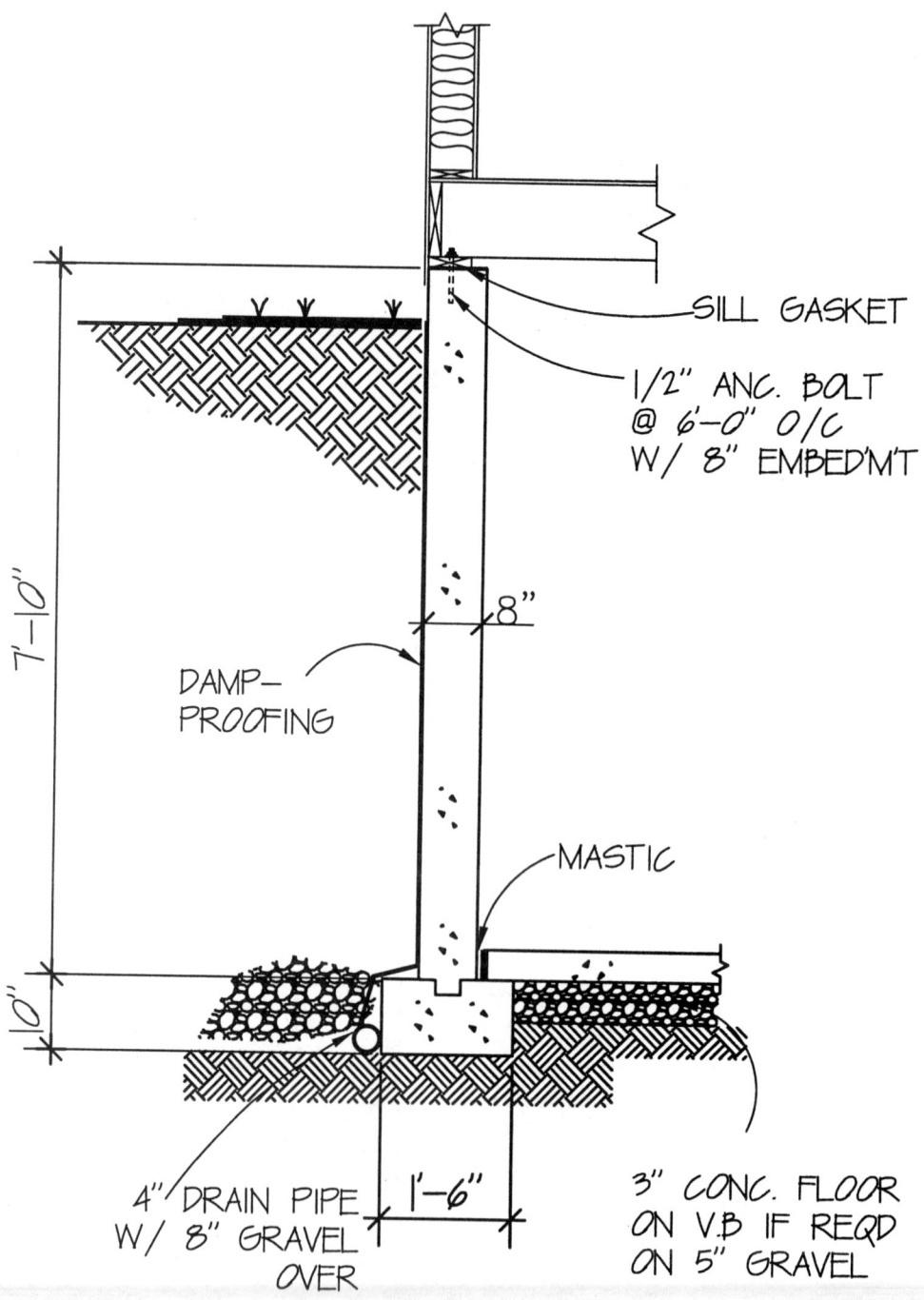

- SILL GASKET
- 1/2" ANC. BOLT @ 6'-0" O/C W/ 8" EMBED'M'T
- 8"
- DAMP-PROOFING
- MASTIC
- 7'-10"
- 10"
- 4" DRAIN PIPE W/ 8" GRAVEL OVER
- 1'-6"
- 3" CONC. FLOOR ON V.B IF REQD ON 5" GRAVEL

TYPICAL WALL SECTION
SCALE: 1/2"=1'-0"

Exercise M16

Take any or all of these and create the isometric views. Note that the difficult part of this object will, of course, be the fillets. Be sure to use different layers and dimension the part when it is finished.

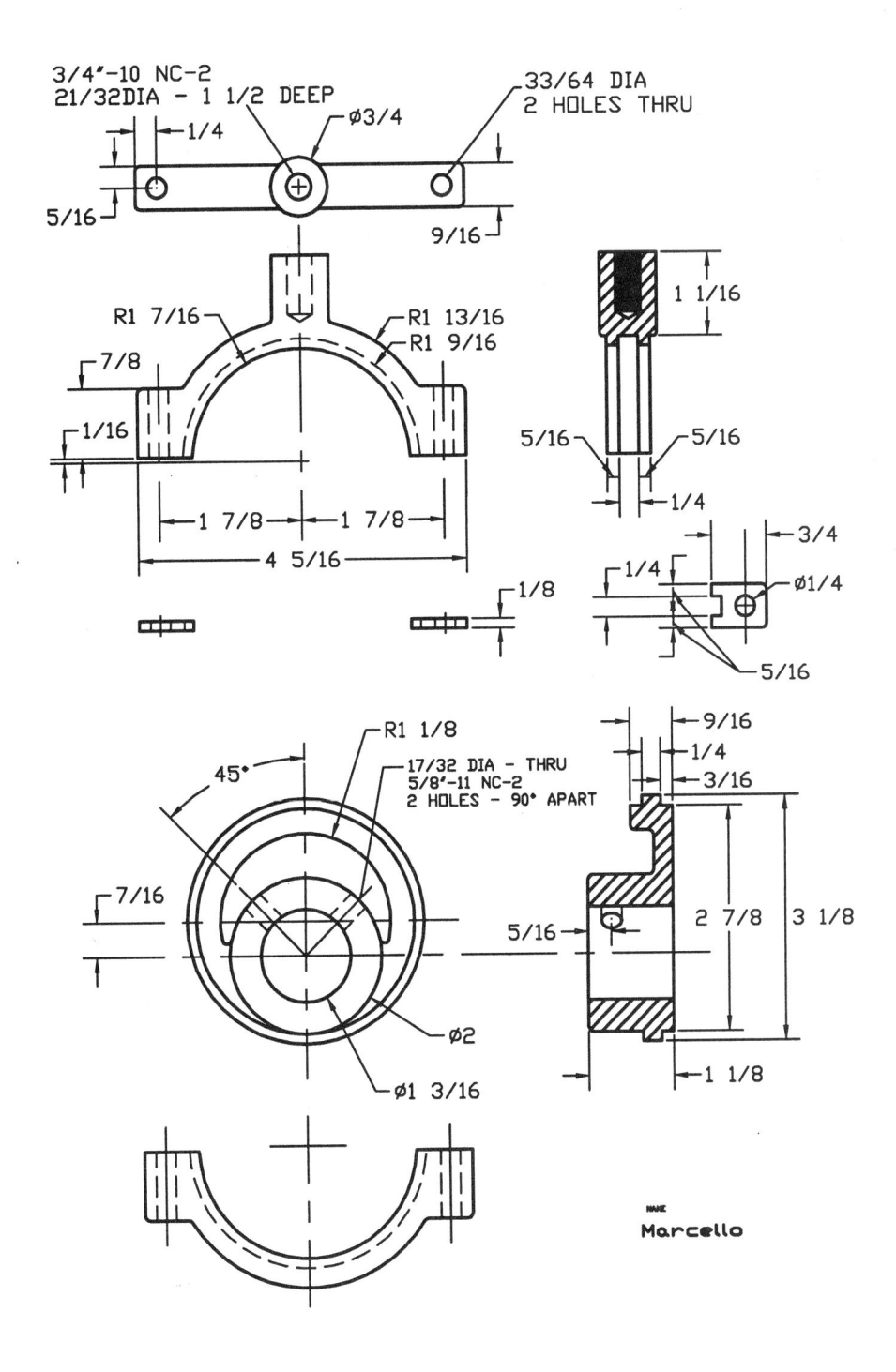

Challenger 16

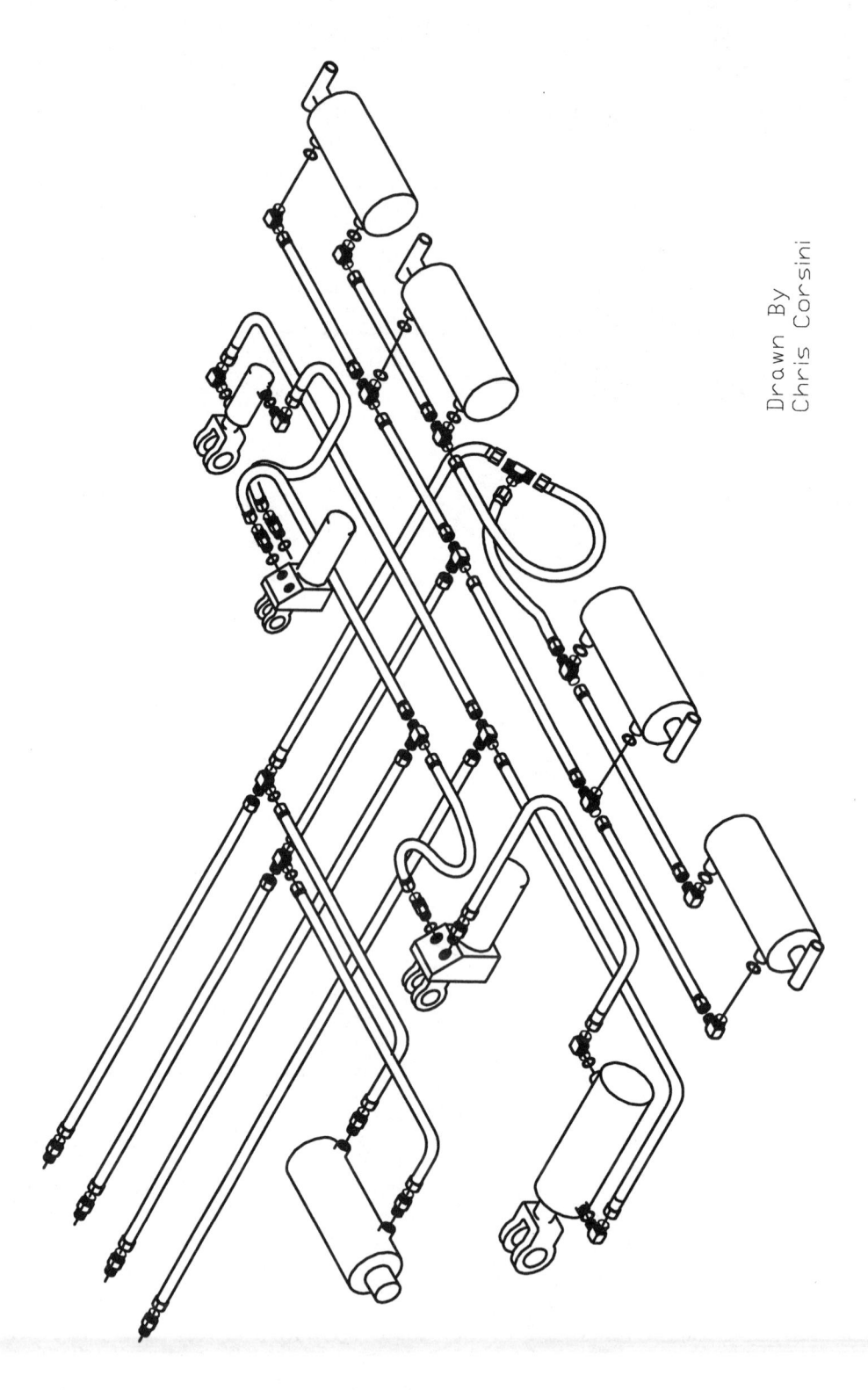

Drawn By
Chris Corsini

17 File Formats and Management

Upon completion of this chapter, you should be able to:

1. Create slides from graphics data using MSLIDE
2. Access on-line slides using VSLIDE
3. Create a SCRIPT file for viewing slides and other purposes
4. Create files for export to other programs
5. Use the GROUP command
6. Use the FILTER command

What Are Slides?

In order to understand slides and script files, it is important to understand what is happening when you are working on a CAD program.

The first step in creating a CAD model or drawing is to use the available commands — LINE, ARC, CIRCLE — to create a *vector file* — one in which all of the geometry is calculated by vectors. The system relates all entered data to a fixed origin, 0,0,0.

Once the vector file is created, the image must be displayed on the screen. To do this the screen must be able to display the vectors.

Each screen is made up of a series of small, addressable spots called *pixels*. Each pixel can display a certain number of colors, depending on the quality of the screen.

The image is relayed to the screen starting from the top left corner and moving in rows down the screen itself, pixel by pixel. This same process displays the image on a television screen, except video images are not usually vector files. This part of the process is referred to as the pixel address format or bit map, because the image is being addressed to the screen as a series of pixels, not as a series of lines.

- **Step 1** The user enters the commands to create the geometry.
- **Step 2** The input data is made into a vector file.
- **Step 3** The image is relayed to the screen pixel by pixel in a bit map file.

Note also that the on-screen menus are addressed in the same manner, so a large part of the image space is taken up by nonimage data. The menus can be taken off the screen, leaving more room for the image.

Up until now you have been using vector files to create and manipulate images. In certain situations, you do not need to work on the CAD file, you only want to see it. Therefore, it is desirable to have just the pixel address file and not the other parts of the file. AutoCAD has the ability to make slides that can be viewed on the screen by extracting only the pixel address portion of the file for viewing.

Slides are useful for several applications:

- To have for easy access a "view" of part of a project; e.g. when working on an elevation of a building, the floor plans can be instantly accessed for consistency
- To provide a slide show of a particular product to clients
- To provide a slide show of your work to a prospective employer
- To have available on file an easily viewed set of images of your own BLOCKs, linefonts, title blocks, etc.
- To have an instructional tool to tell a story or explain a certain concept
- For exchanging images with other graphics and desktop publishing programs
- For creating icon menus

The MSLIDE Command

The procedure for making slides is very simple, but the concepts behind the command are sometimes difficult at first for those who have not worked extensively with computers.

- **Step 1** The first thing you must do is create the graphics for the slide. This is done in the regular Drawing Editor using standard drawing and editing commands.
- **Step 2** Once the drawing is complete, use ZOOM and PAN to center the objects on the screen. The slide that you will be making will take up the entire screen; it is not defined by a Window. Be sure you have the view of the object that you want.
- **Step 3** Now make a slide of the geometry using the command MSLIDE. You need only enter a filename for the desired slide file, and AutoCAD will make a slide of the image on the screen.

MSLIDE creates a slide file of the current viewport. In model space, MSLIDE makes a slide file of the current viewport only. In paper space, MSLIDE makes a slide of a paper space display including all viewports and their contents.

> There is no toolbar or Pull Down choice for this.

The command line equivalent is **MSLIDE**.

This will give you the Create Slide File Dialog box. There is no way to access just the command string. Enter a filename in the File Name box, or select a slide file (.SLD) from the list.

This will create a slide file (CH4FIGS.SLD) in the A: directory. If you do not specify a specific drive and/or directory, the slide will be created in the same directory as the current drawing.

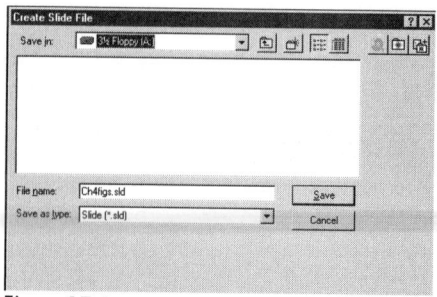

Figure 17-1

Check the directory (**DIR A:**). You should have a file with the extension .SLD; this is your slide file. The extension is added automatically with each MSLIDE command.

The Save As Type button only offers a .sld format. This is the only kind of file you can make from this command.

The slide is now ready to access, and can be accessed at any time in a drawing file by invoking the command VSLIDE. The slide will temporarily replace the information currently on your screen. You can draw on the slide, but when you change the display with either PAN, ZOOM, or REDRAW, your original drawing will reappear. Any objects added onto the slide will appear added to the current drawing.

> **Danger**
> Be careful when editing the information added on top of a slide, because you will also be editing the current drawing underneath the slide.

Editing Slides

You cannot edit slides. You must edit the original drawing and then recreate the slide.

Slide Resolution

When creating slides, always use a full screen set to the highest resolution. Otherwise, slides made in a smaller viewport or at lower resolution may show black lines.

The VSLIDE Command

You can view slides individually with the VSLIDE command or in sequence with the SCRIPT command. (See next section for the SCRIPT command.)

To view a slide, use VSLIDE with the slide filename.

The command line equivalent is **VSLIDE**.

Select a slide to view and choose OK.

The slide file image appears in the graphics area.

To remove the slide from the view, use REDRAW. Type in **R** at the command prompt, or choose REDRAW from the Standard toolbar in Windows or the View menu.

> There is no toolbar or Pull Down menu choice for this.

The command line equivalent is VSLIDE.

```
Command: VSLIDE
```

Again, they have taken out the non-dialog box VSLIDE command, making the process more cumbersome, but the command will bring you this dialog box. A:ch4figs will be retrieved over top of your current drawing. The slide will be displayed in the current viewport if more than one viewport is open.

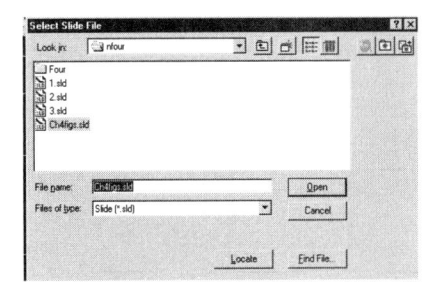

Figure 17-2

> **Notes**
> You have not lost your current drawing; a simple REDRAW will bring it back.

File Formats and Management **417**

Slides from Slide Libraries

Slide libraries allow you to organize your slides.

You can construct a slide library [SLB] from slide files [SLD] by using the slidelib utility program supplied in the AutoCAD support directory.

```
Command: slidelib library [<slidelist>]
```
Where:

Slidelib = the command utility

Library = the slide library file [.slb] into which the slide files [.sld] are added

Slidelist = specifies a list of slide files

Slide Libraries

Managing slides in a specific slide library is an efficient way to avoid cluttering your disk. The library will have an extension of .SLB, and will contain all of your slides for either slide shows or other functions. To modify a slide in a slide library, you must recreate the slide and also recompile the slide library.

Creating the SLIDE LIBrary — An Example

To create the slide library, follow these steps:

Step 1

First create the geometry for the electrical symbols shown. Make each symbol into a separate wblock, then make a slide of each symbol. Use MSLIDE to create the slides.

Once the blocks and slides are complete, exit to DOS. Find the SLIDELIB.EXE file. This should be under the ACAD\SAMPLE or ACAD\SUPPORT directory.

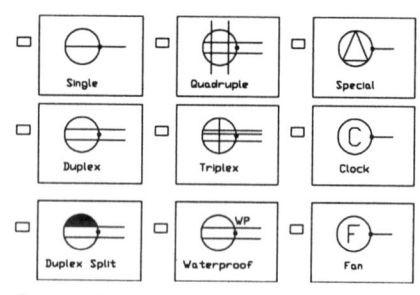

Figure 17-3

Once you have located it, copy it to the directory in which you would like to create your icon file. On the hard drive, create a directory called ICONS. Now copy SLIDELIB.EXE file to this directory.

```
c:\acad2000>MD\ICONS
c:\acad2000>CD\ACAD\SUPPORT
c:\acad2000\support>COPY SLIDELIB.EXE C:\ACAD2000\ICONS
```

If you are working with the A: drive, use the following:

```
c:\acad2000>CD\ACAD\SUPPORT
c:\acad2000\support>COPY SLIDELIB.EXE A:
```
A subdirectory such as ICONS can be used if desired.

```
a:>MD\ICONS
a:>C:
c:\acad2000>CD\ACAD\SUPPORT
c:\acad2000\support>COPY SLIDELIB.EXE A:ICONS
```

Step 2

Once SLIDELIB.EXE is loaded, you can create a slide library. Copy your slides into this directory. Your directory should contain the following:

```
c:\acad2000>DIR A:
SLIDELIB   EXE    24112    07-06-95    12:49a
Single     SLD      547    03-01-95    08:05a
Duplex     SLD      457    03-01-95    08:06a
Triplex    SLD     1138    03-01-95    08:12a
etc.
```

Step 3

The file SLIDELIB.EXE is used to execute a slide library within the directory that it is copied to. At the DOS prompt, create the slide library using the command SLIDELIB as follows:

```
C:\acad>A:
a:>dir *.sld/b > elec
a:>SLIDELIB MLIB ELEC
```

The library file will be called ELEC. After pressing ⏎ you should see the following:

```
SLIDELIB 2.2 (3/8/93)
(c) Copyright 1987-89, 1994, 1995 Autodesk, Inc.
All Rights Reserved.
```

This entry creates the mlib.slb file which contains the names and definitions of the slides listed in elec. Do not delete your slide files, as there is no provision for updating a slide library once it has been created.

The slide library is a list of slide file names that can be used by many utility programs to make menu changes etc.

Script Files

A *script* is a simple text file that contains a set of AutoCAD commands that are executed in succession with a single SCRIPT command. Script files are used to automate or preprogram a process such as viewing slides or running batch plotting.

Creating Script files

Script files are created outside AutoCAD using a text editor, saved in text format, and stored in an external file, like a slide, with the extension .SCR. When invoked, each line of the file is read and executed as if it had been typed in at the command prompt.

As with the template file for ATTEXT, any ASCII-based file can be used to create a script file. The easiest files to use are created with the Editor in DOS and Notepad in Windows.

Scripts to Run in the Drawing Editor

Scripts can be run from within the AutoCAD graphics editor to enter a setup for a file such as the linetype and linetypescale, units, grid, etc., and many other simple routines.

To create a script file, you must be familiar with both the commands and your responses to provide an appropriate sequence of responses in the script file. Every keystroke, every blank space, is significant. AutoCAD accepts either a space or ⏎ as a command or data file delimiter.

For example, a script file to center a drawing called A:ONE.SCR and generate a plot might look like this:

```
ZOOM     (zoom command)
A        (all = ZOOM All)
ZOOM     (zoom command)
.95x     (makes the view a bit smaller than total screen area)
PLOT     (plot command)
D        (plot display)
N        (want to change anything?)
         (blank line represents a return to start plotting)
```

You must turn off the dialog box before using this using **Filedia** <1>:**0**

Once the text file is created, simply run the script.

There are many ways to customize your AutoCAD environment for the projects you will be completing. In many offices, only one standard drawing size is created. If this is true in your case, a prototype drawing is all you need. If there are several different types of drawings, you can create script files that will get you into the desired size and set up for your model or drawing.

For example, if you are working on a part that is 18 × 14, you may find a script file called A2.SCR useful. It could look like this:

```
UNITS    (units command)
2        (decimal linear units)
2        (two decimal places)
1        (decimal angular units)
         (space to accept angle default)
         (measure angles counterclockwise)
LIMITS   (limits command)
-1,-1    (lower limit)
20,16    (upper limit)
ZOOM     (zoom command)
A        (all)
GRID     (grid command)
2        (two unit spacing for grid)
```

```
SNAP    (snap command)
.5      (.5 unit snap spacing)
```

This can be called in as soon as you enter the Drawing Editor. It will give you all the sizes you may need to start the project. A script file can easily take the place of a prototype drawing file if you find this method more suitable to your AutoCAD environment.

The script file can be very useful for creating standardized plots with similar layer/color and layer/linetype adjustments.

The SCRIPT Command

This command invokes the text file created as a script and executes the sequence of commands.

> **Pull Down** From the Tools menu, choose Run Script...

The command line equivalent is **SCRIPT**.

Enter the filename without the extension in the Select Script File dialog box. It will probably default to the ACAD2000 directory if you have not specified one already.

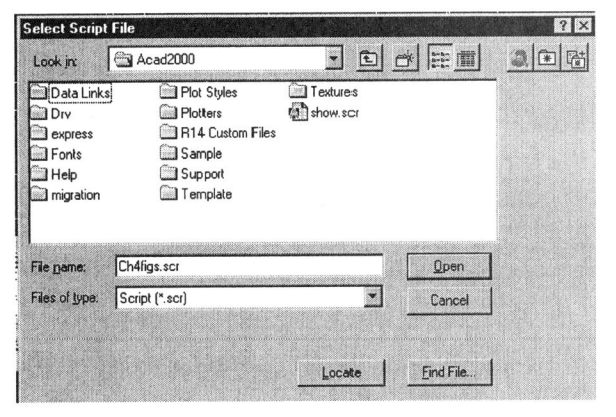

Figure 17-4

Scripts for Slide Shows

In creating a script file for the slide show, you will be preprogramming a series of VSLIDE commands that will allow you to view a series of slides without touching the keyboard. This is a popular technique for trade shows, etc., because it gives the impression that many drawing files are being accessed, one by one. The commands needed to perform the slide show are as follows. Slides 1 and 2 are precreated slides.

```
VSLIDE SLIDE1    (begins the slide show with slide 1)
VSLIDE *SLIDE2   (preloads SLIDE2)
DELAY 1000       (delays 1 sec for viewing (2000 = 2 sec, etc.))
VSLIDE           (displays the preloaded slide)
RSCRIPT          (will repeat the entire program)
```

> **Notes**
> The full script is on page 425.

Stopping the Script File

Use Esc to stop the script file. A backspace will temporarily halt it. Use **RESUME** to continue if the script file has been halted.

Invoking a Script While Loading AutoCAD

Scripts can be used from within the drawing editor and also when you start AutoCAD using a special form of the ACAD command. To invoke a script when you start AutoCAD, use the following command form:

```
drive>ACAD DRAWING-NAME SCRIPT-FILE
```

ACAD is your sign-on code. This may be different with regard to your system setup, e.g. ACAD14, ACAD2000, etc.

The script file must be the second file named on the ACAD program call line; a file type of .SCR is assumed. If AutoCAD can't find the script file, it reports that it can't open the file.

This format is useful for creating setups with grid, ltscale, snap, layer settings, and system variables.

Exporting AutoCAD Files

Word processing and desktop publishing programs can import AutoCAD files. You can also import raster images created by scanners, paint programs, and other applications into an AutoCAD drawing. Copy and Paste routines in Windows can also be used.

> **Notes**
> Copy and Paste do not work from AutoCAD into some systems if the drawing is in paper space.

Exporting in Windows

One major advantage with Windows is the multitasking facility. To take a drawing image from AutoCAD to a word processing format, use Copy and Paste.

1. Open the drawing file in AutoCAD.
2. Under the Edit menu, choose Cut or Copy and identify with a window the image to be exported.
3. Under the File menu, choose Minimize.
4. Open your word processing or desktop publishing document, position cursor at desired spot, usually in a user box.
5. Under the Edit menu, use Paste to place the image.

In Windows, .SLD, .PLT (see Appendix F), and other formats are not necessary except with hidden lines in paper space.

Slides

Some programs will import .SLD files. Within the figure box, graphics box, or user box, try importing the .SLD file. If this is not compatible, try using .PLT files or .HPG files. (The latter extension indicates HPGL or Hewlett Packard Graphics Language files.)

When generating the graphic in AutoCAD, be careful that the sizing of text and dimensions will allow viewing on an 8 1/2" × 11" sheet. Generally, the space given for graphics is about 6" × 6". If your text is barely readable on the screen at 8 1/2" × 11", there is no chance you will see it on a WordPerfect sheet.

Plot Files or HPGL Files

A .PLT or .HPG file can be imported into many software packages. Simply generate a plot file (A:NAME.PLT) for the graphics by using the PLOT command. When in the PLOT command, make sure that you:

- Plot to a file
- Set the driver to an HP driver

Graphics must be generated in a Hewlett Packard plot-file format. Configure the plot for a Hewlett Packard plotter through the Device and Default Selection ... of the Plot Configuration menu.

The HP.DRV (plotter driver file) is standard on any AutoCAD release. If you need to reconfigure to add the plotter driver, use the CONFIG command and add any standard HP plotter driver (the HP 7420 for example) to the plotter options.

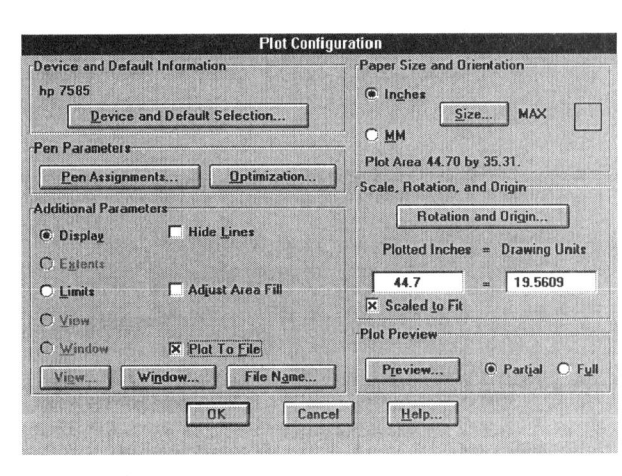

Figure 17-4

> **Notes**
> If using Corel Ventura, this will not work: the files can not be exported into anything except Post Script.

Use the PLOT command in AutoCAD to select the drawing or portion of a drawing to be exported. Make sure the plot is scaled to Fit; otherwise your graphics may be much too large.

Importing Files to AutoCAD

Raster images can be imported into AutoCAD. These images are not vector images and cannot be edited like a drawing file, but they can be useful for tracing or for viewing purposes. Because imported raster files can create large file formats, you should erase the raster image when you no longer need it.

AutoCAD can import the formats GIF (graphics interchange format), PCX, and TIFF (tagged image file format). To start the import, use the following:

> **Toolbar** From the Render toolbar choose the IMAGE button.

The command line equivalent is IMAGEATTACH.

Enter the path and name of file that you want to import.

AutoCAD displays the raster image. Drag the image into position, then specify the scale.

Always test your output device or function before doing your whole document. The display resolution, plotter, and input image can all simply "not work." New graphic programs that will solve your problems for a few hundred dollars are showing up every twenty minutes. Don't trust them until you've actually seen them work on YOUR file.

Prelab 17A Creating Slides and Scripts

Step 1 This splatter file of a young girl blowing a bubble is very simple, but it should illustrate a sequence of events. It also takes up a very small amount of space, so it can be useful in testing out slides and scripts without using up too much time and disk space. If this is too violent for your liking, try another cartoon sequence, making sure that you have a distinct difference between each slide. (Use color 14 for grape bubble gum.)

You can create this series of drawings and create slides of them, generate a similar image or set of images, or use a series of completed drawings to create a slide show of your drawings to date for a perspective employer or client.

Step 2

Create the first view using arcs. Copy the view over and make minor adjustments.

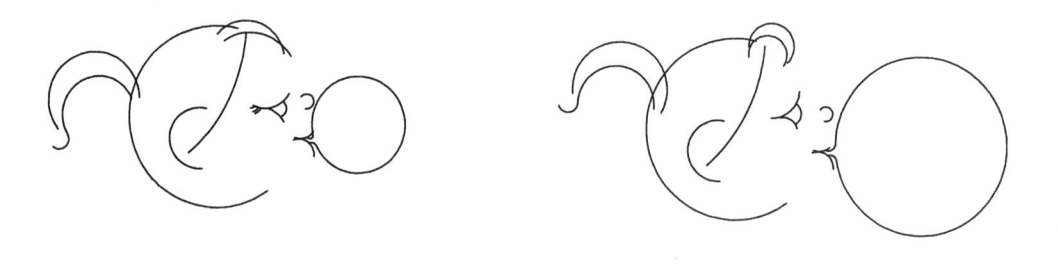

Copy both of the existing files down, and create a sequence of events.

424 CHAPTER SEVENTEEN

Step 3   Now use ZOOM Window to bring each view separately onto the screen, then use MSLIDE to create a slide of each image in sequence. Be careful to number the slides in the proper sequence.

> At the command prompt type MSLIDE.

You should have six slide files when this is completed.

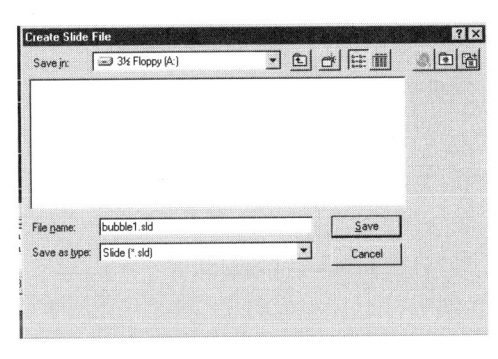

Step 4   Now create a script file in the DOS Editor or Windows Notepad.

```
VSLIDE A:BUBBLE1
VSLIDE *A:BUBBLE2
DELAY 1000
VSLIDE
VSLIDE *A:BUBBLE3
DELAY 1000
VSLIDE
VSLIDE *A:BUBBLE4
DELAY 1000
VSLIDE
VSLIDE *A:BUBBLE5
DELAY 1000
VSLIDE
VSLIDE *A:BUBBLE6
DELAY 1000
VSLIDE
VSLIDE *A:BUBBLE1
RSCRIPT

Save the File as A:Blowup.SCR
Exit the Editor
```

Step 5   The command to load the script is SCRIPT; no extension is needed.

> **Pull Down** From the Tools menu, choose Run Script...

The command line equivalent is **SCRIPT**.

```
Command: Script
```

Managing Larger Files

The organization of a larger model can be a very difficult task even with the use of layers and blocks. AutoCAD has two other ways of organizing files: Groups and Filters.

Layers

There are two controlling factors that are utilized with the Layer function; the first indicates which layer is being drawn on, the second indicates which layers are being displayed and edited. Each object belongs to only one layer. Objects can also be editable or not editable by locking or unlocking the layers.

Filters

Filters allow the user to create a list of properties required of an object for it to be selected. Effectively, it acts like the Lock function of Layering in that it limits selectability of objects by property, such as color or linetype, or by object type, such as arc or polyline.

Filter identifies objects by linetype or color only when these properties have been set up independent of their layer. Filtering by object type is set up by Object Type and relative parameters such as diameter.

Filter lists, like Dimension Styles and Multiline Styles, can be saved in a file and used repeatedly.

The FILTER Command

Filter is used at the command prompt to set up lists for later use at the Select Objects prompt. It can also be set up, like Layer Locking, within the editing command from the dialog box.

> At the command prompt type FILTER.

The command line equivalent is **FILTER**.

The dialog box offers many of the same options as other naming lists.

Delete	erases the selected filter from the list.
Clear List	erases the current filter list.
Named Filters	displays, saves, and deletes filter lists.
Edit Item	moves the selected filter into the Select Filter area for editing. To change a filter, select it and choose Edit item. Edit the filter and values and choose Substitute. The edited filter replaces the selected filter.
Select Filter	adds filters to the current list based on object properties. Additional parameter values can be added.

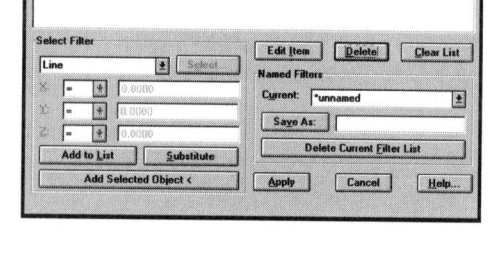

426 CHAPTER SEVENTEEN

Relational Operators	*Operator*	*Meaning*
	<	Less than
	<=	Less than or equal to
	>	Greater than
	>=	Greater than or equal to
	=	Equal to
	!=	Not equal to
	*	Equal to any value

For example, you can have all circles selectable, or just those circles that have a diameter greater than 3, and are on the part of the file that is less than 25 in *X* and 25 in *Y*. Use the following relational operators to set your object filter.

```
Object = Circle
Circle Center  X<=25.00  Y<=25.00  Z<=0.00
Circle Radius >=3.00
```

Grouping Operations	selects filter sets by operands.
Select	displays a dialog box listing all items of the specified type in the drawing.
Add to List	adds the current Select Filter option to the filter list.
Substitute	replaces the selected filter with the one in Select Filter.
Add Selected Object	allows you to select one object in the drawing and add to the filter list.

Groups

A group can be defined simply as a stored selection set. Objects within the model or drawing can belong to several groups, but only one layer. Groups are selection sets that are stored with the model.

Storing objects in groups allows the user to edit a large number of related objects while only selecting them once. The display is not affected by groups. An object can be a member of more than one group.

By picking one object in the group, the whole group is selected. Objects in locked layers are not edited with the other members of the selected group.

The GROUP Command

This creates a named selection set of objects.

> **Pull Down** From the Tools menu, choose Object Group.

The command line equivalent is **-GROUP**.

```
Command:GROUP
[?/Order/Add/Remove/Explode/REName/Selectable/Create]<Create>
```

File Formats and Management

Group Name	displays the names of existing groups
Selectable	indicates whether a selected object will be edited as an individual object or as a group. If the group is Selectable, the object selection pick will select the whole group.

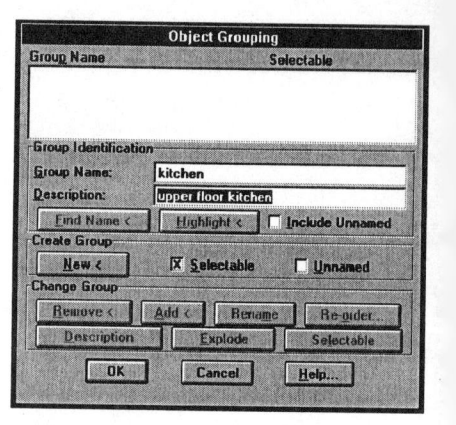

Group Indentification
When a group is selected in the group name list, the group's name and optional description appear in the Group Identification area.

Group Name	displays the name of the selected group.
Description	displays the description of the selected group.
Find Name	lists the groups to which an object belongs.
Highlight	shows the members of the selected group in the graphics area.
Include Unnamed	specifies whether unnamed groups are listed.

Create Group

New	creates a new group from the objects you have selected using the name in the Group Name text box.
Selectable	specifies whether a group is selectable.
Unnamed	indicates that you will accept a sequentially numbered identification for the group.

Change Group

Remove	removes objects from the selection set.
Add	adds objects to the selected group.
Rename	allows the user to rename the group.
Re-order	changes the numberical order of objects within the selected group. This is used for tool path generation. This option will invoke the order group dialog box.

PICKSTYLE

If the PICKSTYLE system variable is set to 1 or 3, the objects in the group will be selected as a group. If the PICKSTYLE system variable is set to 0, the objects will be selected as separate objects.

Prelab 17B Drawing with Layers and Groups

In this example we will draw a bicycle wheel in three different layers, and save it as a group. Then we will draw in the rest of the bicycle, copy the wheel over as a group, and change just the circles to the hidden linetype.

Step 1   Draw in the wheel as shown. Make the tube of the wheel in layer Tube, and the spokes of the wheel in layer Metal.

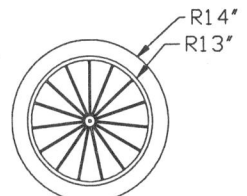

Step 2   Open the Create Group dialog box.

Under Group Identification, enter the word, wheel.

Under Select Group, specify that the group should be selectable.

Choose New.

In the drawing you will be prompted to select the objects. Pick the objects and press OK.

In the Object Group Dialog box, choose OK.

Step 3   At the command prompt, make sure that your PICKSTYLE is set to 1.

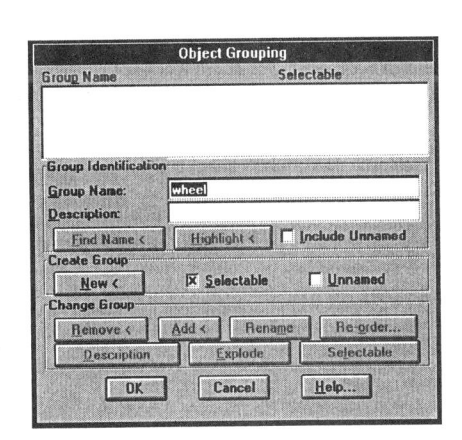

```
Command:PICKSTYLE
New value for PICKSTYLE <0>:1
```

Step 4   Draw in the remainder of the lines in layer Metal. Leave enough room for at least one wheel's width between the two wheel positions.

Step 5   Use the COPY command to copy the wheel from one end of the bicycle to the other.

```
Command:COPY
Select objects: (pick 1)
Select objects:↵
Specify base point or [Multiple]:
```

Notice that the pick point picks the entire wheel, both layers.

Step 6 The circles and spokes are on group wheel. Now filter out only the circles on the drawing, and use Change Properties to change the linetype to hidden. First, you must change the PICKSTYLE system variable to 0 in order to have the individual objects selected.

```
Command: PICKSTYLE
Enter new value for PICKSTYLE<0>:1
```

Step 7 Now invoke the CHPROP command, and use the Object Selection Filters dialog box to identify only the circles.

```
Command: CHPROP
Select objects:
```

Under Select Filter, select Circle.

Select Add to List.

Choose Apply. AutoCAD applies the filter list to whatever you now select.

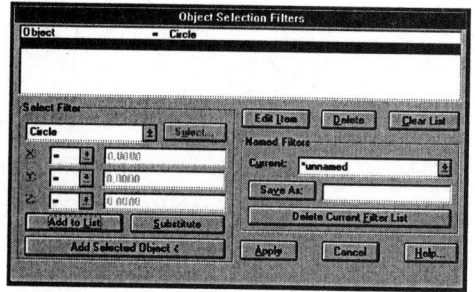

```
Select objects: (pick a window around the entire bicycle)
146 found
136 were filtered out
Select objects:↵
Exiting filtered selection. 10 found.
Specify what property to change (Color/
LAyer/LType/ltScale/Thickness):LT
New Linetype:HIDDEN
Change what property (Color/LAyer/LType/ltScale/Thickness):↵
```

Is the new wheel considered a group with PICKSTYLE set to 1?

Command and Function Summary

FILTER creates lists to select objects based on properties.

GROUP creates a named selection set of objects.

MSLIDE creates a slide file of the current viewport.

SCRIPT executes a sequence of commands from a script.

SLIDELIB creates a slide library for use in icon menus and script files.

Text files are used to compile a series of AutoCAD commands that can be accessed through **SCRIPT**.

VSLIDE displays a raster image slide file in the current viewport.

This is what your clock will look like.

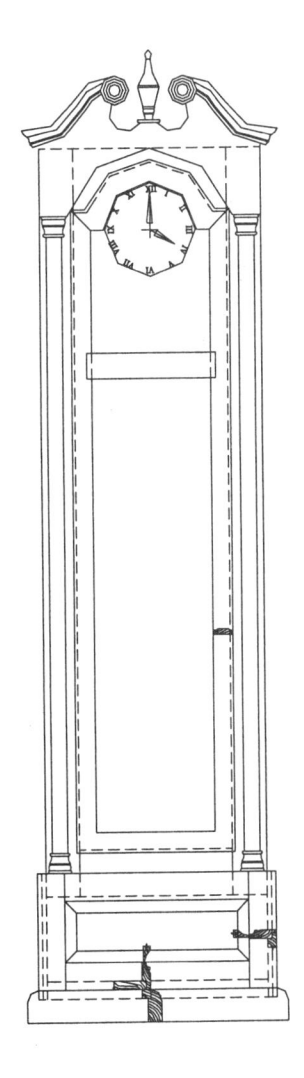

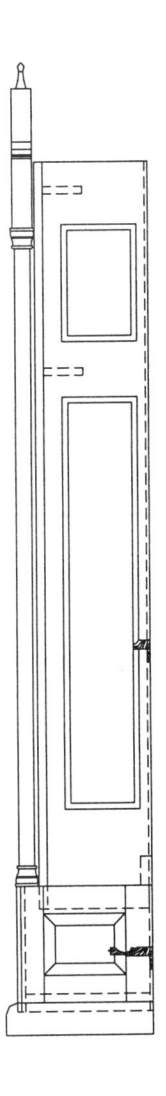

Exercise A17

Attributed block
Building Section
BLOCK NAME: ATTBS

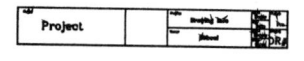

Attributed block
Horizontal Title Block
BLOCK NAME: ATTHT

Attributed block
Wall Section
BLOCK NAME: ATTWS

Block
North Arrow
BLOCK NAME: ARROW

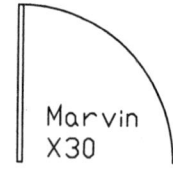

Attributed block
Door
BLOCK NAME: ATTDOOR

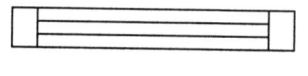

Attributed block
Window
BLOCK NAME: ATTWINDO

Part 1 Take six attributed wblock files. (Create them quickly if you do not have six on file.) Insert them onto a file and add notations as shown in the example. Zoom each one onto the screen individually, and create a slide using MSLIDE for each individual file. You can make the attributes invisible in the block.

Part 2 Generate a script file using either Notebook or the DOS Editor. Save the .SCR file.

Part 3 Use SCRIPT to view the slide show of your blocks.

Exercise C17

Attributed block
Road Section
BLOCK NAME: ATTRS

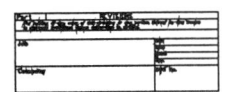

Attributed block
Horizontal Title Block
BLOCK NAME: ATTHT

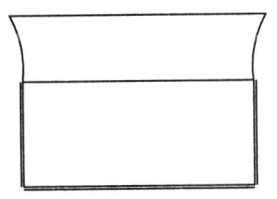

Attributed block
Curb Cut Approach
BLOCK NAME: ATTCCA

Block
North Arrow
BLOCK NAME: ARROW

Attributed block
Turn Arrow
BLOCK NAME: ATTTARR

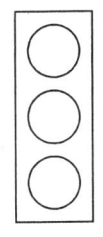

Attributed block
Stop Light
BLCOK NAME: ATTSTOP

Part 1 Take six attributed wblock files. (Create them quickly if you do not have six on file.) Insert them onto a file and add notations as shown in the example. Zoom each one onto the screen individually, and create a slide using MSLIDE for each individual file. You can make the attributes invisible on the block itself.

Part 2 Generate a script file using either Notebook or the DOS Editor. Save the .SCR file.

Part 3 Use SCRIPT to view the slide show of your blocks.

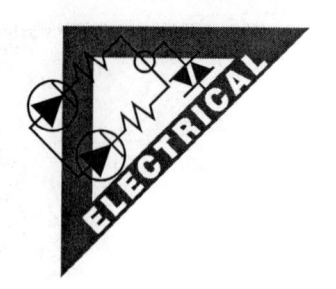

Exercise E17

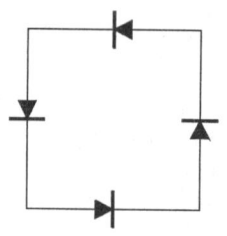

Attributed block
Rectifier
Full Wave Bridge
BLOCK NAME: FWB

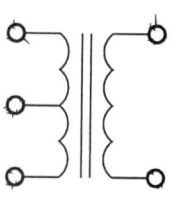

Attributed block
Transformer
Magnetic Core/Single
BLOCK NAME: MCST

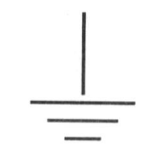

Attributed block
Connecting
Dots
BLOCK NAME: DOTS

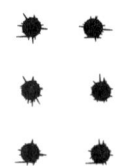

Attributed block
Connecting
Dots
BLOCK NAME: DOTS

Attributed block
Variable
Resistor
BLOCK NAME: VR

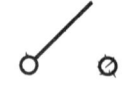

Attributed block
Switch
Single Pole
BLOCK NAME: SPSWITCH

Part 1　　Take six attributed wblock files. (Create them quickly if you do not have six on file). Insert them onto a file and add notations as shown in the example. Zoom each one onto the screen individually, and create a slide using MSLIDE for each individual file. You can make the attributes invisible on the block itself.

Part 2　　Generate a script file using either Notebook or the DOS Editor. Save the .SCR file.

Part 3　　Use SCRIPT to view the slide show of your blocks.

Exercise M17

Attributed block
Section Arrow
BLOCK NAME: ATTSA

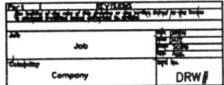

Attributed block
Horizontal Title Block
BLOCK NAME: ATTHT

ACME
sp486

Attributed block
Spring set
BLOCK NAME: ATTSS

Stelco
blt2336

Attributed block
Bolt
BLOCK NAME: ATTBOLT

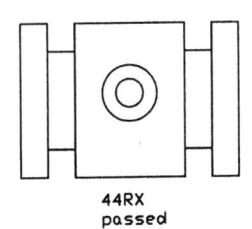

44RX
passed

Attributed block
Centre Pin
BLOCK NAME: ATTPIN

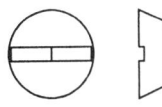

Slotted
.23xx

Attributed block
Slotted
BLOCK NAME: ATTSLOT

Part 1 Take six attributed wblock files. (Create them quickly if you do not have six on file). Insert them onto a file and add notations as shown in the example. Zoom each one onto the screen individually, and create a slide using MSLIDE for each individual file. You can make the attributes invisible on the block itself.

Part 2 Generate a script file using either Notebook or the DOS Editor. Save the .SCR file.

Part 3 Use SCRIPT to view the slide show of your blocks.

Challenger 17

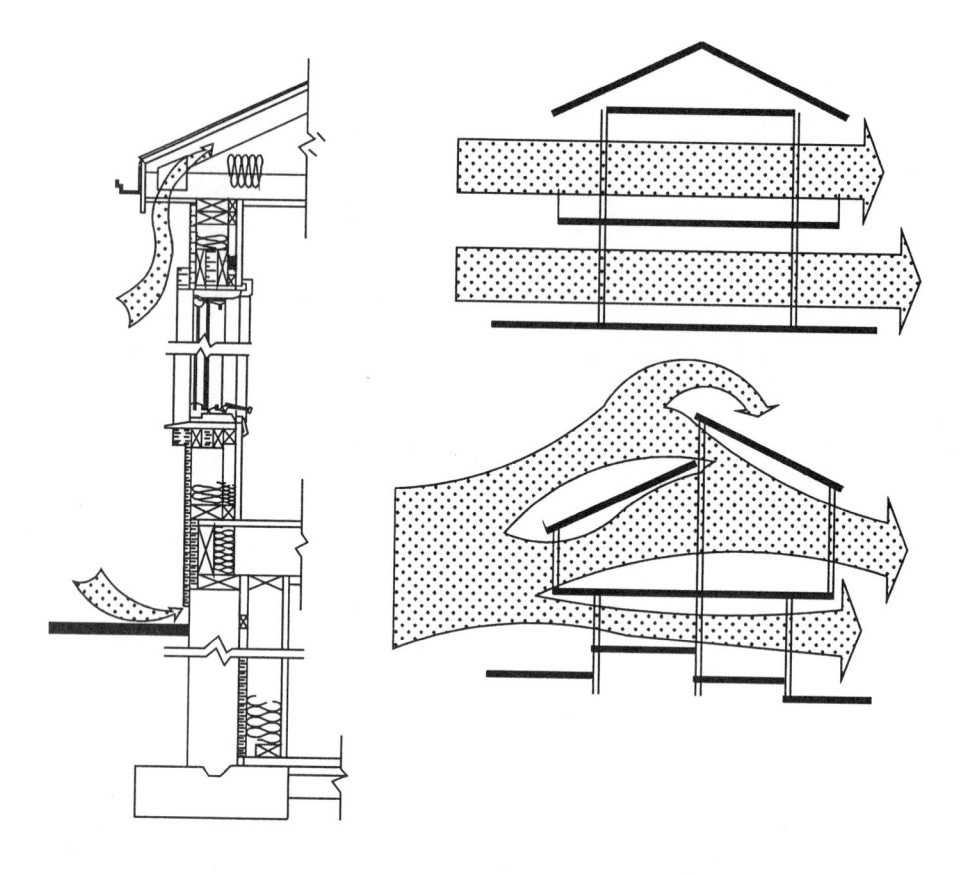

In this drawing of ventilation patterns, we can see how the first view illustrates an insulated house, and the ventilation going into it. The two houses demonstrate ventilation patterns through windows, doors, etc. Using a condition that exists in your discipline, generate a group of views that develop a certain thought process or project and create a slide show for presentation.

- **Mechanical**
    1. Movements of a robotic arm
    2. Drilling a piece of metal
    3. Turning gears

- **Architectural**
    1. Different framing techniques
    2. Movement of a window
    3. Renovation of a kitchen

- **Civil**
    1. Traffic flow problems
    2. Cut and fill before and after
    3. Installation of services in an area

18 Advanced Blocking, Xrefs, And Tracking

Upon completion of this chapter, you should be able to:

1. Create nested blocks
2. Use eXternal REFerences
3. Use Xbind
4. Use AutoTracking

Advanced Blocking

In addition to being used as an assembly tool and as a format for generating attributes, blocks can be compiled for further efficiency of design. One block can contain any number of other blocks so that it can be edited as a group of blocks instead of just a single block object.

Nesting Blocks

Nested blocks are blocks within blocks, or several interconnected blocks. An example would be a workstation in an office layout. In a large company there would certainly be some standards of what desk, storage, and chair arrangements could be used for each position. If each component of the workstation were stored as a separate block, the whole workstation could also be stored as a block and inserted separately as well.

In Figure 18-1, each individual item could be blocked, with or without attribute information, and the whole unit could be blocked for easy insertion into the office layout. Inserting one workstation would obviously be much easier than inserting all of the individual blocks.

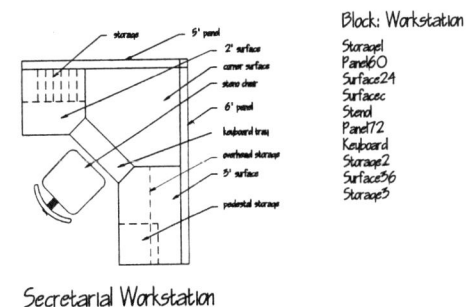

Figure 18-1

The blocks are created individually; then they are blocked as a unit to be part of a single large block. The large block is then inserted as one unit.

Layering, Color, and Linetype with Blocks

When you insert a block into a file, all of the layers associated with the block are inserted as well.

Each object of the block is stored on the layer that it was assigned. If you have planned correctly, you should have control of the objects that are inserted, and the color and linetype of each object should be the same as when it was created. Usually, the color and linetype will be set BYLAYER, but a COLOR or LINETYPE setting will override these.

All objects in layer 0 will take on the current color and linetype, unless they are entered using *BLOCKNAME or exploded. Objects will default to layer 0 when exploded.

When inserting blocks, it is often difficult to determine how best to set up and view the objects. In the example above, two or three manufacturers could be supplying the furnishings for the workstation. You may have the layers set up so that each manufacturer has its own layer. When inserting the workstations, however, you may wish to assign them a color to represent a department. On one floor there could be 12 secretaries representing 4 different departments, and you may wish to have the colors coordinate so that the departments, not the furniture manufacturers, are easily distinguished. If this is the case, the color of the nested block can be set BYBLOCK, and the current layer can be changed while inserting the 12 workstations so that the blocks, when inserted, will take on the color of the department. The layer for each department must be set up, and the BLOCK must be inserted while that layer is current. The block's color and linetype can be changed after it has been inserted by using CHPROP, and the color or linetype can be set BYBLOCK.

If the color and linetype objects are set BYBLOCK, they will take on the settings of the insertion layer at the time of insertion. Remember, if you insert a block on a layer that is frozen, the block will not be visible.

Block Redefinition

Once a block is inserted, you may encounter design changes that will make you want to substitute a different block at the same insertion base point. In the example are shown a coniferous tree symbol on the left and a deciduous on the right. If both trees are blocks, it is possible to substitute one type of tree with another on a layout as long as there are attributes on it.

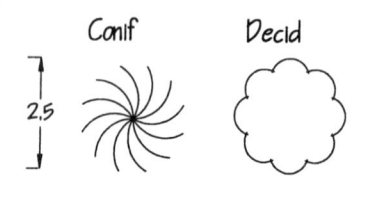

Figure 18-2

```
Command:ATTREDEF
Enter name of block you wish to redefine:CONIF
Select objects for new Block...
Select objects: (pick the objects)
Specify insertion base point of new Block:(pick a point)
```

The previous command has assigned a different block to each of the reference points on the blocks called CONIF. The graphic information of the block DECID will replace the graphic information of the block CONIF. The attribute value Conif will be changed to Decid.

This function can be extremely useful when working on a large drawing or assembly where one of the components which has been entered as an external block has been updated or replaced.

If you have created an office layout with 125 chairs and management decides to change the manufacturer, simply redefine the blocks.

If you are working on an assembly with 150 components of the same type, simply redefine them if the component is upgraded.

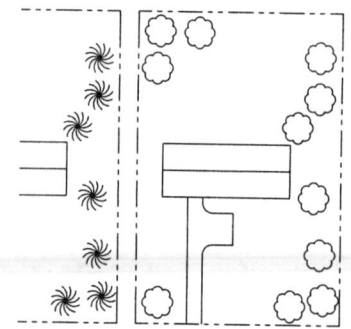

Figure 18-3

Xrefs or External Reference Files

When you insert a block to a file, you are, in fact, adding all of the objects of the block into the current file. When you add an XREF to a file, you are bringing the latest version of a current drawing into your drawing as an external reference. The objects are not actually added to the file. They are referenced for the duration of your editing time and then released. The xrefs are reloaded every time the drawing is loaded. Xrefs don't significantly increase the size of the drawing, because they are not part of the drawing database.

The great advantage of having xref files as opposed to blocks is that the xref files are separate drawing files and thus are subject to change. Every time a file containing an xref is retrieved, it will load the most current version of the referenced file. Any changes in the components of a referenced drawing are automatically shown on the master drawing the next time it is retrieved. This feature is particularly useful when working on a networked system, because many people can access the same drawings for updating.

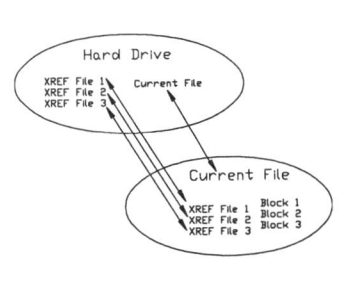

Figure 18-4

In addition, because the xref data is contained in another file, the file size is much smaller than it would be if data were inserted as the same amount of blocks.

Xrefs can be manipulated in exactly the same way as the blocks; the layers can be listed, the object can be edited as a single object, the objects can be used as OSNAP positions, and the colors can be changed. As with blocks, individual items of geometry within the xref cannot be changed. The only difference between an xref and a block is that the xref is not added to the file.

The XREF Command

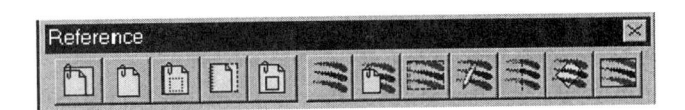

The XREF command offers you seven options.

Toolbar From the Reference toolbar, choose a selection.

Pull Down From the Insert menu, choose External Reference.

The command line equivalent is **XREF** for the dialog box (next page) or **-XREF**.

```
Command:-XREF
Enter an option [?/Bind/Detach/Path/Reload/Overlay/Attach]:
```

Where: **?** = a listing of current xrefs
Bind = an ability to add the xref to the current file, thus making a BLOCK
Detach = a removal of xrefs from the current file
Path = the path that AutoCAD uses when loading one or more xrefs
Reload = an update of an xref without exiting the drawing editor
Overlay = an overlay of an XREF file onto the current file
Attach = an attachment of a new file or a copy of an xref that already exists in the file; much like INSERT

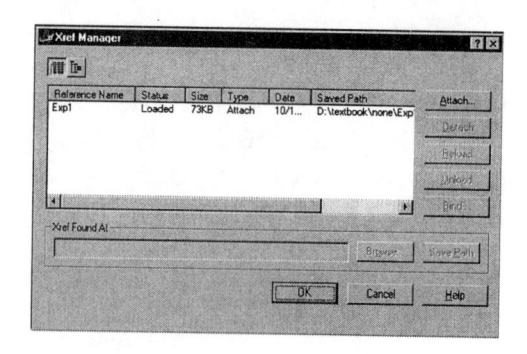

Figure 18-5

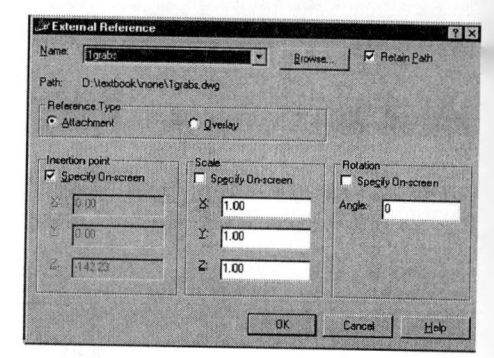

Figure 18-6

XREF Options

Notes

Pick one of the files in the XREF manager to access the other options such as bind.

? will list all the xrefs in a file plus the path to the file. You can display a full listing of files, or just those from a specific path, or you can use * to obtain a wildcard listing with specific drawing names, or to get the Xref Manager.

```
Command:XREF
Enter an option [?/Bind/Detach/Path/Reload/Overlay/Attach]:?

Xref name          Path

Axle               C:\ACAD2000\1999
Tire               C:\ACAD2000\1998

Total Xref(s): 2
```

BIND will change an xref into a block making it a permanent part of a file. This option is most often used when sending files to a client or another user to ensure that all the files are contained in the drawing. It is also useful when archiving files to make sure that all the files are included in the one master file.

When using the Bind option, you can bind the xrefs individually, or you can bind them all by using the * wildcard.

```
Command:XREF
Enter an option [?/Bind/Detach/Path/Reload/Overlay/Attach]:B
Xref(s) to bind:STENO1
     Scanning ...
```

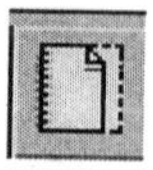

DETACH When you erase an xref, the reference to the exterior file still exists, just as when you erase a block, the block reference still exists. To remove a reference completely from a file use Detach. When you retrieve a drawing with an xref that has been erased but not Detached it will bring the reference into the file but not display it. This takes up valuable space in memory.

Detach will affect an xref whether it is displayed or not, and it will also remove any nested references it finds. Again, the * wildcard can be used to detach all xrefs.

```
Command:XREF
Enter an option [?/Bind/Detach/Path/Reload/Overlay/Attach]:D
Xref(s) to detach:CORNER
     Scanning ...
```

If the xref that you are detaching has multiple insertions, AutoCAD will not perform the function.

PATH If someone has updated or changed the directory of a referenced file, you will need to change the path to enable AutoCAD to locate and retrieve it. The Path option lets you change the path of loaded xrefs.

On a large model it is not unusual to have many or all of the xref source files in a separate directory. Path allows you to assign one or all of your source files to a separate directory. Use the * wildcard to list all of the files.

```
Command:XREF
Enter an option [?/Bind/Detach/Path/Reload/Overlay/Attach]:P
Edit path for which Xref(s):CORNER
     Scanning ...

XREF name: CORNER
Old path: C:\OFFICE\2NDFLR\CORNER
New path: C:\OFFICE\3RDFLR\CORNER
```

The Path option prompts you to enter the names of the xrefs that you want changed. You are then given the old path name and prompted for the new path. You must enter the entire path name correctly. The problem most frequently encountered with this option is the spelling and nomenclature of the path. Pay careful attention to the use of backslashes (\) and colons (:).

RELOAD There are two ways to reload your external files. The first way is simply by retrieving the file; the second is by using the Reload option.

Reload is used most frequently on a networked system where several people are working concurrently on the same project. If user 1 is updating a master file, and user 2 has made significant changes in one of the source files, user 1 may want to update the xref of user 2's file to see what effect the changes have on the master file.

If only one person is working on a project, Reload may be used when making significant changes on a portion of the drawing. If additions are made to a portion of a drawing that is an XREF, it may be WBLOCKed and then reloaded with the current changes. This function helps the file management process. Again, the * wildcard can be used to Reload all of the xrefs.

```
Command:XREF
Enter an option [?/Bind/Detach/Path/Reload/Overlay/Attach]:R
Xref(s) to reload:CORNER
```

OVERLAY attaches a file onto the current file, but doesn't allow the overlaid file to be attached or overlaid on a subsequent file. An overlaid file is not included in a drawing when the drawing itself is attached or overlaid as an xref to another drawing. Overlaid xrefs are designed for data sharing. (See next section, "Attaching Versus Overlaying.")

ATTACH is the default setting. It works much like the INSERT command in that it is used to place an existing xref on the current drawing. As with INSERT, the name of the last xref is used as the default.

```
Command:XREF
Enter an option [?/Bind/Detach/Path/Reload/Overlay/Attach]:A
Xref(s) to attach <CORNER>:A:24PANEL

Attach Xref 24panel:24PANEL
24PANEL loaded.
Insertion point:6,5
```

CLIP allows you to attach portions of an externally referenced file.

```
Command:XREF
Enter an option [?/Bind/Detach/Path/Reload/Overlay/Attach]:C
Enter clipping option [ON/OFF/Clipdepth/Delete/generate
   Polyline/New boundary]<new>:N
Specify clipping boundary:
{Select polyline/Polygonal/Rectangular]<Rectangular>:
Specify first point: (pick the points of the polygon)
```

Attaching Versus Overlaying

An overlaid xref is not included in a drawing when the drawing is itself attached or overlaid as an xref to another drawing.

In Figure 18-7 SCREW.DWG is attached to BUSHING.DWG, which is either attached or overlaid on WORKPART.DWG. All three files are visible, because SCREW.DWG was attached and, whether attached or overlaid, BUSHING.DWG was not more than one level of xref away from WORKPART.DWG.

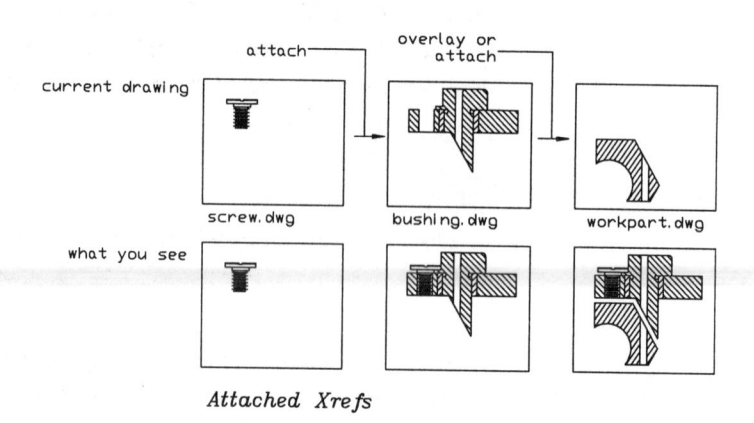

Figure 18-7

In Figure 18-8, SCREW.DWG is overlaid on BUSHING.DWG, which is either attached or overlaid on WORKPART.DWG. When you open WORKPART.DWG, SCREW.DWG is not visible, because it was overlaid, not attached, to BUSHING.DWG and is more than one level of xref away from WORKPART.DWG.

Attached Xrefs

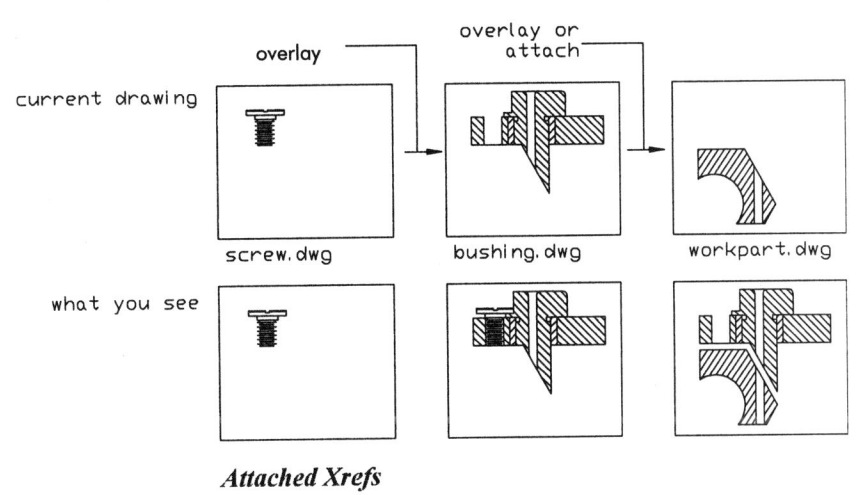

Figure 18-8

Using Xrefs

If you wanted to update a block, you could explode it, update it, and then, if the changes were significant and possibly useful on other files, you could WBLOCK the revised data and reinsert it. (Before inserting, you would need to purge the existing block; use the PURGE command.) If the block was entirely wrong, you could simply erase it.

You can erase an xref, but you can't explode it. Instead, you can access the external source file, update it, and reload it.

> **Notes**
> AutoCAD ignores block attributes and paper space-dependent information in XREFs.

The reinserted wblock would reflect all of the changes that were made on the one update. With xrefs, the revised source file will affect every drawing in which the file is referenced.

Like blocks as well, only the objects created in model space will be loaded into the drawing. No paper-dependent or viewport-dependent objects will be read.

If one or more of the xrefs attached to a drawing is moved or erased, AutoCAD will display an error message when the file is retrieved:

```
"C:\OFFICE\2NDFLR\CORNER" Can't open file
** Error resolving Xref CORNER
```

A block with the name of the xref will be entered at the position the xref was to occupy. This error can be corrected by updating the path name or reloading the referenced file into the original directory.

Xrefs and Layers

All of the properties of the objects of the referenced files will be added to the current file in addition to the objects themselves. Layers, linetypes, colors, and text and dimension styles will be added to the master file.

When these properties are added, they are renamed in the current drawing using a temporary name to avoid confusion and duplication. When new layers are added, the new name will have the xref file name followed by the layer name.

Layer 0 is the exception to this layer renaming. Any objects on Layer 0 will be placed in Layer 0 of the current model, and all objects that are referenced will assume the settings associated with the current Layer 0.

Managing Blocks and Xrefs

If you are transporting a drawing to another machine or site, you must take along the xref files. If the file is not on the disk, it cannot be loaded. Similarly, when someone is backing up and erasing files from the hard drive, it is a good idea to provide him/her with a list of the files that you reference so that they are not backed up to an external hard drive and removed.

When creating files, it is not a bad idea to record file information on paper — such information as:

1. Layers plus creation date
2. Blocks plus first insertion date
3. Xrefs plus first insertion date

If you do not note this information, you can guarantee that you will need it.

As xrefs are inserted, AutoCAD creates an external log (.XLG) file of the inserted file. This ASCII text file, located in the current drawing directory, records all relevant xref information concerning attached files and any subsequent xrefs added. It is updated every time an external reference file is attached.

The XBIND Command

With the XREF command, an external source file is added to a current or master file for the duration of the editing period. When you exit the master file, the source file and all of its dependent "symbols," including linetypes, text styles, layers, and dimension styles, are returned to the original file. While part of the current file, the blocks, the layers, linetypes, etc. are listed and referenced to the current file, but they are not accessible and remain part of the external source file. Therefore you can bind a block from an attached xref.

The XBIND command allows certain of these "symbols" to be added to a current file when it is saved and they can, therefore, be accessed for use. This would allow you to use the customized xref linetype on your current file. At the end of the editing session, the xref would return to its original source file, and the linetype would remain with the current file.

> **Toolbar** From the Reference toolbar, choose Xbind.
>
> **Pull Down** From the Modify menu, choose Object, External Reference, Bind.

The command line equivalent is **XBIND**.

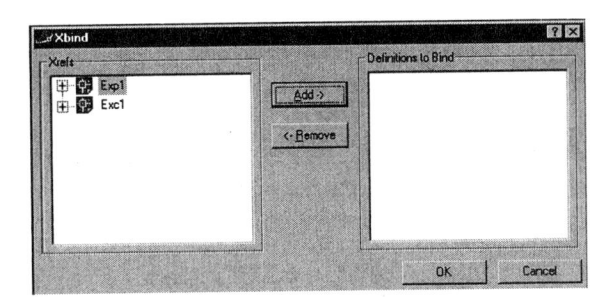

Figure 18-9

The command allows you to attach blocks, layers, linetypes, text and dimensions styles permanently..

```
Command:XBIND
Enter symbol type to bind
    [Block/Dimstyle/LAyer/LType/Style]:
```

Tracking

Tracking is a way to locate a point relative to other points on the drawing. The tracking, or Autotracking, is done along alignment paths that are based on object snap points. For example, in Figures 18-10 through 18-13 you can see how we have created a circle directly vertical from the midpoint of a diagonal line (the X value), at the Y value of a horizontal line.

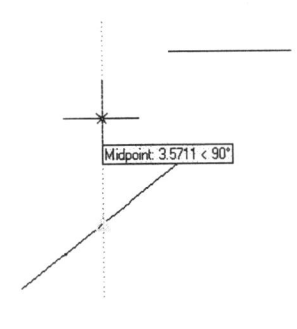

Figure 18-10

Make sure your Autotrack is on, and your OSNAPs are set to MIDpoint and ENDpoint.

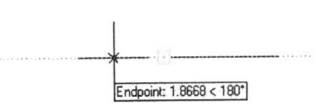

```
Command: Circle
Specify center point for circle or
    [3P/2P/Ttr]: (place your cursor above
    the middle point on the vertical line
    as in Figure 18-10)
(Then move your cursor to the horizontal
    line and pause there, Figure 18-11)
(Then move your cursor left to intersect
    the two lines, Figure 18-12)
                        (Then draw the
                            circle
                            ,18-14)
```

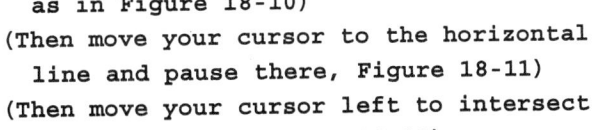

Figure 18-11

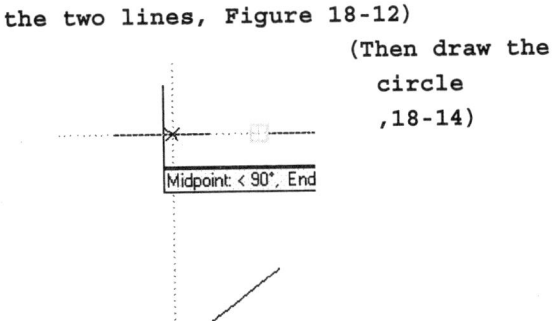

Figure 18-12

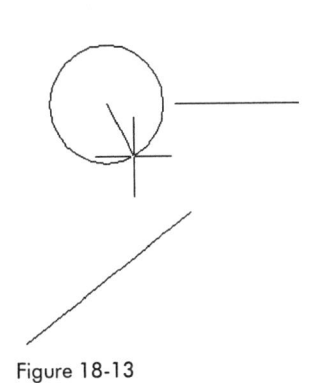

Figure 18-13

Prelab 18 Advanced Blocking and Xrefs

Step 1 Open the file called JIG from Chapter 14. Insert the block called JIGLEG on the right side of the file. If you haven't got this file, quickly draw up just the geometry from page 369.

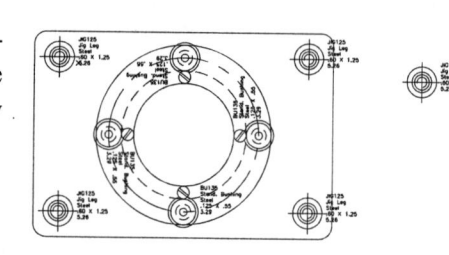

Step 2 Explode the block so that it is separate objects and attribute definitions.

Step 3 Use the ELLIPSE command to add two ellipses to the block. Then BLOCK the data using the same name.

```
Command:BLOCK
Enter block name (or ?):JIGLEG
Block JIGLEG already exists,
    Redefine it?<N>:Y
Insertion base point: (pick the
    intersection of the lines)
Select objects: (pick the block
    and attributes)
```

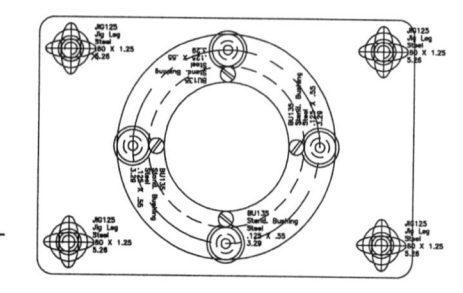

The jiglegs on the part will be automatically updated.

Step 4 Open a new file *without saving the changes in JIG*.

You should have an attributed block file called ATTITLE from Chapter 9. If you don't have this file, quickly create a title block with attributes and WBLOCK it.

INSERT the file ATTITLE and fill in the attributes.

Step 5 Now use the XREF command to reference the JIG file from Chapter 14.

> **Toolbar** From the Reference toolbar, choose Attach.
>
> **Pull Down** From the Insert menu, choose XREF Manager.

The command line equivalent is -**XREF**.

```
Command:-XREF
Enter an option [?/Bind/Detach/Path/Reload/Overlay/Attach]:A
Xref(s) to attach <CORNER>:JIG
```

```
Attach Xref JIG
JIG loaded.
Insertion point: (pick a point)
X scale factor <1>:↵
Y scale factor <1>:↵
Rotation angle <0>:↵
```

Or use the XREF Manager to import the file. You should end up with this.

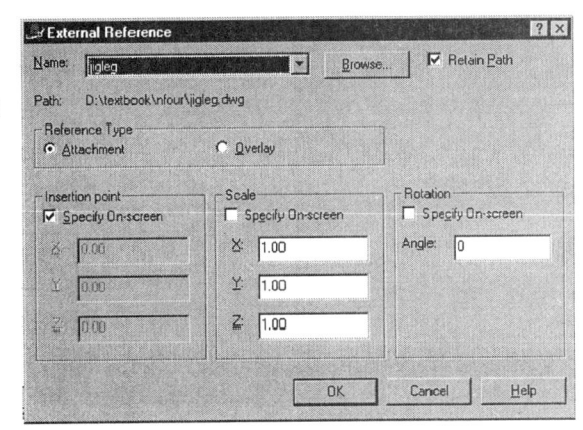

Xrefs can be manipulated in exactly the same way as the blocks: the layers can be listed, the object can be edited as a single object, the objects can be used as OSNAP positions, and the colors can be changed. As with blocks, individual items of geometry within the xref cannot be changed. The only difference between an xref and a block is that the xref is not added to the file.

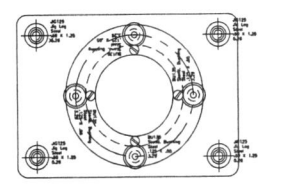

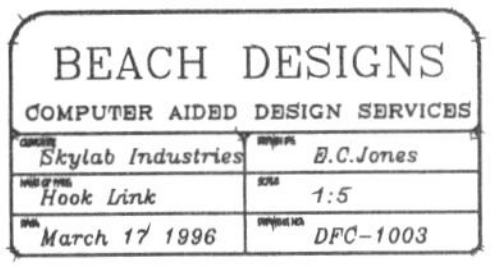

Step 6 SAVE the file as XREF, then open your JIG file.

In the JIG file, use STRETCH to change the size of the JIG. Then use ATTEDIT to change the size of one set of attributes.

```
Command: ATTEDIT
Edit attributes one by one?<Y>:↵
Block name specification <*>:↵
Attribute tag specification
  <*>:↵
Attribute value specification
  <*>:↵
Select attributes:W
First corner: (pick 1)
Other corner: (pick 2)
5 attributes selected.
Value/Position/Height/Angle/
 Style/Layer/Color/Next <N>:H
New height <0.07>:1
Value/Position/Height/Angle/Style/Layer/Color/Next <N>:↵
```

Advanced Blocking and Xrefs **447**

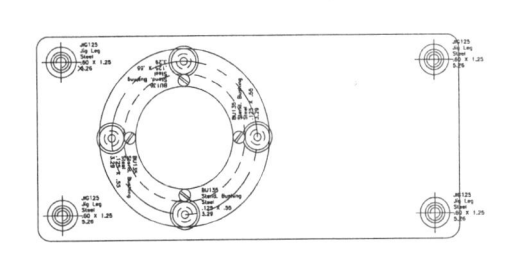

```
Value/Position/Height/Angle/Style/Layer/Color/Next <N>:H
New height<0.07>:1
```

Continue until all heights are changed.

Step 7 SAVE the file and OPEN the file called XREF.

Notice that the XREF has been updated automatically to reflect the new drawing. Both the size of the file and the size of the attributes have been altered.

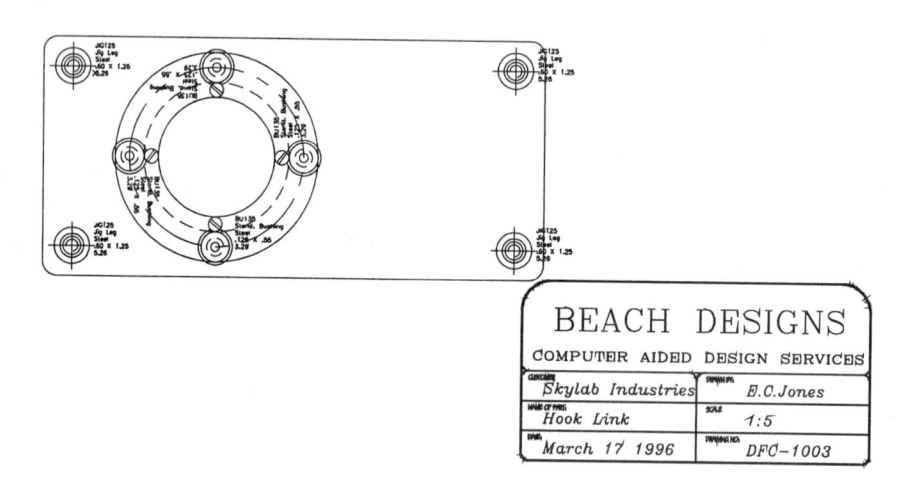

Toolbar From the Reference toolbar, choose Xbind.

Pull Down From the File menu, choose Bind.

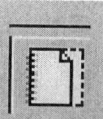

Step 8 Now use the XBIND command to bind the jig to the XREF file.
The command line equivalent is **XBIND**.

```
Command:XBIND
Enter symbol type to bind [Block/Dimstyle/LAyer/LType/Style]:B
Dependent BLOCK name(s):JIG
    Scanning ...
1 Block bound.
```

Use SAVE-AS to create a new file called XREF1. Note the difference in the size of the file XREF and the file XREF1.

Command and Function Summary

XBIND binds a block, layer, linetype, or other object to a file.

XREF allows you to add files to your drawings as external references.

Notes

While doing the following exercises, it is suggested that you note on paper the names of the blocks and xrefs you are using as files.

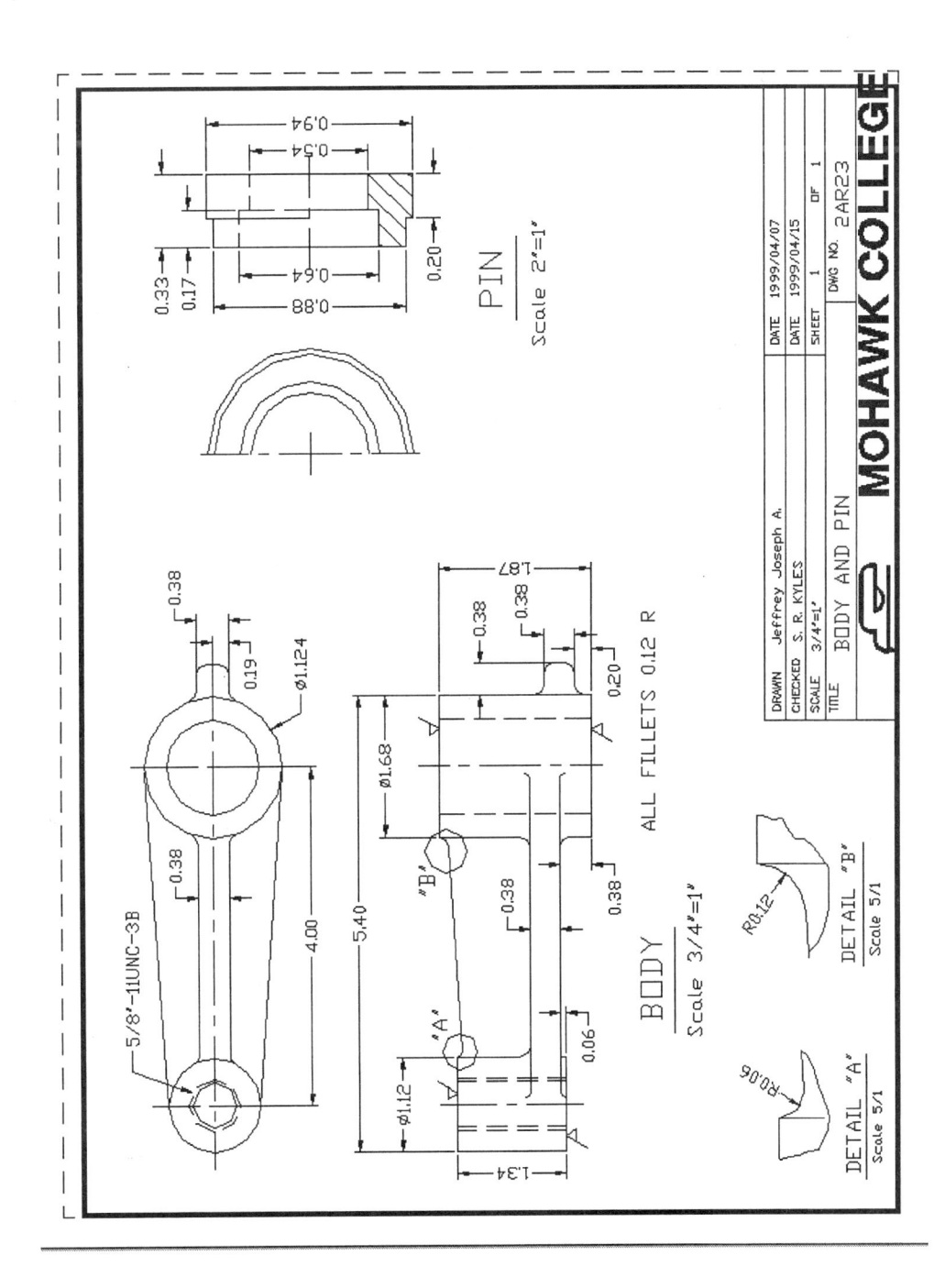

Advanced Blocking and Xrefs

Exercise A18

Step 1 Create the following files:

1. A plain steno chair, filename STENO1
2. A steno chair with arms, filename STENO2
3. A 5′ × 6′ workstation, filename 5X6WST
4. A 6′ × 7′ workstation, filename 6X6WST
5. An executive office, filename MGMT

(Use files from Challenger 4 if you have them.)

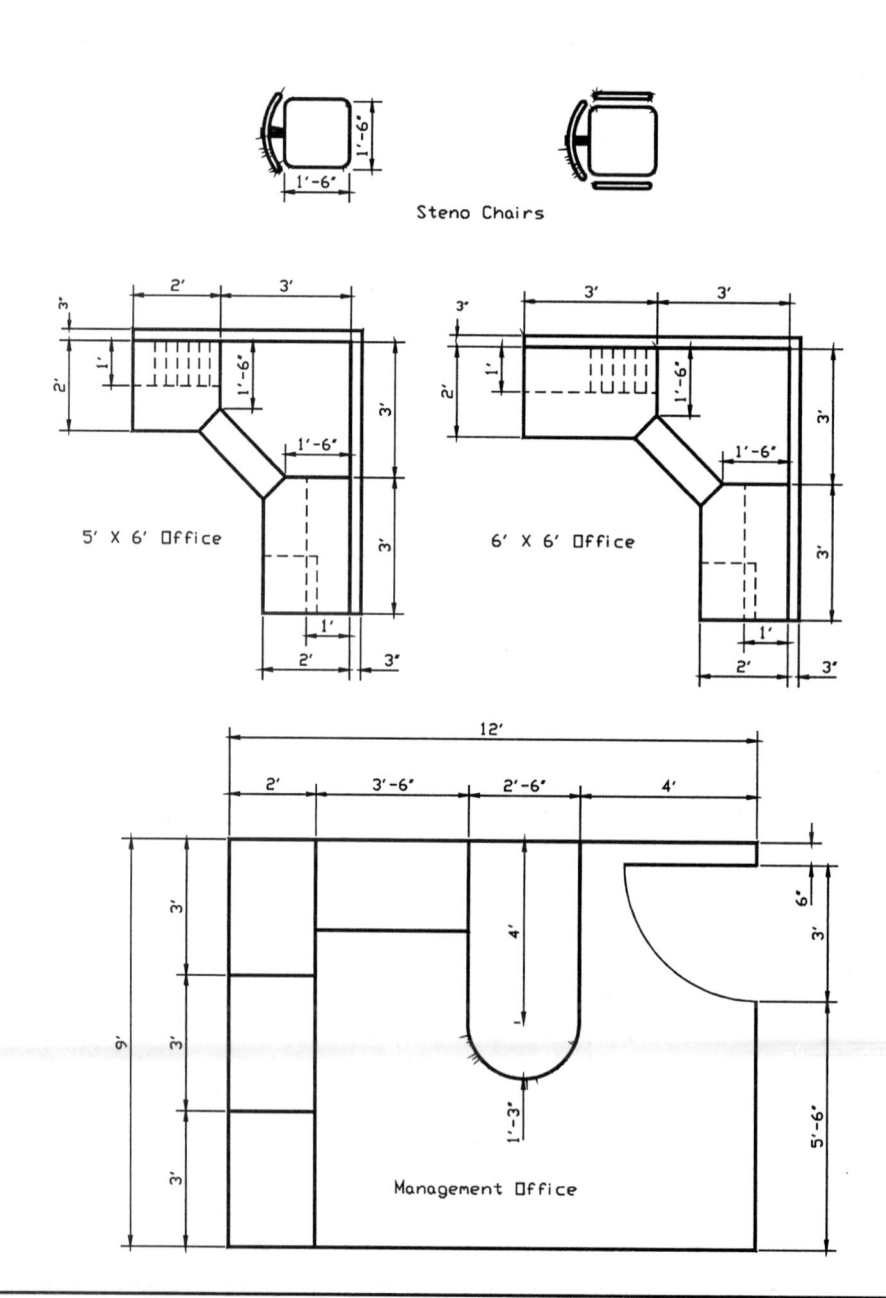

Step 2   Create an office that is 48′ × 28′ with a 6′ double door.

Step 3   Create a bank of eight 5′ × 6′ workstations (filename 5X6WST) in the middle of the room by inserting them as BLOCKs. Add an armless STENO chair (STENO1) to each workstation.

Step 4   Using the XREF command, insert four management offices (MGMT). Insert a STENO chair with arms (STENO2) into each management office.

Step 5   SAVE the file, and note the time and the size of the file as follows:
Filename _____ Time _____ Size _____

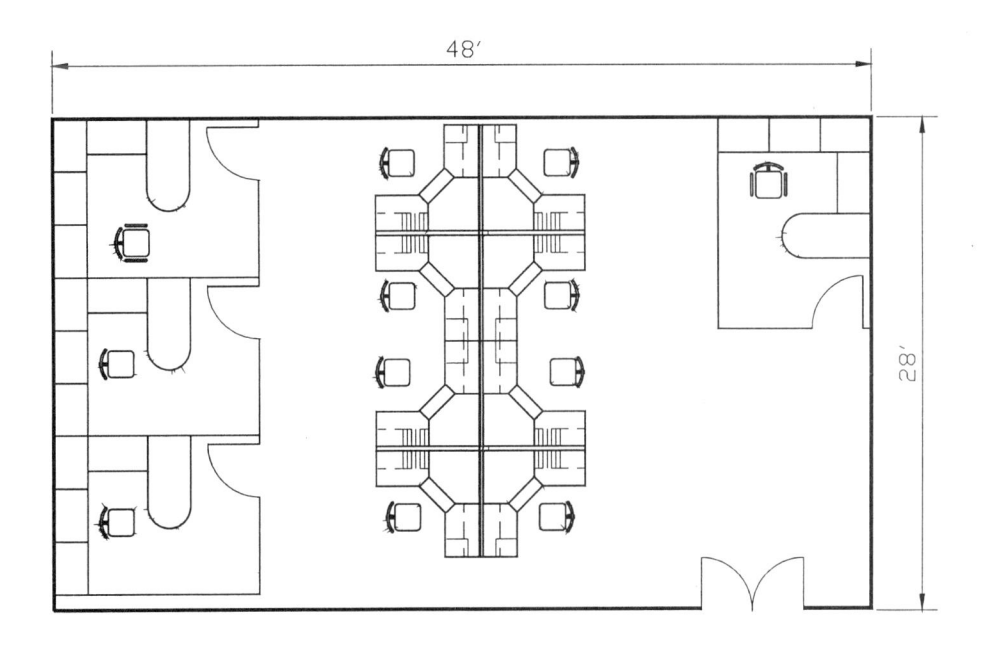

Step 6   Enter the management source file and change the size of the curved desk. Add some filing cabinets and a plant. END the file.

Step 7   Enter your office layout. Note the fact that the management offices have been automatically updated.

Bind the management offices to the office layout. END the file and note its size:

File size _____

Reenter the file and erase the management offices. Detach them from your file and note the size of the file after you have SAVEd:

File size _____

Advanced Blocking and Xrefs   **451**

Exercise C18

Step 1 Create the following files:

1. A deciduous tree, filename DECID
2. A coniferous tree, filename CONIF
3. An 8 m × 8 m house, filename HOUSE
4. A 10 m × 12 m house plus deck, filename HOUSE2
5. A swimming pool, filename POOL

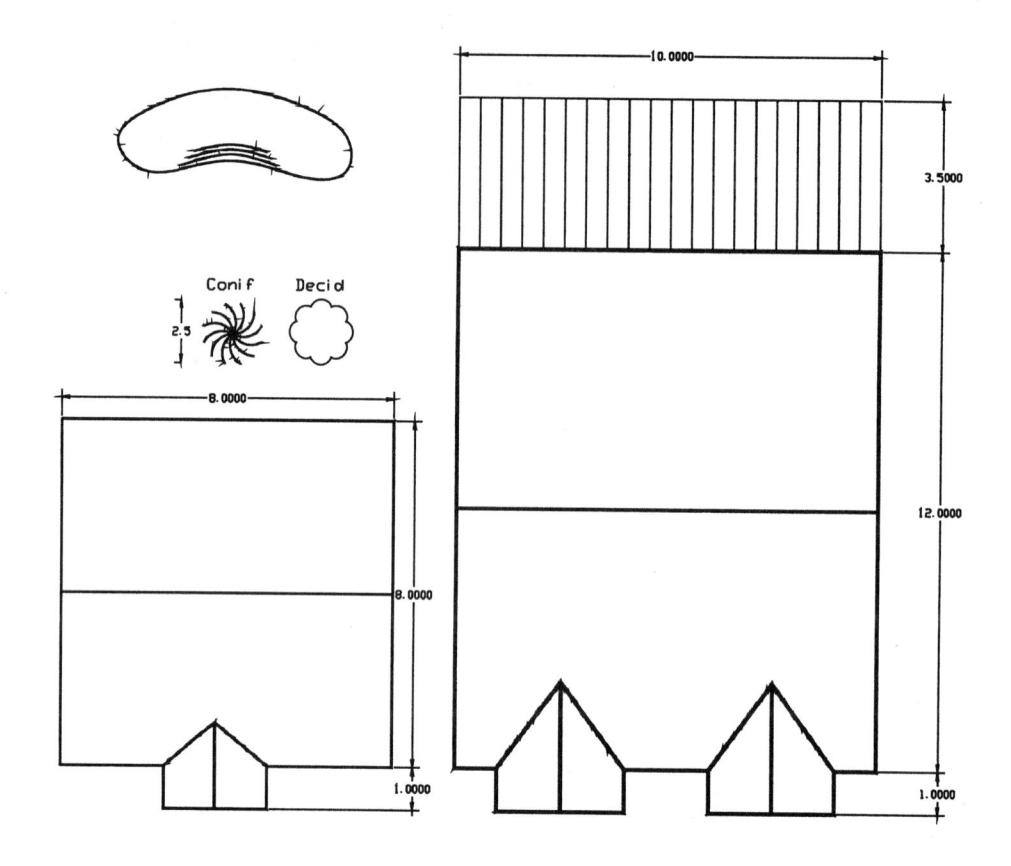

Step 2 Create a plot plan for a single lot that is 20 m × 30 m. In this lot, INSERT the first house (HOUSE1) and at least 12 coniferous trees (CONIF).

Step 3 Using the XREF command, Attach the pool in the backyard   A:POOL.

Step 4   Now SAVE and end the file and note the time the file was saved and the size of the file:
Time _____ Size _____

Step 5   While outside of the file, change the source file for the swimming pool (POOL). Add a diving board and some "natural setting" vegetation.

Step 6   Enter your site plan. Note the fact that the pool has been updated automatically. Bind the pool to the site plan master file.

SAVE the file and note its size.

File size _____

Reenter the file and erase the pool. Detach it from the file and note the size of the file after you have SAVEd:

File size _____

Advanced Blocking and Xrefs   **453**

Exercise E18

Step 1   Create the following files:

1. A fuse, filename FUSE

2. A relay, filename RELAY

3. A temperature control overload, filename OL

Step 2   Using these external blocks, create this 3-phase supply diagram. Then create another file for the control circuit.

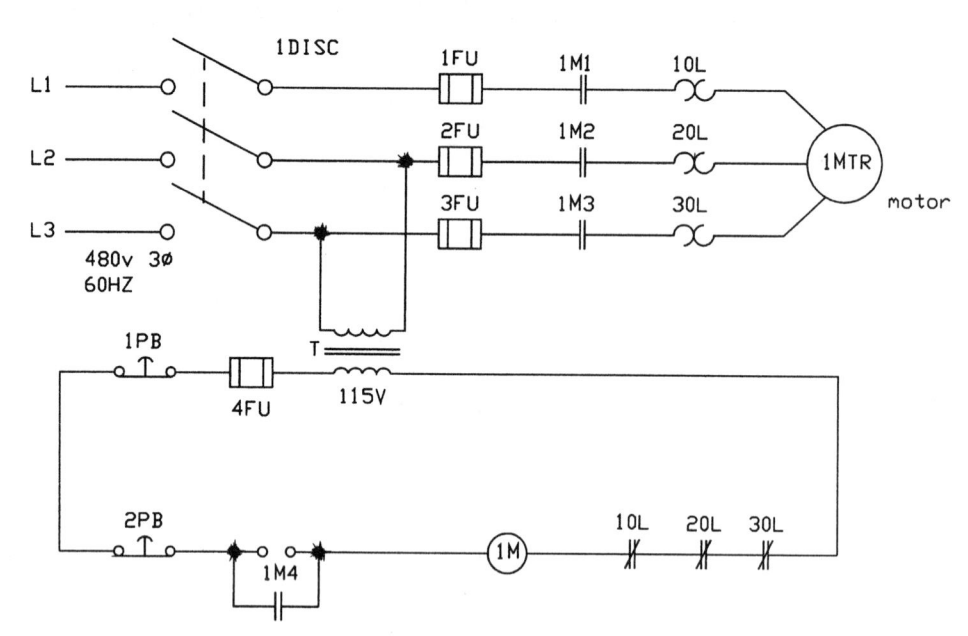

Step 3   Bring up the 3-phase supply diagram and explode one of the fuse blocks. Make some minor changes to the design, and reblock the fuse under the same name.

Step 4   Use XREF to place the control circuit into the 3-phase supply diagram.

Step 5   Save the drawing with the 3-phase supply, and bring up the control circuit file. Redesign the control circuit to a different sequence of operation. Save the file without changing the name.

Step 6   Bring up the 3-phase supply file and note how the file has been updated.

Exercise M18

Step 1 Create the following files:

1. An AutoCAD DOS station, filename ACADDOS

2. An AutoCAD Windows station, filename ACADWIN

3. A machine tool as shown, filename TOOL1

4. Icons for:

   Finite Element Analysis, filename FEA

   Materials, filename MAT

   Existing Parts, filename EXPARTS

   Standard Parts, filename STPARTS

   Machines, filename MACH

   Central Network or Database, filename DATA

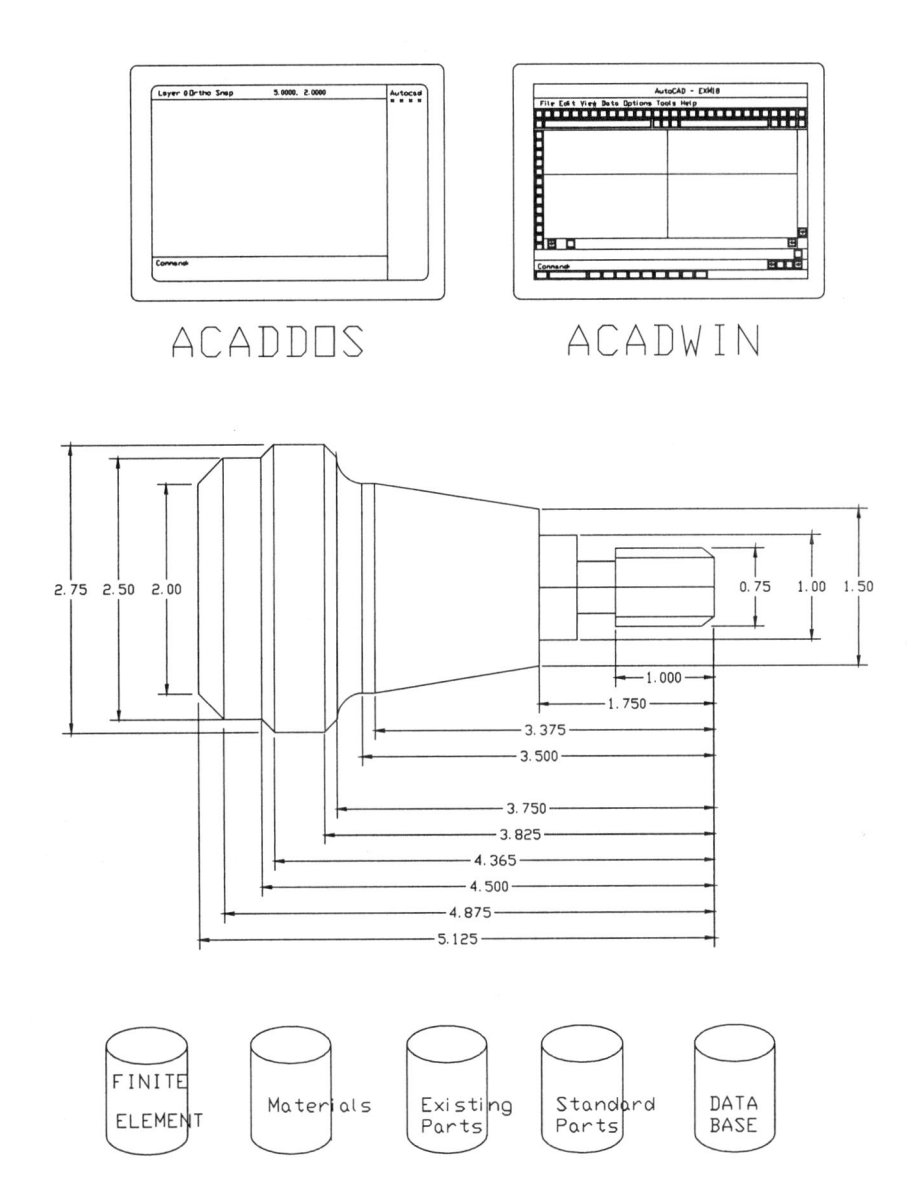

Advanced Blocking and Xrefs

Step 2   Create a data flow management chart as shown.

Step 3   For the first chart, use INSERT to place all of the ICONs. Use XREF to Attach to place the

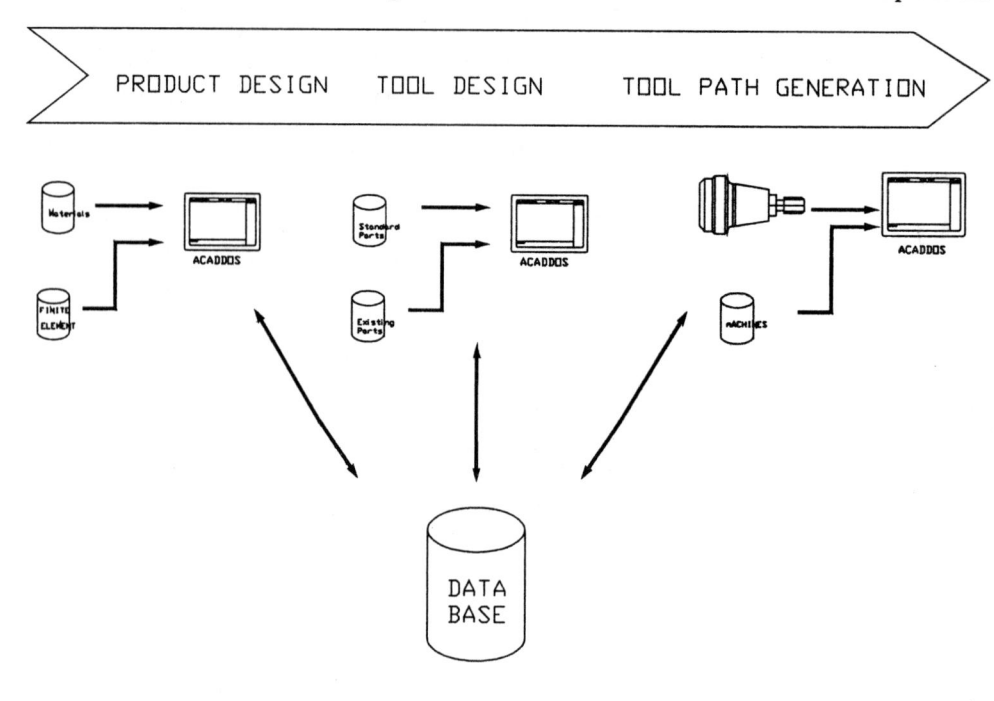

ACADDOS stations at each section of the data flow chart (A:ACAD11). Use XREF also to place the machine tool (A:TOOL1).

Step 4   End the file and note the file size and time:

File size _____ Time _____

Step 5   Enter the file again and Bind the **ACADDOS** files to the Chart.
Once again note the size and time:

File size _____ Time _____

Step 6   Enter the Tool file TOOL1 and use STRETCH to change some of the parameters of the tool. SAVE the file.

Step 7   Enter the flow chart and note the fact that the tool has been automatically updated. Bind your tool file to the flow chart file.

END the file and note the size of the file:

File size _____

Reenter the file, erase the tools and ACAD stations and Detach them from your file. Make sure that they are Detached. Once more, note the file size:

File size _____

Challenger 18A

Using the preceding exercises, create attributes for each BLOCK that is added. Also create new LAYERs for each BLOCK.

Then create a data extract file to extract the files. When you exchange the first set of BLOCKs with the second, generate another data extract file.

Finally, create a file of five nested XREFed drawings (5 lots, 5 office floors, or 5 flow charts). Bind the drawings and save them. Note the size. In each case, use INSERT to create the same drawing and note any difference in the size of the files. Create this drawing with attributes for wall, ceiling, handrail, floor and trim finishes for each separate floor. Block each floor separably, then compile into a finished floor.

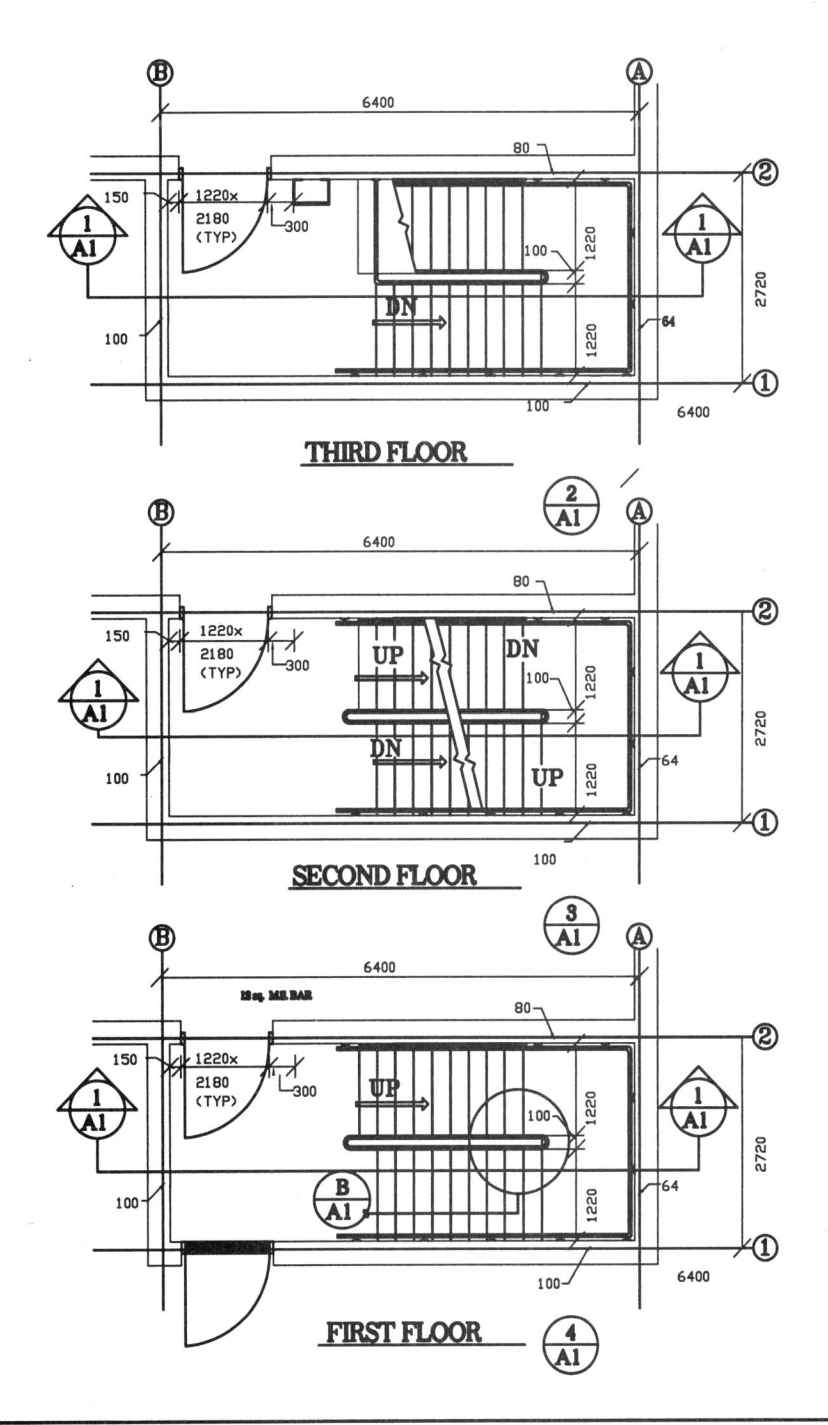

Challenger 18B

For this corner layout, create an attributed A2 title block. On a separate file draw the intersection to scale. Insert the block onto a new drawing, then attach the intersection as an XREF.

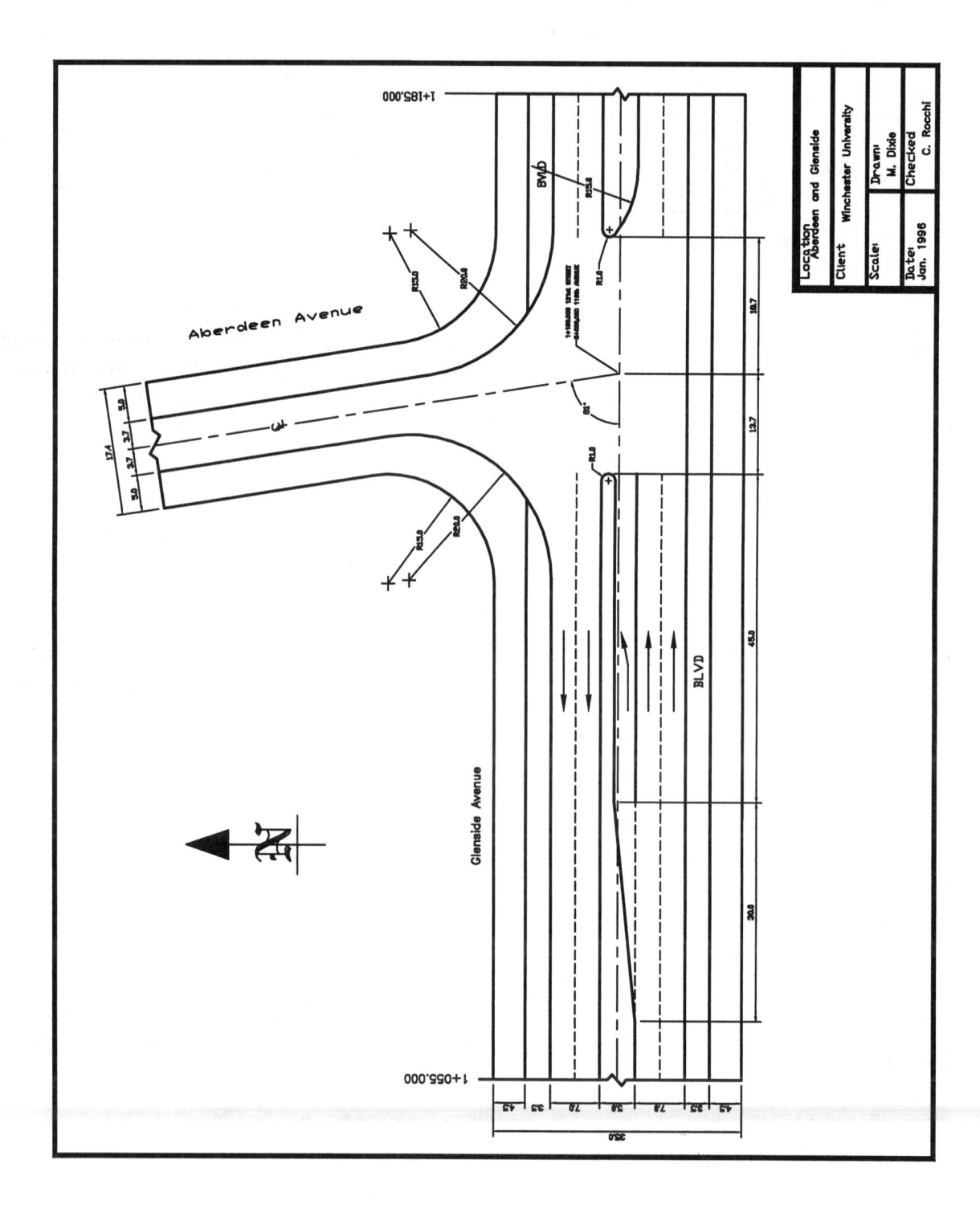

19 Final Tests and Projects

1. On-screen review
2. General review
3. Final drawing projects

The next few pages offer two on-screen problems, 70 questions on the preceding six chapters of this book, and four final projects. Your instructor may offer you these or similar questions as a final exam. If you are not required to write a final exam, these questions will be nonetheless useful in showing you how much you understand.

Section 1: On-Screen Problems

This section is difficult to combine into a Final Project, because there is so little graphic information. Most of this material covers the creation of graphics data and exchanging this data with other types of computer documents.

Final projects are offered after Section 2, to ensure that your understanding of that section is complete and to help you combine all of the skills learned in this section.

Problem 1

Set SNAP to Isometric and draw in the part shown. Use the nominal value of each line — if it says 1.3, make the line 1.3 in length. Use the UNITS command to set the number of digits to the right of the decimal point to 4.

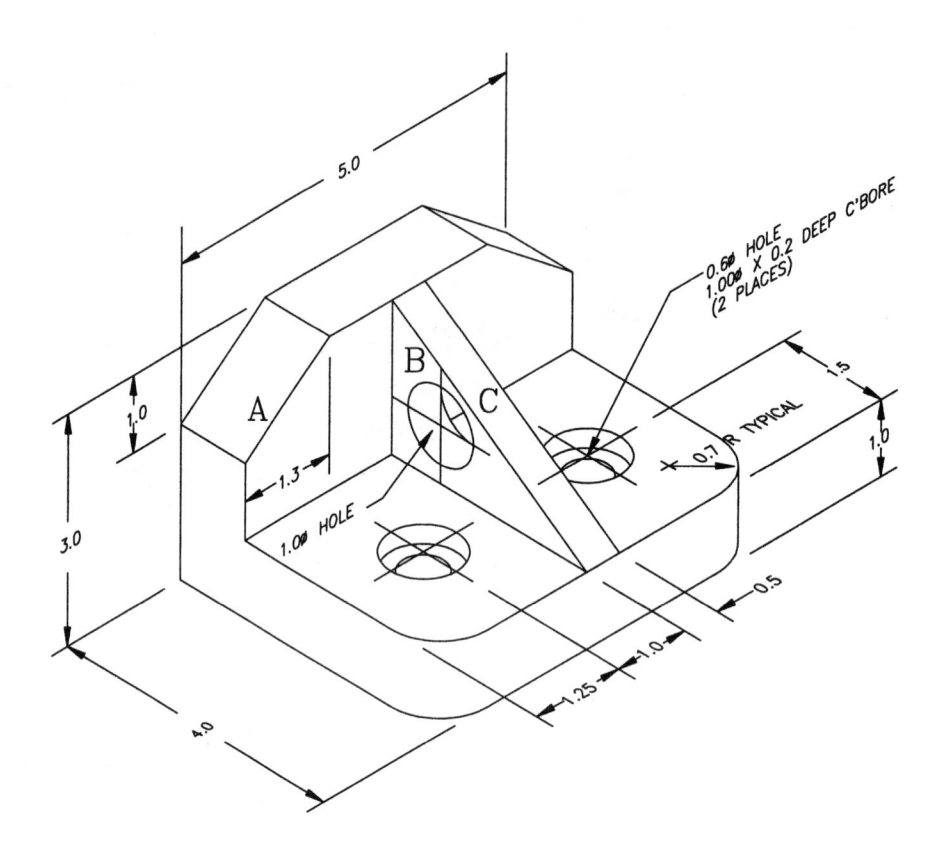

Begin the drawing by setting the back lower left corner of the part at 0,0. Either move the UCS, PAN the screen over, or set your LIMITS so that the 0,0 is on screen.

Refer to your drawing to answer the following questions:

1. The total length of line segment A is:

    a. 1.8775

    b. 2.2015

    c. 1.9975

    d. 1.7500

    e. 2.2565

2. The absolute coordinate value of the center of the circle B is:

    a. 3.4641,2.0000

    b. 3.9672,2.2100

    c. 3.1462,1.5465

    d. 2.6574,2.0000

    e. 3.5837,1.9283

3. The total area of surface C is:

    a. 2.6574

    b. 1.9684

    c. 2.7947

    d. 2.1651

    e. 1.7483

Problem 2

Draw the electrical cover as shown. Start the drawing with the lower left corner at 0,0. Use PAN, UCS, or LIMITS to place the 0,0 on screen.

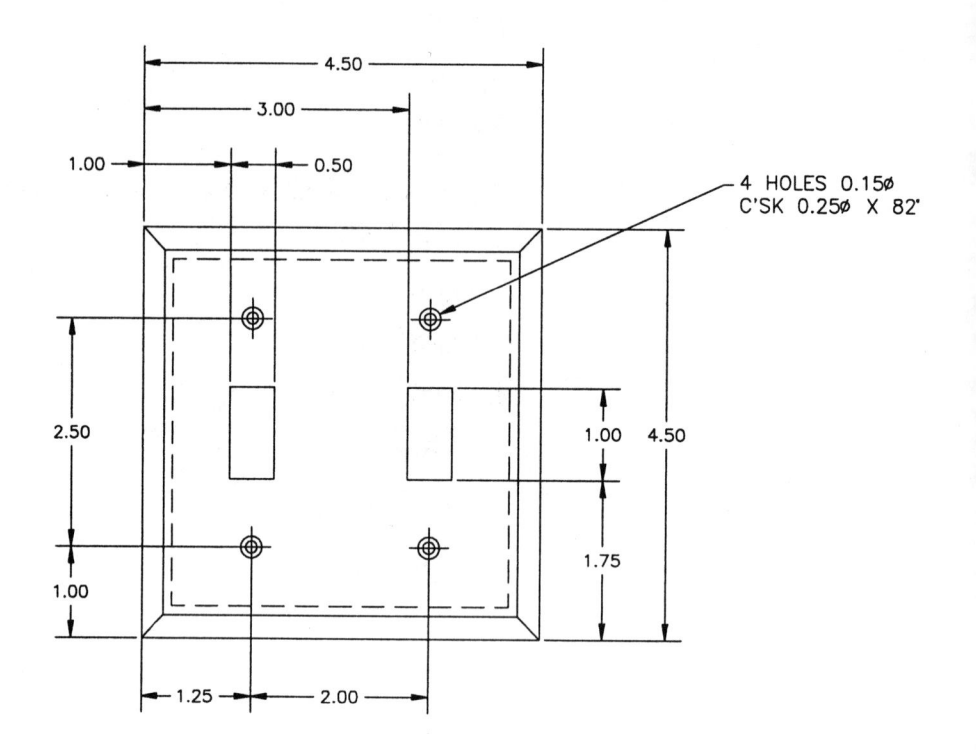

Use the drawing to answer the following questions:

1. The total surface area of the flat portion of the plate minus the bolt holes and rectangular holes is:

    a. 12.5430

    b. 14.8190

    c. 14.2340

    d. 13.3570

    e. 14.9055

2. The total area of the two rectangles and the bolt holes is:

    a. 1.1810

    b. 2.4570

    c. 1.7660

    d. 1.0045

    e. 3.9860

3. The circumference of one of the bolt holes is:

    a. .4520

    b. .8596

    c. .7500

    d. .6725

    e. .7540

4. The absolute coordinate value of the end point of the line at A is:

    a. 4.25,4.25

    b. 4.00,4.00

    c. 3.75,4.00

    d. 3.75,3.75

    e. 4.25,4.00

5. Use the scale command to expand the two rectangles from the center point of the plate by a factor of 1.33. The new surface area of the plate minus the bolt holes and rectangles is:

    a. 15.0990

    b. 12.0422

    c. 14.0422

    d. 13.9586

    e. 15.0958

Section 2: Review

1. Before it can be inserted, an attribute must be:

    a. Blocked

    b. Edited

    c. Extracted

2. When using a Window to choose the series of attributes:

    a. The first attribute defined is offered first.

    b. The attribute closest to the first Window position is chosen first.

    c. The attribute in the highest position in *Y* is chosen first.

3. What happens if you don't define the prompt in the ATTDEF command?

    a. The user will not be prompted.

    b. The tag is used as the prompt.

    c. The default is offered for the prompt.

4. What are you "writing" when you define an ATTRIBUTE?

    a. A program that will help the user define attributes

    b. A script file

    c. An attribute block

5. What happens when you accept the default by hitting ⏎ when asked for the default ATTRIBUTE value?

    a. The default value entered by the person writing the ATTDEF will be chosen.

    b. The system default will be chosen.

    c. The default will be .5.

6. Is an ATTDEF filed with the model even if it hasn't been blocked or inserted?

    a. Yes

    b. No

7. Within the ATTRIBUTE command, what does Invisible refer to?

    a. The lines around the block will be invisible.

    b. The tags will be invisible.

    c. The attributes when inserted will be invisible.

8. Can you change the LAYER of an attributed block?

    a. Yes

    b. No

9. What is the advantage of setting an ATTRIBUTE text height within a title block?

   a. The text will always be the same in all the title blocks.

   b. The text will always have the same justification.

   c. The height will not have to be changed in the STYLE command.

10. Once the ATTRIBUTE is defined, how can you change the prompts?

    a. CHPROP

    b. ATTEDIT

    c. CHANGE

11. Must the ATTRIBUTE be EXPLODEd before it can be moved?

    a. Yes

    b. No

    c. Sometimes

12. How can you modify the color of an ATTRIBUTE?

    a. This is not possible because it has nongraphics data attached.

    b. CHPROP

    c. ATTEDIT

13. If you would like to change the prompting sequence of the ATTRIBUTE instance, what must you do?

    a. CHPROP

    b. EXPLODE and reblock

    c. Change the default

14. What is a "tag"?

    a. The title you give to the attribute definition

    b. The word used to define a prompt

    c. The word for nongraphics data

15. How can an ATTRIBUTEd BLOCK be used in another file?

    a. ATTEXT

    b. By saving it as a WBLOCK

    c. By INSERTing it as an ATTDEF

Final Tests and Projects   465

16. What command do you use to define an ATTRIBUTE?

    a. ATTEXT

    b. ATTDEF

    c. ATTEDIT

17. When you want to attach an attributed BLOCK to a drawing, what command do you use?

    a. BLOCK

    b. INSERT

    c. PURGE

18. What does the term "global" mean when editing attributes?

    a. A global edit affects just the graphics.

    b. A global edit edits all the attributes selected.

    c. A global edit affects just the TAGs.

19. If you don't choose to select the attributes one by one, will all of the attributes on screen be selected?

    a. Yes, if you Window them all.

    b. Yes, they are all inserted from the same block reference.

    c. No, only those selected one by one will be edited.

20. If you have INSERTed many attributed blocks, how do you change the default value and then keep INSERTing it?

    a. It can't be done.

    b. ATTEDIT, then CHANGE

    c. EXPLODE, CHANGE, and reBLOCK

21. What command do you use to modify the value of an ATTRIBUTE instance?

    a. CHANGE and reBLOCK

    b. EXPLODE and CHANGE

    c. ATTEDIT

22. What command do you use to extract the values of all of the ATTRIBUTE instances to an ASCII-based format?

    a. ATTEDIT

    b. ATTEXT

    c. ATTASCII

23. What command is used to change the position of an attribute instance?

    a. ATTEDIT

    b. MOVE

    c. ATTEXT

24. Does QTEXT work on ATTRIBUTES?

    a. Yes

    b. No

25. Why does your attribute extract have to be ASCII-based?

    a. ASCII is an insertable code.

    b. ASCII is the accepted standard.

    c. ASCII has the alphabet that we use.

26. Can you MEASURE a SOLID?

    a. Yes

    b. No

27. What is the quickest method of making five equal portions out of a stretch of geometry that contains two arcs and a circle?

    a. BLOCK it and DIVIDE it

    b. PEDIT and DIVIDE it

    c. PEDIT and MEASURE it

28. Can you use the MEASURE command on an ELLIPSE?

    a. Yes

    b. No

29. What can you do to see the division markers created with the DIVIDE command?

    a. ZOOM Window

    b. Change PDMODE

    c. Change PDSIZE

30. What is the maximum size of the default point?

    a. 10 × 10

    b. No maximum

    c. One pixel

31. If you wanted to have a DONUT shape as opposed to a point displayed as a division marker in the DIVIDE command, how would you do it?

    a. Change the PDMODE

    b. Make the DONUT a BLOCK

    c. Change the PDSIZE

32. Why will the Crossing option not work in the MEASURE command?

    a. Because the LINEs must be picked in a contiguous order

    b. Because the ARCs must be selected first

    c. Because only one object can be selected at a time

33. What is the key element when placing a BLOCK correctly within the MEASURE command?

    a. The scale factor of the block

    b. The insertion base point of the block

    c. The attributes of the block

34. What does the ID command do?

    a. Allows the user to add an ID number to an object

    b. Gives the position of a point relative to the origin

    c. Lists the LAYER, position, and block association of an object

35. If you wanted to find the angle of a LINE relative to 0,0 what command would you use?

    a. LIST

    b. ANGLE

    c. DBLIST

36. If you have UNITS set to two decimal points of accuracy (.00), will a LIST on the objects that you have created with this setting default to two decimal points of accuracy?

    a. Yes

    b. No

37. Can you use OSNAP when you are calculating a DISTance?

    a. Yes

    b. No

38. Does the AREA command calculate volume as well?

   a. Yes

   b. No

39. How would you change the time setting on your computer?

   a. TIME

   b. DATE

   c. TDCREATE

40. Where can you find the position of the last entered point?

   a. ID

   b. LIST

   c. STATUS

41. What does the term "elapsed time" mean?

   a. The time that has elapsed since the user signed onto a file

   b. The time that has elapsed since the user signed onto the system

   c. The time that has elapsed since the file was started

42. What is TDINDWIG?

   a. The time and date indicator in ROM

   b. The elapsed time setting value

   c. The total editing time value

43. What is an EPS file?

   a. Extract Printer Script

   b. Encapsulated PostScript

   c. Enhanced Printer Script

44. What is the difference between a raster file and a bit map?

   a. A raster file only works on a VGA screen.

   b. A raster file accesses the pixels more rapidly.

   c. There is no difference.

45. What is a pixel?

    a. The smallest addressable portion of your screen

    b. The center of your crosshairs

    c. The aperture setting

46. What is a vector file?

    a. A file that relates to the resolution of your screen

    b. A file that records the number of lines on your file

    c. A file that records the position of the objects in your file relative to a fixed origin

47. What three colors make up your screen display?

    a. Red, green, and blue

    b. Red, yellow, and blue

    c. White, black, and green

48. What kind of information is used to make a SLIDE file?

    a. Vector file

    b. Bit map

    c. Window file

49. What command would you use to get a list of slide files?

    a. DIR *.SLD

    b. DIR *.SCR

    c. DIR *.SWR

50. Why does a REGEN take longer than a REDRAW?

    a. A REDRAW will only redraw the vector file.

    b. A REDRAW will only redraw the bit map.

    c. A REDRAW involves the GRID.

51. What does the 1000 stand for in DELAY 1000?

    a. One minute

    b. One nanosecond

    c. One second

52. What does RSCRIPT do?

    a. Redraws the script

    b. Regenerates the script

    c. Repeats the script

53. What is a delimiter?

    a. The limit on the size of your file

    b. The code that indicates the end of an entry

    c. The code that indicates a change in direction

54. What code indicates a preloading of your slides in a script file?

    a. #

    b. *

    c. ^

55. What does the GL stand for in HPGL?

    a. Graphics language

    b. Gather line

    c. Grab line

56. What is a .PLT file?

    a. Perfect line type

    b. Pre-load type

    c. Plot

57. How can you make a .PLT file into an HPGL file?

    a. Rename it (as long as the driver is correct)

    b. Copy it

    c. Extract it

58. What is an image file?

    a. A nongraphics file

    b. A vector file

    c. A bit map file

59. What command do you use to activate the isometric SNAP style?

    a. ISOPLANE

    b. ELLIPSE

    c. SNAP

    d. GRID

60. What pull-down menu is used to set the current drawing plane?

   a. DDLMODE

   b. DDRMODE

   c. DDIMODE

61. What command is used to load a circle on an isometric plane?

   a. ELLIPSE

   b. (Load Isocircle)

   c. ISOCIRCLE

62. What command is used to set the crosshairs to an isometric plane?

   a. F8

   b. SNAP

   c. GRID

   d. ORTHO

63. Can you use CEN to access the center of an isometric circle?

   a. Yes

   b. No

64. Can you draw a SOLID on an isometric plane?

   a. Yes

   b. No

65. What option needs to be changed to add text to an isometric drawing?

   a. Rotation angle

   b. Obliquing angle

   c. Style

66. What command would you use to replace an attributed block with an updated version of another attributed block?

   a. REDEFINE

   b. ATTREDEF

   c. EXPLODE

67. Can a BLOCK contain XREFs?

    a. Yes

    b. No

68. Can an XREF contain BLOCKs?

    a. Yes

    b. No

69. If an XREF contains user-defined HATCH patterns, can these HATCH patterns be used on the file in which the XREF appears?

    a. Yes

    b. No

70. What option is used to add an XREF to the current file?

    a. ATTACH

    b. BIND

    c. BUILD

    d. ADD

Architectural Final

1. Create a floor plan and elevations for the commercial building (opposite page), using MLINE, MLSTYLE, and MLEDIT.

2. Create an ATTRIBUTEd BLOCK with the following:

    a. The area of each room

    b. The final floor finish

    c. The wall color

    d. The trim color

    e. The length of floor trim needed

3. Create another attributed block for the windows and doors containing such information as:

    a. Size of window/door

    b. Rough opening

    c. Glass finish (clear/smoked/triple glaze)

    d. Cost

4. Download this data onto a spreadsheet so that final amount calculations can be made.

5. Create an isometric rendering of the building using Isoplane and SNAP.

6. Document the time taken to create the drawing, the area of the interior, and the size of the file.

7. Accessing the isometric view as an XREF, compile the drawing including the plan, elevations, and an attributed title block.

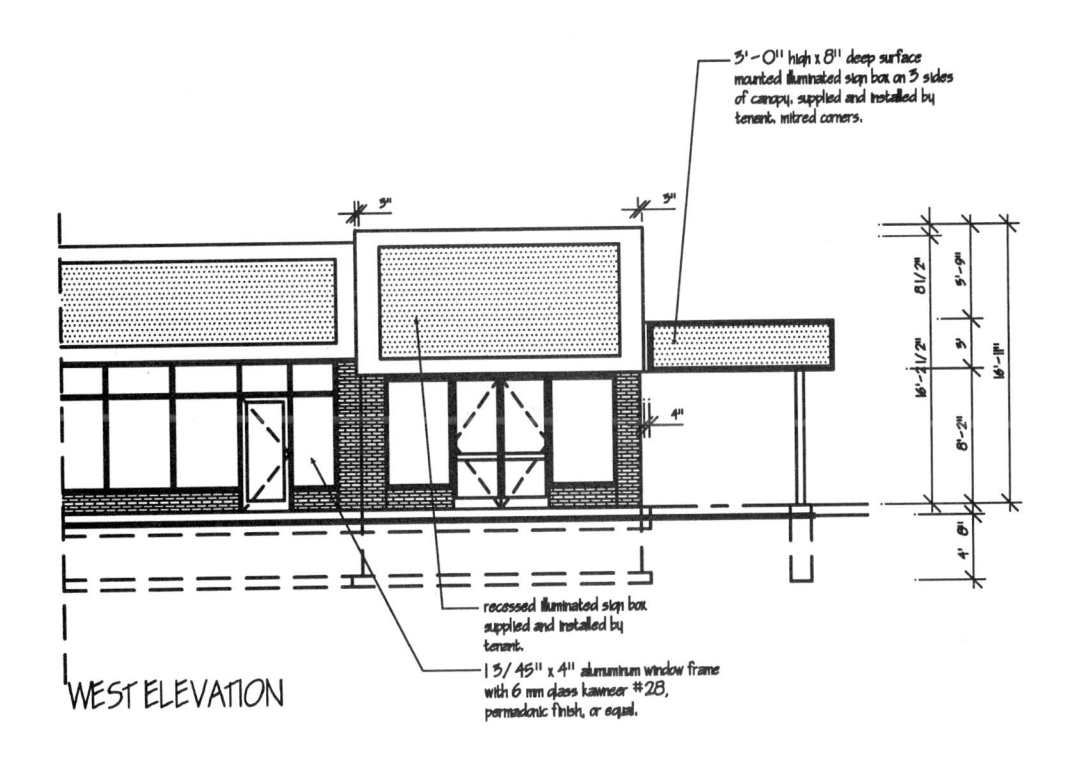

WEST ELEVATION

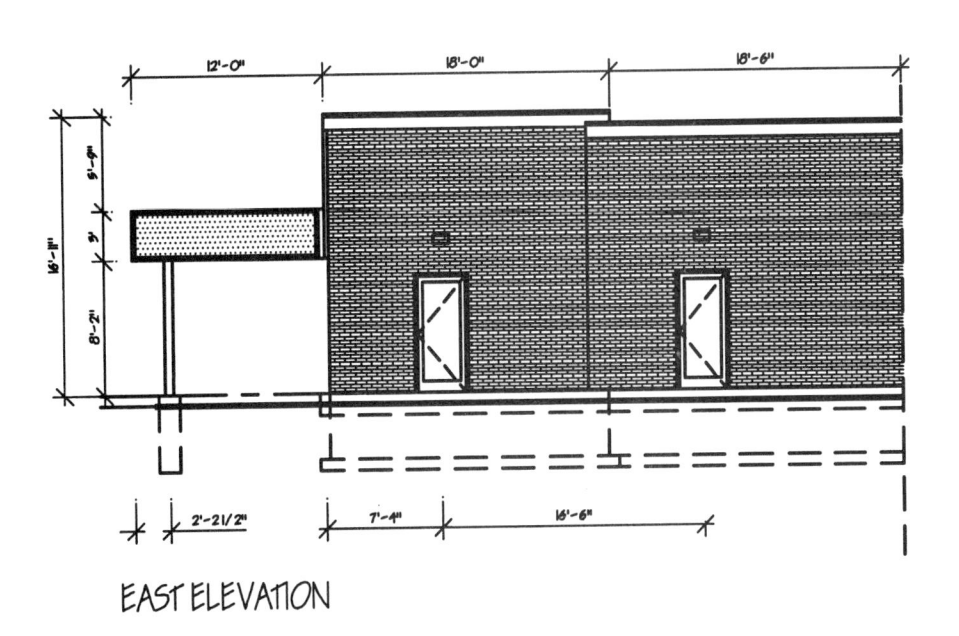

3'-0" high x 8" deep surface mounted illuminated sign box on 3 sides of canopy, supplied and installed by tenant. mitred corners.

recessed illuminated sign box supplied and installed by tenant.

1 3/45" x 4" aluminum window frame with 6 mm glass kawneer #28, permadonic finish, or equal.

EAST ELEVATION

Final Tests and Projects **475**

Civil Final

1. Create two beam details as shown in the drawing (opposite page) with top views as well as front views.

2. Create an ATTRIBUTEd BLOCK of the top view with the following:

    a. The beam title

    b. The material

    c. The finish

    d. The cost

3. Insert both attributed top views to create the roof shown on a third drawing.

4. Download the part data onto a spreadsheet so that cost for the beams can be calculated.

5. Document the time taken to create the drawing, the area of the interior, and the size of the file.

6. Accessing one file as an XREF, compile a drawing including both parts, the overall roof layout, and an attributed title block.

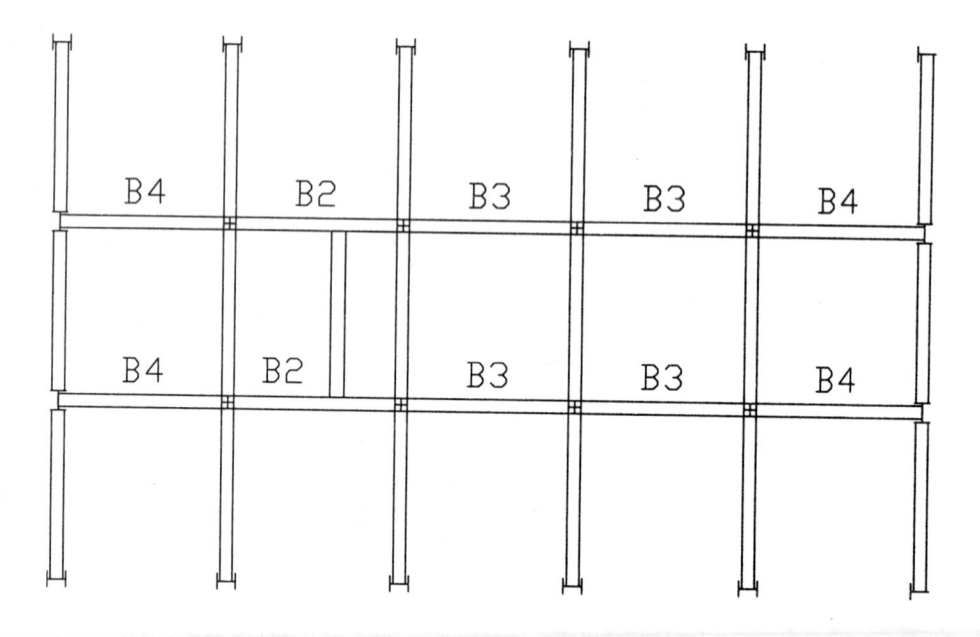

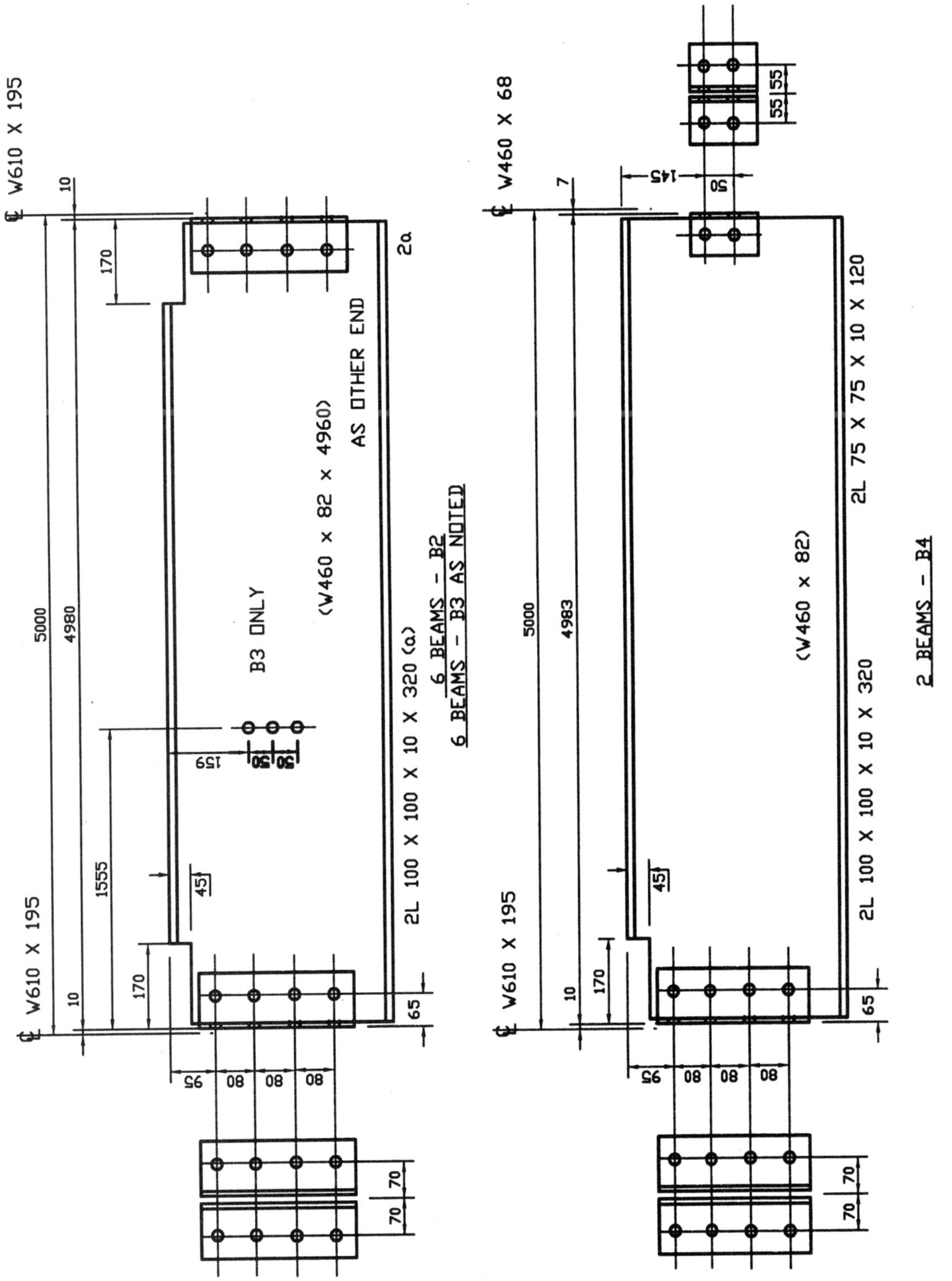
℄ W610 X 195
10
5000
4980
170
1555
45
B3 ONLY
159
50
50
(W460 x 82 x 4960)
AS OTHER END
2a
2L 100 X 100 X 10 X 320 (a)
6 BEAMS - B2
6 BEAMS - B3 AS NOTED
℄ W610 X 195
10
170
65
95
80
80
80
70
70
℄ W460 X 68
7
145
50
55
55
5000
4983
(W460 x 82)
2L 75 X 75 X 10 X 120
2L 100 X 100 X 10 X 320
2 BEAMS - B4
℄ W610 X 195
10
170
45
65
95
80
80
80
70
70

Mechanical Final

1. Draw two separate pulleys from the information provided. On these drawings show a front, a section, an isometric, and a sectioned isometric.

2. Create an ATTRIBUTEd BLOCK of the front view with the following:

    a. The product number

    b. The material

    c. The finish

    d. The cost

3. Insert both attributed front views on a third drawing.

4. Download the part data onto a spreadsheet so that the pulleys can be compared.

5. Document the time taken to create the drawing, the area of the interior, and the size of the file.

6. Accessing one file as an XREF, compile a drawing including both parts as well as an attributed title block.

ROUNDS AND FILLETS R4
KEY SEAT 5D X 10W

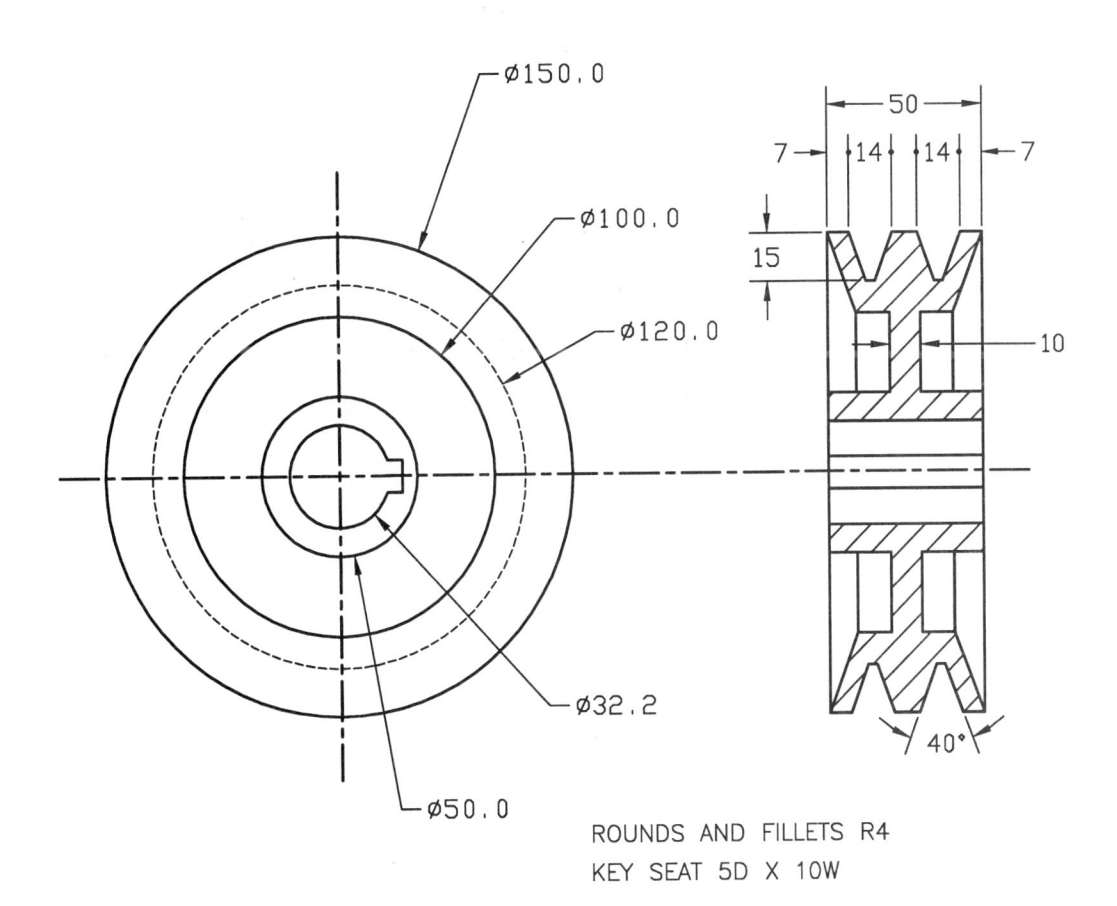

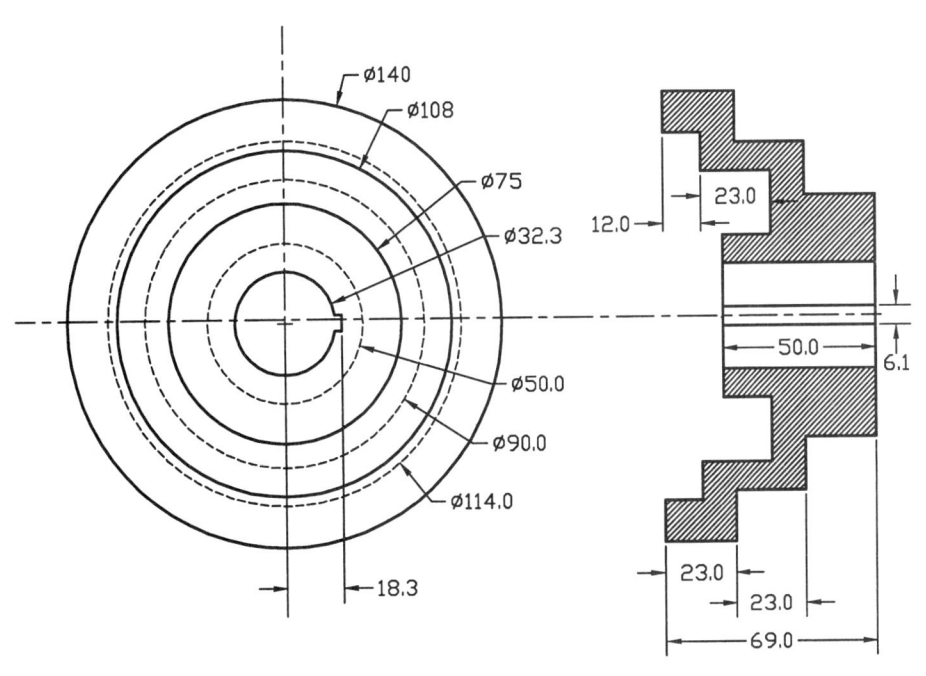

Challenger Final

Using the information on this and page 396, create an exploded isometric view of an assembly as seen in Challengers 10, 16, and 25. Add attributes to each part, and create a part list from that information. Note your time. Create a slide show of each individual part, and the assembly as a whole.

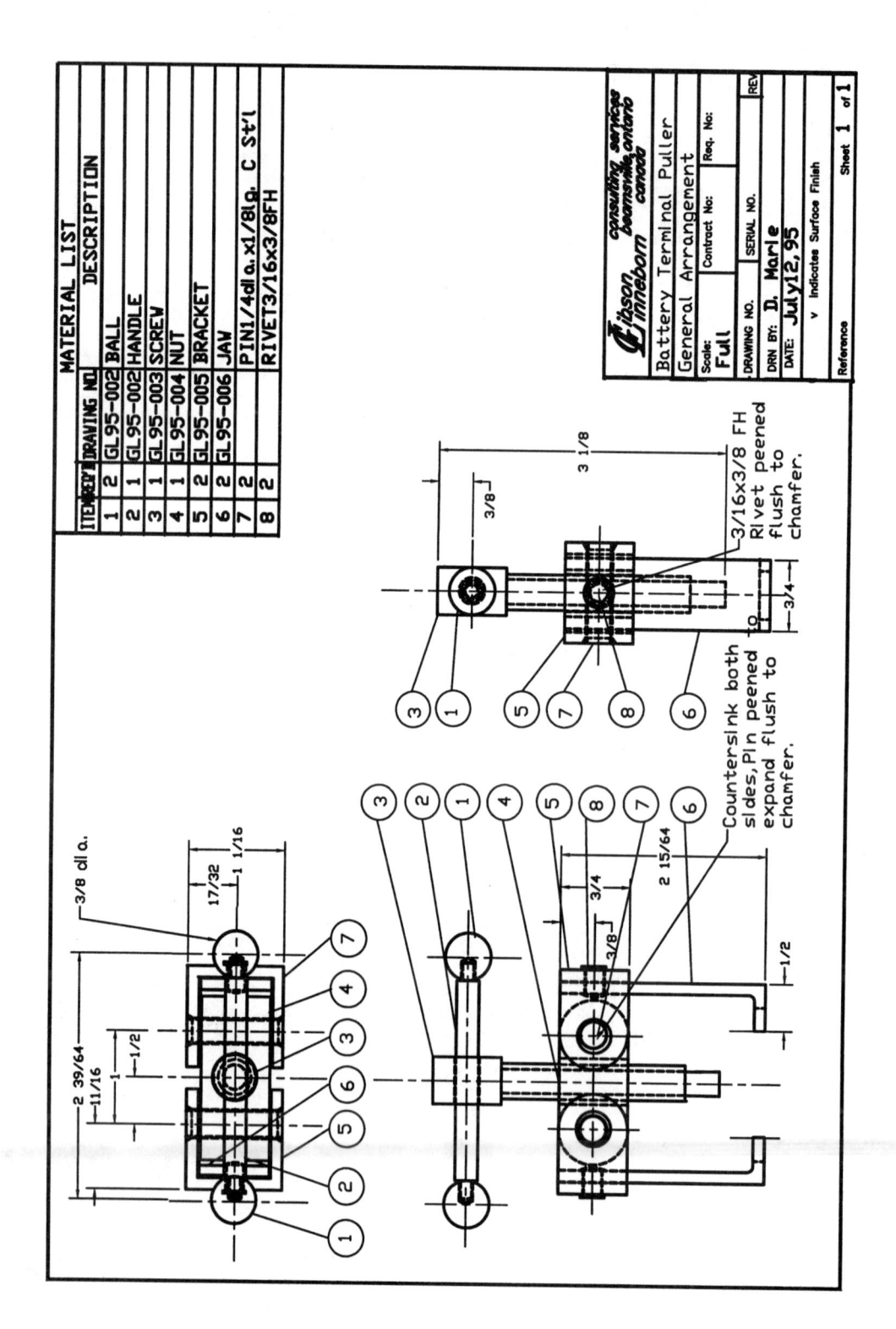

ITEM	QTY	DRAWING NO.	DESCRIPTION
1	2	GL95-002	BALL
2	1	GL95-002	HANDLE
3	1	GL95-003	SCREW
4	1	GL95-004	NUT
5	2	GL95-005	BRACKET
6	2	GL95-006	JAW
7	2		PIN 1/4 dia. x 1/8 lg. C St'l
8	2		RIVET 3/16 x 3/8 FH

Battery Terminal Puller
General Arrangement
Scale: Full
DRN BY: D. Marle
DATE: July 12, 95
Sheet 1 of 1

Gibson consulting services, Innisborn, Ontario, Canada

3/16 x 3/8 FH Rivet peened flush to chamfer.

Countersink both sides, Pin peened expand flush to chamfer.

20 Moving into 3D and Views

Upon completion of this chapter, you should be able to:

1. Use VIEWPORT to set up a multi-view screen
2. Use VIEWPOINT 3D to rotate the views
3. Specify X, Y, and Z coordinates in a 3D coordinate space

Generating 3D Models

Many architectural and engineering offices create two-dimensional drawings of three-dimensional objects in three or four views. While this is an acceptable method, AutoCAD's 3D modeling features save time and offer increased accuracy. A 2D drawing of a model is, after all, a representation of a model in views created independently. A 3D representation of a model can be dimensioned and presented as a drawing, or can be used to extract manufacturing data, volumes, and surface areas, and allow for 3D display possibilities not offered with 2D representations of models.

In this chapter we will concentrate on setting up the screen for maximum access to the model. Then we will learn how to enter the data in point format to gain control of the model. Before getting started it is important to recognize that this is a completely different approach to creating a drawing. Many draftspeople, because of their understanding of the logic in paper "drawing," have difficulty grasping 3D at first. Keep this in mind in order to grasp the concepts more quickly. *You are not making a drawing, you are making a model.*

Think of yourself as being in a model-making class as opposed to a drafting class. Put objects in only where they exist, not as they would be seen in a drawing.

VIEWPORTS or VPORTS

In order to enter your geometry properly, you must be able to see the object not just from one angle, but from many. If you see the object only in one view, it is easier to make mistakes and place objects on the wrong plane.

While performing 3D model construction, independently scaled and oriented views can be placed within the viewports of the screen layout. These views are non-overlapping or tiled, and are in model space.

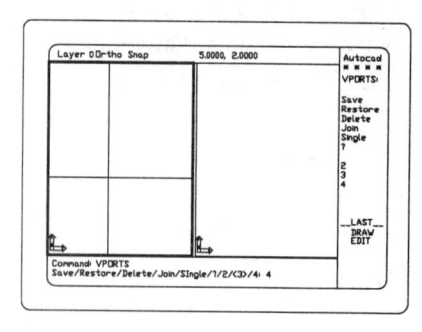

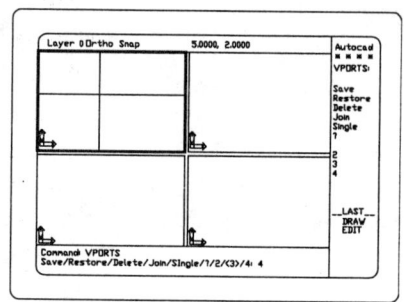

Figure 20-1

For most applications, four viewports will be sufficient. In Figure 20-1, the left screen shows two viewports, the right screen four. The current viewport has the crosshairs, and its outline is also highlighted for clarity. In order to make a viewport current, you simply pick it, or toggle using Ctrl-V.

Before starting any 3D model it is important to set up at least two different views.

While you are creating your model, there is, in fact, only one database being made. If you have two viewports, then you will have two views of the same model. If you have four viewports, then you will have four views of the same model. You will not have four models, but four views.

The VPORTS Command

This command divides the graphics area into multiple tiled viewports. Before you use VPORTS, the Tilemode variable must be set to 1. If you are in paper space, return to model space.

> **Pull Down Menu** From the View menu, choose Viewports, then pick the number of viewports you require.

The Command line equivalent is **-VPORTS**.

```
Command:-VPORTS
Enter an option
  [Save/Restore/Delete/Join/
  SIngle/?/2/3/4]<3>:
```

Figure 20-2

Where: **Save**   = the ability to name and store a VPORT configuration
         Restore = the ability to bring a saved configuration back
         Delete = the ability to delete unwanted viewports
         Join   = join two VPORTS
         SIngle = return to a single viewport
         ?   = a list of saved VPORTS
         2,3,4   = divide current viewport into the selected number

VPORTS 3 is the default. It will configure the screen into 3 areas. You must choose how you would like your screen set up.

```
Command:-VPORTS
Enter an option
   [Save/Restore/Delete/Join/
   SIngle/?/2/3/4]<3>:↵
Enter a configuration option
   [Horizontal/Vertical/Above/
   Below/Left/Right]<Right>:↵
```

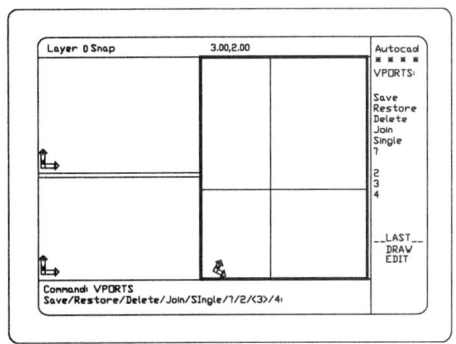

Figure 20-3

The default setting gives you a screen with three viewports. The one on the right is the largest.

This configuration is popular because it allows an isometric view in the large screen, plus top and front views in the smaller screens on the left.

The current view in this case is the large one. These can be accessed through the Pull Down menu as well.

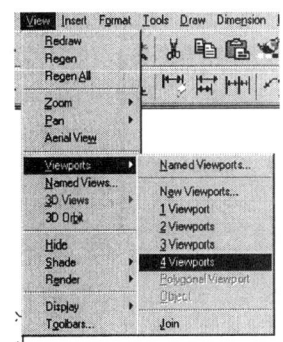

Figure 20-4

> **Danger**
>
> If your screen is divided into three or four views, using the command **VPORTS 3** will cut the screen into three *more* views within the current view. Use **U** or Undo to return to your previous viewport setting.

Using VPORTS

The model remains constant. Whatever configuration is used, there is only one model. Try the following sequence to see how VPORTS operates. Either the dialog box or the command can be used. Choose any model to see how it works.

```
Command:-VPORTS
Enter an option
   [Save/Restore/Delete/Join/
   SIngle/?/2/3/4]<3>:2
Horizontal/<Vertical>:↵
```

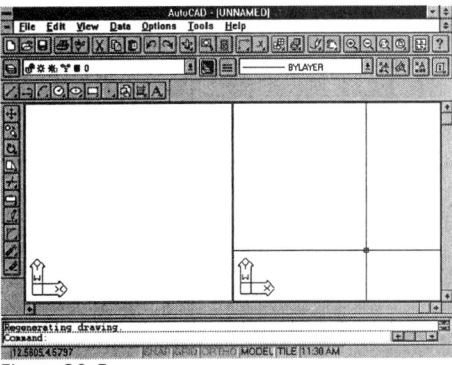

Figure 20-5

This divides the screen into two vertical viewports.

```
Command:VPORTS
Enter an option
   [Save/Restore/Delete/Join/
   SIngle/?/2/3/4]<3>:SI
```

This returns the screen to a single view.

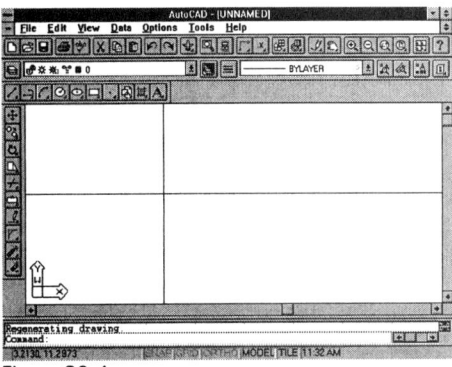

Figure 20-6

Moving into 3D and Views   **483**

```
Command:VPORTS (or space bar)
Enter an option
  [Save/Restore/Delete/Join/
  SIngle/?/2/3/4]<3>:4
```

This divides the screen into four equal viewports.

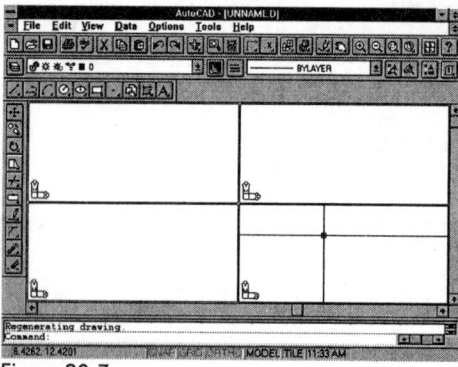

Figure 20-7

Once you have oriented the views, you can save them.

```
Command:VPORTS
Enter an option
  [Save/Restore/Delete/Join/
  SIngle/?/2/3/4]<3>:S
Enter name of new viewport
  configuration:4QUAD
```

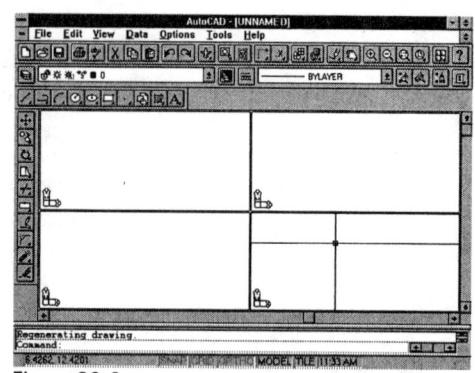

Figure 20-8

This saves this viewport configuration under the name of 4QUAD. In the VPORTS dialog box, use the Named Viewports tab to name and save.

```
Command:VPORTS
Enter an option
  [Save/Restore/Delete/Join/
  SIngle/?/2/3/4]<3>:SI
```

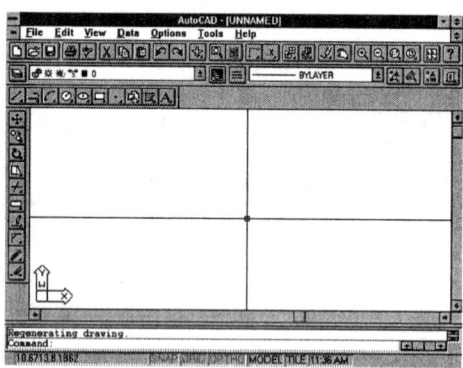

Figure 20-9

This returns the screen to a single view.

```
Command:VPORTS
Enter an option
  [Save/Restore/Delete/Join/
  SIngle/?/2/3/4]<3>:R
Enter name of viewport
  configuration to
  restore:4QUAD
```

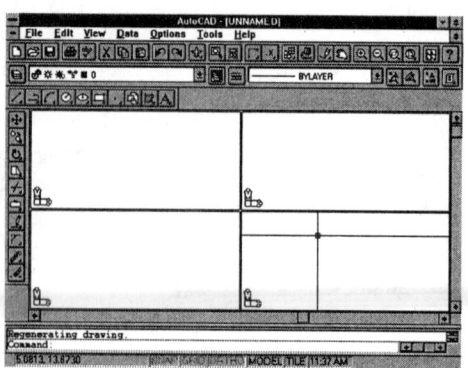

Figure 20-10

This restores the four views.

```
Command:VPORTS
 Enter an option
   [Save/Restore/Delete/Join/
   SIngle/?/2/3/4]<3>:J
 Select dominant viewport
   <current viewport>:(pick 1)
 Select viewport to join:(pick
   2)
```

This joins the two viewports on the right to create one viewport.

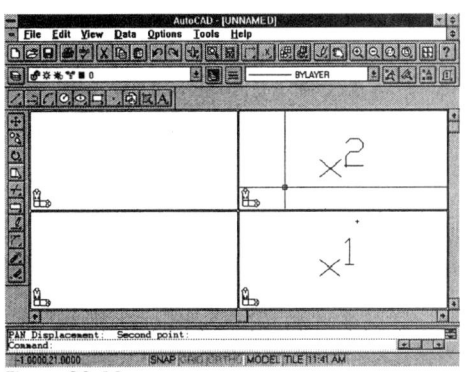

Figure 20-11

Like Layers, the current viewport configuration, and any named configurations are stored with the model.

VPORTS is a View command: the model geometry is not altered by invoking this command.

Viewports can be used in 2D drawings for adding details. Each viewport can have a different zoom factor allowing you to add details but also see the whole picture.

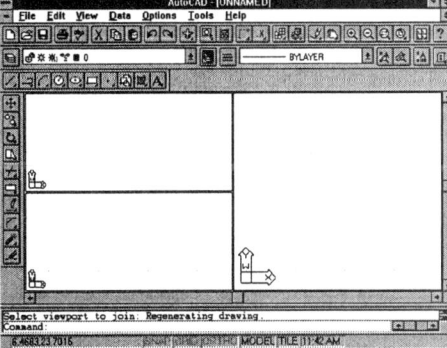

Figure 20-12

Orienting Views Within VPORTS

With several viewports, you can easily view the object from different angles and at different magnification factors. Generally, the Front, Top, Side and Isometric views are used for constructing the model. Use the VPOINT command to orient the object within the views.

Making a VPORT Current

Before orienting a view, make sure that the viewport you want to orient is the current one, the viewport that will be affected by the VPOINT command. Simply pick the viewport to make it current. The crosshairs appear in the current viewport and the viewport's frame is highlighted. *All View commands affect the current viewport unless otherwise specified.*

The VPOINT Command

The VPOINT command sets the viewing direction for a three-dimensional visualization of the model. With the VPOINT command, the operator views the object relative to the origin. VPOINT cannot be used in paper space.

> **Pull Down Menu** From the View menu, choose 3D Views, then choose the view that you need..

The Command line equivalent is **VPOINT**.

The PLAN view will always be the X-Y plane. This is described as 0 in X, 0 in Y, and 1 in Z.

```
Command:VPOINT
Current view direction: VIEWDIR = 0.0000,0.0000,1.0000
Specify a view point or [Rotate],<display compass and tripod>:
```

Moving into 3D and Views

The point coordinates in all commands are read as X,Y,Z. In this diagram you can see that all axes go through 0,0,0. The center point is the origin.

The operator is looking back at the origin from a position of 1 unit in Z, but none in X or Y. The line-of-sight is along the Z axis. This is referred to as the plan view as you are looking at the X-Y view.

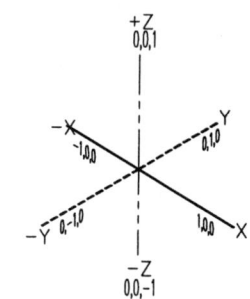

Figure 20-13

Vector

The Vector option is the default option for the Viewpoint command. It allows you to specify a position relative to the origin or 0,0,0 of the model. At the Rotate/<Viewpoint><current>: prompt, enter the X,Y,Z coordinates that describe the position wanted. In order to get a look at the object in 3D, or in a pictorial view, rotate the object so that you can access each part of it.

```
Command:(pick the top right
   viewport)
Command:VPOINT
Current view direction:
   VIEWDIR=0.0000,0.0000,1.0000
Specify a view point or [Rotate]
   <display compass and
   tripod>:1,-1,1
```

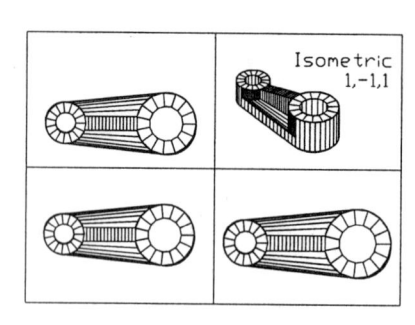

Figure 20-14

Danger

Vector points may not work if you have a Running Object Snap.

If your viewpoint has one value of zero (0) you will be positioned directly on one of the axes; your view will be of one of the planes, not a pictorial.

In a standard layout, the operator views the object from the X-Y plane or top (0,0,1), the X-Z plane or front (0,-1,0), the Y-Z plane or right view (1,0,0) and the isometric (1,-1,1). This allows for enough access to the part.

Remember to pick the view before changing the viewing angle to make it current.

Figure 20-15

To achieve the standard layout you can also choose Top, Front, Left, Right or various views from the 3D Viewport presets under the menu or dialog box. Pick View, then 3D Viewport Presets.

Axis Tripod

In previous releases this was referred to as the *globe icon*. Pick from the menu or press the space bar or ⏎ at the *Specify a view point or [Rotate]*: prompt to get this icon which allows you to define a viewing direction.

The **axis tripod** shows the drawing as a flattened globe of the world. Imagine your model in the middle of this clear globe.

The center point is the North Pole, the inner ring is the equator, and the outer ring is the South Pole. Inside the inner ring is the southern hemisphere, and outside is the northern hemisphere. The crosshairs represent the *X* and *Y* axes, dividing the globe into four quadrants. When you pick a spot on the globe, you are choosing a position from which to view the part.

As you move the cursor, the axes *X*, *Y* and *Z* are shown by a tripod which moves dynamically with the cursor to give an idea of what orientation you will finally have.

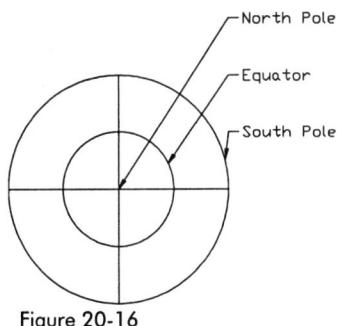

Figure 20-16

The axes rotate according to the position of the point on the globe.

To see the top part, indicate a point between the equator and the North Pole.

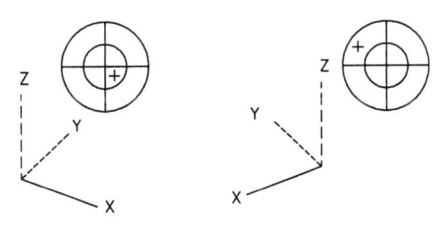

Figure 20-17

Be careful not to pick a point of view from under the object by picking in the outer circle. The pictorial view is generally confusing enough without viewing it from the bottom.

The Axis option is not as accurate as the Vector option. Here are some examples of viewing angles.

Notes

Once the viewpoint is chosen, use **HIDE** to check if you are looking at the model correctly.

```
Command: VPOINT
Enter vpoint <0.0000,0,0000,1.0000>:
```

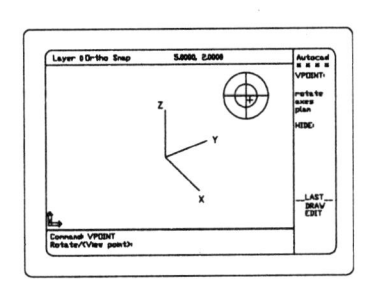

Figure 20-18

In this case the VPOINT coordinates are 2,-2,2.

Preset SE Isometric

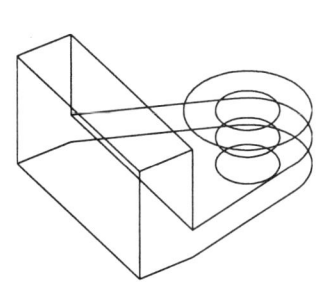

Figure 20-19

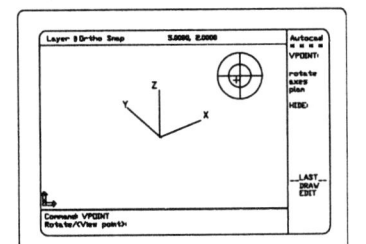

Figure 20-20

In this case the VPOINT coordinates are -2,-2,2.

Preset SW Isometric

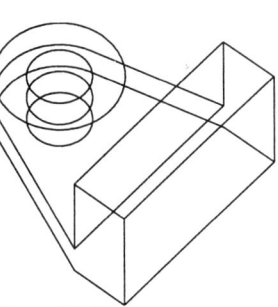

Figure 20-21

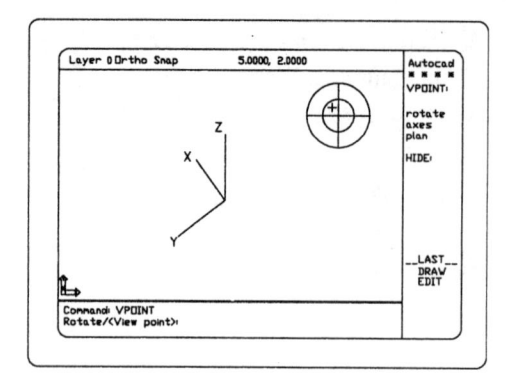

In this case the VPOINT coordinates are -2,2,2.

Preset NW Isometric

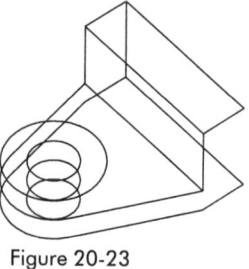

Figure 20-22

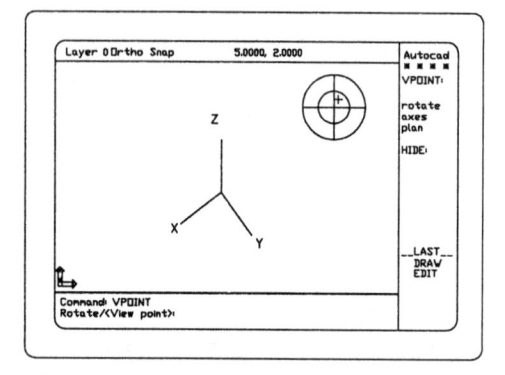

Figure 20-23

In this case the VPOINT coordinates are 2,2,2.

Preset NE Isometric

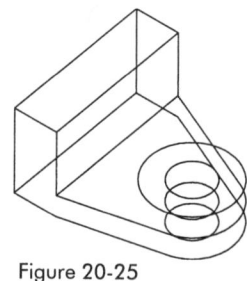

Figure 20-24

Figure 20-25

These orientations can also be found from the preset views.

Whatever view you take, you are always looking back at the image towards the origin or 0,0.

Rotate

This option specifies a new direction using two angles: the angle in the *X-Y* plane and the angle from the *X-Y* plane. For this option, choose Rotate from the 3D Viewpoint command, or from the View menu, 3D Viewpoint, then Select...

The first angle is specified with respect to the *X* axis in the *X-Y* plane, specified as From *X*.

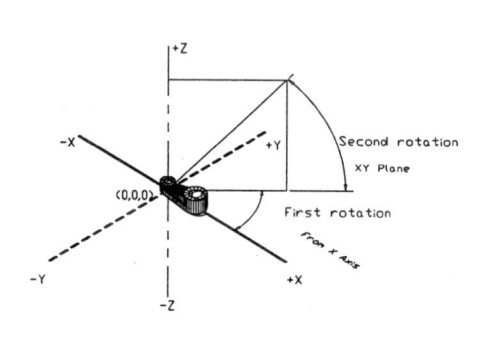

Figure 20-26

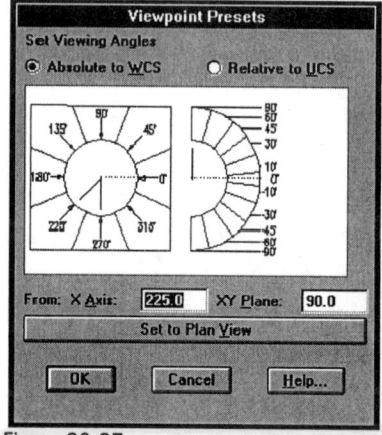

Figure 20-27

The second angle is specified up or down from the *X-Y* plane, specified as the *XY* plane. For a front view choose 270 From *X*, and 90 From *X-Y* plane. For a side view choose 0 From *X*, and 90 From *X-Y* plane. Selecting angles can be done either by clicking your pointing device inside the sector of the image tiles or entering the values.

488 CHAPTER TWENTY

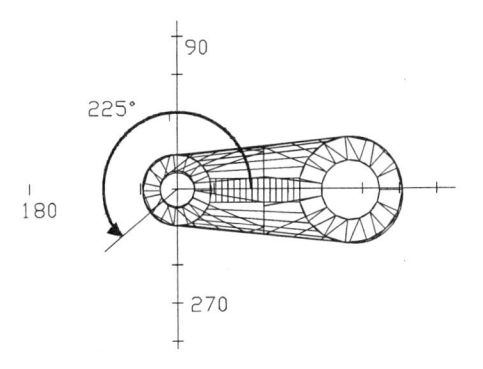

Figure 20-28
Plan View the angle is set to 225 degrees

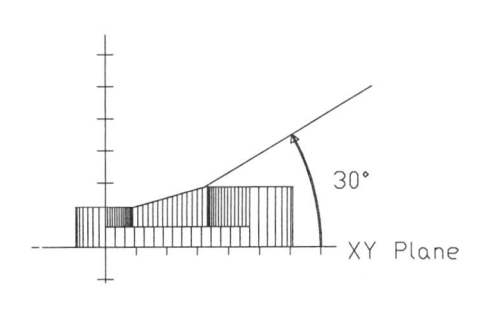

Figure 20-29
Front View the angle is set to 30 degrees

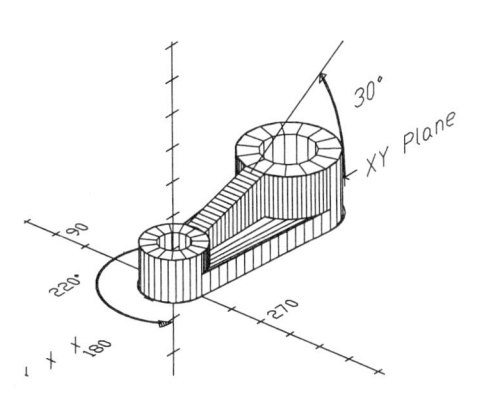

Figure 20-30
Resulting View

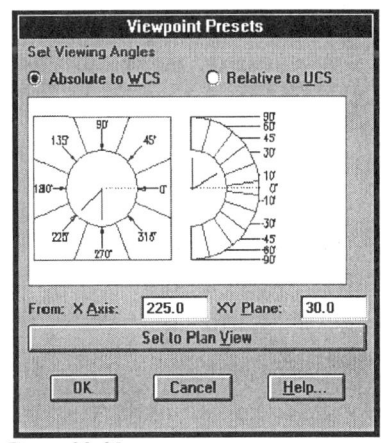

Figure 20-31
Settings on the menu

3D Icons

When multiple viewports with various orientations are used, the icons in each viewport reflect the X-Y plane of that viewport.

In the X-Y plane, the icon will look like this:

This means that this is the X-Y plane. The grid and snap work as they do on previous drawings.

In the pictorial view the icon looks like this and reflects the orientation of the X-Y plane. The grid and snap align with the icon.

In the X-Z and Y-Z views, the X-Y plane is not present. This broken pencil icon reflects that the view has no grid or snap; objects within it must be accessed by OSNAPs.

Imagine drawing on the edge of the paper—you can't, so the pencil is "broken."

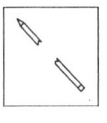

Entering X, Y and Z Coordinates

When entering information by means of the coordinate system, type in the values as before; the third entry is the Z depth. Using incremental entries is no problem in either geometry or editing commands.

Moving into 3D and Views **489**

While working on your part, keep in mind that *the display commands work only in the current viewport.* ZOOM and PAN work very well, as do the others. If you would like to redraw all the viewports, you can use REDRAWALL.

Should you lose your geometry in any one view, use ZOOM All to retrieve it. If you are completely lost, U will undo the past commands.

Keep in mind that it is a *model*, not a drawing.

Coordinate Entry

While working in 2D you are able to enter points in three distinct fashions:
1. Coordinate entry (absolute, incremental, and polar)
2. Selecting a portion of an existing item
3. Picking a point in space.

While in 3D, these concepts remain the same, but you are much more dependent upon points because the object is more complicated, and is viewed from a variety of angles. Before starting a 3D model, always set up your screen for at least two views.

Use the VPORT command to create two viewports.

```
Command:VPORTS
Save/Restore/Delete/Join/?/SI/2/<3>/4:
  2
```

Then use the VIEWPOINT command to make a pictorial view on the right.

Pick the right view to make it current.

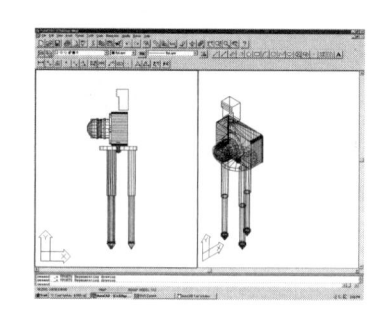

Figure 20-32

```
Command:VPOINT
Current view direction: VIEWDIR=0.0000,0.0000,1.0000
Specify a view point or [Rotate],display compass and
  tripod>:2,-2,2
```

Now use either of the following to enter the lines on the *Z-0* plane as shown in Figure 20-33.

```
Command:LINE            Command:LINE
First point:2,2         First point:2,2
Next point:7,2          Next point:@5,0
Next point:7,4          Next point:@0,2
Next point:6,4          Next point:@-1,0
Next point:6,6          Next point:@0,2
Next point:2,6          Next point:@-4,0
Next point:c            Next point:c
```

You can also set GRID and SNAP and enter the above points by picking the appropriate points on the screen. Any points picked line-of-sight on the screen will be at *Z-0*.

Now that the first plane is in, you can enter the second plane in a variety of ways. The first way is to simply incorporate the *Z*-depth in LINE command.

```
Command:LINE              Command:LINE
From point:2,2,3          From point:2,2,3
Next point:7,2,3          Next point:@5,0
Next point:7,4,3          Next point:@0,2
Next point:6,4,3          Next point:@-1,0
Next point:6,6,3          Next point:@0,2
Next point:2,6,3          Next point:@-4,0
Next point:c              Next point:c
```

With incremental entries, if the Z-axis does not change, you do not need to include it.

This would draw the geometry on the Z-3 plane. An easier way is to use the COPY command.

```
Command:COPY
Select objects:(pick 1 pick 2) (pick
   everything)
Select objects:↵
Specify base point or displacement, or
   [Multiple]:(pick 3) (anywhere)
Second point of displacement:@0,0,3
```

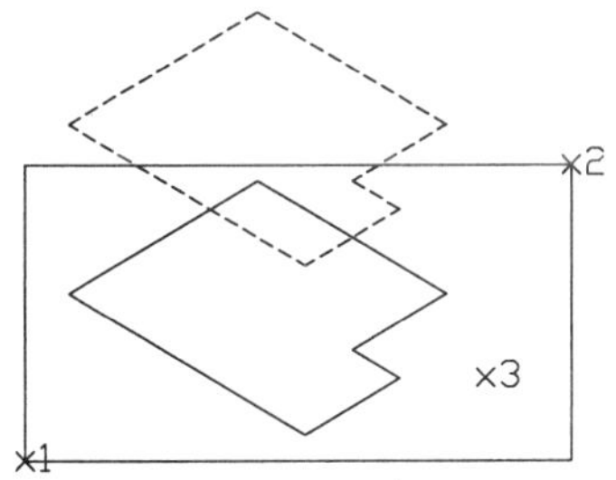

Figure 20-33

This will copy everything to the Z-3 plane.

To complete the part, set your Running Object Snap or OSNAP to END. Enter LINEs from the ends of lines on one plane to the ends of lines on the next plane.

You may notice that if you do not set OSNAP to ENDpoint, your plan view is a mess. This is because *when you are working in a rotated 3D or isometric view, the points you pick on the screen are created on the Z-0 plane*. While lines may look as if they are properly placed from the isometric view, even a slight turn of the part or a view from a different angle shows that it does not work.

In order to access items on a different plane you must use OSNAP or type in the full coordinates, including Z.

Prelab 20   Entering 3D Geometry

This is the object you will draw. The dashed lines indicate the size of the part. It is viewed from the isometric or 1,-1,1 view.

Step 1   Set up the four VPORTS.

> **Pull Down Menu** From the View menu, choose Viewports, then 4 Viewports.

The Command line equivalent is **-VPORTS**.

```
Command:-VPORTS
Enter an option [Save/Restore/Delete/Join/SIngle/?/2/
   3/4]<3>:4
```

Step 2   Set up the viewports so that the top view is on the top left, the front is on the bottom left, the right is on the bottom right, and the isometric is on the top right. Use the menu options or type the vectors as shown.

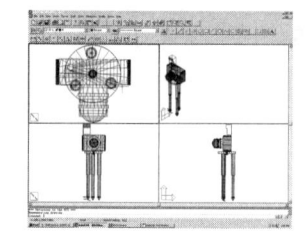

The views are empty, but the icons show that the views have changed.

Step 3   Enter the *Z-0* lines.

```
Command:LINE
First point:0,0
Next point:4,0
Next point:4,2
Next point:6,2
Next point:6,4
Next point:0,4
Next point:0,0
Next point:↵
```

You will need to PAN or ZOOM the views to get them on-screen. Always pick the viewports to make them active before continuing with a View command.

Step 4   Now that the *Z-0* plane is in, extend the next lines vertically from the endpoints; you can see the distance in positive *Z*.

```
Command:LINE
First point:(pick 1)
Next point:@0,0,2
Next point:↵
Command:LINE
First point:(pick 2)
Next point:@0,0,2
Next point:↵
```

Step 5   Now put in the lines on *Y-4* in the same way.

```
Command:LINE
First point:6,4,0
Next point:@0,0,3
Next point:@-6,0,0
Next point:@0,0,-3
Next point:⏎
```

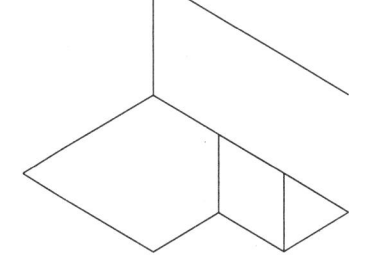

Then add the lines along the top.

```
Command:LINE
First point:(pick 1)
Next point:@0,-1,0
Next point:@6,0,0
Next point: @0,1,0
Next point:⏎
```

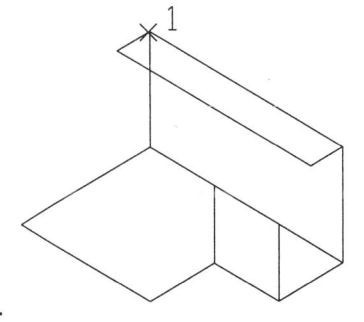

Step 6   Now just join the points together to make a finished part.

```
Command:Running Object Snap at Endpoint
Command:L
First point:(pick 1)
Next point:(pick 2)
Next point:⏎
Command:L
First point:(pick 3)
Next point:(pick 4)
Next point:etc.
```

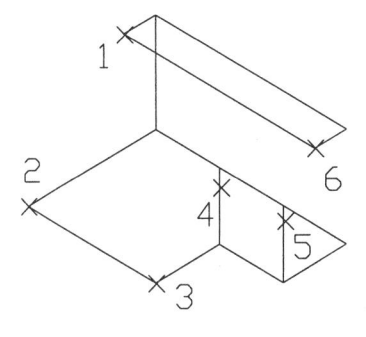

Notes

Use ENDpoint rather than INTersection in 3D because the lines often overlap; and endpoint is generally easier to pick.

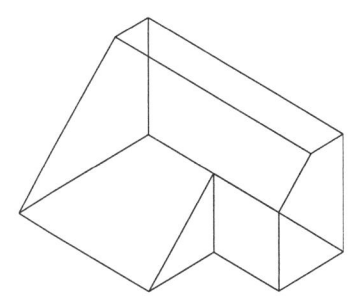

Step 7   Often 1, -1, 1 is difficult to see because the lines overlap. If so, rotate your view using either VPOINT Axis, Vector, or Rotate.

Danger

Always use OSNAPs if the point you are accessing is not on Z-0.

Moving into 3D and Views **493**

Command and Function Summary

VPOINT sets the viewing direction for a three-dimensional visualization of the drawing.

VPORTS divides the graphics area into multiple tiled views.

Danger

Turn OFF your running Object Snap if you are not using it. In the Pictorial view, coordinates may not be entered if the Object Snap is on.

Practice Exercises A20, C20, M20

On the following pages are 20 simple shapes. To gain the practice, set up four VPORTS and VPOINTS for each new part. Do not draw in lines where they do not exist.

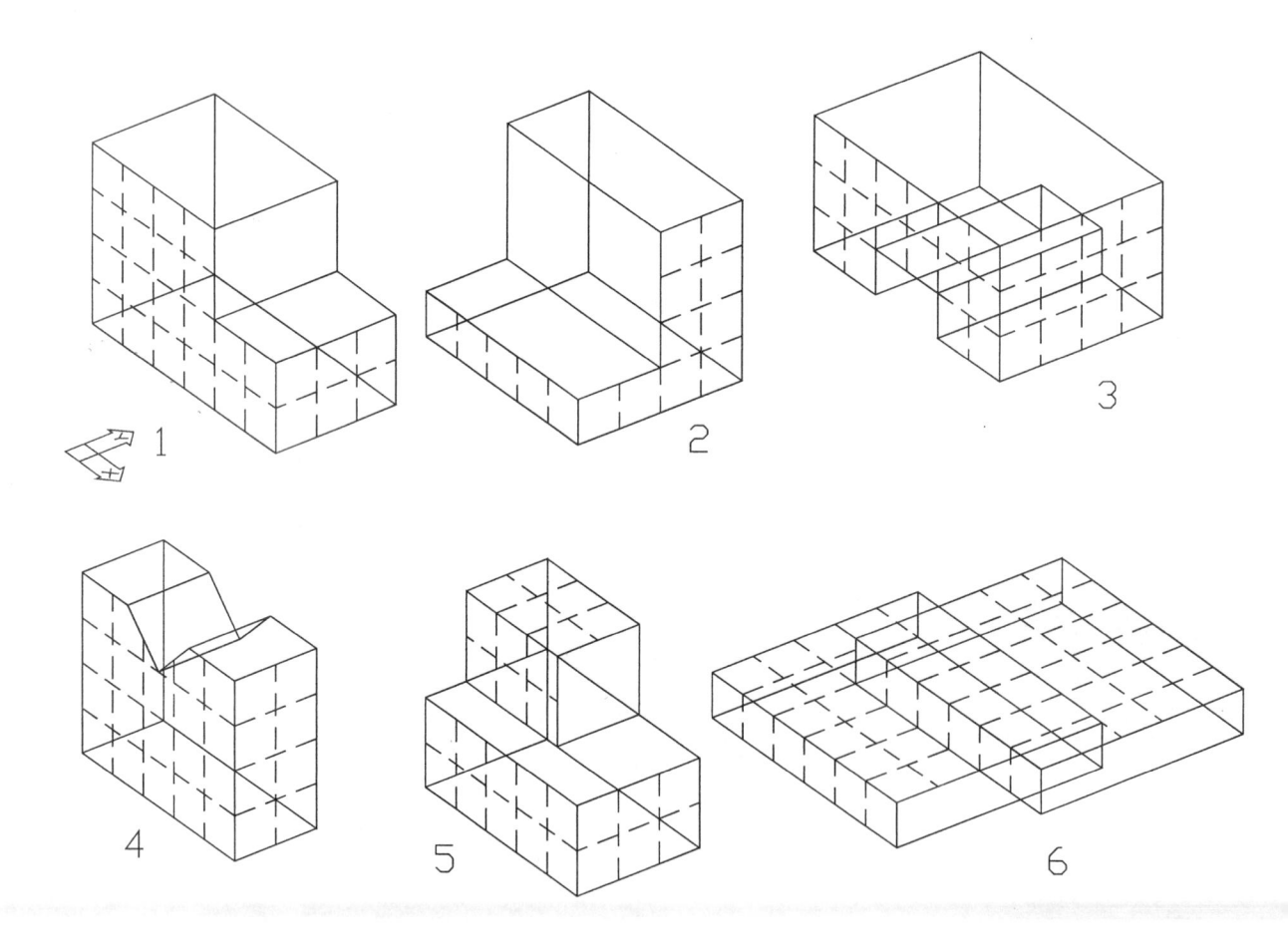

494 CHAPTER TWENTY

Practice Exercises A20, C20, M20 (cont.)

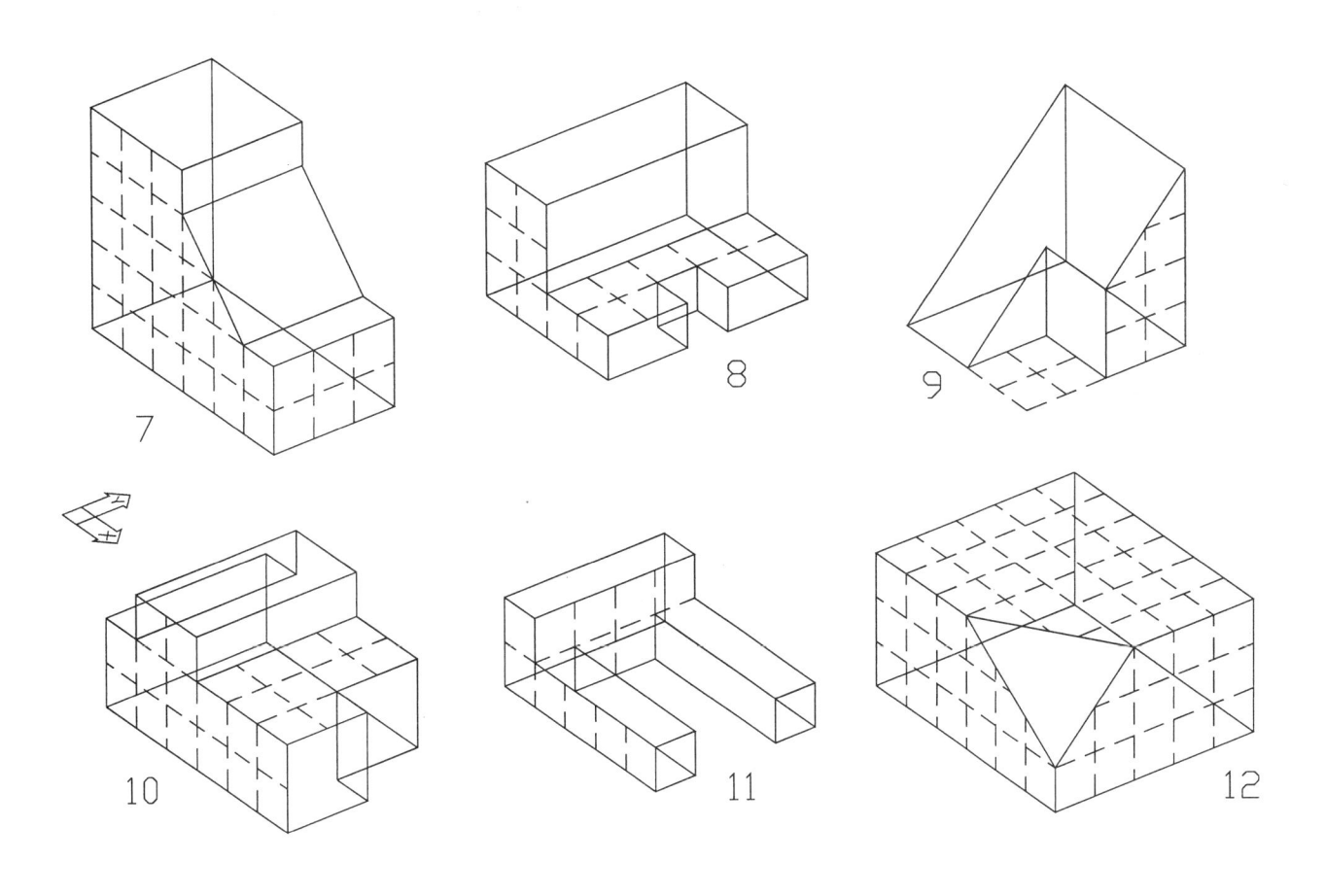

7

8

9

10

11

12

Practice Exercises A20, C20, M20 (cont.)

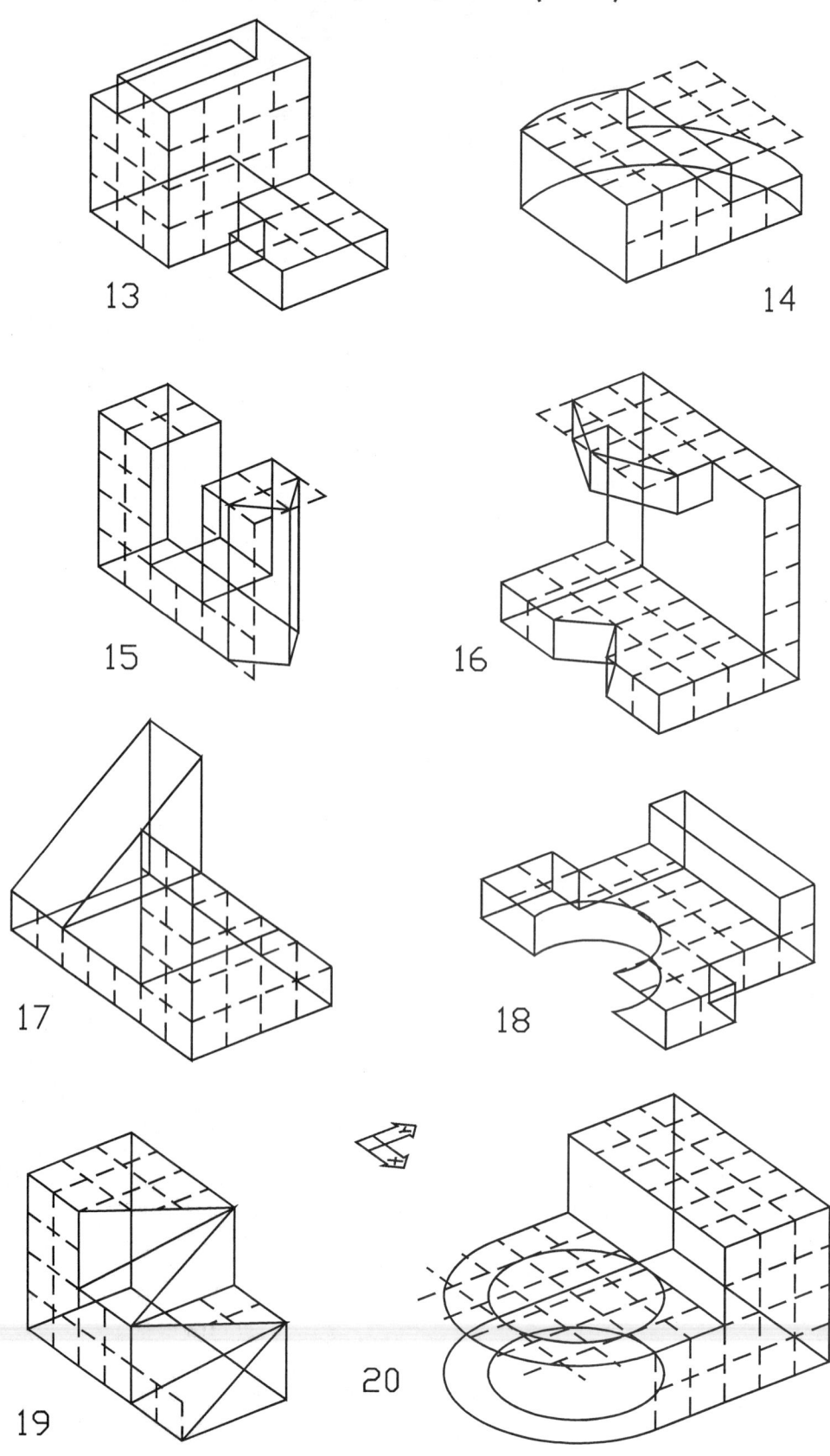

13

14

15

16

17

18

19

20

496 CHAPTER TWENTY

Challenger 20

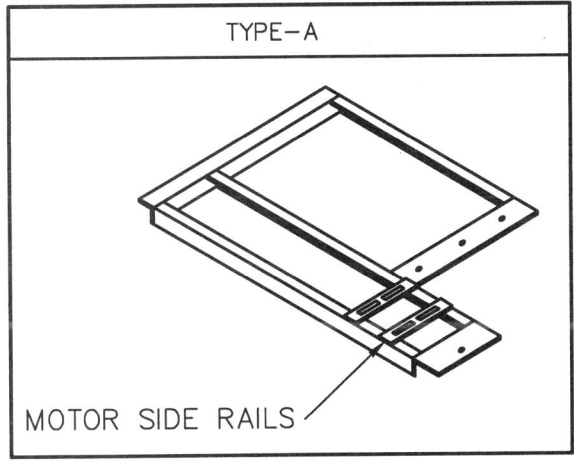

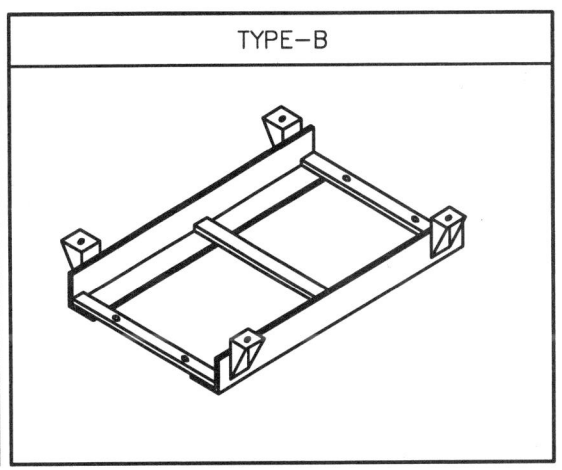

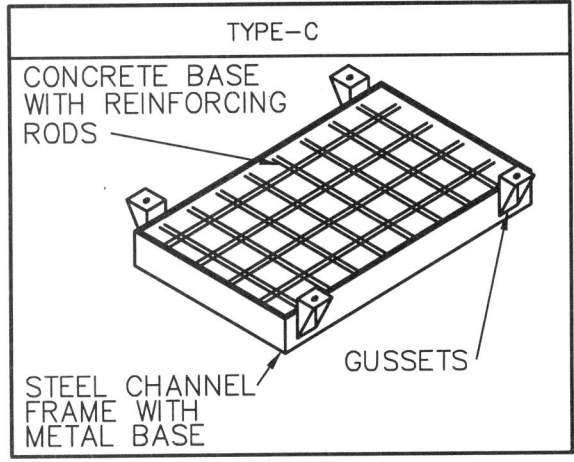

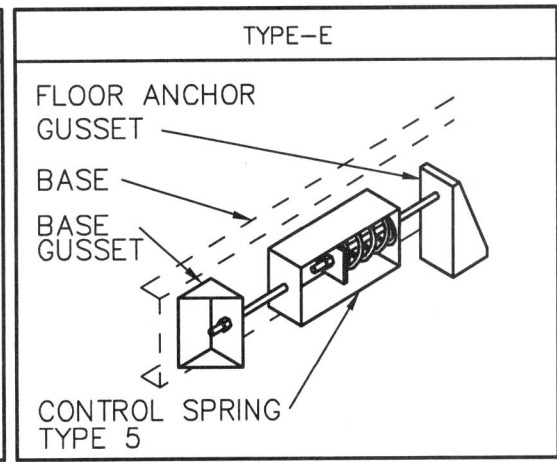

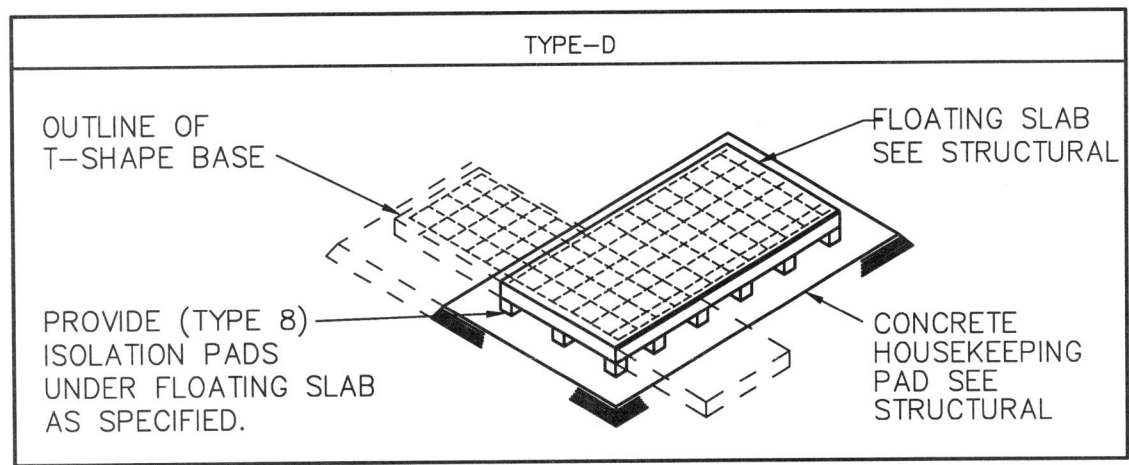

TYPE-A
MOTOR SIDE RAILS

TYPE-B

TYPE-C
CONCRETE BASE WITH REINFORCING RODS

GUSSETS

STEEL CHANNEL FRAME WITH METAL BASE

TYPE-E
FLOOR ANCHOR GUSSET

BASE

BASE GUSSET

CONTROL SPRING TYPE 5

TYPE-D
OUTLINE OF T-SHAPE BASE

FLOATING SLAB SEE STRUCTURAL

PROVIDE (TYPE 8) ISOLATION PADS UNDER FLOATING SLAB AS SPECIFIED.

CONCRETE HOUSEKEEPING PAD SEE STRUCTURAL

Create these roof sections with the proper annotation in the view. These should be created in wireframe.

(Many thanks to UMA for this drawing.)

Moving into 3D and Views **497**

Challenger 20B

Draw the geometry for the part (a). Once completed, surface the object (b). Then use the geometry to make a solid object (c and d); then dimension it (d).

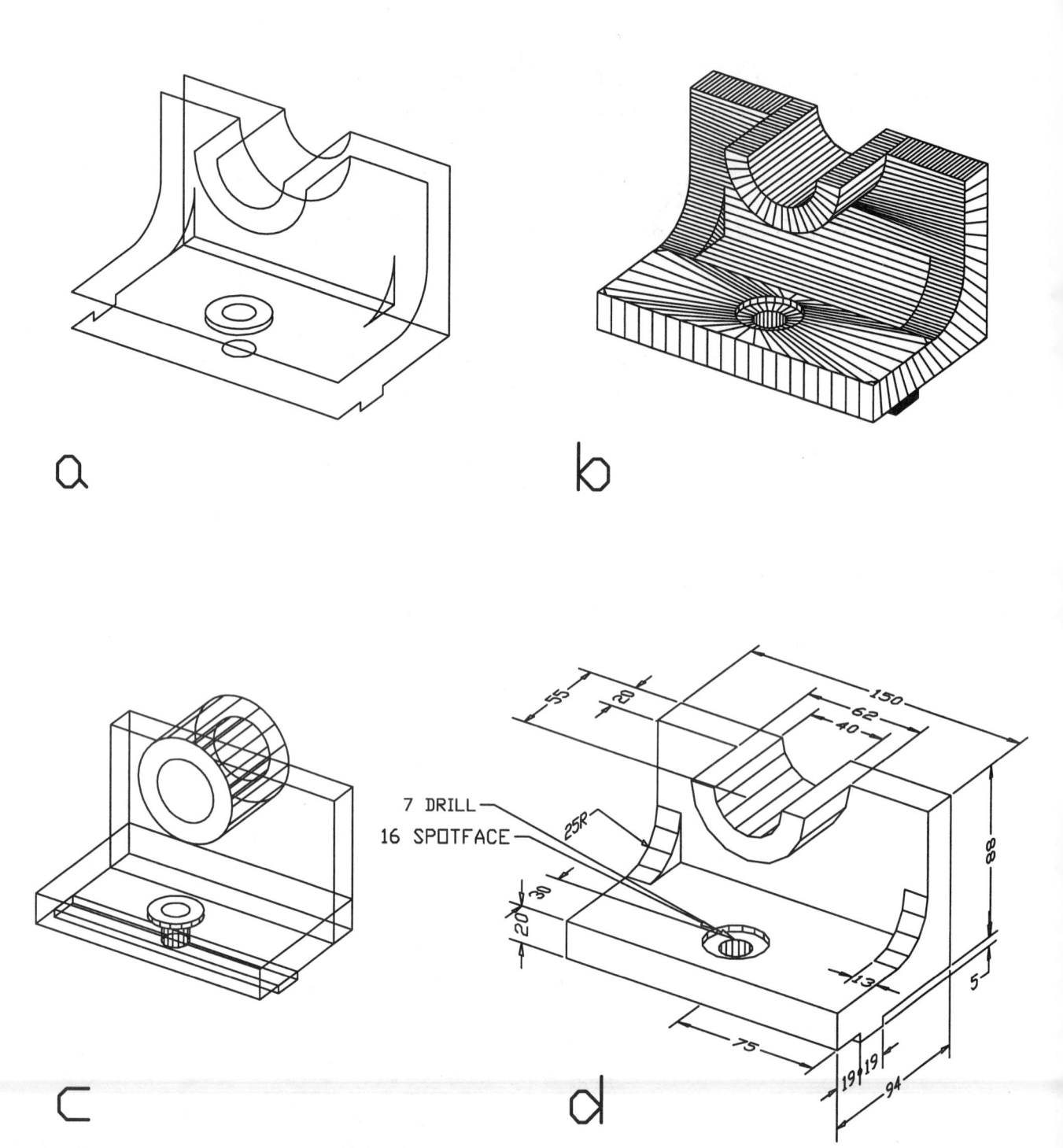

21 User Coordinate System

Upon completion of this chapter, you should be able to:

1. Set the UCS (User Coordinate System) as needed
2. Use the UCS dialog box
3. Save and restore a UCS
4. Create geometry on any given plane

Many geometry and editing commands are dependent upon an *X-Y* plane. Any object with a defined radius—arcs, ellipses, or circles, or width plines, solids or donuts—can only be produced on the *X-Y* plane. This is because such items are planar by definition and may only be made relative to the *X-Y* plane.

Editing commands such as ARRAY, ROTATE, OFFSET, FILLET, and EXTEND are also dependant upon the *X-Y* plane. The resultant objects are calculated normal or perpendicular to the *X-Y* plane.

ROTATE	rotates around *Z*.
ARRAY	creates multiple copies along an *X* or a *Y* axis, never along *Z* because the calculation is normal to *Z*.
OFFSET	offsets along *X* or *Y*.
FILLET	creates a radius.

The User Coordinate System is designed to allow you to change the location of the 0,0,0 origin point and the orientation of the *X-Y* plane and *Z* axis. Once reoriented, you can work relative to any identifiable portion of the part. You identify not only the plane, but the new temporary origin. The axes are always identified from the origin according to positive *X*, *Y*, and *Z*.

Given this, positive *Z* will always be towards the user from the origin.

The Right-hand Rule

As most development in CAD is driven by the Numerical Control or manufacturing industries, it makes sense that many CAD concepts are taken from this technology. A case in point is the concept of the Right-hand Rule, which is derived from mechanical practices and cutting tools.

The Right-hand Rule determines the positive axis direction of the Z axis. If positive X is heading from the origin to the right, and positive Y is heading from the origin straight up, then positive Z is heading towards the viewer. This is referred to as the Right-hand Rule because you can use your right hand to illustrate the position of the axes on any given object.

As you can see in Figure 21-1, the extended right thumb represents X. The pointing index finger represents Y, and the middle finger pointing out represents the proper position of Z every time.

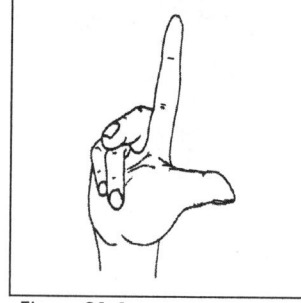

Figure 21-1

You can rotate your hand around any way you want and it will still give you the correct position of Z.

If you are trying to find the position of positive Z, this is the quickest way to do it.

So far we have been working in the X-Y plane of all of our models. When the UCS is not rotated, AutoCAD refers to the orientation as the World Coordinate System. If you want to reorient your UCS, use the UCS command. You can also Save, Restore, and Delete UCSs from your current file with this command.

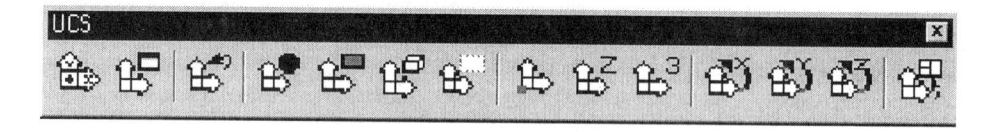

Figure 21-2

The UCS Command

The UCS command allows the user to place and manage the UCS. The new command string is so cumbersome and intricate, that it would appear that Autodesk is determined to have you use the toolbar (above) on this one.

> **Toolbar** From the View Menu, choose toolbars, then UCS.
>
> **Pull Down Menu** From the Tools menu, choose New UCS

The command line equivalent is **UCS**.

```
Command:UCS
Enter an option
  [New/Move/orthoGraphic/Prev/Restore/Save/Del/Apply/?/World]
  <World>:n
Specify origin of new UCS or
  [ZAxis/3point/OBject/Face/View/X/Y/Z] <0,0,0>:
```

Where: New = brings up the list of new UCS positions and allows you to choose one.

Move = shifts the origin of the UCS without changing the rotation of axes.

Ortho	= offers standard planes to set the UCS to.
Previous	= returns to the previous UCS.
Restore	= restores a UCS previously stored and named.
Save	= saves the current UCS with a given name.
Del	= deletes a UCS that has been previously stored and named.
Apply	= applies the current UCS to a specified viewport.
?	= lists the stored UCSs.
World	= sets the UCS to the World Coordinate Space. World is the basis for all user coordinate systems and cannot be redefined.Previous.
ZAxis	= allows you to set the UCS by specifying the origin, then the Z direction.
3point	= allows placement by 3 points: the origin, the X, and then the Y, in that order only.
OBject	= sets UCS according to a planar object and sets the extrusion relative to that object or entity.
Face	= allows the user to place the UCS on the face of a solid object.
View	= sets a new UCS with the Z axis parallel to the viewing direction.
X	= rotates the current UCS around the X axis, keeping the same origin.
Y	= rotates the current UCS around the Y axis, keeping the same origin.
Z	= rotates the current UCS around the Z axis, keeping the same origin.

As with most other commands, only the one or two letters are needed to call up the option wanted. Once you have made your choice, the UCSICON will change direction to reflect your new position. Also, as with other commands, when a point is required, any kind of point entry is acceptable. You can enter the coordinates of that point or use OSNAP with an existing entity or pick a point on the screen.

UCS with OBject

The OBject option of the UCS command allows you to define a new UCS based on a selected new object. For objects other than 3DFACEs (see page 517), the X-Y plane of the new UCS is parallel to the X-Y plane in effect when the object was drawn. However, the X and Y axes can be rotated differently. The following table shows how the UCS is defined.

Object	*UCS Rotation*
Arc	The center of the arc becomes the origin; the X axis passes through the closest endpoint to the point specified.
Circle	The center of the circle becomes the origin; the X axis passes through the point specified.
Line	The closest endpoint of the line becomes the origin; positive X passes through the other end of the line.
Point	The specified point becomes the origin.
Polyline	The startpoint of the PLINE is the new UCS origin; the X axis extends from the startpoint to the next vertex.

3point

Be careful to be specific with the 3point entry or you will get the response, "points are collinear." This means that when entering the points for the origin, X and Y, two points given were the same point. This often happens when indicating an ENDpoint of an item and not picking far enough along the item to have the ENDpoint calculated at the required end. If this happens, use MIDpoint or NEARest.

Selecting a Preset UCS

The UCS dialog box lets you choose a preset User Coordinate System. You can change the current UCS relative to the current UCS or relative to the World UCS.

> **Toolbar** From the UCS menu, choose Display UCS Dialog.

The Command line equivalent is **DDUCS**.

Notes

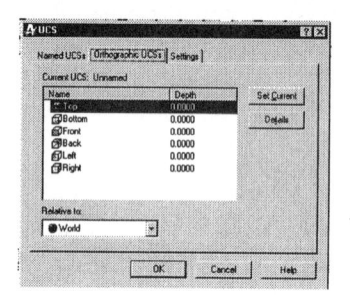

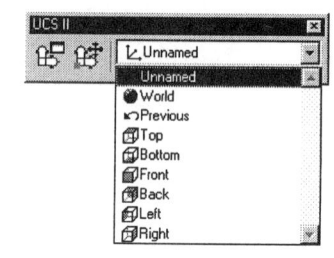

Relative to Current UCS and Absolute to WCS are irrelevant if you restore the World UCS.

Figure 21-3

Figure 21-4

You can also use the UCS II dialog box as shown in figure 21-4.

Saving and Restoring UCS

Once you have oriented a UCS to work on a particular section of your model, you may want to save this orientation for later use.

Saving the UCS

> **Toolbars** From the UCS toolbar, choose UCS dialog box then right click the current UCS and Rename.
>
> **Pull Down Menu** From the Tools menu, choose Named UCS.

To Save your UCS use the Save option of the UCS command.

The command line equivalent is UCS.

```
Command:UCS
Enter an option
  [New/Move/orthoGraphic/Prev/Restore/Save/Del/Apply/?/World]
  <World>:Save
```

The named UCS is now stored and accessible later.

> **Toolbars** From the UCS toolbar, choose UCS dialog box, then right click the current UCS and Rename.
>
> **Pull Down Menu** From the Tools menu, choose Named UCS.

Restoring a UCS

The UCS dialog box makes restoring a UCS quite simple.

The Command line equivalent is **DDUCS**.

The UCS Dialog Box lists the UCSs that you have already created under the named UCSs tab. World Coordinate System is the first entry. If you define other coordinate systems they will be listed here.

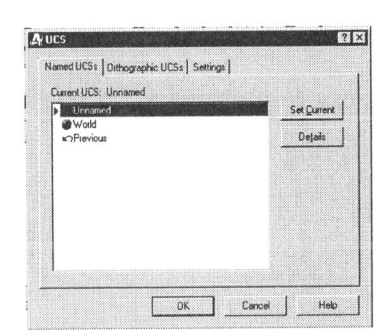

Figure 21-5

Notice that you can be prompted to create a new one or, unlike LAYER, delete one from the current list as well. You can not delete the World or Previous UCSs.

This is handy if you have forgotten what you named your UCSs.

If you define a number of UCSs within one editing session, a *PREVIOUS* entry appears next. You can step back through these coordinate systems by selecting *PREVIOUS* and OK repeatedly. If you do not name the current coordinate system, *NO NAME* is the next entry.

The only trick to retrieving a UCS is remembering what you named it.

Details

This option lists a coordinate system's origin point and the direction of the axes relative to the current UCS.

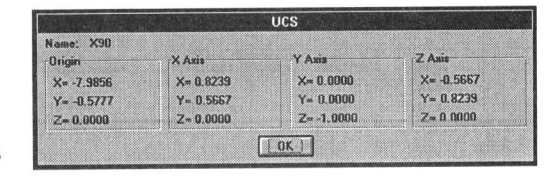

Figure 21-6

Select a UCS name and choose Details.

The UCS Icon

When working in 3D, you are well advised to change your viewports and to use multiple viewports. In each oriented viewport, the UCS is specified by a UCSICON. This icon helps you visualize where the origin of the current UCS is. So far it has always been the *X-Y* plane of the World view.

The current UCS refers to the current orientation of the *X*, *Y* and *Z* axes. The UCSICON echoes this orientation; the cursor rotates as well to the plane of the UCS. The W on the icon stands for World. The other

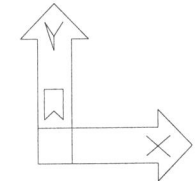

Figure 21-7

If you have a viewport with the broken pencil icon in it, you can indicate items within that viewport by using the OSNAPs available. But you cannot pick a point in space because the *X-Y* plane is perpendicular to the screen and thus difficult to pick.

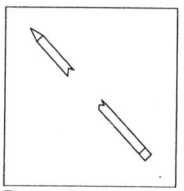

Figure 21-8

Remember that the point you pick or digitize is always placed *line-of-site,* or normal to the *X-Y* plane of whatever plane you are working in. If you pick a point in a plane where the *X-Y* icon is slanted, you will indicate a point *line-of-site* from the screen onto the plane behind it. It is always a good idea to use OSNAP for anything *except your current X-Y plane.*

While working with multiple viewports, you can see how, if all views are rotated, there is only one viewport with an *X-Y* icon perpendicular to your view.

The pictorial view has an icon at an angle and, if two views are different from the *X-Y* (top or front), you will see two broken pencils.

When you change the UCS, the icon changes in every viewport to show you the current UCS.

When we get to paper space in Chapter 26, you will notice another icon, the paper space world coordinate icon.

Figure 21-9

In both the paper space icon and the model space icon, if there is a square in the bottom left corner (Figure 21-10), it means you are looking down the positive *Z* axis. If the box is missing, you are looking at the model from below or up the negative *Z* axis. The + indicates that the icon is located at the origin of the current UCS.

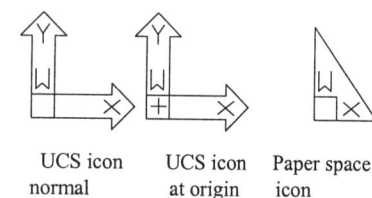

UCS icon normal   UCS icon at origin   Paper space icon

Figure 21-10

The UCSICON Command

The UCSICON command controls the visibility and placement of the UCS icon.

> **Pull Down Menu** From the View menu, choose Display, then UCSICON.

The Command line equivalent is **UCSICON**.

Usually, the icon is placed on the bottom left of the screen, but if you position it on the current origin (Figure 21-10), it will show up there. The command for the icon is as follows:

```
Command: UCSICON
Enter an option [ON/OFF/All/Noorigin/ORigin]
   <ON>: OR
```

Figure 21-11

Notes

The UCSICON will not appear on the origin if placing it there causes it to be trimmed within the view. Use ZOOM .9x to reduce the size of the image within the viewport, and the icon will reappear on the origin.

Where: **ON**   = toggles icon on.
        OFF   = toggles icon off.
        All   = updates all visible viewports.
        Noorigin = displays icon in lower left of screen.
        Origin = displays icon on the origin of the UCS.

UCSFOLLOW

This system variable displays the new UCS in plan view. It generates a plan view whenever you change from one UCS to another. You can change UCSFOLLOW separately for each viewport. If UCSFOLLOW is on for a particular viewport, AutoCAD generates a plan view in that viewport whenever you change coordinate systems.

At the command prompt, type UCSFOLLOW.

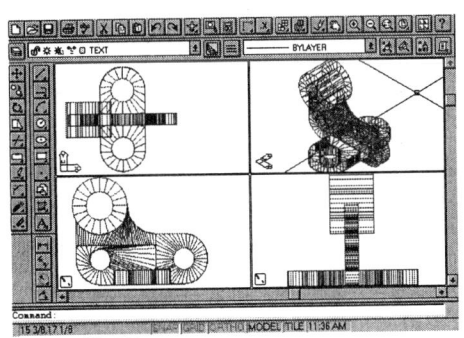

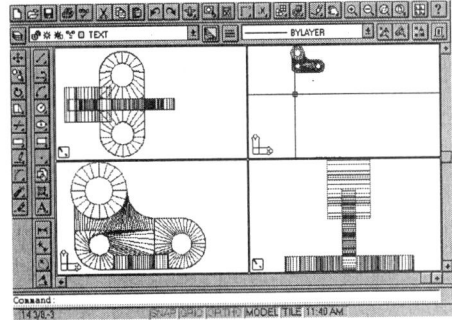

Figure 21-12

Figure 21-13

```
Command: UCSFOLLOW
Enter new value for UCSFOLLOW <0>:1
Command: UCS
Enter an option
  [New/Move/orthoGraphic/Prev/Restore/Save/Del/Apply/?/World]
   <World>:X
Rotation angle about X axis:90
```

The top right view was active when the UCSFOLLOW command was invoked in Figure 21-12. When the UCS was changed, this view shows the current *X-Y* plane.

PLAN

This command also displays the plan view of a User Coordinate System (VPOINT 0,0,1). PLAN *affects the view in the current viewport only.* You can select a plan view of the current User Coordinate System, a previously saved UCS or the World Coordinate System.

```
Command: PLAN
<Current UCS>/Ucs/World:
```

Figure 21-14

Where: **Current UCS** = regenerates a plan view of the display so that the drawing extents fit in the current viewport of the current UCS.

User Coordinate System **505**

UCS	=	changes the plan view of a previously saved UCS and regenerates the display.
World	=	regenerates a plan view of the display so that the drawing extents fit on the screen of the World Coordinate System.
Plan	=	changes the viewing direction and turns off perspective and clipping. This command is useful if you are not sure where the UCS actually is. PLAN will always give you a direct view to work on.

Prelab 21   Changing the UCS

This Prelab gives you experience in setting the UCS. It can also be used as a reference later.

Step 1   Set up your screen to four viewports with a Front, Top, Side, and SW Isometric view.

Draw the object shown using LINE. Make the 0,0 of the part at the bottom left corner.

Use UCSICON to set the UCSICON to the **O**rigin as shown.

```
Command: (pick the isometric viewport)
Command: Zoom A
Command: Z .8x
Command: UCSICON
Enter an option [ON/OFF/All/Noorigin/ORigin] <ON>: OR
```

If the UCSICON still does not appear on the origin, ZOOM down further.

Step 2   Change the position of the origin of the UCS (see figure below) and add a circle at 2,2 with a RAD of 1. The icon is shown at the UCS origin. First change your color to red.

```
Command: COLOR
New color <Bylayer>: 1
Command: UCS
Enter an option
  [New/Move/orthoGraphic/Prev/Restore/Save/Del/Apply/?/World]
  <World>: M
Specify new origin point [or Zdepth] <0.00,0.00,0.00>: (ENDpoint
  pick 1)
Command: C
3P/2P/TTR/<Center point>: 2,2
Diameter/<Radius>: 1
```

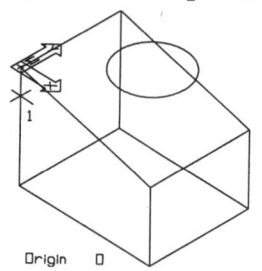

This keeps the same axes and moves the origin to a new location. This is very useful in orienting parts from the new origin point if those coordinates are clear (rather than having to use points relative to the origin).

Step 3   Erase the circle, then change the UCS using ZA and add another circle.

Notes

When specifying a new UCS, you can type in the letter or letters that correspond to the New UCS without having to use N for New first.

```
Command:UCS
Enter an option
  [New/Move/orthoGraphic/Prev/Restore/Save
    /Del/Apply/?/World] <World>:ZA
Specify new origin Point
  <0.00,0.00,0.00>:(ENDpoint pick 1)
Point on positive portion of Z-axis
  <0,0,0>: (ENDpoint pick 2)
Command:C
3P/2P/TTR/<Center point>:2,2
Diameter/<Radius>:1
```

Z Axis ZA

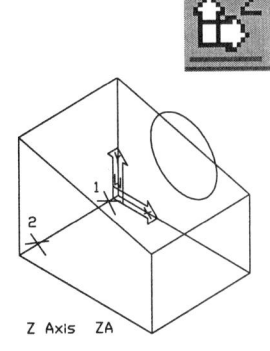

This orients the origin at point 1 and the Z axis through point 2. The X and Y axes relocate relative to the Right-hand rule.

Step 4 Erase the circle, then change the UCS using 3point and add another circle.

```
Command:UCS
Enter an option
  [New/Move/orthoGraphic/Prev/Restore/Save/Del/Apply/?/World]
    <World>:3
Specify new origin Point <0.00,0.00,0.00>:(ENDpoint
  pick 1)
Specify point on positive portion of X-axis
  <0,0,0>: (ENDpoint pick 2)
Specify point on positive Y portion of the
  UCS X-Y plane <0,0,0>:(ENDpoint pick 3)
Command:C
3P/2P/TTR/<Center point>:2,2
Diameter/<Radius>:1
```

3 point

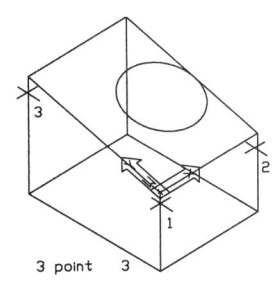

Now save this UCS as SLANT.

```
Command:UCS
Enter an option [New/Move/orthoGraphic/Prev/Restore/
  Save/Del/Apply/?/World] <World>:S
?/Desired UCS name:SLANT
```

Step 5 Leave the current circle, change the UCS using Object and add another circle.

```
Command:UCS
Enter an option
  [New/Move/orthoGraphic/Prev/Restore/
    Save/Del/Apply/?/World]<World>:OB
Select object to align UCS:(pick 1)
```

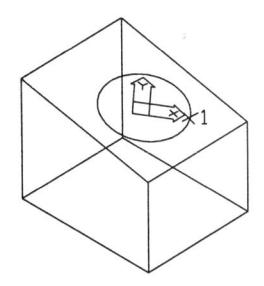

The origin takes the center point of the circle and the X axis is the point picked.

A LINE, DIMension, or SOLID can also be used; the X axis is calculated relative to the origin.

Step 6 Erase any circles on the object and change the UCS to View and add another circle. Try some text as well.

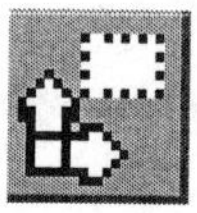

```
Command: UCS
Enter an option
  [New/Move/orthoGraphic/Prev/Restore/
  Save/Del/Apply/?/World]<World>: V
```

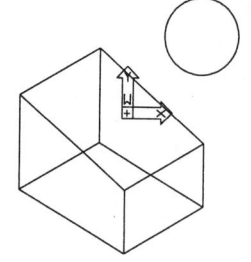

This gives you a UCS perpendicular to your point of view. It is extremely useful for labeling data on a 3D plane. Once the part or data is entered, change the UCS to View and do your notations line-of-sight to make them easy to read.

Step 7 Erase the circle and change the UCS to World, then to an X rotation of 45 degrees. Notice that the X rotation is around the current UCS, in this case World. Add another circle.

```
Command: UCS
Enter an option
  [New/Move/orthoGraphic/Prev/Restore/Save/Del/Apply/
  ?/World]<World>: W
Command: UCS
Enter an option
  [New/Move/orthoGraphic/Prev/Restore/Save/
  Del/Apply/?/World]<World>: X
Specify rotation angle about X axis: 45
```

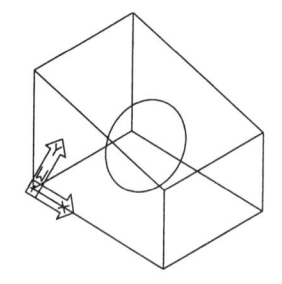

Step 8 Erase the circle and change the UCS to World, then to a *Y* rotation of 45 degrees. Notice that the *Y* rotation is also around the current UCS. Add another circle.

```
Command: UCS
Enter an option
  [New/Move/orthoGraphic/Prev/Restore/Save/Del/Apply/?
  /World]<World>: Y
Specify rotation angle about Y axis: 45
```

Again, a rotation around the current UCS. This is useful for putting cylinders through existing shapes. Once the UCS is rotated, just put a circle in to make sure it's what you want.

The rotation angle is calculated counterclockwise looking down the *Y* axis to the origin.

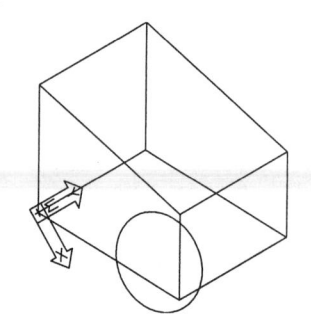

Step 9   Erase the circle and rotate 45 degrees around Z. Add another circle.

```
Command:UCS
Enter an option
   [New/Move/orthoGraphic/Prev/Restore/Sav
   e/Del/Apply/?/World]<World>:Z
Specify rotation angle about Z axis:45
```

A UCS rotation around Z can be useful for rectangular arrays on an angle and for inserting hatches. The hatch lines are calculated relative to the boundary, but also relative to the origin of the part.

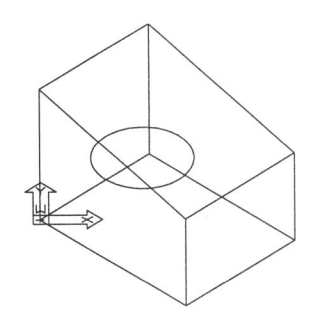

Of course, any orientation of the UCS to an object without the aid of an OSNAP is totally useless.

Step 10   If you want to orient your view in both *X* and *Y*, use the following.

```
Command:UCS
Enter an option
   [New/Move/orthoGraphic/Prev/Restore/Sav
   e/Del/Apply/?/World]<World>:X
Rotation angle about X axis:45
Command:UCS
Enter an option
   [New/Move/orthographic/Prev/Restore/Sav
   e/Del/Apply/?/World] <World>:Y
Rotation angle about Y axis:45
```

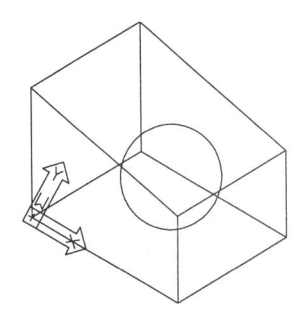

This gives you a rotation in two directions. Remember that this rotates around the last UCS. You can rotate around the World, or around the current UCS.

Step 11   Now access the DDUCS and bring back the SLANT UCS.

> **Toolbar** From the UCS toolbar, choose this button
>
> **Pull Down Menu** From the Tools menu, choose UCS.

The Command line equivalent is **DDUCS**.

The most flexible of the above commands is the 3Point option. As long as you remember that the order is Origin, *X*, and then *Y*, you will have no problem orienting anything.

If you find yourself totally lost, reset to the World UCS and start again.

Press Current to make it current.

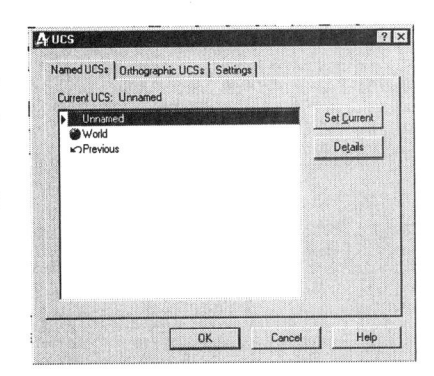

Command and Function Summary

DDUCS allows you to manage the UCSs.

DDUCSP allows you to access preset UCSs.

PLAN displays the plan view of the User Coordinate System.

UCS allows you to reorient the User Coordinate System.

UCSFOLLOW displays the plan view of the current UCS in a given viewport.

UCSICON allows you to place the icon on the object at the origin of the current UCS.

Practice Exercise 21

Once completed, see if you can orient your UCS to any plane on this object.

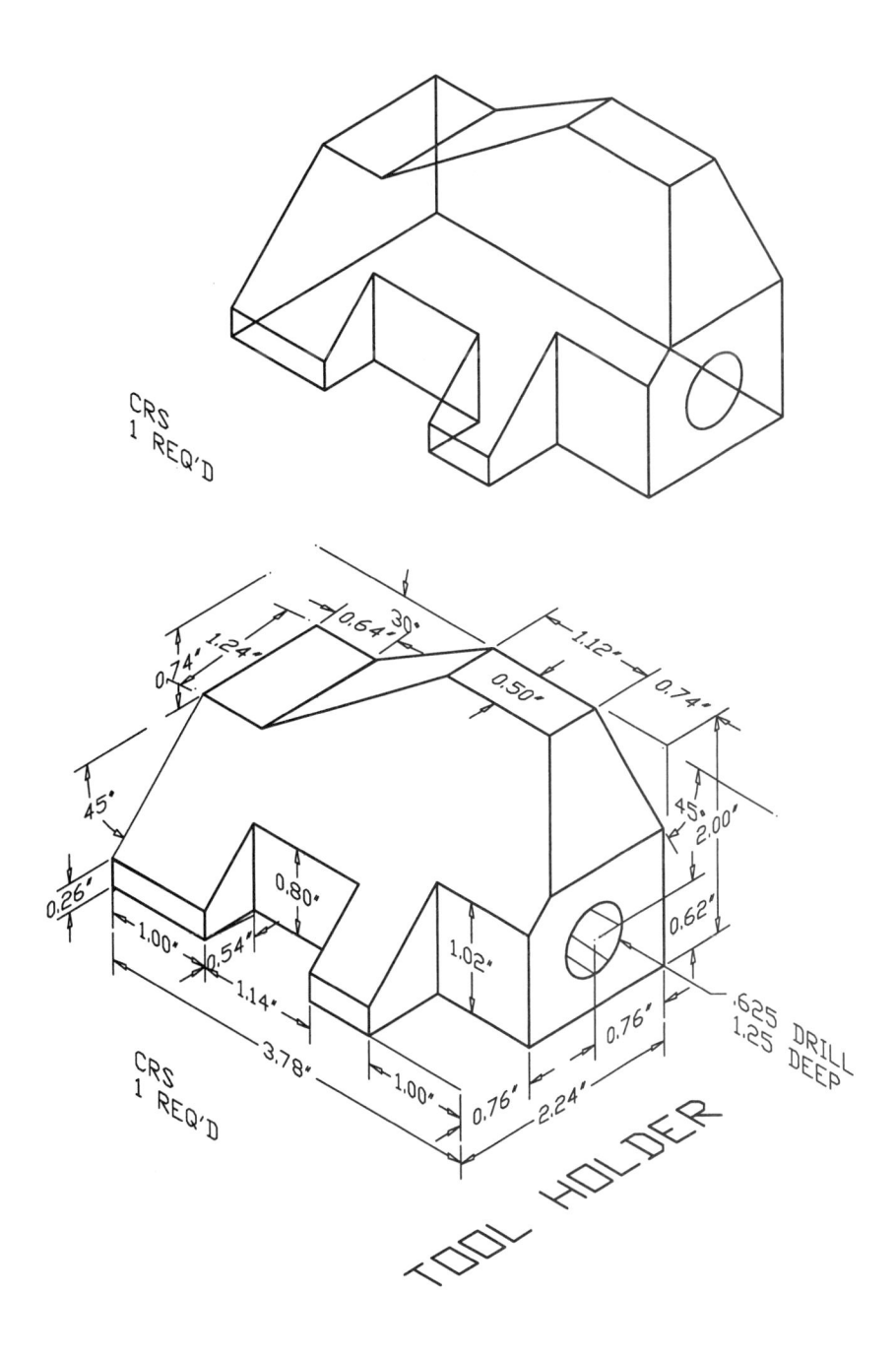

Exercise A21

Construct a food preparation area with the appropriate standard sizes.

Minimum 4" kick space.

Minimum 36" counter height.

Minimum 18" space between counter and upper cabinets.

Minimum 36" for overhead cabinet height.

Change your UCS in order to position the counter top elements and the sinks. Change it again to fit on the stove fan and other details.

A refrigeration center may be added if you have the time.

Use the correct sizes and shapes so that these can be used as prototypes or base drawings for further design in this area.

Save the file—we will be using it later in the file merge chapter.

If you are having difficulty entering objects using your coordinates, try turning OSNAP mode OFF.

There are slight problems with OSNAP ENDpoint on rotated 3D views. Try using INTersection instead.

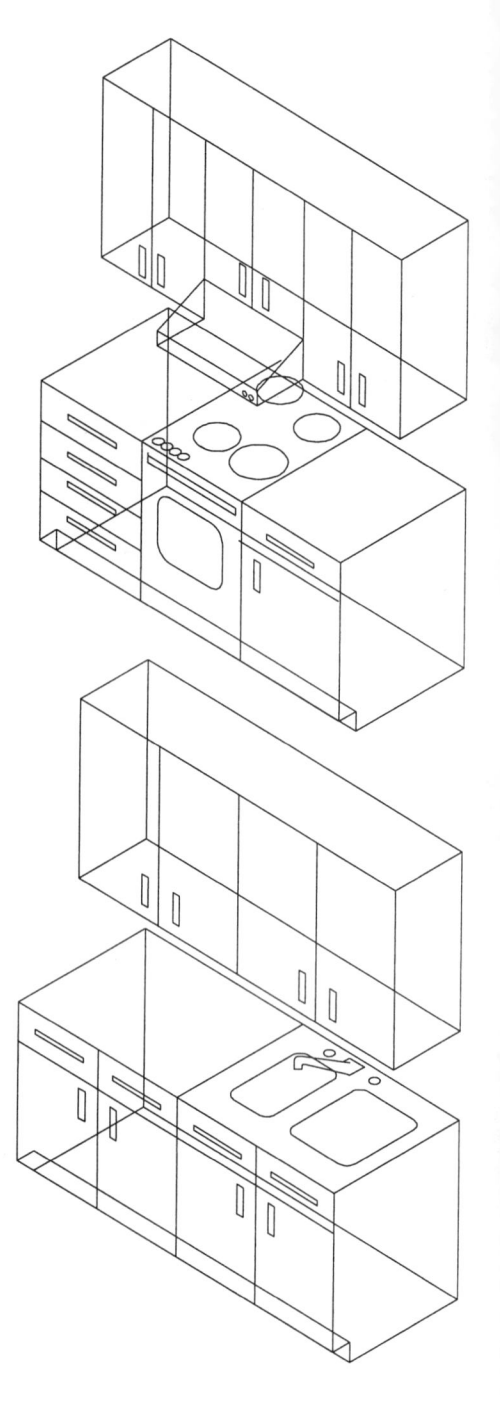

Exercise C21

These shapes provide lots of practice on 3D models. Be sure to change your UCS when needed.

If using UCS with the Entity option, be sure to note the position of the origin. The first few times it is often not where you expect it to be.

When you finish these, try M21.

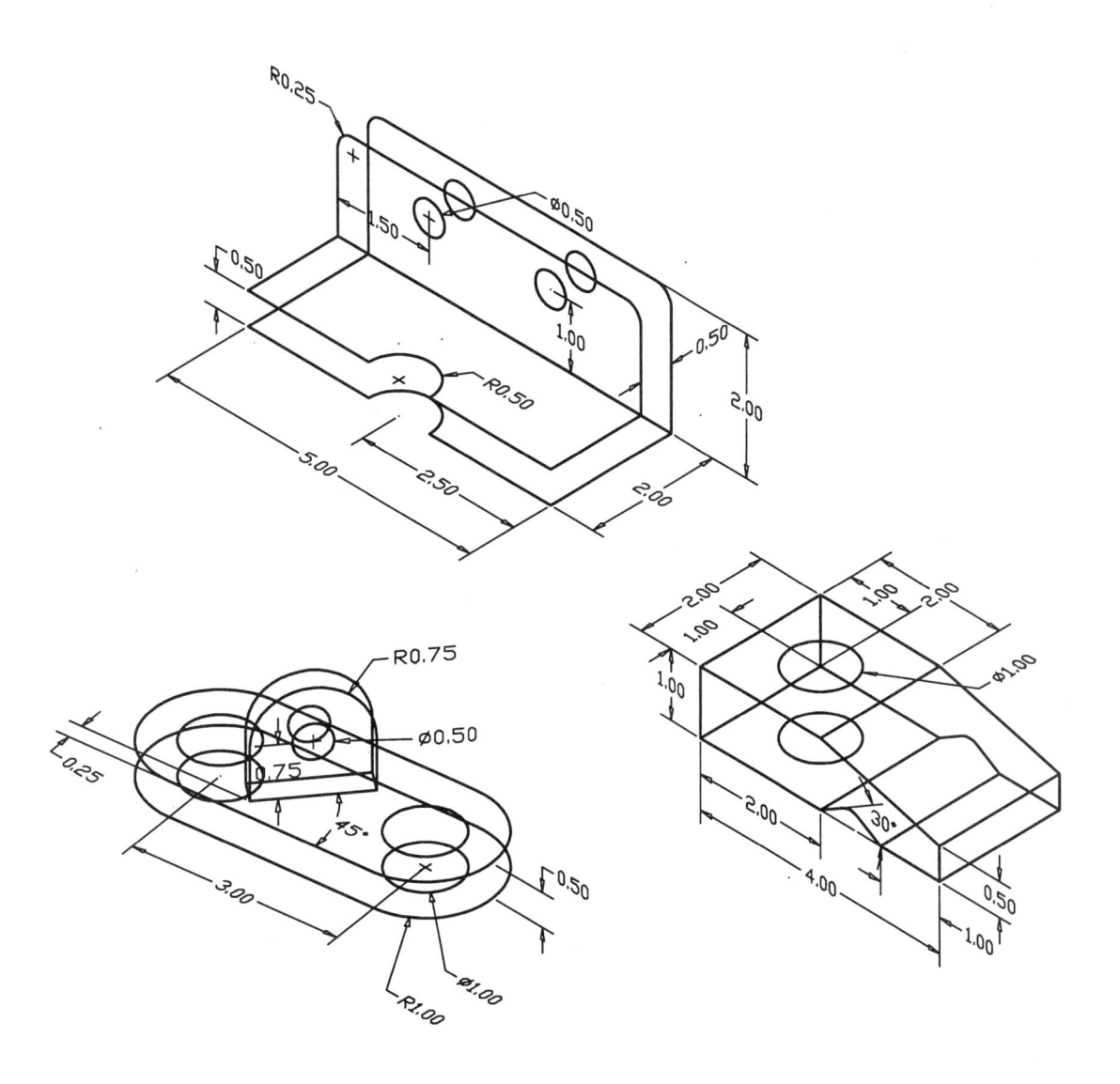

Exercise M21

Draw this object as in the wireframe on the lower right. Save the file so that you can surface it with 3DFACE and RULESURF later.

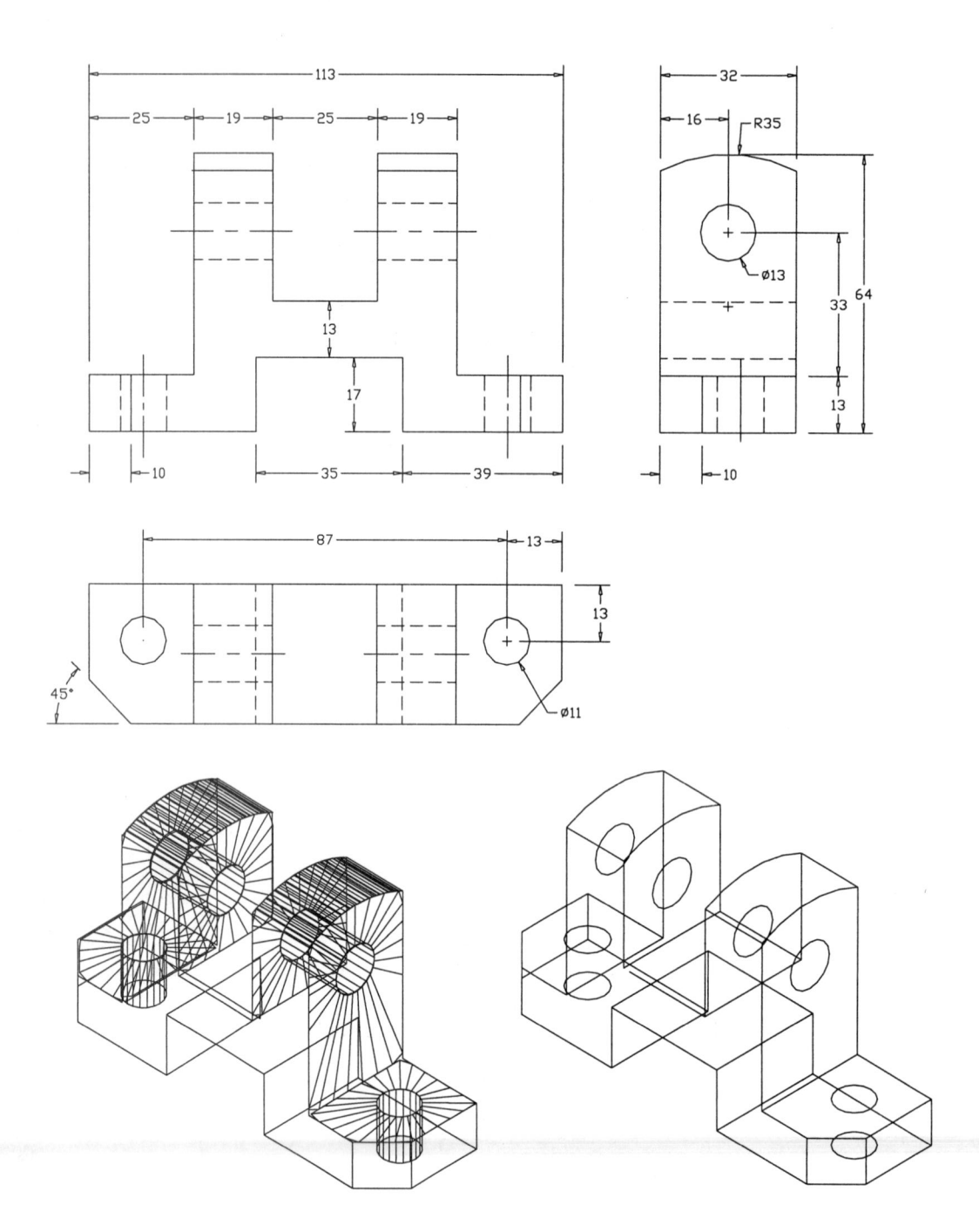

Challenger 21

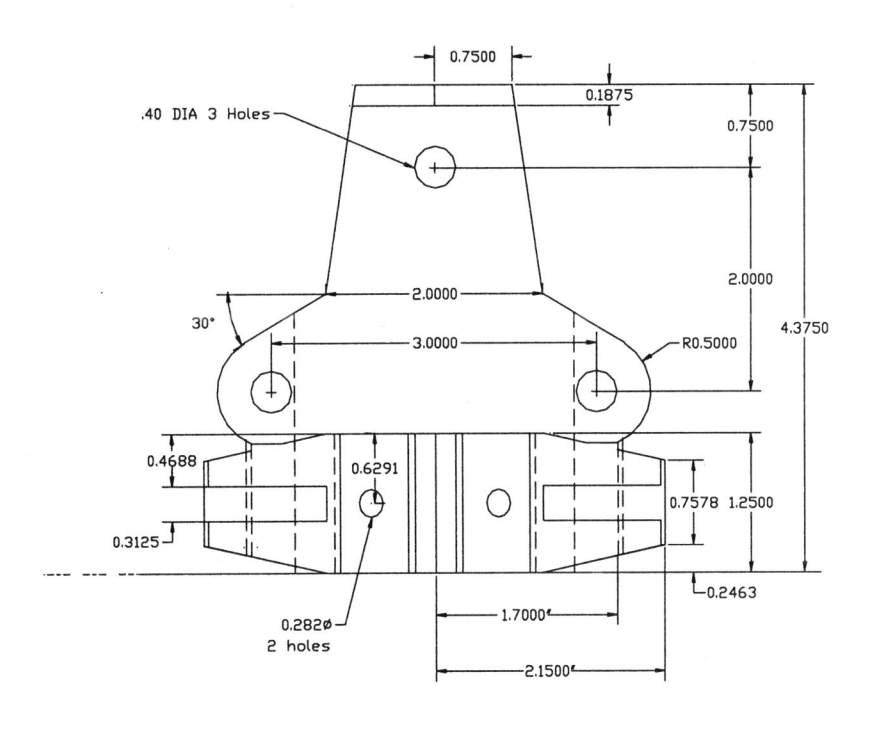

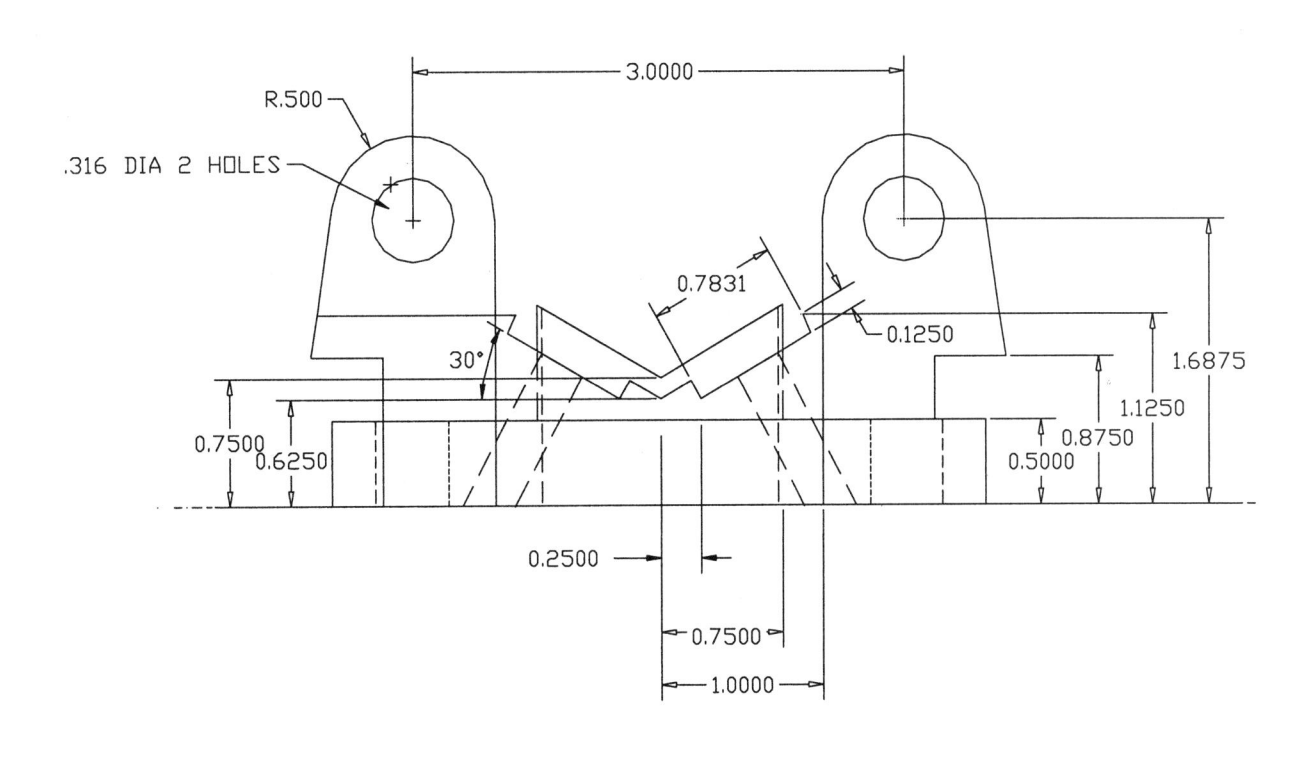

Challenger 21 (cont.)

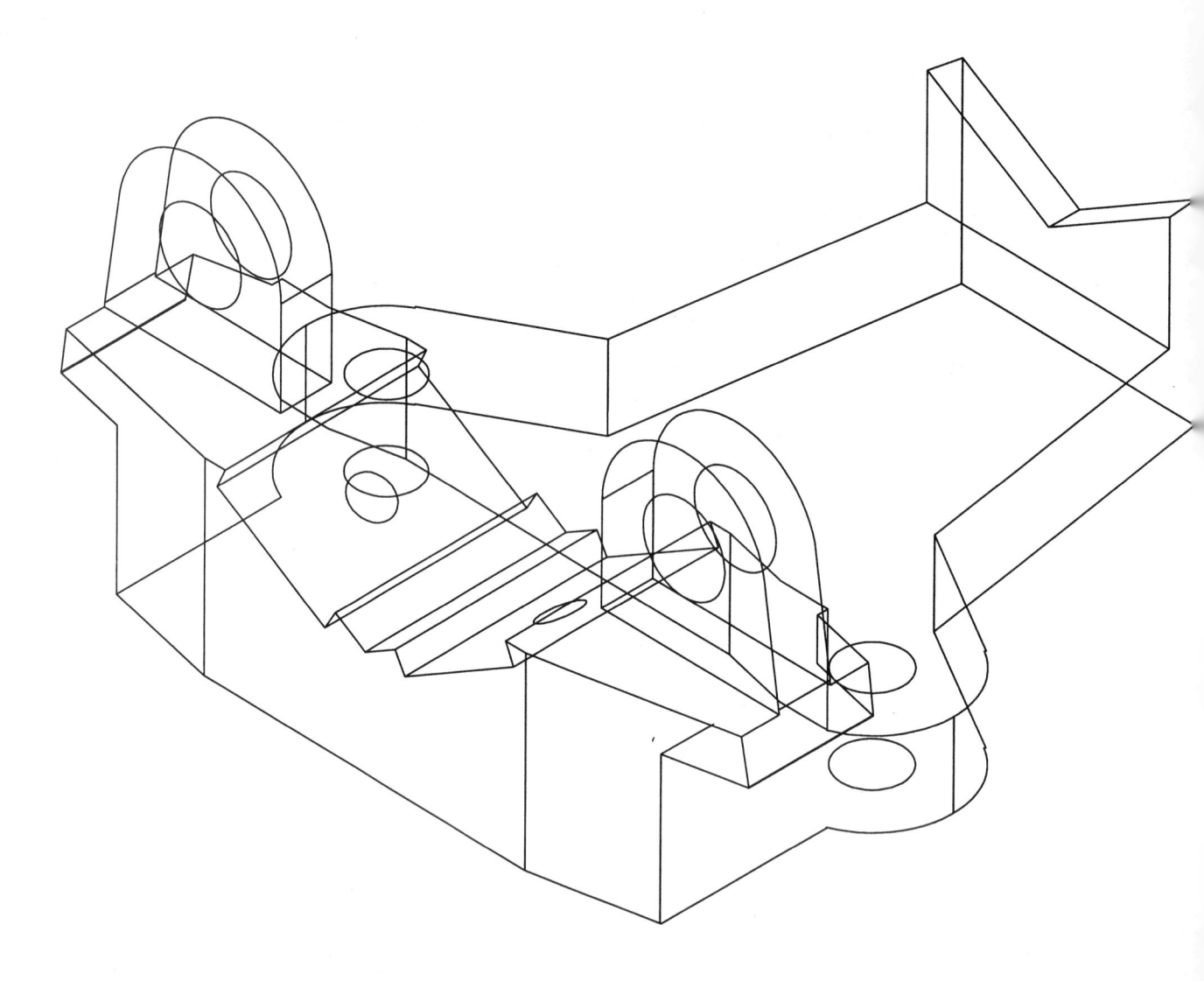

Generate a wireframe of this pipe vise base. If you finish early, the rib and wall thickness is 1/8″, so you can turn it over and add some depth to it.

When finished, save the model so you can practice isometric dimensioning.

While working on this model you may want to save a three-view viewport layout so you can access the front and plan views in more detail.

22 3DFACE, X, Y, and Z Filters, and 3D Autotracking

Upon completion of this chapter, you should be able to:

1. Generate a 3DFACE on any surface
2. Use HIDE to create an image with hidden lines removed
3. Use SHADE to create a shaded image
4. Use X,Y,Z filters

OBJECTIVES

Generating 3D Images

The previous two chapters were developed as a basis for all 3D, but also to give an indication of the "correct" way to develop items in wireframe if your intention is to add surfacing, solids, and anything else that is going to lead to production. In order for a part to be produced, either through CAM or stereo lithography and other 3D part production tools, the part must be described completely in 3D space.

In the first two chapters, only lines were used. Nothing was surfaced. In the next few chapters we will discuss how to fit surfaces onto the lines to create fully described three-dimensional objects.

3DFACE

The 3DFACE command creates an entity that is a planar surface, a section of a plane. The purpose of this command is to have a continuous, coherent plane for viewing an object. The 3DFACE looks like wireframe in that there is no surface display, but it acts as a surface.

For example, instead of having six or seven different extruded plines (see Chapter 23) describing a wall, the 3DFACE can be seen as the final finish, covering the wall so that the construction is not visible. Any or all edges of the surface can be made "invisible" to allow a more visually pleasing surface. This command is used primarily for creating images for viewing (as opposed to creating images for manufacturing), but can be used to create a quick, simple flat "surface" with straight lines between the points describing it.

The 3DFACE is entered in much the same way as SOLID, by pairs of points; but whereas the SOLID is confined to one plane, the 3DFACE is defined by X, Y and Z, and can exist anywhere in space. The 3DFACE can be used to create a hidden or opaque effect. The pick point order in 3DFACE is also a little more natural than that of SOLID; you can choose your points in either clockwise or counterclockwise rotation. The 3DFACE creates a planar effect for creating opaque views, and cannot be extruded like other purely geometric entities.

The 3DFACE Command

The 3DFACE command prompts you for a series of points—first, second, third, and fourth—in the same manner that the SOLID command does. These points can be described by coordinate entry, OSNAPing to existing items or by placing points in space.

Toolbars From the Surfaces toolbar, choose 3DFACE.

Pull Down Menu From the Draw menu, choose Surfaces, then 3DFACE.

The command line equivalent is 3DFACE.

```
Command: 3DFACE
Specify first point or [Invisible]: 0,0
Specify second point or [Invisible]: 4,0
Specify third point or [Invisible]: 4,4
Specify fourth point or [Invisible]
  <create three-sided face>: 0,4
Specify third point or [Invisible]: ⏎
```

Figure 22-1

> **Notes**
> In the interest of saving space and readability, we have shortened the command strings for 3DFACE for the rest of this chapter.

The above command describes a 4-unit square plane starting at 0,0. If the user wanted to continue with the plane, entries could be made in successive pairs of points. If a final single point is needed, instead of a pair, just press ⏎ instead of a point.

```
Command: 3DFACE
Specify first point or [Invisible]: (pick 1)
Second point: (pick 2)
Third point: (pick 3)
Fourth point: (pick 4)
Third point: (pick 5)
Fourth point: (pick 6)
Third point: ⏎
```

Figure 22-2

If you would like to make the line between pick 3 and pick 4 invisible, you can do so by picking the **I** or Invisible option *before the pick that precedes the first point of the line*. In Figure 22-2, you would use an **I** before the first prompt for the third point.

If you forget to use the Invisible option, the EDGE command can be used to make identified edges invisible (see page 520).

In the following example, the line between 3 and 4 is invisible to create the view on the left. Without using I before the third point, you would get the view on the right.

```
Command: 3DFACE
Specify first point or [Invisible]: (pick 1)
Second point: (pick 2)
Third point: I (pick 3)
   (I for invisible)
Fourth point: (pick 4)
Third point: (pick 5)
Fourth point: (pick 6)
Third point: ⏎
```

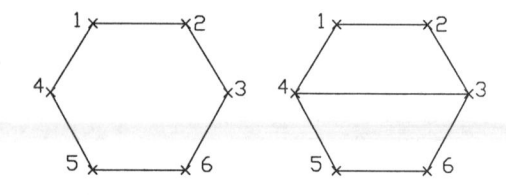

Figure 22-3

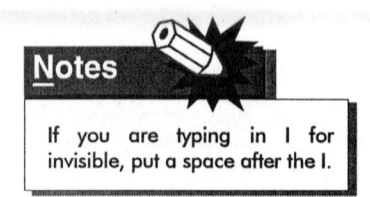

> **Notes**
> If you are typing in I for invisible, put a space after the I.

518   CHAPTER TWENTY-TWO

3DFACE Example

3DFACE can be used to create an opaquing plane to help visualize objects that are already created in wireframe or it can be used to draw planar shapes on its own. In the following exercise the object is created by a series of 3DFACES and nothing else.

You can see how the object is constructed. Change your VPOINT to 2,-2,2 then start with the bottom 3DFACE to create a plane.

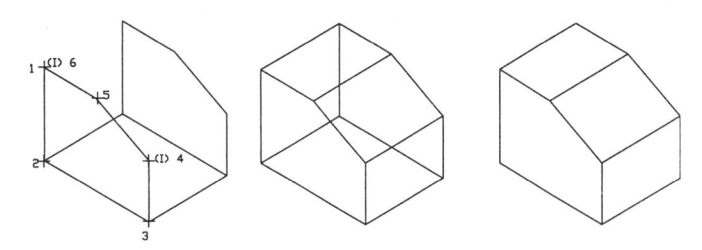

Figure 22-4

```
Command: 3DFACE
Specify first point or [Invisible]: 0,0
Second point: 4,0
Third point: 4,4
Fourth point: 0,4
Third point: ↵
```

Figure 22-5

To construct the front plane you can either change your UCS and pick the points from the screen or you can use coordinates.

If you are using coordinates, try the following.

```
Command: 3DFACE
Specify first point or [Invisible]: 0,0,3
Second point: 0,0,0
Third point: 4,0,0
Fourth point: I 4,0,2
Third point: 2,0,3
Fourth point: I 0,0,3
Third point: ↵
```

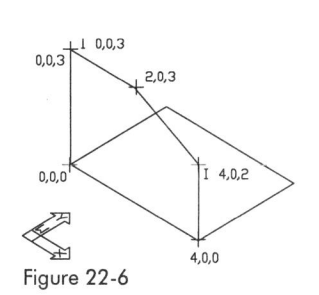

Figure 22-6

The *X* and *Z* change but the *Y* remains constant.

Now you can create the same 3DFACE on Y3.

```
Command: 3DFACE
Specify first point or [Invisible]: 0,3,3
Second point: 0,3,0
Third point: 4,3,0
Fourth point: I 4,3,2
Third point: 2,3,3
Fourth point: I 0,3,3
Third point: ↵
```

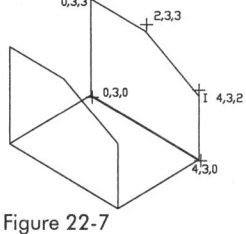

Figure 22-7

You could also COPY the front plane onto the back.

3DFACE and X, Y, and Z Filters **519**

Activate your OSNAP mode to ENDpoint and generate the other three planes using 3DFACE and picking up the appropriate endpoints.

```
Command: 3DFACE
Specify first point or [Invisible]:
ENDpoint of (pick 1)
Second point: ENDpoint of (pick 2)
Third point: ENDpoint of (pick 3)
Fourth point: ENDpoint of (pick 4) etc.
```

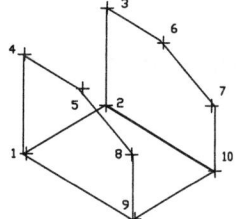

Figure 22-8

Finally, use HIDE and the object will show only those parts visible from your line-of-sight.

If you rotate the VPOINT to 2,2,2 you will have a completely different view of the object and you can try HIDE again to see if it really works.

Other Uses of 3DFACE

If you have a database that contains a lot of items that you would like temporarily blocked out, you can use 3DFACE to create an entirely invisible plane (i.e., none of the outline will appear, it acts only as a screen). This might be handy when you want to show a client only a portion of a part, but not how the rest is progressing or the secrets of your calculations. Another example is in house design—when you want all the interior walls, fixtures, etc., to disappear so that only the outline remains. This is like turning LAYERs off, but blocks out all LAYERs in one specific area.

The EDGE Command

When working on objects that have 3DFACEs, all or some of the edges are often made invisible. If all of the edges are invisible, it is impossible to edit the face. To restore the edges temporarily, use the EDGE command.

Toolbars From the Surfaces toolbar, choose EDGE.

Pull Down Menu From the Draw menu, Surfaces, then EDGE.

The command line equivalent is **EDGE**.

```
Command: EDGE
Specify edge of 3dface to toggle visibility or [Display]:
Enter selection method for Display of hidden edges [Select/All]
```

DISPLAY highlights invisible edges of 3DFACEs so that you can edit them.
SELECT is used to select hidden edges and regenerate selected 3DFACEs.
ALL will regenerate all 3DFACEs.

If you use the Select edge option, you can continue to select edges until all edges that you would like either hidden or visible are identified. If the edges of two or more 3DFACEs are collinear, the visibility of each collinear edge will be altered.

The HIDE Command

HIDE allows the user to create a view of the part with all the hidden lines removed. In 3D construction, we create a wireframe of the model. This allows the designer to create the part from its base geometry. If the user also wants the part to be viewed as a traditional ISOMETRIC view, then all lines that would be hidden in the ISO must be removed. These can be removed from a complex model by using surfacing methods and then HIDE.

> **Toolbars** From the Render toolbar, choose
>
> **Pull Down Menu** From the Tools Menu choose Hide.

The Command line equivalent is **HIDE**.

```
Command:HIDE
Regenerating model.
```

Removing Hidden Lines

HIDE is a very simple command to use—the trick is using it at the correct time. You will note that as you HIDE various lines there is a readout of the number of hidden lines. The drawing is mathematically reconstructed relative to the number of lines that are being hidden. If you hit HIDE when the part is not properly rotated, or you do not have all the objects you need on screen, this command is a real time-waster.

Once objects are hidden, they remain hidden only until the view is regenerated, either by using REGEN or any Display commands such as PAN and ZOOM which regenerate the screen.

HIDE handles circles, traces, plines, regions, 3D faces, polygon meshes, solids, and the extruded edges of objects with nonzero thickness as opaque surfaces which hide objects. If extruded, circles, solids, traces, and wide polylines are treated as solid objects with top and bottom faces.

HIDE and LAYERs

HIDE covers objects that are turned off, and obscures objects behind them. You may have lines obscured by objects that are not on screen but are on LAYERs that are turned off. HIDE will not include LAYERs that are frozen, however; so to avoid losing portions of objects on screen, *Freeze* LAYERS *instead of turning them off*.

HIDE and PLOT

The HIDE command is viewport-dependent. Only objects within the current viewport are hidden. If you plot a viewport, the hidden lines will *not* be removed, even if you have used HIDE on that viewport.

```
Command:TILEMODE
Enter new value for TILEMODE <1>:0
Regenerating layout.
```

Accept the defaults in the dialog box. Now make a view using MVIEW.

> **Notes**
>
> Use MVIEW and Hideplot for plotted images with hidden lines. To create a check plot or small plot of a 3D image with the hidden lines removed, you must use the MVIEW command with the Hideplot option. First make your isometric view current.

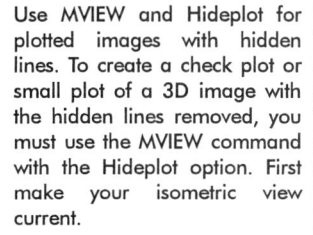

Notes

When using the Copy and Paste routines from the Edit Pull Down menu, you may find that your "paste" will not work if you have "copied" from a paper space environment. Sometimes plotting with an HPGL will be your best solution.

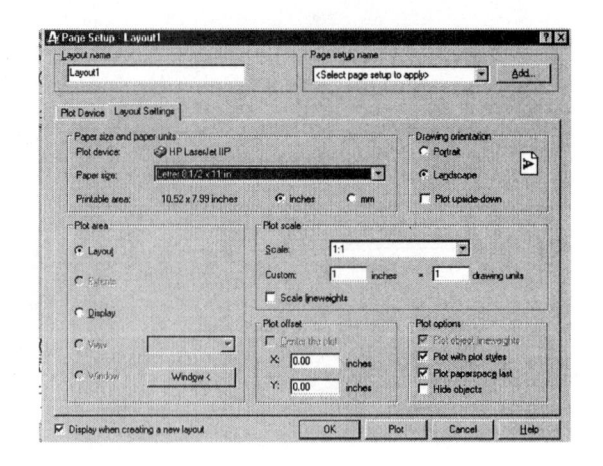

Now turn Hideplot on.

```
Command:MVIEW
Specify corner of viewport or
  [ON/OFF/Hideplot/Lock/Object/Polygonal/Restore/2/3/4/]
  <Fit>:H
Hidden line removal for plotting [ON/OFF]:ON
Select objects:(pick the viewport border)
```

Now plot.

The HIDE command affects the screen display. The MVIEW command with the Hideplot option on affects the plotted image.

Restoring Hidden Lines

To redisplay the lines hidden with the Hide command use REGEN or any display command that will regenerate the screen.

Hiding Lines of Selected Objects

Sometimes you only want a portion of the data on screen to appear with hidden lines removed. To remove hidden lines only on selected objects use the DVIEW command with the Hide option.

> **Toolbars** No button available
>
> **Pull Down Menu** From the View menu, choose 3D Dynamic View.

The Command line equivalent is **DVIEW**.

You will be prompted for the objects that you want affected by the command. Pick these objects, then type in H for hide. The hidden lines will be obscured only temporarily and will be restored as soon as you exit from the command.

The SHADE Command

The SHADE command is used to remove hidden lines from a 3D model and allows the image to be seen as a solid. The HIDE command removes hidden lines and shows the object as a wireframe. The SHADE command displays a flat shaded image of the drawing in the current viewport.

Both HIDE and SHADE are viewport-dependent. That means that the image shows up in the current viewport. Usually the isometric view is best for shaded images.

SHADE can be used on any thickened lines (see Chapter 23), 3DFACES, surfaces, or SOLID models. To SHADE an image:

> **Toolbars** From the Render toolbar, choose
>
> **Pull Down Menu** From the View menu choose SHADE.

The command line equivalent is **SHADE**.

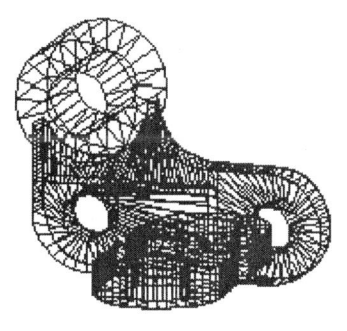

Figure 22-9   Before SHADE   After SHADE

Make sure that you have the isometric viewport current, and then type in SHADE. The shaded image remains in the viewport until the next regeneration of that viewport. The shaded image can be displayed only in that viewport, not on a plot.

SHADEDGE

AutoCAD calculates the shading based on one light source—from directly behind the eye, using the shading method set by the SHADEDGE variable. Use SHADEDGE to change the light source.

SHADEDIF

You can also alter the image with the SHADEDIF system variable which uses the percentage of diffuse reflection and ambient light to create a shaded image.

Color

If you have a computer with 15 colors, there is usually a light and dark version of the same hue. Check the CHROMA slide to see if this is the case. These altering shades can be used to create a very pleasing image that almost simulates a strong light source. For example, you can use color 4 on two sides of a building, and color 12 on the other two sides, giving the impression of a building side in shade.

Notes

Use REGEN to exit from a SHADEd image.

Working with HIDE and SHADE

When working with a view in which you have used HIDE you can still pick up the ENDpoints, MIDpoints, etc. of objects; the image is on screen though the hidden lines have been removed. When working with a view in which SHADE has been used, the image is no longer there, only a rendering of the image is there. You cannot access ENDpoints, MIDpoints or other object snaps on a SHADEd image.

X, Y, and Z Filters

In Chapter 9, X and Y filters were introduced. X, Y, and Z filters are even more important in developing 3D models.

The Z filter is the same as the X and Y filters in that it picks up the value of the point indicated. The Z filter is only a little more difficult to use because it is, for some, more difficult to visualize. In the following, see how the Z filter saves a lot of time placing a circle at the bottom of the object.

First bring up the 3D shape from the 3DFACE exercise. Then set the UCS to the top slanted plane using UCS 3point and ENDpoints.

Now we want to position a circle as a cylinder going through the part.

```
Command: CIRCLE
Specify center point for circle or
  [3P/2P/TTR]:.X of MIDdle of pick 1 (this gets the X value)
(need YZ):.Y of MIDdle of pick 2 (this gets the Y value)
(need Z):0 (positions the circle in the middle of the Z0 plane)
Diameter/<Radius>:.5
```

To get the circle on the bottom plane use:

```
Command: CIRCLE
Specify center point for circle or
  [3P/2P/TTR]:.X of MIDdle of pick 1 (this gets the X value)
(need XZ):.Y of  MIDdle pick 2 (this gets the Y value)
(need Z):.Z of MIDdle pick 3 (this gets the Z value and
  positions the circle at the bottom of the part in line with
  the one above).
Diameter/<Radius>:.5
```

The second circle takes the X of pick 1, the Y of pick 2, and the Z of pick 3.

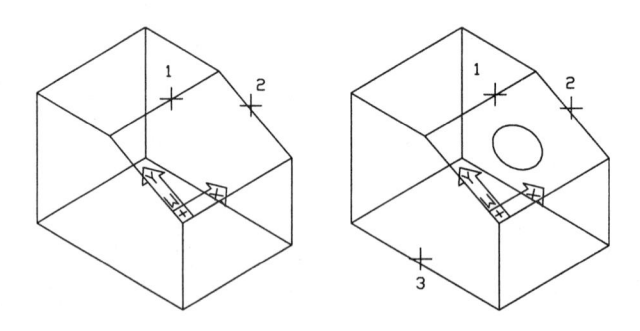

Figure 22-10

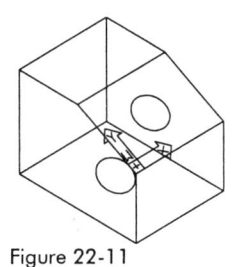

This is a view from the left with both circles in.

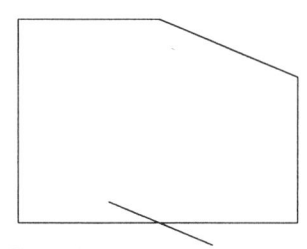

Figure 22-11

Figure 22-12

Figure 22-11 shows both circles in the front view.

Auto Tracking

Now that you can see how the X, Y and Z positions are identified with filters, try doing the same thing with tracking. Make sure your Autotrack is on, and your OSNAPs are set to MIDpoint and ENDpoint. Check the status bar to make sure both are highlighted.

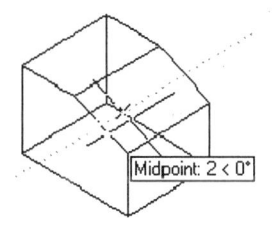

Figure 22-13

```
Command: Circle
Specify center point for circle or
    [3P/2P/Ttr]: (Place your cursor
    above the MIDdle point on the
    diagonal line as in Figure 22-13)
(Then move your cursor to the line
    perpendicular to that and pause
    there at the MIDdle point, Figure
    22-14)
(Then move your cursor to the bottom
    plane, find the MIDdle point of the
    line closest to you, move the cursor
    towards the center until the X is
    shown, Figure 22-15)
(Then pick that spot as the center
    point of your circle.)
```

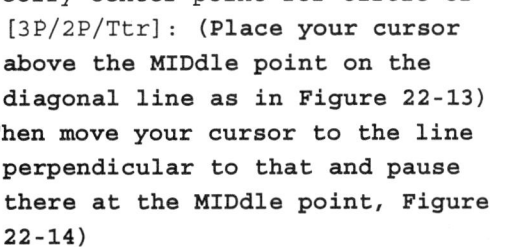

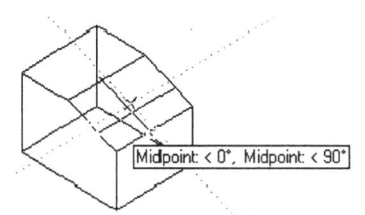

Figure 22-14

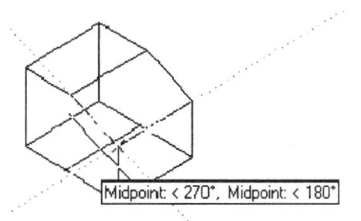

Figure 22-15

Example

Either X, Y, and Z filters or Auto Tracking can be used in any combination. You can choose a filter for an X value and a Y value from a two-dimensional view and then enter the Z coordinate from the keyboard.

Try this example to place the bushing lined up on the axle.

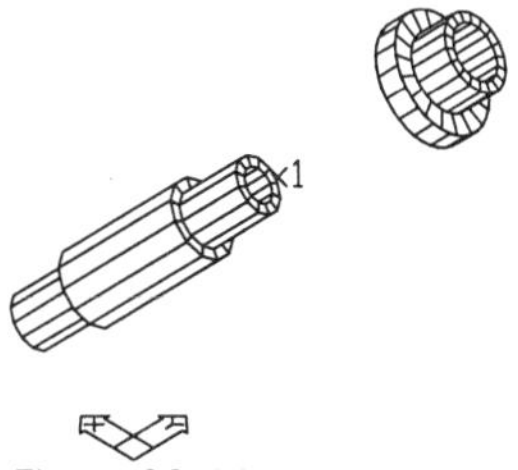

Figure 22-16

Filter values are taken from the current UCS.

3DFACE and X, Y, and Z Filters **525**

Prelab 22 Working with 3DFACE

Step 1 3DFACE can be used on existing wireframe models to add planes for creating hidden lines. Draw the lines and create the wireframe shown. Use four views to get the information in.

The easiest way to draw this is to draw the plan or top view.

Place the bottom left corner at 0,0, then use vertical lines to place the various areas of the model on *Z0*. Draw in the lines at angles, then use TRIM.

Then MOVE or COPY to get the lines up to the *Z* depth.

What we would like is an isometric view with the appropriate lines hidden.

To do this we can place 3DFACEs over the existing geometry.

Once the lines are in, create another layer for the 3DFACES. Make sure the new layer is a different color.

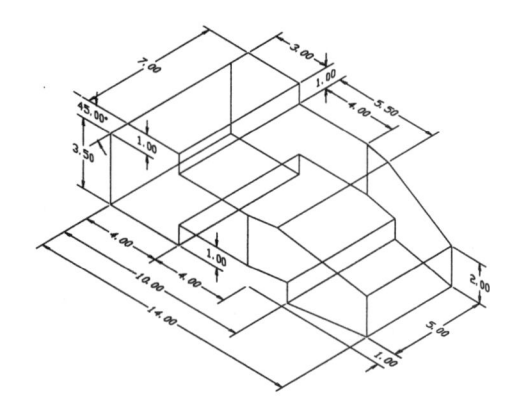

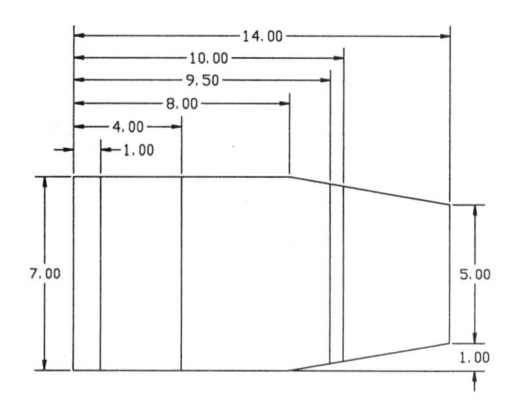

Step 2 Set the Running Object Snap to Endpoint. Then pick 3DFACE. Start with the faces on the back of the part.

> **Toolbars** From the Surfaces toolbar, choose 3DFACE.
>
> **Pull Down Menu** From the Draw menu, Surfaces, then 3DFACE.

The command line equivalent is **3DFACE**.

```
Command:(Create a new layer called 3DFACE, make it a different
   color, and make it current.)
Command:OSNAP
Object snap modes:ENDpoint
Command:3DFACE
Specify first point: (pick 1)
Second point: (pick 2)
Third point: (pick 3)
Fourth point: (pick 4)
Third point: ↵
```

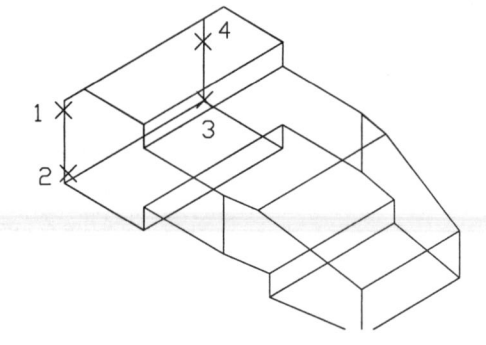

Notes
The 3DFACE command prompts have been modified here for clarity.

Step 3 The top face can be done in one command using the Invisible option.

```
Command: 3DFACE
First point: (pick 1)
Second point: (pick 2)
Third point: I (pick 3)
Fourth point: (pick 4)
Third point: (pick 5)
Fourth point: (pick 6)
Third point: ⏎
```

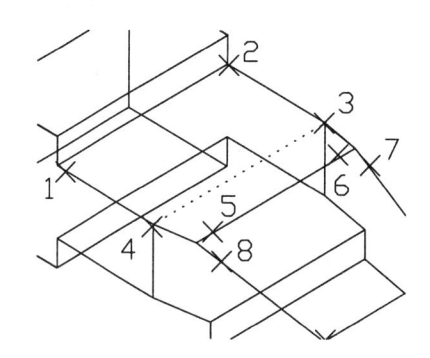

```
Command: 3DFACE
First point: (pick 7)
Second point: (pick 8)
Third point: (pick 9)
Fourth point: (pick 10)
Third point: ⏎
```

Step 4 For the front face, create three different 3DFACEs as shown.

```
Command: 3DFACE
First point: (pick 1)
Second point: (pick 2)
Third point: (pick 3)
Fourth point: I (pick 4)
Third point: ⏎
```

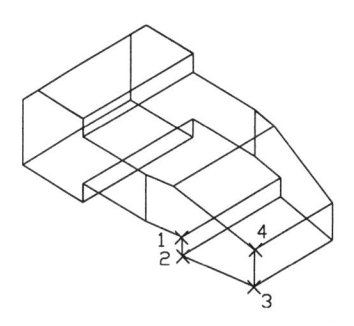

```
Command: 3DFACE
First point: (pick 1)
Second point: (pick 2)
Third point: (pick 3)
Fourth point: I (pick 4)
Third point: ⏎
```

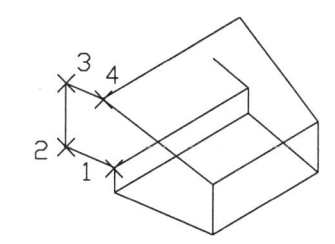

```
Command: 3DFACE
First point: I (pick 1)
Second point: (pick 2)
Third point: I (pick 3)
Fourth point: ⏎
```

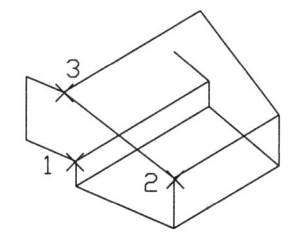

Step 5 You may find that when the 3DFACEs are in they are difficult to erase. Use the EDGE command to show the invisible lines.

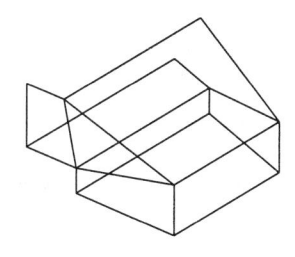

Toolbar From the Surfaces toolbar, choose EDGE.

Pull Down Menu From the Draw menu, Surfaces, then EDGE.

The command line equivalent is EDGE.

```
Command: EDGE
Display/<Select edge>: D
Select/<All>: A
```

The EDGE command can also be used to identify edges that you want to be invisible.

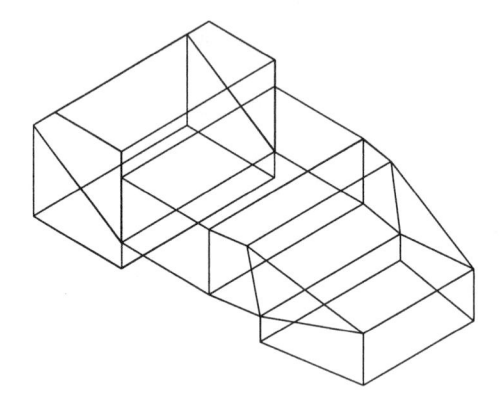

Step 6   Turn them off, and use the SHADE command.

Command and Function Summary

3DFACE creates a three-dimensional face or planar surface on an object.

EDGE changes the visibility of three-dimensional face edges.

HIDE regenerates a three-dimensional model with hidden lines suppressed.

SHADE displays a flat shaded image of the drawing in the current viewport.

Practice Exercise 22

1. Use 3DFACE to create the Box Slide below.
2. Use X, Y, and Z filters when placing the interior shape.
3. Use HIDE to view it properly.
4. Save the file.

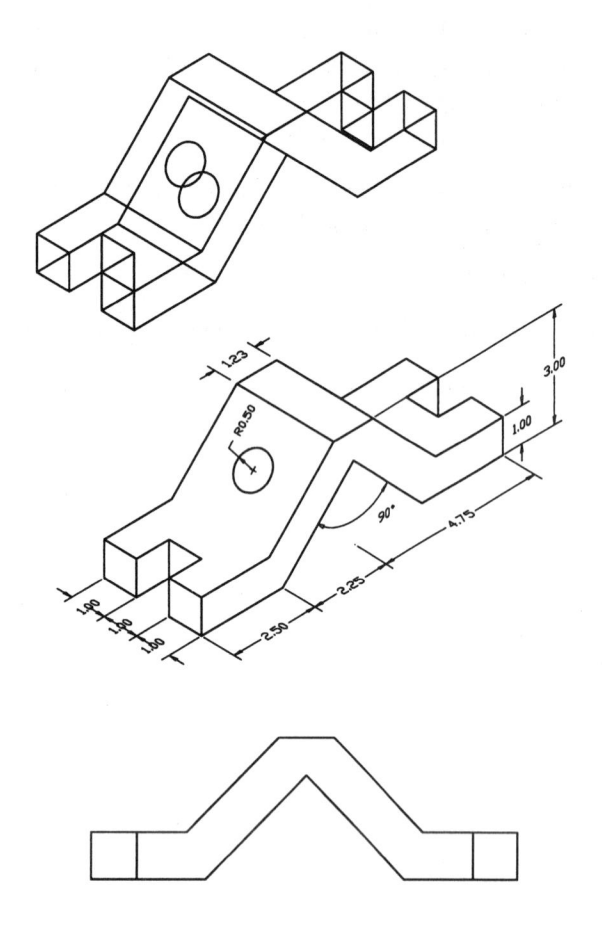

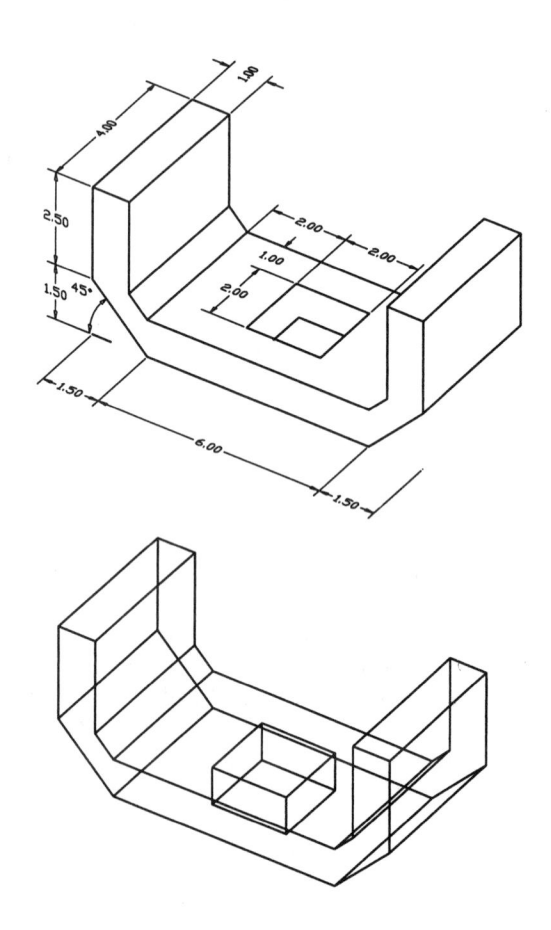

1. Use 3DFACE to create the shape at right.
2. Use HIDE to view it properly.
3. Save the file.

Exercise A22

1. Rotate your view to 1,-1,1 using VPOINT. Using LINE, make a floorplan for an 8′ × 10′ "Bunky" or toolshed.

2. Generate 3DFACE walls on all four sides, leaving two 3′ window openings on the 8′ walls and a 3′ door on the front. You will need more than one 3DFACE per side. One way of entering the 3DFACEs is seen in the example above. Create four 3DFACES with Invisible lines between points 2 and 3 and points 4 and 1, or use EDGE.

3. Using 3DFACE put on a roof. Make sure that the 3DFACE of the roof is *above* the top line of your wall. If it is not, the wall will come through the roof.

4. Use HIDE to create a "solid" building.

5. Using X, Y, and Z filters, place a circular doorknob in the center of the front door.

6. Add a chimney and other details. Add a lawn and garden if you get the urge.

7. Save the file.

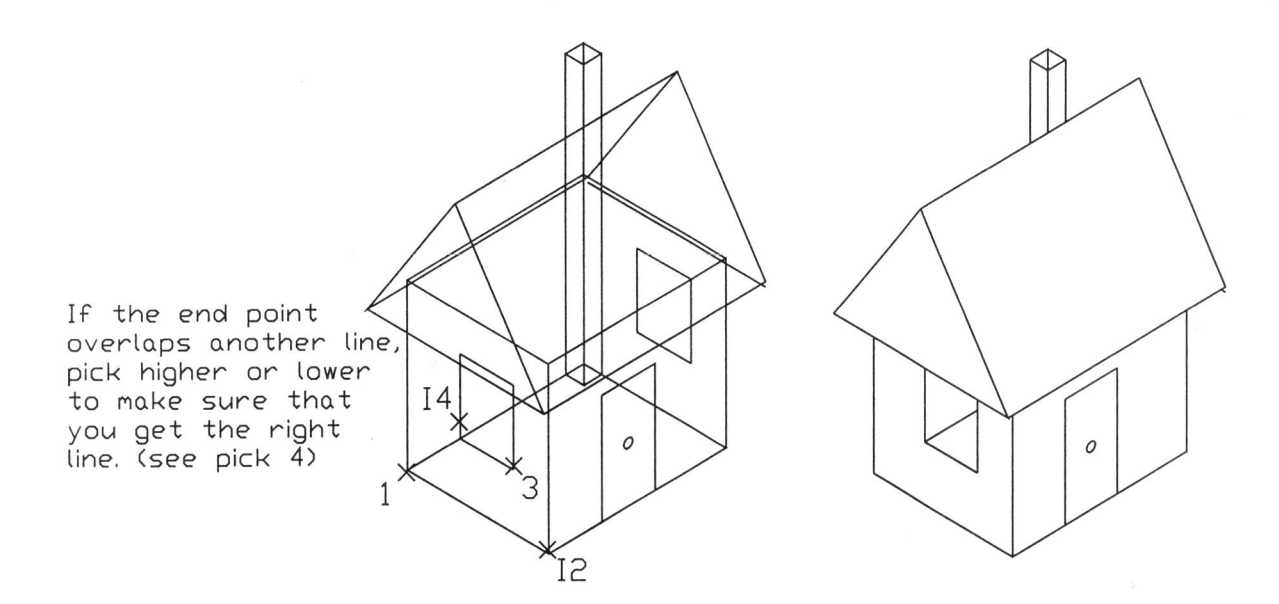

If the end point overlaps another line, pick higher or lower to make sure that you get the right line. (see pick 4)

I2 stands for Invisible 2, choose I on the keyboard, then space then pick.

Exercise C22

Using the dimensions from the footing diagrams in Chapters 7 and 11, create these 3D footings using 3DFACE.

File them as separate models so they can be assembled as a 3D building as the layout in Chapter 9 illustrates.

If you finish early, also create separate files for the footings in Chapter 26.

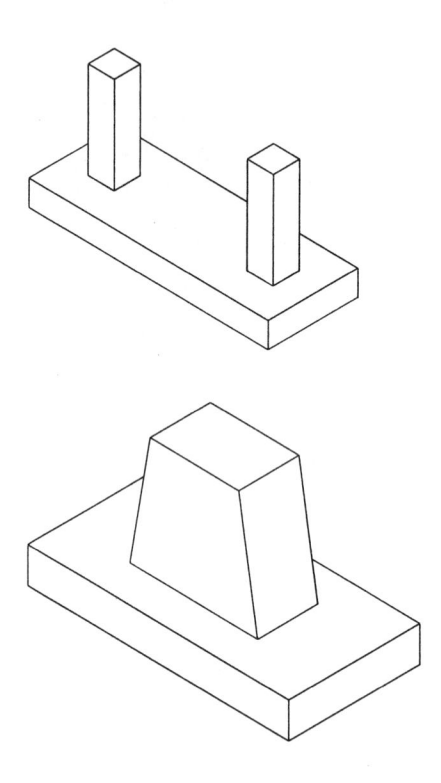

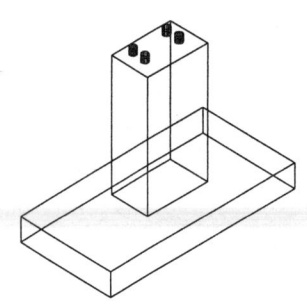

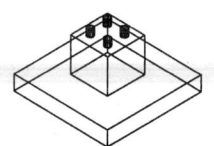

Exercise M22

1. Use 3DFACE to create the camera flash below.
2. Use X, Y, and Z filters to add details to the shape.
3. Use HIDE to view it properly.
4. Save the file.

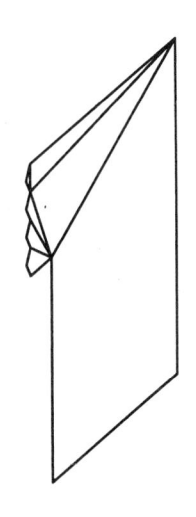

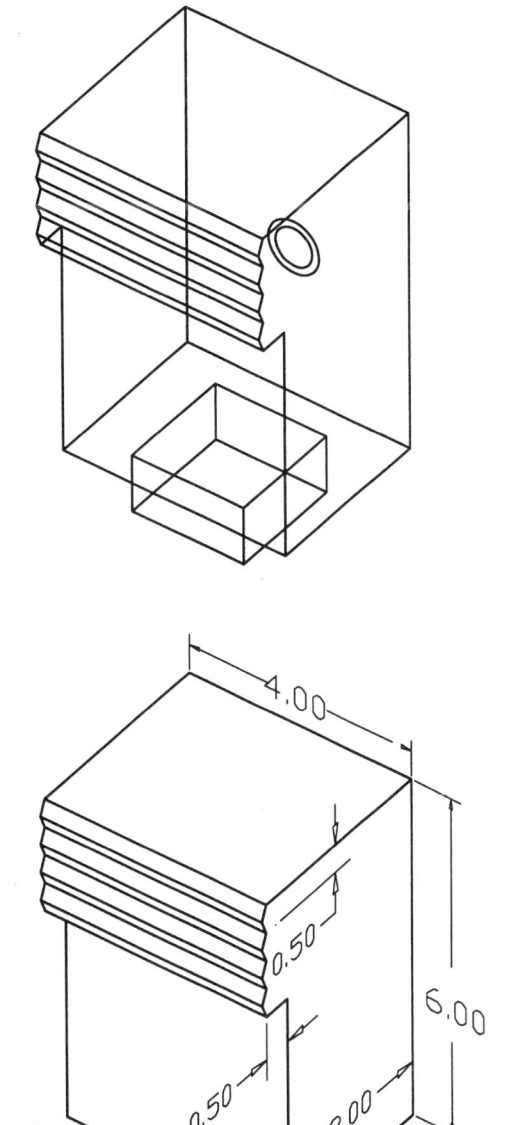

Make sure that the whole plane is covered with 3DFACE. You may need to use more than one.

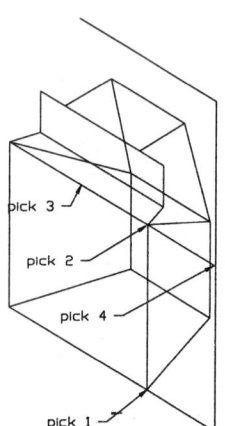

Challenger 22

Taking the actual dimensions of a fireplace from the following chart (in inches), create an interior fireplace. We have used the first set.

Fireplace Opening Width	Height	Depth	Backwall Width	Vertical Backwall Height	Inclined Backwall Height	Flue Out Side	Lining In Side
24	24	16-18	14	14	16	8 1/2 × 13	10
28	24	16-18	14	14	16	8 1/2 × 13	10
36	28	16-18	22	14	18	8 1/2 × 13	12
48	32	18-20	32	14	24	13 × 13	15
60	40	20-22	44	17	30	18 × 18	18
72	40	22-28	51	17	30	18 × 18	18

Create this surface using 3DFACE.

By creating this in a planar or surface mode, you can later take this data with the exterior surface and load it onto AME or analysis software and calculate such things as weight, strength, etc. If you do it strictly with line data, this can not be transferred into a solid or shading mode as quickly.

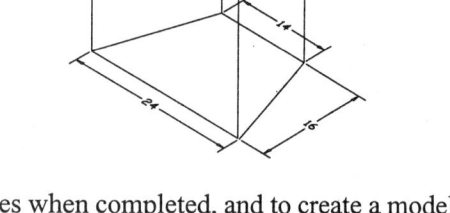

The intent of this model is to have it accessible for experimentation with other facilities when completed, and to create a model for sectioning.

Once the interior is completed, use 3DFACE to create the fireplace's exterior walls, mantle, etc. Remember: using **I** will make unwanted lines invisible. In this case use the following:

```
Command:3DFACE
First point: (pick 1)
Second point:@12,0,0 (taking the
  smallest fireplace)
Third point:i @0,0,24
Fourth point:i END of (pick 2)
Third point: i MID of (pick 3)
Fourth point:i @0,0,24
Third point:@0,0,24
Fourth point:END of pick 4
Third point:↵
```

Challenger 22 (cont.)

Now that the front is finished, create flues, cold-air vents, etc. where they would be on a cold-air-fed fireplace.

Add a ledge by the fireplace opening (slightly cantilevered, 12″) over the floor. Add the mantel details at whatever height you feel is appropriate.

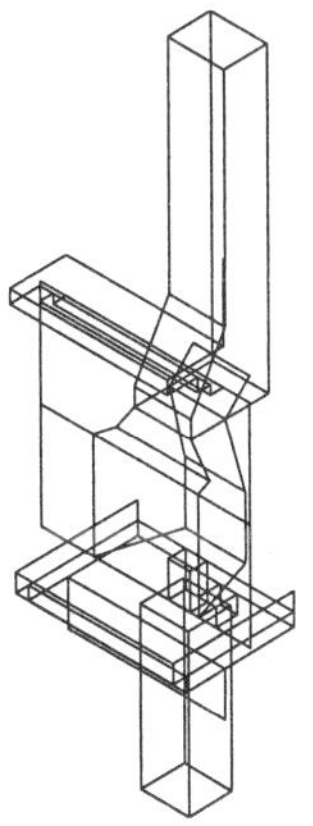

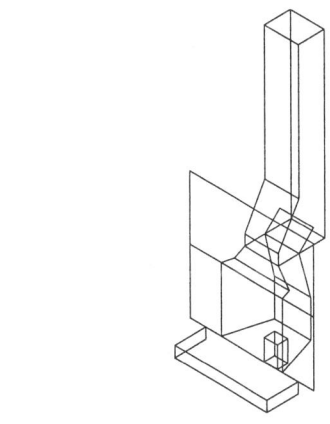

While entering these details, keep in mind that you will want only certain items visible on the final drawing, so keep the parts in different layers for flexibility in the future.

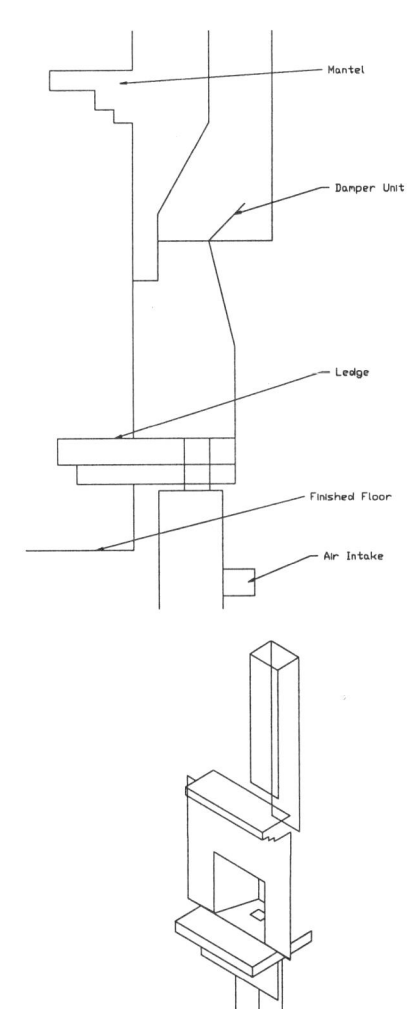

Having completed the fireplace, file the model for use on solids, analysis and AME applications.

Now OFFSET the 3DFACEs to create the firebrick and other masonry details. Use DVIEW with CLip to get a cross section. Make all appropriate dimensions and notations, and create a full drawing.

Having used 3DFACE to create many of your surfaces, you will also be able to generate a nice, fairly comprehensive cut-away view of the finished fireplace with the Hideplot command in MVIEW.

Once your final drawing is assembled, plot it.

Challenger 22B

Create the geometry for this part using circles, lines and fillets, or using solids.

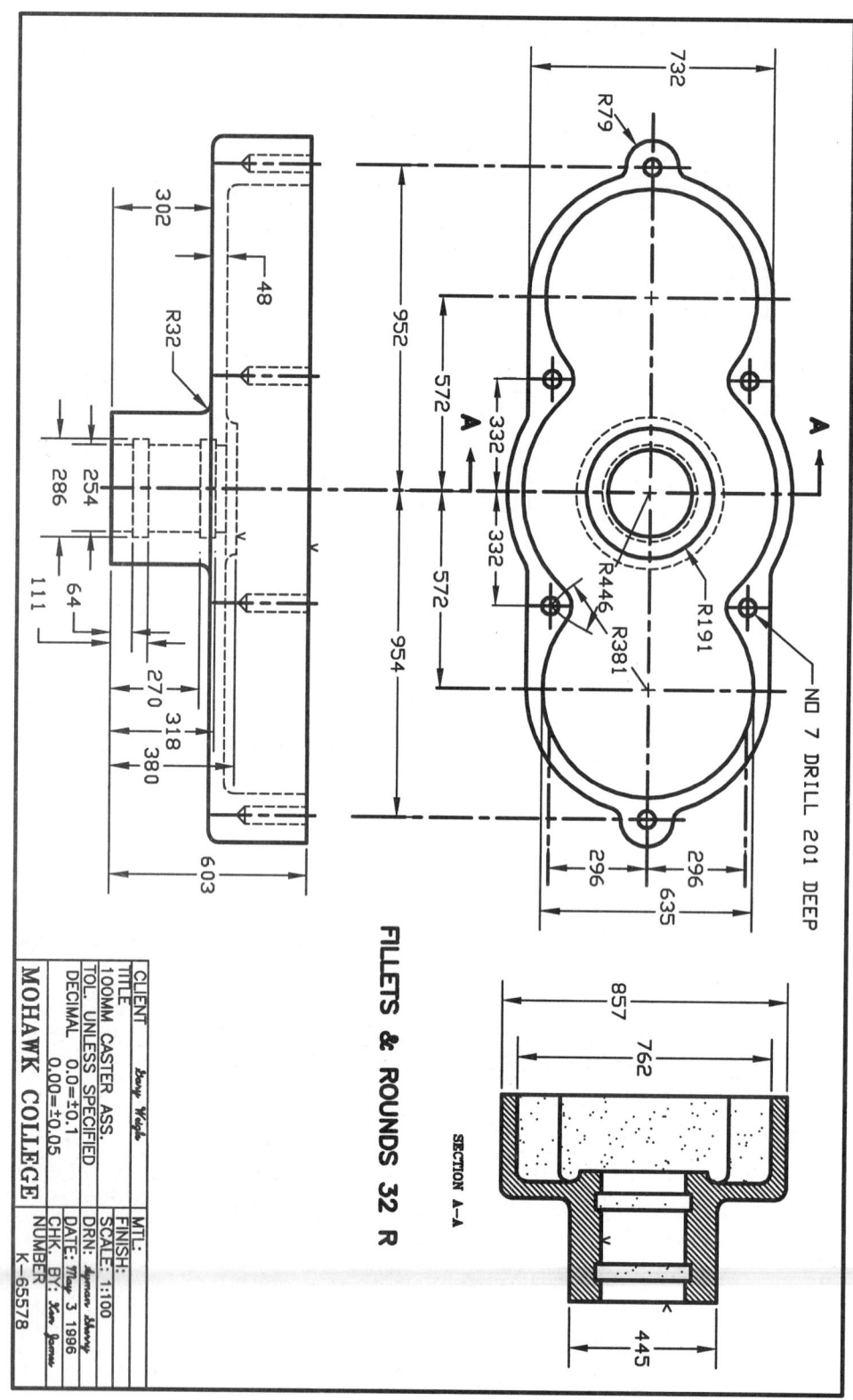

23 Extruding 2D Shapes into 3D Shapes

Upon completion of this chapter, you should be able to:

1. Extrude a 2D image using THICKNESS
2. Change ELEVation to make objects 3D
3. Use HIDE and SHADE on the thickened objects
4. Save and restore your viewports
5. Use the Join option of VPORTS

AutoCAD's ELEVation and THICKNESS commands are very simple tools that simulate 3D meshes. The real advantage is that the ELEVation and THICKNESS can be changed quickly and easily for both new and existing objects.

If your application is not mechanical and you have no intention of producing a 3D model in the near future, you will still need to consider your data as being "fully described" to get analysis and area programs to work, and to get display information.

If you are interested at this point in developing 3D images primarily for display purposes, there are several tools you can use to generate a very agreeable and useful image. The easiest process is an extrusion of the data, developed on the X-Y plane to a specified Z depth.

Any 2D image can be extruded along the Z axis using the ELEVation and THICKNESS commands. The image will be similar to one made with a specified amount of dough and a cookie cutter.

The commands that you use are ELEVation and THICKNESS.

The ELEVation Command

This command sets the elevation and extrusion thickness of new objects. Once the elevation and thickness are set, all subsequent geometry will be produced at the elevation and thickness specified.

The elevation of an object is the Z value of the X-Y plane on which the object is drawn. An elevation of 0 means the base X-Y plane of the existing UCS. An elevation of 36″ would be 36 inches above the X-Y plane of the current UCS.

> At the command prompt, type ELEV.

```
Command:ELEV
Specify new default elevation <0.0000>:2"
Specify new default thickness <0.0000>:6"
```

Elevation is measured from the *X-Y* plane, thickness is measured from the elevation. Thickness can be both above and below the elevation.

The THICKNESS Command

The thickness of an object is the distance that object is extruded above or below its elevation. The thickness is applied uniformly along an object. One object can have only one thickness. To set the thickness of subsequent objects use the following:

> There are no toolbars or pull down menus available for this command.

The Command line equivalent is **THICKNESS.**

```
Command:THICKNESS
Enter new value for THICKNESS <0.0000>:2
```

In the wall on the right you can see that the first panel is put in at an ELEVation of 0 with a THICKNESS of 8'.

In the middle section, the wall supporting the window is at an ELEVation of 0 with a THICKNESS of 3'.

The upper portion of the wall is put in with an ELEVation of 7' and a THICKNESS of 1', taking the height of the wall to 8'.

The upper and lower sections of the wall containing the window are separate objects, either two lines or two plines.

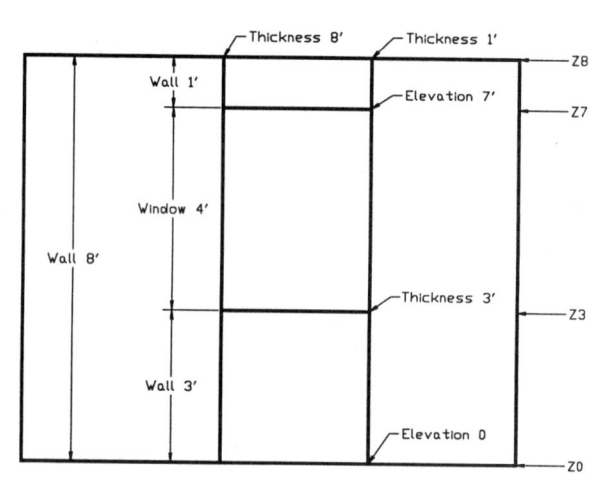

Wall using ELEVATION and THICKNESS

Figure 23-1

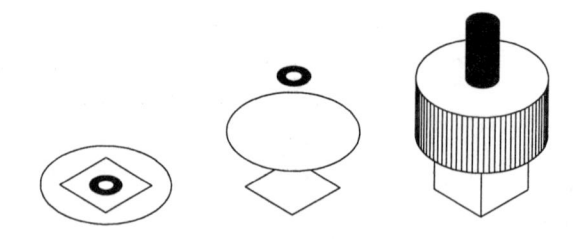

2D Objects   ELEVation changed   THICKNESS changed

Figure 23-2

By changing the ELEVation of an object, you are changing the Z value of the object relative to the current *X-Y* plane. By changing the THICKNESS, you are changing the relative Z depth of the object relative to the current Z value.

Changing Existing ELEVation and THICKNESS

There are two ways of using ELEVation and THICKNESS. The first is to set your ELEVation and THICKNESS, then draw in the geometry. The second is to draw everything onto the *Z-0* plane, then use CHPROP or Modify Properties to change the thickness, and MOVE to get the object to the correct elevation.

If you have a plan view of an object and want to make it into a 3D model, select the objects and use CHANGE or CHPROP to alter the thickness. Figure 22-3 shows a desk unit that was drawn in lines, then in 3DFACE and PLINE. Here is how the 2D object is changed into a 3D object.

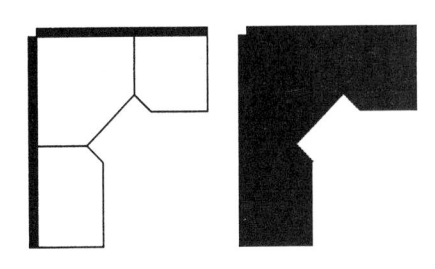

Figure 23-3

Toolbars There is no longer a button for this.

Pull Down Menu From the Modify menu, choose Properties.

The command line equivalent is **CHPROP.**

```
Command: CHPROP
Select objects: (pick the desktops)
Enter property to change
   [Color/LAyer/LType/Ltscale/
   LWeight/Thickness]: T
Specify new thickness <0.0000>: 2
Enter property to change
   [Color/LAyer/LType/Ltscale/
   LWeight/Thickness]: ↵
```

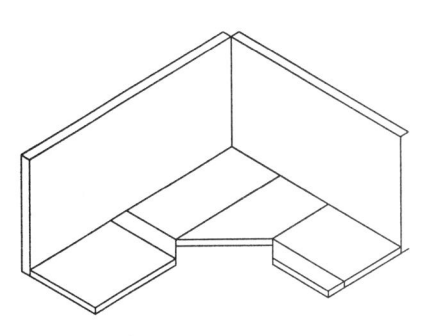

Figure 23-4

The desktops were changed to a thickness of two inches. The panels were changed to a thickness of 36 inches. Then MOVE was used to place the desktops at the correct height.

```
Command: MOVE
Select objects: (pick the objects
   that you want moved)
Specify base point or
   displacement: (pick anywhere on
   Z-0)
Specify second point of
   displacement: @0,0,28
```

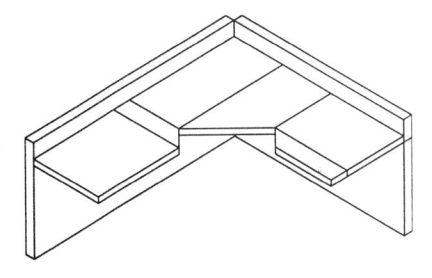

Figure 23-5

This will move the objects to an elevation or *Z* depth of 28 inches.

Use the EDGE command or HideEdge to make lines invisible on your 3DFACE desktop.

Danger

If your objects are *not* showing up where expected, look at your plan view. Use ZOOM All and LIST to find out where your objects are. Always use at least two views.

Thickness of Various Objects

All objects react differently when they are thickened. Circles have a flat, even, solid top. Donuts have a surfaced top which shows the inside and outside radii.

To see how the thickness command works with various objects, set your thickness to 5.

Draw a single line, 4 lines in a square, a circle, a donut, and a pline with a width.

Notice how the items show up in isometric view. Note that it may be easier to place them if you keep your SNAP on.

The objects should look like those shown in Figure 23-6

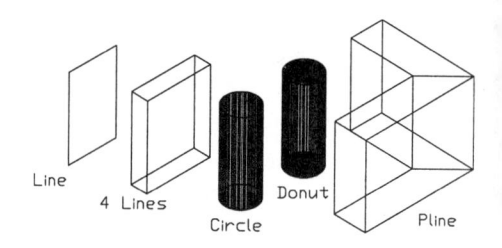

Figure 23-6

They will have a Thickness of 5 and should have a Z value of 0.

Use LIST to find out the thickness of the objects.

3DPOLY

3D faces, 3D polylines, 3D poly meshes, dimensions, and viewports in paper space ignore the current thickness and cannot be extruded. These objects cannot be modified with CHange PROPerties.

Text

When you create new text or attribute definition objects, AutoCAD assigns the objects 0 thickness regardless of the current thickness setting.

Sketch

Line segments produced by SKETCH are extruded after the Record option is selected.

UCS

The current elevation established by the ELEV command remains in effect as you change from one UCS to another, and it defines the drawing plane for the current UCS. The extrusion takes place along the current Z axis.

THICKNESS and ELEVation can be used in conjunction with any other surfacing technique. To have the thickened objects obscure the objects behind them, creating a 3D image, use HIDE.

HIDE and SHADE on Thickened Objects

Since THICKENED objects are used to create a 3D view of an object quickly (as opposed to creating objects that can be manufactured or analyzed with surfacing or Solids), HIDE and SHADE are used frequently. HIDE and SHADE are also very handy to check whether you are looking at the front, back, bottom or top of objects.

Toolbars From the Render toolbar, choose this button.

Pull Down Menu From the Tools Menu, choose HIDE or SHADE.

The command line equivalent is HIDE.

```
Command: HIDE
Regenerating model:
```

Notice the difference between the pline and the 4 lines, as well as the circle and donut object types.

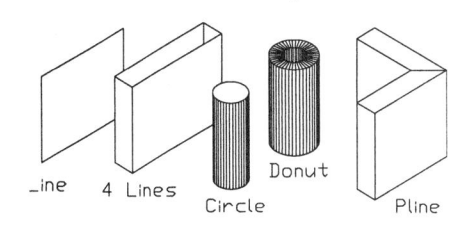

Figure 23-7

Obscuring objects can be time consuming. If you are using THICKNESS just for an object's visual presentation, avoid drawing in all the details that would not be visible at the scale at which you are displaying the objects.

Creating Thickened Objects

To generate an object with fillets and radii in 3D you can first create the plan view of the item in the *X-Y* view.

Then change the ELEVation and THICKNESS for each object. The ELEVation is your absolute *Z* value and the THICKNESS is the incremental distance or the value of the *Z* depth of the item from the smallest *Z* value to the largest.

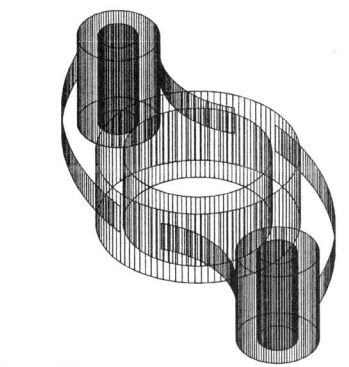

Figure 23-8

As you can see in the illustration, a drawing will look very different, depending upon which objects you choose to HIDE.

Note that the two objects are rendered differently by using circles or donuts. Donuts will surface the top section of the three cylinders but circles will not.

Circles and donuts can both be used for circular or cylindrical shapes. The circle will have a "closed" top, and the donut will have a thick wall, or a top with a midpoint.

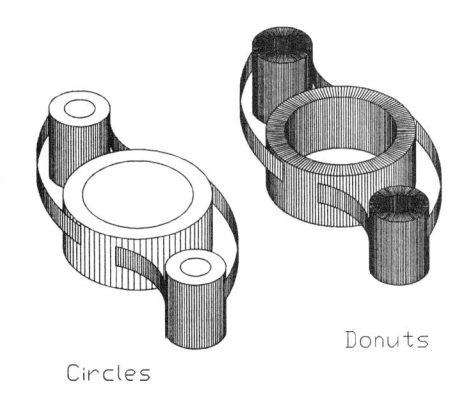

Figure 23-9

VPOINT, VPORTS and VIEW

Now that you are used to setting up your viewports, try using VPORTS and VPOINT with the VIEW command. This series of commands is particularly useful for saving views of objects in the pictorial view that are not rotated with 2,-2,2.

VPOINT

VPOINT allows you to view the object from any angle. The VPOINT command does not control the distance from the object, only the angle at which you view it. Once you change the viewpoint you must then set the ZOOM.

If you have defined a viewpoint and magnification factor or ZOOM which could be useful later, you can save the display by naming it.

Extruding 2D Shapes into 3D Shapes   **541**

> **Toolbar** From the View toolbar, Choose Named Views
>
> **Pull Down Menu** From the View menu, choose Named Views.

The command line equivalent is **-VIEW**.

```
Command:-VIEW
Enter an option
   [?/Orthographic/Delete/Restore/Save/Ucs/Window]:Save
Enter view name to save:Iso
```

Where: **?** = lists the views stored with this model.
Orthogr = allows you to pick a preset orthographic view.
Delete = allows you to delete identified views.
Restore = restores a named view.
Save = allows you to name and save a view.
Ucs = allows you to view the model from the XY plane of a saved UCS.
Window = allows you to name and save a window from the view.

The VIEW dialog box displays the current view name and any views you have named. When a named view is in model space, it is indicated by MSPACE; when in paper space it is indicated by PSPACE.

The options are the same as those indicated above. The New button invokes the New View dialog box where you define a new view.

In the New View dialog box, Current Display uses the current display as the new view.

Define Window allows you to define a portion of your view as the named view. You can either use the coordinates listed in the First Corner and Other Corner area to set the size or indicate the window on the graphics screen by picking Window. You can also save a UCS with your view.

Once you pick Save View, the view will be named and saved.

When you Save and Restore a View, updates to the model will be shown on the updated view.

If you have a layout that includes four viewports and you want an isometric view of the part plus an isometric detail that you have already saved, you can restore the saved view by using the VIEW command.

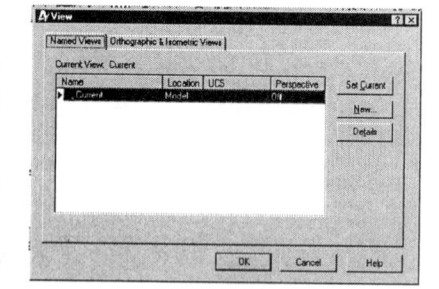

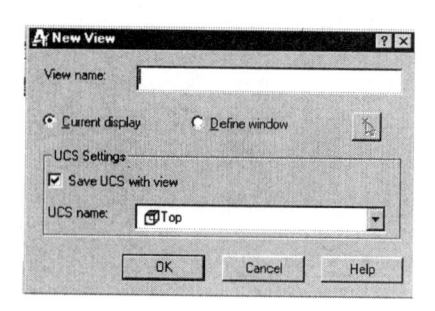

542 CHAPTER TWENTY-THREE

In the illustration to the right, first a 4QUAD viewport layout was restored, then the Save. 4QUAD was restored in the old front view.

```
Command: VPORTS
Enter an option
  [Save/Restore/Delete/
  Join/SIngle/?/2/3/4: R
Enter name of viewport
  configuration to restore: 4QUAD
```

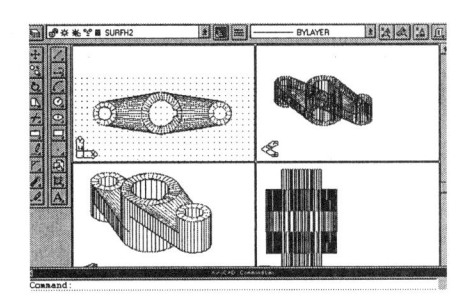

Pick the front view to make it current.

```
Command: View
Enter an option
  [?/Orthographic/Delete/Restore/Save/Ucs/Window]: R
Enter view name to restore: 4QUAD
```

Picking Viewports

During most draw commands you can pick the viewport within the command string. Within the display commands, however, you cannot. Be sure to pick the viewport *before* you activate the display commands.

Picking or Digitizing

When you are picking the screen, try to keep in mind the type of pick you are doing. Basically, there are three types of picks or digitizes.

1. Picking a point in space

When using this type of pick, you are entering a point "line-of-sight" onto the *X-Y* plane or normal to the *X-Y* plane. If your SNAP is on you can pick a point accurately to the SNAP integer. Without the SNAP on, your pick could be anywhere in the general area. If you are picking a point to describe an item (line, circle, ellipse), then you will probably want the SNAP on. If you are picking a point to describe a Window or Crossing, it will not matter if your SNAP is on.

2. Picking a portion of an existing object

When picking using OSNAP or Object SNAP to describe an item, your pick will be very accurate. If your pick is not getting the item you want, it could be because the aperture is too large. If so, change the size using the SETVAR command. If you are set to an OSNAP, you may find it will override a coordinate entry in a 3D isometric view. Turn the OSNAP mode OFF if you are having difficulty entering coordinates, and simply use OSNAP within the command.

3. Picking a ViewPORT

You will need to pick a viewport in order to activate it. This pick can take place before the display commands or within the DRAW or EDIT commands. This pick will not pick up an item if used properly.

Prelab 23 Extruding 2D Shapes

Step 1 Set up a screen with four views: top, front, side and isometric. We are going to create a set of house stairs from one landing to another. The total rise will be 5'. The risers will be 7.5", the treads will be 10".

As most residential staircases are in imperial, change your units to architectural.

Note: Fill OFF may help you visualize this exercise in the plan view.

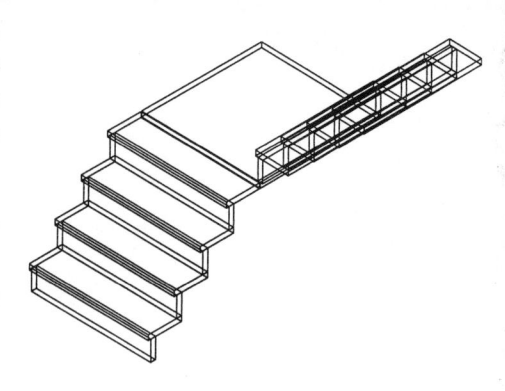

Step 2 First set the thickness to 6". Then enter a pline at a width of 1.5".

At the command prompt type **THICKNESS**.

```
Command: THICKNESS
Set current thickness <0>: 6

Command: PLINE
Specify start point: 0,0
Current line-width is 0
Specify next point or [Arc/Close/
   Halfwidth/Length/Undo/Width]: W
Specify start width <0>: 1.5
Specify end width <0'-1.5">: ↵
Specify next point or [Arc/Close/
   Halfwidth/Length/Undo/Width]: 36,0
Specify next point or [Arc/Close/
   Halfwidth/Length/Undo/Width]: ↵
```

Step 3 Now change the elevation to 6" and the thickness to 1.5" in order to add the tread.

At the command prompt, type ELEV.

```
Command: ELEV
Specify new default elevation <0>: 6"
Specify new default thickness <6">: 1.5"
```

544 CHAPTER TWENTY-THREE

```
Command:PLINE
Specify start point:0,3.5
Current line-width is 0
Specify next point or [Arc/Close/Halfwidth/Length/Undo/Width]:W
Specify start width <0>:10
Specify end width <0'-1.5">:⏎
Specify next point or
   [Arc/Close/Halfwidth/Length/Undo/Width]:36,3.5
Specify next point or
   [Arc/Close/Halfwidth/Length/Undo/Width]:⏎
```

Step 4   Now that one tread is in, array the tread and risers so that there are a total of four. Your front view should be particularly useful for seeing this.

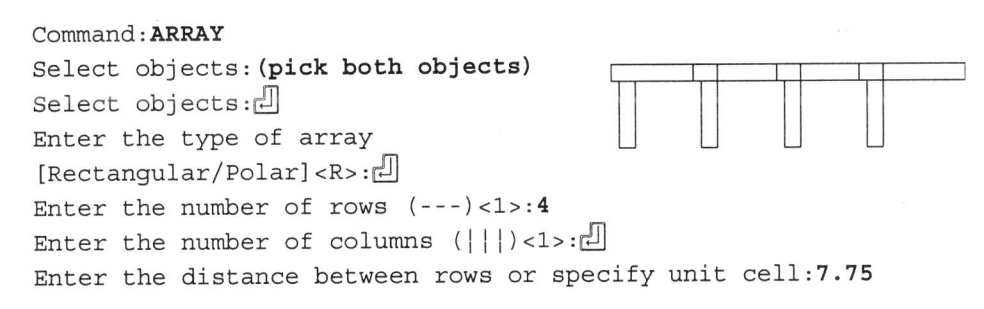

```
Command:ARRAY
Select objects:(pick both objects)
Select objects:⏎
Enter the type of array
[Rectangular/Polar]<R>:⏎
Enter the number of rows (---)<1>:4
Enter the number of columns (|||)<1>:⏎
Enter the distance between rows or specify unit cell:7.75
```

Step 5   Now use MOVE to move them onto a different elevation.

```
Command:MOVE
Select objects:(pick 1, pick 2)
Select objects:⏎
Specify base point: (pick anywhere)
Specify second point
   of displacement:@0,0,7.5
Command:MOVE
Select objects:(pick 3, pick 4)
Select objects:⏎
Specify base point: (pick anywhere)
Specify second point
   of displacement:@0,0,15
```

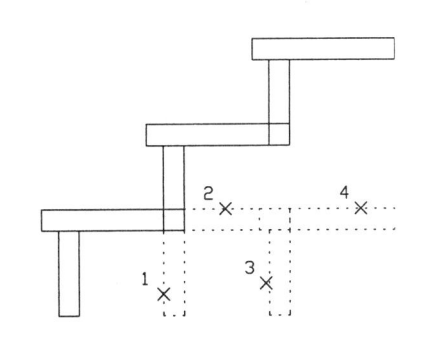

Notes: When moving the stairs, make sure that ObjectSNAP is off.

Continue at 7.5 unit increments. The next step would be displaced 22.5 units (3 × 7.5).

Step 6   In order to create the landing, change your elevation to 2' 4.5'' and your thickness to 1.5''. Draw a SOLID 3'0'' square using SNAP set to 0'2'' or using coordinates.

```
Command:ELEV
Specify new default elevation <6">:2'4.5"
Specify new default thickness <1.5">:⏎
Command:SOLID
Specify first point: (pick 1)
Specify second point: (pick 2)
```

```
Specify third point: (pick 3)
Specify fourth point: (pick 4)
Specify third point: ↵
```

Set your elevation and thickness back to 0.

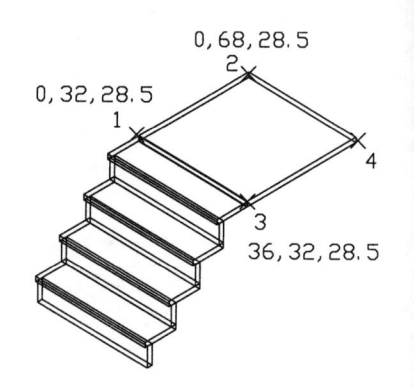

Step 7 Now copy the existing stairs.

```
Command: COPY
Select objects: (pick the stairs)
Select objects: ↵
Specify base point or displacement,
  or [Multiple]: 0,0,0
Specify second point of
Displacement: 36,5'8,2'6
```

Now rotate the stairs 270 degrees. Note that you are rotating around the *X Y* plane. No UCS change is required.

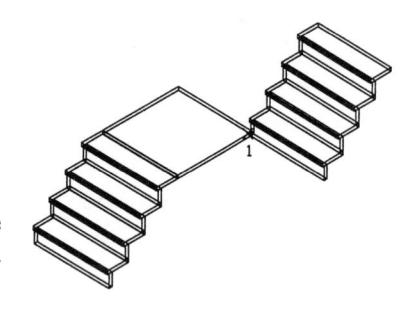

```
Command: ROTATE
Select objects: (pick the upper stairs)
Select objects: ↵
Specify base point: (pick 1)
Specify rotation angle or [Reference]: 270
```

Step 8 Now create the studwall to contain the objects.

Studs can be created from plines and put in on the plan view. Use MOVE to move them up to proper height.

Add some support for the stairs under the landing.

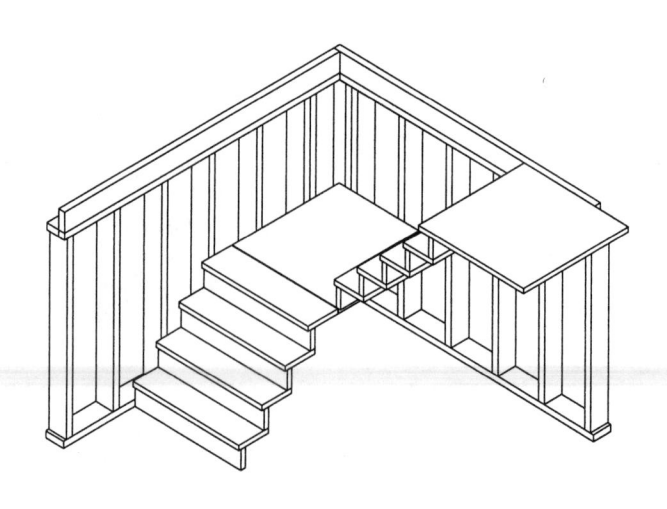

Command and Function Summary

ELEV sets the elevation thickness of new objects.

THICKNESS sets an extrusion thickness for the new objects.

VIEW saves and restores named views.

Exercises

Unless you have done 3D modeling in another system, or are among the ten per cent of people who truly think in 3D, you may find that it takes some time to get used to the concepts and work around a model with any degree of confidence.

A good way to check if you are creating the geometry properly is to have at least two viewports going at all times; change the rotation of your isometric view every now and again to make sure that all the ends meet where they are supposed to.

There are those people who find the concepts in 3D absolutely brutal. If this is the case with you, keep going. Your eyes will bring you to an understanding of the concepts much more quickly than reading any theory.

Practice Exercise 23

Use the dimensions for the clock on pages 373 and 409 to experiment with different ways of creating a mantle clock.

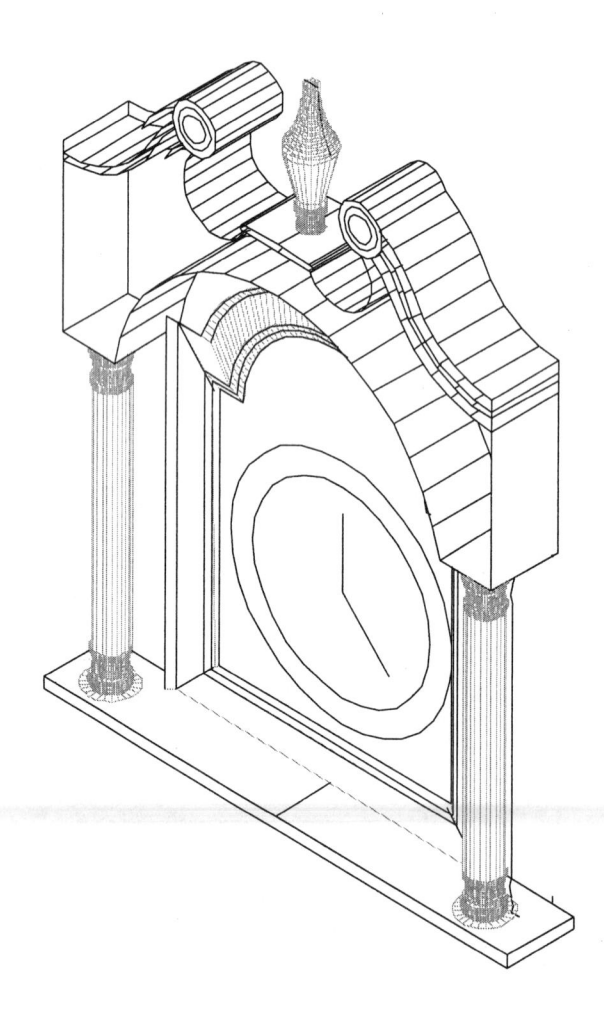

Practice Exercise 23

Using a pline, make a layout for the walls of a house. The walls should be 6-8″ thick. (.5 or .6 at 1 unit = 1 foot). Leave spaces where the windows will be.

Change your VPORTS so that you have at least two. Orient one to plan and the other to 2,-2,2.

Now CHANGE the Thickness of the plines to 8′.

Using a pline again, create the bottom part of the walls underneath the windows.

As the windows will all be different heights, set the thickness and elevation to different heights as you enter them.

Now COPY those plines to a positive Z depth that will leave a space for the windows, but line up with the top of the existing walls at 8′.

Note that you must add two different walls at different ELEVations or Z depths in order to get the wall spaces where the windows will be.

Use HIDE to view this image.

If you have time, add a staircase or some kitchen or bathroom counters.

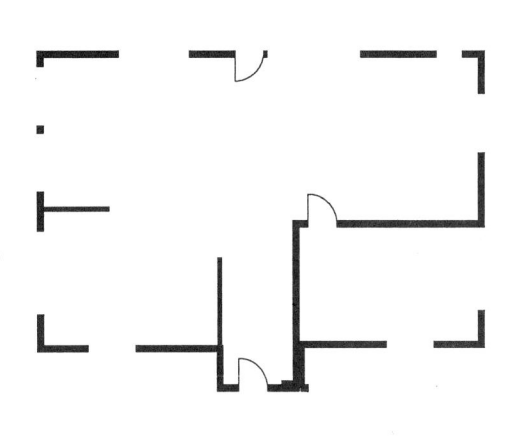

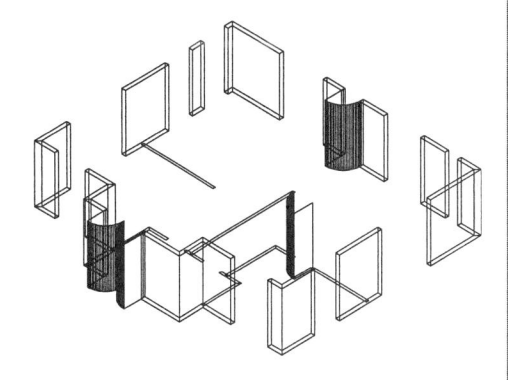

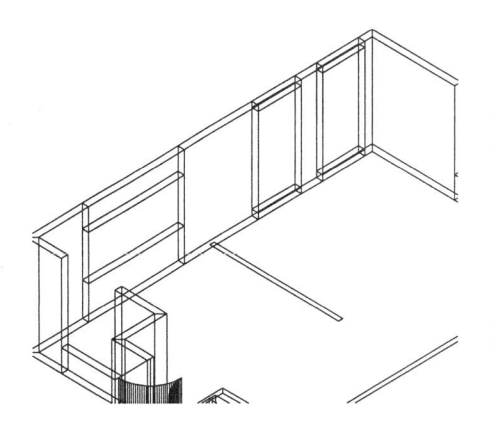

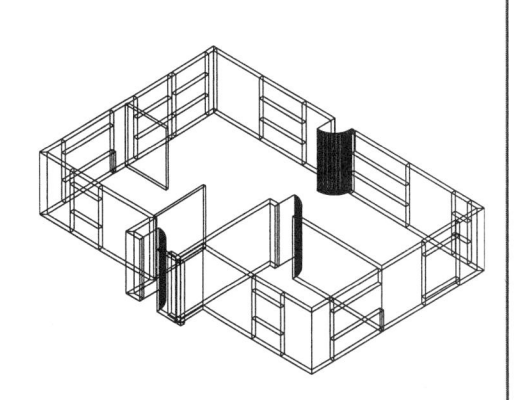

Exercise A23

Using the information in the Challenger Exercise from Chapter 4, create a "pod" of desks using PLINE, LINE, SOLID, and 3DFACE. You will need to use 3DFACE on the desk surfaces, but PLINE will be better for the panels. The height of the panels is 66″. The desk height should be 29″.

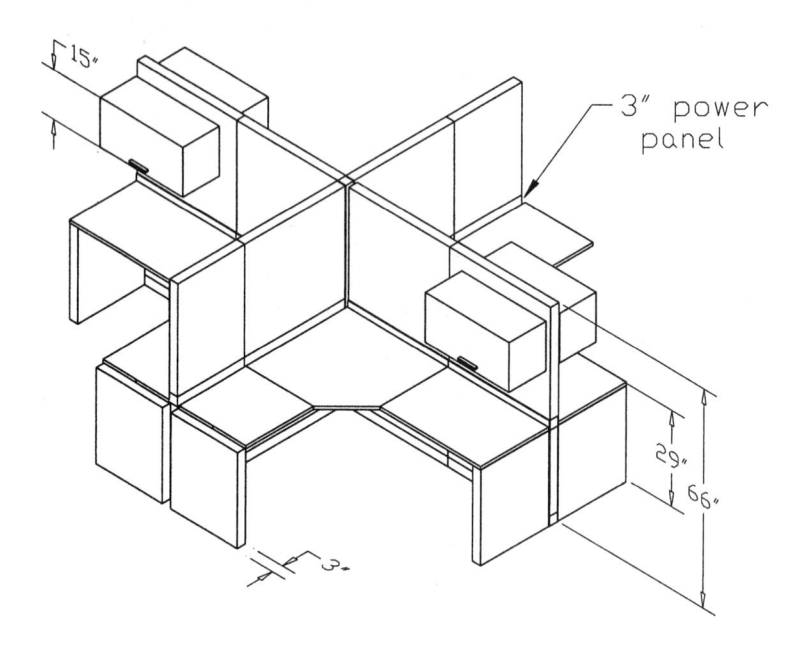

If you have time, create the layout for the entire office.

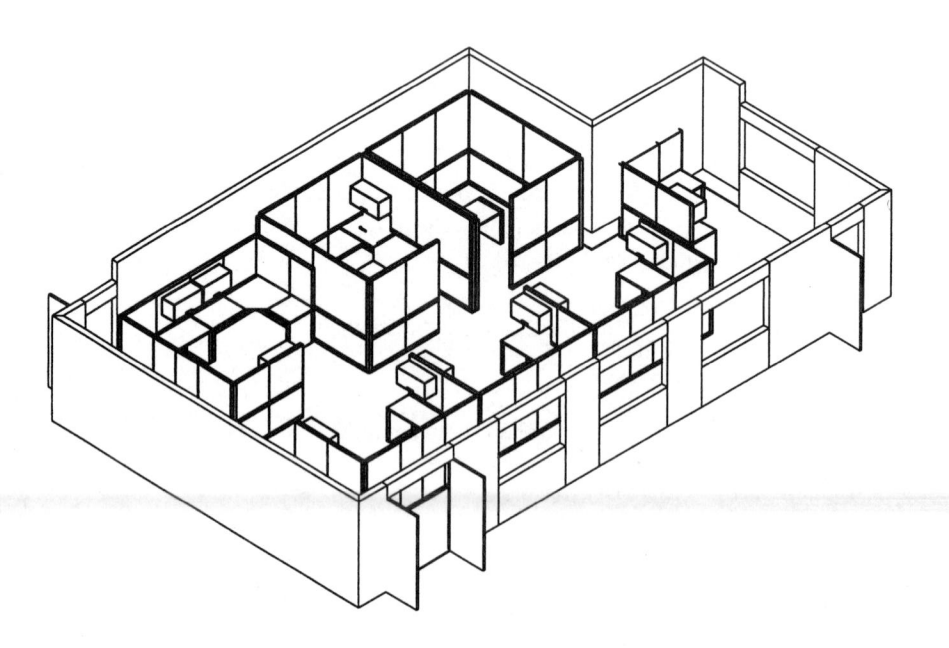

Exercise C23

Using the dimensions listed, draw an outdoor patio, poured concrete bench, and stairway using ELEVation and THICKNESS. Remember 3DFACE. Swimming pool depth should be 12' in the deep end.

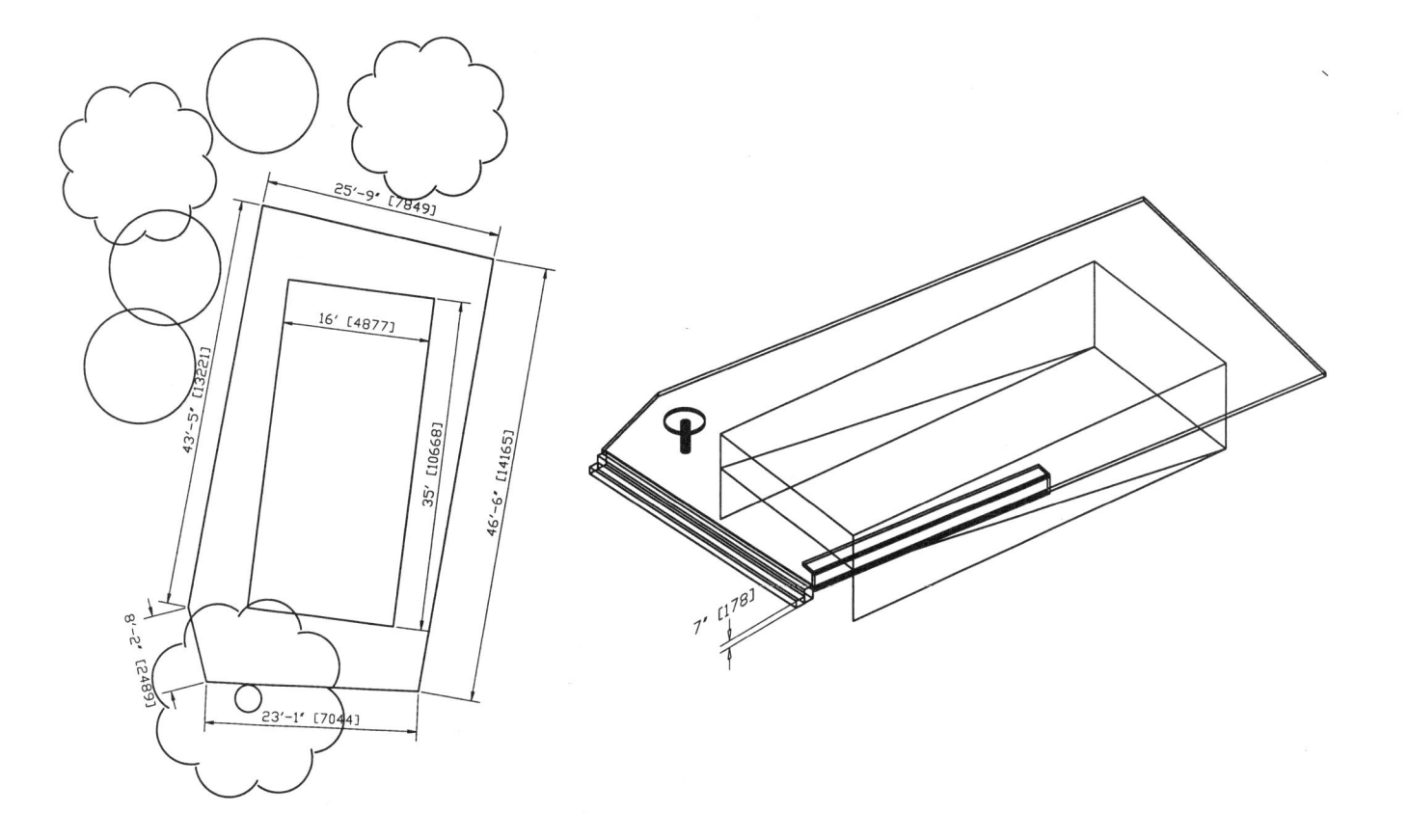

Exercise M23

Try creating some of the illustrations from Chapter 20; see what the constraints of THICKNESS are. Using the model from Chapter 7, change the thickness of the parts' various components. Finally, see how much of the final surfaced model can be created using THICKNESS. The dimensions are on page 193.

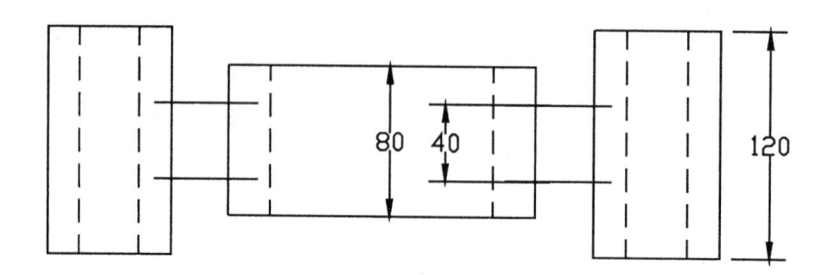

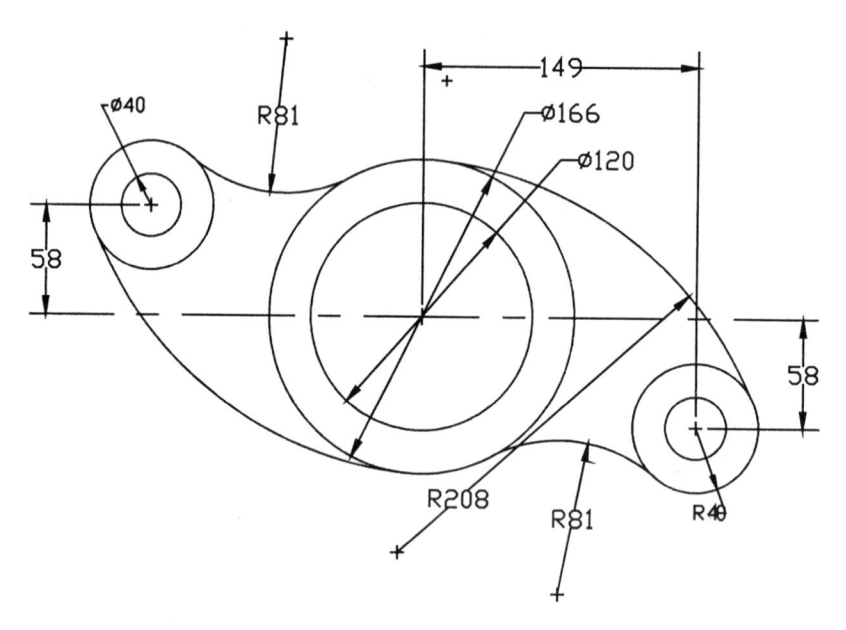

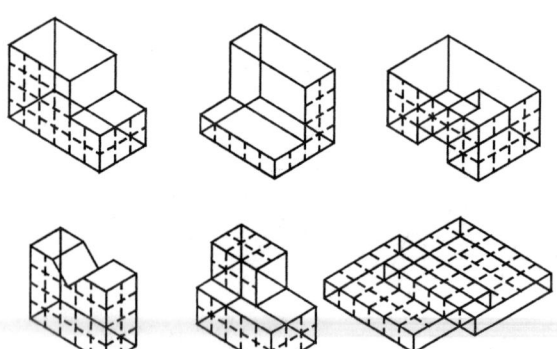

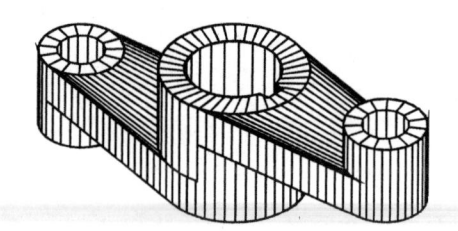

Challenger 23

Using the house constructed in the first 12 chapters and the layout below, create a 3D design of the second floor and ceiling. If you are using extruded lines, you may need to change your UCS. Use either 3D Objects or 3DFACE for joists, etc. Don't forget the ARRAY command.

2nd FLOOR CEILING-JOIST LAYOUT

ALL CEILING JOISTS 2" x 6" @ 16" O/C

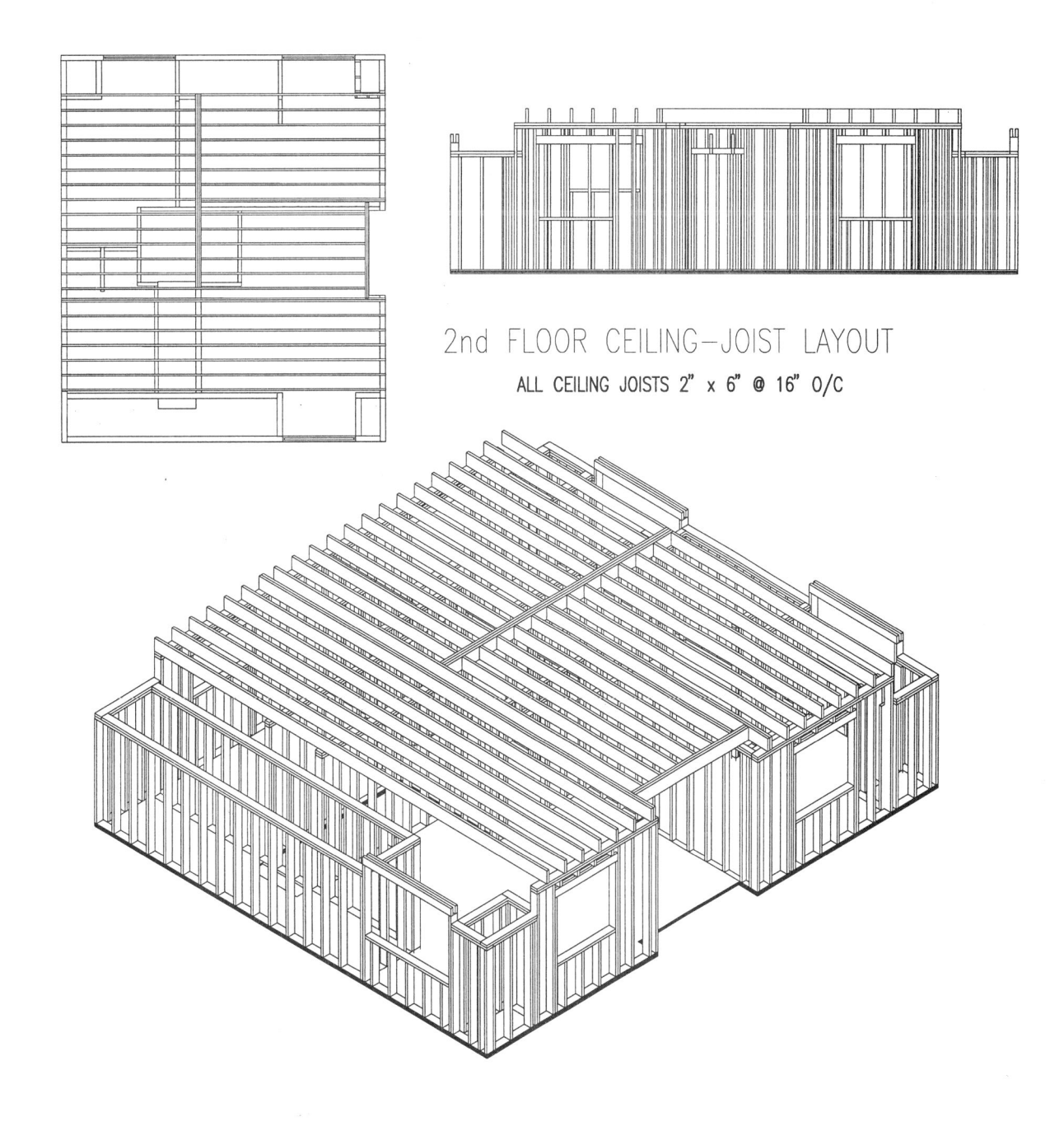

Challenger 23B

Use this section to help construct the floors and roof.

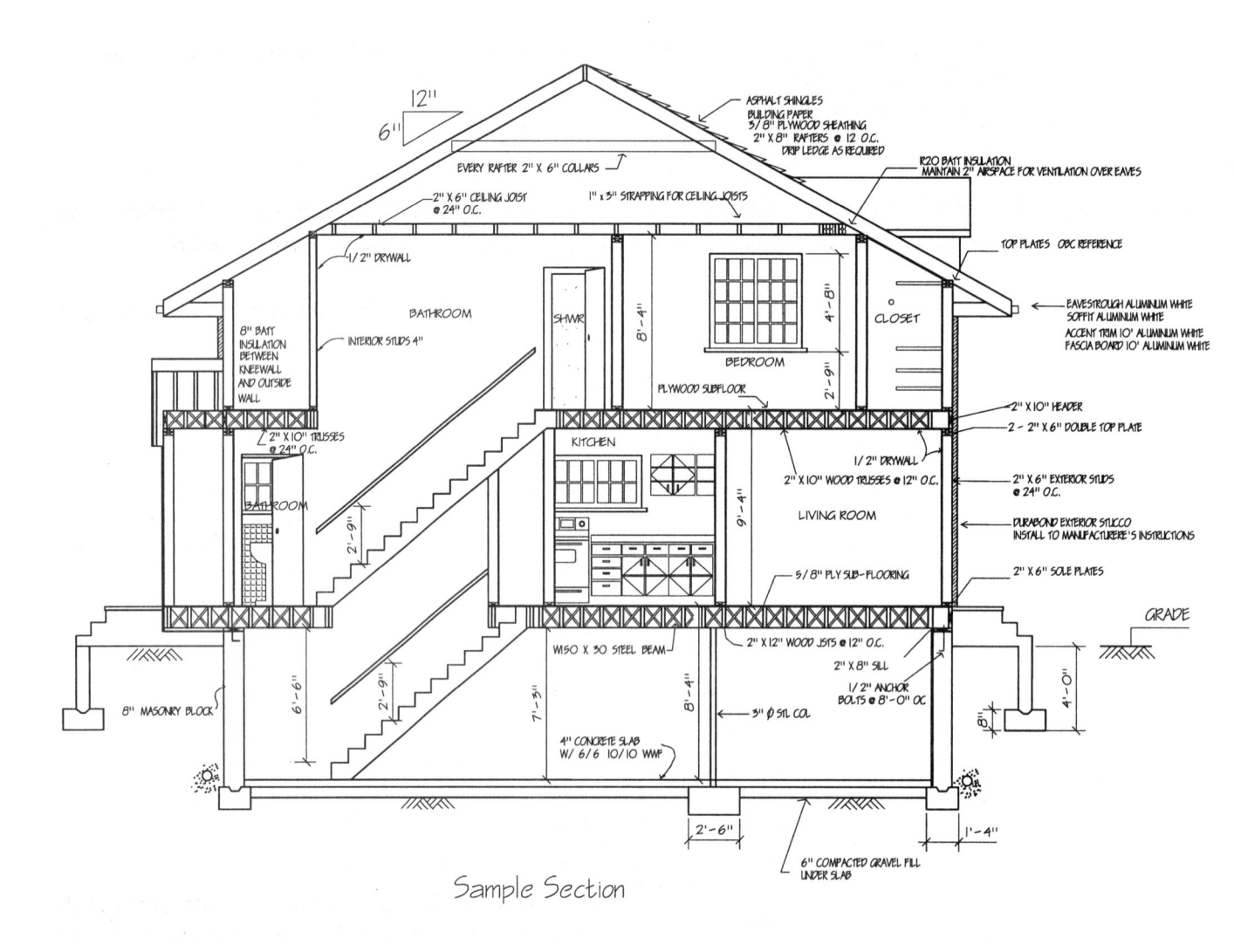

24

Dynamic View, Scripts and Slides

Upon completion of this chapter, you should be able to:

1. Use CAmera, TArget, and POints options of DVIEW to dynamically change the view of an object
2. Generate a perspective view of an object using the Distance option of DVIEW
3. Use MSLIDE, VSLIDE, and SCRIPT to create a slide show of the object

AutoCAD's Model Space

In model space, the object exists as a 3D entity. The views can be seen as different cameras focusing on the object or model itself. VPORTs are used to view the model.

In Figure 24-1 you can see the two viewing angles through which you rotate using the VPOINT command.

The **angle *in X-Y* plane** is essentially a rotation around Z.

The **angle *from X-Y* plane** is essentially a rotation above or below the X-Y plane.

If the **angle *in X-Y* plane** is 0, then you are rotating around Y with the **angle *from X-Y* plane**. You will be looking at the model origin from the 3 o'clock position of a 12-hour clock.

If the **angle *in X-Y* plane** is 90, then you are rotating around X with the **angle *from X-Y* plane.** You will be looking at the model origin from the 12 o'clock position.

Figure 24-1

You can rotate your viewpoint anywhere on the screen with the Rotate option of the VPOINT command. As in everything else in AutoCAD, all angles are counterclockwise. In rotations, this is counterclockwise from the viewpoint looking back towards the origin or 0,0,0.

Many people, particularly in mechanical areas, like to start drawing an item in a regular orthographic view.

Plan

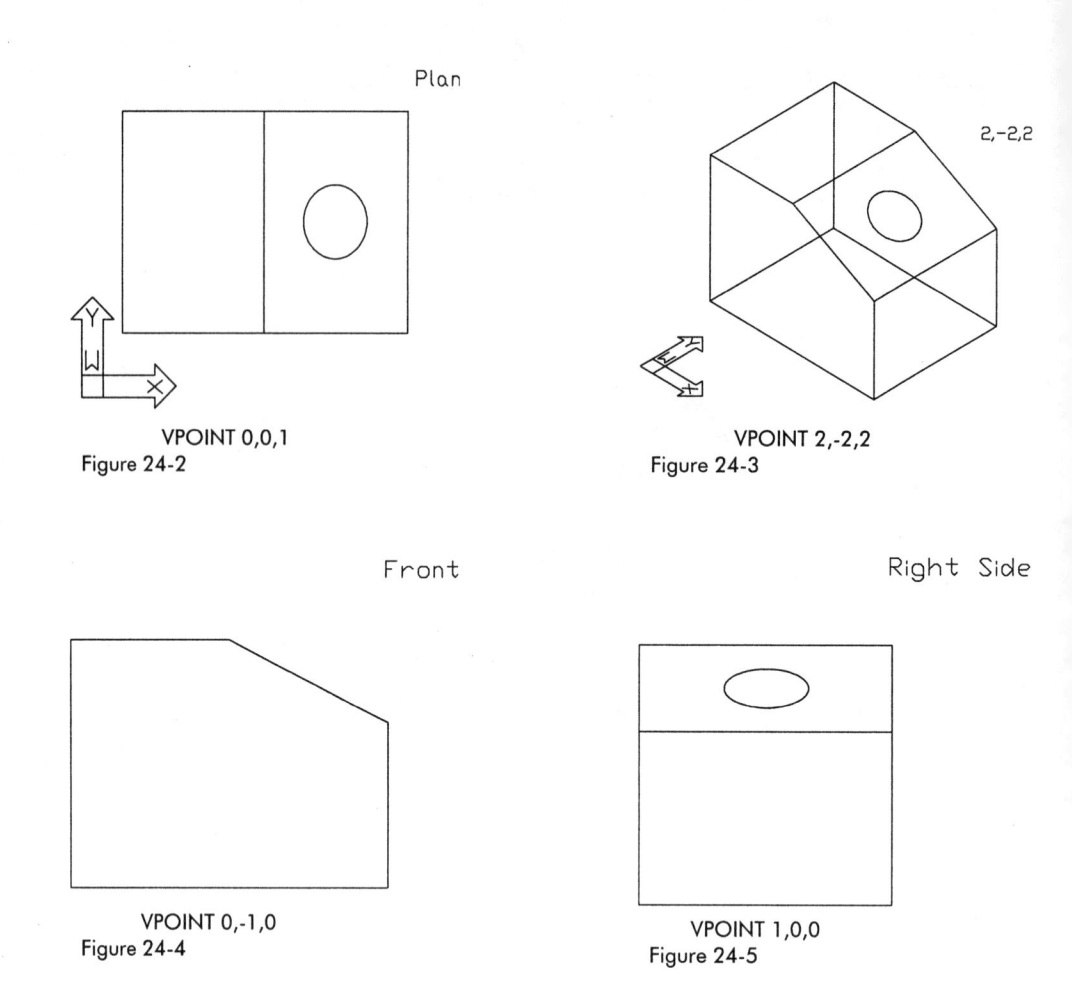

VPOINT 0,0,1
Figure 24-2

2,-2,2

VPOINT 2,-2,2
Figure 24-3

Front

VPOINT 0,-1,0
Figure 24-4

Right Side

VPOINT 1,0,0
Figure 24-5

This layout gives you access to all views and all planes for modification. This is the most practical viewport layout, particularly for mechanical applications, because it allows you to see all necessary views.

Dynamic Viewing

For many reasons, you may wish to rotate views while you are designing the part. This is one of the great advantages of the CAD environment. AutoCAD has developed the DVIEW options (Dynamic VIEW) for this purpose. This command is used most frequently when preparing presentations either on screen or on paper.

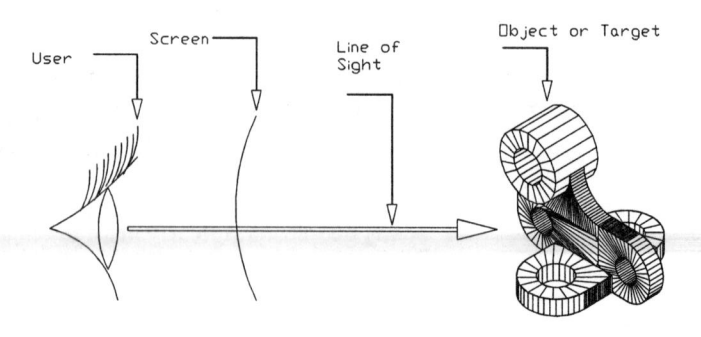

Figure 24-6

The line between the CAmera (user) and the TArget (object) forms the same line-of-sight as that between the user and the object.

You can move the CAmera, object or TArget separately or together to view 3D objects from any angle. Then you can change the distance between the two, ZOOM the object in, PAn it or TWist it. Once positioned, you can CLip and Hide it as well.

In essence, what is happening is that you are making a dynamic use of the rotation capabilities outlined on page 555.

The DVIEW Command

The DVIEW command performs in the same way as a user holding a camera which is focused on a particular point or target on the object. The DVIEW command is as follows:

> **Toolbar** There is no button and no menu choice for this command.

The command line equivalent is **DVIEW**.

```
Command:DVIEW
Select Objects: (pick all)
[CAmera/TArget/Distance/POints/PAn/Zoom/TWist/Clip/Hide/Off/
   Undo]<eXit>:
```

Where: CA = the "camera" angle relative to the part
        CL = the CLip of the object, or sets the front and back clipping planes
        D   = the Distance between the "camera" and the target or object
        H   = a removal of hidden lines within the dynamic view
        O   = perspective off
        PA = pan within the DVIEW command
        PO = points for the "camera" and object or target
        TA = a rotation of the object
        TW = twist; it twists the dynamic view relative to the line of sight
        U   = Undo
        X   = eXit from the DVIEW command
        Z   = Zoom within the DVIEW command; it sets the lens length

Notes

The *options* Pan and Zoom are used *within* the command, whereas the *commands* ZOOM and PAN *are used on their own*.

For most of these options, bringing up a model and playing with the options will help you understand them as quickly as reading the text.

Using DVIEW Options

The DVIEW command affects only the active or current ViewPORT. Once you have entered the command, AutoCAD will prompt you for the objects you would like displayed while rotating. The object select option allows you to minimize the objects to be dynamically viewed. If you have a small (less than 50,000K) file, there is no problem with dynamically viewing it. A large file, however, will take a very long time to drag. With this in mind, AutoCAD developed the default model which is an image of a small house with a chimney. This is the image you get if you do not select any objects to rotate, i.e., if you press enter at the prompt.

AutoCAD searches for a user-defined file or block called DVIEWBLOCK which can be an image appropriate for the application or firm. If this BLOCK is not defined, AutoCAD will bring up this house.

Having selected the objects to drag, AutoCAD now offers you a choice of options. As in most AutoCAD commands, you need only enter the capitalized letters of the option to bring it up. The image will then be manipulated according to your choice of option.

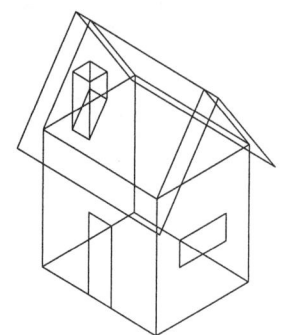

The DVIEW default image.
Figure 24-7

CAmera

Camera establishes the viewing direction, or how you are looking at the object. The image is where it is supposed to be, and you are slowly moving the camera around it until you get the precise position you want.

The CAmera option rotates the object in the same way that the Rotate option of VPOINT does: two angles determine the amount of rotation. The differences are that the CAmera rotates around the target point, not around 0,0,0 and the order of the angle prompts is reversed.

```
Toggle angle in/Enter angle from X-Y plane <90>:
```

Enter **T**, enter an angle, or press ⏎ *(you can drag the image here by moving the mouse).*

Toggle Angle In or From

Switches from viewing *in* the *X-Y* plane to viewing *from* the *X-Y* plane. Entering an angle on the command line locks the cursor movement so you see only the positions available for that angle. The toggle option unlocks the cursor movement for the angle, and you can use the cursor to rotate the camera.

Enter Angle From X-Y Plane

Sets the camera position at an angle above or below the *X-Y* plane. An angle of 90 degrees looks down from above; an angle of -90 degrees looks up from below. A camera angle of 0 degrees means that the camera is parallel to the *X-Y* plane of the current UCS.

Enter Angle In X-Y Plane From X Axis

Sets the camera position at an angle in the *X-Y* plane relative to the *X* axis of the current UCS. This angle is measured from 180 to -180. A rotation angle of 0 means you are looking down the *X* axis; a rotation angle of 90 means you are looking down the *Y* axis.

Once you have toggled or specified the angle from the *X-Y* plane, the prompt returns.

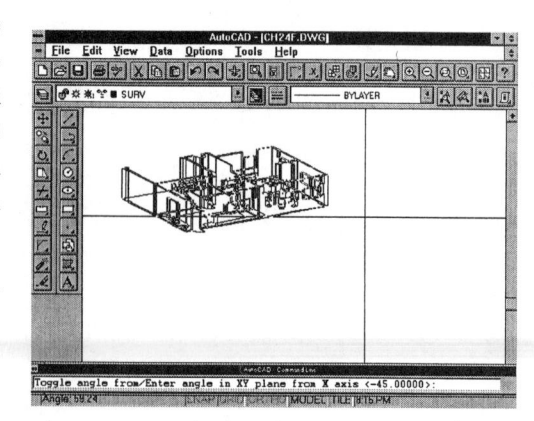

```
Toggle angle in/Enter angle
    from X-Y plane <90>:
```

The image moves along with the cursor; the more items you are dragging, the longer it takes. All of this is dependent on the size of your computer's RAM as well.

```
Command:DVIEW
[CAmera/TArget/Distance/POints/PAn/Zoom/TWist/Clip/Hide/Off/
  Undo]:CA
Specify camera location, or enter angle from XY plane, [Toggle
  angle in]<90>:T
```

With the CAmera option, you are moving the camera around the target or object. Thus you always see the object on the screen if you are not moving the cursor too quickly. The following diagram maps the movement from above.

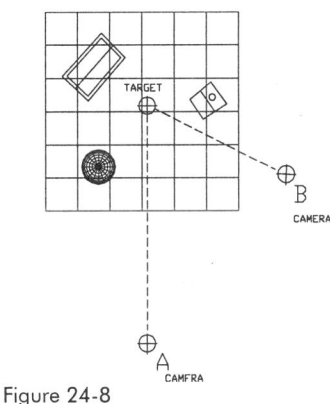

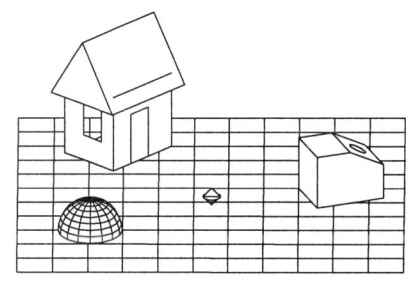

Figure 24-8

Camera at A
Figure 24-9

The CAmera is moving around the set, and the set remains the same.

To create this view, camera spot B is 60 degrees away from camera spot A. Camera spot A, from the target, is -90 degrees; thus camera spot B is -30.

An angle of 90 degrees would be looking at the back of the house. The other objects are a rock and a very trendy compost bin.

Note that the angle used in this and other DVIEW options is the angle of the UCS, not the angle in the WCS.

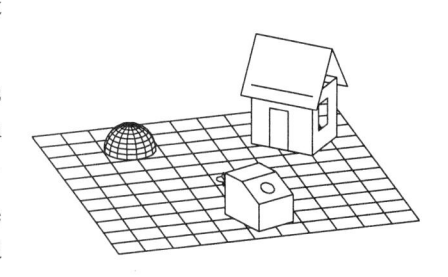

Camera at B
Figure 24-10

The CAmera option is also a very good way to check your 3D images for integrity of design. By picking the CAmera option and turning the part a bit, you can see if it will hold up or if it falls apart at the first rotation. If your parts crumble in CAmera, you are not using OSNAP and UCS properly. The most common error in 3D for beginning students is picking points line-of-sight onto the *X-Y* plane. With CAmera, the objects created this way are immediately apparent.

TArget

The TArget option is similar to CAmera in that it positions the object relative to the camera. TArget is extremely useful for doing walk-throughs of houses, and other activities where you are in the center of the part and want to turn the focus on different areas. Using TArget is like turning your head to view different parts of a scene.

Take the analogy of a movie set once more: instead of the camera moving around the set with the actors stationary (as in CAmera), the actor is moving around the set and the camera is following.

The camera stays in the same place, but the TArget moves. Other than that, the Target option is the same as the Camera option.

```
Command:DVIEW
[CAmera/TArget/Distance/POints/PAn/Zoom/TWist/Clip/Hide/Off/
   Undo]:TA
Specify camera location, or enter angle from XY plane,
   [Toggle angle in]<90> :T
```

Toggle Angle In, Enter Angle From X-Y Plane

See CAmera.

To illustrate the TArget command, we will take the same set. The camera is now at point 0,0 and the objects move accordingly.

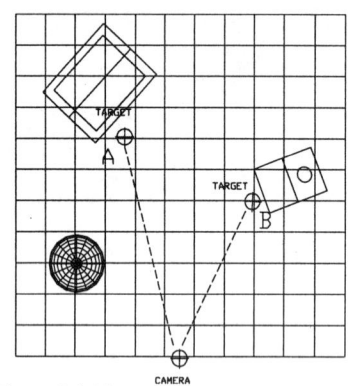

Figure 24-11

Target at A

Figure 24-12

At point B the target is rotated 65 degrees away from 0,0. At point A the target is rotated 105 degrees away from 0,0. Using any angle over 180 degrees will obviously not work as there is nothing behind the camera.

Your default position for target is always 0,0.

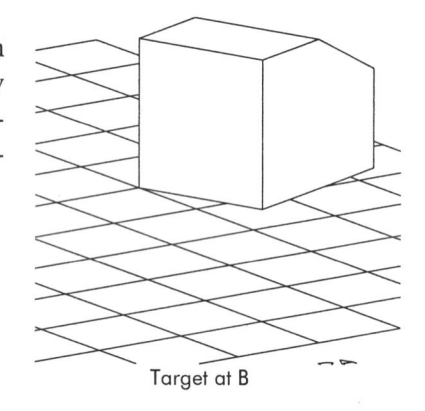

Target at B

Figure 24-13

POints

Another way to set up your screen is to set the line-of-sight with the POints option. This option combines CAmera movement with TArget movement. This option is particularly useful for doing walk-throughs of houses and other buildings to show the various rooms. It also allows you to set the CAmera and TArget for perspective options.

```
Command:DVIEW
[CAmera/TArget/Distance/POints/PAn/Zoom/TWist/Clip/Hide/Off/
   Undo]:PO
Specify target point <7.9248,5.838,0>:4,4,4
Specify camera point <7.9248,5.838,0>:30,30,30
```

Once you have picked the spot for your target, you have a "rubber band" effect with a line from the target to the camera until you have chosen the camera's position.

In Figure 24-14 we have the same layout as in the previous illustrations. From the front the objects look like this. The house is higher than the rock and compost bin.

In Figure 24-15 the target point is the bottom corner of the compost bin and the camera is the top peak of the house's roof. The two points are lined up exactly.

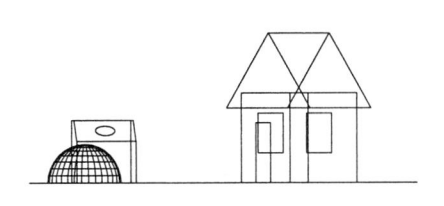

Figure 24-14

In Figure 24-16 the target is the bottom ledge of the window within the house; the camera is the middle point on the right side of the door. This shows that it often is useful to place a point or line at the exact position you want your camera to be. Otherwise you will be looking through the objects as we are looking through the side of the door.

The POints option gives you the possibility of seeing exactly the view you want from the perspective you choose.

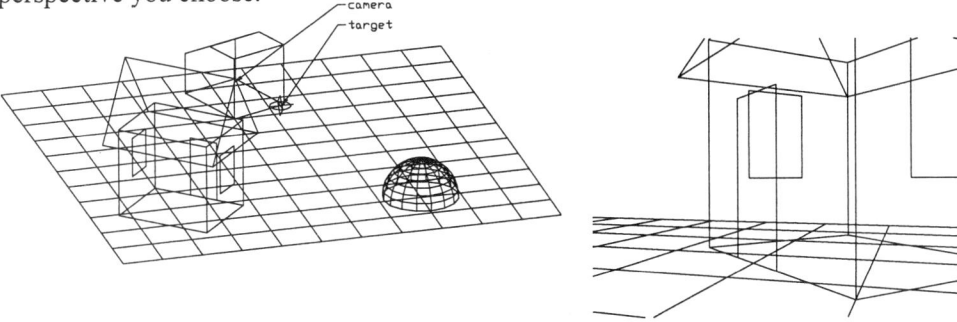

Figure 24-15

Figure 24-16

Distance

Many applications call for a perspective view of a house or object. The perspective command in DVIEW is invoked with the Distance option.

The key to getting Distance to work is to set the TArget and CAmera first. Make sure that you have the TArget on the outside of the house to get an exterior perspective view.

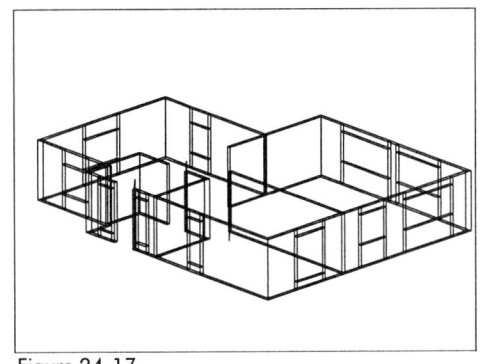

Figure 24-17

The camera is moved along a constant line-of-sight toward or away from the target. The scale this time is from 0X on the left to 16X on the far right, as portrayed by a slider bar on the top of the view. 1X is the current distance.

Figure 24-17 is a view of the object before the Distance option has been employed.

Figure 24-18 has the Distance set at 4X; Figure 24-19 has the distance set at 12X. (Note that the X in this case has nothing to do with the coordinate *X*.)

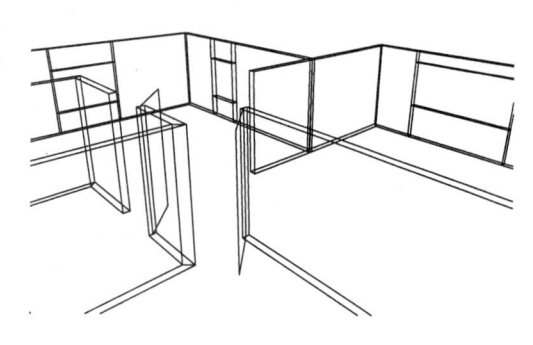

Figure 24-18

The sliding bar in this option will invoke a continuous updating of your screen until you get the view you want. Again, take note of the exact distance for standardized views.

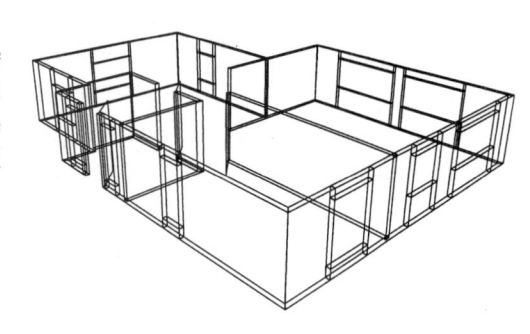

Figure 24-19

Turning Perspective Off

Once you have perspective on, you will notice that many commands are disabled. Also, the icon in the corner of your screen will change to the one in Figure 24-20.

To get back to a view where you can work with the geometry and display commands you need, turn DVIEW OFF.

```
Command:DVIEW
[CAmera/TArget/Distance/POints/PAn/Zoom/
   TWist/CLip/Hide/Off/Undo]:OFF
```

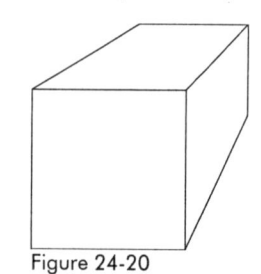

Figure 24-20

CLip

One of the most useful drawing options is CLip. With CLip you can identify a section of the part and extract it for viewing. With many models this is useful for viewing areas obscured by foreground objects. In addition, this offers a relatively easy way to get section views. LAYERs can be used effectively for viewing, but in many cases, the LAYERs are created for ease of viewing and manipulating the whole part, not just one plane. The more complex the wireframe model gets, the more readily you will turn to this command.

The CLipping planes are perpendicular to the line-of-sight, between the camera and the target. In essence, a CLipping plane is like a huge knife or cheese cutter slicing through the part. You can place both a foreground and a background plane at a specific distance from the target. By specifying a positive value, you cut from between the target and the viewer; a negative number cuts behind the target.

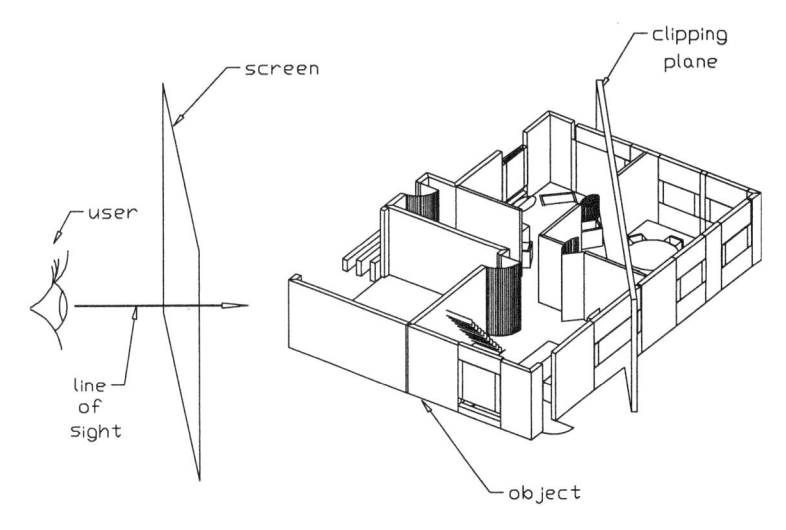

Figure 24-21

In the above illustration, the user is looking line-of-sight at the 3D floor plan. The cutting plane is perpendicular to the user. A Front CLip would take out all objects in front of the CLipping plane leaving only the dining room. A Back CLip would take out everything behind the cutting plane.

```
Command:DVIEW
[CAmera/TArget/Distance/POints/PAn/Zoom/TWist/CLip/Hide/Off/
    Undo]:CL
Enter clipping option [Back/Front/OFF]<Off>:B
Specify distance from target or [ON/OFF]<2.00>:
```

This is a view of a house created with thickened lines. It is a simple 3D layout of a house. The UCS is set to World, but the VPOINT is set to 2,-2,2.

You can see how you get an isometric view of this house.

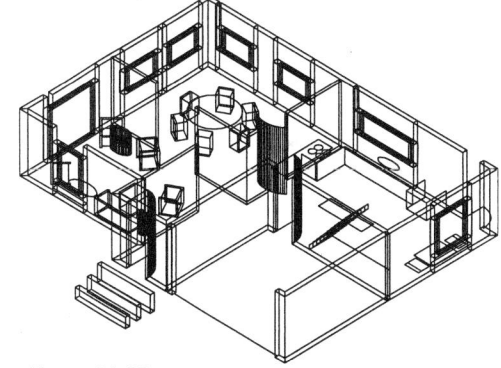

Figure 24-22

In this view the room has been CLipped from the back. The CLipping has been done perpendicular to the line of sight, 19' from the target.

As you can see, the CLipping has taken out part of the back wall. The CLip has gone straight through the house.

This second CLip has taken off almost all of the back portions of the house.

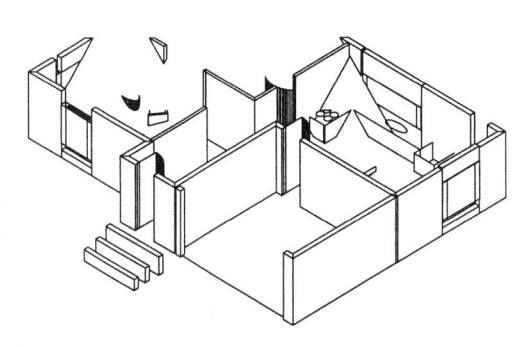

Figure 24-23

Dynamic View, Scripts and Slides

HIDE (Hideplot in MVIEW) has been used in both of these CLips to show the wall cuts. In this view the garage has a section of the back wall taken out.

This type of view could be used on a house for structural presentations. Once the CLip has taken place, the UCS can be changed to View, and notations can be added.

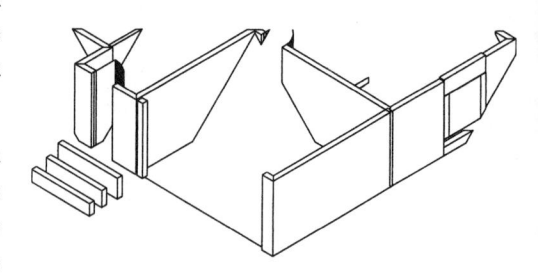

Figure 24-24

CLipping can also be useful for the front sections of houses, particularly for showing sizes of rooms, etc. The Front CLipping plane obscures all objects between the selected plane and the camera. Again, negative and positive numbers can be used as well.

This view has the first 15 feet of the house cut off to show us the inside of the dining room.

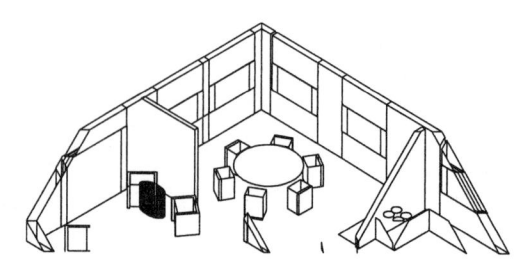

Figure 24-25

Again the slider bar, cut into quarters, drags the front CLipping plane and updates the screen as you move the cursor. The distance from the CLipping plane is shown on the status line above. Positive values indicate a plane between the target and the camera; negative values indicate a plane behind or on the Back of the target, thus defeating the purpose of using Front.

CLipping and Distance

If perspective (Distance) is off, you can change the front CLipping plane at any time. If perspective is on, however, the front CLipping plane remains on until perspective is turned off. If you turn the CLipping plane off while perspective is on, the CLipping plane will move to the camera position, i.e., nothing is clipped.

CLipping to Create Sections

CLipping can be done for presentation or display purposes as seen above, or it can be used to create sections of 3D objects. The most obvious reason for doing this is to make a view for drawing purposes. Another reason is to remove duplicate lines on a view to minimize objects on screen and objects that need to be plotted.

For a complete example of how to CLip a plane accurately, see the Prelab for Chapter 26, page 617.

Figure 24-26

TWist

While we are exploring line-of-sight, another option for viewing is TWist. This rotates the image line-of-sight from the viewer.

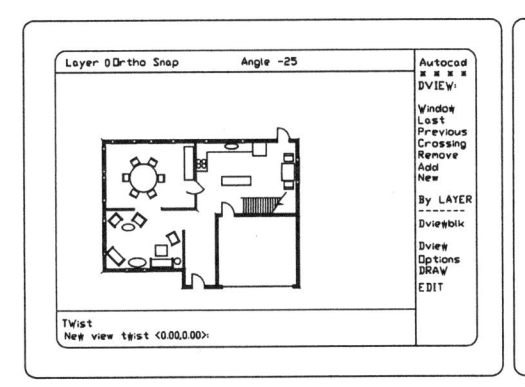

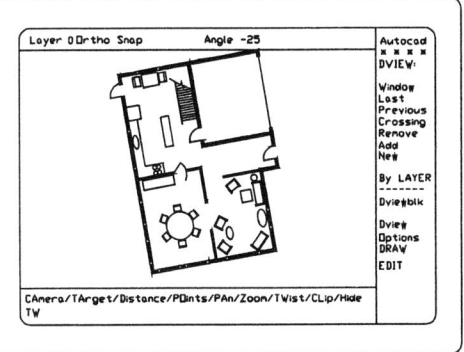

Figure 24-27

```
Command:DVIEW
[CAmera/TArget/Distance/POints/PAn/Zoom/TWist/CLip/Hide/Off/
 Undo]:TW
Specify view twist angle <0.00>:135
```

This looks the same as the editing command ROTATE. The difference is that the geometry has the same coordinates after a TWist, but totally different coordinates after a ROTATE. This is really useful within paper space viewports for orientation.

Zoom and PAn

These commands are the same within the DVIEW command as they have been throughout your AutoCAD experience. The reason they are contained within the DVIEW command is that *they cannot be invoked from without the command if the perspective has been changed*. There are also slight differences in the commands.

Zoom

Zoom will change the magnification of the view of the object, but you are prompted for the lens length or focal distance instead of the scale factor.

```
Command:DVIEW
[CAmera/TArget/Distance/POints/PAn/Zoom/TWist/CLip/Hide/Off/
 Undo]:Z
Specify zoom scale factor <1>:25
```

If you have used the Distance option, you will not be able to use the command ZOOM; you must Zoom with this command. To get a good perspective view you may need to use Distance and Zoom many times before you have the view that you want.

PAn

With PAn, you are asked for a displacement as in the Display command. Again, this takes some practice before you are adept at using Distance without the PAn option.

```
Command:DVIEW
[CAmera/TArget/Distance/POints/PAn/Zoom/TWist/CLip/Hide/Off/
   Undo]:PA
Displacement base point:pick 1
Second point:pick 2
```

Hide, Undo and eXit

These options are also very similar to the commands with the same name.

Hide will give you a view of the objects with all the hidden lines removed. This is included within the command simply for convenience. Note, however, that only the objects selected for viewing within the DVIEW command will have hidden lines removed, and that the full wire frame will return once the DVIEW command has been exited. Use Hide to remove all hidden lines after DVIEW has been done.

Undo will Undo the previous option allowing the user to retain all the options changed within the command already. This is advantageous if there is only one portion of the options that you do not want, and several operations that you do want.

eXit ends the DVIEW command and gets you back to AutoCAD. Keep in mind that if you used Distance to change your perspective, the perspective icon will still be in the bottom left of your viewport, and you will not be able to use certain commands.

You are meant to generate all the parameters of your image within the DVIEW command and have it ready to print when the command is finished. Similar to the CHANGE command, while working in DVIEW you can use one or all options before exiting from the command.

Slides and Scripts

Up until now you have been using vector files to create and manipulate your images. In certain situations you want to record a walk-through of a house on screen or a very simple slide show of a part. To do this, you can create a series of slides using MSLIDE, and then create a SCRIPT file on your disk.

Slides are also useful to import presentation views into other software programs such as CorelDRAW™ or PowerPoint™.

The MSLIDE Command

Essentially a slide extracts only the file's pixel address or bit map file and not other file parts such as the vector file, layers, surfaces, blocks.

3D slides are created the same way as 2D slides. In both cases, the slide takes the information in the current view.

> **Toolbar** There is neither a button nor a Pull Down Menu choice for this command. Type MSLIDE in at the command prompt.

The command line equivalent is **MSLIDE**.

Command:**MSLIDE**

This creates an external file with the extension .SLD. To place it on a separate directory, change the directory at the top.

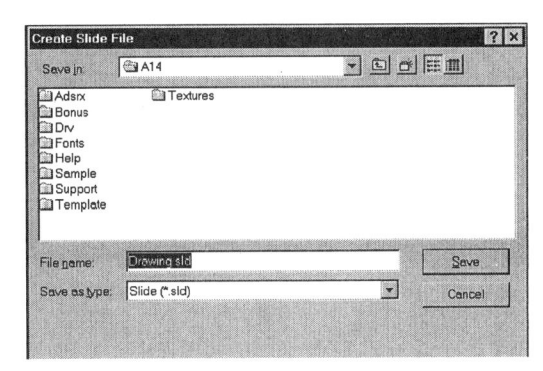

Command:**MSLIDE**

Enter the new directory and name. **D:\slides\front\johnston.sld**

Where: **<Johnston>** = the name of the file you are in
D: = the directory
\slides = the slides subdirectory
front = the name of the slide

The slide that you will be making takes up the entire screen. It is not defined by a Window, so be sure you have the view of the object that you want on screen. Also, use a full or single viewport rather than a portion of a viewport because the resolution of the final image will not be as good if you create a slide in a smaller viewport.

Slides can be viewed while you are in any drawing using the command VSLIDE.

> **Toolbar** There is no button or Pull Down Menu choice for this command.

The VSLIDE Command

To view slides, simply use VSLIDE and the name, as in the following:

Command:**VSLIDE**

The AutoCAD slide **chroma** will be retrieved and placed over your current drawing. You have not lost your drawing, a simple REDRAW will bring it back.

Just as in the INSERT command, you will need to specify the directory or drive if it is not the one that you are currently using.

The SCRIPT Command

Executes a sequence of commands from a script.

A script is a simple text file that contains AutoCAD commands. The script can be run either from inside the Drawing Editor or outside the Drawing Editor from the operating system prompt. Script files are used to automate or preprogram a process such as viewing slides, running plots, or configuring a menu. First the script file is written, then, when invoked, each line of the file is read and executed as if it had been typed in at the command

> **Pull Down Menu** From the Tools menu, choose Run Script.

prompt. The script file essentially records the keystrokes needed to perform a certain function.

The command line equivalent is **SCRIPT**.

```
Command:SCRIPT
Script name:SLIDES
```

Write the script file as shown in Chapter 17.

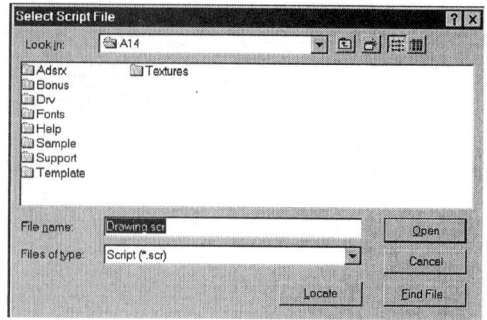

Here is an example of Script file used to show five rooms in a house.

In ASCII type

`VSLIDE A:Front`	Views slide Front
`DELAY 1000`	Delays for 1 second
`VSLIDE A:Hall`	Views slide Hall
`VSLIDE *A:Kitchen`	Preloads Kitchen
`DELAY 1000`	Delays view of Hall
`VSLIDE`	Views immediately Kitchen
`VSLIDE *A:Living`	Preloads Living
`DELAY 1000`	Delays view of Kitchen
`VSLIDE`	Views slide Living
`VSLIDE *A:Bath`	Preloads Bath
`DELAY 1000`	Delays view of Living
`VSLIDE`	Views slide Bath
`DELAY 1000`	Delays view of Bath
`RSCRIPT`	Repeats the script

ESCape will stop the script file. A backspace will temporarily halt it. Use RESUME to continue if the script file has been halted.

AFEGA or AutoFLIX

With every new release of AutoCAD, and indeed many other packages, for every advantage that you gain there are also disadvantages. In previous releases a simple method for showing slides or images was AutoFLIX. This shareware is not included in the AutoCAD base package and runs only in DOS. You may be able to get it from Autodesk, Inc., 2320 Marinship Way, Sausolito, CA 94965. If you can find it, and if you know how to run DOS, and if Windows hasn't totally taken over your oprating system, this is a very useful package.

Prelab 24 Creating a 3D Slide Show

In this prelab we will take a 3D surfaced model, use all of the options in DVIEW to rotate it, create slides of the views, generate a script file, then run the script file. This prelab illustrates the architectural example from Chapter 22, but any other surfaced file will suffice. There are many more sophisticated programs to make automated slide shows from AutoCAD files, but this does the job and needs no external software.

Step 1   Retrieve the file. (For Mechanical people, retrieve the part you surfaced in the past weeks. For Architectural people, retrieve the small "bunky" you created in Chapter 22.) Return to a single viewport, then invoke the DVIEW command and choose the option CAmera. Rotate the view until you are pleased with the angle. HIDE the view, then make a slide on the A drive.

```
Command:DVIEW
[CAmera/TArget/Distance/POints/PAn/
   Zoom/TWist/CLip/Hide/Off/Undo]:CA
 Specify camera location, or enter
   angle from XY plane, or [Toggle
   angle in]<90>: (move the mouse
   until you are happy with the
   view, pick the view)
[CAmera/TArget/Distance/POints/PAn/
   Zoom/TWist/CLip/Hide/Off/Undo]:⏎
Command:HIDE
Command:MSLIDE
(Make Slide file a:1)
```

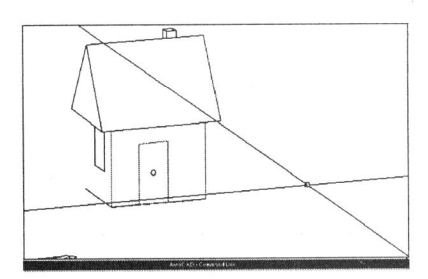

Step 2   Invoke the DVIEW command again and choose the option TA. Hide the image, then make a slide called A:2.

```
Command:DVIEW
[CAmera/TArget/Distance/POints/PAn/
   Zoom/TWist/CLip/Hide/Off/Undo]:TA
 Specify camera location, or enter
   angle from XY plane, or [Toggle
   angle in]<90>:(use the mouse)
```

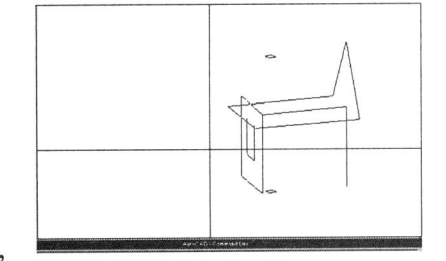

Rotate the view until you are pleased with the angle, then make a slide on the A:drive.

```
Command:MSLIDE
(Make slide file a:2)
```

Dynamic View, Scripts and Slides   569

Step 3 Use the DVIEW option Points to set up the file for a perspective view.

```
Command: DVIEW
[CAmera/TArget/Distance/POints/PAn/
 Zoom/TWist/CLip/Hide/Off/Undo]: PO
Enter target point <25,30,0>: (pick
    the end of the top roof corner)
Enter camera point <0,0,5>:@3',-3',3'
```

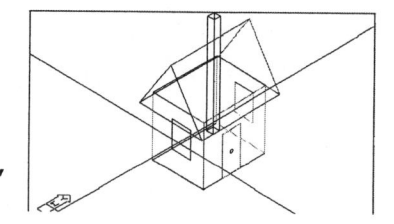

Notes

Make sure that ObjectSNAP is off.

This will give you a view that looks much like the usual isometric view. The difference is that the target and the camera are set.

Step 4 Now use the Distance option to create a perspective. Move the cursor back and forth until you are happy with the view, then exit from the DVIEW command, shade the object and make a slide.

```
Command: DVIEW
[CAmera/TArget/Distance/POints/PAn/
 Zoom/TWist/CLip/Hide/Off/Undo]: D
New Camera/TArget/Distance <2x>: 4x
New Camera/TArget/Distance <5.207>:4
CAmera/TArget/Distance/POints/PAn/
  Zoom/Twist/CLip/Hide/Off/Undo]:⏎
(Use Zoom as needed)
Command: SHADE
Command: MSLIDE
(Make slide file a:3)
```

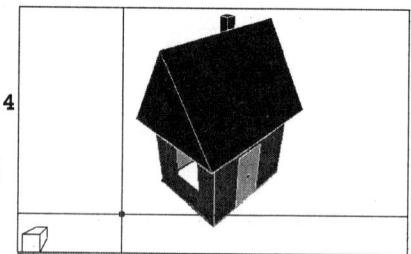

Step 5 Turn off the perspective view. Using the camera and target set now, use clip to take a good look at the interior of the house. If you have not put on a floor, use SOLID to quickly place a floor.

```
Command: REGEN
Command: DVIEW
[CAmera/TArget/Distance/POints/PAn/
 Zoom/TWist/CLip/Hide/Off/Undo]: OFF
CAmera/TArget/Distance/POints/PAn/
  Zoom/TWist/CLip/Hide/Off/Undo]: CL
Enter CLipping option
[Back/Front/OFF]: F
ON/OFF/<Distance from target> <2.00>:
  (move the cursor until you are
   happy with the view)
Command: SHADE
Command: MSLIDE
(Make slide file a:4)
```

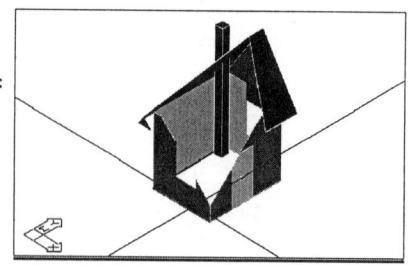

Step 6 Now set up a plan view and have this as the final slide. Use DVIEW with CAmera to set up a plan view.

570 CHAPTER TWENTY-FOUR

```
Command: PLAN
<Current UCS>/Ucs/World: W
Command: SHADE

Command: MSLIDE
(Make slide file a:5)
```

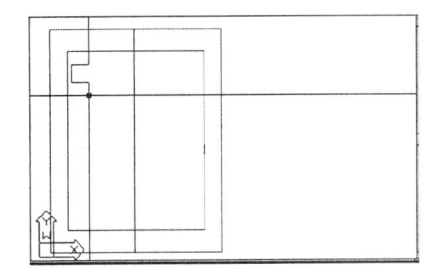

Step 7   Now create a script file. Be sure to name it A:SLIDES.SCR. Type the following, watch for spaces and blank lines—each counts as an extra.

> **Toolbar** From the Accessories program group, choose Notepad. Once finished, under the File menu, choose SAVE, then Minimize. You can also use SHELL, then EDIT.

```
Command: SHELL
OS Command: EDIT a:slides.scr

VSLIDE A:1
DELAY 1000
VSLIDE A:2
DELAY 1000
VSLIDE A:3
DELAY 1000
VSLIDE A:4
DELAY 1000
VSLIDE a:5
DELAY 1000
RSCRIPT
```

Step 8   Use the SCRIPT command to view the slides.

```
Command: SCRIPT
Script file name: A:SLIDES.SCR
```

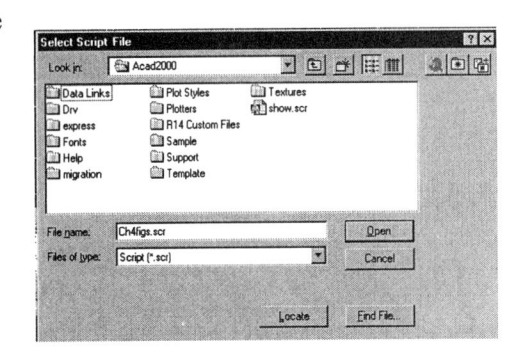

Command and Function Summary

DVIEW defines parallel projection or perspective views.

Practice Exercise 24

Take either of the 3D objects from Chapter 22, and use DVIEW to create a script file with a slide show. Use CAmera, TArget, Distance and CLip.

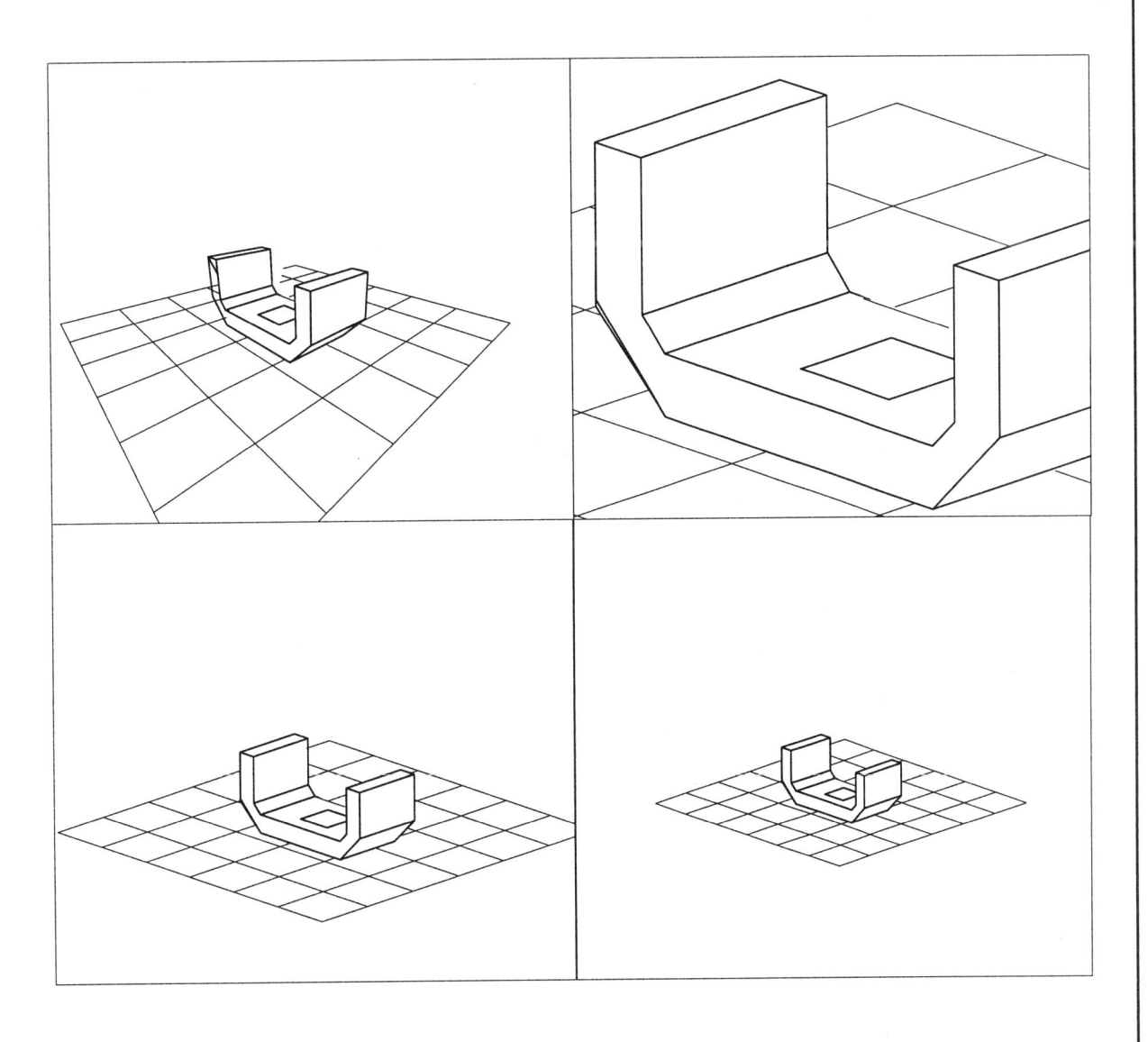

Exercise A24

Step 1 Create a small house using THICKNESS lines, 3DFACES and Surfaces.

Step 2 Using the DVIEW command, create a walk-through of your house looking at each room independent of the others. Remember—there are big bucks in selling real estate. The following are expected views. At least six views will be needed.

   a. Change the TArget and CAmera distance, using POints if it is easier.
   b. Use Distance to create a perspective of each room, and of the house with a roof on.
   c. Use CLipping to get rid of all the rooms that you do not need to see if they are obstructing your view.
   d. Use Zoom and PAn within the DVIEW command to get a perfect view of the object.

Step 3 Create SLIDEs of each room using MSLIDE, and generate a short slide show.

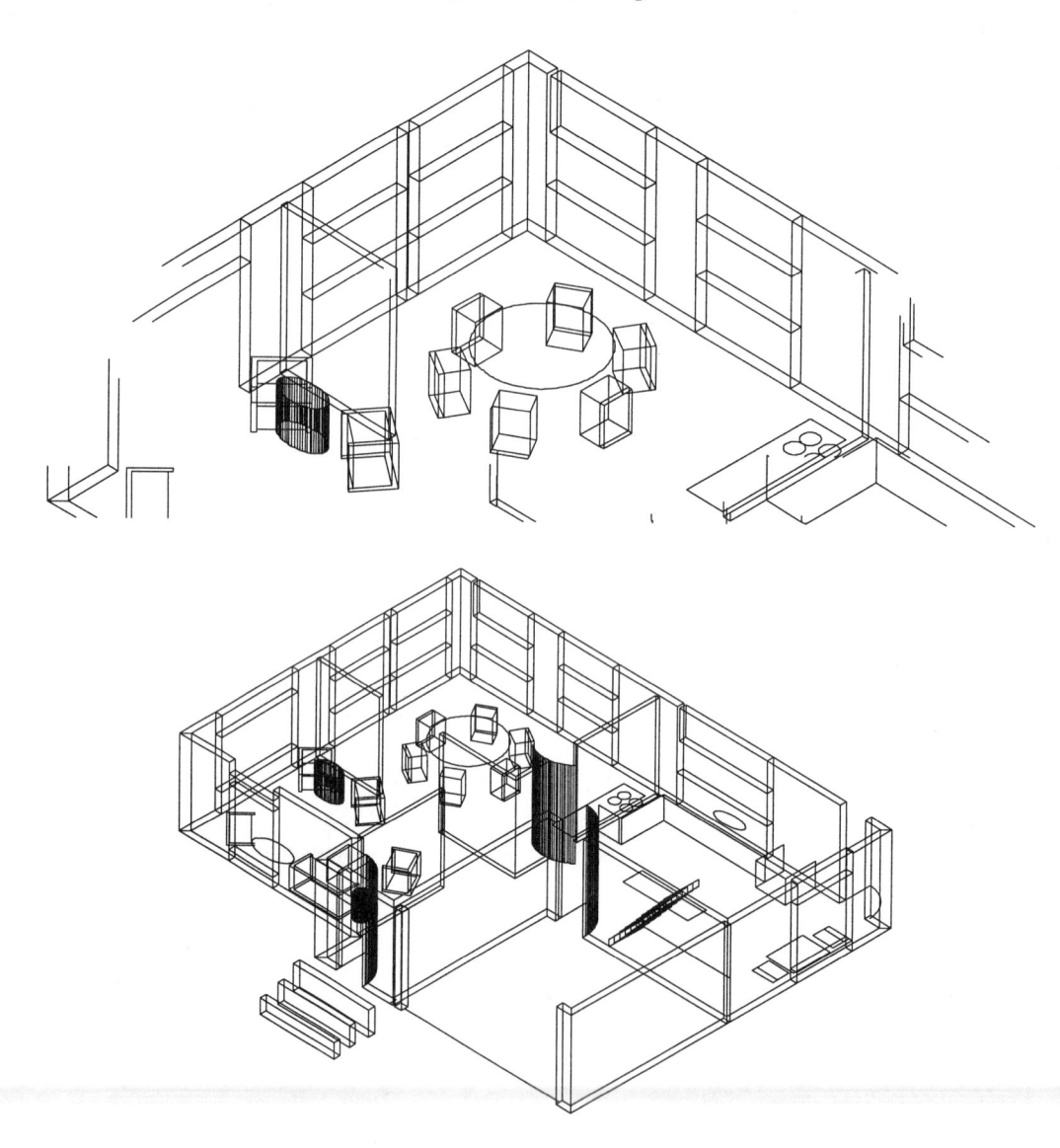

Be careful not to erase objects—they will be needed in other views. Just change your POints and CLip all areas not needed. It is okay to have a few portions of another room present as long as there is no mistaking which room you are actually looking at.

Exercise C24

Using the footings from C22, create a script file of the top, front, side, and pictorial view of each. Make a perspective view, and use CLip to create a section view of each. You should have ten slides minimum. Note that the script and slide files can be taken from two separate drawing files, but will create only one script file.

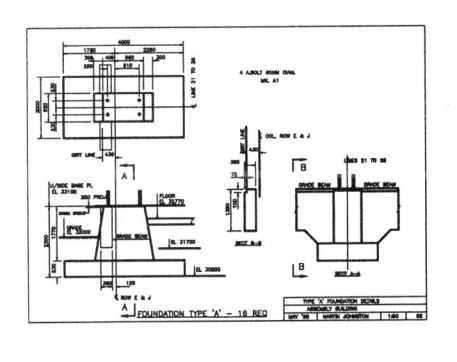

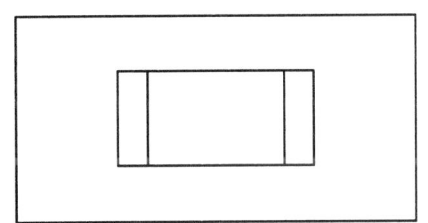

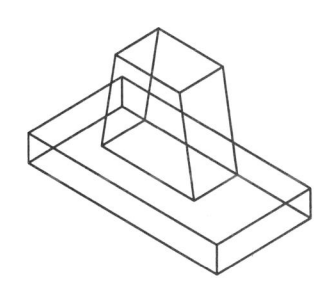

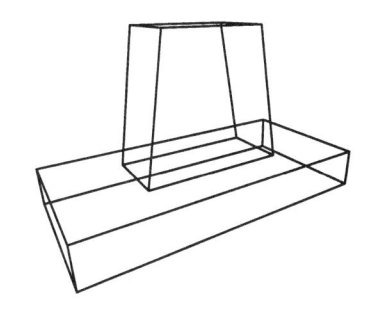

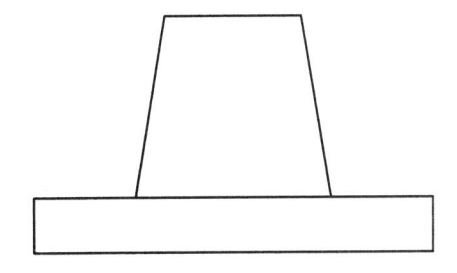

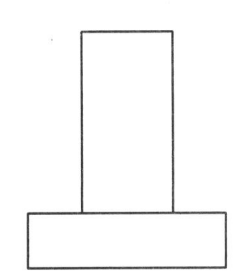

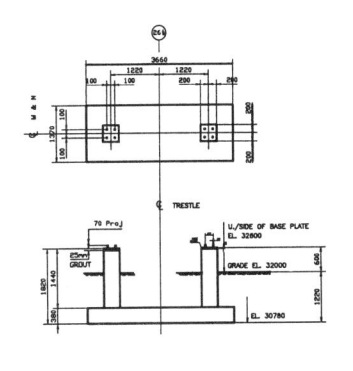

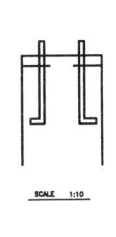

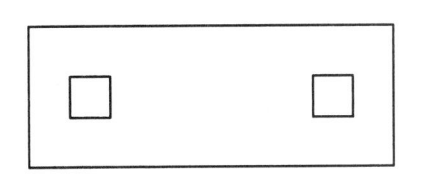

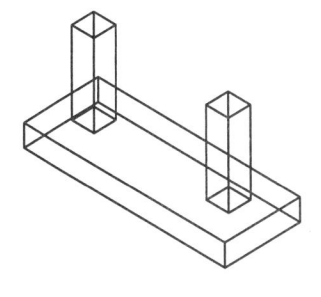

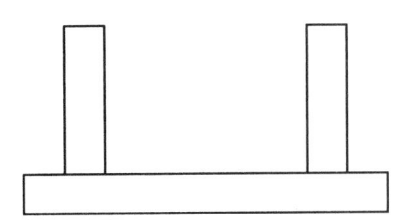

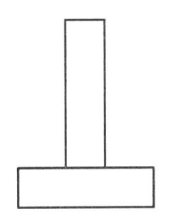

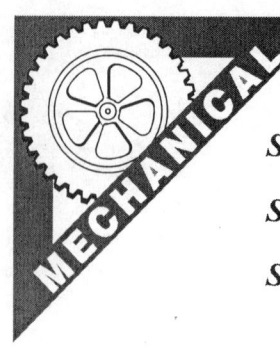

Exercise M24

Step 1　Create a grid the size of Exercise M22 or M23.

Step 2　INSERT your Exercise onto the grid.

Step 3　You are trying to convince the client who has commissioned you to do this part that it is perfect in every detail. You will thus create views of the part from all four sides plus the bottom and top, making use of perspective and Hide to make it look really impressive.

    a.　Change the TArget and CAmera distance, using POints if it is easier.
    b.　Use Distance to create a perspective of each view.
    c.　Use CLipping to create at least one section of the object (See Prelab, Chapter 26).
    d.　Use Zoom and PAn within the DVIEW command to get perfect views of the object.

Step 4　Create slides of each view using MSLIDE, and generate a short slide show.

To aid you in placing the camera or targets, you can create a junk LAYER and add lines from the corners, etc. Once placed, these can be turned off.

Using CLip, try to make a section through the center of the part.

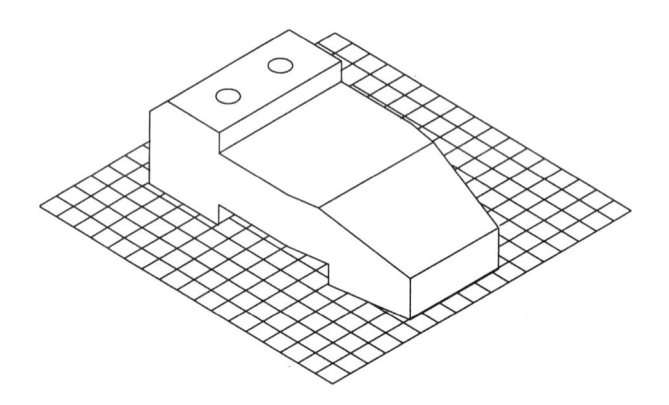

Challenger 24

Construct the walls and roof of the house using 3DFACE as shown.

Block each elevation.

Insert them onto a drawing in the isometric view; change the UCS as needed.

Create new layers for front, back, left, and right.

Add 3DFACEs.

You may need to add lines to aid the entry of the 3DFACE.

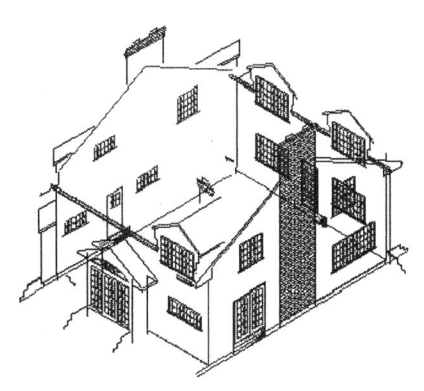

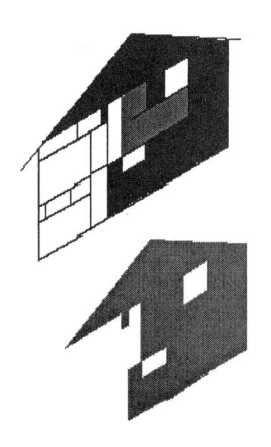

Challenger 24B

Create this New Year's clacker and create a slide file of it.

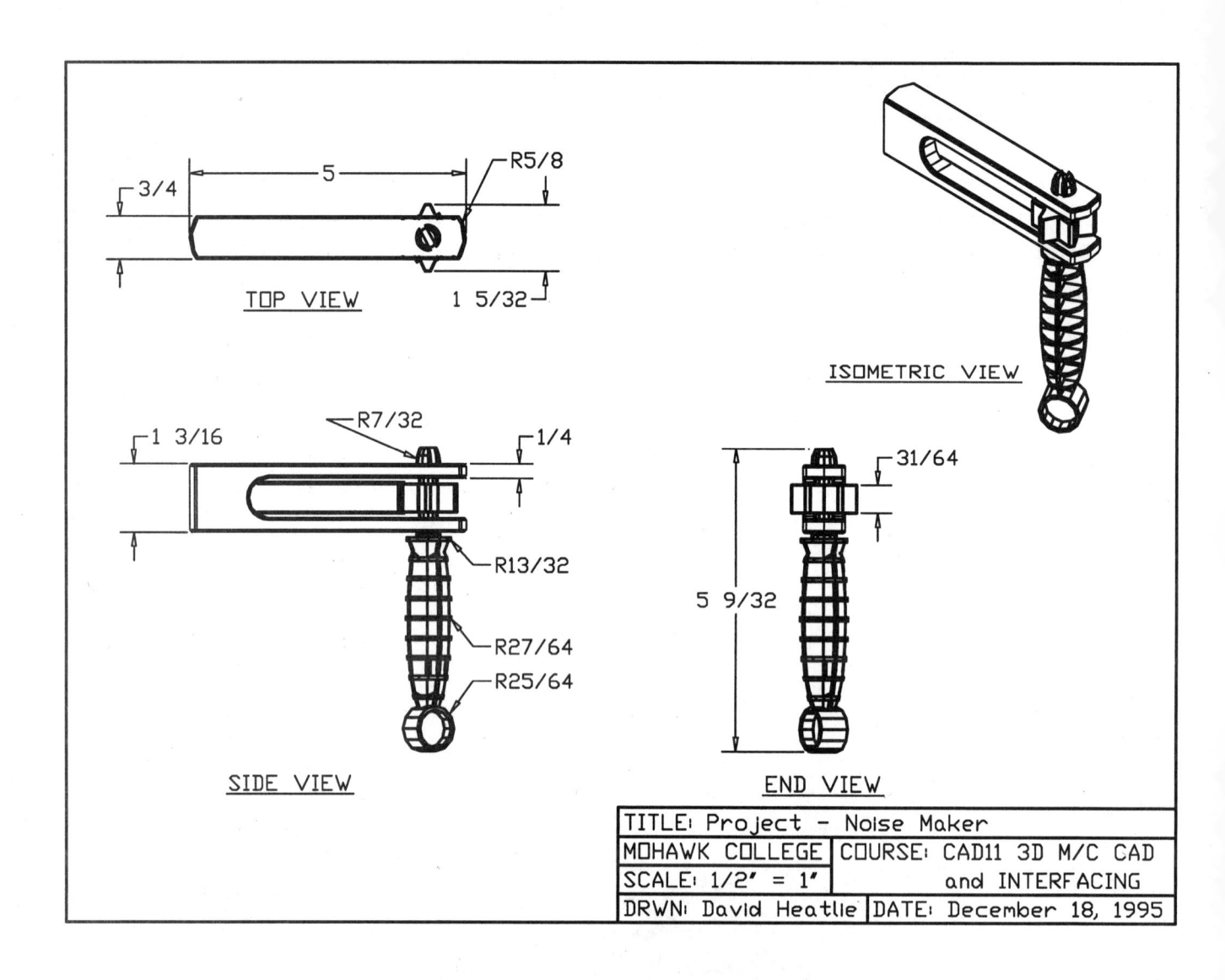

TOP VIEW
- 3/4
- 5
- R5/8
- 1 5/32

SIDE VIEW
- 1 3/16
- R7/32
- 1/4
- R13/32
- R27/64
- R25/64

END VIEW
- 31/64
- 5 9/32

ISOMETRIC VIEW

TITLE: Project – Noise Maker	
MOHAWK COLLEGE	COURSE: CAD11 3D M/C CAD
SCALE: 1/2" = 1"	and INTERFACING
DRWN: David Heatlie	DATE: December 18, 1995

25 Surfacing

Upon completion of this chapter, you should be able to:

1. Create a simple ruled surface (RULESURF), and define the difference between this and a 3DFACE
2. Create a surface of revolution (REVSURF)
3. Create a tabulated surface (TABSURF)
4. Create an edge-defined surface patch (EDGESURF)
5. Create 3D poly or 3D polylines

Surfaces in a CAD Environment

So far you have been working in 3D with linear elements (with the exception of 3DFACE). This means that the information you have entered has a defined start and end, but is *not* surfaced. If you were to hold your model in your hand, you could touch the edges, but your fingers would slip right through the wireframe.

With surfacing, you are "covering" the wireframe with a surface that lets you determine both where the planes actually are and, more importantly, where the inside is relative to the outside.

AutoCAD's hidden line, shading and rendering operations perform differently depending upon the type of surface used. For example, you could use several different methods to create a simple cube shape. You could draw a series of four lines and add thickness; you could draw a pline that has equal length and width and add equal thickness; you could use the BOX command, which essentially adds a series of 3Dfaces; or you could create the cube using 3DFACE. But if you draw a cube only using lines, you will not be able to perform SHADE or HIDE operations because it is only a simple wireframe image in 3D.

Surface Display

The mesh density or number of facets of a surface are defined by a matrix of *m* and *n* vertices. The variable, SURFTAB1 determines the mesh density in the *m* direction; SURFTAB2 determines the mesh density in the *n* direction. This is *not* related to the *X-Y* values.

In Figure 25-1, you can see how the *m* and *n* directions are determined by the direction of the object, *not* the direction of the *X-Y* plane.

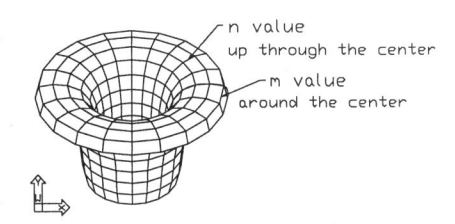

Figure 25-1

While your surface is fully described, you may find it difficult to see because the display lines may be too far apart. Likewise, the part may take on the appearance of a solid because the lines are too close together. Lines are actually edges, so if you explode the surface, you will get a series of 3DFACES.

The SURFTAB1 setting controls the density of the mesh. In Figure 25-2 the object on the left has a mesh setting of 6; the one on the right has a mesh setting of 16. The value repre-

Surfacing 579

sents the number of individual, equally-sized meshes along a defining curve—in this case, in the direction of the revolution.

To change the SURFTAB variables, type the variable at the command prompt. You will need both SURFTAB1 And SURFTAB2.

> **Notes**
>
> SURFTAB1 controls the number of divisions. If the surface does not look smooth, increase the SURFTAB1 value.

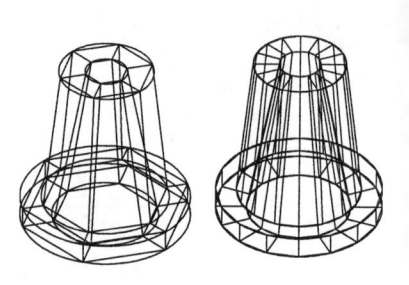

Figure 25-2

> **Toolbars** There are no buttons for SURFTAB1 and SURFTAB2.

The command line equivalent is **SURFTAB1**.

```
Command: SURFTAB1
Enter new value for SURFTAB1 <6>: 20
Command: SURFTAB2
Enter new value for SURFTAB2 <6>: 20
```

3D Polyline Meshes

AutoCAD's surfaces define not only the surface edges, as in 3DFACE and THICKNESS, but *faceted* surfaces using a 3D mesh. These surfaces can describe flat shapes as well as approximating curved surfaces. With the add-on Autodesk product, AutoSURF™ (not detailed in this book), you can create "true" curved surfaces.

RULESURF creates a surface between two lines or curves. The defining linear elements of a RULESURF can be lines, polylines, arcs, circles, ellipses, 3D polylines and splines. The RULESURF can be stretched between any of these elements or any one of these elements and a point.

REVSURF creates a surface by taking a linear element and revolving it around an axis; the defining profile sweeps around the axis, creating a surface. The linear element used to define the surface can be a line, a polyline or an arc or circle. The surface can be a complete 360 degree surface or any portion thereof.

TABSURF creates a surface by taking a defined line and projecting it along a defined line. It approximates a tabulated surface by moving a curve along a vector.

EDGESURF creates a polygon mesh by merging sets of four edges whose endpoints are coincident, approximating a Coon's surface patch.

Ruled Surfaces: RULESURF

By far the easiest type of surface to create is the ruled surface. Again, this is simply a surface generated between two rails, calculated from the nearest endpoint of each rail. To create a RULESURF, use the following:

> **Toolbar** From the Surfaces toolbar, choose Ruled Surface.
>
> **Pull Down Menu** From the Draw menu, choose Surfaces, then Ruled Surface.

The command line equivalent is **RULESURF**.

The two entities can be any kind of linear element: line, arc, circle, pline, ellipse, etc.

A linear element is something you could draw with a pencil without taking your pencil off the paper or overlapping any edges. The linear elements are used extensively to describe items of geometry. In the first half of this book, we used linear elements almost exclusively.

In Figure 25-3, there are two circles and two lines. The surface is generated between these two items simply by picking them.

Figure 25-3

```
Command: RULESURF
Select first defining
  curve: (pick 1)
Select second defining curve: (pick 2)
```

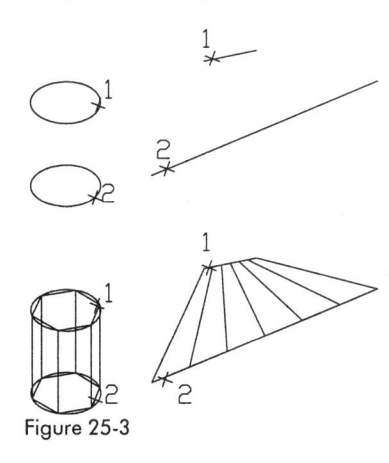

In both cases, the surface that is drawn is much like a surface you would draw by taking a ruler and joining the items with straight lines, starting at one end and working to the other.

In each of these cases, the ruled surfaces are created the same way, using two arcs, two lines, an arc and a point, and two plines.

The only major difficulty with RULESURF is that the system generates the surface between the closest endpoints of the items selected. In Figure 25-4 (the two bottom examples), the two endpoints selected are at different ends of the object, thus the surface is reversed. This is similar to the SOLID command, in that it creates a "bow tie" effect, but in 3D. Try picking the other end of the entity to generate the surface without the "bow tie," or mirror the object.

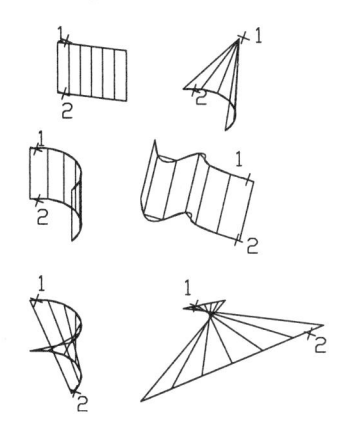

Figure 25-4

You must have a pictorial view while generating surfaces so you can easily pick the end of the item you need to surface.

RULESURF is used extensively to generate surfaces through arcs. Surfaces through a series of arcs, for example, can be drawn using the RULESURF command or the REVSURF command.

In Figure 25-5, ruled surfaces cover the entire surface. This can now be transferred to a solid modeling package or a shading package. NC information can also be generated.

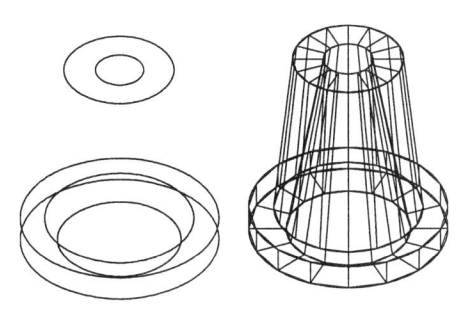

Figure 25-5

RULESURFs *are always done in pairs of rails.*

> **Notes**
>
> You will need several layers to create adjacent surfaces. If you get the response "Entity not usable" you have picked a surface. Freeze it to access the rail underneath.

Surfacing **581**

Problems with RULESURF

In addition to picking the correct end of items, you may encounter problems with closed surfaces. If you are generating a RULESURF with a circle, the second object must be a CIRCLE, a point or another type of closed entity, such as a polyline.

Another problem lies in the direction of the closed entity. While the endpoint of the entity is not considered when generating a ruled surface, *the direction from the endpoint is*. Thus with very little effort you can get a cylinder that resembles an hour glass. This usually occurs when you have been changing the UCS, and you have drawn two circles—one from the bottom of the part, the other from the top. If this occurs, simply Mirror the CIRCLE through its CENter, and delete the original object.

Figure 25-6

On the left (1) is a front face of an object you want to surface. If you added a 3DFACE or extruded the bottom line, you would get part of the face surfaced (2), but still be missing the arced areas. By using RULESURF, you can create a surface between the arcs and the lines (3). Or you can make the lines and arcs on each side into single pline entities. You will have to use this method if the item is asymmetrical.

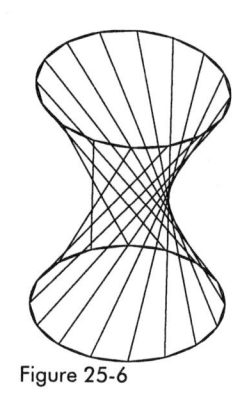

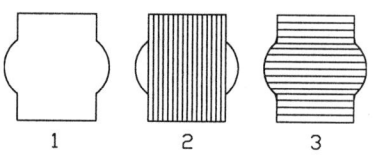

Figure 25-7

If the items on the right side of the face are an arc and two lines, you can change these into a pline or single entity for surfacing by using PEDIT.

```
Command: PEDIT
Select polyline: (pick a line)
Select objects:
Object is not a polyline. Do you want to
   make it into one? <y>:
Enter an option [Close/Join/Width/Edit
   vertex/Fit curve/Spline/Decurve/Ltype
   gen/Undo]: J
Select objects: (pick the arc)
Select objects: (pick the second line)
Select objects:
2 segments added.
```

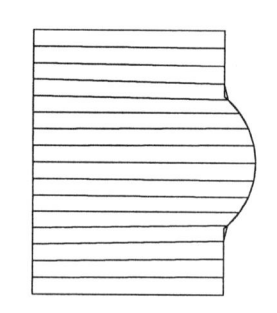

Figure 25-8

If the sides are asymmetrical, the lines or segments describing the item are not always straight. Depending upon your application, you may want to change the amount of segments. To do this, use SURFTAB1. For most applications, this will be close enough.

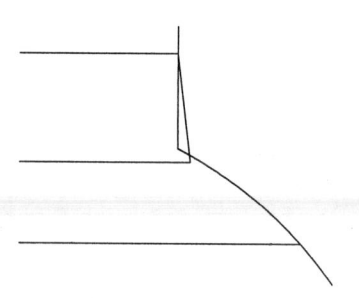

Figure 25-9

582 CHAPTER TWENTY-FIVE

Creating Surfaces with Holes

To create a surface with a hole in it, use RULESURF.

In order to create the surface, you must define the two "curves" as plines; either complex polylines or polyline circles. When defining the plines, you must be sure to line up the two ends of the polylines, and make sure that they are constructed in the same direction. Use List to confirm the radius of the arcs.

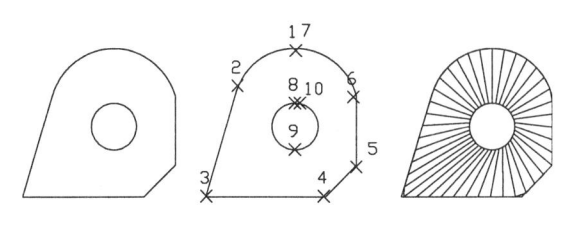

Figure 25-10

If you need to "trace over" the existing objects, create another layer for the pline outline. You may also be able to change the outer shape into a pline with PEDIT.

```
Command:PLINE
Specify start point:QUADrant of (pick 1)
Current line-width is 0.0000
Specify next point or [Arc/Close/Halfwidth/Length/Undo/Width]:A
Angle/CEnter/CLose/Direction/Halfwidth/Line/Radius/
Second pt/Undo]:R
Specify radius of arc:2.5
Specify endpoint of arc or[Angle]:ENDpoint of (pick 2)
Angle/CEnter/CLose/Direction/Halfwidth/Line/Radius/
Second pt/Undo]:L
Specify next point or [Arc/Close/Halfwidth/Length/Undo/Width]
  :ENDpoints of (pick 3, pick 4, pick 5, pick 6)
Specify next point or [Arc/Close/Halfwidth/Length/Undo/Width]:A
Angle/CEnter/CLose/Direction/Halfwidth/Line/Radius/
Second pt/Undo]:QUADrant of (pick 7)
Command:PLINE
Specify start point:QUADrant of (pick 8)
Current line-width is 0.0000
Specify next point or [Arc/Close/Halfwidth/Length/Undo/Width]:A
Angle/CEnter/CLose/Direction/Halfwidth/Line/Radius/
Second pt/Undo]:R
Specify radius of arc:.5
Specify endpoint of arc or [Angle]:QUADrant of (pick 9)
Specify endpoint of arc or
   [Angle/CEnter/CLose/Direction/Halfwidth/Line/Radius/
Second pt/Undo]:QUADrant of (pick 10)

Command:SURFTAB1
New value for SURFTAB1 <6>:40
```

Note: Again, in many cases, you could do this with PEDIT and Join.

```
Command:RULESURF
Select first defining curve:(pick the outer pline)
Select second defining curve:(pick the inner pline)
```

Surfacing 583

If the endpoints do not line up, neither will your surface because it is generated from the end point of the first pline to the endpoint of the second pline counterclockwise to the ends of both plines. The results get even more bizarre if your plines were created in opposite directions. (This often happens if you are using two different UCSs to define a plane.)

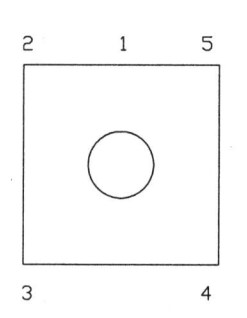

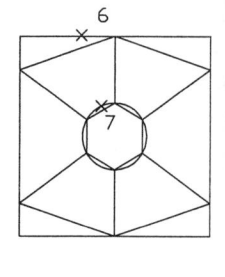

Figure 25-11

In this example, the linear pline was constructed in a counterclockwise direction while the pline circle, either through a change in the UCS or the MIRROR command, was constructed clockwise. In either case, the result is less than desirable.

In addition to keeping the same endpoints and the same direction, the plines must be finished off the same way. If one pline is finished off using CLose, the other must be finished using CLose as well. If not, the surface will be generated incorrectly, if at all.

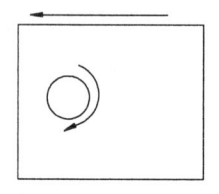

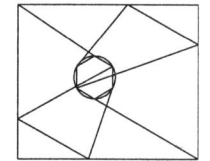

Figure 25-12

3DFACE and RULESURF

When creating 3DFACEs we were, in fact, creating planar surfaces using points to define a boundary. With a 3DFACE the points can be anywhere in space. An extruded 2D solid may look the same as a 3DFACE, but the edges will have a different definition, and the transparency properties will also be different. The major problems with 3DFACE and thickened lines are that they do not support curves. To create a surface between two lines, you can easily create a 3DFACE using the endpoints of the lines for boundary definition. To create a surface between two arcs, you need to identify the arc or radius. An extruded arc will give you a surface relative to an existing arc, but the UCS must be perpendicular to the arc. In addition, once an item is created, the resulting surface is difficult to see and select. This is where RULESURF comes in.

Surface of Revolution or REVSURF

REVSURF offers another extremely easy way to generate a surface. Very simply, REVSURF takes any linear element and rotates it around a defined axis. The linear elements are described as a curve path or profile whether they are curved or not.

Toolbar From the Surfaces toolbar, choose Revolved Surface.

Pull Down Menu From the Draw menu, choose Surfaces, then Revsurf.

The command line equivalent is **REVSURF**.

In Figures 25-13 and 25-14, the profile of the wine glass was entered using PLINE and then PEDIT with SPLINE. In order to visualize the curve, you must be in pictorial view or use DVIEW. The next step is to generate a line that will act as the axis. (Remember to use ORTHO.) The REVSURF command is then invoked and the user picks the entities as prompted.

```
Command: REVSURF
Current wireframe density SURFTAB1=25 SURFTAB2=25
Select object to revolve:(pick 1)
Select object that defines the axis of revolution:(pick 2)
Specify start angle <0>:⏎
Specify included angle (+=ccw, -=cw) <360>:⏎
```

Select object to revolve: this can be one item only. A pline is easier than a set of lines; you must pick the axis. *Do not press enter*.

Select object that defines the axis of revolution: this can be a line or a 2D or 3Dpline. If a pline is chosen, the axis is assumed to be from the first vertex to the last vertex, ignoring all vertices in between.

Start angle: if 0 is chosen, this indicates that the generated surface will start at the path curve. Choosing a non-zero angle will cause the surface to commence at that angle from the curve path.

Figure 25-13

Included angle: the number of degrees that the surface will be wrapped around the axis. A positive number is counterclockwise, a negative number is clockwise (the default is 360 degrees, or a full circle).

If the axis is neither a line or a pline, AutoCAD will prompt with:
```
Entity not usable as rotation
   axis.
```

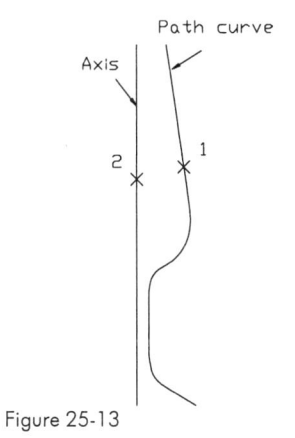

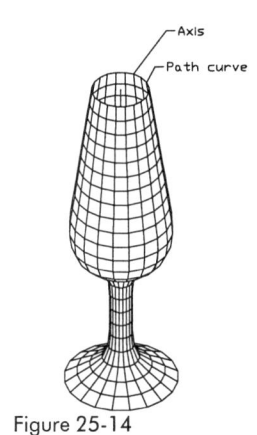

Figure 25-14

Try the simple REVSURF exercise. It takes only a minute, and will help you get a feel for surfacing.

Overlapping Surfaces

Surfaces often overlap when you are trying to pick up a linear element that has been used to describe another surface. By picking the general area, you can pick either the linear element you want or the surface you do not. As is so often the case, Murphy's Law applies here: your pick will probably select the item you do *not* want. Put your surfaces on a series of different layers and freeze them while you are completing the surfacing. This often helps you to better visualize the surface too.

REVSURF and UCS

The REVSURF axis must be parallel to the UCS to give you the curve you require. By having your UCS on the wrong plane, it is quite easy to generate a surface but not know it.

If your surface does not show up, and there is no error prompt, try List on the area to see if a surface has been generated on a rotation different from the one expected. The problem is in the UCS.

Surfacing

In an industrial application, you will probably never have to create a wine glass, except maybe for demonstration purposes. A more practical example would be a corner of an item using a REVSURF for the 90 degree angle.

In this example we have two planes described by four lines each at 90 degrees from one another. We have drawn a line for the axis at one unit in from the first or horizontal plane, and one unit up from the second or vertical plane.

The command to create a curved corner is:

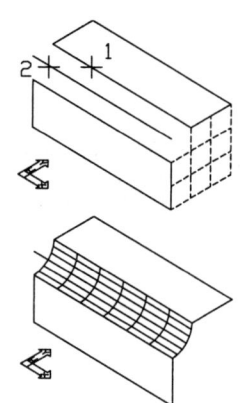

Figure 25-15

```
Command: REVSURF
Current wireframe density SURFTAB1=25 SURFTAB2=25
Select object to revolve: (pick 1)
Select object that defines the axis of revolution: (pick 2)
Specify start angle <0>: ⏎
Specify included angle (+=ccw, -=cw) <360>: -90
```

The line describing one corner of the horizontal plane is taken as the curve path for the curved corner. The start angle remains 0, as this is where we want it to start. The included angle is -90 degrees because we want to have the curve sweeping in a clockwise manner looking down the axis.

We will use the same axis of rotation and the line on the back to create the outside corner.

The angles will remain the same. Notice that the outside curve is much larger than the first because of the distance away from the axis of rotation. This is similar to the size of a circle relative to the radius.

Now we can move or copy the four lines on the vertical and horizontal planes away from the object, and generate surfaces between these lines using RULESURF or 3DFACE.

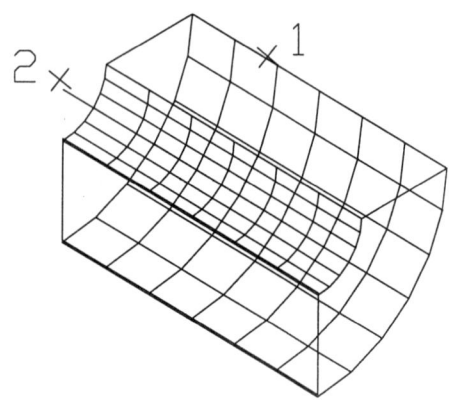

Figure 25-16

Notice that the lines on the mesh displaying the longer edge of the surfaces are farther apart than the lines on the shorter edges. Again, this is because the display, set through SURFTAB1, generates the same number of lines on each surface, relative to the length of the defining line or arc.

Because the surface has more than one direction of lines describing it, you can change both SURFTAB1 and SURFTAB2 to get the image you want. SURFTAB1 changes the display of mesh in one direction; SURFTAB2 changes the display in the other direction.

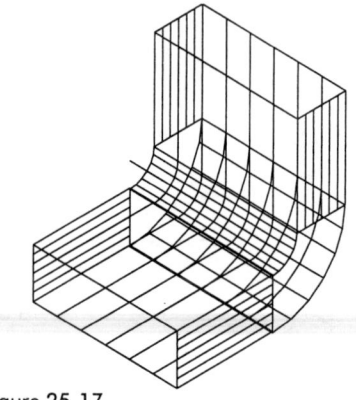

Figure 25-17

Tabulated Surfaces or TABSURF

From the side view we can see that the surfaces, in fact, are placed around the defining axis. At least two viewports are necessary to get the information in where you want it.

TABSURF creates a polygon mesh representing a tabular surface. It is similar to RULESURF and REVSURF in that two objects are needed to define the surface. Like REVSURF, it uses a straight line *not to rotate around, but to stretch along*. The surface, of course, will always have the same shape.

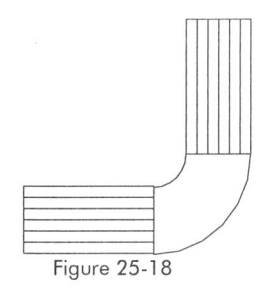

Figure 25-18

In this case, the path is called a *directrix* or *path curve,* and the axis is a *direction vector*, showing the system the magnitude and direction of the required surface. This direction is referred to as a *generatrix* or *direction vector*.

The two objects you need are:

1. a linear element for the curve path or directrix; this can be either a line, an arc, a pline, a circle or any other linear element, and
2. a line or pline along which the outline or directrix will be stretched.

The TABSURF command is then invoked and the user picks the entities as prompted.

> **Toolbar** From the Surfaces toolbar, choose Tabulated Surface.
>
> **Pull Down Menu** From the Draw menu, choose Surfaces, then Tabsurf.

The command line equivalent is **TABSURF**.

The direction vector can be placed away from the path curve and erased after.

```
Command: TABSURF
Select object for path
   curve: (pick 1)
Select direction vector:
   (pick 2)
```

The surface maintains the shape of the original curve. This is a useful surface for predetermined areas or profiles.

The same effect can be achieved with two outlines spaced at the correct distance and using RULESURF. However, TABSURF will often be easier, particularly if a number of items are being tabulated relative to a standard vector.

The display again is dependent on the TABSURF1 setting. The only trick with this surface is to make sure your line or generatrix is, in fact, a line and easily

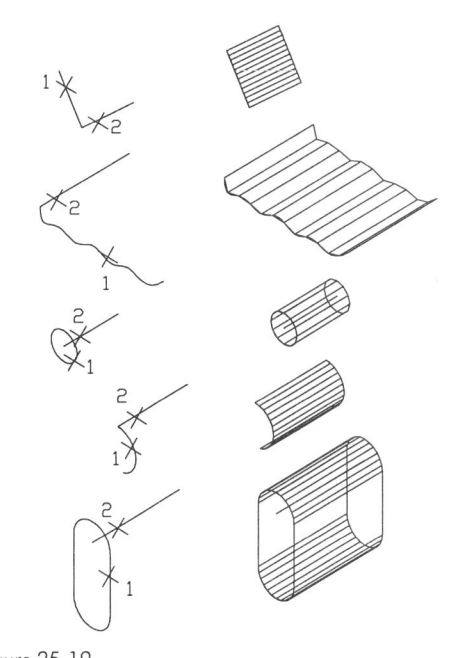

Figure 25-19

Surfacing **587**

picked. If surfaces or other data are overlapping it, you may get the prompt, "Entity not usable as a direction vector."

Edge Surfaces or EDGESURF

This surface is generated by curves which, like the RULESURF curves, can be either curved or straight. It is quite simple to use as long as all four curves are bounded, or "touch at the corners." The surface tabulation is in two directions like REVSURF. It offers much greater flexibility in geometric construction than either RULESURF or TABSURF which essentially are surfaces constructed with straight edges either between two defining curves or along a specific vector.

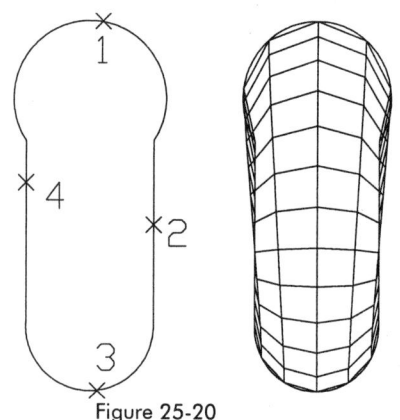

Figure 25-20

Because the surface is tabulated in two different directions, you will need both SURFTAB1 and SURFTAB2 to define the display of the surface.

The surface is generated as a 3D polygon mesh. In this case, the surface is described by four arcs.

The screen was divided into a minimum of three viewports containing a plan view, a right side view and an isometric view. The two arcs picked as 1 and 3 were put in while the UCS was in World.

The UCS was then changed to the right side view using the View option. Then the second two arcs were entered using End to make sure that the ends of all arcs met.

Toolbar From the Surfaces toolbar, choose Edge Surface.

Pull Down Menu From the Draw menu, choose Surfaces, then Edgesurf.

The command line equivalent is **EDGESURF**.

The next step is the command itself.

```
Command: EDGESURF
Current wire frame density:
  SURFTAB1=25 SURFTAB2=25
Select object 1 for surface
  edge: (pick 1)
Select object 2 for surface
  edge: (pick 2)
Select object 3 for surface
  edge: (pick 3)
Select object 4 for surface
  edge: (pick 4)
```

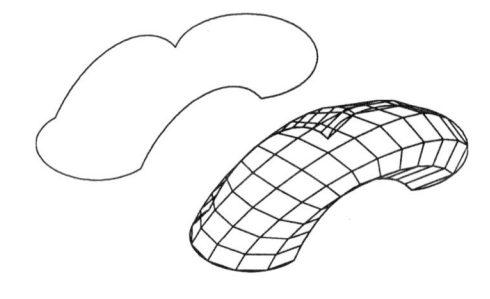

Figure 25-21

As long as all the endpoints meet, the surface will work.

As is often the case when working with surfaces, students have the most difficulty because the screen is not set up properly. Make sure you have at least three views of the object, otherwise you simply will not be able to visualize it.

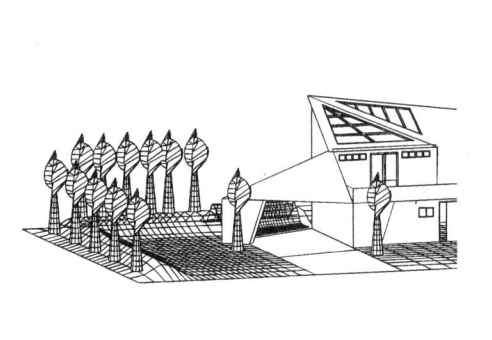

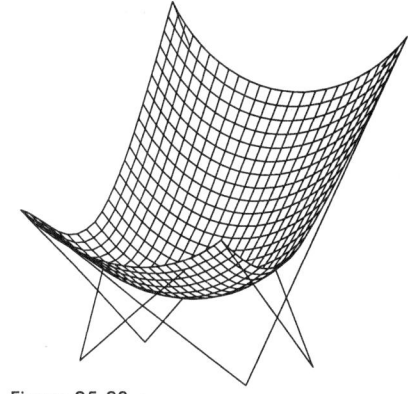

Figure 25-22

Figure 25-23

EDGESURF is very practical in landscaping applications and furniture design.

3DPOLY or 3D PLINEs

You may notice that plines are only two-dimensional entities. For use on surfaces, particularly EDGESURF and 3DMESH (see page 640), you need to have a three-dimensional facility for making plines or polylines.

```
Command:3DPOLY
Specify start point of polyline:0,0,0
Specify endpoint of line or [Undo]:1,1,1
Specify endpoint of line or [Undo] :1,2,2
Specify endpoint of line or [Undo]:2,3,3
Specify endpoint of line or [Undo]:c
```

This will give you a 3D loop. The Close option works the same in this command as in the PLINE command, and the Undo is the same too.

As with the EDGESURF and 3DMESH commands, this is the basis for some very tricky mathematical maneuvers. Your use of 3DPOLY is essentially as good as your use of polynomials. In a manufacturing environment, EDGESURF is extremely useful in industrial, automotive and aerospace design, but not totally necessary in other fields. It helps in fitting three-dimensional b-spline curves to vertices. If this is your specialty, there are very good books available on the mathematics of surfaces.

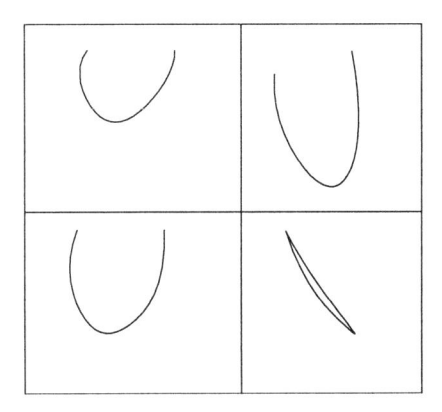

Figure 25-24

In Mapping and Architecture, 3DPOLYs are used to provide contour lines in plot plans in 3D.

Figure 25-24 is an example of a 3DPOLY and how it looks in a top, front, side, and isometric view. In the practice exercise, a 3DPOLY is used to define a linear element along the surface of a curved surface that will act as one of the edges on the EDGESURF.

Prelab 25 Surfacing

This small part will illustrate how to use both REVSURF and RULESURF.

You will need to set up four separate layers: lines, plines, surf1, and surf2.

Set your screen for four viewports as in previous exercises.

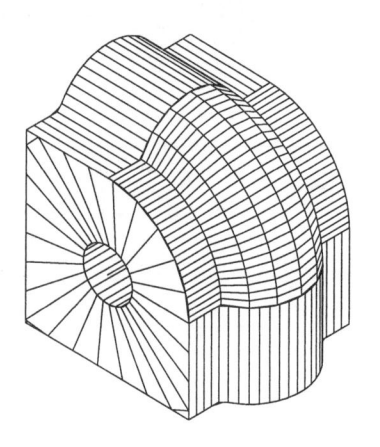

Step 1 In the lines layer, on the *X Y* plane, draw in the first plane as shown on the right.

Notes

Be sure to use different layers and different colors for the outlines and the surfaces. You will need at least two surface layers.

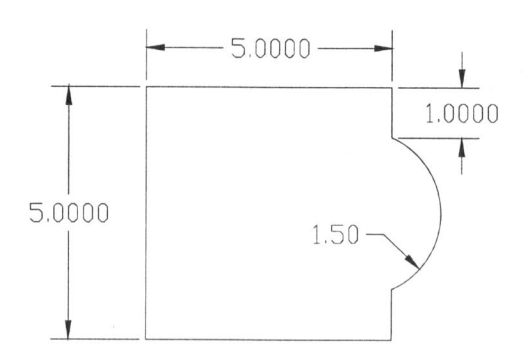

COPY this set of lines and arc. Rotate your UCS around *X* by 90 degrees, then ROTATE this plane 90 degrees using P for previous at your Select Objects prompt.

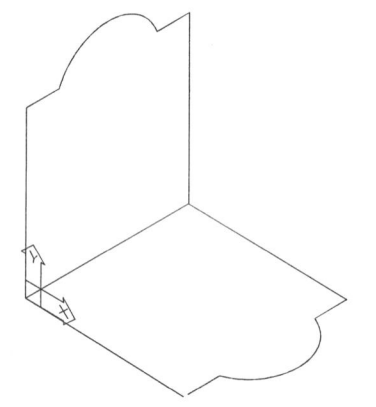

Now put in the front plane and make sure the end points line up. Use the dimensions on the next page.

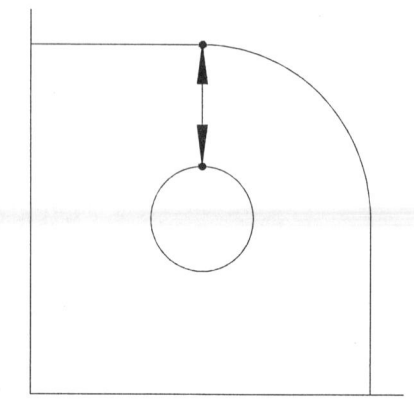

PEDIT with Join can work.

Step 2   Add the other lines and arcs to create the full wireframe part. You will need to rotate your UCS back around *Y*, then back to World. The two small lines and arc (dotted) from the first plane can be copied and rotated. If you did not use pline to draw the plane in, use PEDIT to make them a pline.

```
Command: PEDIT
Select polyline: (pick one of the
   small lines along the top)
Select objects: ⏎
Object is not a polyline. Do you
   want to make it into one? <y>: ⏎
Enter an option [Close/Join/Width/Edit vertex/Fit curve/Spline
   curve/Decurve/Undo]: J
Select objects: (pick the arc)
Select objects: (pick the second line)
Select objects: ⏎
2 segments added.
```

Step 3   Put a line through the centers of the two circles as shown by the thickened polyline (pick 2). First change your surface tabulation.

Then set your layer to Surf1 and use REVSURF to create a surface.

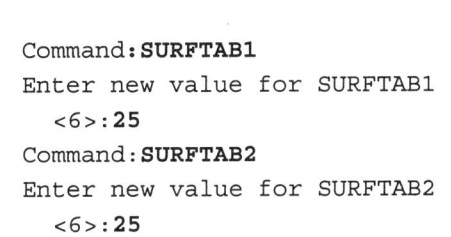

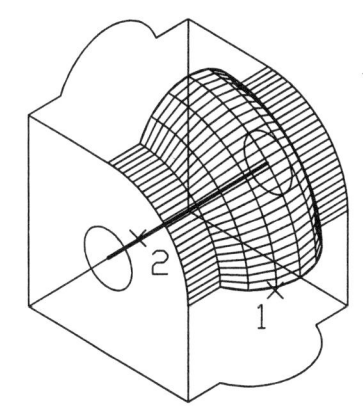

```
Command: SURFTAB1
Enter new value for SURFTAB1
   <6>: 25
Command: SURFTAB2
Enter new value for SURFTAB2
   <6>: 25
```

```
Command: REVSURF
Current wireframe density SURFTAB1=25 SURFTAB2=25
Select object to revolve: (pick 1)
Select object that defines the axis of
  revolution: (pick 2)
Specify start angle <0>: ⏎
Specify included angle (+=ccw, -=cw) <360>: 90
```

Step 4   Now create ruled surfaces. First Freeze layer Surf1 and make Surf2 current. Create a RULESURF between the line on the bottom edge and the lines and arcs along the top and the front edge. First make a pline out of the small lines and arc along the top edge..

Surfacing   **591**

```
Command: RULESURF
Select first defining curve:(pick
  the PLINE along the top)
Select second defining curve:(pick
  the LINE)
```

For the second surface, you may need to Zoom right in to the line. If you get the response, "Entity not usable," you have picked the surface, not the line. You can also use CHPROP to place the first surface on Layer Surf1 which is frozen; then the line will be accessible.

Step 5   For the side surfaces you will need to create polylines and generate the surfaces from these polylines. First change your UCS to this view and work in the Right View. You may need to use CHPROP to put the created surfaces on an undisplayed layer in order to access the points with Osnap.

```
Command: PLINE
Specify start point:ENDpoint of
  (pick 1)
Current line-width is 0.0000
Specify next point or
  [Arc/Close/Halfwidth/Length/
  Undo/Width]:ENDpoints of (pick 3, pick 4, pick 5)
Specify next point or [Arc/Close/Halfwidth/Length/Undo/Width]:a
Angle/CEnter/CLose/Direction/Halfwidth/Line/Radius/
Second pt/Undo]:R
Specify radius of arc:2.5
Specify endpoint of arc or [Angle]:ENDpoint of (pick 6)
Angle/CEnter/CLose/Direction/Halfwidth/Line/Radius/
Second point/Undo/Width]:↵
Command:PLINE
Specify start point:QUADrant of (pick 7)
Current line-width is 0.0000
Specify next point or [Arc/Close/Halfwidth/Length/Undo/Width]:A
Angle/CEnter/CLose/Direction/Halfwidth/Line/Radius/
Second pt/Undo]:R
Specify radius of arc:.75
Specify endpoint of arc or [Angle]:QUADrant of (pick 8)
Specify endpoint of arc or [Angle/CEnter/CLose/
  Direction/Halfwidth/Line/Radius/
  Second pt/Undo]:QUADrant of (pick 9)
Arc/Close/Halfwidth/Length/Undo/Width/<Endpoint of Line>:↵
Command:RULESURF
Select first defining curve:(pick 10)
Select second defining curve:(pick 11)
```

Copy the surface to the back plane. Now freeze the layer that has these surfaces on, and make the other surface layer current.

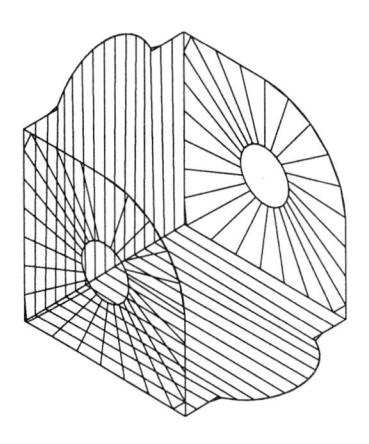

Step 6 For the upper and front surfaces, Thaw the two plines and generate surfaces between the plines. Then use RULESURF to generate surfaces between the two circles.

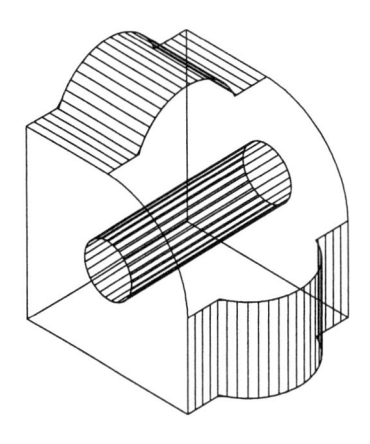

Step 7 Thaw all the layers and the part should be finished.

Freeze the lines, circles and plines before using Hide. If you do not, the circles will create a flat plane.

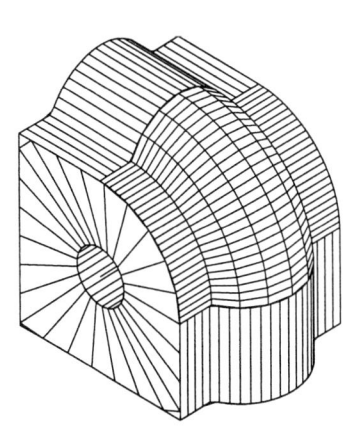

Command and Function Summary

3DPOLY creates a three-dimensional polyline.

EDGESURF creates a three-dimensional polygon mesh.

REVSURF creates a rotated surface around a selected axis.

RULESURF creates a ruled surface between two curves.

SURFTAB1 and **SURFTAB2** control the display of the surfaces.

Practice Exercise 25

Create the parts shown using surfaces and 3DFACEs. You will need to create polylines on the top faces of the surfaces. Dimension the parts if you have time.

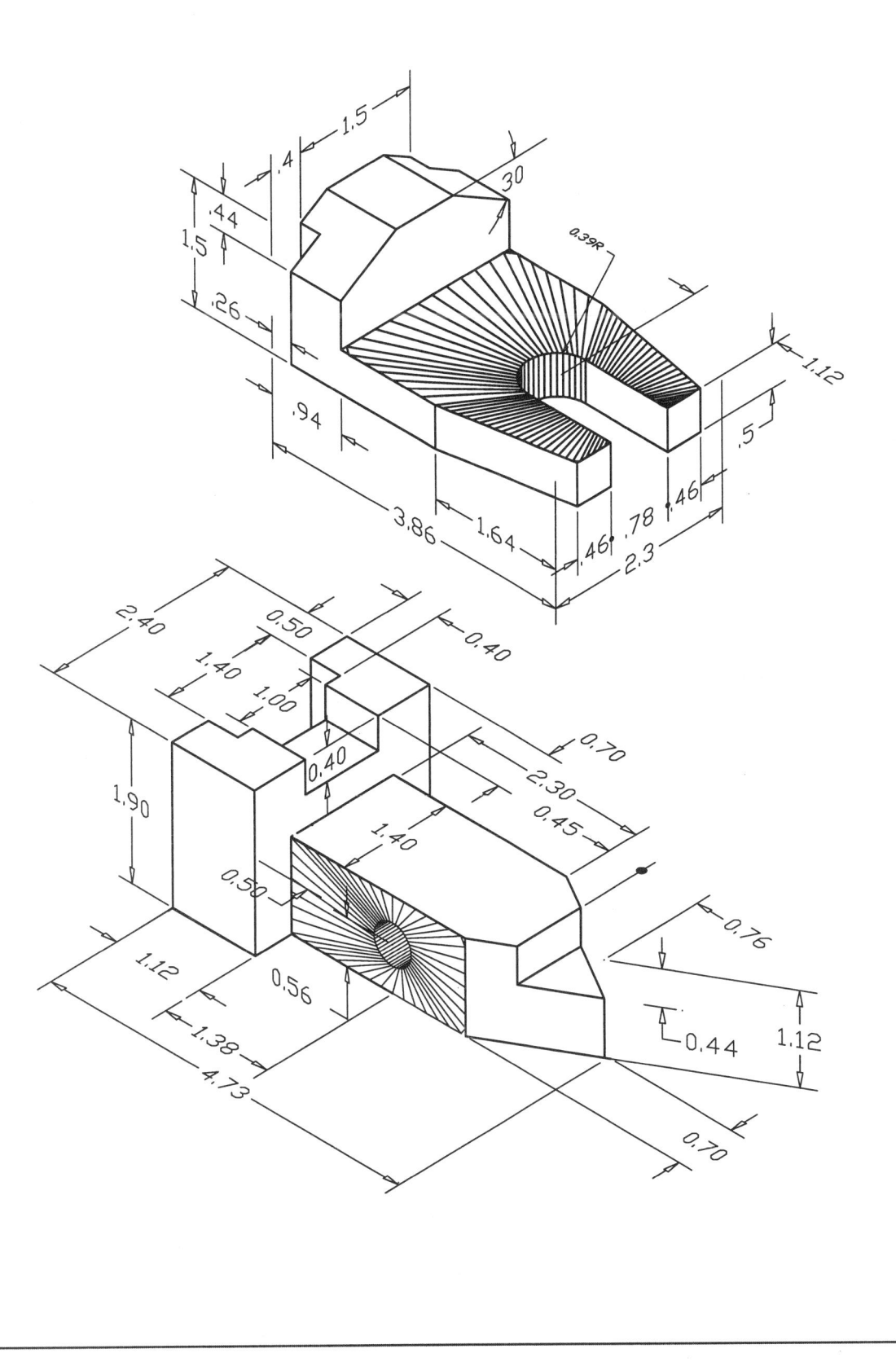

Exercise A25

This classical style gazebo provides good practice.

First draw in a circle which will be the center area of the gazebo. Then place a pillar at a reasonable distance from the center to make a usable room. In the tropics, such facilities are commonly used for dining and recreation, and can easily have a diameter of 20 feet.

Once the outline for the building is in, change your UCS to the top of the pillar and enter some interesting profiles for the detailing on the top of the pillars.

Draw a line for the axis through the pillar, then add another line to act as the *X* value and orient your UCS relative to it.

You will need a central axis of rotation for the curve paths to be rotated around.

You may notice that the curve path must be at the same *Z* depth as the interior of your building; otherwise the revolved surface will be much too big.

Be sure to change your UCS so that the *Z-0* is contained within the model. Use 3point with OSNAP for the best results. LINEs may need to be added to access the origin *X* and *Y*.

Now back in the UCS World and plan view, ARRAY the completed pillars around the center of the gazebo.

Add a ceiling on top of the gazebo, and use RULESURF to give it some depth so that the roof can be supported.

Now add some front steps by placing ARCs at a reasonable distance from the main floor. Use RULESURF to surface all the steps.

You will notice that while Surfaces is on, it is difficult to pick the arcs through which you are generating the surfaces. Just turn your Surface layer off while picking the new surface rails.

Once the steps are completed, you can change the UCS once more and generate a sloping roof over your gazebo.

This is a very simple design, and may take you less than two hours to complete. If so, do some variations on the columns to make them more interesting, and maybe add a platform on the inside of the gazebo.

If the floor is to be made from poured concrete, you may also need to slope it.

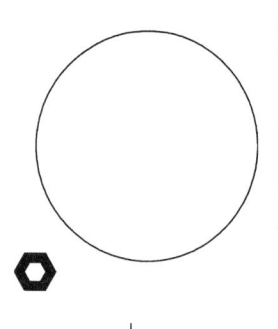

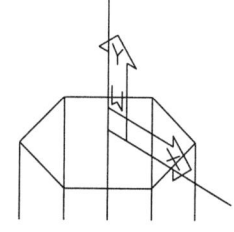

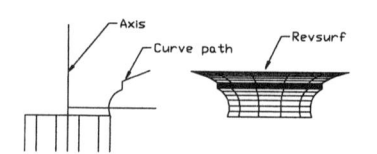

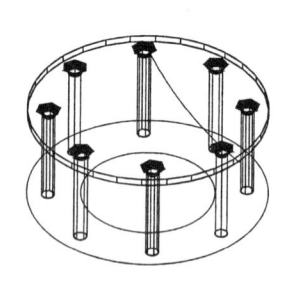

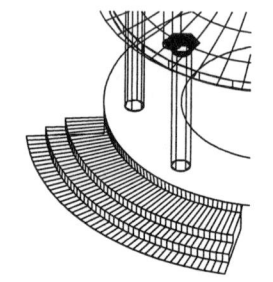

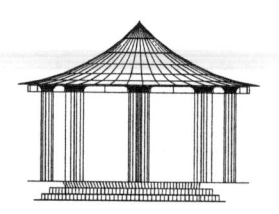

Once finished, use Hide in the isometric view to see what the final design looks like. Save the model.

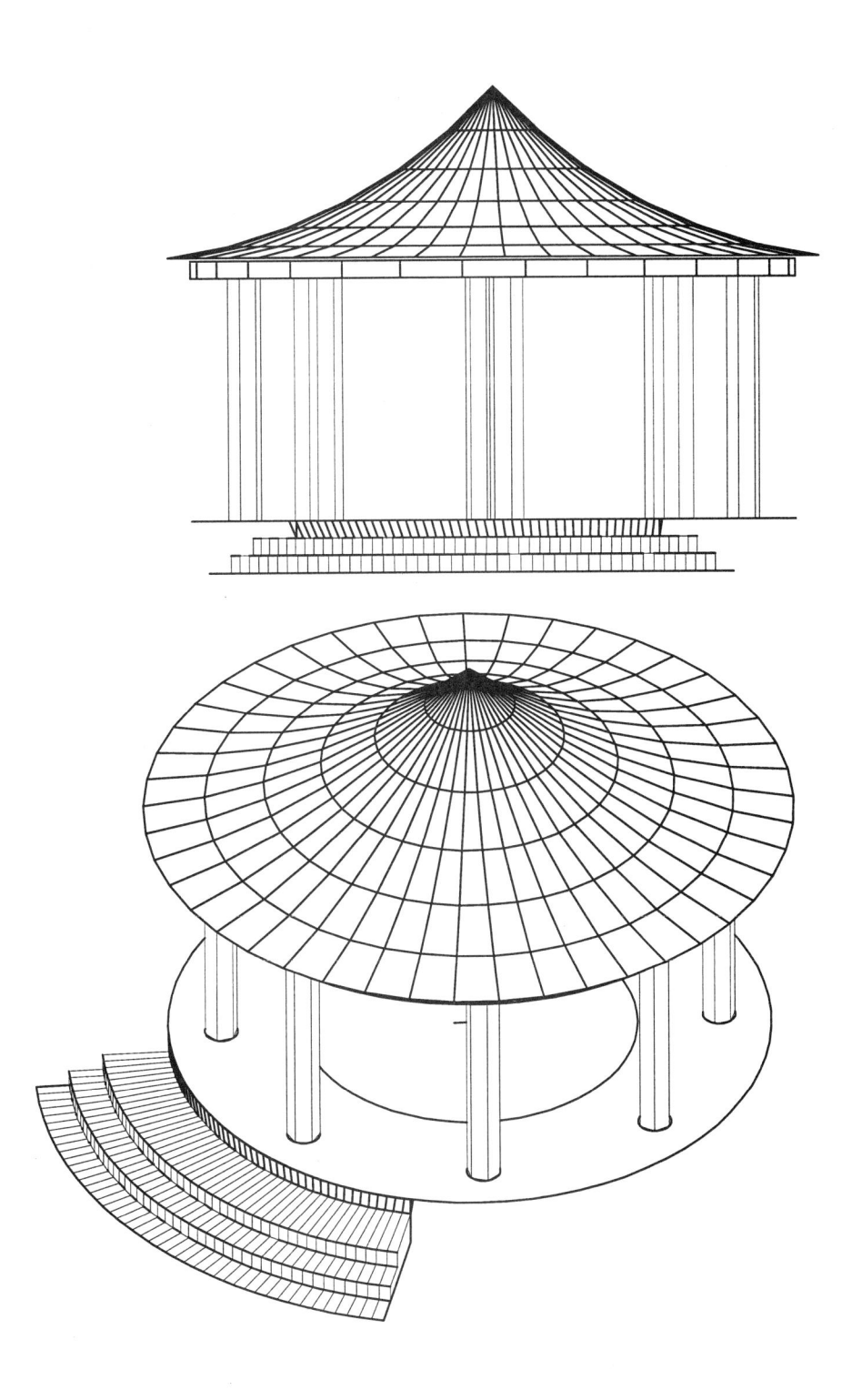

Exercise C25

Before starting, take a look at the last page of this exercise to see what you are going to create; it might help you visualize the various components.

Step 1 Set your screen to three views: front, plan, and 2,-2,2. Then draw in the column base as in the illustration to the right. Use a Snap of 1. Use PEDIT to make it a polyline.

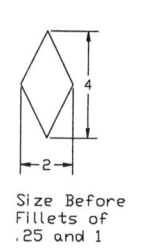

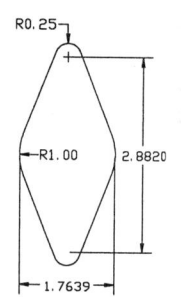

Step 2 Use the COPY command to copy your base from Z0 to Z6.

Create a LAYER for surfaces, and create the surfaces on the columns as in the illustration.

If you encounter the prompt that says you can not surface the item selected, it means that surfaces are overlapping lines and arcs. If so, turn off your LAYER for surfacing, create the surfaces in Layer 0 and use CHPROP to change them to the undisplayed Layer.

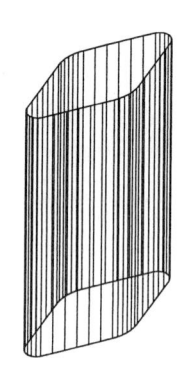

Step 3 With the column base created, change your UCS so that the origin is in the center of the column; the *X* will remain the same, and the *Y* will replace the World space *Z*.

The easiest way to do this is to place a line from the CENter of the arc at the major axis on the top face to the CENter of the arc directly opposite. Then from the MIDpoint of this line, create a line in the direction of *X* .75 units. Now create a line from the MIDpoint of the long line first created in the direction of Z 1 unit.

Use the UCS option, 3point, to pick the Origin, *X* and *Y* of the new coordinate space using the ENDpoints of the LINEs created for placement. The new UCS should be placed as in the illustration. Save the UCS as Column.

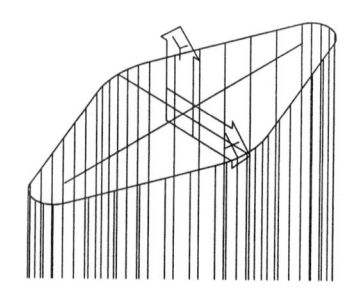

Step 4 Copy the existing column base in the *X* direction 6 units.

Now using the new UCS, create the four arcs and six lines in the example.

First create a line on the second base from the middle of the long line in the direction of *X* -.75 units. Create the first arc using SER from the end of this line to the end of the corresponding line on the other column. Move the UCS to the arc using the OBject option. Now OFFSET this arc at a distance of .5. Set the UCS to Previous.

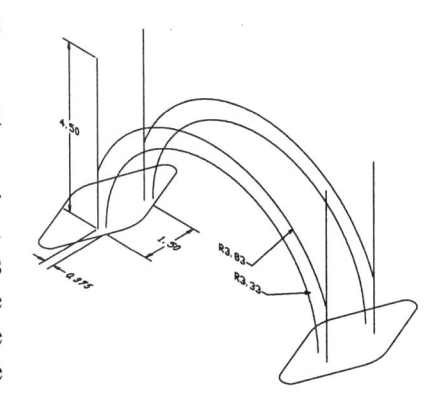

MOVE both arcs and lines in positive *Z* .75 units, then COPY them in *Z* -1.5 units.

Finally, create lines from the ENDpoints of the interior lines in a direction of *Y* 4.5 units and TRIM the arcs to the lines as shown.

Step 5 On your surfacing Layer, add the surfaces as shown.

You may need to change the SURFTAB1 option to get the surfaces at the same distance as in the illustration. In the column base the SURFTAB1 is set to 6. In the illustration below, the SURFTAB1 is set to 20.

The display lines are relative to the length of the objects determining the surface. Since these objects are longer than those in the first set, the SURFTAB1 needs to be a higher number.

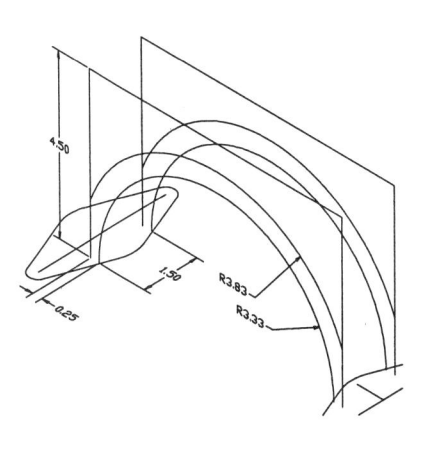

Step 6 On the top face of the column base, create the four lines and two arcs, as in the illustration. Again, FILLET is the easiest command to use. You will, of course, need to rotate your UCS to do this.

3point may be an easy way to create these, and the existing objects can be used again as references.

At this point you may want to create another few layers as well so you can view some of the new surfaces being entered without also viewing the existing surfaces.

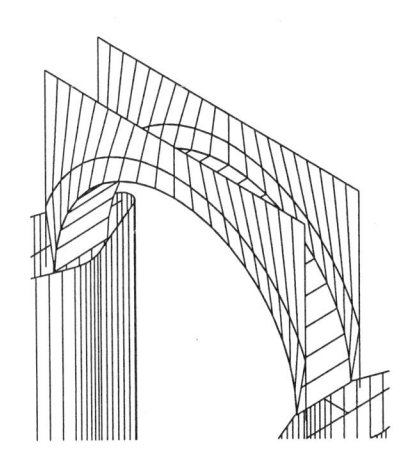

Step 7   Copy the new data in the direction of Z 4.5 units.

Because these objects are quite small, a smaller display factor is required, so change your SURFTAB1 back to 6.

Turn off any layers you do not need to create these surfaces. Then use RULESURF to create the part of the bridge support shown on the left.

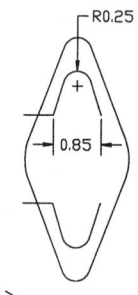

Step 8   Your bridge now needs some finishing.

Take the lines and arcs that define the very top edge of the bridge and OFFSET these by .25 units. If your UCS is still parallel to World, this should be easy.

Now copy these new objects in the direction of Z .5 units. You now have the outline for the top edge of the bridge. Use RULESURF to create the surface between the outlines. Will you need to change the SURFTAB? Would it be easiest to use PEDIT to make these line and arc segments one entity before OFFSETting and COPYing?

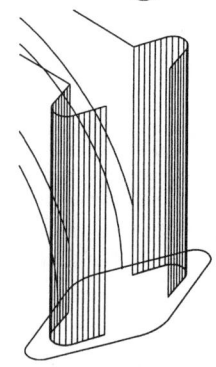

Step 9   Finally, you will need to enter the interior surface of the bridge itself.
If you have changed the lines and arcs in Step 8 to plines, you can copy these plines down in the direction of Z -1 unit.

Turn off any obstructing layers and add a surface for traffic.

You can also finish off the interior of the bridge to your satisfaction.

Add a surface to the top face of the column.

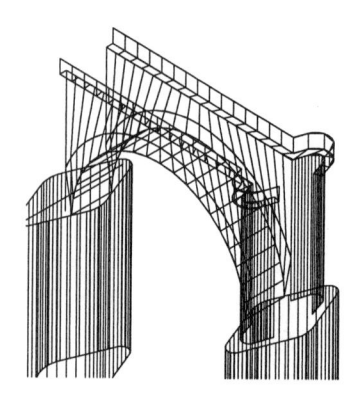

Step 10   Now that you have one complete bridge section, use CHPROP to change one of the column bases to an undisplayed layer.

If you have created the surfaces on LAYERs separate from the linear elements that define them, turn off the linear elements (lines, arcs and plines) before arraying. Since you already have the surface data, these objects are not necessary and will only take up room on the disk.

Save your file, just in case you are running out of room on the disk.

Now use the ARRAY command to create the full bridge as in the example on the next page. With ARRAY, make eight columns at a spacing of six units each as shown in the illustration below.

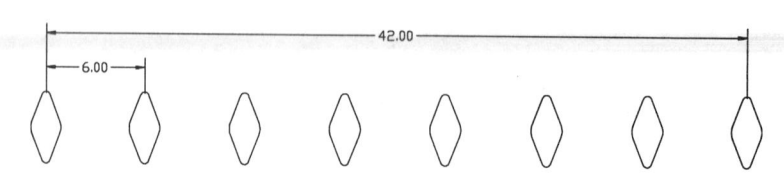

The Alcantara bridge over the Tagus

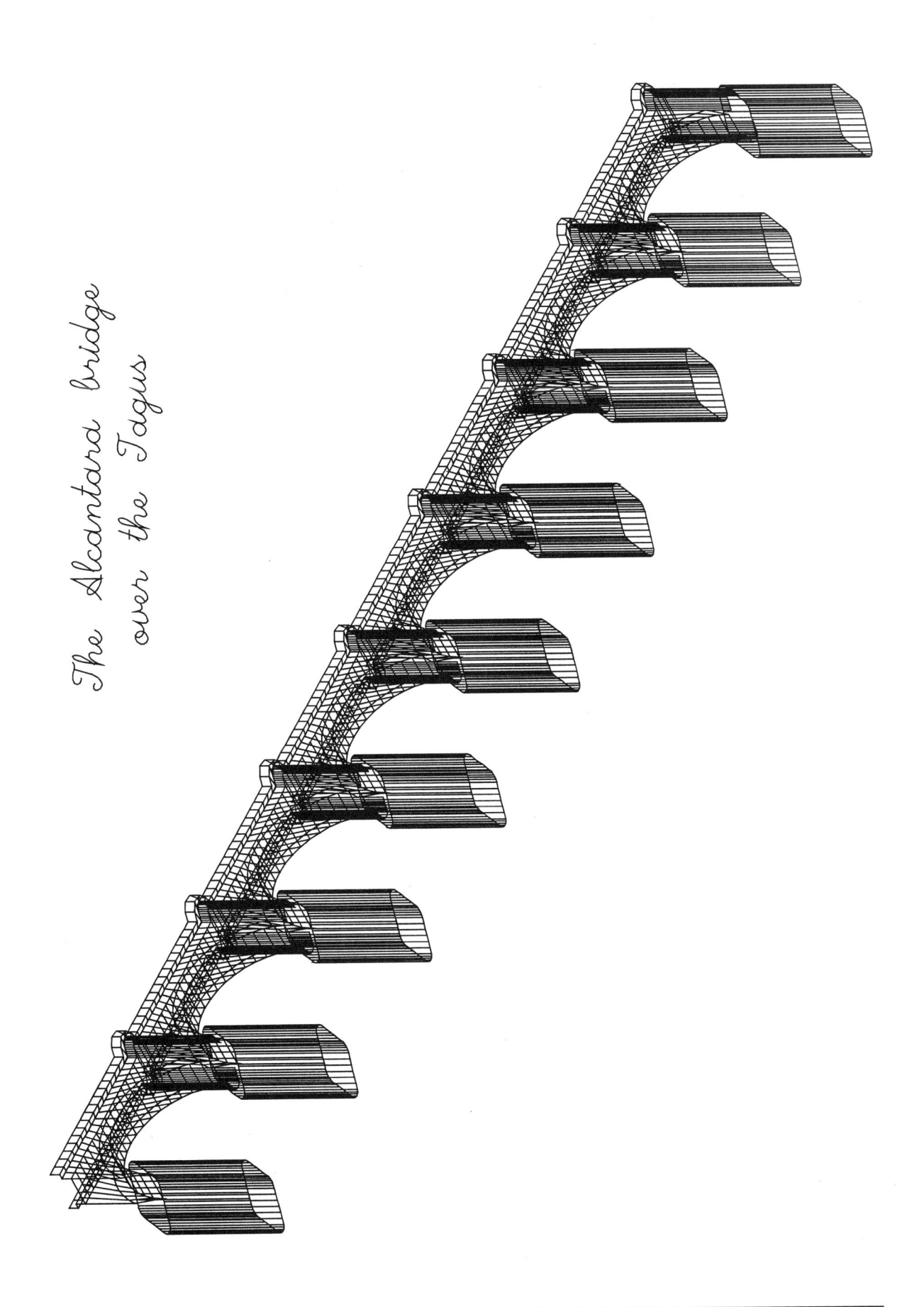

Exercise M25

Create the parts shown using the dimensions found in Chapter 6 (Practice 6) and Chapter 28 (Practice 28). You will need many surfaces to complete them all.

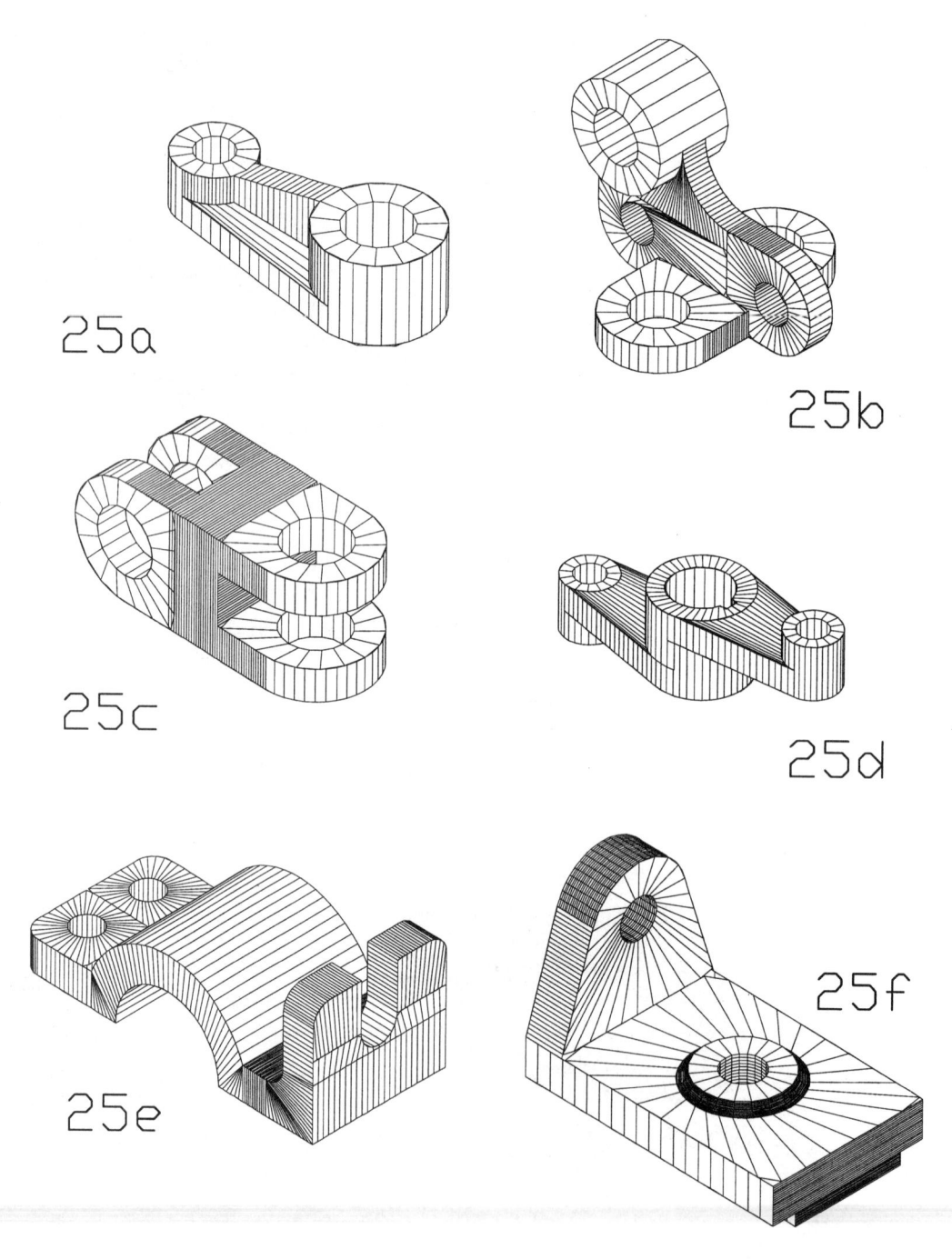

25a

25b

25c

25d

25e

25f

Exercise M25B

This part is slightly more difficult but worth the effort.

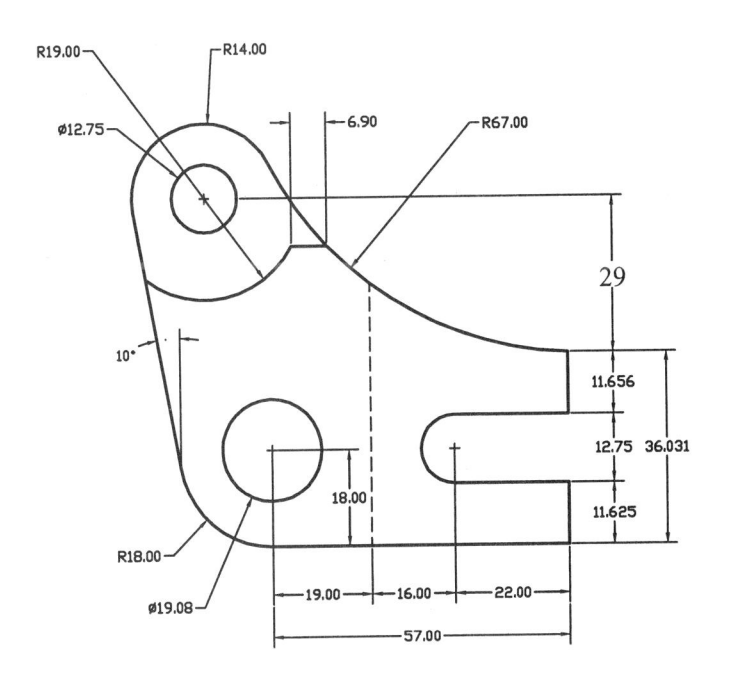

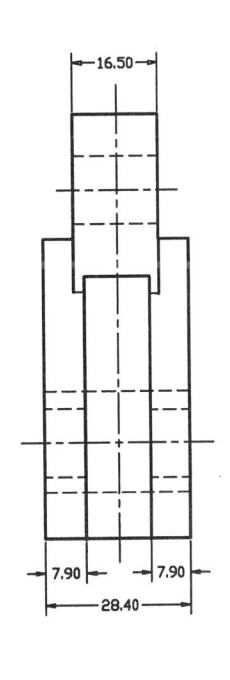

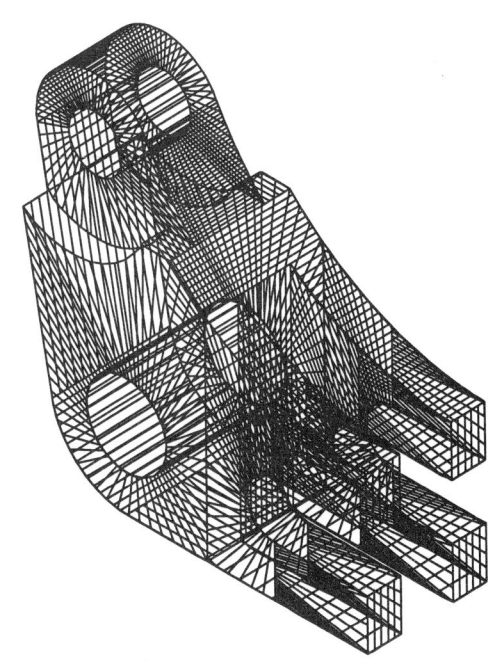

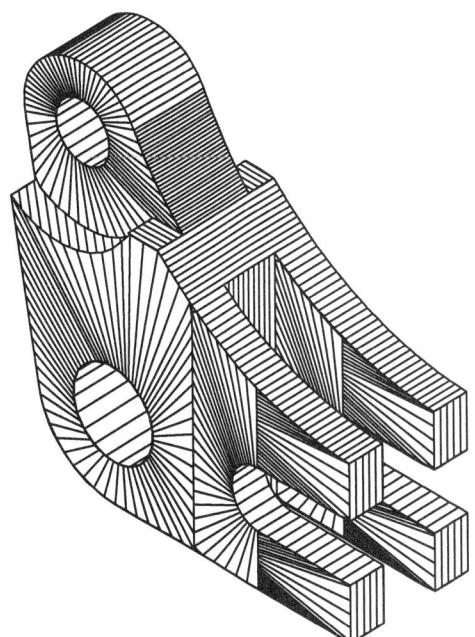

Challenger 25

Using the coordinates from Challenger 10, reference all the individual parts. Create them as individual 3D files, and then insert them as in this assembly view.

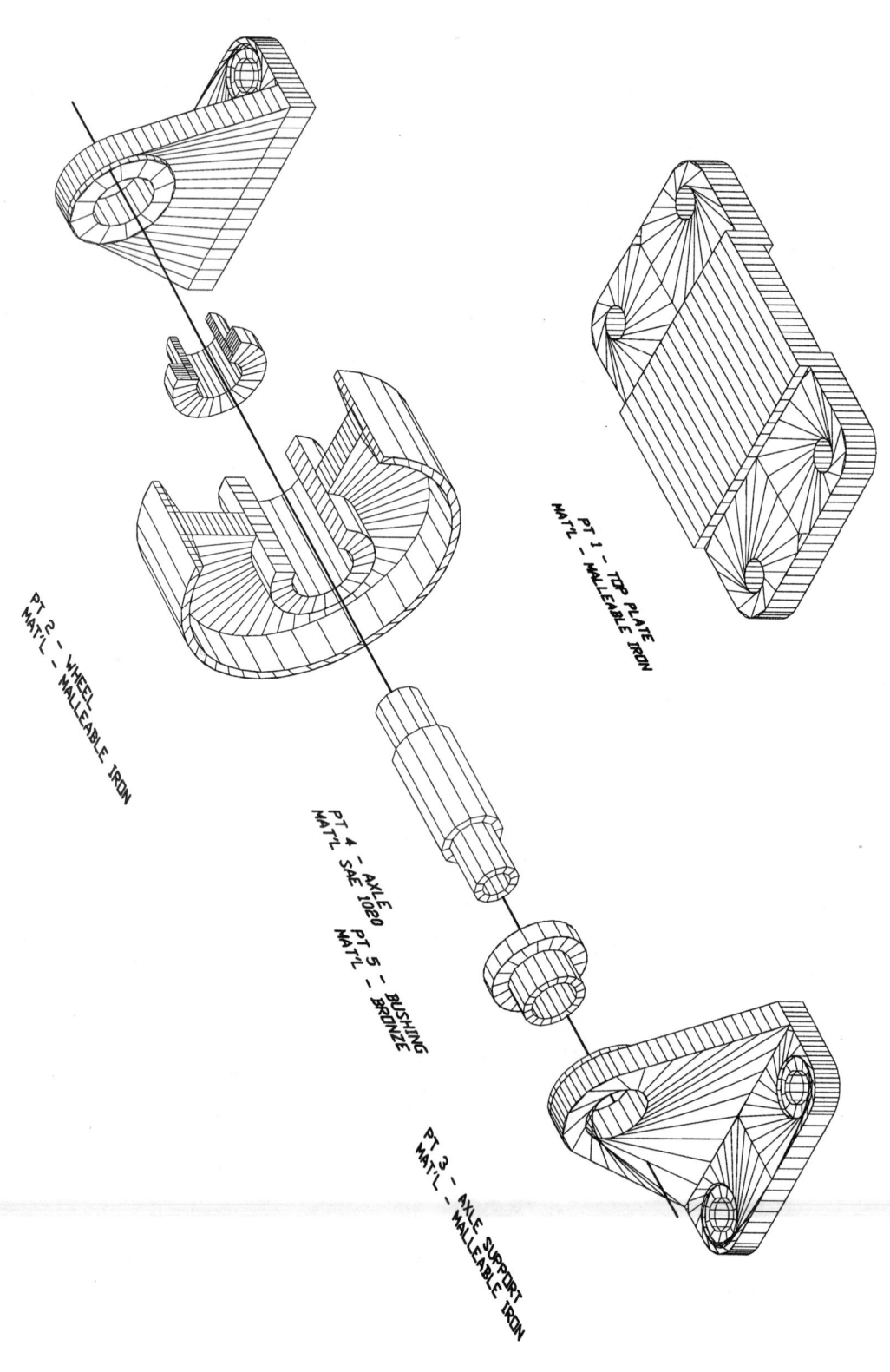

PT. 1 – TOP PLATE
MAT'L – MALLEABLE IRON

PT. 2 – WHEEL
MAT'L – MALLEABLE IRON

PT. 4 – AXLE
MAT'L SAE 1020

PT. 5 – BUSHING
MAT'L – BRONZE

PT. 3 – AXLE SUPPORT
MAT'L – MALLEABLE IRON

26 Paper Space, Model Space and Drawings

Upon completion of this chapter, you should be able to:

1. Change the model space to paper space
2. Use MVIEW to place multiple views on the drawing
3. Use ZOOM XP to scale the views
4. Use VPLAYER to control the layer display
5. Use MVSETUP to automate the plotting process
6. Complete a paper space drawing

OBJECTIVES

Model Space and Paper Space

Model space, paper space, and MVIEW were discussed with regard to 2D drawings in Chapter 11. Here paper space is discussed with regard to 3D models.

Model space is used while creating a model. In model space, multiple viewports are used for accessing a part from any view at any time for means of construction. Once the model is completed, a drawing of the 3D part can be created using the standard views—front, top, side, and iso or pictorial—or any others that properly communicate model data to the viewer.

Paper Space

As discussed in Chapter 11, paper space is a 2D document layout facility. Once the views are completed with all the required dimensioning, paper space takes these views and translates them to a "paper" (much like a "cut and paste" routine), so they can be compiled as a drawing.

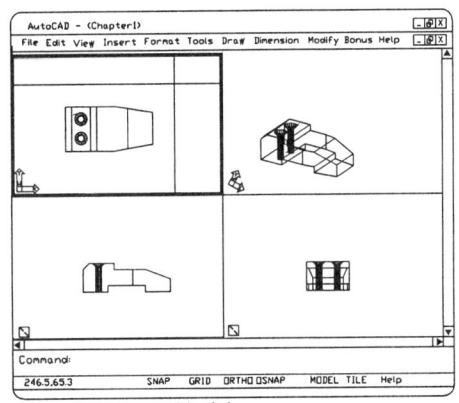

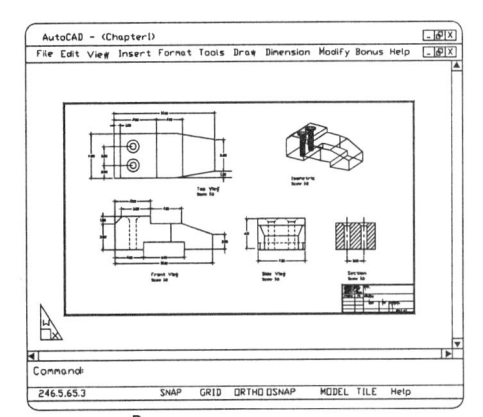

Model space | Paper space

Figure 26-1

In 3D, paper space extends the multiple viewport facility; the multiple viewports used to create the model can automatically be translated to a paper space layout.

You have already been working in model space; in model space you have been describing part geometry. Whether creating a house, a survey, an airplane, or a mold for a contact lens, the CAD operator is relating the physical properties of real world objects to the system.

With paper space, you are adding titles, scales, machining symbols, etc.—data that communicate the size, quality, and surface of the object. The numbers and symbols relate to paper.

In a traditional engineering job shop or architectural office, there are at least two areas where information concerning the final product is created. Draftsmen create drawings of the object and model builders prepare a 3D model. In AutoCAD, as in any other CAD, the process of design takes place on the system in the model stage. Then, once the designer is pleased with the results of the design process, drawings are generated so the object can be constructed or cut.

Before paper space, you would have used blocks to create this type of drawing. Paper space is not only much easier to use than blocks, but also saves a lot of space both on your disk and on the drawing because there are far fewer overlapping lines. When using blocks to compile a drawing, there are four sets of lines in a four-view drawing. With paper space, the data within the file is only one model, thus the storage is much smaller. To get into paper space use TILEMODE, PAPER or the Layout tabs.

Tiled Viewports and Floating Viewports

While in model space, the working environment is referred to as *multi-tiled*. This means that the viewports are placed together edge-by-edge like tiles. While working with the multi-tiled screen, each viewport contains the same information—the same model, the same layers, but in different views and different zoom factors. To access paper space:

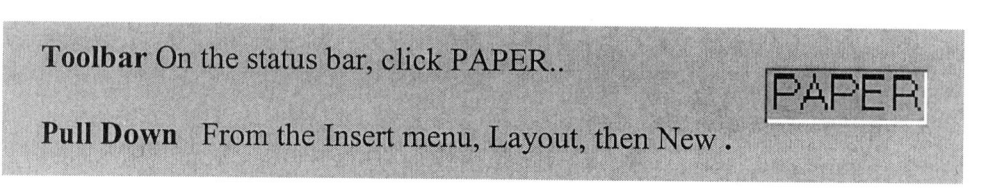

Toolbar On the status bar, click PAPER..

Pull Down From the Insert menu, Layout, then New .

The command line equivalent is **PSPACE** or **PS**.

With model space, you have been describing part geometry. With paper space, you are adding to the part geometry all of those things that relate to paper.

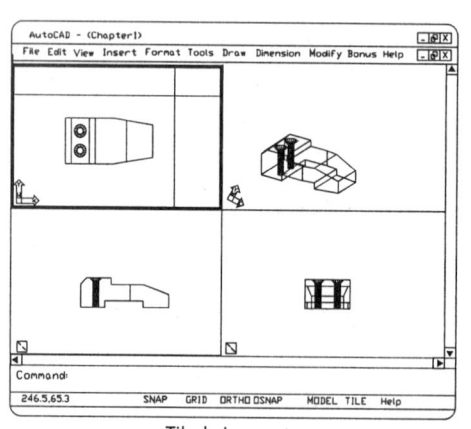

Notes

You must change the TILEMODE variable to 0 to access PSPACE from the command line.

Tiled viewports   Floating viewports

Figure 26-2

Floating viewports differ from tiled viewports, which split the screen into fixed, tiled, model space viewports. With paper space, the viewports can be opened up and/or overlapped. The viewport edges can be frozen so that the views of the object are plotted without the viewport border lines.

To access the floating viewports and a paper space layout, use Paper Space.

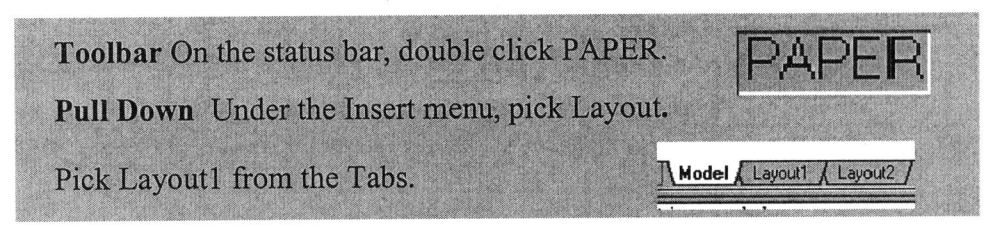

> **Toolbar** On the status bar, double click PAPER.
>
> **Pull Down** Under the Insert menu, pick Layout.
>
> Pick Layout1 from the Tabs.

The command line equivalent is **PSPACE** or **PS**.

Paper space acts like a sheet of paper on which images of the part are compiled, then annotated like a drawing on paper. The page Setup dialog box will occur if no layout has yet been set up.

In order to access the model in a paper space or floating viewports environment, use the MSPACE command.

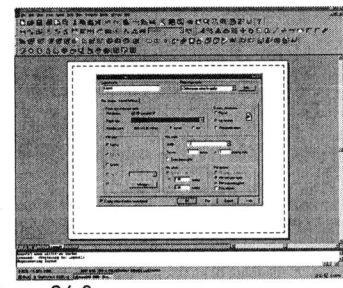

Figure 26-3

Tilemode

When you work in tiled viewports, the TILEMODE system variable is on. Switching to paper space from the menus automatically turns TILEMODE off (0). When TILEMODE is off, you can switch between model space and paper space as needed, using the MSPACE and PSPACE commands.

In order to access paper space from the command line you must use the TILEMODE variable command.

```
Command:TILEMODE
Enter new value for TILEMODE <1>:0
Regenerating layout.
```

Once you have created your views, you can use either TILEMODE or the commands, MSPACE and PSPACE to toggle between the two modes. TILEMODE on (1) will return you to a tiled environment which is the default.

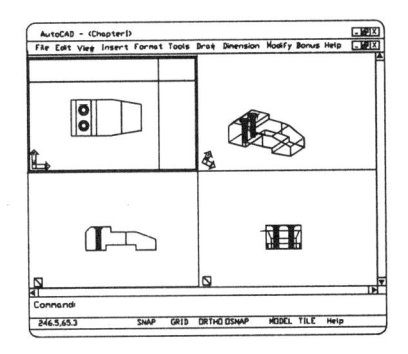

Tilemode on,
model space

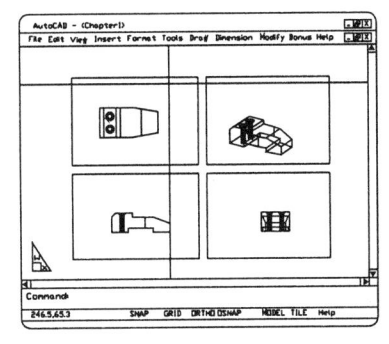

Tilemode off,
paper space

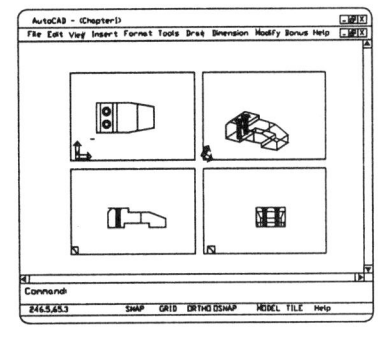

Tilemode off,
model space

Figure 26-4

On the left screen notice that the crosshairs are in one view only. In the middle, the crosshairs cover the screen. On the right, the viewports are not tiled, but the crosshairs are back to one viewport only. In the view on the left, you have a UCS icon in every viewport. In the middle, there is only one UCS paper space icon. On the right, again, there are icons in each corner. In the screen on the left, there are four separate "tiles," four areas totally enclosed and separate from each other. In the middle and on the right, you have one screen cut into four sections.

The viewport with the crosshair is "active." You can make a different view in paper space active by picking with the mouse or using Control-V to toggle between views.

TILEMODE 1 = model space for modeling = MSPACE

TILEMODE 0 = paper space for drawing = PSPACE or MSPACE

By accessing paper space from the pull-down menus, you have switched from an environment that uses tiled views to a floating viewport environment.

When you turn TILEMODE back on, returning to model space, AutoCAD restores the viewport configuration that was active before paper space was entered.

Toggling Between Model Space and Paper Space

To change the Zoom factor or add dimensions, you may wish to toggle to model space without returning to a tiled environment. Use MSPACE or MS to return to model space, and PSPACE or PS to return to paper space without changing the TILEMODE variable.

Once you have accessed paper space, add viewports with the MVIEW command to access your model.

In Release 2000 you are immediately asked for the size of paper when entering paper space. The Page Setup - Layout 1 dialog box allows you to set up all parameters of your final drawing before you even enter the paper environment. You will need to configure a plotter (see page 796) or printer that has drawing size paper before you can access a drawing format. If your printer is set to a standard laser, you won't be able to even draw anything larger than legal size paper.

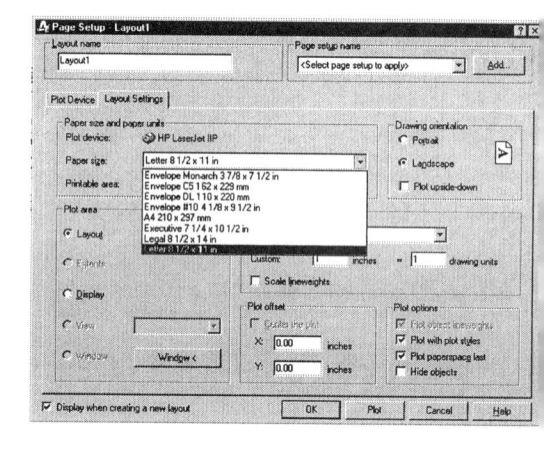

MVIEW

The MVIEW or Make VIEWs command is used to identify views used in paper space. The screen before MVIEWS is like a blank piece of paper. The MVIEW command lets you add viewports to view the model on this "paper" format. Picking from the menus automatically puts you in paper space.

When using the MVIEW command, you can create various configurations of viewports, select viewports for hidden line removal, and have different layers active in different viewports. The default setting is for the user to specify the parameters of a single new viewport. To access MVIEW use the following:

Pull Down From the View menu, choose Viewports, then the number of viewports that you need.

The command line equivalent is **MVIEW**.

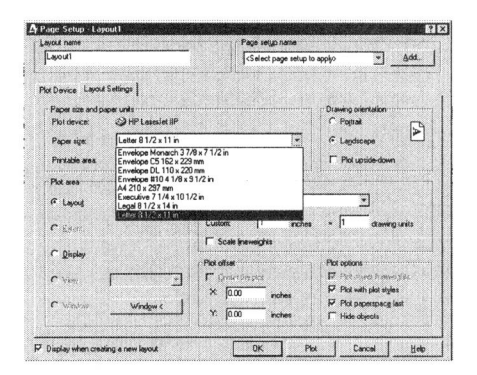

```
Command:MVIEW
Specify corner of viewport or
  [ON/OFF/Fit/Hideplot/Lock/Object/Polygonal/Restore/2/3/4]
  <Fit>: (pick 1)
Other corner: (pick 2)
```

Where: ON = turns on a viewport, making the objects within the borders visible.

OFF = turns off a viewport. When a viewport is off, the enclosed objects do not appear, and the viewport cannot be made current in model space.

Fit = creates one viewport that fills the available display area. The actual size of the viewport depends on the dimensions of the paper space view.

Hideplot = removes hidden lines in a viewport during plotting from paper space.

Lock = locks the selected viewport.

Object = helps you identify a polyline, ellipse, spline, region or circle as the boundary of a viewport.

Polygon = identifies an irregularly shaped polygon as the viewport.

Restore = restores a named viewport configuration.

2 = divides the specified area vertically or horizontally into two viewports.

3 = divides the specified area into three viewports.

4 = divides the specified area into four viewports.

First Point

The default is the placement of one viewport. You can use this single viewport to create a single view of the model for plotting and drawing purposes. This will give you a single view on-screen containing the view of the model that was current in model space. This option is frequently used for removing hidden lines in a check plot.

If you want more than one view, choose another option.

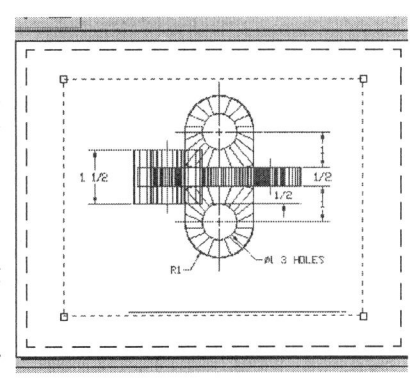

Paper Space, Model Space and Drawings **609**

ON/OFF

The default is to have the drawing show up in the viewports as soon as they are configured. If you would like to have them turned off, usually to save regen and redraw time, just turn the viewport OFF. You can always turn it back on later.

When turning viewports on and off, you are prompted to select objects; the viewports themselves are considered entities and can be turned OFF and ON with one pick on the border of the view.

Hideplot

While in model space, you can use the HIDE command to see your objects with hidden lines in the active viewport. As soon as the viewport is regenerated, however, the items are restored. Using HIDE before the PLOT command in model space will *not* hide the entities in the PLOT. While they may not show on-screen, the entities will show up on paper.

With the Hideplot option, the entities hidden in any particular viewport will remain hidden when you finally PLOT.

```
Command:MVIEW
Specify corner of viewport or [ON/OFF/Fit/Hideplot/Lock/
   Object/Polygonal/Restore/2/3/4]<Fit>:H
ON/OFF:ON
Select objects: (pick one or more viewport frames)
```

While selecting the objects, *remember that the viewport is considered an object*. The geometry is not. Pick the frame or border of the viewport.

Use the OFF option to turn the hidden lines on again in the next plot.

In the PLOT command, the prompt, "Remove hidden lines" will also remove hidden lines, but this usually takes longer than using the Hideplot option.

2/3/4

If you have not saved the layout, use the following to get a regular four-quadrant space.

```
Command:MVIEW
Specify corner of viewport or
   [ON/OFF/Fit/Hideplot/Lock/
   Object/Polygonal/Restore/
   2/3/4]<Fit>:4
Fit/<First point>:F
```

This will create a layout of four quadrants as shown. The view in each quadrant will be the one in your active viewport when you had model space active.

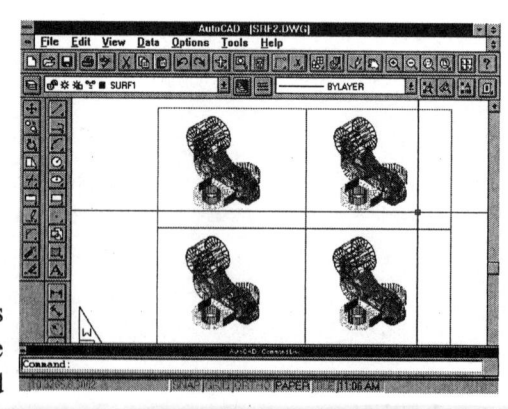

If you want to add three viewports in model space, just ask for the 3 option.

```
Command:MVIEW
```

```
Specify corner of viewport or [ON/OFF/Fit/Hideplot/Lock/
   Object/Polygonal/Restore/2/3/4]<Fit>:3
Horizontal/Vertical/Above/Below/Left/<Right>:
```

Figure 26-5

The preceding are configurations of the 3view MVIEW option. Use Horizontal/Vertical, etc. to place them where you want them.

With the 2View option, you can have the screen in horizontal or vertical sections.

```
Command:MVIEW
Specify corner of viewport or [ON/OFF/Fit/Hideplot/Lock/
   Object/Polygonal/Restore/2/3/4]<Fit>:(pick 1)
Other point:(pick 2)
```

LOCK

Once a viewport is fully detailed, you may want to LOCK it so that no further changes will affect it.

Object and Polygonal

Both of these options offer non-symmetrical viewports. With the Object option, the circle, ellipse, region, or polyline must exist. With polygonal, the polygon is made and then becomes a viewport.

RESTORE

If you have saved the four viewports in VIEWPORTS command, you can bring up the views as they were. If you want to set up four different views you can do this as well, but the first way is simpler. Both methods use MVIEW.

If your configuration of viewports was stored using the VPORTS command under the name **4QUAD**, then you simply restore this screen layout in paper space by using Restore and the name, 4QUAD.

```
Command:VPORTS
Save/Restore/Delete/Join/SIngle/?/2/<3>/4:S
?/Name for new viewport configuration:4QUAD

Command:MVIEW
Specify corner of viewport or [ON/OFF/Fit/Hideplot/Lock/
   Object/Polygonal/Restore/2/3/4]<Fit>:R
Enter name of window configuration to insert <ACTIVE>:4QUAD
Specify the first point or [Fit]:F
```

The Restore option will translate any configuration stored under VPORTS and scale the restored viewport to fit the graphics area. The scaling of each viewport will be discussed shortly. Each view becomes an individual viewport entity.

If you have no stored VPORT, AutoCAD will take the current viewport configuration labeled as Active. You can also display a list of stored viewports with ?.

With the MVIEW command, you can place multiple viewports overlapping each other. The rectangle used to make the view will not show up on the drawing; only the geometry contained within it will. Make sure that your geometry does not overlap. If it does, simply MOVE the viewport over. Each viewport in paper space is considered an entity; it can be picked up on the "frame," not on the enclosed object.

When creating an outline for a drawing, you may also wish to have overlapping views. Viewports created using VPORTS are always non-overlapping or "tiled" views. With MVIEW the viewports can overlap, and with the Polygon and Objects options, they can be of any shape.

Entering the Title Block

Drawings done in paper space should be plotted at a scale of 1:1.

Before you start trying to determine the size of your views, it is a good idea to determine the size of your title block. The MVIEW command allows you to set the size of the views. The paper size is set up using the Page Setup dialog box.

Your title block should then be inserted onto the "paper" so there is enough room on the outer edges to account for the plotter's rollers as they grasp the paper.

Once the title block is placed, the views can be moved and stretched to fit the required space.

Scaling Views Within a Drawing

In model space, as soon as the command ZOOM All is used, you have lost any relation to the actual scale of the part being designed; the image expands to fit the space provided.

In paper space, the views should be offered at an exact scale. The ZOOM option XP allows for scaling of the object relative to the final size of the paper.

The ZOOM option X scales the object relative to its current size within the viewport. In paper space, the scale factor of XP gives you a zoom factor "times the paper scale," or relative to the paper and the actual part. To draw the part at full scale or 1:1 use a ZOOM of 1XP. A setting of .5XP will result in the scaled view being exactly one-half the size of the original. A ZOOM of 2XP will result in a view twice the size of the original.

The charts on page 276 can be used to determine the size of the required zoom. For a final drawing at a scale of 1/4'':1'0'', use 0.020833XP or 1/48XP (4 × 12).

ZOOM plus the paper space size must be performed in model space. Use MS to toggle to model space.

The best time to perform these scale factors is after all the views have been added to the paper.

When the ZOOM command is used in paper space, it affects the entire display. ZOOM .5X will result in a display with the views intact at half the size they were before.

In model space (MSPACE), you can PAN the objects within the viewports. In paper space (PSPACE), the MOVE command will move the views relative to other views. Be careful not to ZOOM the views in model space after scaling them with ZOOM XP. ZOOM Window in PSPACE, then switch to model space to work on your model.

Figure 26-6 shows a screen with four viewports of a simple part in the standard views.

The four views must be lined up and scaled on a 17'' × 11'' sheet of paper.

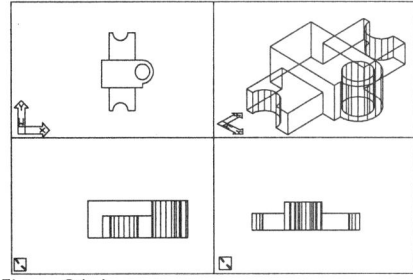

Figure 26-6

Because border lines will show up in the layer created, a new layer called FRAMES was created and made current at this point.

The VPORTS command was used to Save the screen configuration so that it could easily be restored in paper space. The stored name for the viewport was 4QUAD.

Once the page size is established in the Page Setup menu, MVIEW was used to insert the four views at the correct paper size.

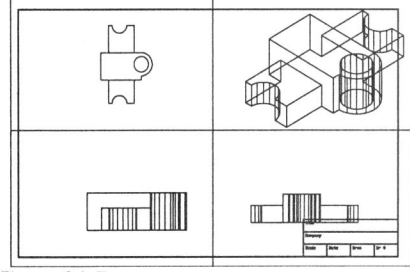

Figure 26-7

In Figure 26-7 the paper size was 17'' × 11''. The configuration of views saved from model space was placed in paper space. A title block was inserted at a size suited to the paper while leaving room for the plotter rollers. Coordinates of .5, .5 × 16.5, 10.5 should work in this case.

Now that the views are on the paper, they are scaled and moved so they line up. To adjust the zoom factor, you must toggle back to model space

```
Command:MS (toggles back
   to model space for
   zooming)
```

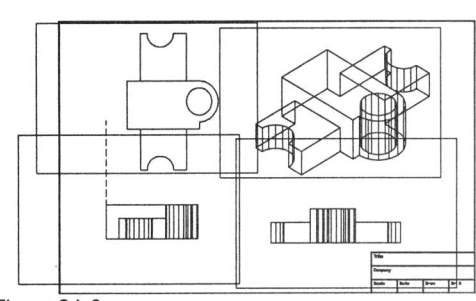

Figure 26-8

> **Notes**
>
> When picking the views to move them across the drawing, pick the border of the view, not the information contained within the view.

Paper Space, Model Space and Drawings **613**

Once back in model space, each viewport will be an independent unit, and you can zoom each one separately. In this case, the part is approximately 10″ × 14″. At a scale of 1:1, the part would not fit on the paper, so the size was reduced by half.

```
Command:ZOOM
Specify corner of window, enter a scale factor (nX or nXP), or
  [All/Center/Dynamic/Extents/Previous/Scale/Window]
  <real time>:.5XP
```

A scale of 1XP was used for the rotated view.

```
Command:ZOOM
All/Center/Dynamic/Extents/Left/Previous/Vmax/Window/
  <Scale(X/XP)>:1XP
```

Locking the Zoom Factor Within a Viewport

In paper space, the views should be offered at an exact scale. The ZOOM option XP allows for scaling of the object relative to the final size of the paper. While you are working in model space, any time you change the zoom factor - ZOOM All, ZOOM Window - you lose your relative zoom size. In Release 2000, once you have established the correct scale you can lock your viewport zoom factor as follows.

1. If your right click options have been disabled, turn them back on using the Tools menu, Options, then the User Preferences Tab. Put a check beside Shortcut menus in drawing area.

2. Move your cursor to the frame or border, pick it and the grips will appear, then right click, and choose Lock Display. This will lock it so that the zoom cannot change.

Editing Floating Viewports

Viewports can be both moved and stretched to allow for full viewing of the objects. Point filters are often used to access the other views for placement (see Prelab, Step 13).

In the example given, PS was used to toggle back to paper space and the MOVE command was used to line the views on the paper.

Use either construction lines (see hidden lines) or point filters to move the information across the screen so that it lines up in paper space. The data contained within the views is accessible for reference either for filters or OSNAPs, but not accessible for editing purposes.

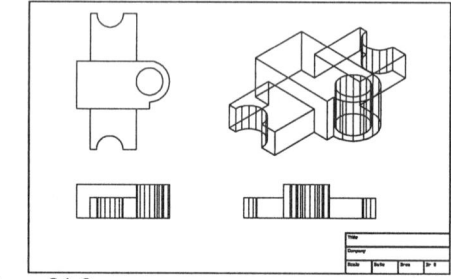

Figure 26-9

Once the views are lined up and scaled to your requirements, the FRAME layer can be turned off and notations and titles can be added to the paper. Add any other text and notes, logos, or symbols in paper space. These will be plotted relative to the paper size.

VPLAYER and MVSETUP are used in 3D as they are in 2D drawings (see page 284).

Plot styles and prototypes can be a real advantage (see page 796).

Prelab 26 3D Paper Space Example

Step 1 **Getting Started**

Retrieve the file created in Chapter 22. Your file should come up with the four views you created in the previous drawing. We will take these four views, add a section, and create a drawing in paper space. First complete the model by adding six surfaces for the countersunk holes as shown below. Erase the top 3DFACE on the top surface.

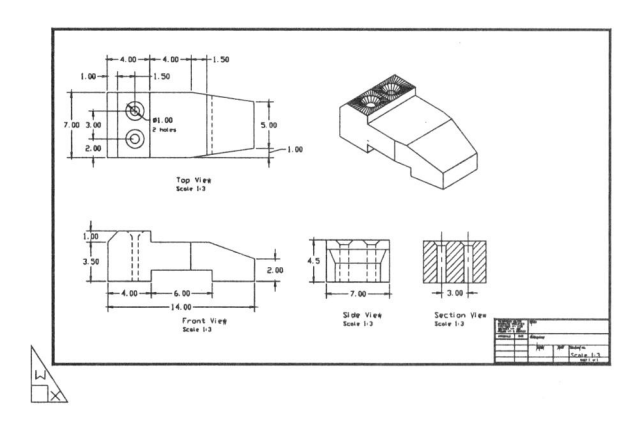

Step 2 **CAmera**

A pictorial view will be placed at a slightly different angle to provide optimum visualization. Use DVIEW and CAmera to obtain a better view in an isometric or pictorial view.

The CAmera option of DVIEW works in the same way as a user holding a camera focused on a particular point or target on the object. The DVIEW command affects only the active or current ViewPORT. Make the pictorial viewport active, then pick DVIEW Options from the Display pull-down menu, and then DVIEW CAmera; or type in DVIEW at the command prompt.

```
Command: (pick in the pictorial viewport)
Command:DVIEW
Select objects or <use DVIEWBLOCK>: (pick everything on screen)
Select objects or <use DVIEWBLOCK>:↵
CAmera/TArget/Distance/POints/PAn/Zoom/TWist/CLip/Hide/Off/
   Undo/<eXit>:CA
```

If you do not select the objects, AutoCAD's default model will show up on the screen. Simply rotate either your own image or the default image to the desired rotation angle.

By moving the cursor you can see how the object changes position by degrees.

If you move the cursor below the middle point of the screen the underside of the object will be shown.

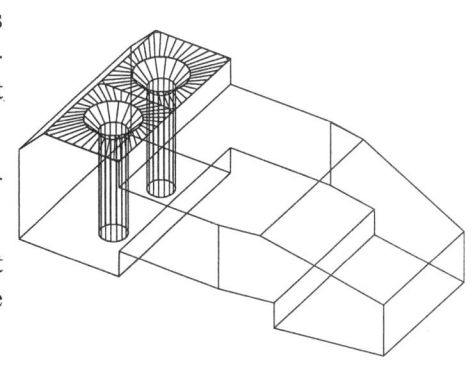

Once you have picked the desired angle, press ↵ to accept the view. Save the view as PIC.

```
Command:-VIEW
Enter an option
  [?/Orthographic/Delete/Restore/Save/Ucs/Window]:S
Enter view name to save:PIC
```

Step 3 POints

Now position the bottom right view to achieve a section view. First position the objects with the POints option of DVIEW, then use the CLip option to section it.

The POints option is similar to CAmera in that it positions the object relative to the viewer. With POints, both the CAmera and the TArget are positioned.

The right side view on the screen is the obvious choice for a section view. The section will be through the countersinks. Since the exact position of the countersinks from the end of the part is known, change the target position to the end of the part and CLip to that distance. In order to access the points as shown in the illustration, first invoke the VPOINT command. This lets you access the parts on the model that describe the desired TArget and CAmera; then use DVIEW and POints.

```
Command: (pick in the bottom right viewport)
Command:VPOINT
Current view direction: VIEWDIR = 0.0000,0.0000,1.0000
Specify a view point or [Rotate] <display compass and
  tripod>:2,-2,2
Command:DVIEW
Select objects or <use DVIEWBLOCK>:(pick everything on screen)
Select objects or <use DVIEWBLOCK>:↵
CAmera/TArget/Distance/POints/PAn/Zoom/TWist/CLip/Hide/Off/
  Undo/<eXit>:POint
Enter target point <13.9865,2.4356,5.3246>:MID of (pick the
  target line shown)
Enter camera point <6.4537,5.4367,3.6845>:MID of (pick the
  camera line shown)
```

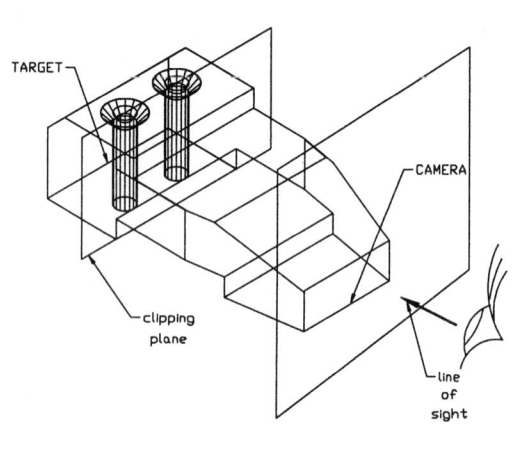

The view will not appear to be different, but this orientation lets you place the cutting plane exactly.

Step 4 **Save the Viewports**

First save the viewport configuration for later use in paper space.

```
Command:-VPORTS
Enter an option[Save/Restore
   Delete/Join/SI/?/2/3/4]:S
Enter name(s) of viewport
   configuration(s) to list
   <*>:4QUAD
```

The four views are ready to be used on a drawing. Now use CLip to clip off the front 11.5 inches.

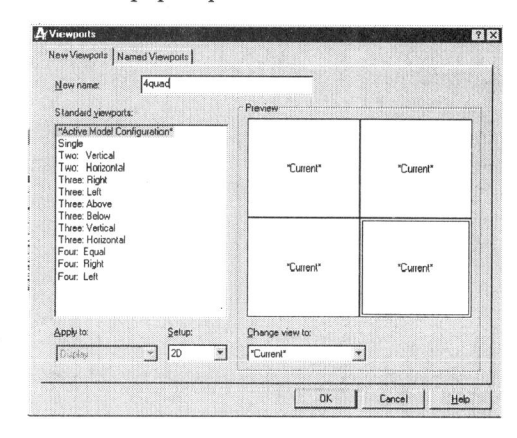

Step 5 **CLip**

Clip is one of the most useful options for creating drawings. With CLip you can identify a section of the part and extract it for viewing.

The CLipping planes are perpendicular to the line of sight, between the camera and the target. In essence, clipping is like a huge knife or cheese cutter slicing through the part. A front CLip will take out all the portions of the object that obscure the two countersinks. A back CLip would take out everything behind the clipping plane.

```
Command:DVIEW
Select objects or <use DVIEWBLOCK>:(pick all objects on screen)
Select objects or <use DVIEWBLOCK>:↵
CAmera/TArget/Distance/POints/PAn/Zoom/TWist/CLip/Hide/Off/
   Undo/<eXit>:CL
Back/Front/<OFF>:F
ON/OFF/<Distance from target> <2.00>:2.5
CAmera/TArget/Distance/POints/PAn/Zoom/TWist/CLip/Hide/Off/
   Undo/<eXit>:↵
```

This will clip to the center of the countersinks. A clip can be achieved by moving the cursor to get the required image, but this is not as accurate.

Step 6 **Creating a Section View**

This is the view that results once the CLip has been performed. Now change the UCS to the front of the plane, and hatch and dimension the section for final drawing purposes. First create a layer called Section, make it a different color and Current, then add the hatches.

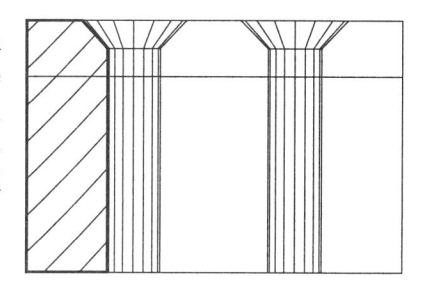

```
Command:UCS
Enter an option
   [New/Move/orthoGraphic/Prev/Restore/Save/Del/Apply/?/World]:V
```

This will rotate the UCS so that the hatch will be produced with the correct orientation. Use the Pick Points option to create the hatch. If this does not work, use PLINEs to create the boundary for the hatch. Lock the layers that you will not be accessing for the hatch. Staggered sections are also much simpler with PLINEs.

```
Command:(in the LAYER command, Lock
  all layers except Section)
Command:OSNAP
Object snap modes:END
Command:PLINE
Specify start point: (pick 1)
[Arc/Close/Halfwidth/Length/Undo/
  Width]: (pick all outlines points
  on boundary)
Command:BHATCH
(See dialog box on the right for
  settings.)
```

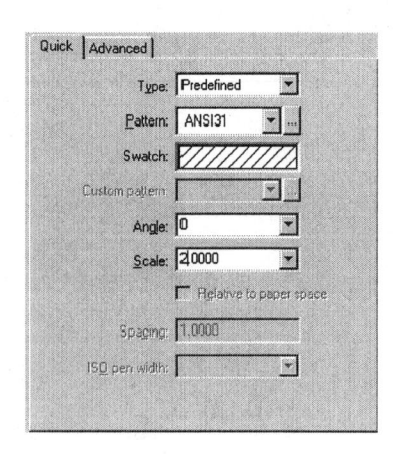

Once the hatch is in, use LINE to add center lines and lines along the top and bottom edges where needed. Keep these in the hatch layer. Use the Layer dialog box to freeze the mesh layer in this viewport. Highlight the layer, then Freeze in the Active viewport.

While creating the hatch and notations, notice that the objects sometimes appear on different Z depths. This is because the section is on the Z 2.5 plane, but any ENDpoint that you pick may be on a different Z depth. Since PLINEs and HATCHs are planar, the first point will determine the Z depth. As long as it looks good from the right side view, this is fine. The information put in is not part of the model itself, but relevant to the drawing only.

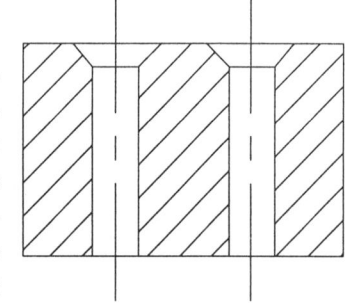

It is drawing- or picture-dependent, and therefore does not need to be coherent in all views.

Step 7 **Saving the View**

Now you can save this view and name it Section.

```
Command:VIEW
Enter an option
   [?/Orthographic/Delete/Restore/Save/Ucs/Window]:S
Enter view name to save:section
```

Step 8 **Preparing the Views for Paper Space**

It may be a good idea to make a simple sketch of the final drawing noting the view scales, DIMSCALEs, and layers current in each view. The final drawing will be plotted on an 11″ × 17″ sheet.

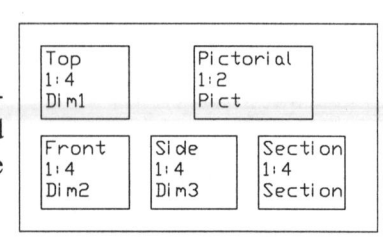

```
Top         Pictorial
1:4         1:2
Dim1        Pict

Front       Side       Section
1:4         1:4        1:4
Dim2        Dim3       Section
```

618 CHAPTER TWENTY-SIX

First restore the viewport configuration that contains the four views. The section layer will appear on all views. For ease in dimensioning, freeze the section layer.

```
Command:VPORTS
Enter an option [Save/Restore/Delete/Join/SI/?/2/3/4]:R
Enter name of viewport configuration to restore or [?]:4QUAD
```

Then create new layers for the dimensions and for the paper space borders called:

DIM1	red
DIM2	yellow
DIM3	green
DIM4	cyan
FRAMES	magenta
PSPACE	blue

The model is on layer 0, Cylinder and 3DFACE.

Step 9 **Dimensioning the Views**

In the top view, generate dimensions on layer DIM1. This is the plan view, so the dimensions will be drawn line-of-sight onto the view. The part is 14 inches long, and will be seen at one-quarter of the original scale when plotted, so the dimensions should be put on with a dimscale of 3. Make sure that these dimensions are created on the layer DIM1.

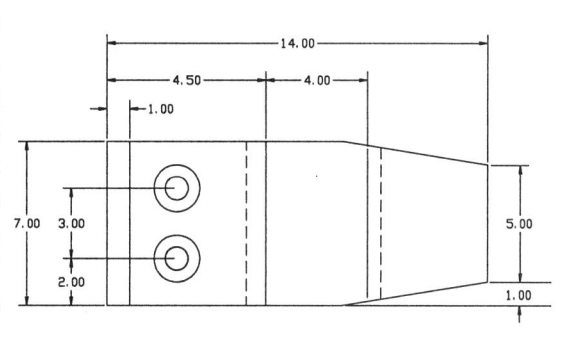

```
Command:(Make DIM1 current)
Command:(Pick in the plan view to make it current)
Command:UCS
Enter an option
   [New/Move/orthoGraphic/Prev/Restore/Save/Del/Apply/?/World]
   <World>:↵
Command:(Set your
   Dimension Style)
Dim:DIMSCALE
Scale factor <1.000>:3
Dim:(add dimensions)
```

> **Notes**
>
> Set UCS to the front face of the part and add the dimensions and hidden lines. Use HIDE to be sure that the lines are not obscured in the plot.

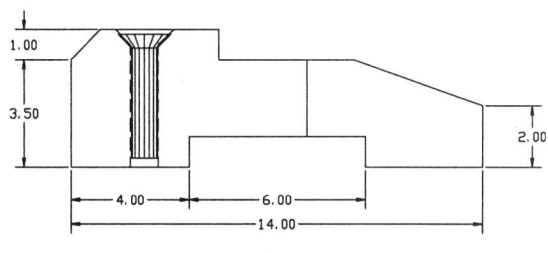

On the front view generate dimensions on DIM2. You will need to change the UCS in order to place the dimensions on the drawing.

Both the View option and the X option can be used. Once changed, dimension the view.

```
Command:(Pick in the front view to make it current)
Command:UCS
Enter an option
   [New/Move/orthoGraphic/Prev/Restore/Save/Del/Apply/?/World]:V
```

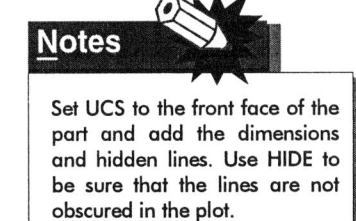

Notes

To freeze a layer in only one viewport, make that viewport active in model space, then freeze the layer using "Active...", the second column from the right.

Use DIM3 and DIM4 for the other views. Compose each view as it will be plotted with any symbols that are necessary at this point. If layers are a problem, use the Layer Properties Manager dialog box to freeze layers in the current viewport. Add hidden lines in the dimensioning layer; the lines obscured by surfaces will not be shown in the final plot.

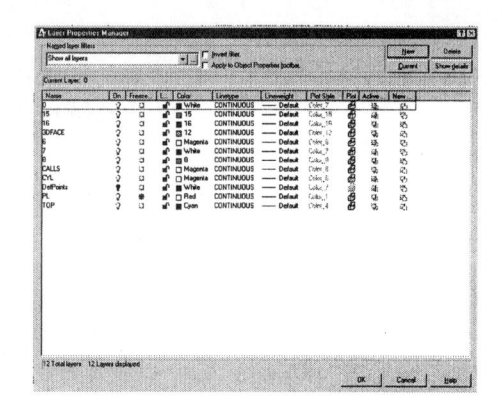

Step 10 **Changing to Paper Space**

Now switch to paper space with TILEMODE off.

> **Toolbar** Pick PAPER on the Status bar.
>
> **Pull Down** From the View menu, pick Paper Space.

The command line equivalent is **TILEMODE**.

AutoCAD displays the Page Setup dialog box. Once you have chosen the page size, the paper space icon will appear. Now you can restore the four viewports and move them around to compile the drawing. If there is a single viewport with a view of your model, just erase it by using ERASE, then picking the frame.

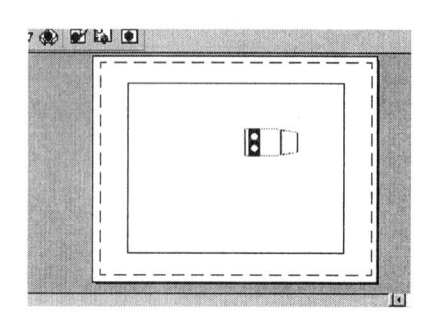

Step 11 **Using MVIEW to Bring up the Views**

The MVIEW or Make VIEWs command is used to place views in paper space. The screen before MVIEW is like a blank piece of paper. The MVIEW command lets you add views of the model to this paper format.

The MVIEW command allows you to create various configurations of viewports, select viewports for hidden line removal, and have different layers active in different viewports.

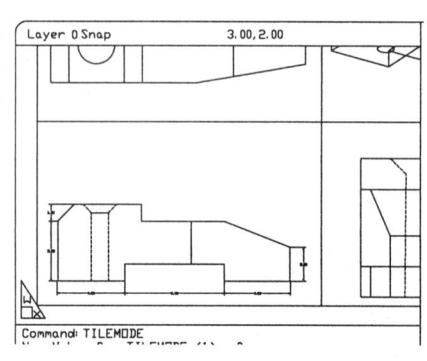

Make the FRAME layer current before starting.

```
Command:(Make FRAME layer current in 'DDLMODES)
Command:MVIEW
Specify corner of viewport or
   [ON/OFF/Hideplot/Lock/Object/Polygonal/Restore/ 2/3/4]
     <Fit>:R
Name of window configuration to insert <ACTIVE>:4QUAD
Fit/ <first point>:1.5,1.5
Other corner:15.5,9.5
```

```
Command: ZOOM
[All/Center/Dynamic/Extents/Previous/Scale/Window]<realtime>:A
```

Specifying 1.5,1.5 for the lower corner and 15.5,9.5 for the view size has left 1.5 inches on all sides of the part. The size of the paper was determined when you entered paper space. If the dialog box did *NOT* appear, use the Insert pull-down menu to open another layout. Choose the plotter, then the paper size.

Each view becomes an individual viewport entity.

If no VPORT configuration is stored, AutoCAD will take the current viewport configuration labeled as ACTIVE. ? will display a list of stored viewports.

Step 12   Using VPLAYER to Freeze Layers in Certain Viewports

Use VPLAYER to freeze the layers not needed in each viewport. DDLMODES or the layer dialog box can be used as well.

> At the command prompt, type in VPLAYER.

```
Command: VPLAYER
Enter an option [?/Freeze/Thaw/Reset/Newfrz/Vpvisdflt]:F
Enter layer name(s) to Freeze:DIM1
Enter an option [All/Select/Current]<current>:S
Select objects: (pick all of
   the views except the plan
   or top view)
Enter an option
[?/Freeze/Thaw/Reset/Newfrz/
   Vpvisdflt]:F
Enter layer name(s) to
   Freeze:DIM2
Enter an option [All/
   Select/Current]<current>:S
Select objects: (pick all
   of the views except the
   front view)
Enter an option [?/Freeze/
   Thaw/Reset/Newfrz/Vpvisdflt]:⏎
```

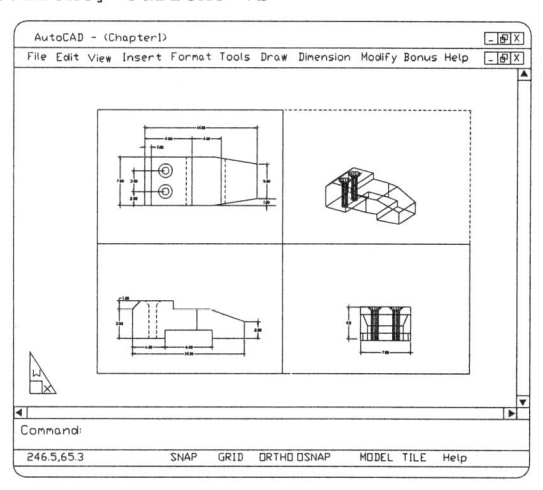

Freeze all layers that should not appear in the viewport.

Step 13   Scale the Views

A setting of 1/4XP will result in the scaled view being exactly one quarter of the size of the original.

ZOOM XP can be used before entering MVIEW or after the views have been added. If you are already in paper space, enter model space to scale your views relative to the final drawing.

```
Command:MSPACE
Command:ZOOM
[All/Center/Dynamic/Extents/
  Previous/Scale/Window]<real
  time>:1/4XP
```

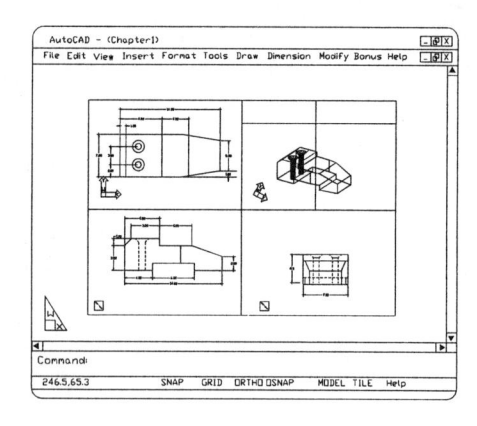

While in this view, PAN the model so that it fits within the boundary. You may need to stretch some dimensions, or return to paper space to stretch the frame of the viewport to contain all of the dimensions.

```
Command:(Pick the next view and continue with ZOOM and PAN)
```

This factor will be needed for all views in this drawing. Be sure to use ZOOM XP on all views, as they may appear correct on-screen if the scale is close to 1:1. Without the ZOOM XP command, perfect scaling cannot be guaranteed.

Step 14 *Lining up the Views*

If the geometry overlaps or conflicts with other views, in paper space simply MOVE the viewport over. Each viewport in paper space is considered an entity—it can be picked up on the "frame" or border—not on the model itself.

```
Command:PSPACE
Command:MOVE
Select objects:(pick the frame
  of the pictorial view)
Select objects:⏎
Specify base point or
  displacement:(pick a point)
Specify second point of
  displacement:
   (pick another point)
```

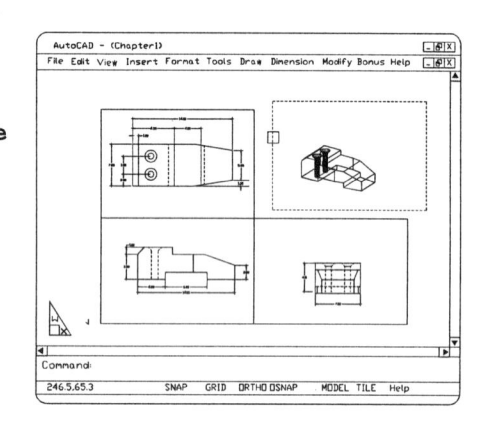

Filters and Autotracking can be used to help line up the views.

```
Command:MOVE
Select objects:(pick 1)
Select objects:⏎
Specify base point or
  displacement:
  END of(pick 2)
Specify second point of
  displacement:
  .x of END of (pick 3)
needs YZ:.Y of END of (pick 4)
needs Z:0
```

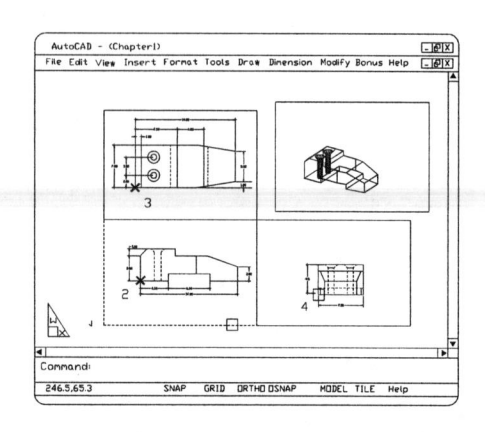

In paper space, points on objects within the view can be accessed as object snaps, but cannot be accessed for editing.

Step 15 **Adding the Section View**

When creating an outline for a drawing, you may also wish to have overlapping views. Viewports created using VPORTS are always non-overlapping or "tiled" views. With MVIEW the viewports can overlap. We now want to place a copy of the section view on the bottom right corner of the screen. We will then have both the right view and the section view. First, move the right view to the left.

```
Command:MOVE
Select objects:(pick the border
   of the right view - pick 1)
Select objects:↵
Specify base point or displacement:(pick 2)
Specify second point of displacement:(pick 3)
```

Now add a viewport.

```
Command:MVIEW
Specify corner of viewport or
   [ON/OFF/Hideplot/Lock/Object/
   Polygonal/Restore/2/3/4]
   <Fit>:(pick 1)
Specify opposite corner:(pick 2)
```

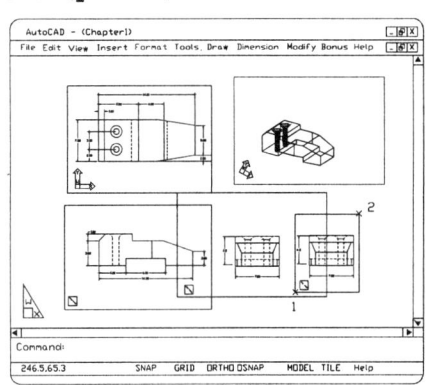

With this command, you can place multiple viewports overlapping each other. The rectangle used to make the view will not show up on the drawing, only the geometry contained within it will. What the new viewport currently contains is an image of the last current viewport. To fill the viewport with the view you want, use VIEW.

In order to add the dimensions or notations onto the section view, restore it in one viewport with the VIEW command.

```
Command:VIEW
  Enter an option
    [?/orthoGraphic/Delete/Resto
    re/Save/Ucs/Window]:R
Enter view name to save:
    SECTION
Restoring model space view.
Select Viewport for view:
    (pick 1)
```

Now add any missing dimensions and notations.

You will notice that you have reverted to model space because of the VIEW command. Use MSPACE with ZOOM 1/4XP to scale the section.

To return to paper space, use the following:

```
Command: PSPACE
(Returning to paper space.)
```

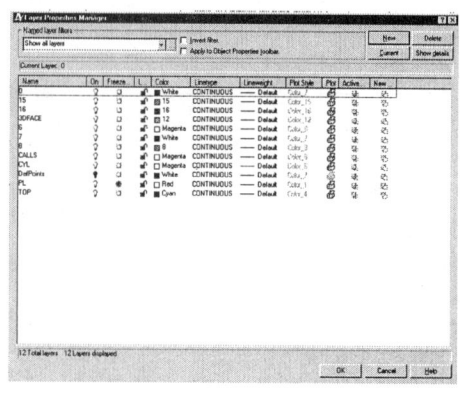

Use the Layer Properties Manager to thaw the section layer globally, then freeze all layers except the section layer in the section view. For single viewports this is by far the easiest method.

Use MOVE to line the section up with the other views.

Finally, use VPLAYER to freeze the section layer in all the other viewports.

> **Notes**
>
> To freeze a layer in only one viewport, make that viewport active in model space, then freeze the layer using "Active...", the second column from the right.

Step 16 — Add the Title Block

In order to see the space you have to work with, add the title block from Practice Exercise 8 so that all views can be scaled and moved to create a balanced drawing. Be sure to change your layer to PSPACE because FRAME will be frozen during plotting.

```
Command: (Use 'ddlmodes to set
    to layer PSPACE)
Command: -Insert
Enter block name or [?]: Title
Specify insertion point: 0,0
Specify X scale factor
    <1>/Corner/XYZ: ⏎
Specify Y scale factor
    (default=X): ⏎
Specify rotation angle <0>: ⏎
```

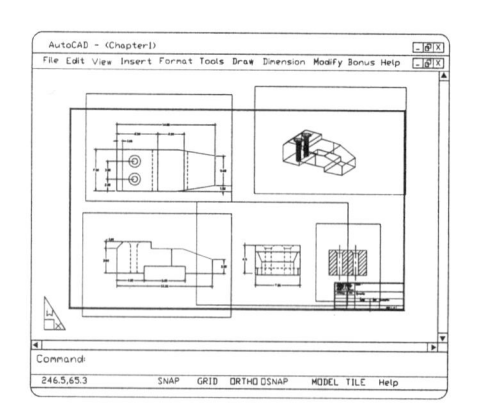

If you have lost the title block file, draw in a pline that would be the same size as the title block, then add the text, etc. in the corner; or use MVSETUP, Title, #9 ANSIB.

Make sure that your title block allows for the plotter rollers; leave at least .5″ on three sides and 1″ on the left side.

Step 17 — Removing Hidden Lines

Using HIDE before the PLOT command in model space will *not* hide the entities in the plot. While they may not show on-screen, the entities will show up on paper.

With the Hideplot option of the MVIEW command, the entities hidden in any particular viewport will be hidden when you finally plot.

The object should be covered with 3DFACEs, so the Hideplot option will make hidden lines disappear. If you are using a pen plotter, also hide the other views to stop the plotter from drawing duplicate lines in the views.

```
Command: MVIEW
Specify corner of viewport or
   [ON/OFF/Hideplot/Lock/Object/
   Polygonal/Restore/2/3/4]
   <Fit>: H
ON/OFF: ON
Select objects: (pick all
   viewports)
```

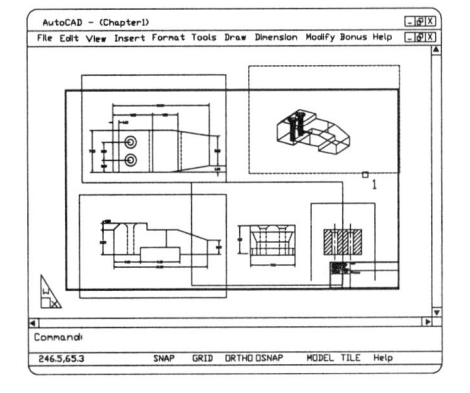

This will provide you with a good pictorial view of the object with hidden lines removed in plotting, plus views that will be plotted with no extra lines.

Step 18 **Turning Off Paper Space Frames or Borders**

The frames or borders for the tiles used to position the views are no longer necessary in the final drawing. Turn off the FRAME layer so that the view borders will be removed, and add any final notations, symbols, or title block information you may need for the final drawing.

```
Command: (Freeze the FRAME
   layer in the Layer
   Properties Manager)
```

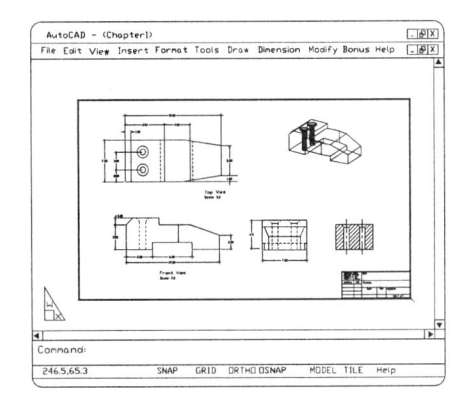

When creating geometry in paper space, the geometry exists on the "paper" itself, not within the view of the part. It is as if the views of the part have been photographed, then placed on transparent decals or slides and arranged on the paper. Any lines, circles, blocks or related data added at this point will enhance the drawing but in no way affect the views. Objects drawn in paper space should be on a separate layer so that they can be frozen when you return to the model. Items drawn in paper space are not accepted as part of the 3D database.

Note that the plines, etc. of the title block are superimposed on the views themselves. The title block is brought in and positioned using INSERT. The text for filling in the details on the title block is put in simply by using the TEXT command.

While you are in paper space you may erase geometry, dimensions, and text that have been entered in the paper space mode. But you cannot erase data that was created in model space and contained within a view.

To switch views when in model space use Ctrl-V or pick the new viewport. If the data is entered in model space, then it is part of your 3D data. To erase it, you must toggle to model space.

Other commands, such as CHANGE and CHPROP, will affect the view as a whole in paper space mode. Again, the entire viewport is accepted as a single entity much the same way that a block is considered a single entity.

Command and Function Summary

CTRL V switches viewports in model space.

Layout is a pull-down menu choice that allows the user to access paper space.

Model space allows for the creation of a model in 2D or 3D space.

MSPACE toggles from model space to paper space viewports.

Paper Space is a 2D drawing layout facility.

PSPACE toggles from paper space to model space.

TILEMODE is a system variable that allows the user to access paper space.

VPLAYER allows layers to be visible or invisible within selected viewports.

Practice Exercise 26

Create this drawing using paper space and MVIEW.

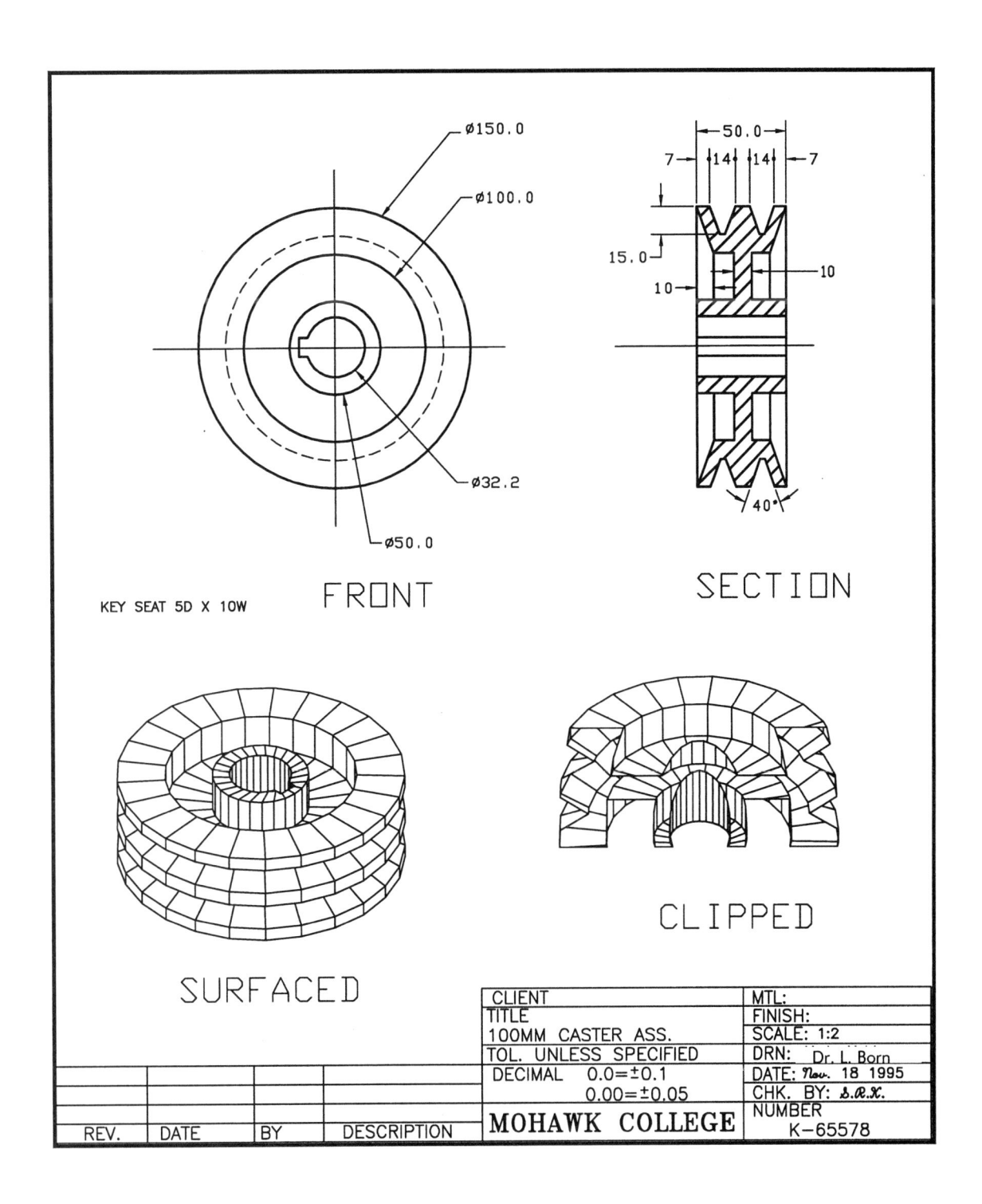

Exercise A26

Create this butterfly chair using EDGESURF, then create a drawing of it in paper space.

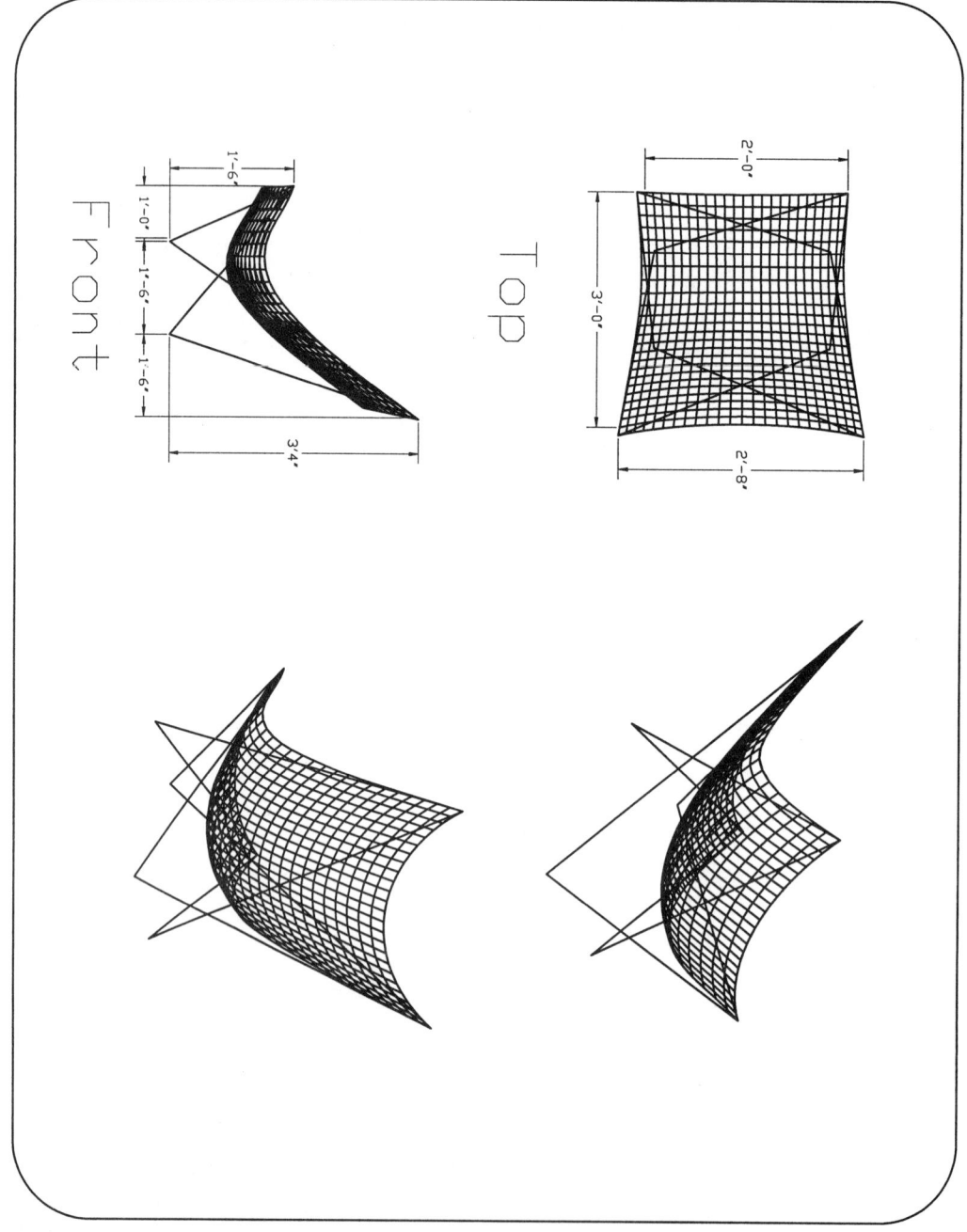

Exercise C26

Create these two footings using 3D objects, then create the drawing using paper space and MVIEW.

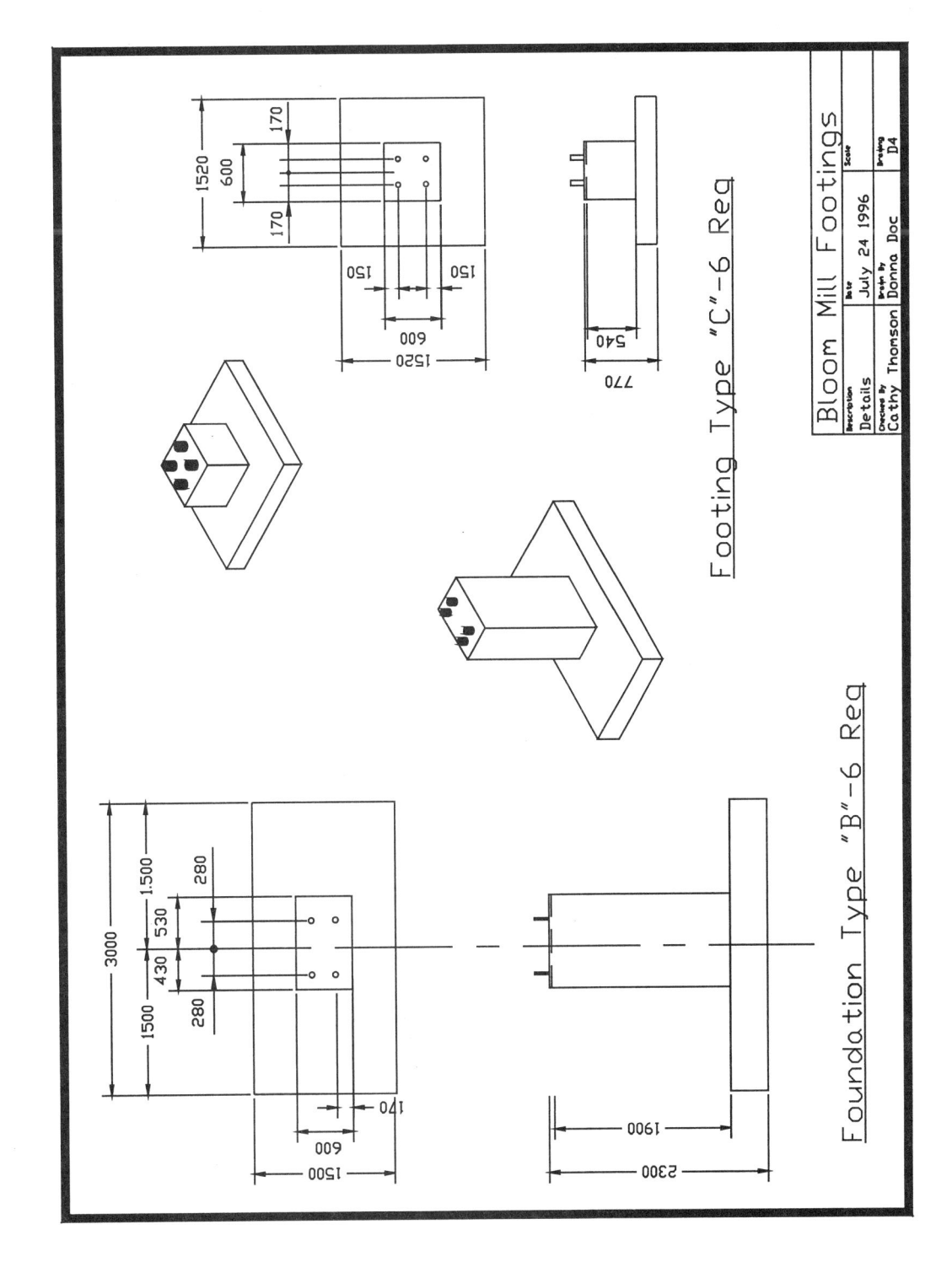

Exercise M26

Create the drawing of this part or a similar part from Chapter 25 using paper space and MVIEW. Remember to use MVIEW with Hideplot to remove the hidden lines in the isometric view.

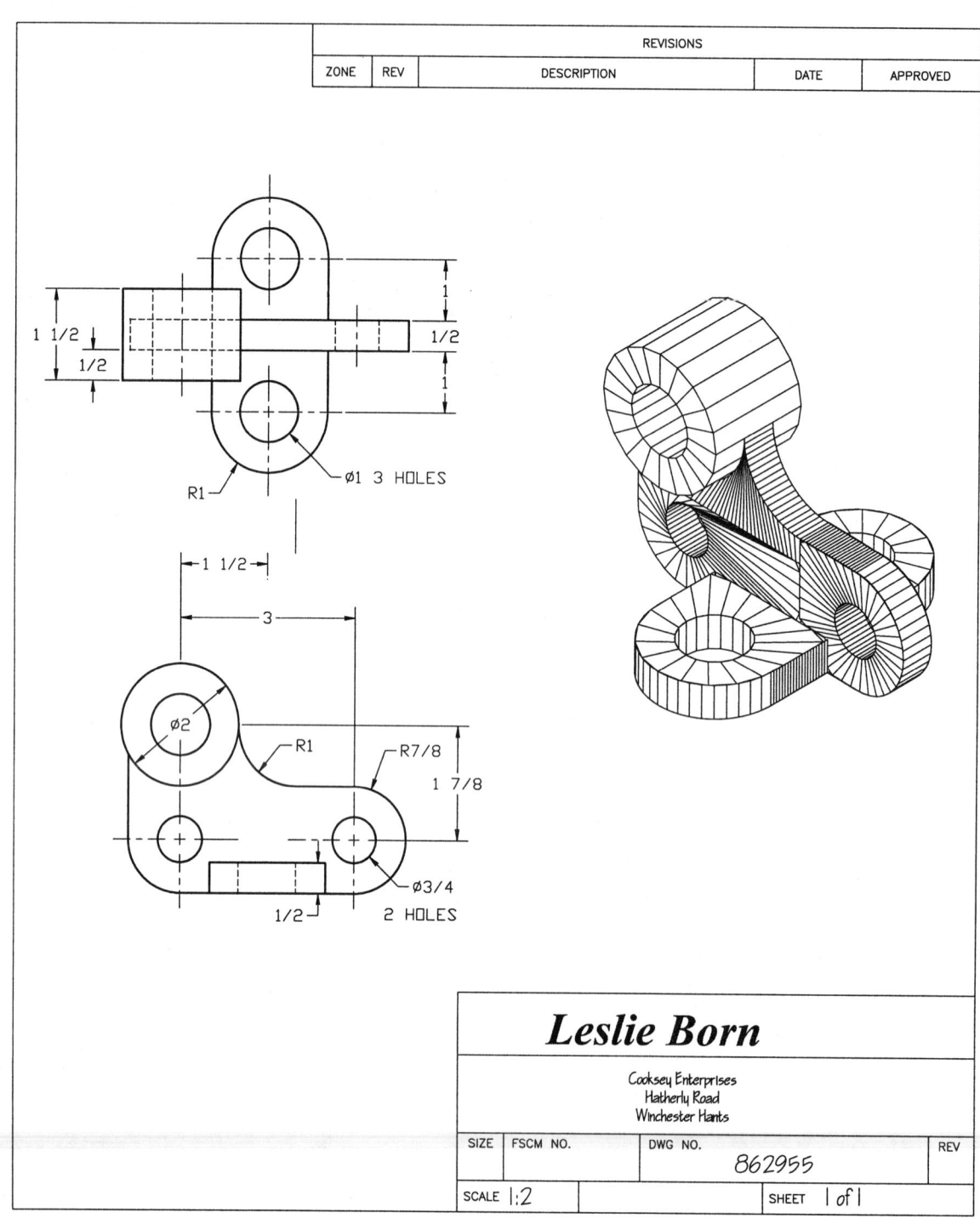

Challenger 26

Design this pulley and provide an assembly view of the object in 3D.

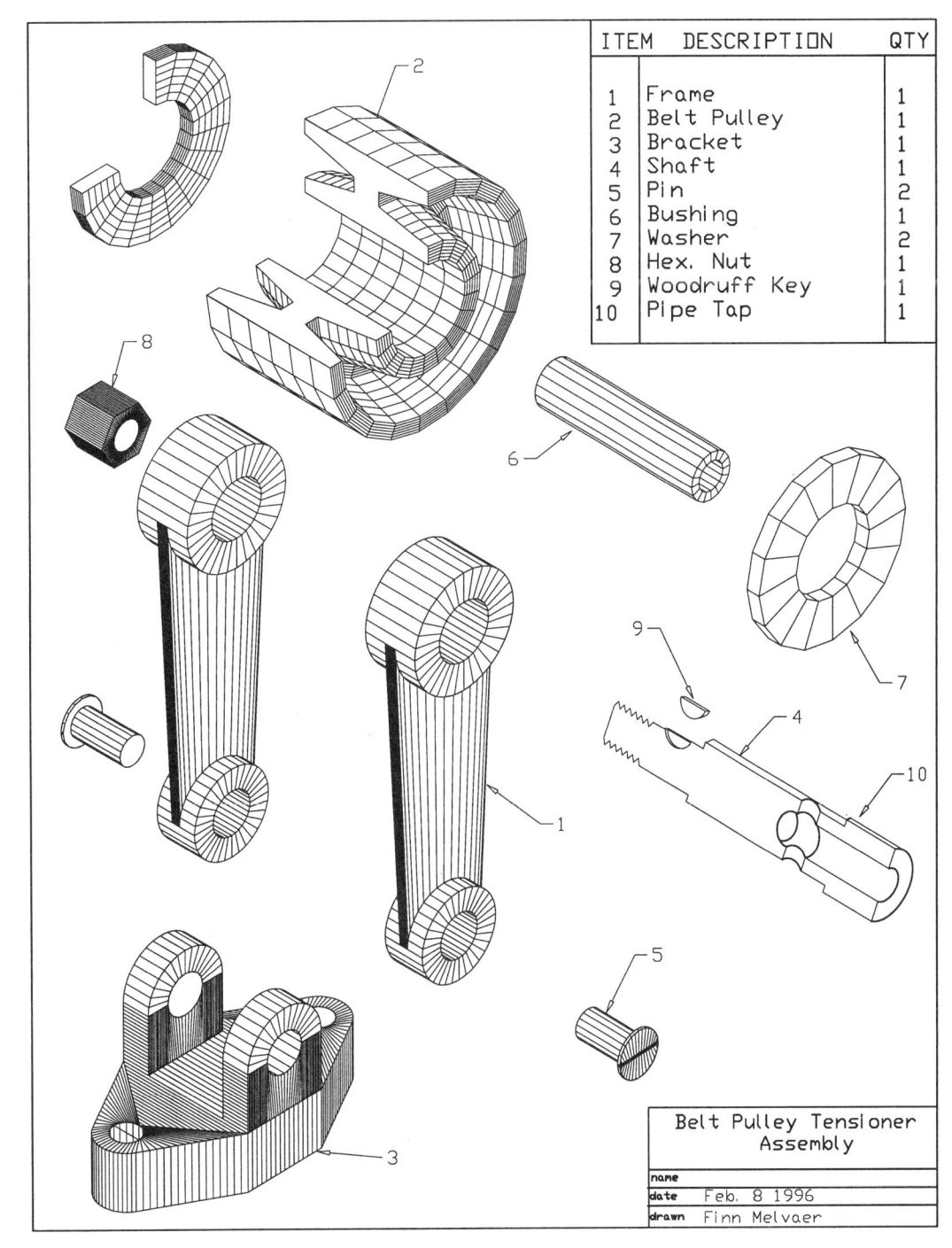

ITEM	DESCRIPTION	QTY
1	Frame	1
2	Belt Pulley	1
3	Bracket	1
4	Shaft	1
5	Pin	2
6	Bushing	1
7	Washer	2
8	Hex. Nut	1
9	Woodruff Key	1
10	Pipe Tap	1

Belt Pulley Tensioner Assembly

name
date Feb. 8 1996
drawn Finn Melvaer

Challenger 26B

Create this C-clamp either surfaced or in solids, then use PSPACE to create the drawing.

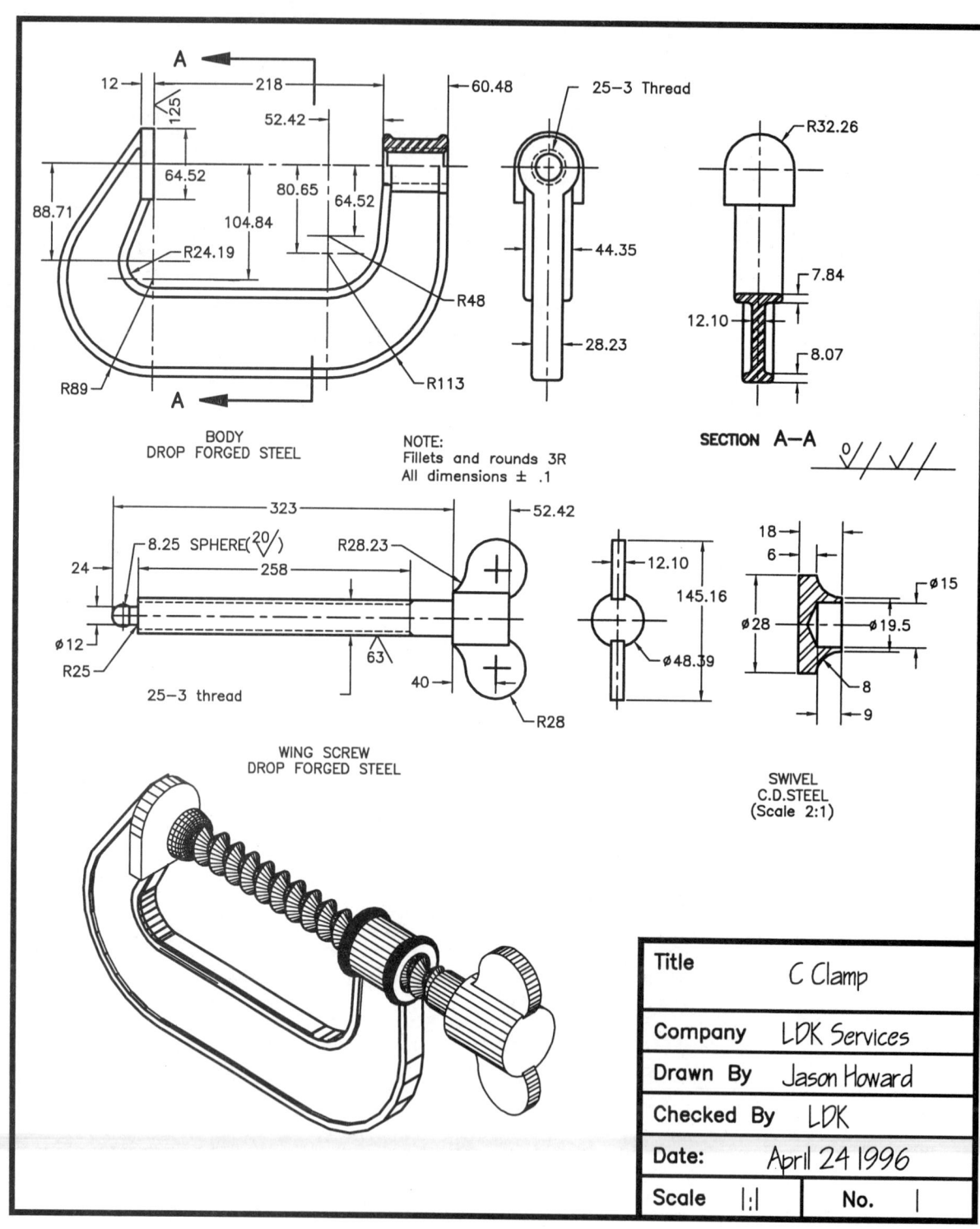

27 3D Shapes, PFACE and Mesh

Upon completion of this chapter, you should be able to:

1. Generate any kind of 3D shape on the AutoCAD menu
2. Manipulate 3D shapes in space
3. Generate a mesh with PFACE
4. Use 3DMESH to create mesh surfaces

OBJECTIVES

More 3D Entities in AutoCAD

So far we have been using AutoCAD to construct objects in space starting from the origin and working with extrusions, the UCS, and basic items of geometry to create objects. We have used lines, arcs, circles, etc., that are extruded in the Z direction, 3DFACEs, and the various surfaces used in 3D.

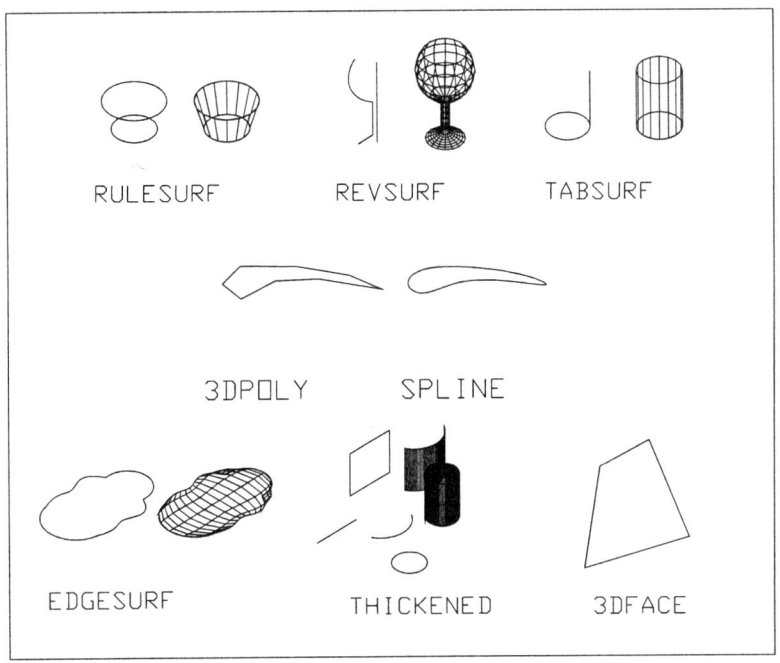

Figure 27-1

3D Commands

In creating 3D geometry with AutoCAD, there is another set of commands that can be quite useful: 3D Objects, accessed through the 3D command. 3D Objects are preprogrammed shapes, three-dimensional polygon mesh objects that look like wireframe objects, but have surfaces. You can enter the shapes listed in the 3D Objects dialog box, as well as create your own shapes and add them to the dialog box.

3D Object commands are quite simple and straightforward to use. They are similar to the Solids commands covered in Chapters 30-33. For those whose computers have limited memory, 3D Object commands are easier to use. 3D Objects can be used to visualize objects in 3D, and to quickly compile 3D images. None of the analysis commands work on 3D Objects.

The 3D Command

The 3D command constructs the following objects which can be shaded or rendered to appear as solid objects.

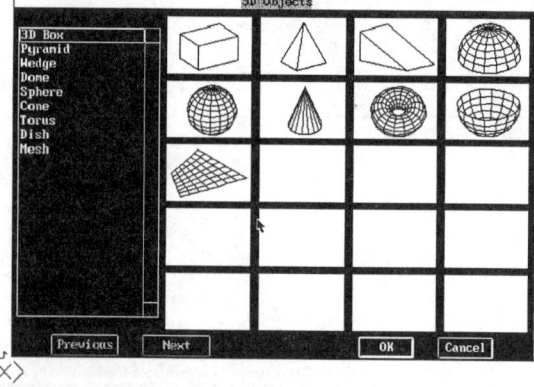

> **Toolbar** From the Surfaces toolbar, select an icon.
>
> **Pull Down Menu** From the Draw pull-down menu, choose Surfaces, then 3D Surfaces, then box, cone, dome, etc.

The command line equivalent is **3D**.

The shapes are selected the same way most icon box items are—with a double pick.

Once you pick the shapes, AutoCAD prompts for the pertinent information needed for completion: diameter, length, etc.

Once the objects are in your drawing, they behave the same as a block. All parts are affected by editing commands, and a single pick identifies the whole shape. Also like blocks, the item can be exploded into its various components with EXPLODE.

Entering 3D at the command prompt will display the following:

```
Command:3D
Box/Cone/DOme/DIsh/Pyramid/Sphere/Torus/Wedge: (enter just the
   first initial(s))
```

3D Objects are used to create objects more quickly than other methods.

The objects drawn are shown in the World Coordinate System with the VPOINT at 2,-2,2. All 3D Objects are drawn relative to the current UCS.

Box

```
Command:3D
Box/Cone/DOme/DIsh/Pyramid/Sphere/
   Torus/Wedge:B
Specify corner point of box: (pick 1)
Specify length of box:3
Specify width of box or [Cube]:5
Specify height of box:1
Specify rotation angle of box about the Z axis or [Reference]:0
```

Figure 27-2

634 CHAPTER TWENTY-SEVEN

If you specify the Cube option, width, length and height each will equal the length input.
Type HIDE to see a closed box.

Wedge

```
Command:3D
Box/Cone/DOme/DIsh/Pyramid/Sphere/
  Torus/Wedge:W
Specify corner point of wedge:0,0
Specify length of wedge:5
Specify width of wedge:3
Specify height of wedge:1
Specify rotation angle  of wedge about the Z axis:0
```

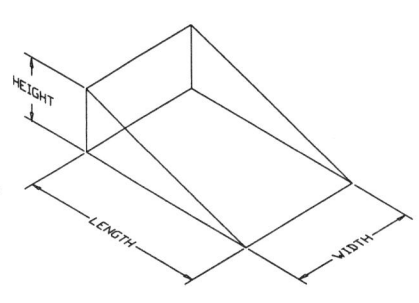

Figure 27-3

The BOX and the WEDGE commands are quite similar in that you first specify the point where the item will start, then the length, width, and height. Finally, in both, you specify the rotation around the Z axis. The height is in the Z direction.

Pyramid

```
Command:3D
Box/Cone/DOme/DIsh/Pyramid/Sphere/
  Torus/Wedge:P
Specify first corner point for base
 of pyramid:0,0
Specify second corner point for base
 of pyramid:3,0
Specify third corner point for base
 of pyramid:3,3
Specify fourth corner point for base
 of pyramid or [Tetrahedron]:0,3
Specify apex point of pyramid or [Ridge/Top]:1.5,1.5,3
```

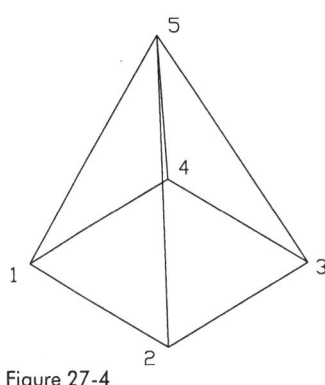

Figure 27-4

This illustrates the default, a quadrilateral base. With the default, you can choose an apex point or two points to define a ridge. If you wanted a tetrahedron, you would specify only the first three points. You would then get a pyramid option for the apex.

```
Command:3D
Box/Cone/DOme/DIsh/Pyramid/Sphere/
  Torus/Wedge:P
Specify first ... pyramid:0,0
Specify second ... pyramid:3,0
Specify third ... pyramid:3,2
Specify fourth ... pyramid or
  [Tetrahedron]:0,2
Specify apex point of pyramid or
  [Ridge/Top]:R
Specify first ridge point:1,1,2
Specify second ridge point:2,1,2
```

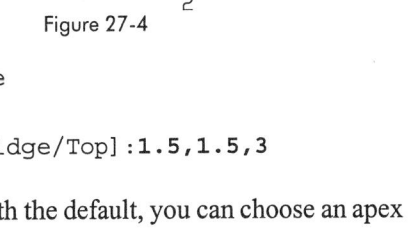

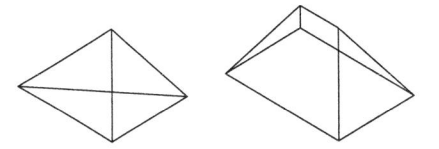

Figure 27-5

3D Shapes, PFACE and Mesh   **635**

Dome

```
Command:3D
Box/Cone/DOme/DIsh/Pyramid/Sphere/
   Torus/Wedge:DO
Specify center of dome: (pick 1)
Specify radius of dome or [Diameter]:.5
Enter number of longitudinal segments for surface <16>:↵
Enter number of latitudinal segments for surface <8>:↵
```

Figure 27-6

Dish

```
Command:3D
Box/Cone/DOme/DIsh/Pyramid/Sphere/
   Torus/Wedge:DI
Specify center of dish: (pick 1)
Specify radius of dish or [Diameter]:.5
Enter number of longitudinal segments for surface <16>:↵
Enter number of latitudinal segments for surface <8>:↵
```

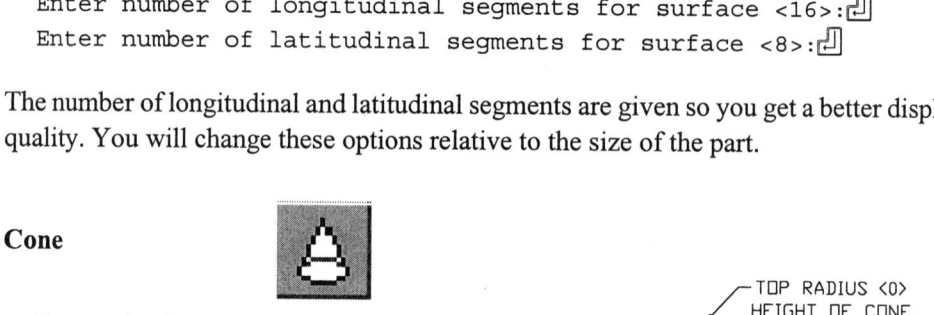

Figure 27-7

The number of longitudinal and latitudinal segments are given so you get a better display quality. You will change these options relative to the size of the part.

Cone

```
Command:3D
Box/Cone/DOme/DIsh/Pyramid/Sphere/
   Torus/Wedge:CO
Base center point: (pick 1)
Diameter/<radius> of base:1
Diameter/<radius> of top <0>:↵
Height:2
Number of segments <16>:↵
```

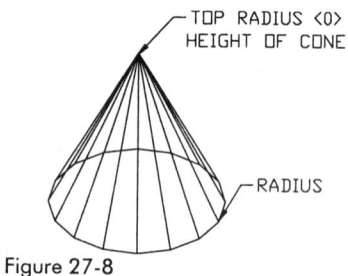

Figure 27-8

Again, the number of segments results in a different display.

Sphere

```
Command:3D
Box/Cone/DOme/DIsh/Pyramid/Sphere/
   Torus/Wedge:S
Specify radius of sphere or
[Diameter]:3,3,3
Enter number longitude segment for surface of sphere:1
Enter number of segments for surface of sphere:16
```

Figure 27-9

Torus

```
Command: 3D
Box/Cone/DOme/DIsh/Pyramid/Sphere/
  Torus/Wedge: T
Specify center point of torus: 4,4,4
Specify radius of torus or [Diameter]: 4
Specify radius of tube or
[Diameter]: .5
Enter number of segments around tube circumference: 10
Enter number of segments around the torus circumference: 12
```

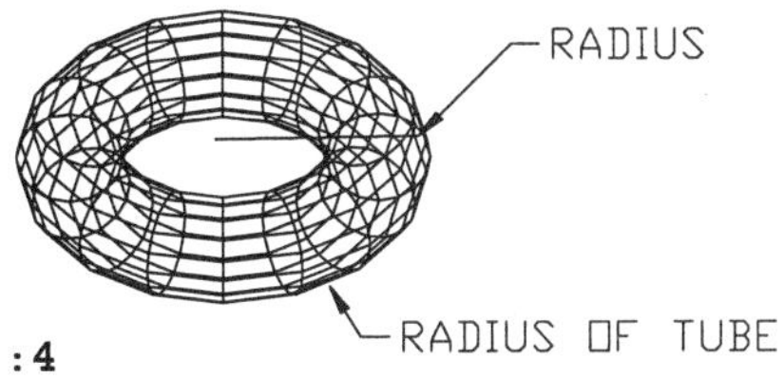

Figure 27-10

Using 3D Objects

The main benefit of using CAD is that it offers a more efficient way of producing drawings and data for manufacturing and analysis purposes. Therefore, it makes sense to use the software in the most efficient way possible.

Consider these automated programs and see how they can be used to speed up surface generation.

BOX versus 3DFACE

If you drew a rectangular shape with 3DFACE, and covered all six sides of the object in the 3DFACE "surface," it would take six 3DFACE commands to do it (one for each face). Even if you wrapped the faces around the rectangle, you would still use three commands.

Note: These points must have X, Y, and Z coordinates given at the numbers.

```
Command: 3DFACE
Specify first point or [Invisible]: 1
Second point: 2
Third point: 3
Fourth point: 4
Third point: 5
Fourth point: 6
Third point: 7
Fourth point: 8
Third point: 1
Fourth point: 2
Third point: ⏎

Command: 3DFACE
First point: 1
Second point: 4
Third point: 5
Fourth point: 8

Command: 3DFACE
First point: 2
Second point: 3
Third point: 6
Fourth point: 7
```

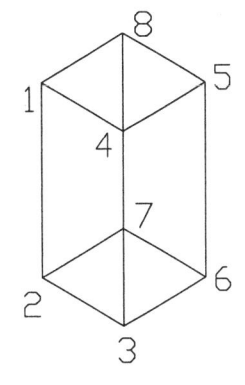

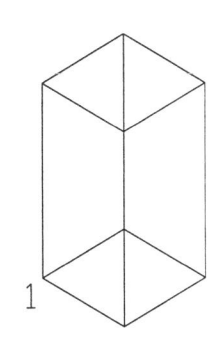

Notes

The 3DFACE command prompts have been truncated for easy reading.

Figure 27-11

The points in the 3DFACEs can be entered using co-ordinates or existing geometry.

3D Shapes, PFACE and Mesh **637**

Or,
```
Command:BOX
Specify corner point of box: (pick 1)
Specify length of box:2
Specify width of box:2
Specify height of box:5
Specify rotation angle of box about the Z axis or [Reference]:0
```

Clearly, the BOX takes less time.

Similarly, with the CONE command, there is much less work than using either RULESURF or TABSURF.

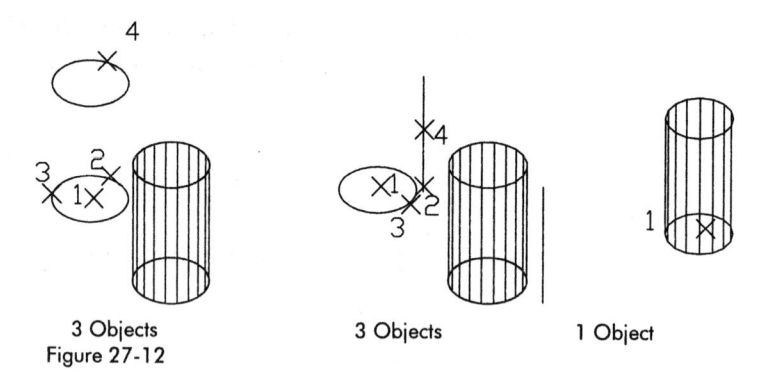

3 Objects
Figure 27-12

3 Objects

1 Object

Notes

The user responses for "picks" have been truncated to (p1) etc. For easy reading.

RULESURF
```
Command:CIRCLE
  <Center point>:(p1)
  <Radius>:.5
Command:COPY
Select objects:L
Select objects:↵
Base point:(p2)
Displacement:@0,0,2
Command:RULESURF

First def.curve:(p3)
Second defining
  curve:(p4)
```

TABSURF
```
Command:CIRCLE
  <Center point>:(p1)
  <Radius>:.5
Command:LINE
From point:(p2)
To point:@0,0,2
To point:↵
Command:TABSURF
Select path
  curve:(p3)
Select direction
  vector:(p4)
```

CONE
```
Command:CONE
Base centerpoint:(p1)
  Dia<Rad>of base:.5
  Dia<Rad>of top:.5
  Height:2
  Number of segments:6
```

You can see by the above example that CONE is by far the easiest way to put in the cylinder (assuming that the geometry is not already existing). If it is existing, the time would be about the same. However, there is another point to be considered: the number of items or objects in the file. In the first two cases, you have two extra items that should be put on a different and nondisplayed layer. In the third example, there is only one object.

If there is a chance that you might accidentally erase the cone, you could have trouble remembering where it was, so the first two examples could save time and trouble. But if the CONE is easily located, it clearly makes for a neater file.

The examples above illustrate the difference between using 3D Objects and AutoCAD's surfacing methods. Again, 3D Objects are simply AutoLISP programs to speed up your processes.

If you are creating a BOX shape, but you want to have one face with a difference series of surfaces, you can explode the BOX and erase the 3DFACE in your way.

The PFACE Command

The next type of surface we will look at is the PFACE mesh. PFACE creates a three-dimensional polyface mesh vertex by vertex. It is a polygon mesh composed of vertices and faces defined by those vertices. Like 3DMESH, PFACE is mostly used in conjunction with AutoLISP or application software.

PFACE is much like the 3DFACE command, but where 3DFACE makes a series of faces with overlapping edges, PFACE makes a single face generated from multiple points. The command asks you to identify the three-dimensional coordinates of each point along the edge of the object you want to describe. The points are, in fact, vertices.

To find the PFACE command:

> **Toolbar** There is no button for PFACE.

```
Command: PFACE
Specify location for vertex 1:0,0,0
Specify location for vertex 2:1,1,1
```
(Continue specifying vertices)
```
Specify location for vertex 10:↵
```

Press ↵ to indicate that you are finished entering vertices. Then you will be prompted to identify which vertices are on which faces, starting with face 1 and continuing until you indicate with ↵ that no more faces are required.

Next the PFACE command will prompt you for the vertices for each face.

```
Face 1, vertex 1: 1
Face 1, vertex 2: 2
Face 1, vertex 3: 3
```

You can enter as many points as you like, and you will be prompted for as many faces as you like. You enter in succession the vertex numbers that define the face you are describing. When you have completed the vertices of one face, press ↵ to advance to the next. When you have completed all the faces, a second ↵ will exit you from the command.

You can also enter the letter C for Color or the letter L for Layer to have the next face shown in a different color or on a different layer. Once you specify the new value, the face and vertex will be requested.

In the following exercise, there are two faces in a simple object described.

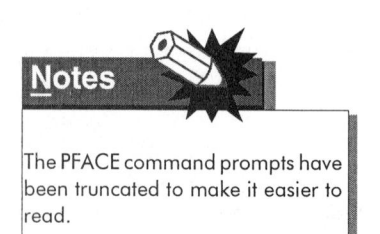

```
Command: PFACE
Vertex 1:0,0,0
Vertex 2:0,2,0
Vertex 3:4,4,0
Vertex 4:4,0,0
Vertex 5:4,0,4
Vertex 6:2,0,3
Vertex 7:0,0,4
Vertex 8:↵
Face 1, vertex 1:1
Face 1, vertex 2:2
Face 1, vertex 3:3
Face 1, vertex 4:4
Face 1, vertex 5:↵
Face 2, vertex 1:color
New color <BYLAYER>:red
Face 2, vertex 1:1
Face 2, vertex 2:4
Face 2, vertex 3:5
Face 2, vertex 4:6
Face 2, vertex 5:7
Face 2, vertex 6:↵
Face 3, vertex 1:↵
```

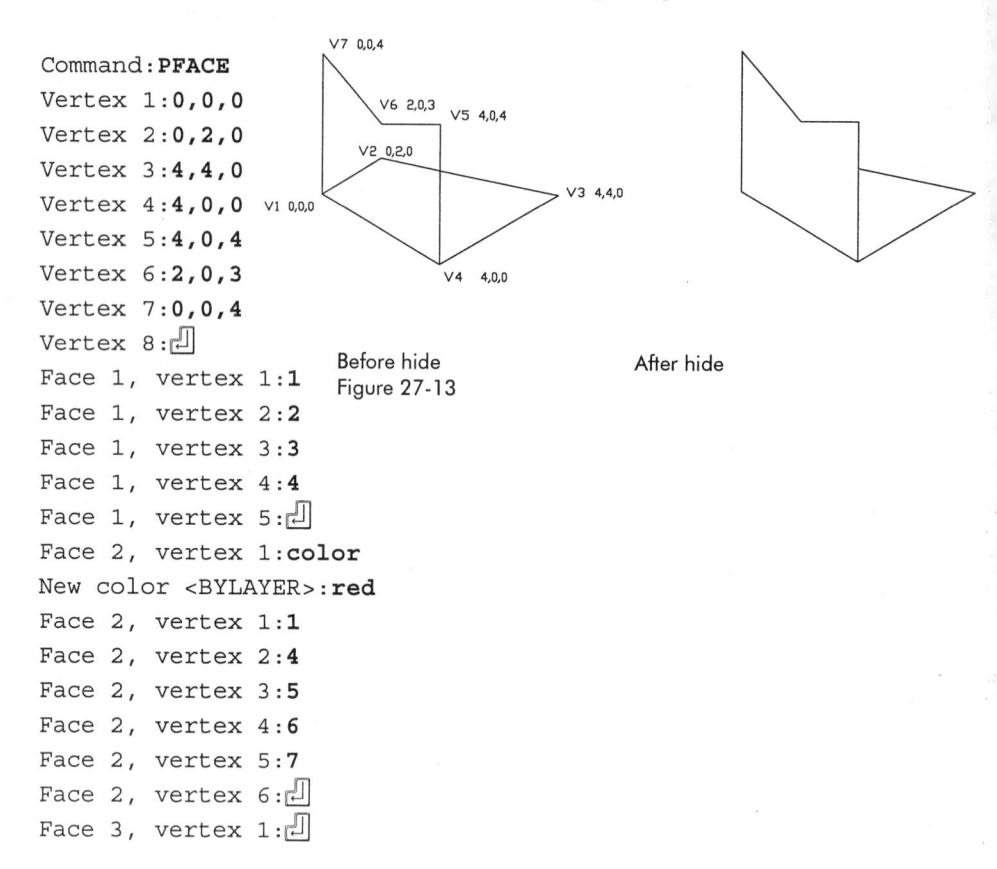

Before hide
Figure 27-13

After hide

> **Notes**
> The PFACE command prompts have been truncated to make it easier to read.

> **Notes**
> If you make a mistake, you must redo the whole sequence. The faces are not shown until complete.

The result is the mesh shown in the illustration. If you would like any edge invisible, enter a negative number for the beginning vertex of the edge.

You cannot edit this mesh with PEDIT, but the other editing commands such as ARRAY, MOVE, COPY, ROTATE, etc., can be used.

The visible entities can be SNAPped.

As you can see from the example, creating a PFACE mesh can be tedious; you may be better off with another type of surface, but if the geometry already exists, you may want to try it.

The trick to using PFACE effectively is to map out the vertices and faces *before* you begin. In the following illustration, face 1 is defined by vertices 1, 5, 6, and 2. Face 2 is defined by vertices 1, 4, 3 and 2. Face 3 is defined by vertices 1, 4, 7, and 5; and face 4 is defined by vertices 3, 4, 7, and 8.

3DMESH

3DMESH creates a three-dimensional wireframe mesh according to defined points which create vertices. The surface is made up of rows and columns of faces which pass through a matrix of points in space creating surface pattern.

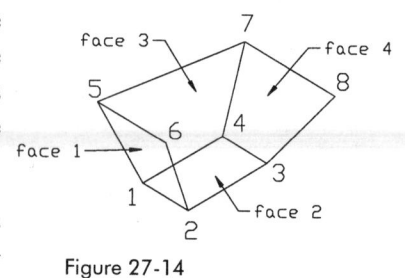

This surface, like EDGESURF, is a polynomial surface, a surface defined in both directions by many numbers or points. The points on mesh surfaces are

Figure 27-14

entered at a specific integer, and are generally worked out using LISP programs to automatically generate the mesh points.

Take a look at most manufactured goods you see everyday—everything from car dashboards, to contact lenses, to razors, to kettles, to airplanes etc.—all are designed with surface programs like these.

The surface in Figure 27-15 was generated by simply picking 16 points: 4 points in the *n* direction and 4 points in the *m* direction. *M* and *n* are indices specifying the number of rows and columns that make up the mesh. In the next mesh, we have entered specific points. To find the 3DMESH command:

> **Toolbar** From the Surfaces toolbar, choose 
>
> **Pull Down Menu** From the Draw menu, choose Surfaces, then 3DMESH.

The command line equivalent is **3DMESH**.

> **Notes**
>
> The 3DMESH command prompts have been truncated to make them easier to read.

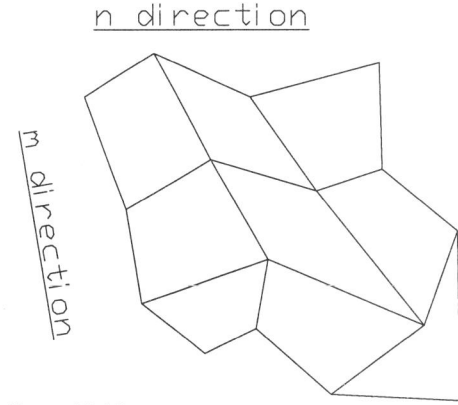

```
Command: 3DMESH
Enter size of mesh in M direction: 4 - 4 rows in one direction
Enter size of mesh in N direction: 4 - 4 rows in the other
Specify location for vertex <0,0>:0,0,0
Vertex <0,1>:10,0,0
Vertex <0,2>:20,0,0
Vertex <0,3>:30,0,0
Vertex <1,0>:0,10,10
Vertex <1,1>:10,10,10
Vertex <1,2>:20,10,10
Vertex <1,3>:30,10,10
Vertex <2,0>:0,15,15
Vertex <2,1>:10,15,15
Vertex <2,2>:20,15,15
Vertex <2,3>:30,15,15
Vertex <3,0>:10,20,20
Vertex <3,1>:20,20,20
Vertex <3,2>:30,20,20
Vertex <3,3>:40,20,20
```

Figure 27-15

The default is to have a mesh of one unit squares. To visualize how this surface is put to use, imagine that you have made a model out of chicken wire (like the base on papier maché figures, Santa Clauses, etc.). The 3DMESH is like the paper that covers the chicken wire. The points are at the junctures of the wire mesh.

It is important that you know this surface exists—it is the major sales feature any CAD system can offer to a manufacturing firm. Since the points must be entered row by row and column by column, the command lends itself to AutoLISP. PFACE is a similar surface, but it uses a smaller and less rigid formula. The major advantage of 3DMESH is that it can be used to make extensive undulating surfaces which can be edited later.

Using PEDIT to Edit 3DMESH

3DMESHs are constructed through a series of points defined in two directions. PEDIT can be used with plines to create either a spline or a Fit curve polyline. PEDIT is used with

3DMESHs in the same way, along two different axes. In addition, PEDIT can be used to edit one or more surface vertices to make the surface fit through a different series of points. In order to understand how PEDIT works, take a look at PEDIT with PLINE.

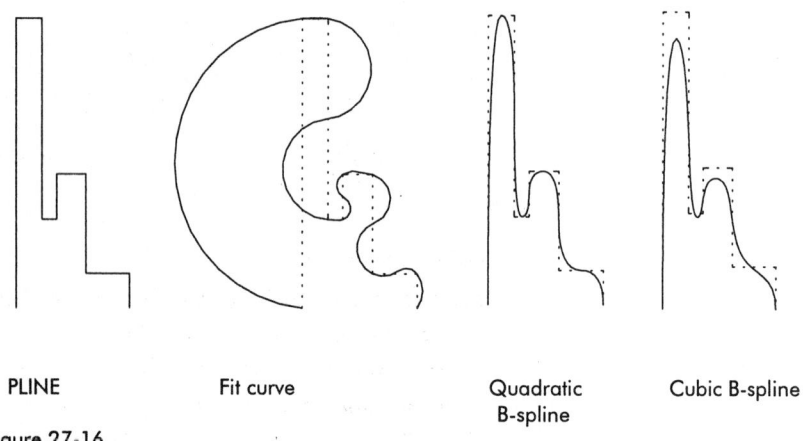

PLINE   Fit curve   Quadratic B-spline   Cubic B-spline

Figure 27-16

As noted in Chapter 3, the PEDIT command creates either a curve segment or a spline using the vertices of the selected plines as the control points for the curves. With the Fit curve option, the curve is constructed by pairs of arcs passing directly through the control points. With the Spline option, the curve fits through the two endpoints of the pline, and is then pulled towards the other points on the pline, but does not necessarily pass through the other control points.

The SPLINETYPE system variable controls the type of spline curve: 5 results in a quadratic B-spline, 6 in a cubic B-spline.

The SPLINESEGS system variable controls the number of line segments between each pair of control points. The greater the number, the more line segments, thus a smoother representation of the spline curve.

With 3DMESHs, the PEDIT command performs the same way, except in two different directions and into the Z depth.

In this example, we have created a 3DMESH through a series of regularly spaced points.

```
Command: 3DMESH
Mesh M size: 4
Mesh N size: 6
Vertex (0,0): 0,0
Vertex (0,1): @4,0
Vertex (0,2): @0,0,4
etc.
```

Figure 27-17

Once completed, the PEDIT command can be used to smooth the surface, either with a quadratic B-spline or a cubic B-spline equation.

Original   Quadratic B-spline   Cubic B-spline

Figure 27-18

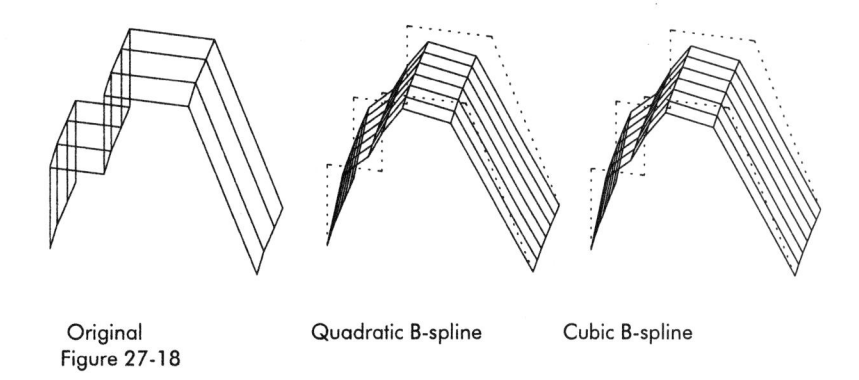

```
Command: PEDIT
Select polyline: (pick the surface)
Enter an option [Edit vertex/Smooth surface/
  Desmooth/Mclose/Nclose/Undo]: S
Generating segment 2...
 Enter an option [Edit vertex/Smooth surface/
  Desmooth/Mclose/Nclose/Undo]:
```

The surface type is determined by the system variable SURFTYPE. The available surface types are as follows:

Surftype	Description
5	Quadratic B-spline
6	Cubic B-spline

The minimum mesh size to create a quadratic B-spline surface is 3 × 3 units. The minimum mesh size for cubic is 4 × 4 units. PEDIT will not be able to calculate any surface with more than 11 vertices in either direction.

The system variable SPLFRAME controls the display of the polygon meshes to which surfaces have been fit (dotted lines in the illustration).

The Decurve option takes the curve out of the surface.

In editing a PLINE, you can use PEDIT to move the position of any of the vertices to create a more pleasing spline. With a 3DMESH, this is even more important as the Edit vertex option can be used to edit the entire surface.

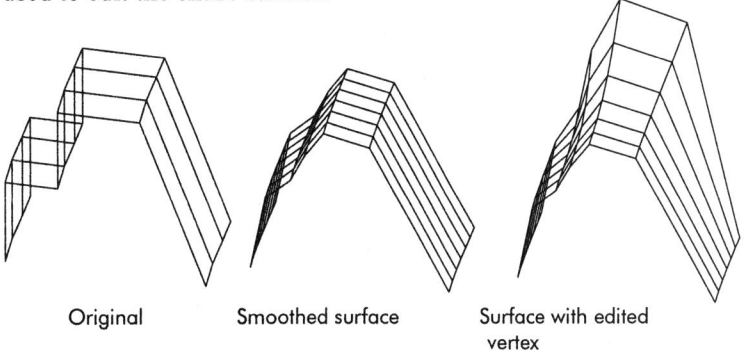

Original   Smoothed surface   Surface with edited vertex

Figure 27-19

3D Shapes, PFACE and Mesh   **643**

```
Command:PEDIT
Select polyline: (pick the surface)
Enter an option [Edit vertex/Smooth surface/
  Desmooth/Mclose/Nclose/Undo]:E
Enter a vertex editing option.
[Next/Previous/Break/Insert/Move/REgen/Straighten/Tangent/Width
  /eXit]:M
Specify new location for marked vertex:
```

You can respond with either a 3D point location or by selecting the point on the screen.

The command will toggle through each control point in the order they were entered. A large X will be shown to highlight your position. The Left and Right options allow you to move in the N direction; Up and Down allow you to move in the M direction. The Move option moves the vertex to a new location.

Prelab 27 3DMESH and 3D Objects

Step 1 In this exercise we will make a small house nestled in a large lot. Use the coordinates listed to create a 25 × 35 meter lot on a surface that slopes 4 meters at some points.

```
Command:3DMESH
Enter size of mesh in M direction: 7 - 7 rows in one direction
Enter size of mesh in N direction: 7 - 7 rows in the other
Specify location for vertex (0,0):0, 0,0
Vertex (0,0):0, 0,0
Vertex (0,1):5,1,0
Vertex (0,2):10,2,0
Vertex (0,3):15,1,0
Vertex (0,4):20,0,0
Vertex (0,5):25,1,.5
Vertex (1,0):0,5,.5
Vertex (1,1):5,5,.5
Vertex (1,2):10,5,1
Vertex (1,3):15,7,1
Vertex (1,4):20,6,1
Vertex (1,5):25,6,1
Vertex (2,0):0,10,.5
Vertex (2,1):5,11,1
Vertex (2,2):10,12,2
Vertex (2,3):15,11,1
Vertex (2,4):20,10,1.5
Vertex (2,5):25,11,2
Vertex (3,0):0,15,1
Vertex (3,1):5,15,1
Vertex (3,2):10,17,2.5
Vertex (3,3):15,16,2
Vertex (3,4):20,15,2
Vertex (3,5):25,16,3
Vertex (4,0):0,20,1.5
Vertex (4,1):5,21,2
Vertex (4,2):10,22,2.5
Vertex (4,3):15,21,3
Vertex (4,4):20,21,2.5
Vertex (4,5):25,20,2
Vertex (5,0):0,25,3
Vertex (5,1):5,26,3
Vertex (5,2):10,27,3.5
Vertex (5,3):15,26,4
Vertex (5,4):20,25,3
Vertex (5,5):25,25,3.5
Vertex (6,0):0,30,3
Vertex (6,1):5,31,3.5
Vertex (6,2):10,31,3.5
Vertex (6,3):15,30,4
Vertex (6,4):20,31,3
Vertex (6,5):25,31,2.5
Vertex (7,0):0,30,3
```

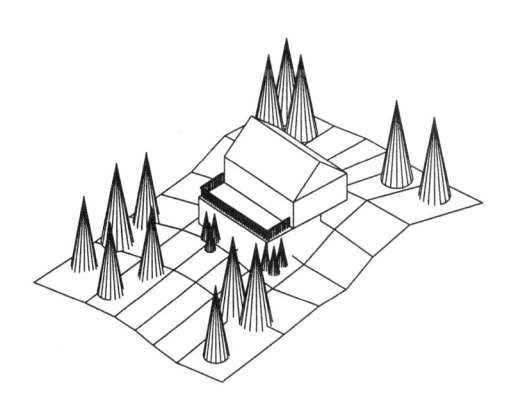

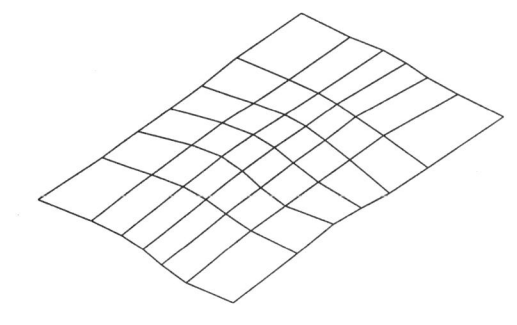

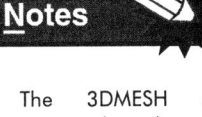

Notes

The 3DMESH command prompts have been truncated to make them easier to read.

```
Vertex (7,1):5,31,3.5
Vertex (7,2):10,31,3.5
Vertex (7,3):15,30,4
Vertex (7,4):20,31,4
Vertex (7,5):25,31,2.5
```

Step 2 This lot looks like the bulldozers have already been on it. Put some more hills on the lot by using PEDIT.

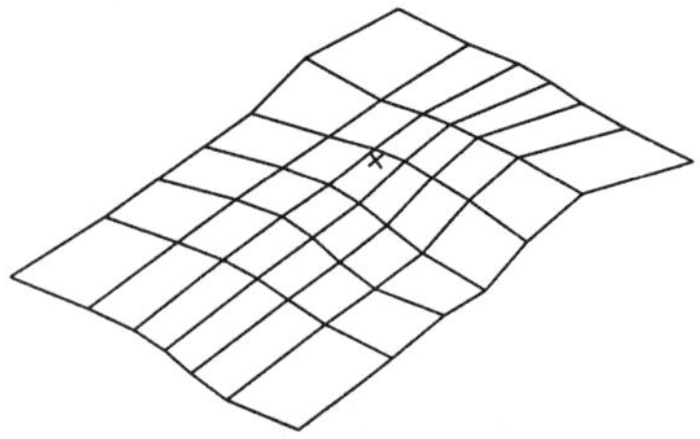

```
Command:PEDIT
Select polyline: (pick the surface)
Enter an option [Edit vertex/Smooth
surface/Desmooth/Mclose/Nclose/Undo]:E
 Enter a vertex editing option.
[Next/Previous/Break/Insert/Move/REgen
/Straighten/Tangent/Width/eXit]:M
Specify new location for marked vertex:
:@0,0,2
```

Step 3 Now use 3D Objects to place the house in the lot. The house will be a back-split; one end of the bottom floor will open onto the back yard, and the other end will be nestled into the hill. Use Z0 to place the house.

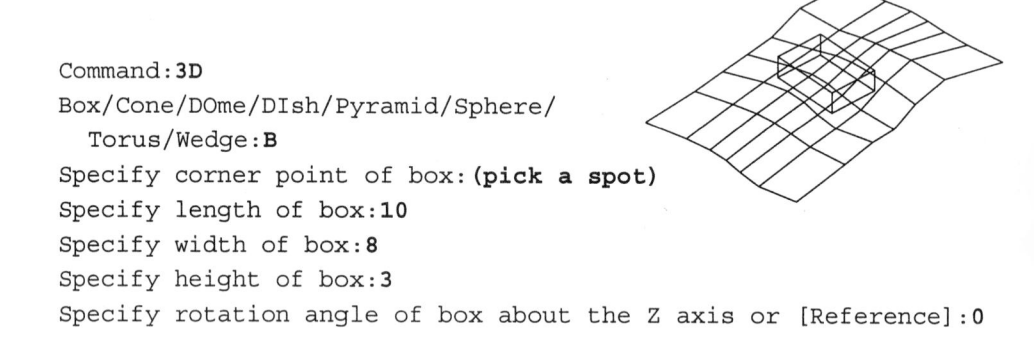

```
Command:3D
Box/Cone/DOme/DIsh/Pyramid/Sphere/
   Torus/Wedge:B
Specify corner point of box:(pick a spot)
Specify length of box:10
Specify width of box:8
Specify height of box:3
Specify rotation angle of box about the Z axis or [Reference]:0
```

Use the same command to place another box on top of the first, midway through the bottom floor so that the top floor opens up onto the higher edge of the hill, and the exposed top of the lower box can be an outdoor patio or terrace.

Step 4 Use the Pyramid option to place the roof. You will need to place a line for the roof ridge first.

If you are planning to use SHADE, use different colrs for the roof and walls.

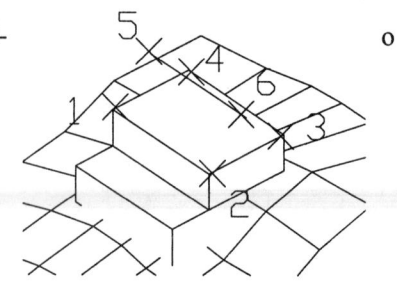

```
Command: 3D
Box/Cone/DOme/DIsh/Pyramid/Sphere/Torus/Wedge: P
Specify first corner point for base of pyramid: (pick 1)
Specify second corner point for base of pyramid: (pick 2)
Specify third corner point for base of pyramid: (pick 3)
Specify fourth corner point for base of pyramid or
    [Tetrahedron]: (pick 4)
Specify apex point of pyramid or [Ridge/Top]: R
First ridge point: (pick 5)
Second ridge point: (pick 6)
```

Step 5 Now that the house is placed, you can use PEDIT again to make sure that the hill meets the house.

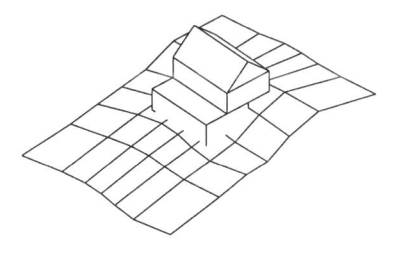

Step 6 Finally use the cylinder option to place trees on the lot.

```
Command: 3D
Box/Cone/DOme/DIsh/Pyramid/
    Sphere/Torus/Wedge: C
Base center point: (pick a point)
Diameter/<radius> of base: 3
Diameter/<radius> of top <0>: ↵
Height: 7
Number of segments <16>: ↵
```

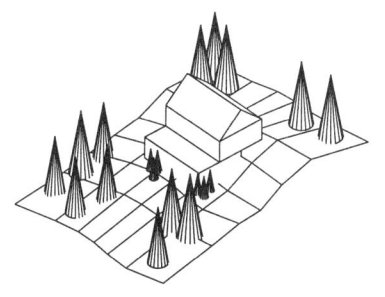

If you have time, make small cones for the balustrades of the railing on the terrace; make the bottom and top .1. Then use UCS and 3point to set the *X* and *Y* values to the terrace, and ARRAY the cones. Finally, add the top of the railings with 3D Box.

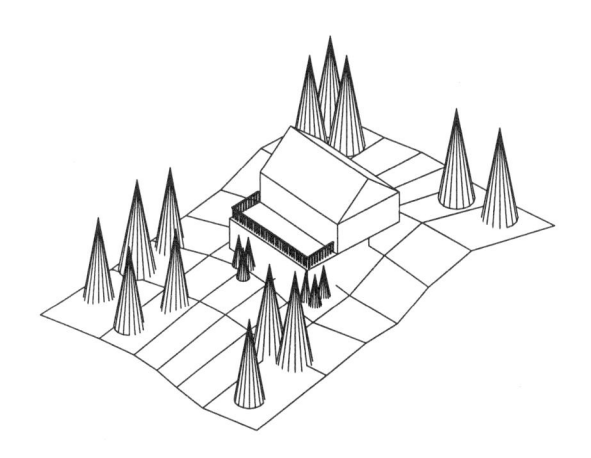

Command and Function Summary

3D Command constructs objects which can be shaded and rendered as solid objects.

Practice Exercise 27

Using the 3D Objects command, create a small suburban house with a few trees and a pool with an inner tube and a beach ball.

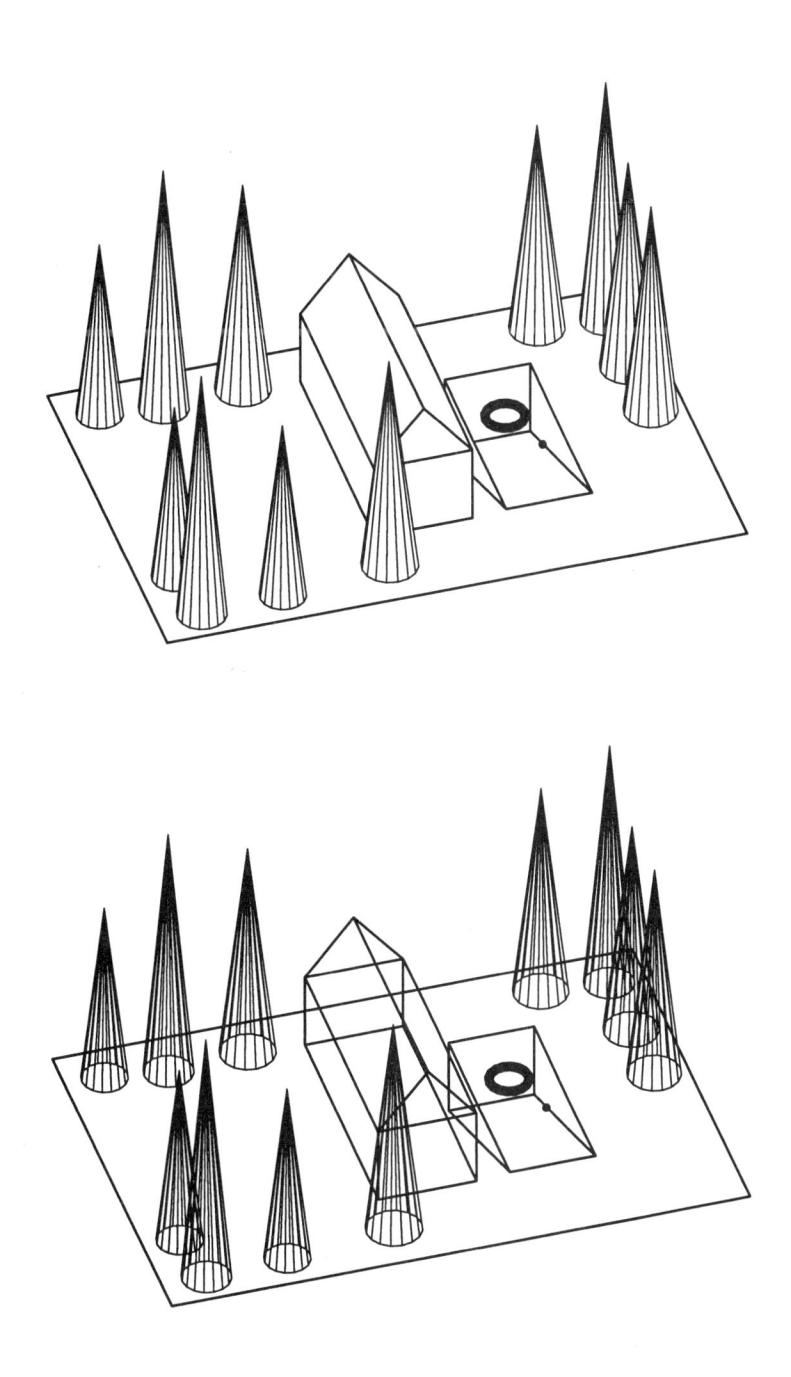

Exercise A27

Using the 3D command with the Box option, create this staircase. Make sure that the railings and tread spacing are to code requirements. You will need to reorient your UCS to place the railings. Use HIDE to view it properly.

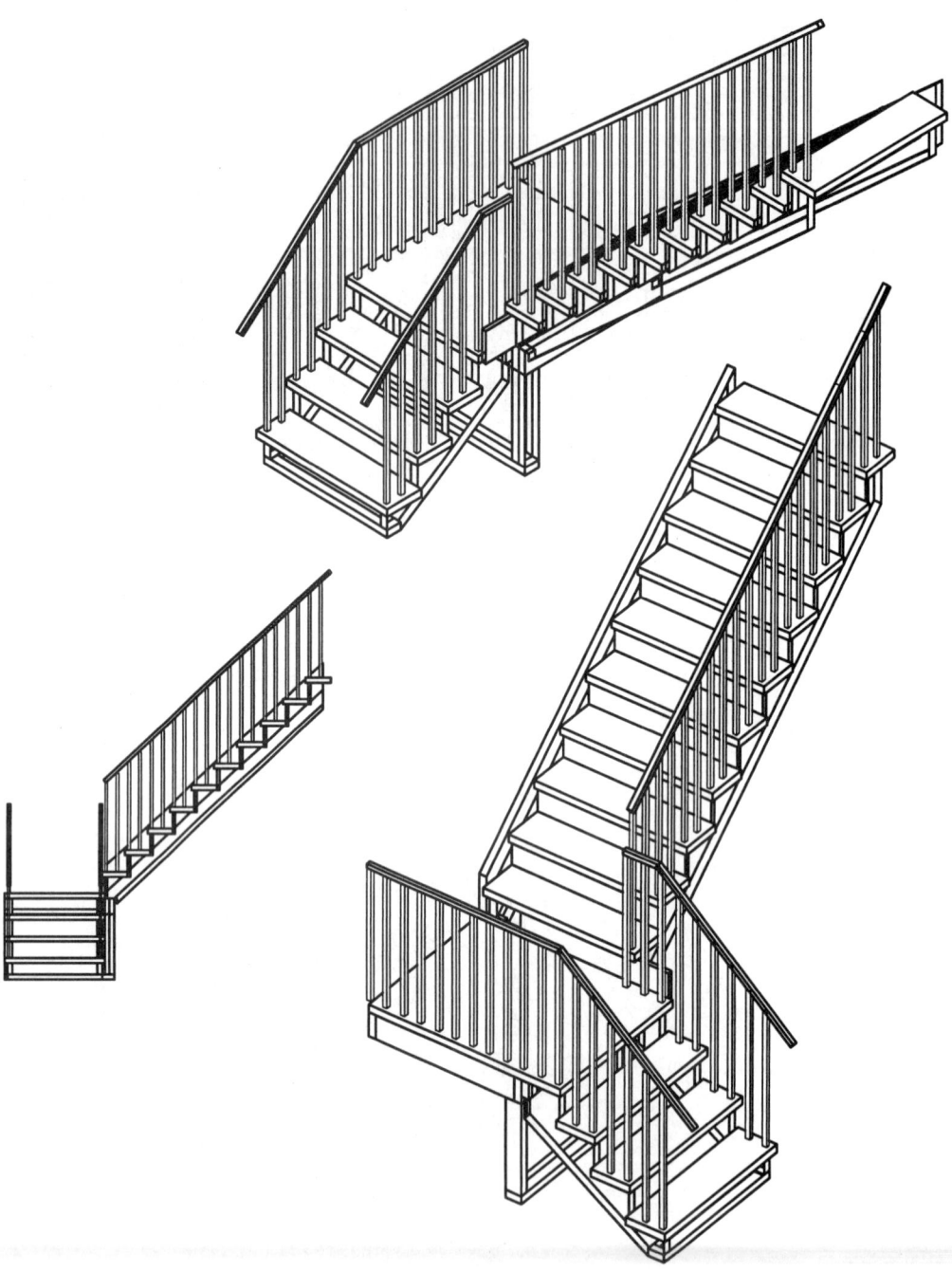

Exercise C27

Use Box, Wedge, and Cone to construct the lookout tower on a bridge as in the illustration. You may need to change the UCS to place the wedges. Use ARRAY to add the cones for the detailing on the top. This exercise will give you good practice in constructing shapes in 3D.

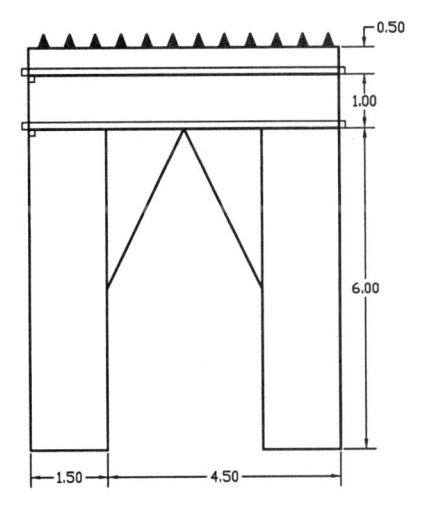

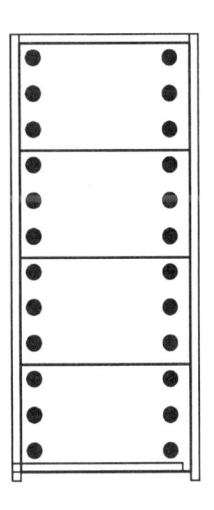

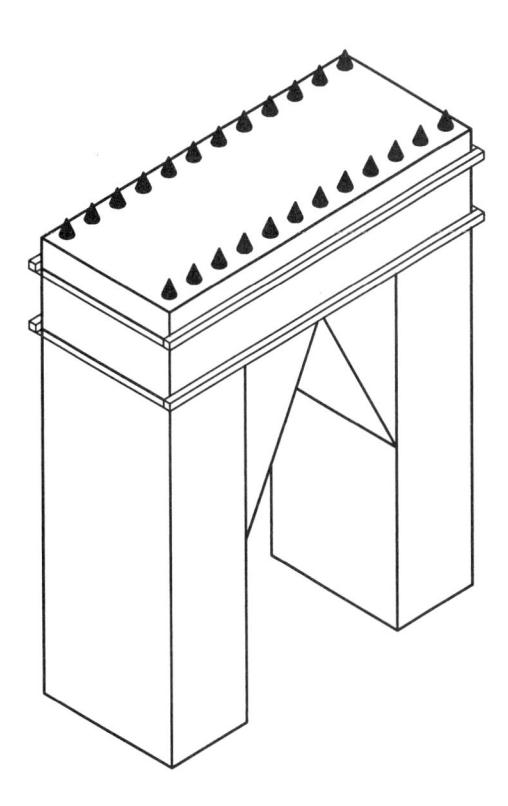

Exercise M27

Using 3D Objects plus the other surfacing commands you know, generate a lens, a lens base, and a viewfinder for the camera. Then, if you have time, create a camera base and surface it. Place the lens, viewfinder, and flash on the camera (see Exercise 22). You can make the lens and the lens base using DOME, CONE, and PLINE. You can make the viewfinder using BOX, WEDGE, and PYRAMID.

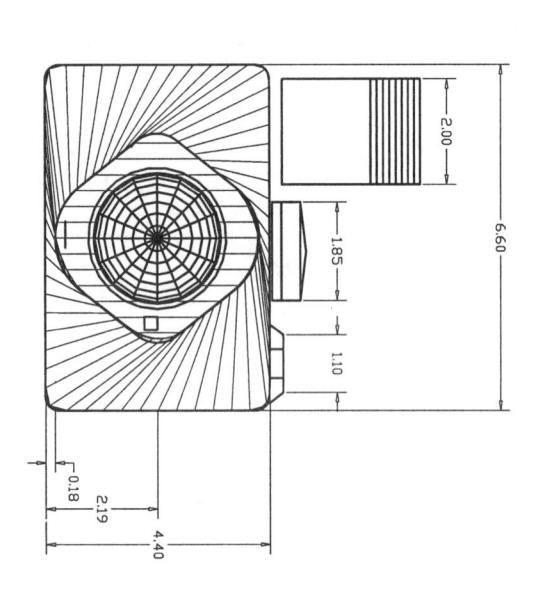

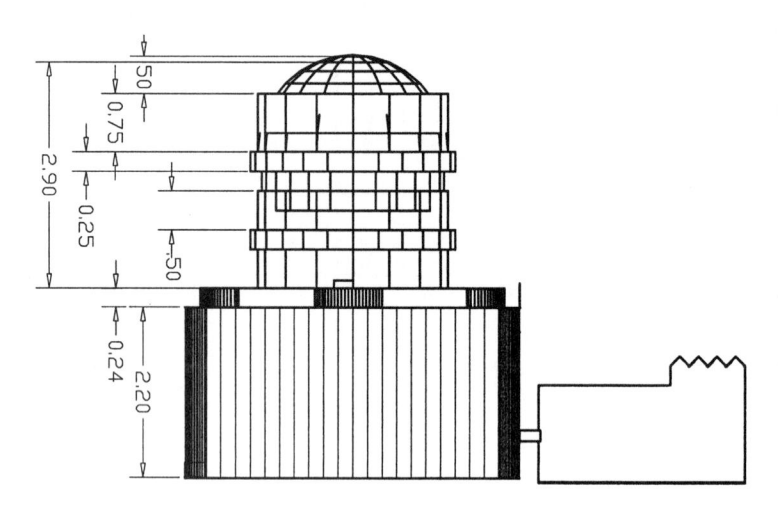

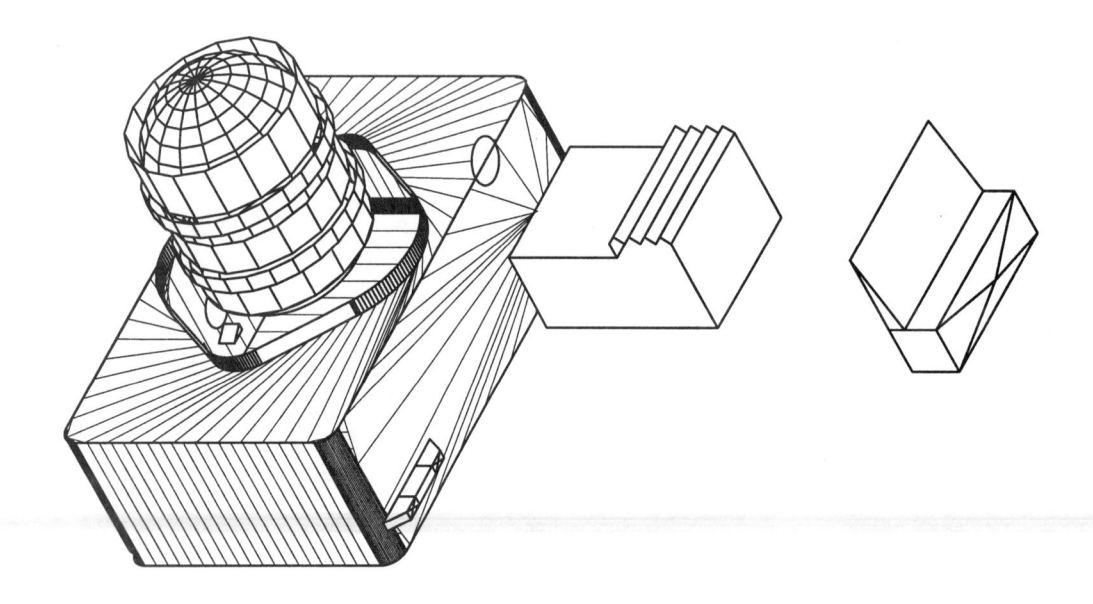

Challenger 27

Create a fireplace with details as shown below.

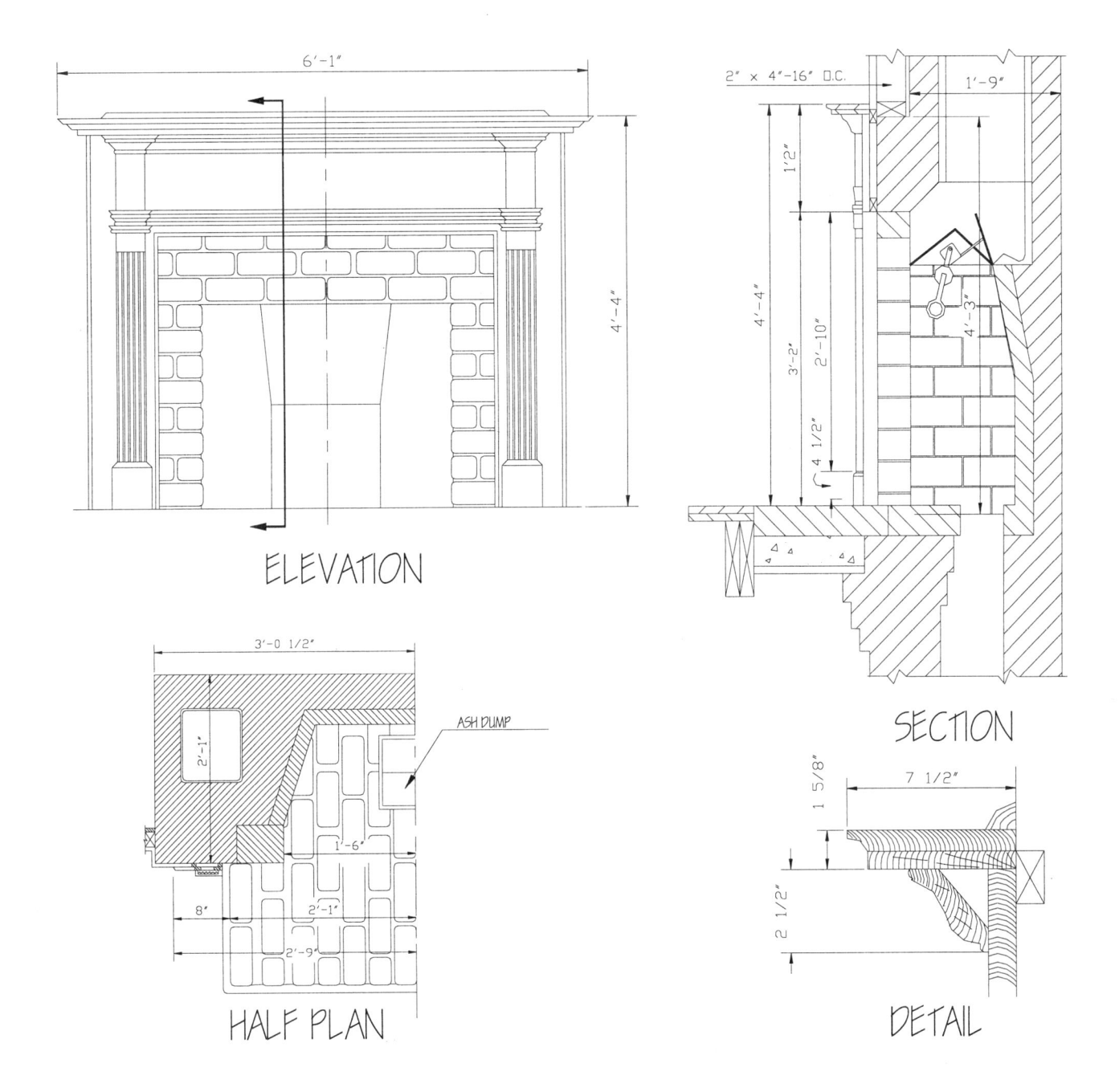

ELEVATION

HALF PLAN

SECTION

DETAIL

3D Shapes, PFACE and Mesh

Challenger 27B

Using 3D objects, construct the second floor of the house, and perhaps the floor boards as well.

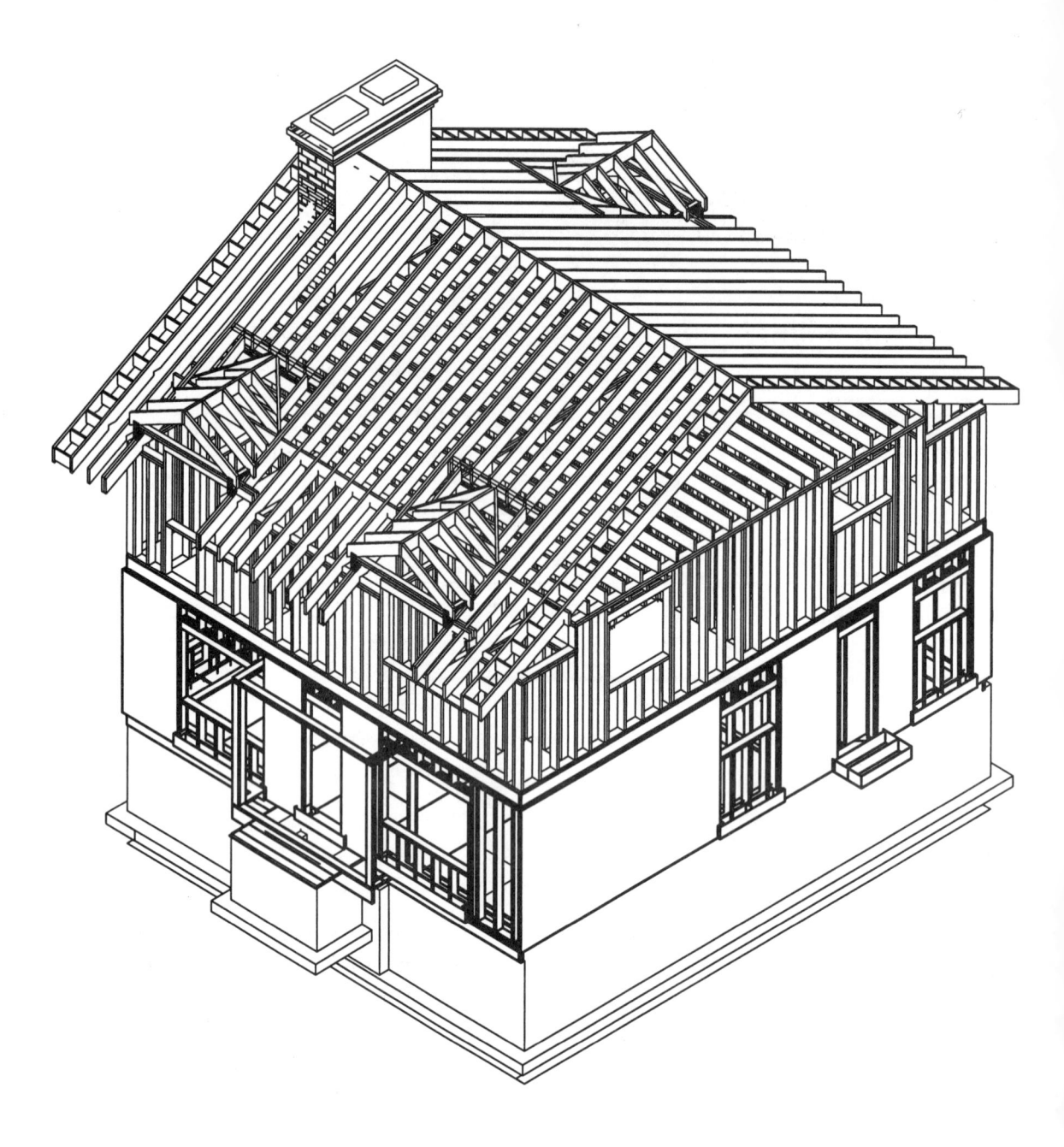

28 Three-Dimensional Solids

Upon completion of this chapter, you should be able to:

1. Create and merge 3D solid objects
2. Subtract solid objects from existing objects
3. Fillet and chamfer 3D objects

What Are Solids?

In the early years of CAD, there were basically two methods of describing 3D parts. The wireframe method used points, lines, and arcs to describe a structure; once described, the object could be covered with a surface. (This approach is covered in Chapters 20-27.) The second method was to create parts by using a series of existing 3D shapes or primitive objects that could be merged into the desired final product. These are 3D solids.

In previous chapters we looked at creating 3D geometry and surfacing it. Now we will look at creating geometry by using shapes or Boolean geometry. AutoCAD's solid modeler creates objects that represent the full volume of an object. It is often easier to create complex solid shapes using this method.

Solids are created from a series of solid shapes: box, wedge, cone, cylinder, etc., that are unioned or combined together to create complex shapes. You can join solids together, subtract them from each other, and also find common volumes.

Like meshes and surfaces, solids are displayed as a wireframe until you hide, shade, or render them. For engineering purposes, the solids can then be analyzed for mass properties. Solids can then be used in NC (numerical control) applications, and also for FEM (finite element modeling).

Line Visibility

The ISOLINES system variable controls the number of tessellation lines used to visualize curved portions of the wireframe. The FACETRES system variable adjusts the smoothness of shaded and hidden line removed objects. System variables are available under the options menu.

Toolbar There is no button for this command.

The command line equivalent is ISOLINES.

```
Command: ISOLINES
Enter new value for isolines <4>:16
```

The isolines will all update to the current isoline value.

Accessing Solids

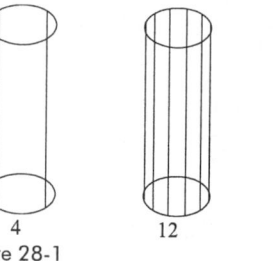

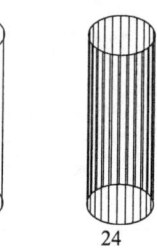

The solids modeler requires a lot of memory. If you are in a lab and saving your files on a floppy disk, write the files to your C: or D: drive (the hard drive), then copy them to a floppy disk later. Don't take a chance on doing something wonderful then watching the whole thing crash because youe floppy disk is not large enough. A Zip drive or similar drive will avoid these problems.

Figure 28-1

Converting AME (Advanced Modelling Extension) Models

In Releases 9 through 12, AutoCAD constructed solids using a function called AME. Should you happen to want towork with solid objects from these releases, they will need to be converted by using AMECONVERT.

AME objects can be converted to AutoCAD solid objects, deleting the AME models. Release 2000's solid modeler has increased accuracy so objects may look slightly different. To convert AME models, use the following procedure.

First open the drawing that contains the AME model, then access the AME Convert command, and select the region (see page 716) or solid you want to convert.

> **Toolbar** There is no button or menu choice for this command.

The command line equivalent is **AMECONVERT**.

Creating Solid Objects

With solids, the process of entering the base geometry is similar to that of 3D Objects (see Chapter 27). With Solids, the user enters boxes, cones, cylinders, and other shapes that are accepted as solid shapes. The shapes that can be created are box, cone, cylinder, solid, torus, and wedge.

When creating 3D objects, always divide your screen into at least two viewports (four is often best), and make sure you always have at least one pictoral view.

Make sure that your point entry is accurate. Once you start processing, there is no easy way of turning back.

Box

With the BOX command, you can create a solid box. The base of the box is always parallel to the *X-Y* plane of the current UCS.

> **Notes**
> Do not pick from the 3D objects dialog box for solids.

> **Toolbar** From the Solids toolbar, choose Box.
>
> **Pull Down Menu** From the Draw menu, Solids; then Box.

The command line equivalent is **BOX**.

```
Command:BOX
Specify corner of box or
   [Center]: (pick 1)
Specify corner or
   [Cube/Length]:L
Specify length:3
Specify width:5
Specify height:1
```

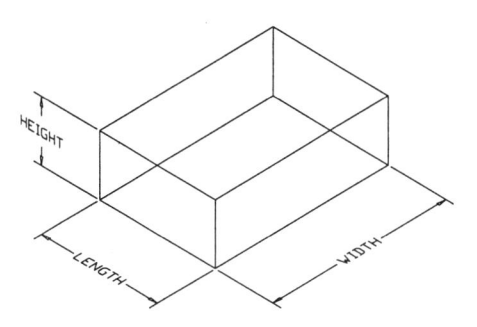

If you specify the Cube option, width, length, and height each will equal your length input.

Figure 28-2

The Center option is used to place a box at its center as shown in Figure 28-3.

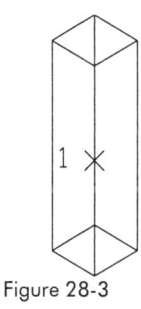

Figure 28-3

Cone

With the CONE command, you can create a solid cone. The base of the cone is always parallel to the *X-Y* plane of the current UCS. The cone has either a circular or elliptical base tapering symmetrically to a point perpendicular to its base.

> **Toolbar** From the Solids toolbar, choose Cone.
>
> **Pull Down Menu** From the Draw menu, choose Solids, then Cone.

The command line equivalent is **CONE**.

```
Command:CONE
Specify center point for base of cone
   or [Elliptical]: (pick 1)
Specify radius for base of cone or
   [Diameter]:1
Specify height of cone or [Apex]:2
```

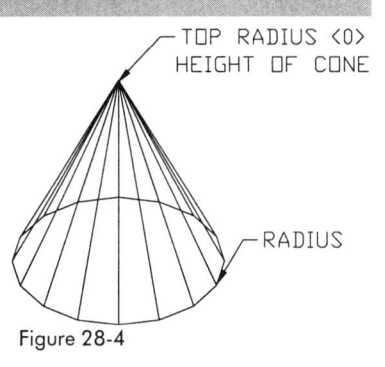

Figure 28-4

A positive value for height will draw the height along the positive *Z* axis; a negative value will draw it upon the negative *Z* axis.

The elliptical option will create an elliptical base for this cone. The major and minor axes specified are prompted.

Cylinder

With the CYLINDER command, you can create a solid cylinder with either a round or elliptical base. The base of the cylinder is always parallel to the *X-Y* plane of the current UCS.

> **Toolbar** From the Solids toolbar, choose Cylinder.
>
> **Pull Down Menu** From the Draw menu, choose Solids, then Cylinder.

The command line equivalent is **CYLINDER**.

```
Command: CYLINDER
Current wire frame density: ISOLINES=4
Center point for base of cylinder or
   [Elliptical]: (pick 1)
Specify radius for base of cylinder or
   [Diameter]:1
Specify height of cylinder or {Center
   of other end]:2
```

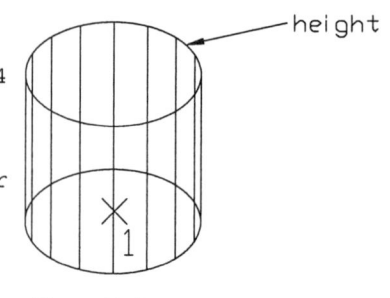

Figure 28-5

A positive value for height will draw the height along the positive Z axis; a negative value will draw it upon the negative Z axis.

The elliptical option will create an elliptical base for this cylinder. The major and minor axes specified are prompted.

Sphere

With the SPHERE command, you can create a solid sphere. The central axis is coincident with the Z axis.

The command line equivalent is **SPHERE**.

> **Toolbar** From the Solids toolbar, choose Sphere.
>
> **Pull Down Menu** From the Draw menu, choose Solids, then Sphere.

```
Command: SPHERE
Current wire frame density:
   ISOLINES=4
Specify center of sphere <0,0,0>:
   (pick 1)
Specify radius of sphere or
   [Diameter]:1
```

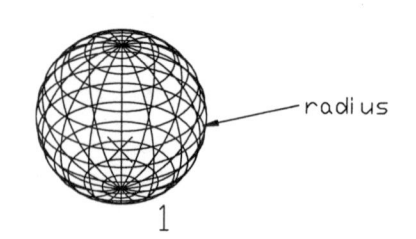

Figure 28-6

To create a dish or dome, combine the SPHERE command with subtract. For a spherical object that has additional detail, create a 2D detail and use the REVOLVE command to define a rotation angle about the Z axis.

Torus

With the TORUS command, you can create a ring shaped solid, similar to a donut. The TORUS is parallel to and bisected by the *X-Y* plane of the current UCS.

> **Toolbar** From the Solids toolbar, choose Torus.
>
> **Pull Down Menu** From the Draw menu, choose Solids, then Torus.

The command line equivalent is **TORUS**.

```
Command: TORUS
Current wire frame density: ISOLINES=16
Specify center of torus <0,0,0>: (pick 1)
Specify radius of torus or [Diameter]:1
Specify radius of tube or [Diameter]:.25
```

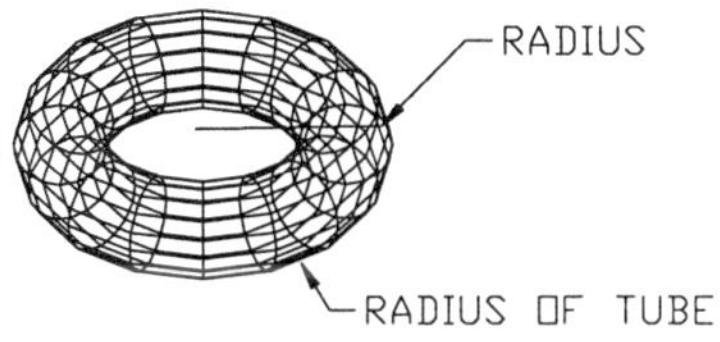

You can also create self-intersecting tori by making the radius of the tube greater than the radius of the torus.

Figure 28-7

This will result in a torus with no central hole.

A negative radius on the torus creates a football-shaped solid.

Wedge

With the WEDGE command, you can create a solid wedge. The base of the WEDGE is parallel to the *X-Y* plane of the current UCS. The height can be negative or positive, and is parallel to the Z axis.

> **Toolbar** From the Solids toolbar, choose Wedge.
>
> **Pull Down Menu** From the Draw menu, choose Solids, then Wedge.

The command line equivalent is **WEDGE**.

```
Command: WEDGE
Specify first corner of wedge or
   [CEnter]<0,0,0>: (pick 1)
Specify corner or [Cube/Length]:(pick
   2)
Specify height:.25
```

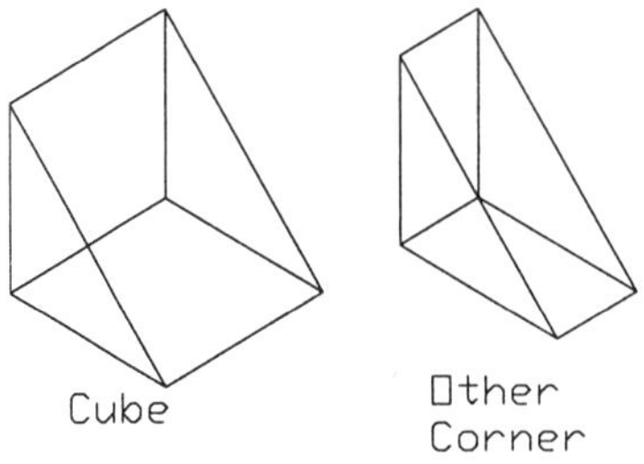

Figure 28-8

The Cube option will create a wedge with sides of equal length. Center creates a wedge by a specified center point. Both negative and positive lengths can be entered. Entering a negative value draws along the negative axis.

Three-Dimensional Solids **659**

Modifying Solid Objects

Once the solid objects are entered, they can be combined and edited using the following commands.

1. **UNION:** One object can be merged with another, thus adding all or part of one object to another.
2. **SUBTRACT:** One object can be subtracted from another, thus removing all or part of one object from another.
3. **INTERSECT**: One object can be made to intersect another, thus preserving only those parts that the objects share.

The UNION Command

Union creates a composite region or solid; it combines the total area of two or more solids or regions. To union objects use the following:

> **Toolbar** From the Solids Editing toolbar, choose UNION.
>
> **Pull Down Menu** From the Modify menu, choose Solids Editing, then UNION.

The command line equivalent is **UNION**.

> **Notes**
>
> Use END not INT as the object snap.

```
Command:BOX
Specify corner of box or
 [Center]: (pick 1)
Specify corner or [Cube/Length]:L
Specify length:(pick 2)
 Second point: (pick 1)
Specify width:(pick 3)
 Second point: (pick 2)
Specify height:3
Command:WEDGE
Specify first corner of wedge or
 [CEnter]<0,0,0>: END of (pick 4)
Specify corner or [Cube/Length]:END of (pick 5)
Specify height:2
```

Figure 28-9

As in 3D Objects, the shapes are determined by length, width, and height.

Once the two objects are created, use UNION to join them or make them into one object.

```
Command:UNION
Select objects: (pick the box)
Select objects: (pick the wedge)
Select objects: ⏎
```

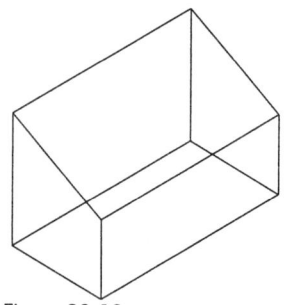

Figure 28-10

The two objects have now become one object. If you edit this object it will MOVE, COPY, etc., as one object.

The SUBTRACT Command

SUBTRACT creates a composite region or solid by subtracting the area of one set of regions or solids from another, and subtracting the volume of one set of solids from another.

> **Toolbar** From the Solids Edit toolbar, choose Subtract. 
>
> **Pull Down Menu** From the Modify menu, choose Solids Editing then Subtract.

The command line equivalent is **SUBTRACT**.

Create another box.

```
Command:BOX
Specify corner of box or [Center]:
  (pick 1)
Specify corner or [Cube/Length]:
  (pick 2)
Specify height:3
```

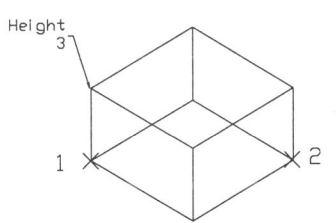

Figure 28-11

Now place a wedge on top of it.

```
Command:WEDGE
Specify first corner of wedge or
  [CEnter]<0,0,0>: END of (pick 4)
Specify corner or [Cube/Length]:END
  of (pick 5)
Specify height:2
```

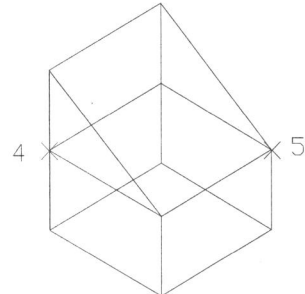

Figure 28-12

Once this is done, create another box inside the first box and wedge; length 1, width 1, height 7.

This box should extend out the top.

Now subtract the third box from the first two solid objects.

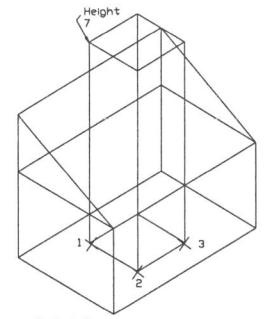

```
Command:SUBTRACT
Select solids and regions to subtract
  from:
Select objects: (pick 5)
Select objects: (pick 6)
Select solids and regions to subtract:
Select objects: (pick 7)
```

Figure 28-13

As you can see from the final image, the large box and wedge have been joined, and the tall, thinner box has been subtracted from them to create one object.

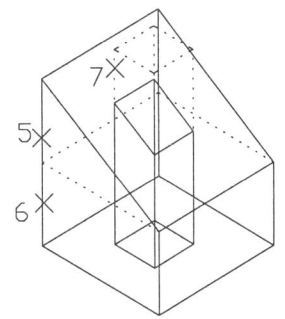

Figure 28-14

Three-Dimensional Solids **661**

The INTERSECT Command

The INTERSECT command creates composite solids or regions from the intersection of two or more solids or regions. Sometimes what you need is the intersection of two objects—just the common part that would remain if you were to subtract everything that does not overlap. In this case, use INTERSECT.

> **Toolbar** From the Modify toolbar, choose Intersect. 
>
> **Pull Down Menu** From the Modify menu, choose Boolean, then Intersect.

The command line equivalent is **INTERSECT**.

Using the examples above, create a box with a wedge on the top. Union the objects. Then place another box in the middle.

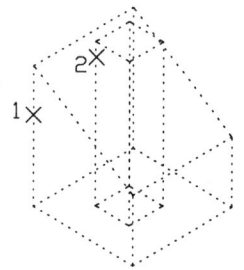

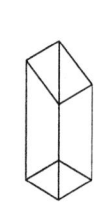

```
Command: INTERSECT
Select objects: (pick the unioned box
   and wedge)
Select objects: (pick the second box)
```

Figure 28-15

What is offered here is the common volume of the two objects.

Filleting and Chamfering Solids

If you are creating complicated geometry with fillets and chamfers etc., using solids will make the process much simpler. Once the object is accepted as one object, one solid with a mass and volume, the fillets and chamfers can be easily extracted.

The CHAMFER Command

CHAMFER bevels the edges of objects, both two-dimensional and solids. If both objects to be chamfered are on the same layer, AutoCAD creates the chamfer line on that layer. Otherwise, AutoCAD creates the chamfer line on the current layer. This is also true for chamfer color and linetype.

> **Toolbar** From the Modify toolbar, choose Chamfer. 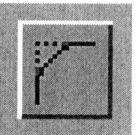
>
> **Pull Down Menu** From the Modify menu, choose Chamfer.

The command line equivalent is **CHAMFER**.

To illustrate this command, create the boxes and use UNION to create one object.

Now use the CHAMFER command to chamfer the edges on both the front and back of the first top surface.

You must indicate both the base surface and the edges to be chamfered within the command.

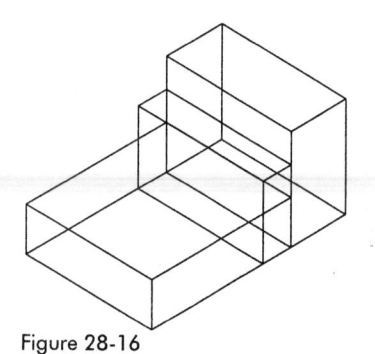

Figure 28-16

You can chamfer any edge on any flat, concave, or convex surface.

```
Command: CHAMFER
(Trim mode) Current chamfer
 Dist1 =0.0000 Dist2 = 0.0000
Select first line or [Polylines/
 Distance/Angle/Trim/Method]:D
Enter first chamfer distance
 <0.0000>:.15
Enter second chamfer distance
 <0.1500>:
Select first line or [Polylines/
 Distance/Angle/Trim/Method]:(pick 1)
Select base surface
Next/<Ok>:
Specify base surface distance <0.15>:
Specify  other surface distance <.15>:
 Select edge or [Loop]: (select an edge)
```

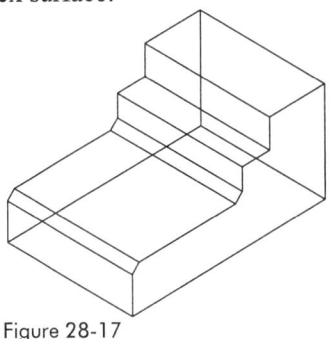

Figure 28-17

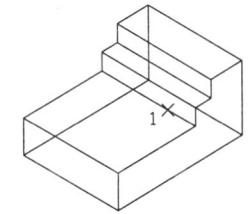

The CHAMFER command creates a bevelled edge on a specified surface, finishing the corners of the bevel on the unbevelled sides as well. Spheres and tori cannot be chamfered because they have no edge, but wedges, cones, and cylinders can.

Only straight and circular edges can be chamfered, so the Ellipse option on the CONE and CYLINDER cannot be used.

If you select an edge not adjacent to the highlighted surface it will not be chamfered.

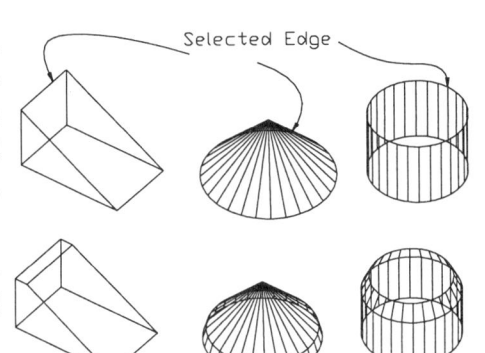

Figure 28-18

If you have used MOVE, COPY, ROTATE, or in any way edited the object, you may see the following response:

```
Surface has been edited
Repeat selection
```

If so, simply choose the base surface again, and it should be picked up.

The FILLET Command

FILLET is similar to CHAMFER in that it edits the edges of an existing object. In addition, both work as 2D and solids commands. Use the same example to show how edges are filleted instead of chamfered.

> **Toolbar** From the Modify toolbar, choose Fillet.
>
> **Pull Down Menu** From the Modify menu, choose Fillet.

The command line equivalent is **FILLET**.

Three-Dimensional Solids

```
Command: FILLET
Current settings: Mode = TRIM,
 Radius = 0.0000
Select first object or [Polylines/
   Radius/Trim]: (pick an edge)
Select fillet radius:2
Select an edge or [Chain/Radius]:
   (pick an edge)
```

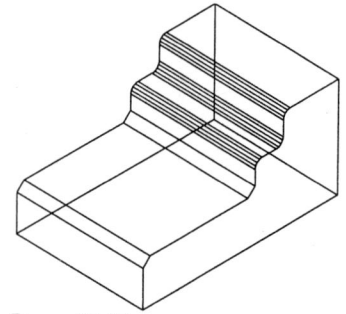

Figure 28-19

As with the CHAMFER command, the edges are edited and finished. Either the Radius or the Diameter can be specified. Cones, wedges and cylinders can also be filleted.

The fillets are always shown in the same color as the selected surface.

You can choose concave or convex edges. The resulting geometry is a solid primitive which is added to or subtracted from the existing solids.

You must pick the edges individually—using window will not work.

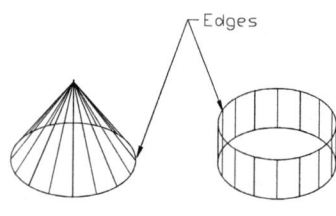

Figure 28-20

Tips and Tricks

When selecting the base surface to perform a chamfer, the object selection pick must be on an edge. In a solid, there are always two surfaces that are attached to each edge. When picking the surface you can be absolutely sure of one thing: the edge you pick will represent the surface you do *not* want. In order to get the surface you want, use the Next option.

```
Command: CHAMFER
(Trim mode) Current chamfer
 Dist1 =0.0000 Dist2 = 0.0000
Select first line or [Polylines/
 Distance/Angle/Trim/Method]:(pick
   edge)
Select first line or [Polylines/
   Distance/Angle/Trim/Method]:(pick 1)
Select base surface
Next/<Ok>:N
Select base surface
Next/<Ok>:↵
Specify base surface distance
   <0.15>:↵
Specify other surface distance
   <.15>:↵
Select edge or [Loop]: (select an edge)
```

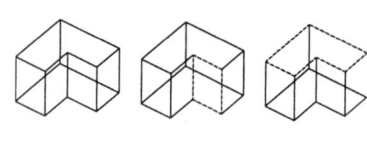

Figure 28-21

Figure 28-22 shows the method for creating a curved interior fillet. The fillets must be created in one command, not two or three. First pick the edge that intersects other edges being filleted, then pick the long edge in one command.

One command   Fillet   Full fillet

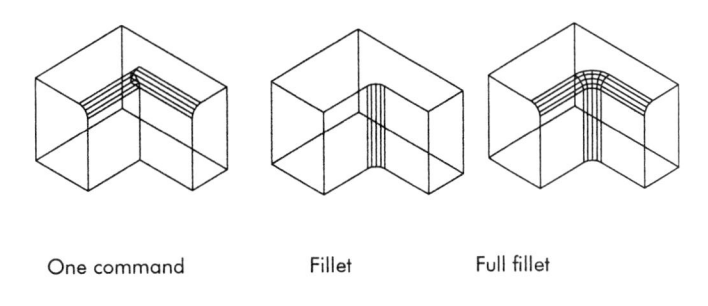

Figure 28-22

Prelab 28 Creating Solid Shapes

This short exercise should make use of most of the introductory solids commands.

Set up your screen so you have at least two viewports with an isometric view in one.

Set your ISOLINES variable to 16.

```
Command:ISOLINES
New value for Isolines <4>:16
```

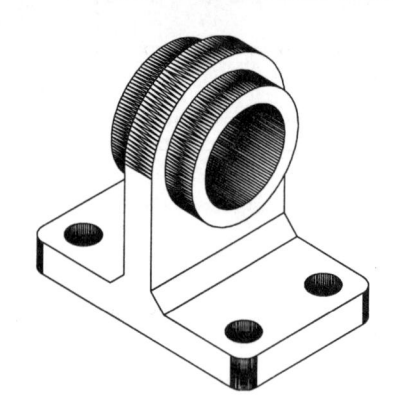

Step 1 Use BOX to create a box that is 8 units by 5 units, and 1 unit high. To make placement easier, start at 0,0,0.

```
Command:BOX
Specify corner of box or
   [Center]: 0,0,0
Specify corner or
   [Cube/Length]:8,5
Specify height:1
```

Then use FILLET to fillet the corners by .5 units. Pick the edges along the edge to be filleted, not along the two adjacent lines as in the 2D version.

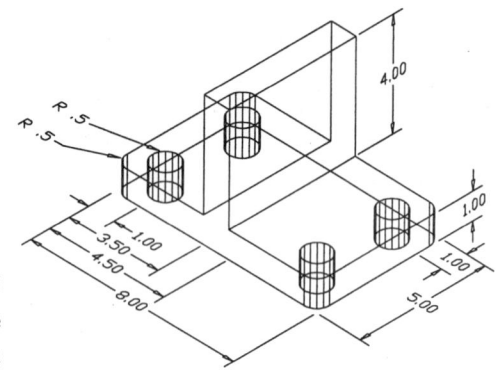

```
Command:FILLET
Current settings: Mode = TRIM, Radius = 0.0000
Select first object or [Polylines/Radius/Trim]: (pick 1)
Select fillet radius:.5
Select an edge or [Chain/Radius]:
   (pick 2, pick 3, pick 4)
```

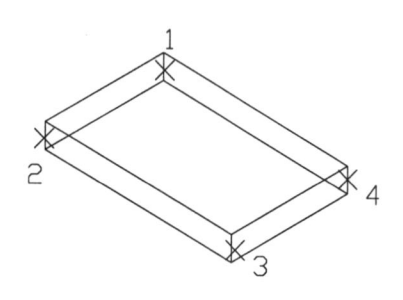

Step 2 Use CYLINDER to create cylinders one unit in from each corner with a .5 radius.

```
Command:CYLINDER
Current wire frame density: ISOLINES=16
Center point for base of cylinder or [Elliptical]: 1,1,0
Specify radius for base of cylinder or [Diameter]:.5
Specify height of cylinder or {Center of other end]:1
```

Use COPY Multiple or ARRAY to place the other cylinders.

Notes

Coordinate entry will not work if you have an OSNAP on.

Use BOX to create another box 1 unit by 5 units, extending 4 units above the original box.

```
Command: BOX
Specify corner of box or [Center]:
   3.5,0,1
Specify corner or [Cube/Length]: 4.5,5,1
Specify height: 4
```

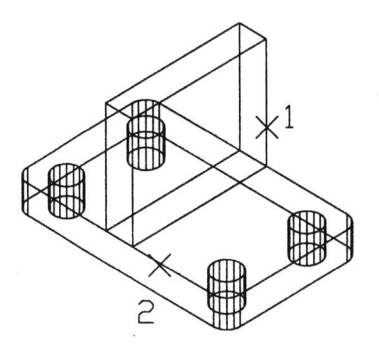

Step 3 Use UNION to join the two boxes.

```
Command: UNION
Select objects: (pick 1)
Select objects: (pick 2)
Select objects: ⏎
```

Step 4 Change your UCS by using 3point so that it is placed as in the illustration below. Use UCSICON with the option OR to check it.

```
Command: UCS
Enter an option [New/Move/orthoGraphic/Prev/Restore/Save/Del/
   Apply/?/World] <World>: 3
Specify new origin point: 4.5,0
Specify point on positive portion of
   the X axis <0,0>: 4.5,4
Specify point on positive portion of
   the Y axis <0,0>: 4.5,0,4
```

Notes

If the cylinder appears on the wrong plane, use MOVE to place it on the correct plane.

Now use CYLINDER to place a cylinder on top of the second box. The radius will be 2.5 and the height will be 1.

```
Command: CYLINDER
Current wire frame density: ISOLINES=16
Center point for base of cylinder or [Elliptical]: MID of (Pick
   the left edge of the top front plane)
Specify radius for base of cylinder or [Diameter]: 2.5
Specify height of cylinder or {Center of other end}: 1
```

You will find that at least two viewports are needed to make sure this data is correct. If you are only using one viewport, use DVIEW CAmera to make sure the objects are being created as desired.

Step 5 Use CHAMFER to create chamfers on the edges connecting the two boxes. The distance in both directions should be .5 units.

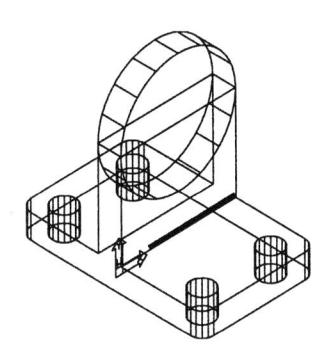

Notes

If you have not used UNION to join the two boxes, the chamfer will be entered in the wrong direction. If they are not joined with UNION, chamfers and fillets will subtract from the existing object instead of joining to an adjacent object. This can be very frustrating if you don't know why it is happening.

```
Command: CHAMFER
(Trim mode) Current chamfer
  Dist1 =0.0000 Dist2 = 0.0000
Select first line or [Polylines/
  Distance/Angle/Trim/Method]: (pick
  edge)
Select base surface
Next/<Ok>:⏎
Specify base surface distance
  <0.15> :.5
Specify  other surface distance
  <.5>:⏎
Select edge or [Loop]: (select an edge)
```

Repeat this command for the other side.

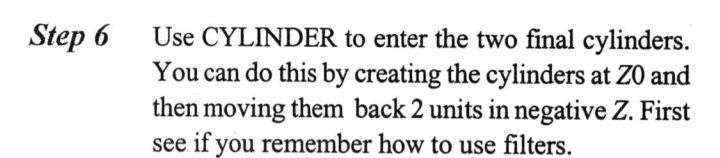

Step 6   Use CYLINDER to enter the two final cylinders. You can do this by creating the cylinders at Z0 and then moving them back 2 units in negative Z. First see if you remember how to use filters.

```
Command: CYLINDER
Current wire frame density:
  ISOLINES=16
Elliptical/<Center point>:.x of
  MID of (Pick the top center of
  the box)
(needs YZ):.y of mid of (Pick the
  same point)
(needs Z):-2
Diameter/<Radius>:2
Height of cylinder:3
```

Enter the second cylinder with a 1.5 radius.

```
Command: CYLINDER
Current wire frame density: ISOLINES=16
Center point for base of cylinder or [Elliptical]: CEN of (Pick
  the last cylinder)
Specify radius for base of cylinder or [Diameter]:1.5
Specify height of cylinder or {Center of other end]:3
```

All the component objects are in. You can now process them using UNION and SUBTRACT. As noted above, it is often necessary to create a UNION before the part is finished.

In this example you will note that the calculations in the later steps take increasingly longer. This can be frustrating if you have limited RAM or your part is extremely large.

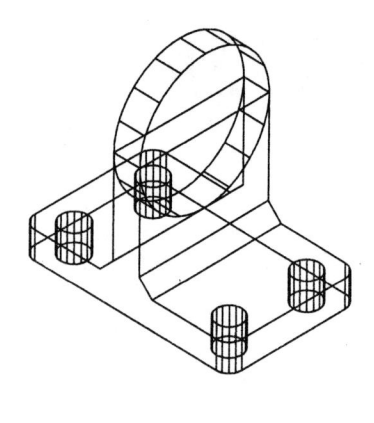

Even with adequate RAM it is a good idea to save a number of processing operations for one or two operations instead of doing five or six seperate operations.

What you want is a composite object, one that contains all the objects you initially entered, subtracting those objects that will create "holes" or spaces in the final part.

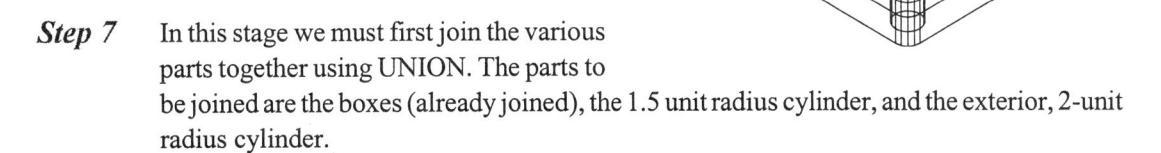

Step 7 In this stage we must first join the various parts together using UNION. The parts to be joined are the boxes (already joined), the 1.5 unit radius cylinder, and the exterior, 2-unit radius cylinder.

```
Command: UNION
Select objects: (Pick the objects indicated)
Select objects:
```

Step 8 Use SUBTRACT to subtract the four cylinders on the base and the cylinder that extends through the center of the upper area.

Again, using one command rather than five in this operation will save a lot of time.

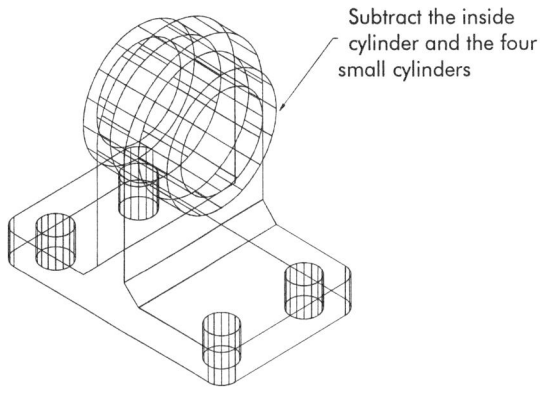

```
Command: SUBTRACT
Select objects from which to subtract. . .
Select objects: (Pick the large object)
Select objects:
Objects to subtract from them
Select objects: (Pick the cylinders indicated)
Select objects:
```

The part is now complete and you can save it for analysis in the next chapter.

The objects you have created are solid objects. What you see are the boundary representations.

Command and Function Summary

BOX allows you to create a solid box.

CHAMFER allows you to create a chamfer on a solid object.

CONE allows you to create a solid cone.

CYLINDER allows you to create a solid cylinder.

FILLET allows you to fillet a solid edge.

INTERSECT allows you to calculate the common volume of two objects.

SPHERE allows you to create a solid sphere.

SUBTRACT allows you to subtract solid objects from existing solid objects.

UNION allows you to combine or UNION two or more solid entities.

This extra part will help you practice. Try to do it in both solids and surfacing.

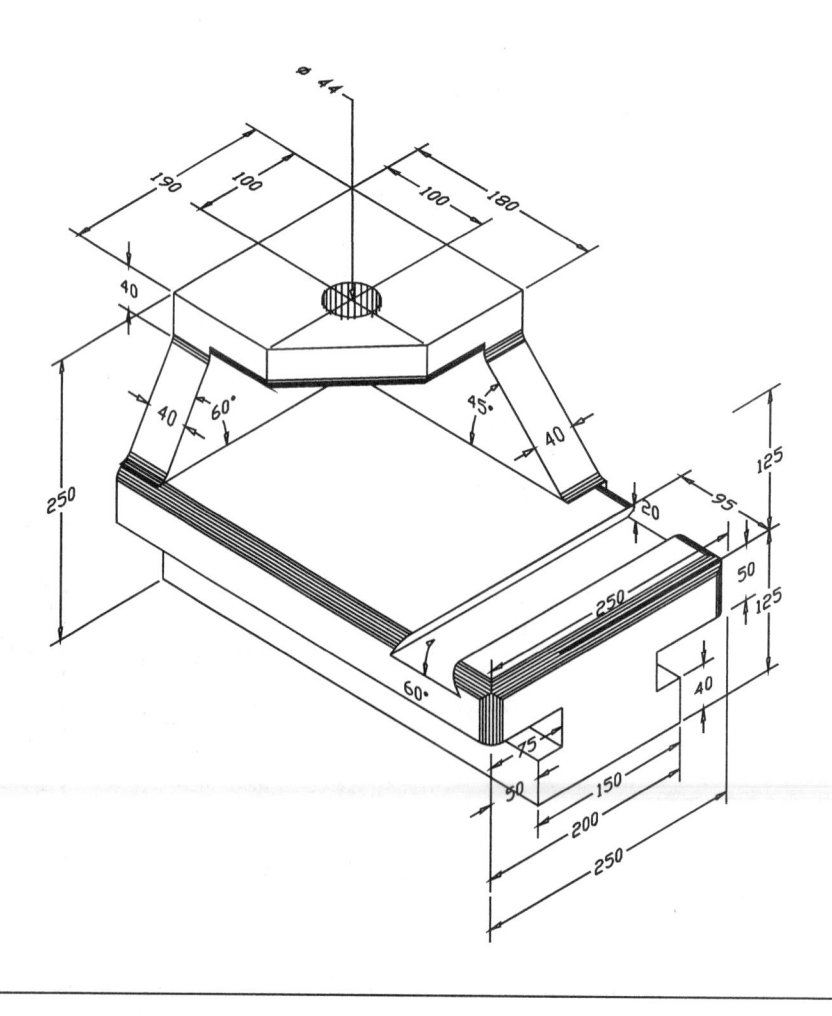

Practice Exercise 28

Create one of these parts using solids plus UNION and SUBTRACT and FILLET, if you need it.

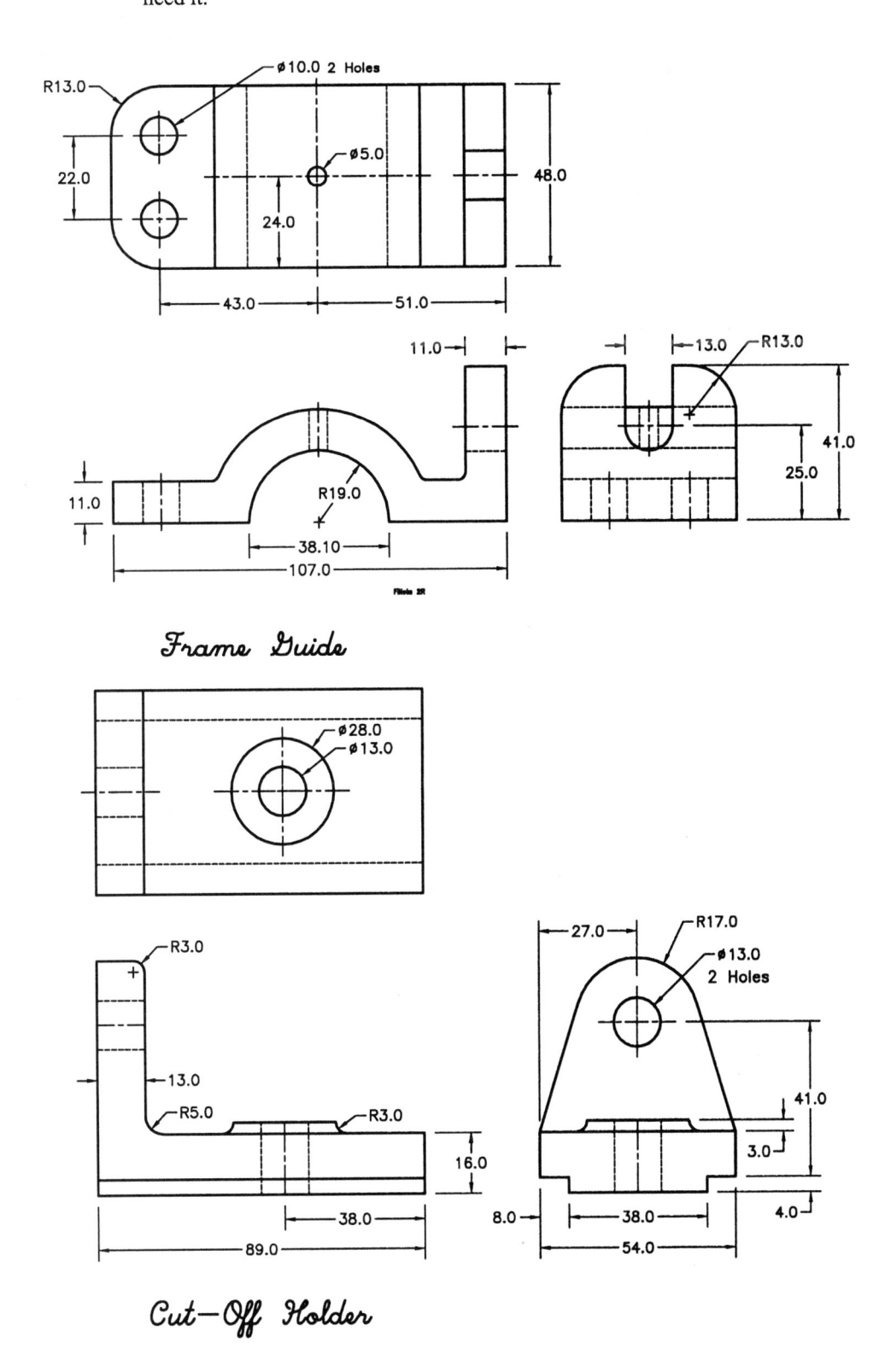

Frame Guide

Cut-Off Holder

Exercise A28

This small domed turret detail will give you an idea of how different solids can be attached to one another. Use this model, or create one of your own with a similar use, but different detailing.

If you are working on the house, create the footings from Exercise A29, and use this as a garden room for the back yard.

A28 HINTS

The turret will be constructed with six sides, each with a window and some detailing on the sides.

Create this geometry using BOX, SPHERE, and CYLINDER. You will not need to change the UCS yet.

Use filters as well as point entry and OSNAPs to place the items.

Be sure to make your dome on top of the window the correct size so that the top of the window curves gracefully.

You will probably need at least three viewports for this design. An isometric view is imperative; use front and plan views as well.

Now use UNION to join all the solids together to form a single wall unit.

It may be quicker to join all these solids into one unit here, then array them and join the arrayed units later.

Once unified, use ARRAY in the plan view to create the room layout. Be sure that the boxes are overlapping—otherwise, you will not be able to join the walls later.

If the inside face of the wall is 6′, the center of the polar array will be 5′6″ from the middle of the wall.

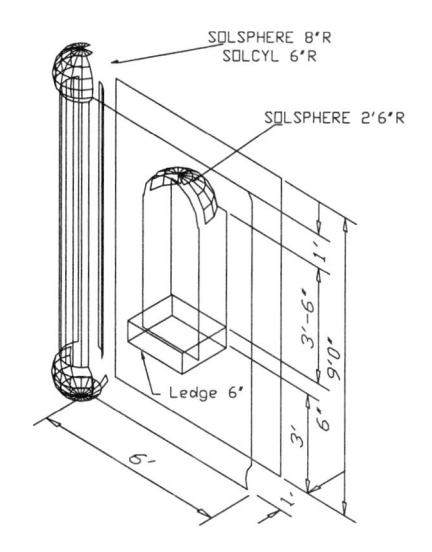

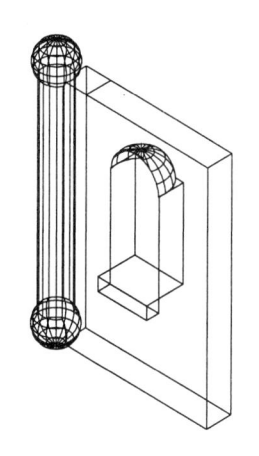

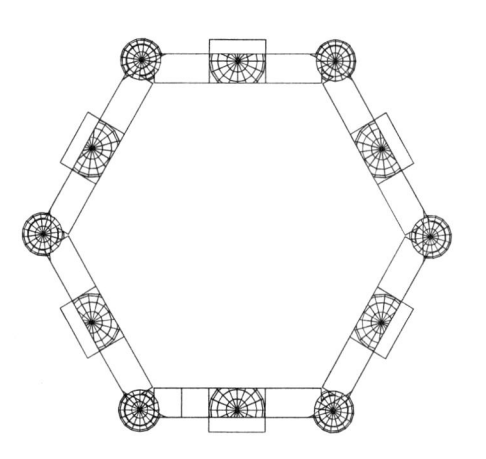

Three-Dimensional Solids **673**

Now the dome must be created. The easiest way to create a dome is by using REVOLVE or revolve a solid. This is very similar to REVSURF in that the curve or pline is revolved around an axis. The difference is that here, we are creating solids, not just a surface.

```
Command: REVOLVE
Select polyline or circle for
   revolution. . .
Select objects:(pick the arced
   PLINE)
Select objects:↵
Axis of revolution -
   Object/x/y/<Start point of
   axis>:E
Select object:(pick the line)
Included angle <full circle>:
   180
```

This command will give you the inside of the dome. Make sure that it fits all the interior corners at the top of the walls.

Again, make sure that the inside surface of the dome is attached to the top of the wall. CYLINDER can be used to make a base for the dome (Use REVOLVE).

The REVOLVE command creates solid entities from the center of the PLINE path.

While TORUS and SPHERE can add lovely detailing, these calculations will take a long time (unless you have 20 megabytes of RAM).

Once assembled, use UNION to join all six walls, the exterior dome, and the exterior cylinder, if you have one.

Use HIDE or DVIEW and Hideplot to create an image with the hidden lines removed.

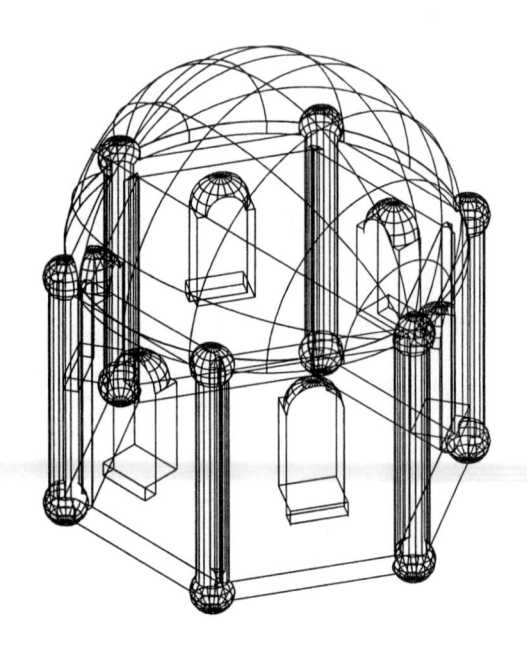

Exercise C28

This bridge will give you some experience in using solids, UNION and SUBTRACT.

Determine the bridge size you want and the arc's open area.

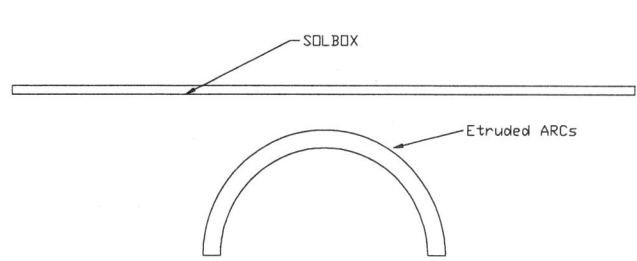

Now start putting in the structure of the bridge. Make sure the supports are evenly spaced and of sufficient height. You can enter one-half of the support and then mirror.

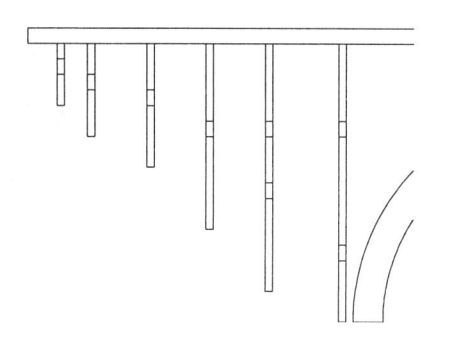

Use DVIEW and HIDE to get a view of the bridge structure from the bottom.

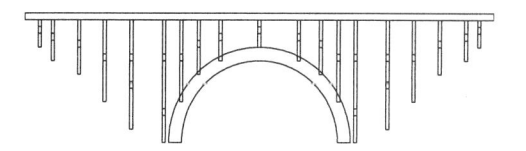

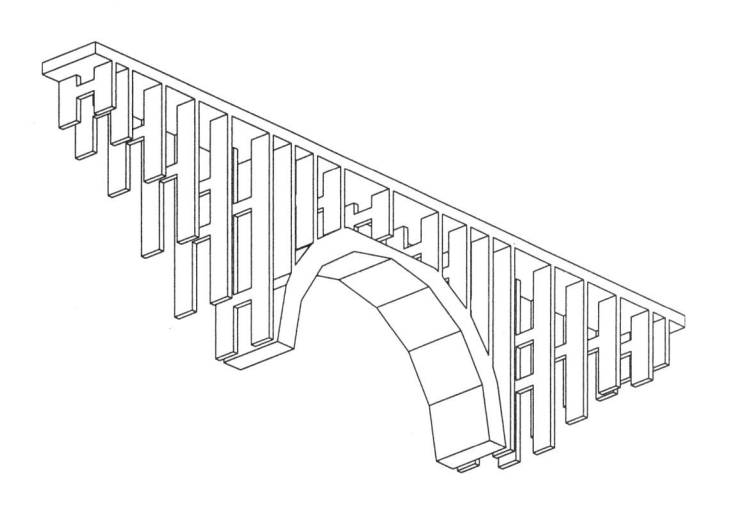

Exercise M28

This slide support is composed of BOXes and CYLINDERs with four FILLETs. Nonetheless, it is a little tricky to create as there are many UCS changes.

We suggest that you enter all the solids first, then process them.

You will need at least three layers: one for base geometry, one for cylinders, and one for additional geometry. If you are planning to dimension this part, add a layer for dimensions as well.

Once completed, create a MESH from the part under the AME DISPLAY menu, and use HIDE to get the final result.

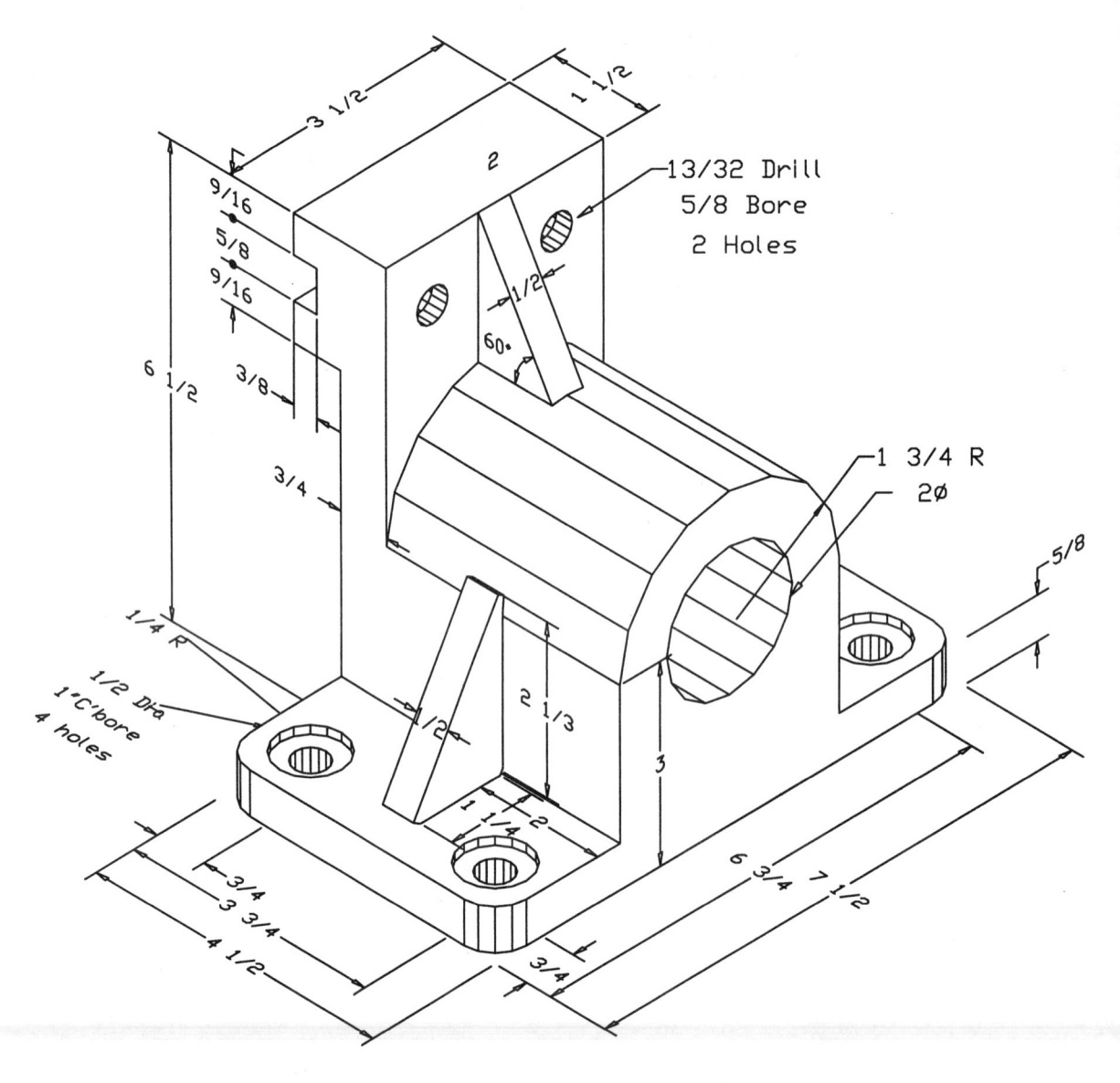

Rounds and Fillets 1/2
Interior Thickness 1/5

Slide Support

M28 Hints

The base geometry is quite simple to enter. Start with a large base. Add the BOXes for the upper surface either by calculating their coordinates or using filters and OSNAPs.

Once in, add the CYLINDERs.

You will find that a plan view, right side, and pictorial view will help you place the cylinders quickly, making sure that the top indentation is at the correct height.

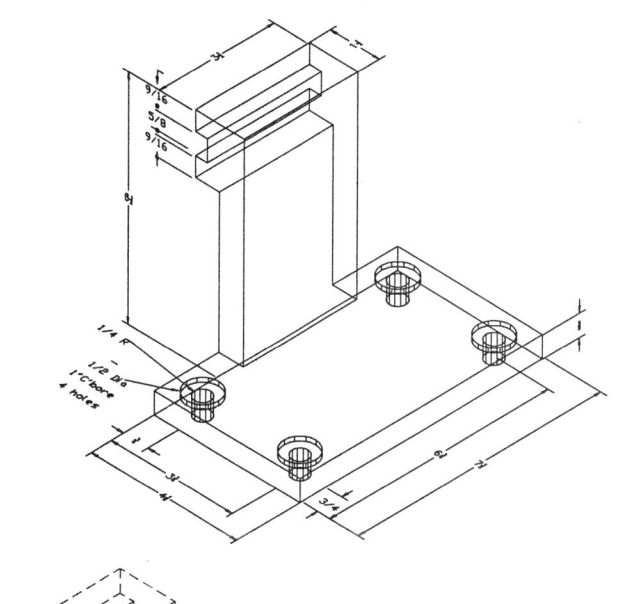

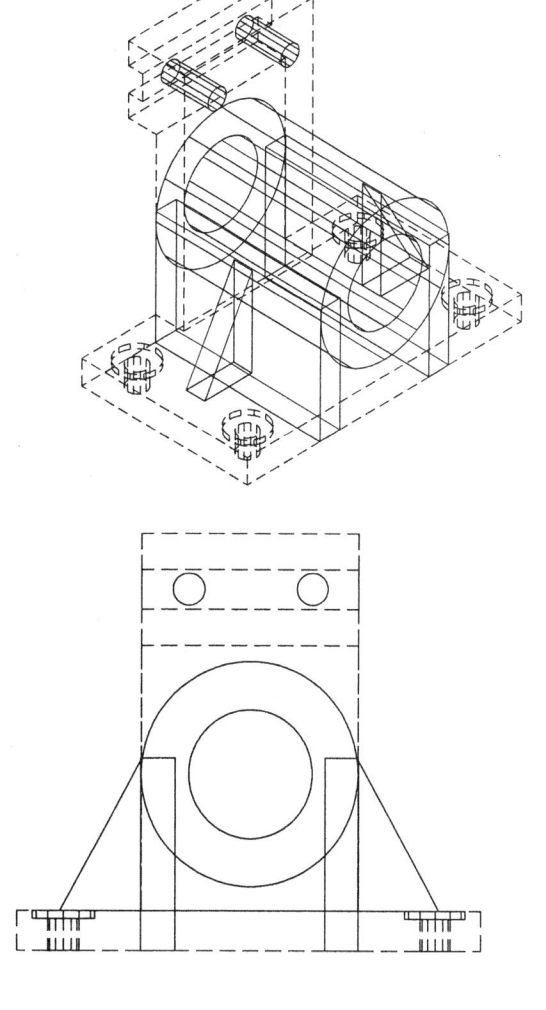

Add the CYLINDERs and two WEDGEs to form the reinforcing veins. The two WEDGEs will be made relative to a different UCS.

Three-Dimensional Solids **677**

Make sure that there are no gaps between the wedges and the cylinder. Once in, the UCS can be changed to Previous, and the wedge can be MIRRORed through the center of the part.

If you have oriented your model the same as in the examples, this will be your front view.

Place the wedge on this surface as shown.

At this stage, it is a good idea to make sure that the cylinders extend through the part.

Check the model from all views before processing because processing takes time; any errors encountered and fixed at this stage will save time later.

Metal parts manufactured in this way are usually hollow on the underside. If not, the stock under the large cylinder would be over an inch thick, thus wasting stock and making an unnecessarily heavy part.

If you created the base box in one piece as in the example, you will need to create a small base part (hidden lines) to erase from the bottom plate. Add a plate for the front face (also in hidden lines).

Add boxes .5 inch in thickness along both sides as shown, leaving the bottom part hollow.

At this point, it is a good idea to save your file if you have not already done so.

For ease in selection, turn off the interior cylinder layer.

Now use UNION to join all the boxes and the large cylinder.

Depending on the capacity of your RAM and processor, this could take a few minutes. (Now may be the time to consider upgrading your computer.)

Now add the cylinder LAYER, and use SUBTRACT to subtract all the interior cylinders from the base part.

Again, this could take some time.

In effect, your part is now complete, except for the fillets.

If you find it difficult to pick, use DVIEW camera to rotate the pictorial view and pick the fillet on the back corner.

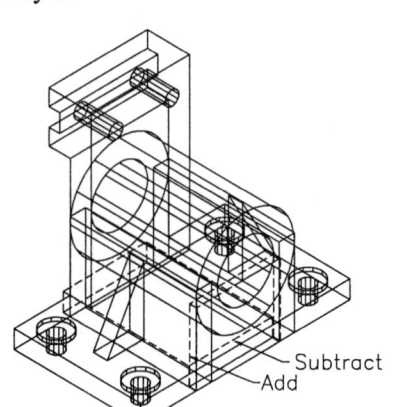

Challenger 28

Using the dimensions from the Challenger 19, create this 3D battery pulley.

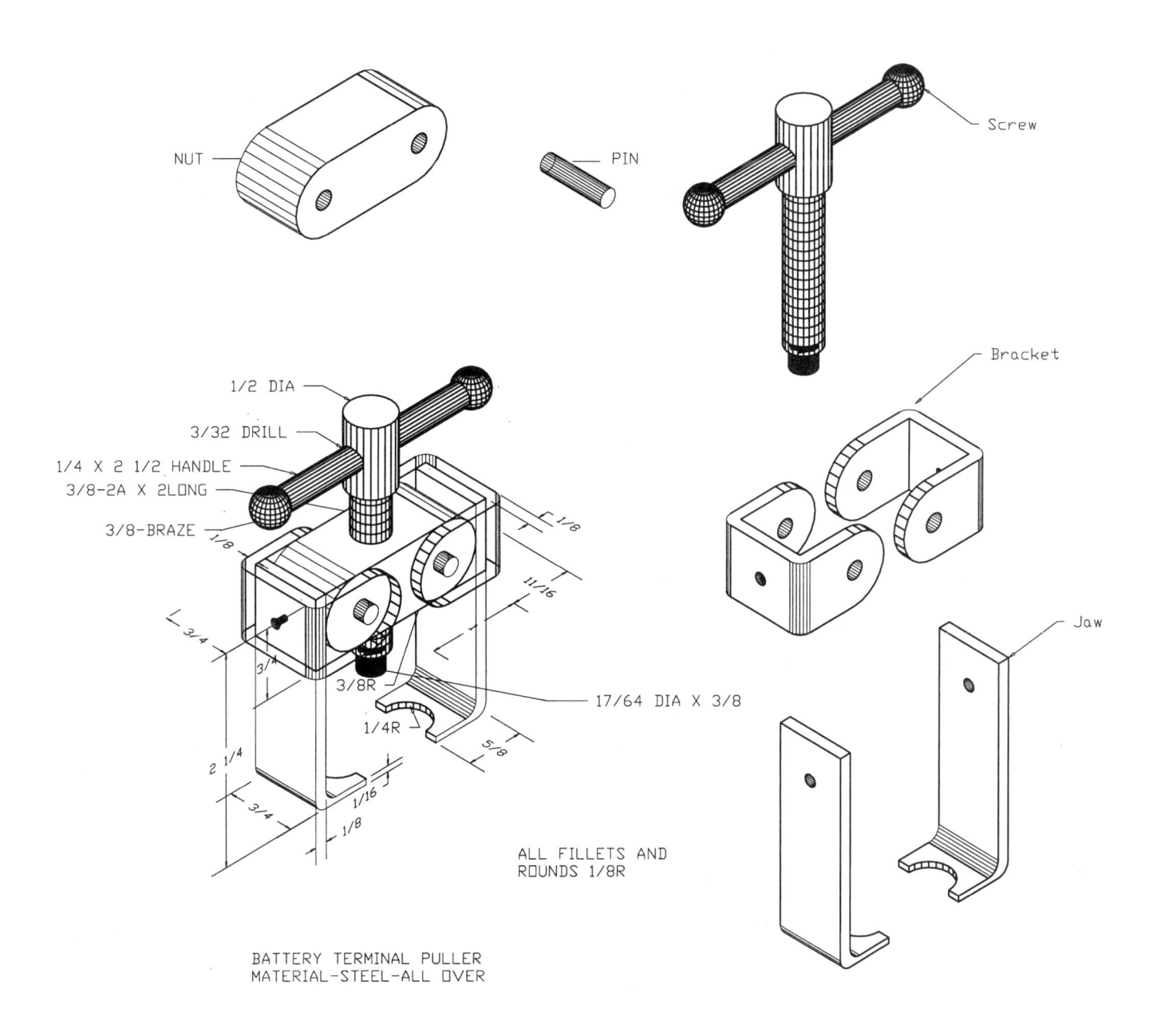

NUT

PIN

Screw

Bracket

Jaw

1/2 DIA
3/32 DRILL
1/4 X 2 1/2 HANDLE
3/8-2A X 2LONG
3/8-BRAZE
1/8
3/4
3/8R
1/4R
1/8
3/4
1/16
2 1/4
3/8
11/16
5/8
17/64 DIA X 3/8

ALL FILLETS AND ROUNDS 1/8R

BATTERY TERMINAL PULLER
MATERIAL-STEEL-ALL OVER

Three-Dimensional Solids 679

Challenger 28B

Create this drawing of a pulley casting, then create the part using solids. Merge the 2D and 3D files to create a paper space drawing.

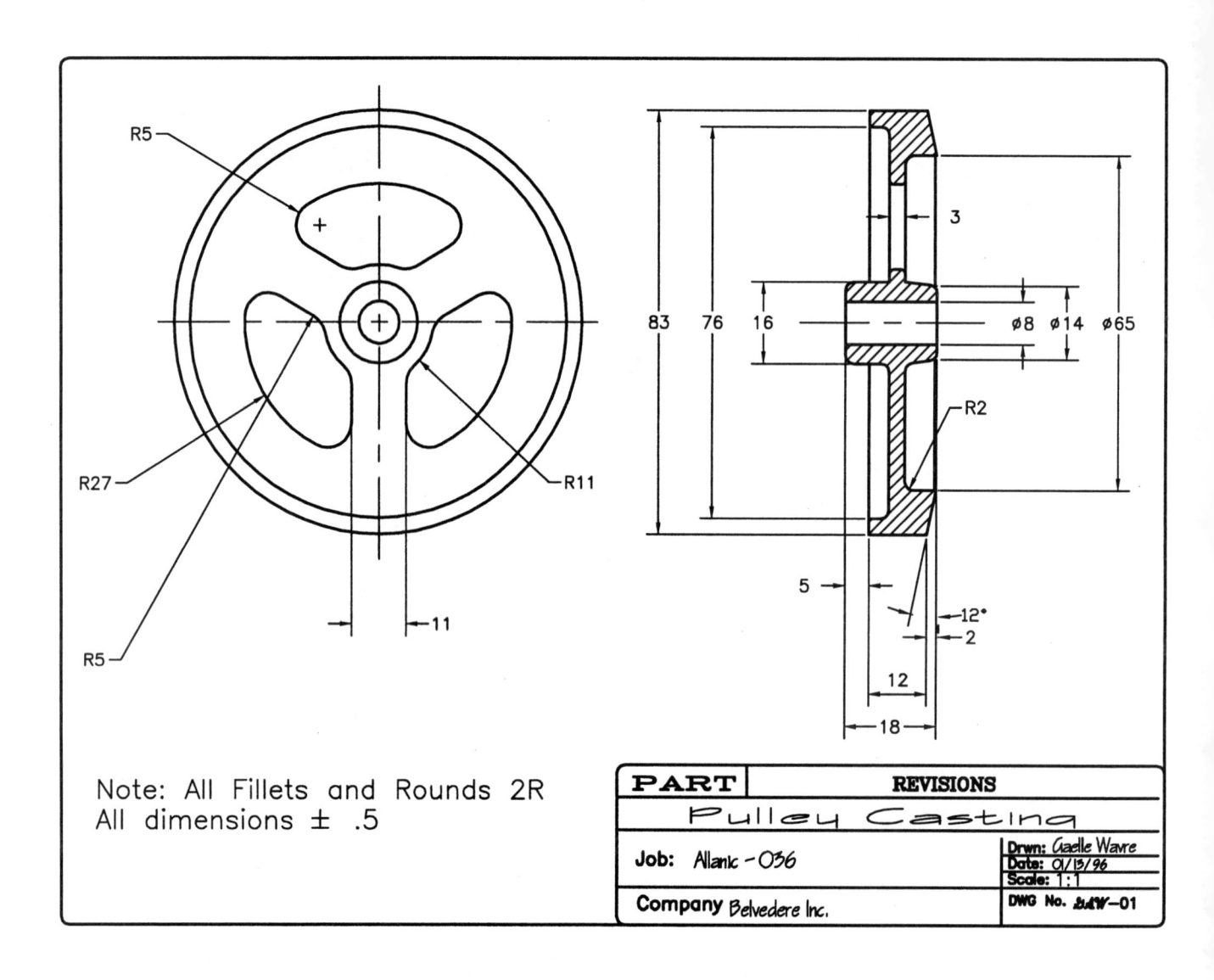

Note: All Fillets and Rounds 2R
All dimensions ± .5

29 Revolving, Extruding and Sectioning in 3D Solids

Upon completion of this chapter, you should be able to:

1. Create solids with revolved surfaces
2. Create solids through extrusions
3. Generate sections of 3D objects
4. Edit solid models

OBJECTIVES

You can create solid models using primitive shapes as well as revolved and extruded shapes. The solid is constructed from a profile using both of the following commands: REVOLVE and EXTRUDE.

The REVOLVE Command

The REVOLVE command is similar to the REVSURF command in that it creates a solid by revolving a two-dimensional object about an axis. The REVOLVE command is useful for making complicated shapes that are possible with BOX, SPHERE, and CYLINDER, but much easier with a revolved solid.

Closed polylines, circles, ellipses, closed splines, donuts, and regions (page 716) can all be used. Polylines that have crossing or self-intersecting segments cannot be revolved. You cannot revolve objects contained within a block. Only one object can be revolved at a time. The Right-hand rule determines the positive direction of rotation. To access REVOLVE:

> **Toolbar** From the Solids toolbar, choose Revolve.
>
> **Pull Down Menu** From the Draw menu, choose Solids, then Revolve.

The command line equivalent is **REVOLVE**.

```
Command: REVOLVE
Current wire frame density:
  ISOLINES=16
Select objects: (pick 1)
Select objects:↵
Specify start point of axis of
  revolution or define by
  [Object/X (axis)/Y (axis)]:
  (pick 2)
End point of axis: (pick 3)
Angle of revolution <360>:↵
```

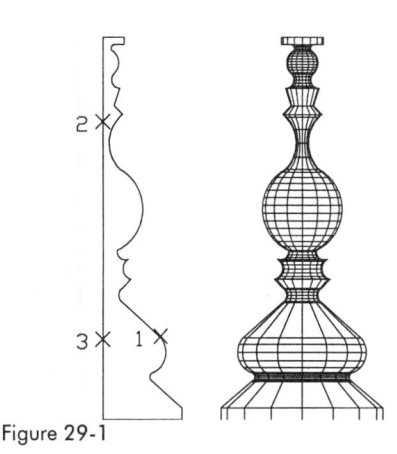

Figure 29-1

Revolving, Extruding and Sectioning in 3D Solids **681**

Startpoint

If there is no existing axis line, you can specify the first and second points of the line. The positive axis direction is from the first to the second point. This is the default.

Object

The Object option lets you use an existing line or single segment polyline as the axis about which to revolve the object. The positive axis direction is from the closest to the farthest endpoint of the line.

```
Command: REVOLVE
Current wire frame density
 ISOLINES=4
Select objects: (pick 1)
Select objects:⏎
Axis of revolution - Object/X/Y/
<Start point of axis>:Object
Select an object: (pick 2)
Angle of revolution <360>:⏎
```

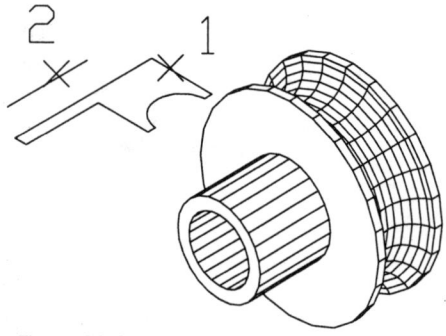

Figure 29-2

X-Y

X uses the positive X axis of the current UCS as the positive axis direction. Y uses the Y axis.

The most common problem with the REVOLVE command is crossing or intersecting. You will get the response:

```
Revolving angle
```

The pline can be revolved a full circle or part of a circle. All methods of selecting the objects are accepted. Only one pline or circle can be used as the object to revolve.

Notes
If the polyline is not closed, this command will not work.

```
Command: REVOLVE
Current wire fframe density:
 ISOLINES=4
Select objects:L
Select objects:⏎
Axis of revolution - Object/X/Y/
<Start point of axis>: (pick 1)
Specify end point of axis: (pick 2)
Specify angle of revolution
   <360>:90
```

Figure 29-3

The EXTRUDE Command

EXTRUDE is a simple method of creating solid primitives by extruding existing two-dimensional objects. EXTRUDE also creates solids by extruding two-dimensional objects along a specified path. Multiple objects can be extruded.

Toolbar From the Solids toolbar, choose Extrude.

Pull Down Menu From the Draw menu, choose Solids, then Extrude.

The command line equivalent is **EXTRUDE**.

```
Command:EXTRUDE
Current wire frame density:
 ISOLINES = 16
Select objects: (pick the PLINE)
Select objects:
Specify height of extrusion or
 [Path]:2
Specify angle of taper for
 extrusion <0>:
```

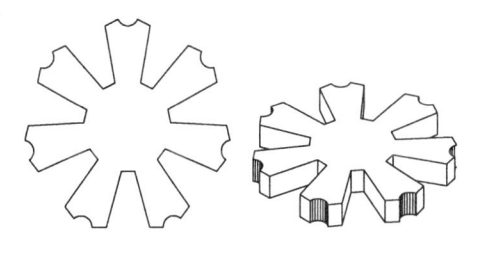

Figure 29-4

As with the REVOLVE command, you can extrude closed polylines, polygons, circles, ellipses, closed splines, donuts, and regions. Polylines that have self-intersecting or crossing segments cannot be extruded.

If the selected polyline has a width or thickness, these properties are ignored.

Extrusion Taper

This tapers an object while it is being extruded along the positive or negative Z axis of the object's coordinate system.

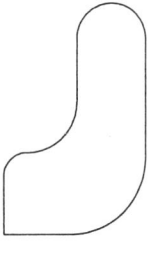

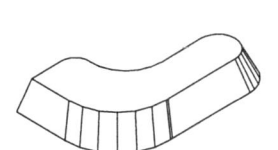

```
Command:EXTRUDE
Current wire frame density:
 ISOLINES = 16
Select objects: (pick the PLINE)
Select objects:
Specify height of extrusion or [Path]:2
Specify angle of taper for extrusion <0>:15
```

Figure 29-5

A large taper angle or a long extrusion height can cause the object, or portions of the object, to taper to a point before reaching the extrusion height.

Path

The path option works similar to the direction vector of the TABSURF command. The surface is extruded relative to a chosen path.

```
Command: EXTRUDE
Current wire frame density:
 ISOLINES = 16
Select objects: (pick the PLINE)
Select objects:↵
Specify height of extrusion or
 [Path]:P
Select path: (pick the line)
```

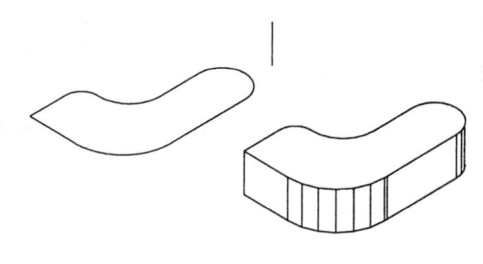

Figure 29-6

The extruded solid starts from the plane of the profile and ends on a plane perpendicular to the path at the path's endpoint. AutoCAD moves the path to the center of the profile if neither of the endpoints of the path are on the plane of the profile.

The SECTION Command

With the SECTION command, you can create a cross section through the solid as a region or a block. The cross section is placed on the current layer. The section takes the form of a region and by default has no associated hatch. The section becomes an independent object and can be isolated for clarity.

> **Toolbar** From the Solids toolbar, choose Section.
>
> **Pull Down Menu** From the Draw menu, choose Solids, then Section.

The command line equivalent is **SECTION**.

Notes

It is difficult to pick CENters and QUADrants in solids, so define your sectioning plane with lines or coordinates.

You can either pick points on the object or use two points through which to identify a sectioning plane.

```
Command: SECTION
Select objects: (pick 1)
Select objects:↵
Specify first point on
  section plane by
  [Object/Zaxis/View/XY/
  YZ/ZX/3 points]:0,0,0
Specify second point on
  plane:10,0,0
Specify third point on plane:10,0,10
```

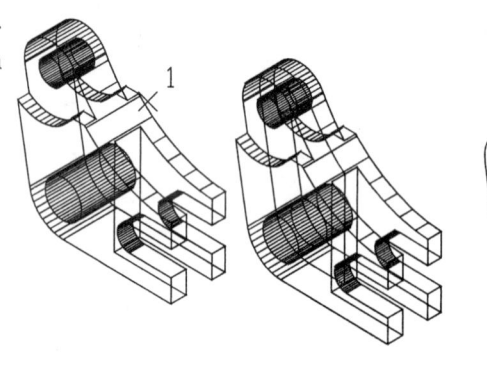

Figure 29-7

Where:
Object = creates a section by a plane.
Zaxis = creates a section along the Z axis.
View = creates a section normal to the current view.
X/Y/Z = create sections along the specified axis.
3 points = creates a section along a plane identified by three points.

Object

Instead of indicating three points for the section plane, you can specify a planar object such as a circle, ellipse, arc, polyline, or spline.

Zaxis

This defines the sectioning plane as specified by an origin point on the Z axis of the plane. Like the Zaxis option of UCS, you specify first the origin, then the point which determines the plane's normal direction.

View

This option aligns the section with the current viewport's viewing plane. Specifying a point defines the location of the sectioning plane.

```
Point on viewing plane <0,0,0>: (pick a point)
```

X-Y

Aligns the sectioning plane with the *X-Y* plane of the current UCS.

Y-Z

Aligns the sectioning plane with the *Y-Z* plane of the current UCS.

Z-X

Aligns the sectioning plane with the *Z-X* plane of the current UCS.

In all three of the above, you are prompted for a point to indicate the position of the plane.

Hatch

The section is not hatched by default. To add the hatch to the region or section use: BHATCH.

Figure 29-8

```
Command: BHATCH
```

The SLICE Command

For constructing a drawing that has a cut-away section, use the SLICE command. SLICE removes the specified side of an object. COPY the object over if you plan to construct a full drawing of the part. The sliced solids retain the layer and color properties of the original solids. The default method of slicing a solid is to specify three points on a plane.

> **Toolbar** From the Solids toolbar, choose Slice.
>
> **Pull Down Menu** From the Draw menu, choose Solids, then Slice.

The command line equivalent is **SLICE**.

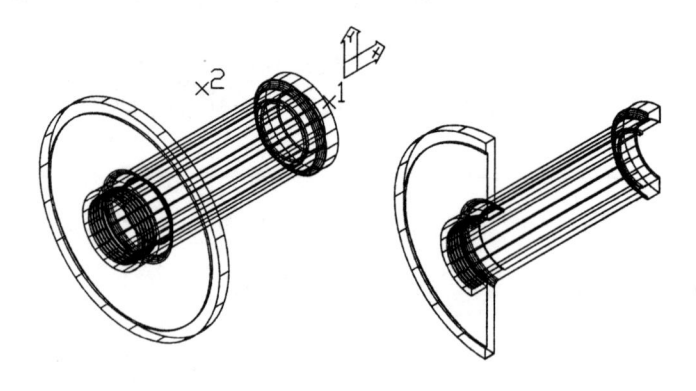

Figure 29-9

```
Command:SLICE
Select objects: (pick 1)
Select objects:↵
Specify first point on slicing plane by
   [Object/Zaxis/View/XY/YZ/ZX/3 points]:0,0,0
Specify second point on plane:10,0,0
Specify third point on plane:10,10,0
Specify a point on desired side of the plane or [keep Both
   sides]:(pick 2)
```

Where: **Object**   = slices the part by a plane
   Zaxis   = slices the part along the *Z* axis
   View   = slices the part normal to the current view
   X-Y/Y-Z/Z-X = slices the part along the specified axis
   3points   = slices the part along a plane identified by three points

If you want both sides of the solid, choose Both and AutoCAD will create one solid on one side of the identified plane, and another on the other side.

Prelab 29 Creating Solids by Revolving 2D Objects

Using the part from the mechanical drawing in Chapter 12 we will create first a 3D solid, then a section, then a sliced view.

This is an excellent part to practice on. The part's lower sections are good practice for extrusions. If you have sufficient time, create the whole part.

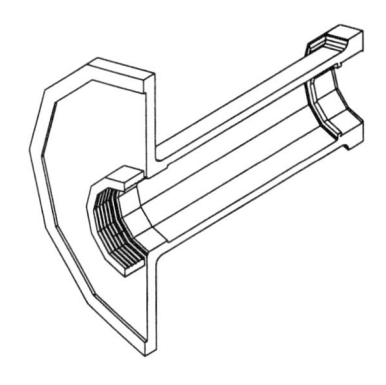

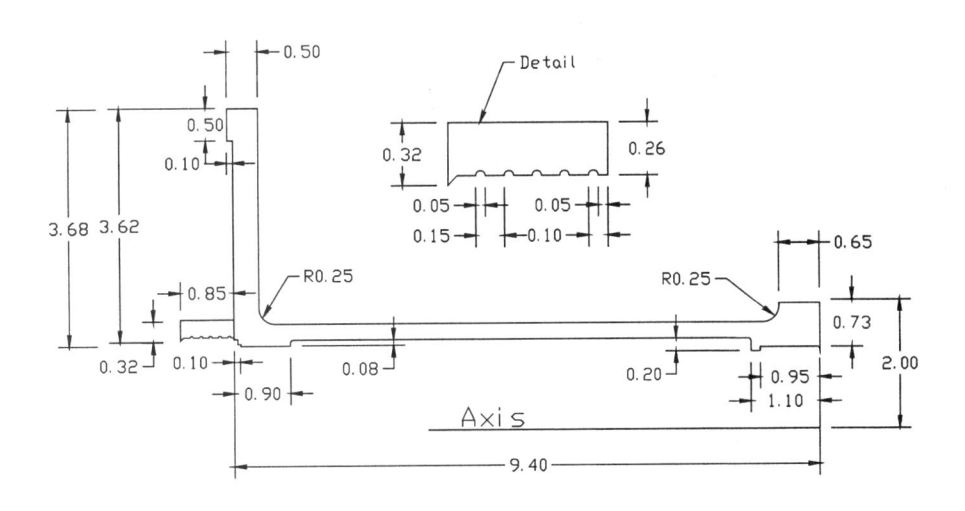

Step 1   Using either the information on page 330 or the drawing above, create two plines for the part, and one line for the axis.

Make the plines on two separate layers, Large and Small.

Step 2   Use REVOLVE to create a 3D solid from the larger polyline and the axis line.

```
Command: REVOLVE
Current wire frame density:
 ISOLINES=16
Select objects: (pick the PLINE)
Select objects:↵
Specify start point of axis of
 revolution or define by
 [Object/X (axis)/Y (axis)/:0
Select an object: (pick the axis
 line)
Angle of revolution <360>:↵
```

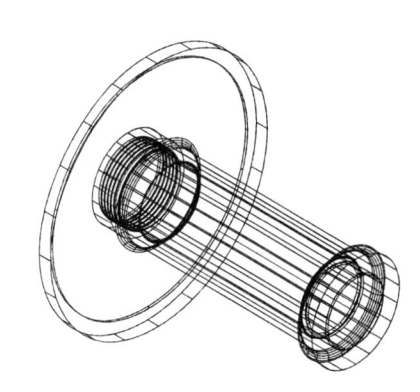

Danger

Do *not* try to create both solids in the one command.

Revolving, Extruding and Sectioning in 3D Solids   **687**

Step 3 Now use the SECTION command to create a section through the part. Create a new layer called Section; make it current and red.

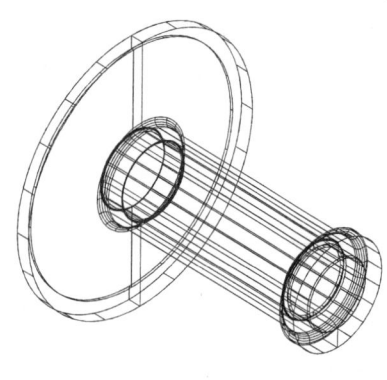

```
Command: SECTION
Select objects: (pick the solid)
Select objects: ⏎
Specify first point on section
  plane by [Object/Zaxis/View/
  XY/YZ/ZX/3points]: 0,0,0
Specify second point on
  plane:10,0,0
Specify third point on plane:10,0,10
```

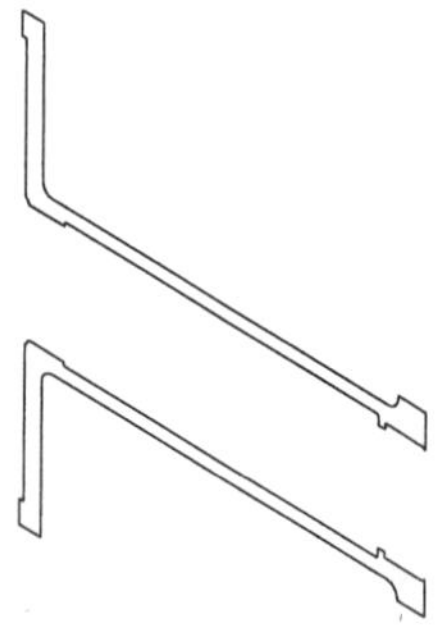

Step 4 Freeze all layers except the Section layer.

The section should be on the current layer.

Thaw the layer containing the solid.

Step 5 Now use the SLICE command to slice the part in half. Copy it over 20 units before slicing.

```
Command: SLICE
Select objects: (pick the solid)
Select objects: ⏎
Specify first point on slicing
  plane by [Object/Zaxis/View/
  XY/YZ/ZX/3 points]:0,0,0
Specify second point on
  plane:10,0,0
Specify third point on
  plane:10,0,10
Specify a point on desired side
  of the plane or [keep Both
  sides]:(pick 1)
```

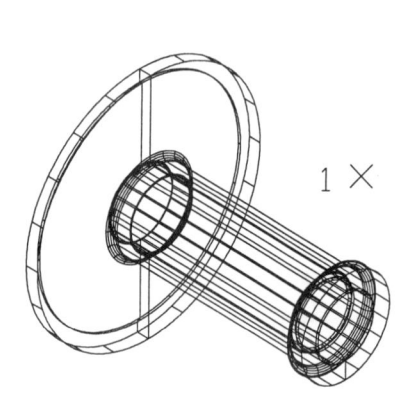

The part will appear on the side that you indicated.

Step 6 Turn off the layer for the existing solid and the section, Large.

Create a new layer for the smaller section.

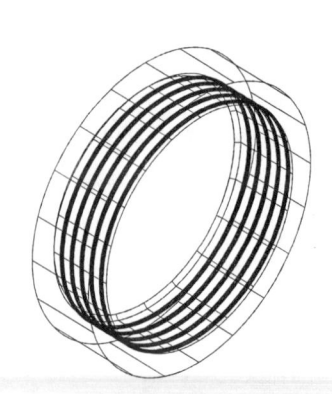

Step 7 Use the SECTION command to create a section of the part.

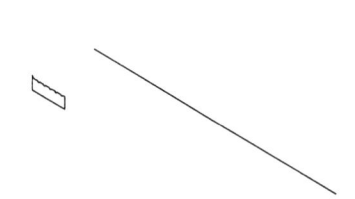

Step 8 Now use the SLICE command to remove the front half of the part.

SAVE the file. Thaw the Large layer, and use HIDE or SHADE to display the part.

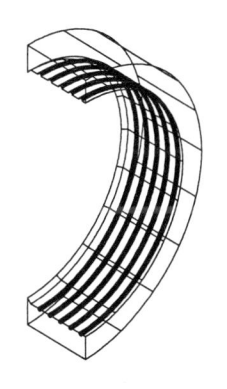

Step 9 Use PSPACE to compile a drawing.

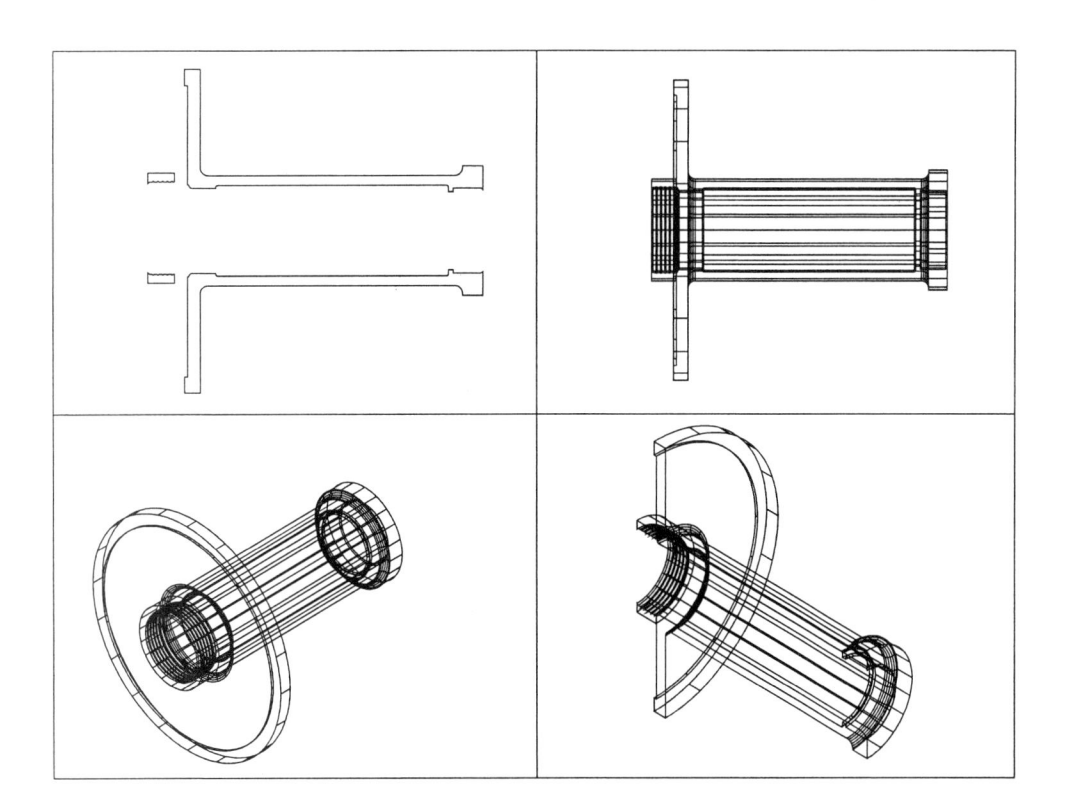

Revolving, Extruding and Sectioning in 3D Solids   **689**

Command and Function Summary

EXTRUDE creates solid primitives by extruding existing two-dimensional objects.

REVOLVE creates a solid by revolving a two-dimensional object about an axis.

SECTION uses the intersection of a plane and solids to create a region.

SLICE slices a set of solids with a plane.

Practice Exercise 29

Draw this template and extrude it by 0.5 units. Create a section of the part and then copy it over and slice off one-half.

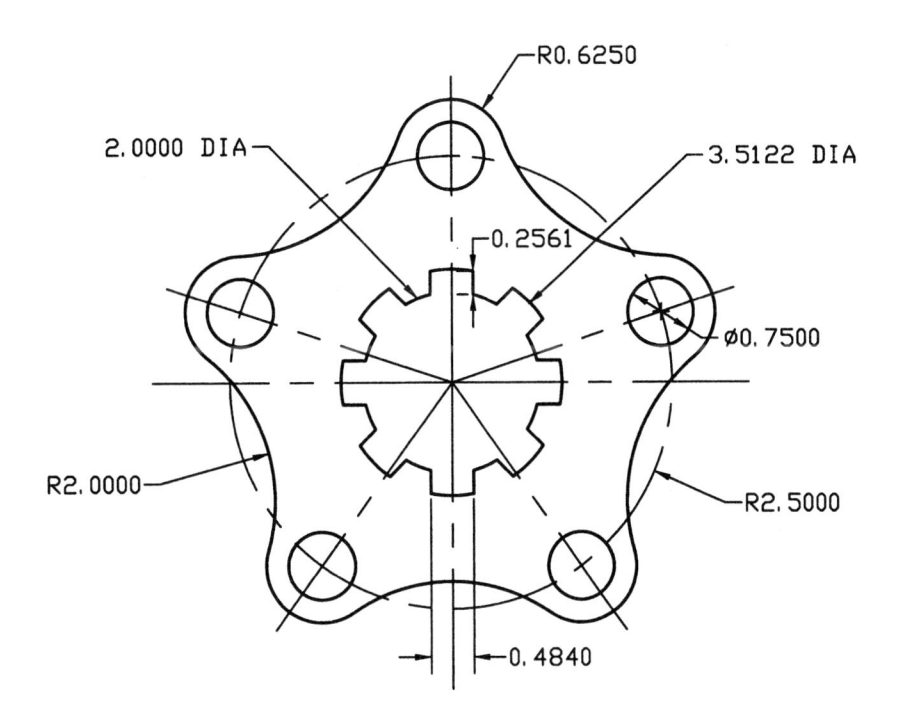

Or use the EXTRUDE command to illustrate the amount of soil to be removed for this basement. The angle of repose can be done with taper.

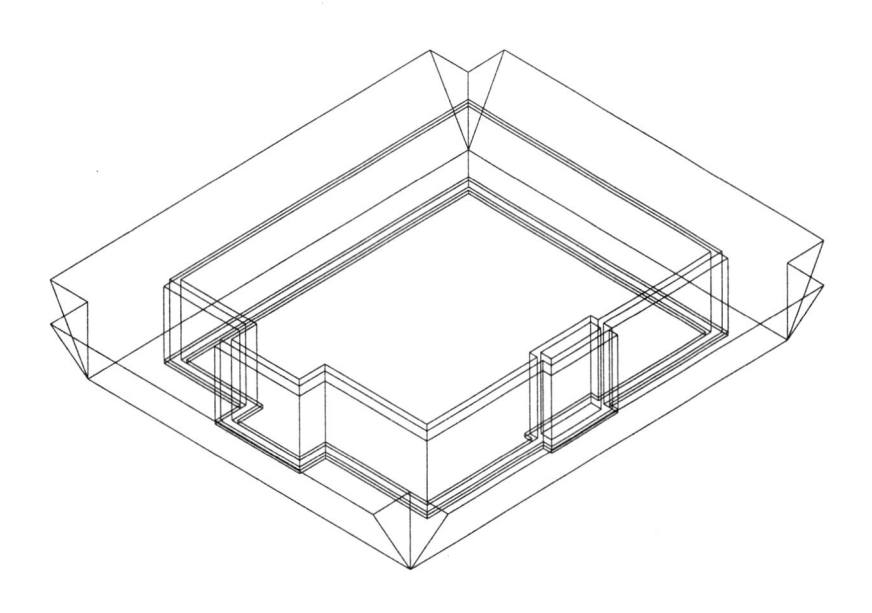

Exercise A29

Using the floor plans for the house created in the first section of this book, create a full 8' basement plus footings for the staircases at the frost line (4' in the north), and a foundation for the fireplace. The footings should be twice the width of the wall (8" usually). The circular fireplace extension from the first floor fireplace is purely cosmetic. Use EXTRUDE to make the job easier.

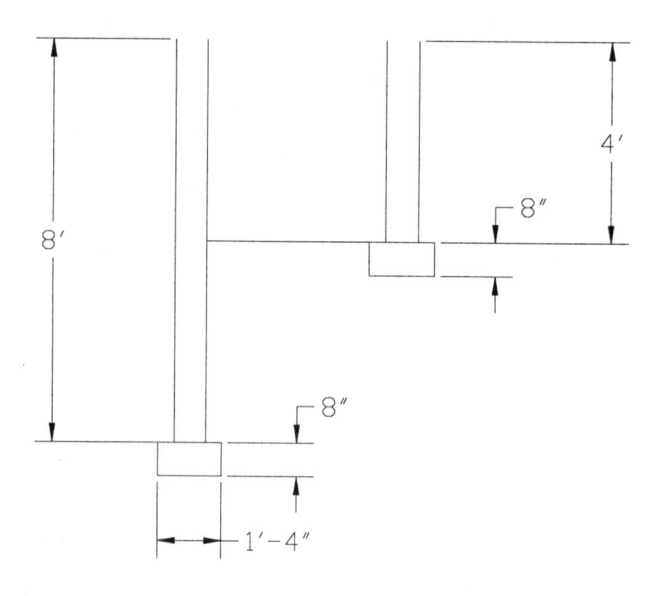

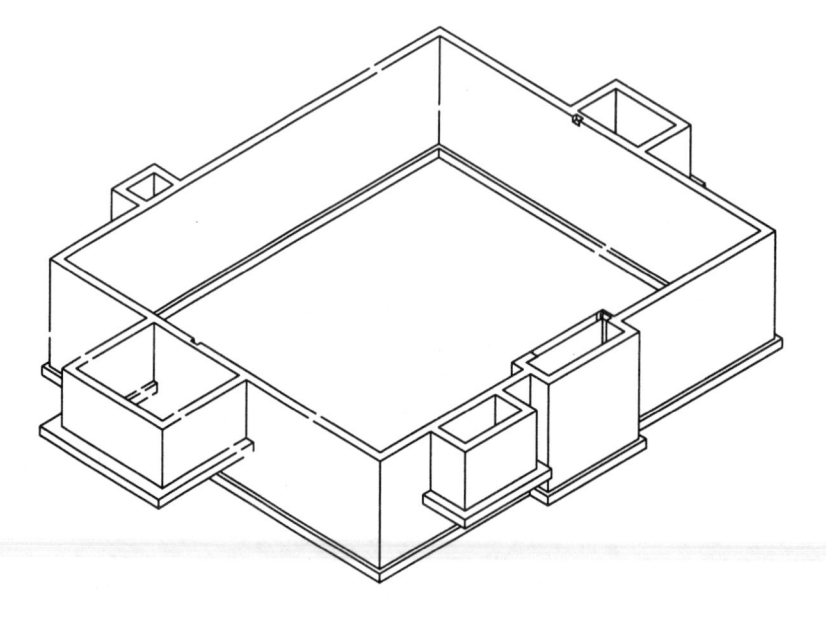

Exercise C29

Use the solids software to design a truss. Any of the examples below are acceptable.

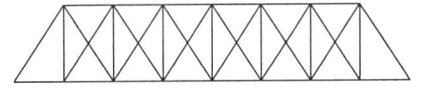

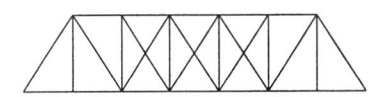

Howe Truss

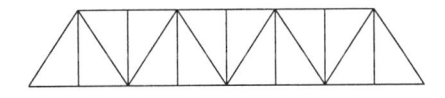

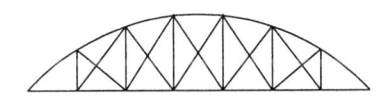

Pratt Truss

Warren Truss

Bowstring Truss

On the right is a simple beam truss design.

Use BOX to create the upper panel, then change your UCS and use CYLINDER to create the support bars.

Because the corners must be rounded and intersecting, you can use either REVOLVE or SPHERE to create partial tori on the ends of the beams as shown.

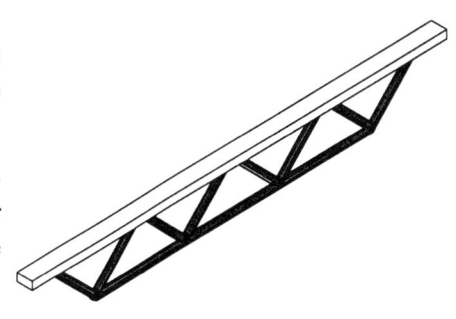

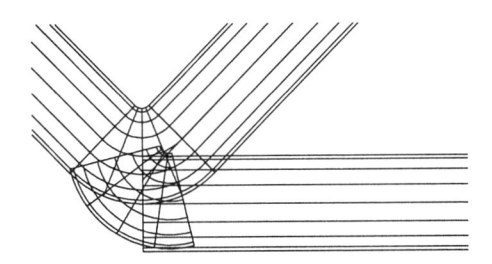

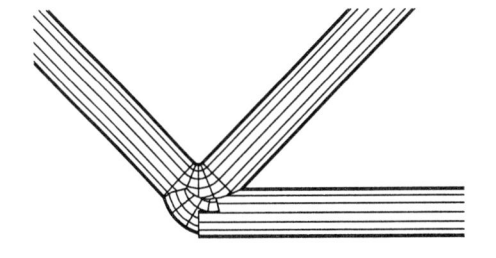

Once the information is in, use UNION to complete the part.

Exercise M29

29a will give you more practice with EXTRUDE and REVOLVE. Once finished, use SLICE to create a sectioned view of the part you have drawn. If you have limited time, 29B is a lot easier.

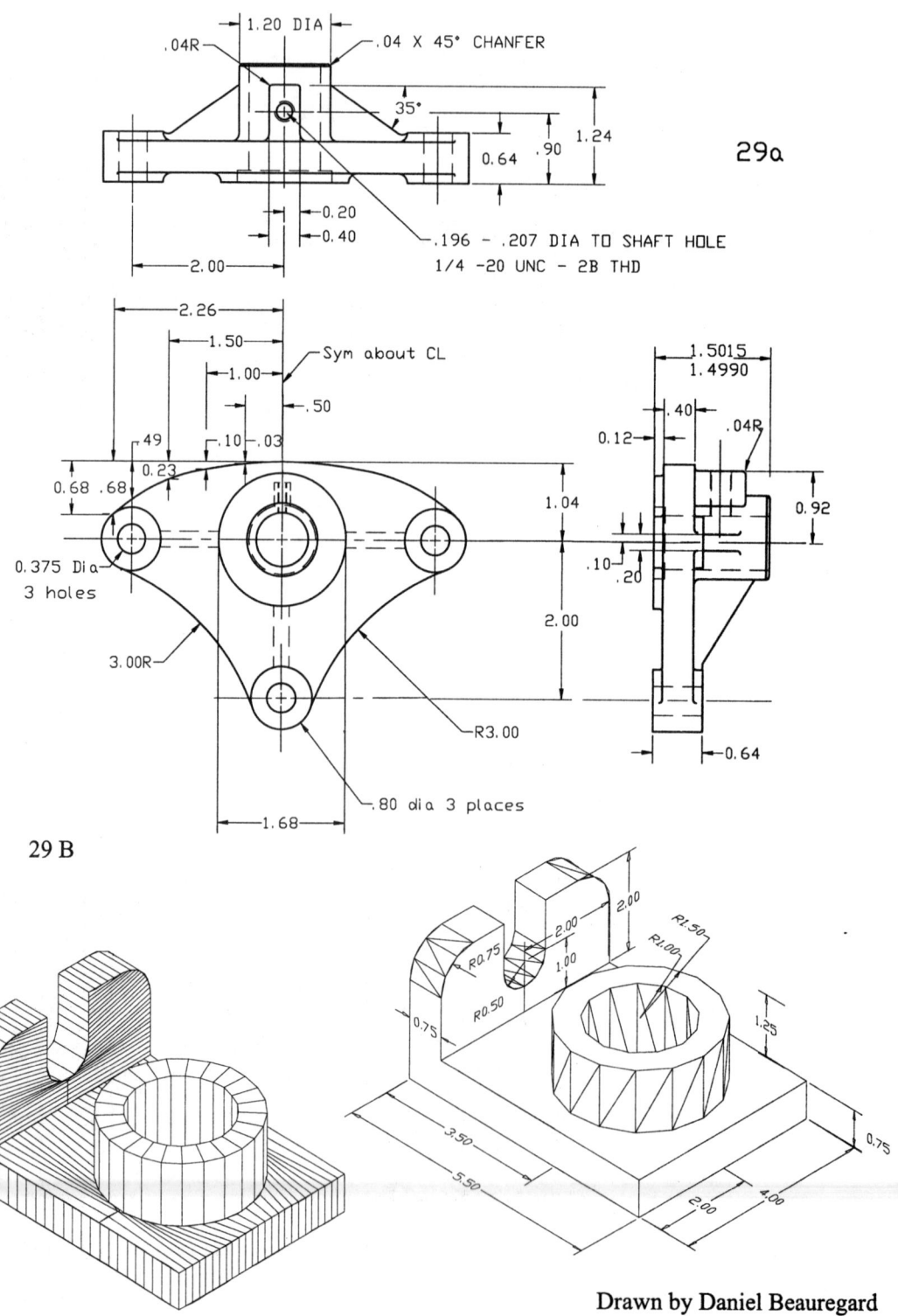

Drawn by Daniel Beauregard

Challenger 29

Create this part using 3D solids; in particular, use the EXTRUDE command.

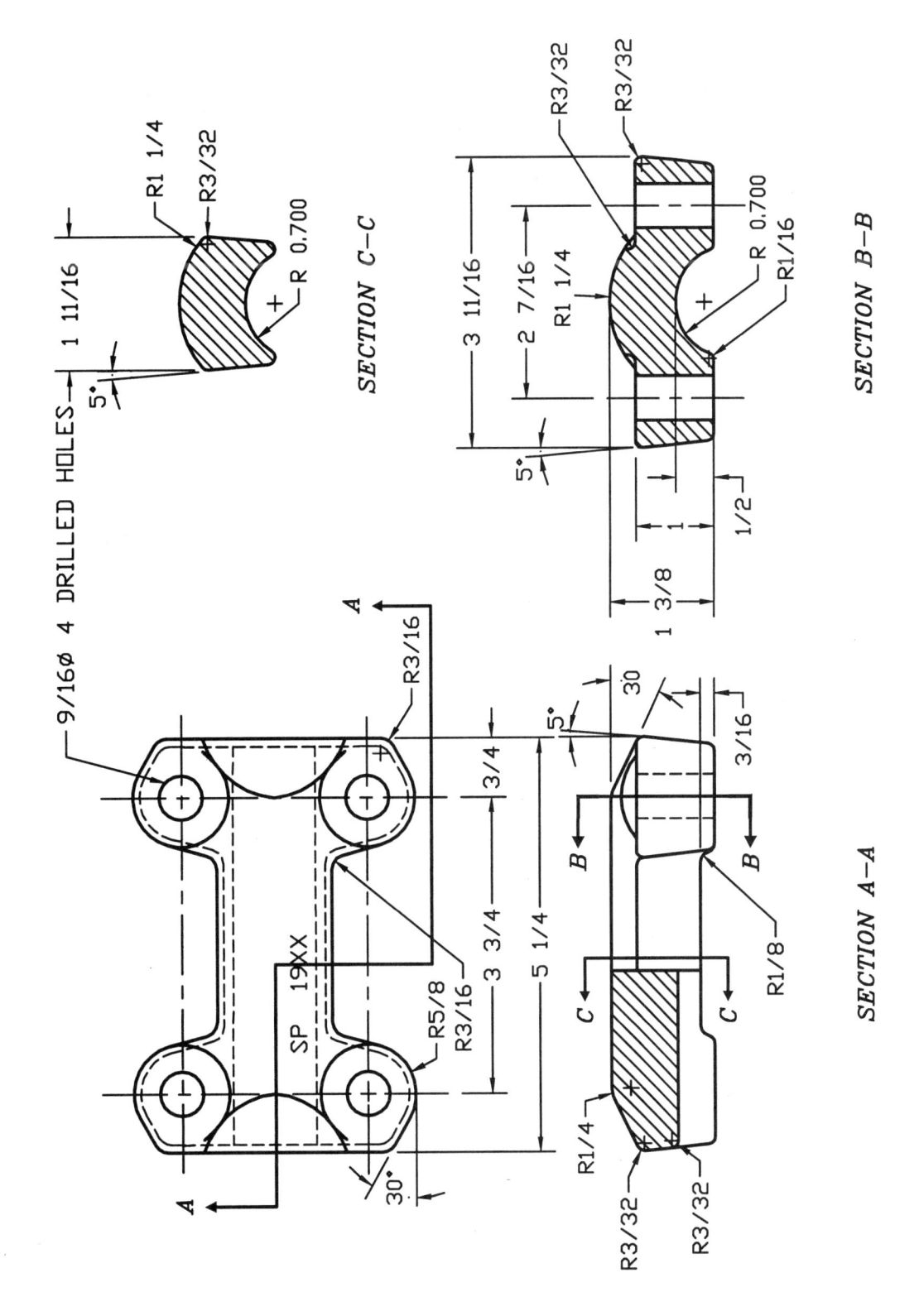

Challenger 29B

Create a dome design. This could be a gazebo or an airport.

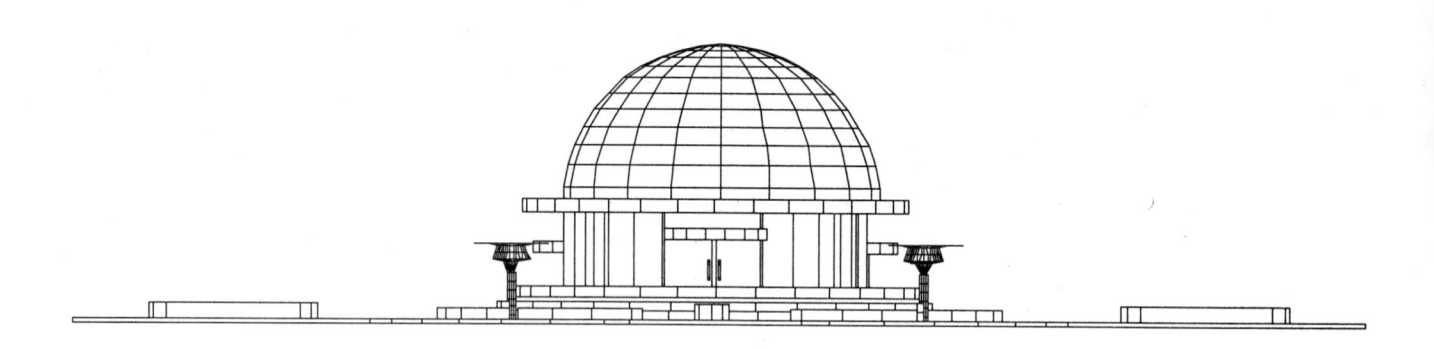

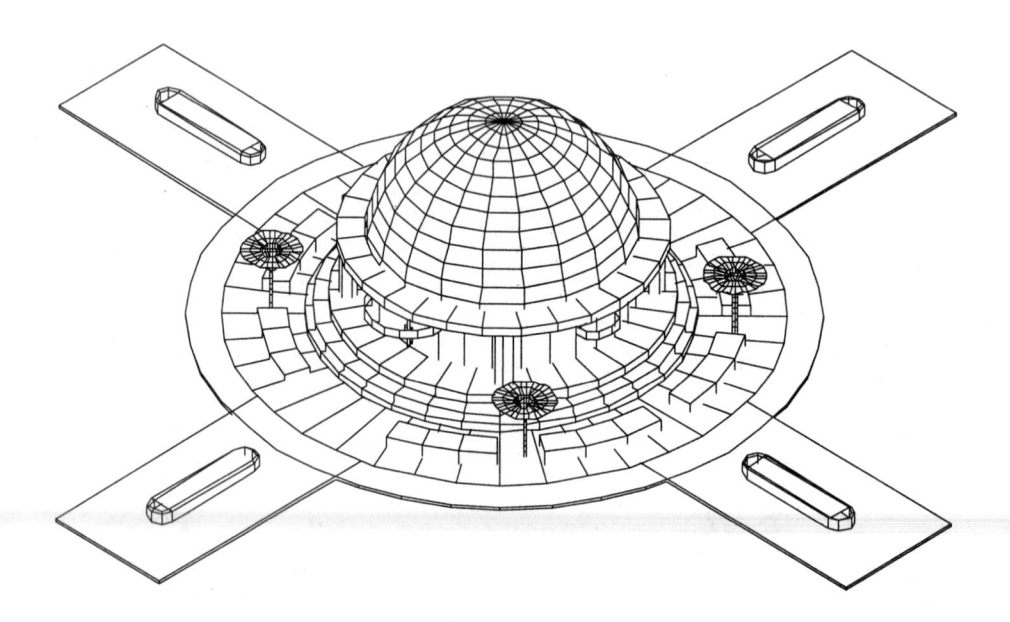

30
Editing Solids, Regions, and 3D Objects

Upon completion of this chapter, you should be able to:

1. Use ARRAY, ROTATE, MOVE, COPY, and MIRROR in 3D mode
2. Use TRIM and EXTEND in 3D mode
3. Use FILLET in 3D mode

There are two ways of editing objects in 3D: the first is to change the UCS so that whatever command you invoke is relative to the current UCS plane; the second is to use the commands created for use in 3D.

The 3DARRAY Command

With the ARRAY command, you can create a rectangular or polar array of objects normal to the X-Y plane of the current UCS. With the 3DARRAY command you can create three-dimensional arrays of objects without changing the UCS. In addition to specifying the number of objects in the X direction, the Y direction or in the final array, you specify the number of levels or the number of copies in the Z direction.

Rectangular 3D Arrays

To create a rectangular 3DARRAY, first create the base object, then find the 3DARRAY command. The arrayed objects are still relative to the current UCS, but you can have them arrayed along the Z axis.

> **Toolbar** There is no button for this command.
>
> **Pull Down Menu** From the Modify menu, choose 3D Operation, then 3DARRAY.

The command line equivalent is **3DARRAY**.

```
Command:3DARRAY
Select objects:(pick 1)
Other corner:(pick 2)
Select objects:↵
Enter the type of array
[Rectangular/Polar]<R>:↵
Enter number of rows (--)<1>:5
Enter number of columns (|||)<1>:1
Enter number of levels (...)<1>:2
Specify distance between the rows:50
```

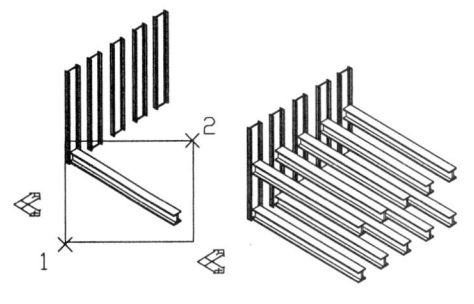

Figure 30-1

Editing Solids, Regions and 3D Objects   **697**

```
SpeciFy distance between the levels:75
```
This copies objects in a matrix of rows (*X* axis), columns (*Y* axis), and levels (*Z* axis). Positive values generate the array along the positive *X*, *Y*, and *Z*, whereas negative values generate the array along the negative *X*, *Y*, and *Z*.

> **Notes**
>
> In the examples, the *HIDE* command has been invoked for clarity.

Polar 3D Arrays

To create a polar array, first create the base object, then execute 3DARRAY. You must have an axis about which to generate the array; this is always from the center point of the rotation. This command operates independent of the current UCS.

> **Toolbar** There is no button for this command.
>
> **Pull Down Menu** From the Modify menu, choose 3D Operation, then 3DARRAY.

The command line equivalent is **3DARRAY**.

```
Command:3DARRAY
Select objects:(pick 1)
Select objects:
Enter the type of array
  [Rectangular/Polar] <R>:P
Enter the number of items
in the array:6
Specify the angle to fill
(+=CCW,-=CW) <360>:
Rotate arrayed objects <Y>:
Specify center point of array:MIDdle of (pick 2)
Specify second point on axis of rotation:END of (pick 3)
```

Figure 30-2

The specified angle determines the number of degrees by which AutoCAD rotates the objects about the axis of rotation.

A negative number produces a clockwise rotation.

ARRAYs Along Different UCSs

For staircases and other elements with angled rows, and columns, rotate the UCS to the specified angle, then use a 2D ARRAY.

> **Toolbar** From the Modify toolbar, choose Array.
>
> **Pull Down Menu** From the Modify menu choose Array.

The command line equivalent is **ARRAY**.

It is probably a good idea to put in construction lines as in Figure 30-3.

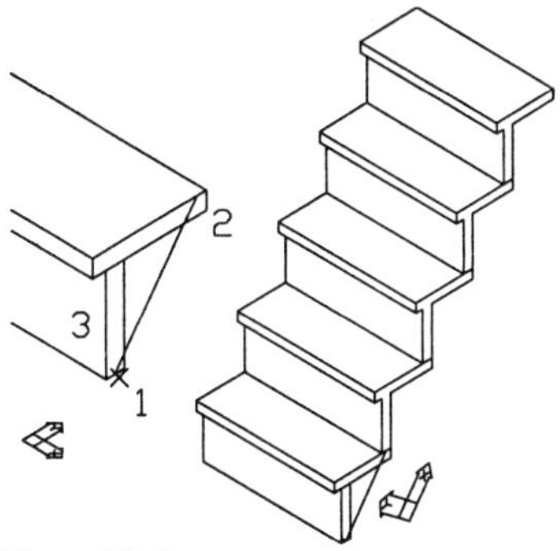

```
Command:UCS
Enter an option [New/Move/
 orthoGraphic/Prev/Restore/
 Save/Del/?]<World>:3
Specify new origin:(pick 1)
Specify ...X axis:(pick 2)
Specify...Y axis:(pick 3)
Command:Array
Select objects:(pick the stair)
Select objects:⏎
Enter type of array [Rectangular/Polar]:⏎
Enter number of rows (---)<1>:⏎ (accepts the default of 1)
Enter number of columns (|||)<1>:5
Specify distance between the columns:11.92
```

Figure 30-3

Use the LIST command or the DISTance command to find the distance between the two points, in this case 11.92 (9″ run × 7 7/8″ rise).

The MIRROR3D Command

With the MIRROR3D command you can create a mirror image of the object or objects through a specified plane. The mirroring plane can be one of the following:

1. The plane of a planar object
2. A plane parallel to the X-Y, X-Z, or Y-Z plane of the current UCS that passes through a point you select
3. A plane defined by three points that you select

To create mirrored objects use the following:

Toolbar There is no button for this command.

Pull Down Menu From the Modify menu, choose 3D Operation, then MIRROR3D.

The command line equivalent is **MIRROR3D**.

```
Command:MIRROR3D
Select objects: (pick the objects)
Specify first point of mirror plane (3 points) or
   [Object/Last/Zaxis/View/XY/YZ/ZX/3 points] <3points>:
```

Where: **Plane by Object** = an existing object
       3 point = A plane defined by three points
       Last = the last mirroring plane
       Zaxis = a plane specified by this axis
       View = the viewing plane in the current viewport
       X-Y/X-Z/Y-Z = aligns the plane with one of the standard planes defined by a point, relative to the current UCS

This object will illustrate how some of the rotations work. To make it, use BOX, WEDGE, and SPHERE. To place the sphere on the top face, use point filters. Once placed, use UNION and SUBTRACT to make it into one object.

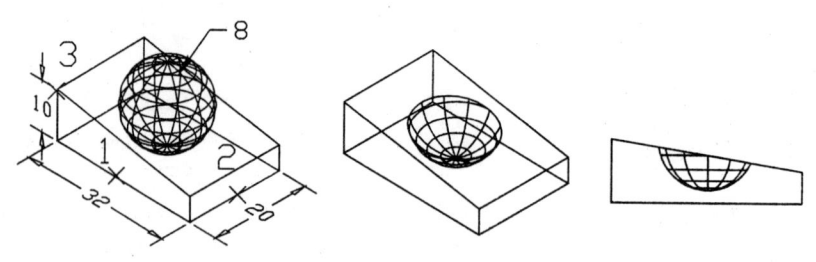

Figure 30-4

```
Command:SPHERE
Current wire frame density: ISOLINES=12
Specify center of sphere <0,0,0>:.x of MID of (pick 1)
Need YZ:.y of MID of (pick 2)
Need Z:END of (pick 3)
Specify radius of sphere or [Diameter]:8
```

In the illustrations, HIDE has been used to enhance clarity.

3 Point

This option defines the mirroring plane by three points. Be sure to use OSNAPs.

```
Command:MIRROR3D
Select objects: (pick the object)
Specify first point of mirror
 plane (3 points) or [Object/Last/
Zaxis/View/XY/YZ/ZX/3 points]
 <3points>:↵
Specify first point on plane:
 (pick 1)
Specify second point on plane:(pick 2)
Specify third point on plane:(pick 3)
Delete source objects? <N>:↵
```

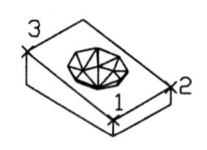

Figure 30-5

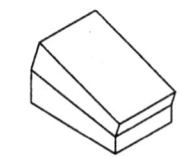

Object

This option specifies the mirroring plane by an existing object. The objects must be planar; circles, plines, ellipses, solids, etc.

Notes

Depending on the version of AutoCAD, the Object option may be Entity. The help files still reflect both.

```
Command:MIRROR3D
Select objects: (pick the object)
Specify first point of mirror
 plane (3 points) or [Object/Last/
Zaxis/View/XY/YZ/ZX/3 points]
 <3points>:Object
Select a circle, arc or 2D polyline segment: (pick 1)
Delete source objects? <N>:↵
```

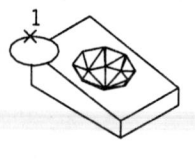

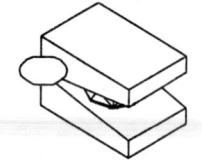

Figure 30-6

Zaxis

This option specifies a plane by a point on the plane and a point normal to the plane from the first point..

Notes

Object cannot be picked if SHADE has been used: use REGEN to return to selectable objects.

```
Command:MIRROR3D
Select objects: (pick the object)
 Specify first point of mirror
 plane (3 points) or [Object/Last/
Zaxis/View/XY/YZ/ZX/3 points]
 <3points>:Z
Specify point on mirror plane: (pick 1)
Specify point on Z axis (normal)
 of mirror plane:(pick 2)
Delete source objects? <N>:⏎
```

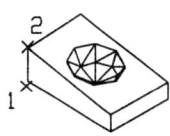

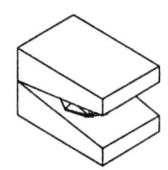

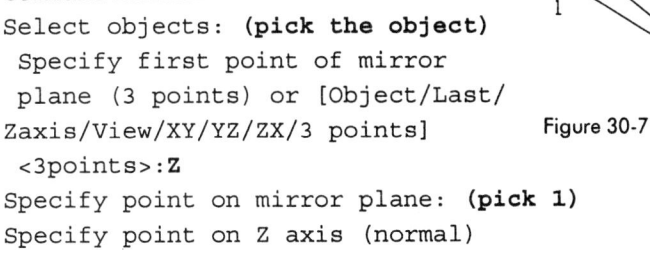

Figure 30-7

The results will be opposite if the pick sequence is reversed.

```
Command:MIRROR3D
Select objects: (pick the object)
Specify first point of mirror
 plane (3 points) or [Object/Last/
Zaxis/View/XY/YZ/ZX/3 points]
 <3points>:Z
Specify point on mirror plane: (pick 1)
Specify point on Z axis (normal) of
   plane: (pick 2)
Delete source objects? <N>:⏎
```

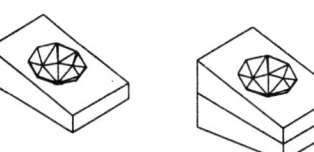

Figure 30-8

The ROTATE3D Command

The ROTATE3D command allows you to rotate objects in 3D without moving the UCS. The ROTATE command allows rotation of 3D objects, but only around the Z axis of the current UCS. Using ROTATE3D, you can specify the axis of rotation using two points, an object, the *X*, *Y*, or *Z* axes, or the *Z* direction of the current view.

To rotate objects in 3D use the following:

> **Toolbar** There is no button for this command.
>
> **Pull Down Menu** From the Modify menu, choose 3D Operation, then ROTATE3D.

The command line equivalent is **ROTATE3D**.

Remember to use the Osnap options when specifying the axis.

Again, depending on the version of the release, the Object option may be Entity.

Editing Solids, Regions and 3D Objects **701**

```
Command: ROTATE3D
Current positive angle:
 ANGDIR=counterclockwise ANGBASE=0
Select objects: (pick the object
   to be rotated)
Select objects:⏎
Specify first point on axis or
 define axis by [Object/Last/View/Xaxis/Yaxis/Zaxis/2 points]:
 (pick 1)
Specify second point on axis: (pick 2)
Specify rotation angle or [Reference]:90
```

Figure 30-9

Axis by Object or Entity

Axis by object or entity aligns the axis of rotation with an existing entity. The object or entity must be a line, circle, arc, or 2D pline.

```
Command: ROTATE3D
Select objects: (pick the object to
   rotate)
Select objects:⏎
Specify first point on axis or
 define axis by [Object/Last/
 View/Xaxis/Yaxis/Zaxis/2 points]:
 Object
Select a line, circle, arc, or
2D-polyline segment: (pick the circle)
Specify rotation angle or [Reference]:90
```

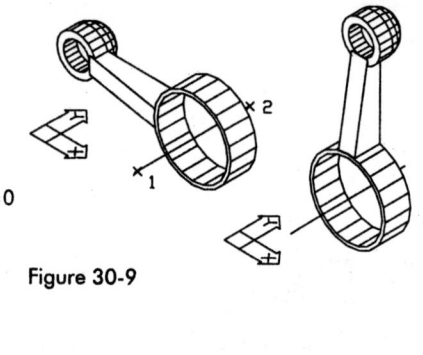

Figure 30-10

AutoCAD aligns itself with objects as follows:

Line aligns with the line itself.

Circle aligns with the 3D axis of the circle.

Arc aligns with the 3D axis passing through the center of the arc.

Pline treats a straight segment as a line segment, and an arc segment as an arc.

Axes

The *X, Y,* or *Z* axes can all be used as rotation axes.

```
Command: ROTATE3D
Select objects: (pick the object)
Select objects:⏎
Specify first point on axis or
 define axis by [Object/Last/View/
 Xaxis/Yaxis/Zaxis/2 points]:X
Specify point on X axis <0,0,0>: (pick 1)
Specify rotation angle or [Reference]:90
```

Figure 30-11

Last

This option aligns the axis with the last axis used.

View

This option aligns the axis of rotation with the viewing direction of the current viewport that passes through the selected point.

MOVE and COPY in 3D

MOVE and COPY are used in 3D the same way as in 2D drawings. If an object selection is used to identify the direction vector, the objects will align with the specified point on the existing object. If specifying points in 3D space, the *X*, *Y* and *Z* axes may be specified. If using incremental entries, the position of the first point (base point) is irrelevant.

```
Command:MOVE
Select objects:(pick the object)
Select objects:↵
Specify base point: (pick 1)
Specify displacement:@0,0,5
```

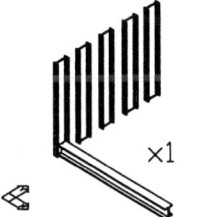

Figure 30-12

Danger
Incremental entries will often not work if there is a running object snap.

```
Command:COPY
Select objects:(pick the objects)
Select objects:↵
Specify base point or
  [Multiple]: (pick 1)
Specify second point of
displacement:@0,0,5
```

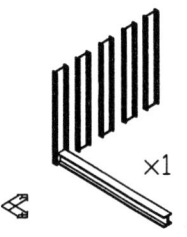

Figure 30-13

The incremental entries will be accepted relative to the current UCS.

Trimming and Extending in 3D

The system variables PROJMODE and EXTEDGE allow you to choose one of three projections for a trim or extend operation: the *X-Y* plane of the current UCS, the current viewing plane, or true 3D, which is not a projection. Without using these variables, you will only be able to trim to the current UCS.

In a true 3D extend or trim operation, objects must intersect with the boundaries in 3D space. If the two objects do not intersect and you trim or extend in the current UCS *X-Y* plane, the trimmed or extended boundary might not end precisely at the boundary in 3D space.

You can trim or extend an object to any other object on screen, regardless of whether it is or is not on the same plane or parallel to the cutting or boundary edges.

Editing Solids, Regions and 3D Objects **703**

```
Command: TRIM
Current settings:  Projection mode = UCS, Edge = None
Select cutting edges
Select objects:(pick 1)
Select objects:⏎
Select object to trim or [Project/Edge/Undo]:P
Enter a projection option [None/Ucs/View]<Ucs>:U
Select object to trim or [Project/Edge/Undo]:(pick 2)
Select object to trim or [Project/Edge/Undo]:(pick 3)
Select object to trim or [Project/Edge/Undo]:⏎
```

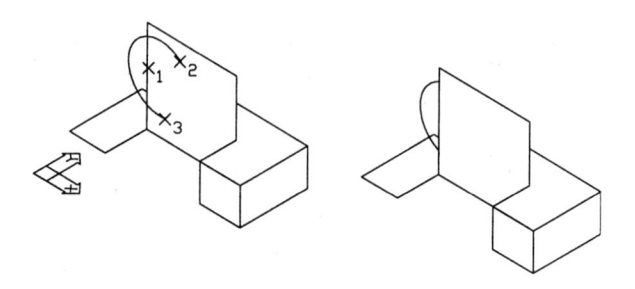

Figure 30-14

```
Command:EXTEND
Current settings: Projection mode = UCS, Edge = None
Select cutting edges
Select objects:(pick 1)
Select objects:⏎
Select object to extend or [Project/Edge/Undo]:E
Enter an implied edge extension mode [Extend/No extend] <No
   extend>:⏎
Select object to extend or [Project/Edge/Undo]:(pick 2)
Select object to extend or [Project/Edge/Undo]:(pick 3)
Select object to extend or [Project/Edge/Undo]:⏎
```

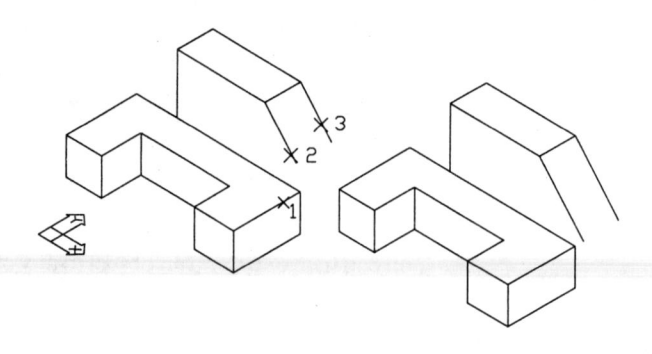

Figure 30-15

Prelab 30 Editing Solids

In this prelab we will simply experiment in Solids with some of the editing commands.

Step 1   Draw up the part as shown. Use Solids. Once all the components are in, use SUBTRACT on the interior cylinders and UNION on all objects to join them together.

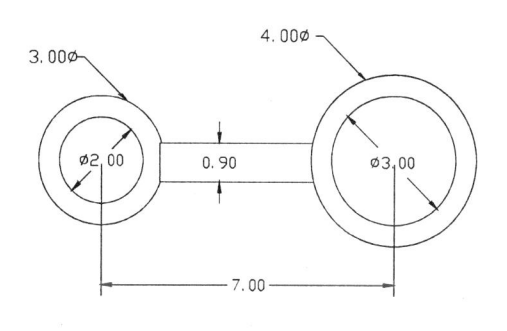

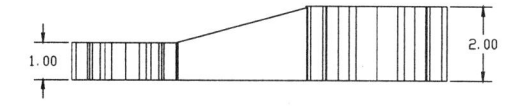

Step 2   Now change your UCS by rotating it around *X* by 90 degrees.

Once in, create a circle on the *X-Y* plane.

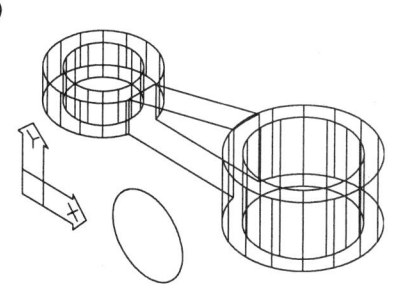

Now use ROTATE3D to rotate the part 90 degrees.

```
Command:ROTATE3D
Select objects: (pick 1)
Select objects:↵
Specify first point on axis or
  define axis by [Object/Last/
  View/Xaxis/Yaxis/Zaxis/2 points]:
 Object
Select a line, circle, arc, or
2D-polyline segment:(pick 2)
Specify rotation angle or
   [Reference]:90
```

The object has been rotated around the circle.

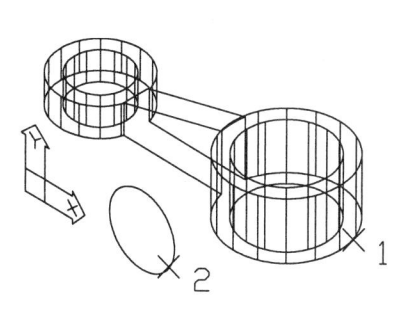

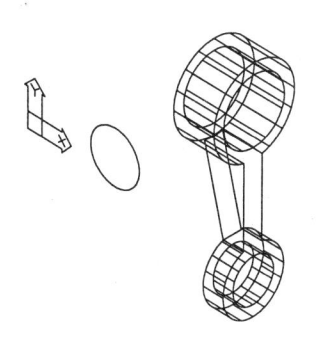

Step 3 Now draw a line through the center of the large cylinder out from the object five units. Use ORTHO. Then access the 3DARRAY command to array the objects.

```
Command: 3DARRAY
Select objects: (pick 1)
Select objects:
Enter the type of array
 [Rectangular/Polar] <R>: P
Enter the number of items
 In the array: 6
Specify the angle to fill
 (+=CCW,-=CW) <360>:
Rotate arrayed objects <Y>:
Specify center point of
array: MIDdle of (pick 2)
Specify second point on axis of rotation: END of (pick 3)
```

Now use UNION to make all the parts into one object.

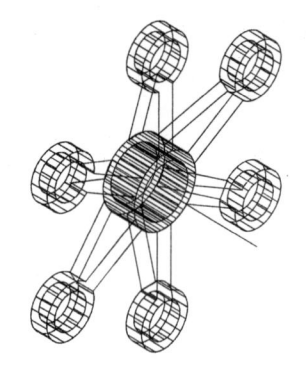

Step 4 Now use MIRROR3D to mirror the objects around one another so that they are facing. Use MIRROR3D with the Zaxis option.

```
Command: MIRROR3D
Select objects: (pick 1)
 Specify first point of mirror plane (3 points) or
  [Object/Last/Zaxis/View /XY/YZ/ZX/3 points]<3points>: Z
Specify point on mirror plane: MIDpoint of (pick 2)
Specify point on Z axis (normal) of mirror plane:
 END of (pick 3)
Delete source objects? <N>:
```

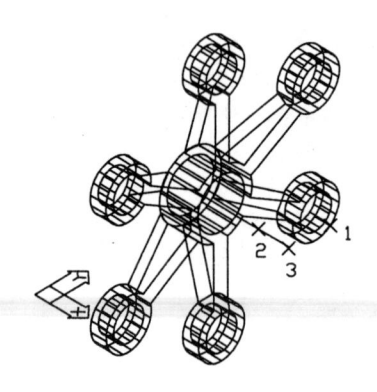

Command and Function Summary

3DARRAY creates arrays of objects in 3D.

MIRROR3D creates mirrored objects through 3D planes.

Practice Exercise 30

Create one sprocket of this Geneva gear on the *X-Z* plane as a solid with a thickness of .15. Use 3DARRAY to array all the sprockets. Draw in the keyway and subtract it.

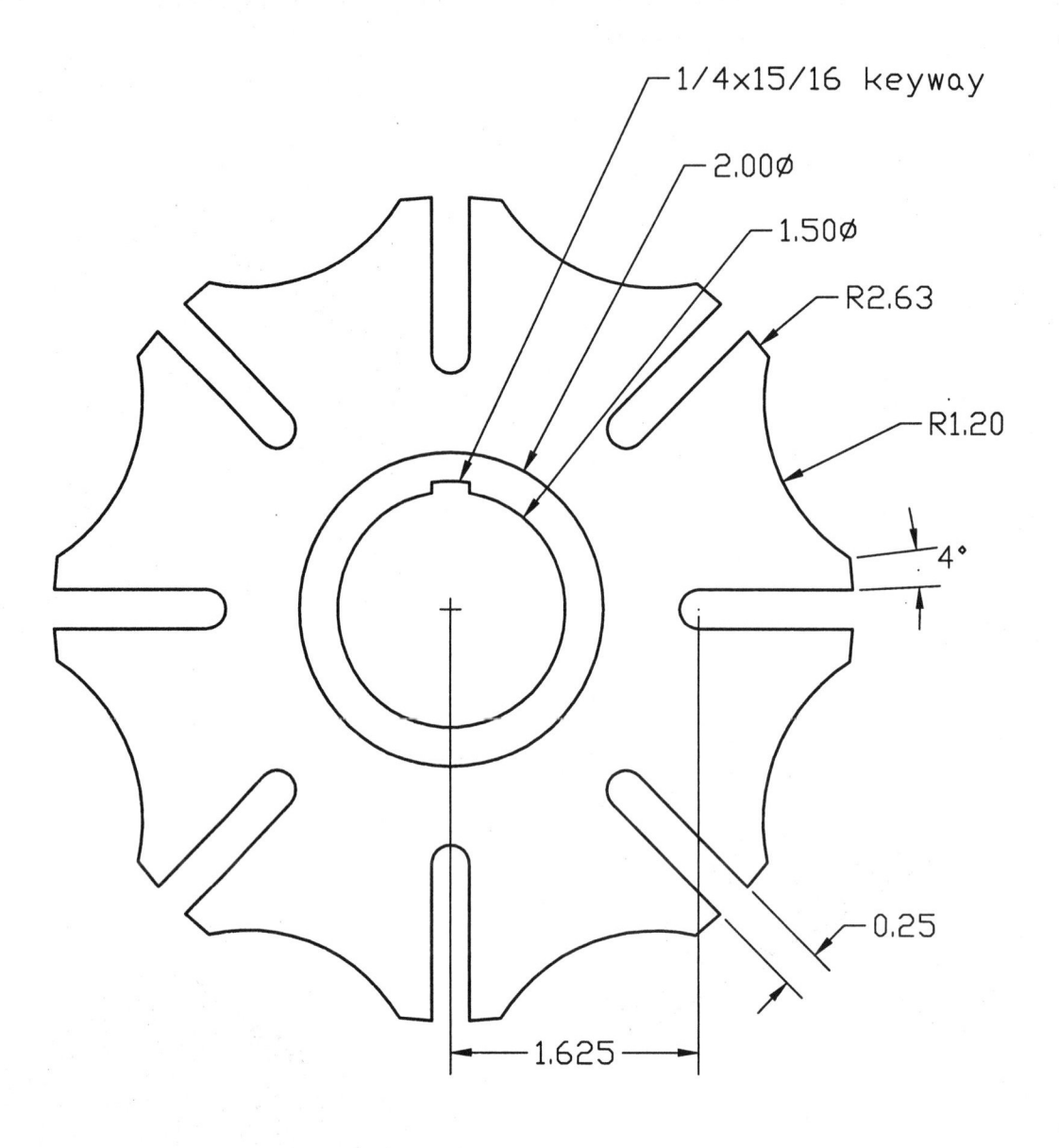

Exercise A30

Using the floor plan for the house from the first section of the book, create the floor joists and the plywood covering in solids. Use ARRAY and 3DARRAY when needed.

Note: Using 3D objects will make a much smaller file than using solids. Unless you need to calculate the weight or strength of the floor, use 3D objects.

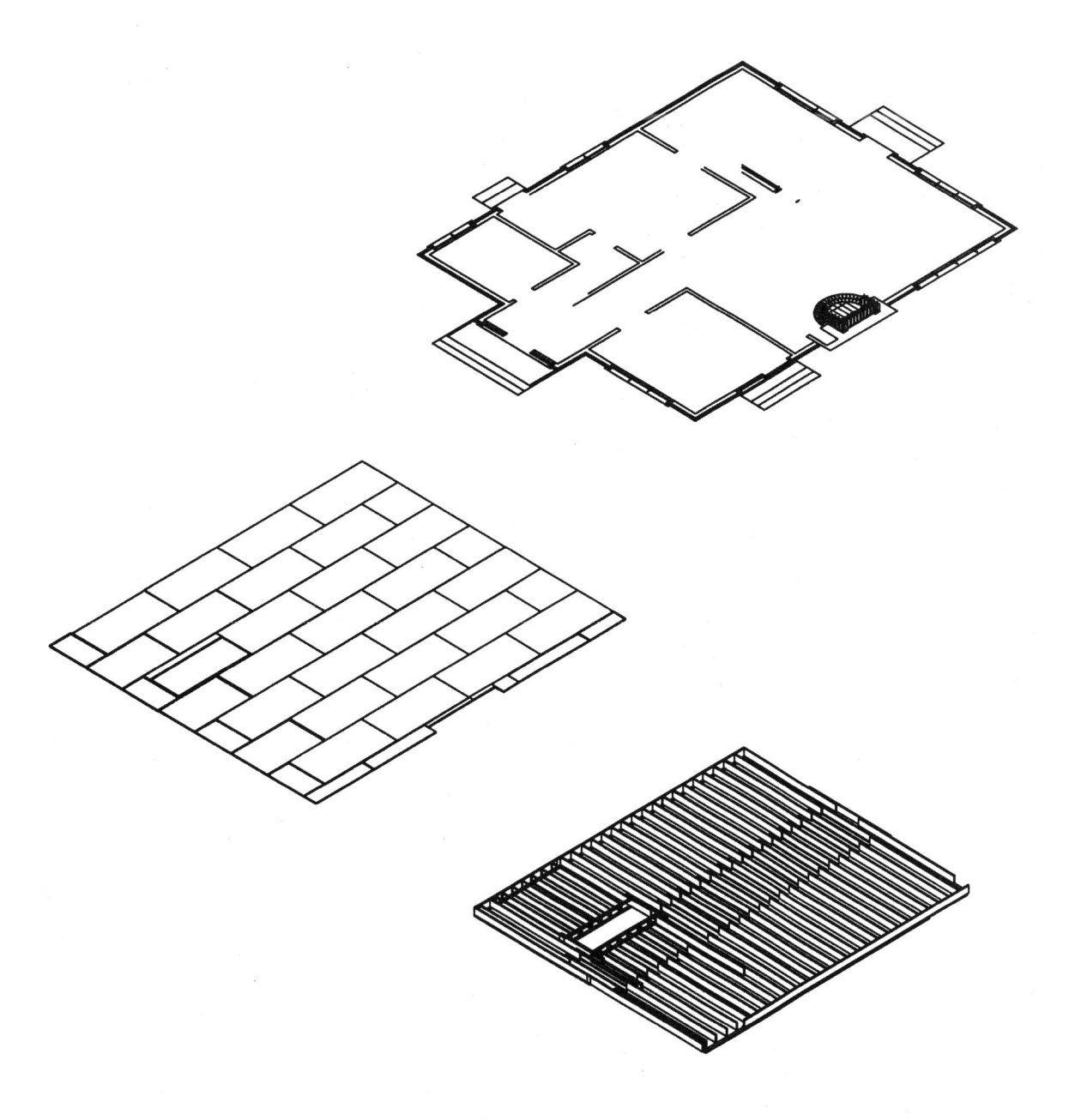

Exercise A30 (cont.)

Use solids or 3D objects to create the frame of the first floor on top of the subfloor from the previous page. This will take up much space on your disk and may require more than two hours to complete.

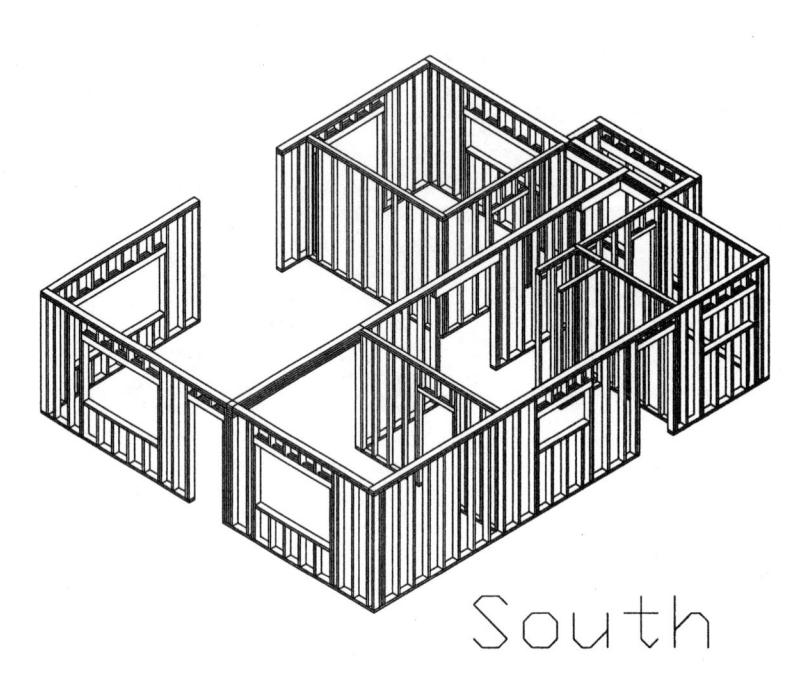

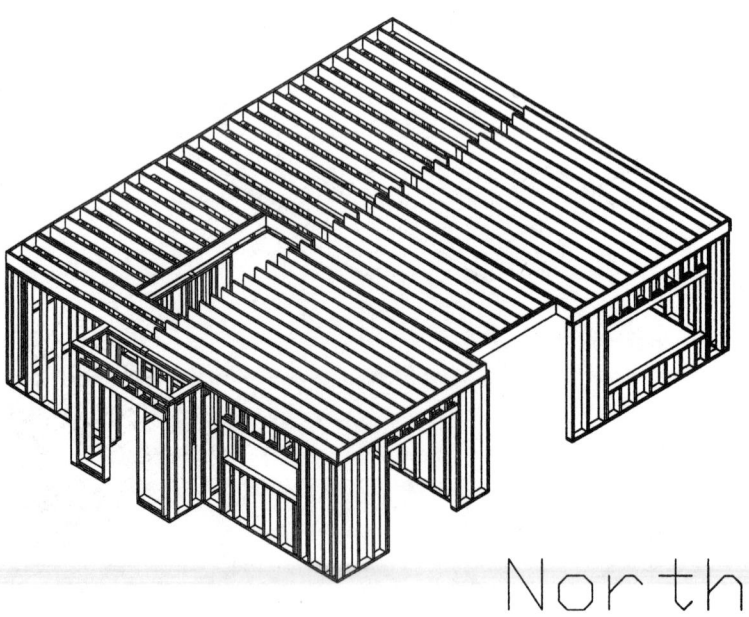

South

North

Exercise C30

Draw this industrial stairwell using local code requirements. Use ARRAY or 3DARRAY for the stairs.

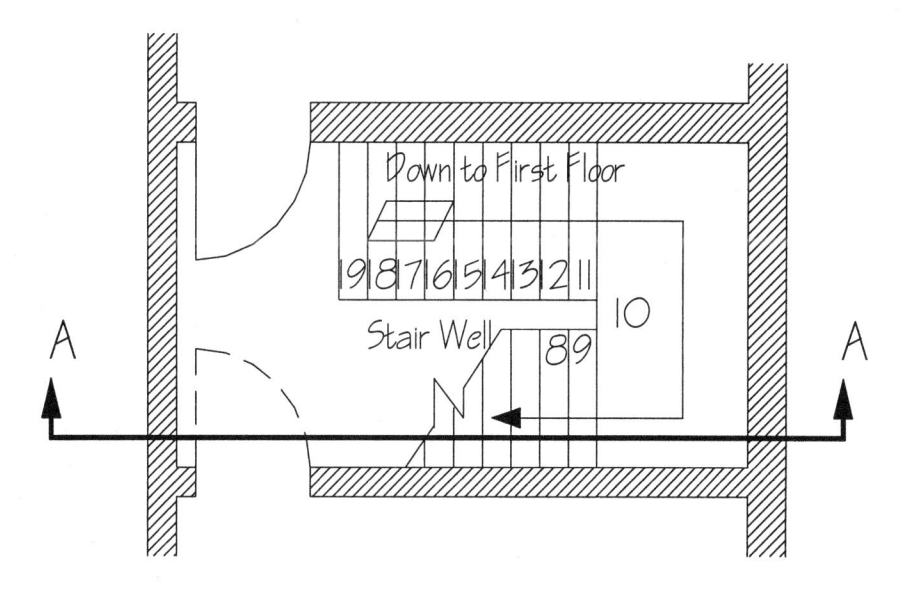

Second Floor Plan

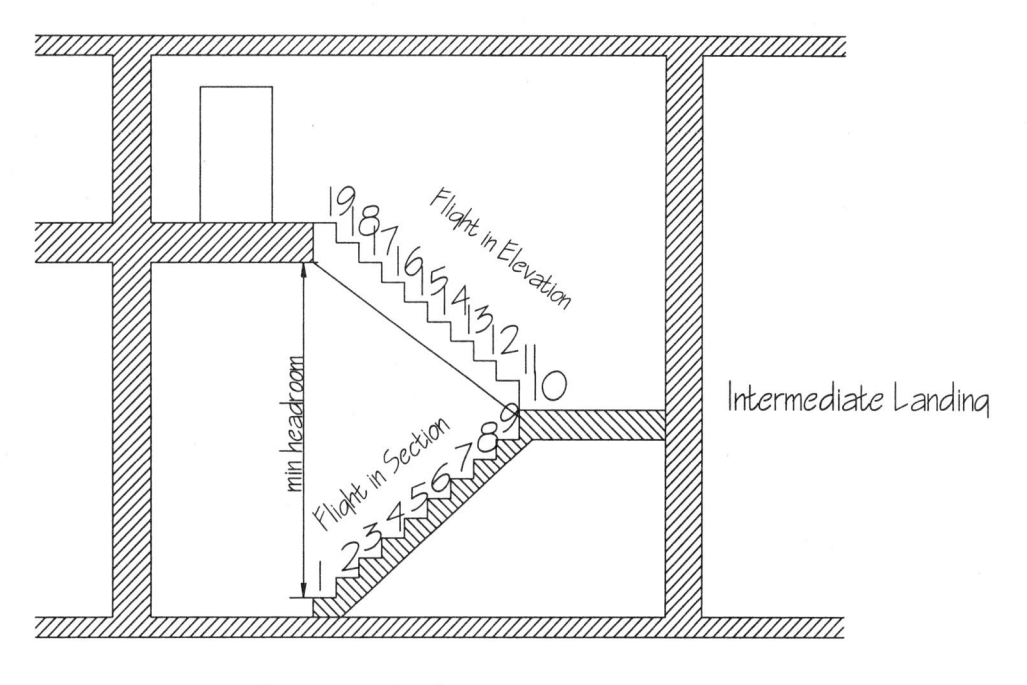

Section A-A

Exercise M30

Draw the bushing in 30A using 3DARRAY and Solids.

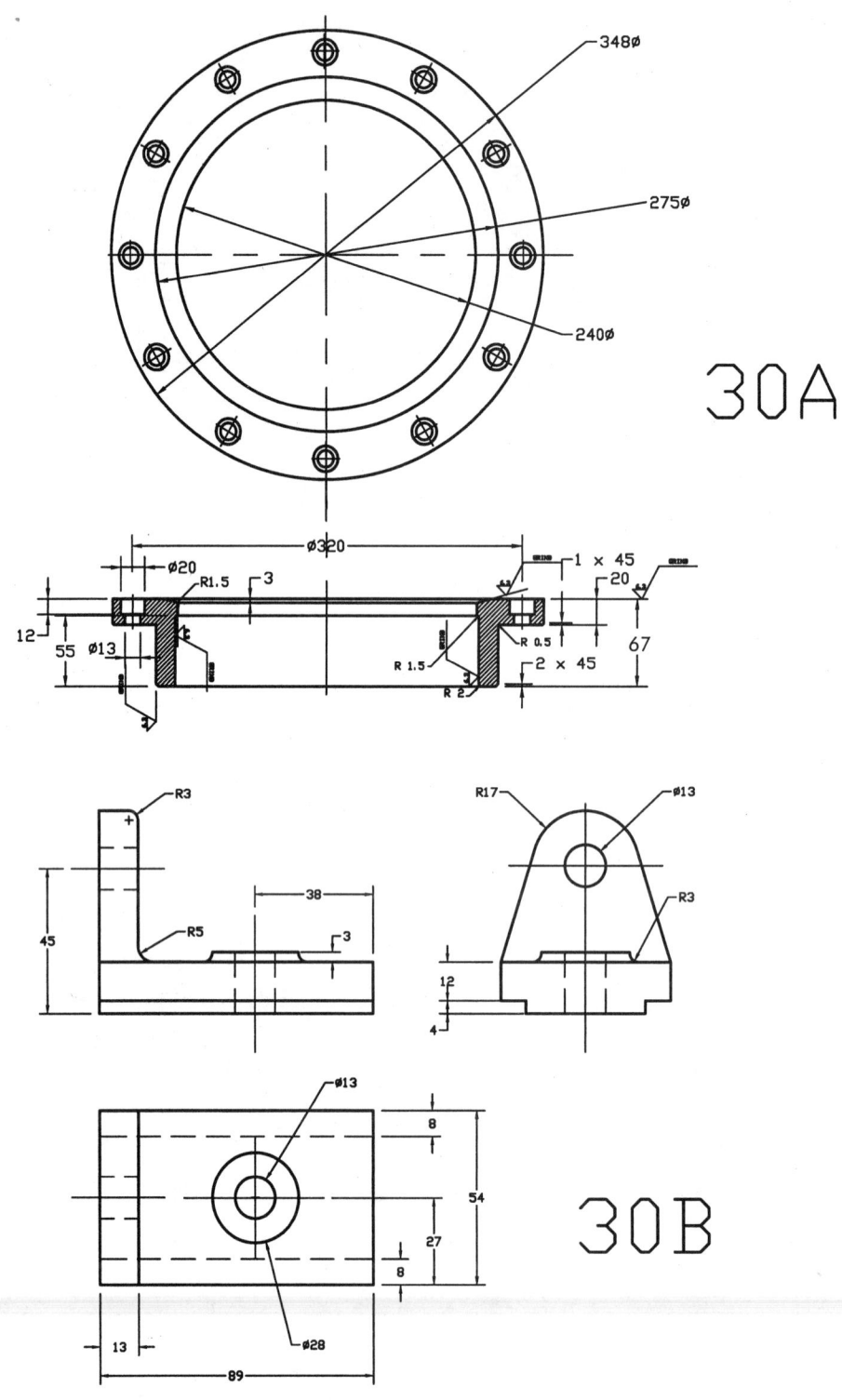

Challenger 30

Create this petroleum nozzle in 3D. Use Solids to calculate the weight of the parts in A (bronze), and B (steel).

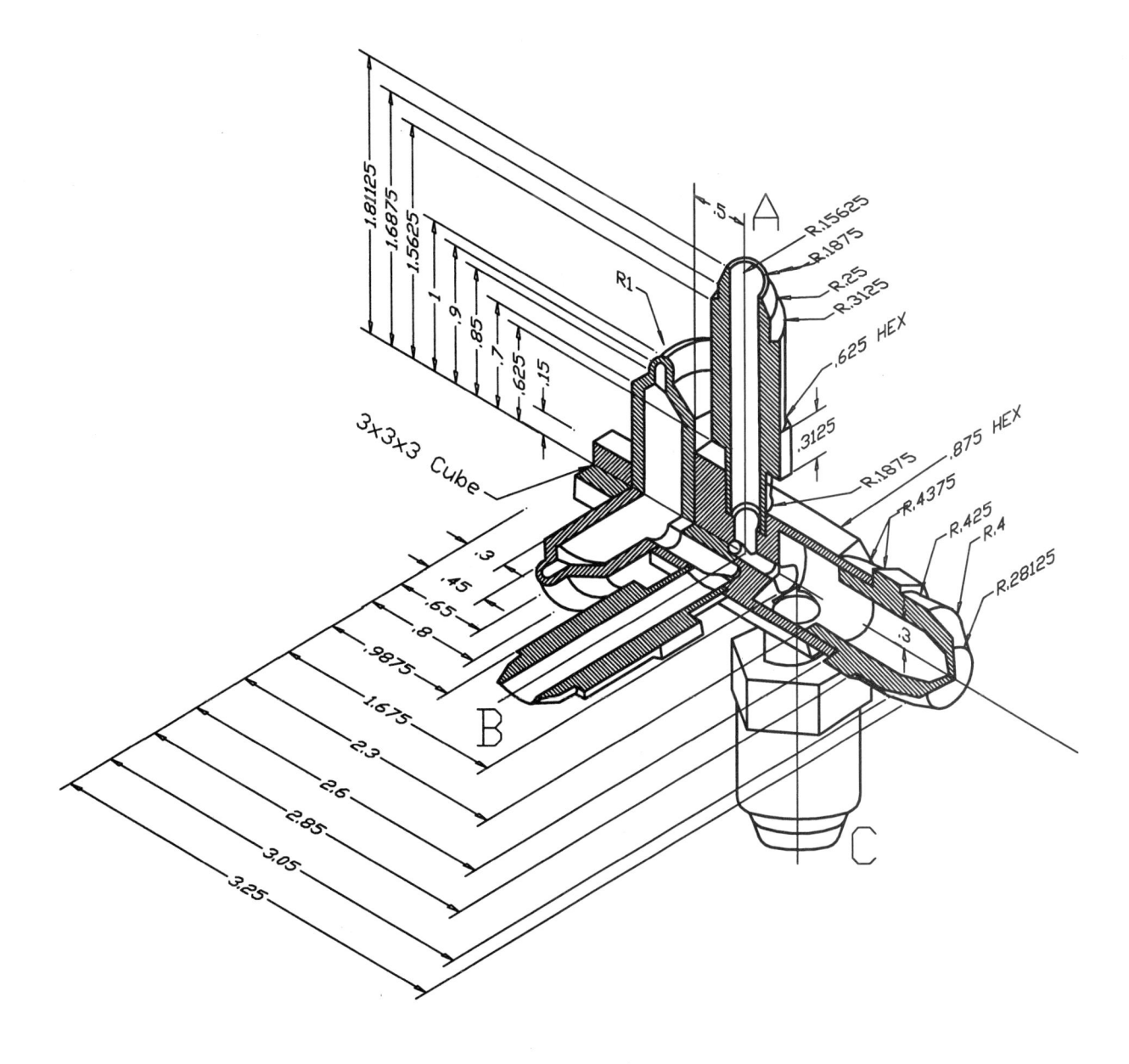

Challenger 30 (cont.)

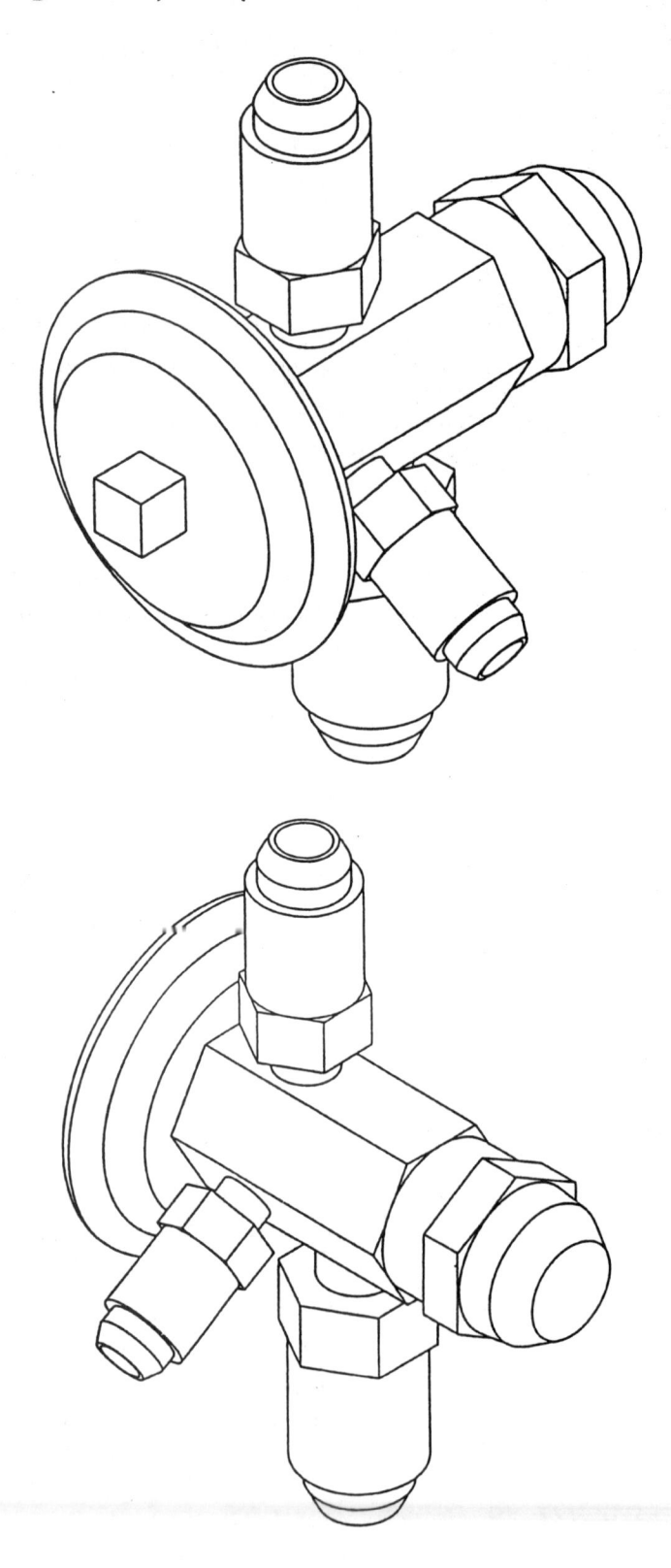

31 Regions and Mass Properties Calculations

Upon completion of this chapter, you should be able to:

1. Create two-dimensional regions
2. Calculate the surface area of solids
3. Calculate the mass properties of regions and solids

Regions

AutoCAD uses the term *region* to define a series of 2D objects (lines, circles, arcs, plines, etc.) that are picked as one solid object. The region can be a simple outline or it can contain "holes." The outer edge of the region is called the "outer loop" and the "holes" are called "inner loops." The objects that make up the loops must either be closed or form closed areas by sharing endpoints with other objects. They must also be coplanar.

Objects such as 3D polylines and face meshes can be converted into regions by being exploded. You cannot form regions from open objects that intersect and form a closed area; for example, intersecting arcs or self-intersecting curves.

Regions can be used for area analysis, section analysis, and can be extruded or revolved to create complex solids. You can apply hatching and shading to regions for display purposes.

We will use four different examples to show how this works, because the applications and uses are much different.

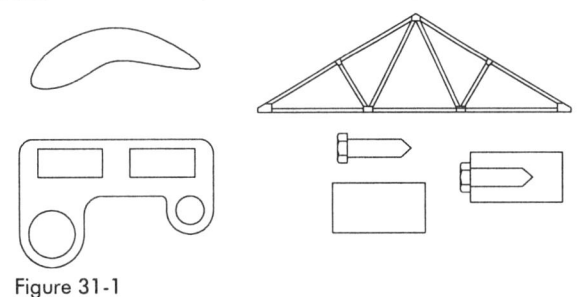

Figure 31-1

1. When designing turbine blades, propeller blades, etc., the method is to generate a series of cross sections (as in the closed spline), calculate the centroids (page 722), stack the sections, and rotate them according to the required blade angle. We will calculate the centroid of the closed spline.
2. We will use a simple template to create a composite region and then calculate the area.
3. Moments of inertia, weight, and other relevant factors can be generated from the simple truss region.
4. The volume of an intersection, such as this bolt in some stock, can also be calculated.

The REGION Command

The REGION command creates a region from existing objects. Regions can exist anywhere in space, but are 2D entities. To create a region, use the regular 2D commands to generate the outline, then use the REGION command.

> **Toolbar** From the Draw toolbar, choose Region.
>
> **Pull Down Menu** From the Draw menu, choose Region.

The command line equivalent is **REGION**.

Create a spline and make it into a region. Make sure the spline is closed.

```
Command: REGION
Select objects: (pick 1)
1 loop extracted
1 region created
```

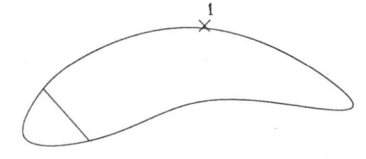

Figure 31-2

Creating Composite Regions

You can create composite regions by subtracting, combining, or finding the intersection of regions.

SUBTRACT with Regions

Retreive this object from Chapter 1 or draw it now. Use REGION to create a region.

```
Command: REGION
Select objects: (pick 1 through 12)
1 loop extracted
1 region created
```

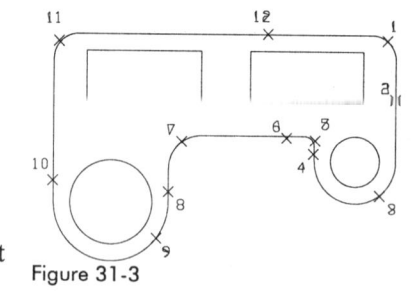

Like PEDIT with the Join option, the objects must have "touching" endpoints.

Figure 31-3

First select the objects to be solidified on the "outer loop." The outline must be solidified first. When you have created the "outer loop" of the region, change the inner sections to regions.

```
Command: REGION
Select objects: (pick 1 through 10)
4 loops extracted
4 regions created
```

Now use SUBTRACT to subtract the interior boundaries or "inner loops."

Figure 31-4

The command line equivalent is **SUBTRACT**.

Toolbar From the Solids Editing toolbar, choose Subtract.

Pull Down Menu From the Modify menu, choose Solids Editing, then Subtract.

```
Command: SUBTRACT
Select solids and regions to
   subtract from.
Select objects: (pick 1)
Select objects: ⏎
Select solids and regions to
   subtract....
Select objects: (pick 2, 3, 4, 5)
Select objects: ⏎
```

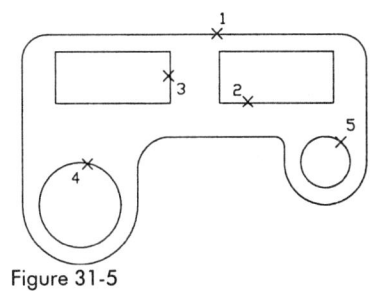

Figure 31-5

To make sure that the shape has become a region, use SHADE.

```
Command: SHADE
```

UNION with Regions

Draw this simple truss using PLINE. Use REGION to make regions of each section. To make sure that each section becomes one complete object, use UNION.

Toolbar From the Solids Editing toolbar, choose Union.

Pull Down Menu From the Modify menu, choose Solids editing, then Union.

The command line equivalent is **UNION**.

```
Command: UNION
Select objects: (pick 1
   through 18)
1 loop extracted
1 region created
```

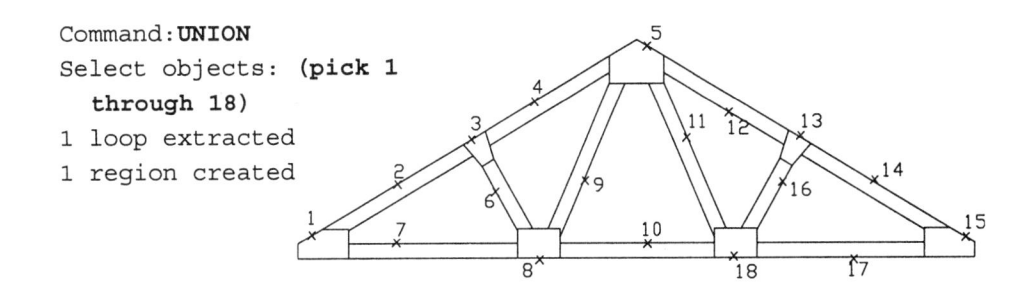

Figure 31-6

INTERSECTION with Regions

To calculate the area and mass properties of intersecting objects, use INTERSECTION. Draw the piece of stock, and the bolt in Figure 31-7. Make each into a region. Move the bolt onto the stock, then use INTERSECTION to extract the intersection.

Regions and Mass Properties Calculations **717**

> **Toolbar** From the Solids Editng toolbar, choose Intersection.
>
> **Pull Down Menu** From the Modify menu, choose Solids Editing, then Intersection.

The command line equivalent is INTERSECT.

```
Command: INTERSECT
Select object to intersect:
  (pick 1)
Select object to intersect:
  (pick 2)
```

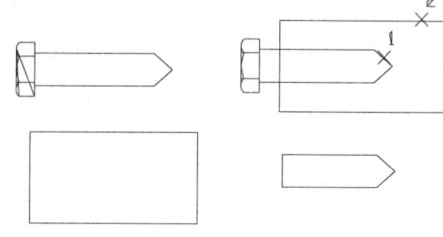

Figure 31-7

You can select in any order the regions whose intersection you want to find. The resulting object is also a region.

The regions are now completed and we can use the AREA and Mass Properties calculations.

The AREA Command

You often need to find the total surface area of an object in order to calculate quantities of finish materials and sizes. To calculate the surface area of either a region or a 3D solid model, use the AREA command.

> **Toolbar** From the Inquiry toolbar, choose Area.
>
> **Pull Down Menu** From the Tools menu, choose Inquiry, then Area.

The command line equivalent is **AREA**.

For the template, choose the Object option.

```
Command: AREA
Specify first corner point or
  [Object/Add/Subtract]:O
Select objects: (pick the template)
Area = 12182.6150
Length = 1345.7876
```

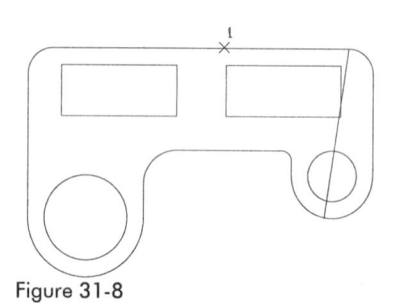

Figure 31-8

If the Architectural units are set to current, your readout should be:
```
Area = 12182.6 square inches (84.601 square feet), length = 112
   feet, 1.75 inches.
```

The same command is used for the 3D solid object. Use the Prelab from Chapter 30 as an example.

```
Command: AREA
Specify first corner point or [Object/Add/Subtract]:O
Select objects: (pick the object)
Area = 218.3255   Length = 0.0000
```

Many objects can be calculated together and a sum total can be achieved by using the Add option.

The readout for the area is determined by your units. If the Architectural units are set to current, your readout should be:

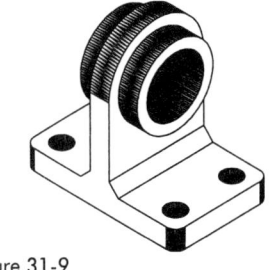

```
Area = 218.33 (1.5161 square feet),
    length = 0 feet, 0 inches
```

Figure 31-9

Mass Properties

The solids capabilities of AutoCAD Release 2000 are useful for many reasons. Some people find model creation to be much simpler in solids than in wireframe. Shading and rendering in solids often give more pleasing results. Finally, in creating solid objects, the user can extract volumetric information such as volume, center of gravity, principal axes, and moments of inertia.

The MASSPROP Command

Mass properties calculations can be performed on both 2D regions and 3D solids. To access the mass properties command use the following:

> **Toolbar** From the Inquiry menu, choose Massprop.
>
> **Pull Down Menu** From the Tools menu, choose Inquiry, then Mass Properties.

The command line equivalent is **MASSPROP**.

Using the same objects, try using the MASSPROP command. First try the template.

Mass Properties on 2D Regions

MASSPROP can be used on 2D Regions as shown in the following example.

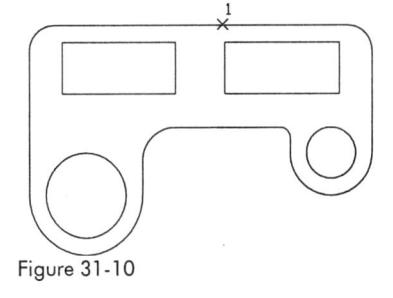

Figure 31-10

```
Command:MASSPROP
Select objects: (pick the object)
```

	Regions
Area:	12182.6150
Perimeter:	1345.7876
Bounding box:	X: 646.8903 — 856.8903
	Y: -30.8733 — 104.1267
Centroid:	X: 742.5765
	Y: 54.1376
Moments of inertia:	X: 48380997.1792
	Y: 6771657089.4622
Product of inertia:	X-Y: 495102141.5872

Regions and Mass Properties Calculations

Radii of gyration: X: 63.0184

    Y: 745.5508

Principal moments and X-Y directions about centroid:

    I: 11993764.2744 along [0.9920 0.1265]

    J: 54602188.1137 along [-0.1265 0.9920]

These commands are a bit risky—if you are not familiar with mass properties calculations, the numbers can be in the wrong unit readout or entirely incorrect, and you will not know it. Just remember, the computer will not "make a mistake" if you input the correct information.

Mass Properties of 3D Solids

3D objects are just as simple to calculate. Use the example from Prelab 30 to create this mass properties calculation.

```
Command:MASSPROP
Select objects: (pick the object)
```

MASSPROP displays the object mass properties on screen, then asks if you want to write the mass properties to a text file.

```
Write to a file?<N>:Y
```

If you enter Y, MASSPROP prompts you to enter a file name. The file is written in ASCII and can be entered transparently into any DOS or Windows-based word processing software.

```
Command:MASSPROP
Select objects: (pick the object)
```

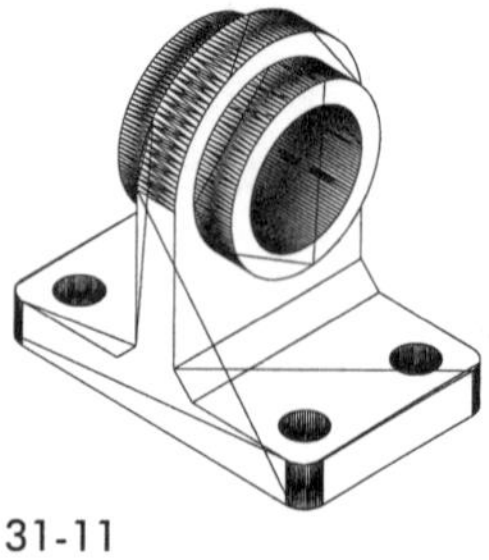

Figure 31-11

	Solids
Mass:	67.9050
Volume:	67.9050
Bounding box:	X: 0.0000 — 8.0000
	Y: -11.0000 — -4.0000
	Z: -2.5000 — 2.5000
Centroid:	X: 4.0000
	Y: -8.9271
	Z: 0.0029

Moments of inertia:	X: 5841.2083
	Y: 1421.0077
	Z: 6983.5969
Products of inertia:	X-Y: -2424.7815
	Y-Z: -2.0617
	Z-X: 1.3744
Radii of gyration:	X: 9.2747
	Y: 4.5745
	Z: 10.1412

Principal moments and *X-Y-Z* directions about centroid:

I: 429.6273 along [0.9999 0.0000 0.0105]
J: 334.5268 along [0.0000 1.0000 -0.0020]
K: 485.5499 along [-0.0105 0.0020 0.9999]

Again, if you are using Architectural units, the readout will reflect the changes.

Solids

Mass:	71.6384 pounds
Volume:	71.6384 cubic inches
Bounding box:	X: -2.9749 — 5.8033 inches
	Y: -2.1258 — 6.9770 inches
	Z: -5.8931 — 3.0764 inches
Centroid:	X: 1.4142 inches
	Y: 2.2195 inches
	Z: -1.0286 inches
Moments of inertia:	X: 944.8942 pounds square inches
	Y: 620.2851 pounds square inches
	Z: 954.9010 pounds square inches
Products of inertia:	X-Y: 210.9050 pounds square inches
	Y-Z: -82.2022 pounds square inches
	Z-X: -84.4788 pounds square inches
Radii of gyration:	X: 3.6318 inches
	Y: 2.9425 inches
	Z: 3.6510 inches

Principal moments (pounds, square inches) and *X-Y-Z* directions about centroid:

I: 492.0448 along [0.7076 -0.4080 0.5769]
J: 343.6783 along [0.0000 0.8165 0.5774]
K: 540.3855 along [-0.7066 -0.4086 0.5777]

To interpret the readout, use the following:

Mass

The measure of a body's inertia. Because AutoCAD uses a density of one, mass and volume have the same value.

Volume

The amount of 3D space that a solid encloses.

Bounding Box

Defined by the diagonally opposite corners of a 3D box that encloses the solid.

Centroid

A 3D point that is the center of mass for solids. AutoCAD assumes a solid of uniform density.

Moments of Inertia

The mass's moments of inertia are used when computing the force required to rotate an object about a given axis, such as a wheel rotating about an axle. The formula for mass moments of inertia is: mass_moments_of_inertia_=mass*radius axis^2

Products of Inertia

This property is used to determine the forces causing motion in an object. It is always calculated with respect to two orthogonal planes (*Y-Z* and *X-Z*). The formula for product of inertia is: product_of_inertiaYZ=mass*distcentroid_to YZ*distcentroid_to_XZ.

Radii of Gyration

Gyration radii is another way of indicating a solid's moments of inertia. The formula for the radii of gyration is: gyration_radii=(moments_of_inertia/body_mass)1/2.

Principal Moments and X-Y-Z Directions About a Centroid

At the centroid of an object there is a certain axis through which the moment of inertia is highest. Another axis, normal to the first axis and also through the centroid, has about it a moment of inertia which is lowest. A third value included in the results is somewhere between the high and the low. These are the principal moments of inertia, which are derived from the products of inertia and have the same units.

Calculations Based on the Current UCS

The variables used to control the units in which the mass properties are calculated are as follows:

Variable	Used to Calculate
Density	Mass of solids
Length	Volume of solids
Length*Length	Area of regions and surface area of solids
Length*Length*Length	Bounding box, radii of gyration, centroid, and perimeter
Density*Length*Length	Moments of inertia, products of inertia, and principal moments

Prelab 31 Mass Properties

Step 1 Create the object shown using AutoCAD's Solids. Use UNION and SUBTRACT to create one object.

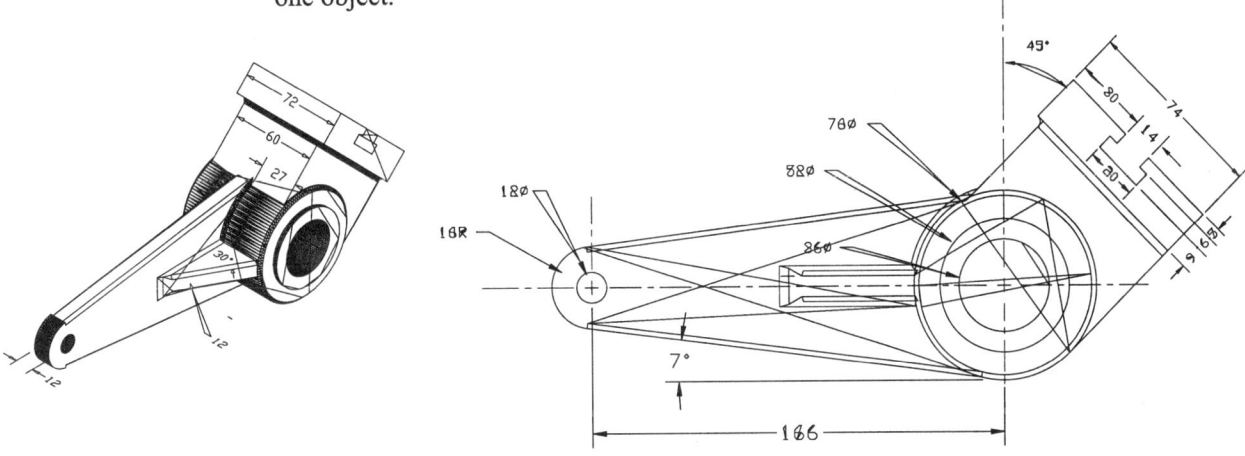

Step 2 Once completed, use the AREA command to find the total surface area.

```
Command:AREA
Specify first corner point or [Object/Add/ Subtract]:O
Select objects: (pick the object)
Area = 662.60 Length = 0.0000
```

Step 3 Now use the MASSPROP command to find the volume of the part.

```
Command:MASSPROP
Select objects: (pick the object)
Write to a file?<N>:Y
```

Name the file a:prelab.mpr

Step 4 Now access Notepad in Windows or the DOS editor, and display the information from the mpr file.

Solids	+
Mass:	518477.7256
Volume:	518477.7256
Bounding box:	X: -41.0000 — 31.0000
	Y: -100.0667 — 162.0149
	Z: -41.0000 — 75.7211
Centroid:	X: -5.6057
	Y: 81.2347
	Z: 10.1680

Moments of inertia:	X: 5185221949.1881
	Y: 585696872.2914
	Z: 4959448764.3820
Products of inertia:	X-Y: -202571339.5967
	Y-Z: 683047583.6635
	Z-X: -25100908.4924
Radii of gyration:	X: 100.0043
	Y: 33.6102
	Z: 97.8029
Principal moments and X-Y-Z directions about centroid:	+
	I: 1711138504.7403 along [0.9993 -0.0323 0.0199]
	J: 454042681.3661 along [0.0268 0.9723 0.2321]
	K: 1582444749.9835 along [-0.0269 -0.2314 0.9725]

Command and Function Summary

AREA calculates the area and perimeter of objects or of defined areas.

MASSPROP calculates and displays the mass properties of regions or solids.

REGION creates a region from existing 2D objects.

For practice, draw this simple part in both solids and surfaces. The surfaced item is .5 units in depth, and the solid is 1 unit. If you wanted to change the solid to .5, how would you do it? If you wanted to change the surfaced item, would that be easier?

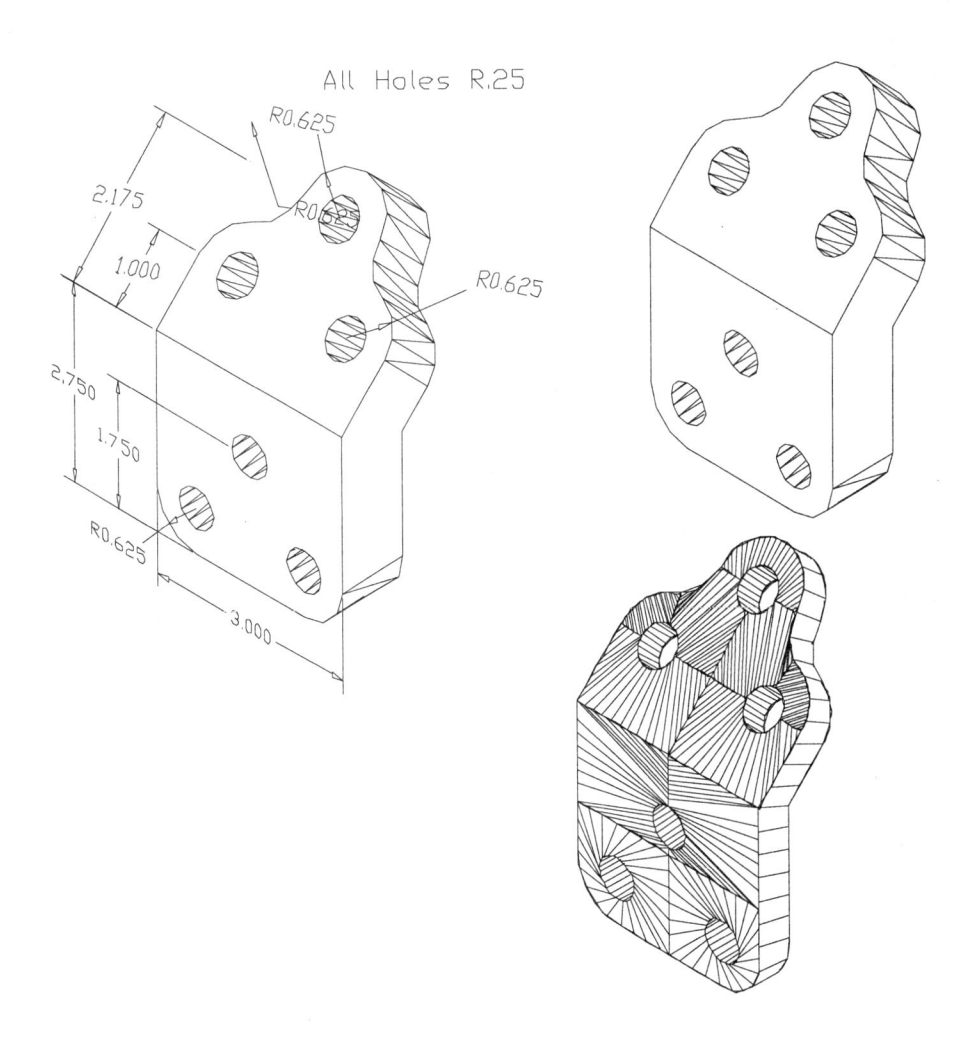

Regions and Mass Properties Calculations

Practice Exercise 31

Start with a five-sided polygon with a circle inside. Use EXTRUDE to make them solid, and subtract the circle from the polygon (1). Change the UCS and copy the part, then rotate it (2,3). Return to UCS World, and ARRAY the part to create five objects. Change your UCS, and MIRROR the objects (4). Rotate the original objects and move them into place.

UNION all of the objects, and calculate the volume and area.

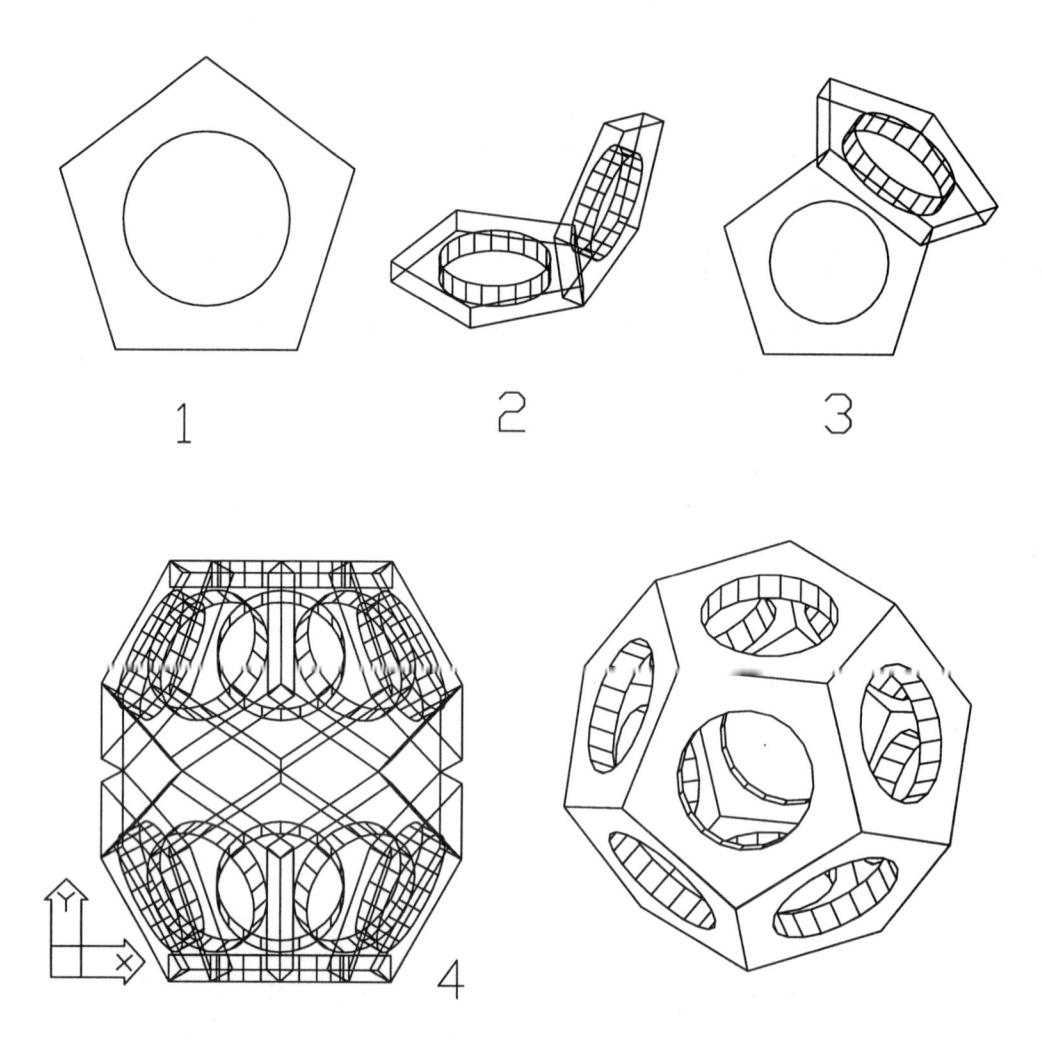

Exercise A31

Continuing on the house plan, create a roof plan of the model as shown, using 3D solids. Then UNION the objects for the roof together, and find the area and the mass properties of the roof members only. Save your file regularly. Solids are not as easy to work with once you have a lot of them.

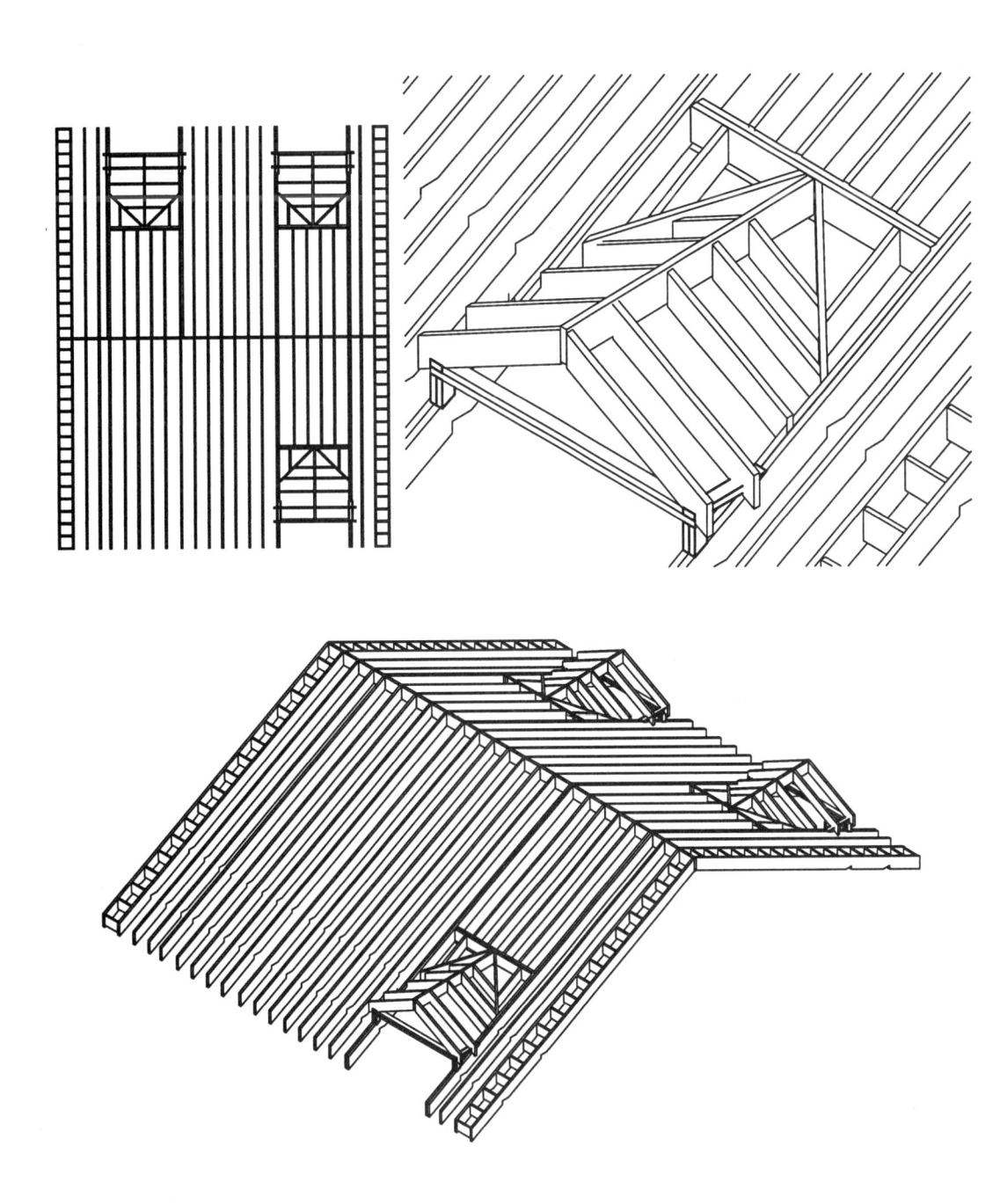

Exercise C31

Using the beam example from Chapter 11, create a 3D beam using AutoCAD's Solids. Then create a joining beam. Place the beams as in the illustrated roof. Use UNION to join all the roof beams. Calculate the total surface area and then the volume.

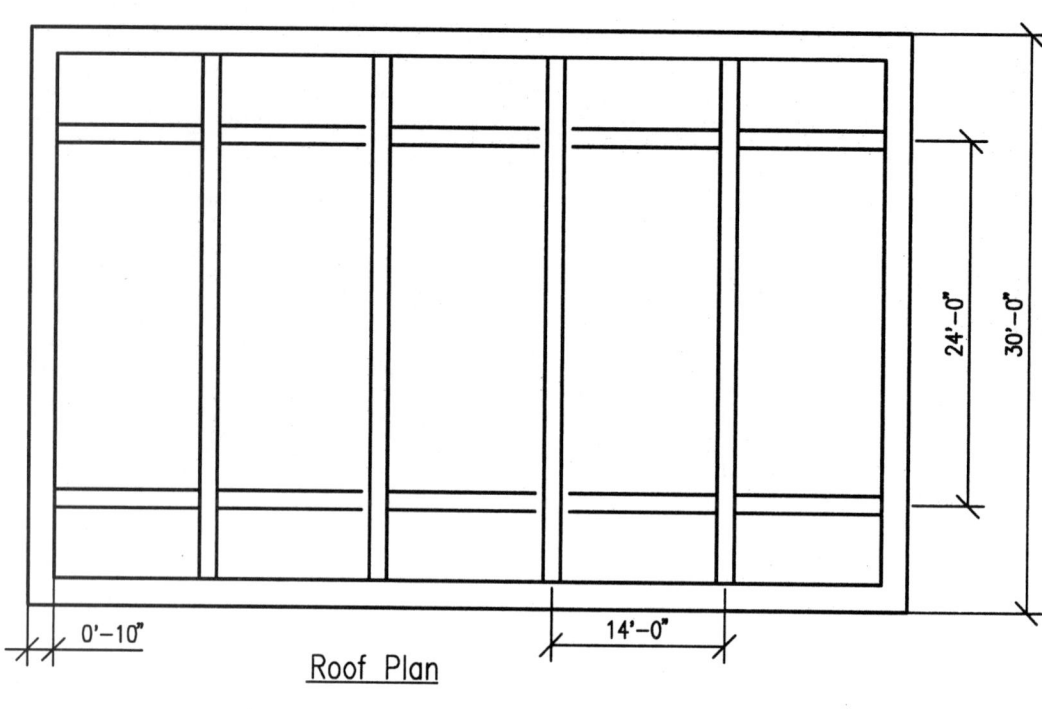

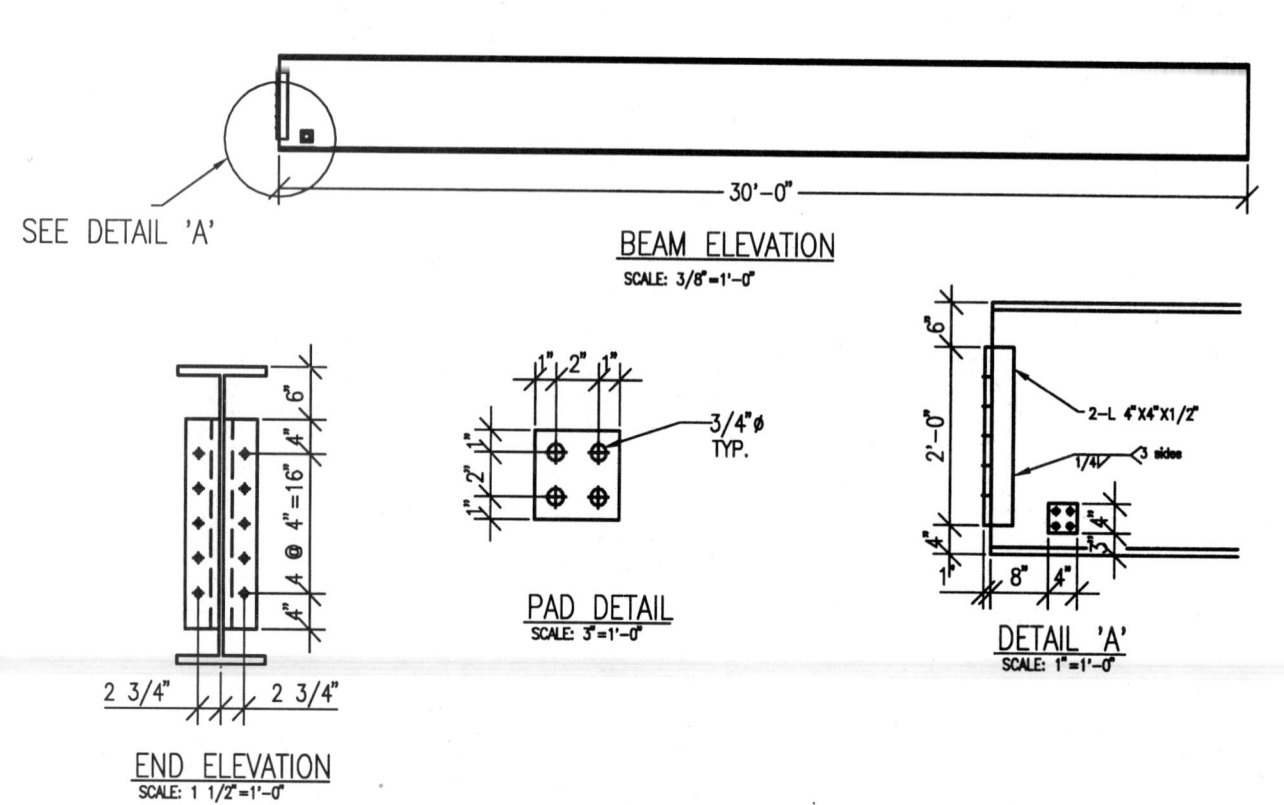

Roof Plan

BEAM ELEVATION
SCALE: 3/8"=1'-0"

END ELEVATION
SCALE: 1 1/2"=1'-0"

PAD DETAIL
SCALE: 3"=1'-0"

DETAIL 'A'
SCALE: 1"=1'-0"

Exercise M31

Create this block and clamp assembly using Solids. Then calculate the total surface area and volume.

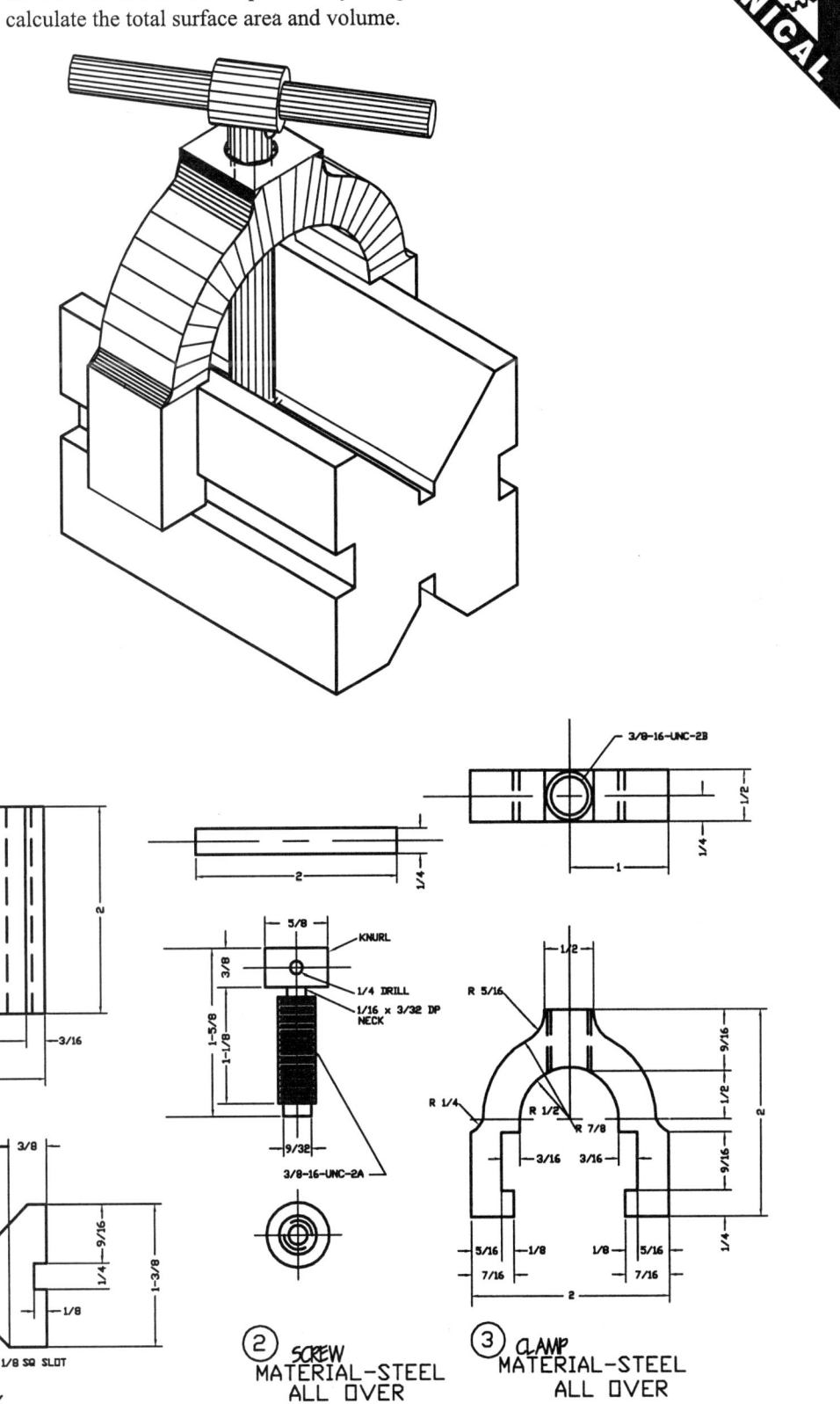

① V-BLOCK
MATERIAL STEEL
ALL OVER

② SCREW
MATERIAL-STEEL
ALL OVER

③ CLAMP
MATERIAL-STEEL
ALL OVER

Challenger 31

Using the dimensions from Chapter 10's Challenger, create the caster as shown, then calculate the total surface area and the total volume. In Chapter 25 this exercise is done in surfacing. Note the differences in file size and the time it takes to construct it.

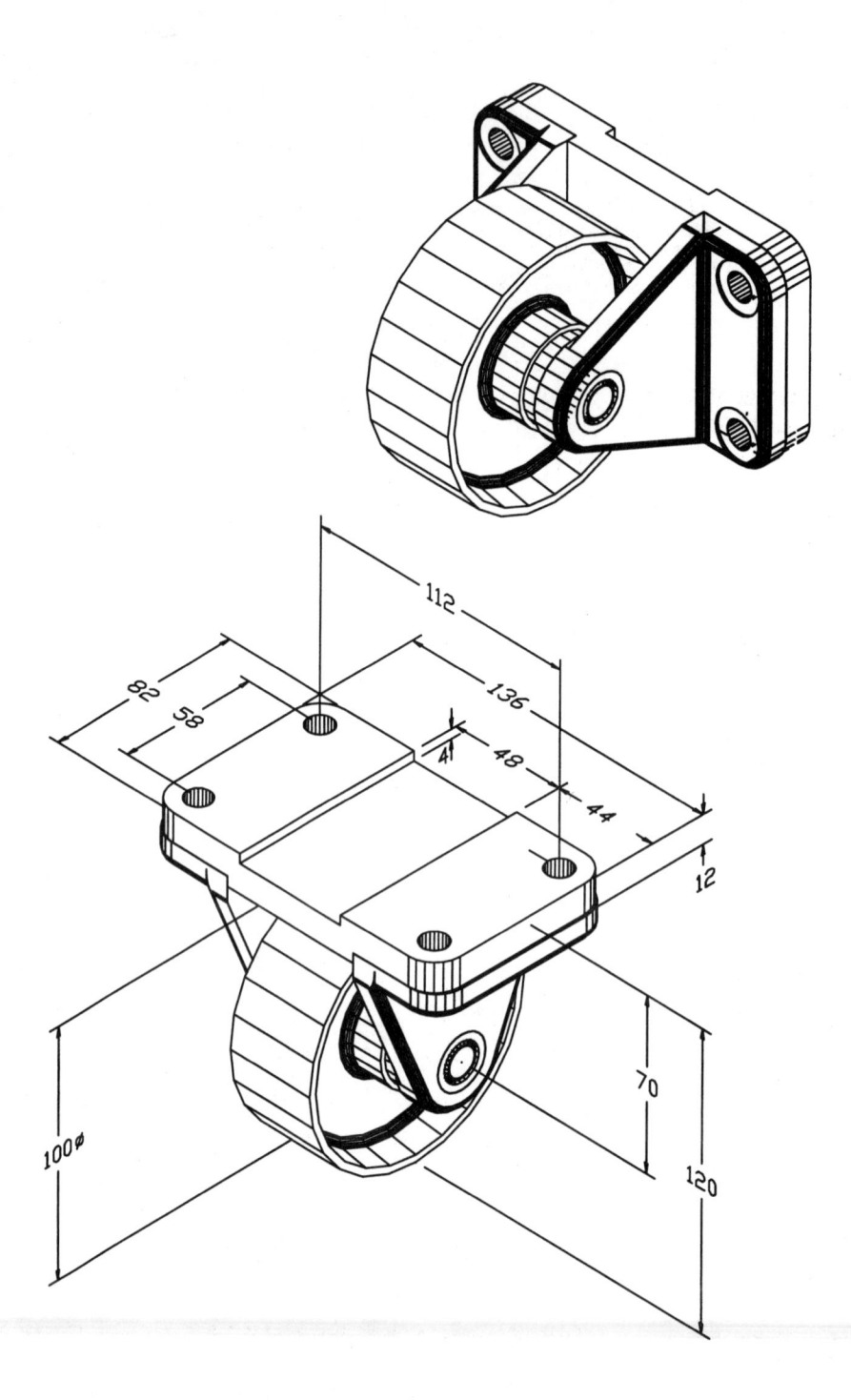

32 Managing and Exporting Models

Upon completion of this chapter, you should be able to:

1. List the properties of objects and the components of a file
2. Use filters and layer locking for editing objects
3. Transfer large files with zip routines and backups
4. Import and export .dxf files, .ps, .tif, .gif, and .pcx files
5. Use .mnx and .shx files for proper file transfer

OBJECTIVES

Components of Large Models

Whether in 2D or 3D, managing large models can be very difficult, even with the use of groups, layers, blocks, and Xrefs. View commands make the process much easier, but if there is no management involved, things can quickly get out of hand. In small models it is difficult to remember the names of layers, dimension styles, text styles, views, viewport configurations, blocks, and Xrefs. In a large model, the process becomes much more complex, particularly if you have one operation using the file for manufacturing or construction purposes, and one operation using the file for creating drawings. Detailed documentation is required to produce the model, but doubly important if the file is being transferred to someone else. If no documentation is available, here is how you would list the elements of a file:

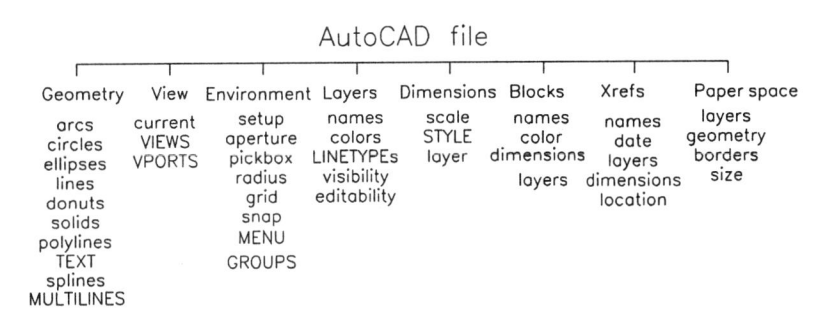

```
                          AutoCAD file
┌──────────┬────────┬─────────────┬──────────┬──────────┬─────────┬──────────┬────────────┐
Geometry   View    Environment   Layers     Dimensions Blocks   Xrefs      Paper space
arcs       current setup         names      scale      names    names      layers
circles    VIEWS   aperture      colors     STYLE      color    date       geometry
ellipses   VPORTS  pickbox       LINETYPEs  layer      dimensions layers   borders
lines              radius        visibility            layers   dimensions size
donuts             grid          editability                    location
solids             snap
polylines          MENU
TEXT               GROUPS
splines
MULTILINES
```

Figure 32-1

Every file is composed of several different areas. First there is the geometry. This is the vector file you are creating. It is shown in AutoCAD through the View parameters. The environment is how you actually look at the model: the setting variables, limits, grid, snap, etc. The layers, like the groups, exist to help you organize the model. Blocks and Xrefs help you save space on your disk, and access other models for reference. Finally, paper space objects exist only in a paper environment to help you create plots.

Figure 32-1 shows how the model can be conceived. All capitalized headings, plus many more, can contain named, stored, and often externally referenced parameters. For example, the MULTILINES used in this drawing can be part of a .mls file used in many other files. The .mnu or MENU file used in this drawing can be used in many other files, but may not be the only MENU file available.

Suppose you had to take over someone else's drawing—what would you need to know? And how do you get this information? Keeping this in mind, how can you assure that the files you create can be accessed by other people in case you win a lottery and disappear from work for a few days?

Listing the Parameters of the Database

To list the parameters of the database—ie., Limits, OSNAPs, current point, current modes, etc.—use STATUS.

> **Pull Down Menu** From the Tools menu, choose Inquiry, then Status..

The command line equivalent is **STATUS**.

Listing Database Information for Objects

To list the X, Y, Z positions, plus the properties of an object, use LIST.

> **Toolbar** From the Inquiry toolbar, choose List.
>
> **Pull Down Menu** From the Tools menu, choose Inquiry, then List.

Listing Blocks, Dimension Styles, Groups, Layers, Multiline Styles, Text Styles, UCSs, Views, Vports, and Xrefs

For all of these file components, there are often two ways of getting a listing. First, through the command line, choose the ?. Second, use the dialog box to list the available components in each category.

Blocks Use INSERT or DDINSERT.

```
Command: INSERT
Block name (or ?):?
```

Pick the down arrow as shown to list internal blocks; pick Browse . . . to list drawings that have been inserted.

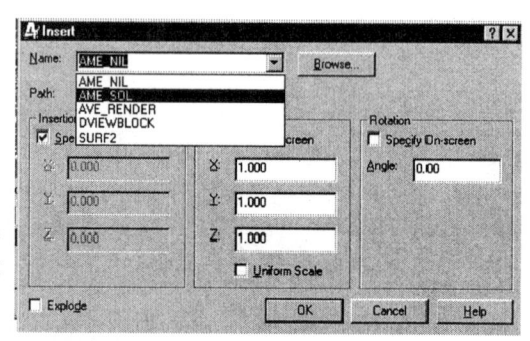

> **Toolbar** From the Insert toolbar, choose this icon.
>
> **Pull Down Menu** From the Insert menu, choose Block.

Dimension Styles   Use DIMSTYLE and DIM - STATUS.

```
Command: DIMSTYLE
Text style (or ?):?
```

List other styles by picking the top line with the arrow.

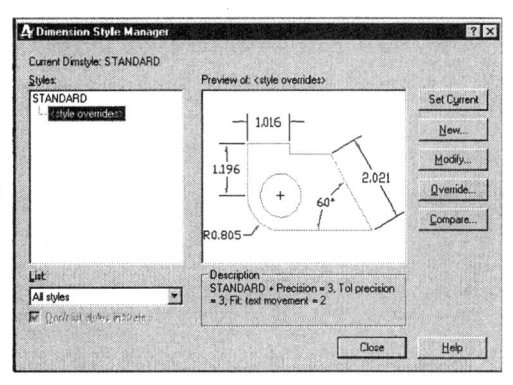

> **Toolbar** From the Dimension menu, choose Style.

Groups   Use Group, which gives the dialog box.

```
Command: GROUP
```

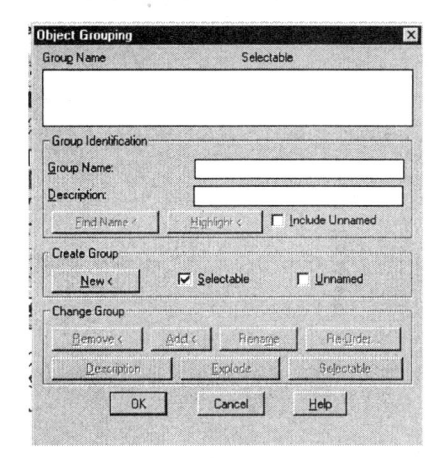

> **Toolbar** There is no button for this command.
>
> **Pull Down Menu** There is no menu choice for this command.

Layers   Use LAYER to get the Layer Properties Manager.

```
Command: LAYER
```

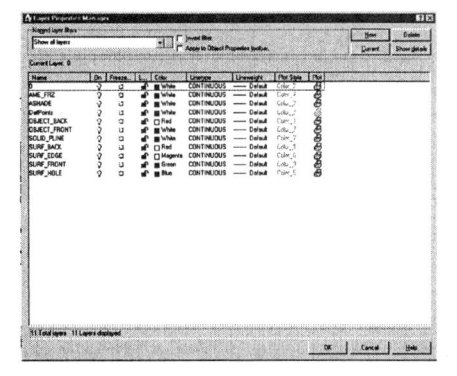

> **Toolbar** From the Standard toolbar, choose this icon.
>
> **Pull Down Menu** From the Format menu, choose Layers.

Managing and Exporting Models   **733**

Multiline Styles   Use MLSTYLE, which gives the dialog box.

        Command: **MLSTYLE**

List other styles by picking the top line with the arrow.

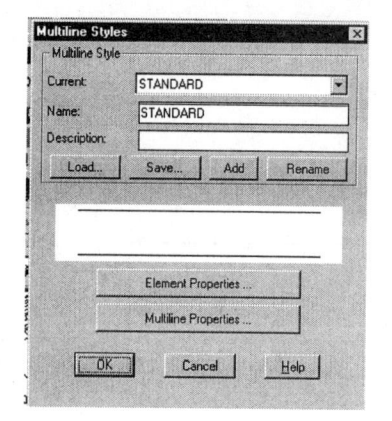

> **Pull Down Menu** From the Format menu, choose Multiline Style...

UCS   Use UCS or DDUCS.

        Command: **UCS**
        Origin/ZAxis/3point/OBject/View/
          X/Y/Z/Prev/Restore/Save/Del/?/
          <World>: **?**

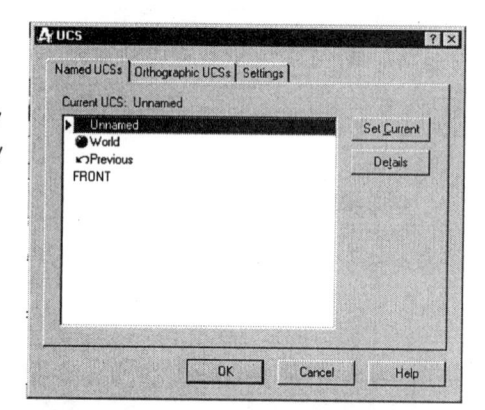

> **Toolbar** From the UCS toolbar, choose Display UCS
>
> **Pull Down Menu** From the Tools menu, choose Named UCS.

View   Use View or DDVIEW.

        Command: **VIEW**
        ?/Delete/Restore/Save/Window: **?**

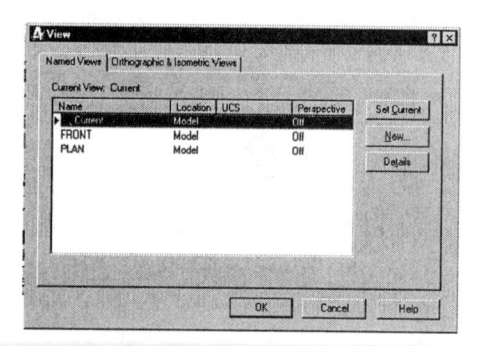

> **Toolbar** From the Viewpoint toolbar, choose this icon.
>
> **Pull Down Menu** From the View menu, choose Named Views.

VPORTS Use VPORTS.

> **Pull Down Menu** From the View menu, choose Tiled Viewports.

Xrefs Use the Xref command to list the available Xrefs.

> **Toolbar** From the Reference toolbar, choose this icon.
>
> **Pull Down Menu** From the Insert menu, choose Xref Manager.

```
Command:XREF
Enter an option
   [?/Bind/Detach/Path/Reload/Overlay/Attach]<Attach>:?
```

Listing Other Types of Files (see file extensions in Appendix B)

If you are using .mnx, .shx or .scr files that need to be transferred from one system to another, or if you are searching for .pcx, .tif, .plt, or .hpg files on a disk, use the FILES command or the directory listing to do a global search. In DOS you can perform a simple file search with DIR. In Windows, use the FIND command on the Start button.

> **Command Prompt** Use SHELL to get to DOS, then type in DIR, then the directory, name or wildcard, and extension of the listing. (See Wildcards, page 736.)

```
Command:DIR
Files to list:A:*.tif
```

Where: **a:** = the directory
             *   = all files in that directory
           .tif = the extension for TIFF files.

> **File Management** In Release 2000, all file management is assumed to be under the Windows format. Shell to DOS and list files plus their extensions and dates if your system is too slow for the Windows format.

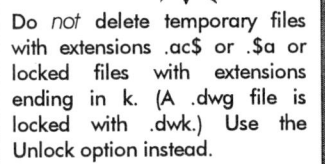

Danger
Do *not* delete temporary files with extensions .ac$ or .$a or locked files with extensions ending in k. (A .dwg file is locked with .dwk.) Use the Unlock option instead.

Windows Explorer helps with file management as well.

Always keep at least one backup of everything you do.

In Windows, use the **My Computer** menu, then File to copy, delete, and rename files. Use the right click button when identifying a file to make this process easier. Open the folder, pick the file, then right click.

Delete: Point to the file you want to delete, right click, then pick Delete.

Copy: Point to the file you want to copy, right click, then pick Copy.

Paste: Point to the folder where you want the copy, right click, then pick Paste..

Rename File: Point to the file or activate it, then pick rename, then type in the new name.

Wildcards

Many functions in AutoCAD use lists. To make lists more efficient the characters below can be used. Blocks, layers, linetypes, views, custom hatches, etc., can all be listed using wildcards.

Character	Name	Purpose	Example
*	asterisk	matches any string	
*	anything		
n*	anything starting with an n		next, nines, n12
*mn	anything ending in mn		column, 098mn
mn	anything with mn in the string		smnstr, armnh, mn1
~*mn*	anything not having mn in the string		wheel, gear
`*mn	anything with mn in the string		omni, mn345
@	at	matches any alpha character	
@	anything with only one alpha character or letter		a, t, n
@n	anything that has two letters ending in n		wn, rn, jn
#	pound	matches any numeric value	
#	any number		2, 7, 6
#nm	anything starting with a number and ending with nm		5nm, 7nm
nm#	anything starting with nm and ending with a number		nm5, nm2
~	tilde	matches anything but the pattern	
~#	anything not ending in a number		wall, fireplc
~*fat*	anything without fat		celry, grpfrt, 12
~.	anything that is alphanumeric		wall2, floor, 324
.	period	matches any non-alphanumeric character	
?	question	matches any single character	
[-]	hyphen	inside square brackets specifies a range for a single character	
[m-z] x	matches anything starting with letters between m and z, ending in x		tx, wx, px
[~m-z] x	matches anything except strings starting with letters between m and z, ending in x		ax, dx, lx

[...]	matches any one of the characters enclosed	
[~...]	matches any character not enclosed	
[~aeiou]	matches any string without a vowel	
'	**reverse quote**	**reads the character that follows as a literal character**

Making Listing Easier

Five minutes of documentation is worth hours of editing. Once you have a complete file that will be used as a block or an XREF, note on the drawing or model where the origin is. Then use either a hardcopy or screen method to save it. These can be used for stored UCSs and groups too.

Hardcopy Method

Simply print the file out, with the name of the file plus the directory and date, and the origin noted. On the back of the page, note the layers, MLINEs, Dimension or Text styles, and any other stored information that may be imported with the file. Keep this hardcopy file by your workstation for future reference. If you do not use this file for six months or a year, you could be surprised by how much you may forget.

Screen Method

This method is much more "environmentally friendly." When the file is completed, if you have a pictorial view, change your UCS to View, then note with a Leader where the origin is. Add the name of the file, plus the date. Then note to the side a listing of the layers, dimension and line styles, etc. Then, save the file as a slide (see page 416). Make a script file of all your slides and save that to your hard drive, or on a clearly labeled floppy. This way you will be able to flip through your slides and find the one you want much more quickly. Otherwise, you will have to bring each file up and keep repeating this process for each separate file.

AutoCAD's drawing preview file search in Release 2000 is a great advantage, as are some of the other management programs available. These features show you (and anyone else) not only what the files are called, but when they were last filed, plus any imported information that could be overridden or added to your current file.

Model Documentation

Documentation can be in either a hardcopy or on-screen format. "Read-me" files are very useful but, believe it or not, there are many people who still do not know how to use them. If you are working on big models, you may need the following information whether you are creating files in Windows that can be accessed transparently or actually printing documentation on paper. Whether you are working on a part that is going to be manufactured or you are a student working on a joint school project this information should be available to you. Standard forms, either on-screen or on paper, are a good idea. If you regularly exchange files, you can very quickly end up with duplicate layer and group names.

Designers	- Judy Born, Gunter Born
Data files used	- AR355 house plans
Layers	- firstf, secondf, thirdf, footing
	- mill1 - toolpath for mill
Groups	- fireplace, kitchen, foyer (add slides)

	- veins, wedges, handle (add slides)
Blocks	- powderrm, laundry, porch (add slides)
	- mdlbolt1, sideblt2, gear, (add slides)
Symbols	- symdiode, title, section
Views	- terracSE, kitchNW
	- handdet, bolt3det
VPORTS	- 3view - floorpl, kitch, bath
	- 4Quad - fr, top, rside, det
Drawings	- plans, elevations, firplace det, window det,
	- drw handle
Slides	- kitchen blocks, concrete blocks
	- bolts, pins, and gears
Menu	- SRKarch.mnu

Management Considerations

Layers

Each object belongs to one, and only one layer. The layer of an object is therefore a property of that particular object. The layer displayability is also a property of each viewport in the floating viewports. This is extremely important for organization within the model. Make sure that you are using this displayability for such operations as adding surfaces and dimensioning.

Groups

Groups allow the user to edit a large number of related objects while only selecting them "manually" once. The display cannot be controlled by group. Because the individual objects can be manipulated either singly or as a unit, make sure that all layer levels are displayed before editing the group.

A group can contain other groups as well, just as a block can be composed of several blocks. Be sure that your layers, groups, and blocks are being edited correctly.

Filters

When graphically selecting an object, the proximity of the cursor determines which object is chosen. Object filtering controls selectability. Using global selectability for layers and object types can greatly improve your productivity. Consider the option of object selectability before setting up your layers. If there is a way to pick only arcs, then there is no reason to have an Arc layer.

Transferring Large Drawings

Files should be created on the hard drive, then transferred by floppy disk or tape to other systems. If your floppy disk has a capacity of 1.4MB, you often cannot open a file larger than 600K from that disk. The system can be configured to place a temporary directory within AutoCAD's working directory, but this is not always possible in classroom settings. In many cases there must be at least as much room left on the diskette as there is in the file.

If your file is less than 1.4 MB, create a subdirectory on a workstation, copy the file to that subdirectory, work on the drawing, then copy the file back before you leave.

Exporting Files

If the drawing is larger than the capacity of the disk, you can use Zip programs to backup and restore the drawing.

You can use drawings and images created in other versions of AutoCAD and other software packages. AutoCAD handles some form of conversion for .DXF, .DXB, .GIF, .TIF, .PCX, .SAT, 3DSTUDIO, WMF, PostScript, and AME models. The most common file type for graphics is .DXF.

.DXF Files

.DXF files are the ASCII-code or DOS-text files for the graphics or vector statements. These are the clean files that can be transferred to other graphics packages or to word processing, analysis, or accounting files.

.DXF and Graphics Packages

.DXFs or Drawing Interchange Format files are the easiest way to transfer AutoCAD files to a similar or more specialized CAD program. Judging by market share, AutoCAD is the most accessible PC-based CAD program available. The DXF capability allows users to access this fairly inexpensive system, AutoCAD, for data entry and then have the graphics data entered into an expensive system (IDEAS, CV, KATIA, UNIGRAPHICS), thereby greatly reducing the cost-per-seat in a CAD lab. In addition, it makes the graphics data of AutoCAD available for third-party or specialized software programmers.

.DXF and Text Editors

.DXF files are also handy for editing large strings of text and notes because the text editors in word processing software are much more powerful than AutoCAD's vector format.

DXFOUT and DXFIN

DXFOUT takes the AutoCAD drawing file out of AutoCAD and make it accessible to other systems. DXFIN imports .DXF files into AutoCAD.

DXFIN

In the File dialog box, find the .dxf file you want to import, then choose OK.

DXFOUT

If you type DXFOUT at the command prompt, you will get the Save As menu. If you access Save As from the File Pull Down menu, you can specify the file type as DXF and export that way.

> **Toolbar** At the command prompt, enter DXFOUT.
>
> **Pull Down Menu** From the File menu, choose Save As.

Note: Be sure you have a lot of space for this file.

DXF Graphics Transfer Example

Exporting DXF Files

Try this example:

1. In AutoCAD, create a file called A:DXTEST. Change the limits, snap, and grid from the defaults to any other value, just so you can see that they have been changed. Enter at least one line, one arc, and one circle. Create a new layer called 1 with color 1 (red). Enter the text style Romanc, and then enter three lines of text.
2. Save this file creating an A:DXTEST.DWG on your disk or, if you are not using floppies, on your C: drive.
3. While still in the graphics editor, pick Save As from the File Pull Down Menu, then DXF under Save As Type.

Command: **DXFOUT**

The Options button will allow you to save a portion of the file instead of all of it, or you can choose a different release of AutoCAD or a different file type to export as.

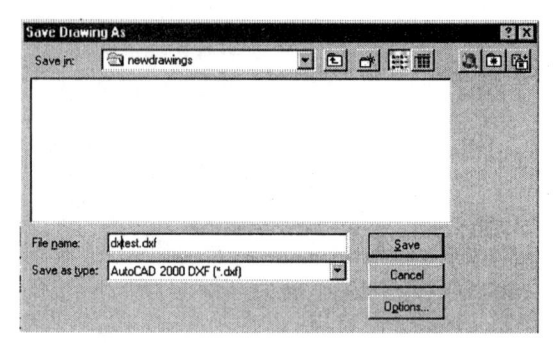

If you type in DXFOUT, AutoCAD will automatically use the extension .DXF for the file. The default is the file that you are currently using, so you have created DXTEST.DXF.

AutoCAD will now create the DXF file A:DXTEST.DXF. This DXF file can now be inserted into many other CAD and third-party programs. (That's the theory, it doesn't always work.)

This file can be opened up as a text file in any word processing package. If you are curious, open it up and try to find your text and lines. You may be surprised at how much information goes into setting up this file.

Importing DXF Files

To AutoCAD

If you are fortunate enough to have a different CAD software package at your site, use this instead of AutoCAD. If you do not have another CAD package on site, import the file into AutoCAD. If you have an earlier release of AutoCAD (Release 9), try importing to it.

Example – DXF Import

Exit from the current file (it is not necessary to save it again), and continue as follows:

1. Create a new file in AutoCAD called TEST1.
2. Go to the File menu and select Open, then specify the file type as DXF or type in DXFIN.

Command: **DXFIN**

AutoCAD will load the DXTEST file complete with the settings used. What is the difference between this and a block insert?

1. When inserting a block, you are prompted to change the size or rotation of the block insert, so it fits into the current file. With DXF imports, you are not prompted for this information because the imported file forms the complete file.
2. With block inserts you are prompted for the location of the origin of the block; but with DXFs you are entering the entire file, not just a set of objects, therefore 0,0,0 is the origin.
3. All settings are included in the DXF file. Limits, grid, snap, all DIMVARS and SETVARs, etc., will be included in the imported file.

When importing a DXF file, always use an "empty drawing," that is, before any BLOCKS, LAYERS, LINETYPES, VIEWPORTS, fonts, or geometry have been entered. In this way you will get a complete DXF. If the current drawing file is not empty, you will have added only the entities. If you enter a previously altered file, you will see this prompt:

```
Not a new drawing — only entities section will be printed
```

This tells you that only the geometry data has been added. In fact, the data imported to a previously started file is much like a block—it contains no variables or settings. To make sure that your files are empty, use TEST= when starting.

This exercise was performed in AutoCAD to give you a sense of how it works. But the purpose of the command is to transfer AutoCAD data to another CAD package. The process should be as easy as the one outlined above.

Using GIF, PCX, and TIFF files

These are *raster files*, and will be imported only as raster images. They are brought in as a block composed of 2D solid objects. If you want the image to be accepted as arcs, lines, and circles, you will need to trace it with the regular geometry commands. Because imported raster files can create large drawing files, you should erase the raster image when you no longer need it.

Toolbar From the Insert toolbar, pick Image.

Pull Down Menu From the Reference menu, pick Attach Image.

Enter the path and file name of the file you want to import. Drag the image into position. You must have a large amount of RAM available for the image to appear.

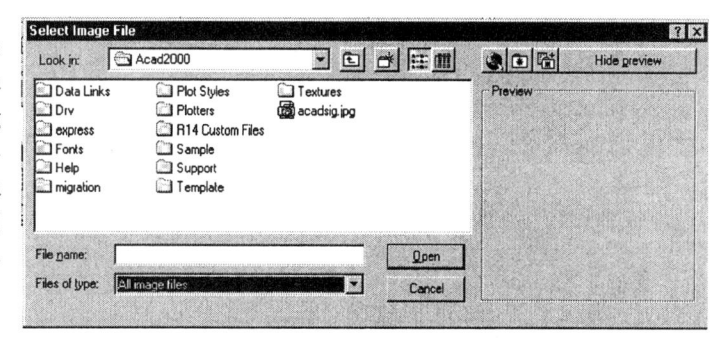

Like plotting and printing, the industry is moving far too quickly to have any real handle on image formats from month to month. This week's leading edge format may not be compatible with the machines of 50% of the people you need to send it to. If you are e-mailing images, make sure that the person receiving the image has space on their disk for it. If you have not transferred a certain file type or a certain image before, assume it won't work until it actually does.

Files You May Want to Transfer with the Drawing File

Many companies have their own customized menu file. In addition, people use many text font files that are not part of AutoCAD's basic font files. When you load an AutoCAD drawing file, you may be requested to identify a font file or menu file if your original one is not present.

Menu Files

If you are loading a drawing file and you get a message that the menu file is not found, it means that the file's menu is customized and cannot be loaded into this file. In this case, access the Support menu of the current AutoCAD release and load the default ACAD.MNU.

Font Files

AutoCAD Release 2000 substitutes a standard font if a customized font is not available. If your system gives an error message, it means that there is a font file (or many font files) that are not part of AutoCAD's setup. You will be prompted for a font file to replace the one indicated. Choose a font file such as Roman and the text will be shown in this font. If you press Ctrl-C at this point, no text will appear either in the title block or in the dimensions where this font was present.

Plotter and Printer Files

Release 2000 has a fully renovated plotting and printing set up. In addition to being able to use many different printers and plotters, you now have the capability to save your printer set-ups and to set up your default files for each specific printer. See Appendix D for the printing and plotting files that you may want to take with you.

Taking the Menu and the Fonts with You

If you are taking a file somewhere, or if you are giving the file to someone else, also give them a copy of the .shp or .shx file that comprises your fonts, and the .mnu or .mnx file that comprises your menu. With these files, the person receiving the drawing can load it problem-free.

Purging Files

If you find that a file that someone else has drawn is very large and takes a lot of time to load, use PURGE to erase all unnecessary information. If the file is still very large, open a new file, insert the drawing, open the dimension style you require, and explode the file. This may make it smaller.

Model Management

There are many tricks and tips to make assembling large drawings easier. These tricks can be summed up by getting three things right:
1. Origin should be well placed.
2. Scale should be 1:1.
3. LAYERs should be well organized.

Origin

If your origin is not well placed on the model you are trying to insert, you could spend a long time Moving it, ZOOMing in on it, and generally messing about with it.

If you are using blocks of 3D models extensively, you should create either an icon menu or a slide that will show you the exact size and origin of the part.

Scale

If the objects are entered at a 1:1 scale, there will be no problem inserting them. Again, to make the process easier, make sure your data is well documented on-line.

LAYERs

You may have noticed that the models inserted into your file come with all their respective LAYERs. XREFd files will also have LAYERs that are added to your list.

Prelab 32 Merging 3D Files

While working on large projects, it is often desirable to have two or more separate files of different parts of the final object or assembly. These can either be inserted as blocks or referenced as XREFs when the part is ready to be merged and drawn. Having several files saves time and space both in RAM and on back-up disks.

Once completed, the various parts of the assemblies can be loaded onto the same file and compiled in paper space for drawing purposes.

This also allows you to have component parts that can be used, not just in one drawing or project, but many.

Step 1   Open the three files for the camera as shown. (These should be part of the instructor's package. If not, take the time to draw the parts as shown.)

We will compile a group of parts that can be merged into a single model.

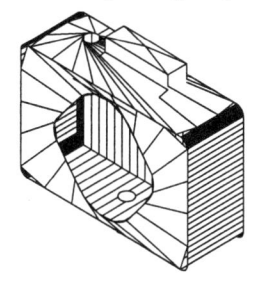

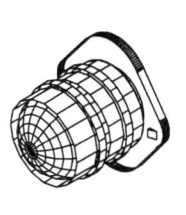

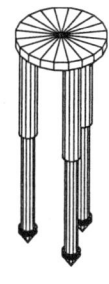

Step 2   These camera parts are all on different files and will now be merged as a whole. Because we want to compile a drawing with these objects in it, open each file and note:

1. The origin
2. The layers
3. The groups
4. The menu
5. The text files
6. The font files

Step 3   Before starting to merge, make sure you are aware of the origin and axes of all your files.

Make sure that your insertion point or 0,0,0 is found on the model itself. Use the BASE command if it is not. The direction of positive Z must also be noted so the files will fit in the correct direction. If the origin is not in a logical spot on the model, either MOVE your model so that it is, or WBLOCK the model, changing the insertion point.

Once everything is ready, place your models onto a blank base model using INSERT or XREF Attach. XREF will help keep the file small. Create a fully assembled part from the various separate files.

If the model is entering at an incorrect angle, change the UCS to accommodate the base model's origin.

There are really only two things to consider when INSERTing: the scale of the model and the origin and axes.

The 3point UCS is often easiest to use when lining something up because even on slanting surfaces you can be exact.

Step 4   Create a drawing of the finished part using paper space. Compile a drawing that has a 3D view of the whole part, an exploded assembly of the whole part, a detail of each part with dimensions and a title block. Save your file every half-hour or 15 minutes. You can change your AUTOSAVE variable to do this.

Step 5   Create a data file with information concerning the part as outlined above.

Part Name

Start Date: Back-up dates:
Company:
Part no:
Designer:
Directories:

Layer	*Date created*	*Group*	*Block*
Body	June 4 1995	Frame	Cabody
SURF1	July 1 1995	Surfs	Cabody
Flash	Aug. 23 1995	Frame	Caflash
3Dface	Aug. 24 1995	Surfs	Caflash

It is a good idea to back-up your documentation at the same time you back-up your model.

Insert your attributed title block.

Practice Exercise 32

Using the information from the mechanical exercise in Chapter 6, create a surfaced image. In paper space, open an isometric view. Be sure to freeze all layers that have circles. Use Filters to do this. Now insert the drawing from Chapter 6, plus a title block from Chapter 8.

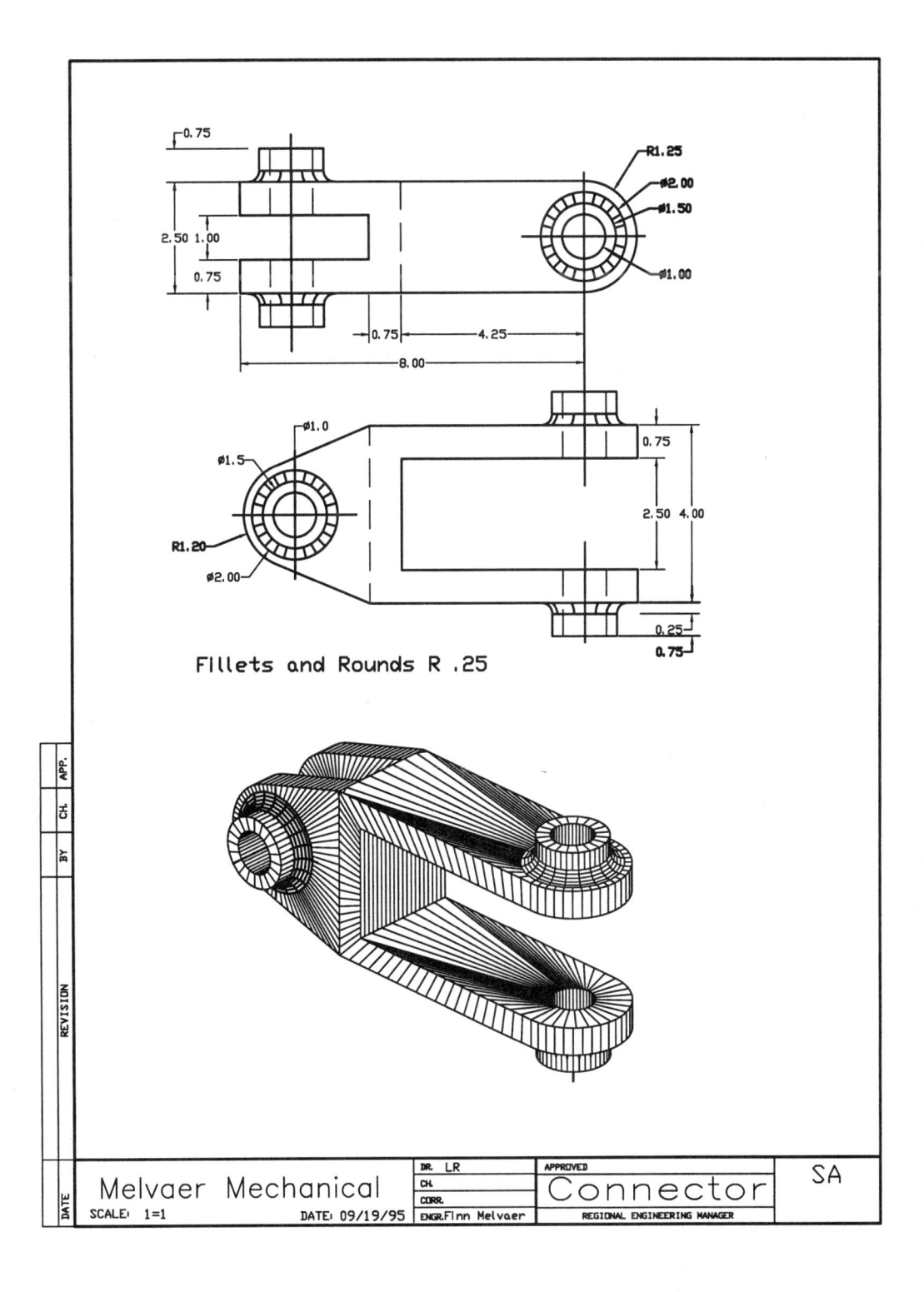

Exercise A32

Using the model you have been working on, compile a drawing with floor plans, elevations, a few sections, a 3D rendered image, an image of the framework, and a few details. This may take longer than the required class time, but the effect is worth having.

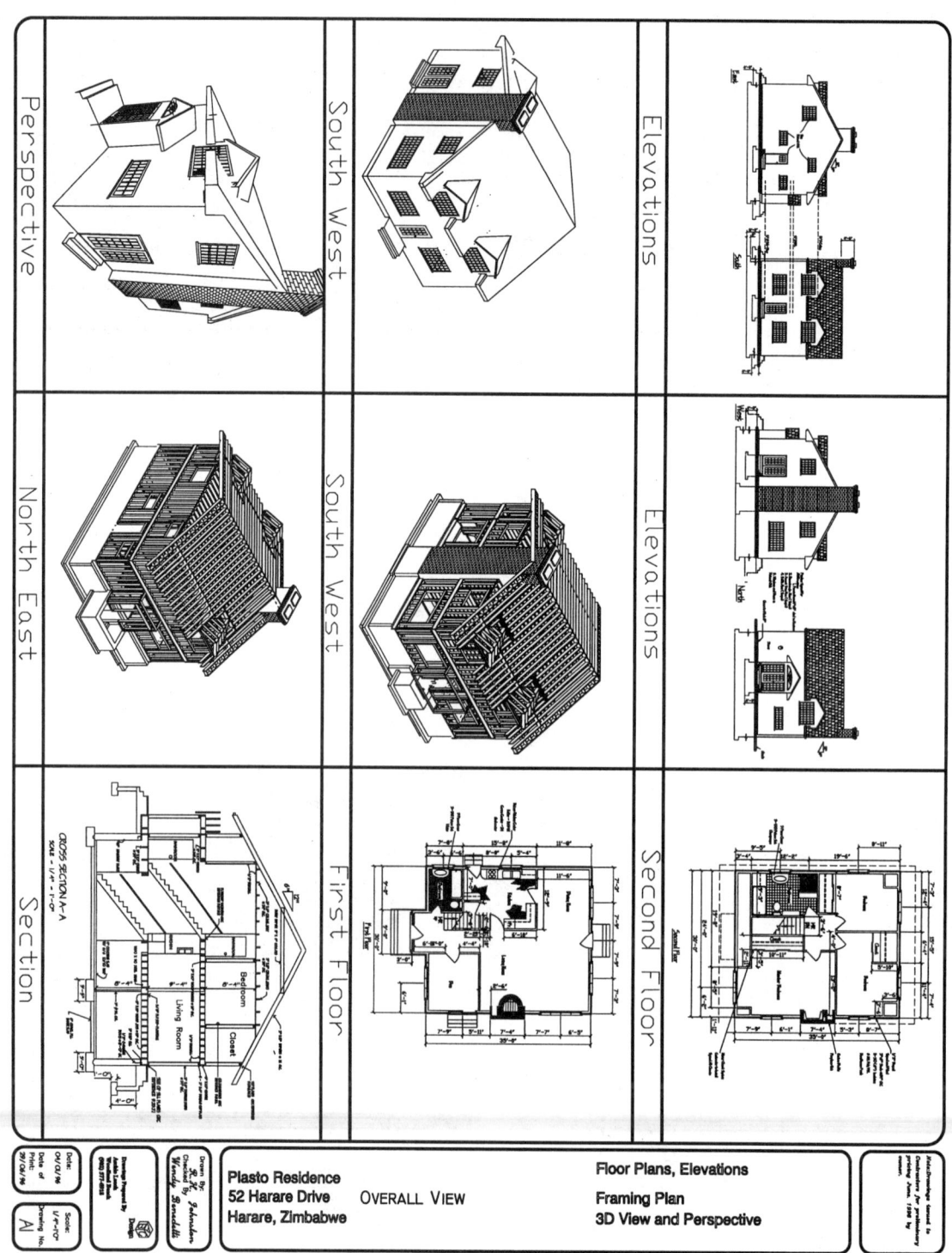

746 CHAPTER THIRTY-TWO

Exercise C32

Create 3D footings from Chapters 7, 11, and 26, plus the layout from Chapter 8. Construct a drawing as shown. Keep a detailed record of which layers, groups, and file names you have.

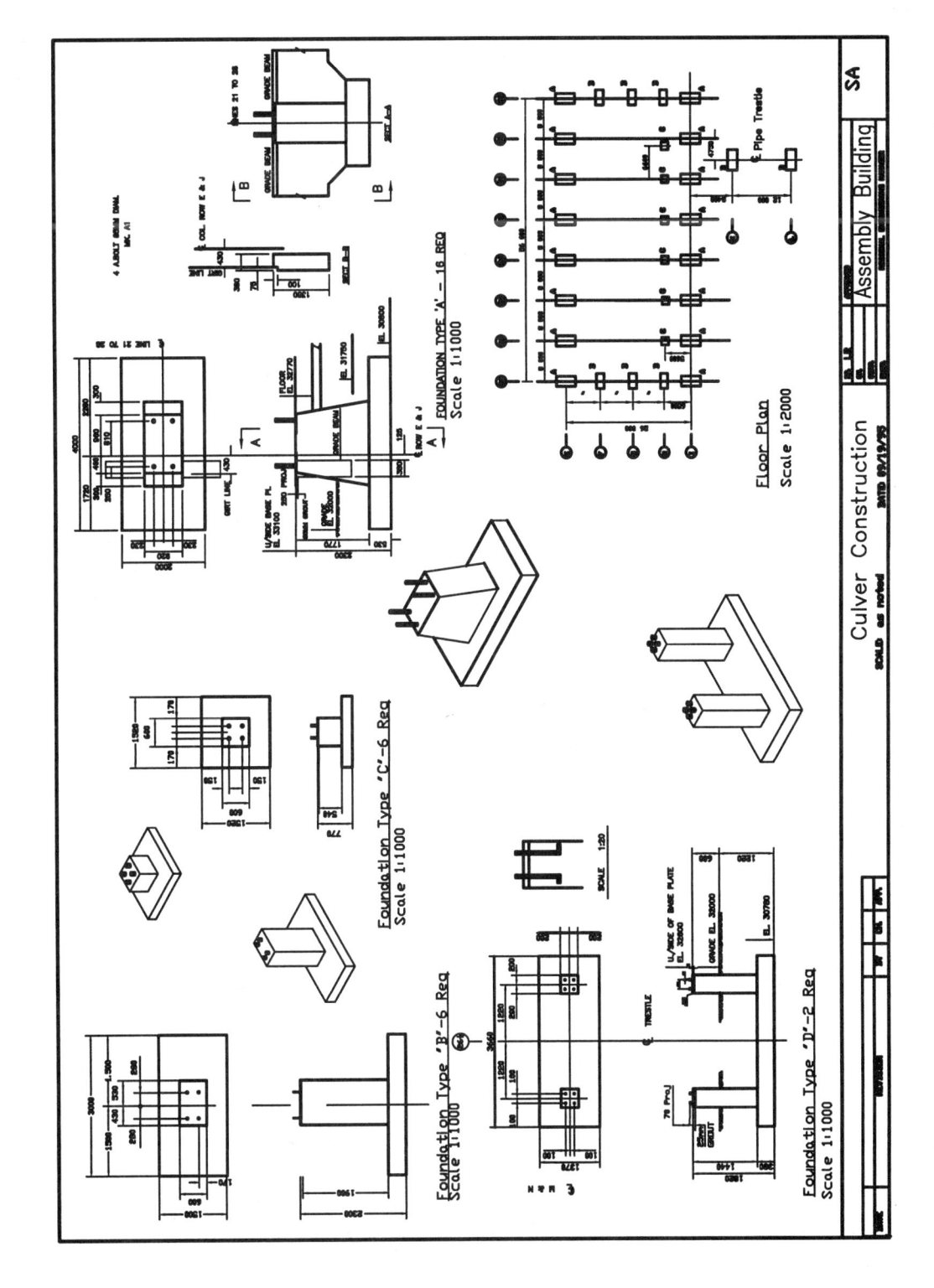

Exercise M32

Using the information from the practice exercises in Chapters 1, 2, 3, 4, 6, 7, and 9, plus the assembly drawing in Chapter 10 and the Challenger 3D model in Chapter 25, compile a complete drawing.

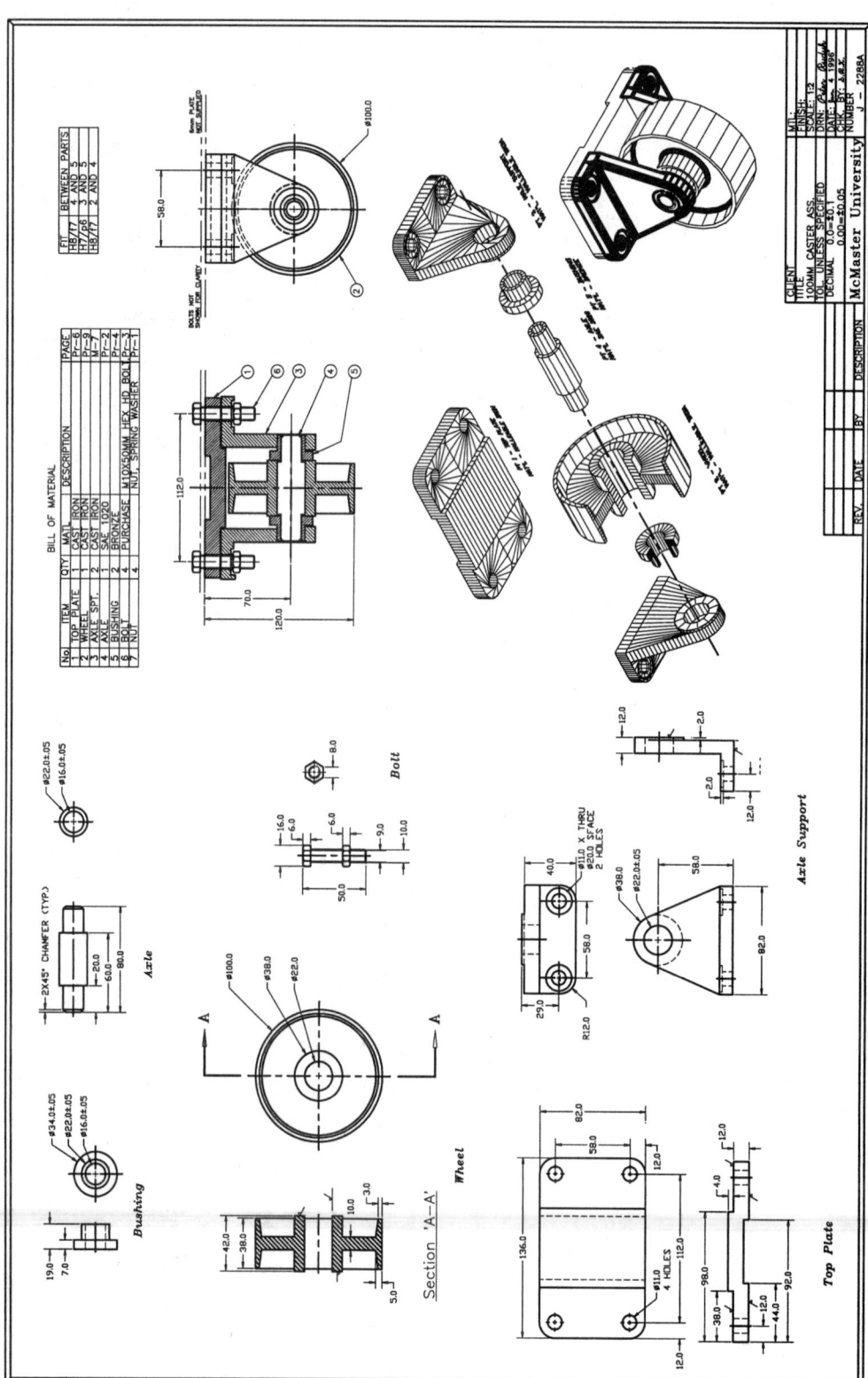

Challenger 32

Create a composite drawing of this or another residence, or a small building.

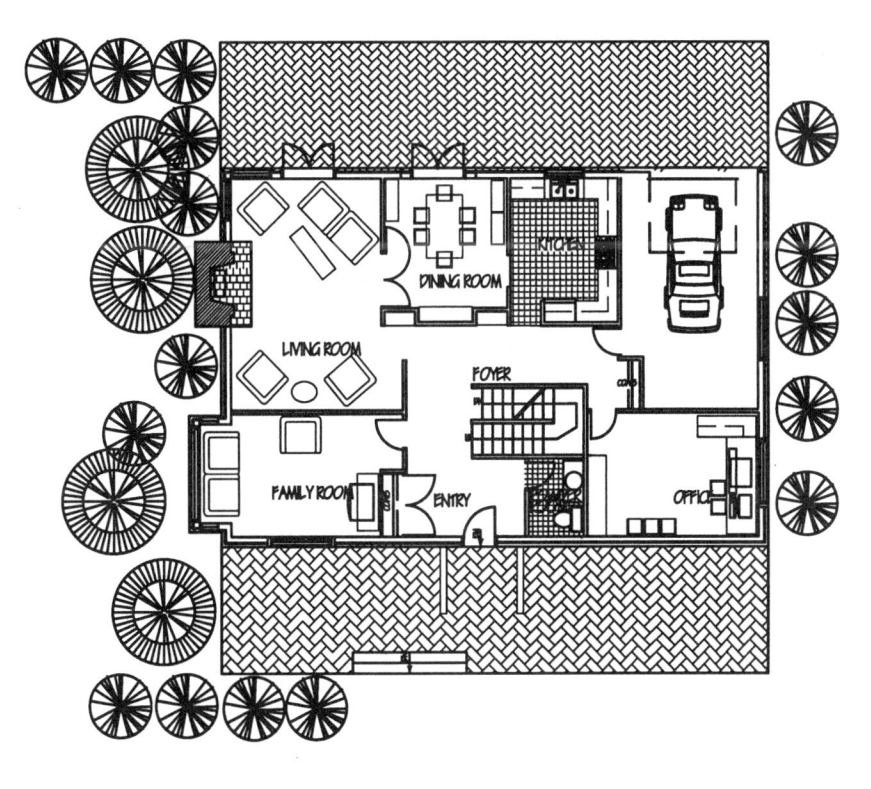

Challenger 32B

Create a small commercial building in 3D showing the four areas as illustrated: structural foundation, structural first floor, architectural basement/foundation, architectural floor plan. Create a slide show of the structure and floor plans as the building is rotated. Note: This drawing is for illustration only; you would never actually combine drawings like this.

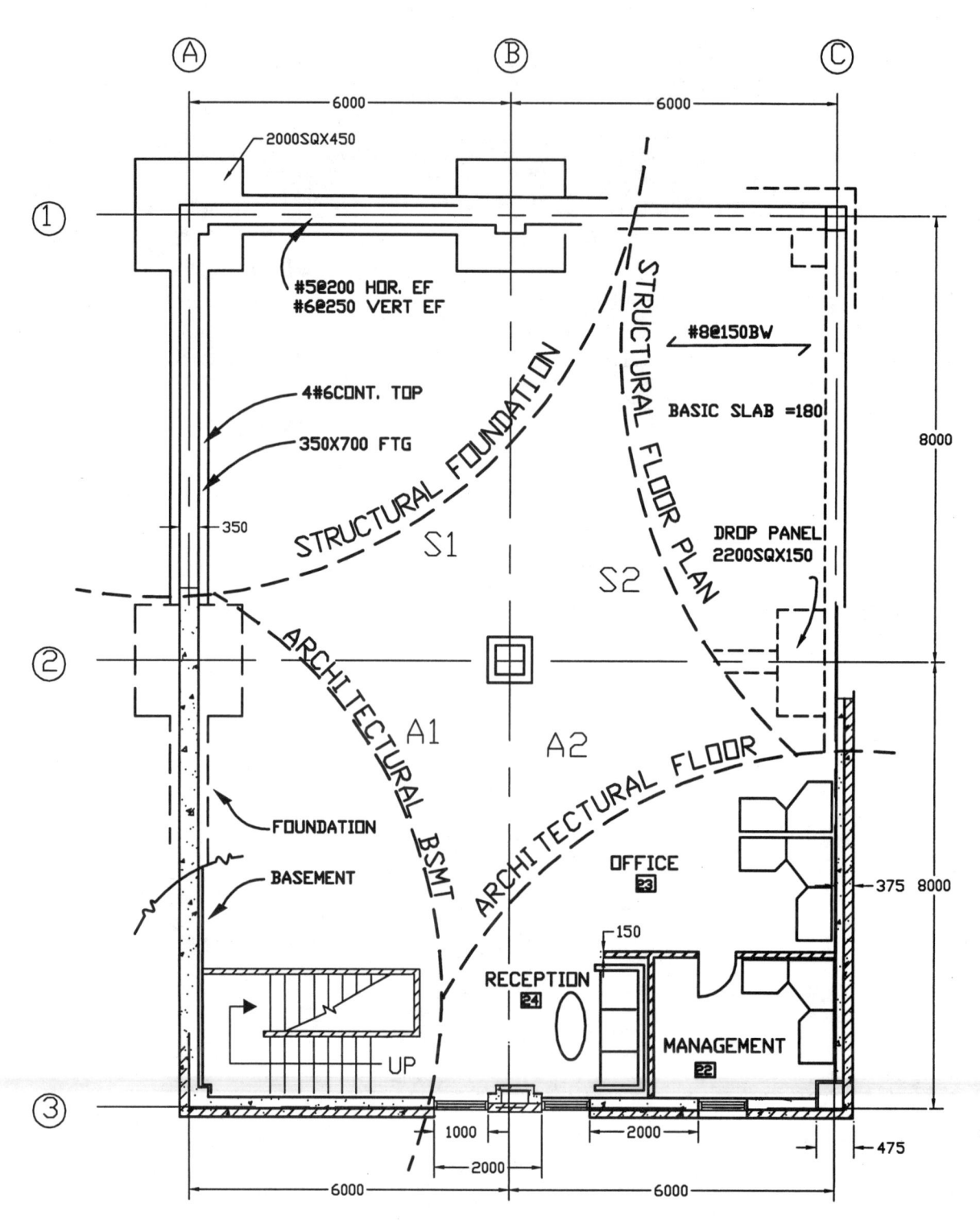

33 Dimensioning 3D Parts

Upon completion of this chapter, you should be able to:

1. Set the UCS for dimensioning a 3D part
2. Use the Oblique option for associative dimensions
3. Change the Dimension style for 3D dimensioning

3D Dimensioning

There are two ways of creating 3D dimensions: first, simply align the UCS to the plane on which you would like your dimensions; second, use blocks for arrowheads at the correct angles for an exact representation, and create a text font with the correct obliquing angle for an isometric view in 2D; then use the Oblique option under the dimensions menu.

On a true 3D object, changing the UCS is often the simplest method.

Dimensioning by Aligning the UCS

Using this method of 3D dimensioning offers several advantages over the other method:

1. The UPDate command will not offer so many surprises should you need to update text font for any reason.
2. For many people, it takes less time to set up a UCS than to create BLOCKs and deal with the changes in dimension style.

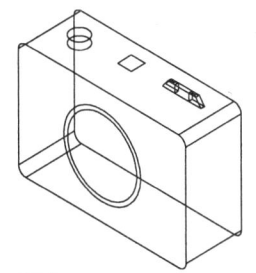

Figure 33-1

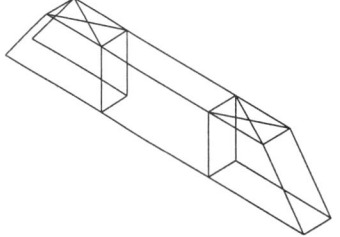

Figure 33-2

The method for isometric dimensions is quite simple. In this camera box, the shutter release button is created using 3DFACE. Then it is dimensioned in isometric by changing the UCS to the plane on which the dimensions are to appear.

Change the UCS using the UCS command option 3POINT, and use END as an OSNAP on the 3DFACEs to make sure you have the correct plane.

Figure 33-3

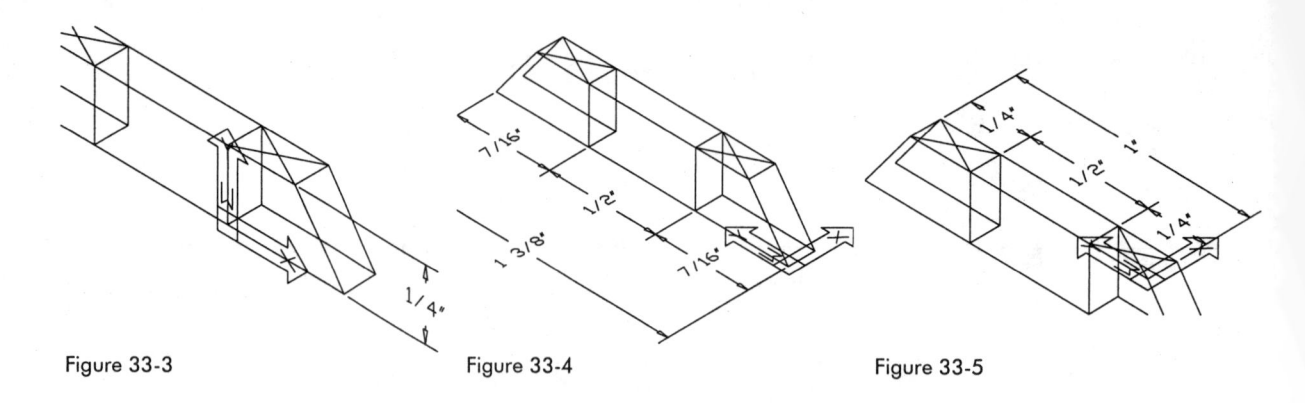

Figure 33-4

Figure 33-5

- In each case the UCS has been changed to the plane shown by the UCS icon. The dimension text, arrowhead, lines, and all related data line up according to the UCS plane. This method is also useful when your view is not exactly 30 degrees.

It is a good idea to create separate layers for each plane for orientation of dimensions.

Isometric Dimensioning by Changing the Dimension Variables

In the following method, you would need to adjust the BLOCKs or the text to fit slightly off-center views.

The trick to this method of dimensioning is to change your SNAP to Style Isometric. The SNAP must be on in the view that you want to dimension (i.e., if you are doing the top of a model, the SNAP must be aligned to this view). Use Ctrl-E to change Isoplanes.

This way, the lines you draw will snap to a 30 or 150 degree angle.

```
Command: SNAP
Specify snap spacing or [ON/OFF/Aspect/Rotate/Style/Type]
  <1.5>: S
Enter snap grid style [Standard/Isometric] <S>: I
Specify vertical spacing <1.5>: .25
```

Then change the obliquing angle of the dimension text that you use to fit this angle. Make sure that you have DIMBLK set for the arrowhead orientation, and your text STYLE has the correct obliqued angle set (text slant); dimension using ALIGNED. If your text orientation is incorrect, use TROTATE. You will, of course, need to change the STYLE and DIMBLK for each orientation.

Changing the Text Slant

While putting in the dimension, your text may have the wrong slant. You need to define and name two text styles with 30 degree and -30 degree obliquing angles. If you are using a prototype drawing, these can be defined and then left with the drawing. The first one will be used with an arrowhead that slants to the left. The second can be used with an arrowhead that slants to the right. Save your text style with its changes under a specific style name.

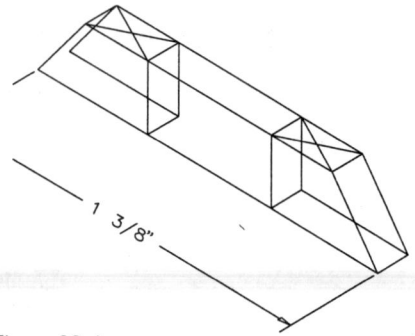

Figure 33-6

752 CHAPTER THIRTY-THREE

Defining Arrowheads

In many applications, regular arrowheads will do.

If your arrowheads (meant for orthographic view), do not have the sloped backs needed for isometric drawings, they are easy to create. To define your arrowheads, create a solid or use 3 lines that take up the area defined by 0,0, -.9,.15, and -1.0915,-.182. Another style uses 0,0, .12, .33, and 1.1, .18.

Once you have created either the lines or the solid, make a BLOCK of it. Now mirror the first one over and use it for another BLOCK.

Once you have both the text and the arrowhead blocks created, you simply need to set your text to the desired font (using a 30 or -30 obliquing angle) and change the DIMBLK option for the desired arrowhead block (see dialog box below).

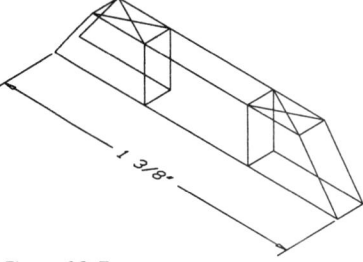

Figure 33-7

Loading the Changes into Dimension Styles

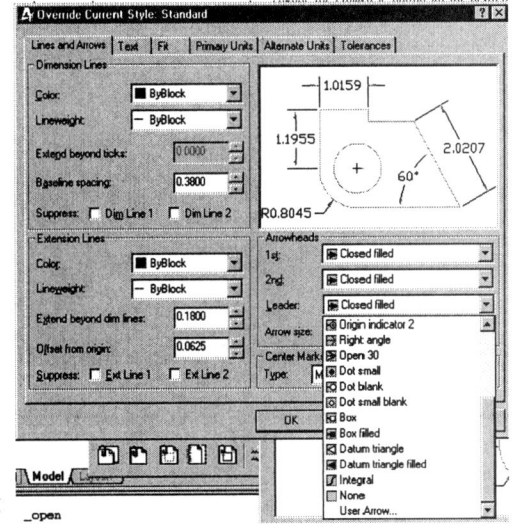

Now place the changes in your Dimension Styles. First access the Text tab of the Modify menu for the text, then the Lines and Arows tab for the arrowheads.

Under Arrowheads, pick the down arrow and then User to load the arrow block name. Once it is loaded, you can use it for anything.

Save the style under the name Oblique.

Now dimension your drawing using ALIGNED or ROTATE with the dimension line set to 30 degrees. Next use the Oblique command to change the angle of the extension lines to 150 degrees; it should look like Figure 33-7 at the bottom.

There are many Auto LISP routines that will make the dimensioning of such parts easier. If you find these options useful, consider using AutoLISP to automate the process you have just completed because it takes time to exit DIM to change both text fonts and DIMBLK. Also consider these for a prototype drawing.

In the following exercise, line up your UCS with the plane on which you would like your dimensions, then create the dimensions.

Now try a second exercise changing your dimension variables. Determine which method you find preferable.

Dimensioning 3D Parts   **753**

Prelab 33 3D Dimensioning

Step 1 Open the Prelab exercise from Chapter 31. We will be placing dimensions on it as shown in this illustration.

Set your dimension scale to 40 and the unit readout to 0 decimal points.

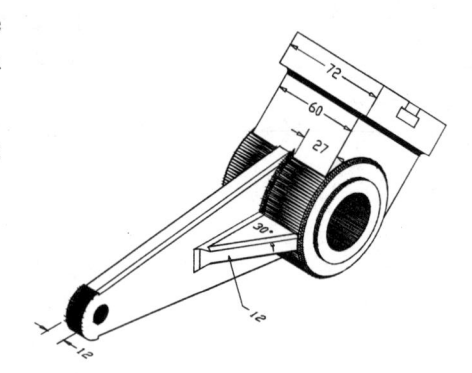

Step 2 With the UCS still at World, enter the width of the end as shown.

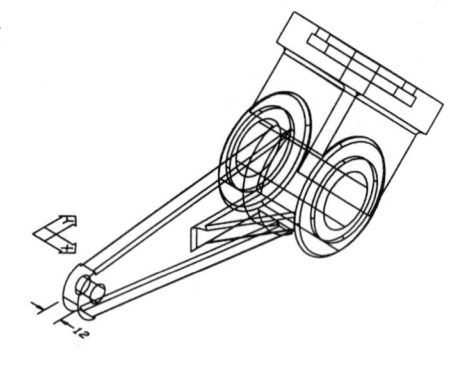

Step 3 Now place your UCS on the top face using the 3points option.

Once this is in, enter the dimension as shown. It is not necessary to change the dimension style again.

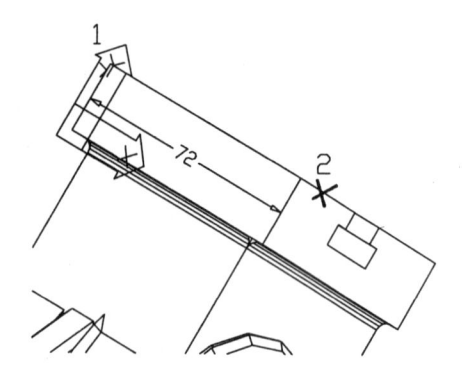

Step 4 Using the UCS command, place the origin of the UCS on the next level down.

Use ENDpoint to actually access the front face of the plane. Then place the two dimensions on this plane. You will need to use ENDpoint OSNAPs again.

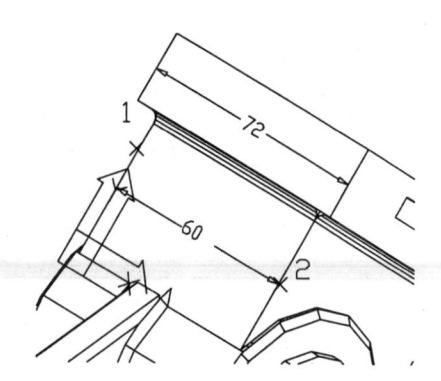

Step 5 Finally, using the 3point option of UCS, place the angular dimension on the face shown here. You may need to zoom in considerably to get the dimension to fit.

If you have time, create two 30-degree arrowheads. Block them under different names, then load them as the User Arrowhead.

Add two text styles: one with 30 degrees obliquing angle, the other with -30 degrees obliquing angle.

Try entering dimensions this way as well.

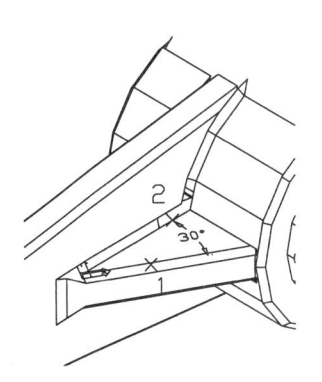

Exercises

3D dimensioning is quite simple once you understand the concept, so try dimensioning some of your existing files or spend some time creating these files, then dimension them. The more experience you have, the better.

Practice Exercise 33

Create this file in solids as shown. Then add dimensions.

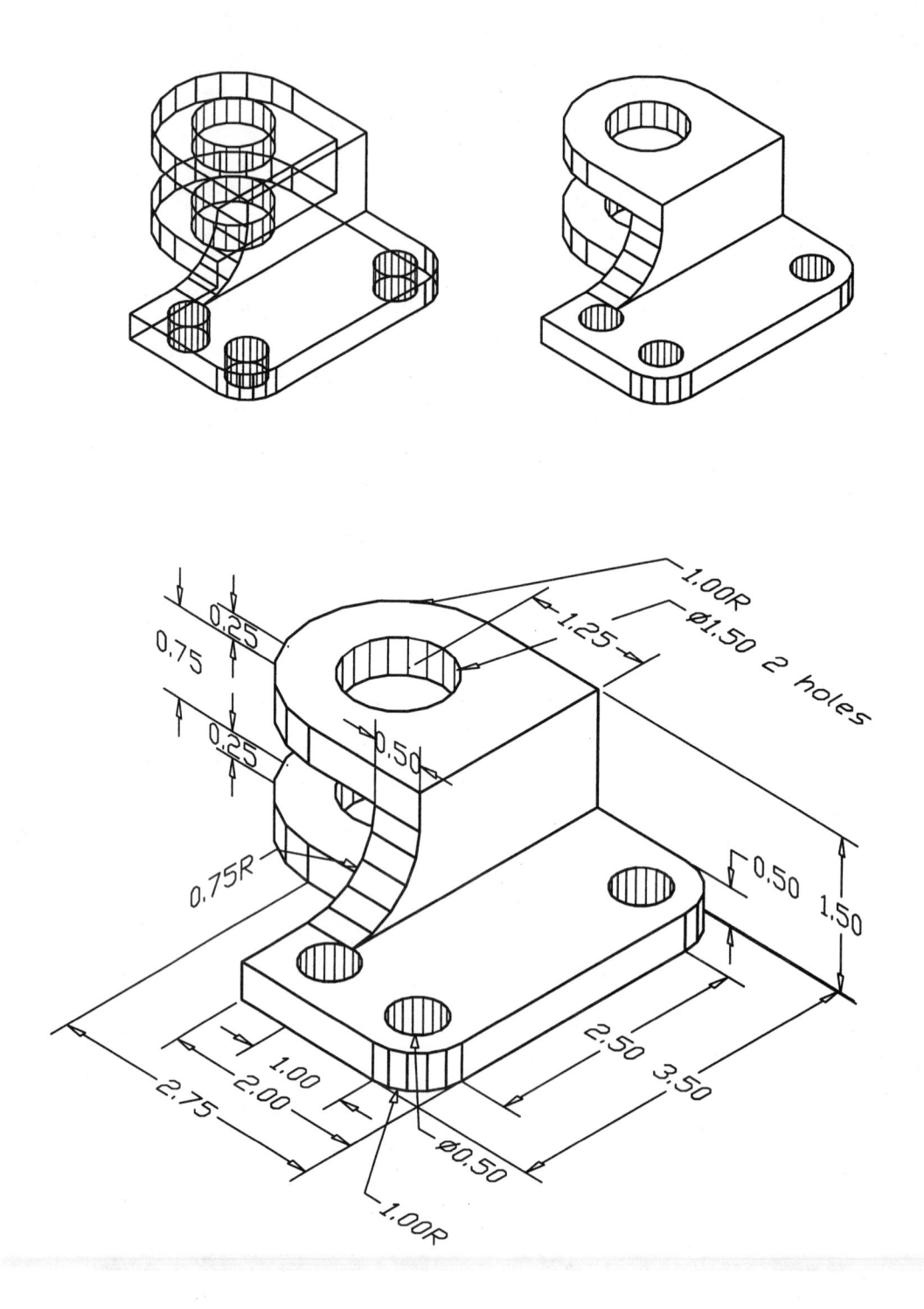

If you are changing your UCS for these dimensions, be sure to change the origin as well as the orientation.

Exercise A33

Sections are important, and 3D sections can give *all* the information needed in a wall or partition. Create this:

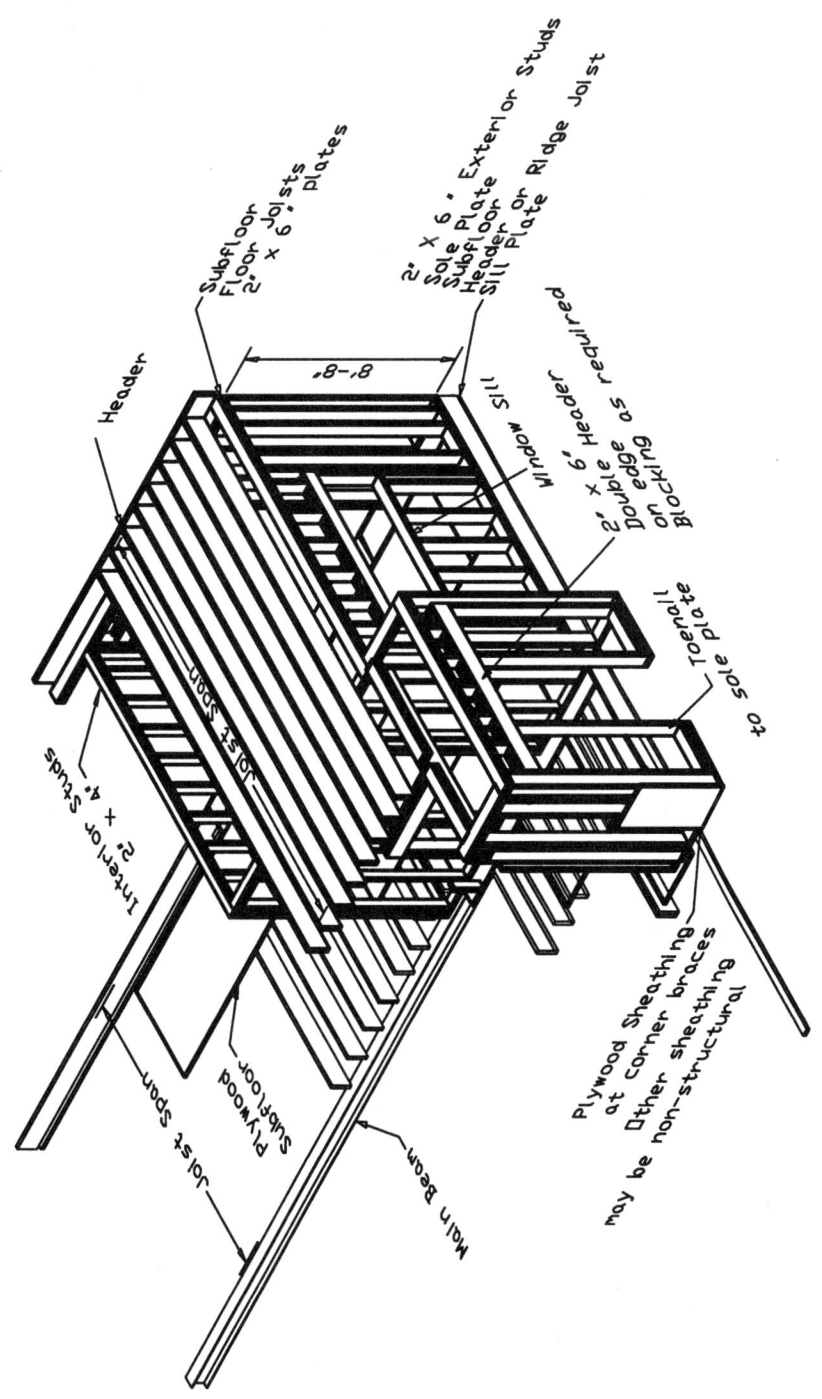

Exercise C33

Draw these calipers and add overall dimensions. Save the file regularly.

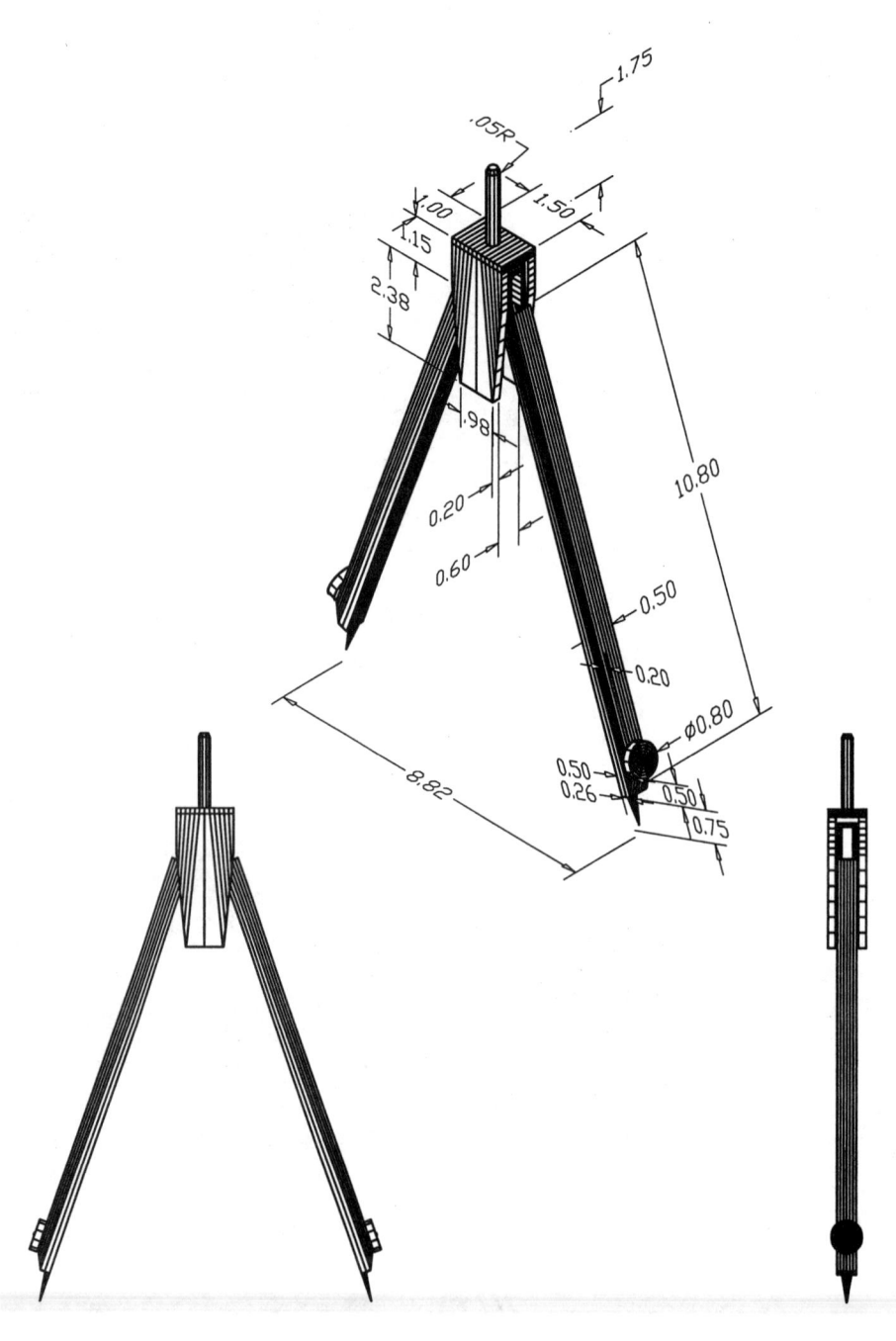

Exercise M33

Draw this wood vise, then dimension it.

Challenger 33

Using standards from the *Machinist's Handbook*, create a standard thread drawing (a). Use POINTS with ARRAY to array the points around the center point, creating one "loop" for each surface edge (b). Move the points up to reach the vertical pitch distance (c). Use 3DPOLY to create a polyline between each edge (d). Use either 3DMESH or RULESURF to create the thread (e). Add the thread end with 3DMESH (f). Then add the stock.

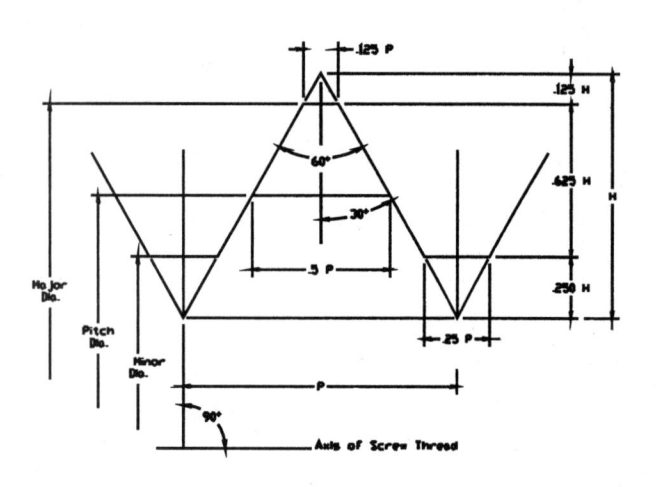

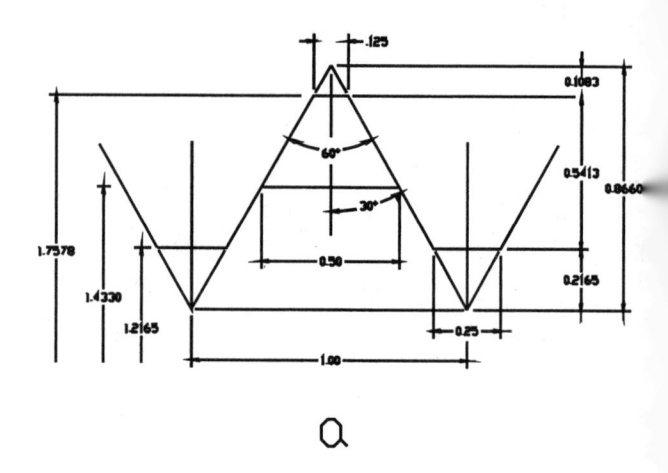

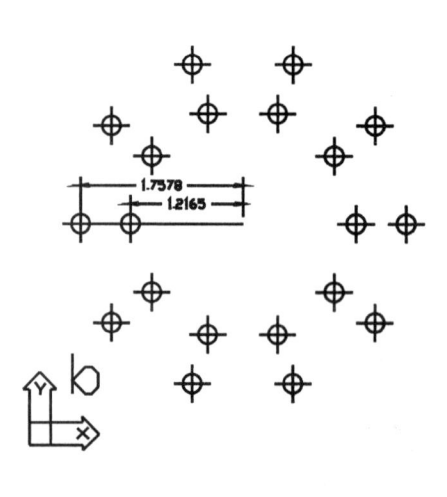

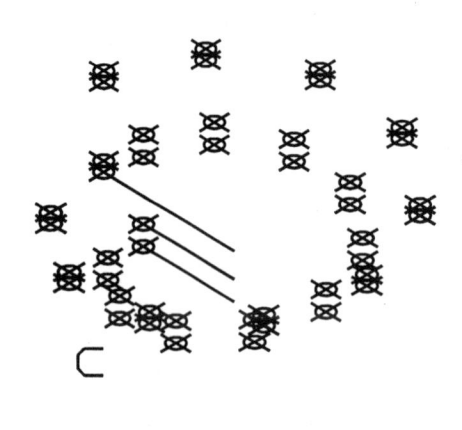

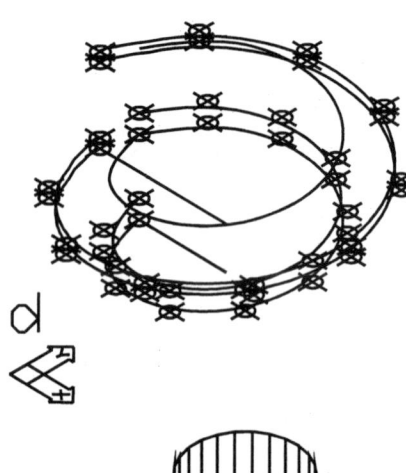

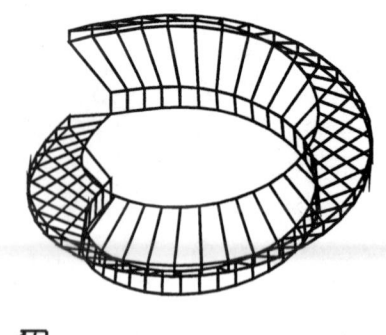

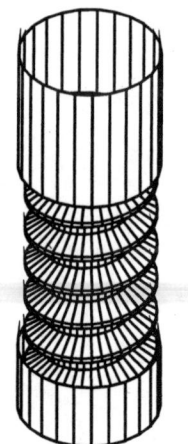

760 CHAPTER THIRTY-THREE

34 Final Projects

OBJECTIVES
1. On-screen review
2. General Review
3. Final Drawing Projects

In the second half of this book there have been basically two different AutoCAD-based subjects: 3D modeling, and engineering analysis. In the next few pages the final projects incorporate both these aspects of the software with a 3D model accompanied by documentation on the project itself. If you are not using solids, simply create the 3D models.

If you have been working through the projects as outlined herein, you should have no trouble completing the final projects. *It may be a good idea to start the final project six or seven weeks before the end of term so you will have adequate time to get it finished, plotted, and presentable.*

Again, there are three projects presented: architectural, civil, and mechanical.

As a college instructor, it is always interesting to follow graduating students through their various careers. First, it is important to assess the value of what we are teaching students. Second, it is interesting to see where life picks up after schooling is completed. I am often astounded to see students who were heading toward brilliant careers in residential house design doing work on piping layouts and exhaust fan molds; and the opposite—mechanically trained students doing presentation drawings for architectural purposes.

Notes
Don't forget to keep a back-up.

Whether you are trained as a technologist, a technician, an engineer or an architect, it is always a good idea to learn how to read drawings produced in other disciplines. The more proficient you are with AutoCAD or any other CAD package, the more marketable your skills will be. If the building industry is suffering a slump, there is nothing wrong with taking a job in a different area until the market turns around.

Final Tests

The next few pages will offer you one on-screen problem with four questions followed by 100 questions pertaining to the last 13 chapters of this book. Your instructor may offer you these or similar questions as a final exam. If you are not required to write a final exam, these questions can still give you an idea of how much you understand.

Problem 1

Draw the object shown in solids starting with the 0,0,0 at the point indicated. Set Units to Decimal with no numbers after the decimal point.

Make sure the geometry is perfect.

Refer to the model to answer the following questions.

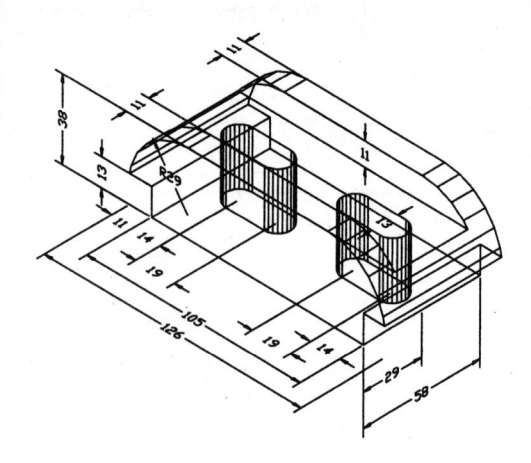

1. What is the mass of the object shown?

    a. 14609

    b. 180240

    c. 1367623

    d. 180248

    e. 28375363

2. What are the radii of gyration?

    a. 73,255,264

    b. 12,647,564

    c. 73,25,35

    d. 487,89,324

3. What is the absolute value of point A?

    a. 110,47,27

    b. 112,48,27

    c. 109,47,27

    d. 110,48,27

4. What is the area of the model?

    a. 43875.37 sq mm

    b. 32832.84 sq mm

    c. 28283.86 sq mm

    d. 30683.46 sq mm

    e. 30517.22 sq mm

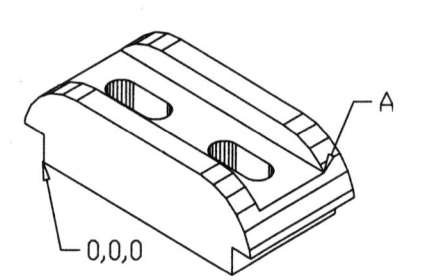

3D Review

Choose the answer that is most correct.

1. A UCS

    a. Identifies a plane in 3D for you to work on

    b. Creates a 2D plane that looks like a 3D plane

    c. Creates a UCSICON in 3D

2. Changing the UCS

    a. Can be useful for making circles on oblique surfaces

    b. Can be useful for placing text on an oblique surface

    c. Can be useful for creating cylinders

    d. All of the above

3. How many areas can the screen be divided into?

    a. 4

    b. 12

    c. 16

    d. No limit

4. What command do you use to divide the screen into various tiled viewports?

    a. VPORTS

    b. VPOINT

    c. VIEWRES

    d. MAKEVIEW

5. What does Restore mean in the above command?

    a. Restore a named view

    b. Restore a named screen layout

    c. Restore the previous screen

6. What is the "Right-hand rule"?

    a. Always use your right hand on the mouse.

    b. If X is your index finger and Y is your middle finger, Z will be perpendicular to them.

    c. If your thumb is X and your index finger fully extended is Y, then your middle finger pointed straight out from your palm will be positive Z.

7. What does the middle circle stand for in the Globe Icon?

    a. The equator

    b. The center of the screen

    c. *Z-0*

8. How do you find the Globe Icon?

    a. Use the space bar after the VPOINT command.

    b. Use the pull-down menu for Set Viewports.

    c. Use the Axis Tripod option in the VPOINT command.

    d. Both a and b

9. Can you use polar coordinates in an isometric view?

    a. No

    b. Yes

    c. Sometimes

10. On what plane will a point show up if you pick it in the isometric view?

    a. On the *Z-0* plane of the world coordinate space

    b. On the *Z-0* plane of the UCS

    c. Line-of-sight onto the *X* plane

11. Why is OSNAP important in the isometric view?

    a. Because you cannot enter coordinates in 3D

    b. Because points are entered on the *X-Y* plane without OSNAP

    c. Because existing geometry is readily accessible

12. What command do you use to extrude an existing object?

    a. THICKNESS

    b. SETVAR

    c. CHANGE

13. What command do you use to change the *Z* coordinate of an existing object?

    a. MOVE

    b. CLIP

    c. ELEVATION

    d. a and b

    e. a and c

14. If you have extruded a line to 4 units, can you break a section out of the bottom of the image (Z-0) but keep the top (Z-4) intact?

    a. No

    b. Yes

15. What command do you use to make hidden lines invisible in a plot?

    a. LAYER HIDDENXXX

    b. PLOT HIDDENNAME

    c. MVIEW with HIDEPLOT

16. Will a REDRAW update your screen after HIDE?

    a. Yes

    b. No

17. What can you do to make sure your next five items will be on the Z depth of 5?

    a. Set your THICKNESS.

    b. Set your ELEVATION.

    c. Change your UCS to X5.

18. Why can't a CIRCLE be placed on an X-Z plane?

    a. Circles must be normal to the UCS Z-0 plane.

    b. Circles must be placed on an ISOPLANE.

    c. Circles must be on a Y-Z plane.

19. How do you change the UCS from the World Coordinate space orientation to the Y-Z plane?

    a. Rotate around X.

    b. Rotate around Y.

    c. Rotate around Z.

20. What command do you use to get back to the World Coordinate space?

    a. UCS U

    b. UCS W

    c. UCS P

21. What does the broken pencil icon mean?

    a. The *X-Y* plane is not visible within that viewport.

    b. The *X-Z* plane is active.

    c. The UCS has been changed.

22. If you change the *X* option of the UCS command to 90 degrees, what plane do you want to have the UCS on?

    a. *X-Z*

    b. *X-Y*

    c. *Y-Z*

23. How many times can you change the UCS before filing?

    a. Only 8

    b. 16

    c. Unlimited

24. What does the + mean in the bottom of the UCS icon?

    a. You are looking at the top of the object.

    b. You are looking at the bottom of the object.

    c. You have the icon on the origin of the UCS.

25. What does the UCS option 3POINT do?

    a. Lets you orient the UCS relative to 3 points

    b. Lets you orient the UCS relative to 1 point and an origin

    c. Lets you orient the UCS using OSNAP

26. What does the term "toggle" mean?

    a. This turns an item off.

    b. This turns a function on or off.

    c. This turns the grid off.

27. What does the O option stand for in the UCS command?

    a. Object

    b. Opposite

    c. Outside Boundaries

28. What does the P option stand for in the UCS command?

    a. Pline

    b. Previous

    c. Partial

29. What does the response "lines are collinear" mean?

   a. You have chosen the same point twice.

   b. You have described a line that already exists.

   c. You have entered a null code.

   d. All of the above

30. Of what use is the UCS dialog box?

   a. To access orthographic preset UCSs

   b. To save stored orientations of the UCS

   c. To access stored UCSs

   d. All of the above

31. If you are working in the isometric view and you use the STRETCH command, how is the object STRETCHed?

   a. Relative to the line-of-sight

   b. Relative to the world coordinates

   c. Relative to the UCS

   d. All of the above

32. Can you use 3DFACE on a curved surface?

   a. Yes, if you have EXPLODEd it

   b. Yes, if you have stored it

   c. No

33. Can you use 3DFACE on a PLINE?

   a. Yes, as long as there are no curves

   b. Yes, as long as you use PEDIT

   c. No

34. What is 3DFACE used for?

   a. Creating planes for describing 3D objects

   b. Creating planes for viewing

   c. Creating obliquing planes

   d. All of the above

35. How do you indicate that you would like to enter an *X* filter?

   a. .X

   b. @.x

   c. x of

36. Can you enter both an *X* and a *Y* filter?

    a. Yes

    b. No

37. What happens to *Z* when you have entered filters for both *X* and *Y*?

    a. *Z* needs to be specified.

    b. *Z* remains at 0.

    c. *Z* takes the current *Z* depth.

38. What command do you use to make lines that were hidden with HIDE reappear?

    a. REGEN

    b. REDRAW

    c. ZOOM A

    d. All of the above

39. What happens if you PLOT a view in which LINEs have been hidden in the HIDE command?

    a. The lines are hidden on the plot.

    b. The lines are shown in a different color.

    c. The lines are not hidden on the plot.

40. What happens if you print a view in which you have used HIDE?

    a. The lines are hidden on the print.

    b. The lines are shown in a different color.

    c. The lines are not hidden on the print.

41. What is model space?

    a. The default space in AutoCAD

    b. The space used for creating 3D models

    c. The space used for creating drawings

    d. All of the above

42. Which of these commands gets to paper space?

    a. TILESPACE

    b. TILECHANGE

    c. TILEMODE

43. What is paper space for?

    a. It is a facility for hiding lines in plots.

    b. It is a 2D layout facility.

    c. It is for creating drawings of 3D parts.

    d. All of the above

44. Does a file using paper space take up much more room on the disk?

    A. Depends on the file

    b. Always takes more room

    c. Never takes more room

45. What does the D stand for in DVIEW?

    a. Drawing

    b. Dynamic

    c. Delta

    d. Difficult

46. What does a Target do?

    a. Positions the viewer relative to the object

    b. Positions the objects relative to the viewer

    c. Changes the size of the view file

47. How do you change the orientation of an object for viewing?

    a. DVIEW POints

    b. DVIEW CAmera

    c. PAN

    d. All of the above

48. How do you get a perspective view?

    a. DVIEW PE

    b. DVIEW D

    c. DVIEW I

49. Why can't you change the ZOOM if you have created a perspective view?

    a. The objects have been modified so that the vector files are no longer accessible for magnification.

    b. The objects have been expanded to fit the screen.

    c. The objects are not accessible by a simple magnification process because they have been edited.

50. What do the letters PA stand for in the DVIEW option?

   a. Point Advance

   b. PAn

   c. Point Access

51. What effect does TWist have on the view?

   a. Rotates the view relative to the UCS Z

   b. Rotates the view relative to the screen

   c. Rotates the objects like a ROTATE command

52. If you have made a total mess of your view, how do you get back to where you were in the DVIEW command?

   a. U

   b. DVIEW Undo

   c. DVIEW erase

   d. All of the above

53. How does the POints option in DVIEW work?

   a. Lets you set the TArget and CAmera positions

   b. Gives two points which act as the X and Y of your screen

   c. Lets you rotate the view along the X-Y plane and from the X-Y plane

54. What is the difference between TWist and ROTATE?

   a. TWist is a display function and Rotate moves the objects relative to the origin.

   b. There is no difference.

   c. Rotate is counterclockwise and TWist is clockwise.

55. How do you place dimensions on a surface that is not perpendicular to the viewer in a 3D model?

   a. Change the view with DVIEW.

   b. Change the UCS.

   c. Use the DIM VARS.

56. What is VPLAYER?

   a. The LAYER control within a viewport in PSPACE

   b. The LAYER accessed in the HIDEPLOT option

   c. The LAYER used for viewing objects

   d. All of the above

57. What does MVIEW provide?

   a. Multiple, overlapping viewports

   b. Single paper space viewports

   c. Compiled views of drawings

   d. All of the above

58. What is the difference between Hideplot and HIDE?

   a. HIDE is file-dependent and HIDEPLOT is drawing-dependent.

   b. HIDE is view-dependent and HIDEPLOT is viewport-dependent.

   c. HIDE is used only for prints and HIDEPLOT is used for both plots and prints.

59. What does the term TILEMODE mean?

   a. A mode that turns your screen off

   b. The ability to plot hidden lines in a different color

   c. The partitioning of your screen for 2D layout or 2D and 3D design

   d. A mode that enables paper space

60. What does the option Restore do in the MVIEW command?

   a. Restores a saved drawing

   b. Restores a saved viewport

   c. Restores a saved orientation of DVIEW commands

   d. Restores a saved viewport configuration or the viewport configuration that was current in MSPACE

61. What does Vpvisdflt mean?

   a. Viewport visible display fit

   b. Viewport visibility default

   c. View parity display default

62. How can you get a surface that curves?

   a. REVSURF

   b. RULESURF

   c. THICKNESS

   d. All of the above

63. Which surface needs a minimum of two objects to complete?

   a. REVSURF

   b. RULESURF

   c. THICKNESS

   d. Both a and b

64. What command uses a central axis?

    a. REVSURF

    b. RULESURF

    c. THICKNESS

    d. All of the above

65. How do you change the number of segments on a surface?

    a. TABSURF1

    b. SURFTAB1

    c. VIEWRES

    d. All of the above

66. What do you need for a tabulated surface?

    a. A path curve and a direction vector

    b. A PLINE and a LINE

    c. An axis and a curve path

67. When will you get the response "Entity not usable as rotation axis" in the REVSURF command?

    a. When the object used as an axis is not on the same Z depth as the curve path

    b. When the axis is an arc

    c. When the axis is not a pline

68. If you have a line that you would like to act as one rail of a surface, and an arc and a line as the other rail, how do you accomplish this?

    a. Make the arc a closed entity

    b. Make the line and arc one object using PEDIT

    c. Make the line a pline

69. How many edges can you have in an EDGESURF?

    a. 4

    b. 8

    c. Any multiple of 4

    d. No limit

70. How many vectors can you have in a 3DMESH?

    a. Maximum 16

    b. Maximum 32

    c. No limit

71. Which surface would you use to create a dashboard of a car?

    a. REVSURF

    b. RULESURF

    c. 3DMESH

72. What is the similarity between 3DFACE and the other surfaces?

    a. They all hide objects behind them in HIDE.

    b. They all are composed of a minimum of two linear elements.

    c. They all have a maximum of 16 edges.

    d. All of the above

73. What happens if you give a negative number for the included angle in a REVSURF?

    a. The REVSURF will be clockwise instead of counterclockwise.

    b. The REVSURF will not work.

    c. The REVSURF will have a negative Z value.

74. Why do you need to surface an object to use AutoSHADE?

    a. The object must be accepted as a solid.

    b. The system needs to determine the inside and outside of objects.

    c. The object must have a volume.

    d. All of the above

    e. None of the above

75. What is the advantage of using 3D objects?

    a. To simplify the design process

    b. To cut down on the number of objects on the screen

    c. To create polynomial surfaces

76. How can you define your own 3D Objects and have them available?

    a. Make them into BLOCKs.

    b. Create LISP routines for the shapes you need.

    c. Create script files.

    d. Any of the above.

77. How many objects are there in a completed sphere using the 3D objects routine?

    a. One

    b. Two

    c. Three

78. How does SURFTAB1 affect the 3D Object CONE command?

    a. It tabulates the surface along the cone's height.

    b. It changes the display of the cone.

    c. There is no effect.

79. How many faces can you have in a PFACE?

    a. Any multiple of 2

    b. Any number

    c. Any multiple of 4

80. Can you move a surface without moving the associated rails or base objects?

    a. Yes

    b. No

81. What is the secret to inserting 3D models?

    a. Know your axes and origin.

    b. Change your UCS.

    c. Record the scale of the object.

    d. All of the above

82. How many models can you merge?

    a. As many as your RAM can take

    b. As many as your drive or directory can take

    c. As many as the .ac$ file can hold

    d. As many as the XREFS can support

83. Which of the following are affected by the size of your RAM?

    a. Solids

    b. SURFTAB

    c. PSPACE

    d. All of the above

84. Why would you use solids modeling rather than 3D objects?

    a. To perform analysis on final models

    b. To subtract interior spaces

    c. To save RAM

    d. Both a and b

85. Are dishes available as a primitive in solids?

    a. Yes

    b. No

86. Which command can change a pline into a solid?

    a. EXTRUDE

    b. SOLIDIFY

    c. Both of the above

87. If you were trying to add one half of a sphere to a rectangular solid how could you do it?

    a. SPHERE plus UNION

    b. REVOLVE plus UNION

    c. EXTRUDE plus UNION

88. Which of the following calculates a centroid in a solid or region?

    a. AREA

    b. MASS

    c. MASSPROP

89. Why should you avoid extruding splined plines with EXTRUDE?

    a. There is a limit to the number of vertices the command can accept.

    b. You cannot extrude a curved shape.

    c. You cannot extrude a pline.

90. What command would you use to remove the volume of a cylinder from a box?

    a. SEPARATE

    b. SUBTRACT

    c. CHPROP

    d. All of the above

91. What command will let you reposition a solid?

    a. MOVE

    b. EXTRUDE

    c. ROTATE

    d. All of the above

92. Can you BREAK a Solid?

    a. No

    b. Yes

93. Can you change the color of a solid?

    a. No

    b. Yes

94. Can a Region be considered a composite?

    a. No

    b. Yes

95. How can you create a hidden solid in a plot?

    a. Use HIDE.

    b. Use MVIEW and Hideplot.

    c. Use PSPACE and Hideplot.

96. How can you create a 3D donut shape?

    a. Use TORUS.

    b. Use DONUT.

    c. Use SPHERE.

97. What is the default setting for Z on a Region?

    a. Non-specified

    b. Current UCS

    c. WCS Z-0

98. Which operation are you unable to perform with a pline that has thickness?

    a. EXTRUDE

    b. ROTATE

99. If you try REVOLVE on a pline, when will you get the response, "Lines Intersect"?

    a. When your axis is not as long as the curve path

    b. When the pline is closed

    c. When the direct line from the open ends of the pline intersect the axis of rotation

100. What does the EXPLODE command do in solids?

    a. Separates the solid into primitives

    b. Retraces the steps of the solids

    c. Changes the solid to a mesh

Final Projects

Final Project: Design

This will be a Design-Draft project that will allow you to work through the part from a parametric perspective.

Final Project: Architecture

Use the 3D solids commands to design the foyer of a large public building. The foundations of the building should be adequate for support, and the interior of the foyer should be a minimum of two stories in height.

When designing, make maximum use of LAYERs so that final calculations can be made for volumes of different materials, and mass properties calculations can be made on all structural elements.

Once created, analyze the building with regard to strength and weight. Use mass properties to determine the total volume of concrete required, and the total volume of structural steel or wood frame required.

Along with your presentation-quality drawings, submit the following: the interior area of the foyer (for calculations concerning cost of finish), mass properties of the foyer, the volume of concrete used in the foundations (for estimating calculations), and a list of materials for estimating purposes.

Final Project: Civil

Using a typical residential survey, provide two 3D layouts of 22 houses on varying lot sizes. On the first drawing indicate the new developer's access route. On the second survey, illustrate the alternate access route preferred by residents.

Include with your drawings a report on how much cut and fill needs to be done with both designs. Use solids to help you in your calculations.

Final Project: Mechanical

Use the 3D and solids to create a 3D model of the fandrive in Chapter 12.

Make maximum use of LAYERs so you can submit with your drawings a full mass properties analysis and bill of materials.

Design Exercise 34

This is a design project as opposed to a drafting project. No dimensions are given because you are to make them up. The idea here is to make the object shown in solids, using brass, and to make it so that the weight is more or less 5 pounds. Both sides must be completely symmetrical. Once this is done, transfer the solid into surfaces. Why? Because your manufacturing software is suddenly and inexplicably incompatible with this version of AutoCAD, and you have to get the part out *TONIGHT*. This is a real world exercise.

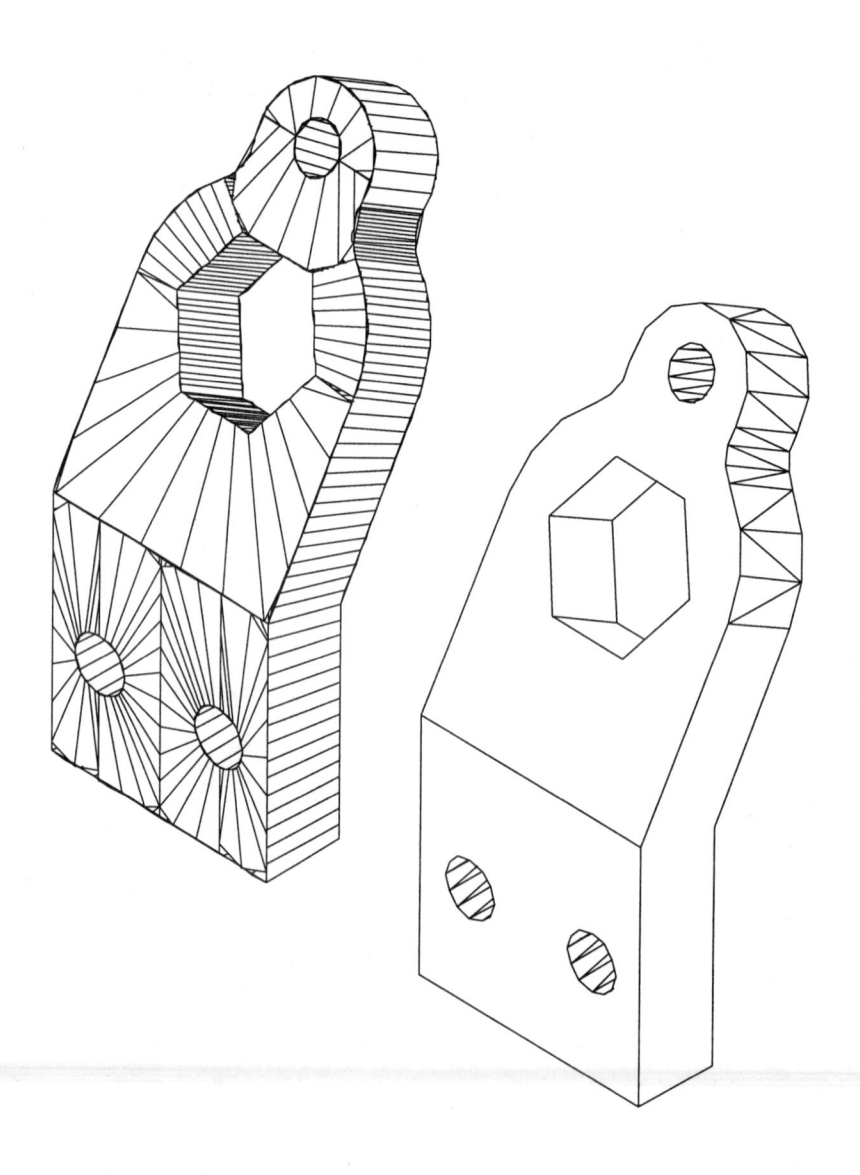

Exercise A34

Use the 3D commands and solids to design the foyer of a large public building.

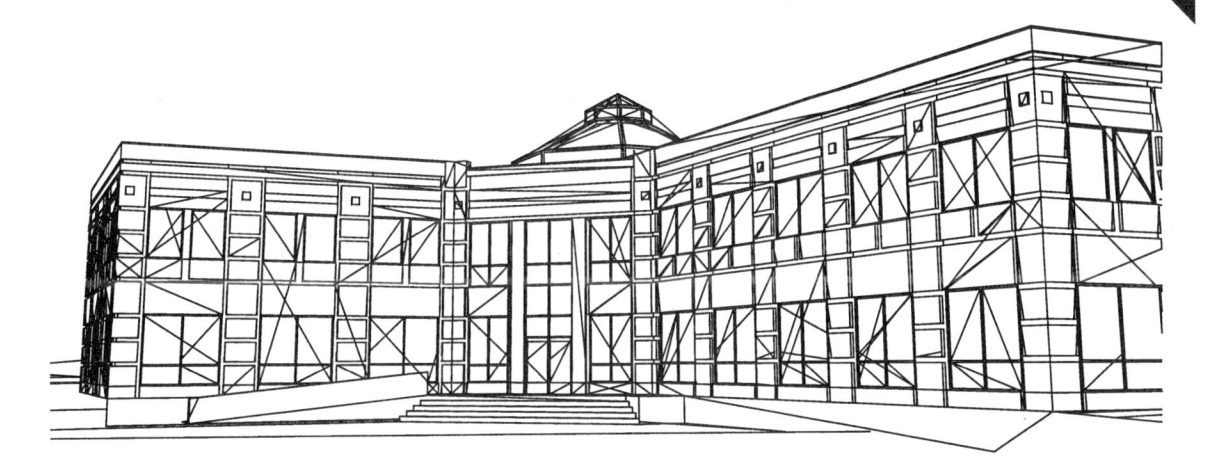

Niagara Falls, New York
Water Treatment Plant
Consultant: Brinkeroff, Gore and Storey
Drawn by Dave Umbach

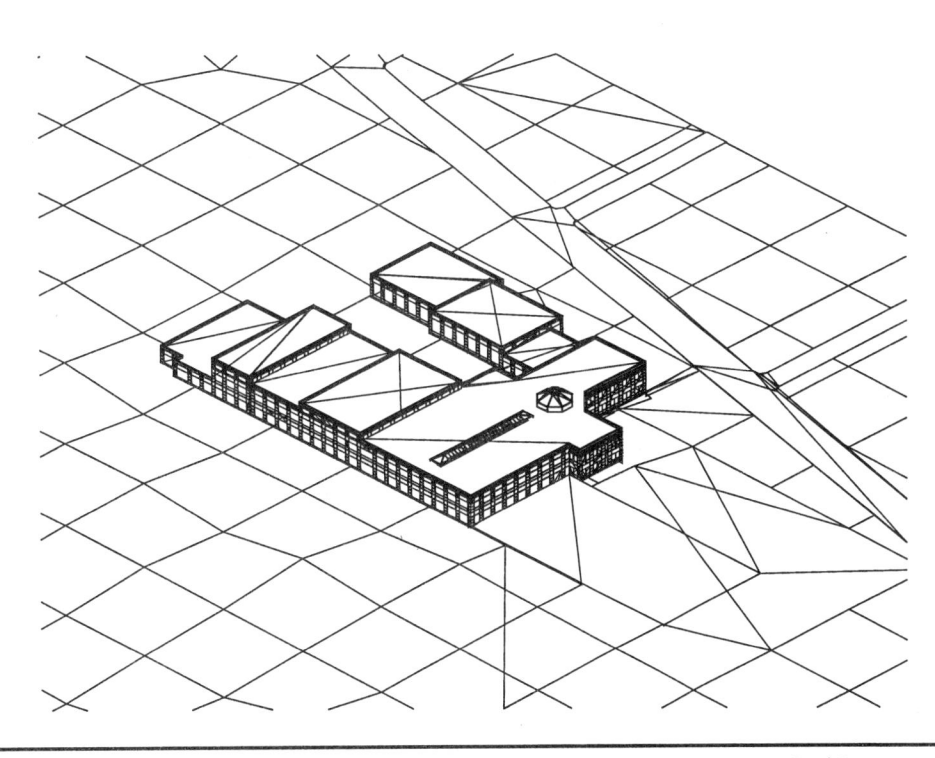

Client: City of Niagara Falls, New York

Final Projects

Exercise A34 (cont.)

XREFs are helpful in limiting the size of the file.

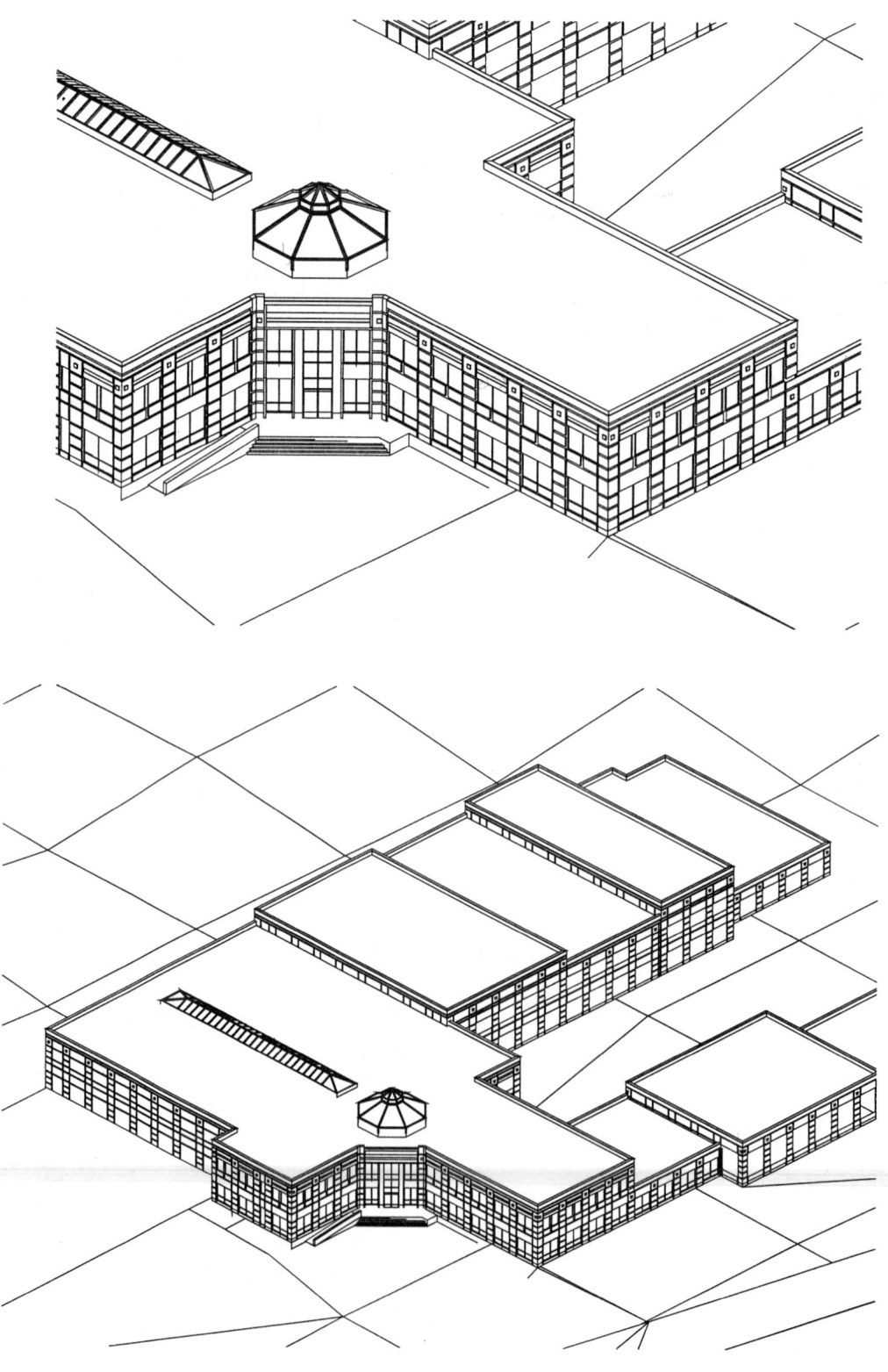

Exercise C34

Using a typical residential survey, provide two 2D layouts of 22 houses on varying lot sizes. Make sure that all contours of the land are maintained, and that trees block the view of the houses from the main thoroughfare. Each house should have at least five mature trees on the lot. No two houses should be alike.

Include with your drawings a report on how much cut and fill needs to be done with both road designs.

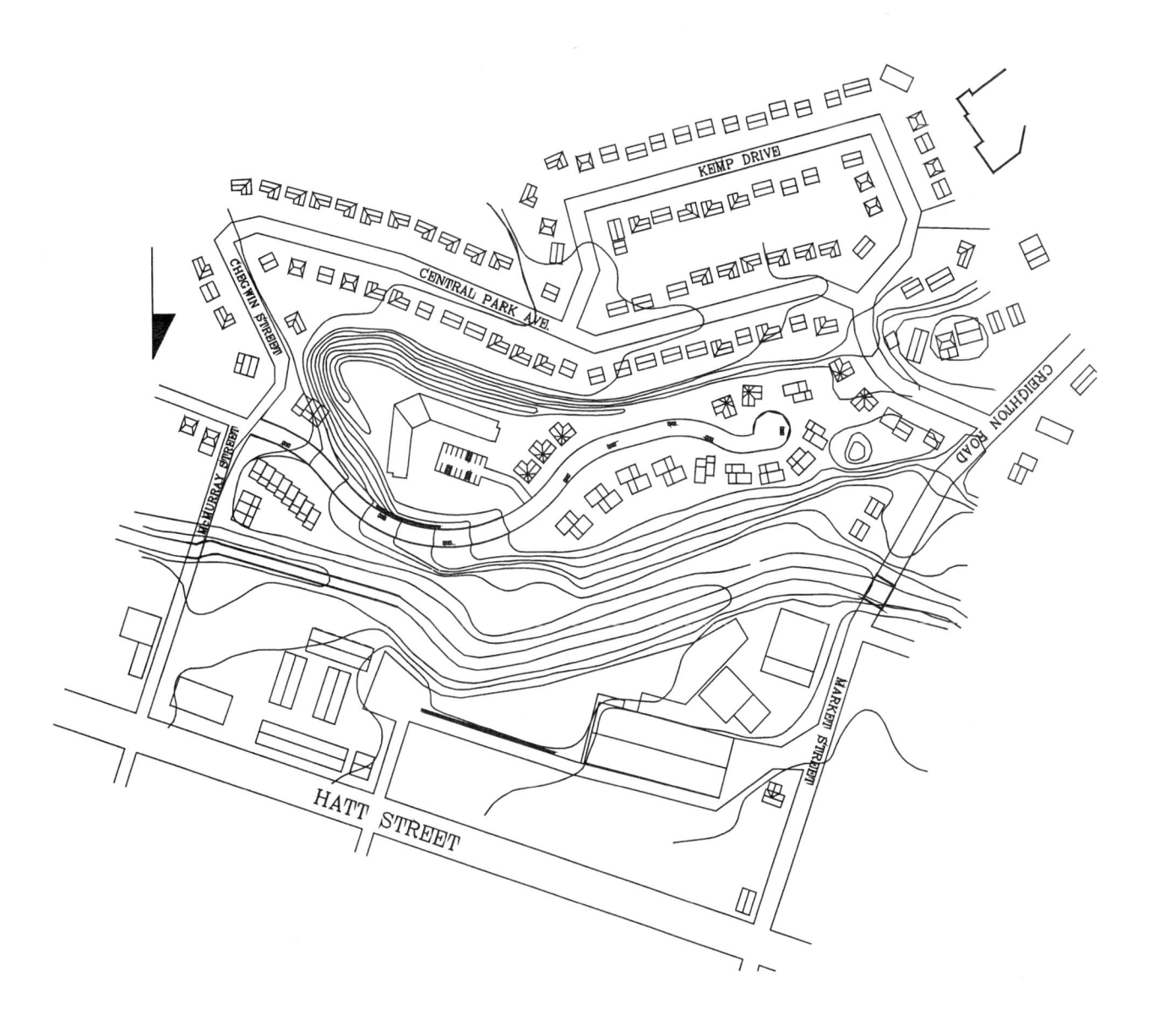

The drawing above shows the contour lines plus the main arteries. These would remain the same in both designs. (Example courtesy of Andy Slupecki.)

Exercise C34 (cont.)

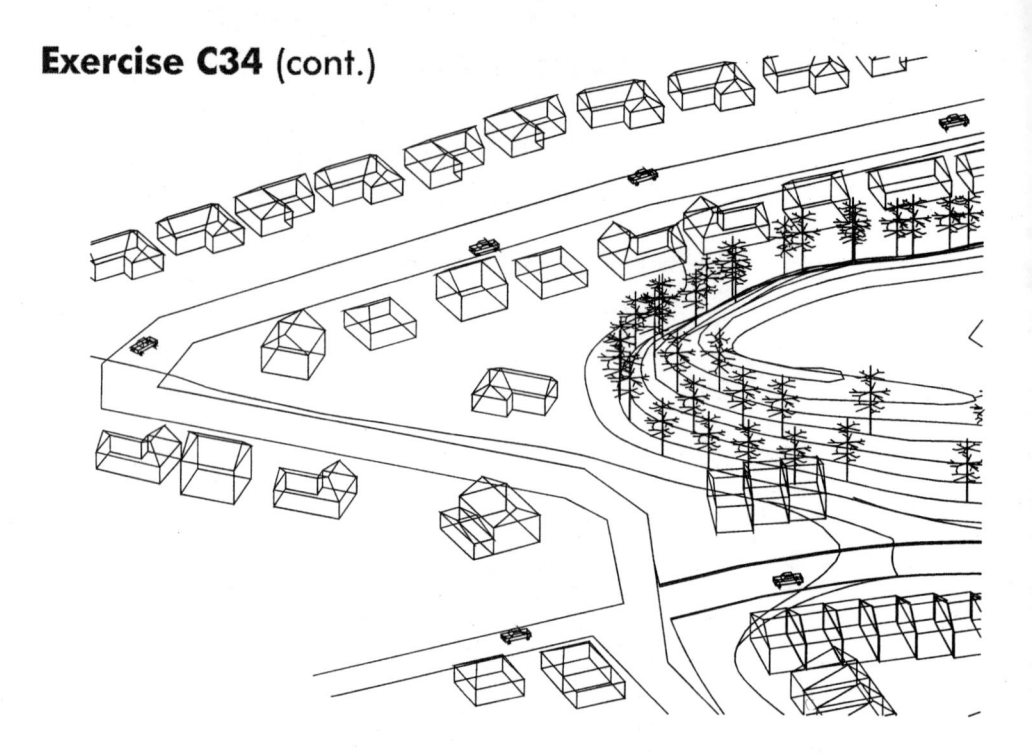

Trees and cars can be added to give the design a realistic look.

For the final presentations, rotate the image so that it is viewed in isometric; then add a title block and notations with the UCS at View.

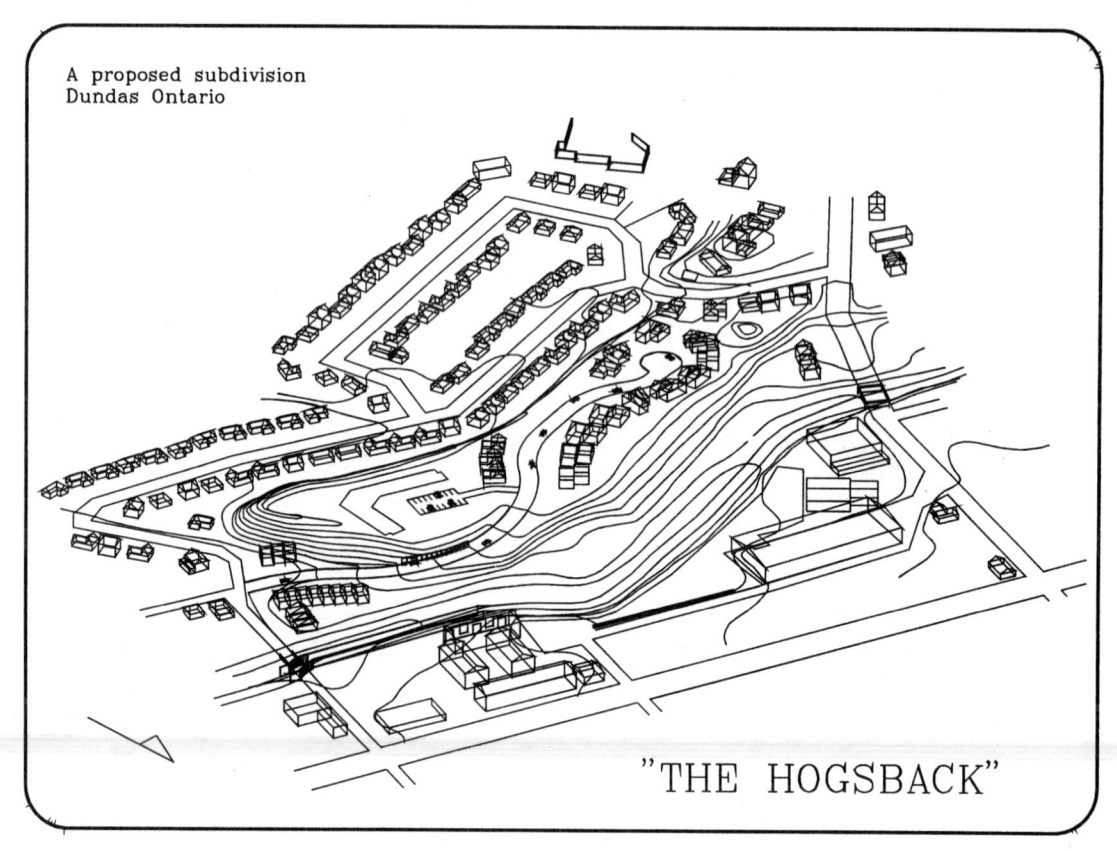

A proposed subdivision
Dundas Ontario

"THE HOGSBACK"

(Example courtesy of Andy Slupecki.)

Exercise M34

Dimensions for this part are on pages 330, 331 and in the *Instructor's Manual*.

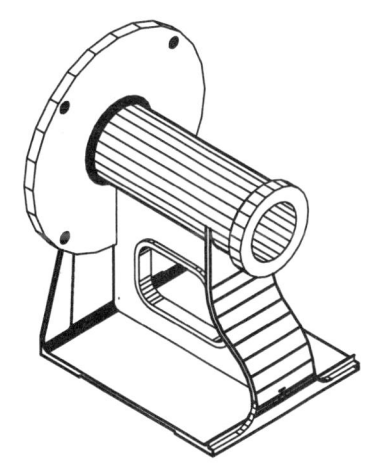

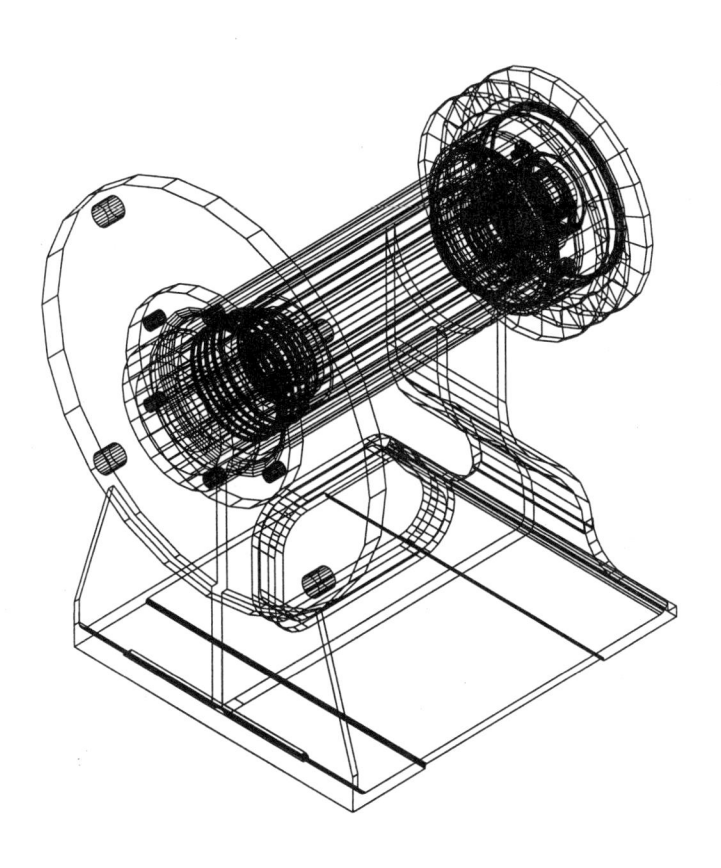

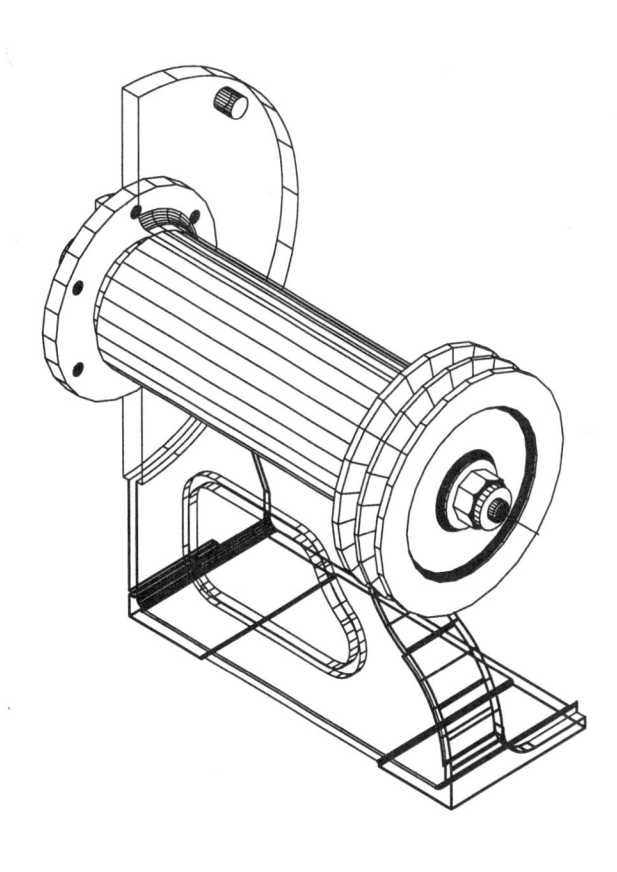

Exercise M34 (cont.)

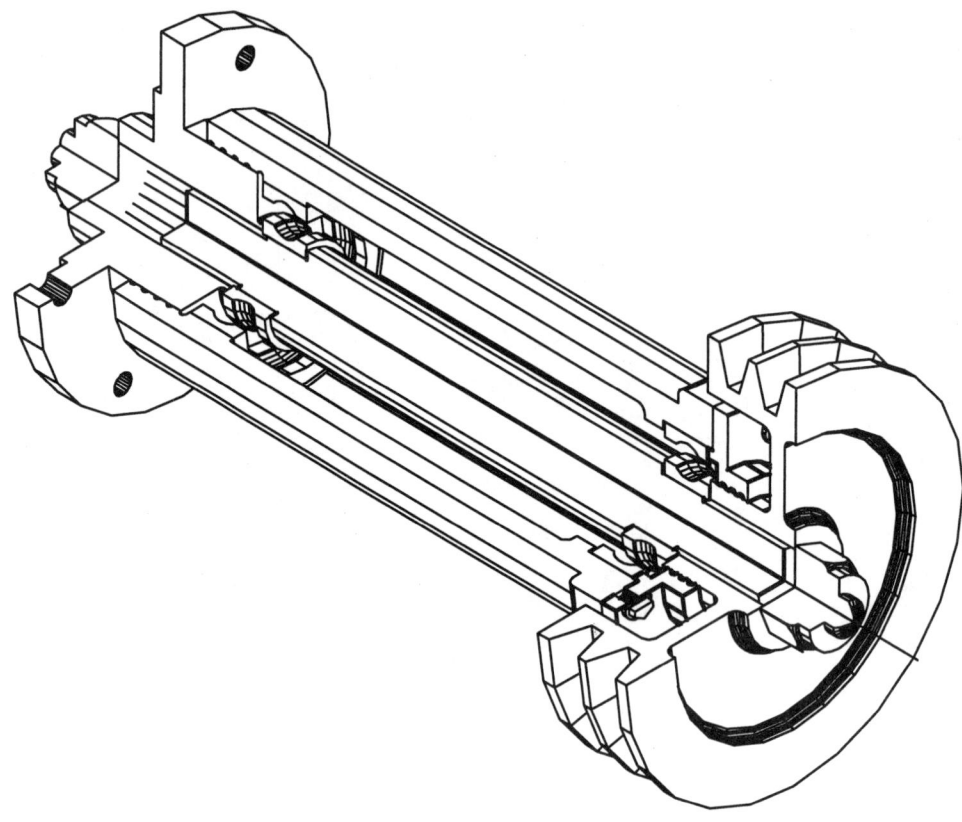

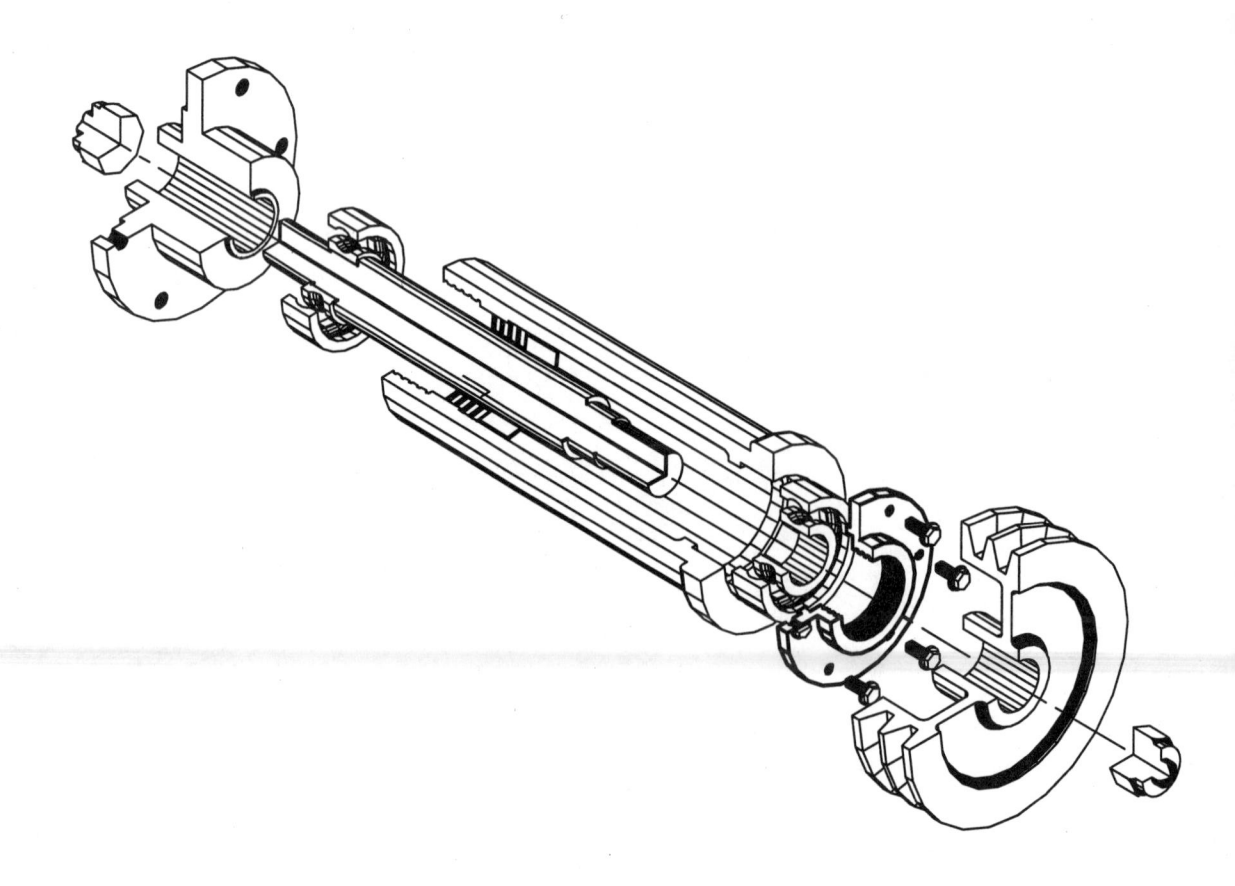

Appendix A
Glossary of Terms

a, A **absolute coordinates** Points located in space relative to the file's fixed origin, used to locate points on objects.

ADS (AutoCAD development system) A programming interface that allows third-party developers to include applications written in high-level languages such as C.

Alias Shorthand for an AutoCAD command. (See Appendix C, Abbreviations and Aliases.)

alpha character Any letter from A to Z.

alphanumeric Any letter or number. Alphanumeric screens are ones that show only alphanumeric characters and no graphics.

annotations Text, dimensions, tolerances, symbols, and notes.

ASCII (American standard code for information interchange) **code** The code which describes each alphanumeric or special character in computer language. This code translates an M or a 2 or an * into a series of 0s and 1s that most computer languages can interpret.

aspect ratio The image height-to-width ratio on a CAD display screen.

associative dimension A dimension that adapts as the associated geometry is modified.

attribute definition An AutoCAD object that serves as a template for assigning attribute values to drawing objects. (For attributes, see Chapter 14.)

AutoDESK The company that produces AutoCAD.

AutoLISP A programming language built into the AutoCAD program. It is an open program and users are encouraged to learn AutoLISP in order to create their own programs. To enter an AutoLISP program, use the following with ( ) and "".

```
Command:(load "d:\path\file name")
```

b, B **basepoint** 1. In the context of editing grips, the grip that turns to a solid color when picked to specify the focus of the subsequent editing operation. 2. A point for relative distance and angle when copying, moving, and rotating objects.

Bezier curve A polynomial curve used in B-spline curve calculations, defined by a set of control points representing an equation of an order one less than the number of points being considered.

bit map A digital representation of a display image as a pattern of bits, where each bit maps one or more pixels. Multiple bit maps may be used in color graphics to assign values to each pixel, which are used as indices to the color look-up table, if one exists.

blip marks or blips Temporary screen markers displayed by AutoCAD when you indicate a point on-screen.

block The name, base point, and set of objects you create with the BLOCK command.

block reference Insertions of a block created by the INSERT command. Also called a *block instance*.

b-spline A mathematical representation of a smooth curve.

b-spline curve A curve defined by a set of control points. Also called a *NURBS curve*.

b-spline surface A mathematical description of a 3D surface which passes through a set of B-splines, e.g., Bezier or Coon's.

c, C

Cartesian coordinate system A coordinate system defined using three perpendicular axes (*X,Y,Z*) to specify locations in 3D space.

center line Line that radiates from the center mark of a dimensioned circle.

character A numeral, letter, or other linguistic, mathematical, or logical symbol.

character font The style of a character set.

chord A line segment joining two points in a circle or arc.

circular array Multiple copies of drawing objects around an arc or circle.

circular external reference An externally referenced drawing (XREF) that references itself directly or indirectly. The XREF that creates the circular condition is ignored.

command line A text area reserved for keyboard input, prompts, and special messages.

constructive solid geometry (CSG) The method of using intersection, union, and subtraction operations to construct composite solids.

coordinates Cartesian coordinates overlaid on the number space of the display screen. A pair of numbers (*X, Y*) or a triplet of numbers (*X, Y, Z*) that correspond to a point on a plane (*X-Y*) or in space (*X,Y, Z*).

crosshair Crossed horizontal/vertical lines representing a cursor, with the intersection being used to indicate desired device coordinates.

cross section A view of a part formed by the intersection of the part and a cutting plane.

cursor A symbol or a pair of intersecting lines on a video display screen that can be moved around to place textual or graphic information. Also called *graphics cursor*.

d, D

database A comprehe nsive collection of information having predetermined structure and organization suitable for communication, interpretation, or processing.

default Predefined value used for a program input or parameter, shown in AutoCAD within angle brackets <>.

definition points Points for creating an associative dimension. AutoCAD refers to the points to modify the appearance and value of an associative dimension when the associated object is modified. Also called *defpoints*.

digitize To enter graphical points into a computer from a data tablet with a puck or stylus.

digitizer A device that tracks the relative position of the cursor for the purpose of recording the relative location of objects.

diskette A magnetic data storage device; also known as a disk.

dithering To increase the variations of color or intensity on raster displays by trading picture resolution for patterns of pixel arrays.

DOS (disk operating system) The Microsoft program that controls the CPU (central processing unit), output peripherals, etc.

drag To move an object across the display screen using a puck, mouse, or stylus.

.DWG File name extension of a drawing file.

e, E

electrostatic printer/plotter A computer output peripheral that prints and plots by placing electrostatic charges on small areas of treated paper in desired patterns, upon which toner is spread and baked.

endpoints Either of the points that mark the end of a line, arc, circle, or other primitive.

entity Fundamental building blocks which the designer uses to represent a product—lines, arcs, ellipses, text, splines, etc. Also known as an *item* or *object*.

f, F

face A finite, planar, cylindrical, conical, spherical, or toroidal surface on a solid model.

fill To fill an area of the display surface bounded by vectors with a solid color or pattern.

font The style of a letter or character. A character set, comprising letters, numbers, punctuation marks, and symbols, of a distinctive size and design. Also called *typeface*.

freeze To ignore the objects on specified layers when regenerating a drawing, thereby shortening regeneration time. Objects on frozen layers are not displayed, regenerated, or plotted.

function keys Keys on the keyboard that can be used to toggle or program functions.

g, G

graphics screen The area of the AutoCAD screen used for creating and editing graphics.

gray scale An ordered description of the tonal levels of an input image.

grid Uniformly spaced points which create a visual drawing aid to determine distance.

grips Small squares that appear on objects you select. After selecting the grip, you edit the object by dragging it with the mouse rather than entering editing commands.

h, H

half-space The portion of 3D space that lies on one side of a surface. If the surface is planar, the half-space is known as a planar half-space.

handle A unique alphanumeric representation of an object in the AutoCAD database.

hard copy Any printed or plotted printout.

hatch Regular pattern filling an enclosed area.

hidden lines The line segments which would not be visible to a viewer of a 3D display item because they are "behind" other parts of the same or other display items.

hidden surfaces Surfaces obscured by other surfaces from a specific viewpoint.

hole 1. A closed hatch boundary within another closed hatch boundary. 2. A feature of a solid.

i, I

icon A graphic image of a function or facility to help either choose or recognize your position and options. The UCS icon in the bottom left corner of your screen is an example.

icon menu A menu that contains multiple image tiles and can be customized by editing the ACAD.MNU file.

IGES (initial graphic exchange specification) An ANSI-standard format for the digital representation and exchange of information between CAD/CAM systems.

image file An AutoCAD command in pictorial format.

ink jet plotter A plotter which uses electrostatic technology to first atomize a liquid ink and then control the number of droplets that are deposited on the plotting medium.

initial environment The variables and settings for new drawings as defined by the default prototype drawing, such as ACAD.DWG.

instance When used in conjunction with blocks, a copy of a BLOCK created and stored apart from the actual drawing or model. Every time the BLOCK is INSERTed, it is one instance or copy of the block, but the block remains intact in memory. This is like a rubber stamp, the impression of the stamp being an instance. Also called a *block reference*.

integer value Many commands have options available by choosing a whole number such as 0, 1, 2, etc. These are integer values for the command.

interactive graphics The use of a computer terminal to generate graphics command-by-command, as opposed to batch processing.

interpolation points Points that a curve or surface pass through to define the curve or surface. Also called *fit points*.

island An enclosed area within the hatch area.

isometric drawing A drawing of an object with the *X*, *Y*, and *Z* axes spaced 120 degrees apart and the *Z* axis projected vertically.

k, K

key Specification for a database location associated with a key value for searching the database.

l, L

laser plotter A plotter which produces images through the use of a laser (light amplification through stimulated emission of radiation).

layer A logical grouping of data, like transparent acetate overlays on a drawing. You can view layers individually or in combination.

linetype Specification for the display of a line or other type of curve. For example, a continuous line has a different linetype from a dashed line. Also called *line font*.

link An SQL connection between an AutoCAD object and an external database record.

lock file A binary file, created when you open an AutoCAD data file, that contains permissions, which determine if other AutoCAD users can read or write to the opened file.

loop A closed statement that repeats.

m, M   **macro**   A single command made up of a group of commands.

mass properties   Calculation of physical engineering information about a part, e.g., perimeter, centroid, volume, weight, and moments of inertia.

***M* direction, *N* direction**   In the matrix that determines a polygon mesh, the *M* direction is established from the first to the second row, and the *N* direction is established from the first to the second column.

menu   A list of options or functions displayed on the video screen.

mnemonic   An abbreviated command entry scheme for simplifying command input. For example, CP can be a mnemonic for the COPY command and Z for the ZOOM command. (See also *alias.*)

model   A geometrically accurate representation of an object. In AutoCAD, graphic data is often referred to as a model as opposed to a drawing because the data is not always used to create drawings, particularly in 3D applications.

model space   The original position of the origin and axes with regard to the model. With the world coordinate system you are using model space.

mouse   A data entry device that echoes the position of the cursor on the screen and helps the user to define a point or item that is desired. Much like a *puck*.

n, N   **nesting**   Embedding data in levels of other data so that certain routines or data can be executed or accessed continuously or in a loop.

node   A point object. Used as an object snap in MEASURE and DIVIDE commands.

null response   To accept the default by pressing the space bar or ⏎.

o, O   **object**   A primitive, such as a line, circle, or polyline, treated as a single element for creation, manipulation, and modification.

object snap (OSNAP)   Modes for selecting commonly needed points on an object while you create or edit an AutoCAD drawing.

on-line documentation   Information about the commands within the database.

operating system   The microcomputer software program which controls the CPU and the input/output peripherals, and provides the working of programs.

origin   The fixed $X0$, $Y0$, $Z0$ of the model. The point on the coordinate system whose values are all zero.

ortho mode   An AutoCAD setting that limits pointing device input to horizontal or vertical relative to the current snap angle.

p, P   **pan**   To move from one zoomed-in view to another without changing size. A horizontal translation.

paper space   An AutoCAD state for creating a finished layout for printing and plotting, as opposed to doing drafting or design work. Model space is the state for creating the drawing. Although both 2D and 3D objects can exist in paper space, commands that render a 3D viewpoint are disabled.

pixel   The smallest section of your screen; the dot resolution of an image. The discrete display element of a raster display represented as a single point with a specified color or intensity.

platform   A computer system, for example, the DOS platform, or Windows platform.

pline   Polynumeral line. A line composed of many different vertices.

polygon window   A multi-sided selection window for selecting objects in groups.

primitive   1. The simplest and most basic geometry you can create: LINEs, CIRCLEs, ARCS, etc., are all primitives. 2. A solid or region building block such as a box, wedge, cone, cylinder, sphere, and torus.

prompt   Any message or symbol from the computer system informing the user of possible actions or operations. A guide to the operator, indicating possible actions or options.

prototype drawing   A drawing file with preestablished settings for new drawings, such as ACAD.DWG or ACADISO.DWG. Any drawing can be used as a prototype drawing. (See also *initial environment*.)

puck   A mouse, the moveable cursor assembly used with a digitizing tablet to locate points accurately for input.

Pull Down Menu   A list of commands you can display and execute beside the AutoCAD window while the graphics screen is active. The Pull Down Menu is automatically displayed in DOS but needs to be invoked with the ACAD.MNU in Windows.

r, R

raster scan   Line-by-line sweep across the entire display surface to generate elements of a display image.

read-only   A readout that can be read but not edited.

redraw   To quickly refresh or clean up the current viewport without updating the file's database.

relative coordinates   Incremental coordinates. Coordinates specified relative to previous coordinates.

rendering   A shaded and hidden line image of solid objects.

resolution   The number of horizontal and vertical rows of pixels that can be displayed by a particular graphics controller or monitor. For example, a standard VGA graphics controller and color monitor has a resolution of 640 columns and 480 rows of pixels.

RGB colour   A colour described in terms of its red, green, and blue intensity levels.

right-hand rule   A method of determining which is the positive direction of the axes at the origin by using the right hand to point to the *X* (thumb), *Y* (index finger), and *Z* (middle finger).

ROM (read only memory)   Contains the commands that start the computer and address the various peripherals. This is a read-only chip and cannot be changed.

rubber band   A line that stretches dynamically in conjunction with your cursor during many editing and drawing commands.

running object snap   Setting an object snap mode so it continues for subsequent selections.

s, S

scale factor   A number which multiplies the vector endpoint coordinates to produce scaling.

script file   A set of one or more AutoCAD commands executed sequentially with a single SCRIPT command. Script files are created outside AutoCAD using a text editor, saved in text format, and stored in an external file with the extension .SCR.

selection set   One or more AutoCAD objects specified for processing as a unit.

selection window   A rectangular area drawn in the AutoCAD graphics area to select objects in groups.

slide file   A file that contains a raster image or snapshot of the display on the graphics screen. Slides have the extension .SLB.

slide library   A collection of slide files organized for convenient retrieval and display. Slide library names have the extension .SLB and are created with the SLIDELIB.EXE utility.

snap   A drawing aid function which allows you to place entities at a preset spacing.

standard toolbar   In Windows, the portion of the AutoCAD user interface that appears under the title bar by default in the graphics window. It contains a layer control field, a coordinate display field, a box displaying the current color, and a series of macro buttons.

string   A sequence of characters.

stylus   A device analogous to a pencil which is used in conjunction with a data tablet to input coordinate information.

swap files   Files needed by AutoCAD to create your temporary file, typically with hexadecimal numbers and the extension .SWR. Normally, these files are erased when you exit the program, but if the system locks for any reason, you can erase these files from your directory.

system variable   A name that AutoCAD recognizes as a mode, size, or limit. Read-only system variables such as DWGNAME cannot be modified directly by the user.

t, T

tablet   An input device which digitizes coordinate data indicated by stylus position.

temporary files   Data files created during an AutoCAD session and deleted when you exit the file. If the session ends abnormally, either by power failure or by removing the diskette from the drive while addressing that drive, temporary files might be left on the disk.

tessellation lines   Lines displayed on a curved surface to help you visualize the curved surface better.

text style   A named, stored collection of settings that determines the appearance of text characters.

third-party developers   Companies offering software enhancements to AutoCAD users that are based on AutoCAD software. AutoCAD has maintained an open policy toward such developers, offering a great deal of support to those who would like to customize their software for specific purposes.

toolbar   Part of the AutoCAD interface containing icons that represent commands.

transparent command   A command started while another is in progress. Transparent commands must be preceded with an apostrophe (').

u, U

UCS (user coordinate system)   he three-axis coordinate system that can be rotated and placed at any location in order to help you with the creation of your model.

unit   A user-defined distance, such as kilometers, inches, metres, and miles, used as a standard of measurement in a drawing. The default is inches.

v, V

vector   A mathematical straight line which has both magnitude and direction.

vertex A topologically unique point in space used to define boundaries.

viewport A bounded area that displays some portion of a drawing's model space. The TILEMODE system variable determines the type of viewport created. (See *paper space*.)

virtual screen A pixel map of the current regenerated view. This is stored in memory and determines the speed of REDRAWs with regard to the percentage of the drawing that is regenerated in addition to the actual on-screen image.

w, W

window A selected rectangle for image display or processing.

wire frame A representation of a solid object that displays edges and tessellation lines.

world coordinate system (WCS) The original position of the origin and axes on the model.

WPolygon A multisided polygon window used to select objects within its borders.

wraparound The phenomenon whereby a vector which overflows the number space is continued on the opposite edge of the drawing.

x, X

Xref A file referenced to the current file but still on the main disk. (See Chapter 18.)

z, Z

Zoom The process of reducing or increasing the apparent magnification of graphics on the display screen.

Appendix B
File Extensions

.3ds	3D Studio file
.ahp	AutoCAD Help files ACAD.AHP
.bak	Drawing file backup
.bat	Batch file
.bin	Binary image file
.bxn	Emergency backup file
.c	ADS source code file
.cc	ADS source code file
.cfg	Configuration file ACAD.CFG
.com	Machine language command file
.ctb	Color Style Table used for saing plotting styles
.dcl	Dialog box definition file ACAD.DCL
.dcc	Dialog box color control files (DOS only)
.dct	Dictionary files
.drv	Plotter Driver fil;e
.dwg	Drawing file (ACAD.DWG is the standard prototype drawing)
.dwk	Locked drawing file
.dxb	Binary drawing interchange file
.dxf	Drawing interchange file (ASCII or binary)
.dxx	Attribute extract file in DXF format
.eps	Encapsulated Post Script file
.err	Error file ACAD.ERR (error log file)
.exe	DOS executable file (ACAD.EXE)
.hpg	Hewlett Packard Graphics Language file
.hlp	Windows Help file ACAD.HLP
.lib	ADS library files
.lin	Linetype library file (ACAD.LIN is the standard line library)
.lsp	AutoLISP application file
.lpt	Line printer file
.mnc	Compiled menu file (DOS only) ACAD.MNC
.mnu	Menu template file (ACAD.MNUis the standard menu template file)
.mnx	Compiled menu source file

.msg	Message file (ACAD.MSG such as message displayed by ABOUT command)
.old	Original version of converted drawing file
.pat	Hatch pattern library file (ACAD.PAT has the standard patterns)
.pgp	Program parameters file (ACAD.PGP is the standard parameters)
.pfb	PostScript font file
.pfm	PostScript font metric file
.plt	Plot file
.prp	ADI printer plotter output file
.pwd	Login file
.scr	Script file
.shp	AutoCAD shape file
.shx	Shape/font-definition source file
.slb	Slide library file (ACAD.SLB is the standard slide library file)
.sld	Slide file
.stb	Named Style Table for plotting
.tif	Tagged image file
.ttf	TrueType font file
.txt	Attribute extract or template file
.unt	Units file ACAD.UNT (units conversion file)
.xlg	External references log file
.$ac	AutoCAD temporary file
.$a	AutoCAD temporary file

Appendix C
Abbreviations and Aliases

AutoCAD's .PGP file is an ASCII-based text file containing AutoCAD program parameters. Within this file you can abbreviate frequently used AutoCAD commands by defining aliases for them. You can make any command, device-driver command, or external command into an alias.

Any ASCII editor can be used to edit the ACAD.PGP file. Any AutoCAD, AutoLISP, ADS, Solids, operating system or graphics display-driver command can be abbreviated. Once you have altered the .PGP file, simply SAVE it and the commands will be accessible through the alias.

These two comma-delimited fields define a command alias in the ACAD.PGP file:

    Abbreviation,   *command

abbreviation   is the abbreviation of the command that you enter at the command prompt.

command   is the command that it invokes.

For example, in the .PGP file, type in:

m,*move   This will make the MOVE command accessible from typing in only the letter m.

The following is a partial list of AutoCAD and Solids commands for creating abbreviations or aliases:

A,	*ARC	P,	*PAN
C,	*CIRCLE	PS,	*PSPACE
CP,	*COPY	PL,	*PLINE
DV,	*DVIEW	R,	*REDRAW
E,	*ERASE	Z,	*ZOOM
L,	*LINE		
LA,	*LAYER	SUB,	*SUBTRACT
M,	*MOVE	CONE,	*CONESOLID
MI,	*MIRROR	SOL,	*SOLIDIFY
MS,	*MSPACE	UN,	*UNION

Appendix D
Plotting and Printing

Once your drawing is finished and you want a hardcopy or plot, make sure that your title block is complete, then use the Print or PLOT command to create either a plot or a .plt file that can be taken to a plotter. If your computer is linked directly to a plotter or printer, simply plot directly. If your computer is not linked directly to a plotter, create a .plt file on a floppy disk, and take it to load onto the plotter.

AutoCAD has a completely new plotting setup in Release 2000 which, will prove to be much more comprehensive and flexible once you get to know it. In the meantime, it is a good idea to keep Release 13 or 14 on your computer so you can plot something in a hurry if you need to (Use Save As Type to save into R14 or R13). None of the drivers in Release 2000 work the same way as in Release 14, and there will be some set up time needed for configuration and fine tuning.

Plotters and Output Peripherals

Before we consider how to get your drawing or data actually plotted, it is a good idea to outline some of the common plotters to see what they are and how they are used.

There are many types of plotters and printers available, and prices are coming down while capabilities advance. The most common plotters and printers include pen plotters, electrostatic plotters, dot matrix, and laser printers. If you need a full drawing, a pen plotter or an electrostatic plotter will be necessary. If you want an image of your drawing in 8 ½ x 11", then a laser is fine.

Plotting at 8.5 x 11 and Work Arounds

If you only need a small plot, your computer may be hooked up to a laser printer that will print you an image that will not be to scale. When you set up Release 2000, make sure you add the driver to your plotter and do a few test plots before you actually need them.

If you are in a networked situation, or you are sharing your computer with other people, it is always good to have two or three different ways to get out a small plot. Even the most intellegent and well intentioned people have a tendency to "readdress the plotter" or change the drivers when you are least expecting it. If you can't simply plot to your printer, there are a few ways to bring the image into word processors and plot that way.

COPY AND PASTE The Windows Copy and Paste functions work quite well with a few minutes of fine tuning. Use COPY under the Edit pull down menu to grab the image, then paste it into the page layout document. Make sure your Viewres is set high in AutoCAD or your circles will become octagons in the target document. Images made in paper space do not copy. To get a hidden image you must be in model space and use HIDE. All paper space dependant information will be lost.

Danger

To print HPGLs in Corel Ventura, you must use a PCL driver: HPGLs are no longer compatible after Release 6.

HPGLs or Hewlett Packard Graphics Language Files For this you set up an early driver from HP such as the 75858B and simply create a plot file by saving as a .plt. This works for both paper space and model space images, and gives you the advantage of being able to trace the images. (With Copy and Paste, the images on their own can't be saved.) HPGLs can be printed in either PCL or post script, and are compatible with most word processing and desktop software.

With both of the above, simply copy the image into a word processing file, and the drawing can be printed from a machine that is not running AutoCAD.

Plotting large drawings

AutoCAD's Release 2000 has a tutorial on plotting, and it is a very good idea to read it. If you are plotting for the first time, it is a good idea to have someone with you who has had success with that particular plotter before. There are so many variables and options such as line width and rotation of the plot on the paper, that you could waste a lot of time and money before getting a good plot.

When a plotter is installed in a company, it is also a good idea to have someone test it and set up the parameters for each paper size. Every plotter has a different mechanism for moving the paper and for placing the paper in the plotter. Do not assume that your plot will work the first time you do it on a new plotter.

The PLOT Command

While the drawing is on screen, access the PLOT or PRINT command:

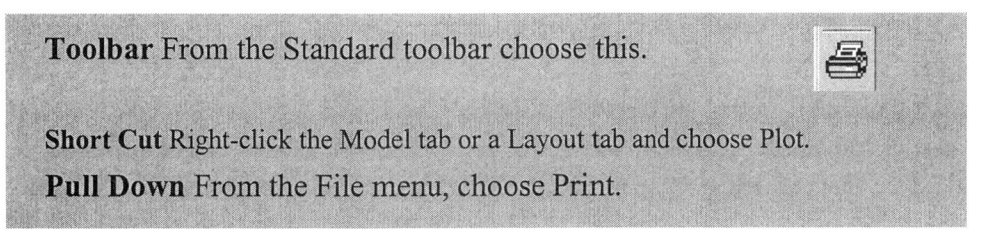

Toolbar From the Standard toolbar choose this.

Short Cut Right-click the Model tab or a Layout tab and choose Plot.

Pull Down From the File menu, choose Print.

The command line equivalent is **PLOT**.

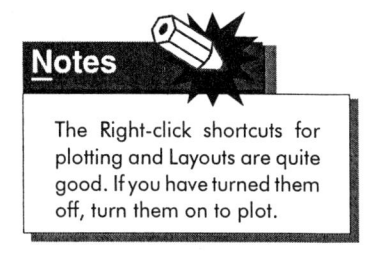

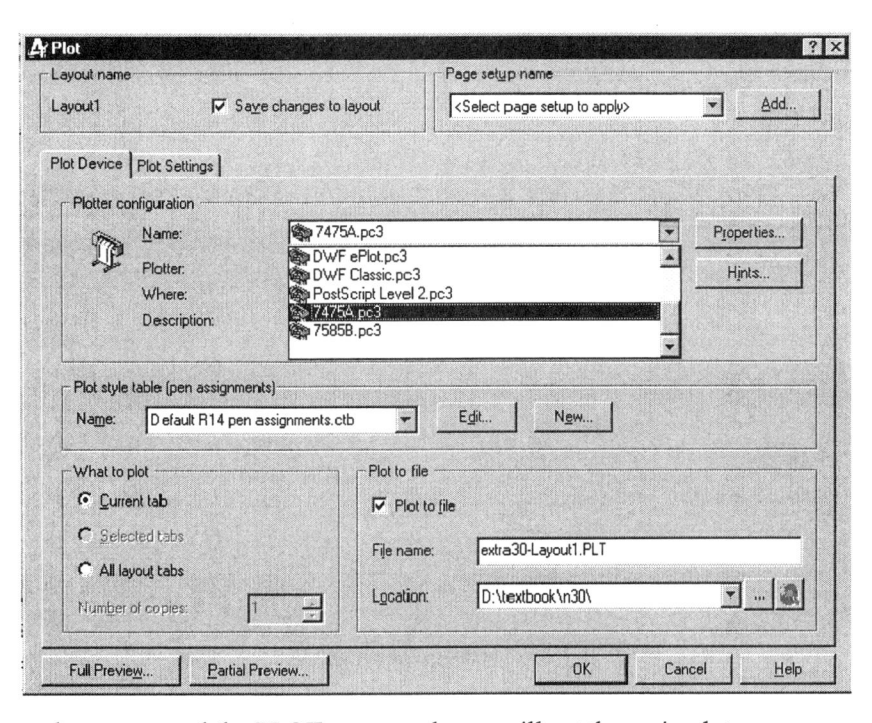

Notes

The Right-click shortcuts for plotting and Layouts are quite good. If you have turned them off, turn them on to plot.

Once you have accessed the PLOT command, you will get the main plot menu.

Plotting and Printing **797**

If you want to accept all of the defaults, press OK and your plot will be produced. If your system is set up to plot anything on screen to a laser printer, then you should be able to simply pick up your print. Should you wish to change any of the defaults or print to another plotter, pick the related button.

Plot Device

The Plot Device tab lets you set up your device and your style (see below). It also allows you to have the plot written to a file as opposed to being sent straight to the plotter.

Device and Default Selection

There is a large selection of plotters available. To access a new plotter, pick the Plot Device tab and use the arrow beside Name: to access the other plotters.

This screen will offer you a list of the loaded plotters. Pick one and continue. If you have a check in the Plot to File box, you can create a plot file that can be taken to a different plotter. If the plotter you need is not listed, then you must load it by CONFIGuring it.

Configuring a New Plotter

If the plotter you need is not on the list provided, use the CONFIG command to load a new one. At the command prompt, type in CONFIG. Then answer the questions for loading the new plotter driver. You will need to pick the driver you want, and provide a name for it. If there are questions you are not sure of, accept the default; it will probably work on the new plotter if it worked on the last one.

Note: Selecting another plotter may change the settings of other parameters in the plotting dialog box.

Notes
Plotters come with plotter drivers. If you buy a used plotter, be sure to get the driver with it. If the salesman doesn't have the driver, don't buy the plotter.

If you prefer the Windows method of loading a driver, use the Plotter Manager option under the File pull down menu, then choose Add a Plotter Wizard and work your way through all the dialog boxes.

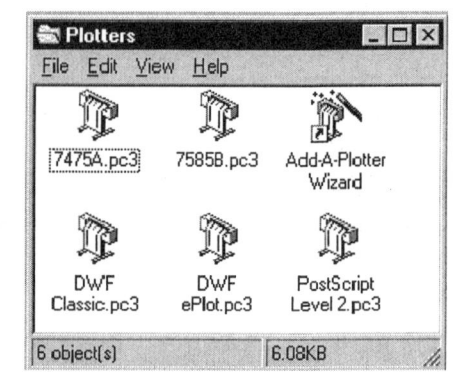

Plot Style Table (Pen Assignments)

There is a large selection of plotters available. You can have these set up with your Plot Style, or you can set them with the Edit button.

The Plot Style Table will default to whatever your previous setup was. As you can see, there are enough options to keep you busy for hours. Choose the ones that work and then just save the settings as a plot style.

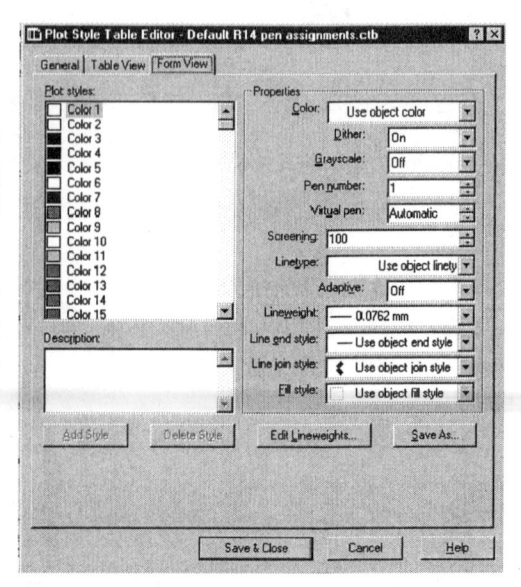

Plot to File

Plot to File will create a .plt file for transfer into either a word processing file using a HP driver or to a plotter not connected to your machine. Always take a copy of your drawing file with you if you are plotting off site in case there are errors.

Plot Preview

This will give you an idea of how big your plot is, and how it fits on paper. Use either the Full Preview or the Partial Preview before you spend the time or money on a paper plot.

Plot Settings

The Plot Settings tab lets you specify the drawing scale, orientation, and area. These settings are specific to the plot you are currently creating.

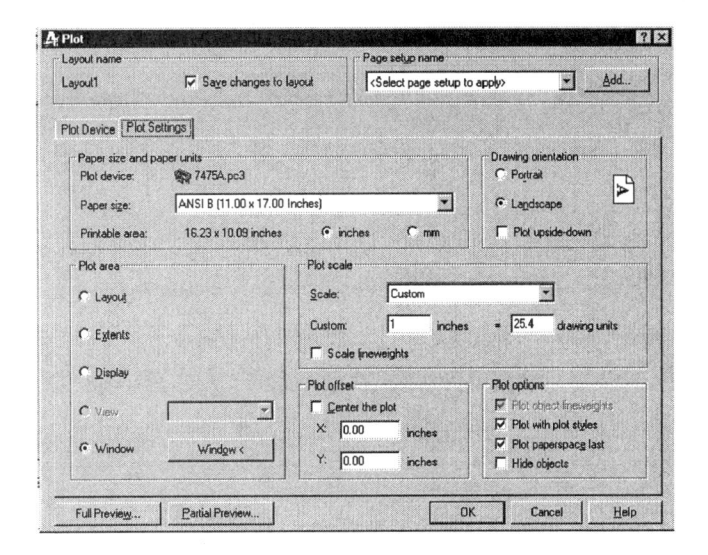

Plot area

This section allows you to plot either a portion or all of the image on screen.

Display takes everything on screen; in paper space from all viewports, in model space only from the current viewport.

Extents takes all portions of the drawing that contain entities. By using ZOOM Extent before plotting, you will be able to check that there is no "floating geometry" outside the limits which will be plotted.

Layout takes only that portion of the file contained in the specified layout. This is for paper space drawings only.

Window allows you to select a rectangular portion of the file, a detail, or the whole view. It can only be used if you are in the Drawing Editor.

View takes a stored view of the data. Like Window, it can be all or a portion of the file. In order to plot a View, you must save a view prior to using the PLOT command. This option is particularly useful when you are plotting from the Main Menu because you can be sure of what you will get.

> **Danger**
>
> This is where most students have problems. Do you know what size the paper is? Does the plotter require two or three inches to compensate for rollers?

Paper Size and Paper Units

First decide if you want to plot in inches or millimetsre. Then choose the size of paper you need.

Depending on the size of drawing you require, pick the preset drawing size, or set a user-defined size.

The drawing sizes may have been set up during your software installation to agree with the available sizes of your plotter. The standard sizes should agree with national standards, and there will be an option for larger or custom size plots. Simply choose the letter designation in response to the plotting size prompt.

Drawing Orientation

Always do a plot preview using the Full Preview... Button before creating your plot file. If this shows only a portion of your file, use the drawing orientation options to set the file correctly.

Scale

The drawing will be set in terms of plotted inches : drawing inches or plotted millimetres : drawing units. Try to start plotting directly with the proper scale so that your plots will always be correct. Use Fit only when the actual scale of the drawing is not needed.

The plot origin is always assumed to be the bottom left corner of the paper. If you want to relocate the origin of the plot to another portion of the paper, reset this parameter by changing the X and Y values in the edit box. This is usually done to place a title block onto an existing drawing or to place a missing view onto an otherwise completed drawing. Some skill is needed here, so try placing the view or plot onto a test sheet before placing it on the final paper—especially if there are drawings on the paper that could be ruined.

The default on a plotter is to have the drawing's X value perpendicular to the bar of the plotter, and the Y value parallel to the plotting bed (as the drawing usually looks on screen). For printers, however, the X value of the drawing is taken to be the 8.5'' edge of the paper, and the Y value is taken to be the 11'' edge of the paper. Therefore, you will probably *not* want to change this on a pen plotter, but *will* want to change it for a printout. The rotation you choose will become the default for the next plot. The final readout before printing will tell you the size of your plotting area, and will give you the option of checking the plot rotation.

Plot offset

The Plot Offset option is used when you have a plot that covers only a portion of a paper, or a plot that you want to specify as not being near the edge of the paper. Again, use Full Preview... before wasting paper.

Plot options

Plot options allows you to try to set object lineweights, or to use a Plot Style. You can also try to have the hidden lines removed. The easiest and most successful way to use Release 2000's new plotting functions is to set up a Plot Style that suits your plotter and your drawing style, and take it with you.

Plot Styles

Like Dimension Styles, the Plot Style is set up to ultimately give you consistnet quality plots. Plot styles let you set up and save a series of parameters that will plot objects with a different appearance (color, linetype, lineweight, etc.) than their appearance in the drawings. Using different *plot style tables* you can plot the same drawing with different sets of effects . Plot styles are used to control:

- Color, linetype and lineweight
- End, join and fill styles for multilines
- Dithering and gray scaling
- Pen assignments

When a plot style table is used, the objects are plotted as defined by the plot style table. You can use a color plot style table (by using the Edit button on your Plot Device tab), a named plot style (as shown below), or neither.

Plot style tables can be used for any output device. A black and white plotter will not be able to print in color, but the colored lines may show up in varying grey scales. Always test your plots before you need to submit them.

Drawings from earlier releases of AutoCAD will have a default color style table taken from the pen setup for the plotter when the drawing was filed.

Plot styles are set up in files with extensions .stb (named style table) and .ctb (color-dependant style table). These files are saved in the Plot Tables folder. Only one color style table can be used per drawing, but several named style tables can be used in each drawing. This would allow the drawing to be printed with different effects, or several different layouts with different style tables to be part of a file.

Color Plot Style Tables

A color-dependant plot style is similar to the pen tables in R14.; there are 255 styles, one for each color. Each color in the file has a pen associated with it. You can change the pen color and pen width for each color. For example, color two or yellow may have a thin black pen associated with it instead of the yellow default.

The color style table is set up in the Plot Device tab under the Plot style table area. Only one color table can be associated with each drawing.

Named Plot Style Tables

You can define any number of named plot styles for use in any number of drawings. Like LAYERs, it is a good idea not to get too carried away, and to have a definite protocol set up in your office or group.

Named plot styles can be set up by layer or by object. To assign a plot style to a layer, open the Layer Properties Manager, and pick on the plot style icon of the layer you want to set.

To set a plot style to an object, use the Properties dialog box. Understandably, if there are many plot styles associated with many different objects in a drawing, the plotting process can get quite complicated.

Using Plot Styles

Color plot style tables are set to control the plot style of the file. The color table is set up in the plot command, and the plot is created according to these effects.

Named plot styles can be set up according to the file or according to specific layers and/or objects.

Creating Plot Style Tables

There are two "Wizards" used to create plot styles; the color plot style wizard and the named plot style wizard. Both are found under the Tools pull down menu, under Wizards.

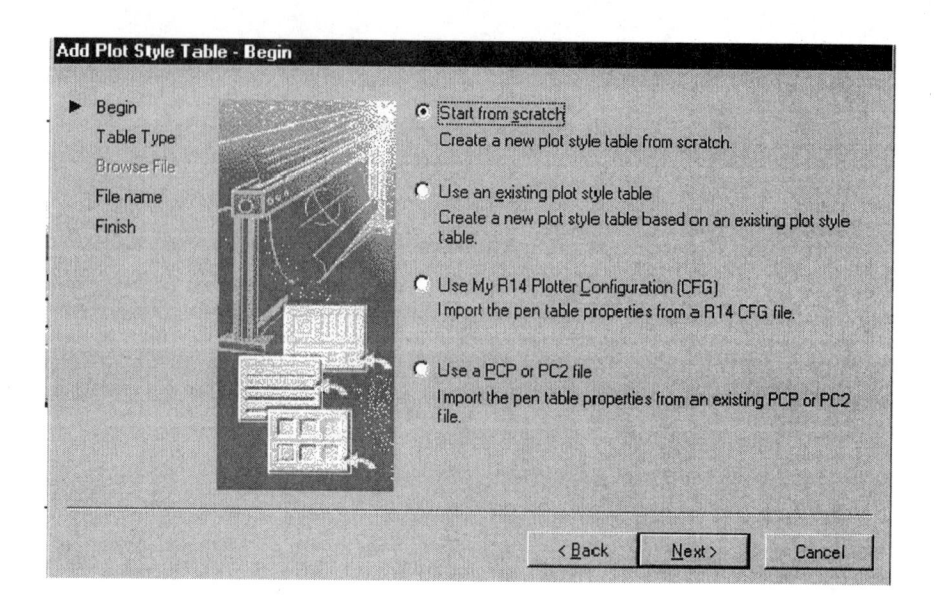

If your plotter was set up properly under a previous release, you can save your plot style using the defaults from your last plotter configuration. There is a good chance this will work.

If you had a different plotter configuration set up with your plotter, the PCP or PC2 file that was set up can also be used.

If you have some time to set up a whole new set of parameters, you can start from scratch. You will be prompted to give a name for the plot style once you have everything set up.

Once it is set up, this is an independant file that can be taken to other machines or used by other people accessing the same plotter.

Trouble Shooting

Make sure you have a backup copy of the file before you plot (in case you get an error message on the disk). Remember to leave enough available space on the disk; available space must at least equal the size of the file you wish to plot. You cannot plot a file from a floppy disk that occupies more than 1/3 of the disk.

Ideally, you should plot from a hard drive whenever feasible. But due to the size of many classes, this is not always possible.

Technical Difficulties

Plotter maintenance is mandatory. Pens will dry out if not recapped between plots. Cap them and put them away. In addition, pens run out of ink and, if felt-tipped, wear down. When making plots, remember that continuous lines improve plot speed. There is no point in having a hidden line if LTSCALE is too small to read. If your plot is taking a very long time, you may have forgotten to change the LTSCALE.

Practice at least one plot before your final project is due. Plots seldom work perfectly the first time.

Appendix E

AutoCAD's Standard Hatch Patterns

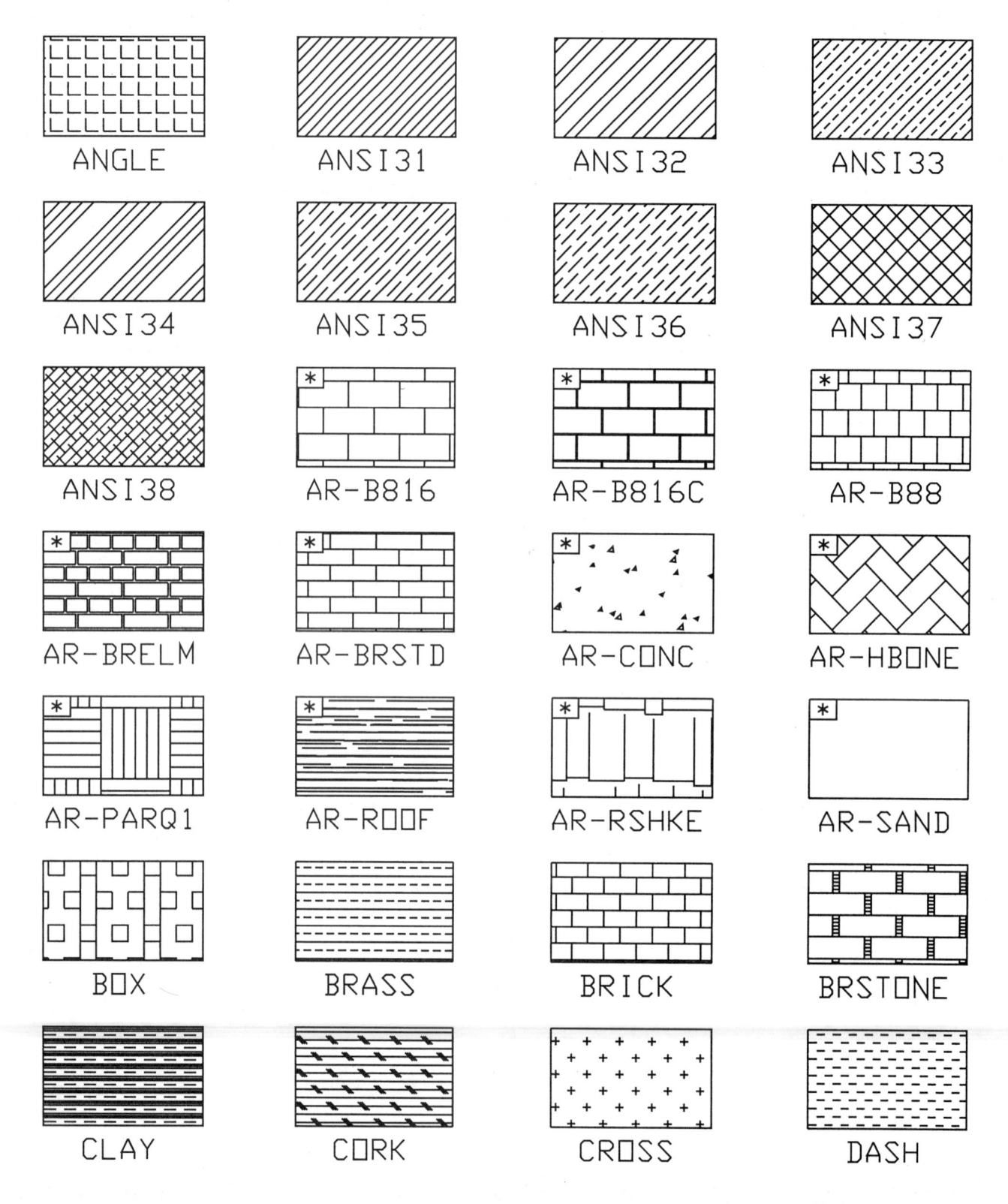

ANGLE	ANSI31	ANSI32	ANSI33
ANSI34	ANSI35	ANSI36	ANSI37
ANSI38	AR-B816	AR-B816C	AR-B88
AR-BRELM	AR-BRSTD	AR-CONC	AR-HBONE
AR-PARQ1	AR-ROOF	AR-RSHKE	AR-SAND
BOX	BRASS	BRICK	BRSTONE
CLAY	CORK	CROSS	DASH

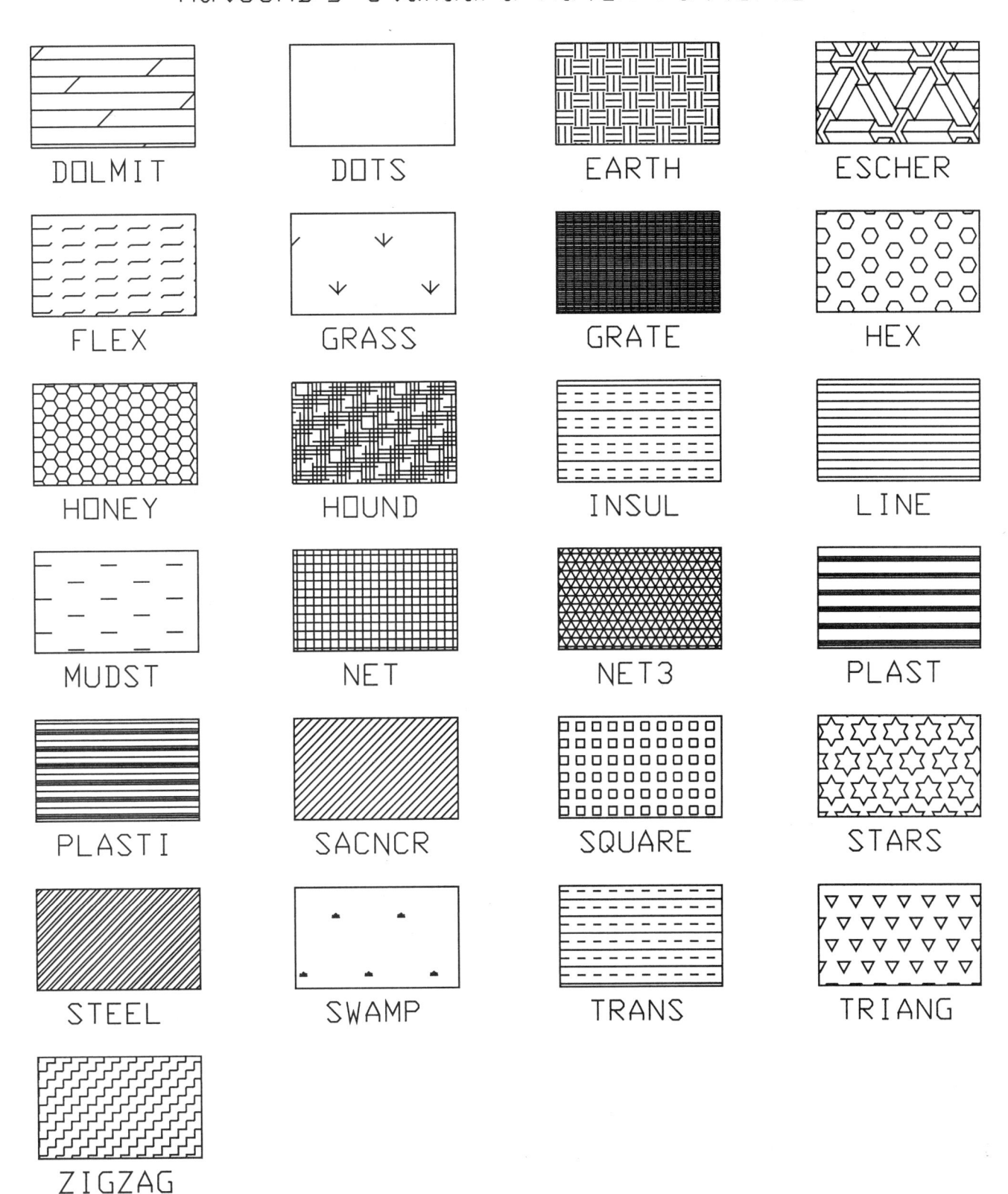

AutoCAD's Standard Hatch Patterns

DOLMIT	DOTS	EARTH	ESCHER
FLEX	GRASS	GRATE	HEX
HONEY	HOUND	INSUL	LINE
MUDST	NET	NET3	PLAST
PLASTI	SACNCR	SQUARE	STARS
STEEL	SWAMP	TRANS	TRIANG
ZIGZAG			

AutoCAD's Standard Hatch Patterns

Appendix F

AutoCAD Standard Fonts

STANDARD	To enter text use TEXT or DTEXT . ABC 123
MONO	To enter text use TEXT or DTEXT . ABC 123
ROMANS	To enter text use TEXT or DTEXT . ABC 123
ROMAND	To enter text use TEXT or DTEXT . ABC 123
ROMANC	To enter text use TEXT or DTEXT . ABC 123
ROMANT	To enter text use TEXT or DTEXT . ABC 123
SCRIPTS	To enter text use TEXT or DTEXT . ABC 123
SCRIPTC	To enter text use TEXT or DTEXT . ABC 123
ITALICC	To enter text use TEXT or DTEXT . ABC 123
ITALICT	To enter text use TEXT or DTEXT . ABC 123
ΓΡΕΕΚΣ	Το εντερ τεξτ υσε ΤΕΞΤ ορ ΔΤΕΞΤ . ΑΒΧ 123
ΓΡΕΕΚΧ	Το εντερ τεξτ υσε ΤΕΞΤ ορ ΔΤΕΞΤ . ΑΒΧ 123
GOTHICE	To enter text use TEXT or DTEXT . ABC 123
GOTHICG	To enter text use TEXT or DTEXT . ABC 123
GOTHICI	To enter text use TEXT or DTEXT . ABC 123
ВШСИЛЛИВ	Уо днудс удчу фπд УДЧУ ос ГУДЧУ . АВВ 123
CYRRILTLC	To enter text use TEXT or DTEXT . ABC 123
SYASTRO	... 123
SYMAP	... 123
SYMATH	⊂(√Σ{√] }√∫} {{√ ⊂±∈⊂ () ‖⊂±∈⊂ . 123
SYMETEO	... 123
SYMUSIC	... 123

Additional Fonts

CITYBLUEPRINT	To enter text use TEXT or DTEXT . ABC 123
COUNTRYBLUEPRINT	To enter text use TEXT or DTEXT . ABC 123
SANSSERIF	To enter text use TEXT or DTEXT . ABC 123
TECHNIC	To ENTER TEXT USE TEXT OR DTEXT . ABC 123

Index

(period or dot) extensions, 793

3D command, 633
3DARRAY command, 697
3DFACE command, **517**, 526, 584, 637
3DMESH command, 640
3DPOLY command, 540, **589**
3D Polyline Meshes, 580
3D Solids, 655

A
Absolute coordinates, 6
acad.dwg file, 1
Add entry selection method, 114
ALIGN command, **128**
Aligned dimensions, 168
ALL entry selection method, 83
Alternate units dimensioning, 176
AMECONVERT command, 656
Angle brackets, 38
Angles
    degrees/minutes/seconds, 20
    dimensioning, 171
    grads, 20
    input, 8
    overview, 8
    radians, 20
ANGULAR dimensions, 171
ANSI drafting standards, 275
Apparent Intersection snap, 45
APERTURE command, xxii, 47
ARC command, **11**, 25
Architectural, 18
Arcs
    add to polyline, 65, 66
    dragging, 12
    methods of specification, 24
    options, 12, 24
    radial dimensions, 170
AREA command, 338, 718
ARRAY command, **125**
    array polar, 125
    array rectangular, 126, 127, 129
    array 3D, 697
Arrow blocks, 172
Arrowheads, dimensioning, 172
ASCII, 420
Associative dimensioning, 180
ATTDEF command, 360
ATTDIA system variable, 363
ATTDISP command, 364
ATTEDIT command, 379
ATTEXT command, 385
Attribute definition, 360

Attribute extract, 365
Attributes
    blocking, 362
    defining, 360
    dialog boxes, 361
    displaying of, 364
    editing of, 362
    extraction of, 384
    options, 364, 380
    overview, 359
    visibility, 364
    with Xrefs, 443
Autoflix, 568
AutoSNAP, 47
Autotracking, 525
Axis Tripod, 486

B
Backup files, 489
BASELINE dimensions, 169
Begin AutoCAD session, 1, xi, xii
BHATCH command, **222**, 227, 236
    angle, 224
    advanced options, 227
    dialog box, 222
    editing, 228
    Irregular shapes, 69, 229
    overview, 222
    patterns, 223
    scale, 223, 224
    styles, 223
BLIPs, 17
BLOCK command, **252**
Blocks,
    advantages, 251
    arrow, 172
    attributes and, 362
    color, 260, 437
    defining, 252
    editing, 258
    external, 254
    frozen layers with, 437
    insertion, 253
    instance, 254, 437
    layers, 260, 437
    linetypes, 260, 437
    listing, 254
    naming conventions, 261
    nested, 437
    output to disk, 255
    overview, 252
    place into drawings, 253
    redefining, 257
    removing from file, 261

    scaling, 257
    updating, 257, 259
    with XREFs, 439
Borders
    in PAPERSPACE, 290, 296
BOUNDARY command, 341, 350
Boundary
    Boundary Hatch dialog box, 222
    boundary set, 225
Boundary set, 5, 225, 227
BOX command, **656**
Box option of 3D command, 634
BREAK command, **47**
Browse Search dialog box, xviii
B-spline curves, 337
Buttons (mouse), xiii
BYBLOCK
    color, 260
    linetype, 260
BYLAYER
    color, 146
    linetype, 147

C
Calculating
    area, 338
    distance, 341
    point on a line, 15
Cartesian coordinates, 1
CDF attribute extract, 383
Center lines, 147
Center marks, 173, 184
CENter object snap, 42
CHAMFER command, **49**
Chamfering solids, 662
CHANGE command, 149, **204**, 210
Change Properties, 149, 156
Changing Linetypes, 149, 205, 156
Changing colors outside of layers, 146
CHPROP command, **149**, 156, 539
CIRCLE command, **11**, 25, 53
Circles
    creating, 6, 11
    isometric, 398
    filled, 69
    options, 11, 25
    solid filled, 69
    tangent to, 25
Circular (polar) arrays, 125
Clipping 3D objects, 562
Closing lines, 9, 10
Closing polylines, 62
COLOR command, **146**
Color

Blocks and, 261
BYBLOCK, 261
BYLAYER, 146
changing, 149
changing display, xii
current, 146
Commands
    aliases, xxii
    accessing, xx
    entering from keyboard, xiv, xix
    entry, xiv, xix
    repeated, 12
    transparent, 16
Command lines, xix
Compatability with older versions of Auto-CAD, vii
CONE command, **657**
Cone option of 3D command, 636
CONTINUE dimension, 169
Converting old drawings, xix
Coordinates
    absolute, 6
    digitizing, 9
    display, 4
    entering, xiv, 6
    incremental, 7
    polar, 8
    relative, 7
    User Coordinate System, 2
    X, Y, Z point filters, 230
COPY command, **86**, 102
COPY Multiple, 86
Crosshatching, 221
Crossing polygon system variable, 48, 84
Crossing window entity selection method, xx, 48, 84
Current Layer, 145
Current text style, 201, 202
Current UCS, 1
Cursor
    and paper space, 283
    target size, 47
Curves
    B-spline, 337
    fitting, 65
    spline, 337
Cylinder Command, 658

D

Data entry
    angles, 8
    coordinates, 6, 7
    feet and inches, 18
    file names, xxi
    numeric values, 6, 7
    specifying points, 6, 7
    variables and arithmetical expressions, xi

X, Y, Z point filters, 230
DDATTDEF command, 361
DDATTEXT command, 385
DDCHPROP command, 149
DDEDIT command, 205
DDGROUP command, 428
DDIM command, 171
DDINSERT command, 253, 732
DDLMODES command, 143
DDLMODIFY command, 205
DDLTYPE command, 147
DDOSNAP command, 47
DDPTYPE command, 333
DDRMODES command, 41
DDUCS command, 502, 734
DDUNITS command, 18
DDVIEW command, 542, 734
Decimal, 18
Default working environment, 1
Definition points, 166
DEFPOINTS layer, 152
Deleting
    line segments, 48
    multiline vertices, 347
    objects, 48
    toolbars, xvii
    unused blocks, 262
Dialog boxes, xxi
DIAMETER dimensions, 170
Digitizing, 9
Dimension styles, 178, 753
Dimension text,
    angle, 174
    editing, 180, 753
    styles, 177
    variables, setting, 177
Dimensioning, 165
    2D, 165
    aligned, 168
    alternate units, 176
    and paper space scaling, 286
    angular, 171
    arcs, 170, 183
    arrow blocks, 172
    arrows, 172
    baseline increment, 169
    basic, 171
    center lines, 173, 184
    commands, 165
    continued, 169
    definition points, 166
    diameter, 170
    dimension line, 166
    editing, 180
    entities, 166
    extension line, 166, 173
    format, 173, 183

horizontal, 163
leaders, 207
Linear, 166, 181
lines, 166
mode, 166
Radius, 170
scale factor, 172
selection grips, 95
stretching, 180, 185
styles, 171, 177, 179, 182, 186
text, 174, 175, 177
text format, 172
text location, 174
tick, 172
tolerances, 177
units of measure, 176, 182
updating, 178, 179
vertical, 167
Dimensioning in 3D, 751
Dimensioning variables
    DIMALT, 176
    DIMALTD, 176
    DIMALTF, 176
    DIMAPOST, 175
    DIMASO, 180
    DIMASZ, 172
    DIMBLK, 172
    DIMBLK1, 172
    DIMBLK2, 172
    DIMCEN, 173
    DIMCLRD, 172
    DIMCLRE, 172
    DIMCLRT, 172
    DIMDLE, 172
    DIMDLI, 172
    DIMEXE, 172
    DIMEXO, 172
    DIMGAP, 172
    DIMLFAC, 172
    DIMLIM, 177
    DIMOVERRIDE, 178
    DIMPOST, 175
    DIMRND, 177
    DIMSCALE, 172
    DIMSE1, 173
    DIMSE2, 173
    DIMSTYLE, 178, 179, 182
    DIMTAD, 174, 175
    DIMEDIT, 180
    DIMTIH, 179
    DIMTIX, 174
    DIMTM, 177
    DIMTOFL, 174
    DIMTOH, 174
    DIMTOL, 177
    DIMTP, 177
    DIMTSZ, 172

DIMTXT, 177
DIMZIN, 176
Dimstyle, 733
Dir command, 735
Dish option of the 3D command, 636
Display
    cleaning up of, 17
    colours, xii
    grid, 40
    linetype, 147
    panning, 14
    zooming, 13
Displaying toolbars, xviii
DIST command, 341
DIVIDE command, 334
Documentation, 737
Dome option of the 3D command, 636
DONUT command, 69
Dot extensions, 489
Drafting standards, 275
Dragging
    Arcs, 11
    during mirror, 89
Drawing
    aids, 41
    changing directories, xviii
    changing name, 4
    compiling, 279
    conversion, vii, xx
    converting an old, vii, xx
    export of, 255
    extents, 5
    inserting, 254
    isometric, 397
    opening existing, xvii
    prototype, 99
    recovering, xvii
    scale, 338
    starting, xvii
    units, 17
DTEXT command, **197**, 209
duplicate items, see COPY, 86
DVIEW command, 557
DXF
    DXFIN, 740
    DXFOUT, 740
Dynamic
    text, 197
    view, 556
    zoom, 13

E

EDGE command, **520**, 539
EDGESURF command, 580, **588**
Editing
    attribute definitions, 363
    attributes in blocks, 379
    commands, 83
    dimensions, 180
    floating viewports, 283, 293
    hatches, 228
    meshes, 634
    Multiline text, 346
    paragraph text, 205
    polylines, 65
    selecting objects for, 83
    snap angle, 40
    solids, 697
    splines, 338
    text, 205
    tiled viewports, 485
ELEV command, 537
Elevation
    changing, 539
    defined, 537
ELLIPSE command, 399
END command, xxi
ENDpoint object snap, 42
Engineering, 19
ERASE command, **48**
Exiting AutoCAD, xix, xxii
EXPLODE command, **259**
Exploding
    blocks, 258
    dimensions, 180
    polylines, 258
Exporting files, 255, 422
EXTEND command, **120**, 121, 131
Extend to Implied Intersection, 121
Extending in 3D, 703
Extension line (dimensions), 173
Extensions (file), 489
External references, 439
Extracting attributes, 385
EXTRUDE command, 683
Extrusion direction, 683

F

F1 key, 2
Feet and inches, 18
Fence, 85
Filenames, xxi
File
    ASCII, 420
    extensions, 489
    formats, 489
    listing, 735
    managing, 309
    plotting to, 423
    recovery, xx
    renaming, xxi
    saving, xxi
    script, 420
    searching for, xxi
    slide, 416
    temporary, xxi, 490
FILES command, 735
FILLET command, **12**, **663**
Filleting,
    arcs, 23
    circles, 101
    in 3D, 663
    lines, 12, 25
    setting radius for, 25
FILTER command, 426
Filters X, Y, Z, 230, 523
Flip screen, 2
Floating
    command window, xvii
    toolbars, xvi
    viewports, 281, 290
Floppy disks, xi
Flyout properties, xvi
Font files, 203, 742
    assigning, 202
    PostScript, 203
    TrueType, 203
Fractional units display, 19
Freezing layers
    in single views, 144
    in paper space, 285
Frozen layers, 144
Function keys, xiii

G

Geometry Commands, 1
GIFIN command, 423, 741
Graphics area, xii
Grid
    Isometric, 398
    standard, 1, 4, 21, 39
GRID command, **40**
Grips, 48, 94
GROUP command, **427**, 733

H

Hatch
    area, 225
    associative, 228
    boundaries, 225
    editing, 228
    from command line, 221
    patterns, 223
    previewing, 226
    selecting objects, 226
    styles, 223
HATCH command, **221**
HATCHEDIT command, **228**
HELP command, **37**
Hexagons, 67
Hidden lines

in paper space, 275
in plotting, 609
restoring, 523
suppressing, 521
HIDE command, **521**, 487
Hideedge system variable, 521
Hideplot, 609
Hiding lines in plotted viewports, 609
Highlighting group members, 428
HORIZONTAL dimensions, 167
HPGL files, 423I
Icon display, 489
ID command, 343
Implied intersection, 121
Importing images,
    to AutoCAD, 423
    to word processing, 422
Inches, zero suppression, 176
Included angle, 126
Incremental point entry, 7
Inquiry commands, 338
INSERT command, **253**
Insertion
    base insertion point, 252
    multiple, 257
    of 3D blocks, 743
    scale, 253, 279
INTERSECT command, 662
INTERSECT with regions, 717
Intersection object snap, 42
Intersections
    editing multilines, 346
    trimming to implied, 121
Invisible attributes, 364
ISOLINES system variable, 655
Isometric
    circles, 398
    grid and snap, 40
    text, 206
ISOPLANE command, 398

J
Joining PLINEs, 66
Justification of text, 71, 196

K
Keyboard entry, xii
Keys (function), x, xii, xiii

L
Last entity selection method, 85
LAYER command, **143**
Layer control dialog box, 143, 733
Layers
    "0" layer zero, 152
    Blocks and, 260
    changing, 145, 149
    colors, 144, 146, 149, 151

controlling visibility, 151
creating, 144, 153
current, 144, 145
DDLMODES, 143
Defpoints, 152
filtering, 152
freeze and thaw, 144, 151
freeze and thaw in paperspace, 284, 290
hide with, 521
linetypes, 151
list, 152
lock and unlock, 144, 151
modifying, 145
naming conventions, 152
new, 151
on and off, 151
overview, 143
properties, 146
renaming, 145
thaw and freeze, 144, 151
turning off, 151
turning on, 151
visibility
    and layers, 151
    and viewports, 144
LEADER command, **207**
Left justified text, 70
Limits, 1, 3, 21
LIMITS command, **2**, 21, 39
.lin files, 97
Line width (PLINE), 63
LINE command, **6**
Lines
    center, 147
    chamfering, 49
    extension, 173
    filleting, 12
    freehand, 229
    multiple, 71
    using and entering, 6
    visibility with 3D solids, 655
    with undo, 10
LINETYPE command, 97, 98, **147**
Linetypes
    and layers, 147
    assigning, 147
    by Block, 260
    by object, 98
    by Layer, 147, 149
    changing, 99
    current, 98
    listing library files, 98
    scaling, 99
    scaling in paper space, 286
    standard, 97
LIST command, **15**, 342, 732

Listing
    dimension styles, 171
    filenames and files, 735
    frozen layers, 151
    properties of objects, 15, 149
    viewport configurations, 734
Loading
    files, xix
    linetypes, 98
Locking layers, 151
LTSCALE command, 99

M
Mass properties, 719
MASSPROP command, 719
MEASURE command, **335**
Menu
    bars, xiii, xvi
    buttons, xiii, xvi
    command entry, xvi, xviii
    files, xviii
    icon, xvi
    pop-up, xvi
    pull-down, xvi
    screen, xvi
    standard, xvi, 490
    transferring, 742
MENU command, xvii
Mesh,
    edge-defined, 641
    open, 641
MIDpoint object snap, 42
MINSERT command, **258**
Minus tolerancing, 177
MIRROR command, **89**, 100
MIRROR3D command, 699
Mirror grip mode, 97
Mirroring
    and dimensioning, 189
    existing objects, 89, 103
    with grips, 97
MIRRTEXT system variable, 91
MLEDIT command, 346
MLINE command, **71**, 75
MLSTYLE command, 344, 734
.mnu files, xvii, 490
Model space, 282, 605
    dimensioning in, 282
    switching to, 281, 608
Modes,
    grid, 40
    grip, 95
    ortho, 10
    Snap, 39
Modify polyline, 65
Modify toolbar, xiii
Mouse, xii

MOVE command, **87**, 100
Moving objects to 0,0, 88
Move grip mode, 97
Moving viewports, 283
MSLIDE command, **416**
MSPACE command, **282**
MTEXT command, **199**, 200, 213
Multiline editing, 346
Multiline Styles dialog box, 345
Multiline
    adding vertices, 346
    creating styles, 344
    deleting vertices, 346
    drawing, 71
    editing, 346
    elements of, 71
    joints, 347
    using existing styles, 346
Multiline text, 198
Multiple
    copies, 86, 87
    inserts, 257
    linetypes, 347
    viewports, 281, 608
MVIEW command, 281, 522, 608
MVSETUP, 286, 298, 614

N
Naming
    groups, 428
    layers, 144
    views, 542
NEARest object snap, 42
Nested blocks, 437
NEW command, xx
New File Name dialog box, xx
NODE object snap, 42
NONE object snap, 42
Null response text, 198

O
Object Grouping Dialog box, 428
Objects
    changing properties of, 149
    creation of, 6
    editing of, 83
    ignoring, xx
Object selection filters, 426
Object selection methods
    Add, 144
    All, 83
    Cpoly, 83, 84
    Crossing Polygon, xx, 83, 85, 115
    Crossing Window, xx, 83, 88
    Cycling, 48
    Fence, 83, 85
    Last, 83, 85
    Multiple, 83
    Previous, 83, 85
    Remove, 113, 117
    Single, 84
    Window, 83
    WPolygon, 83, 85
Object snap
    Apparent Intersection, 42, 45
    CENter, 42, 44
    disabling, 42
    ENDpoint, 42, 44, 52
    From, 42, 45
    in 3D, 493
    INSERTion, 42,
    INTersection, 42, 46
    MIDpoint, 42, 52
    Multiple, 47
    NEARest, 42
    NODE, 42
    NONE, 42, 46
    PERpendicular, 42, 44
    QUADrant, 42, 43, 50
    QUICK, 42, 46
    TANgent, 42, 43
OFFSET command, **122**
OOPS command, **48**
OPEN command, xxi
Options Dialog Box, xxi
Origin of model or drawing, 1, 3
ORTHO command, **10**
Ortho mode, 10
Orthographic projection, 404
OSNAP command, **41**, 46

P
PAN command, **15**
Paper space
    dimensioning, 286
    floating viewports, 281, 605
    freezing layers, 284
    objects, 263
    overview, 280
    plotting hidden lines, 609
    scaling views in, 284
    switching to, 280, 608
Parallel, 42, 46
Paragraph text, 199, 200, 206
Parallel lines, 71
Parent dimension style, 177
PCX files, 423, 741
PDMODE system variable, 333, 348
PDSIZE system variable, 333, 348
PEDIT command, **65**, 641
Pen assignment for plots, 495
Period extensions, 489
PERpendicular object snap, 42
Perspective views, 561
PFACE command, 639
Pick button, xii
PLINE command, **62**
Pline (see polyline)
Plot
    colors, 799
    configuration, 798
    display, 800
    extents, 800
    limits, 800
    origin, 800
    preview, 801
    rotation, 801
    scale, 800
    to file, **62**, 799
    to printer, 799
    view, 801
    Window, 800
    with hidden lines removed, 521
PLOT command, **797**, 494
Plot dialog box, 62
Plus tolerancing, 177
POINT command, **348**
Point filters, 230, 234
Pointing devices, xx
Points
    3D, 489
    display modes, 333
    entering, 6, 41
    locating, 343
Polar
    arrays, 125
    coordinates, 8
POLYGON command, **67**
Polygon window, 85
Polylines
    3D, 540
    arc segment options, 65
    calculating area of, 338, 718
    closing, 63
    corners, 64, 102
    drawing, 62, 72
    editing, 65, 66
    exploding, 258
    filleting, 65
    joining, 66
    splined, 66, 130
    width, 62, 64
PostScripts, 203
Preview
    hatch, 226
    plot, 497
Print dialog box, 800
Prompts, x
Prototype drawing, 99
PSPACE command, **282**, 605
Pull-down menus, xviii

PURGE command, **262**
PYRAMID option, 3D command, 635

Q
QSAVE command, xx
QTEXT command, **204**
Quadrant, 42
Quick object snap, 42
QUIT command, xix

R
RADIAL dimensions, 170, 183
Radius
    arc, 24
    circle, 25
    setting for fillets, 25
ray casting, 227
Record (SKETCH option), 229
Rectangular arrays, 126
Redefining blocks, 259
REDO command, 94
REDRAW command, 16
REGEN command, 16, 17
REGION command, 716
Relative coordinates, 7
Releases of AutoCAD, vii, xviii, 1
Remove entity selection method, 113
Return key, x
REVOLVE command, **681**
Revolved solids, 681
REVSURF command, **580**, 584
Right-click, xxi
Right-hand-rule, 499
ROTATE command, **91**, 92, 103
Rotate and copy, 92
ROTATE3D command, 701
Rotate grip mode, 96
Rscript, 421, 425
Ruled Surfaces, 580
RULESURF command, **580**
Running object snap, 47
Running object snap dialog box, 47

S
SAVE command, xviii
SAVEAS command, xviii
Save drawing as dialog box, xviii
Saving your work, xviii
SCALE command, **93**
Scaling
    dimensions, 172
    drawings, 93, 275, 276, 284
    hatches, 223, 275
    linetypes, 148
    plots, 497, 612
    text, 70, 277, 278
    title blocks, 275
    viewports, 275
    views, 612

with grips, 97
Scientific, 19
Screen
    color, xxi
    Windows, xiii
Screen menus, xvii
.SCR files, 422
SCRIPT command, **421**
Script files, 419, 567
Scrollbars, xvi, xxi
SDF attribute extract, 383
SECTION command, **684**
Sections, 232, 234, 236
Selection set (see object selection methods)
Setting up, 5, 6
SHADE command, **522**, 523
SHADEDGE system variable, 523
SHADEDIF system variable, 523
SHELL command, 388
Showedge system varaible, 521
.SHP files, 490
.SHX files, 490
Sign on code, xi
Single entity selection methods, 42
SKETCH command, 229
SKPOLY variable, 230
SLICE command, **685**
SLIDELIB utility program, 419
Slider bars, xvii
Slides, 416, 566
Slide shows, 421
Snap
    base point, 40
    isometric, 40
    rotation angle, 40
SNAP command, 1, 4, 21, **39**, 397
SOLID command, **68**, 74
Solids
    creating, 655
    modifying, 660
Sphere option of the 3D command, 636
SPHERE command, **658**
SPLINE command, 337
SPLINETYPE command, 67
Spline curves, from polylines, 66
Starting AutoCAD, x, xii, 1, 5, 6
STATUS command, **732**
Status line, xii
STRETCH command, **115**, 131
    dimensioning, 180, 185
Stretch grip mode, 95
STYLE command, **202**, 403
Styles
    dimensioning, 179
    hatching, 223
    isometric snap, 40

linetype, 147
text, 202
SUBTRACT command, **661**
Suppressing zeros
    in dimensions, 176
    in units readout, 18
Surface display, 579
Surfaces
    and wireframe, 579
    of revolution, 681
    ruled, 581
    tabulated, 587
SURFTAB1 system variable, 580
SURFTAB2 system variable, 580
Surveying units, 18, 20
Symbol library, 263

T
TABSURF command, 580, **587**
Tabulated surfaces, 587
Tangent with circles, 25, 51
TANgent object snap, 42, 43
Target point, 559
Temporary files, xxi, 490
Text
    alignment options, 70, 196
    ASCII, 420
    dimension orientation, 174, 177
    display, 204
    dynamic, 197
    editing, 204
    fonts, 201
    height, 70
    importing, 203
    justification, 70, 175, 196
    linear, 69
    mirroring, 91
    multiline, 198
    overscore, 198
    paragraph, 199
    slant in dimensioning, 752
    special characters, 198
    styles, 201, 209
    underscored, 198
    vertical, 202
TEXT command, 69, **195**
Text editor, 201
Text files, 385
Text styles, 201
Thawing layers
    in paper space, 284
Thickness
    changing, 539
    current, 537
    of an object, 539
    setting, 538
THICKNESS system variable, **538**, 540

TIFF format, 423
TIFFIN command, 423
Tiled viewports, 281
    in model space, 282
    in paper space, 607
Tilemode
    commands affected by, 281, 285
    MVIEW command, 281
    and paper space, 281, 606
    turning on and off, 281
TILEMODE command, **281, 607**
Title blocks, 275
Toggle keys, xiv
Toolbars
    accessing, xiv
    docking, xv
    moving, xv
TORUS command, 659
TRACE command, **61**
Tracking, 445
Transparent commands, 16
TRIM command, 45, 51, 52, **118**, 119, 120, 130
Trim to implied intersection, 121
Trimming in 3D, 703
TrueType fonts, 203

U
U command, 10, 121
UCS command, 2, 500
UCS
    dimensioning with, 752
    editing with, 698
UCSICON command, 504
UNDO command, 121
UNION command, 660, 717
UNITS command, **17**
Units of measure
    alternate, 176
    display format, 18
    drawings, 17
    setting style, 18
    surveyors, 20
Unlocking layers, 151
Updating dimensions, 180
User coordinate system, 1
User Responses, x

V
Values
    absolute, 6
    relative, 7
Variables
    dimensioning (see Dimensioning variables)
Vector files, 415
Vertical dimensions, 167
Vertical text, 201

VIEW command, **542**
Viewpoint, 541
Viewports
    floating, 606, 613
    freezing layers in, 614
    layer visibility, 614
    restoring, 611
    thawing layers in, 614
    tiled, 606
    using, 543
Views
    3D, 610
    paper space, 608
    saving, 542
VPLAYER command, **285**
VPOINT command, **541**
VPORTS command, 543
VSLIDE command, **417**, 567

W
WBLOCK command, **255**, 443
WCS (see World Coordinate System)
WEDGE command, **659**
Wedge option of the 3D command, **635**
Width of Polylines, 62
Wild card character, 736
Window entity selection method, 48, 84
Windows
    switching from DOS to, xix
    using, xiii
Wire frame modelling, 579
World Coordinate System (WCS), 2
WPolygon entity selection method, 85

X
X Zoom scale factor, 15
XBIND command, 444
XP zoom scale factor, 284
XREF command, 439
Xrefs
    adding to drawings, 442
    attaching to drawings, 442, 445
    binding to drawings, 440, 445
    layers, 439, 444
    overview, 439
    reloading, 441
    removing from drawings, 440
    updating, 441
X, Y, Z point filters, 230, 524

Z
Zero suppression
    in dimensioning, 176
    in screen display, 18
Zoom
    full plot preview, 497
    in paper space, 284
    overview, 13

scale factor X, 15
scale factor XP, 284
transparent, 16
ZOOM command, **13**
    All, 4, 14
    Center, 13
    Dynamic, 13
    Extents, 13
    In, 14
    Out, 14
    Previous, 13
    Scale, 13, 14
    Vmax, 13
    Window, 14
    XP, 284, 612

Modify Toolbar

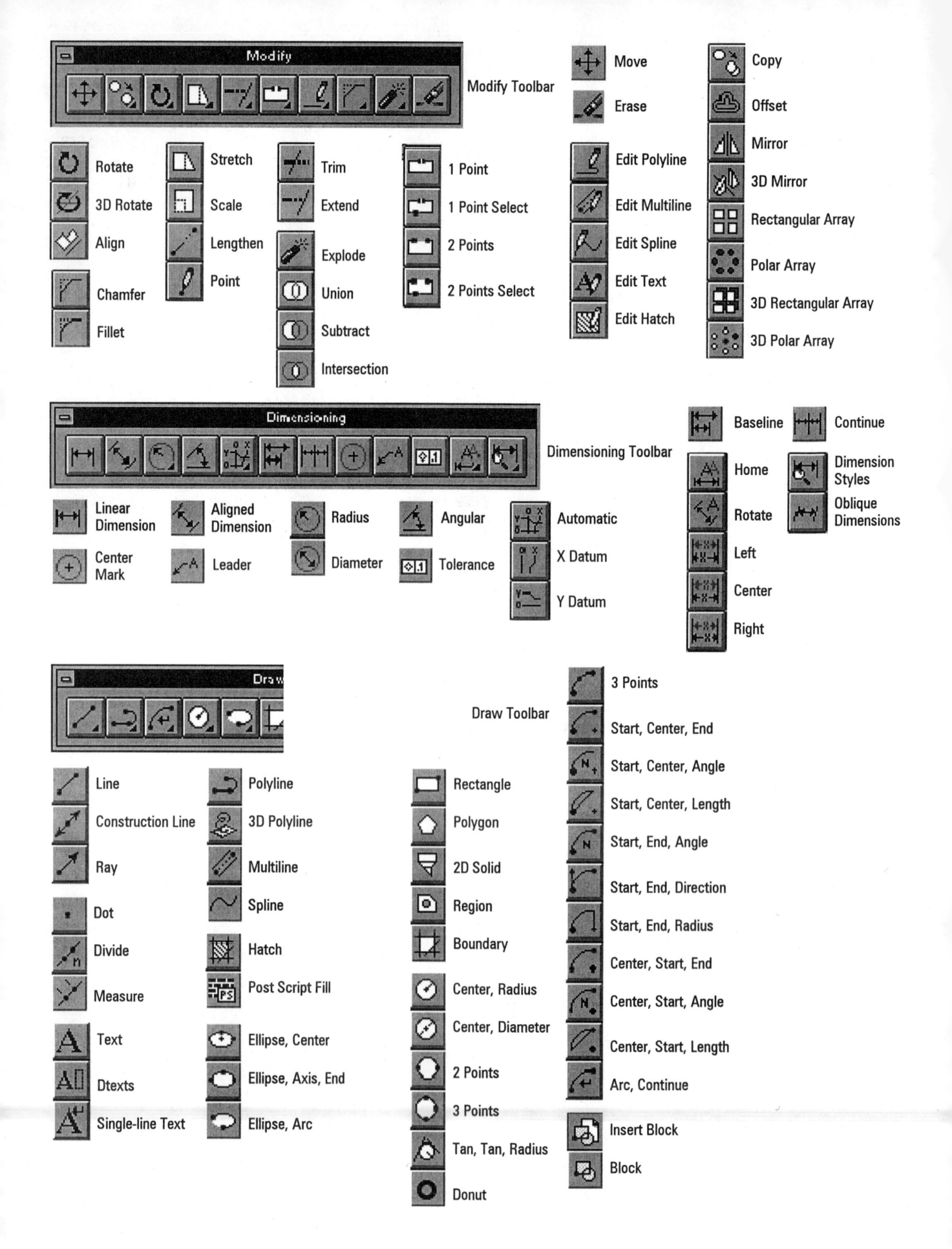

- Rotate
- 3D Rotate
- Align
- Chamfer
- Fillet
- Stretch
- Scale
- Lengthen
- Point
- Trim
- Extend
- Explode
- Union
- Subtract
- Intersection
- 1 Point
- 1 Point Select
- 2 Points
- 2 Points Select
- Move
- Erase
- Edit Polyline
- Edit Multiline
- Edit Spline
- Edit Text
- Edit Hatch
- Copy
- Offset
- Mirror
- 3D Mirror
- Rectangular Array
- Polar Array
- 3D Rectangular Array
- 3D Polar Array

Dimensioning Toolbar

- Linear Dimension
- Center Mark
- Aligned Dimension
- Leader
- Radius
- Diameter
- Angular
- Tolerance
- Automatic
- X Datum
- Y Datum
- Baseline
- Home
- Rotate
- Left
- Center
- Right
- Continue
- Dimension Styles
- Oblique Dimensions

Draw Toolbar

- Line
- Construction Line
- Ray
- Dot
- Divide
- Measure
- Text
- Dtexts
- Single-line Text
- Polyline
- 3D Polyline
- Multiline
- Spline
- Hatch
- Post Script Fill
- Ellipse, Center
- Ellipse, Axis, End
- Ellipse, Arc
- Rectangle
- Polygon
- 2D Solid
- Region
- Boundary
- Center, Radius
- Center, Diameter
- 2 Points
- 3 Points
- Tan, Tan, Radius
- Donut
- 3 Points
- Start, Center, End
- Start, Center, Angle
- Start, Center, Length
- Start, End, Angle
- Start, End, Direction
- Start, End, Radius
- Center, Start, End
- Center, Start, Angle
- Center, Start, Length
- Arc, Continue
- Insert Block
- Block

Windows Icons

Windows Icons

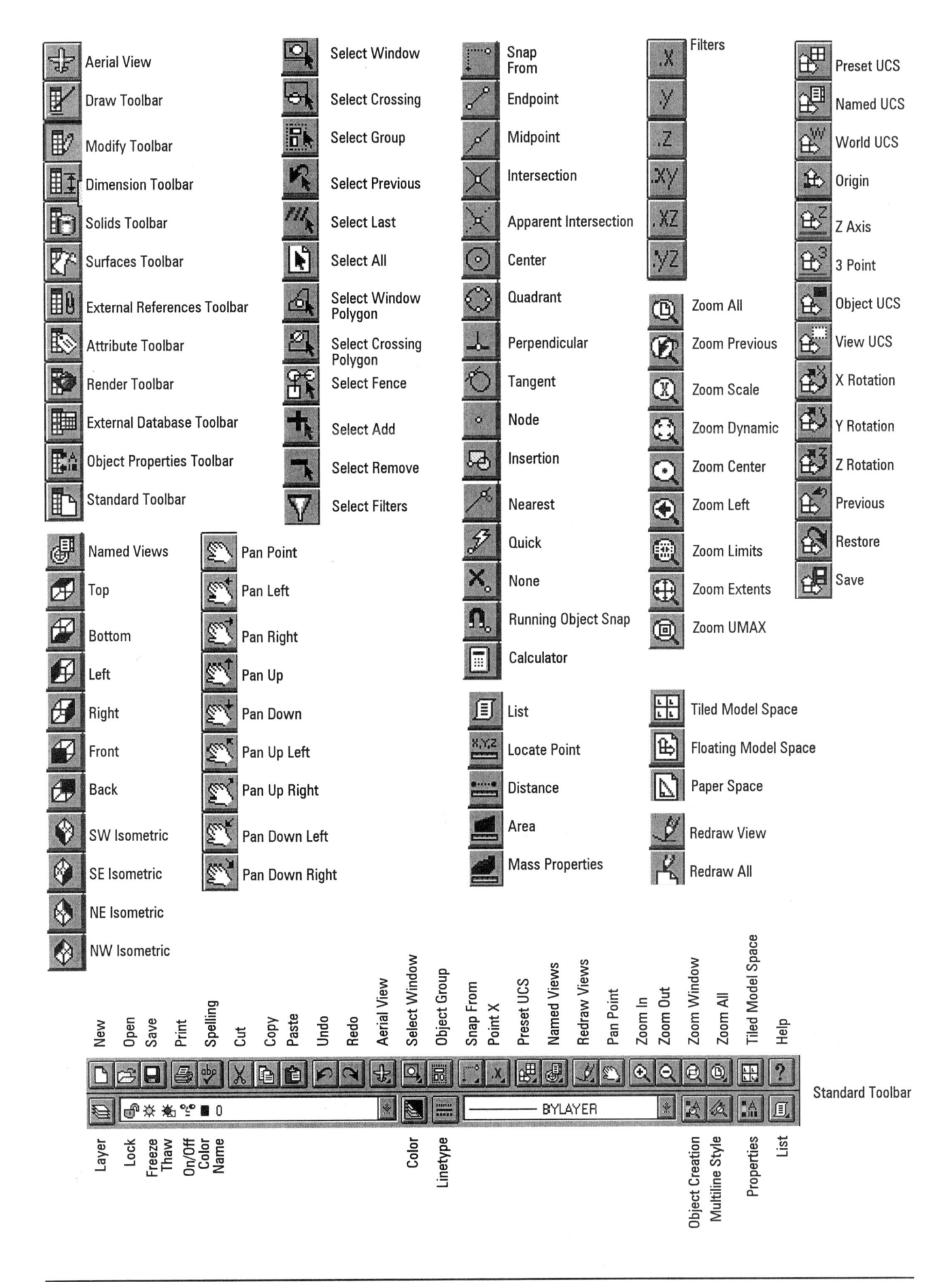

Toolbars
- Aerial View
- Draw Toolbar
- Modify Toolbar
- Dimension Toolbar
- Solids Toolbar
- Surfaces Toolbar
- External References Toolbar
- Attribute Toolbar
- Render Toolbar
- External Database Toolbar
- Object Properties Toolbar
- Standard Toolbar

Views
- Named Views
- Top
- Bottom
- Left
- Right
- Front
- Back
- SW Isometric
- SE Isometric
- NE Isometric
- NW Isometric

Pan
- Pan Point
- Pan Left
- Pan Right
- Pan Up
- Pan Down
- Pan Up Left
- Pan Up Right
- Pan Down Left
- Pan Down Right

Select
- Select Window
- Select Crossing
- Select Group
- Select Previous
- Select Last
- Select All
- Select Window Polygon
- Select Crossing Polygon
- Select Fence
- Select Add
- Select Remove
- Select Filters

Object Snap
- Snap From
- Endpoint
- Midpoint
- Intersection
- Apparent Intersection
- Center
- Quadrant
- Perpendicular
- Tangent
- Node
- Insertion
- Nearest
- Quick
- None
- Running Object Snap
- Calculator

Inquiry
- List
- Locate Point
- Distance
- Area
- Mass Properties

Filters
- .x
- .y
- .z
- .xy
- .xz
- .yz

Zoom
- Zoom All
- Zoom Previous
- Zoom Scale
- Zoom Dynamic
- Zoom Center
- Zoom Left
- Zoom Limits
- Zoom Extents
- Zoom UMAX

Model/Paper Space
- Tiled Model Space
- Floating Model Space
- Paper Space
- Redraw View
- Redraw All

UCS
- Preset UCS
- Named UCS
- World UCS
- Origin
- Z Axis
- 3 Point
- Object UCS
- View UCS
- X Rotation
- Y Rotation
- Z Rotation
- Previous
- Restore
- Save

Standard Toolbar
New, Open, Save, Print, Spelling, Cut, Copy, Paste, Undo, Redo, Aerial View, Select Window, Object Group, Snap From, Point X, Preset UCS, Named Views, Redraw Views, Pan Point, Zoom In, Zoom Out, Zoom Window, Zoom All, Tiled Model Space, Help

Layer, Lock, Freeze Thaw, On/Off Color Name, Color, Linetype, Object Creation, Multiline Style, Properties, List